Dictionary of Literary Biography

1 *The American Renaissance in New England,* edited by Joel Myerson (1978)

2 *American Novelists Since World War II,* edited by Jeffrey Helterman and Richard Layman (1978)

3 *Antebellum Writers in New York and the South,* edited by Joel Myerson (1979)

4 *American Writers in Paris, 1920-1939,* edited by Karen Lane Rood (1980)

5 *American Poets Since World War II,* 2 parts, edited by Donald J. Greiner (1980)

6 *American Novelists Since World War II, Second Series,* edited by James E. Kibler Jr. (1980)

7 *Twentieth-Century American Dramatists,* 2 parts, edited by John MacNicholas (1981)

8 *Twentieth-Century American Science-Fiction Writers,* 2 parts, edited by David Cowart and Thomas L. Wymer (1981)

9 *American Novelists, 1910-1945,* 3 parts, edited by James J. Martine (1981)

10 *Modern British Dramatists, 1900-1945,* 2 parts, edited by Stanley Weintraub (1982)

11 *American Humorists, 1800-1950,* 2 parts, edited by Stanley Trachtenberg (1982)

12 *American Realists and Naturalists,* edited by Donald Pizer and Earl N. Harbert (1982)

13 *British Dramatists Since World War II,* 2 parts, edited by Stanley Weintraub (1982)

14 *British Novelists Since 1960,* 2 parts, edited by Jay L. Halio (1983)

15 *British Novelists, 1930-1959,* 2 parts, edited by Bernard Oldsey (1983)

16 *The Beats: Literary Bohemians in Postwar America,* 2 parts, edited by Ann Charters (1983)

17 *Twentieth-Century American Historians,* edited by Clyde N. Wilson (1983)

18 *Victorian Novelists After 1885,* edited by Ira B. Nadel and William E. Fredeman (1983)

19 *British Poets, 1880-1914,* edited by Donald E. Stanford (1983)

20 *British Poets, 1914-1945,* edited by Donald E. Stanford (1983)

21 *Victorian Novelists Before 1885,* edited by Ira B. Nadel and William E. Fredeman (1983)

22 *American Writers for Children, 1900-1960,* edited by John Cech (1983)

23 *American Newspaper Journalists, 1873-1900,* edited by Perry J. Ashley (1983)

24 *American Colonial Writers, 1606-1734,* edited by Emory Elliott (1984)

25 *American Newspaper Journalists, 1901-1925,* edited by Perry J. Ashley (1984)

26 *American Screenwriters,* edited by Robert E. Morsberger, Stephen O. Lesser, and Randall Clark (1984)

27 *Poets of Great Britain and Ireland, 1945-1960,* edited by Vincent B. Sherry Jr. (1984)

28 *Twentieth-Century American-Jewish Fiction Writers,* edited by Daniel Walden (1984)

29 *American Newspaper Journalists, 1926-1950,* edited by Perry J. Ashley (1984)

30 *American Historians, 1607-1865,* edited by Clyde N. Wilson (1984)

31 *American Colonial Writers, 1735-1781,* edited by Emory Elliott (1984)

32 *Victorian Poets Before 1850,* edited by William E. Fredeman and Ira B. Nadel (1984)

33 *Afro-American Fiction Writers After 1955,* edited by Thadious M. Davis and Trudier Harris (1984)

34 *British Novelists, 1890-1929: Traditionalists,* edited by Thomas F. Staley (1985)

35 *Victorian Poets After 1850,* edited by William E. Fredeman and Ira B. Nadel (1985)

36 *British Novelists, 1890-1929: Modernists,* edited by Thomas F. Staley (1985)

37 *American Writers of the Early Republic,* edited by Emory Elliott (1985)

38 *Afro-American Writers After 1955: Dramatists and Prose Writers,* edited by Thadious M. Davis and Trudier Harris (1985)

39 *British Novelists, 1660-1800,* 2 parts, edited by Martin C. Battestin (1985)

40 *Poets of Great Britain and Ireland Since 1960,* 2 parts, edited by Vincent B. Sherry Jr. (1985)

41 *Afro-American Poets Since 1955,* edited by Trudier Harris and Thadious M. Davis (1985)

42 *American Writers for Children Before 1900,* edited by Glenn E. Estes (1985)

43 *American Newspaper Journalists, 1690-1872,* edited by Perry J. Ashley (1986)

44 *American Screenwriters, Second Series,* edited by Randall Clark, Robert E. Morsberger, and Stephen O. Lesser (1986)

45 *American Poets, 1880-1945, First Series,* edited by Peter Quartermain (1986)

46 *American Literary Publishing Houses, 1900-1980: Trade and Paperback,* edited by Peter Dzwonkoski (1986)

47 *American Historians, 1866-1912,* edited by Clyde N. Wilson (1986)

48 *American Poets, 1880-1945, Second Series,* edited by Peter Quartermain (1986)

49 *American Literary Publishing Houses, 1638-1899,* 2 parts, edited by Peter Dzwonkoski (1986)

50 *Afro-American Writers Before the Harlem Renaissance,* edited by Trudier Harris (1986)

51 *Afro-American Writers from the Harlem Renaissance to 1940,* edited by Trudier Harris (1987)

52 *American Writers for Children Since 1960: Fiction,* edited by Glenn E. Estes (1986)

53 *Canadian Writers Since 1960, First Series,* edited by W. H. New (1986)

54 *American Poets, 1880-1945, Third Series,* 2 parts, edited by Peter Quartermain (1987)

55 *Victorian Prose Writers Before 1867,* edited by William B. Thesing (1987)

56 *German Fiction Writers, 1914-1945,* edited by James Hardin (1987)

57 *Victorian Prose Writers After 1867,* edited by William B. Thesing (1987)

58 *Jacobean and Caroline Dramatists,* edited by Fredson Bowers (1987)

59 *American Literary Critics and Scholars, 1800-1850,* edited by John W. Rathbun and Monica M. Grecu (1987)

60 *Canadian Writers Since 1960, Second Series,* edited by W. H. New (1987)

61 *American Writers for Children Since 1960: Poets, Illustrators, and Nonfiction Authors,* edited by Glenn E. Estes (1987)

62 *Elizabethan Dramatists,* edited by Fredson Bowers (1987)

63 *Modern American Critics, 1920-1955,* edited by Gregory S. Jay (1988)

64 *American Literary Critics and Scholars, 1850-1880,* edited by John W. Rathbun and Monica M. Grecu (1988)

65 *French Novelists, 1900-1930,* edited by Catharine Savage Brosman (1988)

66 *German Fiction Writers, 1885-1913,* 2 parts, edited by James Hardin (1988)

67 *Modern American Critics Since 1955,* edited by Gregory S. Jay (1988)

68 *Canadian Writers, 1920-1959, First Series,* edited by W. H. New (1988)

69 *Contemporary German Fiction Writers, First Series,* edited by Wolfgang D. Elfe and James Hardin (1988)

70 *British Mystery Writers, 1860-1919,* edited by Bernard Benstock and Thomas F. Staley (1988)

71 *American Literary Critics and Scholars, 1880-1900,* edited by John W. Rathbun and Monica M. Grecu (1988)

72 *French Novelists, 1930-1960,* edited by Catharine Savage Brosman (1988)

73 *American Magazine Journalists, 1741-1850,* edited by Sam G. Riley (1988)

74 *American Short-Story Writers Before 1880,* edited by Bobby Ellen Kimbel, with the assistance of William E. Grant (1988)

75 *Contemporary German Fiction Writers, Second Series,* edited by Wolfgang D. Elfe and James Hardin (1988)

76 *Afro-American Writers, 1940-1955,* edited by Trudier Harris (1988)

77 *British Mystery Writers, 1920-1939,* edited by Bernard Benstock and Thomas F. Staley (1988)

78 *American Short-Story Writers, 1880-1910,* edited by Bobby Ellen Kimbel, with the assistance of William E. Grant (1988)

79 *American Magazine Journalists, 1850-1900,* edited by Sam G. Riley (1988)

80 *Restoration and Eighteenth-Century Dramatists, First Series,* edited by Paula R. Backscheider (1989)

81 *Austrian Fiction Writers, 1875-1913,* edited by James Hardin and Donald G. Daviau (1989)

82 *Chicano Writers, First Series,* edited by Francisco A. Lomelí and Carl R. Shirley (1989)

83 *French Novelists Since 1960,* edited by Catharine Savage Brosman (1989)

84 *Restoration and Eighteenth-Century Dramatists, Second Series,* edited by Paula R. Backscheider (1989)

85 *Austrian Fiction Writers After 1914,* edited by James Hardin and Donald G. Daviau (1989)

86 *American Short-Story Writers, 1910-1945, First Series,* edited by Bobby Ellen Kimbel (1989)

87 *British Mystery and Thriller Writers Since 1940, First Series,* edited by Bernard Benstock and Thomas F. Staley (1989)

88 *Canadian Writers, 1920-1959, Second Series,* edited by W. H. New (1989)

89 *Restoration and Eighteenth-Century Dramatists, Third Series,* edited by Paula R. Backscheider (1989)

90 *German Writers in the Age of Goethe, 1789-1832,* edited by James Hardin and Christoph E. Schweitzer (1989)

91 *American Magazine Journalists, 1900-1960, First Series,* edited by Sam G. Riley (1990)

92 *Canadian Writers, 1890-1920,* edited by W. H. New (1990)

93 *British Romantic Poets, 1789-1832, First Series,* edited by John R. Greenfield (1990)

94 *German Writers in the Age of Goethe: Sturm und Drang to Classicism,* edited by James Hardin and Christoph E. Schweitzer (1990)

95 *Eighteenth-Century British Poets, First Series,* edited by John Sitter (1990)

96 *British Romantic Poets, 1789-1832, Second Series,* edited by John R. Greenfield (1990)

97 *German Writers from the Enlightenment to Sturm und Drang, 1720-1764,* edited by James Hardin and Christoph E. Schweitzer (1990)

98 *Modern British Essayists, First Series,* edited by Robert Beum (1990)

99 *Canadian Writers Before 1890,* edited by W. H. New (1990)

100 *Modern British Essayists, Second Series,* edited by Robert Beum (1990)

101 *British Prose Writers, 1660-1800, First Series,* edited by Donald T. Siebert (1991)

102 *American Short-Story Writers, 1910-1945, Second Series,* edited by Bobby Ellen Kimbel (1991)

103 *American Literary Biographers, First Series,* edited by Steven Serafin (1991)

104 *British Prose Writers, 1660-1800, Second Series,* edited by Donald T. Siebert (1991)

105 *American Poets Since World War II, Second Series,* edited by R. S. Gwynn (1991)

106 *British Literary Publishing Houses, 1820-1880,* edited by Patricia J. Anderson and Jonathan Rose (1991)

107 *British Romantic Prose Writers, 1789-1832, First Series,* edited by John R. Greenfield (1991)

108 *Twentieth-Century Spanish Poets, First Series,* edited by Michael L. Perna (1991)

109 *Eighteenth-Century British Poets, Second Series,* edited by John Sitter (1991)

110 *British Romantic Prose Writers, 1789-1832, Second Series,* edited by John R. Greenfield (1991)

111 *American Literary Biographers, Second Series,* edited by Steven Serafin (1991)

112 *British Literary Publishing Houses, 1881-1965,* edited by Jonathan Rose and Patricia J. Anderson (1991)

113 *Modern Latin-American Fiction Writers, First Series,* edited by William Luis (1992)

114 *Twentieth-Century Italian Poets, First Series,* edited by Giovanna Wedel De Stasio, Glauco Cambon, and Antonio Illiano (1992)

115 *Medieval Philosophers,* edited by Jeremiah Hackett (1992)

116 *British Romantic Novelists, 1789-1832,* edited by Bradford K. Mudge (1992)

117 *Twentieth-Century Caribbean and Black African Writers, First Series,* edited by Bernth Lindfors and Reinhard Sander (1992)

118 *Twentieth-Century German Dramatists, 1889-1918,* edited by Wolfgang D. Elfe and James Hardin (1992)

119 *Nineteenth-Century French Fiction Writers: Romanticism and Realism, 1800-1860,* edited by Catharine Savage Brosman (1992)

120 *American Poets Since World War II, Third Series,* edited by R. S. Gwynn (1992)

121 *Seventeenth-Century British Nondramatic Poets, First Series,* edited by M. Thomas Hester (1992)

122 *Chicano Writers, Second Series,* edited by Francisco A. Lomelí and Carl R. Shirley (1992)

123 *Nineteenth-Century French Fiction Writers: Naturalism and Beyond, 1860-1900,* edited by Catharine Savage Brosman (1992)

124 *Twentieth-Century German Dramatists, 1919-1992,* edited by Wolfgang D. Elfe and James Hardin (1992)

125 *Twentieth-Century Caribbean and Black African Writers, Second Series,* edited by Bernth Lindfors and Reinhard Sander (1993)

126 *Seventeenth-Century British Nondramatic Poets, Second Series,* edited by M. Thomas Hester (1993)

127 *American Newspaper Publishers, 1950-1990,* edited by Perry J. Ashley (1993)

128 *Twentieth-Century Italian Poets, Second Series,* edited by Giovanna Wedel De Stasio, Glauco Cambon, and Antonio Illiano (1993)

129 *Nineteenth-Century German Writers, 1841-1900,* edited by James Hardin and Siegfried Mews (1993)

130 *American Short-Story Writers Since World War II,* edited by Patrick Meanor (1993)

131 *Seventeenth-Century British Nondramatic Poets, Third Series,* edited by M. Thomas Hester (1993)

132 *Sixteenth-Century British Nondramatic Writers, First Series,* edited by David A. Richardson (1993)

133 *Nineteenth-Century German Writers to 1840,* edited by James Hardin and Siegfried Mews (1993)

134 *Twentieth-Century Spanish Poets, Second Series,* edited by Jerry Phillips Winfield (1994)

135 *British Short-Fiction Writers, 1880-1914: The Realist Tradition,* edited by William B. Thesing (1994)

136 *Sixteenth-Century British Nondramatic Writers, Second Series,* edited by David A. Richardson (1994)

137 *American Magazine Journalists, 1900-1960, Second Series,* edited by Sam G. Riley (1994)

138 *German Writers and Works of the High Middle Ages: 1170-1280,* edited by James Hardin and Will Hasty (1994)

139 *British Short-Fiction Writers, 1945-1980,* edited by Dean Baldwin (1994)

140 *American Book-Collectors and Bibliographers, First Series,* edited by Joseph Rosenblum (1994)

141 *British Children's Writers, 1880-1914,* edited by Laura M. Zaidman (1994)

142 *Eighteenth-Century British Literary Biographers,* edited by Steven Serafin (1994)

143 *American Novelists Since World War II, Third Series,* edited by James R. Giles and Wanda H. Giles (1994)

144 *Nineteenth-Century British Literary Biographers,* edited by Steven Serafin (1994)

145 *Modern Latin-American Fiction Writers, Second Series,* edited by William Luis and Ann González (1994)

146 *Old and Middle English Literature,* edited by Jeffrey Helterman and Jerome Mitchell (1994)

147 *South Slavic Writers Before World War II,* edited by Vasa D. Mihailovich (1994)

148 *German Writers and Works of the Early Middle Ages: 800-1170,* edited by Will Hasty and James Hardin (1994)

149 *Late Nineteenth- and Early Twentieth-Century British Literary Biographers,* edited by Steven Serafin (1995)

150 *Early Modern Russian Writers, Late Seventeenth and Eighteenth Centuries,* edited by Marcus C. Levitt (1995)

151 *British Prose Writers of the Early Seventeenth Century,* edited by Clayton D. Lein (1995)

152 *American Novelists Since World War II, Fourth Series,* edited by James R. Giles and Wanda H. Giles (1995)

153 *Late-Victorian and Edwardian British Novelists, First Series,* edited by George M. Johnson (1995)

154 *The British Literary Book Trade, 1700-1820,* edited by James K. Bracken and Joel Silver (1995)

155 *Twentieth-Century British Literary Biographers,* edited by Steven Serafin (1995)

156 *British Short-Fiction Writers, 1880-1914: The Romantic Tradition,* edited by William F. Naufftus (1995)

157 *Twentieth-Century Caribbean and Black African Writers, Third Series,* edited by Bernth Lindfors and Reinhard Sander (1995)

158 *British Reform Writers, 1789-1832,* edited by Gary Kelly and Edd Applegate (1995)

159 *British Short-Fiction Writers, 1800-1880,* edited by John R. Greenfield (1996)

160 *British Children's Writers, 1914-1960,* edited by Donald R. Hettinga and Gary D. Schmidt (1996)

161 *British Children's Writers Since 1960, First Series,* edited by Caroline Hunt (1996)

162 *British Short-Fiction Writers, 1915-1945,* edited by John H. Rogers (1996)

163 *British Children's Writers, 1800-1880,* edited by Meena Khorana (1996)

164 *German Baroque Writers, 1580-1660,* edited by James Hardin (1996)

165 *American Poets Since World War II, Fourth Series,* edited by Joseph Conte (1996)

166 *British Travel Writers, 1837-1875,* edited by Barbara Brothers and Julia Gergits (1996)

167 *Sixteenth-Century British Nondramatic Writers, Third Series,* edited by David A. Richardson (1996)

168 *German Baroque Writers, 1661-1730,* edited by James Hardin (1996)

169 *American Poets Since World War II, Fifth Series,* edited by Joseph Conte (1996)

170 *The British Literary Book Trade, 1475-1700,* edited by James K. Bracken and Joel Silver (1996)

171 *Twentieth-Century American Sportswriters,* edited by Richard Orodenker (1996)

172 *Sixteenth-Century British Nondramatic Writers, Fourth Series,* edited by David A. Richardson (1996)

173 *American Novelists Since World War II, Fifth Series,* edited by James R. Giles and Wanda H. Giles (1996)

174 *British Travel Writers, 1876-1909,* edited by Barbara Brothers and Julia Gergits (1997)

175 *Native American Writers of the United States,* edited by Kenneth M. Roemer (1997)

176 *Ancient Greek Authors,* edited by Ward W. Briggs (1997)

177 *Italian Novelists Since World War II, 1945-1965,* edited by Augustus Pallotta (1997)

178 *British Fantasy and Science-Fiction Writers Before World War I,* edited by Darren Harris-Fain (1997)

179 *German Writers of the Renaissance and Reformation, 1280-1580,* edited by James Hardin and Max Reinhart (1997)

180 *Japanese Fiction Writers, 1868-1945,* edited by Van C. Gessel (1997)

181 *South Slavic Writers Since World War II,* edited by Vasa D. Mihailovich (1997)

182 *Japanese Fiction Writers Since World War II,* edited by Van C. Gessel (1997)

183 *American Travel Writers, 1776-1864,* edited by James J. Schramer and Donald Ross (1997)

184 *Nineteenth-Century British Book-Collectors and Bibliographers,* edited by William Baker and Kenneth Womack (1997)

185 *American Literary Journalists, 1945-1995, First Series,* edited by Arthur J. Kaul (1998)

186 *Nineteenth-Century American Western Writers,* edited by Robert L. Gale (1998)

187 *American Book Collectors and Bibliographers, Second Series,* edited by Joseph Rosenblum (1998)

188 *American Book and Magazine Illustrators to 1920,* edited by Steven E. Smith, Catherine A. Hastedt, and Donald H. Dyal (1998)

189 *American Travel Writers, 1850-1915,* edited by Donald Ross and James J. Schramer (1998)

190 *British Reform Writers, 1832-1914,* edited by Gary Kelly and Edd Applegate (1998)

191 *British Novelists Between the Wars,* edited by George M. Johnson (1998)

192 *French Dramatists, 1789-1914,* edited by Barbara T. Cooper (1998)

193 *American Poets Since World War II, Sixth Series,* edited by Joseph Conte (1998)

194 *British Novelists Since 1960, Second Series,* edited by Merritt Moseley (1998)

195 *British Travel Writers, 1910-1939,* edited by Barbara Brothers and Julia Gergits (1998)

196 *Italian Novelists Since World War II, 1965-1995,* edited by Augustus Pallotta (1999)

197 *Late-Victorian and Edwardian British Novelists, Second Series,* edited by George M. Johnson (1999)

198 *Russian Literature in the Age of Pushkin and Gogol: Prose,* edited by Christine A. Rydel (1999)

199 *Victorian Women Poets,* edited by William B. Thesing (1999)

200 *American Women Prose Writers to 1820,* edited by Carla J. Mulford, with Angela Vietto and Amy E. Winans (1999)

201 *Twentieth-Century British Book Collectors and Bibliographers,* edited by William Baker and Kenneth Womack (1999)

202 *Nineteenth-Century American Fiction Writers,* edited by Kent P. Ljungquist (1999)

203 *Medieval Japanese Writers,* edited by Steven D. Carter (1999)

204 *British Travel Writers, 1940-1997,* edited by Barbara Brothers and Julia M. Gergits (1999)

205 *Russian Literature in the Age of Pushkin and Gogol: Poetry and Drama,* edited by Christine A. Rydel (1999)

206 *Twentieth-Century American Western Writers, First Series,* edited by Richard H. Cracroft (1999)

207 *British Novelists Since 1960, Third Series,* edited by Merritt Moseley (1999)

208 *Literature of the French and Occitan Middle Ages: Eleventh to Fifteenth Centuries,* edited by Deborah Sinnreich-Levi and Ian S. Laurie (1999)

209 *Chicano Writers, Third Series,* edited by Francisco A. Lomelí and Carl R. Shirley (1999)

210 *Ernest Hemingway: A Documentary Volume,* edited by Robert W. Trogdon (1999)

211 *Ancient Roman Writers,* edited by Ward W. Briggs (1999)

212 *Twentieth-Century American Western Writers, Second Series,* edited by Richard H. Cracroft (1999)

213 *Pre-Nineteenth-Century British Book Collectors and Bibliographers,* edited by William Baker and Kenneth Womack (1999)

214 *Twentieth-Century Danish Writers,* edited by Marianne Stecher-Hansen (1999)

215 *Twentieth-Century Eastern European Writers, First Series,* edited by Steven Serafin (1999)

216 *British Poets of the Great War: Brooke, Rosenberg, Thomas. A Documentary Volume,* edited by Patrick Quinn (2000)

217 *Nineteenth-Century French Poets,* edited by Robert Beum (2000)

218 *American Short-Story Writers Since World War II, Second Series,* edited by Patrick Meanor and Gwen Crane (2000)

219 *F. Scott Fitzgerald's* The Great Gatsby: *A Documentary Volume,* edited by Matthew J. Bruccoli (2000)

220 *Twentieth-Century Eastern European Writers, Second Series,* edited by Steven Serafin (2000)

221 *American Women Prose Writers, 1870-1920,* edited by Sharon M. Harris, with the assistance of Heidi L. M. Jacobs and Jennifer Putzi (2000)

222 *H. L. Mencken: A Documentary Volume,* edited by Richard J. Schrader (2000)

223 *The American Renaissance in New England, Second Series,* edited by Wesley T. Mott (2000)

224 *Walt Whitman: A Documentary Volume,* edited by Joel Myerson (2000)

225 *South African Writers,* edited by Paul A. Scanlon (2000)

226 *American Hard-Boiled Crime Writers,* edited by George Parker Anderson and Julie B. Anderson (2000)

227 *American Novelists Since World War II, Sixth Series,* edited by James R. Giles and Wanda H. Giles (2000)

228 *Twentieth-Century American Dramatists, Second Series,* edited by Christopher J. Wheatley (2000)

229 *Thomas Wolfe: A Documentary Volume,* edited by Ted Mitchell (2001)

230 *Australian Literature, 1788-1914,* edited by Selina Samuels (2001)

231 *British Novelists Since 1960, Fourth Series,* edited by Merritt Moseley (2001)

232 *Twentieth-Century Eastern European Writers, Third Series,* edited by Steven Serafin (2001)

233 *British and Irish Dramatists Since World War II, Second Series,* edited by John Bull (2001)

234 *American Short-Story Writers Since World War II, Third Series,* edited by Patrick Meanor and Richard E. Lee (2001)

235 *The American Renaissance in New England, Third Series,* edited by Wesley T. Mott (2001)

236 *British Rhetoricians and Logicians, 1500-1660,* edited by Edward A. Malone (2001)

237 *The Beats: A Documentary Volume,* edited by Matt Theado (2001)

238 *Russian Novelists in the Age of Tolstoy and Dostoevsky,* edited by J. Alexander Ogden and Judith E. Kalb (2001)

239 *American Women Prose Writers: 1820-1870,* edited by Amy E. Hudock and Katharine Rodier (2001)

240 *Late Nineteenth- and Early Twentieth-Century British Women Poets,* edited by William B. Thesing (2001)

241 *American Sportswriters and Writers on Sport,* edited by Richard Orodenker (2001)

242 *Twentieth-Century European Cultural Theorists, First Series,* edited by Paul Hansom (2001)

243 *The American Renaissance in New England, Fourth Series,* edited by Wesley T. Mott (2001)

244 *American Short-Story Writers Since World War II, Fourth Series,* edited by Patrick Meanor and Joseph McNicholas (2001)

245 *British and Irish Dramatists Since World War II, Third Series,* edited by John Bull (2001)

246 *Twentieth-Century American Cultural Theorists,* edited by Paul Hansom (2001)

247 *James Joyce: A Documentary Volume,* edited by A. Nicholas Fargnoli (2001)

248 *Antebellum Writers in the South, Second Series,* edited by Kent Ljungquist (2001)

249 *Twentieth-Century American Dramatists, Third Series,* edited by Christopher Wheatley (2002).

250 *Antebellum Writers in New York, Second Series,* edited by Kent Ljungquist (2002).

251 *Canadian Fantasy and Science-Fiction Writers,* edited by Douglas Ivison (2002).

252 *British Philosophers, 1500–1799,* edited by Philip B. Dematteis and Peter S. Fosl (2002).

253 *Raymond Chandler: A Documentary Volume,* edited by Robert Moss (2002).

254 *The House of Putnam, 1837–1872: A Documentary Volume,* edited by Ezra Greenspan (2002).

Dictionary of Literary Biography Documentary Series

1 *Sherwood Anderson, Willa Cather, John Dos Passos, Theodore Dreiser, F. Scott Fitzgerald, Ernest Hemingway, Sinclair Lewis,* edited by Margaret A. Van Antwerp (1982)

2 *James Gould Cozzens, James T. Farrell, William Faulkner, John O'Hara, John Steinbeck, Thomas Wolfe, Richard Wright,* edited by Margaret A. Van Antwerp (1982)

3 *Saul Bellow, Jack Kerouac, Norman Mailer, Vladimir Nabokov, John Updike, Kurt Vonnegut,* edited by Mary Bruccoli (1983)

4 *Tennessee Williams,* edited by Margaret A. Van Antwerp and Sally Johns (1984)

5 *American Transcendentalists,* edited by Joel Myerson (1988)

6 *Hardboiled Mystery Writers: Raymond Chandler, Dashiell Hammett, Ross Macdonald,* edited by Matthew J. Bruccoli and Richard Layman (1989)

7 *Modern American Poets: James Dickey, Robert Frost, Marianne Moore,* edited by Karen L. Rood (1989)

8 *The Black Aesthetic Movement,* edited by Jeffrey Louis Decker (1991)

9 *American Writers of the Vietnam War: W. D. Ehrhart, Larry Heinemann, Tim O'Brien, Walter McDonald, John M. Del Vecchio,* edited by Ronald Baughman (1991)

10 *The Bloomsbury Group,* edited by Edward L. Bishop (1992)

11 *American Proletarian Culture: The Twenties and The Thirties,* edited by Jon Christian Suggs (1993)

12 *Southern Women Writers: Flannery O'Connor, Katherine Anne Porter, Eudora Welty,* edited by Mary Ann Wimsatt and Karen L. Rood (1994)

13 *The House of Scribner, 1846-1904,* edited by John Delaney (1996)

14 *Four Women Writers for Children, 1868-1918,* edited by Caroline C. Hunt (1996)

15 *American Expatriate Writers: Paris in the Twenties,* edited by Matthew J. Bruccoli and Robert W. Trogdon (1997)

16 *The House of Scribner, 1905-1930,* edited by John Delaney (1997)

17 *The House of Scribner, 1931-1984,* edited by John Delaney (1998)

18 *British Poets of The Great War: Sassoon, Graves, Owen,* edited by Patrick Quinn (1999)

19 *James Dickey,* edited by Judith S. Baughman (1999)

See also DLB 210, 216, 219, 222, 224, 229, 237, 247, 253, 254

Dictionary of Literary Biography Yearbooks

1980 edited by Karen L. Rood, Jean W. Ross, and Richard Ziegfeld (1981)

1981 edited by Karen L. Rood, Jean W. Ross, and Richard Ziegfeld (1982)

1982 edited by Richard Ziegfeld; associate editors: Jean W. Ross and Lynne C. Zeigler (1983)

1983 edited by Mary Bruccoli and Jean W. Ross; associate editor Richard Ziegfeld (1984)

1984 edited by Jean W. Ross (1985)

1985 edited by Jean W. Ross (1986)

1986 edited by J. M. Brook (1987)

1987 edited by J. M. Brook (1988)

1988 edited by J. M. Brook (1989)

1989 edited by J. M. Brook (1990)

1990 edited by James W. Hipp (1991)

1991 edited by James W. Hipp (1992)

1992 edited by James W. Hipp (1993)

1993 edited by James W. Hipp, contributing editor George Garrett (1994)

1994 edited by James W. Hipp, contributing editor George Garrett (1995)

1995 edited by James W. Hipp, contributing editor George Garrett (1996)

1996 edited by Samuel W. Bruce and L. Kay Webster, contributing editor George Garrett (1997)

1997 edited by Matthew J. Bruccoli and George Garrett, with the assistance of L. Kay Webster (1998)

1998 edited by Matthew J. Bruccoli, contributing editor George Garrett, with the assistance of D. W. Thomas (1999)

1999 edited by Matthew J. Bruccoli, contributing editor George Garrett, with the assistance of D. W. Thomas (2000)

2000 edited by Matthew J. Bruccoli, contributing editor George Garrett, with the assistance of George Parker Anderson (2001)

Concise Series

Concise Dictionary of American Literary Biography, 7 volumes (1988-1999): *The New Consciousness, 1941-1968; Colonization to the American Renaissance, 1640-1865; Realism, Naturalism, and Local Color, 1865-1917; The Twenties, 1917-1929; The Age of Maturity, 1929-1941; Broadening Views, 1968-1988; Supplement: Modern Writers, 1900-1998.*

Concise Dictionary of British Literary Biography, 8 volumes (1991-1992): *Writers of the Middle Ages and Renaissance Before 1660; Writers of the Restoration and Eighteenth Century, 1660-1789; Writers of the Romantic Period, 1789-1832; Victorian Writers, 1832-1890; Late-Victorian and Edwardian Writers, 1890-1914; Modern Writers, 1914-1945; Writers After World War II, 1945-1960; Contemporary Writers, 1960 to Present.*

Concise Dictionary of World Literary Biography, 10 volumes projected (1999-   ): *Ancient Greek and Roman Writers; German Writers; African, Caribbean, and Latin American Writers; South Slavic and Eastern European Writers.*

Dictionary of Literary Biography® • Volume Two Hundred Fifty-Four

The House of Putnam, 1837–1872

A Documentary Volume

Dictionary of Literary Biography® • Volume Two Hundred Fifty-Four

The House of Putnam, 1837–1872
A Documentary Volume

Edited by
Ezra Greenspan
University of South Carolina

A Bruccoli Clark Layman Book
The Gale Group
Detroit • San Francisco • London • Boston • Woodbridge, Conn.

Library of Congress Cataloging-in-Publication Data

The house of Putnam, 1837–1872: a documentary volume / edited by Ezra Greenspan.
    p. cm.–(Dictionary of literary biography; v. 254)
"A Bruccoli Clark Layman book."
Includes bibliographical references and index.
ISBN 0-7876-5248-2 (alk. paper)
1. Putnam, George Palmer, 1814–1872. 2. G. P. Putnam & Sons–History. 3. Putnam, George Palmer, 1814–1872–Bibliography. 4. G. P. Putnam & Sons–Bibliography. 5. Publishers and publishing–United States–Biography. 6. Publishers and publishing–United States–History–19th century. 7. Authors and publishers–United States–History–19th century. I. Greenspan, Ezra. II. Series.

Z473.P95 H68 2001
070.5'092–dc21   2001053223

10 9 8 7 6 5 4 3 2 1

To Barbara and LeRoy Greenspan: Builders of Our House

Contents

Plan of the Series. xv

Preface. xvii

Acknowledgments. xix

George Palmer Putnam: A Biographical Sketch 3

    John Francis letter to Putnam, 13 September 1855

    Obituary, *Publishers' and Stationers' Weekly Trade Circular,*
        26 December 1872

    Announcement, *Publishers' and Stationers' Weekly Trade Circular,*
        25 January 1872

    Resolution, *The Publishers' Weekly,* 16 January 1873

Historical Overview of the House of Putnam 13

Transatlantic Business. 13

    Lewis Gaylord Clark, excerpt from "Editor's Table,"
        Knickerbocker Magazine, March 1837

    Wiley and Putnam & South Carolina College

        Wiley and Putnam letter to Reverend Robert Henry,
            17 February 1845

        Wiley and Putnam letter to Reverend Henry,
            22 July 1845

    Putnam Trade Catalogues

    Putnam letter to Henry Stevens, 1 August 1846

A New Beginning 20

    A London Alliance

        Announcement, *The Publishers' Circular,* 15 December 1848

    Publishing The Crystal Palace

        Putnam letter to Theodore Sedgwick, 13 November 1852

    Announcement, *New-York Tribune,* 15 July 1853

    Advertisement, *The New York Times,* 10 May 1854

Financial Difficulties and Recovery. 30

    Charles Sedgwick letter to Putnam, 12 December 1855

A Family Business. 32

    The End of an Era

        Announcement, *The Publishers' Weekly,* 2 January 1873

Illustrated Chronology 35

>   Notice, *Knickerbocker Magazine,* November 1838

Selected Correspondence 55

James Lenox 55

>   Putnam letter to Lenox, 4 January 1847
>   Putnam letter to Lenox, 19 February 1847
>   Putnam letter to Lenox, 18 May 1847

Asa Gray 57

>   Putnam letter to Gray, 28 February 1844
>   Putnam letter to Gray, 26 January 1846
>   Putnam letter to Gray, 3 May 1848
>   Putnam letter to Gray, 29 September 1851
>   Putnam letter to Gray, 14 March 1854
>   Putnam letter to Gray, 16 July 1857
>   Putnam letter to Gray, 8 August 1857

James Fenimore Cooper 60

>   Putnam letter to Cooper, 3 March 1849
>   Memorandum of Agreement between Cooper and Putnam,
>   March 1849
>   Putnam letter to Cooper, April 1849
>   Putnam letter to Cooper, 20 April 1849
>   Putnam letter to Cooper, 27 July 1849
>   Bentley letter to Putnam, 22 December 1849
>   Putnam letter to Cooper, 14 February 1850
>   Putnam letter to Cooper, 19 February 1850
>   Putnam letter to Cooper, 28 March 1850
>   Putnam letter to Cooper, 17 April 1850
>   Putnam letter to Cooper, 5 June 1850
>   Putnam letter to Cooper, 22 November 1850
>   Putnam letter to Cooper, 13 January 1851
>   Putnam letter to Cooper, 21 January 1851
>   Putnam letter to Cooper; 29 March 1851
>   Putnam letter to Cooper, 5 May 1851
>   Putnam letter to Cooper, 9 August 1851
>   Putnam letter to Susan Fenimore Cooper,
>   2 December 1851

Harper and Brothers 67

>   Putnam letter to Harper & Brothers, 29 January 1851
>   Harper & Brothers letter to Putnam, 30 January 1851
>   Putnam letter to Harper & Brothers, 30 January 1851
>   Harper & Brothers letter to Putnam, 24 February 1851
>   Review, *Holden's Dollar Magazine,* April 1851
>   Putnam letter to Harper & Brothers, 14 December 1853

Ticknor and Fields 70

   William D. Ticknor letter to Putnam, 2 January 1849
   Ticknor, Reed, and Fields letter to Putnam, 25 October 1851
   James T. Fields letter to Putnam, 12 November 1852
   Ticknor letter to Putnam, 16 December 1852
   Ticknor and Fields letter to Putnam, 30 March 1854
   Ticknor letter to Putnam, 12 January 1858
   Ticknor and Fields letter to Putnam, 15 January 1858

Executives and Editors Associated with the House of Putnam 73

John Wiley 73

   Wiley letter to Library Committee, 22 June 1855

Evert A. Duyckinck. 74

   Edgar Allan Poe, excerpt from "The Literati of New York City,"
      Godey's Lady's Book, July 1846
   Putnam letter to Duyckinck, 10 November 1854

Orville Roorbach. 75

   Notice, *The Literary World,* 25 November 1848
   Introduction, *Bibliotheca Americana,* March 1849

Frederick Saunders 78

   Sketch, *The Literary World,* 5 January 1850

Charles Frederick Briggs 82

   Poe, excerpt from "The Literati of New York City,"–No. 1
      Godey's Lady Book, June 1846

Parke Godwin 83

   Godwin letter to Putnam, summer 1854
   Godwin letter to Putnam, summer 1854
   Godwin letter to Putnam, summer 1854
   Godwin letter to Putnam, 26 June 1854

George William Curtis 85

   Curtis letter to Putnam, 12 July 1854
   Curtis letter to Putnam, 3 July 1855
   Frederick S. Cozzens letter to Putnam, 8 July 1856

Frederic Beecher Perkins. 87

   Perkins, excerpt from "Reading and Courses of Reading,"
      The Best Reading

George Haven Putnam 88

   Putnam letter to Bayard Taylor, 31 December 1872
   Putnam letter to Taylor, 4 February 1873
   Putnam, excerpt from *Memories of a Publisher, 1865–1915*

Putnam Authors 91

Edgar Allan Poe 91

    George Haven Putnam, excerpt from *A Memoir*
        of George Palmer Putnam, 1903

Andrew Jackson Downing. 93

    Downing letter to Putnam, 28 March 1850

Caroline M. Kirkland 94

    Putnam letter to Kirkland, 15 August 1852

Herman Melville 95

    Fitz-James O'Brien, excerpt from *Putnam's Monthly,*
        February 1853

William Gilmore Simms 101

    Lewis Gaylord Clark (?), excerpt from *Knickerbocker Magazine,*
        October 1845

    Walt Whitman, excerpt from *Brooklyn Daily Eagle,*
        9 March 1846

Thomas Carlyle 102

    Whitman, excerpt from *Brooklyn Daily Eagle,*
        31 January 1846

    Wiley and Putnam, excerpt from *Wiley & Putnam's*
        Literary News-Letter, October 1846

    Carlyle letter to E. P. Clark, 18 March 1847

Washington Irving 106

    George Innes letter to Putnam, 30 July 1849

    Announcement, *The Literary World,* 10 June 1848

    Excerpt from *The Literary World,* 2 September 1848

    Irving letter to Charles R. Leslie, 19 October 1848

    Robert Cooke letter to Putnam, 29 August 1849

    Irving letter to Putnam, 27 December 1852

    Notice, *American Literary Gazette and Publishers' Circular,*
        2 November 1863

    Announcement, *American Literary Gazette and Publishers' Circular,*
        June 1871

James Fenimore Cooper 113

    Cooper, excerpt from introduction to *The Pioneers* (1851)

    Review, *The Literary World,* 5 May 1849

    Francis Parkman, excerpt from *The North American Review,*
        January 1852

Catharine Maria Sedgwick 121

    Review, *The Literary World,* 6 October 1849

    Sedgwick letter to Putnam, 20 November 1856

John Pendleton Kennedy. 124

    Kennedy letter to Putnam, 20 December 1851

Bayard Taylor...125

    Taylor letter to Putnam, 18 October 1862

    Taylor letter to Donald Grant Mitchell, 14 February 1865

Asa Gray...128

    Review, *Wiley and Putnam's Literary News-Letter,* August 1845

George Palmer Putnam...129

    Clark, review, *Knickerbocker Magazine,* February 1838

    Review, *American Monthly Magazine,* April 1838

    Putnam letter to *The New York Times,* undated

Henry Tuckerman..132

    Notice, *Publishers' and Stationers' Weekly Trade Circular,*
        18 January 1872

Susan Warner..133

    Warner, journal entry, 25 September 1850

    Warner letter to Putnam, 27 December 1870

Fredrika Bremer..134

    Bremer, dedication, *Hertha* (1856)

Susan Fenimore Cooper...136

    Notice, *The Literary World,* 23 November 1850

Notable Putnam Publications......................................137

The Narrative of Arthur Gordon Pym (Edgar Allan Poe, 1838)..............137

    Review, *Court Gazette,* 13 October 1838

Letters and Notes on the Manners, Customs, and Condition
    of the North American Indians (George Catlin, 1842).................138

Tales (Poe, 1845)..139

    Margaret Fuller, review, *New-York Tribune,* 11 July 1845

    Poe, reaction to Fuller remarks, *The Broadway Journal,*
        4 October 1845

    Review, *Graham's Magazine,* September 1845

The Raven and Other Poems (Poe, 1845)...............................140

    Poe, preface to *The Raven and Other Poems* (1845)

    Fuller, review, *New-York Tribune,* 26 November 1845

Typee (Herman Melville, 1846).......................................142

    Gansevoort Melville letter to Herman Melville, 3 April 1846

    Nathaniel Hawthorne, notice, *Salem Advertiser,* 25 March 1846

    Fuller, review, *New-York Tribune,* 4 April 1846

    Walt Whitman, remark, *Brooklyn Daily Eagle,* 15 April 1846

Mosses from an Old Manse (Hawthorne, 1846)........................145

    Duyckinck letter to Hawthorne, 21 March 1845

    Melville, essay, *The Literary World,* 17 and 24 August 1850

Papers on Literature and Art (Fuller, 1846) 155

    Fuller letter to Evert Duyckinck, 30 October 1846

    Duyckinck, notice, *Wiley and Putnam's Literary News-Letter,*
        August 1846

    Putnam, notice, *Wiley and Putnam's Literary News-Letter,*
        November 1846

    Frederick Henry Hedge (?), review, *Christian Examiner,* January 1847

Views A-foot (Bayard Taylor, 1846) 157

    Taylor letter to John B. Phillips, 16 October 1846

    Review, *Knickerbocker Magazine,* January 1847

Modern Painters (John Ruskin, 1847) 159

    Review, *The Literary World,* 24 July 1847

Eureka: A Prose Poem (Poe, 1848) 161

    Review, *The Literary World,* 29 July 1848

A Fable for Critics (James Russell Lowell, 1848) 164

    Lowell letter to Charles Frederick Briggs, 12 May 1848

    Briggs letter to Lowell, 25 October 1848

Poole's Index to Periodical Literature (William Frederick Poole, 1848) 165

    Poole, notice, *The Literary World,* 29 April 1848

The California and Oregon Trail (Francis Parkman, 1849) 167

    Putnam letter to Parkman, 30 March 1849

    Parkman letter to Putnam, 8 September 1849

    Putnam letter to Parkman, 3 January 1850

    Putnam letter to Parkman, 26 November 1851

    Putnam letter to Parkman, 12 March 1870

Nineveh and Its Remains (Austen Henry Layard, 1849) 169

    Edward Robinson letter to Putnam, *The Literary World,*
        17 March 1849

The Wide, Wide World (Susan Warner, 1850) 172

Queechy (Warner, 1852) 172

    Review, *New-York Tribune,* 1 May 1852

    Review, *Southern Literary Messenger,* April 1854

Homes of American Authors (1853) 175

    George William Curtis letter to Putnam, 1852

    Hammat Billings letter to Putnam, 2 July 1852

    Caroline Kirkland letter to Putnam, 21 August 1852

    Review, *Southern Literary Messenger,* December 1852

    Review, *Graham's Magazine,* May 1853

Homes of American Statesmen (1854) 178

    Putnam letter to Nathaniel Parker Willis, 28 February 1853

    Putnam, introduction to *Homes of American Statesmen*

Life of George Washington (Washington Irving, 1855–1859) 179

Review, *Norton's Literary Gazette and Publishers' Circular,*
1 June 1855

*Personal Narrative of a Pilgrimage to El-Medinah
and Meccah* (Richard Burton, 1856) 181

Taylor, introduction to *Personal Narrative of a Pilgrimage
to El-Medinah and Meccah* (1856)

Review, *Putnam's Monthly,* November 1856

Life and Letters of Washington Irving (Pierre Irving, 1862–1864) 184

Review, *Putnam's Magazine,* April 1870

Book of the Artists. American Artistic Life (Henry Tuckerman, 1867) 185

Notice, *New-York Tribune,* 12 December 1867

Putnam Series 186

Wiley and Putnam's Library of Choice Reading (1845–1847) 186

Announcement, *New York Evening Post,* 22 March 1845
Review, *Broadway Journal,* 22 March 1845
Excerpt from review, *Democratic Review,* April 1845
Putnam letter to Evert Duyckinck, 19 May 1845
Review of series, *Democratic Review,* March 1847

Wiley and Putnam Library of American Books (1845–1847) 193

Review, *New York Morning News,* 21 June 1845
Evert Duyckinck letter to Ralph Waldo Emerson,
13 August 1845
Notice, *Democratic Review,* October 1845
Putnam, notice, *Wiley and Putnam's Literary News-Letter,*
October 1845
Walt Whitman, notice, *Brooklyn Daily Eagle,* 21 February 1846

Wiley and Putnam's Foreign Library (1846–1847) 197

Putnam, notice, *The Literary World,* 1 June 1850

Putnam's Railway Classics (1851–1860s) 199

Putnam's Semi-Monthly Library (1852–1854) 200

Putnam's Home Cyclopedia (1852–1853) 201

Rebellion Record (1861–1868) 203

Putnam, note, *Putnam's Magazine,* undated
Susan Warner letter to Putnam, 10 October 1862
Notice, *Putnam's Magazine,* January 1868

Putnam Magazines 204

Wiley and Putnam's Literary News-Letter and Monthly Register
and *The Literary World.* 204

Wiley and Putnam letter to Evert Duyckinck, 21 April 1847
Evert Duyckinck letter to George A. Duyckinck, 14 June 1847

Putnam's Monthly (January 1851–April 1853) 205

    Ralph Waldo Emerson letter to *Putnam's Monthly,* 11 October 1852

    Henry James Sr. letter to *Putnam's Monthly,* 5 November 1852

    Announcement, *Graham's Magazine,* February 1853

    Charles Frederick Briggs letter to *Putnam's Monthly,* 20 February 1853

    Announcement, *Putnam's Monthly,* June 1852

    Notice, *Washington National Era,* 18 August 1853

    James Russell Lowell letter to Briggs, September 1853

    Notice, *Putnam's Monthly,* December 1853

    Putnam letter to William Cullen Bryant, 28 December 1853

    Notice, *Southern Literary Messenger,* April 1854

    Putnam letter to Herman Melville, 13 May 1854

    Notice, *Putnam's Monthly,* undated

    Parke Godwin, "Our Parties and Politics," *Putnam's Monthly,*
        September 1854

    George Sumner letter to Putnam, undated

    James Avis Bartley letter to Putnam, 14 September 1854

    Notice, *Putnam's Monthly,* 1 December 1854

    Notice, *Liberator,* 8 December 1854

    George William Curtis letter to Henry Wadsworth Longfellow,
        8 March 1855

Putnam's Magazine (January 1868–November 1870) .229

    Briggs, notice, *Putnam's Magazine,* undated

    Curtis letter to Briggs, January 1868

    Briggs, excerpt from editorial, *Putnam's Magazine,* January 1868

    Notice, *Putnam's Magazine,* December 1868

    Notice, *Putnam's Magazine,* November 1870

George Palmer Putnam's Writings on the Profession of Publishing 242

A Few Preliminary Notes and Statistics 242

    Putnam, "A Few Preliminary Notes and Statistics,"
        American Book Circular, 1843

    Putnam letter to George Bancroft, 23 August 1843

    George Sumner letter to Putnam, 18 December 1843

Recollections of Irving 251

    James T. Fields letter to Putnam, 29 September 1860

    "Letter from New York," *Boston Post,* 30 October 1860

    Putnam, "Recollections of Irving," *Atlantic Monthly,* November 1860

Rough Notes of Thirty Years in the Trade 261

    Putnam, "Rough Notes of Thirty Years in the Trade,"
        American Publishers' Circular and Literary Gazette,
        15 July, 1 August, and 15 August 1863

Rough Notes of the English Book-Trade 272

    Putnam, "Rough Notes of the English Book-Trade,"
        American Publishers' Circular and Literary Gazette, 15 October 1863

Some Things in London and Paris 276

   Putnam, "Some Things in London and Paris–1839–1869,"
      Putnam's Magazine, June 1869

Leaves from a Publisher's Letter-Book 289

   Putnam, "Leaves from a Publisher's Letter-Book," *Putnam's Magazine,*
      October–December 1869

George Palmer Putnam's Public Statements 310

Dispute on International Copyright 310

   Putnam letter to A. Hart, *Norton's Literary Gazette*
      and Publishers' Circular, 15 April 1853

   Hart's letter to Putnam in reply, *Norton's Literary Gazette*
      and Publishers' Circular, 15 June 1853

Crystal Palace Speech 318

   Putnam, "Intoductory Statistical Sketch/Regular Toasts," *American*
      Publishers' Circular and Literary Gazette, 29 September 1855

Speech at Boston Harbor. 324

   Putnam, "The Boston Book Trade Sale," from unknown
      Boston newspaper, August 1859

Eulogy for Charles Scribner 325

   Putnam, "In Memoriam," *Scribner's Monthly,* November 1871

Nineteenth-Century Assessments of Putnam and His Company 328

Sketches of the Publishers Series 328

   Putnam, "Sketches of the Publishers. George P. Putnam,"
      The Round Table, 10, 17 February 1866

Notes on Books and Booksellers 333

   William Cullen Bryant, notice, *American Literary Gazette*
      and Publishers' Circular, 1 January 1868

A Daughter's Appreciation 334

   Mary Putnam Jacobi, "George P. Putnam: An Appreciation,"
      from *A Memoir of George Palmer Putnam,* January 1873

James C. Derby on Putnam. 338

   Derby, "George Palmer Putnam," from
      Fifty Years among Authors, Books and Publishers, 1884

Books for Further Reading 347

Cumulative Index 349

Plan of the Series

The advisory board, the editors, and the publisher of the *Dictionary of Literary Biography* are joined in endorsing Mark Twain's declaration. The literature of a nation provides an inexhaustible resource of permanent worth. Our purpose is to make literature and its creators better understood and more accessible to students and the reading public, while satisfying the needs of teachers and researchers.

To meet these requirements, *literary biography* has been construed in terms of the author's achievement. The most important thing about a writer is his writing. Accordingly, the entries in *DLB* are career biographies, tracing the development of the author's canon and the evolution of his reputation.

The purpose of *DLB* is not only to provide reliable information in a usable format but also to place the figures in the larger perspective of literary history and to offer appraisals of their accomplishments by qualified scholars.

The publication plan for *DLB* resulted from two years of preparation. The project was proposed to Bruccoli Clark by Frederick G. Ruffner, president of the Gale Research Company, in November 1975. After specimen entries were prepared and typeset, an advisory board was formed to refine the entry format and develop the series rationale. In meetings held during 1976, the publisher, series editors, and advisory board approved the scheme for a comprehensive biographical dictionary of persons who contributed to literature. Editorial work on the first volume began in January 1977, and it was published in 1978. In order to make *DLB* more than a dictionary and to compile volumes that individually have claim to status as literary history, it was decided to organize volumes by topic, period, or

genre. Each of these freestanding volumes provides a biographical-bibliographical guide and overview for a particular area of literature. We are convinced that this organization—as opposed to a single alphabet method—constitutes a valuable innovation in the presentation of reference material. The volume plan necessarily requires many decisions for the placement and treatment of authors. Certain figures will be included in separate volumes, but with different entries emphasizing the aspect of his career appropriate to each volume. Ernest Hemingway, for example, is represented in *American Writers in Paris, 1920–1939* by an entry focusing on his expatriate apprenticeship; he is also in *American Novelists, 1910–1945* with an entry surveying his entire career, as well as in *American Short-Story Writers, 1910–1945, Second Series* with an entry concentrating on his short fiction. Each volume includes a cumulative index of the subject authors and articles.

Since 1981 the series has been further augmented by the *DLB Yearbooks,* which update published entries, add new entries to keep the *DLB* current with contemporary activity, and provide articles on literary history. There have also been nineteen *DLB Documentary Series* volumes which provide illustrations, facsimiles, and biographical and critical source materials for figures, works, or groups judged to have particular interest for students. In 1999 the *Documentary Series* was incorporated into the *DLB* volume numbering system beginning with *DLB 210: Ernest Hemingway.*

We define literature as the *intellectual commerce of a nation:* not merely as belles lettres but as that ample and complex process by which ideas are generated, shaped, and transmitted. *DLB* entries are not limited to "creative writers" but extend to other figures who in their time and in their way influenced the mind of a people. Thus the series encompasses historians, journalists, publishers, book collectors, and screenwriters. By this means readers of *DLB* may be aided to perceive literature not as cult scripture in the keeping of intellectual high priests but firmly positioned at the center of a nation's life.

DLB includes the major writers appropriate to each volume and those standing in the ranks behind them. Scholarly and critical counsel has been sought in deciding which minor figures to include and how full their entries should be. Wherever possible, useful references are made to figures who do not warrant separate entries.

Each *DLB* volume has an expert volume editor responsible for planning the volume, selecting the figures for inclusion, and assigning the entries. Volume editors are also responsible for preparing, where appropriate, appendices surveying the major periodicals and literary and intellectual movements for their volumes, as well as lists of further readings. Work on the series as a whole is coordinated at the Bruccoli Clark Layman editorial center in Columbia, South Carolina, where the editorial staff is responsible for accuracy and utility of the published volumes.

One feature that distinguishes *DLB* is the illustration policy—its concern with the iconography of literature. Just as an author is influenced by his surroundings, so is the reader's understanding of the author enhanced by a knowledge of his environment. Therefore *DLB* volumes include not only drawings, paintings, and photographs of authors, often depicting them at various stages in their careers, but also illustrations of their families and places where they lived. Title pages are regularly reproduced in facsimile along with dust jackets for modern authors. The dust jackets are a special feature of *DLB* because they often document better than anything else the way in which an author's work was perceived in its own time. Specimens of the writers' manuscripts and letters are included when feasible.

Samuel Johnson rightly decreed that "The chief glory of every people arises from its authors." The purpose of the *Dictionary of Literary Biography* is to compile literary history in the surest way available to us—by accurate and comprehensive treatment of the lives and work of those who contributed to it.

The *DLB* Advisory Board

Preface

Dictionary of Literary Biography 254: The House of Putnam, 1837–1872 tells the interrelated story of one of the great publishing firms of nineteenth-century America and of one of the founding figures of modern American publishing. It adopts this dual-focused mode of presentation for two reasons: (1) George Palmer Putnam played a central role not only in founding and running his publishing house but also in organizing book publishers into a more centralized industry with a more self-conscious sense of its calling, and (2) Putnam concentrated the publishing activities of his house around a commitment to patronizing American authorship and improving the standards (in all senses) of American bookmaking.

DLB 254: The House of Putnam, 1837–1872 not only tells the story but also documents and illustrates it, drawing on the rich archives of Putnam printed and illustrated materials concentrated at Princeton University Library, the Library of Congress, the New York Public Library, and smaller collections of Putnam materials scattered around the country, as well as on the collections of authors and editors associated with the Putnam house and family. It also draws heavily for its documentation on the extensive print record made possible by contemporaneous newspaper and magazine journalism, since the rapid expansion of book publishing was directly interconnected to that of newspaper and magazine publishing. By no coincidence, two of the most important members of Putnam's professional circle were William Cullen Bryant and Horace Greeley, editors, respectively, of the *New York Evening Post* and the *New York Tribune*.

Like volumes 13, 16, and 17 in the DLB documentary series that cover the House of Scribner from 1846 to 1984, *DLB 254: The House of Putnam, 1837–1872* combines publishing history, biography, and family history. No less than the House of Scribner, the House of Putnam was a family-owned-and-run company well into the twentieth century. Indeed, G. P. Putnam became G. P. Putnam and Sons in 1870, then G. P. Putnam's Sons immediately after the founder's death in 1872. For that matter, the practice was much the same among many of the other great nineteenth-century houses, including the houses of Appleton, of Harper, and of Lippincott, as sons followed fathers into the company offices in a pattern that replicated itself in many industries during this early era of expansive capitalism.

The time span that is the focus of this volume corresponds to the publishing career of George Palmer Putnam. It begins with the partnership of Wiley and Putnam, founded in 1837 when Putnam joined with the young New York publisher John Wiley to form an aggressive new bookselling and publishing house, which thrived until Putnam went off on his own in 1848 to form G. P. Putnam. The decision to include that initial decade in *The House of Putnam* was a simple one because Putnam recycled much of the Wiley and Putnam publishing list in the initial list of G. P. Putnam.

The organization of the volume is designed to highlight the biography of the firm, its founder, chief authors and editors, major works, important series, and leading in-house magazines. The volume begins with illustrated synopses of the life of the publisher and of the firm, "George Palmer Putnam: A Biographical Sketch" and "Historical Overview of the House of Putnam," followed by a time line of the firm's history, "Illustrated Chronology," which provides a detailed, year-by-year time line of G. P. Putnam. The next sections present samples of Putnam's correspondence with authors, collectors, and publishers ("Selected Correspondence") and brief synopses of the men who were associated with the firm, "Executives and Editors Associated with The House of Putnam." Longer sections, "Putnam Authors" and "Notable Putnam Publications," focus on the chief authors handled by the firm and on some of the significant works published by it—each author and work illustrated and/or documented. Each of these two sections is organized chronologically—the works, by date of publication by G. P. Putnam; the authors, by date of first publication by G. P. Putnam. There follow sections on the firm's libraries, "Putnam Series," and on its major magazines, "Putnam Magazines," which played an important role not only in the affairs of the house but also in the development of mid-century American letters. The volume concludes with "George Palmer Putnam's Writings on the Profession of Publishing," "George Palmer Putnam's Public Statements," and a final section, "Nineteenth-Century Assessments of Putnam and His Company," which highlights his and his firm's centrality in the expansion and professionalization of the American publishing industry.

Acknowledgments

This book was produced by Bruccoli Clark Layman, Inc. Karen L. Rood is senior editor. George Parker Anderson was the in-house editor.

Production manager is Philip B. Dematteis.

Administrative support was provided by Ann M. Cheschi, Amber L. Coker, and Angi Pleasant.

Accountant is Ann-Marie Holland.

Copyediting supervisor is Sally R. Evans. The copyediting staff includes Phyllis A. Avant, Brenda Carol Blanton, Worthy B. Evans, William Tobias Mathes, Rebecca Mayo, and Elizabeth Jo Ann Sumner. Freelance copyeditor is Brenda Cabra.

Editorial associates are Michael S. Allen, Michael S. Martin, and Pamela A. Warren.

Database manager is José A. Juarez.

Layout and graphics supervisor is Janet E. Hill. The graphics staff includes Karla Corley Brown and Zoe R. Cook.

Office manager is Kathy Lawler Merlette.

Photography supervisor is Paul Talbot. Photography editor is Scott Nemzek.

Digital photographic copy work was performed by Joseph M. Bruccoli.

The SGML staff includes Jaime All, Frank Graham, Linda Dalton Mullinax, Jason Paddock, and Alex Snead.

Systems manager is Marie L. Parker.

Typesetting supervisor is Kathleen M. Flanagan. The typesetting staff includes Jaime All, Patricia Marie Flanagan, Mark J. McEwan, and Pamela D. Norton. Freelance typesetter is Wanda Adams.

Walter W. Ross did library research. He was assisted by Jaime All, Steven Gross, and the following librarians at the Thomas Cooper Library of the University of South Carolina: circulation department head Tucker Taylor; reference department head Virginia W. Weathers; Brette Barclay, Marilee Birchfield, Paul Cammarata, Gary Geer, Michael Macan, Tom Marcil, Rose Marshall, and Sharon Verba; interlibrary loan department head John Brunswick; and interlibrary loan staff Robert Arndt, Hayden Battle, Barry Bull, Jo Cottingham, Marna Hostetler, Marieum McClary, Erika Peake, and Nelson Rivera.

I first thank my colleagues at the University of South Carolina. I thank Mila Tasseva-Kurktchieva for her expertise and patience in scanning the illustrations for this volume. I thank Professor Patrick Scott, Associate University Librarian for Special Collections at the Thomas Cooper Library of the University of South Carolina, for his expert help and generosity in locating materials, making them available, and opening up the facilities of his division to me. His cooperation greatly expedited the completion of this project. Joel Myerson assisted me in locating what otherwise might have been hard-to-find pictures by digging into his own collections. I also thank my research assistants, Tracy Bealer and Brian Harmon, for their able assistance with photocopying and typing documents.

I thank the following institutions for permission to publish manuscript materials and/or illustrations in their collections: American Antiquarian Society; Bowdoin College; Cornell University; Duke University Archives; Free Library of Philadelphia; Gray Herbarium Archives, University Archives, and Houghton Library, Harvard University; Library of Congress; Massachusetts Historical Society; Morristown National Historical Park, New Jersey; New York Public Library; New York Society Library; Pierpont Morgan Library; Princeton University; Union College, New York; University of California, Los Angeles; University of South Carolina Archives; University of Vermont; University of Virginia; Wesleyan University; and Yale University Archives. I also acknowledge the permission of Mr. Henry Cooper to reproduce the G. P. Putnam–James Fenimore Cooper correspondence in this volume.

The House of Putnam, 1837–1872

A Documentary Volume

Dictionary of Literary Biography

George Palmer Putnam: A Biographical Sketch

(7 February 1814 – 20 December 1872)

See also the Putnam entries in *DLB 3: Antebellum Writers in New York and the South; DLB 79: American Magazine Journalists, 1850–1900;* and *DLB 250: Antebellum Writers in New York.*

To speak about the House of Putnam is in effect to speak about its founder, George Palmer Putnam. Putnam simultaneously oversaw the operation of his publishing house and served as one of the driving forces behind the emergence of modern publishing in the United States.

He descended on his father's side from a line of Yankee Putnams, who had settled first in Salem, Massachusetts, in the mid seventeenth century, then moved in the early eighteenth century to the recently incorporated town of North Reading. His mother's family, the Palmers, arrived in Massachusetts a century after the Putnams. The earliest was his great-grandfather, General Joseph Palmer, who settled in Quincy and prospered but lost his fortune as a result of unreturned loans made to the nation during the Revolutionary War.

More immediately, his father, Henry, was a Harvard-educated lawyer; his mother, Catherine Hunt Palmer, was a one-time student in the Young Ladies' Academy of Susanna Rowson (best known today as author of *Charlotte Temple,* 1791). They married outside Boston in 1807 and soon afterward moved to the small college town of Brunswick, Maine, where their five children—two boys and three girls—were born (George was the fourth born and the only son to survive childhood). The mainstay of the family was Catherine, who operated a well-regarded private school out of the family house; Henry, a shadowy figure in the family annals, worked only occasionally in his profession and probably not consistently in any other. In 1820 he published a small local history, *A Description of Brunswick, (Maine)* with

The earliest known likeness of George Palmer Putnam
(Library of Congress)

the local printer, Joseph Griffin, at whose shop his son might have gotten his first introduction to printing. Young Putnam was not long for Brunswick, however; the family sent him off in 1825 to do an apprenticeship at the Boston carpet store of his father's brother-in-law, John Gulliver. That arrangement proved short-lived; Putnam felt stymied by the mundane work and managed to get himself released from its conditions in 1829, at which time he left

Married,

On Thursday evening, March 11, by Rev. Mr. Pease, Mr. T. W. Reeve and Miss Julia Jane, only daughter of Francis Ferry, all of this city.

On Sunday evening, March 14, by Rev. Mr. Higby, Mr. SMITH A. PARKES and Miss HARRIET MATILDA, youngest daughter of Samuel Maverick, Esq.

On Saturday morning, March 13, by Rev. Orville Dewey, Mr. Geo. Palmer Putnam and Miss Victorine Haven, all of this city.

Announcement of Putnam's marriage in New World *(quarto ed. 2, 20 March 1841, p. 192). Putnam and his wife entertained often in their modest home in London; their guests included Washington Irving, Giuseppe Mazzini, and Louis Napoleon (later Napoleon III).*

the Gullivers and reunited with his mother, who by then was living in New York City.

Putnam arrived in the city with little formal education and no professional orientation but quickly found work as a clerk at the bookstore of George Bleecker on lower Broadway, near Maiden Lane. There the fifteen-year-old Putnam learned the rudiments of the bookselling business and boarded above the store with his employer. He moved several years later to a better situation as general clerk in the larger bookstore of Jonathan Leavitt, located just a block up the avenue at the corner of John Street. During his years with Leavitt (1831–1836), Putnam quickly advanced from performing menial chores to carrying out serious responsibilities, such as copying letters, taking inventory, and—eventually—compiling book catalogues. He also took care of his own growing intellectual needs by educating himself via an intensive course of reading, much of it provided by books from the Mercantile Library, which he frequently patronized until late at night after work.

Talented and ambitious, Putnam conceived and executed two serious literary projects during his spare time at Leavitt's. The first was a handy reference manual he called *Chronology; or, An Introduction and Index to Universal History, Biography, and Useful Knowledge* and persuaded his employer to publish. Popular from the start, it proved a steady seller and advanced through successive printings and updated editions from the time of its initial publication in 1833 through the end of the century. The other was his inception of the first publishers' trade journal in the United States, the *Booksellers' Advertiser and Monthly Register of New Publications*, which he began in January 1834 and carried on as a one-person operation before abandoning the demanding project at year's end.

He had no sooner resumed the *Booksellers' Advertiser* in winter 1836 than he suspended it again—this time as a result of an enticing offer to join the firm of Wiley and Long as a junior partner. Operating from a storefront at 161 Broadway, the partners engaged in the sale of books in both the domestic and international markets, as well as in general publishing. Their desire to gain an advantage in the growing transatlantic traffic in books and magazines led them within weeks of Putnam's joining the firm to send him to Europe on a six-month reconnaissance tour, during which he made the acquaintance of the trade throughout Great Britain and the Continent and made arrangements that gave his firm advantages in securing European works for sale and reprinting in New York.

When George Long retired in early 1837, the two remaining partners reorganized the firm as Wiley and Putnam, the name under which they were to do business for a decade. Buoyed by the results of Putnam's 1836 trip, the two men decided in 1838 to open a permanent office in London, the first overseas branch of an American publishing house and a sign that the American publishing sector was moving beyond its fledgling status. Running that operation became Putnam's chief responsibility, which he handled with considerable success.

Putnam made himself a fixture among London literary professionals of all sorts and his firm an established presence in the English booktrade during the decade of his residence. In spring 1841 Putnam returned briefly to the United States to marry sixteen-year-old Victorine Haven, a student in his mother's private school. During the course of their marriage the couple raised ten children, including three sons—George Haven, John Bishop, and Irving—who eventually succeeded their father in his business. In the final three years of his London assignment Putnam turned his

It is indispensably necessary for the security of the Holder that this Letter be kept apart from the Circular Notes.

LETTRE d' INDICATION.

London and Westminster Bank,

Londres, ce 19 Febr 1847.

Messieurs

Le Porteur de cette Lettre M. George Palmer Putnam pour le quel nous réclamons vos attentions, est muni de nos billets de Change Circulaires pour son Voyage. Nous vous prions de lui en fournir la valeur sur son double acquit au cours du Change à Usance sur notre Place, et sans déductions de frais d'après nos instructions.

Si la Ville ou il en touchera le montant n'a pas de Change direct sur Londres vous voudrez bien en combiner un avec la Place Cambiste la plus voisine.

Vous observerez que tout Agio sur espèces d'or, ou d'argent, et tous frais extraordinaires dans le Cas d'un remboursement indirect doivent être supportés par le Porteur, et ne peuvent être à notre charge.

Cette Lettre devant accompagner nos Billets Circulaires doit rester dans les mains de leur Porteur jusqu'à leur épuisement.

Nous avons l'honneur d'être

Messieurs

Vos très humbles et très

obéissants Serviteurs,

Villes	Correspondans	Villes	Correspondans
ABBEVILLE	M.M. Grdvelle & Cie.	ATHENES	M.M. F. Strong
AIX LA CHAPELLE	Oeder & Cie.	AUGSBOURG	P. de Stettin
AIX EN PROVENCE	Guitton Talamel	AVIGNON	Thomas Frerès
ALEPPO	Wm. & Robt. Black & Co.	AVRANCHES	F. Hullin
ALEXANDRIE	Briggs & Cie.		
AMIENS	Grimaux & Coderille		
AMSTERDAM	Hope & Cie.	BADEN BADEN	F. S. Meyer
ANCONE	G. Terni & Fils		S. Haber & Fils
ANVERS	Osy & Cie.	BAGNERES DE BIGORRE	Villeneuve & Cie.

A letter of passage Putnam used when he and his wife made a farewell tour of Europe before returning to the United States. One member of their traveling party in Italy was Margaret Fuller, a recent Wiley and Putnam author.

PASSENGERS ARRIVED

In packet-ship Margaret Evans, from London and Portsmouth—G P Putnam, lady, 3 children and 2 servants, Mrs Lawrence and 3 children, N York; A Haeiner, P Blesch, J Blesch, L Hagmann, F Hammel, lady and servant, Lieut Von Grone, of Germany; Mrs Gipps, Wm Pitt, Geo Dickinson, J Chaffey, Miss Ryan, Miss Clemants, of London; Capt Baldwin, British Navy; Dr Richardson, Toronto, U C; Mrs Harman, Miss Harman, Miss G Harman, of Jersey; H Goldberg, Ohio; J Punshon and lady, L Punshon, J Harris, Sidney Stook, Wm Bates, N Bates, Geo Dennington, Miss Naish, Miss Warner, H Fennenly, lady and 4 children, Mrs Loder, of England, and 300 in the steerage.

Announcement in the New York Tribune *(22 June 1847) of passengers arrived from England, including Putnam and his family*

"American Literary Agency" into an outpost of American progress by fitting out a room with the latest American books, magazines, and newspapers.

Putnam returned to the United States with his young family in June 1847 and took up his share of Wiley and Putnam's responsibilities at 161 Broadway. Within months of his return, however, he decided to leave Wiley and open his own publishing house. In the final weeks of the year he arranged to rent a storefront at 155 Broadway just down the street from Wiley, who had kept the old store, and opened his doors to business in March 1848 as G. P. Putnam. He remained in New York as head of the firm the rest of his life, except for one brief interlude during the Civil War when he took the important and lucrative position of federal tax collector for central Manhattan.

At the time of going into business on his own, Putnam was already one of the most highly regarded, broadly experienced members of the profession. During the remaining quarter century of his career, he exercised a bold, energetic advocacy not only of his own firm but also of the entire publishing profession that earned him the status of one of the great nineteenth-century publishers. He championed a variety of causes important to the trade: centralization of the publishing profession, patronization of American authors and letters, formation of institutions and organizations for promoting the arts and letters in the United States, and support for an international copyright treaty or legislation. To name just a few of the missions in which he played

a leading role—he established the International Copyright Association (1868) in his attempt to encourage Congress to enter into an international copyright agreement with England; he organized the New York Book Publishers' Association, the most ambitious trade organization to date in the United States, and sponsored under its auspices the great Crystal Palace authors-publishers dinner of 1855; and he chaired the committee that founded the Metropolitan

---

Among the dozens of responses sent to Putnam as organizer of the New York Crystal Palace authors-publishers dinner came this 13 September 1855 congratulatory note from John Francis, one of the city's most venerable literary figures and one of the few people to attend both the Crystal Palace celebration and its 1837 predecessor at New York's City Hotel, which Putnam also helped to organize.

The first time I had the pleasure of witnessing a general gathering of American Publishers, was at the Old City Hotel, Broadway, in 1802 . . . I believe, and under the auspices of the remarkable Mathew Carey. About thirty years after I was one of the large assembly brought together by the brothers Harper.

—George Palmer Putnam Collection, Manuscripts and Archives Division, The New York Public Library, Astor, Lenox and Tilden Foundations

N. Y. PUBLISHERS' ASSOCIATION.

FALL TRADE SALE.

NEW YORK, *June* 20, 1855.

DEAR SIRS,

We have this day arranged with MESSRS. BANGS, BROTHER & Co. to conduct our first Sale, under the regulations of the Association, as annexed, to commence on the 18th September.

Will you therefore please to forward your invoices immediately, or not later than the 10th July, addressed to G. P. PUTNAM, Secretary of the Publishers' Association.

You will observe by the list of contributors already received, and hereto annexed, that the Sale will embrace the invoices of a large proportion of all the Publishers in the United States. It is understood to be the general intention to contribute liberal numbers, and to make this Sale in every way attractive. We have reason to believe that the list of contributors will also include many who have not yet given their names, owing to the supposed uncertainty of our arrangements up to this day. The time now fixed—Sept. 18th—is generally regarded as the best, to secure a large attendance of the Trade from every part of the country, who will then be prepared to purchase liberally.

It is understood that Messrs. BANGS BRO. & Co. have advertised *their own Sale on the 4th Sept.* To prevent mistakes please observe that the SALE OF THE PUBLISHERS' ASSOCIATION will commence on the 18th; and invoices should be forwarded *as above specified*, so that their places may be drawn for, according to the 1st regulation. This will be done at the regular Meeting on the 11th July.

By order of the Executive Board,

G. P. PUTNAM, *Secretary.*

Circular announcing the 1855 trade sale, the first organized under the auspices of the New York Booksellers' Association, with a personal note from Putnam to publisher J. D. DeBow of New Orleans (Rare Book, Manuscript, and Special Collections Library, Duke University)

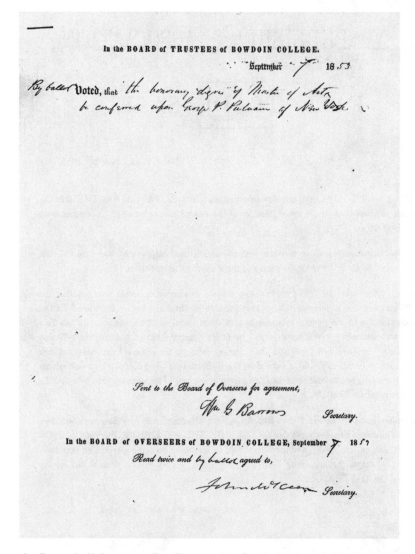

In the BOARD of TRUSTEES of BOWDOIN COLLEGE.

September 7 18 53.

Voted, that the honorary degree of Master of Arts be conferred upon George P. Putnam of New York.

Sent to the Board of Overseers for agreement,

Wm. C. Barrows   Secretary.

In the BOARD of OVERSEERS of BOWDOIN COLLEGE, September 7 18 5?

Read twice and by ballot agreed to,

John McKeen   Secretary.

An honorary degree presented to Putnam by his hometown college. Putnam, whose formal education ended in elementary school, took pride in receiving honorary degrees (Votes of the Boards [1.1.5], Special Collections and Archives, Bowdoin College Library).

Museum (1869–1870) and served as the first superintendent of the museum in the year of his death. In addition, Putnam often put his pen at the service of the profession, providing highly informative annals of American publishing on an infrequent basis; at one time he considered writing a full-fledged professional memoir, which unfortunately for posterity he abandoned long before completion.

All this time he was running G. P. Putnam. He did so with a spirit of optimism that matched his idealism. Despite his primary-school education, he was one of the most literate publishers of his generation and well read especially in the arts and letters, the areas in which his house concentrated its publications and became a national leader, especially in the antebellum years. He published many of the leading authors of his time in the fields of history, literature, art, science, travel, and religion; and he made a particular name for himself and his firm as a patron of works by American writers.

By the time of his sudden death in 1872, Putnam was widely regarded as one of the senior figures of the profession. That status was affirmed by the Publishers' Board of Trade, which in the days after his death adopted resolutions honoring his contribution to the profession as "a publisher whose life added to our calling and whose memory is among the best traditions" and commemorating his career as "one of great advantage to American letters." Although his positions on such core professional issues as international copyright, trade associations, and pricing were far less popular with his peers than he sometimes believed, he was an authoritative spokesman of his generation on the role of publishing as a force in the creation of modern American culture.

Putnam's death certificate. With his sudden death during the Christmas shopping season, the House of Putnam entered the new year with uncertain prospects (New York Department of Records and Information Services).

Putnam died at work in his office on 20 December 1872. Appearing six days later, his obituary in Publishers' and Stationers' Weekly Trade Circular *was more accurate in its broad strokes than in its details.*

George Palmer Putnam.

America sustains a sore loss in George P. Putnam, one of its most trusty representative men, but no man had ever better earned, by a long, earnest, Christian, effective life, that promotion from this world to that which is to come, which those whom he leaves would for their own sakes have had long deferred. He was a very quiet man, in all his doing, but his long life was crowned with work of quite as much importance to the nation and to the world as that of many who made much more stir among men.

One of the veterans of the American book trade, he was as young in thought and activity, up to the very moment of his death, as the freshest lad whom he admired and encouraged with his kindly and warm heart. During this busy season of Christmas time, Mr. Putnam had been at the store, and in the best of health and spirits, active and busy as always, all through. At five o'clock, Friday afternoon, the 20th inst., as he was showing "The Gallery of Landscape Painters" to Rev. W. H. Van Doren, he turned away suddenly, as though faint, and failing in an endeavor to rally himself, gave a deep groan, and sank to the floor, striking his head against a shelf as he fell. Two of Mr. Putnam's sons were in the store. He was immediately raised and placed on one of the book tables, restoratives were applied, and Drs. Ferguson and Brink immediately summoned, but only to discover that he was dead, the result apparently of an apoplectic stroke.

George Palmer Putnam was born at Brunswick, Me., February 21, 1814. Revolutionary blood of the best sort flowed in his veins, for he was the grandson of Gen. Joseph Palmer, and grandnephew of the famed Gen. Israel Putnam. He was what is called a self-made man, having received but a common-school education in his native place and in Boston, and made his start in life at the age of 14, as a clerk in the book store of Daniel Leavitt, in New York.

At this early date, he began to be a bookmaker in the other sense as well, and commenced in 1828 a compilation of dates which resulted finally in that well-known book of reference "The World's Progress," first published as a "chronology," in 1833. After remaining with Mr. Leavitt some years, he entered the employ of Mr. John Wiley, and in 1840 the well-known firm of Wiley & Putnam was formed. In 1838, he had issued another volume of his own, "The Tourist in Europe." In 1841, he went to London and established there a branch of the firm in Paternoster Row and a pleasant home in St. John's Wood, which many Americans still remember

with delight. He remained a Londoner seven years, meantime issuing "The American Bookseller," 1843, and a compilation of "American Facts," 1845, meant partly as a reply to Mr. Dickens' "American Notes." This did much to acquaint Englishmen with the United States and its people, and Mr. Putnam was always proud of the beneficial influence he had thus exerted. He was almost the first to introduce American books into the mother country, and was also a pioneer in the importation of English books.

In 1848 he came back to New York, and soon after engaged in business by himself. In 1850 he published his chronology, revised, and "The World's Progress," of which he has since issued numerous editions, revising it every few years to date. This was the most important literary work especially his own. The establishment, in 1852, of *Putnam's Magazine,* was however the special work and pride of his life, for it did perhaps as much as any one thing to foster the growth of a native literature, to gather our then isolated writers into a connection in which each might be encouraged and helped by working alongside his fellows. Geo. William Curtis and James Briggs were his associates in this work, which occupied a then unique place as a strictly American and original magazine. "Maga" became a considerable success, but it was sold in 1856, and its new publishers failed in the crisis of 1857. In 1863, Mr. Putnam gave up business to become a Collector of Internal Revenue, a position which he filled with ability and credit till 1866, when, in connection with his eldest son G. Harris Putnam, the present house of G. P. Putnam & Sons was founded, the plural of the second part arising from the admission later of his second son, J. Bishop Putnam. The "old pea-green" magazine was revived by the new house in 1867, and continued successfully until it was merged with *Scribner's Monthly* on the establishment of the latter in 1870.

Shortly after Mr. Putnam went into business under his own name, he began the publication of Washington Irving's works, and thus was commenced a close, vital friendship between author and publisher, which is one of the pleasantest episodes in the history of literature. He early encouraged the literary ambition of Bayard Taylor, and, indeed, it is difficult to estimate how many men of letters are indebted to Mr. Putnam for kind encouragement, when that to them was all in all. He was the publisher, also, of Poe, Cooper, Kennedy, Curtis, Godwin, and other noted American authors, and the helpful and appreciated friend of all.

Singularly winning in manner, and even in temper, a radiance of genial feeling always on his pleasant face and a cordial greeting always in his grasp of the hand, no one who had ever met him but saw why he had been the life-long and intimate friend of such men as those and others who are left to mourn him. For these outward qualities were the expression of a beautiful soul, a warm heart, a

The recently launched trade paper Publishers' and Stationers' Weekly Trade Circular *(soon to be renamed* Publishers Weekly) *carried the announcement of Putnam's position at the newly founded Metropolitan Museum of Art.*

MR. GEO. P. PUTNAM, the veteran publisher, and one of the most active of the Trustees of the Metropolitan Art Museum, has consented to accept the position of Managing Trustee or Honorary Superintendent of that Institution for the first year. He will devote considerable time to its organization–of course without withdrawing from the business with which he has so long been identified.

– *Publishers' and Stationers' Weekly Trade Circular,*
1 (25 January 1872): 44

mind well-stored and vigorous. As unassuming as the humblest could be, while the peer of the proudest, no person of whatever class met Mr. Putnam without feeling that here was one whose acquaintance was a delight, whose friendship an honor. It was chiefly in personal influence upon individuals that his life-work was done, for with his somewhat hesitating speech, a peculiarity which gave weight to his conversation, he was not much given to public address. Yet there were few men who had done more leadership in the literary and art development of his country. In all such undertakings he was trustingly looked to for

enthusiastic help, and he never failed in effective response to the trust.

In social and club life Mr. Putnam has always been a leader. His literary receptions in the earlier days at his pleasant home, where any and every one dropped in for a sure and kind welcome, and Irving, Bryant, and the other leaders of literature were often to be met, will always be remembered. He was one of the early members of the Century and of the Union League Clubs, serving for many years on the Art Committee of the latter. His art tastes were always strong, and he gave early attention to the publication of fine American illustrated books, the artist's edition of the Sketch-Book, even now seldom equalled, being a pioneer in that field. He was always a great friend of artists, was one of the founders of the Metropolitan Museum of Art, of which he was during the past year Honorary Superintendent, giving his services freely and without charge; and his position in American art circles was worthily recognized by General Van Buren in his appointment of Mr. Putnam as Chairman of the Committee on Art in connection with the Vienna Exposition.

The history of Mr. Putnam's career as a publisher was one altogether of measures toward the best interests of his country and his readers. He felt deeply the responsibility of the publisher, and never did anything issue from his press which he thought would injure in any way or degree, man, woman, or child. His conscientiousness and his Christianity were thus vital, permeating every moment

Notice placed by friends of Putnam in the 23 December 1872 issue of the New-York Tribune

and every act of his life. As a writer and compiler he had done much and good service, as all readers know. As a supporter of American art no one was before him; it is impossible to estimate how much art in this country is indebted to Mr. Putnam. He was self-sacrificing always, but never more cheerfully and continuously than in his years of voluntary rule in connection with that long series of efforts now crowned in the Metropolitan Museum of Art. We trust that some fitting record of his memory may be made in connection with this enterprise, which commanded his last efforts, and with which we believe he would like best to have his name especially associated.

We do not propose to write a memoir of Mr. Putnam; that is a work which might well be, which we trust the public will demand shall be, undertaken at length by the eldest son who so worthily represents his father. Few lives have included so much worth the telling, and we imagine sufficient material for the book is easily to be gathered. But whatever worthy memorial, in monument of art or on the printed page, shall be made of Mr. Putnam, none will be so thorough a testimonial to his worth as the affectionate remembrance in which he is today held in many hundred hearts.

The funeral of Mr. Putnam took place on Monday, 23d inst., from the Madison Avenue Baptist Church, corner of Thirty-first street, of which he was a leading member. The Rev. Dr. Elder, pastor of the church, opened the services with prayer, after which the Rev. Dr. Tyng read a chapter from I Corinthians, and the Rev. Drs. Elder, Crosby, and Prentiss made feeling addresses, bearing testimony with one accord to the true greatness of their friend as a man and Christian, in his business as in his personal life. William Cullen Bryant, John Taylor Johnston, Daniel Huntington, John Wiley, Charles Collins, John O. Sargent, Vincent Collyer, A. D. F. Randolph, Henry Holt, Andrew C. Armstrong, Sandford R. Gifford, and Richard Butler, were the pall-bearers, and among many other prominent friends of the deceased present in the large assemblage, were J. A. J. Cresswell, Parke Godwin, Professor Butler, D. Van Nostrand, George A. Leavitt, Smith Sheldon, Wm. H. Appleton, R. R. McBurney, Albert Mason, the Rev. Dr. T. D. Anderson, the Rev. Dr. Samuel B. Osgood, and the Rev. O. B. Frothingham, Maunsell B. Field, formerly Assistant Secretary of the Treasury; Tetsnoske Tomita, Japanese Consul, a warm personal friend of the late publisher, and Pierre M. Irving, nephew of Washington Irving. The remains were conveyed to Woodlawn Cemetery.

The following card to the public was issued, by the timely thoughtfulness and practical sympathy of members of the trade, on Saturday: The undersigned, members of the book trade, realizing that to the affliction of the family of the late Mr. Geo. P. Putnam ought not to be added the very serious financial detriment of an interruption to the business of the deceased at this most important season, have taken upon themselves the responsibility of conducting it at the store of G. P. Putnam & Sons, corner Fourth avenue and Twenty-third street, until the surviving members of the firm can assume control.

Henry Holt,
Andrew Armstrong,
Alfred Houghton,
John Wiley.

The memorial meeting of the trade was called for this (Thursday) afternoon at the Trade Sales Rooms.

— *Publishers' and Stationers' Weekly Trade Circular,*
2 (26 December 1872): 697–698

The official trade resolution commemorating Putnam was issued by his young friend and occasional coworker Henry Holt, a future pillar of the publishing establishment.

The Committee on Resolutions respecting Mr. Putnam's death offered the following report, which was unanimously adopted, and ordered to be printed in the daily papers, and transmitted to the family of the deceased.

Resolved: That this Board regards with deep sorrow the death of Mr. George P. Putnam—a publisher whose life added dignity to our calling, and whose memory is among its best traditions.

Resolved: That we, as his business associates, wish to join our testimony to that already so copiously given by the press, that Mr. Putnam's career was one of great advantage to American letters, and that his example is worthy of the best emulation of those whose function it is to decide what literature shall go before the public.

Resolved: That while his sudden death well reminds us of the uncertainty of our term of active effort, it equally reminds us that it is impossible entirely to obliterate the influence of a good and useful life.

HENRY HOLT,
Secretary.
—*The Publishers' Weekly,* 3 (16 January 1873): 42

Historical Overview of the House of Putnam

See also the G. P. Putnam's Sons and John Wiley and Sons entries in *DLB 49: American Literary Publishing Houses, 1638–1899;* the G. P. Putnam's Sons entry in *DLB 106: British Literary Publishing Houses, 1820–1880;* and the entry on the G. P. Putnam archives in *DLB Yearbook: 1992.*

The House of Putnam originated with the formation of the partnership between two young New Yorkers, John Wiley and George Palmer Putnam, as Wiley and Putnam in March 1837. From humble beginnings as a relatively small player in the retail booktrade and general publishing, the partnership prospered as it grew over the course of the early and mid 1840s into one of the largest, most successful firms in New York City.

The business matured as the trade, as Putnam still thought of it throughout his lifetime, was rapidly evolving into a modern industry, one of New York City's largest during the years in which Putnam was in partnership with Wiley. Increasingly, publishers such as Wiley and Putnam, not authors or printers, took the lead in initiating and overseeing the production of printed works and did so by attempting to systematize the means of production, beginning with the establishment of long-term relations with authors engaged on professional terms. Nevertheless, operating capital remained a serious problem for all but the largest and most aggressive firms. The issue of capital was a particular contraint for Wiley and Putnam (as later for G. P. Putnam), which found its means often stretched to the limit in its attempt to expand its publishing and retail operations.

Like most other midcentury publishers (Harper and Brothers being the most notable exception), Wiley and Putnam and its successors did not manufacture its own works; rather, it shipped out printing, stereotyping, and binding orders to specialist firms around the city. In order to ensure that its books were well made, the firm generally patronized the best printers and stereotypists in town, such as John Trow and Robert Craighead. Its own offices at 161 Broadway consisted of little more than a bookstore and attached rooms in which clients were received, correspondence conducted and accounts kept. The office staff consisted of proba-

Company Names
1837–1847: Wiley and Putnam
1848–1852: G. P. Putnam
1852–1857: G. P. Putnam and Company
1857–1866: G. P. Putnam
1867–1870: G. P. Putnam and Son
1870–1872: G. P. Putnam and Sons
1873–1931: G. P. Putnam's Sons

bly no more than a half dozen people, whose positions were loosely defined and who handled the main office work. More expert work, such as editorial oversight, normally called for temporary hires, as when Evert A. Duyckinck was brought in to oversee the management of the Wiley and Putnam libraries from 1845 to 1847.

Transatlantic Business

A major factor in the success of the Wiley and Putnam partnership was Putnam's work in London, where he moved in 1838 to open a branch office. Putnam had first visited London in 1836, within months of accepting a junior position with Wiley and Long. His partners had quickly dispatched him on an extended reconnaissance tour of the major book publishing and retailing centers of Great Britain and the European continent. The purpose of Putnam's trip, one of several transatlantic forays made that year by American publishers, was to assess the state of the international book market and to position his firm to play a larger role in the rapidly growing international trade in books and magazines. Two years later, after he had become a full-fledged partner in the reconstituted house of Wiley and Putnam, Putnam crossed the ocean again to open the firm's new office in London.

The new London office proved so successful that the firm maintained its two-country presence and became a pioneer among American publishing houses in entering fully into international publishing and bookselling. During this period Putnam distinguished himself as the leading American book professional in England and made his firm the principal American intermediary for the international book market. Operating out of a series of offices in Pater-

IMPORTERS OF ENGLISH AND OTHER FOREIGN BOOKS,

No. 161, BROADWAY, NEW YORK; AND No. 67, PATERNOSTER ROW, LONDON.

WILEY & PUTNAM

HAVE established at No. 67, Paternoster Row, London, an Agency conducted by one of the house under the same firm, for the purchase of choice ENGLISH, FRENCH, and GERMAN PUBLICATIONS, for Universities and Private Libraries; and for the sale of American Books, Periodicals, and Copyrights.

Such an arrangement, it has been often suggested, would be very desirable for Authors and Publishers on this side, who wish either to effect sales of their own editions of original works suited to the English market, or to secure a London Copyright therefor: while to Literary Institutions, and Individuals about making additions to their libraries, it offers the following inducements; viz.

I. All orders will be personally and carefully attended to by one of the firm, who is well acquainted with the British and Continental Book Market: purchases made of the Publishers, direct, without the usual commissions of a London Agent; and in many cases, rare and voluminous works would be obtained, at the Library Auction Sales and otherwise, at prices much depreciated.

II. If funds to three-fourths the amount of any considerable order are furnished in advance, the commission charged for all purchases is but 10 per cent. on the original cost at the lowest wholesale prices; and as our purchases are often made in quantities for the Trade, or in exchange for American Books, we can usually deliver English Books in New York at prices as low, and sometimes much less, than those of the London Publishers.

III. Books for Incorporated Literary Institutions we engage to furnish *free of duty*; and in most cases, they will be received in New York within seventy days from the date of the order.

. Orders for FRENCH & GERMAN BOOKS executed on the same terms, and the Goods shipped direct from Havre or Hamburgh.

The MAGAZINES and PERIODICALS of every description forwarded by the Steamers, or by the Liverpool Packets, of the 1st of each Month, the day of Publication in London.

ENGLISH AND FOREIGN CATALOGUES FURNISHED.

Orders should be addressed as above, 161, Broadway, New York; or 67, Paternoster Row, London.

One of many circulars mailed by Wiley and Putnam as it strove to become the leading American intermediary in the transatlantic book business. The London address is that of the firm's first office in the English capital (Willbur Fisk Papers, Special Collections & Archives, Wesleyan University Library).

Putnam enjoyed exceptionally warm relations with Lewis Gaylord Clark, the editor of the important Knickerbocker Magazine, *which often resulted in free publicity for his business. A case in point is this excerpt from Clark's "Editor's Table."*

While on the subject of foreign literature, we would refer the reader to the advertisement of Messrs. WILEY AND PUTNAM, in reference to importing books from abroad. The last-named gentleman has recently returned from a bibliographical tour through Great-Britain, France, and Germany, during which he made arrangements for executing orders for private libraries, as well as for universities and literary institutions, which receive their importations free of duty. The library of Columbia College and the Mercantile Library have lately been enriched by many rare and valuable works imported by this house; and we deem ourselves performing an acceptable service to the public, by a reference to the advantages and facilities at their command.

—*Knickerbocker Magazine,* 9 (March 1837): 316

noster Row, Stationers' Court, and Waterloo Place, he combined full-scale retail operations with publishing and did so, of course, in conjunction with the same dual activities pursued by the firm out of its New York offices on Broadway.

Maintaining the London office was expensive, especially when the cost of supporting the fast-growing Putnam household was included, and the work was demanding. The need for the coordination of the New York and London offices was constant, but transatlantic communication during the period was cumbersome. To ensure maximal efficiency and coordination between the offices, Putnam returned to New York on a nearly annual basis, sometimes staying for months and meeting customers and canvasing for orders to take back with him to London. Both the New York and London offices were necessarily wary of cut-throat competition and piracy that arose from a lack of international copyright regulation. In addition, the conduct of business was frequently complicated by the requirements of dealing with two separate government bureaucracies.

Because London was at the time a much larger and more vital publishing center than New York, Putnam at first concentrated on buying British and Continental books and magazines for sale in the United States, whether on commission for institutional or private purchasers or for retail at the Broadway store. Putnam played a major role in improving the New York branch's retail stock of European books and magazines, helping to turn it into one of New

York City's finest bookstores. The store was popular with the literati of the time. It was there, for instance, that publisher J. C. Derby initially met Edgar Allan Poe, recently famous following the 1845 newspaper and magazine publication of "The Raven." Also among its customers were Herman Melville and Margaret Fuller, as well as the entire Young America circle of cultural nationalists gathered around Evert Duyckinck (whose extensive library was heavily stocked with Wiley and Putnam purchases, many placed through Putnam in London).

Putnam's considerable skill as a purchaser of rare and fine books and manuscripts also helped to make Wiley and Putnam the primary American agency for the purchase of such items, a position his company held until dislodged by Henry Stevens, Putnam's friend-turned-rival, in the mid 1840s. The firm routinely advertised its services in New York and London newspapers and magazines, and it counted among its clients many of the leading libraries and educational institutions in the United States, such as Harvard and Yale, and lesser known schools such as South Carolina College. Moreover, through his close relations with Stevens, Putnam obtained voluminous business for his firm during the mid 1840s as a supplier of Americana for the British Museum.

Although publishing was a secondary activity in the early years of Wiley and Putnam, from the beginning of the partnership Putnam supplied the firm with texts for reprinting in the United States. In 1845 the firm set out to move into the ranks of the leading literary publishers in the country. With the conclusion of a cheap-publications war— a period from the late 1830s through the early 1840s during which publishers flooded the market with inexpensive books—prices stabilized and conditions for publishing greatly improved. Wiley initiated his firm's new direction by signing Evert Duyckinck to oversee the two new Wiley and Putnam series titled Library of Choice Reading and Library of American Books.

As the focus of Wiley and Putnam shifted from bookselling to publishing, Putnam purchased the rights to many attractive books and manuscripts for simultaneous publication or simply republication in the United States. At a time when the lack of international copyright and the underdevelopment of American authorship encouraged American publishers to prefer foreign to native works, Putnam committed Wiley and Putnam to the competition for republication of European works currently being waged by larger houses in New York and Philadelphia. He made arrangements with the leading publishers of London, especially John Murray, Edward Moxon, and Richard Bentley, for American reprinting rights to their works. Among the authors whose works he secured for his firm in New York were Thomas Carlyle, George Borrow, Anna Jameson, Thomas Hood, and Leigh Hunt. In fact, many of the titles

W. & P. having made special arrangements with the Proprietors of the *English Editions* of the following leading Periodicals, propose to supply them to the American Public at greatly reduced prices—in some instances for less than one-half the old rates, and nearly one-half less than they can *now* be furnished by any other house. The Periodicals will always be received by the steamers, and will be mailed or delivered usually—the Monthlies about the 20th of each month, and the Quarterlies about the 20th of the month of publication. All orders, *postpaid,* accompanied by a remittance, will receive prompt attention.

No subscription can be taken unless payment is made strictly in advance. It is desirable that all who wish to commence their subscriptions with the January number for 1843, should forward their orders so that they may reach us by the 25th November.

No subscription taken for less than six months—and they must commence either with the January or the July number. Odd numbers can be furnished to complete sets at same prices.

I. THE QUARTERLY REVIEW—Edited by J. G Lockhart, Esq. $4 00 per annum.

II. THE EDINBURGH REVIEW—Edited by Francis Napier. $4 00 per annum.

III. THE BRITISH CRITIC. $4 00 per annum.

IV. THE LONDON AND WESTMINSTER REVIEW—Edited by Mr. Mill. $4 00 per annum.

V. THE FOREIGN QUARTERLY REVIEW—Conducted by a new Editor. $4 00 per annum.

VI. THE BRITISH AND FOREIGN REVIEW—Edited by John Kemble. $4 00 per annum.

VII. BRITISH AND FOREIGN MEDICAL REVIEW—Edited by John Forbes and John Conolly, M D. $5 00 per annum.

VIII BLACKWOOD'S MAGAZINE—Edited by John Wilson. $5 00 per annum.

IX. FRAZER'S MAGAZINE—Edited by Dr. Maginn. $6 00 per annum.

X. THE MONTHLY MAGAZINE—Edited by Mr. Tomline. $6 00 per annum.

XI. NEW MONTHLY MAGAZINE—Edited by Thomas Hood. $1 00 per annum.

XII. TH. UNITED SERVICE JOURNAL AND NAVAL AND MILITARY MAGAZINE. $10 00 per annum.

XIII. DUBLIN UNIVERSITY MAGAZINE—Edited by "Harry Lorrequer," (Dr. Lever.) $5 00 per annum.

XIV. AINSWORTH'S MAGAZINE—A Monthly Miscellany of Romance, General Literature, and Art; *Illustrated* by Cruikshank. $3 00 per annum.

XV. THE CIVIL ENGINEER AND ARCHITECT'S JOURNAL. $5 00 per annum.

XVI THE (Glasgow) PRACTICAL MECHANIC AND ENGINEER'S MAGAZINE. $2 50 per annum.

☞ All the Periodicals published either in England or France, can be promptly supplied at the most reasonable prices.   o15

Wiley and Putnam advertisement in the 15 October 1842 issue of New World. *Wiley and Putnam attempted to capture the New York market for European magazines but abandoned the field to the competition after several years of having their authorized importations undersold by local printers.*

Wiley and Putnam & South Carolina College

This 17 February 1845 Wiley and Putnam letter to Reverend Robert Henry, the president of South Carolina College, one of the firm's best institutional clients, gives an unusually detailed account of how book orders got filled on the nineteenth-century international book market.

Rev. R. Henry DD
President of So Carolina College
D Sir

We have the pleasure now of giving you an Invoice of a part of the Books ordered by you a little while since.–They appear to be in very good order & we trust will give entire satisfaction–We look for more on a/c of the same order soon–Some have been ordered from Germany and some from Italy–and we expect also to get many of them in London–those now sent come from France[.] We supposed that the order could be executed on better terms & more fully on the continent & therefore sent there first–after a thorough search there our agents were instructed to communicate with Mr. Putnam & this by their last advice they were about to do–they also say that after Mr P has done what he can they will take the list again & in the course of a few months will be able doubtless to furnish others–

Very Respectfully Yours
Wiley and Putnam
New York Feb 17–1845

In a 22 July 1845 letter, Wiley and Putnam acknowledged receipt of $1,000 for the most recent shipment of books, most from Europe. This unusually heavy purchase resulted from the school's attempt to stock its new South Caroliniana Library, the first freestanding college library in the United States.

Rev. Robert Henry DD
D Sir

Your kind favor of the 16th Inst. with check for One Thousand dollars is safely received & the amt is passed to the credit of So Carolina College at your request.–

All shipments will be insured to Charleston & you may be assured that we will use all dispatch in filling up as far as possible the deficiencies in your orders yet in hand–

We now had sent an Invoice of Luthers Wks–
Very Respectfully yours
Wiley and Putnam
New York July 22 1845
NB We shall send you a few more books from France & London in a day or two–
–University Archives, University of South Carolina

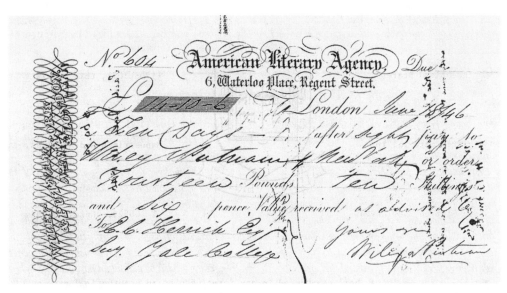

A receipt from the London office that was attached to an invoice for books and magazines purchased by Putnam in Europe for Yale College Library. It accompanied his letter to the college librarian, explaining delivery delays and omissions (Yale Collection of American Literature, Beinecke Rare Book and Manuscript Library).

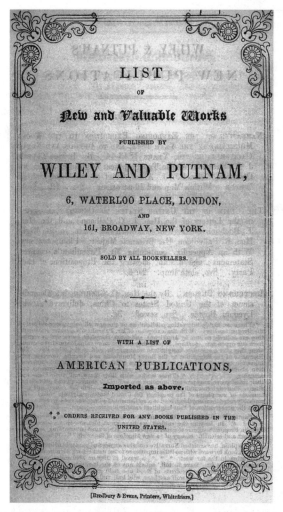

Cover for an 1845 trade catalogue that advertised a wide variety of house publications, as well as books and magazines imported from North America and sold at the Waterloo Place Bookstore. The English public was invited "to make free use, at any time, of the various sources of Information Respecting the United States, Literary, Political, Commercial, and for the use of Travellers, which are made available" at the firm's self-styled "American Literary Agency." Bradbury and Evans, the London printing shop that produced this fifty-two page catalogue, printed many of the works published by the overseas office of Wiley and Putnam, beginning with Edgar Allan Poe's The Narrative of Arthur Gordon Pym *in 1838 (Collection of Ezra Greenspan).*

Putnam Trade Catalogues

Even before joining Wiley and Long in 1836, Putnam produced trade catalogues for his employers. The making of catalogues—an endeavor that in earlier times was undertaken by printers who doubled as publishers such as Benjamin Franklin and Isaiah Thomas—became increasingly indispensable to the publishing profession as it moved fully into an age of mechanical reproduction and expanding publishing lists. Individual firms produced catalogues of their own publications, and industry-wide lists were compiled at the times of trade sales, where large job lots were offered and sold, generating revenues that increased apace with the rapid capitalization of the industry. The growth of the publishing industry also inspired pioneering bibliographical projects, such as William

Frederick Poole's Index to Periodical Literature *(1848), soon known as* Poole's Index, *and Orville A. Roorbach's* Bibliotheca Americana *(1849).*

List making was a personal specialty of Putnam's, and some of the finest trade catalogues in the profession were produced by Wiley and Putnam over the course of the 1840s. These catalogues, usually published annually and sometimes hundreds of pages in length, listed not only the firm's own works but also foreign and domestic texts generally. They were greatly valued by individual purchasers, members of the trade, and librarians of large institutions around the country. A nearly full set of Wiley and Putnam catalogues, ordered by historian Jared Sparks, survives at Harvard.

that appeared in Wiley and Putnam's Library of Choice Reading were secured by Putnam.

During its two-year life the Library of Choice Reading, which featured reprints mostly of British texts, came to include works by Carlyle, William Makepeace Thackeray, Charles Dickens, Hood, William Hazlitt, Alexander William Kinglake, and other leading belletristic authors of the time. The somewhat less voluminous Library of American Books, by contrast, presented original—and, therefore, copyrighted—works by American authors, including Herman Melville's *Typee* (1846), Nathaniel Hawthorne's *Mosses from an Old Manse* (1846), Poe's *Tales* (1845) and *The Raven and Other Poems* (1845), Margaret Fuller's *Papers on Literature and Art* (1846), and William Gilmore Simms's *The Wigwam and the Cabin* (1845) and *Views and Reviews in American Literature, History and Fiction* (1845). Though probably only modestly profitable, the two libraries were the result of the marketing strategy that characterized Wiley and Putnam and later G. P. Putnam: lively reading intended chiefly for the middle class, priced moderately, and presented in handsome bindings. In their individual titles as well as collectively, these two Wiley and Putnam series offered some of the best reading then available in the United States.

While providing the American market with European material, Putnam also positioned Wiley and Putnam as the main intermediary in books and periodicals passing from the United States to Britain. A patriotic businessman, Putnam combined ideology and economic self-interest in turning his London store and agency into a center for the sale of American publications. At the height of his success in 1845, he stocked a room of his offices at Waterloo Place, which he proudly called the American Literary Agency, with American newspapers, magazines, books, and paintings. During the mid 1840s in particular, he not only imported many American works from publishers across the country but also published London editions of some of his most attractive American authors. Among them were single or multiple works by Andrew Jackson Downing, Margaret Fuller, Edgar Allan Poe, and Asa Gray. More often than not, however, he ceded the publication of his American authors to better positioned London houses.

By 1847 the profitability of Wiley and Putnam's two-country arrangement was decreasing as the firm faced mounting pressure for customers and profits from American competitors sending American agents overseas to represent them. Wiley had importuned Putnam by 1846 to consider spending at least as much time in New York as in London, and finally in spring 1847 Putnam was ready to accede. He moved his business to smaller quarters and left it in the hands of his chief clerk, David Davidson.

Putnam returned home to New York permanently in June and settled for the first time in ten years into shared offices with his more conservative colleague.

This arrangement apparently did not suit the enterprising Putnam, who within a few months decided to venture out on his own. According to the agreement they reached late that year, Wiley retained the old store and the two men split the assets, the largest part of which was in stock and plates. Despite extremely limited capital, Putnam proudly opened for business as G. P. Putnam in March 1848 at 155 Broadway.

Recently landed in the United States, Putnam reports to Henry Stevens, his contact with the British Museum, on his progress traveling up and down the eastern seaboard purchasing books, manuscripts, and maps for the museum's fast-growing collection of Americana.

New York Augt 1, 1846
My dear Stevens
I am crowded into the very last moment—You know the old story. Suffice it to say that I have not lost a minute since I landed & have worked hard on the Museum business, as I am determined it shall be done thoroughly & faithfully & as economically as possible—to your credit & my own (to you.)—I have been to Washington—saw Webster, Marsh, Force, Polk, Bancroft & all the Senators—printed a circular about Pub. Doc. to Secs. of all the states & another to the Senators from the respective states. I enclose one for your information & hope you will approve of it. I shall send duplicates to the States &c & shall *visit* the Secs. of R. Island, Connt., Mass., Maine, N Hampshire & N. York—& hope to get all the *recent* Docs. gratis—the others & the scarce books I advd. for—(see commercial—)—& we have letters from all quarters—This was the true system & will save the Museum 10% if not more.—I *ransacked* Washington, Phila. & Baltimore & shall do ditto here & at the East—shall buy of Gowans, Drake, &c all that they offer as cheap—but not more—Have sent three cases odds & ends to begin with. Invoice enclosed. Insured here. Humberston advised to keep them for advice from Museum—I am waiting for the *T.* & *W.* packet [?] steamer & shall then write you more at large.—Tariff bill passed & I was there to see.—
In great haste Thine   *G. P. Putnam*
News from Mr Lenox enclosed—Be moderate in prices to him
    —*Special Collections, University of Vermont*

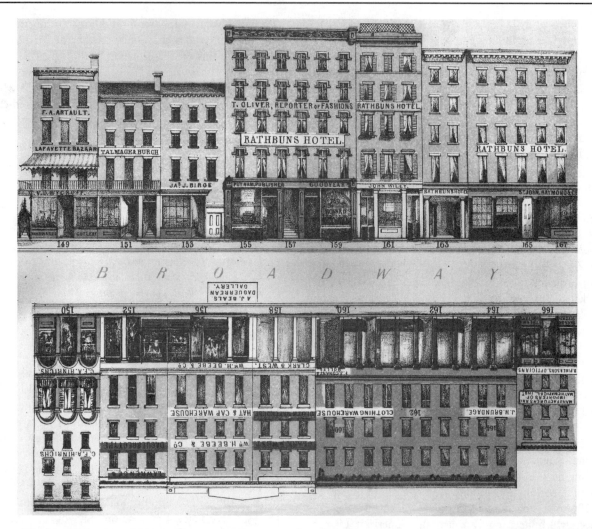

Page from the Illuminated Pictorial Directory of New York *(1848) showing the first G. P. Putnam store, two doors down from John Wiley's office. These locations were at the center of New York's antebellum bookselling district on lower Broadway (courtesy of the New York Public Library).*

A New Beginning

In characteristic fashion, Putnam moved quickly and aggressively to stake his own claim in the print marketplace. Much of his initial list necessarily came from the Wiley and Putnam backlist, but in his first months of solo operation he also used his extensive network of contacts to lay the foundation of his own outstanding belletristic list. His most important initiative was in reaching an agreement with Washington Irving, the most esteemed author in the country, to publish an "author's revised edition" of all his old works, which were then out of print in the United States, and any new ones he might write. Putnam's partnership with Irving, which lasted beyond the author's death, proved hugely successful and earned both men tens of thousands of dollars. Putnam's earnings enabled him to bankroll his general operations for nearly a generation. He followed this agreement with similar multiple-works deals with James Fenimore Cooper and Catharine Maria Sedgwick, as well as contracts to publish attractive new works that became classics, including Poe's *Eureka* (1848), *Poole's Index* (1848–   ), James Russell Lowell's *Fable for Critics* (1848), and Francis Parkman's *Oregon Trail* (1849). Contracting for books from both the United States and Britain helped to establish G. P. Putnam quickly not only as an important force within the trade but also as a nationally and internationally recognized literary publisher.

Putnam entered the new decade of the 1850s with great expectations for his own firm and for American publishing generally. Economic conditions were favorable for an expansion of publishing operations, and Putnam was eager to position his company to take full advantage of them. G. P. Putnam continued to publish works by authors old and new. Chief among them was Irving, whose name

GEO. P. PUTNAM

Has the pleasure of announcing that, agreeably to his contract with the distinguished author, he will shortly commence the publication of

A NEW, UNIFORM, AND COMPLETE EDITION

OF THE

WORKS OF WASHINGTON IRVING,

Revised and enlarged by the Author,

IN TWELVE ELEGANT DUODECIMO VOLUMES.

Beautifully printed with new type, and on superior paper, made expressly for the purpose.

Price $1 25 per vol., neatly bound in cloth.

The first volume of the Series will be

THE SKETCH-BOOK, complete in one volume,

which will be ready on the first day of September,

KNICKERBOCKER'S HISTORY OF NEW YORK,

with revisions and copious additions,

will be published on the 1st of October,

THE LIFE AND VOYAGES OF COLUMBUS,

Vol. I. on the 1st of November,

and the succeeding volumes will be issued on the first day of each month until completed;—as follows:

THE SKETCH BOOK, in one volume.
KNICKERBOCKER'S NEW YORK, in one volume.
TALES OF A TRAVELLER, in one volume.
BRACEBRIDGE HALL, in one volume.
THE CONQUEST OF GRENADA, in one volume.
THE ALHAMBRA, in one volume.

THE CRAYON MISCELLANY, in one volume
Abbotsford, Newstead, The Prairies, &c.
THE SPANISH LEGENDS, in one volume.*
LIFE AND VOYAGES OF COLUMBUS, and THE COMPANIONS OF COLUMBUS, 2 vols.
ADVENTURES OF CAPT. BONNEVILLE, one vol.

ASTORIA, one volume.

* *These Volumes will comprise several papers now first collected.*

THE ILLUSTRATED SKETCH-BOOK.

In October will be published,

THE SKETCH-BOOK. BY WASHINGTON IRVING.

In one volume, square octavo.

Illustrated with a Series of highly-finished Engravings on wood, from designs by DARLEY and others, engraved in the best style by CHILDS, HERRICK, &c. This Edition will be printed on paper of the finest quality, similar in size and style to the New Edition of "Halleck's Poems." It is intended that the illustrations shall be superior to any Engravings on wood yet produced in this country, and that the mechanical execution of the volume, altogether, shall be worthy of the author's reputation. It will form an elegant and appropriate gift-book for all seasons.

THE ILLUSTRATED KNICKERBOCKER,

With a Series of Original Designs, in 1 vol. 8vo. is also in preparation.

MR. PUTNAM has also the honor to announce that he will publish at intervals (in connexion, and uniform with the other collected Writings),

MR. IRVING'S NEW WORKS,

NOW NEARLY READY FOR THE PRESS; INCLUDING

THE LIFE OF MOHAMMED, THE LIFE OF WASHINGTON,

New Volumes of MISCELLANIES, BIOGRAPHIES, &c.

*** This being the first uniform and complete edition of Mr. Irving's Works, either in this country or in Europe, the publisher confidently believes that the undertaking will meet with a prompt and cordial response. To say this, is perhaps superfluous and impertinent; for it is a truism that no *American* book-case (not to say *library*) can be well filled without the works of WASHINGTON IRVING; while the English language itself comprises no purer models of composition.

N. B. *Caution to the Trade.*—Justice both to the author and publisher requires that the importation of foreign editions of Irving's Works (or any part of them), which has heretofore been suffered because the American editions were long out of print, should now be STRICTLY PROHIBITED. *All foreign copies imported or offered for sale hereafter, will be liable to forfeiture, and the vendor will incur the usual penalty.*

Orders from the trade will receive prompt attention, on liberal terms.

G. P. PUTNAM has also made arrangements for the early commencement of new works or new editions of the works of

MISS C. M. SEDGEWICK,
CHARLES FENNO HOFFMAN,
GEORGE H. CALVERT,
J. BAYARD TAYLOR,
JAS. RUSSELL LOWELL,
S. WELLS WILLIAMS,
A. J. DOWNING,

PROF. A. GRAY,
MRS. E. OAKES SMITH,
MRS. C. M. KIRKLAND,
MARY HOWITT,
T. K. HERVEY,
ELLIOT WARBURTON,
LEIGH HUNT,

THOMAS CARLYLE,
R. MONCKTON MILNES,
MRS. JAMESON,
CHARLES LAMB,
SIR FRANCIS HEAD,
W. A. THACKERAY,
THOS. HOOD.

Advertisement in the 10 June 1848 issue of The Literary World *in which Putnam signals his clear intention to establish his firm as a national leader in the publication of belles lettres*

A London Alliance

His long experience in the international book trade persuaded Putnam at the time of his separation from Wiley that he needed a continuing connection to the European market. Shortly after going out on his own as G. P. Putnam in 1848, he made a transatlantic alliance with his old acquaintance John Chapman, a British publisher who was eager to get into the increasingly lucrative American trade: each to serve as an outlet for the other's publications. Chapman's announcement of the alliance appeared in the London trade paper Publishers' Circular.

Mr. John Chapman begs to announce that he has made an arrangement with Mr. G. Putnam, (of the late firm of Wiley and Putnam, American Booksellers), to continue the business of supplying American Publications of every description, both for the trade in quantities, and for special orders, whereby he has secured the valuable co-operation of Mr. Putnam, who, in consequence of his residence in New York, his long-established business, and extensive experience, possesses every facility for selecting and sending full supplies by each steamer of all new and desirable books published in every part of the United States, immediately after publication.

The above arrangement, in addition to Mr. Chapman's already extensively established connection in various parts of America, places him in the most advantageous position to execute orders in every department of American Literature with the greatest promptitude, and on the most favourable terms.

Libraries and Public Institutions in England, or on the Continent, requiring American Works, carefully supplied; and if desirable, when books are ordered in quantities, shipments can be made direct from the United States to their appointed destination.

American Periodicals punctually furnished to subscribers, and those not generally imported, *as well as all works not in stock,* may be obtained in about five or six weeks after the date of the order.

Catalogues and Lists of American Books, *as well as of Mr. Chapman's English Publications,* will be sent *gratis* on application. Persons ordering from them, direct or through other Booksellers, will please to state if such works shall be

John Chapman, an aggressive publisher whom Putnam knew well from his London years, became Putnam's overseas trade partner during the late 1840s.

obtained from America should they not be in stock.

Parcels and Cases are made up and forwarded by each Steamer and regular sailing Packet to New York, Boston, and Philadelphia, in which works for Review may be inclosed.

Mr. Chapman invites the attention of the Literary Public to the extensive Stock in his American Department, which is conveniently displayed for inspection in a spacious room, affording the desirable facility of leisurely examining such books as visitors may wish to see before giving their orders.

LONDON, 142, STRAND.
December 10, 1848.
–*The Publishers' Circular,* 11 (15 December 1848): 409

Device used by G. P. Putnam in the early 1850s, indicating the firm's association with leading American writers

was by now associated with the company. The "author's revised edition," which the company published in a wide variety of formats–illustrated and unillustrated, sets and individual volumes, large and small pages, fancy and simple–in order to maximize coverage of the reading audience, remained popular throughout the decade. At the same time, the publisher was enthusiastic about the particular work both he and Irving hoped would be recognized as the author's magnum opus: his five-volume biography of the first president of the United States, *Life of George Washington* (1855–1859).

Other writers who quickly became identified as Putnam authors included Bayard Taylor, James Fenimore Cooper, and Asa Gray. Taylor's first book, *Views A-Foot* (1846), had been published in the Wiley and Putnam Library of American Books, and his subsequent travel writings, all published by G. P. Putnam, sold well throughout the decade. The company's arrangement with Cooper was complicated by the availability of an edition of his most popular novels published by Stringer and Townsend that was cheaper than a similar edition published by Putnam. In fact, at the time of Cooper's death in 1851, the company was probably profiting

more from its dealing with Cooper's daughter Susan, author of *Rural Hours* (1850), than with him. Several works by Harvard botanist Asa Gray, who like Taylor was a former Wiley and Putnam author, proved steady sellers throughout the decade.

The company added several popular authors and works to its list during the late 1840s and early 1850s. Undoubtedly the most important was Susan Warner, who brought the firm the single best-selling book–and perhaps the most unexpected bonanza–it was ever to publish: *The Wide, Wide World* (1850). Sales of the novel began slowly but gradually grew over the course of 1851 into the tens of thousands, and they continued strong for several more years. Sales of her next novel, *Queechy* (1852), were also strong although they leveled off far more quickly than did the sales of *Wide, Wide World*. Other popular authors who entered the Putnam list during these years were Caroline M. Kirkland, whose *Western Clearings* (1845) had been published in the Wiley and Putnam Library of American Books; William Cullen Bryant; George William Curtis; Elizabeth F. Ellet; Emma Willard; and Caroline H. Gilman.

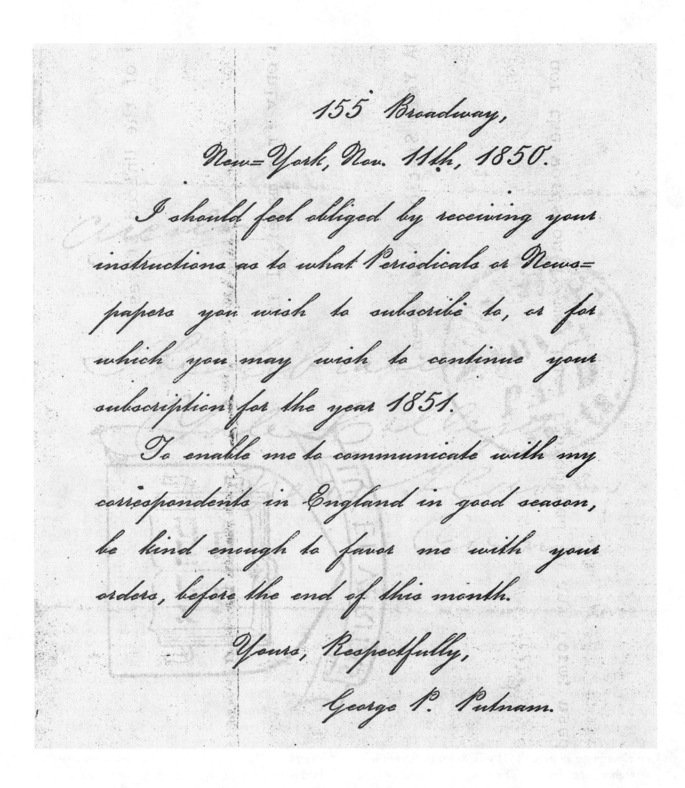

Circular sent by Putnam to potential periodical buyers. He typically solicited book and periodical orders before making overseas trips (Yale Collection of American Literature, Beinecke Rare Book and Manuscript Library).

TRADE LIST

OF

GEORGE P. PUTNAM'S PUBLICATIONS.

155 Broadway, New-York:
March, 1851.

* American Historical and Literary Curiosities, folio, half morocco	$6 00
* Ancient Monuments of the Mississppi Valley, 4to. clth	10 00
Bethune's Orations and Discourses, 12mo. cloth	1 25
Borrow's Lavengro, an autobiography; with portrait, 7th thousand, 12mo. cloth	1 25
Do do paper covers	50
* Bosworth's Anglo Saxon and English Dictionary, 8vo. cloth	3 00
Bremer's Works, author's revised edition:	
The Neighbors, with portr. and vignette, 12mo., cloth	1 00
Home, ——	1 00
Brown's Turkish Evening's Entertainments, 12mo.	1 25
Do do cloth extra gilt	1 75
* Bunyan's Pilgrim, illustrated, 300 eng's, 8vo. clth gt	3 00
*Do do do cloth ex gt edges	3 75
*Do do do mor extra	5 00
Bryant's Letters of a Traveller, 12mo. cloth or sheep	1 25
†Do do do illustrated edition, with steel engravings, 8vo. cloth gilt	4 00
†Do do do mor extra	6 00
Beranger's Lyrics, by Young, 12mo. cloth	1 25
Do do cloth gilt	1 75
†Do do splendid illust. edition, 8vo. cloth	4 50
†Do do cloth, extra, gilt edges	5 00
Calvert's Scenes and Thoughts in Europe, 12mo. cloth	50
Chase's Polk Administration, 8vo. ——	2 50
Chaucer, Selections from, by Deshler, 12mo.	63
Do do do cloth gt	1 00
Do do do sheep	75
Do and Spenser, 12mo. cloth	1 25
Do do do gilt	1 75
Coe's Drawing Cards, 10 packets, each	25
Do New Drawing Book,	75
Church's Calculus, new enlarged edition, 8vo. half bd	1 50
Clarke's (Mary Cowden) Heroines of Shakspeare, 15 parts, each illustrated with engravings on steel:—	
Portia, The Heiress of Belmont; with portrait,	25
The Thane's Daughter; with a view of Cawdor Castle,	25
Helena, The Physician's Orphan; with portrait,	25
Desdemona, The Magnifico's Child; with view of Venice,	25
Meg and Alice, The Merry Maids of Windsor; with view of Windsor,	25
Isabella, The Votaress; with portrait,	25
Katharine and Bianca, The Shrew and the Demure; with a view of Padua,	25
Ophelia, The Rose of Elsinore; with a view of Elsinore,	25
Rosalind and Celia, The Friends; with a view of the Forest of Ardennes,	25
Juliet, The White Dove of Verona; with a view of Verona,	25
Beatrice and Hero, The Cousins; with a view Messina,	25
Olivia, The Lady of Illyria; with a scene on the Illyrian Coast,	25
Hermione, The Russian Princess; with a forest scene in winter,	25
Viola, The Twin; with a view on the Adriatic,	25
Imogen, The Peerless; Sketch of an Ancient Briton,	25
Do do do 2 vols. cloth gilt	

Coleridge's Biographia Literaria, 2 vols. 12mo. cloth	$2 00
Companion (the); after Dinner Table Talk, 12mo. cloth	75
Cooper's choice works in 12 vols. 12mo. cloth ex	15 00
Do do do sheep extra	15 00
Do do do half calf extra	24 00
Do do do calf extra	30 00
Comprising the following works, each complete in 1 vol. sold separately.	1 25

The Spy,	The Red Rover,	The Pilot,
The Water Witch,	Wing and Wing,	Two Admirals,
Last of Mohicans,	Deerslayer,	Pathfinder,
The Pioneers,	The Prairie.	Ways of the Hour.

Cooper's Men of Manhattan, with ills. 1 vol. 8vo. cloth	
Cooper, Miss, Rural Hours, 12mo. cloth or sheep	1 25
Do do do do gilt	1 75
Do do do do half calf	1 75
Do do do do calf extra	2 50
†Do do do illustrated with colored engravings, 8vo. cloth gilt extra	5 00
†Do do do do mor. extra	7 00
†Do do do do bevelled	8 00
†Do do do do papier mache elegant	9 00
Do do do new work, 12mo. cloth	
Copway's (Kah-ge-ga-gah-bowh) Ojibeway Conquest, 12mo. cloth	50
Do do do cloth gilt	1 00
Counting House Manual: French and English correspondence, 12mo. cloth	75
Curzon's Monasteries of the Levant, with eng's 12mo. clo	1 50
Do do do without plts. hlf roan	1 00
Dana's system of Mineralogy, new edition, rev'd 8vo. clo	4 00
Dwight's Ancient Mythology, now edition, do —	1 50
Do do do abridged, 12mo. half roan	75
Downing's Landscape Gardening and Rural Architecture. 5th edition, illustrated, 8vo. cloth	3 50
†Ehninger's Designs to Hood's Bridge of Sighs, 4to. paper	2 00
†Do do do cloth	2 50
†Do do to Irving's Dolph Heyliger, 4to. do	4 00
Eliot's History of Roman Liberty, with ills.2 vols. 8vo clo	4 50
Ellet's Family Pictures from the Bible, 12mo. cloth	75
Do do do do do sheep	87
Do do do do do with frontispiece, gilt extra	1 25
Do Illustrated Scripture Gift Book, with fine engravings, square 8vo. cloth gilt	3 00
Do do do do imitation mor	3 50
Do do do do mor extra	5 00
Fairfax's Tasso's Jerusalem Delivered, 12mo. clo or shp	1 25
Do do do do gilt extra	1 75
Do do do do half calf	1 75
Do do do do full calf extra	2 50
Fadette, a domestic story, 12mo. cloth	75
Do do do cloth extra gilt	1 25
First of the Knickerbockers, 12mo. cloth	75
Ford's Spaniards and their Country, 12mo. clo or sheep	1 00
Do do do do do half calf	1 50
Do do do do do full calf extra	2 50
Fosgate on Sleep, etc. 12mo. cloth	75
Fouqué's Undine and Sintram, 12mo.	50
Do do do gilt extra	1 00
Game of Natural History, in case. plain	50
Do do do colored	1 00
Game of Anna, (poetical) in case.	50
Goethe's Autobiography, 2 vols. 12mo. cloth	1 75

This three-page 1851 trade list of G. P. Putnam publications shows the company's focus on belles lettres and well-made books. The majority of the titles are by contemporary Anglo-American writers. The works of prominent Wiley and Putnam authors—Washington Irving, James Fenimore Cooper, Catharine Maria Sedgwick, and Bayard Taylor—are all available in multiple bindings. Perhaps the most popular title on the list was Susan Warner's The Wide, Wide World, advertised, according to her wishes, as "by Elizabeth Wetherell."

Goethe and Schiller's Correspondence, 12mo.	cloth $1 00
Glimpses of the Wonderful, illustrated,	—— 50
Do do do 12mo.	—— 75
Goodrich's Poems, illustrated by 40 designs, 8vo.	2 00
Do do plain	1 50
Godwin's (Parke) Vala: or the Nightingale, with designs, 4to.	cloth 2 00
Goldsmith's complete Works by Prior, with engraved vignettes, 4 vols. 12mo.	cloth 5 00
Do do do do do sheep	6 00
†Do do do do do half mor	8 00
†Do do do do do gilt tops	9 00
†Do do do do do full elf ex	10 00
Goldsmith's Vicar of Wakefield, 12mo.	cloth 50
Do do do fine edition with eng's. cloth extra gilt	1 25
†Gray's Botanical Text Book, new edition, with 1200 engravings, 8vo.	cloth 1 75
*Gray's Genera of Plants of the U. S. illustrated, 2 vols. royal 8vo.	cloth 12 00
Green on Bronchitis, 2d edition, 8vo.	—— 3 00
Do the Croup, 12mo.	50
Greene's (G. W.) Historical Studies, 12mo. clo or sheep	1 25
†Do do do do half calf	1 75
†Do do do do full calf	2 50
Gibbs' Chemical Text Book, (in press)	
Gilbart on Banking, notes by McCulloch, 1 vol.	cloth
Gilman's (Mrs.) The Sibyl, 12mo.	cloth gt 1 50
Hawks' Egypt and her Monuments: with tinted plates, 8vo.	cloth 2 50
Do do do half mor gt edges	3 50
Do do do school edition, without large plates, 12mo.	hf roan 1 00
Do Monuments of Central and Western America, 8vo. (in press)	
Hervey's Book of Christmas, 12mo.	cloth 50
Do do	cloth ex gt 1 00
Home Treasury: with plates, 12mo.	cloth 50
Homer's Iliad, by Cowper, Notes by Southey: with Flaxman's designs, 8vo.	cloth 3 00
Do do do	cloth gt edges 3 50
Do do school edition, 12mo. hf roan or cloth	1 25
Hood's Poems, 12mo.	cloth 50
Do do do	cloth gt 1 00
Do Prose and Verse, 12mo.	cloth 1 00
Do do do	cloth gt 1 50
Howitt's Songs and Ballads, 12mo.	cloth 76
Do do do with fine portrait,	cloth gt 1 25
Hows' Practical Elocutionist, 12mo.	hf roan 1 00
Hunt's (Leigh) Imagination and Fancy, 12mo.	cloth 63
Do do do	sheep 75
Do do do	cloth gilt 1 00
†Do do do	half calf 1 25
†Do do do	calf extra 2 00
Do Italian Poets, 12mo.	cloth or sheep 1 25
Do do	cloth gilt 1 75
†Do do	half calf 1 75
†Do do	calf extra 2 50
†Irving's (Washington) Complete Works, fine edition, 15 vols. square 12mo.	blue cloth gilt backs 19 00
†Do do do	hf calf 30 00
†Do do do	full calf ex 37 50
†Do do do	hf mor gt tops 32 25
Do do school library edition 12mo. shp ex	22 50
†Do The Alhambra, 12mo.	dark green cloth 1 25
†Do Astoria,	1 50
†Do Bonneville's Adventures,	1 25
†Do Bracebridge Hall,	1 25
†Do do do	cloth gt ex 1 75
†Do Crayon Miscellany,	cloth 1 25
†Do Columbus, 3 vols.	4 50
†Do do fine library edition, 3 vols. royal 8vo.	cloth 6 00
†Do Life of Goldsmith,	1 25
†Do do	cloth gt ex 1 75

Irving's (Washington) Conquest of Granada,	cloth $1 25
†Do Mahomet and his Successors, 2 vols.	—— 2 50
†Do The Sketch Book,	—— 1 25
†Do do	cloth ex gt 1 75
†Do The Traveller,	cloth 1 25
†Do do	cloth gt 1 75
†Do Knickerbocker's New-York,	cloth 1 25
†Do do	cloth gt 1 75
(The above volumes, cloth gilt, are adapted for school prizes, &c.)	
Irving's Works, illustrated with designs, by Darley, &c.	
†The Sketch Book, square 8vo.	cloth 3 50
†Do do do	cloth gt 4 00
†Do do do	mor extra 6 00
†Do do do	bevelled 7 00
†Do Knickerbocker, do	cloth 3 50
†Do do do	cloth gt 4 00
†Do do do	mor extra 6 00
†Do do do	bevelled 7 00
†Do Traveller, do	cloth 3 50
†Do do do	cloth gt 4 00
†Do do do	mor extra 6 00
†Do do do	bevelled 7 00
†Do Goldsmith's Life, 8vo.	cloth 2 50
†Do do do	cloth gt ex 3 00
†Do do do	mor extra 5 00
Do Life of George Washington, with illustrations, (in press).	
Do Crayon Reader, 12mo.	half roan 75
Do Book of the Hudson,	paper cover 25
Do do do	cloth 37
Do do do with fine illus's, 12mo.	50
†Irving's (Theodore) Conquest of Florida, 12mo.	—— 1 25
†Do do do	cloth gilt 1 75
†Do do do	half calf 2 00
†Do Fountain of Living Waters,	cloth 50
Do do do	cloth gilt 75
*Johnston's National Atlas, 41 splendid Maps, large folio, new and improved edition,	half morocco 24 00
Keats' Poetical Works, 12mo.	cloth or sheep 1 00
Do do do	cloth gilt 1 50
Do do do	half calf 1 50
Do do do	calf extra 2 25
Do Life and Letters, by Milnes, 12mo. cloth or sheep	1 25
Do do do do cl. gilt ex. or hlf. calf	1 75
Do do do 'do	full calf 2 50
King of the Hurons, 12mo.	cloth 1 00
Do do	paper covers 75
Kinglake's Eothen: or Traces of Travel in the East, 12mo.	cloth 50
Do do do	cloth gilt 1 00
Do Oriental Life Illustrated, with Engravings on steel,	cloth gilt 1 50
Kingsbury's Artillery and Infantry Practice, 12mo. cloth	75
Kirkland's Spenser's Faery Queene, 12mo.	cloth 63
Do do do	sheep 75
Do do do cloth gilt ex. or hlf. calf	1 25
Do do do	calf extra gilt 2 00
Klipstein's Anglo Saxon Grammar, 12mo.	cloth 1 25
Do do Gospels,	cloth 1 25
Do Analecta Saxonica, 2 vols.	cloth 3 50
Do Ælfric's Homily,	cloth 50
Do Glossary to Analecta Saxonica, (in press.)	
Lamb's Dramatic Poets, 12mo.	cloth 1 25
Do do do	cloth gilt or half calf 1 75
Do do do	calf extra 2 50
Do Essays of Elia,	cloth 1 00
Do do	cloth gilt or half calf 1 50
Do do	full calf 2 00
Lanman's Letters from the Alleghanies, 12mo.	cloth 75
Layard's Nineveh and its Remains, 9th thousand, 2 vols. 8vo., with 113 Illustrations,	cloth 4 50
Do do do	sheep extra 5 00
Do do 2 vols in one, hlf. mor. gilt	5 00
Do do with woodcuts only	
(School Library ed.,) 2 vols. 12mo. hf. roan	1 75

Lowell's Fable for Critics. 12mo. . . cloth .63
Lynch's (Anne C.) Poems, with designs by Darley, 8vo clo $1.50
　Do　　　　do　　　　. . . cloth gilt 2 00
MacFarlane's History of Steam Navigation, 12mo. cloth 75
Martha Martell's Second Love, or the World's Opinion,
　12mo. . . . . cloth 1 00
　Do　　　　do　　　do . . cloth gilt 1 50
Montague's Selections from Taylor, Burton, Hooker,
　&c., 12mo. . . . . cloth 63
　Do　　　do　　　do　 . . . sheep 75
　Do　　　do　　　do . . cloth gilt extra 1 25
McCulloch's Essays on Currency, &c., 8vo. . sewed
Manual of the Fine Arts, Critical and Historical,
　12mo. . . . . cloth 1 25
　Do　　(for School libraries and Classes) sheep 1 25
†Do　　　　　　　　　 . . . . half calf 1 75
†Do　　　　　　　　　 . . . . calf extra 2 50
Mayo's (W. S.) Kaloolah, a Romance, 4th ed. 12mo. cloth 1 25
　Do　　　do　　　 . . . . cloth gilt 2 00
　Do　　　do　　cheap ed. in 8vo. paper covers 50
　Do　　The Berber: a Romance of Morocco, 3rd
　　edition. 12mo. . . . . . cloth 1 25
　Do　　Romance Dust, 12mo. . . . cloth 1 00
*Memorial, (The) a Souvenir of Genius and Virtue, with
　fine engravings on steel, 8vo. . . cloth gilt 3 50
　*Do　　do　　 . . . . morocco extra 5 00
Owen's Hints on Public Architecture, with 113 tinted
　plates, 1 vol. 4to. . . . . . cloth 6 00
Parkman's Prairie and Rocky Mountain Life, 12mo,
　　　　　　　　 . . . . cloth or sheep 1 25
　Do　　do　　do . . . half calf 1 75
†Do　　do　　do . . . calf extra 2 50
Putnam's World's Progress: a Dictionary of Dates, 5th
　thousand, small 8vo. . . . . cloth 2 00
†Do　　do　　do . . . sheep extra 2 25
　Do　　do　　do half moroc. marbled edge 2 75
　Do　　do　　do　　do . gilt tops 3 00
　Do　　do　　do . . . calf extra 3 50
　Do　　do　　do . . antique morocco 3 75
Putnam's Book-Buyer's Manual, with a classified index,
　8vo. . . . . half bound 75
　Do　　Home-Manuals or Cyclopædias—uniform with
　　the World's Progress,
　Do　　Hand-Book of Science, . . (in press.)
　Do　　do　　of Literature and Fine Arts, do
　Do　　do　　of Biography, . . do
　Do　　do　　of the Useful Arts, . do
Pragay's Hungarian War, 2d edition, 12mo. cloth 75
Peacock's Headlong Hall and Nightmare Abbey, 12mo.
　　　　　　　　 . . . . . . cloth 50
Ridner's Artist's Hand-Book, 12mo. . . cloth 75
Robinson's (Mrs.) Literature of the Slavic Nations, 12mo.
　　　　　　　　 . . . . . . cloth 1 25
Roscoe's Life of Benvenuto Cellini, new edit., 12mo. cloth 1 25
Richards' Shakspeare Callendar, 18mo. . . cloth 38
　Do　　do　　do　 . . . gilt extra 63
Robinson Crusoe's Farm Yard, 16mo. . half bound 50
*Roorbach's Bibliotheca Americana, 8vo. . cloth 4 00
　*Do　　do　　Supplement to do. 8vo. cloth 1 50
Sedgwick's (Miss C. M.) Clarence: A Tale, 12mo.
　　　　　　　　 . . . . cloth or sheep 1 25
†Do　　do　　do　 . . . half calf 1 75
†Do　　do　　do　 . . . calf extra 2 50
　Do　　do　Redwood, 12mo. clo or sheep 1 24
†Do　　do　　do　 . . . half calf 1 75
†Do　　do　　do　 . . . calf extra 2 50
　Do　　Morals of Manners, 16mo. . cloth 25
　Do　　Facts and Fancies, do . . do 50
　Do　　A New England Tale, 12mo.

Sedgwick's (Miss C. M.) A New Work, (in press.)
Smyth's Unity of the Races, 12mo. . . cloth $1 25
Smith's New Elements of Geometry, 8vo. —— 1 00
Spencer's, The East, with 8 fine illustrations, 8vo. —— 3 00
　Do　　do　　 . . half mor gilt edges 4 00
　Do　　do　　school edition, 12mo. half roan 1 50
Squier (Hon. E. G.) Nicaragua, with illustrations, 8vo. clo
Stuart (Prof. M.) Commentary on Ecclesiastes, 12mo. ——
St. John's Lybian Desert, 12mo. . . . cloth 75
　Do　　do　　do　 . . . half roan 75
St. Leger, or the Threads of Life, 3d ed. 12mo. cloth 1 00
　Do　　do　　do　 . . . half calf 1 50
　Do　　do　　do　 . . . calf extra 2 25
Sweetser's Mental Hygiene, 12mo. . . cloth 1 00
Taylor's (Bayard) Eldorado, 3d edition, with tinted plates,
　2 vols, 12mo. . . . . . . cloth 2 00
　Do　　do　　do　　do　 . sheep 2 00
　Do　　do　　do　without plates 1 vol. 12mo.
　　　　　　　　 . . . . cloth or sheep 1 25
　Do　　do　　do　 . . . half calf 1 75
　Do　　do　　do　 . . . calf extra 2 50
　Do　　Views a-foot, 12th ed. 12mo. . cloth 1 25
　Do　　do　　do　school library edition, sheep 1 25
　Do　　do　　do　 . . . half calf 1 75
　Do　　do　　do　 . . . calf extra 2 50
　Do　　Rhymes of Travel, 12mo. . . cloth 75
　Do　　do　　do　 . . . gilt extra 1 25
Tuckerman's, The Optimist, 12mo. . . cloth 75
　Do　　do　　 . . . . half calf 1 25
　Do　　do　　 . . . . calf extra 1 75
Turnbull's Genius of Italy, 3d edition, 12mo. cloth 1 00
　Do　　do　　do　 . . . sheep 1 25
　Do　　do　　do　 . . . half calf 1 50
†Do　　do　　do　 . . . calf extra 2 25
　Do　　do　　do with 8 illustrations, gilt extra 2 00
Tuthill's (Mrs.) Nursery Book, 18mo. . . cloth 50
　Do　　Success in Life, The Merchant, with plates,
　　12mo. . . . . half bound 63
　Do　　do　do　　do　 . gilt extra 1 00
　Do　　The Lawyer, with plates, 12mo. half bound 50
　Do　　do　　do　 . . . gilt extra 1 00
　Do　　The Mechanic, with plates, 12mo. half bound 63
　Do　　do　　do　 . . . gilt extra 1 00
　Do　　The Artist, (in press.)
Tschudi's Travels in Peru, 12mo. . . cloth 1 00
　Do　　do　　do　 . . . sheep 1 25
　Do　　do　　do　 . . . half calf 1 75
　Do　　do　　do　 . . . calf extra 2 25
Ungewitter's Europe, Past and Present, with index, 3d
　edition, large 12mo. . . . . cloth 1 50
　Do　　do　　do　　do　 . half roan 1 50
　Do　　do　　do　　do　 . sheep 1 75
Walton's Lives of Hooker, Donne, &c., 12mo. cloth 1 00
　Do　　do　　do　 . . . sheep 1 25
　Do　　do　　do　 . . . half calf 1 75
　Do　　do　　do　cloth gilt extra 1 50
　Do　　do　　do　 . . . calf extra 2 25
Warburton's Crescent and the Cross, 12mo. cloth 1 25
　Do　　do　　do　 . . . half roan 1 25
　Do　　do　　do　 . . . sheep 1 25
　Do　　do　　do　 . . . half calf 1 75
　Do　　do　　do　 . . . calf extra 2 50
Wide, Wide World, by Elizabeth Wetherell, 2d edition,
　2 vols, 12mo. . . . . . . cloth 1 50
　Do　　do　　do　2 vols. in 1, gilt extra 2 00
Willard's Last Leaves of American History, 12mo. cloth 1 00
　Do　　do　　do　for libraries, sheep 1 00
Young Naturalist's Rambles, 16mo. . . cloth 50
Young American's Primer; numerous engravings, 12mo.
　　　　　　　　 . . . . . . sewed, 25

Baker, Godwin & Co., Printers, No. 1 Spruce-st., N. Y.

Several of Putnam's successful ventures were with foreign authors. Through his long-standing connection with the English publisher John Murray, Putnam obtained the rights to publish the pioneering Assyriologist Sir Austen Henry Layard's *Nineveh and Its Remains* (1849), which proved so successful that the company followed it up with *Discoveries in the Ruins of Nineveh and Babylon* (1853). Another popular writer picked up by the company was the Swedish novelist Fredrika Bremer. By coming to terms with her to republish and pay royalties for *The Home* and *The Neighbors,* which had been published in the United States by Harper and Brothers in the 1840s with no offer of royalties, Putnam was doing what he considered a justice to her. The Harpers, however, retaliated by underselling Putnam with cheaper editions not only of Bremer's books but also of Layard's *Discoveries in the Ruins of Nineveh and Babylon.*

As was the pattern among other successful firms, many of G. P. Putnam's publications during this period were generated in-house. Some were series publications such as Putnam's District School Library, Putnam's Semi-Monthly Library, Putnam's

Railway Library, and Putnam's Home Cyclopedia (one of the six reference volumes of this last series included an updated edition of Putnam's *Chronology*). Among the most inventive and original projects the company produced were the three historically significant gift books that Putnam himself initiated and edited: *The Home Book of the Picturesque* (1852), *Homes of American Authors* (1853), and *Homes of American Statesmen* (1854). All of these G. P. Putnam books were finely produced, drawing on the work of the leading writers and illustrators of the day and incorporating the latest technology of bookmaking.

In fall 1852 Putnam took on his first partner, John Leslie, a young businessman who had already been with the firm for several years, and changed the name of the business to G. P. Putnam and Company. Putnam continued to oversee the publishing operations and assigned Leslie chief responsibilities for the accounts. Putnam's decision to go into partnership might well have been related to the two major initiatives that the firm was then considering and that became realities early in 1853: the undertaking of *Putnam's Monthly* and the bid to gain the status of

Publishing the Crystal Palace

Foreseeing an extraordinary publishing opportunity for his company, Putnam wrote in 1852 to Theodore Sedgwick, the president of the organizing committee of the 1853 New York Exhibition of the Industry of all Nations. In offering the services of his firm as official publisher of the exhibition, Putnam, who came to terms with Sedgwick in early 1853, was making a mistake that eventually resulted in serious financial losses.

Nov 13th 2

Theodore Sedgwick Esq

President of the Assocn. for Exhbt. of Industry etc.

Sir, We beg leave to submit the following proposition for printing publishing & selling the Catalogues of the Exhibition of the Industry of all Nations, viz.

We will print and publish at our own expense a plain edition of the Catalogue in such form and at such price as shall be approved by your Board of Directors.

We will also print & publish at our own expense an Illustrated edition of such Catalogue subject also to similar approval.

For the exclusive right to print these Catalogues and vend the same in the Exhibition building &

elsewhere, we will bind ourselves to pay to your association say one tenth of the gross sales, and in addition, to said tenth we will pay one third the nett profit of said Catalogues up to the time of closing the Exhibition.

In connection, and as a collateral arrangement, we would ask the privilege of placing in the Exhibition a steam printing press of great power, on which we propose to print an Illustrated journal devoted to the Exhibition and to kindred subjects. If your Board should see fit to give us the exclusive right to print such paper in the Building we will pay the Association one-half of the nett profits arriving [?] in the sale of the paper.

In regard to our responsibility and standing we presume that they are not unfavorably known—but, if necessary for the satisfaction of your Board, a suitable guarantee could be given, for our creditable fullfilment of the undertaking.

Very respectfully, Sir,

Your Obdt. Servt.

Geo P. Putnam &c

—*Manuscripts Division, Department of Rare Books and Special Collections, Princeton University Library. Published with permission of the Princeton University Library.*

Illustration in the 13 August 1853 issue of the London Illustrated News *showing the crowds, including President Franklin Pierce and members of his cabinet, attending the inauguration of New York's Crystal Palace, which was modeled after the Crystal Palace erected in London for the Great Exhibition of 1851.*

authorized publisher to the first world's fair held in the United States, the 1853 Exposition of the Industry of All Nations held in New York's Crystal Palace. The former was a major critical and a moderate commercial success; the latter, a financial disaster. The two initiatives ended within months of each other in late 1854 to early 1855 as the firm struggled to balance its books. The need for capital had become so severe by spring 1854 that the firm went to auction several times within months to sell off retail stock and even the plates of many of its leading properties. This sudden emergency must have caught Putnam by surprise, and at the time he was evidently unaware that an additional cause of his firm's problems—beyond its having made too many investments with too little capital—was the likely embezzlement of company funds by Leslie.

Financial Difficulties and Recovery

On 15 September 1854 Putnam called his creditors together and presented a case for his solvency. He must have been persuasive, since the firm's chief authors–Irving, Taylor, and Warner–remained loyal and its main creditors continued to be supportive. Although he was able to keep G. P. Putnam and Company in operation, he was forced to contract its activities, selling the magazine and drawing in his list more tightly around his core authors. This new cautionary strategy proved so effective that as finances stabilized the company resumed a more active publishing strategy. The first two volumes of Irving's *Life of George Washington* appeared in 1855 and sold well, as did the latest travel narratives by the prolific Taylor. The firm also published Melville's *Israel Potter* (1855), which had been first serialized in *Putnam's Magazine;* new editions of several of John Pendleton Kennedy's most popular novels, *Swallow Barn* (1851) and *Horse-Shoe Robinson* (1852); Susan Cooper's *The Rhyme and Reason of Country Life* (1854); and a condensed one-volume edition of Richard Burton's *Personal Narrative of a Pilgrimage to El-Medinah and Meccah* (1856), which included an introduction by Taylor, the first American edition of Burton's work.

The renewed prosperity of G. P. Putnam and Company ended suddenly in summer 1857, catching Putnam completely unawares. After Leslie's death by drowning on 4 July, Putnam inspected the firm's account books and discovered that his partner had embezzled large sums from the company, leaving it virtually insolvent. Worse yet, the firm's exigency coincided with a spiraling financial panic overtaking the entire economy. Unable to replicate the arrangement he had made in 1854, Putnam had no choice but to declare bankruptcy. He was fortunate, at least, to receive a favorable settlement that allowed him to pay off his major creditors and resume limited operations.

His firm's financial crisis compelled Putnam to take the drastic measure of selling off many of the company's assets in stereotype plates and stocks. One of the authors whose properties he parted with was Catharine Maria Sedgwick, an old friend and longtime client of both Wiley and Putnam and G. P. Putnam. Putnam thought enough of her to assemble in the late 1840s and early 1850s a revised author's edition of some of her leading works, just as he was doing with Irving, Cooper, and Kennedy. Finding confusion ensuing from the transfer of her works to the publisher J. C. Derby, Charles Sedgwick, the author's brother, appealed to Putnam for clarification in his 12 December 1855 letter.

Lenox Dec 12. 1855

G. P. Putnam Esq

Dr Sir

In yr letter to my Sister of Mar. 30. 1854. you inform her of the Transfer by you to J. C. Derby of the stereotype plates of the "New England Tale" "Clarence" & "Redwood" & the Transfer to Evans & Dickerson of "Facts & Fancies & Morals of manners" & that these publishers were to assume yr Responsibilities & to acct. to my sister in like manner as you had done–In the same letter you requested my sister to send you her copy of the agreement with her consent to the Transfer–This was promptly done & you refd. to a certificate of Evans & Dickerson of their purchase & an undertaking by them to fulfill yr agreement–The Certificate of Mr. Derby was not forwarded but you may recollect that you promised to do so, & that afterwards I called at yr office & you said that there wd be no difficulty respecting it & that it should be attended to–now my Dr. Sir, as neither Derby nor Evans & Dickerson have never [*sic*] done a thing abt these Books–& as the Transfer to them has operated to deprive my sister of the Income of the Books which she deserved from you, you perceive that it is important she should be put in possession of the papers that she may understand perfectly her *rights*–as well as her obligations & liabilities to Derby & Evans & Dickerson–I have therefore to request that you will have the kindness to return me the copy of the contract forwarded at yr request & the assent to the transfer by Mr. Derby if it has been or can be procured & if not your certificate of the facts that I may know the legal relation that subsists between my Sister and Mr. J. C. Derby.

I am truly sorry to trouble you for I know yr. hands are full–but it is really important to my Sister to make a final disposition of these Books.–I am Dr. Sir

Truly and Respy.

Yr Friend

Chas. Sedgwick

–Manuscripts Division, Department of Rare Books and Special Collections, Princeton University Library. Published with permission of the Princeton University Library.

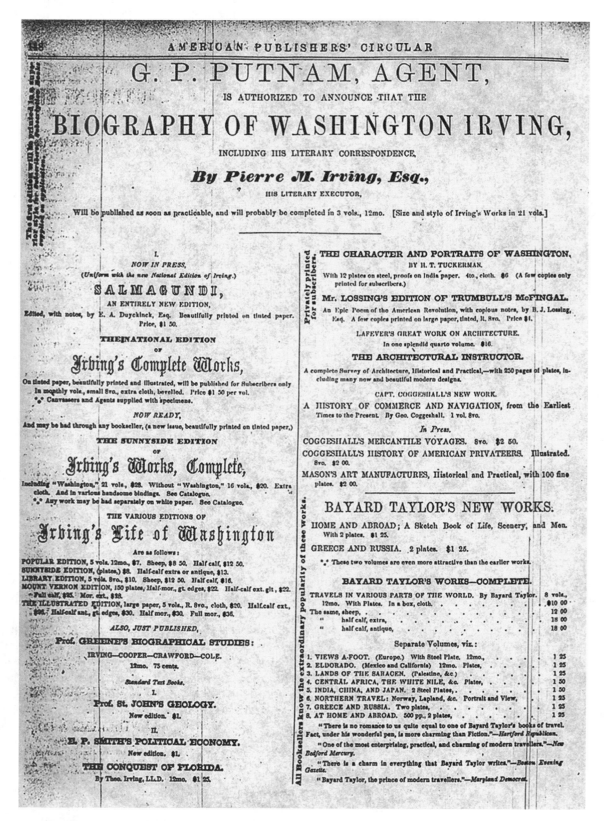

Announcement of the Putnam firm's activities and plans in the 24 March 1860 issue of American Publishers' Circular and Literary Gazette. *Unable to persuade Irving to write his autobiography, Putnam was determined to publish a full-scale biography of the author by his nephew and literary executor.*

G. P. Putnam reopened for business in September 1857, its list anchored by the works of the still loyal Irving and Taylor. The profits from these writers' continued productivity and the enduring popularity of their old works, combined with scaled-back business expenses, achieved by taking smaller offices and laying off personnel, made viable Putnam's posture as an all-purpose publisher and agent to Irving and Cooper. With improved financial conditions in the country and greater stability for the house came better times.

The publication of the last volume of *Life of George Washington* in 1859 boosted interest in Irving's complete oeuvre, which was reinforced when the author died late that year. The firm took full advantage of the renewed interest in Irving by marketing his works aggressively during the years from 1859 to 1861, giving them greater attention than the works of any other American writer had ever received. Furthermore, just a few months after Irving's death Putnam reached an agreement with his nephew and literary executor, Pierre Irving, for a biography, *The Life and Letters of Washington Irving* (1862–1864), which was published in four volumes and proved a strong seller. In 1863 Putnam gambled on the continuing popularity of Irving's most famous title by producing a lavish "Artist's Edition" of his *Sketch Book,* which included 120 illustrations by the leading artists of the country. The cost to produce this volume was reportedly $20,000–an unprecedentedly high expense for a single volume–which he shared with young Henry Holt, who was just beginning his distinguished career.

G. P. Putnam had reestablished its financial stability before the beginning of the Civil War, which Putnam, in contrast to his peers, saw less as an obstacle than as a challenge. Despite the loss of Southern markets and the steep rise of prices, he set an ambitious publishing course within weeks of the outbreak of hostilities on 12 April 1861. Later in that month he announced the publication of the *Rebellion Record,* an illustrated serial archive of printed materials relating to the conflict that evolved into one of the most important compendia to come out of the war. He was careful, however, to keep that project and related ones distinct from the affairs of the company, publishing them instead via the partnership he formed with two other New York City literary professionals, journalist Frank Moore and publisher Charles T. Evans. He also published a wide variety of topical books relating to the war. In addition, he did his best to keep the works of Irving and Taylor before the public. Although facing a depressed market for books, he was aided in selling the works of his two

prime authors by the success of Pierre Irving's biography of his uncle and by Taylor's turn toward fiction and the completion of the first of three popular novels, *Hannah Thurston* (1863).

Putnam dramatically altered the course of his own career in 1864 and, with it, the status of his house. Since his appointment as the United States Revenue Collector for the Eighth District of New York in 1862, he had been working two full-time jobs simultaneously, dividing his time between his government office at 921 Broadway and his publishing office at 441 Broadway. Already fifty years old at the time of his appointment, Putnam soon found his multiple responsibilities too demanding. In 1863 he brought in help, hiring J. C. Derby, one of the most experienced and energetic bookmen in the country, to assist with the promotion of the Artist's Edition of *The Sketch Book* and probably other G. P. Putnam publications. In spring 1864 he negotiated an arrangement with the firm of Hurd and Houghton, his neighbors a block down Broadway, to take over his publishing assets effective 1 August 1864. The agreement with Hurd and Houghton had been partially anticipated by Putnam's decision the previous year to enter into a marketing arrangement with Ticknor and Fields of Boston for the distribution of books in their respective cities. At the time, he contracted with their printer, Henry Houghton, the proprietor of the renowned Riverside Press of Cambridge, for the production of a new "blue and gold" edition of *The Sketch Book* similar to the ones he was producing for Ticknor and Fields. Putnam must have been sufficiently impressed by Houghton to feel comfortable assigning his properties to Houghton and his new partner.

A Family Business

Putnam's arrangement with Hurd and Houghton continued for several years, with Putnam leaving the day-to-day management to his partners, though he occasionally checked in and consulted with them. But suddenly in autumn 1866 Putnam ended the partnership–a decision that was precipitated when President Andrew Johnson fired him from his post after Putnam refused to make a government appointee's expected donation in support of the chief executive. Left with no means of support, Putnam lost no time in the last weeks of the year taking back his plates and stock from Hurd and Houghton, renting second-floor offices at 661 Broadway, and preparing to reopen for business. By the time he was ready to open his door to business in January 1867, his house was for the first time a family business: G. P. Putnam and Son, the son being his eldest, George Haven Putnam, his eventual successor as head of the firm.

Illustration on G. P. Putnam and Son stationery showing their offices in the new YMCA building, where the company moved in 1870 (George Palmer Putnam Collection, Manuscripts Division, Princeton University Library)

G. P. Putnam and Son ran a tight ship; Putnam handled the publishing affairs of the house, George Haven the accounts, and several employees the secretarial and general office work. In 1868 the second oldest son among the ten Putnam children, John Bishop Putnam, was brought into the business and given primary responsibility for overseeing the production of the house's publications, which remained entirely an external function. In 1870 Putnam formally recognized John Bishop's contribution to the firm by renaming the company G. P. Putnam and Sons. In 1872 Putnam's third oldest son, Irving Putnam, was brought into the business; his responsibilities were initially limited, although after his father's death he became head of the retail operations of G. P. Putnam's Sons and took responsibility in later years for its new bookstore.

The years from 1867 to 1872 were precarious for the reconstituted house. The Putnams began with little operating capital and were hampered throughout this period by insufficient funds. Furthermore,

they entered the market at a competitive disadvantage to better established houses with deeper pockets, connections to the leading writers of the younger generation, and successful house periodicals. What the Putnams did have from the start was George Palmer Putnam's good name with writers, editors, publishers, bankers, and the general public; his longstanding ties throughout the profession; and the core properties–especially the works of Irving and Taylor–left over from his earlier company's backlist. They immediately secured from Pierre Irving rights to his uncle's works for an additional five-year period and reached terms with Taylor for the publication of his newest work, *Colorado* (1867), and the reprinting of his earlier works. They also reprinted other works on their backlist, including four volumes of fiction and nonfiction compiled from *Putnam's Monthly*. New works they published included *No Love Lost* (1869), an early novel by William Dean Howells, and *Book of the Artists* (1867), a new study by longtime Putnam author Henry Tuckerman, which returned the house to its historic strength as a publisher of art books.

Putnam also decided during the first year of operation to take on the challenge of resuscitating *Putnam's Monthly,* which was retitled *Putnam's Magazine.* He had been tempted to do so right from the start but restrained the urge until he thought company finances were sufficient to sustain a general magazine. Relying on many of the people who had made *Putnam's Monthly* a success, especially Charles Frederick Briggs, whom he brought back as editor, Putnam published the first number in January 1868. Despite his best efforts to engage first-rate editorial and authorial talent, *Putnam's Magazine* was a shadow of its former self and proved a feeble competitor to a new generation of better written, better illustrated, better financed American magazines, such as *Atlantic Monthly, Harper's Monthly,* and *The Nation.* Putnam postponed the inevitable for several years before resigning himself to failure and reaching an agreement in autumn 1870 with his old friend Charles Scribner to merge *Putnam's* with Scribner's planned new magazine *Scribner's Monthly.*

The firm moved in 1870 to new quarters in the recently built Young Men's Christian Association (YMCA) building at the corner of Twenty-third Street and Fourth Avenue–by far the most northern location any G. P. Putnam office had occupied and one well situated in the reconfigured business district of the fast-growing city. Increased space allowed the Putnams to reinstate a retail operation that had been in suspension since the mid 1850s; they kept the store well stocked with a wide selection of American and European works as well as with choice bibliographical and artistic items picked up by Putnam during his periodic trips to England. He had resumed in 1867 his earlier custom of traveling overseas about once a year (or sending George Haven in his place) to attempt to make arrangements for American publication of British works. These European trips were less successful than those he had made in the antebellum years, and he found no best-selling author or work for his company. Putnam had fewer connections to writers, particularly younger ones, than he had enjoyed in his dynamic days; the company list of the late 1860s–early 1870s was heavily oriented toward the past. Fortunately for the Putnams, they did still have important assets on which to draw, such as Irving and Taylor, whose works they continued to print in multiple editions, and they made effective use of their still serviceable backlist.

The financial situation of G. P. Putnam and Sons was especially tenuous through much of 1872,

when George Haven several times had trouble paying bills. The sudden death of Putnam on 20 December left the future of the company in immediate doubt. To ease the burden on the family and business, fellow publishers kept the store open during the holiday shopping season while the brothers remained home in mourning. On their return, they reorganized the company as G. P. Putnam's Sons and managed to survive not only the panic of 1873 but several additional years of difficulty. In the mid 1870s the brothers began to take the series of actions that turned the business into a far more financially secure, better rounded enterprise than it had ever previously been. No longer content to continue the longstanding practice of working with independent printing houses in the city, John Bishop in 1874 established an in-house printing office, which for the first time gave the company integrated manufacturing and selling functions. Two decades later he took the initiative one step further by building a full-scale book manufacturing plant in New Rochelle, the Knickerbocker Press. During the same period George Haven greatly expanded the house's publishing list, built up a new core of Putnam authors and series, and opened a branch office in London that proved an important asset in improving the firm's status in both international publishing and bookselling. By the 1880s and 1890s, G. P. Putnam's Sons was once again one of the most thriving houses in American publishing.

The End of an Era

In the days following their father's sudden death, the sons planned the restructuring of the family firm and came out with a formal announcement of its change of name.

New York City.–The partnership heretofore existing between George P. Putnam, George Haven Putnam, and John Bishop Putnam, all of New York, under the firm name of G. P. Putnam & Sons, was dissolved on the 20th of December, by the death of George P. Putnam. The business of the firm will be continued without change or interruption at its present location, 308 4th ave. and 54 E. 23d st., by George Haven Putnam and John Bishop Putnam, under the firm name of G. P. Putnam's Sons.

–The Publishers' Weekly, 3 (2 January 1873): 11

Illustrated Chronology

This chronology presents a selected list of significant events and publications in the career of George Palmer Putnam and the history of his publishing house.

1837

March　　John Wiley and George Palmer Putnam form the partnership of Wiley and Putnam. The firm operates out of rented quarters at 161 Broadway in the heart of the bookselling sector of Manhattan and engages in general bookselling and publishing, as well as acting as a purchasing agent for individual and institutional book buyers.

April–December　　Putnam's European travelogue, based on his reconnaissance tour the previous year on behalf of Wiley and Long, is published as "Random Leaves from a Journal of Travels in England, Scotland, France, and Germany" in eight monthly installments (May excepted) in the *Knickerbocker Magazine*.

1838

August　　Putnam arrives in London to open a Wiley and Putnam office, the first overseas branch of an American publishing house. He takes up quarters at 67 Paternoster Row, advertises his firm in the local and professional papers, and quickly makes the acquaintance of people in the trade.

October　　Putnam initiates the publication of a Wiley and Putnam London edition of Edgar Allan Poe's recently published novel *The Narrative of Arthur Gordon Pym*, quite possibly the firm's first publication in England.

No doubt as a favor to Putnam, Lewis Gaylord Clark printed a friendly notice of Wiley and Putnam's recently opened London office and its transatlantic services.

AMERICAN PUBLISHING HOUSE IN LONDON.—We ask attention to the catalogue annexed to the present number, of the new American Publishing and Bookselling House of Messrs. WILEY AND PUTNAM, 67 Paternoster-Row, London. This establishment supplies an important desideratum to our people, as well as London, (and London is England, and something more.) The increasing demand for information concerning this country, our literature, especially, can now be freely and expeditiously supplied, while the libraries of our colleges and other public institutions, not less than those of private individuals, may now be supplied, with unfailing despatch, and with but a trifling advance from English prices. Rare books, prints, and other works of art, also, new or old, may be received here, within an incredibly brief space of time, and we may add, also, at an incredibly small expense, compared with prices demanded but a short time ago. Of the partner in England, GEORGE P. PUTNAM, Esq., we may say, generally, (and we speak from a long and intimate acquaintance,) that Americans abroad will find him to unite the courteous bearing and unassuming manners of a gentleman, with the spirit and feeling of a true American, whose pride and pleasure it will be, to serve the interests of his countrymen; and all who may have occasion to test his business qualities, in the execution of foreign orders, may rely upon his faithful and effective discharge of even the most difficult literary trust.

—*Knickerbocker Magazine,* 12 (November 1838): 468–469

LONDON BOOK AGENCY.

WILEY & PUTNAM,

WHOLESALE DEALERS IN

ENGLISH AND OTHER FOREIGN BOOKS,

No. 35 Paternoster Row, LONDON, and No. 161 Broadway, NEW-YORK.

THE Subscribers have established at No. 35 Paternoster Row, London, an Agency conducted by one of the house under the same firm as in New-York, for the purchase of choice ENGLISH, FRENCH, and GERMAN PUBLICATIONS, for Universities and Private Libraries ; and for the sale of American Books, Periodicals, and Copyrights.

Such an arrangement, it has been often suggested, would be very desirable for Authors and Publishers on this side, who wish either to effect sales of their own editions of original works suited to the English market, or to secure a London Copyright therefor : while to Literary Institutions, and Individuals about making additions to their libraries, it offers the following inducements, viz. :

I. All orders, either for the Trade or for Gentlemen wishing but a single Book, will be personally and carefully attended to by one of the firm, who is well acquainted with the British and Continental Book Market; purchases are made of the Publishers, direct, without the usual commissions of a London Agent : and in many cases, rare and voluminous works are obtained, at the Library Auction Sales and otherwise, at prices much depreciated.

II. If funds to three-fourths the amount of any considerable order are furnished in advance, the commission charged for all purchases is but 10 per cent. on the original cost at the lowest wholesale prices ; and as our purchases are often made in quantities for the Trade, or in exchange for American Books, we can usually deliver English Books in New-York at prices as low, and sometimes much less, than those of the London Publishers.

III. Books for Incorporated Literary Institutions we engage to furnish *free of duty;* and in most cases, they will be received in New-York within seventy days from the date of the order.

Having been favored with orders from the following Institutions, we have the pleasure of referring to their Directors, viz. :

Columbia College, New-York.	Connecticut Institute.
University of the City of New-York.	Athenæum, Salem, Mass.
Mercantile Library Association, New-York.	Williams College, Mass.
Society Library and Athenæum, New-York.	United States' Naval Lyceum, Brooklyn.
Geneva College, Geneva, N.Y.	United States' War Department, Washington.
Military Academy, West Point, N.Y.	University of Virginia.
Michigan University and State Libraries, Detroit.	University of Alabama.
Dartmouth College, Hanover, N.H.	University of Georgia.
Yale College, New Haven, Conn.	University of Louisiana.
Hartford Institute, Conn.	

*** Orders for FRENCH & GERMAN BOOKS executed on the same terms, and the Goods shipped direct from Havre or Hamburgh.

The MAGAZINES and PERIODICALS of every description forwarded by the Steamers, or by the Liverpool Packets, of the 1st of each Month, the day of Publication in London.

ENGLISH AND FOREIGN CATALOGUES FURNISHED.

Your orders are respectfully solicited, addressed as above, 161 Broadway, New-York ; or 35 Paternoster Row, London.

WILEY & PUTNAM.

Advertisement for its London agency that Wiley and Putnam sent to institutional clients throughout the United States (courtesy of the Harvard University Archives)

1839

Spring   Putnam hosts Evert Duyckinck, one of the firm's best clients, who is visiting London. The two men board for the duration of Duyckinck's stay in the same rooming house on the Strand.

June   Wiley and Putnam relocates to 35 Paternoster Row.

1840

Winter   Putnam arrives back in New York for a visit that lasts nearly half a year.

Spring   Putnam becomes engaged to Victorine Haven, but his fiancée's guardians consider her too young to enter immediately into marriage. He travels down to Washington, D.C., on book-related business, possibly to confer with lobby members of Congress about international copyright. On his return journey up the eastern seaboard he offers Wiley and Putnam's London services to libraries and private book buyers.

25 July   Putnam sails back to England alone from New York.

August   In London, Putnam hosts the prolific historian and Harvard professor Jared Sparks and the Bible scholar Edward Robinson, an important Wiley and Putnam author.

1841

January   Needing more space, Wiley and Putnam relocates its London office to Amen Corner, Stationers' Court, another address in the heart of the bookselling district.

February   Putnam returns to New York for a brief trip, the main purpose of which is to marry Victorine Haven.

15 March   Putnam marries Haven at her sister's house in Manhattan, with Reverend Orville Dewey presiding. The young couple journey briefly to Washington, D.C., where they are introduced to the newly installed president, William Henry Harrison, before returning back north.

1 April   The Putnams sail from Boston for London.

September   The company initiates publication in New York of *Wiley and Putnam's Literary News-Letter and Monthly Register of New Books Foreign and American*. Though oriented toward the firm's own publications, it serves as the leading American trade publication until it merges in 1847 with the newly launched *Literary World*.

1842

April/May   Wiley and Putnam publish the first American edition of George Borrow's *The Zincali*. The book is undersold by cheaper, pirated editions.

August   Mary Putnam, the first of the Putnams' ten children, is born in the family house at Euston Square.

1843

Summer   Putnam returns to the United States for an extended stay.

23 August   Putnam takes part in the formation of the American Copyright Club in New York, a group whose purpose is to promote the adoption of international copyright laws.

Notice appearing in the March 1841 issue of Knickerbocker Magazine.

Advertisement in the 15 July 1841 issue of American Publishers' Circular and Literary Gazette. *Wiley and Putnam often publicized its services in the press, especially the trade journals, on both sides of the Atlantic.*

| Fall | Putnam spends weeks traveling the eastern seaboard from the South to New England collecting names for a petition in support of an international copyright agreement, which he presents to Congress in December shortly before his departure for England. |

1844

| March | Wiley and Putnam relocates its London office, which Putnam renames the American Literary Agency, to spacious quarters at Waterloo Place. Putnam establishes a reading room with American newspapers, magazines, books, and paintings. |
| April | George Haven Putnam, George Palmer Putnam's first son and future head of G. P. Putnam's Sons, is born in the house on St. John's Wood Road, to which the family recently moved. |

AMERICAN FACTS.

NOTES AND STATISTICS

RELATIVE TO THE

GOVERNMENT, RESOURCES, ENGAGEMENTS, MANUFACTURES,
COMMERCE, RELIGION, EDUCATION, LITERATURE,
FINE ARTS, MANNERS AND CUSTOMS

OF THE

UNITED STATES OF AMERICA.

BY GEORGE PALMER PUTNAM,

MEMBER OF THE NEW YORK HISTORICAL SOCIETY; HON. MEM. OF THE CONNECTICUT
HIST. SOC.; HON. SECRETARY OF THE AMERICAN ART-UNION.

AUTHOR OF AN INTRODUCTION TO HISTORY, ETC.

WITH PORTRAITS AND A MAP.

LONDON:
WILEY AND PUTNAM, 6, WATERLOO PLACE,
AND 161, BROADWAY, NEW YORK.

1845.

Title page for book that Putnam wrote to dispel European ignorance about the United States. For its time Putnam's book was one of the most complete compendia of information about his native country.

1845

February	Wiley hires Evert Duyckinck as literary adviser and launches the Wiley and Putnam Library of Choice Reading. A decision is soon made to publish a separate American series, the Library of American Books, which is to consist exclusively of new works by American writers. Putnam arranges to publish many of the titles from the Library of American Books series in England.
April	Wiley and Putnam publishes Putnam's *American Facts* in London.
June	Wiley and Putnam publishes Poe's *Tales* in its Library of American Books.
September	Wiley and Putnam publishes William Gilmore Simms's *The Wigwam and the Cabin,* first series, in the Library of American Books.
November	Wiley and Putnam publishes Poe's *The Raven and Other Poems.*
December	Wiley and Putnam publishes the first American edition of Thomas Carlye's *Oliver Cromwell's Letters and Speeches.*

1846

Winter — Arriving in London short of funds after a European tour, Bayard Taylor makes the acquaintance of Putnam and takes temporary work in the Wiley and Putnam office. He remains until May, when his earnings allow him to book passage to the United States.

January — Gansvoort Melville, acting as his brother's literary agent and accompanied by Washington Irving, comes to Putnam's London office to offer Wiley and Putnam American rights to Herman Melville's *Typee,* which is being published by Murray in England. Putnam and Melville agree to terms within days, and Putnam sends to New York a set of proofs, corrected from the London edition, on the 4 February steamer.

February — Wiley and Putnam publishes the second series of Simms's *The Wigwam and the Cabin* in the Library of American Books.

March — Wiley and Putnam publishes *Typee* in the Library of American Books.

April — Wiley and Putnam publishes Simms's *Views and Reviews in American Literature, History and Fiction* in the Library of American Books.

Putnam visits Carlyle at his home and offers the services of Wiley and Putnam as his American publishers. They begin complicated negotiations that last six weeks.

June — Wiley and Putnam publishes Nathaniel Hawthorne's *Mosses from an Old Manse* in the Library of American Books.

18 June — Carlyle signs a contract at the Waterloo offices of Wiley and Putnam for the publication of new editions of *Sartor Resartus* (1836), *The French Revolution: A History* (1837), *Chartism* (1839), *On Heroes, Hero-Worship & the Heroic in History* (1841), *Past and Present* (1843), and *Oliver Cromwell's Letters and Speeches* (1845–1846), the last of which is the newly expanded edition.

BOOKS WANTED.—We invite the attention, not only of book-sellers, but especially of those who own private libraries, to an advertisement of Messrs. Wiley & Putnam, who are charged with a commission to fill up a long list of American books for the British Museum. Doubtless many of these books are now to be found only in private libraries; but the purpose of the British Museum—to obtain a complete collection of American books—is so liberal and laudable that some inconvenience may well be submitted to, in order to promote an object thus entitled to our respect and approbation.

Notice in the 23 July 1846 issue of the New York Commercial Advertiser. *The British Museum, which was then amassing the largest collection of Americana in the world, was one of Wiley and Putnam's best customers.*

NEW YORK, JULY 26, 1846.

SIR:

We beg leave most respectfully to invite your attention to the enclosed Circular to the Secretary of State of your State, respecting the Public Documents, &c. for the Library of the British Museum.

Should it meet your approbation we should feel obliged if you will forward it, and will kindly use your influence in promoting its object in either one or the other of the modes proposed.

We are, sir, with the highest respect,

Your obedient servants,

WILEY & PUTNAM.

Cover letter sent as part of an effort to solicit American documents for Henry Stevens, agent to the British Museum. Putnam spent much of summer 1846 working on this project. (Department of Special Collections, Young Research Library, UCLA)

Summer	Putnam returns to the United States for several months and travels extensively up and down the eastern seaboard as an agent for rare-book dealer Henry Stevens, who commissioned him on behalf of the British Museum to buy rare works of Americana for its collections. While in Washington, D.C., Putnam negotiates—without success—to have Wiley and Putnam named the official agent of the newly founded Smithsonian Institution.
September	Wiley and Putnam publishes Margaret Fuller's *Papers on Literature and Art* in the Library of American Books. Shortly after his return to England, Putnam arranges the publication of a London edition of the work. He sells it as well as Fuller's *Woman in the Nineteenth Century* (1845) at his store, which the author visits that fall during her stay in England.
December	Wiley and Putnam publishes Taylor's *Views A-foot,* the record of his European tour, in the Library of American Books.

1847

15 January	Evert Duyckinck signs a contract to edit a new weekly magazine, *Literary World,* which is to be published jointly by Wiley and Putnam and Appleton's.
February	The Putnams depart on a three-month trip through Europe, during which Putnam buys rare books, including Bibles, for the firm's most important individual client, James Lenox of New York, who is amassing one of the greatest American book collections of his time. While traveling through Italy the Putnams meet up with and become the traveling companions of Fuller.
6 February	The first issue of the *Literary World* is published.
March	Putnam's chief assistant in London, David Davidson, purchases a fine copy of the Gutenberg Bible auctioned at Sotheby's for the record price of £500. Putnam authorized the purchase on behalf of Lenox, who initially balks at the price and refuses the item.
April	Dissatisfied with Duyckinck's involvement of his friend Cornelius Mathews in editorial policies, Wiley and Appleton fire Duyckinck and replace him as editor of *Literary World* with Charles Fenno Hoffman.

Advertisement in the 15 May 1847 issue of Literary World *for one
of the printers often used by Wiley and Putnam. Craighead,
who operated one of the best printing and stereotyping
shops in antebellum New York, printed books by
such authors as Poe and Melville
for the company.*

6 May	The Putnams return to England from their tour of the Continent. During the next few weeks Putnam makes final preparations to return to the United States. He leaves the London office in the hands of Davidson, who in Putnam's absence has already overseen the firm's move from its Waterloo Place address to smaller offices on Paternoster Row.
24 May	The Putnams sail from Portsmouth for New York.
July	Wiley and Putnam publishes the first volume of John Ruskin's *Modern Painters*.
17 July	John Bishop Putnam, the second son and future head of the manufacturing branch of G. P. Putnam's Sons, is born in the family house on Staten Island.

| Summer | Putnam settles into the office at 161 Broadway. He manages to persuade Lenox to purchase the Gutenberg Bible that the firm bought with him in mind back in March. |
| Fall | Putnam decides to go into business for himself and reaches an agreement with Wiley late that year or early the next about the division of their assets. |

Announcement of Putnam's new business, opening in March 1848

Notice of the 1848 dissolution of Wiley and Putnam. Putnam decided to end his nearly ten-year partnership with Wiley within months of his permanent return from their London office.

1848

March	G. P. Putnam opens for business at 155 Broadway.
March–April	Putnam negotiates with Washington Irving for the right to publish a revised edition of his old works and any new works he may write.
May	Putnam makes a brief trip to England, where he arranges for publisher John Chapman, 142 Strand, to become his London partner and his friend Thomas Delf to be his London agent.
June	G. P. Putnam publishes William Frederick Poole's *An Alphabetical Index to Subjects* (subsequently known as *Poole's Index*).
July	G. P. Putnam publishes Poe's *Eureka*.
26 July	Irving signs a contract for the publication of all his works, new and old, with G. P. Putnam.
August	G. P. Putnam launches the "author's revised edition" of Irving's works with the publication of *History of New York*. The *Sketch Book* follows in October, then other Irving titles in rapid order over the next year, generally in both illustrated and unillustrated editions.
October	G. P. Putnam publishes James Russell Lowell's *A Fable for Critics*.

1849

March | G. P. Putnam publishes Francis Parkman's *California and Oregon Trail*.

Putnam reaches a preliminary agreement with James Fenimore Cooper for publication of a new edition of some of his most popular novels, beginning with *The Spy*. From 1849 through 1851 he publishes thirteen of Cooper's works, including all the Leatherstocking novels and the new novel *The Way of the Hour* (1850).

G. P. Putnam publishes the first American edition of Austen Henry Layard's *Nineveh and Its Remains*.

Fall | Putnam successfully negotiates with Catharine Maria Sedgwick for the right to publish a new edition that includes some of her most popular works. The agreement remained in effect through 1854.

October | Putnam hosts popular Swedish writer Fredrika Bremer at his home on Staten Island and reaches an agreement with her to republish several of her most popular novels. Putnam editions of *The Neighbours* and *The Home* appear early the next year.

1850

May | G. P. Putnam publishes William Cullen Bryant's *Letters of a Traveller*.

November | Putnam hosts Cooper at his house on Staten Island and soon reaches an agreement with him to publish "The Towns of Manhattan," a social history of New York City that Cooper struggles to write despite illness but leaves incomplete at the time of his death in September 1851.

December | G. P. Putnam publishes Susan Warner's *The Wide, Wide World*.

1851

November | G. P. Putnam publishes *Home Book of the Picturesque*.

1852

Winter | Irving Putnam, the third son and future head of the retail branch of G. P. Putnam's Sons, is born in the family house on Staten Island.

April | G. P. Putnam publishes Warner's *Queechy,* which in its opening month sells more quickly than any of the firm's previous books. Also, in late April or early May, the company publishes *Memorial of James Fenimore Cooper.*

May | G. P. Putnam relocates from 155 Broadway to 12 Park Place.

Fall | G. P. Putnam and Company is formed as Putnam takes employee John Leslie as a partner.

October | Putnam sends out a circular to dozens of American authors inviting them to contribute to his forthcoming magazine, *Putnam's Monthly.*

November | G. P. Putnam and Company publishes *Homes of American Authors.*

13 November | Putnam proposes to the president of the committee planning the 1853 world's fair in New York (formally known as the Exhibition of the Industry of All Nations) that G. P. Putnam and Company be appointed the official publisher of the event. His proposal is accepted in early 1853.

G.P. Putnam, American and Foreign
Bookseller, and Purchasing Agent for the
Trade, and Public Institutions.
155, Broadway New York. Agencies in
London, Paris and Leipsic.

New York May 5th 1851.

Dear Sir

I propose to leave for London,
and Paris, on the 31st inst. and to return in
July. Should you have occasion to send for
any Foreign Books, or Works of Art, and
you see fit to entrust me with your commissions
you may rely upon careful personal attention
to them, with whatever advantage results from
twenty years experience. A small percentage will
be charged on the net wholesale cost of the books
in Europe.

Orders received before the 31st will be executed by
myself during my visit, but my new arrangements
in Europe are such as to enable me, at any time to
execute Orders for Foreign books generally, with
much greater expedition than has been usual heretofore.

I am, Sir

Yours respectfully
Geo. P. Putnam.

Circular sent by Putnam to prospective clients before one of his European trips. Putnam made nearly annual trips to England to renew relations with publishers, stock his store, and purchase on commission select books and periodicals for American customers (Duyckinck Family Papers, Manuscripts and Archives Division, The New York Public Library, Astor, Lenox and Tilden Foundations).

Announcement of G. P. Putnam's move to new offices in the 14 May 1852 issue of the New York Tribune.
*The company moved frequently during its early history, in bad times to economize and in good times for
more space and for a better location vis-à-vis the northward expansion of commerce in the city.*

1853

January	The first number of *Putnam's Monthly* is published.
February	The second number of *Putnam's Monthly* generates a sales-increasing controversy with its publication of John Hanson's "Have We a Bourbon among Us?" in which he speculates that the "legitimate" heir to the French throne is living in the United States.
June	G. P. Putnam and Company publishes the long-delayed American edition of Layard's *Discoveries in the Ruins of Nineveh and Babylon*. This authorized text is soon undersold by Harper and Brothers' pirated edition.
14 July	Putnam is present at the inaugural ceremony of the Crystal Palace. In accordance with his agreement with the building's supervisors, his firm's *Illustrated Record* of the Exhibition is printed on steam-powered presses positioned in plain sight of spectators.

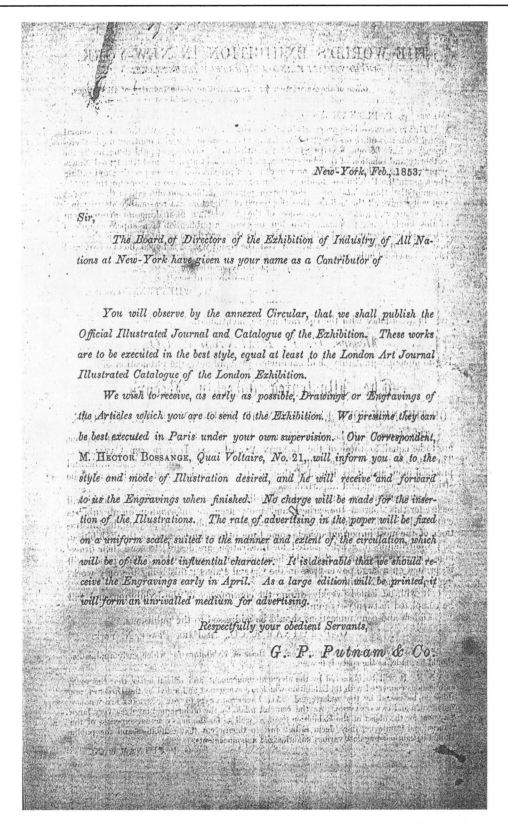

New-York, Feb., 1853.

Sir,

The Board of Directors of the Exhibition of Industry of All Nations at New-York have given us your name as a Contributor of

You will observe by the annexed Circular, that we shall publish the Official Illustrated Journal and Catalogue of the Exhibition. These works are to be executed in the best style, equal at least to the London Art Journal Illustrated Catalogue of the London Exhibition.

We wish to receive, as early as possible, Drawings or Engravings of the Articles which you are to send to the Exhibition. We presume they can be best executed in Paris under your own supervision. Our Correspondent, M. Hector Bossange, Quai Voltaire, No. 21, will inform you as to the style and mode of Illustration desired, and he will receive and forward to us the Engravings when finished. No charge will be made for the insertion of the Illustrations. The rate of advertising in the paper will be fixed on a uniform scale, suited to the manner and extent of the circulation, which will be of the most influential character. It is desirable that we should receive the Engravings early in April. As a large edition will be printed, it will form an unrivalled medium for advertising.

Respectfully your obedient Servants,

G. P. Putnam & Co.

Form letter soliciting advertising for G. P. Putnam and Company's publications promoting the world's fair. The company hoped that selling advertisements would help defray the costs of its heavy investment in its exhibition publications (George Palmer Putnam Collection, Manuscripts Division, Princeton University Library).

November	G. P. Putnam and Company publishes *Homes of American Statesmen.*
	G. P. Putnam and Company initiates publication of Susan and Anna Warner's juvenile series *Ellen Montgomery's Book Shelf* with *Mr. Rutherford's Children,* the first of five volumes published by the firm during the mid 1850s.

1854

May	Badly in need of operating capital, G. P. Putnam and Company sells off its entire retail stock at auction.
August	Rumored to be near bankruptcy, G. P. Putnam and Company sells off the majority of its stock and stereotype plates at auction.
15 September	Putnam gathers his creditors in a meeting and successfully pleads a case for debt extension, which permits him to keep the company solvent.
October	Putnam fires Charles Frederick Briggs as editor of *Putnam's Monthly* and assumes the position himself, with help from Frederic Beecher Perkins.

1855

March	After months of looking for a buyer, Putnam finally sells *Putnam's Monthly* to the new publishing firm of Dix and Edwards.
	G. P. Putnam and Company publishes Melville's *Israel Potter.*

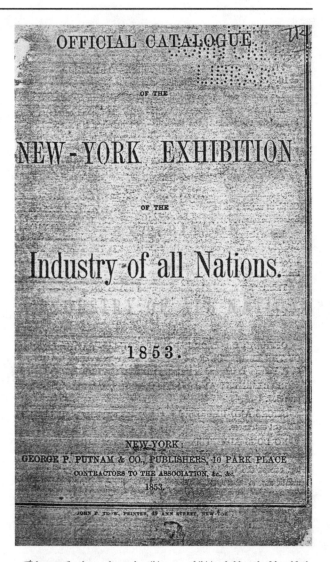

Title page for the catalogue describing an exhibition held at the New York Crystal Palace. The involvement of G. P. Putnam and Company with the exhibition proved so costly and unremunerative that it nearly drove the firm into bankruptcy.

Spring	Putnam leads efforts that culminate in the formation of the New York Book Publishers' Association and its trade journal, *American Publishers' Circular and Literary Gazette.*
May	G. P. Putnam and Company publishes first volume of Irving's *Life of George Washington.*
September	The "Complimentary Fruit and Floral Festival to Authors," organized by Putnam and hosted by the New York Book Publishers' Association, meets the evening of 27 September in the Crystal Palace.

1856

February	David Wells, who invests $10,000 in the firm, becomes a junior partner at G. P. Putnam and Company; the company relocates to 321 Broadway.

NEW YORK.

G. P. PUTNAM & COMPANY,

NEW COPARTNERSHIP.

G. P. PUTNAM & CO. beg to announce to their friends and the public, that from the 1st of February, 1856, Mr. DAVID A. WELLS will be associated with them in their Bookselling and Publishing Business, which will be continued as heretofore under the same firm.

REMOVAL.

ON THE 15TH JANUARY, THE UNDERSIGNED WILL REMOVE TO THEIR NEW PREMISES, No. 321 BROADWAY, (Up Stairs, nearly opposite Pearl St.)

In this central location, with more room and other facilities, we propose in addition to our own publications, to devote especial attention to those of the principal houses in Boston and Philadelphia. We have made arrangements to supply the trade especially with the publications of

Messrs. Ticknor & Fields	*Boston.*	Messrs. H. C. Baird,	Philadelphia.
Crosby, Nichols & Co.,	"	Lindsay & Blakiston,	"
Whittemore, Niles & Hall,	"	E. H. Butler & Co.,	"
J. B. Lippincott & Co.,	*Philadelphia.*	W. P. Hazard,	"
H. Cowperthwait & Co.,	"	J. W. Moore,	"
Lea & Blanchard,	"	Hayes & Zell,	"
Parry & McMillan,	"	Childs & Peterson,	"

IMPORTATION OF FOREIGN BOOKS.

Special orders for the Trade and for Private Libraries will be executed as heretofore, at a moderate rate of commission. Any book published in Great Britain or France will be supplied by the return steamer. Orders forwarded by every steamer.

Public Libraries, Lyceums, &c., supplied at Wholesale Prices with any Books published in the United States or Europe.

We intend to devote particular and careful attention to this department, and we respectfully solicit orders. An experience of twenty years will enable us to fill them satisfactorily.

Announcement in the 12 January 1856 issue of American Publishers' Circular and Literary Gazette. *Putnam's partnerships were rarely successful; his association with David Wells lasted only one year.*

April	G. P. Putnam and Company publishes Bremer's novel *Hertha*.
September	G. P. Putnam and Company publishes the first American edition of Richard Burton's *Personal Narrative of a Pilgrimage to El-Medinah and Meccah*.

1857

January	Wells withdraws his investment and leaves the company.
March	G. P. Putnam and Company publishes Josiah Holland's first novel, *The Bay Path*.
4 July	John Leslie dies by drowning. In going through the company accounts Putnam discovers that Leslie has embezzled from the company and that the firm is unable to pay its debts. He is forced to declare bankruptcy and to put G. P. Putnam and Company into the hands of receivers.
September	The reconstituted G. P. Putnam opens for business, mainly as the publisher and agent for Washington Irving and Bayard Taylor.

1858

Spring   In a cost-cutting move, G. P. Putnam relocates to smaller quarters at 506 Broadway.

1859

February   Putnam arranges with Sheldon and Company, a leading firm of schoolbook publishers and jobbers, to handle his books, hoping to increase their distribution across the country.

May   G. P. Putnam relocates to 115 Nassau Street.

                      G. P. Putnam publishes the fifth and last volume of Irving's *Life of George Washington.*

28 December   Washington Irving dies.

1860

Winter   Putnam negotiates a biography of Irving by his nephew, Pierre Irving, who as literary executor has access to his uncle's correspondence and papers.

November   Putnam publishes his "Recollections of Irving" in *Atlantic Monthly.*

1861

January   G. P. Putnam relocates to new quarters at 532 Broadway.

12 April   The Confederate army fires on Fort Sumter, beginning the Civil War. Within weeks Putnam enters into an agreement with journalist Frank Moore to publish the *Rebellion Record,* a weekly serial of Civil War materials. Their partnership is kept separate from the accounts of G. P. Putnam.

1862

March/April   G. P. Putnam publishes the first volume of Pierre Irving's *Life and Letters of Washington Irving,* which runs to four volumes.

Late Spring   Putnam is appointed United States Revenue Collector for the Eighth District of New York. He splits his time for the next two years between his G. P. Putnam office at 532 Broadway (441 Broadway after April 1863), his government office at 921 Broadway, and the Loyal Publication Society headquarters at 831 Broadway (whose publications he oversees).

1863

April   G. P. Putnam relocates to rooms on the upper floor of 441 Broadway, next door to Appleton's, Putnam's longtime friends and colleagues.

November   G. P. Putnam publishes the "Artist's Edition" of Irving's *Sketch Book.*

December   G. P. Putnam publishes the fourth and final volume of Pierre Irving's *Life and Letters of Washington Irving.*

1864

August   Putnam temporarily assigns to Hurd and Houghton responsibility for manufacturing and selling the works of G. P. Putnam.

NEW YORK.

532 Broadway, New York, October 24, 1862.

TO THE TRADE.

GENTLEMEN:

In consequence of the increased cost of Paper and Binding, it is necessary that the prices of Books should also be increased.

The Discount to the Trade on the various editions of Irving, Taylor, Hood, Kimball, &c., must be modified to meet the present cost of manufacture; but until the first of December orders will be filled as heretofore.

"THE REBELLION RECORD," "HEROES AND MARTYRS," and "AMONG THE PINES," are supplied either by G. P. PUTNAM or C. T. EVANS, on PRECISELY THE SAME TERMS.

G. P. PUTNAM will be glad to receive orders for these books or any books in the market.

Cash settlements monthly, as heretofore.

Respectfully yours,

G. P. PUTNAM.

G. P. PUTNAM

HAS JUST ISSUED THE FOLLOWING:

"AMONG THE PINES; or, SOUTH IN SECESSION TIME."

By EDMUND KIRKE. 24th thousand,	cloth,	$0 75
	paper,	0 50

FRANCIS' HISTORY OF THE BANK OF ENGLAND.

8vo.	cloth,	3 00

RUTTAN ON WARMING AND VENTILATING Public and Private Buildings, Railway Cars, &c.

Illustrated. Royal 8vo. Net cash price.		3 00

SALOME, THE DAUGHTER OF HERODIAS. A Dramatic Poem.

12mo.	cloth,	0 75

THE REBELLION RECORD.

Four Volumes. Royal 8vo.	cloth,	15 00
	sheep,	16 00
	half calf, antique,	20 00
	half morocco,	20 00

*** The Fourth Volume will be ready November 1, and also Monthly Part 24. Orders should be sent at once. Price of each volume: Cloth, $3 75; sheep, $4; half calf or morocco, $5.

Announcement in the 1 November 1862 issue of American Publishers' Circular and Literary Gazette of G. P. Putnam's rising prices, which were the result of steep inflation during the Civil War

PUTNAM'S NEW PUBLICATIONS—Continued.

II.

COMPLETION OF THE

LIFE AND LETTERS

OF

WASHINGTON IRVING.

BY PIERRE M. IRVING.

IN FOUR VOLUMES.

The Publisher has the satisfaction of announcing that the fourth volume of this delightful and attractive work is completed. It includes a

Copious Index to the Four Volumes,

Prepared by S. AUSTIN ALLIBONE, LL.D., Author of the "Dictionary of Authors."

*** This work is not a bald biographical account of an individual, but chiefly consists of a series of sprightly and charming LETTERS, written in various parts of Europe and the United States, and graphically describing notable events, national characteristics, and distinguished statesmen and literary men, whose names are "familiar in our mouths as household words"—the whole extending over a period of more than SIXTY YEARS, and including the times of the First Napoleon, the times of Jefferson, and Madison, and Aaron Burr;—associations and correspondence with Scott, Lockhart, Moore, Rogers, Leslie, James, Dickens, and a host of others in England, France, and Spain: while the literary and political incidents and characteristics of the whole of the present century, at home and abroad, are recalled by the vivid biographical touches of these familiar letters. The genial humor, and the magnetic characteristics of the writer are especially drawn out in the domestic and family letters, which form a large part of the volumes. No epistolary or biographical collection in the English language, or perhaps in any other, is comparable with this in the variety, scope, and interest of the topics, and the characters introduced. It may be described as "the Autobiography of Washington Irving as [unconsciously] related in several hundred familiar letters to friends; with pen-pictures of the times in which he lived."

The materials for this work, if more freely used, would have filled six or eight volumes. The editor, who received from his distinguished relative these materials, with the request that he should use them as he thought best, has selected and compressed into four volumes, the matter most essential to the narrative, and most illustrative of the author's characteristics. It was at first hoped that this might be done in three volumes, but this was found to be impracticable, and many intelligent readers have urgently asked for as many more.

In consequence of the great advance a few months since in the price of paper and binding—more than 33⅓ per cent.—the publisher was reluctantly compelled to add about 10 per cent. to the price of this and other books, as was done generally by other publishers. In order to meet the wishes of the Trade, and of the large numbers of owners of Irving's Works who will require this work as a companion to their sets, the price, now that the work is complete, and the expense of manufacture somewhat modified, is fixed at

$1 50 per Volume.

The prices in the Publisher's Catalogue are therefore to be corrected as follows:—

Irving's Life, 4 volumes, cloth, extra,	.	.	.	.	.	.	.	$6 00.
" " half calf, extra,	.	.	.	.	.	.	.	10 00.
" " half calf, antique,	.	.	.	.	.	.	.	10 00.

40,000 sets will be wanted to accompany the revised editions of Irving's Works already printed and sold. This edition matches all those sets.

*** The more expensive editions of this work are:—

The National Edition, 4 volumes, superfine paper,	.	.	.	.	$7 00.
" " " half calf, extra,	.	.	.	.	11 00.
" " " half calf, antique,	.	.	.	.	11 00.
The Laid Paper Edition, uncut, 4 volumes,	.	.	.	.	7 00.
" " half morocco, gilt tops,	.	.	.	.	12 00.
A few copies on large paper, with 70 extra plates, morocco extra,	.	.	32 00.

Announcement of the completed Washington Irving biography in the 1 December 1863 issue of American Publishers' Circular and Literary Gazette. *Putnam believed that the biography spurred sales of the revised editions of Irving's works.*

Announcement of Hurd and Houghton's taking over Putnam's publishing list in the 1 June 1864 issue of American Publishers' Circular and Literary Gazette. *Putnam made the arrangement on a temporary basis so that he could devote himself to his position of United States Revenue Collector.*

1865

July	Putnam employs his son, George Haven Putnam, recently discharged from army service, as Deputy Collector for the Eighth District of New York.

1866

Fall	Putnam is fired from his government position for refusing to pay the expected contribution to President Andrew Johnson's campaign.
Winter	G. P. Putnam relocates to 459 Broome Street, an emerging center for New York City book publishers.
1 December	Putnam advertises his decision to reopen his publishing house.

1867

Winter	John Bishop Putnam leaves Pennsylvania Agricultural School to join the firm.
January	Putnam and his son George Haven Putnam open G. P. Putnam and Son for business at 661 Broadway.
August	G. P. Putnam and Son negotiates a deal to become the exclusive supplier of textbooks to the Empire of Japan.
Fall	Putnam makes preparations to resume publication of a general monthly magazine, naming it *Putnam's Magazine* to distinguish it from its predecessor, *Putnam's Monthly*.
December	G. P. Putnam and Son publishes Henry Tuckerman's *Book of the Artists*.

1868

January	The first number of *Putnam's Magazine* is published.

1869

Summer	G. P. Putnam and Son enters into an agreement with J. B. Lippincott and Company of Philadelphia for the manufacture of several editions of the works of Washington Irving from existing Putnam plates and for their joint distribution.

1870

April/May	Recognizing his son John Bishop's contribution, Putnam makes him a partner and renames the company G. P. Putnam and Sons.
Winter	G. P. Putnam and Son relocates far uptown to more spacious quarters in the Young Men's Christian Association Building at the corner of Twenty-third Street and Fourth Avenue. The move puts the firm closer to the new business center located near Madison Square.

| November | Unable to repeat his success with *Putnam's Monthly,* Putnam publishes the last number of *Putnam's Magazine* and merges it with *Scribner's Monthly,* whose first number appears in December. |

1871

| October | G. P. Putnam and Sons publishes Tuckerman's *The Life of John Pendleton Kennedy* as part of a ten-volume *Collected Works.* |

1872

| Winter | Irving Putnam leaves Amherst College to join G. P. Putnam and Sons. |
| 20 December | George Palmer Putnam dies suddenly. Members of the trade keep the store open through the holiday season while the family mourns. Shortly after their resumption of business, the three brothers rename the company G. P. Putnam's Sons. |

No. 51, Jan. 2, 1873.]   *The Publishers' Weekly.*   15

NOTICE TO THE TRADE.

G. P. PUTNAM'S SONS,

Publishers, Booksellers, Stationers, and Importers,

308 Fourth Ave. and 54 East 23d St.

New York, December 27th, 1872.

The Firm of G. P. Putnam & Sons having been dissolved by the death of George P. Putnam, we have the honor to inform you that the business will be continued without change or interruption, by the undersigned, under the firm name of G. P. PUTNAM'S SONS.

Trusting to receive a continuance of the confidence and favors so liberally extended to the former firm, we remain,

Yours Respectfully,

GEO. HAVEN PUTNAM.
JNO. BISHOP PUTNAM.   **G. P. PUTNAM'S SONS.**

Notification of a new era for the company. Led by Putnam's three eldest sons, the reconstituted firm operated on a scale and profitability it had never experienced under his control.

Selected Correspondence

With few exceptions, the correspondence and business records of nineteenth-century publishing houses are spotty. The reasons are many: few firms survived intact into the age of research libraries, publishers rarely treated their archives as repositories of interest to posterity, and frequent physical moves and fires thinned whatever materials did survive. The House of Putnam is only a partial exception. Few of its financial accounts are extant, and most of those that are have been preserved in the archives of other firms or writers. Likewise, only a small, if significant, portion of its once voluminous correspondence has survived. The following section prints selected samples of the surviving Putnam archive, which are intended to document the company's dealings with authors, book collectors, and fellow publishers. Most of the material is in manuscript form, which sometimes makes exact transcription difficult.

James Lenox, who was Putnam's most important private client in the mid 1840s. In 1847 Putnam purchased for him the first Gutenberg Bible brought to the United States.

James Lenox

Putnam represented dozens of American clients, private and institutional, during his decade in London. The only individual account that approached the size of his institutional dealings was that of James Lenox of New York City, a wealthy bibliophile then in the process of amassing one of the greatest book and manuscript collections in the United States. Putnam courted Lenox's business especially in the mid 1840s but eventually lost out to Henry Stevens. Lenox's huge collection, including a copy of the Gutenberg Bible and dozens of other rare books purchased for him by Putnam, became one of the two pillars on which the New York Public Library was built in the late nineteenth century. All of the letters in this section come from the James Lenox Papers, Manuscripts and Archives Division, The New York Public Library, Astor, Lenox and Tilden Foundations.

* * *

In this excerpt from a letter to Lenox, Putnam discusses the details for a proposed European book-buying tour on his behalf, which would take him to major private and public book collections in France, Italy, and Germany.

(New York)

London Jany 4th 1847

Dear Sir,

Your esteemed favors of 25th Novr. & 13th Decr. were duly recd.—

The mode which you mentioned as the most fair & proper one for dividing the Durazzo library in case the purchase was effected is undoubtedly the only correct way of doing it, so far as the <u>principle</u> is concerned—If, however, the whole catalogue was previously priced by Payne & Foss, so as to amount to just the nett cost, they might not be willing, perhaps, that the first selection should be yours in all cases—especially if the amount selected was but a minor part of the whole: i.e. they might wish to have some of those which you selected & consider that the claim would be better than yours inasmuch as they take the larger portion. I do not know that this would happen; but it is better of course, to have a proper understanding about it in the outset. There might be perhaps a few items only in this position, which you would prefer to have even at a small advance upon the first estimate. Of course I should not tell them which items you have selected until the catalogue is priced throughout—though I did sometime since mention to Mr Foss your general remark, that you wished most of the Bibles, some of the Mss. and some Aldines.

In regard to the expense of the journey to Genoa I should consider it proper, in case the purchase is not effected, that you should be at the expense only of a business journey there & back. I do not know precisely what this would cost: the nearest I can learn is from £25. to £35.: but to be exact, I would limit the sum to £30. : and in this case I would be ready to attend to any other commissions for you, there or on the way, without other charge. If the purchase is made I should charge our usual coms. upon the amount (10%–) without any other expenses than those of packing & shipping the books.—I propose this, because, as I mentioned, I am anxious to visit Italy, & go beyond Genoa—but I should not do this at present unless I had your commission.

* * *

Putnam here informs Lenox of his plans to make various choice purchases for him, chief among them a fine copy of the Gutenberg Bible (the Mazarine) soon to be sold at auction at Sotheby's. Many of the other purchases that he hoped to make for Lenox were to be effected through his partnership with the London firm Payne & Foss.

James Lenox Esq.
(New York)   London Feby 19th 1847
Dear Sir,

. . . .

Your esteemed favor of Jany 30 per Hibernia was duly recd., together with the list of articles which you wish to have from the Durazzo library in case the purchase of the whole can be effected jointly by Mr Payne & myself. I have arranged with Mr Foss to meet Mr Payne in Rome & return with him to Genoa and shall leave on Monday next, (22d.).—Mr Payne is a person of high character as well as bibliographical knowledge, and I am quite sure that if we succeed in purchasing the collection, it will be done in a manner which will recieve [sic] your entire approval. I shall certainly take the utmost pains to serve you faithfully & satisfactorily.

A library of rather extraordinary character is to be sold here by Sotheby, March 12 to 24. It contains some very fine & rare Mss. & illuminated books, several Caxtons & Wynkyn de Wordes; the first four

editions of Shakespeare; first editions of Milton, & many other rarities. The sale is not yet advertised, but by particular favor Mr. Sotheby has given me an opportunity to examine the books, with an early copy of the Catalogue, which I send you herewith. You will percieve [sic] that among the Bibles is a beautiful copy of the Mazarine Bible—the first book ever printed with moveable types. Only 13 other copies are known to exist, eight of which are in public libraries. This copy is in wonderful condition; & probably an opportunity to purchase another might not occur again for many years. There is also the first Paris edition, also in fine condition—and these, together with five or six other Bibles being on your list, I have left special directions with our Mr Davidson to attend the sale & purchase them for you.—

* * *

Frustrated by Lenox's refusal to accept the Gutenberg Bible at the £500 price bid for him by Wiley and Putnam, Putnam informs Lenox that he still has it on hand and is trying to sell it to the underbidder, the English collector Sir Thomas Phillipps. Phillipps likewise declined it, but Putnam succeeded in selling the Bible to Lenox shortly after returning to the United States in June.

London May 18, 1847
James Lenox Esq.
(N. York)
Dear Sir,

I regret exceedingly to learn from Mr. Wiley that you do not approve of the purchase of the Mazarin Bible. It has not yet been sent out, and I have written to the next highest bidder respecting it—but as he resides in Worcester-shire, his reply will not arrive 'till after this steamer has sailed. The gentleman referred to is Sir Thos. Phillips, Bart., and his bid having been £495, I trust he will be glad to take it without any material loss. I am told that the reasons for this high price were—1st the beautiful condition of this copy—and 2ndly, the fact that it is the only copy now existing out of a public library—and therefore its value is greatly enhanced over all copies heretofore sold. Those best informed on the subject assure me that under the circumstances the price, great as it is, is not extravagant.—

As I sail for New York this week, I defer a more particular account of these & other commissions, until I have the favor of seeing you there.

With high respect,
Your obt. Servt. G P Putnam

Asa Gray

Established Harvard professor Asa Gray assiduously preserved his long professional correspondence with Putnam; the result is one of the most complete Putnam files in existence. Given their warm personal relations and many-sided professional dealings, sometimes requiring Putnam to serve Gray not only as a publisher but also as an overseas purchasing agent for books, equipment, and specimens, the Putnam and Gray correspondence is also one of the most revealing company files. The following letters give a sampling of the kinds of issues, arrangements, and frustrations that nineteenth-century literary professionalism typically brought to author and publisher alike. All of the letters in this section come from the Archives of the Gray Herbarium, Harvard University.

* * *

In this 28 February 1844 letter Putnam explains to Gray the transcontinental arrangements offered by his firm for sending books to the United States and invites him to visit the new Putnam offices and the family home. Putnam's conjecture that he would soon have a son proved true when George Haven was born a month later.

London, Feby 28/44

My dear Professor,

Your favor of Feby 1 was duly recd. in spite of your frozen thermometer.

. . . .

We have <u>now</u> a regular correspondent in Hamburg & can obtain whatever you may require promptly. If any books pass through England they of course cost somewhat more, but they reach you by the steamers much sooner. Any bulky orders can be shipped however direct from Hamburg to New York. –

We can obtain any thing from St. Petersburgh through Dulan & Co.–but have no direct correspondence there.

I send a ream of note paper & envelopes, for you to W. & P. New York.–

I shall be quite delighted to take chops with you again–not at Dolly's–<u>but at our house No 31 Euston Square–with lunch at our new business in Waterloo Place</u> (!!! near the Duke of York's big column. We have a famous place there <u>& shall remove on the 15th March.–Do</u> come & make us a visit–You shall see that the "American agency" is becoming famous & Mrs. Putnam will be proud to show you her <u>Conservatory</u> & her <u>Son</u>(?) & Daughter –

Meanwhile believe me dear Sir

Very Faithfully yours

<u>G. P. Putnam</u>

Prof. A. Gray

* * *

In his letter of 26 January 1846 to Gray, Putnam discusses the promotion of the second edition of Gray's standard The Botanical Text-Book for Colleges, Schools, and Private Students *(1842) and brings his friend up to date about the Putnam family, whom Gray met during a visit to London.*

6 Waterloo Place

London Jany 26/46.

My dear Professor Gray,

Your favor of 29th Decr. was duly recd. & the letter to Prof. Arnott promptly posted. He wrote for the book before I had time to explain before hand that we had not got it!–It is very strange, but Wiley has never sent me a copy of 2nd edn.–it has been overlooked in some way I wrote specially about it two or three months ago–I hope they are <u>now</u> on the way. I have advd. it conspicuously in our new catalogue & have no doubt it will sell well. It will of course be a capital thing for Mr Arnott to introduce it at Glasgow. I have written to him explaining that there has been some oversight–& that a copy shall be sent to him the moment it arrives.

Our two daughters & son & Mamma flourish finely in <u>Knickerbocker</u> Cottage. This is the climate for hardy <u>plants.</u>

I am dear sir, Yours faithfully

<u>Geo P. Putnam</u>

* * *

Hoping to retain Gray as a client, Putnam wrote to him soon after going into business on his own.

155 Broadway New York

May 3 1848

My dear Professor,

Wherein have I offended thee?–

Could you not have given me the glorification of having my name connected in some way with <u>either</u> of your new works?–

So far as the last one is concerned, I had not the slightest intimation in any way that it was coming out. Of course you would do as you think best & it is not for me to find you erroneous in so doing–but as you know how proud I should be to sail under your name–& how much pains I shd. take to please you I <u>did</u> think you would not forget me altogether.

Pray excuse me for saying so much–but I find these new arrangements of <u>yours</u> make it <u>necessary</u> for me to speak for <u>myself</u>–even more than my modesty would warrant.

My agency is continued in London in a new & I trust more satisfactory shape–Mr. Thos. Delf acting for me "<u>Putnam's Agency at Chapman's 342 Strand</u>

London." Delf purchases English books for me & in my name–& Chapman will do my business in American books.

If you knew <u>all</u>, you would admit that I am entitled to a fair share of all the "former famous" etc.–

Whenever I <u>can</u> do any thing for you, pray give me an opportunity, & believe me,

Dear Sir,

       Very truly Yours

         <u>Geo. P. Putnam</u>

Profr. Asa Gray,

* * *

In this detailed explanation of delays and mistakes made in packing books purchased in Europe and shipping them to Putnam's clients in the United States, Putnam, typically pressed for time in handling his office correspondence, uses the abbreviations "ex" for "from," as when he references the steamship Copernicus, *and "CH." for customhouse. The "Dr Torrey" mentioned is John Torrey, the co-author with Gray of* A Flora of North America *(1838–1843).*

New York Sept 29, 1851

Prof. A. Gray,

(Cambridge),

My dear Sir.

I delayed replying to your last letter simply because the goods <u>ex</u> Copernicus were promised the "next day"–and it has been "tomorrow and tomorrow" till <u>now</u>–They are at length through the CH. & are sent by Kinsleys express this day.

There is another package–<u>ex-Canada</u> from <u>Havre</u> now at Boston–which will be delivered to you by the broker at Boston,–tomorrow or next day.

The cases I referred to as having been sent to Mr. Cunningham some <u>weeks</u> ago were those <u>ex</u> Howard from Hamburgh, in April last & <u>ex</u> "Franklin" from Havre in May last. Annexed herewith are the particulars of expense, so that you may see what the contents were[.] A letter of advice was sent to Mr Cunningham at the time these cares were sent so that I think these could not be the ones that are missing–I do not find any record or advice of any other cases than these two, the one now at Boston & the three packages sent today.–

The missing packages for Dr Torrey & Mr Curtis must have been sent to Florida in Dr Boardman's parcel–at least Mr Curtis thinks so:–but if so they must have been packed together by Delf in London, & with only Dr Boardman's address. It is <u>very</u> hard to get clerks in the way of attending to such things carefully & promptly–but I will always do my best. For a month past I have been in a <u>whirlpool</u> of business.

       Yours G P Putnam

Economizing on paper, Putnam added a postscript that ran up the left margin.

P.S. It happens that another parcel <u>should</u> be forthcoming from the "Isaac Newton" from Hamburgh–which arrived sometime since–but the case was not found in the vessel. A full report about this shall be sent tomorrow–

* * *

The following is a form letter Putnam sent to Gray and several other of his "author-friends" to inform them of his decision to auction some of their literary properties. In a note in Putnam's hand attached to a second copy, Putnam assured Gray that his company meant to part only with Gray's Genera flora Americana boreali-orientalis illustrata *(2 volumes, 1848, 1849), not more profitable works. Gray apparently accepted Putnam's explanation; he remained a loyal Putnam author until the firm's 1857 bankruptcy.*

March 14 1854

Dear Sir,

The announcement contained in the enclosed will doubtless occasion some surprise. It is somewhat sudden, but the measure was not decided upon without careful deliberation and the conviction that it was dictated by an honest regard for the mutual interests of those concerned.

We should not have made this announcement without previous consultation with all our author- friends, had it not been necessary to secure the present opportunity of the New York Trade sale, which is now going on; and the decision was not made until this day. We hope to show you that we have had your interests in view, as well as our own, and you will find that the sale of the plates of your work will not be completed without due care that our own contracts for the copyright of future editions are properly understood & assumed by the purchaser.–

For all copies <u>already printed</u> we shall account to you as usual.

We shall be glad to see you at the sale, if you can make it convenient

We can but hope & believe that under the new administration of your work it may recieve [*sic*] a new impulse, and yield a better return for the author than we have been able to render heretofore. It is with great reluctance that we part with it.

       With high respect, dear Sir

       Very truly yours

       G. P. Putnam and Co

* * *

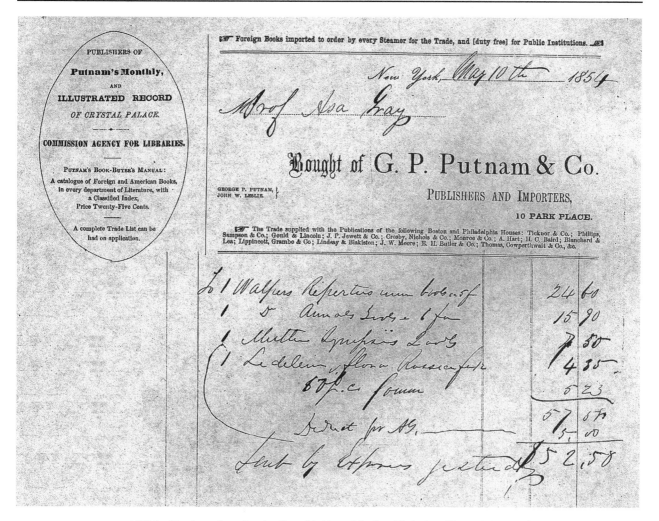

A bill detailing items charged to Asa Gray (Archives of the Gray Herbarium, Harvard University)

Two weeks after the death of John Leslie, his young partner and the financial officer of G. P. Putnam and Company, Putnam reported to Gray on the disarray he was finding in the accounts.

Prof. A Gray

July 16, 1857

My dear Sir

The plates—(35 copies of 72 plates) will be packed this P. M. & sent you as directed. I am thankful this is complete.

Leslie's sudden death has given me serious trouble & great anxiety, for he had (unfortunately) so entirely the management of our accounts & finances, that I have not been able to unravel some important matters known only to himself, or to keep engagements which he had made without my knowledge. Thus I have been completely <u>cornered</u>. But I am just completing a full transcript—& it is probable that all will be put in good shape in a day or two.

* * *

In his attempt to salvage his publishing house after discovering the severe damage done by Leslie's fraud, Putnam writes seeking Gray's assent to his decision to sell the rights to three of Gray's books to the large New York educational publisher Ivison and Phinney. Putnam's dealings with Gray thereby came to an end.

Prof. A. Gray, Cambridge

Augt 8th 1857

My dear Professor,

Ivison & Phinney have so much to say about the unsatisfactory nature of divided interests in the text books that I have been induced to consent to give up these three books to them entirely—your assent being first obtained.

As they are wealthy & thoroughly well established in the schoolbook trade, I presume you will be fully satisfied to have these books entirely in their hands. They will manage them judiciously & you will recieve [*sic*] your money promptly as the contract requires.

Will you be kind enough to send your assent as pr memo. enclosed, by return mail, to enable me to complete the arrangement with them?–

I shall render your a/c of stewardship of Genera & Flora [.] The plates wanting to Exp. Expn shall be sent to-day.

Truly yours G. P Putnam

Putnam added a postscript that ran up the left margin.

I & P. will account to Metcalf & Co. for the plates of Text Book as soon as finished. Your draft $250. was paid this day

---

James Fenimore Cooper

Putnam became Cooper's publisher in 1849 at a time when Putnam was eagerly pursuing control of the works of several American writers of the older generation. In addition to his prize author, Washington Irving, Putnam recruited Cooper as well as Catharine Maria Sedgwick and John Pendleton Kennedy. He remained Cooper's publisher until the author's death in 1851, bringing out many of his most popular older works and several of his more recent ones. Their collaboration, however, proved considerably less successful than either man had hoped because Cooper had signed away the copyright to some of his most popular works (including the Leatherstocking novels), and cheaper editions of his works were already in circulation, undercutting sales of the Putnam editions.

Cooper kept the incoming letters from Putnam during the two and one-half years of their professional relationship, and much of that file is reprinted below. These letters reveal a more strictly business relationship than Putnam kept with most of his long-term clients, who frequently became author-friends. All of the letters in this section come from the Yale Collection of American Literature, Beinecke Rare Book and Manuscript Library.

* * *

With this letter Putnam enclosed a draft contract for Cooper's inspection. In the last paragraph Putnam refers to promissory notes, in effect the money he is contracting to pay for leasing Cooper's plates. The new work being contracted for is The Ways of the Hour *(1850).*

155 Broadway
March 3, 1849

Dear Sir,

I have made a draft of agreement respecting the new work which is more in accordance with the usual

practice of the trade, and with my own rules in business. I trust it will be equally satisfactory to you.

If you will be good enough to look it over and mark any alterations that you wish, I will consider them and have two fair copies made to be signed whenever convenient to yourself.

I presume the obligation to give my notes on the completion of the plates will be equally binding (in case of accident to me,) as the notes themselves. The nature and scope of the work itself, I leave of course, to your own judgment and discretion with entire confidence.

With high respects,
J. Fenimore Cooper Esq.   Dear Sir,
Your obt. Servt.
<u>Geo. P. Putnam</u>

* * *

Putnam's dealings with Cooper were never simple, as this proposed contract written in Putnam's hand shows. Cooper insisted on keeping in his possession whatever copyrights he had not already given away and on producing his own stereotype plates for works new and old, which he leased on stipulated terms and for designated periods to his publishers. The unusually detailed language of this draft contract gives a rough indication of how many conditions Cooper set on his publishers and the way he adhered to an older, author-dominated model of publication.

Memorandum of Agreement made this   day of March, 1849 between J. Fenimore Cooper of Cooperstown, State of New York, and Geo. P. Putnam, Publisher of New York city, witnessith

That said Cooper undertakes and agrees to deliver to said Putnam in the city of New York on or before the day of   next, the Stereotype Plates of a new work of fiction, to be written by said Cooper, and to contain the usual or average quantity of matter which is comprised in former similar work by said Cooper. The said stereotype plates shall be made from new types, and in a style similar in form and equal in execution to those of the "Sketch Book" published by said Putnam.

That said Cooper, for and in consideration of certain payments to be made to him by said Putnam, as herein after named, agrees to give the said Putnam the sole right for the period of two years to print and publish from said stereotype plates as many copies or editions as he, the said Putnam may find expedient–always provided, that the number of copies on hand or at the disposal of said Putnam, at the expiration of the term of this agreement shall not exceed Five Hundred.

That said Cooper, in consideration of said payment as beforementioned, further agrees that he will not publish or cause to be published any other new work of Fiction of similar form or character during the period of eight months commencing four months prior to the publication of the work specified in the present agreement: and no other publication, in any form, of the work herein agreed upon shall be permitted or authorized by said Cooper.

For and in consideration of the use of the copyright of stereotype plates for two years from the day of publication, of said new work of Fiction being conveyed to said Putnam as aforesaid, the said Putnam hereby agrees and binds himself to give his promissory notes, payable to said Cooper for the sum of One thousand Dollars, that is to say: On the delivery to said Putnam in New York of the Stereotype Plates, complete, the said Putnam agrees to pay to said Cooper his notes dated on the day of such delivery as follows; one note each at, four, five, six, seven and eight months, each for Two Hundred Dollars.

Said Putnam further agrees, that whenever during the said two years, the sale of the said work shall have exceeded four thousand copies, he shall then pay the said Cooper at the rate of twenty five cents per copy for all that he may have sold over and above the first four thousand copies: amount for said sale to be rendered in February and August of each year.

Said Putnam further agrees, that at the expiration of two years from the day of publication of said work the stereotype plate shall be returned to said Cooper in good condition, ordinary wear and tear excepted, and that all the rights of said Putnam in said Book shall terminate with the exception of his retaining his right to dispose of the copies on hand, subject to the conditions of this agreement, and which copies shall not exceed five hundred.

* * *

In this letter Putnam refers to the plates of The Spy, *the first of Cooper's revised editions Putnam published, which were then still arriving from the Philadelphia printing shop of John Fagan, customarily used by Cooper. At the time Cooper was also preparing a history of New York City and had asked Putnam's opinion of prospective titles.*

New York, April 1849

J. Fenimore Cooper Esq.
(Cooperstown)

Dear Sir,

Your esteemed favor of 31ˢᵗ Mch was duly recd.–I will see that a copy of the Title page of The Spy is sent to you in good season, before the book is printed.

Fagan has not yet sent all the plates, but I expect them in a few days. I am waiting to have the vol. more nearly ready before I say much to the trade. I showed a sheet of it at the Trade Sale, and about 100 copies were called for, but there was no general sale of it, the book

not being ready for delivery. I hope to give it a full and suitable currency as soon as it is issued.

In regard to the title of the work, I shd. hardly know which to choose, of those you mention: viz
The Tombs of Manhattan–No. 4
The <u>Men of Manhattan</u>–No. 1
The Minds of Manhattan–No. 3
The Ways of Manhattan–No. 2

I have numbered them in the order they strike me–i.e.–No. 1 seems to me best–No. 2 next best etc.–I think "The Tombs" has become a cant phrase, which would not give a good impression.
With high respect, Sir,
Very truly yours,
Geo. P. Putnam

* * *

Putnam's sending Cooper a sample title page for inspection is an unusual step–reserved for his most important clients.

J. Fenimore Cooper Esq.　　　　New York, Apl. 20 1849
Dear Sir,

I enclose the Title-page of "The Spy" as you requested. I expect to publish it on Monday or Tuesday of next week. There is a good, honest, full-sized page, but I hope it will make a respectable and neat looking book.
Very respectfully, Dear Sir,
Your Obt. Servt.
Geo. P. Putnam
–Yale Collection of American Literature, Beinecke Rare Book and Manuscript Library

* * *

In the early years of his career, Cooper had amassed considerable sums from the sale of printing rights to his works to London publishers. (He was paid $6,000, for example, for his 1831 novel, The Bravo.*) He hoped to do well also with his new novel,* The Ways of the Hour *(1850), but, as Putnam forewarns him here, a recent change in English copyright law had undermined the ability of foreign writers to receive protection. As a result, English publishers were growing ever more cautious about bringing out editions of foreign works.*

New York, July 27, 1849
J. Fenimore Cooper Esq.
(Cooperstown)
Dear Sir,

I beg to acknowledge your esteemed favor of 23d.–

From my knowledge of the London publisher–and the business I have transacted there, I should not be at all sanguine of effecting with them such an arrangement as you would expect. They have always had more or less "doubts" about the safety of copyright originating on this side–and I

Richard Bentley, a leading London publisher and dealer in American books, whom Putnam believed sometimes treated American writers shabbily. First with his partner, Henry Colburn, and then on his own, Richard Bentley was generally James Fenimore Cooper's English publisher of choice, beginning with The Borderers *(Colburn and Bentley, 1829). Bentley paid Cooper well for his copyrights through the 1830s, but these payments declined over the 1840s as Cooper's works fell increasingly into the hands of pirates.*

In this letter, Richard Bentley offers Putnam a reciprocal deal: each to have priority of foreign publication to the other's works. At the time the London publisher of Herman Melville, James Fenimore Cooper, and other American writers, Bentley was eager to take further advantage of recent favorable legal rulings liberalizing English copyright protection to foreign authors. Putnam, who already was dealing extensively with the House of Murray, his choice among English publishers, answered Bentley promptly but presumably agreed to enter into only a strictly limited arrangement for particular books.

New Burlington Street
Dec. 22, 1849

Sir,

Observing in "The Literary Week" the list of your new works by American authors and being myself, as you are aware largely engaged with your native writers, I have thought it desirable to address you, with the view to an arrangement which might give me here the priority of copyright. It will afford me pleasure to offer you either a specific sum for any particular work, or to agree to publish such works as I think would succeed in my hands on the principle of dividing equally with you the net profits of such publications, after deducting [?] and always holding you in all such cases harmless in the event of loss. Some such arrangement may perhaps suit you, and I think in return I could sell you early copies of my books, & you could enter into any arrangement like that I have above indicated.

I am Sir,
Yours faithfully,
Richard Bentley

George Putnam Esq.

—George Palmer Putnam Collection, Manuscripts and Archives Divison, The New York Public Library, Astor, Lenox and Tilden Foundations

fear the late decision would influence them still more agt. assuming any risk on this point. I judge so especially because a London publisher who has a special interest in the question wrote to me by the last steamer that the question was now <u>settled positively</u> that an American could <u>not</u> have a copyright.

I shall of course be ready to send out your proposal to be fairly placed before the leading publishers: I think however that it would be much better if <u>you</u> would write <u>personally</u> to such of the publishers as are engaged in this branch—and my agent will call on them with your letter. This would expedite the business and secure a prompt decision. I presume the following are all that it would be worth while to write to viz:

> Henry Colburn
> T.C. Newby
> Chapman and Hall?
> Smith, Elder and Co.

If the first accepts, the other letters would not be delivered. If <u>neither</u> shd. accept, my agent (Mr. Thos. Delf) would call on Bentley, if you wish. Please give your <u>ultimatum</u> in these instructions for Mr. Delf.

Do you still think "The Ways of the Hour" a good title?

> With high respect, Sir, Yours obediently
> <u>Geo. P. Putnam</u>

* * *

As Putnam feared, most London publishers were reluctant to accept Cooper's The Ways of the Hour. *The exception was Richard Bentley, a leading publisher of American works, whom Cooper viewed as a last resort because he had made an offer the author at first considered unacceptable.*

> New York, Feby 14, 1850

My dear Sir,

My agent again writes me from London that after a full and thorough trial he can obtain no offer in London for the Ways of the Hour, better than that of Bentley. In the present state of things there, I feel sure that Bentley's proposal is the best that can be obtained.

Will you be good enough to let me know what is the prospect about the pubn. of the work—and when the stereotyping will probably be finished? I should be glad to know, with reference to Trade Sale. It is very desirable that I shd. have it in time for that,—say 25ᵗʰ March. Cannot this be effected?

> With high respect, Dear Sir,
> Yours faithfully
> <u>G. P. Putnam</u>

J. Fenimore Cooper Esq.

* * *

Putnam wrote Cooper a follow-up note on the Bentley arrangement for The Ways of the Hour *five days later.*

> New York, Feby 19ᵗʰ 1850

Dear Sir,

Will you be kind enough to write a memo. for the government and my agent in London respecting "Ways of the Hour" or will you merely have it sent to Bentley as a matter of course—accepting his proposal?

It appears to me from all I can learn that there is no chance of doing better than to accept Bentley's offer—under the present state of things.—

In this case will you be good enough to write to Bentley, per the steamer of tomorrow?

> Very truly yours,
> <u>Geo. P. Putnam</u>

* * *

Putnam postponed the publication date of The Ways of the Hour *in order to protect Cooper's English copyright, which depended on its prior publication in that country. By this time Putnam had contracted to publish Susan Fenimore Cooper's* Rural Hours, *whose oversight Cooper was taking upon himself. The "file of proofs" Putnam refers to are a copy of the corrected proofs of* Rural Hours, *which Bentley had also agreed to bring out in London.*

> New York, March 28ᵗʰ 1850

J. Fenimore Cooper Esq.
> (Cooperstown, N.Y.)

Dear Sir,

It was altogether a mistake that the "Ways" was announced for Saturday. I <u>did</u> intend as I wrote yesterday to publish next week, having forgotten your wish to put it forward—but I will now announce that it will be postponed for a few days. I should be glad to publish by the <u>18ᵗʰ</u> however, if you think that will be sufficiently late to protect the work in London. Will you be good enough to let me know if this will do? Of course I shall be careful that no copies go out in any way.

The notes were made without special reference to day of publ. but as an average of the whole—My book keeper finding that some were a little in advance. I think you will find the <u>average</u> right.

I will see that the proofs of Rural Hours are sent more frequently—and I hope the delay may be avoided.

I will send the file of proofs to Mr. Bentley by next steamer as mentioned yesterday.

> Very respy yours, <u>Geo. P. Putnam</u>

* * *

The frustrations of serving as Cooper's publisher are clear in this letter. While dealing with Putnam for the revised editions of his works, Cooper also had a binding arrangement with Stringer and Townsend, a rival New York publisher, to bring out less fancy, unrevised editions. The two publishers were supposed to stick to different market niches, but, as this letter attests, Putnam did not believe his rival was being true to the agreement.

N. York, Apl. 17, 1850

J. Fenimore Cooper Esq.

Dear Sir,

By this mail I sent at last a file of the revises [?] of "Rural Hours." If you wish I presume the whole could be sent to Mr. Bentley by the new steamer "Atlantic" which sails on the 27ᵗʰ. I regret that these proofs have been so long delayed, but I could not possibly get them from the stereotypers before.

In regard to the parcel of "Ways of the Hour" sent to Mr. Bentley through my agent Mr. Delf, I am quite sure there could not have been any delay after they reached him. As they were enclosed in a case of books—the delay probably occurred at the Liverpool Custom House.—I have written to Mr. Delf about it.

A copy of "Ways of the Hour" was sent to Miss Cruger and two copies to yourself (by Mr. Phinney) as you directed. A second impression is now on the press—(the first having been only 1000 copies, to save time.)

The new advt. of our freinds [*sic*] Stringer and Townsend conveys an impression which is decidedly injurious to the interests of the revised edns. of "Pilot," "Spy," "Red Rover" etc. The spirit of our arrangement and in fact the words of the agreement implied that no other edns. were to be allowed except the cheap edns. as then published—i.e. in paper at 50 cts. But when they advertise new editions on "superior paper," "2 vols. in one at 75cts"—the public certainly infer that a direct rivalry exists between the two edns. and that theirs is similar to mine though much cheaper. I do not of course object to their advertising complete "sets in cloth at $24," but I think you will agree with me that the present advt. is not quite right. Mr Townsend admitted this, on my calling his attention to it and promised to withdraw it—or rather to alter it—but now on second thought he declines to do it—and therefore I mention it, hoping you will sustain my view of the case.

I remain, Dear Sir, very respectfully yours,

Geo. P. Putnam

* * *

In this note Putnam addresses Cooper about his reading of proofs for one of the works being published in the author's revised edition. In this emergent era of professional authorship, publishers were rapidly coming to regard authorial correction of proof as a necessity rather than a courtesy to the writer.

June 5/50

Dear Sir,

The Printer says the last prints sent were first plate proofs for the author's revision. I have 30 or 40 more and a like number tomorrow. Will you send them on or read them yourself.

Respectfully Yours for

G. P. Putnam

F. Saunders

Fenimore Cooper Esq.

* * *

Putnam here sets a date for Cooper's visit to his family home on Staten Island, which was to combine business and pleasure.

My dear Sir,

May we expect the pleasure of your visit at the island on Monday? I hope you will find that day convenient.

Very truly and respy yours,

Geo. P. Putnam

Nov. 22/50

J. Fenimore Cooper Esq.

When you pass this way I shd. be glad to consult you about the alterations in "Rural Hours"

* * *

Inquiring about the status of Cooper's history of New York City, Putnam also asks for details of Susan Fenimore Cooper's next work—as well he should, following the surprising success of Rural Hours, *which was far outselling the revised editions of her father's works.*

New York, Jan. 13/51

Dear Sir,

Enclosed you will please find Engravers' proofs of 4 Illustrations to "Men of Manhattan," wh. I send that you may assign their proper destination in the text. I shall esteem it a favor if you will give me an idea when the work can be given to the press, as the printers are at leisure comparatively, and it would be well perhaps to be early in the field with the work. Please return the

Map of Manhattan and surroundings that Cooper drew for his projected history of New York City. The author died before the project could be completed (Yale Collection of American Literature, Beinecke Rare Book and Manuscript Library).

proofs (for the printer) at your convenience and also please indicate the time when we may expect copy.

Very respy yours,
Geo. P. Putnam

PS. Please also let us know as speedily as may be, what additional Illustrations will be required: Also when may we look for Miss Cooper's new work and what will be its title. By this mail you will see our first announcement of your new work (in the Evening Post)

* * *

Putnam writes to work out more details regarding illustrations and the approximate publishing date for Cooper's still incomplete history of New York City. As was customary in the profession, Putnam was timing the publication either toward the spring or fall trade sales or publishing seasons.

New York, Jany 21/51

J. Fenimore Cooper Esq.
My dear Sir,

I have your esteemed favor returning proofs of Engraving. I should certainly prefer to publish the book in March, and trust that this may be effected—

but if it is not practicable it will doubtless be best to postpone 'till Augt or Sept.—in which case the notes would be retired and exchanged.—

In regard to Maps. Does your text call for a <u>new</u> one—i.e. N.Y. and environs as they <u>are</u> or as they were in early times? Or both?—I can have an outline map of the <u>old</u> N. York, and another taken from the last guide book, giving the present outline of the city and its suburbs—harbor, L. I.—etc etc.

So also with other buildings, both old and new—If you will be kind enough to let me know which are most essential—as mentioned in the text, I will have them engraved. The engravings already done have cost a considerable sum, and as it is necessary to fix a limit to the expense, so as not to have the vol. too costly, it is desirable to apportion the expenses to the best advantage. Perhaps all this will be in time, however, when you came to town in February. I presume Miss Cooper's book will be ready for publishing in March?

Very resp'y.
Geo. P. Putnam

* * *

A pioneer in the publication of American art books, Putnam invites Cooper to contribute an article to the Home Book of the Picturesque, *an illustrated landscape book brought out in fall 1851. Cooper agreed.*

155 Broadway NY
Mar 29/51

My dear Sir,

Can I prevail upon you to write an article for the Book of American Landscape, to be published in the early Autumn? The subjects of the Engravings are mentioned on the other side. I should be glad to have an article of from 6 to 30 pages, either upon some of these subjects in particular, or upon the general features of American scenery, local incidents, or the history or present state of American Art,—as you may prefer. The topics already promised are indicated in the subjoined list. It would be desirable to have the article by the 13th of June, or earlier. The book is something of an experiment, but I shall endeavor to meet your views promptly, as to the pecuniary value of your contribution. Another year, I hope to something better, if the volume succeeds.

Very truly yours,
Geo. P. Putnam

Fenimore Cooper Esq.

If you will have the kindness to let me know as early as possible, I shall feel greatly obliged.

List of Engravings

Bay of New York	Kirk
*Cascade bridge on the Eric railroad	Talbott
West Rock W. New Haven	Church
*View on the Alleghanies N.C.	Richards
Winter Scene on the Housatonic	Gignoux
Fall in the Catskills	Kensett
Schroon Lake	Cole
War-War-Yondah Lake	Cropsey
The Adirondack Mountains	Durand
View on the Iunietta, Pa	Talbott
The Clove, Catskills	Durand
View on the Rondout	Huntington

* This first engraved by Bayard Taylor Esq.

* The scene by the artist himself

* * *

Rushed for time before an overseas trip, Putnam discusses details concerning Cooper's proposed landscape article for Home Book of the Picturesque *and his still not definitively titled history of New York City.*

Broadway, May 5th, 1851

My dear Sir,

As I expect to go to London, this month, to be absent six weeks, pray excuse me for reminding you of the article for our book of Landscapes. If you will kindly let me know within a week or two, what will be the topic and its title, and about how many pages, I can then leave the whole matter in train—I should be glad if you could find it convenient to have the article ready soon after the first of June—

The other articles will be by W. Irving, W. Bryant, W. Halleck, N. Willis, Rev. Dr. Bethune, Rev. W. Magoon, and H. T. Tuckerman Esq. and W. Bayard Taylor. They will make from 10 to 20 pages each, the size is small folio, large pica type, leaded—

I am dear Sir,
Very Truly Yours
Geo. P. Putnam

The subject you proposed,—comparative characteristics of Amer. and European Scenery would be very interesting and desirable.

J. Fenimore Cooper Esq.

I should be glad to have the copy also of the "Men of Manhattan" before I leave on the 31st, if you can have it ready. I will leave in train whatever more is necessary in the way of illustration, if you can indicate what is necessary. Do you still prefer the title—the "Men of Manhattan"?

This letter is the last one that Putnam wrote to Cooper. Unaware of how seriously ill Cooper was, Putnam inquires about the readiness of the history of New York City, which he was eager to get to press in time for the Christmas season. Cooper died less than five weeks after this letter was written, on 14 September 1851, leaving his last book incomplete.

155 Broadway, NY
Augt 9/51

My dear Sir,

I have had a rough outline for a map made by a draftsman merely to ascertain about what <u>scale</u> will suit your purpose and how much space it must cover. It can be made on a larger scale if you wish. When you decide about the scale and the outline, the draftsman will make another sketch more in detail, and with accurate measurements, and send it for you to insert your own additions, etc.

You did not mention in your last what are the prospects in regard to <u>time</u>. I fear the necessary delay of the proofs–(the first is not yet recd. back) will make it impossible to publish this season.

The number of copies "Rural Hours" reported sold by Bentley (180) certainly seems very small–but I shd. be more incredulous if the book had been printed in a different form and at a moderate price.

In 2 vol at a guinea and without illustrations, it could only reach the circulating libraries–at least the chief sale would be to them–and the <u>work</u> is perhaps too quiet and high-toned to have any great run among readers for mere amusement. I shd. be surprised certainly, if no more has been done–but I can hardly suppose Bentley would make a false return.

With high respect and best wishes for your early and entire recovery, I remain yours obty <u>G. P. Putnam</u>

* * *

After her father's death, Susan Fenimore Cooper tried to prepare a manuscript of "Towns of Manhattan" for press. Putnam was eager to cooperate, as this letter attests, but repeated requests for alterations and a series of misfortunes in the printing and editorial offices, which resulted in the loss of parts of the manuscript, doomed the project. Nor was Susan Fenimore Cooper's "The Shield" ever published. In 1852 Putnam did publish her sister Charlotte Fenimore Cooper's translation of Ida Pfeiffer's A Journey to Iceland and Travels in Sweden and Norway.

155 Broadway, New York, Decr. 2, 1851

Miss J. Fenimore Cooper

(Cooperstown)

Dear Madam,

Your favor of Nov. 28 with proofs of Towns of Manhattan and "The Shield" was duly recd.–

In regard to the cut–the early view of New Amsterdam, I was puzzled myself for it did not seem to agree fully with the description–and yet I supposed it must be the one referred to. I presume the passage you have substituted will make it allright.

Your proposal respecting the re-modeling of the whole work is exceedingly difficult for me to answer, because I cannot judge how far the work would differ from that now prepared. If you had proposed to re-write or remodel it before we commenced printing I should doubtless have preferred that you should do so: but under the present circumstances, my own impression is in favor of proceeding as we are, with your notes to the original work. For many reasons it seems to me that this will be best now.

This is a bustling season, and I have a vast deal to think of and to be anxious about, so that I cannot consider such a matter so calmly and carefully as I could

wish–But I trust you will on the whole feel willing to proceed and to make your father's plan as complete as possible by your own additions.

The expense of the sheets already printed would probably be about $150 or $175.–

If you wish to suggest any more wood cuts or illustrations, to be engraved, it would be desirable to put them in hand as early as possible. You are aware that we have a general bird's eye view of New York in 1851– taken from <u>Union Square</u>–and can have another taken from the <u>harbour</u> if it is desirable–We have also cuts of Trinity Church (the second one), the Government House and the Old City Hall.

I shall proceed with Mde. Pfeiffer's work and The Shield as rapidly as possible–presuming you can finish the copy as rapidly as it is wanted.

Pray excuse this hurried letter–and believe me

Faithfully yours,

<u>Geo. P. Putnam</u>

Harper and Brothers

Putnam's attitude toward Harper and Brothers, a New York firm that was the most successful publisher in the country, was ambivalent. A man who rightfully prided himself for his collegiality, Putnam admired the scale of their operations and their success, which he saw as reflecting well on the development of both the publishing profession and literary culture in the United States. He looked less favorably, however, on the favoritism they showed for foreign authors and their methods, which sometimes included piracy and sharp dealings with fellow American publishers. When those methods were turned against him, Putnam reacted with a combination of innocent surprise and self-righteous anger.

The disagreement that arose between the two houses concerned American rights to several popular European authors, especially George Borrow and Fredrika Bremer. Putnam had gained rights to Borrow's work from the author's English publisher John Murray, and to Bremer's books through an agreement negotiated by their common friend, Andrew Jackson Downing. The Harpers, who had until then been Bremer's American publisher, simmered as Putnam–to their minds, unethically–took over one of their best-selling authors; they reacted–to his mind, with inexplicable aggression–by reprinting a cheaper edition of Borrow's Lavengro.

The following exchange of letters chronicles the dispute between G. P. Putnam and Harper and Brothers, a symptomatic outbreak of infighting between rival publishers made virtually inevitable by the lack of an international copyright agreement defining the rights to foreign texts. It played itself out quickly, as most episodes of the sort did, though it made a lasting impression on Putnam, who always thereafter regarded the Harpers as his foil in American literary publishing. Nevertheless, Putnam's final letter in the exchange is a statement of commiseration for the destruction of their business complex, revealing his underlying ethos of collegiality. All of the letters in this section come from the George Palmer Putnam Collection, Manuscripts Division, Department of Rare Books and Special Collections, Princeton University Library, and are published with permission of the Princeton University Library.

* * *

155 Broadway   Jan 29, 1851
Messrs. Harper & Brothers–
Dear Sirs,

I have observed that you have again announced that you shall reprint Borrow's "Lavengro."–

Considering that my arrangements with Mr. Murray to republish this work from an early copy, were made as long ago as November 1848, (the proposition originating with him,) and that at least one of your house was aware of that fact, I have been unwilling to suppose that you really intended to reprint another edition.–If any good reason why the ordinary usages of the trade should be departed from in this instance, may I ask you to be good enough to mention it?–

I am not aware that I have given you any cause for complaint–I have carefully avoided all interference with your publishing arrangements and have not even sought or proposed for a single English book for re-publication for two years past; while I have declined several proposals made to me for such reprints from early copies.

If there be nevertheless any good reason why it is right and proper, according to equity and usage, for you to reprint Borrow's work; in rivalry to my edition (which will be printed from an early copy obtained at my considerable cost,) I should feel greatly obliged if you would let me know what that reason is–

I am, Dear Sirs
Very truly Yours
Geo P. Putnam

* * *

No. 82 Cliff St.
Jany 30, 1851
Dear Sir –

In reply to your favor received last evening, (but without date,) and as a reason why we shall publish "Lavengro," we beg to say –

Fletcher, James, John, and J. Wesley Harper, photographed by Mathew Brady in his studio, circa 1850 (Library of Congress). The Harper brothers were the most successful book publishers in mid-nineteenth-century America.

That you have, without cause, reprinted <u>two</u> of our publications upon us.

There is still another reason but as the above is deemed quite sufficient, it is unnecessary to give it at present, especially as we have reason to <u>know</u> that you have for some time been familiar with our complaints, and with our intentions to defend our invaded rights.

With these views we must say that your <u>motive</u> in addressing to us the apparently friendly Note referred to is beyond our comprehension.

We are, dear Sir,

    Yours respectfully

      <u>Harper & Brothers</u>.

* * *

155 Broadway, Jan 30th 1851.

Messrs. Harper & Brothers –

Dear Sirs –

I have your note of this morning. It is true that in accordance with the special request of a personal friend of Miss Bremer, I have printed library editions of two of her works, the profits of which were to be divided with the author: an undertaking which seemed to be an appropriate compliment to that lady, on the occasion of her visit to this country. But that this was an infringement, in the slightest degree, of your rights, either legal or according to usage, I never for one moment supposed–In the first place, there had been at least two other editions of those works, besides yours;–and secondly, my book, published at a dollar, can hardly be deemed a rival to yours, which had been published for years, in thousands, at <u>one shilling</u>.

I can truly say that in acceding to this proposal on behalf of Miss Bremer, I did not consider there was the slightest interference with yours and other cheap editions, so long in the market,–and it never appeared to me that for my part in this matter you had the smallest grounds for complaint.

This, and this only, can be the foundation of your charge, that I have "reprinted two of your publications."

You say that there is another reason, but omit to give it, as you "have reason to know that I have been some time familiar with your intention to defend your invaded rights."

I know of no other reason, unless it be that you make objections to the <u>mode</u> in which my arrangement was made with Mr. Murray.–Now I may take a wrong view of the subject, but it appears to me, that so long as the fact remains that I pay for

an early copy of the book, and for the express authority to reprint it, the particular <u>mode</u> or <u>amount</u> of the payment, can be of no concern to anybody else.

I cannot admit, that I am "familiar" with your complaints. On the contrary, although I have been told in general terms that you felt aggrieved in some way, I have dismissed such remarks as idle, <u>knowing</u> that I have not consciously given you any cause for complaint, but on the contrary, have <u>felt</u> a <u>right</u> to claim your confidence, courtesy, and good-will, and have never dreamed of meddling with your business arrangements, in any way which could be deemed objectionable.

Your last remark, that my "apparently friendly note" is beyond your comprehension, seems to me quite uncalled for. I wrote in good faith, to ask simply, whether you really intended to reprint Borrow after knowing the circumstances,–and secondly, if you did, why? Surely it was not amiss that I should wish to know the nature of your complaints, if you had any. I must repeat that as yet I know of no good or just cause for your charge that I have invaded your rights. I should be truly sorry to find that you had just cause for complaint against me, for I have ever felt a friendly deference to your houses, and have neither the means nor the disposition to enter into rivalry with it.

In this case, if you persist in your intention, I shall certainly feel aggrieved, and may deem it proper to state the case publicly as it stands.

    Very truly yours

    <u>Geo P Putnam</u>

* * *

This next extant letter indicates that Putnam took the case for his edition of Lavengro *to the newspapers.*

No. 82 Cliff St.

February 24, 1851.

Mr. Geo. P. Putnam,

Dear <u>Sir</u>, We see by the morning's papers that you advertise your edition of "Lavengro" as "the only one that comprises the whole of the original work." Our object in addressing to you this Note is, to deny the statement, and to inquire whether it has your authority and sanction.

    Yours, Very respectfully,

      Harper & Brothers

* * *

This excerpt from the editor's column "Familiar Talk with Our Readers" appeared just after the publication of the Harper edition of Lavengro, *by which time an outraged Putnam had made his dispute with the larger house a matter of public knowledge.*

Should we turn back with you, reader, from this moving memorial of departed Eminence, to the living world, of which we, as writers and editors, are members, and talk to you of the clashing interests of rival printing-offices, rival publishers, rival magazines (and we could say a good and bad word for each and every of them), what a tumult we should have—with the shock between original magazines, "bone of our bone and flesh of our flesh," and those monstrous ornamental goîtres, the great reprints:— there are the two editions of BORROW, whose kind, scholarly face you have on our first page—the one issued by Mr. PUTNAM "from early proof-sheets received from London, by an express arrangement with Mr. Murray" (the author's London publisher), the other by our good friends the Brothers HARPER, hurried out with such Caesarean enterprise as to have left one leg—we mean one leaf, behind it: very cheap, however, and not badly printed.

–*Holden's Dollar Magazine*, 7 (April 1851): 192

In a major fire that broke out on 10 December 1853, the Harper complex at 82 Cliff Street, the largest printing plant in the United States, was destroyed, with nearly complete loss of plates, stock, and manuscript. The Harper brothers immediately set about rebuilding.

Washington Dc. 14/53

Messrs. Harper & Brothers

In thinking of the severe disaster which your business has suffered, it seems natural to suppose that the prompt sympathy, especially of the trade, will be cordially expressed, without exception or qualification—and the question necessarily comes to me why should not I be one of the thousands who will express their good will on this occasion?

The answer is equally obvious,—there has been an appearance, at least, of ill-will between your house & myself—and I might reasonably doubt how far any wish on my part to remove this ill will, might be met & responded to.

It is not because I suppose that even this great calamity, disastrous though it be, can have any effect on your ample resources so serious as to call for anything else than a friendly expression, on all sides, of deep regret at this great destruction of property. I only

thought the opportunity a suitable [one] for me to say, that anything else than cordial good will and friendly relations between myself and all engaged in the trade & especially those at the head of the trade, is deeply repugnant to my feeling—and that however I may have considered myself aggrieved and however you may have thought I had done amiss, and however warm I have been in speaking of a supposed grievance as I honestly felt—this may be a time when all these things may be properly and easily buried and forgotten. If you feel so disposed—and from this time if such be your disposition it may surely be easy to avoid all grounds for complaint on either side.

I write this, hastily, from impulse while absent from home. It is a small [?] amid the engrossing & important affairs of your great business—but I trust that as the motive for these lines has been candidly [?] stated, they will not be recieved [*sic*] in any other light.

Very respectfully, gentl.

Yours

Geo P Putnam

Ticknor and Fields

The good professional relations between Ticknor and Fields and G. P. Putnam and Company, leaders in literary publishing in Boston and New York, respectively, were enhanced by the cordial personal relations between James T. Fields and George P. Putnam. Each firm dealt primarily in the belles lettres, and each served its locale as a major outlet for the other's books. Business between them was brisk in the 1850s, but the position of each firm with respect to its market shifted over the decade, as the activities of G. P. Putnam contracted and those of Ticknor and Fields expanded. All the correspondence below, except for James Fields's letter, is preserved in Ticknor and Fields's pressed-letter books. The writing in these books has so faded that occasional words or phrases in the documents are difficult to read or indecipherable.

* * *

The natural alliance between the houses led Ticknor in his 2 January 1849 letter to Putnam to propose favorable discount terms between them.

We have frequent calls for your Publications from the Trade who will not buy at all unless we can make 10 or 15 percent discount. We think it will be for your interest to allow us a larger discount[,] such a one as will enable us to offer your publications to country booksellers & others who buy & sell again. If you could send us your books in large quantities & make our house a depot[?] where your books could always be found, or not as your principle

James T. Fields, a leading literary publisher in Boston and the country, who was one of Putnam's closest colleagues in the profession

---

A Brief History

The line of descent of the Boston publishing house best known as Ticknor and Fields began in 1832 when William D. Ticknor formed a partnership with John Allen and became involved first in bookselling and then in publishing. Allen left the firm to form his own imprint, John Allen and Company, in 1834. For the next thirty years Ticknor continued his career as a publisher, changing the name of his company in 1843, 1849, and 1854 to acknowledge the contributions of first John Reed and then James T. Fields, who had begun his career as a clerk with Allen and Ticknor.

Allen and Ticknor (1832–1834)
William D. Ticknor (1834–1843)
William D. Ticknor and Company (1843–1849)
Ticknor, Reed and Fields (1849–1854)
Ticknor and Fields (1854–1868)

Fields became half owner of the firm in 1854. A notable literary publisher, the house brought out Nathaniel Hawthorne's The Scarlet Letter *(1850) and continued as his publisher until 1863; it also published Henry David Thoreau's* Walden *(1854). William D. Ticknor died in 1864, and his son Howard Ticknor was bought out in 1868 as a new house was born—Fields, Osgood and Company.*

---

agent here (as other houses in N.Y. & Phil. do who make us their dist.) we could always be sure of selling to the Trade & making Booksellers here in New England a proper dist. We of course should speak to make the same dist. from our Publ. Please write us in[?] this month & say what increase of [missing] you think it cost for your interest to make this your amt in future . . .

—reproduced by permission of the Houghton Library, Harvard University, MS Am 2030.2 (52)

* * *

Distribution problems plagued the publishing industry throughout the nineteenth century, and complaints such as this 25 October 1851 note from Ticknor, Reed and Fields to Putnam were common. The item in question was G. P. Putnam's recently published giftbook.

We make it a matter to have you supplied with our books, when published, as soon as any other house. We begin to think that you do not do as well by us, for looking into a periodical store this morning, we espied accidentally the "Home Book of Beauty" published by you, and were told that it was an old book on <u>their</u> counters. We are somewhat sensitive in the matter of not having new publications as soon as our neighbors, (and particularly your publications) and our interest in their sales hinges on this point.

—reproduced by permission of the Houghton Library, Harvard University

* * *

In this typically friendly 12 November 1852 note, Fields explains the various services he is doing for G. P. Putnam books in Boston. The book he was distributing to local newspaper editors was presumably Homes of American Authors.

My Dear Putnam.

<u>The</u> Bk. has arrived & many thanks rise up to acknowledge yr. kindness. I will see that the <u>victims</u> receive theirs. It is a fine thing surely & must succeed. I advise that your five copies for Boston Editors be sent as follows

√ Dr. Brewer	(Atlas)
√ Saml. Kettell Eq	(Courier)
√ Chas. G. Greene Esq	(Post)
√ N. Hale Esq	(D. Addn.)
√ Robt. Carter	(Commonwealth)
√ John S. Sleeper Esq	(Misc. Jl.)

I wish I could "drop in" at No. 16 but business forbids. I have sent by todays Express the Portraits I promised you and wish they were all on larger paper. I was obliged to send to Miss Mitford the Cooper, Bryant &

Irving you gave me and must pay for <u>another</u> set. Dont refuse me. Please say to Mr. Saunders I have made bargains with our papers for inserting those Advts. & that you get the same [?] we get ourselves.

Send a supply of the "<u>Homes</u>" as early as possible as I shall make it a speciality to sell a good many. I do not know of a book so captivating to the eye and heart of an American.

With best compliments to Mrs. Putnam and best wishes for the health and happiness of the handsome "half dozen"–

Very Sincerely Yrs.
J. T. Fields

If I can ever be of any service to you here tell me how & it shall be rendered. Send us (nice copies) of "The Homes" good impressions, say to start with–25 cloth.

10 mor.[?]

–Manuscripts Division, Department of Rare Books and Special Collections, Princeton University Library. Published with permission of the Princeton University Library.

* * *

In his 16 December 1852 letter Ticknor negotiates discount terms for a large order of Putnam's acclaimed new gift book, Homes of American Authors.

In your letter of Nov. 29 you say "If you will make up your order at once for a hundred copies, we will give you a discount of <u>5</u>% for your note at 4 mos." Now if this does not mean 38 1/3 % it means nothing at all. This is the <u>letter</u> & the point of the remarks, & we had no other thoughts in sending the order.

. . . .

This letter of Nov 29 seems to have been an unfortunate one, taking it altogether. We think, however, touching the "Home Book" you can't but see that we are entirely correct.

–reproduced by permission of the Houghton Library, Harvard University, MS Am 2030. 2 (54)

* * *

In this 30 March 1854 letter to Bangs Bros. and Company, New York auctioneers, Ticknor and Fields disputes terms of purchase for auctioned copies of Putnam's edition of Horatio Bridge's Journal of an African Cruiser, *originally published as the lead title in the Wiley and Putnam Library of American Books and now an item in Putnam's general sale of stock and plates.*

We have your a/c.–As you charge for packing & shipping we expect you to attend to this as usual. There is one item to which we object, Viz. 500 "African

Cruiser" sheets. Mr. Putnam announced at the sale that there were <u>145</u> copies on hand–these we agreed to take when we purchased but not the 500 now added. We must decline receiving these, as we do not want them at any price.

We should not have paid even <u>$50</u>–for the plates had we understood that there were this no. on hand. The other items are correct. & can be forwarded by you,–or we will attend to this & deduct from your bill your charge for packing &.

–reproduced by permission of the Houghton Library, Harvard University, MS Am 2030. 2 (55)

* * *

In his 12 January 1858 order from Putnam's list, Ticknor includes a hefty order of Washington Irving's four-volume, still uncompleted biography of George Washington and of Elisha Kane's Arctic expedition travelogue, as well as various other works by Irving and George William Curtis.

You may send us, as you proposed
    50 Dr Kane clo.
also, 25 Irving's Washn. 4 vols. 12mo clo.
    10 Do Do   Do ½ [?] clf Ext.
    5 Irving's Works 15 Vols. clo
    5 Do.   Do.   Do. ½ light clf
    3 Irving Sketch Bk–illustrated
    3 Curtis's Writings [5] vols cl.
Send the above by Fall River freight line–bill by mail.– Where is Bayard Taylor's new vol.?–We see it announced as ready in New York.–Let us have it as soon as possible.

–reproduced by permission of the Houghton Library, Harvard University, MS Am 2030. 2 (57)

* * *

On 15 January 1858 Ticknor and Fields followed up on their recent order.

We rec<u>d</u> this morning an invoice of a portion of the books ordered.–We were very sorry not to have recd. the Washington Complete, as we are in immediate want of several sets.–Send them as soon <u>as possible</u>. You proposed to send us 50 Kane at $3.50.–You send only 20, & charge these at 3.75. We charge back the difference–$5.00. which please credit to us. We ordered 5 Irving Wks 15 Vols.–you sent only <u>3</u>–[gave] no reason for not sending the 10 Cops Washn [per]clf (light) Extra.–If you can't send them bound–send 10 sets folded & collated.–Send a few bound if you can, as we want them at once.–

–reproduced by permission of the Houghton Library, Harvard University, MS Am 2030. 2 (57)

Executives and Editors Associated with the House of Putnam

The growing scale of operations required that nineteenth-century publishing houses employ a variety of both junior and senior coworkers. The following section consists of sketches of the most important associates—partners, editors, and collaborators—of the House of Putnam during the thirty-six-year span of Putnam's connection with the firm.

John Wiley

The son of Charles Wiley, the leading literary publisher of the Knickerbocker generation of James Fenimore Cooper, Washington Irving, James Kirke Paulding, and Richard Henry Dana, John Wiley (1812–1891) was exposed early to the world of professional letters. Even as a teenager John Wiley was involved in various publishing, retailing, and jobbing relationships in New York City. In 1832, with George Long, he formed the firm of Wiley and Long. Putnam was taken in as a junior partner in 1836, and Long soon afterward retired, precipitating the reorganization of the firm as Wiley and Putnam in 1837.

With Wiley running the New York office and Putnam the London office from 1838 to 1847, the firm grew into one of the leading participants in the rapidly expanding transatlantic trade in books and periodicals. During this period the New York office remained the center of the firm's operations, and Wiley set its overall policies. Wiley, for instance, made the crucial decision in winter 1845 to become more actively involved in publishing by hiring Evert A. Duyckinck to serve as literary adviser, with responsibility to oversee production and marketing of the important Wiley and Putnam libraries of 1845–1847.

The permanent return of Putnam to New York in June 1847 reunited the partners for the first time in a decade, an arrangement that proved constricting to the more adventurous younger partner. By year's end, Putnam took steps to open his own publishing house, and in March 1848 the partnership of Wiley and Putnam was disbanded, Wiley keeping the old office at 161 Broadway and Putnam opening a new one just down the block. Wiley remained in active business as publisher, retailer, and jobber to the end of his life. Although he kept a lower publishing profile than during the years of his partnership

John Wiley, the senior partner of Wiley and Putnam. Although the two men were not close personally, they remained on collegial terms even after the breakup of their partnership.

with Putnam, he intelligently reoriented his new firm's publishing activities toward his own interests in science and engineering, an important, emergent sector of modern publishing. At his death he left behind the family-owned company, John Wiley and Sons, which, like G. P. Putnam's Sons, grew in succeeding generations into one of the mainstays of twentieth-century American publishing.

* * *

For years after the breakup with Putnam, Wiley maintained a London office at Paternoster Row and continued to engage in the rare book and import trade. When he wrote this solicitation in 1855, he was advertising himself as "Importer, Publisher, and Bookseller"; the 10 percent commission he charges for his services as overseas agent was standard.

To the Library Committee
                    &
Librarian of New York Society Library
          Gentl
          In answer to your application I shall be most happy to act as the agent of your association for the supply of American & Foreign Publications—Periodicals included. My facilities for procuring cheaply & promptly all works issued in this & other countries are as good at least I think as those of any other House—I should supply all books <u>at actual</u> cost & it would be my endeavor to procure them at the lowest possible price—for my trouble or agency I should charge a commission of <u>ten per cent on</u> the net amount of each Invoice—Foreign Books & Periodicals will be received <u>Free of Duty</u>—
          Very Respectfully   <u>John Wiley</u>
New York June 22–1855–

                    –*The New York Society Library*

Evert A. Duyckinck, who directed Wiley and Putnam literary series from 1845 to 1847. Duyckinck and Putnam cooperated over many years on various publication schemes and in the fight for American acceptance of international copyright (Wallach Division of Art, Portrait File, New York Public Library).

Evert A. Duyckinck

Like John Wiley, Evert A. Duyckinck (1816–1878) was born to professional letters. His father, an occasional partner in joint publication projects with Charles Wiley, was a successful New York City publisher and bookseller during the first decades of the nineteenth century. Educated at Columbia College and left an income by his father, Duyckinck during the early 1840s edited several short-lived Manhattan literary journals. In 1845 he persuaded John Wiley to finance two series, one featuring European reprints and a second composed of original American works. Brought out under Duyckinck's expert literary direction, the Wiley and Putnam Library of Choice Reading and Library of American Books became the leading American literary publishing projects of the decade. These series filled the void in the American market of high-quality, moderately priced books. Furthermore, the American series served to introduce many young American writers to a national and—with Putnam's help in London—international audience. In addition, Duyckinck and his younger brother George financed jointly with the publisher the shorter-lived Wiley and Putnam Foreign Library.

Toward the end of his editorship of the library series in winter 1847, Duyckinck reached an agreement to edit a new weekly journal, the Literary World, *under the financial control of Wiley and Putnam and their fellow publisher Daniel Appleton. Duyckinck hoped to turn the* Literary World *into an American equivalent of the London Athenæum, but he initially held his editorial post for only slightly more than two months. The publishers, who had previously stated their strong objection to Duyckinck's involvement of his controversial friend Cornelius Mathews in editorial policy, presented him with an ultimatum: distance Mathews from the operation, buy the journal himself, or leave. When Duyckinck refused even to accept the necessity of the choice, Wiley and Appleton, acting without the absent Putnam's knowledge, summarily fired him and hired Charles Fenno Hoffman as editor. That arrangement lasted only until September 1848, when Evert and his brother George bought the periodical. From 1848 until 1853, when the brothers disbanded the publication, the* Literary World *catered intelligently and with a high degree of sophistication both to the publishing industry and to letters. In subsequent years, Putnam enlisted his old friend's support for projects ranging from* Putnam's Monthly *to the International Copyright Association.*

* * *

In this excerpt from his "The Literati of New York City," Edgar Allan Poe praises Duyckinck's supervision of Wiley and Putnam's Library of Choice Reading. Poe, of course, had reason to support Duyckinck, who had chosen two of his books for the Library of American Books.

Not the least important service rendered by him was the projection and editorship of Wiley and Putnam's "Library of Choice Reading," a series which brought to public notice many valuable foreign works which had been suffering under neglect in this country, and at the same time afforded unwanted [or unwonted] encouragement to native authors by publishing their books, in good style and in good company, without trouble or risk to the authors themselves, and in the very teeth of the disadvantages arising from the want of an international copyright.

—*Godey's Lady's Book*, 33 (July 1846): 15–16

* * *

The relationship between Putnam and Duyckinck began in the 1830s and continued until Putnam's death. Putnam hosted Duyckinck in London in the late 1830s during the latter's grand tour, supplied him with rare books over many years, and consulted him on various projects. In this letter he asks for his better educated friend's judgment of a poem submitted to Putnam's Monthly *by William Gilmore Simms, whom Duyckinck aided in placing works in New York publications.*

Nov. 10 1854

My dear Sir

I shall consider you the god-father of this poem—& therefore I venture to trouble you with the question whether some of the verses may not be properly & judiciously omitted. I am no critic, but I cannot feel convinced that all the verses or at least all the <u>lines</u> are pure gold —I don't wish to offend Mr. Simms by omissions—but he will remember that <u>we</u> give this poem anonymously and therefore the magazine only is responsible

In haste yours truly,

E. A. Duyckinck   <u>G P Putnam</u>

Putnam added a postscript that ran up the left margin.

<u>Entre-nous</u> is this a great <u>poem</u>? If <u>you</u> say so I rest content.

—*Duyckinck Family Papers, Manuscripts and Archives Division, The New York Public Library, Astor, Lenox and Tilden Foundations*

Orville Roorbach

A pioneering American bibliographer and well-regarded professional bookman, Orville Roorbach (1803–1861) managed the wholesale department of Wiley and Putnam. Roorbach continued in that role for a year or so with G. P. Putnam after the 1847–1848 breakup of the old firm. During his time as manager Roorbach had been working on his life project of compiling a bibliography on American books. He initially failed to find a publisher for his Bibliotheca Americana *and wound up paying for its publication himself in 1849. Putnam, who presumably originally declined to publish Roorbach's book, did serve as its New York and London distributor; also, in 1850 he published Roorbach's addendum. By that time, Roorbach had left Putnam's employ and set up his own bookstore and agency in rooms above G. P. Putnam at 155 Broadway.*

* * *

This prepublication notice was probably written by Duyckinck. Mungo Park and Branta Mayer were well-known travel writers.

A new bibliographical work is in preparation, by O. A. Roorbach of this city, a gentleman well known throughout the country from a thirty years' connexion with the book trade as publisher, and latterly from his active engagement with one of the largest New York houses; circumstances which peculiarly qualify him for the work he has now undertaken. This is to issue, in a comprehensive volume, A Complete Alphabetical List of all American publications since 1820, and incidentally all works of a prior date, of a scientific character, of which there has been no reprint since 1820, and *all* works relating to America that may come within the writer's research, with the number of Volumes, size, style of binding, price, and publisher, on the same page.

The original plan was to make a book of reference for the trade only; but on after consideration, it was concluded that with a little more labor a book could be prepared useful also to literary institutions and individuals. There will be no classification except Biography and Law, but one continuous Alphabetical List will be furnished, giving the books under the Author's Name, the General Title of the Work, and the country to which it relates, an arrangement by which a person can scarcely fail to find the work sought for. If he wants information, for instance, on Africa, Mexico, or any other country, he will find all that has been published in the way of History, whether by Mungo Park or Brantz Mayer.

CATALOGUE

OF

AMERICAN PUBLICATIONS,

FROM

1820 TO 1848.

"A Manual for the Booksellers and the Bookbuyers."

COMPILED AND ARRANGED

By O. A. ROORBACH.

The Subscriber will put to Press, in the course of the present Month, a

CATALOGUE OF AMERICAN PUBLICATIONS,

INCLUDING

REPRINTS AND ORIGINAL WORKS,

FROM

1820 TO 1848 INCLUSIVE,

AND

ALL WORKS RELATING TO AMERICA, THAT MAY COME
WITHIN HIS SEARCH.

The Catalogue will be one continuous Alphabetical List (except Law and Biography,
which will be classed separately), under the Author's Name, the General
Title of the Work, and also the Country to which it may Relate,
with the Size, Number of Volumes, Style of Binding,
and Publisher, on the same Page.

By this arrangement the book sought for can readily be found, and to the distant
Bookseller it will be peculiarly useful as a Manual of Reference, as he can at once
inform his customer whether such a book has been published, and the price at which
he can supply it; by knowing the publisher, he will readily know at what rate of
discount he can purchase. Of such books as have been published years since, and
to be found only in the hands of collectors of second hand and rare books, the size,
publisher, and date of publication only is given, as the present value is regulated by
the scarcity or intrinsic value of the work.

Four-fifths or more of the Titles enumerated in the Catalogue are from personal
inspection, or a knowledge of the book, and care has been taken to give the real
publisher.

The book will be printed in One Volume, full-sized Octavo, of from 300 to 325
pages, containing about 15,000 Titles, and an Alphabetical List of all (over 600)
the Publishers named, with their Residences.

PRICE IN FULL CLOTH, $4 00.

ORVILLE A. ROORBACH.

Subscriptions received by Mr. G. P. PUTNAM, 155 *Broadway,*
New York.

Advertisement for Roorbach's Bibliotheca Americana *in the*
13 January 1849 issue of The Literary World

Flag of a 15 November 1851 Norton's Literary Advertiser, *whose design showcases Orville A. Roorbach's* Bibliotheca Americana, *an indication of the spirit of professionalism and cultural nationalism that was transforming publishing in the United States at midcentury*

Mr. Roorbach has devoted all his leisure time for the last two years to this work, and expects to go to press in January with over 15,000 Titles, in an octavo of 350 or 400 pages.

–*The Literary World,* 3 (25 November 1848): 855–856

* * *

Roorbach's introduction to Bibliotheca Americana, *in which he requests cooperation in keeping his bibliography accurate and updated, shows that, like Putnam, he believed in the corporate nature of the publishing profession.*

The purpose of this book is to supply Booksellers with a practical Manual of information respecting all books printed in this country during the last thirty years; in other words, all American editions now in the market. Some few of the more important or curious works printed prior to 1820 are also mentioned.

The aim has been to make the arrangement such as will give the desired information with as little search as possible. The prices are taken from the publishers' Trade Lists. Of such books as are now scarce, or out of print, and which are to be found only in the hands of collectors of second-hand and rare books, the size, publisher, and date of publication are given, as the present price is regulated by the scarcity or intrinsic value of the work.

As far as could be ascertained, all reprints from English works (excepting the Law list) are noted by (*), American translations of Foreign works by (+), and reprints, having notes or additions by American editors, are indicated by (#).

Biographical and Law books are classed separately at the end of the volume. The general list contains both the authors' names (when they are given in the books) and also the title of the book, repeated in its place in the alphabetical arrangement.

It is proposed to continue this Catalogue by Supplements, at intervals, in which any errors which may have occurred in this volume will be corrected. It is also intended to publish a Classified Index.

Believing that such a book of reference as this will be found of essential value to every one connected with the Trade, the compiler trusts that every Bookseller will at once coincide in this opinion; and as only a small edition is printed, specially for their use, it is hoped that the Trade will promptly join in repaying the very considerable trouble and expense incurred.

Orville A. Roorbach

New York, <u>March</u>, 1849

* Authors, Publishers, etc., will confer a favor and insure a correct description of their publications in the Supplement by sending the full title, size, style of binding, and price, to

O. A. R., New-York.

Frederick Saunders

Frederick Saunders (1807–1902) was the son of William Saunders, the managing partner of the British publishing house Saunders and Otley. His father sent him in 1837 to the United States to set up a branch office and to seek protection in Congress for the firm's authors—especially Bulwer-Lytton—against American piracy, particulary that of Harper and Brothers. He later went to work as a house adviser to the Harpers and, after a stint at the New York Tribune, served in a similar capacity at G. P. Putnam. In 1852 he helped Putnam compile Homes of American Authors; *he also wrote for* Putnam's Monthly *and published several of his many books with G. P. Putnam.*

Saunders's career overlapped Putnam's in many regards. Both were involved early in their careers in transatlantic publishing, both labored for the passage of international copyright legislation, and both took part in the 1855 Crystal Palace dinner. On at least one occasion their personal lives also intersected in a completely unexpected way when their eldest sons both were captured late in the Civil War and sent off to Southern prisons. By chance the sons made each other's acquaintance at Libby Prison in January 1865.

* * *

Saunders was one of the few people in the United States whose knowledge and experience in domestic and international publishing was comparable to that of Putnam. In the following essay, "The Publishing Business," Saunders welcomes the new half century with an historical survey of the history of printing and publishing in the West, which he sees as leading up to the new era of improved technology, large-scale production, and widespread literacy—in short, what he and Putnam alike would have called progress.

The enterprises of Publishers constitute an important feature in the history of literature. Booksellers and Publishers are the public purveyors of our literary aliment. They sustain intermediate relations between the public and authors, whose interests, next to their own, it is their province to foster and defend. The book-business of modern times has assumed an importance unknown to the days of its infancy, when the monks monopolized the *Commercium librorum.*

The profession is said to have taken its rise, indeed, even in classic times, when an extensive traffic was carried on in MSS. by the Scribes and Copyists; and to have flourished also during the Saxon era, many eminent names being on record of transcribers in the seventh and eight centuries. Books in their present form were first invented, it is said, by Attalus, King of Pergamus, in 887.

The diffusive spread of knowledge, and the founding of monasteries, gave increased importance to this branch of commerce, although the earliest mention of a "public dealer in books" is one of Peter de Blois, who lived about 1170. He was a distinguished scholar—the craft in his day having been more remarkable for erudition than it has been in some subsequent epochs of its history. Booksellers then exercised their calling under the supervision and censorship of the Universities; and books themselves were then, moreover, rare and costly luxuries,—the prerogative of the privileged few; now they have become the common property of mankind.

During the middle ages, the booksellers were called *Stationarii* at the Universities of Paris and Bologna; but the first regularly matriculated bookseller was doubtless Faustus, for he is said to have carried the books for sale to the Monasteries in France, and elsewhere. The first bookseller, it is stated, who purchased MSS. for publication, and speculated in the enterprise, not possessing a press of his own, was John Otto of Nuremberg, who flourished in 1516. Caxton, the father of the English press, however, who lived 1471–1491, and who had twenty-four presses in his office at Westminster Abbey, doubtless issued many new and original productions at his own risk, as well as older works, and the emanations of his own pen.

The history of the publishing business, from the invention of the "divine art" to the close of the seventeenth century, is graced with a luminous train of illustrious names, as author-booksellers, whose literary attainments and critical acumen shed lustre alike on both the pursuits of author and publisher.

From the days of Caxton to the accession of James I., the press appears to have been to no inconsiderable extent devoted to the printing of classical works; this preference for the literary stores of antiquity, however, was not restricted to the English press, it prevailed to a still greater degree among the printers of Germany, Italy, and France. The labors of the Alduses, the Stephenses, and the Plantins were thus consecrated, till at the dawn, and during the era of the Reformation, the printing of the Sacred Scriptures, in a great measure, divided the attention of the printers. The celebrated names of Wynkin de Worde, Pynson, Weir, Day, Dunton, Lintot, Tonson, and Ballard, with others, form a luminous train of illustrious bibliopoles, whose literary enterprises occupy a conspicuous feature in early literary history, for some of them contributed in no small degree to enrich numerically the estate of English literature. Wynkin de Worde, the able associate and successor of Caxton, having printed four hundred and eight distinct works, while Pynson, Day, and others, issued more than half that number each. Between the years 1474 and 1600, it has been estimated about 350 printers flourished in England and Scotland, and that the products of their several presses amounted in the aggregate to 10,000 distinct productions. At the great fire of London, in 1666, the booksellers of Paternoster Row sustained a serious loss—as heavy a calamity to them as the destruction of the Alexandrian Library was to the ancients. Dwelling in such close proximity to St. Paul's, they were accustomed to deposit large quantities of books, for their supposed greater safety, in the vaults of the Old Cathedral; these, at the time of the fire, were valued by Evelyn at £200,000.

The number of new publications issued from 1800 to 1827, exclusive of pamphlets, according to the London Catalogue, was 19,860, or an average of 600 new works per annum: in the eleven previous years 4096; and for the intervening period—1789 to 1666—it has been supposed the annual issues of new books averaged 100. This estimate is exclusive of the legion of pamphlets, which are too numerous to compute, as may safely be inferred from the fact of the 2000 volumes—consisting of 30,000 tracts issued between 1640 and 1660, which were presented to the British Museum by George the Third.

The most potent auxiliary in the multiplication of books, since the discovery of "the divine art," has undoubtedly been the invention of the steam-press. By its economic process, the affluent resources of genius and the literary wealth of the world have been rendered universally accessible. To compute the benefits it has conferred upon the present, as well as the immunities it will convey to all subsequent times, transcends all human calculations. The Press is like the caloric of nature—it overspreads and circulates throughout the whole social system. With this numerical increase of books has been a corresponding increase of authors and readers; it has been also characterized by a prolific growth of pseudo-authorship.

True books—books that are books—are comparatively few; they are the pure gold of our literary currency, which is represented by a prodigal distribution of paper counterfeits. In 1827, a new system of cheap publications commenced,—"Constable's Miscellany," and the issues of the "Society for the Diffusion of Useful Knowledge," taking the lead, which were followed in 1832 by the "Penny Magazine," "Chamber's Journal," "The Family Library," "Penny Cyclopædia," &c., which last work cost something like £200,000 in its production. It has been supposed that the annual periodical issues of the British press at that time exceeded the amount of printed sheets published throughout Europe, from the period of Guttemberg's discovery to the year 1500. The weekly circulation of "Punch" alone is said to have been about 300,000; and the gross amount of magazines and other periodicals sold on "Magazine-day," in Paternoster Row, monthly, has been esti-

mated at 500,000 copies. The annual returns of periodical works alone are estimated at £300,000.

The "Pictorial History of England," which cost its publishers, Charles Knight & Co., £50,500, was one of the liberal enterprises of the age, although inferior to many other literary speculations; like the Penny Cyclopædia, it was a great gift to the masses, who were excluded from the benefits of more expensive works. Publishers even in the days of Pope were the medium of liberal payments to authors, as Lintot's munificent payment of £5,000 for the translation of Homer attests. Rees's great Cyclopædia was also produced at the cost of £300,000. Scott received for his romances something like £100,000, and Byron nearly £25,000 for his various copyrights. Henry G. Bohn's great catalogue of 300,000 volumes, comprising the most superb and extensive literary stock in existence, also exhibited the fruits of enterprise by publishers to an immense extent.

Among the more prominent publishers of costly embellished works, the names of John Boydell and John Nichols take foremost rank;—these worthies are said to have expended jointly the princely sum of £350,000 in the promotion of art. Boydell's Shakspeare, and Dugdale's *Monasticon Anglicanum,* were among their magnificent speculations,—the former, unfortunately, subjecting its publisher to a loss of £100,000. We might also refer to the superb work of Pistolesi on the Vatican, and the numerous works of art that have been produced during the century, as evidences of the importance of the bibliographic craft. Bohn and Tegg have each made large fortunes by buying up "remainders" of editions of works, the sales of which had begun to subside: so enormous are their respective collections that their wealth in books surpasses, it is believed, even that of Longmans.

Longman & Co. are the largest publishers in the world, taking into the account the enormous amount of capital they have constantly embarked in copyrights. Moore received from this establishment £3,000 for his *Lalla Rookh,* and for several years £300 per annum, on account of his *Irish Melodies.* They also pay £600 a year for ten years for Mr. Macaulay's History of England, volumes 1 and 2.

But it is needless to specify instances of this kind. They have in their employ about two hundred persons in their establishment; and some idea may be formed of the prodigious extent of their business, from the fact that a messenger is kept constantly occupied in conveying their letters to and from the Post-office, at frequent intervals. Murray, Bentley, and Colburn, are styled the aristocratic publishers; they do not, as Longmans, sell other books as well as their own publications,—these are, however, so numerous and important, that they may be said to rank next to Longmans as to the magnitude of their pecuniary operations.

The Messrs. Chambers, of Edinburgh, are considered unrivalled for the extent and completeness of their establishment,—some five hundred persons being employed in its several departments, of type-setting, stereotyping, printing, and binding. It is impossible to ascertain the gross pecuniary amount of their operations per annum. Some idea of their prodigious extent may be inferred from the fact that for one item—the paper used for their series of cheap tracts, they paid £25,766—more than $125,000. They also paid the enormous sum of £40,000 merely for advertising their Cyclopædia of Literature,—proof sufficient of the prodigal liberality of their business policy. Their establishment is eleven stories high; their presses throw off 150,000 whole sheets a day. It was Robert Chambers, we believe, who recently paid out from the business, £20,000 for a country seat, without sensibly affecting its funds. This reminds us of the fact that both Longmans, Murray, Tegg, and others, have not only amassed large fortunes, they also possess splendid town and country residences, and live in a style of great affluence. It is the boast of the Chambers that they pay liberally for literary service, nor have they ever been known to print a pirated edition of any work. These enterprising brothers have done more, perhaps, than any other two individuals of the age for the promotion of sound and useful knowledge, and the cultivation of an improved standard of popular taste for reading, by their Edinburgh Journal and other publications; and they have accomplished all without patronage, having on their first arrival in Edinburgh some twenty years ago, been obliged to vend small pamphlets about the streets for their support.

The literary enterprises of the Continental publishers have received such interruption by the political excitements which have prevailed the past two years that we have not made any special inquiry as to their present condition. Even Dumas, like his no less fecund contemporary, James, has well nigh ceased to write or indite; and Thiers seems to prefer politics to his pen, although his History of the Consulate of Napoleon produced him 500,000 francs, from his publisher, Gosselin. Eugene Sue, Souliè, Lamartine, Scribe, and others, have derived princely sums from their works. Scribe for example received, it is said, in all, 2,400,000 francs for his numerous dramatic productions, and Chateaubriand 500,000 francs for his Memoirs, while Lamartine made his pen no less prolific of pecuniary results, although his improvidence seems to have exhausted them all. Didot, who is very rich, Galignani, and Gosselin, are among the most prominent of the publishers of Paris. There are others, however,—Baudry, the republisher of the classics bearing his name,—Masson, who issues mostly medical books,—Ballière, who has a house also in London, the publisher of medical works; also Roret, Matthias, and Bachelier, who issue chiefly works of a scientific character. Didot estimated that during the first eight months of the year 1840 the issues of the French press were 87,000 new works, 3,700 reprints, and about 4,000 translations.

Brockhaus's establishment of Leipzic is, with the exception of Chambers's, the most important and complete of its kind in Europe. Its several departments are devoted to the paper-making, type-making, stereotyping, printing, and binding; it has also apartments for the accommodation of a corps of editors—all included within the walls of the huge building. They have over 100 agents and correspondents in the various German States; Longmans, we believe, have, however, nearly double that number.

About 325 clerks and artisans are regularly engaged in this establishment; and the utmost regularity and system prevail throughout its multiform operations. Eight steam power and 42 iron presses are there used, which print off 110,000 sheets of 24 pages per day; in addition to which, there are usually engaged about 36 artists and engravers on steel and wood, who likewise occupy rooms in the establishment. Brockhaus, like the Harpers, sell only their own publications. They also issue a daily paper—Deutsch Allgem. Zeitung. Cotta is the publisher of the works of Schiller, Goethe, and other classics; Goethe received 30,000 crowns for his copyright; and of Schiller's works, over 80,000 copies had been sold some time since.

Among the publishers of the United States Messrs. Harper & Brothers of course take the precedence; they may be indeed regarded as the most important as to the numerical extent of their operations, of any in the world. Compared with Longmans, however, their pecuniary disbursements for copyrights are doubtless far inferior,—most of the works they republish being available to their purpose gratuitously. This being the case, the numerical extent of their issues cannot be judged by those of Longmans, who embark an immense amount of capital in authorship. Another item of expense, advertising, bears a small proportion in their case to the great London firm—the charges for advertising being at least four times as much in England as they are in the United States. The Harpers pay about $4,000 a year for their advertising. The duty on paper forms also a no inconsiderable item in the estimates of the English publisher. As an instance of the relative copyright payments, we might refer to that of Mr. Macaulay's History of England,—Longmans pay the author $6,000-$30,000 for the first ten years' lease of his two volumes,—the Harpers £200-$1,000. Still the Harpers pay by far the largest premiums for the priority of English works, and to some of their popular American authors they have been enabled to give munificent sums. Mr. Prescott has received in the neighborhood of $30,000; Mr. Stephens about the same; Rev. Mr. Barnes nearly as much, and Prof. Anthon more; while of Morse's Geography, over half a million copies have been printed. They also pay $6,000 for the literary labor of Prof. Andrews's forthcoming Latin Lexicon. The Harpers are possessed of unrivalled resources and facilities. Within their own establishment, all the details and machinery of publishing are carried on, with the exception of paper making and type founding. Their extensive range of buildings, equal to six or seven five story houses, they divide into the several departments of composing rooms, stereotype foundry, press rooms, warehouses, bindery, &c. Nineteen double medium power presses, besides Napier presses, are constantly throwing off printed sheets, to the extent of some 70 reams per diem, while in the bindery 50 barrel of flour are required for making paste every year, as well as 1,200 dozen sheepskins, 750 pieces of muslin of 40 square yards each, and sixty tons of pasteboard. Over 40,000 lbs. of metal are used per annum for casting stereotype plates, of which their vaults contain about $300,000 worth; they also have about 70,000 lbs. of various founts of type in their composing rooms. Even the cuttings from the edges of the books, in the process of binding, amount to 18 tons of shavings per annum, which are sold to the paper-makers. Their annual sales have been estimated in round numbers at 2,000,000 volumes, including pamphlets. There are attached to this establishment usually from 300 to 350 employees, in the various departments of the business, among that number about 100 being females, who fold and sew the sheets of books.

Mr. Putnam, of Broadway, bids fair to elevate the standard of bibliographic taste among us by his numerous and splendid issues; and Messrs. Appleton deserve also the thanks of all lovers of elegant books for the beautiful style in which most of their publications are produced. Carey & Hart, of Philadelphia, as well as Lea & Blanchard, are also well known as extensive publishers; and the worthy bibliopoles of our "Modern Athens" are not likely to be forgotten in a survey of the doings of the craft; but our subject seems to expand rather than diminish, as we progress with it, and we must therefore refrain from further specifications.

Before closing our sketch, we must, however, refer to the fact of a new book market which seems to have sprung up almost spontaneously into existence,–that of Cincinnati. Four or five large bookselling and publishing firms are there in full operation, for the supply of the great West. The pecuniary operations of two or three of these amount already to something like $175,000 per annum; the names of Messrs. Derby & Co., James & Co.,

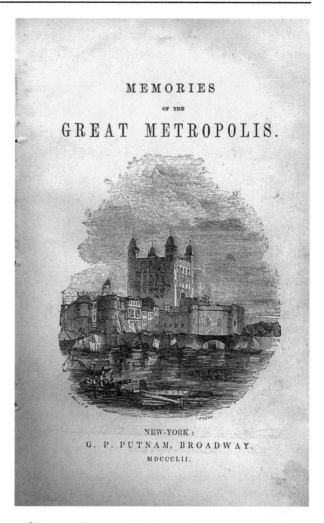

Title page for Frederick Saunders's London guidebook, whose covers were embossed with gold-engraved sketches of London buildings. Putnam was known throughout the trade for the quality of his bookmaking, and he took particular care with Saunders's work.

W. B. Smith & Co., will at once recur to the reader. Over one million per annum is said to be already devoted to this branch of western enterprise; and the amount must necessarily every year be increased.

There is one consideration that naturally recurs to the mind in reviewing the progressive advancement of literary enterprise,–it is the desirableness of an international copyright on the products of mind; let this be effected, and the rights of the author be respected, and his labor paid for wherever it is appreciated, and equity and law will in this respect at least have become equivalent terms.

–*The Literary World,* 6 (5 January 1850): 11–13

Charles Frederick Briggs, an experienced literary journalist who edited both Putnam's Monthly *in the 1850s and* Putnam's Magazine *in the 1860s*

Charles Frederick Briggs

One of the premier journalists in antebellum New York City, Charles Frederick Briggs (1804–1877) worked in senior positions on many magazines, including the New-York Mirror, Broadway Journal, *and* Holden's Dollar Magazine, *and wrote for* The New York Times *and other dailies before forming an alliance with Putnam in 1852. The summer of that year he helped oversee production of* Homes of American Authors, *as he had earlier helped Putnam with the publication of his good friend James Russell Lowell's* A Fable for Critics *(1848). His main collaboration with Putnam began in fall 1852 when he initiated the idea of* Putnam's Monthly *and then played a leading role in its planning. He served as its senior editor for its first year and a half, writing a considerable portion of its fiction, essays, and reviews, set its high-minded, liberal editorial line, and solicited invitations from leading writers around the country. Briggs's editorship ended in summer or autumn 1854 when Putnam grew dissatisfied with his failure to meet responsibilities in a timely manner. Relations between the two men must have remained respectful, however, because Putnam immediately hired Briggs as editor in 1867 when he resuscitated the periodical as* Putnam's Magazine. *The reprise venture, though, proved unprofitable from the first, and Briggs was let go (or resigned) long before the magazine was sold to Charles Scribner in 1870.*

* * *

This sketch of Briggs, which appeared in the longer essay "The Literati of New York City–No. 1," was written by Poe, who worked with Briggs at the Broadway Journal *in 1845. Relations between the men–different in background, temperament, and politics–soured over the course of their collaboration, leaving little goodwill by the time that Briggs abandoned the paper to Poe. Some residue of that animosity may well color this grudging portrait.*

Mr. Briggs is better known as Harry Franco, a *nom de plume* assumed since the publication, in the "Knickerbocker Magazine," of his series of papers called "Adventures of Harry Franco." He also wrote for "The Knickerbocker" some articles entitled "The Haunted Merchant," and from time to time subsequently has been a contributor to that journal. The two productions just mentioned have some merit. They depend for their effect upon the relation in a straightforward manner, just as one would talk, of the most commonplace events–a kind of writing which, to ordinary and especially to indolent intellects, has a very observable charm. To cultivated or to active minds it is in an equal degree distasteful, even when claiming the merit of originality. Mr. Briggs's manner, however, is an obvious imitation of Smollett, and, as usual with all imitation, produces an unfavourable impression upon those conversant with the original. It is a common failing, also, with imitators, to out-Herod Herod in aping the peculiarities of the model, and too frequently the faults are more pertinaciously exaggerated than the merits. Thus, the author of "Harry Franco" carries the simplicity of Smollett to insipidity, and his picturesque low-life is made to degenerate into sheer vulgarity. A fair idea of the general tone of the work may be gathered from the following passage:–

. . . .

If Mr. Briggs has a *forte,* it a Flemish fidelity that omits nothing, whether agreeable or disagreeable; but I cannot call this *forte* a virtue. He has also some humour, but nothing of an original character. Occasionally he has written good things. A magazine article called "Dobbs and his Cantelope" was quite easy and clever in its way; but the way is necessarily a small one. Now and then he has attempted criticism, of which, as might be expected, he made a farce. The silliest thing of this kind ever penned, perhaps, was an elaborate attack of his on Thomas Babington Macaulay, published in "The Democratic Review;"–the force of folly could no farther go. Mr. Briggs has never composed in his life three consecutive sentences of grammatical English. He is grossly uneducated.

In connection with Mr. John Bisco he was the originator of the late "Broadway Journal"–my editorial association with that work not having commenced until the sixth or seventh number, although I wrote for it occasionally from the first. Among the principal papers contributed by Mr. B. were those discussing the paintings at the last exhibition of the Academy of Fine Arts in New York. I may be permitted to say that there was scarcely a point in his whole series of criticisms on this subject at which I did not radically disagree with him. Whatever taste he has in art is, like his taste in letters, Flemish.

Mr. Briggs's personal appearance is not prepossessing. He is about five feet six inches in height, somewhat slightly framed, with a sharp, thin face, narrow and low forehead, pert-looking nose, mouth rather pleasant in expression, eyes not so good, gray and small, although occasionally brilliant. In dress he is apt to affect the artist, priding himself especially upon his personal acquaintance with artists and his general connoisseurship. He is a member of the Art Union. He walks with a quick, nervous step. His address is quite good, frank and insinuating. His conversation has now and then the merit of humour, but he has a perfect mania for contradiction, and it is impossible to utter an uninterrupted sentence in his hearing. He has much warmth of feeling, and is not a person to be disliked, although very apt to irritate and annoy. Two of his most marked characteristics are vacillation of purpose and a passion for being mysterious. His most intimate friends seem to know nothing of his movements, and it is folly to expect from him a direct answer about anything. He has, apparently, traveled; pretends to a knowledge of French (of which he is profoundly ignorant); has been engaged in an infinite variety of employments, and now, I believe, occupies a lawyer's office in Nassau street. He is married, goes little into society, and seems about forty years of age.

    – *Godey's Lady's Book,* 32 (June 1846): 294–295

Parke Godwin

A leading journalist and editor at the New York Evening Post, *Parke Godwin (1816–1904) became involved in autumn 1852 in the planning of* Putnam's Monthly. *He then joined Briggs and George William Curtis as the editorial triumvirate of the magazine, with Goodwin taking special responsibility for political affairs. A man of strong views–his antislavery convictions and contempt for current presidential and congressional incompetence matched those of Putnam and the other editors–Goodwin set the political tone of the journal with his sharp pen. His outspoken essays gradually attracted widespread attention in the press and among readers, making for the magazine friends among progressives and enemies among conservatives, particularly in the South, where* Putnam's Monthly, *despite calling itself a "national" magazine, became increasingly unpopular and associated with "black republicanism." Godwin remained with the magazine even after Put-*

nam sold it to Dix and Edwards in winter 1855 and continued to pound away at the injustices and corruptions he saw in American political life.

At Putnam's request, Godwin returned for a stint as managing editor of Putnam's Magazine *early in 1870, at a time when the magazine was suffering from both poor circulation and inferior general quality. But Godwin, with his elitist tastes and deep convictions about America's "political degeneracy," was hardly the man to steer a magazine to popularity, and if anything* Putnam's Magazine *declined even more steeply during the period of his control. In summer 1870 Putnam had no choice but to sell the magazine to Charles Scribner, reluctantly explaining to Godwin that their high-brow formula of "sober literature alone" without pictures and other light touches had failed to attract the postbellum reading public.*

In addition to his work as an editor, Godwin was an important contributor of books to the G. P. Putnam list. With Charles A. Dana, he translated and edited Tales from the German of Heinrich Zschokke *(1845) for the Wiley and Putnam Library of Choice Reading; he also edited the first American edition of* The Auto-Biography of Goethe *(1846–1847), which was included in the Wiley and Putnam Foreign Library. He was the author of books such as* Hand-Book of Universal Biography *(1852), which was later republished with a supplement as* The Cyclopaedia of Biography *(1878), and* Out of the Past: Critical and Literary Papers *(1870).*

* * *

Parke Godwin, an associate editor of Putnam's Monthly, *as he was rendered by Elias Hicks in the October 1854 issue. Godwin later served as the last editor of* Putnam's Magazine.

The following three letters from Godwin to Putnam, though undated by month and year, can be judged by context to have been written in late June–early July 1854. All three letters concern Goodwin's antislavery provocative essay "Our Parties and Politics," which was published in the September issue of Putnam's Monthly, *and a portrait of Godwin by Elias Hicks that also appeared in the magazine. "Mr. Bryant" refers to William Cullen Bryant, Godwin's father-in-law and Putnam's longtime friend and occasional client.*

Roslyn   Friday morning

My dear Mr. Putnam,

I have finished the article on Politics, but on reading it over am determined not to send it in. These delicate subjects ought not to be touched, unless it is done with <u>caution</u>, and at the same time <u>strength</u>, but I have hardly succeeded in either, or rather there is much to say, which I have not said to my satisfaction, and which it would take a few days more reflection to get into shape. It seems to me therefore better to postpone the matter to the September number. Briggs has material enough for August without it, while September would be a better month for it to produce an effect. If, however, it must be had sooner, let me know by return mail, i.e. by Mr. Bryant who comes here this evening 3 1/2 o'clock. The Editorial Notes shall all be sent or brought on Monday. In case the "Politics" is not to appear till Sept. how would it do to say in Ed. Notes of August some thing to the effect that "our political readers may expect next month an article on 'Our Parties and Politics' by the author of 'Our New President,' which we think will create scarcely "less sensation than that essay."

I have no time to come to town this week. It costs a <u>day</u> which I can employ more profitably. Next week I shall be in to see you. If Maga for July is out, will you send me a copy by Mr. Bryant, or else by mail. Tell Briggs that he and his daughter couldn't do better for the 4th holidays than to come out & see us. We can give him [?] feed, if nothing else.

Yours truly,

Parke Godwin

—Manuscripts Division, Department of Rare Books and Special Collections, Princeton University Library. Published with permission of the Princeton University Library.

* * *

Putnam complied with Godwin's request that his article appear toward the "head" of the magazine in order to attract lyceum organizers.

Roslyn   Monday

My dear Mr. Putnam,

I send you the article, not being able to bring it,–as indeed I don't know when I shall get to town, as I expect Hicks here to take my phiz. Will you be kind enough to read the proof of editorial notes? The proof of the article I must see myself; if sent by mail any day before 9 o'clock it will reach me in a couple of hours & may be returned early next day. Or if sent by steamer George Law, (foot of Fulton Street, E. R. sailing at 4 1/2 PM) it will reach me at night in time to be returned by 9 o'clock next day. If you conclude to print, which I am now free to hope that you will, please don't cut out or amend until after I shall have seen the proof, as there may be words here and there to correct which may modify your judgments.

It would be a most essential service to me <u>pecuniarily</u> to get the Head in the Sept. Number or to get it announced for the October, as it will doubtless attract the attention of the Lyceum & Associations to me as a lecturer next winter. Considering the <u>amount</u> that I have written for Maga, (if not the quality) I ought to come among the earliest contributors. Hicks will have his sketch ready at the end of the week & it can be done in three weeks by the engraver.

My wife wants to know how Mrs. Putnam is, and desires also to be remembered to her & to yourself. She is better pleased with my ("Politics etc") than I am myself, though I am not dissatisfied with it in its present shape.

Yours truly,

Parke Godwin

—Manuscripts Division, Department of Rare Books and Special Collections, Princeton University Library. Published with permission of the Princeton University Library.

* * *

After receiving Putnam's favorable judgment of the article, Godwin worries about his portrait—which was done in time and printed on the verso of the first page of the article.

Roslyn Saturday

My dear Mr. Putnam,

I am glad you like the article, the more so, as I am not myself entirely satisfied. Much remains "unsaid" in the remarks, but I had no idea in writing it, that we could get out of the controversy with this single shot. We shall be compelled, now that we have broken the ice, to follow it up, with another shot. –how soon depends on circumstances.

–I have been disappointed in not seeing Hicks this week. He could not come down, but is to be here on Monday. The portrait I am anxious about, as so much of my <u>living</u>, i.e. lecturing may depend upon its coming out in time. –I hope to be in town Monday tho I can't promise, as it costs me somewhat to get in and out, and the Peruvian is not abundant in these diggings.

Mrs. Godwin desires to be remembered at home. –I want to make a short Review of Horace Mann's Inaugural Address at Antioch, but can't do it till next week; will that be in time for Sept. –say for a five pager? I shall <u>criticise</u> it.

Yours truly

Godwin

–Manuscripts Division, Department of Rare Books and Special Collections, Princeton University Library. Published with permission of the Princeton University Library.

* * *

Putnam took a different tack with each of his editors. With the anxious Godwin, he was typically reassuring, as in this 26 June 1854 letter in which he anticipates receiving "Our Parties and Politics."

My dear Godwin,

I am sorry to find that you have misapprehended so much of my hasty note. Its chief object was to <u>suggest</u> to you whether you would not <u>prefer</u> to give to some other part of the Magazine the same time you had given to the <u>Notes</u>–but I certainly had no intention to initiate any "Turkish" proceedings or any other that you would deem improper. I value your co-operation & your writings too much to urge, even if justice & courtesy did not forbid, any changes in existing arrangements between us that were not satisfactory & pleasant on both sides. However I will not discuss these points in a letter but leave them till you come to town–merely remarking, by the way, that we <u>need all</u> the co-operation and force you can give us, so as to make our <u>Maga. A.1</u> in <u>all</u> respects & have it out much <u>earlier</u> than heretofore.

I will send the books per railway today as you request & hope to get your article tomorrow–& the Notes by Saturday. When shall you come to town?

Truly yours   <u>G. P. Putnam</u>

–Manuscripts Division, Department of Rare Books and Special Collections, Princeton University Library. Published with permission of the Princeton University Library.

George William Curtis

One of the most talented and popular literary essayists and journalists of his time, George William Curtis (1824–1892) was a close friend of Putnam and an invaluable professional ally. Putnam appealed to him in 1852 to edit Homes of American Authors *but had to settle for his authorship of several of the essays in the volume. Curtis was a founding editor of* Putnam's Monthly *and not only played a major role in its general editing but also contributed some of its most charming writing, including his serialized novels* The Potiphar Papers *and* Prue and I. *When looking to replace Briggs in 1854 as managing editor, Putnam naturally offered the position to Curtis but was refused. Curtis did stay on for the remainder of Putnam's tenure as publisher and even beyond; he was the only person involved with the magazine from its founding until its demise in 1857.*

Curtis published The Potiphar Papers *(1853) in book form and several other works with G. P. Putnam, but his primary publisher and employer during his long career was Harper and Broth-*

George William Curtis, an associate editor of Putnam's Monthly, *as he was rendered by H. B. Hall in the July 1854 issue*

ers. This fact must have saddened Putnam, who found Curtis (along with Bayard Taylor) the most congenial literary man in the country and a multitalented writer-editor whom he attempted many times to attract to senior positions in G. P. Putnam. Although Curtis invariably declined such positions, he remained Putnam's friend and was especially close to the two oldest children, George Haven Putnam and Mary Putnam Jacobi.

* * *

The fluidity for which Curtis's magazine pieces were famous also characterized his letters. Replying to Putnam's attempt to draw him into closer connection with G. P. Putnam and Company and its magazine, Curtis, who was also working editorially at the time for Harper and Brothers, courteously maintained his distance.

He also maintained his distance geographically. He conducted much of his editorial and authorial work—and received payment for them—through the mails. A favorite summering spot of his was Newport, though the specific incident he is referring to is obscure.

Newport July 12, '54

My dear Sir,

I thank you for your prompt reply. Your letter and the a/c reached me safely this morning.

"Think not of any severance of our lives." The best that I do, I give to you, because I feel that, in a way, it does me no great good as an author to work elsewhere. But I cannot forget that my interest (every author's interest to stand well with his Publishers) and the perfectly fair treatment I have always received from them, binds me in a certain degree.

The circumstances of the "Newport" were personal and peculiar.

You must not suppose that I am in any degree weaned from you & yours, although I have less direct supervision of the Magazine. I am an outpost, now, a sentry upon the lines challenging all who do not acknowledge the flag. But I am, to say truth, rather a lazy outpost, and don't send in as many prisoners, nor as much aid & comfort, as a braver warrior would.

How goes the new arrangement?

Your always truly
George Wm. Curtis

Will you send me, at convenience, the Potiphar a/c to the first July?

—Manuscripts Division, Department of Rare Books and Special Collections, Princeton University Library. Published with permission of the Princeton University Library.

* * *

Putnam followed the serialization of Curtis's popular Potiphar Papers *in* Putnam's Monthly *with its book publication. He doubtless wanted to do the same following the serialization of* Prue and I, *but this letter from Curtis indicates that the author was already then entertaining a proposition. It presumably came from the Harpers, who published* Prue and I *in 1856.*

Providence
July 3, 1855

My dear Sir,

I have received a proposition to publish the papers I have written in "Putnam"—the "Prue" articles. I replied that I could make no final arrangement until I had communicated with you, because although there was no agreement between us, I did not wish, under the circumstances, to do anything in the matter without hearing from you.

I wish you would drop me a line at your earliest convenience.

The tropics be upon us. But I suppose upon the river the Dog Star also rages. I beg to be most kindly remembered to Mrs. Putnam, & am always

Most truly Yours
George Wm. Curtis

—Manuscripts Division, Department of Rare Books and Special Collections, Princeton University Library. Published with permission of the Princeton University Library.

* * *

Putnam's friend Frederick S. Cozzens, author of The Sparrowgrass Papers serial in Putnam's Monthly, *writes of his willingness to host Curtis, familiarly known as "the Howadji," for his popular travel books to the Middle East, and William Cullen Bryant, two ardent Republicans set to speak on behalf of presidential candidate John C. Frémont at a rally to be held near the Yonkers, New York, homes of Putnam and Cozzens. "Old Buck" was the nickname of Democratic candidate James Buchanan, who defeated Frémont and became the last president of the antebellum U.S.*

July 8/56

My dear Putnam,

I should be delighted to take care of Curtis and Bryant both if you will allow me so to do, or if not, Curtis. I should see the Howadji this evening and will entertain him but not his principles. Fremont's case must be rather weak I should think to require <u>two</u> such speakers to urge his claims. Old Buck will go in without talking.

Yours
Fred. S. Cozzens

—Manuscripts Division, Department of Rare Books and Special Collections, Princeton University Library. Published with permission of the Princeton University Library.

* * *

Frederic Beecher Perkins

The connections of Frederic Beecher Perkins (1828–1899) to the world of letters were multiple, both through blood (Harriet Beecher Stowe was his cousin; Edward Everett Hale, his brother-in-law; and Charlotte Perkins Gilman, his daughter) and through personal accomplishment. He was involved with many periodicals and libraries, often in senior roles. Putnam invited him to edit Putnam's Monthly *in 1854 after firing Charles Briggs, and Perkins remained with the magazine until Putnam sold it in early 1855. He returned to the reconstituted firm of G. P. Putnam and Son in 1867 as a general adviser and also played a role as assistant editor of* Putnam's Magazine *during its short life. In addition, he published a biography of Charles Dickens with the firm in 1870 and oversaw its successful bibliography,* The Best Reading *(1872), which became a standard reference for self-education for the remainder of the century.*

* * *

In this excerpt from his long essay "Reading and Courses of Reading," Perkins offers middle-class American readers suggestions to improve their knowledge of their country's history and culture. The essay was printed as an appendix to The Best Reading.

Now prepare for the splitting off of the American Colonies into an independent historical career. Read the Federalist, to show what the men meant who founded our polity, and De Tocqueville's Democracy in America, for a marvellous and only not prophetic exposition of what their purpose turned out to be. (While you are about it, shape our own history at once by reading Bancroft's mammoth preparation to begin our history, and Hildreth's dense and full annals.)

Make a backward step for France. Read De Tocqueville's Ancient Régime, to show you why the French Revolution broke out; and then Thiers and Carlyle, to show what it did. Follow with Thiers' Consulate and Empire; read Napier's Peninsular War, a wonderfully clear and vigorous narrative of the military achievements which were the real entering wedge toward Napoleon's downfall; and avoid Scott's Life and Abbot's Life of Napoleon. For German literature in these days, read Goethe (Taylor's Faust, the rest of his works as you can get them); Schiller–I mean both the Works and the Life of both.

Then take up the literary harvest of England in the first part of this century. Read Scott's Works, and Lockhart's Scott; Byron, Wordsworth, Coleridge, Keats, and Shelley; and read after the writings of each a biography of each. Read also Lamb's Writings, and those of Thomas de Quincey.

Then open out the vast arena of the present epoch, with its innumerable writers and its numerous entirely new departments of investigation. There is a sufficient conventional excuse for not venturing to even attempt to blaze out

Frederic Beecher Perkins, who, at different times in the 1850s and 1860s, edited G. P. Putnam magazines, as well as various books and series for the firm

a path through such a crowded and luxuriant forest. Yet, let the notice be ventured that the present age is notable most of all for advances in science, and what is closely related thereto: and in belles-lettres, for prose fiction. I barely name Humboldt's Cosmos, Darwin's Origin of Species and Descent of Man, Sir William Hamilton's Metaphysics and Logic, the writings of Herbert Spencer, Charles Dickens, W. M. Thackeray, and Nathaniel Hawthorne. As for all the rest, any one who has read according to this series down to this point, or half-way down to it, with fair abilities and steady, careful attention, is by that time better able to choose both departments and authors for himself than I or any other guide.

Then please to consider what a store of deep and broad and noble and beautiful thoughts, what a wide range of classes of literature, what a vast mass of facts, the knowledge of that series of books implies; and yet it is a pretty short "Course of Reading," as courses of reading go.

But I will not say I recommend it. I will say that I would dearly love to begin at the beginning of it this very day, and go straight through to the end.

George Haven Putnam, who was his father's right-hand man following the post–Civil War reorganization of the company.
He became the central figure in G. P. Putnam's Sons after his father's death and a leader of the
publishing industry for more than half a century.

George Haven Putnam

George Haven Putnam (1844–1930) was not only his father's namesake but also his finest legacy to the profession. Singled out by Putnam for employment in his firm during the early years of the Civil War, George Haven secured permission instead to volunteer for the army. Following completion of military service in 1865, George Haven joined his father as deputy revenue collector and continued in that role until Putnam was fired in late 1866. He then became a junior partner in G. P. Putnam and Son and made himself invaluable in running the business. At first George Haven's chief responsibility was for the accounts of the firm, but he gradually took a broadened role, representing the firm overseas and dealing with authors, manufacturers, and creditors.

Following his father's death, George Haven Putnam became president of the reconstituted firm G. P. Putnam's Sons, with his brother John Bishop directing manufacturing and his brother Irving overseeing the retail end of the business. In the nearly fifty years of his leadership, George Haven led the firm to renewed prosperity and vastly expanded its national and international operations, making G. P. Putnam's Sons one of the leading publishers in the industry. Like his father, he became a central figure in the profession as a publishing historian and champion for international copyright.

* * *

George Haven Putnam's report to family friend and longtime client Bayard Taylor of details of Putnam's death and the status of the family business might also be read as implicitly requesting Taylor's continued loyalty to the firm. Taylor had worked intermittently as editor or foreign correspondent over many years for the New York Tribune.

New York, Dec. 31 1872

Bayard Taylor Esq.

Gotha, Germany

My dear Mr Taylor,

The papers will have given you, before you receive this letter, the news of the terrible loss we have sustained; a loss in which I know we are assured of your heartfelt sympathy.

It is now ten days since my father's death, but so great has been the pressure of care and work brought suddenly upon me that I have hardly had a moment for thought or for grief.–Bishop's heart has been much shaken by the death of his wife and child, whom we buried hardly a fortnight ago, and it may be some little time before he is strong enough to give me efficient help, so that for the time I am alone in the office, and feel <u>very much alone</u>.–Father had been much saddened by the death of Hattie, (Bishop's wife) of whom we were all very fond, and was anxious about Bishop–The day before his death he had attended the funeral of his old friend Kensett, from which he returned quite tired and with a slight attack of bronchitis.–But he was as busy and active as usual, and we saw [paper torn] to be anxious for him. He was taken with hardly a moment's warning, dying in his office in my arms, and his death was apparently as painless as it was peaceful.–We are told it was caused by some form of heart disease. Great as is the shock to us of so sudden a loss, we are glad he was spared the burden of a lingering illness, and there was perhaps a certain fitness [in] his passing away from us while in the midst of the business to which his life had been devoted, and among the books he loved so well.–My mother has so far stood the shock bravely.– She has all her children with her, with whom it is hard to feel lonely, and there is to her a consolation also in feeling how fully the <u>community</u> sympathizes with our loss, in coming to know more fully how wide was the circle in which my father was held in respect, friendship and affection. The kind and appreciative words that have come to us during the past week, are a pleasant remembrance to associate with our sorrows.

My father left little property besides a small life insurance and his interest in the business, which goes to mother, and the legacy of his <u>good name</u>, which his sons will endeavor to make good use of.–Much as we shall miss in the business the benefit of his experience, counsel and supervision, and the weight of his personal influence with his wide circle of business and literary friends and acquaintants, we do <u>not</u> feel utterly at a loss about the conduct of affairs.–

I have had for some years the active management of a large part of the business, and Bishop has had charge of the <u>manufacturing</u> department, and we are fully acquainted with all the details of the work before us.–I am thankful that father was spared until we boys had acquired some business knowledge and experience. Without wishing to appear over-confident, I <u>do</u> feel myself to be competent to manage to good advantage the interests now in my hands, and I hope to be able to retain all my father's old associations and connections, especially those in which he had taken a special pride, and a personal interest.–I am arranging for the use of some little additional capital, and I hope to commence the year freed from some of the financial anxieties that had too often worn upon my dear father.

I enclose the notice of the change of firm. I have altered the old name as little as possible, and I would have retained it just as it was if the law had permitted.

While I am not desirous, for some little time at least, of entering upon many new enterprizes, I shall be very much indebted to any of our literary friends who will take an interest in making suggestions, or who will give me an opportunity to take hold of desirable undertakings.–

I have been wishing for some days to write to you, but the pressure of daily work has been so great that my correspondence has been much delayed.

I have heard that you were coming home to take some active part in the management of the "Tribune," and hope much the rumor may be true.–

With my best regards to Mrs Taylor, and Miss Lilian, and to such of your father-in-law's family as may remember me

The closing and a postscript ran up the left margin.

I am Yours faithfully

Geo. Haven Putnam

I enclose an article from "The Mail" that may interest you

–Division of Rare Books and Manuscript Collections,
Cornell University Library

* * *

In response to a letter from Taylor, George Haven sent a follow-up expression of regard and professional reassurance.

New York, Feby. 4 1873

My dear Mr Taylor,

I have just received your very kind letter of Jany. 17th.

Fearing that you may not have received mine of Dec. 31st., and wishing to show you that you were among the first to whom I had wished to write, I enclose a copy of this. Your letter to mother I forward to her in Florida, whither she has gone in care of Bishop, whose heart continues in a very unsatisfactory condition.

I send in another cover the notice of the change of our firm, and the list of spring publications, which last will show you that although I am for the time left alone, I do not intend to let the business come to a stand-still.–

I am much touched by your kind suggestion in regard to delaying the payment of copyright, in case my finances are straightened.–Fortunately although I have had a good deal on my shoulders, I have thus far been able to meet all claims as they fell due, and have not found myself obliged to ask for an extension or accommodations.

I expect to have your copyright a/c ready by the 24ᵗʰ, and to send a check for it to your father.

It is very gratifying to me to have you speak so warmly of your long association with my father. He had always thoroughly enjoyed his relations with you, and had taken pleasure in the thought that you were not only a successful author who whom he had done business, but a near personal friend.

–Division of Rare Books and Manuscript Collections,
Cornell University Library

* * *

George Haven Putnam published this commemoration of his father in the second volume of his autobiography, Memories of a Publisher, 1865–1915, *which G. P. Putnam's Sons published in 1915.*

The Death of My Father. In December, 1872, came the sudden death of my father, which left upon myself and my younger brother the responsibility for the management of the publishing concern. My father was at the time but fifty-eight years of age, and he ought to have been spared for a longer term of service for his own home circle and for the community in which he had made for himself an honourable place. The nature of his service I have attempted to estimate in an earlier volume.

I could not but feel that my own experience had been too limited to qualify me properly for my new responsibilities. I had had no business training excepting what could be secured in the work of a regiment in active service and what had come to me during the six years since the war. My father had creative capacity and literary taste, and he had always been fortunate in his relations with his authors, nearly all of whom became his personal friends. He had no good knowledge, however, of the details of the commercial side of a publishing business, and it had been necessary for me in taking hold with him as a junior partner to instruct myself in order that I might be in a position to check off the work of subordinates and to free my father, as far as possible, from the details of office work.

From my earliest boyhood, my relations with my father had been close. He was by nature keenly sympathetic, and I could always feel assured without spoken words that he understood what I had at heart and that he made my hopes and aims his own. I know that during the six years of our working together, with the many business problems and perplexities, I was on my part, as I arrived at a fuller understanding of his high purposes and of his simple-hearted straightforward standard of action, more than ready to identify myself with his hopes and wishes. It is to me a great satisfaction to remember that the last six years of close business and personal association passed without a jar or a friction. If there had been any such instances, the fault must have rested with myself, for there was really no merit in working harmoniously with a partner of his temperament.

Putnam Authors

Loyalty was a common expectation that nineteenth-century publishers had of their authors. Putnam also thought of most of his authors as friends. Particularly in the pre-Civil War portion of his career, he was able to count a number of the leading authors in the country as both clients and friends. The following group of "Putnam authors" is selected on the basis of its long-term (or, in several cases, continuous) ties to G. P. Putnam and the importance of its books to American literary culture. The authors are presented in the order of their initial chronological appearance under the Putnam imprint.

Edgar Allan Poe

The career of Edgar Allan Poe (1809–1849) was so troubled and inconstant that it may be misleading to claim that he was a "Putnam author." He did, however, publish more books—and more of his premier works—with Putnam than with any other publisher. The first book Poe published with Putnam was The Narrative of Arthur Gordon Pym, of Nantucket, *whose New York edition was published by the Harpers in summer 1838 just as Putnam was setting out to open the London office of Wiley and Putnam. Within several months Putnam brought out a slightly revised London edition of the novel, with a publisher's statement added and the final scene of the novel eliminated.*

The result of the solicitation of editor Evert Duyckinck was that two more Poe works were published in 1845 in the Wiley and Putnam Library of American Books. Duyckinck, in fact, made the selections for Tales, *which brought together some of Poe's finest prose. Encouraged by that work, he persuaded Poe later that year to publish a small volume of poems,* The Raven and Other Poems, *presumably designed to capitalize on the fame of its recently published title piece.*

Eureka: A Prose Poem *was published in summer 1848 as one of the first titles to appear on the list of the new firm of G. P. Putnam. It was addressed "To the few who love me and whom I love." Although Putnam recalled an excited Poe coming to his office with the manuscript and requesting an edition of 50,000 copies, Putnam published 750.*

PUTNAM BOOKS BY POE: *The Narrative of Arthur Gordon Pym, of Nantucket . . . ,* anonymous (New York: Harper, 1838; London: Wiley & Putnam, 1838);

Tales (New York: Wiley & Putnam, 1845; London: Wiley & Putnam, 1845);

Edgar Allan Poe

The Raven and Other Poems (New York: Wiley & Putnam, 1845; London: Wiley & Putnam, 1846);

Eureka: A Prose Poem (New York: G. P. Putnam, 1848; London: Chapman, 1848).

* * *

George Haven Putnam's account of Poe's decade-long dealings with his father in A Memoir of George Palmer Putnam *(1903) combines fact, error, and legend. The year given for Poe's bringing the manuscript of* The Narrative of Arthur Gordon Pym *to his father, for example, is a decade late. Poe did not visit London in his maturity, and he did not authorize its London publication. Although Poe presumably did bring the manuscript of* Eureka *to Putnam's recently established Broadway office, the description of the episode may well include as much fancy as fact.*

The catalogue of the first year included a third name which has remained known in literature,—that of Edgar A. Poe. Poe also had come to be known by my father during his sojourn in London, and it was in London that had been printed as a separate sketch the narrative of a seaman of Nantucket. It was probably in 1847 that Poe, who had been introduced to my father as a man of letters or a journalist, brought into his office in Waterloo Place a manuscript which had, as he related, been sent to him by some friends in Nantucket, and which purported to be the journal of a Nantucket seaman who had gone out in one of the whalers on a trip to the Arctic seas. The seaman had never returned, but, according to Poe's story, the manuscript containing the account of his last journey had in some fashion made its way back to his Nantucket home. It was sent to London rather than to New York for the reason that in 1847, in connection with the expeditions in search of Sir John Franklin, there was a very wide-spread public interest in all matters relating to the Arctic regions. My father began the reading of the seaman's narrative and found himself not a little impressed with it. The literary style was in accordance with what might have been expected from an intelligent New Englander who, while without any experience in writing, knew how to describe in a simple and graphic fashion what he had seen. The readers who are familiar with the story as now printed in *Poe's Works* will remember that through two thirds of the narrative the record proceeds quietly enough, the incidents being no more exceptional than might naturally have been looked for during such a voyage as was described. It seems that my father was interrupted in his reading, but, judging that in any case the sketch was well worth bringing into print and would be likely in the present tendency of English interest to attract public attention, he sent it to the printers. It was not until he read in one of the critical journals of the time a rather sharp reference to the "methods of Yankee publishers" that he took time to examine the closing pages of the "narrative of Gordon Pym, seaman, from Nantucket." It will be remembered that the last words in the manuscript described the drawing of the vessel into the whirl of a great vortex supposed to be situated at the Pole, and the account ends with some such words as, "And we are going down, down, down." There is no reference to the coming up again of either the author or any of his companions, and it was naturally difficult to understand how this very curious narrative had made its way back to Nantucket and from Nantucket to London. Mr. Poe had been paid for his story some money, which was, he said, very much needed by the widow of the unfortunate seaman who was left alone in Nantucket.

My father does not record having had any opportunity of receiving from the versatile author any explanation of the matter, but Poe must have secured forgiveness in some way, because in 1848 he was a visitor at the Broadway office, where he was putting into shape what he described as the great discovery of the age.

He came into the office one afternoon in the half-intoxicated condition in which, if I understand the record of his life, much of his literary work had been done. He demanded a desk, pen, ink, and paper. "Oh, Mr. Putnam," he said, "you do not yet realize how important is the work that I am here bringing to completion. I have solved the secret of the universe." He wrote furiously during the hours of daylight that remained, until the time came for my father to take his boat for Staten Island. The author was then turned over to the care of the book-keeper and remained writing until the book-keeper also had departed for home. The porter had patience for a little time longer and then, more interested in the plans for his own supper than in the secrets of the universe, put the poet out notwithstanding protests. The next day the performance was repeated on practically the same lines. On the third day, the completed manuscript was brought by the poet to the publisher's desk and was handed over with most glowing prophecies as to the revolution that was to be brought about in the conceptions of mankind.

> Mr. Putnam [said Poe, his eye with fine frenzy rolling], here is a revelation that will make fame for myself and fortune for my publisher. The world has been waiting for it. To me has come as an inspiration a conception that has not yet been reached by scientific investigators. For such a result the name *Eureka* is certainly fitting. I judge that you ought to make your first edition not less than one million copies. You would not wish to have a reading public on both sides of the Atlantic in a state of irritation because copies could not be secured.

My father took the manuscript (which, as was the case with even the most intoxicated effusions of Poe, was in a beautiful and very legible script), and found himself impressed with the eloquence of the fantasy, but not quite so clear in his mind as to its importance as a scientific discovery. His views of the immediate demand from the public were, in any case, not fully up to the expectations of the author. He printed of *Eureka* a first edition of 750 copies, and a year later at least a third of these copies were still on hand. The essay will now be found in its place with the other prose writings of Poe.

I am not sufficiently familiar with the chronology of astronomical investigation to know at just what date the nebular hypothesis originated. It is probable, however, that Poe, who was not a student of astronomy, could have known little or nothing of the results secured by Herschel and others, even if these results were at the time in print. He may fairly, therefore, be entitled to the credit of having secured in some inspirational fashion of his own a conception expressed by him as a fantasy, which did happen to be in line with the results of scientific investigation.

Here is a Poe document that can be termed characteristic, and which is properly to be connected with the history of *Eureka:*

> Received of George P. Putnam Fourteen Dollars, money loaned, to be repaid out of the proceeds of the Copyright of my work entitled *Eureka, a Prose Poem;* and I hereby engage, in case the sales of said work do not cover the expenses, according to the account rendered by said Putnam in January, 1849, to repay the said amount of Fourteen Dollars and I also engage not to ask or apply for any other loans or advances from said Putnam in any way, and to wait until January, 1849, for the statement of account as above, before making any demand whatever.
>
>   Edgar A. Poe
>
> New York, May, 1848.
> Witnesses,
>   Maria Clemur [*sic*].
>   Marie Louise Shaw.
>
> *—A Memoir of George Palmer Putnam,*
> volume 1, pp. 232–237

Andrew Jackson Downing

Andrew Jackson Downing (1815–1852) was the leading American landscape architect and designer of his generation. He came to the subject naturally, working in his father's nursery and acquiring an autodidact's knowledge of botany and gardening, supplemented by the growing literature on the subject in England. Indeed, he later edited several important British works on landscape gardening that were published by Wiley and Putnam in New York.

Except for The Architecture of Country Houses *(1850), he published all of his major books and most of his minor ones with Wiley and Putnam and its successor firms. His first important work was* A Treatise on the Theory and Prac-

tice of Landscape Gardening *(1841), which established the author as an international authority on landscape gardening. The subtitle of the volume,* Adapted to North America, *indicated a pride of place that undoubtedly solidified his reputation in the United States. He followed that study with the well-received* Cottage Residences *(1842), which opened the subject of rural design to a broader, less affluent stratum of homeowners. Perhaps his most influential work was* The Fruits and Fruit Trees of America *(1845), which remained in print throughout the century.*

Wiley and Putnam generally published Downing's early works in both New York and London. When Putnam formed his own company in 1848, John Wiley retained rights to most of Downing's works and kept many of them in print for decades. Putnam, though, kept up a friendship with Downing. After the author died in a steamboat explosion in 1852, Putnam secured rights to his last work, Rural Essays, *probably through the mediation of their mutual friend Fredrika Bremer; it was published in 1853.*

PUTNAM BOOKS BY DOWNING: *A Treatise on the Theory and Practice of Landscape Gardening* (New York: Wiley & Putnam, 1841; London: Wiley & Putnam, 1841);

Landscape Gardening and Rural Architecture (New York: Wiley & Putnam, 1841; London: Wiley & Putnam, 1841);

Andrew Jackson Downing

Cottage Residences (New York: Wiley & Putnam, 1842;
    London: Wiley & Putnam, 1842);
Gardening for Ladies, by Jane Loudon, edited by
    Downing (New York: Wiley & Putnam, 1843);
The Fruits and Fruit Trees of America (New York: Wiley
    & Putnam, 1845; London: Wiley & Putnam,
    1845);
Rural Essays (New York: G. P. Putnam and Com-
    pany, 1853).

OTHER: *The Theory of Horticulture,* by John Lindley,
    annotated by Downing and Asa Gray (New
    York: Wiley & Putnam, 1841);
Hints to Young Architects, by George Wightwick, with
    additions by Downing (New York: Wiley &
    Putnam, 1847; London: Wiley & Putnam,
    1847).

* * *

*Complaints by nineteenth-century authors about non-
payment, tardy payment, or insufficient payment were common. In this letter to Putnam, Downing states his frustration
with Wiley's failure to pay him the previous year's royalties,
presumably on the old Wiley and Putnam account, and seeks
to regularize his income on a semiannual basis, which was
then becoming standard in the profession.*

Newburgh   March 28, 1850

My dear Sir,

The arrangement Mr. Leslie made would have
perfectly satisfied me—but that I am just now minus
the whole past year's settlement of copy right a/c
which I expected from Mr. Wiley this spring. I will
therefore take it as an especial favor to be allowed to
continue the other note if you will have the goodness to return yours for the enclosed.

I will make arrangements by which both these
notes be paid at next maturity,—and I must also
effect some arrangement by which my other copy
rights will hereafter produce me a semi-annual
income.

Yours very sincerely
A. J. Downing
Geo. P. Putnam, Esq.
    —*Manuscripts Division, Department of Rare Books and
    Special Collections, Princeton University Library. Published
    with permission of the Princeton University Library.*

Caroline M. Kirkland

Caroline M. Kirkland

*Caroline M. Kirkland (1801–1864) was one of the most
prolific female writers of her generation, as well as the first editor
of the* Union Magazine. *Although she published most frequently during the 1840s and 1850s with the firm of Charles
Scribner, she also published occasional books with Wiley and Putnam—two books in the Library of American Books—and G. P.
Putnam. Her relationship with Putnam was also personal; the
Putnams occasionally hosted her at their home. Kirkland collaborated on various of the house gift books, including* Home Book
of the Picturesque, Homes of American Authors, *and*
Homes of American Statesmen. *She was involved in the
early meetings held at the Putnams' house in the planning of*
Putnam's Monthly *and became a valued contributor to the
magazine.*

PUTNAM BOOKS BY KIRKLAND: *Western Clearings,*
    as Mrs. Mary Clavers (New York: Wiley & Put-
    nam, 1845; London: Wiley & Putnam, 1846);
The Book of Home Beauty (New York: G. P. Putnam,
    1852).

OTHER: *Spenser and the Faëry Queen,* edited by Kirkland
    (New York & London: Wiley & Putnam, 1847);

Garden Walks with the Poets, edited by Kirkland (New York: G. P. Putnam and Company, 1852);

"Bryant," in *Homes of American Authors; Comprising Anecdotical, Personal, and Descriptive Sketches, by Various Writers* (New York: G. P. Putnam and Company, 1853).

* * *

Putnam wrote to Kirkland about the chapter she contributed to Homes of American Authors *on William Cullen Bryant. Her payment of $25 was the standard sum for contributors.*

N. York Augt. 15/52

My dear Mrs. Kirkland,

Your "Bryant" is "first rate"—as Tom Thumb said to the Queen about her picture gallery. I am not sure yet whether the proof can be sent to you before 21st.

At any rate you shall see the plate proofs—for all essential corrections.

Whenever you have occasion for $25 it will be ready for you. I wish it were more—but it is still not <u>too</u> easy for me to be <u>just</u>—to say nothing about generous.

Hope you are enjoying yourself. Pray come home <u>safe</u>. Respy. & truly yours,

<u>G. P. Putnam</u>

Mrs. C. M. Kirkland

—Manuscripts Division, Department of Rare Books and Special Collections, Princeton University Library. Published with permission of the Princeton University Library.

Herman Melville

Herman Melville (1819–1891), who was a Harper and Brothers author for most of the intermediate stage of his career, published his first novel, Typee *(1846), with Wiley and Putnam. His brother Gansvoort, secretary to the American legation in London, initially arranged for the publication of* Typee *with John Murray in London. In early 1846, while the work was being prepared for publication, Gansvoort and Washington Irving left a copy of the text with Putnam at the Wiley and Putnam office at Waterloo Place. Putnam spent the weekend reading the novel and immediately accepted it for the Library of American Books. Publication and royalty details were soon worked out between Gansvoort and Putnam, and proof sheets of the Murray edition were sent by steamer to New York to allow for nearly simultaneous transatlantic publication.*

Melville published his succeeding novels from Omoo *(1847) to* Pierre *(1852) with the larger house of Harper and Brothers. By 1853, however, with his popularity falling off*

Herman Melville, who published his first novel and some of his finest short fiction with Putnam

sharply and indebted to the Harpers for advances, he reoriented himself from the novel to short fiction, which he placed with the two leading literary periodicals of the mid 1850s, Putnam's Monthly and Harper's Monthly. *His stories for* Putnam's Monthly *included "Bartleby, the Scrivener," "Benito Cereno," and "The Encantadas, or Enchanted Isles." He also serialized* Israel Potter *(1855) in the magazine, which subsequently came out with G. P. Putnam and Company in book form. Putnam remained in loose social contact with Melville during the 1860s and approached him for magazine contributions when he made plans in fall 1867 to resuscitate the house journal as* Putnam's Magazine, *but no Melville piece ever appeared in the new periodical.*

PUTNAM WORKS BY MELVILLE: *Narrative of a Four Months' Residence among the Natives of a Valley of the Marquesas Islands: Or, A Peep at Polynesian Life* (London: Murray, 1846); republished as *Typee: A Peep at Polynesian Life. During a Four Months' Residence in a Valley of the Marquesas, With Notices of the French Occupation of Tahiti and the Provisional Cession of the Sandwich Islands to Lord Paulet,* 2 volumes (New York: Wiley & Putnam / London: Murray, 1846); revised edition, with "The Story of Toby," 2 volumes (New York: Wiley & Putnam / London: Murray, 1846);

Israel Potter: His Fifty Years of Exile (New York: G. P. Putnam and Company, 1855; London: Routledge, 1855);

Clarel: A Poem and Pilgrimage in the Holy Land, 2 volumes (New York: G. P. Putnam's Sons, 1876).

OTHER: "Bartleby, the Scrivener," "The Encantadas, or Enchanted Isles," "Benito Cereno," "The Lightning-Rod Man," and "The Bell-Tower," in *Putnam's Monthly,* 1853 to 1856.

* * *

This long overview of Melville's career was the second entry (following one on Donald Mitchell) in a series on contemporary American writers initiated by the Putnam's Monthly *editors as part of their effort to do justice to American authorship. The author was Fitz-James O'Brien, a popular magazinist and short-story writer who contributed frequently to* Putnam's *and* Harper's *monthlies. O'Brien's verdict here was the common one: Melville was stronger in his early, fact-based works, weaker in his later, more purely imaginative ones. His warning that Melville should return to his earlier style would have been all too familiar to the author.*

OUR YOUNG AUTHORS–MELVILLE.

WHEN Typee first appeared, great was the enthusiasm. The oddity of the name set critics a wondering. Reviewers who were in the habit of writing an elaborate review of a work, from merely glancing over the heads of the chapters, and thinking a little over the title-page, were completely at fault. TYPEE told nothing. It had no antecedents. It might have been an animal, or it might have been a new game, or it might have been a treatise on magic. Did they open the book, and look over the chapters, they were not much wiser. Barbarous congregations of syllables, such as Kory-Kory, Nukuheva, Moa Artua, met their eyes. The end of it was, that the whole tribe of London and American critics had to sit down and read it all, before they dared speak of a book filled with such mysterious syllables. From reading they began to like it. There was a great deal of rich, rough talent about it. The scenes were fresh, and highly colored; the habits and manners described had the charm of novelty; and the style, though not the purest or most elegant, had a fine narrative facility about it, that rendered it very pleasurable reading, after the maudlin journeys in Greece–travels in the Holy Land, full of Biblical raptures, and yacht-tours in the Mediterranean, where monotonous sea-dinners and vulgar shore-pleasures were faithfully chronicled, with such like trash that had been inundating the literary market for years previous. TYPEE was successful. It could scarcely be otherwise. Prosy to the last degree, in some portions, there yet

were scenes in it full of exquisite description, and novel characters, who, like Fayaway, were in themselves so graceful, that we could not help loving them. Mr. Melville found that he had opened a fertile field, which he was not slow to work. Sea novels had, as it were, been run into the ground by Marryatt, Chamier, and Cooper. People were growing weary of shipwrecks and fires at sea. Every possible incident that could occur, on board men-of-war, privateers, and prizes, had been described over and over again, with an ability that left nothing to be desired. The whole of a sailor's life was laid bare to us. We knew exactly what they ate, what they drank, and at what hours they ate and drank it. Their language, their loves, their grievances, and their mutinies, were as familiar as the death of Cock Robin. Even staid, sober, land-lubbering people, who got sea-sick crossing in a Brooklyn ferry-boat, began to know the names of ropes and spars, and imagined no longer that a "scupper" was one of the sails. Mr. Melville came forward with his books, to relieve this state of well informed dulness. By a happy mixture of fresh land scenery, with some clever ship-life, he produced a brilliant amalgam, that was loudly welcomed by the public. Who does not relish Dr. Long-ghost all the better, for leaving the Julia, albeit prisoner-wise, and going ashore to that funny Calabooza Beretanee where he has epileptic fits, in order to get a good dinner, and makes a fan out of a paddle, to keep off the mosquitoes. Does not the wild voluptuous dance of the "back-sliding girls," in the Valley of Martair, contrast magnificently with that terrible night off Papeetee, when the Mowree tried to run "Little Jule" ashore upon the coral breakers. In this contrast, which abounds in Mr. Melville's books, lies one of his greatest charms. Sea and shore mingling harmoniously together, like music-chords. Now floating on the wide blue southern seas–the sport of calms and hurricanes–the companion of the sullen Bent, the Doctor and Captain Guy. Anon clasping to our bosoms those jaunty, impassioned creatures, yclept Day-born, Night-born, and the Wakeful; or watching Fayaway laving her perfect, shining form in the cool lake, by whose green bank the cocoa sheds its fruit, and the bread-fruit tree towers. All this is delicious, to those who have been playing vulgar midshipman's tricks with Chamier and Marryatt, and comes to us pleasantly even after Cooper's powerful and tender sea-tales.

It is no easy matter to pronounce which of Mr. Melville's books is the best. All of them (and he has published a goodly number, for so young an author) have had their own share of success, and their own peculiar merits, always saving and excepting Pierre– wild, inflated, repulsive that it is.

For us there is something very charming about Mardi, all the time fully aware of its sad defects in taste and style. Of course, we give Mr. Melville every credit for his deliberate plagiarisms of old Sir Thomas Browne's gorgeous and metaphorical manner. Affectation upon affectation is scattered recklessly through its pages. Wild similes, cloudy philosophy, all things turned topsy-turvy, until we seem to feel all earth melting away from beneath our feet, and nothing but Mardi remaining. Reading this wild book, we can imagine ourselves mounted upon some Tartar steed, golden caparisons clank around our person, ostrich plumes of driven whiteness hang over our brow, and cloud our vision with dancing snow. Lance in hand, from which the horse-tail quivers in the wind, we stand beneath the shadow of our desert-tent, dreaming of golden caravans. Suddenly a thirst for motion fills us with uncontrollable desire. Our steed paws the sand, and our lance trembles to its very steel point, in grasp of nervous eagerness. Away, away, along the sandy plain! Clouds of sand, that shine in the sun like gold, are flung up around us. The swift ostrich stares to see us pass it in our headlong flight. Pilgrims, wending Mecca-ward, tremble when they behold the advancing pillar of dust in which we and our steed are shrouded, and fall on their faces prostrate before what they believe to be the terrible Simoom. Still onward, onward! We have outrun our very breath, and left it miles behind, and no longer panting, we race onward, unearthly calm. Every now and then we come to an oasis. Ho! pull up, good steed, and drink. We stop. Soft steals the moist fountain-wind through the tall, still palm-trees; tenderly the rich green grass sinks and rises as we tread. Cooly, freshly, diamondly, the desert-spring wells out and cools our parching lips. But waste not time. Again in saddle; again speeding along the desert we know not whither. A wide black gulf, deep and edgeless, bars our path. What! coward steed! Dost thou think to stop and tremble? No, not even if it were the gulf of death, shored with dismal banks of night. On, on! Strike the stirrup-spurs deep into the flanks! lift the heavy golden bridle! Smite, smite heavily with the elastic lance-shaft! The quivering, frightened steed paws, and rears, and bounds. Down, down we sink through yielding air. Clouds, shapeless, formless clouds, fly up as we fly down. And the ocean that sounds below lifts up its billowy arms to receive us. Moonbeams cover the sea with a silver shroud. Caves murmur. Spirits float midway between the waves and heaven. We, steed and all, sail grandly onwards like an ocean centaur. But it is not always calm. Hoarse syllables of storm mutter in the North, and waves rise angrily to answer them.

What shall we do, with weary desert steed against the legion of winds?

Scatter them with our lance?

Out-blow them with a breath, and burst their lungs?

All vain! They are too strong. They pour upon us from every side. The star Arcturus frowns red disaster from the sky. If we seek not harbor we are lost. A golden hope looms upon us from the distance! Let us fly. Now desert-steed, paw the waves as once thou didst the sand. O'erleap the fencing billows, and make for that white spot that looms distantly. The winds gallop fast behind, and will smite us unseen. The sea-gulls ride before, like stewards of the airy course, to clear the way. The desert-steed strains every nerve, wave after wave clears he, and paws onward to the white island that is to be our Salvator. We near it just as the tempest scents us, and bays upon our track.

But what is this we see?

No island, no sheltering harbor, no white fortress to defend the fugitive:

But a great, white, world-wide placard, with these words traced upon its surface:

MARDI

AND

A VOYAGE THITHER.

BY HERMAN MELVILLE.

A greater difference could hardly exist between two men than between Mr. Mitchell and Mr. Melville, albeit we have chosen to link them together in our chain. Mitchell writes essentially from the heart. He is continually gazing inward, picking up what he finds there, and displaying it with a childlike, innocent pleasure to the world. From forms, and forms alone does Melville take his text. He looks out of himself, and takes a rich outline view of what he sees. He is essentially exoterical in feeling. Matter is his god. His dreams are material. His philosophy is sensual. Beautiful women, shadowy lakes, nodding, plumy trees, and succulent banquets, make Melville's scenery, unless his theme utterly preclude all such. His language is rich and heavy, with a plating of imagery. He has a barbaric love of ornament, and does not mind much how it is put on. Swept away by this sensual longing, he frequently writes at random. One can see that he uses certain words only because they roll off the pen lusciously and roundly, just as a child, who is entirely the sport of sense, grasps at the largest apple. In Mardi is this peculiarly obvious. A long experience of the South sea islanders has no doubt induced this. The languages of these groups are singularly mellifluous and resonant, vowels enter largely into the composition of every word, and dissyllabled words are rare. Mr. Melville has been attracted by this. Whenever he can use a word of four syllables where a monosyllable would answer just as well, he chooses the former. A certain fulness of style is very attractive. Sir Thomas Browne, from whom Mr. Melville copies much that is good, is a great friend of magnificent diction. And his tract on urn burial is as lofty and poetical as if Memnon's statue chanted it, when the setting sun fell aslant across the Pyramids. But we find no nonsense in Sir Thomas. In every thing he says there is a deep meaning, although sometimes an erroneous one. We cannot always say as much for Mr. Melville. In his latest work he transcended even the jargon of Paracelsus and his followers. The Rosetta stone gave up its secret, but we believe that to the end of time Pierre will remain an ambiguity.

Mardi, we believe, is intended to embody all the philosophy of which Mr. Melville is capable, and we have no hesitation in saying that the philosophical parts are the worst. We do not for a moment pretend to say that we understand the system laid down by the author. Whether there be a system in it at all, is at least somewhat problematical, but when Mr. Melville does condescend to be intelligible, what he has to say for himself in the way of philosophy, is so exceedingly stale and trite, that it would be more in place in a school-boy's copy-book, than in a romance otherwise distinguished for splendor of imagery, and richness of diction. The descriptive painting in this wild book is gorgeous and fantastic in the extreme. It is a tapestry of dreams, worked with silken threads, dyed in the ocean of an Eastern sunset. Nothing however strange startles us as we float onwards through this misty panorama. King Media looms out from the canvas, an antique gentleman full of drowsy courtesy. Babbalanja philosophizes over his calabash, or relates the shadowy adventures of shadows in the land of shades. From out the woods, canopied with flowers, that let the daylight in only through courtesy, comes Donjalolo, the Southern Sardanapalus. Women droop over his pale enervate figure, and strive to light its exhausted fires with their burning eyes. He looks up lazily, and opens his small, red mouth to catch a drop of honey that is trembling in the core of some over-hanging flower. Fatigued with this exertion, he sinks back with a sigh into the soft arms interlaced behind. Then comes Hautia, Queen of spells that lie in lilies, and mistress of the music of feet. Around her float flushing nymphs, who love through endless dances, and die in the ecstasy of mingled motion. While far behind, throned in mist, and with one foot dabbling in the great ocean of the Future, stands the lost Yillah; problem of beauty to which there is no solution save through death.

All these characters flit before us in Mardi, and bring with them no consciousness of their unreality and deception. As shadows they come to us, but they are sensual shades. Their joys thrill through us. When they banquet in drowsy splendor—when they wander upon beaches of pearls and rubies—when they wreath their brows with blossoms more fragrant and luscious than the buds that grow in Paradise, our senses twine with theirs, and we forget every thing, save the vision of their gorgeous pleasures. It is this sensual power that holds the secret of Mr. Melville's first successes. No matter how unreal the scenery, if the pleasure be but truly painted, the world will cry "bravo!" We draw pictures of Gods and Goddesses, and hang them on our walls, but we take good care to let their divinity be but nominal. Diana, Juno, Venus, are they known, but they loom out from the canvas, substantial, unadulterated women. Seldom does there live an Ixion who loves to embrace clouds. Call it a cloud if you will, and if it have the appearance of flesh and blood, the adorer will be satisfied. But we doubt if there is to be found any man enthusiast enough to clasp a vapor to his heart, be it schirri-shaped or cumulous, and baptized with the sweetest name ever breathed from the Attic tongue. Mr. Melville therefore deals in vapors, but he twines around them so cunningly all human attributes, and pranks them out so lusciously with all the witcheries of sense, that we forget their shadowy nomenclatures, and worship the substantial incarnation.

It must not be imagined from this, that Mr. Melville is incapable of dealing with the events of more matter-of-fact life. He is averse to it, no doubt, and if we may judge by Pierre, is becoming more averse to it as he grows older. But he sometimes takes the vulgar monster by the shoulders and wields it finely. In Omoo, which by the way contains some exceedingly fine passages, occurs the following account of the attempt of a South sea savage named Bembo to run the ship ashore on a coral reef, because he had been insulted by one of the ship's crew is very graphic [sic].

. . . .

Typee, the first and most successful of Mr. Melville's books, commands attention for the clearness of its narrative, the novelty of its scenery, and the simplicity of its style, in which latter feature it is a wondrous contrast to Mardi, Moby Dick, and Pierre. The story of Typee is plain enough. The hero becomes discontented with his ship, while among the Marquesas islands, and comes to the determination of effecting his escape. This he does in company with Toby, a fellow-sailor, a rough, jolly mortal, who grumbles and enjoys himself all the time, as most grumblers do. The island on which they effect their escape is divided into two great clans, who each occupy a valley, and between whom a deadly enmity exists. These are the Typees and the Happars. Like our own Christian sects they are not given to speaking well of each other. The Happars call the Typees cannibals, and the Typees vow that the amount of babies consumed annually in Happar is quite incredible. Tom and Toby fall into the hands of the Typees, where their position is very precarious, until Tom discovers that the way to their affection is to abuse the Happars. He accordingly launches out against this unfortunate race, of whom he knows nothing, and is in consequence treated with the utmost courtesy and affection by their foes. In this valley of savages, where the flowers and the women are beautiful beyond conception, Tom and Toby pass their days pleasantly. Swimming in the clear lakes with Typee girls, who cleave the water like dolphins; feasting in sacred temples off of suckling pig, lolling beneath the bread-fruit trees with Fayaway, or making "Tappa" with the housekeepers and matrons, they spend as agreeable a life as ever town-imprisoned merchant's clerk sighed for. In Typee there were no debts, consequently no duns. The charming inhabitants dispensed with all clothing, and tailors were unknown. No detestable bills to mar one's new year's pleasures with items of "seven fancy vests, $85; three coats, $120; gloves, ties, &c., &c., &c., &c., &c., $200." Tom had no hotel bill to pay. A piece of Tappa, or a quid of tobacco was current coin, and if the girls of the valley got up a ball, there was no subscription list, no lady patronesses, and no enmities gathering out of rejected applications for tickets.

It does not appear either that there were any "sets," or *cliques* in Typee. Mr. Melville does not mention that they had their Fifth Avenue, or their Bleecker Rubicon. Society was not divided into petty circles, each revolving round some insignificant centre, and fancying themselves the central sun of the universe of fashion. Typee ladies did not receive their visitors in drawing-rooms resplendent with gilt vulgarity, and if they had ever been so fortunate as to travel, we doubt if they would have talked one down with the Grand Duke of Fiddeldedeestein "whom they met at Baden-Baden," and who—let it be whispered *sub rosa*—cheated the *pater-familias* at écarte. Would that the world could be Typee-ized. Would that we could strip every vain pretender of the plumage that chance has given him, and turn him out upon the world with nothing to clothe him save his own merits. How your vulgar Argus, with a million of dollars on his tail, would find his level in Typee. The friends of the Grand Duke of Fiddeldedeestein, would not rise an inch higher in Mehevi's estimation for having known the ducal swindler, and then—then what do you say to the inexpressible, almost unimaginable, never-to-be-realized delight of paying off your

tailor's bill for the last time, in cowrie-shells and Tappa!

In this primitive valley of Typee we meet with Fayaway. Charming, smooth-skinned siren, around whose sun-browned form the waves lap and dimple, like the longing touches of a lover's fingers. What luxury untold it must have been to live with thee beneath the shady places of Typee. To dance with thee in the moonlight in front of the deep-eaved hut; to hunt with thee for strange flowers in the deep, silent woods, or sail with thee on the lake when the sunset painted our tappa sail with finer hues than the work of Gobelins. How Tom could ever have left thee, surpasseth human understanding. Left thee, graceful, artless child of the forest and the stream, to dwell among civilized women—dancing machines; flirting machines, built of whalebone and painted red.

And sadly we leave Fayaway lamenting her white lover.

White Jacket is a pure sea-book, but very clever. It is a clear, quiet picture of life on board of a man-of-war. It has less of Mr. Melville's faults than almost any of his works, and is distinguished for clear, wholesome satire, and a manly style. There is a scene describing the amputation of a sailor's leg by a brutal, cold-blooded surgeon, Patella, that Smollett might have painted. We would gladly quote it, but that it rather exceeds the limits usually afforded in an article so short as ours.

There is one chapter in which the hero details the loss of the White Jacket, from wearing which, he and the book take their name, that strikes us as a very fine piece of descriptive writing. We give it entire.

. . . .

This is fine. We have often met with descriptions, some well painted enough, of dizzy aerial adventures, but never one like this. Our ears tingle as we read it. The air surges around us as we fall from that fearful height. The sea divides, the green mist flashes into a thousand hues, and we sit for an instant a stride of Death's balance. Weight, unutterable weight presses upon our shoulders, and we seem as if about to be crushed into nothingness. Then a sudden change. A revulsion which is accompanied with soft, low music; and we float upwards. We seem gliding through an oiled ocean, so smoothly do we pass. It breaks, it parts above our head. The next moment we shoot out from a cloud of feathers, and are battling with the waves.

In Redburn, we find an account of the death of a sailor, by spontaneous combustion. Well described, poetically described, fraught with none of the revolting scenery which it is so easy to gather round such an end. In the last number of Bleak House, Mr. Dickens has attempted the same thing. He has also performed what he attempted. But, if ever man deserved public prosecution for his writing, he does, for this single passage. A hospital student could not read it without sickening. A ghoul, who had lived all his days upon the festering corruption of the grave-yard, could have written nothing more hideously revolting than the death of Krook. It is as loathsome to read it as to enter one of the charnels in London city. We do not believe that a woman of sensitive nerves could take it up without fainting over the details. For ourselves, we fling the book away, with an anathema on the author that we should be sorry for him to hear.

Mr. Melville does not improve with time. His later books are a decided falling off, and his last scarcely deserves naming; this however we scarce believe to be an indication of exhaustion. Keats says beautifully in his preface to Endymion, that "The imagination of a boy is healthy, and the mature imagination of a man is healthy, but there is a space of life between, in which the soul is in a ferment, the character undecided, the way of life uncertain, the ambition thick-sighted."

Just at present we believe the author of Pierre to be in this state of ferment. Typee, his first book, was healthy; Omoo nearly so; after that came Mardi, with its excusable wildness; then came Moby Dick, and Pierre with its inexcusable insanity. We trust that these rhapsodies will end the interregnum of nonsense to which Keats refers, as forming a portion of every man's life; and that Mr. Melville will write less at random and more at leisure, than of late. Of his last book we would fain not speak did we not feel that he is just now at that stage of author-life when a little wholesome advice may save him a hundred future follies. When first we read Pierre, we felt a strong inclination to believe the whole thing to be a well-got-up hoax. We remembered having read a novel in six volumes once of the same order, called "The Abbess," in which the stilted style of writing is exposed very funnily; and, as a specimen of unparalleled bombast, we believed it to be unequalled until we met with Pierre. In Mardi there is a strong vein of vague, morphinized poetry, running through the whole book. We do not know what it means from the beginning to the end, but we do not want to know, and accept it as a rhapsody. Babbalanja philosophizing drowsily, or the luxurious sybaritical King Media, lazily listening to the hum of waters, are all shrouded dimly in opiate-fumes, and dream-clouds,

and we love them only as sensual shadows. Whatever they say or do; whether they sail in a golden boat, or eat silver fruits, or make pies of emeralds and rubies, or any thing else equally ridiculous, we feel perfectly satisfied that it is all right, because there is no claim made upon our practical belief. But if Mr. Melville had placed Babbalanja and Media and Yoomy in the Fifth Avenue, instead of a longitude and latitude less inland; if we met them in theatres instead of palm groves, and heard Babbalanja lecturing before the Historical Society instead of his dreamy islanders, we should feel naturally rather indignant at such a tax upon our credulity. We would feel inclined to say with the Orientals, that Mr. Melville had been laughing at our beards, and Pacha-like condemn on the instant to a literary bastinado. Now Pierre has all the madness of Mardi, without its vague, dreamy, poetic charm. All Mr. Melville's many affectations of style and thought are here crowded together in a mad mosaic. Talk of Rabelais's word-nonsense! there was always something queer, and odd, and funny, gleaming through his unintelligibility. But Pierre transcends all the nonsense-writing that the world ever beheld.

Thought staggers through each page like one poisoned. Language is drunken and reeling. Style is antipodical, and marches on its head. Then the moral is bad. Conceal it how you will, a revolting picture presents itself. A wretched, cowardly boy for a hero, who, from some feeling of mad romance, together with a mass of inexplicable reasons which, probably, the author alone fathoms, chooses to live in poverty with his illegitimate sister, whom he passes off to the world as his wife, instead of being respectably married to a legitimate cousin. Everbody is vicious in some way or other. The mother is vicious with pride. Isabel has a cancer of morbid, vicious, minerva-press-romance, eating into her heart. Lucy Tartan is viciously humble, and licks the dust beneath Pierre's feet viciously. Delly Ulver is humanly vicious, and in the rest of the book, whatever of vice is wanting in the remaining characters, is made up by superabundant viciosities of style.

Let Mr. Melville stay his step in time. He totters on the edge of a precipice, over which all his hard-earned fame may tumble with such another weight as Pierre attached to it. He has peculiar talents, which may be turned to rare advantage. Let him diet himself for a year or two on Addison, and avoid Sir Thomas Browne, and there is little doubt but that he will make a notch on the American Pine.

– *Putnam's Monthly,* 1 (February 1853): 155–164

William Gilmore Simms, who followed Poe as the second major Southern writer published by Wiley and Putnam. Simms gladly accepted Evert Duyckinck's offer to publish with the firm as a means of reaching beyond the South to a national audience.

William Gilmore Simms

An ambitious, prolific professional writer who made rich, artistic use of Southern materials, William Gilmore Simms (1806–1870) published two books with Wiley and Putnam when he was at the height of his powers. The connection, mediated by his friend Evert Duyckinck, was mutually beneficial. Simms, who suffered financially because of his isolation from northern literary centers, welcomed Duyckinck's invitation to publish his work in the Library of American Books. Wiley and Putnam, for its part, acquired two of the best titles in its series, the short-story collection The Wigwam and the Cabin *(1845–1846) and the critical work* Views and Reviews in American Literature, History and Fiction *(1846–1847).*

PUTNAM BOOKS BY SIMMS: *The Wigwam and the Cabin,* first and second series (New York: Wiley & Putnam, 1845–1846; London: Wiley & Putnam, 1845–1846);

Views and Reviews in American Literature, History and Fiction, first and second series (New York: Wiley & Putnam, 1846–1847; London: Wiley & Putnam, 1846–1847).

* * *

This swipe at Simms, "a very voluminous author . . . ," and the South was probably made by Lewis Gaylord Clark, who was settling personal scores with various New York City literati, including Evert Duyckinck, William Jones, and, perhaps most especially, Poe, who had recently championed the works of his fellow Southerner Simms.

. . . 'Mr. JONES,' we say, has an article in the last number of our 'Democratic' contemporary [Democratic Review], upon the subject of 'American Humor,' which we quite concur with the 'Broadway Journal' in characterizing as 'contemptible, both in a moral and literary sense;' and as 'the production of an imitator and a quack.' It is quite baseless, moreover; being suggested by an article in a Southern magazine, of small circulation and smaller influence, written by a very voluminous author, now in the decadence of a limited sectional reputation; a writer who, having no shadow of humor of his own, is poorly qualified to judge of the humor, or lack of humor, of any body else. He might with equal fitness and propriety have indited a didactic paper upon the scholarship of the country. Yet such is the writer who broadly asserts that we are 'without any humorous literature;' that our 'published humor is a blank,' etc.

– *Knickerbocker,* 26 (October 1845): 378

* * *

This moralistic assessment of the stories in The Wigwam and the Cabin, *second series, was by Walt Whitman, the earnest young editor of Brooklyn's leading newspaper.*

Simms is unquestionably one of the most attractive writers of the age; and yet some of his characters— to our mind at least—are in excessively bad taste. It *may* be all well enough to introduce a "foul rabble of lewd spirits," in order to show that "Virtue can triumph even in the worst estates," but it is our impression that ladies and gentlemen of refinement—to say nothing of heads of families—would rather take the maxim upon trust than have it exemplified to them or their children through the medium of a picture so very coarse and indelicate in its details, as that drawn by Mr. Simms in his "Cayloa." The last chapter of this story is rendered particularly objectionable by the introduction of a revolting drunken scene—and the tale as a whole is certainly calculated to reflect upon American literature, either at home or abroad.

There are several other tales in the volume, of an unexceptionable and highly entertaining character.

– *Brooklyn Daily Eagle,* 9 March 1846

Thomas Carlyle in 1847 (reproduced by permission of the Houghton Library, Harvard University, bMS Am 1280.235 [703.13])

Thomas Carlyle

In 1845 Putnam began courting Thomas Carlyle (1795–1881), hoping to become his American publisher. Carlyle, who like other popular foreign authors suffered from American piracy, had previously settled for catch-as-catch-can publication deals for individual works arranged largely through Ralph Waldo Emerson. Putnam in fall 1845 reached an agreement with Carlyle's English publishers, Chapman and Hall, for a Wiley and Putnam edition of Oliver Cromwell's Letters and Speeches, *which was published in December. In April 1846 Putnam discussed with Carlyle terms for a general agreement. Following complicated negotiations that included Putnam's consultation with Wiley and Evert Duyckinck in New York and Carlyle's with Emerson in Concord, the two men reached final terms in June 1846 for Wiley and Putnam editions of* Chartism, Past and Present, Sartor Resartus, The French Revolution, *and* On Heroes, Hero-Worship, and the Heroic in History. *Most of these titles appeared in the Wiley and Putnam Library of Choice Reading (*Chartism *and* Past and Present *were bound together as one volume) in 1846–1847. When the partners split up in early 1848, the stereotype plates for most of the works were purchased by Harper and Brothers. The former partners continued to sell off their remaining stock of Carlyle's works.*

PUTNAM BOOKS BY CARLYLE: *Oliver Cromwell's Letters and Speeches,* 2 volumes, edited by Carlyle (New York: Wiley & Putnam, 1846);

On Heroes, Hero-Worship, and the Heroic in History (New York: Wiley & Putnam, 1846); **first edition,** *On Heroes, Hero-Worship & the Heroic in History* (London: Fraser, 1841; New York: Appleton, 1841);

Sartor Resartus (New York: Wiley & Putnam, 1846); **first edition,** *Sartor Resartus* (Boston: Munroe, 1836; London: Saunders & Otley, 1838);

The French Revolution (New York: Wiley & Putnam, 1846); **first edition,** *The French Revolution: A History* (3 volumes, London: Fraser, 1837; 2 volumes, Boston: Little & Brown, 1838);

Past and Present and *Chartism* (New York: Wiley & Putnam, 1847); **first edition,** *Past and Present* (London: Chapman & Hall, 1843; Boston: Little & Brown, 1843) and *Chartism* (London: Fraser, 1839; Boston: Little & Brown, 1840).

* * *

In his "Books Worth Reading" column Whitman writes enthusiastically about the recently published Wiley and Putnam edition of Oliver Cromwell's Letters and Speeches, *which he notices in the context of a review of the Library of Choice Reading. In all likelihood, the firm had sent the newspaper a review copy of Carlyle's work.*

Carlyle's Cromwell: A dashy, rollicky, most readable book that sets at defiance all the old rules of English composition. It has also another distinguishing difference from nearly all European works relating to that era—the era of the great Cromwell—*it tells the truth.*

    —*Brooklyn Daily Eagle,* 31 January 1846

* * *

In this excerpt from its trade journal Wiley and Putnam announces its intent to publish an authorized edition of Carlyle's works, no doubt hoping to forestall competition. Piracy against its edition nevertheless ensued, reducing profits to both author and publisher.

Messrs. Wiley and Putnam have concluded a copyright contract with Thomas Carlyle, for the publication of a complete series of his works in this country, with the exception of the Miscellany, for which Messrs. Carey and Hart of Philadelphia have already made a similar arrangement. In accordance with this contract, W. and P. have just issued a new edition of "Heroes and Hero Worship," thoroughly revised by the author, with additions. The remaining works, The French Revolution, Sartor Resartus, Past and Present, &c., will follow in rapid succession.

    — *Wiley & Putnam's Literary News-Letter,* 5 (October 1846): 74

* * *

Carlyle, who expected considerable royalties from the Wiley and Putnam editions, writes to E. P. Clark, a Boston bank clerk recommended by Emerson, to request his supervision of the account with the publisher. Clark apparently executed his job professionally; a copy of the records of the various Wiley and Putnam printings, which Carlyle had specifically asked him to collect, survives in the Ralph Waldo Emerson Memorial Association of Harvard. Carlyle came away from the deal embittered, convinced that he received only a small portion of the royalties owed him.

5 Cheyne Row, Chelsea, London
18 March, 1847

My dear Sir,

Tho' I have long known you, in a very kind manner, thro' Mr Emerson and otherwise, and have even made use of you as a practical Friend, our relation, very genuine in itself, has been hitherto a silent one. But now, it would appear, the time for speech too has come. I have a piece of real business to entrust you with; and I must ask you, as a very necessary favour, to take it up in the shape of business, (if you will be so good) to transact and articulately report accordingly.

Last year, as you are aware, in a Contract made with the Messrs. Wiley & Putnam Booksellers of New-York, of which Contract my portion is now in your hands, I took the liberty to nominate you as my representative with them in all pecuniary matters that were to arise in consequence. The Contract is sufficiently explicit: Corrected Copies of my Book with exclusive sanction to print the same; this on my side was the thing promised: on theirs was to be paid a Twentieth-part (I think it is) of the Selling-price of all the copies sold by them; and, what was a very special condition, particularly insisted on as the preliminary of all,—an account as well, and fully payment on the same terms, of all the Copies already sold (from the very first, as well as henceforth) of my Book on Cromwell, concerning which, owing to mistakes between my London Bookseller and them, there had not till then been any bargain between us. These conditions I think you will find clearly set forth in the written Papers, drawn up by Mr Putnam here and signed by both him and me, of which you now hold one, and Mr Wiley (I suppose) the other precisely of the same import.—I have on my side, a good many months ago, furnished Copies of all the Books, with due corrections etc., with an Index to one of them (which was a more considerable improvement); and most of them, I suppose, are now on sale as Printed Books in the United States. On the Messrs. Wiley & Putnam's side I have yet had no results, no money or accounts, or

distinct intimation of such:—solely, about a month ago, Mr Putnam here (whom I hardly ever have occasion to see), writing that a time of settlement was coming, in the "month of June" which is now approaching us. This is the state of the Bargain: all performed on my side, and brought into the preterite tense; on their side, al[l] still waited for (very naturally, I suppose), and to be demanded with due rigour of inspection from the future tenses.

Of Messrs. W. & P.'s intention to keep these terms, as regular merchants and honourable men, I have no reason to entertain the slightest doubt. But it becomes important for me, as you will perceive,—apart even from the probably very considerable pecuniary interests involved in the business,—to ascertain for myself, with the completest possible assurance, that the terms are accurately kept; that no portion of the concern which is really mine in this matter be in any way huddled into twilight and confusion, but that it be all really seen into, managed, and made the best of,—as it beseems all the concerns of a reasonable man, in this exact world, to be. The thing I want, and ought to want, is very clear to you.

Now if you, as a real man of business, will undertake this charge for me, I shall, at all times, with the completest satisfaction I could have in it, be able to assure myself that it is actually getting itself done; that I personally need give myself no more trouble about it. The function to be performed is this simple one: To ascertain in some way that will be convincing to you, How many Copies of my several Books the Messrs Wiley & Putnam do print (for which they zealously promise all manner of facilities, access to their Printers, Papermakers, to their Accounts etc etc); and then at the due term to exact payment for the same. In this country it is not difficult to ascertain in a convincing manner how many copies a Bookseller prints; but it is a thing, too, which cannot be done without trouble, without exertion, scrutiny and locomotion; in fact the whole charge I am struggling to put upon you is founded on work, on trouble.

For which reason, and according to an old principle of mine, I find it altogether indispensable that the man who undertakes this service for me must exact and receive his due professional wages. This is the grand, indeed this is the one condition I shall require of you; if you concede this, I shall full surely understand with myself that this includes all: but, for the same reason, this I say is indispensable. Tell me you undertake the business professionally, for due wages, then the matter is already settled, and you are fully installed and authorized, and I shall be free of care thenceforth;—and over above all wages, you will have done me a favour which I shall deeply acknowledge. About all which, I should hope, there need be no difficulty. But if, for whatever reason, you cannot accept the charge on these terms, then I will request you to consult with Mr Emerson and fix upon a man for me that will; to whom I may straightway consign it in due form; and so, in some good way, be fairly rid of the affair.—This is all I have leave to say for the present; except that (with many real regards and wishes) I am—Yours always truly

T. Carlyle

— reproduced by permission of the Houghton Library, Harvard University, Autograph File

CARLYLE'S WORKS.

Just Published—one vol. cloth, $1.

PAST AND PRESENT, AND CHARTISM.

This Book, "Past and Present," I have read over and revised into a correct state, for Messrs. Wiley and Putnam of New York, who are hereby authorized, they and they only, so far as I can authorize them, to print and vend the same in the United States.   THOMAS CARLYLE.
London, 1846.

2 vols. cloth, $2 50.

FRENCH REVOLUTION.

" An extraordinary work, and one that will be extensively read—for the work possesses all the characteristics of an epic or dramatic poem, founded on historical facts."—*Albion.*

Price 50 cents.

SARTOR RESARTUS.

"Sartor Resartus is the most philosophical and original of any of the works of this strange but powerful writer. Men may find as much fault with Carlyle as they please, but he will be read and admired, not for his crabbed and inverted style of writing, but for the strength, point, and boldness of his thoughts, and the novelty with which he invests the most common-place truths."—*New York Observer.*

Price 50 cents.

HEROES AND HERO WORSHIP.

" A book full of original, fiery thought to stir the souls of men. We could copy whole pages—but everybody will read it whether the press notice it or not."—*Journal of Commerce.*

Two vols. red cloth, $2 50.

CROMWELL'S LETTERS AND SPEECHES.

"'Tis unquestionably the most marked and important book of the season."—*Courier.*

" The work should be largely read, were it only to clear away the mists which poets, dramatists, and novelists throw over the period, in their pictures of cavaliers and roundheads; or to restore Cromwell to his true position as a man of action, in stirring times, without making him, on the one hand, a cold, remorseless hypocrite, or, on the other, a special messenger of vengeance."—*Anglo-American.*

Wiley & Putnam, 161 Broadway.

Advertisement for Wiley and Putnam editions of Carlyle's works in the 17 April 1847 issue of The Literary World

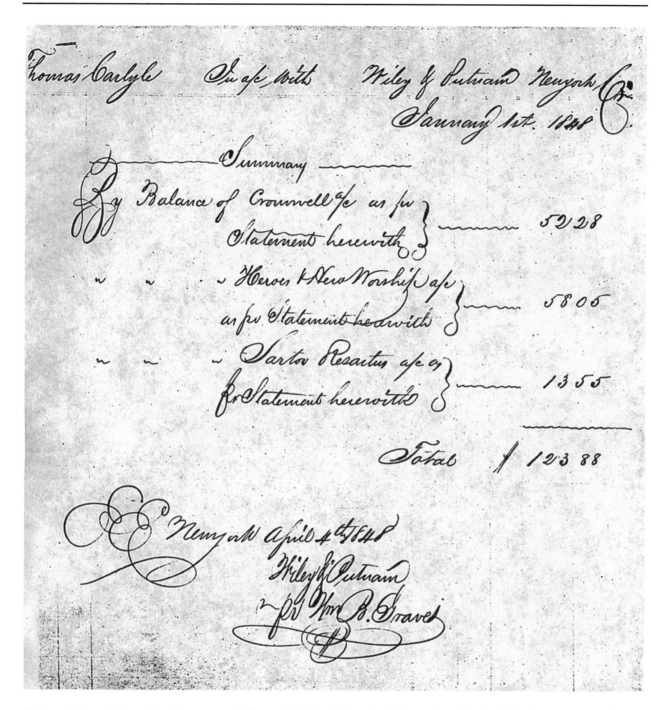

Wiley and Putnam's statement for their account with Thomas Carlyle, in which are listed the author's royalties for the first American edition of Oliver Cromwell's Letters and Speeches, *published in two volumes in 1846, and for the new editions of* On Heroes, Hero-Worship and the Heroic in History *and* Sartor Resartus *(reproduced by permission of the Houghton Library, Harvard University, bMS Am 1280.235 [217]).*

Washington Irving, the House of Putnam's greatest asset and the most respected American writer of his era. The notations at the bottom of the engraving, printed in G. P. Putnam's Homes of American Authors, *are in Putnam's hand.*

Washington Irving

The business relationship between Putnam and Washington Irving (1783–1859) was one of the most profitable, long-lived connections between a publisher and a writer in nineteenth-century America. During his entire career Putnam was recognized as "Irving's publisher." It is no exaggeration to claim that the House of Putnam was built in large part on the profits produced by Irving's enormous and enduring popularity through the middle decades of the century.

Putnam had made Irving's acquaintance as early as the New York Booksellers' Association dinner of March 1837; he met him at various events and places in London, including at his home and office, over the course of the next decade. In the half-dozen years following the 1842 breakup of Irving's longstanding connection with Carey and Hart of Philadelphia, Putnam (or his firm) approached Irving several times with the offer of printing a new edition of his collected works, but Irving politely declined. Finally, in spring 1848, Putnam, just recently in business for himself, made a timely offer for an "author's revised edition" that Irving accepted. Details were finalized and Irving in July signed a contract that gave G. P. Putnam five-year rights to print a revised edition of all of his old works as well as to publish any new works he might write.

With much to gain, the two men lost no time in commencing their venture. Irving worked as fast as he could to provide the revised texts and Putnam as quickly printed them. The first title, A History of New-York, was published on or around 30 August, and other books rapidly followed, though not quite at the monthly rate that Putnam had envisioned. Arrangements were also made for authorized editions to be published by John Murray in London, although that deal was eventually undermined by piracy. In New York, Putnam had sensibly warded off possible competition by warning the trade against importing foreign editions. For the duration of Putnam's career he was effectively Irving's only American publisher.

Putnam exploited his privileged position masterfully, giving Irving's works a breadth of circulation unprecedented for an American fiction writer. G. P. Putnam editions of Irving's books poured off presses in the 1850s and 1860s—illustrated and unillustrated, cheap and expensive, trade and subscription. Putnam was as aggressive in the marketing of Irving's new works as his old ones, especially his long-awaited Life of George Washington (5 volumes, 1855–1859). The arrangement resulted in sales of more than a million volumes, earning the author tens of thousands and his publisher hundreds of thousands of dollars.

PUTNAM BOOKS BY IRVING: *A History of New York*, republished as volume 1 of *The Works of Washington Irving* (New York: G. P. Putnam, 1848; London: G. P. Putnam, 1848); revised edition (New York: G. P. Putnam, 1857); **first edition**, *A History of New York . . .* , 2 volumes, as Diedrich Knickerbocker (New York & Philadelphia: Inskeep & Bradford / Boston: M'Ilhenny / Baltimore: Coale & Thomas / Charleston: Morford, Willington, 1809; revised edition, New York & Philadelphia: Inskeep & Bradford, 1812; London: Murray, 1820);

The Sketch Book of Geoffrey Crayon, republished as volume 2 of *The Works of Washington Irving* (New York: G. P. Putnam, 1848; London: G. P. Putnam, 1848); **first edition**, *The Sketch Book of Geoffrey Crayon, Gent.*, 7 parts, as Geoffrey Crayon (New York: Printed by C. S. Van Winkle, 1819–1820); revised edition, 2 volumes (volume 1, London: John Miller, 1820; volume 2, London: Murray, 1820); revised edition (Paris: Baudry & Didot, 1823);

The Life and Voyages of Christopher Columbus, republished as volumes 3–5 of *The Works of Washington Irving* (New York: G. P. Putnam, 1848–1849; London:

G. P. Putnam, 1848–1849); **first edition,** *Voyages and Discoveries of the Companions of Columbus* (London: Murray, 1831; Philadelphia: Carey & Lea, 1831);

Bracebridge Hall, republished as volume 6 of *The Works of Washington Irving* (New York: G. P. Putnam, 1849; London: G. P. Putnam, 1849); **first edition,** *Bracebridge Hall, or the Humourists. A Medley,* 2 volumes, as Geoffrey Crayon (New York: Printed by C. S. Van Winkle, 1822; London: Murray, 1822);

Tales of a Traveller, republished as volume 7 of *The Works of Washington Irving* (New York: G. P. Putnam, 1849; London: G. P. Putnam, 1849); **first edition,** *Tales of a Traveller,* 2 volumes, as Geoffrey Crayon (London: Murray, 1824; abridged edition, Philadelphia: Carey & Lea, 1824; unabridged edition, New York: Printed by C. S. Van Winkle, 1825);

Astoria, revised as volume 8 of *The Works of Washington Irving* (New York: G. P. Putnam, 1849); **first edition,** *Astoria, or, Enterprise Beyond the Rocky Mountains,* 3 volumes (London: Bentley, 1836); republished as *Astoria, or Anecdotes of an Enterprise Beyond the Rocky Mountains,* 2 volumes (Philadelphia: Carey, Lea & Blanchard, 1836);

A Book of the Hudson (New York: G. P. Putnam, 1849);

The Crayon Miscellany, republished as volume 9 of *The Works of Washington Irving* (New York: G. P. Putnam, 1849; London: G. P. Putnam, 1849)—includes **first edition,** *A Tour on the Prairies,* number 1 of *Miscellanies,* as The Author of *The Sketch Book* (London: Murray, 1835); republished as number 1 of *The Crayon Miscellany* (Philadelphia: Carey, Lea & Blanchard, 1835); **first edition,** *Abbotsford and Newstead Abbey,* number 2 of *Miscellanies,* as The Author of *The Sketch Book* (London: Murray, 1835); republished as number 2 of *The Crayon Miscellany* (Philadelphia: Carey, Lea & Blanchard, 1835); and **first edition,** *Legends of the Conquest of Spain,* number 3 of *Miscellanies,* as The Author of *The Sketch Book* (London: Murray, 1835); republished as number 3 of *The Crayon Miscellany* (Philadelphia: Carey, Lea & Blanchard, 1835);

The Adventures of Captain Bonneville, republished as volume 10 of *The Works of Washington Irving* (New York: G. P. Putnam, 1849; London: G. P. Putnam, 1849); **first edition,** *The Rocky Mountains: Or, Scenes, Incidents, and Adventures in the Far West; Digested from the Journal of Captain B. L. E. Bonneville, of the Army of the United States, and Illustrated from Various Other Sources,* 2 volumes (Philadelphia: Carey, Lea & Blanchard, 1837); republished as *Adventures of Captain Bonneville, or, Scenes beyond the Rocky Mountains of the Far West,* 3 volumes (London: Bentley, 1837);

Oliver Goldsmith: A Biography, revised and enlarged version of *The Miscellaneous Works of Oliver Goldsmith,* published as volume 11 of *The Works of Washington Irving* (New York: G. P. Putnam, 1849 / London: Murray, 1849); **first edition,** *The Miscellaneous Works of Oliver Goldsmith, with an Account of His Life and Writings,* 4 volumes (Paris: Galignani/Didot, 1825); biography revised in *The Life of Oliver Goldsmith, with Selections from His Writings,* 2 volumes (New York: Harper, 1840);

Mahomet and His Successors, volumes 12–13 of *The Works of Washington Irving* (New York: G. P. Putnam, 1850);

A Chronicle of the Conquest of Granada, republished as volume 14 of *The Works of Washington Irving* (New York: G. P. Putnam / London: Murray, 1850); **first edition,** *A Chronicle of the Conquest of Granada,* 2 volumes, as Fray Antonio Agapida (Philadelphia: Carey, Lea & Carey, 1829; London: Murray, 1829);

The Alhambra, revised as volume 15 of *The Works of Washington Irving* (New York: G. P. Putnam, 1851); **first edition,** *The Alhambra,* 2 volumes, as Geoffrey Crayon (London: Colburn & Bentley, 1832); as The Author of *The Sketch Book,* 2 volumes (Philadelphia: Carey & Lea, 1832); revised as *The Alhambra: A Series of Sketches of the Moors and Spaniards by the Author of "The Sketch Book"* (Philadelphia: Carey, Lea & Blanchard, 1836);

Wolfert's Roost and Other Papers, republished as volume 16 of *The Works of Washington Irving* (New York: G. P. Putnam and Company, 1855); **first edition,** *Chronicles of Wolfert's Roost and Other Papers* (Edinburgh: Constable, Low / London: Hamilton, Adams / Dublin: MGlashan, 1855);

Life of George Washington, 5 volumes (New York: G. P. Putnam, 1855–1859; London: Bohn, 1855–1859);

Salmagundi (New York: G. P. Putnam and Company, 1857); **first edition,** *Salmagundi; or, the Whim-whams and Opinions of Launcelot Langstaff, Esq. & Others,* by Irving, William Irving, and James Kirke Paulding, 20 parts, republished in 2 volumes (New York: D. Longworth, 1807–1808; London: Printed for J. M. Richardson, 1811; revised edition, New York: D. Longworth, 1814; revised by Irving, Paris: Galignani, 1824; Paris: Baudry, 1824);

Spanish Papers and Other Miscellanies, Hitherto Unpublished or Uncollected, 2 volumes, edited by Pierre M. Irving (New York: G. P. Putnam / Hurd & Houghton, 1866; London: Low, 1866).

* * *

In this letter to Putnam, George Inness (1825–1894) reports on the assignment he was given to draw a sketch of Sunnyside, Irving's house overlooking the Hudson River. Innes, who became one of the foremost American landscape painters of the nineteenth century, was in the earliest stage of his career in the late 1840s.

                                        Tarrytown   July 30th 1849

Sir

I have after a great deal of difficulty furnished a drawing of Mr. Irving's house. The situation of the house and grounds made it necessary for me to make rather a compilation from several different points than an ordinary sketch first to the front within 30 feet of the house then to another and more distant point[,] and so changing from point to point and distance to distance and arranging all the different perspectives in one constant whole rendered the drawing a very tedious and lengthy operation. I also send you the drawing of West Point. I hope you will be pleased with both. I do not wish to charge you anything extravagant but they have taken so much of my time and been so considerable in expense that $20 each will not pay at as good a rate as $5 would for my largest drawings done at home[;] if however you think it more than you can afford as I know you have already spent considerable on the Irving place I shall be satisfied with the ordinary price. If you can send me the money within a few days I shall be very much obliged to you as I have not enough to finish my summer trip. As you are anxious to have the minutiae of the house I will send you my larger sketch in a few days. Tell the engraver not to work on the building until he gets it as it may assist him very materially. Yours most respectfully,

                                        Geo. Inness

– George Palmer Putnam Correspondence, Manuscripts and Archives Division, The New York Public Library, Astor, Lenox and Tilden Foundations

                                        * * *

Putnam was quick to announce his ambitious undertaking with Irving and to ply the press with information about it as the series progressed, as in the following announcement. In contrast to what is reported here, A History of New York *at the last moment replaced* The Sketch Book of Geoffrey Crayon *as the initial volume to accommodate Irving. The Irving edition eventually stretched to twenty-one volumes, including the five-volume* Life of George Washington.

GEORGE P. PUTNAM, New York, has in preparation a complete and uniform edition of Washington Irving's works, the first volume of which, to contain the Sketch Book, will be issued the 1st of September. The whole series, revised and enlarged by the author, will be comprised in twelve duodecimo volumes, and will be illustrated by engravings on wood from designs by Darley. Mr. Irving has been some time preparing the Life of Mohammed, the Life of Washington, and several new volumes of Miscellanies and Biographies, which will be issued at intervals, in connexion with the other writings.

                                        – The Literary World, 3 (10 June 1848): 370

                                        * * *

Newspapers and magazines gave extensive coverage to the author's revised edition, volume by volume, beginning with the appearance of A History of New York *in September 1848.*

PUTNAM'S Edition of this celebrated work, forms the first volume of Irving's works now about to be issued complete from the press of the same publisher. "Knickerbocker's History" laid the corner stone of Washington Irving's fame; and our last perusal of the work convinces us that his genius can never be rightly understood or appreciated by one not familiar with the work. It not only contains the germs of everything that is characteristic of his later writings, but it also conveys an idea of powers far beyond anything he has ever accomplished, justly high and permanent as is his reputation in letters.

It has often occurred to us that there are two stages in the life of an author in which the peculiarities of his genius come out to the best advantage. The one is, when yet unknown to fame, his "utterances" (as Miss Martineau would call them) are instinctively from himself; the other comes, when heartsick with writing up to a reputation, his pen is resorted to only to enforce some favorite theme, or relieve his unoccupied feelings. With reputation, springs up consciousness; and the real man never comes out while he thinks of an audience, or attempts to write up to expectation. Hence it is that some of the best productions of Genius after it has attained celebrity, have been given to the word anonymously.

But we will venture further. We are strongly disposed to think then, that writing for pecuniary profit is more favorable to strong and healthy production than writing for fame. Were it otherwise, why would not amateur writers have left something behind them to compete in value with the works of professional authors? The pursuit of fame must necessarily bring that *consciousness* with it, which, as we

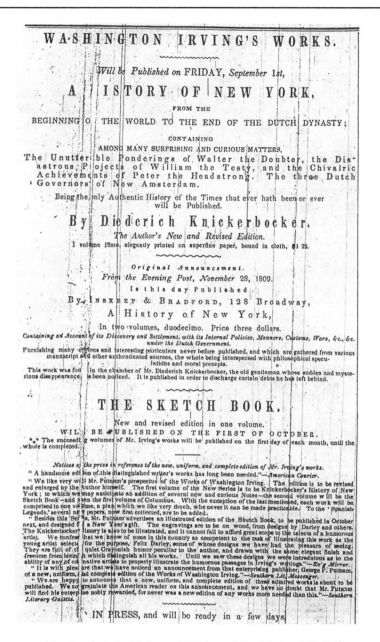

Advertisement in the 26 August 1848 issue of The Literary World

have before said, is fatal to single-minded effort. But how is it, when "vile lucre" is the object? Why the author avenges himself for subjection to the hard needs of life by the indulgence of his own mental writings. Shakspeare wrote his poems for Fame, and those poems speak only the taste and the thoughts of the age in which he lived. He wrote his dramas for money, and they transcend the taste, and speak to the thoughts of all time. In one of his Sonnets, the player-poet says:–

> "Oh, childe thou no' because my nature is subdued,
> Even like the dyer's hand, by what it works in."

"What it works in" being the grub-street duty of furbishing up old plays, or dramatising the novels of the day for the Globe Theatre. Prisoned into this work-house of literary toil, the poet avenged himself on his destiny by giving all freedom to the play of his imagination and feelings–until the common materials out of which he was called upon to produce his fabric were enwrought so richly from the exhaustless prodigality of his own mind, that they came forth new and fresh creations to the wondering world.

Yet had Shakspeare been called upon to write a prize poem for the Drury Lane Theatre of that day, he would not perhaps have soared above half a dozen writers of his time.

We are aware that all this is directly in the teeth of the popular notion of the action of genius. That spoilt and conceited animal, the public, always insists upon believing that genius works as directly with reference to its approval as does a street-pavior for that of the Board of Aldermen. But it is a great mistake to suppose that because there must be design in every great work of literature or art, that the *intention* of it is a design upon public approval. The patriot, Tell, would wish to be remembered and applauded by his countrymen. But when he seized the sword and lifted his Country's flag he struck not for honor or reputation-sake; but the emotion which impelled him made him willing to die unforgotten in her meanest ditch, if by his death he could serve her. He would have been a player and not a patriot, had he struck for the world's applause, instead of lifting his arm as he did for a cause and from a feeling which transcends all reference to men's praises. Exactly so it is with the true artist, whether poet, author, or painter, in their happiest efforts. They work *from* themselves—and not *at* the world, however grateful they may be for its cheer when faint and weary with their spirit-tasking, and needing some external stimulus for a fresh effort.

But the reader marvels how all this solemn didacticism can be suggested by a burlesque history like that of Knickerbocker. The connexion, if not already implied, is a most simple one; for *spontaneity* of feeling characterizes throughout this early production of the now illustrious pen to which that quality is not generally accorded by the warmest admirers of the Sketch-Book. The very origin of the work originated in impulsive whim, as is told by its author in the following introduction, written this summer. . . .

— *The Literary World,* 3 (2 September 1848): 604–607

* * *

Putnam published Irving's works in a variety of formats designed to reach every stratum of book buyers. One of his most successful strategies was to produce illustrated as well as standard editions of the major works. As a result, he hired some of the leading artists of the day. In the following letter, Irving appeals to Charles R. Leslie for a sketch to be used in the forthcoming illustrated edition of A History of New York.

New-York, Octr 19th. 1848

My dear Leslie,

Mr Putnam of this city is publishing a revised edition of my works, which meets with success beyond my expectations[.] Next Spring he will put forth an illustrated edition of Knickerbocker[.] I wish you would give me a pen or pencil sketch of Diedrich for a frontispiece[.] I think you could hit off my idea of the little Dutch Historian better than any one else. There is a vile caricature of him which was published with an American edition while I was in Europe, and which is copied on all the Knickerbocker Omnibuses Steam boats &c &c. I wish a genuine likeness of him to supplant it

I scrawl this in great haste just as Mr Putnam is on the point of embarking

With kind remembrances to Mrs Leslie and your family

Yours ever my dear Leslie / Most affectionately

Washington Irving

— *Clifton Waller Barrett Library of American Literature, Special Collections Department, University of Virginia Library*

* * *

Eager to serve Irving on all fronts, Putnam arranged for the English publication of some of the volumes in the author's revised edition series with John Murray, the leading literary publisher in London. The deal brought together Irving with his original London publisher and Putnam with his chief partner in transatlantic publishing. Although potentially lucrative to both Irving and Murray, the arrangement proved vulnerable to the inherent difficulties of international publishing. In this letter to Putnam a senior associate of Murray, Robert Cooke, expresses some of the concerns of his firm. Frustrating as the situation then was, it soon grew worse as local pirates began to infringe on Irving's London copyright, which was dependent on prior English publication.

Albemarle St.   London
Aug. 29, 1849

My dear Sir,

Mr. Murray is in receipt both of your letter communicating the new life of Goldsmith by Mr. Irving and also of the sheets themselves & I therefore lose no time in acknowledging them & also making known Mr. Murray's acceptance of the offer made by you of the stereotyped plates of the same for £60, with the understanding of paying the author 10% on the same conditions as agreed for the Lives of Mahomed & Washington.

The only drawback we see to the entire success of these Biographies in this country, is the rapidity in which they are appearing. The public are taken too suddenly & cannot understand an author writing at such speed, forgetting that they are works which have been in hand so long. We do not wish to publish Goldsmith before <u>December</u> & yet you say it will be issued after the work has been forwarded to us. It will compel us to send it forth earlier.

Can you give us any idea as to when Mahomed or Washington will be ready. We have not yet published Columbus or Knickerbocker. We have only a season of 6 months—now we are doing nothing & it is a certain loss & failure to publish at all. When you can do give us notice & breathing time. . . .

I am My dear Sir

faithfully Yours

Robt. Cooke

Mr. G. P. Putnam

> *—Manuscripts Division, Department of Rare Books and Special Collections, Princeton University Library. Published with permission of the Princeton University Library.*

* * *

Putnam kept Irving's holiday thank-you note in his scrapbook. Widely reprinted after Irving's death, the letter became a central document in the emerging narrative of friendly relations between Victorian authors and publishers in the United States.

Sunnyside   Dec 27ᵗʰ 1852

My dear Sir,

Your parcel of books reached me on Christmas morning; your letter not being addressed to Dearman went to Tarrytown and did not come to hand until to-day.

My nieces join with me in thanking you for the beautiful books you have sent us, and you and Mrs Putnam for your wishes for a merry Christmas and a happy New Year.

For my own especial part let me say how sensibly I appreciate the kind tone and expressions of your letter, but as to your talk of obligations to me I am conscious of none that have not been fully counterbalanced on your part; and I take pleasure in expressing the great satisfaction I have derived, throughout all our intercourse, from your amiable, obliging and honorable conduct. Indeed I never had dealings with any man, whether in the way of business or friendship more perfectly free from any alloy.

That these dealings have been profitable is mainly owing to your own sagacity and enterprise. You had confidence in the continued vitality of my writings when [name excised] had almost persuaded me they were defunct. You called them again into active existence and gave them a circulation that I believe has surprised even yourself. In rejoicing at their success my satisfaction is doubly enhanced by the idea that you share in the benefits derived from it.

Wishing you that continued prosperity in business, which your upright, enterprising, truthful and liberal mode of conducting it merits, and is calculated to ensure; and again invoking on you and yours a happy New Year

I remain very truly & heartily

Yours,

Washington Irving

Geo. P. Putnam Esq

> *—Manuscripts Division, Department of Rare Books and Special Collections, Princeton University Library. Published with permission of the Princeton University Library.*

* * *

Despite his firm's limited finances and the economic instability caused by the Civil War, Putnam gambled on the enduring popularity of The Sketch Book of Geoffrey Crayon, *bringing out one of the most lavishly illustrated and finely manufactured editions he ever published. The following notice appeared in the trade journal.*

G. P. PUTNAM, of New York, has had in preparation for several years an illustrated edition of Irving's "Sketch Book," which is now on the eve of completion, and which promises to leave nothing to be desired in the way of printing, engraving, or binding. It is appropriately termed "The Artist's Edition," and contains original designs from nearly every American artist of distinction. These have been printed with the utmost care by Mr. Alvord, whose workmanship is of the best, and has received commendation as such from Mr. Burton, in his "Book Hunter." The binding, in Levant morocco, is by Mathews; the paper is of especial manufacture; and the whole work will be the embodiment of the taste, experience, and judgment of Irving's friend and publisher, Mr. Putnam. The sole drawback is that owing to the great embarrassments that beset publishers at this time in our country, from the scarcity of skilled labor, only a limited edition can be supplied this season, and those wishing the work should make their wants known as early as possible. The same publisher has prepared for subscribers a large paper edition of Irving's works, and of his Life and Letters by his nephew, of which but one hundred copies have been printed, and a small portion only remain unappropriated. The Hudson Legends, comprising "Sleepy Hollow" and "Rip Van Winkle," have been prepared in small quarto, and may be had, either separately in paper covers, or together in a neat volume, choicely illustrated.

> *— American Literary Gazette and Publishers' Circular,* octavo series, 2 (2 November 1863): 7

* * *

Advertisement in American Literary Gazette and Publishers' Circular *for one of the most expensive books ever produced by G. P. Putnam. The firm shared the expenses with Henry Holt, who was just beginning his publishing career.*

This brief account of Irving's publication history was occasioned by Putnam's recent article on Irving, "Memories of Distinguished Authors, Washington Irving," which was published in the 27 May 1871 issue of Harper's Weekly.

Mr. Geo. P. Putnam, of New York, has contributed to the illustrated series, "Memoirs of Distinguished Authors," now appearing in "Harper's Weekly," a sketch of Washington Irving, with portraits and views of Sunnyside, and neighboring places associated with the personality of "Geoffrey Crayon." It occupies over four pages, and is full of information—as it ought to be, for Mr. Putnam was Irving's friend as well as publisher—and chronicles the gratifying fact that the uniform edition of his works, commenced in 1848, at a time when it was generally supposed any republication would scarcely pay expenses, has yielded $150,000 to Irving and his representatives. Precisely in the same manner, in 1829, when the chief marketable value of the "Waverley Novels" was supposed to have ceased, Mr.

Robert Cadell induced Scott to write new Introductions and Notes, and the sale was, and still is, enormous. The American publishers of Irving's works have been successively: 1. D. Longworth, at the "Shakspeare Gallery," who produced "Salmagundi," in little yellow-covered weekly numbers, in 1807. 2. Inskeep & Bradford, 128 Broadway, who issued "Knickerbocker," in 1809. 3. C. S. Van Winkle, who printed (for the author) "The Sketch Book," in handsome octavo numbers, in 1820. ("Bracebridge" and "The Traveller" were first published in New York, in numbers, for the author.) 4. G. & C. Carvill, corner of Broadway and Wall Street, issued "Columbus," in two octavo volumes, in 1829. 5. Carey & Lea, Philadelphia, published the first editions of "Alhambra," "Granada," "Crayon," "Bonneville," and "Astoria," and reprints of the earlier works.

– *American Literary Gazette and Publishers' Circular,* 17 (1 June 1871): 60

James Fenimore Cooper, who became a Putnam author near the end of his career. This engraving, which was made from a Mathew Brady photograph, was published in Homes of American Authors.

James Fenimore Cooper

James Fenimore Cooper (1789–1851) began his career as a loyal client of Charles Wiley, the father of Putnam's future partner in Wiley and Putnam. After his father's death, the younger Wiley published Cooper's A Letter to His Countrymen *(1834), but he lacked the financial wherewithal to lure Cooper away from Carey and Lea of Philadelphia (from 1839, Lea and Blanchard), with whom the author published from 1825 until the mid 1840s.*

Shortly after reaching his agreement with Washington Irving, Putnam made Cooper a similar offer to bring out revised versions of his earlier works in well-made, uniform hardbound editions. Tempted but wary, Cooper agreed to a more limited arrangement whereby he leased printing rights to G. P. Putnam for some of his earlier works while also allowing the New York firm of Stringer and Townsend to publish competing editions. Putnam's series of revised editions of Cooper's works was launched in

April or May 1849 with The Spy. *A dozen more titles followed over the course of the next two years, including the Leatherstocking series. The firm also brought out Cooper's latest—and, as it turned out, last—novel,* The Ways of the Hour, *in April 1850. The cheaper editions produced by Stringer and Townsend ulitimately undermined the profitable basis of Putnam's editions and made them less successful financially than the revised editions of Irving's works. Putnam chose not to request an extension after the lapse of the original contract.*

Putnam was widely identified with Cooper by the time of the author's death in September 1851. The publisher honored Cooper by organizing testimonials in New York and by compiling and seeing to press a collection of tributes, Memorial of James Fenimore Cooper *(1852). Cooper, who was already regarded as a founding figure in the history of American letters, was also celebrated later that year in* Homes of American Authors.

PUTNAM BOOKS BY COOPER: *The Spy,* revised edition (New York: G. P. Putnam, 1849); **first edition,** *The Spy,* anonymous, 2 volumes (New York: Wiley & Halstead, 1821; London: Whittaker, 1822);

The Pilot, revised edition (New York: G. P. Putnam, 1849); **first edition,** *The Pilot,* anonymous, 2 volumes (New York: Charles Wiley, 1823; London: Miller, 1824);

The Ways of the Hour, anonymous (New York: G. P. Putnam, 1850; London: Bentley, 1850);

The Red Rover, revised edition (New York: G. P. Putnam, 1850; **first edition,** *The Red Rover,* 2 volumes (Philadelphia: Carey, Lea & Carey / London: Henry Colburn, 1827);

The Deerslayer, revised edition (New York: G. P. Putnam, 1850); **first edition,** *The Deerslayer,* anonymous, 2 volumes (Philadelphia: Lea & Blanchard / London: Bentley, 1841);

The Last of the Mohicans, revised edition (New York: G. P. Putnam, 1850); **first edition,** *The Last of the Mohicans,* anonymous, 2 volumes (Philadelphia: Carey & Lea / London: Miller, 1826);

The Pioneers, revised edition (New York: G. P. Putnam, 1851); **first edition,** *The Pioneers,* anonymous, 2 volumes (New York: Wiley / London: Murray, 1823);

The Pathfinder, revised edition (New York: G. P. Putnam, 1851); **first edition,** *The Pathfinder,* anonymous (3 volumes, London: Bentley / 2 volumes, Philadelphia: Lea & Blanchard, 1840);

The Prairie, revised edition (New York: G. P. Putnam, 1851); **first edition,** *The Prairie,* anonymous (3 volumes, London: Colburn / 2 volumes, Philadelphia: Carey, Lea & Carey, 1827);

The Wing-and-Wing, revised edition (New York: G. P. Putnam, 1851); **first edition,** *The Jack O'Lantern,*

3 volumes (London: Bentley, 1842); republished as *The Wing-and-Wing,* anonymous, 2 volumes (Philadelphia: Lea & Blanchard, 1842);

The Water-Witch, revised edition (New York: G. P. Putnam, 1851); **first edition,** *The Water-Witch,* anonymous (3 volumes, Dresden: Walther / 2 volumes, London: Colburn & Bentley, 1830; 1 volume, Philadelphia: Carey & Lea, 1831);

The Two Admirals, revised edition (New York: G. P. Putnam, 1851); **first edition,** *The Two Admirals* (3 volumes, London: Bentley / anonymous, 2 volumes, Philadelphia: Lea & Blanchard, 1842);

History of the Navy of the United States of America, republished by Putnam (New York: G. P. Putnam and Company, 1853); **first edition,** *The History of the Navy of the United States of America,* 2 volumes (Philadelphia: Lea & Blanchard / London: Bentley, 1839).

* * *

Although Cooper was expected to write new introductions and to revise the texts for the author's edition, his changes were often minimal and never extensive. For his introduction to the 1851 Putnam edition of The Pioneers, *for example, he interpolated the paragraphs below near the end of his introduction to the 1831 edition of the novel.*

It may be well to say here, a little more explicitly, that there was no intention to describe with particular accuracy any real characters in this book. It has been often said, and in published statements, that the heroine of this book was drawn after a sister of the writer, who was killed by a fall from a horse now near half a century since. So ingenious is conjecture that a personal resemblance has been discovered between the fictitious character and the deceased relative! It is scarcely possible to describe two females of the same class in life, who would be less alike, personally, than Elizabeth Temple and the sister of the author who met with the deplorable fate mentioned. In a word, they were as unlike in this respect as in history, character, and fortunes.

Circumstances rendered this sister singularly dear to the author. After a lapse of half a century, he is writing this paragraph with a pain that would induce him to cancel it, were it not still more painful to have it believed that one whom he regarded with a reverence that surpassed the love of a brother was converted by him into the heroine of a work of fiction.

* * *

Like many of his contemporaries, this anonymous reviewer for The Literary World *linked Cooper with Irving as the premier American fiction writers and applauded the handsome new revised editions being brought out by G. P. Putnam, whose uniform format for the works of the two authors reinforced the coupling.*

IT is pleasant to see the names of Cooper and Irving brought together again, by Mr. Putnam, in the new uniform editions of their works. We have always been accustomed to associate them in our own minds, and have never liked to see them separated. The Spy and the Sketch-Book were the first American books, which were universally acknowledged to contain a performance as well as a promise. We well remember the enthusiasm with which they were received, and the proud expectations which they awakened among the liberal-minded abroad and the patriotic at home. Irving was soon allowed a seat by the sides of Goldsmith and Addison; and Cooper was translated in every country of the Continent, where any interest was felt in a foreign literature. It was a noble beginning, and has been nobly maintained: for after all that we have done, and we certainly have done much when the whole question is considered, these are still the great names of American literature.

We know that it has been somewhat the fashion of late years to quarrel with Cooper. There is an element of combativeness in the great novelist's character, which has been pretty fully developed. He has told a great many unwelcome truths, and seldom taken pains to sweeten the edge of his bowl. When a statesman writes his memoirs, or a historian proposes a history of his own times, if he be rich in worldly wisdom, he generally leaves his manuscript to his heirs and keeps his contemporaries quiet by the dread of a possible castigation or the hope of future praise. But woe to the unhappy man if a chapter or a page ever finds its way into the world before he has made his way out of it. Friends and foes fall upon him together. Sincerity is no protection. Uprightness and honesty no good. Even truth itself can shield him with only a very few. He is bigoted; he is blind; and these are the least of his offences. We do not love the truth, and how can we be expected to love those who tell it?

Now, this has been the case with Mr. Cooper. He has indulged in contemporary history, and he has paid the penalty. But if high motives could atone for so grave an offence, he might well hope to be excused. There never was a more thorough-hearted American man than he; one who felt more deeply the dignity of Republican citizenship, or who sustained it more worthily. If all of Mr. Cooper's European life were known, his uniform kindness to all of his countrymen who needed it, his liberal encouragement of American artists, his judicious defence of American principles, and his manly adherence to them under all circumstances and in spite of allurements a hundredth part of which would have shipwrecked the Republicanism of three-fourths of our travellers, he would be acknowledged to have written much of that which has galled us so deeply, more in sorrow than in bitterness.

We trust that Mr. Putnam is going to set all this right by bringing out all of Cooper's works together, in that elegant and tasteful style which he understands so well. We shall then see if there is any work, or series of works, in which American character appears so well as a whole, and yet is drawn so fearlessly, and with such masterly skill. We are looking forward to some very happy hours from this republication. One of the happiest half-hours a book ever gave us, we owe to that admirable custom which our newspapers once followed, of giving us a foretaste of every new publication while it was on its way through the press. It was when all the world was looking eagerly for something new from the author of the Spy. The "Pioneers" was announced, and before it got fully into the world, the "wild cat" scene was published in a New York daily. It was our first glance into an American forest, and our first shake of the hand with Leatherstocking. We were somewhat younger then than we are now, and had not reached that privileged age in which you are allowed to be the first to seize upon the newspaper. But we were allowed to hear it read, and never shall we forget the feelings with which we watched the efforts of poor old "Brave" (for it seemed as if we were looking on, instead of listening), nor the terror which we felt, as the wild cat turned from his dead body to glance at that of her young, and then back again to the defenceless maiden, nor the thrill of delight with which we heard old "Leatherstocking's" words–"Stoop your head lower, gall, your bonnet hides the creature's head." And next we had the "Devil's Grip," in the same way, and then the glorious "Bunker's Hill," the only truly graphic description of that most American of battles that has ever been written.

Mr. Putnam begins as, in fact, Cooper's fame did, with the Spy–the first work which opened the rich veins of American life and scenery for the historical novelist, and which, through all the lights and shades of the author's popularity, has kept its place firmly. Harvey Birch is a shadowing forth of Natty Bumpo–"a coming event casting before" one of those shadows which men never forget; and nowhere, out of history, has Washington ever been introduced with anything like success, but in Harper.

The new edition of Mr. Cooper's novels is to be revised, corrected, and illustrated, with a new introduction, notes, &c. From the interesting preface to the "Spy" before us, we glean a few facts which may gratify the lovers of the "curiosities of literature". . . .

– *The Literary World,* 4 (5 May 1849): 393–394

* * *

Francis Parkman

The author of this unsigned overview of Cooper's career in The North American Review, *occasioned and perhaps made possible by Cooper's recent death, is the distinguished historian Francis Parkman, who had made a national reputation as an expert on the geography and ethnography of the American West with* California and Oregon Trail *(G. P. Putnam, 1849). Parkman provides one of the most comprehensive, astute contemporaneous analyses of Cooper's strengths and weaknesses as a writer as well as an assessment of what he sees as a still "provincial" literary culture.*

No American writer has been so extensively read as James Fenimore Cooper. His novels have been translated into nearly every European tongue. Nay, we are told–but hardly know how to believe it–that they may be had duly rendered into Persian at the bazaars of Ispahan. We have seen some of them, well thumbed and worn, at a little village in a remote mountainous district of Sicily; and in Naples and Milan, the book-stalls bear witness that "*L'Ultimo dei Mohecanni*" is still a popular work. In England, these American novels have been eagerly read and transformed into popular dramas; while cheap and often stupidly mutilated editions of them have been circulated through all her colonies, garrisons, and naval stations, from New Zealand to Canada.

Nor is this widely spread popularity undeserved. Of all American writers, Cooper is the most original, the most thoroughly national. His genius drew aliment from the soil where God had planted it, and rose to a vigorous growth, rough and gnarled, but strong as a mountain cedar. His volumes are a faithful mirror of that rude transatlantic nature, which to European eyes appears so strange and new. The sea and the forest have been the scenes of his countrymen's most conspicuous achievements; and it is on the sea and in the forest that Cooper is most at home. Their spirit inspired him, their images were graven on his heart; and the men whom their embrace has nurtured, the sailor, the hunter, the pioneer, move and act upon his pages with all the truth and energy of real life.

There is one great writer with whom Cooper has been often compared, and the comparison is not void of justice; for though, on the whole, far inferior, there are certain points of literary excellence in regard to which he may contest the palm with Sir Walter Scott. It is true, that he has no claim to share the humor and pathos, the fine perception of beauty and delicacy in character, which adds such charms to the romances of Scott. Nor can he boast that compass and variety of power, which could deal alike with forms of humanity so diverse; which could portray with equal mastery the Templar Bois Guilbert, and the Jewess Rebecca; the manly heart of Henry Morton, and the gentle heroism of Jeanie Deans. But notwithstanding this unquestioned inferiority on the part of Cooper, there were marked affinities between him and his great contemporary. Both were practical men, able and willing to grapple with the hard realities of the world. Either might have learned with ease to lead a regiment, or command a line-of-battle ship. Their conceptions of character were no mere abstract ideas, or unsubstantial images, but solid embodiments in living flesh and blood. Bulwer and Hawthorne—the conjunction may excite a smile—are writers of a different stamp. Their conceptions are often exhibited with consummate skill, and, in one of these examples at least, with admirable truthfulness; but they never cheat us into a belief of their reality. We may marvel at the skill of the artist, but we are prone to regard his creations rather as figments of art than as reproductions of nature,—as a series of vivified and animate pictures, rather than as breathing men and women. With Scott and with Cooper it is far otherwise. Dominie Sampson and the Antiquary are as distinct and familiar to our minds as some eccentric acquaintance of our childhood. If we met Long Tom Coffin on the wharf at New Bedford, we should wonder where we had before seen that familiar face and figure. The tall, gaunt form

of Leatherstocking, the weather-beaten face, the bony hand, the cap of fox-skin, and the old hunting frock, polished with long service, seem so palpable and real, that, in some moods of mind, one may easily confound them with the memories of his own experiences. Others have been gifted to conceive the elements of far loftier character, and even to combine these elements in a manner equally truthful; but few have rivalled Cooper in the power of breathing into his creations the breath of life, and turning the phantoms of his brain into seeming realities. It is to this, in no small measure that he owes his widely spread popularity. His most successful portraitures are drawn, it is true, from humble walks and rude associations; yet they are instinct with life, and stamped with the impress of a masculine and original genius.

The descriptions of external nature with which Cooper's works abound bear a certain analogy to his portraitures of character. There is no glow upon his pictures, no warm and varied coloring, no studied contrast of light and shade. Their virtue consists in their fidelity, in the strength with which they impress themselves upon the mind, and the strange tenacity with which they cling to the memory. For our own part, it was many years since we had turned the pages of Cooper, but still we were haunted by the images which his spell had evoked;—the dark gleaming of hill-embosomed lakes, the tracery of forest boughs against the red evening sky, and the raven flapping his black wings above the carnage field near the Horican. These descriptions have often, it must be confessed, the grave fault of being overloaded with detail; but they are utterly mistaken who affirm, as some have done, that they are but a catalogue of commonplaces,—mountains and woods, rivers and torrents, thrown together as a matter of course. A genuine love of nature inspired the artist's pen; and they who cannot feel the efficacy of its strong picturing have neither heart nor mind for the grandeur of the outer world.

Before proceeding, however, we must observe that, in speaking of Cooper's writings, we have reference only to those happier offspring of his genius which form the basis of his reputation; for, of that numerous progeny which of late years have swarmed from his pen, we have never read one, and therefore, notwithstanding the ancient usage of reviewers, do not think ourselves entitled to comment upon them.

The style of Cooper is, as style must always be, in no small measure the exponent of the author's mind. It is not elastic or varied, and is certainly far from elegant. Its best characteristics are a manly directness, and a freedom from those prettinesses, studied turns of expression, and petty tricks of rhetoric, which are the pride of less masculine writers. Cooper is no favorite with *dilettanti* critics. In truth, such criticism does not suit his case. He should be measured on deeper principles, not by his manner, but by his pith and substance. A rough diamond, and he is one of the roughest, is worth more than a jewel of paste, though its facets may not shine so clearly.

And yet, try Cooper by what test we may, we shall discover in him grave defects. The field of his success is, after all, a narrow one, and even in his best works he often oversteps its limits. His attempts at sentiment are notoriously unsuccessful. Above all, when he aspires to portray a heroine, no words can express the remarkable character of the product. With simple country girls he succeeds somewhat better; but when he essays a higher flight, his failure is calamitous. The most rabid asserter of the rights of woman is scarcely more ignorant of woman's true power and dignity. This is the more singular, as his novels are very far from being void of feeling. They seldom, however–and who can wonder at it?–find much favor with women, who for the most part can see little in them but ghastly stories of shipwrecks, ambuscades, and bush fights, mingled with prolix descriptions and stupid dialogues. Their most appreciating readers may perhaps be found, not among persons of sedentary and studious habits, but among those of a more active turn, military officers and the like, whose tastes have not been trained into fastidiousness, and who are often better qualified than literary men to feel the freshness and truth of the author's descriptions.

The merit of a novelist is usually measured less by his mere power of description than by his skill in delineating character. The permanency of Cooper's reputation must, as it seems to us, rest upon three or four finely conceived and admirably executed portraits. We do not allude to his Indian characters, which it must be granted, are for the most part either superficially or falsely drawn; while the long conversations which he puts into their mouths, are as truthless as they are tiresome. Such as they are, however, they have been eagerly copied by a legion of the smaller poets and novel writers; so that, jointly with Thomas Campbell, Cooper is responsible for the fathering of those aboriginal heroes, lovers, and sages, who have long formed a petty nuisance in our literature. The portraits of which we have spoken are all those of white men, from humble ranks of society, yet not of a mean or vulgar stamp. Conspicuous before them all stands the well known figure of Leatherstocking. The life and character of this personage are contained in a series of five independent novels, entitled, in honor of him, The Leatherstocking Tales. Cooper has been censured, and even ridiculed, for this frequent reproduction of his favorite hero, which, it is affirmed, argues poverty of invention; and

yet there is not one of the tales in question with which we would willingly part. To have drawn such a character is in itself sufficient honor; and had Cooper achieved nothing else, this alone must have insured him a wide and merited renown. There is something admirably felicitous in the conception of this hybrid offspring of civilization and barbarism, in whom uprightness, kindliness, innate philosophy, and the truest moral perceptions are joined with the wandering instincts and hatred of restraint which stamp the Indian or the Bedouin. Nor is the character in the least unnatural. The white denizens of the forest and the prairie are often among the worst, though never among the meanest, of mankind; but it is equally true, that where the moral instincts are originally strong, they may find nutriment and growth among the rude scenes and grand associations of the wilderness. Men as true, generous, and kindly as Leatherstocking may still be found among the perilous solitudes of the West. The quiet, unostentatious courage of Cooper's hero had its counterpart in the character of Daniel Boone; and the latter had the same unaffected love of nature which forms so pleasing a feature in the mind of Leatherstocking.

Civilization has a destroying as well as a creating power. It is exterminating the buffalo and the Indian, over whose fate too many lamentations, real or affected, have been sounded for us to renew them here. It must, moreover, eventually sweep from before it a class of men, its own precursors and pioneers, so remarkable both in their virtues and their faults, that few will see their extinction without regret. Of these men Leatherstocking is the representative; and though in him the traits of the individual are quite as prominent as those of the class, yet his character is not on this account less interesting, or less worthy of permanent remembrance. His life conveys in some sort an epitome of American history, during one of its most busy and decisive periods. At first, we find him a lonely young hunter in what was then the wilderness of New York. Ten or twelve years later, he is playing his part manfully in the Old French War. After the close of the Revolution, we meet him again on the same spot where he was first introduced to us; but now every thing is changed. The solitary margin of the Otsego lake is transformed into the seat of a growing settlement, and the hunter, oppressed by the restraints of society, turns his aged footsteps westward in search of his congenial solitudes. At length, we discover him for the last time, an octogenarian trapper, far out on the prairies of the West. It is clear that the successive stages of his retreat from society could not well be presented in a single story, and that the repetition which has been charged against Cooper as a fault was indispensable to the development of his design.

The Deerslayer, the first novel in the series of the Leatherstocking Tales, seems to us one of the most interesting of Cooper's productions. He has chosen for the scene of his story the Otsego lake, on whose banks he lived and died, and whose scenery he has introduced into three, if not more, of his novels. The Deerslayer, or Leatherstocking, here makes his first appearance as a young man, in fact scarcely emerged from boyhood, yet with all the simplicity, candor, feeling, and penetration, which mark his riper years. The old buccaneer in his aquatic habitation, and the contrasted characters of his two daughters, add a human interest to the scene, for the want of which the highest skill in mere landscape painting cannot compensate. The character of Judith seems to us the best drawn, and by far the most interesting, female portrait in any of Cooper's novels with which we are acquainted. The story, however, is not free from the characteristic faults of its author. Above all, it contains, in one instance at least, a glaring exhibition of his aptitude for describing horrors. When he compels his marvellously graphic pen to depict scenes which would disgrace the shambles or the dissecting table, none can wonder that ladies and young clergymen regard his pages with abhorrence. These, however, are but casual defects in a work which bears the unmistakable impress of genius.

The Pathfinder forms the second volume of the series, and is remarkable, even among its companions, for the force and distinctness of its pictures. For ourselves—though we diligently perused the despatches—the battle of Palo Alto and the storming of Monterey are not more real and present to our minds than some of the scenes and characters of The Pathfinder, though we have not read it for nine years;—the little fort on the margin of Lake Ontario, the surrounding woods and waters, the veteran major in command, the treacherous Scotchman, the dogmatic old sailor, and the Pathfinder himself. Several of these scenes are borrowed in part from Mrs. Grant's Memoirs of an American Lady; but in borrowing, Cooper has transmuted shadows into substance. Mrs. Grant's facts—for as such we are to take them—have an air of fiction; while Cooper's fiction wears the aspect of solid fact. His peculiar powers could not be better illustrated than by a comparison of the passages alluded to in the two books.

One of the most widely known of Cooper's novels is The Last of the Mohicans, which forms the third volume of the series, and which, with all the elements of a vulgar popularity, combines excellences of a far higher order. It has, nevertheless, its great and obtrusive faults. It takes needless liberties with history; and though it would be folly to demand that an historical novelist should always conform to received authorities, yet it is certainly desirable that he should not unneces-

sarily set them at defiance; since the incidents of the novel are apt to remain longer in the memory than those of the less palatable history. But whatever may be the extent of the novelist's license, it is, at all events, essential that his story should have some semblance of probability, and not run counter to nature and common sense. In The Last of the Mohicans, the machinery of the plot falls little short of absurdity. Why a veteran officer, pent up in a little fort, and hourly expecting to be beleaguered by a vastly superior force, consisting in great part of bloodthirsty savages, should at that particular time desire or permit a visit from his two daughters, is a question not easy to answer. Nor is the difficulty lessened when it is remembered, that the young ladies are to make the journey through a wilderness full of Indian scalping parties. It is equally difficult to see why the lover of Alice should choose, merely for the sake of a romantic ride, to conduct her and her sister by a circuitous and most perilous by-path through the forests, when they might more easily have gone by a good road under the safe escort of a column of troops who marched for the fort that very morning. The story founded on these gross inventions is sustained by various minor improbabilities, which cannot escape the reader unless his attention is absorbed by the powerful interest of the narrative.

It seems to us a defect in a novel or a poem, when the heroine is compelled to undergo bodily hardship, to sleep out at night in the woods, drenched by rain, stung by mosquitos and scratched by briars,—to forego all appliances of the toilet, and above all, to lodge in an Indian wigwam. Women have sometimes endured such privation, and endured it with fortitude; but it may be safely affirmed, that for the time, all grace and romance were banished from their presence. We read Longfellow's Evangeline with much sympathy in the fortunes of the errant heroine, until, as we approached the end of the poem, every other sentiment was lost in admiration at the unparalleled extent of her wanderings, at the dexterity with which she contrived to elude at least a dozen tribes of savages at that time in a state of war, at the strength of her constitution, and at her marvellous proficiency in woodcraft. When, however, we had followed her for about two thousand miles on her forest pilgrimage, and reflected on the figure she must have made, so tattered and bepatched, bedrenched and bedraggled, we could not but esteem it a happy circumstance that she failed, as she did, to meet her lover; since, had he seen her in such plight, every spark of sentiment must have vanished from his breast, and all the romance of the poem have been ingloriously extinguished. With Cooper's heroines, Cora and Alice, the case is not so hard. Yet, as it does not appear that, on a journey of several weeks, they were permitted to carry so much as a valise or a carpet bag, and as we are expressly told, that on several occasions, they dropped by the wayside their gloves, veils, and other useful articles of apparel, it is certain, that at the journey's end, they must have presented an appearance more adapted to call forth a Christian sympathy than any emotion of a more romantic nature.

In respect to the delineation of character, The Last of the Mohicans is surpassed by several other works of the author. Its distinguishing merit lies in its descriptions of scenery and action. Of the personages who figure in it, one of the most interesting is the young Mohican, Uncas, who, however, does not at all resemble a genuine Indian. Magua, the villain of the story, is a less untruthful portrait. Cooper has been criticized for having represented him as falling in love with Cora; and the criticism is based on the alleged ground that passions of this kind are not characteristic of the Indian. This may, in some qualified sense, be true; but it is well known that Indians, in real life as well as in novels, display a peculiar partiality for white women, on the same principle by which Italians are prone to admire a light complexion, while Swedes regard a brunette with highest esteem. Cora was the very person to fascinate an Indian. The coldest warrior would gladly have received her into his lodge, and promoted her to be his favorite wife, wholly dispensing, in honor of her charms, with flagellation or any of the severer marks of conjugal displeasure.

The character of Hawkeye or Leatherstocking is, in the Mohicans as elsewhere, clearly and admirably drawn. He often displays, however, a weakness which excites the impatience of the reader,—an excessive and ill-timed loquacity. When, for example, in the fight at Glenn's Falls, he and Major Heywood are crouching in the thicket, watching the motions of four Indians, whose heads are visible above a log at a little distance, and who, in the expression of Hawkeye himself, are gathering for a rush, the scout employs the time in dilating upon the properties of the "long-barrelled, soft-metalled rifle." The design is, no doubt, to convey an impression of his coolness in moments of extreme danger; but under such circumstances, the bravest man would judge it the part of good sense to use his eyes rather than his tongue. Men of Hawkeye's class, however talkative they may be at the camp-fire, are remarkable for preserving a close silence while engaged in the active labors of their calling.

It is easy to find fault with The Last of the Mohicans; but it is far from easy to rival or even approach its excellences. The book has the genuine game flavor; it exhales the odors of the pine woods and the freshness of the mountain wind. Its dark and rugged scenery rises as distinctly on the eye as the images of the painter's canvas, or rather as the reflection of nature herself. But it is not as the mere rendering of material forms, that these wood paintings are most highly to be esteemed. They are instinct with life, with the very spirit of the wilderness; they breathe the sombre poetry of solitude and danger. In these achievements of his art, Cooper, we think, has no equal, unless it may be the author of that striking romance, Wacousta or the Prophecy, whose fine powers of imagination are, however, even less under the guidance of a just taste than those of the American novelist.

The most obvious merit of The Last of the Mohicans consists in its descriptions of action, in the power with which the author absorbs the reader's sympathies, and leads him, as it were, to play a part in the scene. One reads the accounts of a great battle—aside from any cause or principle at issue—with the same kind of interest with which he beholds the grand destructive phenomena of nature, a tempest at sea, or a tornado in the tropics; yet with a feeling far more intense, since the conflict is not a mere striving of insensate elements, but of living tides of human wrath and valor. With descriptions of petty skirmishes or single combats, the feeling is of a different kind. The reader is enlisted in the fray, a partaker, as it were, in every thought and movement of the combatants, in the alternations of fear and triumph, the prompt expedient the desparate resort, the papitations of human weakness, or the courage that faces death. Of this species of description, the scene of the conflict at Glenn's Falls is an admirable example, unsurpassed, we think, even by the combat of Balfour and Bothwell, or by any other passage of the kind in the novels of Scott. The scenery of the fight, the foaming cataract, the little islet with its stout-hearted defenders, the precipices and the dark pine woods, add greatly to the effect. The scene is conjured before the reader's eye, not as a vision or a picture, but like the tangible presence of rock, river, and forest. His very senses seem conspiring to deceive him. He seems to feel against his cheek the wind and spray of the cataract, and hear its sullen roar, amid the yells of the assailants and the sharp crack of the answering rifle. The scene of the strife is pointed out to travellers as if this fictitious combat were a real event of history. Mills, factories, and bridges have marred the native wildness of the spot, and a village has usurped the domain of the forest; yet still those foaming waters and black sheets of limestone rock are clothed with all the interest of an historic memory; and the cicerone of the place can show the caves where the affrighted sisters took refuge, the point where the Indians landed, and the rock whence the despairing Huron was flung into the abyss. Nay, if the lapse of a few years has not enlightened his understanding, the guide would as soon doubt the reality of the battle of Saratoga, as that of Hawkeye's fight with the Mingoes.

The Pioneers, the fourth volume of the series, is, in several respects, the best of Cooper's works. Unlike some of its companions, it bears every mark of having been written from the results of personal experience; and indeed, Cooper is well known to have drawn largely on the recollections of his earlier years in the composition of this novel. The characters are full of vitality and truth, though, in one or two instances, the excellence of delineation is impaired by a certain taint of vulgarity. Leatherstocking, as he appears in The Pioneers, must certainly have had his living original in some gaunt, gray-haired old woodsman, to whose stories of hunts and Indian fights the author may perhaps have listened in his boyhood with rapt ears, unconsciously garnering up in memory the germs which time was to develop into a rich harvest. The scenes of the Christmas turkey-shooting, the fish-spearing by firelight on Otsego lake, the rescue from the panther, and the burning of the woods, are all inimitable in their way. Of all Cooper's works, The Pioneers seems to us most likely to hold a permanent place in literature, for it preserves a vivid reflection of scenes and characters which will soon have passed away.

The Prairie, the last of the Leatherstocking Tales, is a novel of far inferior merit. The story is very improbable, and not very interesting. The pictures of scenery are less true to nature than in the previous volumes, and seem to indicate that Cooper had little or no personal acquaintance with the remoter parts of the West. The book, however, has several passages of much interest, one of the best of which is the scene in which the aged trapper discovers, in the person of a young officer, the grandson of Duncan Heywood and Alice Munro, whom, half a century before, he had protected when in such imminent jeopardy on the rocks of Glenn's Falls and among the mountains of Lake George. The death of Abiram White is very striking, though reminding the reader too much of a similar scene in the Spy. The grand deformity of the story is the wretched attempt at humor in the person of Dr. Obed Battius. David Gamut, in The Mohicans, is bad enough; but Battius outherods Herod, and great must be the merit of the book which one such incubus would not sink beyond redemption.

The novel, which first brought the name of Cooper into distinguished notice, was The Spy; and this book, which gave him his earliest reputation, will contribute largely to preserve it. The story is full of interest, and the character of Harvey Birch is drawn with singular skill.

The Pilot is usually considered the best of Cooper's sea tales. It is in truth a masterpiece of his genius; and although the reader is apt to pass with impatience over the long conversations among the ladies at St. Ruth's, and between Alice Dunscombe and the disguised Paul Jones,

yet he is amply repaid when he follows the author to his congenial element. The description of the wreck of the Ariel, and the death of Long Tom Coffin, can scarcely be spoken of in terms of too much admiration. Long Tom is to Cooper's sea tales what Leatherstocking is to the novels of the forest,—a conception so original and forcible, that posterity will hardly suffer it to escape from remembrance. The Red Rover, The Water-Witch, and the remainder of the sea tales, are marked with the same excellences and defects with the novels already mentioned, and further comments would therefore be useless.

The recent death of the man who had achieved so much in the cause of American literature has called forth, as it should have done, a general expression of regret; and the outcries, not unprovoked, which of late have been raised against him, are drowned in the voice of sorrow. The most marked and original of American writers has passed from among us. It was an auspicious moment when his earlier works first saw the light; for there was promise in their rude vigor,—a good hope that from such rough beginnings the country might develop a literary progeny which, taking lessons in the graces, and refining with the lapse of years, might one day do honor to its parentage; and when the chastened genius of Bryant arose, it seemed that the fulfilment of such a hope was not far remote. But this fair promise has failed, and to this hour the purpose, the energy, the passion of America have never found their adequate expression on the printed page. The number of good writers truly American, by which we mean all those who are not imitators of foreign modes, might be counted on the fingers of the two hands; nor are the writers of this small class, not excepting even Bryant himself, in any eminent degree the favorites of those among their countrymen who make pretensions to taste and refinement. As in life and manners the American people seem bent on aping the polished luxury of another hemisphere, so likewise they reserve their enthusiasm and their purses for the honeyed verse and the sugared prose of an emasculate and supposititious literature.

Some French writer,—Chateaubriand, we believe,—observes that the only portion of the American people who exhibit any distinctive national character are the backwoodsmen of the West. The remark is not strictly true. The whole merchant marine, from captains to cabin-boys, the lumbermen of Maine, the farmers of New England, and indeed all the laboring population of the country, not of foreign origin, are marked with strong and peculiar traits. But when we ascend into the educated and polished classes, these peculiarities are smoothed away, until, in many cases, they are invisible. An educated Englishman is an Englishman still; an educated Frenchman is often intensely French; but an educated American is apt to have no national character at all. The condition of the literature of the country is, as might be expected, in close accordance with these peculiarities of its society. With but few exceptions, the only books which reflect the national mind are those which emanate from, or are adapted to, the unschooled classes of the people; such, for example, as Dr. Bird's Nick of the Woods, The Life of David Crockett, The Big Bear of Arkansas, with its kindred legends, and, we may add, the earlier novels of Cooper. In the politer walks of literature, we find much grace of style, but very little originality of thought,–productions which might as readily be taken for the work of an Englishman as of an American.

This lack of originality has been loudly complained of, but it seems to us inevitable under the circumstances. The healthful growth of the intellect, whether national or individual, like healthful growth of every other kind, must proceed from the action of internal energies, and not from foreign aid. Too much assistance, too many stimulants, weaken instead of increasing it. The cravings of the American mind, eager as they are, are amply supplied by the copious stream of English current literature. Thousands, nay, millions of readers and writers drink from this bounteous source, and feed on this foreign aliment, till the whole complexion of their thoughts is tinged with it, and by a sort of necessity they think and write at second hand. If this transatlantic supply were completely cut off, and the nation abandoned to its own resources, it would eventually promote, in a high degree, the development of the national intellect. The vitality and force, which are abundantly displayed in every department of active life, would soon find their way into a higher channel, to meet the new and clamorous necessity for mental food; and in the space of a generation, the oft-repeated demand for an original literature would be fully satisfied.

In respect to every department of active life, the United States are fully emancipated from their ancient colonial subjection. They can plan, invent, and achieve for themselves, and this, too, with a commanding success. But in all the finer functions of thought, in all matters of literature and taste, we are still essentially provincial. England once held us in a state of political dependency. That day is past; but she still holds us in an intellectual dependency far more complete. Her thoughts become our thoughts, by a process unconscious, but inevitable. She caters for our mind and fancy with a liberal hand. We are spared the labor of self-support; but by the universal law, applicable to nations no less than individuals, we are weakened by the want of independent exercise. It is a matter of common remark, that the most highly educated classes among us are far from being the most efficient either in thought or action. The vigorous life of the nation springs from the deep rich soil at the bottom of society. Its men of greatest influence are those who have studied men before they studied books, and who, by hard battling with the world, and boldly following out the bent of their native genius, have hewn their own way to wealth, station, or knowledge, from the ploughshare or the forecastle. The comparative shortcomings of the best educated among us may be traced to several causes; but, as we are constrained to think, they are mainly owing to the fact that the highest civilization of America is communicated from without instead of being developed from within, and is therefore nerveless and unproductive.

–*The North American Review*, 74 (January 1852): 147–161

Catharine Maria Sedgwick

Catharine Maria Sedgwick (1789–1867) was approached by Putnam in 1849 with nearly the same proposal he made that year to Cooper: the publication of a handsomely produced, revised edition of the author's earlier works. Putnam's relationship with Sedgwick extended back nearly a dozen years; when he was in London, Putnam had done various professional favors for her, including representing her with local publishers and helping her to find accommodations in the city.

Catharine Maria Sedgwick, who published with Putnam intermittently over a span of two decades

In asking Sedgwick to join his project of bringing out revised editions of the works of established American novelists, Putnam had the advantage not only of enjoying a cordial personal relationship with her but also of having already been involved in the publication of her work. Wiley and Putnam had published Morals or Manners *in 1846 and–one of the firm's last publications–*Facts and Fancies for School-Day Reading *in 1848. The Putnam revised edition of Sedgwick's works began with the publication of* Clarence *in September 1849, which was followed by* Redwood *(1850),* A New England Tale *(1852), and* Morals or Manners *(1854). All of these books were brought out in the same duodecimo format as the revised editions of Irving and Cooper, although Putnam also published* Morals or Manners *and* Facts and Fancies for School-Day Reading *in less elaborate, 16mo editions priced at 25¢ or 50¢ and designated for district school libraries. Putnam's regard for Sedgwick is further shown by his choosing her as the only female author included in* Homes of American Authors.

PUTNAM BOOKS BY SEDGWICK: *Morals or Manners; or, Hints for Our Young People* (New York: Wiley & Putnam, 1846; London: Wiley & Putnam, 1846);

Facts and Fancies for School-Day Reading (New York: Wiley & Putnam, 1848; London: Wiley & Putnam, 1848);

Clarence, revised edition (New York: G. P. Putnam, 1849); **first edition,** *Clarence; or, A Tale of Our Own Times,* 2 volumes (Philadelphia: Carey & Lea, 1830; London: Colburn & Bentley, 1830);

Redwood, republished by Putnam (New York: G. P. Putnam, 1850); **first edition,** *Redwood: A Tale,* 2 volumes (New York: Bliss & White, 1824);

A New England Tale, enlarged edition, *A New England Tale and Miscellanies* (New York: G. P. Putnam, 1852); **first edition,** *A New-England Tale; or, Sketches of New-England Character and Manners* (New York: Bliss & White, 1822; London: Miller, 1822).

* * *

In this assessment of the first Sedgwick novel published by Putnam in the revised edition, the reviewer for Literary World *argues that her novel not only belongs alongside works by Irving and Cooper but also deserves to be measured against the standards of the leading writers of Europe.*

Clarence; or, a Tale of Our Own Times. By the Author of Hope Leslie, *&c Author's Revised Edition. Geo. P. Putnam: 1849.*

MISS SEDGWICK has been aptly instanced as an American writer whose success and popularity have not been the result of transatlantic favor, and whose reputation does not depend upon the *dicta* of foreign critics, inasmuch as it was acquired at the first without their aid. Ever since her first entrance into the world of letters her literary productions have been mainly, in every sense of the word, American. Not only have the scenes and incidents of her works of fiction been drawn from the history of this country or its domestic manners, but her more directly useful and perhaps most praiseworthy efforts have all been in illustration of its social habits and tendencies. Besides this, there are perhaps none of our writers whose works in their spirit and style more completely reflect the prominent characteristics of the American mind. They are marked less by the refinements of highly cultivated taste and imagination than by a rigorous straightforwardness of purpose and a practical energy, of which the principal ingredient is that rare quality in authorship, good common sense.

We do not intend to be understood as limiting our praise of Miss Sedgwick's writings to their indigenous character, any more than we would convey the idea that Americanism by itself is their most satisfactory ingredient. We are not so anxious for the establishment of that "national literature" for which so many ardent appeals are advanced by annual orators and weekly essayists, as to desire its advance at the expense of principles of taste and judgment, which lie far behind the circumstances of locality or nationality. We are not disposed to make ourselves uncomfortable with American books any more than with American broadcloth, so long as better are to be had. It is no consolation in the midst of the stupidities of a trashy novel or an unreliable history, to be assured that it is the production of native talent. We have every reason to believe that in the department of authorship, as in every other branch of invention, we may compete successfully with the old world, but never with anything that deserves the name of success, so long as our literature is tested by any other rules than those which have determined long ago the merit and the value of works which are by common consent the ripest fruits of the literature of our language.

If, then, Miss Sedgwick's works came to us with no other recommendation than that which she modestly advances in her preface–their American origin, we should hardly recognise their claim. We should not be amongst the readers whom she "hopes to find, who will relish a book for its *home* atmosphere—who will have something of the feelings of him who said he would rather have a single apple from the garden of his father's house than all the fruits of France." This is a proper and commendable feeling within certain limits; but it would hardly be safe, even for Miss Sedgwick, secure though she be in the friendship and admiration of all American readers, to risk the permanency of her literary reputation upon the slender basis of its nationality.

We think, as we have already intimated, that it has a surer foundation—the foundation of good sense, active and enlightened sympathies, a genial warmth of sentiment, and an earnest energy of thought, ingredients which, while they would give the assurance of success to literary efforts of almost any description which taste or inclination might prompt, receive a higher impulse and a more satisfactory recompense when applied to advance the real and immediate interests of society, and to promote the culture of a *genuine* nationality.

CLARENCE is, we believe, one of Miss Sedgwick's earlier works. It is a domestic novel; one of a class which the modern improvements in fiction have rather elbowed out of popularity. It is called "A Tale of our own Times," but we outgrow our own recollection so fast in this country that its local descriptions and incidents have entirely lost their contemporary freshness. A description of Broadway some twenty years ago, in the first chapter, would hardly be recognised by a New Yorker; and the author is forced to introduce a note at the end of the chapter, apologizing for the air of antiquity which has unconsciously overgrown her subject. But the story is a good one. We remember reading it with interest years ago, in a dingy two volume edition, and being very much interested in the fortunes of its characters. It is not one of those books which makes the reader wonder that it could ever have been written by a woman, for Miss Sedgwick, fortunately, has never allied herself to that class of authoresses who studiously ignore in their writings the Providence that has made them women. There is all through Clarence a happy feminine grace which adds vastly to its interest and effect.

Mr. Putnam has done well in adding the works of his gifted countrywoman to his series of American authors. The volume is uniform with the works of Irving and Cooper, in the neatest style of execution. Only in one particular, in the worst possible taste. The book in its general appearance

bears indications enough of having issued from the tasteful hands of Mr. Putnam, without the necessity of his autograph on the titlepage. This species of authentication and ornament should be left to the undisturbed possession of quack doctors.

– *The Literary World*, 5 (6 October 1849): 297–298

* * *

Sedgwick's professional relationship with Putnam ended in 1854, when the publisher, facing bankruptcy, sold at auction the plates and stock of her works to New York publisher J. C. Derby. Nevertheless, as this 1856 letter to Putnam shows, Sedgwick maintained ties and continued to seek his professional advice.

My dear Mr. Putnam,

You may perhaps remember my sending you an article while you had the conduct of your magazine which you preferred to delay the publication of till the [?] should come round. In the meantime the work passed from your hands, & the article in question having never appeared is probably among the Editors' waste-papers. If not irreclaimable, & not costing you too much trouble, I should be glad to get it into my possession again. As I have had no communication with the Editors on the subject I feel no right to apply to them.

I was in town for a few days last month & hoped to have <u>made</u> an opportunity of seeing you— & learning the present condition of that capital of yours, intact I trust, & to whose state I can never be indifferent. The health and happiness of your family—God preserve it to you, my friend—When other changes may come, & be met by a manly & christian spirit.

As my books are lying on Mr. Derby's dead-shelf—& he utterly declines complying with the terms of his contract, I think of throwing the whole, provided I can make a good arrangement with him with Harper's hands—but I wished, first of all, to communicate with you on the subject.

Will you remember me kindly to Mrs. Putnam & your young people

& believe me truly yours,
C. M. Sedgwick

Lenox 20 Novr. '56

John Pendleton Kennedy

A leading novelist of the generation of Cooper, Irving, and Sedgwick, John Pendleton Kennedy (1795–1870) was another writer whose works Putnam sought to reintroduce to a new generation of readers. In Kennedy's case, however, Putnam brought out new editions of only three of the author's best-known novels of the South: Swallow Barn *in 1851,* Horse Shoe Robinson *in 1852, and* Rob of the Bowl *in 1854. Shortly after Kennedy's death in 1870, G. P. Putnam and Sons published a ten-volume edition of his works, edited by Henry Tuckerman, that also included these novels as well as Kennedy's previously unpublished* At Home and Abroad: A Series of Essays.

PUTNAM BOOKS BY KENNEDY: *Swallow Barn,* revised edition (New York: G. P. Putnam, 1851); **first edition,** *Swallow Barn, Or A Sojourn in the Old Dominion,* 2 volumes (Philadelphia: Carey & Lea, 1832);

Horse Shoe Robinson, revised edition (New York: G. P. Putnam, 1852); **first edition,** *Horse-Shoe Robinson: A Tale of the Tory Ascendency,* 2 volumes (Philadelphia: Carey, Lea & Blanchard, 1835);

Rob of the Bowl, revised edition (New York: G. P. Putnam and Company, 1854); **first edition,** *Rob of the Bowl: A Legend of St. Iginoe's,* 2 volumes (Philadelphia: Lea & Blanchard, 1838);

Occasional Addresses (New York: G. P. Putnam and Sons, 1872);

Memoirs of the Life of William Wirt (New York: G. P. Putnam and Sons, 1872); **first edition,** *Memoirs of the Life of William Wirt,* 2 volumes (Philadelphia: Lea & Blanchard, 1849);

Political and Official Papers (New York: G. P. Putnam and Sons, 1872);

Quodlibet (New York: G. P. Putnam and Sons, 1872); **first edition,** *Quodlibet* (Philadelphia: Lea & Blanchard, 1840);

At Home and Abroad: A Series of Essays (New York: G. P. Putnam and Sons, 1872).

* * *

Eager to see his works brought out in the usual handsome Putnam style, Kennedy writes to Putnam for assurance and to state his preference for an illustrator–F. O. C. Darley, the leading illustrator of his time, who illustrated Irving's works.

Baltimore   Dec. 20, 1851

My dear Sir,

In the expectation of being able to make a visit to New York to participate in the celebration of the Cooper Testimonial, I have hitherto foreborne to send you the copy of Horse Shoe Robinson from which I wished

John Pendleton Kennedy, as he was represented in the September 1854 issue of Putnam's Monthly

the new edition to be printed. It was my purpose to take it with me and to see you personally. I am unfortunately compelled to forego the pleasure of this visit, being now confined to the house with an inflammation of the eye which will not allow me to risk the exposure of the journey.

I shall, therefore, send you the revised volumes either by express, or by a private hand in a few days. In the meantime, I wish you to give me a memorandum that you have undertaken the republication of this work on the same terms as that of Swallow Barn, to be enacted in the same manner to match that volume.

I should like to have a frontispiece for each volume from Darley–some appropriate scene of the tale designed in his best style. The publication must be in two volumes, and I would confer with Darley upon the two pictures. I had a moment's conversation with him on this matter when I saw him in October, and presume he would be able to do what we may suggest without delay. I wish you to speak to him on the subject, and engage him in the undertaking.

What is the condition of the Swallow Barn publication? How many copies have you now printed—and how does it keep its ground?

Very truly

yours

J. P. Kennedy

P.S. I want the <u>short</u> copy of Adams' works—and also a copy of Hamilton's—both as far as published. Can you send them to me—by Waters or Murphy?—

—Manuscripts Division, Department of Rare Books and Special Collections, Princeton University Library. Published with permission of the Princeton University Library.

Bayard Taylor, as he was represented in the August 1854 issue of Putnam's Monthly

Bayard Taylor

Bayard Taylor (1825–1878) was second to Irving in popularity but first in longevity among G. P. Putnam authors. The basis of Taylor's relationship with the House of Putnam was the author's warm friendship with Putnam, who shared his tastes, opinions, and views. The two men first met in London in 1846 when Taylor, short of funds after a long tour of the European Continent, came to the Wiley and Putnam office looking for temporary employment. Putnam set him to work at one of his office desks, and they soon struck up a friendship. A professional relationship ensued when Taylor returned to the United States, composed his travels under the title Views A-foot *(1846), and offered the work to the New York office of Wiley and Putnam. Appearing in the Library of American Books, Taylor's book sold well, going through multiple printings over the next decade and remaining in print the rest of the century.*

The success of Views A-foot *laid the groundwork for a lifelong collaboration between Putnam and Taylor. It was soon followed by* Rhymes of Travel, Ballads and Poems *(1849), the first of many Taylor works to be published under the recently formed G. P. Putnam imprint. Next came* Eldorado *(1850), a book of travels in Mexico, which was followed during the next two decades by nearly a dozen more travelogues published with his friend, including an account of his accompanying Commodore Perry on the historic expedition to Japan,* A Visit to India, China, and Japan, in the Year 1833 *(1855). Expanding his repertoire in the Civil War years, Taylor wrote fiction, beginning with* Hannah Thurston *(1863). In addition, he co-edited with George Ripley the* Hand-Book of Literature and Fine Arts *(1852) in the six-volume* Putnam's Home Cyclopedia *and contributed to many of the finest collective projects carried out by the house, including* The Home Book of the Picturesque, Putnam's Monthly, Putnam's Magazine, *and the* Rebellion Record.

PUTNAM BOOKS BY TAYLOR: *Views A-foot; or, Europe Seen with Knapsack and Staff* (New York: Wiley & Putnam, 1846); augmented as *Pedestrian Tour in Europe. Views A-foot; or, Europe Seen with Knapsack and Staff* (New York: G. P. Putnam, 1848); revised edition (New York: G. P. Putnam and Company / London: Sampson Low, Son, 1855);

Rhymes of Travel, Ballads and Poems (New York: G. P. Putnam, 1849);

Eldorado; or, Adventures in the Path of Empire: Comprising a Voyage to California, via Panama; Life in San Francisco and Monterey; Pictures of the Gold Region, and Experiences of Mexican Travel, 2 volumes (New York: G. P. Putnam, 1850; London: Richard Bentley, 1850);

A Journey to Central Africa; or, Life and Landscapes from Egypt to the Negro Kingdoms of the White Nile (New York: G. P. Putnam and Company, 1854); republished as *Life and Landscapes from Egypt to the Negro Kingdoms of the White Nile: Being A Journey to Central Africa* (London: Sampson Low, Son, 1854);

The Lands of the Saracen; or, Pictures of Palestine, Asia Minor, Sicily, and Spain (New York: G. P. Putnam and Company, 1855 [i.e., 1854]); republished as *Pictures of Palestine, Asia Minor, Sicily, and Spain; or, The Lands of the Saracen* (London: Sampson Low, 1855 [i.e., 1854]);

A Visit to India, China, and Japan, in the Year 1853 (New York: G. P. Putnam and Company / London: Sampson Low, Son, 1855);

Northern Travel: Summer and Winter Pictures of Sweden, Lapland, and Norway (London: Sampson Low, Son, 1858 [i.e., 1857]); republished as *Northern Travel: Summer and Winter Pictures of Sweden, Denmark, and Lapland* (New York: G. P. Putnam, 1858 [i.e., 1857]);

Travels in Greece and Russia, with an Excursion to Crete (New York: G. P. Putnam, 1859; London: Sampson Low, Son, 1859);

At Home and Abroad: A Sketch-Book of Life, Scenery, and Men (New York: G. P. Putnam, 1860 [i.e. 1859]; London: Sampson Low, Son, 1860 [i.e., 1859]);

At Home and Abroad: A Sketch-Book of Life, Scenery, and Men . . . , Second Series (New York: G. P. Putnam, 1862; London: Sampson Low, Son, 1862);

Hannah Thurston: A Story of American Life (New York: G. P. Putnam, 1863; 3 volumes, London: Sampson Low, Son, 1863);

John Godfrey's Fortunes; Related by Himself. A Story of American Life (New York: G. P. Putnam / Hurd & Houghton, 1864; 3 volumes, London: Sampson Low, Son & Marston, 1864);

The Story of Kennett (New York: G. P. Putnam / Hurd & Houghton, 1866; 2 volumes, London: Sampson Low, Son, 1866);

Colorado: A Summer Trip (New York: G. P. Putnam and Son, 1867);

By-Ways of Europe (New York: G. P. Putnam and Son, 1869); also published as *Byeways of Europe*, 2 volumes (London: Sampson Low, Son & Marston, 1869);

Joseph and His Friend: A Story of Pennsylvania (New York: G. P. Putnam and Sons / London: Sampson Low, Son & Marston, 1870);

Beauty and the Beast: And Tales of Home (New York: G. P. Putnam and Sons, 1872; London: Sampson Low, Marston, Low & Searle, 1872);

Egypt and Iceland in the Year 1874 (New York: G. P. Putnam's Sons, 1874; London: Sampson Low, Marston, Low & Searle, 1875);

Boys of Other Countries (New York: G. P. Putnam's Sons, 1876); enlarged (New York: G. P. Putnam's Sons, 1901; London: G. P. Putnam's Sons, 1901);

Studies in German Literature, edited by Marie Hansen-Taylor (New York: G. P. Putnam's Sons, 1879; London: Sampson Low, Marston, Searle, 1879);

Critical Essays and Literary Notes, edited by Hansen-Taylor (New York: G. P. Putnam's Sons, 1880; London: Sampson Low, Marston, Searle & Rivington, 1880).

OTHER: *Hand-Book of Literature and Fine Arts,* edited by Taylor and George Ripley (New York: G. P. Putnam, 1852).

Congratulating Putnam on his recent appointment as tax collector in Manhattan, Taylor discusses his own ambitions to be appointed minister to Russia. Knowing that the influence of William Cullen Bryant had helped Putnam to gain his position, he urges Putnam to encourage Bryant and other well-placed men to persuade President Abraham Lincoln to make his appointment. Whatever their intervention, Taylor was passed over. His discussion of the timing of his next major book presumably concerns Hannah Thurston.

<u>private</u>   U. S. Legation
St. Petersburg
Oct. 18, 1862

My dear Putnam:

I have just received yours of the 23d ult. First of all I must tell you how much I am delighted with your appointment. The times have tried us all pretty severely, and it is a great satisfaction to know that you are now tolerably secure. I have been sometimes a little importunate, in our business relations, but always through necessity; and if I can but be as lucky as you (although, pecuniarily, this post is less valuable than yours) I promise, henceforth, never to ask for money except when you can conveniently give it.

I have now been, for a month, the only official representative of the U. S. in St. Petersburg, having both the Legation and the Consulate in my hands. My relations with the Imperial Government are of the most satisfactory kind: the place exactly suits me, and there will be a break in the harmony of the universe if I am not allowed to remain. I wrote a poem on the 1000th anniversary of the Russian Empire, for which I have received the special thanks of the Emperor—you will have seen it in the Tribune. Prince Gorkekacow tells me that the whole Imperial Family were delighted, and the Emperor holds on to the MS. refusing to give it to anybody. I have also established very cordial relations with the diplomatists here—especially Lord Napier and the Duc de Montebello,—and am in a position to be of real service to the country, if our good Pres't could only be made to understand it. I have no scruples with regard to opposing Clay's claims. His object is unworthy an American representative. He has his gas business (which, alone, disqualifies him,) and moreover, a liaison of a low order, which everybody here knows, and whereby all American residents are scandalized. Moreover, he may stay here ten years, and he will never know anything of Russia. There is really nothing of him except his Anti-Slavery, and it is needed at home.

But, really, I am so agreeably situated here, and so thoroughly satisfied with that I have done and am doing that I am afraid I shall not be allowed to stay. My friends must lose no time. An application must be made at once. Cameron comes home by the steamer which takes this letter, and the succession will be decided immediately afterwards. A simultaneous use of all the interest which I may be able to obtain, in addition to Cameron's testimony, may be sufficient to move the Pres't. Bryant has not answered my letter, and I therefore beg that you will speak to him on my behalf. Everett has promised me his influence, and I think he, with Hamlin, Bryant, Bancroft and Cameron, would be enough. Seward can testify, from my dispatches, that I am fully capable of conducting the Legation.

With regard to the book, I think it should not appear, in any case, this fall or winter. A sale of 5000 would not be a success, but I want to bring it out when it can command 20,000. The material is fresh and very entertaining, and I would rather wait awhile, than have but a partial success. I know that, in order to complete the new series, it ought to be ready—but there will be less loss in delaying the completion than in bringing out the last vol. before its proper time. I shall be obliged to copy the entire MS on thin paper and forward it by mail. I have not yet been able to do this, on account of much business, and besides the very uncertainty of my position disturbs me. You can easily invent some apology for the delay, and, under the circumstances, must have a little patience with me.

My "Home and Abroad" has just been translated into Swedish.

I write in a hurry, to catch the "Scotia,"—I have much more to say, but the immediate necessity of my friends doing all they can in my behalf brooks no delay. If I stay, I shall serve the country faithfully, and produce a work when I come back, which shall drive all others on Russia out of the market. Give my kindest regards (in which my wife joins) to Mrs. Putnam, Minnie, and all the children. My Lilian is very well, wife also. We all like St. Petersburg and the Russians. Remember me to all good friends.

Ever yours,
Bayard Taylor

* * *

Donald Grant Mitchell, who wrote as "Ik Marvel" and was one of the most popular writers of his generation. His Reveries of a Bachelor *(1850) was a best-selling book in the 1850s.*

In an unusually frank reply to the popular author Donald Grant Mitchell, Taylor discusses his long-term experience as an author. Over the course of his career Taylor published his prose primarily with G. P. Putnam, whose list at the time of this letter was being overseen by Hurd & Houghton, and his poetry primarily with Ticknor and Fields. Taylor was one of the most professionally minded writers of his generation, and his businesslike attitude and expectations toward the profession of authorship anticipated publisher-author relations in the last third of the century. In fact, his remarks point to the emergence of author associations later in the century.

No. 139 East 8th St.
New York.
Feb. 14, 1865.

My dear Mr. Mitchell:

My engagements (I am still forced to lecture) have prevented my immediate reply to your note. I have often wished that there could be a general understanding among American authors in regard to the value of copyright, and the amount of percentage proper to be paid by publishers. As it is, each one must now make the best terms he can. The publishers seem to consider 10 per cent of the retail price as a sort of par, above which they only allow an author to rise when he is sufficiently popular to enforce better terms. This, of course, is considerably less than half-profits (in ordinary times)–which ought to be the standard. Mr. Putnam estimated that 12 1/2 percent. is about equivalent to half profits, and W. Irving and myself accepted this estimate, the publisher paying for the plates and owning them. Afterwards, when Putnam became embarrassed, we arranged to purchase the plates, and a new contract was made, by which I received 25 cents per vol. the retail price being $1.50. Afterwards, Mr. P. thinking this too high, I voluntarily reduced it to 20 cents, until last summer. In July I made a new contract when Hurd & Houghton undertook the details of publication, and the price of the vols. was raised to $1.75. By this contract I get 25 cts. on each volume, except "John Godfrey" for which I receive 30 cts. the retail price being $2.25. This is an average of about 14 per cent. But as I own the plates, engravings, etc.–a dead capital of about $8,000,–the interest of which should be deducted from my receipts–it is almost equivalent to the old arrangement of 12 1/2 per cent. You do not state whether you pay for your own plates, which is a point of some importance. I think the scale of half-profits is a fair one, provided the estimate is fairly made. For instance, some publishers, I know, take their lowest rate of discount to the trade (40 per cent. off) as the basis of the calculation– when the usual rate is 33 1/3 per cent. and when, moreover, they sell hundreds or thousands of volumes at the retail price.

My experience with Ticknor and Fields is similar to your own. They actually insist on reducing the copyright on their blue-and-gold editions to 7 per cent. on the retail price. This I have not submitted to, alth' they assure me that Longfellow, Holmes and Whittier have accepted. I am not of the opinion that coffee, tin, turpentine and whiskey should go up, and an author's copyright go down at the same time. I believe, however, that publishers are earning less now than formerly, because they have so long delayed increasing the price of books. But that is their business, and an author should not be made to suffer for it.

With regard to advertising, I have always insisted that the statement of the sale of a vol. should be correct, and therefore returned in the account, and thus far, I have been paid according to the advertised number. I am sure that a publisher could be legally held to pay the author the copyright on the number of vols. which he advertises as having been sold.

We now have to depend entirely on the publisher's returns, which we cannot verify without seeming to doubt his honesty. I am fortunately situated in this respect, and I believe you are, so far as Mr. Scribner is concerned: but the plan is bad, for all that. I wish some arrangement could be devised by which the author could have control over,–or, at least, cognizance of–the exact number of copies printed and bound.

If we could do this, and then ascertain the exact percentage which represents the actual half-profit, our interests

would stand on a much more satisfactory basis. First of all there should be a full and free comparison of experiences among authors, and to this end I have sent you mine. If it is not as complete as you need, pray let me know. I have written hastily and may have overlooked some points.

Very sincerely yours,
Bayard Taylor.

Asa Gray

The leading botanist of antebellum America, Asa Gray (1810–1888) published several of the standard works in his field with G. P. Putnam. Wiley and Putnam published A Flora of North America *(1838–1841), which Gray co-authored with John Torrey; his closer connection with the firm came through his developing relationship with Putnam. The two men first met in the late 1830s in London, where Gray had come to purchase specimens and to buy books for the fledgling library of the University of Michigan. A friendship quickly ensued, which brought Wiley and Putnam Gray's* Botanical Text-Book, *a work that Putnam published in updated editions well into the next decade. He continued to serve as Gray's main publisher until his financial constraints ended their relationship in 1857.*

PUTNAM BOOKS BY GRAY: *A Flora of North America,* 2 volumes (New York & London: Wiley & Putnam, 1838, 1843);

Asa Gray in 1838, shortly after he had met Putnam in England

The Botanical Text-Book for Colleges, Schools, and Private Students,
revised edition (New York: Wiley & Putnam / Boston:
Little, Brown, 1842); revised as *Introduction to Structural
and Systematic Botany, and Vegetable Physiology* (New York:
Ivison, Blakeman, Taylor, 1857); revised as *Structural
Botany, or Organography on the Basis of Morphology* (New
York & Chicago: Ivison, Blakeman, Taylor, 1879); **first
edition,** *Elements of Botany* (New York: G. & C. Carvill,
1836);

Genera Florae Americae (New York: G. P. Putnam, 1849; London: G. P. Putnam, 1849); **first edition,** *Genera flora
Americana boreali-orientalis illustrata,* 2 volumes, illustrations by Isaac Sprague and descriptions by Gray (Boston: J. Monroe / New York & London: Wiley, 1848,
1849);

Manual of the Botany of the Northern United States, revised edition
(New York: G. P. Putnam and Company, 1856;
revised again, New York: G. P. Putnam and Company / Ivison & Phinney, 1856; revised again, New
York: G. P. Putnam, 1859; revised again, 1863;
revised again, New York: Ivison, Blakeman, 1867);
first edition, *A Manual of the Botany of the Northern United
States* (Boston: J. Munroe / London: Chapman, 1848);

First Lessons in Botany and Vegetable Physiology (New York: G. P.
Putnam and Company / Ivison, Phinney, 1857);
revised as *The Elements of Botany for Beginners and for
Schools* (New York: American Book Company, 1887).

* * *

This Newark Advertiser *review of Gray's botanical textbook,
which Wiley and Putnam had recently published in an updated and
expanded edition, was incorporated into the firm's advertisements.*

It augers well for the intellectual and moral character
of the age, that there is everywhere a growing taste for the
cultivation of natural science; and happily there are new
helps constantly furnished for the prosecution of these
highly important and practical studies. Such, in a high
degree, is Dr. Gray's Botanical Text-book; a second edition
of which, revised and enlarged, is now just from the press.
We report the opinion of the most competent judges of the
merits of this book, when we say that, though it professes to
be only an elementary treatise, it exhibits the science in a
most improved state, and is not less remarkable for its apt
illustrations than its felicitous arrangement. It is brought out
in an exceedingly handsome form, possibly with some reference to the taste of the ladies, many of whom, in later years,
have been found among the most diligent students of the science of which it treats.

— *Wiley and Putnam's Literary News-Letter,*
4 (August 1845): 354

George Palmer Putnam in 1859 (Collection of Ezra Greenspan)

George Palmer Putnam

*Author, annalist, editor, journalist, and compiler, George
Palmer Putnam (1814–1872) was the most prolific author-publisher
of his time—cumulatively one of his own firm's most productive
authors. His earliest work was a reference volume,* Chronology; or, An Introduction and Index to Universal History, Biography, and Useful Knowledge *(1833), which he
compiled as a teenage bookstore clerk and that outlived him,
remaining in print and coming out in new editions into the twentieth century. The next year he compiled and edited the first American publishers' trade paper,* Booksellers' Advertiser and
Monthly Register of New Publications *(January–December
1834, January 1836), which he abandoned upon joining Wiley
and Long in 1836. Perhaps the book he took most pride in was*
American Facts *(1845), a handy reference book of information
about the United States that he published through the London
office of Wiley and Putnam.*

*Putnam also published two travelogues with Wiley and
Putnam. He combined the earlier one,* Memoranda During a
Tour of Eight Months in Great Britain and on the Con-
tinent, *in 1836, with his European guidebook* The Tourist in

Europe, *in one volume published in 1838. The second travelogue he published was* A Pocket Memorandum Book During a Ten Weeks' Trip to Italy and Germany in 1847 *(1848), which chronicled the European business trip/vacation he made buying rare books for the collector James Lenox and touring for pleasure in the company of his wife and friends.*

In a more strictly professional vein, Putnam oversaw the London portion of the editing and compilation of Wiley and Putnam's Literary News-Letter and Monthly Register of New Books. *He also compiled many book catalogues—typically among the most professional such catalogues of the time—for both Wiley and Putnam and G. P. Putnam of domestic and foreign books. One standout catalogue was his firm's* Catalogue of Foreign and American Books *(alternately known as "Putnam's Book-Buyer's Manual"), a two-hundred-page compendium of G. P. Putnam's mostly contemporary works that he marketed to the trade in 1850. He continued to produce trade-oriented works of that sort to the end of his career, one of the finest being* The Best Reading (1872). *Putnam also edited important gift books for his company, including* Home Book of the Picturesque *(1852),* Homes of American Authors *(1853), and* Homes of American Statesmen *(1854).*

PUTNAM BOOKS BY PUTNAM: *The Tourist in Europe; or, a Concise Summary of the Various Routes, Objects of Interest, &c in Great Britain, France, Switzerland, Italy, Germany, Belgium and Holland; with Hints on Time, Expenses, Hotels, Conveyances, Passports, Coins, &c; Memoranda During a Tour of Eight Months in Great Britain and on the Continent, in 1836* (New York: Wiley & Putnam, 1838);

American Facts: Notes and Statistics Relative to the Government, Resources, Engagements, Manufactures, Commerce, Religion, Education, Literature, Fine Arts, Manners and Customs of the United States of America (London: Wiley & Putnam, 1845);

A Pocket Memorandum Book During a Ten Weeks' Trip to Italy and Germany in 1847 (New York, 1848);

The World's Progress: A Dictionary of Dates: with Tabular Views of General History, revised and enlarged edition (New York: G. P. Putnam, 1850; revised, 1851); republished as *Handbook of Chronology and History: The World's Progress, A Dictionary of Dates: with Tabular Views of General History* (New York: G. P. Putnam, 1852); republished as *The World's Progress: A Dictionary of Dates, with Tabular Views of General History* (New York: Barnes / Cincinnati: Derby, 1854); republished as *The World's Progress: A Dictionary of Dates; With Tabular Views of General History and a Historical Chart* (New York: G. P. Putnam, 1857); revised and enlarged as *Cyclopedia of Chronology; or, The World's Progress: A Dictionary of Dates, with Tabular Views of General History and an Historical Chart* (New York: Barnes & Burr, 1860);

revised and enlarged as *The World's Progress: A Dictionary of Dates, Being a Chronological and Alphabetical Record of All Essential Facts in the Progress of Society, from the Creation of the World to the Inauguration of Lincoln* (New York: G. P. Putnam, 1864); revised and enlarged as *The World's Progress: A Dictionary of Dates: Being a Chronological and Alphabetical Record of All Essential Facts in the Progress of Society, from the Creation of the World to August, 1867* (New York: G. P. Putnam and Son, 1867); **first edition,** *Chronology: or, An Introduction and Index to Universal History, Biography, and Useful Knowledge; Comprising a Chronological, Contemporary, and Alphabetical Record, of Important and Interesting Occurrence, from the Earliest Period to the Present Time* (New York: Leavitt / Boston: Crocker & Brewster, 1833);

Memorial of James Fenimore Cooper (New York: G. P. Putnam, 1852);

Catalogue of A Private Collection of Autograph Letters, Documents, Portraits and Curiosities (New York: G. P. Putnam, 1858);

Suggestions for Household Libraries of Essential and Standard Books (Exclusive of Scientific and Religious Works) (New York: G. P. Putnam and Sons, 1870); revised as *The Best Reading: Hints on the Selection of Books; on the Formation of Libraries, Public and Private* (New York: G. P. Putnam's Sons, 1873).

OTHER: *Home Book of the Picturesque* (New York: G. P. Putnam, 1852);

Homes of American Authors (New York: G. P. Putnam and Company, 1853);

Homes of American Statesmen (New York: G. P. Putnam and Company, 1854);

Ten Years of the World's Progress, Being a Supplement to the Work of That Title, edited by Putnam (New York: G. P. Putnam, 1861);

Haydn's Dictionary of Dates, edited by Benjamin Vincent with a supplement by Putnam (New York: G. P. Putnam and Son, 1867).

* * *

Knickerbocker Magazine editor Lewis Gaylord Clark gives a generous "puff" to Putnam's guidebook The Tourist in Europe. *Clark does not mention that he serialized portions of the book in his magazine.*

THE TOURIST IN EUROPE.—We have examined the MSS. of a work under this title, now in the press of Messrs. WILEY AND PUTNAM, the plan and execution of which combine the useful and entertaining, in a very happy manner. In addition to the memoranda made during a tour of eight months in Great Britain and on the Continent, in 1836, which alone comprise a mass of valuable facts and interesting descriptions, in a style at once spirited and unassuming, this volume will contain a variety of valuable information for Americans going to Europe; such as outlines of the various routes; references to places and things most worthy of notice; hints on time, distances, hotels, conveyances, passports; tables of actual expenses during recent tours in Great Britain, France, Switzerland, Germany, Belgium and Holland; table of coins of those countries, and their relative value; list of travels, 'guide books;' and other details, carefully collected from original sources, and personal observation. Thus, while of special value to the tourist, this book will be no less attractive to the general reader.

–Knickerbocker Magazine, 11 (February 1838): 189

* * *

Another friendly review of Putnam's The Tourist in Europe *appeared in* American Monthly Magazine.

WE have just space enough left, in which to commend this excellent, unpretending little volume. It is, we understand, from the pen of Mr. George Putnam, a partner in the publishing house by which it was issued. It is a highly creditable production. The letters are written in an off-hand, easy, and amusing style, which, without evincing any attempt at display, shows that the author was willing to draw freely upon his resources for the gratification of the reader. It is a most valuable guide-book for travellers, and to such we recommend it, as well to those who may be disposed to live over again in imagination the time of their sojournings abroad.

– American Monthly Magazine, 5 (April 1838): 384

* * *

Putnam was quick to protect his literary properties against pirates. One means of defense he frequently took was to expose unethical or illegal acts in the local or trade press. This attempt to forestall a "raid" on his Irving properties by exposing it in The New York Times *survived as a clipping in Putnam's scrapbook.*

To the Editor of the New-York Times:

A paragraph copied in the <u>Times</u> from a letter in the Boston <u>Post,</u> makes a statement in regard to some unknown person's intention to "do a little freebooting" on some volumes of Irving's earlier works. To call this proposed proceeding "privateering," as the writer does elsewhere, is perhaps scarcely correct, if privateering means licensed and authorized warfare on an enemy's property. This "intention" does not appear to have any

such warrant. No <u>enmity</u> or open warfare is pretended–no reprisals for damage done, or public or personal injury sustained–but simple, plain, open, or rather secret "freebooting"; for the "enterprising" and "adventurous freebooter" is apparently so doubtful of the character of his proposed "raid" on the private interests and property of two families, (no member of which I am quite sure has ever done him an injury, whoever he is,) that he hesitates to give his own name, but suggests the "ventilation" of his free and easy project through an anonymous correspondent of a journal in another city.

The legal, moral, commercial, or other aspects of the proposed invasion, or–whatever it may be properly designated, need not be discussed at present. It is just possible that though the "freebooter" may have power to inflict some damage on me and those dependent upon me, as well as on the large family circle of the author in question, he may find it will prove of less benefit to himself than he now supposes.

I would scarcely beg leave at present, to state that I am still the publisher of <u>all</u> of Irving's works; that my contract for them, has just been renewed for five years; that there are no "new publishers" to be attacked, for my interest in the books are the same as ever; that the present editions of the works contain a large amount of new matter which the "freebooter" might find it unpleasant to steal; and that the attempt to reprint the incomplete and unrevised edition of the two or three volumes which, <u>in these imperfect editions,</u> have ceased to be protected, is a gross injustice to the memory of the author, as well as an unjustifiable raid on the private interests and means of his family. This, at least, is my honest impression, albeit a selfish view of the case.

Even if there were no copyright, if the books were <u>foreign,</u> but had been reprinted for a long series of years in every variety of form which the public demanded–the involvement of time and money in the mere manufacture, would seem to be entitled to some courtesy, to say the least. No publisher, however, who claims any position in the trade or the community worthy of true respect, would need any argument on this point.

I would merely add that even the excuse that the "raided" article may be sold <u>cheaper,</u> will not hold in this case. Editions of all these volumes, in the revised and <u>complete</u> form, are either ready or in active progress, to be sold at the minimum rates of non-copyright books. Yours respectfully,

G. P. Putnam

–Manuscripts Division, Department of Rare Books and Special Collections, Princeton University Library. Published with permission of the Princeton University Library.

Henry Tuckerman, who contributed to G. P. Putnam books and magazines for more than two decades

Henry Tuckerman

Henry Tuckerman (1813–1871) was a leading critic of arts and letters in mid-century America. A longtime friend of Putnam's, he began their professional association with the publication of The Optimist *in 1850. During the next few years he was particularly active with the house, contributing a landscape sketch to* Home Book of the Picturesque *(1852), writing the Washington Irving sketch in* Home of American Authors *(1853), and compiling* A Memorial of Horatio Greenough *(1853). Tuckerman also contributed to both* Putnam's Monthly *and* Putnam's Magazine, *serving the latter, as well, as an assistant editor covering the fine arts. Finally, he edited for the firm a posthumous edition of the writings of John Pendleton Kennedy and wrote a biography of the author,* The Life of John Pendleton Kennedy *(1871).*

Tuckerman's outstanding publication with G. P. Putnam was Book of the Artists. American Artist Life *(1867), which marked the culmination of his interest in the history of the arts in America. In his book he called formally for the establishment of a major art museum in New York City and subsequently worked with Putnam to further this cause. Tuckerman died just months before the Metropolitan Museum of Art opened its doors in February 1872.*

PUTNAM BOOKS BY TUCKERMAN: *The Optimist* (New York: G. P. Putnam, 1850); republished as *The Optimist: A Series of Essays* (New York: G. P. Putnam, 1852);

Sicily: A Pilgrimage (New York: G. P. Putnam, 1852); **first edition,** *Isabel; or, A Pilgrimage in Sicily* (Philadelphia: Lea & Blanchard, 1839);

A Memorial of Horatio Greenough (New York: G. P. Putnam and Company, 1853);

The Character and Portraits of Washington (New York: G. P. Putnam, 1859);

Book of the Artists. American Artist Life (New York: G. P. Putnam and Son, 1867);

Maga Papers about Paris (New York: G. P. Putnam and Son, 1867);

The Life of John Pendleton Kennedy (New York: G. P. Putnam and Sons, 1871).

OTHER: "Over the Mountains; or, The Western Pioneer," in *Home Book of the Picturesque: or, American Scenery, Art, and Literature* (New York: G. P. Putnam, 1852).

* * *

In the last years of his life Tuckerman not only wrote a biography of John Pendleton Kennedy but also supervised G. P. Putnam's new editions of Kennedy's works, which updated and expanded upon the revised editions of Kennedy's chief novels that the firm brought out in the early 1850s.

THE last act of the late H. T. Tuckerman was to pen a brief note, the Saturday night before he died, to his friend and publisher, Mr. G. P. Putnam, in reference to the works of Hon. John P. Kennedy, which he had just finished editing. He was then failing rapidly, and the precious memento is but an undecipherable scrawl. Mr. Tuckerman refused to accept remuneration, either for his biography of Mr. Kennedy, an old and dear friend, one of whose literary executors he was, or for the editing of his works. Of the latter, three volumes remain, to be published next month by the Messrs. Putnam: his "Journey in Europe and other Journals," "Political Papers," and "Miscellanies," uniform with those preceding. On these Mr. Tuckerman's last literary work was done. The Putnams will also print immediately, chiefly for private circulation, a memorial of the late critic, containing Dr. Bellows's funeral address and a fine portrait.

– *Publishers' and Stationers' Weekly Trade Circular*, 1 (18 January 1872): 8

Susan Warner, a best-selling author in the 1850s, whether as "Elizabeth Wetherell" or under her own name

Susan Warner

Susan Warner (1819–1895) is most widely recognized as a G. P. Putnam author for her hugely successful sentimental novel The Wide, Wide World *(1850), which is also widely regarded as her first book of any kind. She had, however, previously collaborated with her sister Anna on a children's book published by G. P. Putnam in late 1849,* Robinson Crusoe's Farmyard, *which was accompanied by a set of related playing cards colored by the sisters.*

Putnam accepted The Wide, Wide World *for publication—after it had been turned down by various other New York City houses—in summer 1850. He and his wife invited Warner to their Staten Island home for several weeks in late September and early October while she read proof. The novel was published in December and in the following year became a runaway best-seller. Warner then published a second domestic sentimental novel with Putnam,* Queechy, *which, though not quite as popular or as well received as its predecessor, also sold tens of thousands of copies. Unfortunately for Putnam,* Queechy *was the last adult novel that she was to produce for the house.*

The close working relations between Warner and Putnam continued for another four years, during which time Warner turned to writing books for children. Beginning in 1853 she collaborated with her sister on a series called Ellen Montgomery's Book Shelf *that built*

on the popularity of the lead character of The Wide, Wide World. *G. P. Putnam published the first title in the series,* Mr. Rutherford's Children, *as well as three more titles over the next three years. The connection between the Warners and the house ended, however, in 1856, as the sisters became more involved with the leading religious publisher in New York City, Robert Carter, even though their friendship with Putnam continued to the end of his life.*

PUTNAM BOOKS BY WARNER: *The Wide, Wide World* (2 volumes, New York: G. P. Putnam, 1850; 1 volume, London: Nisbet, 1852);
Robinson Crusoe's Farmyard (New York: G. P. Putnam, 1851);
Queechy, 2 volumes (New York: G. P. Putnam, 1852; London: Nisbet, 1852);
Mr. Rutherford's Children, 2 volumes (New York: Putnam, 1853–1855);
Carl Krinken: His Christmas Stocking, by Warner and Anna Warner (New York: G. P. Putnam and Company, 1853); republished as *The Christmas Stocking* (London: Nisbet, 1853);
Wych Hazel, by Warner and Anna Warner (New York: G. P. Putnam's Sons, 1876; London: Nisbet, 1876);
The Gold of Chickaree, by Warner and Anna Warner (New York: G. P. Putnam's Sons, 1876; London: Nisbet, 1876);
Diana (New York: G. P. Putnam's Sons, 1877; London: Nisbet, 1877).

* * *

The following passage, a 25 September 1850 journal entry that Susan's sister Anna published in her biography Susan Warner *(1909), details Warner's first meeting with Putnam, which took place at his 155 Broadway office. She was to accompany Putnam and his wife to their Staten Island home, where she would be their guest while correcting proof of* The Wide, Wide World.

I was introduced in due form, as you have doubtless heard, to my host and hostess, and established in one of the two armchairs behind the screen, in the great bookstore, to await the time when we might walk down to Whitehall to take the one o'clock boat for Staten Island. Little Minny Putnam was introduced to me as, I believe, the lady who had written "Robinson Crusoe's Farmyard," but I did n't rush into explanations at the very first burst. Mr. Putnam shewed me a beautiful illustrated copy of "Rural Hours"; exquisite birds and pretty flowers; but *I* would have given more general illustrations. He also shewed me some papier maché covers for the same work,—adorned very handsomely with mother-of-pearl wreaths of flowers—all different. That book has taken very well; is n't it odd? Then I turned over the leaves of a most splendid Pilgrims Progress which Mr. Putnam had received as a present from England. Full of illustrations beautifully done, in all but the *mind's* part; so on the whole to my taste poor. Mr. P. had left us, after shewing me a bundle of proofs and telling me if I was tired of waiting there I might amuse myself with them. Not *there,* many thanks to him. I sat looking over the Pilgrims Progress, too much out of my latitude to enjoy it, and sometimes exchanging a few words with Mrs. Putnam. By and by appeared Mr. Putnam, and surprised me greatly by saying to me that he had been so fortunate as to secure a ticket for me for Jenny Lind's concert that evening,—he could only get such and such a place, but it was the last ticket to be had. Mrs. Putnam then and afterwards expressed great pleasure that he had succeeded; she had been afraid they would have to do a rude thing,—go off and leave me alone. . . .

— Susan Warner, pp. 287–288

* * *

Warner commissions Putnam to sell her family's portrait of George Washington.

The Island
West Point N. Y.
Dec. 27, 1870

Dear Mr Putnam

I asked one of your boys, the other day, Mr Irving I think, to ask you to be so kind as to send the Washington to me again—which you have kindly kept for me so long. But now I am going to ask you instead to <u>sell</u> it for me. I want money. I must part with the picture, if I can for any <u>reasonable</u> price. I will not stand on $1000. I will take less—& I will allow you or any of your boys a good commission for selling it. Can it be done? Of course before you should close with any purchaser I should like to be communicated with—<u>unless</u> you should have a good price offered that there would be no question about accepting.

— Clifton Waller Barrett Library of American Literature, Special
Collections Department, University of Virginia Library

Fredrika Bremer

A Swedish fiction writer, essayist, and memoirist with an international reputation and following, Fredrika Bremer (1801–1865) became one of the most popular writers in mid-century America. Originally published by Harper and Brothers in the 1840s, she made Putnam's acquaintance in 1848 or 1849 at the home of Andrew Jackson Downing. The author and the publisher soon developed a warm friendship and a professional relationship. Following a visit with the Putnams at their Staten Island home in October 1849, she entered into an agreement to allow his firm to reprint two of her most popular novels, The Home (1850) *and* The Neighbours (1850). *In return,*

Fredrika Bremer, whose alliance with Putnam after years of publishing with the Harpers led to tension between the houses

Putnam agreed to pay her a royalty on all copies sold, a better deal than she had previously had with the Harpers.

Because of Putnam's arrangement with Bremer, the Harpers took revenge in 1851 by publishing a cheaper version of G. P. Putnam's edition of George Borrow's Lavengro, *which they brought out in cooperation with the author and his London publisher. Putnam, however, did not back down; five years later he pursued his special relationship with Bremer by publishing an authorized edition of her new novel,* Hertha (1856). *To protect both her and himself, he printed advance advertisements in the press that excerpted her letter authorizing him as her American publisher.*

PUTNAM BOOKS BY BREMER: *The Home,* translated from the Swedish by Mary Howitt (New York: G. P. Putnam, 1850); **first American edition,** *The Home* (New York: Harpers, 1843);

The Neighbours (New York: G. P. Putnam, 1850); **first American edition,** *The Neighbors* (New York: Harpers, 1843);

Hertha, translated by Howitt (New York: G. P. Putnam and Company, 1856).

* * *

Bremer's gratitude to Putnam for his various professional services in promoting her as both an author and a lecturer was deep and long-lasting. She expressed it publicly in the protofeminist "Dedication for the American Edition" of Hertha, *published by G. P. Putnam and Company in 1856. Andrew Jackson Downing, the landscape architect and author, became one of Bremer's dearest American friends during her 1849 visit in the country.*

To the
Blessed Memory of
A. J. Downing,
This book is dedicated in love and grateful remembrance
By the Author

"The women must regenerate us socially," was a favorite saying of yours, my friend, a saying precious to me as coming from a spirit so just, so observing, and discriminating as yours; and as it seemed to me to express a feeling inherent though half conscious in the people of your country, the great New World, the land of promise and of hope to millions of hearts in Europe.

It also corresponded deeply to the faith of my own heart. But if woman shall be able to accomplish the great work which we believe intrusted to her by the great author of life; our laws and customs, institutions and education, must not counteract the normal development of her noblest faculties, of her will and aspirations; they must rather be to her the very soil and sun in which the tree of life can grow, and develop its branches and bear its fruits, in full correspondence to its inward essence. You will certainly assent to this, my friend, you whose skilful hand loved to raise plants of every kind so as to propitiate their full growth and God-given beauty or grace. But is it so with regard to human institutions—for the growth of woman's mind, and the full development of her God-given gifts?

You know, my friend, that it is not so; you observed it already on earth, and you must know it better still in that blessed society where men and women commune as angels before the face of God. Even in your native land, which a friend and countryman of mine calls, "The promised land of woman, and the child," and where the women are indulged and left fancy-free certainly more than in any other country on earth, it is not so. There, even there, indulgence has not yet become justice, and the love for woman not reverence to her mission, so as to command a training for her mind, and opportunities for its development corresponding to that mission—training and opportunities which alone can make her acquire her full worth. Nor has she yet been propitiated so far in any country on earth, though superior natures have in almost all countries shown the worth and influence she is capable of.

Of her situation in my own land with reference to our laws and social customs, I have drawn a picture in the work which bears the name of *Hertha,* and which I dedicate to you; then by men such as you, and to you congenial, I should wish my work to be judged. Its bitter parts must be excused on the score of bitter pain, not of a selfish kind. The

patriarchal bonds which keep back the growth of woman's mind and social life in Sweden, and which sometimes amount to the most crushing tyranny, I have shadowed forth in these pages often with a heavy heart.

But I have done it for love for the moral growth and worth of my people, in strong faith and hope that when its noble spirit came to look facts in the face, and know the sufferings and debasement, or the bitterness of spirit arising from this state of things, it will rise and carry out in the liberation of woman, the noble motto of our present King, "*Truth and Justice.*"

My people was the first among the Scandinavian nations to liberate its slaves, when the blessed voice of the Redeemer was heard in the North, proclaiming the brotherhood of all men and the freedom in the *father* God. Certainly it cannot long be one of the last to liberate the loving companions of man, *woman,* from a state of tutelage and bondage, which other Christian countries have already shaken off for her. More than this liberation I do not at present hope for. But when the day will come, when the sons of the earth will better know their true welfare, they will give much more still to her who is to be the Mother and first teacher, in fact, the inspiring Egeria of the future generations, the coming Man! From your heavenly home, my friend, methinks I see you smiling down, "Amen."

Since we parted on America's shores, the homes of my country have drawn nearer to those of your land in sympathy and love for their noble hearts, their beautiful life, and I am happy to know that I have some part in this, though only as the well who gives back the images of the flowers and stars looking down in her mirror.

Your noblest poets and prose writers have begun to be translated in my native tongue. Uncle Tom's Cabin has been read passionately by rich and poor, in the palaces and cabins of my land; Longfellow's poems are translated by a graceful Swedish muse, and Washington Irving's Wolfert's Roost is now read in our daily papers throughout the land, with that peculiar pleasure and charm awakened by this delightful writer, ever young, ever pure, writing as no other romantic interest with classical purity and elegance, beloved by all classes, read in all lands.

Even your books, my friend, are spreading in my country, and are at this moment helping my brother-in-law to build a house and plant a garden for his summer residence.

At my parting with you, I promised to give the right of publication in America of a work of mine to a friend of yours, whose generous spirit even I had learned to know and to appreciate. In now giving my Hertha in the hands of Mr. George P. Putnam, I am conscious that I intrust to him the work, which, of all my writings, has the deepest root in my own life and consciousness,—a work which sacred duty commanded me to write. And I am happy to fulfil my engagement to him and a wish of yours.

F. B.

Susan Fenimore Cooper, seated in group at left. Her father, James Fenimore Cooper, stands behind her (detail in painting by Samuel F. B. Morse; Gallery of the Louvre, 1833).

Susan Fenimore Cooper

Until recently, Susan Fenimore Cooper (1813–1894) was remembered—to the extent that she was remembered at all—as the dutiful daughter and de facto literary executor of her famous father. Critics, though, have rediscovered her Rural Hours *(1850), an impressive work of naturalist sketches that quickly earned her a reputation with her contemporaries. It also earned substantial profits for her and G. P. Putnam, who rushed to publish an illustrated edition and kept the book in print for many years.*

Cooper planned a subsequent work, "The Shield," which she discussed with Putnam several times. Although the publisher advertised the book during the early 1850s as being "in progress," it was never completed. As an editor, Cooper did complete a second book for the company, The Rhyme and Reason of Country Life *(1854).*

PUTNAM BOOKS BY COOPER: *Rural Hours. By a Lady* (New York: G. P. Putnam, 1850; anonymous, 2 volumes, London: Bentley, 1850); republished as *Journal of a Naturalist in the United States* (London: Bentley, 1855); enlarged as *Rural Hours* (New York: G. P. Putnam and Son, 1868).

OTHER: *The Rhyme and Reason of Country Life; or, Selections from Fields Old and New,* edited, with a preface, introduction, and headnotes, by Cooper (New York: G. P. Putnam and Company, 1854).

* * *

Putnam took particular pride in his firm's illustrated edition of Rural Hours, *which he showed to Warner when she came to his store in September 1850. It was one of several illustrated Putnam editions on sale for the Christmas season that came in for notice in the following review.*

Another illustrated edition from Mr. Putnam's stock of American Classics, is Miss Cooper's Rural Hours, to which there are twenty-one happily-executed colored pictures of American birds and flowers, lithographed from the best designs, and all of them novel to the public in this popular form. There are few books which can have greater recommendations than this for the ensuing season. It is written by an American lady, in the purest style, and with the truest observation; full of the knowledge and love of things about us which constitute the essential holiday spirit.

– *The Literary World,* 7 (23 November 1850)

Notable Putnam Publications

Only a middle-sized publishing house operating generally with scarce captial, G. P. Putnam nevertheless had a national reputation for both the content and appearance of its publications. The strength of the house was in belles lettres, especially art, literature, travel, and history, and its list was geared to the tastes of the well-heeled middle class. The following list of select G. P. Putnam books presents many of the best-known works published by the house during its founder's era. Although there were a few best-sellers and a number of steady sellers among them, some of these books did not even meet expenses and others brought little profit to the house. This pattern was the same among most contemporaneous publishing houses, for losers often outnumbered winners; best-sellers were rare; and profit margins were tight.

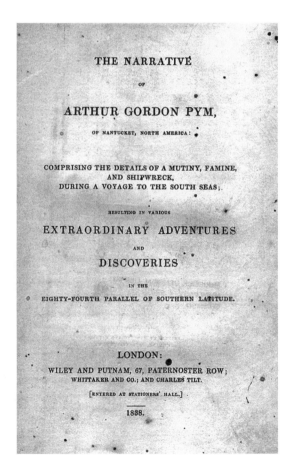

THE NARRATIVE

OF

ARTHUR GORDON PYM,

OF NANTUCKET, NORTH AMERICA:

COMPRISING THE DETAILS OF A MUTINY, FAMINE,
AND SHIPWRECK,
DURING A VOYAGE TO THE SOUTH SEAS;

RESULTING IN VARIOUS

EXTRAORDINARY ADVENTURES

AND

DISCOVERIES

IN THE

EIGHTY-FOURTH PARALLEL OF SOUTHERN LATITUDE.

LONDON:
WILEY AND PUTNAM, 67, PATERNOSTER ROW;
WHITTAKER AND CO.; AND CHARLES TILT.
[ENTERED AT STATIONERS' HALL.]

1838.

Title page for what was probably the first book published by the London office of Wiley and Putnam (courtesy of Special Collections, Thomas Cooper Library, University of South Carolina)

The Narrative of Arthur Gordon Pym (1838)

The New York edition of Edgar Allan Poe's only novel, The Narrative of Arthur Gordon Pym, *was published by Harper and Brothers in July 1838 when Putnam was already en route to establish the London office of Wiley and Putnam. One of the first titles he brought out—quite possibly, the first—once he set up operations was Poe's novel, which he had printed from a copy of the Harper edition. Although frequently labeled a pirated edition, the Wiley and Putnam* Narrative of Arthur Gordon Pym *did not infringe on any existent English copyright. To judge from the statement on the title page that the work was registered at Stationers' Hall, it is likely that Putnam personally sought local protection for his edition. Unwilling to wager too heavily on its profitability, he arranged for the work to be brought out jointly with his New York friends, the Appletons, as well as with two local firms, Charles Tilt and Whittaker and Company, which presumably offered distributional advantages attractive to a London newcomer.*

The Wiley and Putnam edition differed textually in several respects from the Harper edition. It included an introductory note, probably written by Putnam, that was signed "The Publishers. 67 Paternoster-row, London." Furthermore, it seriously bowdlerized the narrative by excising the culminating spectral vision with which the Harper edition ended.

* * *

The Wiley and Putnam edition was fairly widely reviewed in England. This reaction in the Court Gazette *is one of the earliest reviews, printed within days of its London publication. Like many others, the reviewer discusses the veracity of the narrative, which the London publishers affirmed in the preface. And like Putnam in his promotional notice and the majority of reviewers, the writer compares Poe's work to Daniel Defoe's* Robinson Crusoe *(1719).*

This is a book which, as the title setteth forth, comprises "the details of a mutiny, famine, and shipwreck, which occurred to the author during a voyage to the South Seas, resulting in various extraordinary adventures and discoveries in the eighty-fourth parallel of southern latitude." We apprehend it has been produced as a sort of practical exposition and proof of Byron's assertion, that "truth is stranger than fiction." It is, in fact, a book of wonders, originally published in an American periodical, without any warranty of truth. It now appears that the exciting interest of the story which is told, and the intrinsic evidence of its veracity and general accuracy, have induced the London publishers to present it to the public in an entire form. The style of the narrative is not an indifferent imitation of that adopted by De Foe, in his best novel, "Robinson Crusoe." In matters of surprise, if not in those which appertain to philosophy and morals, the volume will remind the reader of that popular work. We present the opening page. . . .

—*Court Gazette*, 13 October 1838

Letters and Notes on the Manners, Customs, and Condition of the North American Indians (1842)

The publication of George Catlin's classic study of Native American life, Letters and Notes on the Manners, Customs, and Condition of the North American Indians, *grew out of the friendship established in* London in the early 1840s between Catlin and Putnam. Catlin, a self-described "Nimrodical lawyer," gave up his profession to study painting. He spent much of the 1830s in the West studying, sketching, and painting the Native Americans of the Great Plains. Unable to sell his large collection of paintings to the United States government, he packed up his work and took it overseas, exhibiting his Indian Gallery to considerable crowds in London and Paris. Putnam first saw the exhibition in 1841 and quickly struck up a warm friendship with Catlin. As Catlin hoped to find a publisher willing to bring out an extensive compendium of his letters and sketches, their friendship inevitably turned to business. Several London publishers had rejected Catlin's offer outright, and Putnam, too, was initially reluctant to take on so risky and expensive a venture. He did agree, however, to make Wiley and Putnam the American distributor of the edition of the work that Catlin had printed in London in 1841. Wiley and Putnam published the expanded 1842 and 1844 American editions from sheets printed in London.

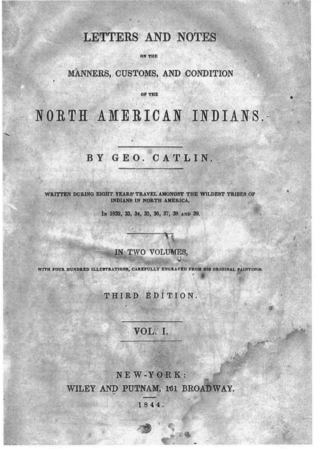

Frontispiece and title page for an expanded edition of the book Catlin originally had published himself in 1841. The illustration misrepresents the artist's method, for he usually produced a quick sketch of his subjects that he later turned into a painting (courtesy of Special Collections, Thomas Cooper Library, University of South Carolina).

Tales (1845)

The publication of Poe's Tales *originated in an offer made to the author in spring 1845 by Evert A. Duyckinck, who was then initiating the production of the Wiley and Putnam Library of American Books. Poe allowed Duyckinck to choose the stories, and the editor selected some of Poe's best work.* Tales *appeared as the second title in the series after Horatio Bridge's* Journal of an African Cruiser, *which was edited by Nathaniel Hawthorne. Wiley and Putnam brought out the work in June in a one-volume format bound in paper or cardboard, and Putnam soon thereafter published a London edition compiled from sheets of the New York edition fitted with a cancel title page.*

* * *

Margaret Fuller reviewed Poe's work several times in 1845, a year in which they both frequently appeared in print as authors and critics. Poe likewise discussed her work, even including her in a long, generally favorable sketch in 1846 as part of his coverage of "The New York Literati." Fuller's brief review of Tales *provides some of the most discerning contemporaneous analysis of Poe's skills as a short-fiction writer.*

Tales: By Edgar A. Poe. Wiley and Putnam's Library of American Books. No. II.

Mr. Poe's tales need no aid of newspaper comment to give them popularity; they have secured it. We are glad to see them given to the public in this neat form, so that thousands more may be entertained by them without force of injury to their eye-sight.

No form of literary activity has so terribly degenerated among us as the tale. Now that every body who wants a new hat or bonnet takes this way to earn one from the magazines or annuals, we are inundated with the very flimsiest fabrics ever spun by mortal brain. Almost every person of feeling or fancy could supply a few agreeable and natural narratives, but when, instead of using their materials spontaneously, they set to work, with geography in hand, to find unexplored nooks of wild scenery in which to locate their Indians, or interesting farmers' daughters, or with some abridgment of history to hunt up monarchs or heroes yet unused to become the subjects of their crude coloring, the sale-work produced is a sad affair indeed and "gluts the market" to the sorrow both of buyers and lookers-on.

In such a state of things, the writings of Mr. Poe are a refreshment, for they are the fruit of genuine observations and experience, combined with an invention, which is not "making up," as children call *their* way of contriving stories, but a penetration into the causes of things which leads to original but credible results. His narrative proceeds with vigor, his colors are applied with discrimination, and where the effects are fantastic they are not unmeaningly so.

The "Murders of the Rue Morgue" especially made a great impression upon those who did not know its author

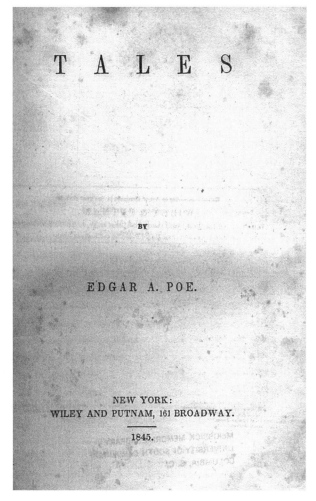

Title page for the collection of Poe's stories chosen by Putnam editor Evert A. Duyckinck (courtesy of Special Collections, Thomas Cooper Library, University of South Carolina)

and were not familiar with his mode of treatment. Several of his stories make us wish he would enter the higher walk of the metaphysical novel, and, taking a mind of the self-possessed and deeply marked sort that suits him, give us a deeper and longer acquaintance with its life and the springs of its life than is possible in the compass of these tales.

As Mr. Poe is a professed critic, and of all the band the most unsparing to others, we are surprized to find some inaccuracies in the use of words, such as these [:] "he had with him many books, but rarely *employed* them."—"His results have, in truth, the *whole air* of intuition."

The degree of skill shown in the management of revolting or terrible circumstances makes the pieces that have such subjects more interesting than the others. Even the failures are those of an intellect of strong fibre and well-chosen aim.

—New-York Tribune, 11 July 1845, p. 1

* * *

Poe's reaction to Fuller's remarks appeared in The Broadway Journal.

In a very complimentary notice, by Miss Fuller, of "Tales by Edgar A. Poe," the critic objects to the phrases "he had many books but rarely *employed* them"–and "his results, brought about by the very soul and essence of method, had, in fact, the *whole air* of intuition." We bow to the well-considered opinions of Miss Fuller, whom, *of course,* we very highly respect–but we have in vain endeavored to understand, in these cases, the grounds of her objections. Perhaps she will explain.

–*The Broadway Journal,* 2 (4 October 1845): 200

* * *

This appreciative analysis of Tales *appeared in* Graham's, *a magazine for which Poe had recently worked. Several of the tales reprinted in the collection had first appeared in* Graham's.

These tales are among the most original and characteristic compositions in American letters. In their collected form, they cannot fail to make a forcible impression on the reading public. We are glad to see them in a "Library of American Books." "The Gold Bug" attracted great attention at the time it appeared, and is quite remarkable as an instance of intellectual acuteness and subtlety of reasoning. "The Fall of the House of Usher" is a story of horror and gloom, in which the feeling of supernatural fear is represented with great power. The pertinacity with which Mr. Poe probes a terror to its depths, and spreads it out to the reader, so that it can be seen as well as felt, is a peculiarity of his tales. He is an anatomist of the horrible and ghastly, and trusts for effect, not so much in exciting a vague feeling of fear and terror, as in leading the mind through the whole framework of crime and perversity, and enabling the intellect to comprehend their law and relations. Metaphysical acuteness characterizes the whole book. "The Murders in the Rue Morgue," and "The Mystery of Marie Roget," are fine instances of the interest which may be given to subtle speculations and reasonings, when they are exercised to penetrate mysteries which the mind aches to know. "A Descent into the Maelstrom," "Mesmeric Revelation," "The Purloined Letter," "The Man of the Crowd," "The Black Cat," are all characterized by force and refinement of intellect, and are all effective as tales. The volume is a great stimulant to reflection. It demands intellectual activity in the reader. There are some hardy paradoxes in it, uttered with unhesitating confidence, and supported with great ingenuity. These "stir and sting" the mind to such a degree, that examination and reasoning become necessary to the reader's peace.

–*Graham's Magazine,* 28 (September 1845): 143

The Raven and Other Poems (1845)

Tales *sold well enough to justify the inclusion of a second Poe work in the Library of American Books. Cautious generally about the profitability of verse, the publishers included few volumes of poetry in either the Library of American Books or the Library of Choice Reading. They made an exception with Poe's poems, no doubt encouraged by the fame generated by "The Raven" following its newspaper and magazine publication in early 1845. The volume was published in November as the eighth title in the series. A London edition was published early the next year, printed, as was the firm's practice, from the New York sheets and fitted with a cancel title page. As with a few other brief works in their libraries, Wiley and Putnam produced a composite volume of Poe's work by binding some copies of* The Raven and Other Poems *with sets of sheets of* Tales.

* * *

In the preface to the Wiley and Putnam edition Poe calls poetry his "passion."

These trifles are collected and republished chiefly with a view to their redemption from the many improvements to which they have been subjected while going at random "the rounds of the press." If what I have written is to circulate at all, I am naturally anxious that it should circulate as I wrote it. In defence of my own taste, nevertheless, it is incumbent upon me to say, that I think nothing in this volume of much value to the public, or very creditable to myself. Events not to be controlled have prevented me from making, at any time, any serious effort in what, under happier circumstances, would have been the field of my choice. With me poetry has been not a purpose, but a passion; and the passions should be held in reverence; they must not–they cannot at all be excited with an eye to the paltry compensations, or the more paltry commendations, of mankind.

E. A. P.

* * *

Margaret Fuller wrote on Poe a second time in 1845 with this long review of his poetry in the New-York Tribune.

THE RAVEN AND OTHER POEMS: By Edgar A. Poe, 1845: (No. VIII. of Wiley and Putnam's Library of American Books.)

Mr. Poe throws down the gauntlet in his preface by what he says of "the paltry compensations or more paltry commendations of mankind." Some champion might be expected to start up from the "somewhat sizeable" class embraced, or more properly speaking, boxed on the ear, by this defiance, who might try whether the sting of Criticism was as indifferent to this knight of the pen as he professes its honey to be.

Were there such a champion, gifted with acumen to dissect, and a swift glancing wit to enliven the operation, he could find no more legitimate subject, no fairer game than Mr. Poe, who has wielded the weapons of criticism, without relenting, whether with the dagger he rent and tore the garment in which some favored Joseph had pranked himself, secure of honor in the sight of all men, or whether with uplifted tomahawk he rushed upon the new-born children of some hapless genius, who had fancied and persuaded his friends to fancy that they were beautiful and worthy a long and honored life. A large band of these offended dignitaries and aggrieved parents must be on the watch for a volume of "Poems by Edgar A. Poe," ready to cut, rend and slash in turn, and hoping to see his own Raven left alone to prey upon the slaughter of which it is the herald.

Such joust and tournament we look to see and, indeed, have some stake in the matter so far as we have friends whose wrongs cry aloud for the avenger. Natheless we could not take part in the *melée,* except to join the crowd of lookers-on in the cry—Heaven speed the right!

Early we read that fable of Apollo who rewarded the critic, who had painfully winnowed the wheat, with the chaff for his pains. We joined the gentle Affirmative School, and have confidence that if we indulge ourselves chiefly with the appreciation of the good qualities, Time will take care of the faults.—For Time holds a strainer like that used in the diamond mines;—have but patience and the water and gravel will all pass through and only the precious stones be left. Yet we are not blind to the uses of severe criticism, and of just censure, especially in a time and place so degraded by venal and indiscriminate praise as the present. That unholy alliance, that shameless sham, whose motto is

"Caw me

And I'll caw thee."

That system of mutual adulation and organized puff which was carried to such perfection in the time and may be seen drawn to the life in the correspondence of Miss Hannah More, is fully represented in our day and generation. We see that it meets a counter-agency, from the league of Truthtellers, few, but each of them mighty as Fingal or any other hero of the sort. Let such tell the whole truth, as well as nothing but the truth, but let their sternness be in the spirit of Love. Let them seek to understand the purpose and scope of an author, his capacity as well as his fulfilments, and how his faults are made to grow by the same sunshine that acts upon his virtues, for this is the case with talents no less than with

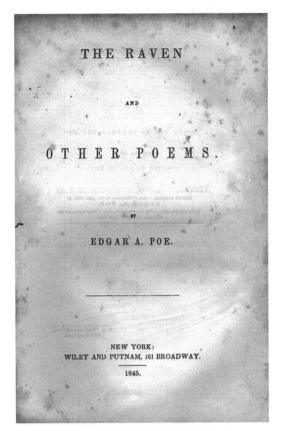

Title page for the collection Wiley and Putnam published after "The Raven" proved enormously popular earlier in 1845 (courtesy of Special Collections, Thomas Cooper Library, University of South Carolina)

character. The rich field requires frequent and careful weeding; frequent, lest the weeds exhaust the soil; careful, lest the flowers and grain be pulled up along with the weeds.

Well! but to return to Mr. Poe; we are not unwilling that cavil should do her worst on his book, because both by act and word he has challenged it, but as this is no office for us, we shall merely indicate, in our usual slight way, what, naturally and unsought, has struck ourselves in the reading of these verses.

It has often been our case to share the mistake of Gil Blas, with regard to the Archbishop. We have taken people at their word, and while rejoicing that women could bear neglect without feeling mean pique, and that authors, rising above self-love, could show candor about their works and magnanimously meet both justice and injustice, we have been rudely awakened from our dream, and found that Chanticleer, who crowed so bravely, showed himself at last but a dunghill fowl. Yet Heaven grant we never become too worldly-wise thus to trust a generous word, and we surely are not so yet, for we believe Mr. Poe to be sincere when he says:

"In defence of my own taste, it is incumbent upon me to say that I think nothing in this volume of much value to the public or very creditable to myself. Events not to be controlled have prevented me from making, at any time, any serious effort in what, under happier circumstances, would have been the field of my choice."

We believe Mr. Poe to be sincere in this declaration; if he is, we respect him; if otherwise, we do not. Such things should never be said unless in hearty earnest. If in earnest, they are honorable pledges; if not, a pitiful fence and foil of vanity. Earnest or not, the words are thus far true: the productions in this volume indicate a power to do something far better. With the exception of The Raven, which seems intended chiefly to show the writer's artistic skill, and is in its way a rare and finished specimen, they are all fragments—*fyttes* upon the lyre, almost all of which leave us something to desire or demand. This is not the case, however, with these lines . . .

[*Excerpts from "To One in Paradise" omitted.*]

This kind of beauty is especially conspicuous, then rising into dignity, in the poem called "The Haunted Palace."

The imagination of this writer rarely expresses itself in pronounced forms, but rather in a sweep of images, thronging and distant like a procession of moonlight clouds on the horizon, but like them characteristic and harmonious one with another, according to their office.

The descriptive power is greatest when it takes a shape not unlike an incantation, as in the first part of "The Sleeper," where

> "I stand beneath the mystic moon,
> An opiate vapor, dewy, dim,
> Exhales from out a golden rim,
> And, softly dripping, drop by drop,
> Upon the quiet mountain top,
> Steals drowsily and musically
> Into the Universal valley."

Why *universal*?—"resolve me that, Master Moth."
And farther on, "The lily *lolls* upon the wave."

This word lolls, often made use of in these poems, presents a vulgar image to our thought; we know not how it is to that of others.

The lines which follow about the open window are highly poetical. So is the "Bridal Ballad" in its power of suggesting a whole tribe and train of thoughts and pictures by few and simple touches.

The Poems written in youth, written, indeed, we understand, in childhood, before the author was ten years old, are a great psychological curiosity. Is it the delirium of a prematurely excited brain that causes such a rapture of words? What is to be gathered from seeing the future so fully anticipated in the germ? The passions are not unfrequently felt in their full shock, if

not in their intensity, at eight or nine years old, but here they are reflected upon,

> "Sweet was their death—with them to die was rife
> With the last ecstacy of satiate life."

The scenes from Politian are done with clear, sharp strokes; the power is rather metaphysical than dramatic. We must repeat what we have heretofore said, that we could wish to see Mr. Poe engaged in a metaphysical romance. He needs a sustained flight and a fair range to show what his powers really are. Let us have from him the analysis of the Passions, with their appropriate Fates; let us have his speculations clarified; let him intersperse dialogue or poem, as the occasion prompts, and give us something really good and strong, firmly wrought, and fairly blazoned. Such would be better employment than detecting literary larcenies, not worth pointing out if they exist. Such employment is quite unworthy of one who dares vie with the Angel.

[*The review concludes with the printing of "Israfel."*]
    —*New-York Tribune*, 26 November 1845, p. 1

Typee (1846)

Herman Melville's first novel, Typee, *was published by John Murray in London in the Colonial and Home Library and by Wiley and Putnam in New York in the Library of American Books. The manuscript by the unknown author came to Putnam in his London office just weeks after he had put Poe's* Raven and Other Poems *to press. A quick reading of the work, which reminded him of* Robinson Crusoe *(it was soon to be called "a second* Robinson Crusoe*" in one London review), persuaded Putnam to make an offer to Gansevoort Melville, the author's agent and brother, to publish it in New York. Terms were quickly worked out and Putnam sent a corrected copy of the Murray proof sheets by steamer to New York, where Wiley and Duyckinck rushed it into print. The Wiley and Putnam edition appeared in March and soon attracted widespread public attention.*

The March publication of the novel was only the beginning of the story of the New York publishing history of Typee. *Wiley's own examination of the text, prompted by reports about its salacious and sacrilegious character from his pastor and in the press, moved him later that spring to demand extensive expurgations from Melville before the book could be reprinted. On the defensive about the veracity of his text even before its publication in London and New York, Melville acceded broadly to Wiley's demand. But even before a revised New York edition could be prepared for press, the situation was complicated by the sudden emergence in early*

July of the real-life Richard Tobias Greene ("Toby" in the novel), whose own narrative Melville wished to add as a corroborating appendix to the revised edition. The heavily expurgated version of Typee, *with attacks against missionaries and graphic depictions of the sensual ease of Marquesan life eliminated or toned down—but its basic plot substantiated by the inclusion of "The Story of Toby"—was printed on 31 July 1846 and remained the text seen by the American public through the remainder of Melville's life.*

* * *

Gansevoort Melville in this excerpt discusses business details relating to Typee *with his brother. He enclosed a copy of the terms he had worked out with Wiley and Putnam for the American edition.*

London April 3rd 1846.
My dear Herman,
Herewith you have copy of the arrangement with Wiley & Putnam for the publication in the U S

of your work on the Marquesas. The letter of W & P under date of Jan 13th is the result of a previous understanding between Mr Putnam & myself. As the correspondence speaks for itself, it is quite unnecessary to add any comment. By the steamer of tomorrow I send to yr address several newspapers art & critiques on your book. The one in the "Sun" was written by a gentleman who is very friendly to myself, and who may possibly from that reason have made it unusually eulogistic–

Yours of Feb 28 was recd a few days ago by the sailing packet Joshua Bates. I am happy to learn by it that the previous intelligence transmitted by me was "gratifying enough." I am glad that you continue busy, and in my next or the one after that will venture to make some suggestions about your next book . . .

–reproduced by permission of the Houghton Library, Harvard University, MS Am 188 (163)

* * *

Frontispiece and title page for the only Melville novel published by Wiley and Putnam. After the dissolution of his partnership with John Wiley, Putnam published Melville stories in Putnam's Monthly *and a second novel,* Israel Potter *(courtesy of Special Collections, Thomas Cooper Library, University of South Carolina).*

Copyright entry for Typee *from the ledger of the lower Manhattan district court closest to the Wiley and Putnam office. Copyright law required the depositing of single copies of works at the local district court (reproduced by permission of the Houghton Library, Harvard University).*

In this unsigned notice in the Salem Advertiser, *Nathaniel Hawthorne joins many other contemporary reviewers in praising the power and freedom of Melville's writing. Shortly after he first met Hawthorne four years later, Melville was similarly enthusiastic about Hawthorne's contribution to the Library of American Books.*

Wiley and Putnam's Library of American Books, Nos. XIII and XIV. The present numbers of this excellent and popular series, contain a very remarkable work, entitled *Typee, or a Peep at Polynesian Life*. It records the adventures of a young American who ran away from a whale ship at the Marquesas, and spent some months as the guest, or captive, of a native tribe, of which scarcely anything had been hitherto known to the civilized world.–The book is lightly but vigorously written; and we are acquainted with no work that gives a freer and more effective picture of barbarian life, in that unadulterated state of which there are now so few specimens remaining. The gentleness of disposition that seems akin to the delicious climate, is shown in contrast with traits of savage fierceness;–on one page, we read of manners and modes of life that indicate a whole system of innocence and peace; and on the next, we catch a glimpse of a smoked human head, and the half-picked skeleton of what had been (in a culinary sense) a *well-dressed* man. The author's descriptions of the native girls are voluptuously colored, yet not more so than the exigencies of the subject appear to require. He has that freedom of view–it would be too harsh to call it laxity of principle–which renders him tolerant of codes of morals that may be little in accordance with our own; a spirit proper enough to a young and adventurous sailor, and which makes his book the more wholesome to our staid landsmen. The narrative is skilfully managed, and in a literary point of view, the execution of the work is worthy of the novelty and interest of its subject.

–*Salem Advertiser,* 25 March 1846, pp. 67–68

* * *

In this instance of one Library of American Books author reviewing another, Margaret Fuller praises Melville's South Sea narrative while also engaging the current controversy surrounding the book provoked by its harsh criticism of missionaries, a controversy she archly passes on to the young ladies of country sewing societies.

Typee would seem, also, to be the record of imaginary adventures by someone who had visited those regions. But it is a very entertaining and

pleasing narrative, and the Happy Valley of the gentle cannibals compares very well with the best contrivances of the learned Dr. Johnson to produce similar impressions. Of the power of this writer to make pretty and spirited pictures as well [as] of his quick and arch manner generally, a happy specimen may be seen in the account of the savage climbing the cocoa-tree, p. 273, vol. 2d. Many of the observations and narratives we suppose to be strictly correct. Is the account given of the result of the missionary enterprises in the Sandwich Islands of this number? We suppose so from what we have heard in other ways. With a view to ascertaining the truth, it would be well if the sewing societies, now engaged in providing funds for such enterprises, would read the particulars they will find in this book beginning p. 249, vol. 2d, and make inquiries in consequence, before going on with their efforts. Generally, the sewing societies of the country villages will find this the very book they wish to have read while assembled at their work. Othello's hairbreadth 'scapes were nothing to those by this hero in the descent of the cataracts, and many a Desdemona might seriously incline her ear to the descriptions of the lovely Fay-a-way.

–*New-York Tribune,* 4 April 1846, p. 1

* * *

Walt Whitman briefly remarked on Typee *in a column titled "Literary News, Notices, etc."*

Typee.–A strange, graceful, most readable book this. It seems to be a compound of the "Seward's Narrative," and "Guidentio de Lucca," style and reading. As a book to hold in one's hand and pore dreamily over of a summer day, it is unsurpassed.–(Wiley & Putnam, 161 Broadway.)

–*Brooklyn Daily Eagle,* 15 April 1846

Mosses from an Old Manse (1846)

When Duyckinck initiated the Library of American Books, in part to publicize the accomplishments of American authors, he had Hawthorne particularly in mind. He was pleased to have Hawthorne's involvement in preparing for print the first title in the library, Horatio Bridge's Narrative of an African Cruiser, *but he wanted to include an original work by Hawthorne that would allow him to cast national attention on this still largely unknown author. To Duyckinck's delight, Hawthorne accepted his proposal in spring 1845 to prepare a book of tales to be published in the Wiley and Putnam series.*

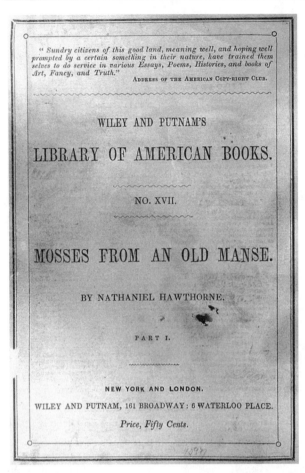

"Sundry citizens of this good land, meaning well, and hoping well prompted by a certain something in their nature, have trained them selves to do service in various Essays, Poems, Histories, and books of Art, Fancy, and Truth."
ADDRESS OF THE AMERICAN COPY-RIGHT CLUB.

WILEY AND PUTNAM'S

LIBRARY OF AMERICAN BOOKS.

NO. XVII.

MOSSES FROM AN OLD MANSE.

BY NATHANIEL HAWTHORNE.

PART I.

NEW YORK AND LONDON.

WILEY AND PUTNAM, 161 BROADWAY: 6 WATERLOO PLACE.

Price, Fifty Cents.

Title page for the 1846 collection of stories that was Hawthorne's well-received contribution to Wiley and Putnam's Library of American Books (courtesy of the American Antiquarian Society)

Mosses from an Old Manse did not appear in the Library, however, for a year after their agreement. The delay was occasioned by Hawthorne's protracted difficulty in composing the opening sketch "The Old Manse," accounts of which filled the letters Hawthorne wrote Duyckinck during the interval. The book finally appeared in a two-volume format in the Library of American Books in June 1846, with the London edition published by Putnam about a month later.

* * *

While he was awaiting the manuscript of Journal of an African Cruiser *that Hawthorne was editing, Duyckinck wrote to Hawthorne to offer terms for the publication of a story collection. One sign of the firm's eagerness to publish such a book was the uncharacteristic offer of an advance. Hawthorne, who doubtless was excited by the prospect of gaining a national audience for his work, quickly accepted the offer. John O'Sullivan, influential editor of the* Democratic Review, *was eager to see his friend's work finally earn a national reputation.*

20 Clinton Place March 21, 1845

Dear Sir,

I have to acknowledge the receipt of your letter–but that might have been done some fortnight ago. I was waiting to receive the promised MSS book of travels and reply then. But within a few days I have been dipping into that fountain–the genius of M. Aubepine (What I found there is written in the next 'Democratic') and the result of a renewed intimacy with the author is that it is desirable for Messrs Wiley & Putnam to publish something in their series from Mr. Hawthorne himself and that if Mr H has not a new book to publish a volume of once Told Stories will meet the requirement.

Mr Wiley is of the same opinion and on conference with Mr O'Sullivan, who has on his mind and in his heart the literary welfare of Mr Hawthorne, the publication of a volume of such tales seemed advisable. There is one other important person to consult and that is Mr H himself. Can you let Messrs W & P have some twelve or fifteen of your Tales not published in the two volumes and if possible a few more [?] and a Preface–if you choose to write one. The terms Messrs W & P offer are eight cents a copy on the edition, fully equal to one half the profits. The book to be stereotyped and vigorously pushed and for a couple of unpublished Tales to go in the number they would advance you at once One Hundred dollars on a semi-annual settlement. One of the advantages of this mode of publication, a very neat and elegant one, by the way,–of which I send you a specimen in a [?] by mail,–might be–if this first volume be successful and I see no reason to doubt it–the gradual collection and publication of all your Tales in successive volumes. The library is to be conducted with spirit–the works of Leigh Hunt, Lamb, Hazlitt and others of a similar genuine stamp included. Mr Wiley is in treaty with [Nathaniel Parker] Willis and has already secured a volume from Poe.

The following occur to me–Buds and Bird Voices; The Procession of Life; The New Adam & Eve; The Celestial Railroad; Egotism or the Bosom Serpent; Fire Worship; Roger Malvin's Burial; The Two Widows; The Artist of the Beautiful; Writings of M Aubepine; Young Goodman Brown; The History of a Bell (in the Knickerbocker) & some late ones in the Democratic.

The copyright of course yours & the arrangement made for a definite time.

I have now laid the whole matter before you and await your early answer. I am also looking out for the MSS Travels.

–Duyckinck Family Papers, Manuscripts and Archives Division, The New York Public Library, Astor, Lenox and Tilden Foundations

* * *

Written four years after the publication of Mosses from an Old Manse, *Melville's essay in* The Literary World *is the most famous and enduring nineteenth-century review not only of the collection but also of any of the works published in Wiley and Putnam's Library of American Books. It is also one of the most powerful expressions of the cultural nationalism pervasive among the series's editors, publishers, and authors alike.*

Hawthorne and His Mosses

By A Virginian Spending July in Vermont

A papered chamber in a fine old farm-house–a mile from any other dwelling, and dipped to the eaves in foliage–surrounded by mountains, old woods, and Indian ponds,–this, surely is the place to write of Hawthorne. Some charm is in this northern air, for love and duty seem both impelling to the task. A man of a deep and noble nature has seized me in this seclusion. His wild, witch-voice rings through me; or, in softer cadences, I seem to hear it in the songs of the hill-side birds that sing in the larch trees at my window.

Would that all excellent books were foundlings, without father or mother, that so it might be, we could glorify them, without including their ostensible authors! Nor would any true man take exception to this;–least of all, he who writes, "When the Artist rises high enough to achieve the Beautiful, the symbol by which he makes it perceptible to mortal senses becomes of little value in his eyes, while his spirit possesses itself in the enjoyment of the reality."

But more than this, I know not what would be the right name to put on the title-page of an excellent book; but this I feel, that the names of all fine authors are fictitious ones, far more so than that of Junius;–simply standing, as they do, for the mystical, ever-eluding spirit of all beauty, which ubiquitously possesses men of genius. Purely imaginative as this fancy may appear, it nevertheless seems to receive some warranty from the fact, that on a personal interview no great author has ever come up to the idea of his reader. But that dust of which our bodies are composed, how can it fitly express the nobler intelligences among us? With reverence be it spoken, that not even in the case of one deemed more than man, not even in our Saviour, did his visible frame betoken anything of the augustness of the nature within. Else, how could those Jewish eyewitnesses fail to see heaven in his glance!

It is curious, how a man may travel along a country road, and yet miss the grandest, or sweetest of prospects, by reason of an intervening hedge, so like all other hedges, as in no way to hint of the wide landscape beyond. So has it been with me concerning the enchanting landscape in the soul of this Hawthorne, this most excellent Man of Mosses. His "Old Manse" has been written now four years, but I never read it till a day or two since. I had seen it in the book-stores–heard of it often–even had it recommended to me by a tasteful friend, as a rare, quiet book, perhaps too deserving of popularity to be popular. But there are so many books called "excellent," and so much unpopular merit, that amid the thick stir of other things, the hint of my tasteful friend was disregarded; and for four years the Mosses on the Old Manse never refreshed me with their perennial green. It may be, however, that all this while, the book, likewise, was only improving in flavor and body. At any rate, it so chanced that this long procrastination eventuated in a happy result. At breakfast the other day, a mountain girl, a cousin of mine, who for the last two weeks has every morning helped me to strawberries and raspberries, which, like the roses and pearls in the fairy tale, seemed to fall into the saucer from those strawberry-beds, her cheeks–this delightful creature, this charming Cherry says to me–"I see you spend your mornings in the haymow; and yesterday I found there 'Dwight's Travels in New England.' Now I have something far better than that, something more congenial to our summer on these hills. Take these raspberries, and then I will give you some moss." "Moss!" said I. "Yes, and you must take it to the barn with you, and good-by to 'Dwight.'"

With that she left me, and soon returned with a volume, verdantly bound, and garnished with a curious frontispiece in green; nothing less than a fragment of real moss cunningly pressed to a flyleaf. "Why, this," said I, spilling my raspberries, "this is the 'Mosses from an Old Manse.'" "Yes," said cousin Cherry, "yes, it is that flowery Hawthorne." "Hawthorne and Mosses," said I, "no more: it is morning: it is July in the country: and I am off for the barn."

Stretched on that new mown clover, the hill-side breeze blowing over me through the wide barn-door, and soothed by the hum of the bees in the meadows around, how magically stole over me this Mossy Man! and how amply, how bountifully, did he redeem that delicious promise to his guests in the Old Manse, of whom it is written–"Others could give them pleasure, or amusement, or instruction–these could be picked up anywhere–but it was for me to give them rest. Rest, in a life of trouble! What better could be done for weary and world-worn spirits? What better could be done for anybody, who came within our magic circle, than to throw the spell of a magic spirit over him?"–So all that day, half-buried in the new clover, I watched this Hawthorne's "Assyrian dawn, and Paphian sunset and moonrise, from the summit of our Eastern Hill."

An engraving of the Old Manse that appeared in Homes of American Authors *as Hawthorne's place of residence, though Hawthorne neither owned nor had lived in the house for a decade*

The soft ravishments of the man spun me round about in a web of dreams, and when the book was closed, when the spell was over, this wizard "dismissed me with but misty reminiscences, as if I had been dreaming of him."

What a wild moonlight of contemplative humor bathes that Old Manse!–the rich and rare distilment of a spicy and slowly-oozing heart. No rollicking rudeness, no gross fun fed on fat dinners, and bred in the lees of wine,–but a humor so spiritually gentle, so high, so deep, and yet so richly relishable, that it were hardly inappropriate in an angel. It is the very religion of mirth; for nothing so human but it may be advanced to that. The orchard of the Old Manse seems the visible type of the fine mind that has described it–those twisted and contorted old trees, "that stretch out their crooked branches, and take such hold of the imagination, that we remember them as humorists and odd-fellows." And then, as surrounded by these grotesque forms, and hushed in the noon-day repose of this Hawthorne's spell, how aptly might the still fall of his ruddy thoughts into your soul be symbolized by "the thump of a great apple, in the stillest afternoon, falling without a breath of wind, from the mere necessity of perfect ripeness!" For no less ripe than ruddy are the apples of the thoughts and fancies in this sweet Man of Mosses–

"Buds and Bird-Voices"–

What a delicious thing is that! "Will the world ever be so decayed, that Spring may not renew its greenness?" And the "Fire-Worship." Was ever the hearth so glorified into an altar before? The mere title of that piece is better than any common work in fifty folio volumes. How exquisite is this:–"Nor did it lessen the charm of his soft, familiar courtesy and helpfulness, that the mighty spirit, were opportunity offered him, would run riot through the peaceful house, wrap its inmates in his terrible embrace, and leave nothing of them save their whitened bones. This possibility of mad destruction only made his domestic kindness the more beautiful and touching. It was so sweet of him, being endowed with such power, to dwell, day after day, and one long, lonesome night after another, on the dusky hearth, only now and then betraying his wild nature, by thrusting his red tongue out of the chimney-top! True, he had done much mischief in the world, and was pretty certain to do more, but his warm heart atoned for all; He was kindly to the race of man."

But he has still other apples, not quite so ruddy, though full as ripe:–apples, that have been left to wither on the tree, after the pleasant autumn gathering is past. The sketch of "The Old Apple Dealer" is conceived in the subtlest spirit of sadness; he whose "subdued and nerveless boyhood prefigured his abortive prime, which, likewise, contained within itself the prophecy and image of his lean and torpid age." Such touches as are in this piece cannot proceed from any common heart. They argue such a depth of tenderness, such a boundless sympathy with all forms of being, such an omnipresent love, that we must needs say, that this Hawthorne is here almost alone in his generation,–at least, in the artistic manifestation of these things. Still more. Such touches as these,–and many, very many similar ones, all through his chapters–furnish clues, whereby we enter a little way into the intricate, profound heart where they originated. And we see that suffering, some time or other and in some shape or other,– this only can enable any man to depict it in others. All over him, Hawthorne's melancholy rests like an Indian-summer, which, though bathing a whole country in one softness, still reveals the distinctive hue of every towering hill and each far-winding vale.

But it is the least part of genius that attracts admiration. Where Hawthorne is known, he seems to be deemed a pleasant writer, with a pleasant style,–a sequestered, harmless man, from whom any deep and weighty thing would hardly be anticipated–a man who means no meanings. But there is no man, in whom humor and love, like mountain peaks, soar to such a rapt height as to receive the irradiations of the upper skies;–there is no man in whom humor and love are developed in that high form called genius; no such man can exist without also possessing, as the indispensable complement of these, a great, deep intellect, which drops down into the universe like a plummet. Or, love and humor are only the eyes, through which such an intellect views this world. The great beauty in such a mind is but the product of its strength. What, to all readers, can be more charming than the piece entitled "Monsieur du Miroir;" and to a reader at all capable of fully fathoming it, what, at the same time, can possess more mystical depth of meaning?–Yes, there he sits and looks at me,–this "shape of mystery," this "identical Monsieur du Miroir." "Methinks I should tremble now, were his wizard power of gliding through all impedi-

ments in search of me, to place him suddenly before my eyes."

How profound, nay appalling, is the moral evolved by the Earth's Holocaust; where–beginning with the hollow follies and affectations of the world,–all vanities and empty theories and forms are, one after another, and by an admirably graduated, growing comprehensiveness, thrown into the allegorical fire, till, at length, nothing is left but the all-engendering heart of man; which remaining still unconsumed, the great conflagration is naught.

Of a piece with this, is the "Intelligence Office," a wondrous symbolizing of the secret workings in men's souls. There are other sketches still more charged with ponderous import.

"The Christmas Banquet," and "The Bosom Serpent," would be fine subjects for a curious and elaborate analysis, touching the conjectural parts of the mind that produced them. For spite of all the Indian-summer sunlight on the hither side of Hawthorne's soul, the other side–like the dark half of the physical sphere–is shrouded in a blackness, ten times black. But this darkness but gives more effect to the ever-moving dawn, that for ever advances through it, and circumnavigates his world. Whether Hawthorne has simply availed himself of this mystical blackness as a means to the wondrous effects he makes it to produce in his lights and shades; or whether there really lurks in him, perhaps unknown to himself, a touch of Puritanic gloom,–this, I cannot altogether tell. Certain it is, however, that this great power of blackness in him derives its force from its appeals to that Calvinistic sense of Innate Depravity and Original Sin, from whose visitations, in some shape or other, no deeply thinking mind is always and wholly free. For, in certain moods, no man can weigh this world, without throwing in something, somehow like Original Sin, to strike the uneven balance. At all events, perhaps no writer has ever wielded this terrific thought with greater terror than this same harmless Hawthorne. Still more: this black conceit pervades him through and through. You may be witched by his sunlight,–transported by the bright gildings in the skies he builds over you; but there is the blackness of darkness beyond; and even his bright gildings but fringe, and play upon the edges of thunder-clouds.–In one word, the world is mistaken in this Nathaniel Hawthorne. He himself must often have smiled at its absurd misconception of him. He is immeasurably deeper than the plummet of the mere critic. For it is not the brain that can test such a man; it is only the heart. You cannot come to know greatness by inspecting it; there is no glimpse to be caught of it, except by intuition; you need not ring it, you but touch it, and you find it is gold.

Now it is that blackness in Hawthorne, of which I have spoken, that so fixes and fascinates me. It may be, nevertheless, that it is too largely developed in him. Perhaps he does not give us a ray of his light for every shade of his dark. But however this may be, this blackness it is that furnishes the infinite obscure of his back-ground,—that back-ground, against which Shakspeare plays his grandest conceits, the things that have made for Shakspeare his loftiest but most circumscribed renown, as the profoundest of thinkers. For by philosophers Shakspeare is not adored as the great man of tragedy and comedy.—"Off with his head; so much for Buckingham!" this sort of rant, interlined by another hand, brings down the house,—those mistaken souls, who dream of Shakspeare as a mere man of Richard-the-Third humps and Macbeth daggers. But it is those deep far-away things in him; those occasional flashings-forth of the intuitive Truth in him; those short, quick probings at the very axis of reality;—these are the things that make Shakspeare, Shakspeare. Through the mouths of the dark characters of Hamlet, Timon, Lear, and Iago, he craftily says, or sometimes insinuates the things which we feel to be so terrifically true, that it were all but madness for any good man, in his own proper character, to utter, or even hint of them. Tormented into desperation, Lear, the frantic king, tears off the mask, and speaks the same madness of vital truth. But, as I before said, it is the least part of genius that attracts admiration. And so, much of the blind, unbridled admiration that has been heaped upon Shakspeare, has been lavished upon the least part of him. And few of his endless commentators and critics seem to have remembered, or even perceived, that the immediate products of a great mind are not so great as that undeveloped, and sometimes undevelopable yet dimly-discernible greatness, to which those immediate products are but the infallible indices. In Shakspeare's tomb lies infinitely more than Shakspeare ever wrote. And if I magnify Shakspeare, it is not so much for what he did do as for what he did not do or refrained from doing. For in this world of lies, Truth is forced to fly like a scared white doe in the woodlands; and only by cunning glimpses will she reveal herself, as in Shakspeare and other masters of the great Art of Telling the Truth,—even though it be covertly and by snatches.

But if this view of the all-popular Shakspeare be seldom taken by his readers, and if very few who extol him have ever read him deeply, or perhaps, only have seen him on the tricky stage, (which alone made, and is still making him his mere mob renown)—if few men have time, or patience, or palate, for the spiritual truth as it is in that great genius;—it is then no matter of surprise, that in a contemporaneous age, Nathaniel Hawthorne is a man as yet almost utterly mistaken among men. Here and there, in some quiet armchair in the noisy town, or some deep nook among the noiseless mountains, he may be appreciated for something of what he is. But unlike Shakspeare, who was forced to the contrary course by circumstances, Hawthorne (either from simple disinclination, or else from inaptitude) refrains from all the popularizing noise and show of broad farce and blood-besmeared tragedy; content with the still, rich utterances of a great intellect in repose, and which sends few thoughts into circulation, except they be arterialized at his large warm lungs, and expanded in his honest heart.

Nor need you fix upon that blackness in him, if it suit you not. Nor, indeed, will all readers discern it, for it is, mostly, insinuated to those who may best understand it, and account for it; it is not obtruded upon every one alike.

Some may start to read of Shakspeare and Hawthorne on the same page. They may say, that if an illustration were needed, a lesser light might have sufficed to elucidate this Hawthorne, this small man of yesterday. But I am not willingly one of those, who as touching Shakspeare at least, exemplify the maxim of Rochefoucault, that "we exalt the reputation of some, in order to depress that of others;"—who, to teach all noble-souled aspirants that there is no hope for them, pronounce Shakspeare absolutely unapproachable. But Shakspeare has been approached. There are minds that have gone as far as Shakspeare into the universe. And hardly a mortal man, who, at some time or other, has not felt as great thoughts in him as any you will find in Hamlet. We must not inferentially malign mankind for the sake of any one man, whoever he may be. This is too cheap a purchase of contentment for conscious mediocrity to make. Besides, this absolute and unconditional adoration of Shakspeare has grown to be a part of our Anglo-Saxon superstitions. The Thirty-Nine articles are now Forty. Intolerance has come to exist in this matter. You must believe in Shakspeare's unapproachability, or quit the country. But what sort of belief is this for an American, a man who is bound to carry republican progressiveness into Literature, as well as into Life? Believe me, my friends, that men not very much inferior to Shakspeare, are this day being born on the banks of the Ohio. And the day will come when you shall say, Who reads a book by an Englishman that is a modern? The great mistake seems to be, that even with those Americans who look forward to the coming of a great literary genius among us, they somehow fancy he will come in the costume of Queen Elizabeth's day; be a writer of dramas founded upon old English history or the tales of Boccaccio. Whereas, great geniuses are parts of the times; they themselves are the times, and possess a correspondent coloring. It is of a piece with the Jews, who while their Shiloh was meekly walking in their streets, were still praying for his magnificent coming; looking for him in a chariot, who was already among them on an ass. Nor must we forget that, in his own lifetime, Shakspeare was not Shakspeare, but only Master William Shakspeare of the shrewd, thriving business firm of Condell, Shakspeare & Co., proprietors of the Globe Theatre in London; and by a courtly author, of the name of Chettle, was looked at as an "upstart crow," beautified "with other birds' feathers." For, mark it well, imitation is often the first charge brought against real originality. Why this is so, there is not space to set forth here. You must have plenty of sea-room to tell the Truth in; especially when it seems to have an aspect of newness, as America did in 1492, though it was then just as old, and perhaps older than Asia, only those sagacious philosophers, the common sailors, had never seen it before, swearing it was all water and moonshine there.

–*The Literary World*, 7 (17 August 1850): 125–127

* * *

Now I do not say that Nathaniel of Salem is a greater than William of Avon, or as great. But the difference between the two men is by no means immeasurable. Not a very great deal more, and Nathaniel were verily William.

This too, I mean, that if Shakspeare has not been equalled, give the world time, and he is sure to be surpassed, in one hemisphere or the other. Nor will it at all do to say, that the world is getting grey and grizzled now, and has lost that fresh charm which she wore of old, and by virtue of which the great poets of past times made themselves what we esteem them to be. Not so. The world is as young to-day as when it was created; and this Vermont morning dew is as wet to my feet, as Eden's dew to Adam's. Nor has nature been all over ransacked by our progenitors, so that no new charms and mysteries remain for this latter generation to find. Far from it. The trillionth part has not yet been said; and all that has been said, but multiplies the avenues to what remains to be said. It is not so much paucity as superabundance of material that seems to incapacitate modern authors.

Let America, then, prize and cherish her writers; yea, let her glorify them. They are not so many in number as to exhaust her good-will. And while she has good kith and kin of her own, to take to her bosom, let her not lavish her embraces upon the household of an alien. For believe it or not, England, after all, is in many things an alien to us. China has more bonds of real love for us than she. But even were there no strong literary individualities among us, as there are some dozens at least, nevertheless, let America first praise mediocrity even, in her

own children, before she praises (for everywhere, merit demands acknowledgment from every one) the best excellence in the children of any other land. Let her own authors, I say, have the priority of appreciation. I was very much pleased with a hot-headed Carolina cousin of mine, who once said,–"If there were no other American to stand by, in literature,–why, then, I would stand by Pop Emmons and his 'Fredoniad,' and till a better epic came along, swear it was not very far behind the 'Iliad.'" Take away the words, and in spirit he was sound.

Not that American genius needs patronage in order to expand. For that explosive sort of stuff will expand though screwed up in a vice, and burst it, though it were triple steel. It is for the nation's sake, and not for her authors' sake, that I would have America be heedful of the increasing greatness among her writers. For how great the shame, if other nations should be before her, in crowning her heroes of the pen! But this is almost the case now. American authors have received more just and discriminating praise (however loftily and ridiculously given, in certain cases) even from some Englishmen, than from their own countrymen. There are hardly five critics in America; and several of them are asleep. As for patronage, it is the American author who now patronizes his country, and not his country him. And if at times some among them appeal to the people for more recognition, it is not always with selfish motives, but patriotic ones.

It is true, that but few of them as yet have evinced that decided originality which merits great praise. But that graceful writer, who perhaps of all Americans has received the most plaudits from his own country for his productions,–that very popular and amiable writer, however good and self-reliant in many things, perhaps owes his chief reputation to the self-acknowledged imitation of a foreign model, and to the studied avoidance of all topics but smooth ones. But it is better to fail in originality, than to succeed in imitation. He who has never failed somewhere, that man cannot be great. Failure is the true test of greatness. And if it be said, that continual success is a proof that a man wisely knows his powers,– it is only to be added, that, in that case, he knows them to be small. Let us believe it, then, once for all, that there is no hope for us in these smooth pleasing writers that know their powers. Without malice, but to speak the plain fact, they but furnish an appendix to Goldsmith, and other English authors. And we want no American Goldsmiths; nay, we want no American Miltons. It were the vilest thing you could say of a true American author, that he were an American Tompkins. Call him an American, and have done, for you cannot say a nobler thing of him. But it is not meant that all American writers should studiously cleave to nationality in their writings; only this, no American writer should write like an Englishman or a Frenchman; let him write like a man, for then he will be sure to write like an American. Let us away with this leaven of literary flunkeyism towards England. If either must play the flunkey in this thing, let England do it, not us. While we are rapidly preparing for that political supremacy among the nations which prophetically awaits us at the close of the present century, in a literary point of view, we are deplorably unprepared for it; and we seem studious to remain so. Hitherto, reasons might have existed why this should be; but no good reason exists now. And all that is requisite to amendment in this matter, is simply this: that, while fully acknowledging all excellence everywhere, we should refrain from unduly lauding foreign writers, and, at the same time, duly recognise the meritorious writers that are our own;– those writers who breathe that unshackled, democratic spirit of Christianity in all things, which now takes the practical lead in the world, though at the same time led by ourselves– us Americans. Let us boldly contemn all imitation, though it comes to us graceful and fragrant as the morning; and foster all originality, though at first, it be crabbed and ugly as our own pine knots. And if any of our authors fail, or seem to fail, then, in the words of my Carolina cousin, let us clap him on the shoulder, and back him against all Europe for his second round. The truth is, that in one point of view, this matter of a national literature has come to such a pass with us, that in some sense we must turn bullies, else the day is lost, or superiority so far beyond us, that we can hardly say it will ever be ours.

And now, my countrymen, as an excellent author of your own flesh and blood,–an unimitating, and, perhaps, in his way, an inimitable man–whom better can I commend to you, in the first place, than Nathaniel Hawthorne. He is one of the new, and far better generation of your writers. The smell of your beeches and hemlocks is upon him; your own broad prairies are in his soul; and if you travel away inland into his deep and noble nature, you will hear the far roar of his Niagara. Give not over to future generations the glad duty of acknowledging him for what he is. Take that joy to yourself, in your own generation; and so shall he feel those grateful impulses on him, that may possibly prompt him to the full flower of some still greater achievement in your eyes. And by confessing him you thereby confess others; you brace the whole brotherhood. For genius, all over the world, stands hand in hand, and one shock of recognition runs the whole circle round.

In treating of Hawthorne, or rather of Hawthorne in his writings (for I never saw the man; and in the chances of a quiet plantation life, remote from his haunts, perhaps never shall); in treating of his works, I say, I have thus far omitted all mention of

his "Twice told Tales," and "Scarlet Letter." Both are excellent; but full of such manifold, strange, and diffusive beauties, that time would all but fail me, to point the half of them out. But there are things in those two books, which, had they been written in England a century ago, Nathaniel Hawthorne had utterly displaced many of the bright names we now revere on authority. But I am content to leave Hawthorne to himself, and to the infallible finding of posterity; and however great may be the praise I have bestowed upon him, I feel that in so doing I have more served and honored myself, than him. For, at bottom, great excellence is praise enough to itself; but the feeling of a sincere and appreciative love and admiration towards it, this is relieved by utterance; and warm, honest praise, ever leaves a pleasant flavor in the mouth; and it is an honorable thing to confess to what is honorable in others.

But I cannot leave my subject yet. No man can read a fine author, and relish him to his very bones while he reads, without subsequently fancying to himself some ideal image of the man and his mind. And if you rightly look for it, you will almost always find that the author himself has somewhere furnished you with his own picture. For poets (whether in prose or verse), being painters of nature, are like their brethren of the pencil, the true portrait-painters, who, in the multitude of likenesses to be sketched, do not invariably omit their own; and in all high instances, they paint them without any vanity, though at times with a lurking something that would take several pages to properly define.

I submit it, then, to those best acquainted with the man personally, whether the following is not Nathaniel Hawthorne,–and to himself, whether something involved in it does not express the temper of his mind,–that lasting temper of all true, candid men–a seeker, not a finder yet:–

A man now entered, in neglected attire, with the aspect of a thinker, but somewhat too rough-hewn and brawny for a scholar. His face was full of sturdy vigor, with some finer and keener attribute beneath; though harsh at first, it was tempered with the glow of a large, warm heart, which had force enough to heat his powerful intellect through and through. He advanced to the Intelligencer, and looked at him with a glance of such stern sincerity, that perhaps few secrets were beyond its scope.

"'I seek for Truth,' said he."

* * * * *

Melville's Berkshire farmhouse, Arrowhead (circa early 1860s), where he wrote his review of Hawthorne's Mosses from an Old Manse

Twenty-four hours have elapsed since writing the foregoing. I have just returned from the hay-mow, charged more and more with love and admiration of Hawthorne. For I have just been gleaning through the Mosses, picking up many things here and there that had previously escaped me. And I found that but to glean after this man, is better than to be in at the harvest of others. To be frank (though, perhaps, rather foolish), notwithstanding what I wrote yesterday of these Mosses, I had not then culled them all; but had, nevertheless, been sufficiently sensible of the subtle essence in them, as to write as I did. To what infinite height of loving wonder and admiration I may yet be borne, when by repeatedly banqueting on these Mosses, I shall have thoroughly incorporated their whole stuff into my being,—that, I cannot tell. But already I feel that this Hawthorne has dropped germinous seeds into my soul. He expands and deepens down, the more I contemplate him; and further and further, shoots his strong New England roots into the hot soil of my Southern soul.

By careful reference to the "Table of Contents," I now find that I have gone through all the sketches; but that when I yesterday wrote, I had not at all read two particular pieces, to which I now desire to call special attention,—"A Select Party," and "Young Goodman Brown." Here, be it said to all those whom this poor fugitive scrawl of mine may tempt to the perusal of the "Mosses," that they must on no account suffer themselves to be trifled with, disappointed, or deceived by the triviality of many of the titles to these sketches. For in more than one instance, the title utterly belies the piece. It is as if rustic demijohns containing the very best

and costliest of Falernian and Tokay, were labelled "Cider," "Perry," and "Elder-berry wine." The truth seems to be, that like many other geniuses, this Man of Mosses takes great delight in hoodwinking the world,—at least, with respect to himself. Personally, I doubt not that he rather prefers to be generally esteemed but a so-so sort of author; being willing to reserve the thorough and acute appreciation of what he is, to that party most qualified to judge—that is, to himself. Besides, at the bottom of their natures, men like Hawthorne, in many things, deem the plaudits of the public such strong presumptive evidence of mediocrity in the object of them, that it would in some degree render them doubtful of their own powers, did they hear much and vociferous braying concerning them in the public pastures. True, I have been braying myself (if you please to be witty enough to have it so) but then I claim to be the first that has so brayed in this particular matter; and therefore, while pleading guilty to the charge, still claim all the merit due to originality.

But with whatever motive, playful or profound, Nathaniel Hawthorne has chosen to entitle his pieces in the manner he has, it is certain that some of them are directly calculated to deceive—egregiously deceive, the superficial skimmer of pages. To be downright and candid once more, let me cheerfully say, that two of these titles did dolefully dupe no less an eagle-eyed reader than myself; and that, too, after I had been impressed with a sense of the great depth and breadth of this American man. "Who in the name of thunder" (as the country-people say in this neighborhood), "who in the name of thunder," would anticipate any marvel in a piece entitled 'Young Goodman Brown?'" You would of course suppose that it was a simple little tale, intended as a supplement to "Goody Two Shoes." Whereas, it is deep as Dante; nor can you finish it, without addressing the author in his own words—"It is yours to penetrate, in every bosom, the deep mystery of sin." And with Young Goodman, too, in allegorical pursuit of his Puritan wife, you cry out in your anguish:

"'Faith!' shouted Goodman Brown, in a voice of agony and desperation; and the echoes of the forest mocked him, crying—'Faith! Faith!' as if bewildered wretches were seeking her all through the wilderness."

Now this same piece, entitled "Young Goodman Brown," is one of the two that I had not all read yesterday; and I allude to it now, because it is, in itself, such a strong positive illustration of that blackness in Hawthorne, which I had assumed from the mere occasional shadows of it, as revealed in several of the other sketches. But had I previously perused "Young Goodman Brown," I should have been at no pains to draw the conclusion, which I came to at a time when I was ignorant that the book contained one such direct and unqualified manifestation of it.

The other piece of the two referred to, is entitled "A Select Party," which, in my first simplicity upon originally taking hold of the book, I fancied must treat of some pumpkin-pie party in Old Salem, or some chowder-party on Cape Cod. Whereas, by all the gods of Peedee, it is the sweetest and sublimest thing that has been written since Spenser wrote. Nay, there is nothing in Spenser that surpasses it, perhaps, nothing that equals it. And the test is this: read any canto in "The Faery Queen," and then read "A Select Party," and decide which pleases you most,—that is, if you are qualified to judge. Do not be frightened at this; for when Spenser was alive, he was thought of very much as Hawthorne is now,—was generally accounted just such a "gentle" harmless man. It may be, that to common eyes, the sublimity of Hawthorne seems lost in his sweetness,—as perhaps in this same "Select Party" of his; for whom he has builded so august a dome of sunset clouds, and served them on richer plate than Belshazzar when he banqueted his lords in Babylon.

But my chief business now, is to point out a particular page in this piece, having reference to an honored guest, who under the name of "The Master Genius," but in the guise "of a young man of poor attire, with no insignia of rank or acknowledged eminence," is introduced to the man of Fancy, who is the giver of the feast. Now, the page having reference to this "Master Genius," so happily expresses much of what I yesterday wrote, touching the coming of the literary

Shiloh of America, that I cannot but be charmed by the coincidence; especially, when it shows such a parity of ideas, at least, in this one point, between a man like Hawthorne and a man like me.

And here, let me throw out another conceit of mine touching this American Shiloh, or "Master Genius," as Hawthorne calls him. May it not be, that this commanding mind has not been, is not, and never will be, individually developed in any one man? And would it, indeed, appear so unreasonable to suppose, that this great fulness and overflowing may be, or may be destined to be, shared by a plurality of men of genius? Surely, to take the very greatest example on record, Shakspeare cannot be regarded as in himself the concretion of all the genius of his time; nor as so immeasurably beyond Marlowe, Webster, Ford, Beaumont, Jonson, that those great men can be said to share none of his power? For one, I conceive that there were dramatists in Elizabeth's day, between whom and Shakspeare the distance was by no means great. Let anyone, hitherto little acquainted with those neglected old authors, for the first time read them thoroughly, or even read Charles Lamb's Specimens of them, and he will be amazed at the wondrous ability of those Anaks of men, and shocked at this renewed example of the fact, that Fortune has more to do with fame than merit,—though, without merit, lasting fame there can be none.

Nevertheless, it would argue too ill of my country were this maxim to hold good concerning Nathaniel Hawthorne, a man, who already, in some few minds, has shed "such a light, as never illuminates the earth save when a great heart burns as the household fire of a grand intellect."

The words are his,—"in the Select Party;" and they are a magnificent setting to a coincident sentiment of my own, but ramblingly expressed yesterday, in reference to himself. Gainsay it who will, as I now write, I am Posterity speaking by proxy—and after times will make it more than good, when I declare, that the American, who up to the present day has evinced, in literature, the largest brain with the largest heart, that man is Nathaniel Hawthorne. Moreover, that whatever Nathaniel Hawthorne may hereafter write, "The Mosses from an Old Manse" will be ultimately accounted his master-piece. For there is a sure, though a secret sign in some works which proves the culmination of the powers (only the developable ones, however) that produced them. But I am by no means desirous of the glory of a prophet. I pray Heaven that Hawthorne may *yet* prove me an impostor in this prediction. Especially, as I somehow cling to the strange fancy, that, in all men, hiddenly reside certain wondrous, occult properties—as in some plants and minerals—which by some happy but very rare accident (as bronze was discovered by the melting of the iron and brass in the burning of Corinth) may chance to be called forth here on earth; not entirely waiting for their better discovery in the more congenial, blessed atmosphere of heaven.

Once more—for it is hard to be finite upon an infinite subject, and all subjects are infinite. By some people this entire scrawl of mine may be esteemed altogether unnecessary, inasmuch "as years ago" (they may say) "we found out the rich and rare stuff in this Hawthorne, whom you now parade forth, as if only *yourself* were the discoverer of this Portuguese diamond in our literature." But even granting all this—and adding to it, the assumption that the books of Hawthorne have sold by the five thousand,—what does that signify? They should be sold by the hundred thousand; and read by the million; and admired by every one who is capable of admiration.

–*The Literary World*, 7 (24 August 1850): 145–147

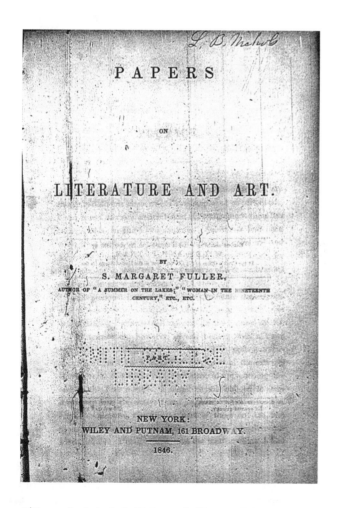

Title page for the book of critical essays by Margaret Fuller published by Wiley and Putnam (Smith College Library)

Papers on Literature and Art (1846)

Margaret Fuller was living in New York and writing book reviews and social and cultural commentary for the New-York Tribune *when Duyckinck solicited a contribution from her for the Library of American Books. She gladly accepted the offer and compiled a manuscript culled from her journalism.* Papers on Literature and Art *was published in the Library a month after* Mosses from an Old Manse. *Its path to print, however, was far from smooth, for Wiley, who was demanding changes of Melville that spring for the new edition of* Typee, *insisted that Fuller cut the size and narrow the range of her manuscript. She reluctantly consented.*

Papers on Literature and Art *appeared in New York in a two-volume edition just as Fuller departed the city for her fateful trip to Europe. She arrived in London shortly before the sheets of the book reached Putnam, who issued the work out of his London office and store (which Fuller visited, as she did Putnam's home that fall). It was attracting attention in the London press at the time of her visit, and she wrote him from Paris in November to request that he send her five copies of that book and as many as he could find of* Woman in the Nineteenth Century *(1845) for distribution in France.*

* * *

In a letter to Evert Duyckinck, Fuller complains about having to conform to John Wiley's requirement that Papers on Literature and Art *fit the length and standards of other works in the Library of American Books.*

London
30th Octr 1846

Dear Mr Duyckinck,

The letter which I intended to write you dwindles into a note, for many as were my interruptions in N.Y. they scarcely enabled me to form a notion of those inevitable to a London life. The only way of escape is to hide;—this is what I tried to do today in order to write some notes by Mr Welford, yet here it is three o clock before I can put pen to paper.

Yet I like London, like England <u>very</u> much and have already formed so many interesting connections that I do not feel that I could be content to return to the U.S. without passing some time here again. Indeed I may come and pass some time here for the purpose of writing. Several fine openings have been made for me where I might have taken up important subjects and published my view in excellent places, but I cannot now possibly get time to write without sacrificing many valuable opportunities of learning. A year hence will not be too late.

I have been recd here with a warmth that surprized me; it is chiefly to Women in the 19th etc. that I am indebted for this; that little volume has been read and prized by many. It is a real misfortune to me that Mr. Wiley took the course he did about my miscellanies; the vols have been kindly read but every one mentions their being <u>thin</u>; the arrangement, too, that obliged me to leave out all I had written on Continental life was very unfortunate for me. I have reason to feel daily how much use it would have been to me if these essays and others of a radical stamp were now before the readers and that a false impression has been given here of the range and scope of my efforts. However it is of some use to have those that are printed with me now, though I have constantly to regret the absence of some I intended to insert as now is just the time for them to make their mark here.

. . . .

Now I must stop for lack of time, though much there is to say. Will you write to me at Paris. I shall be there in a week, your brother, if there, can hear of me at Galignani's. I shall leave my address there, and shall stay a month or more. In Rome Torlonia is our banker. Will you be so kind as to send three sets of the "Papers on Literature and Art" to <u>Richard F. Fuller, 6 State St. Boston</u>. I will write him what to do with them. Please give my best regards to Mr Mathews. I should like much to hear from him, too, if he has time[.] Letters are a true favor to me, now when <u>I</u> have no time to earn them.

                                                    Margaret Fuller

—Duyckinck Family Papers, Manuscripts and Archives Division, The New York Public Library, Astor, Lenox and Tilden Foundations

* * *

This generous prepublication comment was probably the work of the series editor, Evert Duyckinck.

Miss S. Margaret Fuller's New Work, "Papers on Literature and Art," will also be published within the month. It will be one of the most striking and independent critical works ever issued by an American author. It will contain several papers on American literature. It will form two new numbers of the Library of American Books.

                                    —Wiley and Putnam's Literary News-Letter,
                                             5 (August 1846): 58

* * *

These remarks about Fuller in the English press were reported by Putnam, who often saw her in London. He worked devotedly to promote her books in Great Britain and on the Continent.

"Papers on Literature and Art," by Miss Margaret Fuller, have just been published in London in two 12 mo. volumes, and very flatteringly received by the critics. The Spectator—the highest authority, speaks thus: "These two volumes, slender in bulk but rich in matter, are all we have yet seen of the writings of the author. If this be a fault in us, it is one which we long to repair, for we have seen enough to convince us that Margaret Fuller is worthy to hold her place among the highest order of female writers of our day. The present volumes present to us the thoughts of a full and discerning mind, delicately susceptible of all impressions of beauty; earnest, generous, and singularly graceful and appropriate. The criticism in these volumes, if not always faultless, is at least always elevated and genial. It is of that best kind which expands the mind of the student, and prompts him to new trains of thought," etc, etc. This is indeed praise, especially from such a wet blanket of a paper as the *Spectator.*

The Critic says—"All of these papers contain passages of striking beauty, everywhere we recognize the welcome and unmistakable tokens of a mind whose forceful activity conventionalities have been unable to fetter, and whose aspirations and sympathies, equally lofty and pure, do honor to humanity. As a critic of Literature, we accord to Margaret Fuller a high position. She possesses most of the requirements essential to that office—quickness of apprehension, varied and extensive reading, a sound judgment, and a discriminating taste."

                                    —Wiley and Putnam's Literary News-Letter, 5
                                             (November 1846): 81

* * *

This review, signed "H," was presumably written by Fuller's good friend Frederic Henry Hedge, a fellow transcendentalist.

These volumes, consisting mostly of selections from Miss Fuller's writings, including, as she informs us in her Preface, some of her earliest, as well as latest, productions, form part of "Wiley and Putnam's Library of American Books." They bear marks throughout of a vigorous mind, discriminating thought, varied and ever ready power, with candid and fearless expression. In the use of language—freedom, copiousness, richness, and precision of words—Miss Fuller has few superiors. By this alone one is repaid for reading these pages, differ as he may from the opinions he finds there. And besides this there is a fulness of meaning, and a kindness as well as boldness of utterance, which make us forget differences, or care not for them. Indeed, in regard to this writer, extravagant as have seemed to us some of her views and words (much less so, however, in this publication, than in the others referred to in the title-page), we are inclined to use the generous language in which she herself has summed up her remarks on the British poets:– "For myself, I think that where there is such beauty and strength, we can afford to be silent about slight defects; and that we refine our taste more effectually by venerating the grand and lovely, than by detecting the little and mean." The last epithets have no application here; but the others are strictly appropriate.

We therefore do not stop to point out defects, or consider objections frequently heard. We have run through this collection of pieces with pleasure and profit. That which pleases us least, and the only one, perhaps, that will give much offence, is the view of "American Literature." That she does that literature injustice, most will feel; that she is greatly unjust to one of our living historians, and several of our poets, many will earnestly say. And none, we think, will fail to notice an oracular air and magisterial decision, hardly indicative of meekness, nor helping to inspire in those ignorant of the writer entire confidence in the soundness of her judgment. But for perspicuity of style, for which she has not always been noted, for freedom and freshness of thought, for delicacy and affluence of imagination, with evident truthfulness of heart, these publications deserve to be known and read.

–*Christian Examiner*, 42 (January 1847): 140–141

Views A-foot (1846)

Putnam first met J. Bayard Taylor when he arrived in London in early 1846 sorely in need of funds and made his way to the London office of Wiley and Putnam. Taylor had just completed a poor man's equivalent of the grand tour on a minimum of funds, a circumstance that he later cleverly exploited as the basis of the resultant travelogue, Views A-foot. *Putnam immediately took to his visitor—years later he named a son after him— and offered him temporary employment while Taylor awaited compensation from American newspapers for travel letters sent to them.*

After arriving back in the United States, Taylor rapidly composed a narrative of his European travels and before the end of the year reached terms with John Wiley for its publication. The volume appeared in December as one of the later titles in the Library of American Books *and quickly emerged as one of the most popular books published in any of the Wiley and Putnam libraries. Its popularity may be accounted for in part by its subtitle,* Europe Seen with Knapsack and Staff, *for the book*

captured the public fancy as not only a vivid account of European travel but also as a key that opened the experience of travel to more than just the privileged few. G. P. Putnam kept Views A-foot *in print in multiple editions and formats throughout the rest of the century, and it remained a popular item on the company list into the twentieth century.*

* * *

In New York to read proof, Taylor discusses his work on Views A-foot *with his friend John B. Phillips. He had little sense at the time of its imminent popularity or of the professional prospects it would open up to him. The preface he refers to, by Nathaniel Parker Willis, one of the best-known periodical writers in the country, could only have helped the book get a hearing.*

New York, Oct. 16, 1846.
while reading proof
Views-a-foot

My dear John:

According to promise, I sit down to write you, <u>very soon</u>, after getting here. You must not scold, for indeed I have been and still am, very busy, endeavoring to push this troublesome book through the press. The public generally think authors have delightful times—nothing to do but sit down at their leisure and spin out their yarns, but I tell you as far as mere exhausting labor is concerned, I would rather plough all day. It is the exciting glow of conception and the delight of self-expression which compensates the writer for his toil. He possesses his reward within him, even if the world never acknowledges his claim to the "faculty divine." There are many secrets the mass has not yet learned and perhaps never will—nor does the true author wish it. So that whatever emanates from his soul meet with a response from the few who like him live in the spirit of <u>coming</u> ages, he can endure to be called a drone and a dreamer.

I hardly know how I slipped into this train of thought—I certainly had no idea of it when I began to write, but a letter to you unlocks my whole soul, and you must be content to take the tides as they come. The stream may be occasionally turbid, but it is never slow or scanty.

When I say I have been busy, I must explain myself by telling you that in addition to reading the proof, as fast as the Chapters are printed, I am entirely revising the whole work. I see much to strike out and much to alter, every time I review it and although this is not a work about the reputation of which I care much, still I want it to go before the world in a decent garb. I find that I need to study the principles of language much more than I have done. There is a great deal more art about it than persons suppose—in fact, nothing but <u>years</u> of careful and constant practice can make a ready and yet elegant writer. The printers have been delayed with my book in the commencement, so I shall probably have to stay here a week longer than I expected. I have made a bargain with Wiley,—not as good perhaps as an established writer could make, but still, a fair beginning—$100 for every thousand copies sold—under the condition, of course, that it pays expenses;—if not, I get—nothing. Willis is going to give me the preface in a few days. We have a title which will, I think, be striking and attractive. It is: "Views A-Foot; or a Pedestrian's Observations of People and Places in Europe." The first part of it did not please me at first, but since it has become familiar I like it very much. . . .

—*Pierpont Morgan Library*

* * *

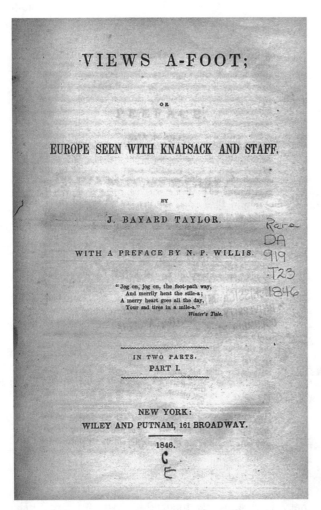

VIEWS A-FOOT;

OR

EUROPE SEEN WITH KNAPSACK AND STAFF.

BY

J. BAYARD TAYLOR.

WITH A PREFACE BY N. P. WILLIS.

"Jog on, jog on, the foot-path way,
And merrily hent the stile-a;
A merry heart goes all the day,
Your sad tires in a mile-a."
Winter's Tale.

IN TWO PARTS.
PART I.

NEW YORK:
WILEY AND PUTNAM, 161 BROADWAY.

1846.

Title page for one of the most popular travel books of its era (courtesy of Special Collections, Thomas Cooper Library, University of South Carolina)

The Knickerbocker *reviewer expresses the reaction of many contemporary readers who responded positively both to Taylor and his tale of making the grand tour "a-foot."*

Truthful and graphic in description, and teeming with evidences of mind of no merely common order, this book of travels addresses itself not only to our interest and admiration, but to our sympathies, which are elicited in a remarkable degree by the novel taste and aspirations of the young printer. The strong will and the magnetic hope which so certainly insure success; the enthusiasm and energy which buoyed up the firm traveller under the toils and fatigues of long journeys 'afoot;' and above all, under the most disheartening of evils, a 'lean purse,' excite our wonder and compel our praise. The character of the man first strikes us. We are constantly attracted by his industrious research and his profound love of the intellectual; his strong interest in the useful sciences, and his spiritual appreciation of the wonderful and the beautiful. We repeat, the writer is the leading object of interest in the book; and this because of the novelty of his character and purpose. As a book of travels the work might not be striking. As a collection of new and multifarious anecdotes, incidents and descriptions, it ranks with the best of its kind. In short, it is a volume to which one turns when the brain is racked and wearied in the contest with the 'higher powers;' when the 'Zanonis' and the 'Lucretius' are laid upon the shelf; when the appetite for the marvellous is satiated in 'Typee,' or when, disgusted with the heaps of puerile 'light' works which are piled up around us, our eye falling upon these volumes, the attractive title leads to the more attractive page, and we become pleased, engaged, and—rested.

We meet with but one disappointment in glancing at these 'Views Afoot.' We lament an oversight which seems incongruous in the character of the author; an oversight which will deprive the great majority of his readers of that information which would have been to him the surest harbinger of fame. We inferred that the traveller "afoot" would at least stumble over those lights and shadows of *simple life* which are the subject of so much fiction, but of which no *real* portraiture ever has been given. For example, we should have liked to know something *true* of the French grisette; not a history of caps, flounces and ribbons, nor of love-scenes, assignations, and the like; but of the young-hearted girl of Normandy or Languedoc; her peasant-home, her hopes, her first affections, before she has been seduced away to far-off Paris to be ruined or to die. Again, we should like to have peeped in through the windows of some good, honest German vrouw, and inquired, if we chose, the ingredients of her sour-krout, or have a hob-a-nob with some of the stout lasses, her daughters. We thought to find in the work natural and simple pictures of natural and simple things; a panoramic view, which would have made us familiar with foreign *people,* whose lands, governments, institutions and wonders have been described and embellished, and almost demolished by every previous traveller. Yet, notwithstanding those grains of abatement, we must invoke for our young author's good volumes a cordial reception; and we may venture to predict for him a 'name,' even though this book of travels do not win it for him. The subjoined reflections, suggested by hearing the chimes of Mary-le-bone-Chapel, will afford the reader some impression of the writer's meditative current of thought. They come to us, we scarcely know how, like the reveries of our own mind on hearing the chimes of Trinity. . . .

　　　　　　　　　—Knickerbocker, 29 (January 1847): 77–78

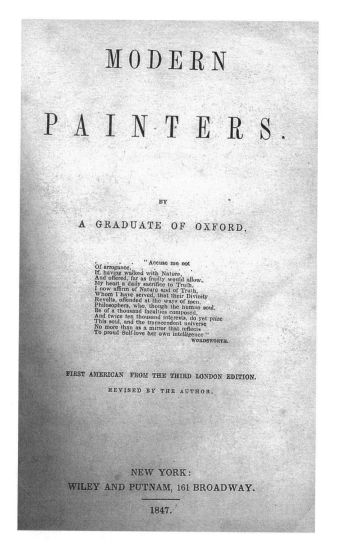

Title page for the first of five volumes of John Ruskin's Modern Painters, *which was initially published in England in 1834 (courtesy of Thomas Cooper Library, University of South Carolina)*

Modern Painters (1847)

It is unlikely that either Putnam or Wiley knew who the "Graduate of Oxford" was when their firm acquired American printing rights to the first volume of John Ruskin's Modern Painters *in spring or summer 1847. It is equally unlikely that they recognized it at the time as a potential classic. But when the work quickly earned critical praise and registered strong sales, they soon came to regard it as a valuable addition to their list. Despite Putnam's affinity for the fine arts, Wiley received the publishing rights to Ruskin in his share of the assets following the company breakup, and he remained Ruskin's American publisher for most of the nineteenth century.*

* * *

This anonymous reviewer for The Literary World *was one of many critics and readers who immediately recognized Ruskin's work as a seminal study of modern Western painting.*

Modern Painters. By a Graduate of Oxford. Parts I. and II. First American from the third London edition. Revised by the Author. New York: Wiley & Putnam. 1847.

An elegant and ingenious treatise, which abounds in an original vein of speculation and remarkable graphic ability. The great idea of the author is, that painting as a mechanical art is only a species of language, and is to be judged not by the material dexterity but the spiritual significance of its results. This is finely elucidated. The sources of pleasure derivable from art are analysed, and then their philosophy applied to fact. Many of the views of this graduate of Oxford are noble, just, and eminently worthy the serious consideration both of artists and lovers of painting. No discriminating reader, indeed, can fail to be kindled and informed by a thoughtful perusal of the work, and we, therefore, earnestly commend it as rich, persuasive, and liberal, as well as elevating in its influence. At the same time it is to be borne in mind that the author is an enthusiast, and consequently goes to extremes. His admiration of Turner is extravagant, and betrays him into occasional dogmatism; while he judged Claude and Salvator from too confined a point of observation. The rigid application of almost any theory, either to art or literature, necessarily involves more or less injustice. In his general reasoning on art in its comprehensive sense, and his descriptions of individual pictures by way of illustrating his argument—there is a positive genius; but in his zeal for the moderns, he permits himself to pass too slightingly the claims of the old masters. With due allowance for the influence of personal feeling and opinions, the Modern Painters is the most interesting and valuable work on art which has appeared for many years.

　　　　　　　　　—The Literary World, 1 (24 July 1847): 591

Advertisement in the *17 July 1847* issue of The Literary World

Eureka: A Prose Poem (1848)

Many years after Poe brought the manuscript of Eureka *to his Broadway office, Putnam recalled the event and pictured Poe as highly excited as he sat in the Putnam office and worked over his manuscript, for which he had expectations of popular and critical success. Putnam printed 750 copies in July, which was far more than the market required for a work that was commonly dismissed as nonsense. It sold much less well than Poe's works in the Wiley and Putnam Library of American Books.* Eureka *was published in England by Putnam's London dealer, John Chapman.*

* * *

Poe's Eureka *was published during a time of increasing conflict between science and religion; the reviewer for* The Literary World, *while concluding that the work is original and provocative, finds that much of it is "arrant fudge" and suspects it is a literary hoax.*

This is a strange work—a very strange work, and will excite quite a sensation in certain circles, both at home and abroad. It presents a two-fold appearance—as a poem, and as a work of science. It is only as the former, the author tells us, he would wish his work to be judged after he is dead;—leaving us at liberty, as it may be inferred, to judge of it as the latter so long as he shall still be on earth to see that it has fair play. In both respects much might be said both for and against various portions of Eureka, but except an occasional allusion, we shall let the Poetry take care of itself, and confine our remarks to the work in so far as it purports to be Truth—Scientific, Metaphysical, or Theological.

The book opens, after the introduction, with an extract from a letter purporting to have been found in a bottle floating on the *Mare tenebrarum,* an ocean "but little frequented in modern days unless by the Transcendentalists and some other divers for crotchets." Now it is singular that with the sensible and supreme contempt expressed by Mr. Poe for the Transcendentalists, he should have gone to the Shadowy Sea frequented but by them, for a defence on which his whole discovery rests. This letter is a keen burlesque on the Aristotelian and Baconian methods of ascertaining truth, both of which the writer ridicules and despises, and pours forth his rhapsodical ecstasies in glorification of the third mode—the noble art of *guessing.* Now we have nothing to say against guessing in scientific matters. It certainly has antiquity and universality in its favor, especially as regards the formation of Cosmogonies, and our witty correspondent from the "Sea of Shadows," so far from making any new discovery, has only been advertising what has ever been more or less the practice all the world over, being always in highest vogue where ignorance and barbarism most prevailed. All the nonsense put forth by Hindoos, Scandinavians, Greeks, Romans, North American Indians, and Negroes, to say nothing of the philoso-

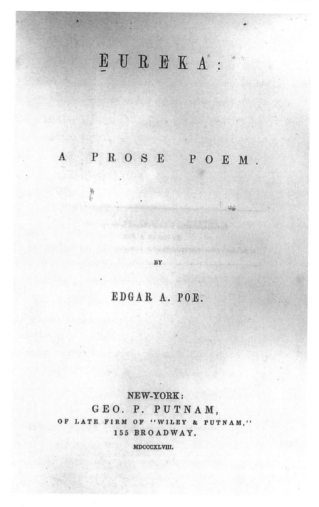

EUREKA:

A PROSE POEM.

BY

EDGAR A. POE.

NEW-YORK:
GEO. P. PUTNAM,
OF LATE FIRM OF "WILEY & PUTNAM,"
155 BROADWAY.
MDCCCXLVIII.

Title page for the Poe work that did not sell out Putnam's initial printing of 750 copies (courtesy of the American Antiquarian Society)

phers and poets, has been the result of this ancient and noble art of guessing, and surely they all had as much right to guess as Mr. Poe. It must be granted, however, that *guessing* is as good a plan as any other,—provided it *hits;* but in order to tell whether it hits or not, we are compelled to resort to that slow and troublesome process called "demonstration," a plan much decried by those who excel rather in wit than wisdom. We hope that on some of his subsequent excursions to the Ocean of Shadows, Mr. Poe may find another bottle which may enable him to *guess* his *demonstrations* also. That would be something *new.*

As we have already said, we think a guess as good as anything else, provided it *hits.* The question is: does Mr. Poe's guess hit? We think that partly it does, and partly it does not. And here we can do nothing but indicate the *results* of our reflection on the theories propounded by Mr. Poe. To argue the point would require a volume far larger than Eureka. The great point of the Discovery claimed by Mr. Poe, is his mode of accounting for the principle of the Newtonian Law of Gravity. This may be stated in general

MEMORANDUM OF AGREEMENT between GEORGE P. PUTNAM, of the city of New-York, Publisher, of the first part and *Edgar A. Poe of New York* of the second part in consideration of the sum of one dollar each to the other mutually paid.

The said party of the second part, *his* executors, administrators, and assigns, in consideration aforesaid, doth agree to the party of the first part, his executors, administrators, and assigns, to have a certain manuscript book entitled *"Eureka, a Prose Poem"* ready for publication *on the day of the date hereof.*

AND the said party of the first part doth also agree with the party of the second part, to publish the said manuscript work, and to pay and advance all the expenses of printing, binding, advertising, and all the necessary expenses incurred thereon, and to issue and publish the same on or before *15th day of June next*

AND it is hereby mutually understood and agreed by and between the parties aforesaid, that if, on the—— (day of) after the publication, it shall appear that the sales of said work shall not have produced the full amount of expenses paid out and incurred by the said party of the first part in publishing the same, that then the said party of the second part shall pay or secure to be paid the sum sufficient to cover or secure such deficiency. *This article erased, G.P.P.*

AND it is further agreed between the parties hereto, that when it is ascertained that the said party of the first part has been fully repaid or reimbursed for all expenses laid out or incurred in the publication of said work, that then the said party of the first part shall pay to the said party of the second part, at the rate of *ten per cent upon the retail price of all copies that have been or may be sold.*

and continue so to pay as long as said work is published by said party of the first part : which said payment shall be made in February and August, of each year by a note at *three* months to be given by the said party of the first part to the party of the second part.

AND it is further agreed by and between the parties, that, the said party of the second part, shall not print or publish or cause to be printed or published, the same or any other edition of the said work revised, corrected, enlarged, or otherwise, or any work of similar character, tending to interfere with or injure the sales of the said work, under penalty of forfeiture of all interest or profit he may have in the same under this agreement.

In witness whereof, the said parties have affixed their hands and seals on this *22d* day of *May* the year of our Lord one thousand eight hundred *& forty eight*

Signed and Sealed in presence of

Edgar A Poe

Chas. ? Mavy

Wm. P. Putnam

Contract for Eureka: A Prose Poem. *The specification of 10 percent royalties was a standard payment for Putnam authors (courtesy of the Free Library of Philadelphia).*

terms as follows: The Attraction of Gravitation, which acts with a force inversely proportional to the squares of the distances, is but the reaction of the original act of creation, which was effected by irradiating the atoms of which the universe is composed from one centre of unity, with a force directly proportional to the squares of the distances (reaction being action conversed), and that this was the mode of distributing the original matter is shown on geometrical principles. The development of electricity, and the formation of stars and suns, luminous and non-luminous, moons and planets with their rings, &c., is deduced, very much according to the nebular theory of La Place, from the principle propounded above.* In this, and perhaps in some other parts, such as the scheme for the final destruction of the Universe, the guess seems to *hit,* or at least comes apparently near the mark. Kepler's laws, it is well known, were guessed, and have been received as true, not because the principle of those laws was demonstrated by him or by anybody else, but merely because observed and known facts all agreed with them. And Mr. Poe's *guess* is in some parts substantiated by the *same kind and the same degree of proof as the other,*—that is, *perfect harmony with all ascertained facts.* So far as this can be *shown,* his theory must and will stand. Where it fails, his guess will return to the Sea of Shadows from whence it came.

In many respects it would be very easy to show a close correspondence between this theory and the Mosaic account. It would require no more ingenuity than has been already displayed by the geologists in accommodating Scripture to their Science. But there are several points which Mr. Poe discusses in which he reminds us of his own forcible account of a certain class of philosophers who, like himself, draw largely on the Ocean of Shadows. "There are people, I am aware, who, busying themselves in attempts at the unattainable, acquire very easily, by dint of the jargon they emit, among those thinkers—that—they—think with whom darkness and depth are synonymous, a kind of cuttle-fish reputation for profundity; but the finest quality of thought is its self-cognisance;"—and to judge by the accuracy of the description, Mr. Poe possesses this "finest quality of thought" in a high degree of perfection. If further proof of this be needed, look at the system of Pantheism which is more or less inwoven into the texture of the whole book, but displays itself most broadly at the end. Yet the whole is most absurdly inconsistent. On pp. 28, 29, Mr. Poe speaks of "God" and "the Godhead" as a Christian or a deist might speak—as being One. On p. 103 he has the "hardihood" to assert that we have a right to infer that there are an infinity of universes (?) such as ours, of which "Each exists, apart, and independently, in *the bosom of its proper and particular god."* This makes Mr. Poe a polytheist—a believer in an *infinite* number of *proper and particular* gods, existing *apart and independently.* On page 141 it appears that this infinity of gods is forgotten, and Mr. Poe

cannot conceive "that anything exists *greater than his own soul;"* he feels "intense overwhelming dissatisfaction and rebellion at the thought; he asserts that this feeling is superior to any demonstration;" and that each soul is therefore "*its own god, its own creator."* All this is extraordinary nonsense, if not blasphemy; and it may very possibly be *both.* Nay we have Mr. Poe's own authority for saying so—authority which seems to be "divine" with him. After all these contradictory propoundings concerning "God" we would remind him of what he lays down on page 28. "Of this Godhead, in itself, he alone is not imbecile—he alone is not impious, who propounds—*nothing."* A man who thus conclusively convicts himself of imbecility and impiety needs no further refutation.

To conclude our brief and imperfect notice of this strange and in many respects original production, we should say that much of its physical portion may be true,— and we commend this particularly to the attention of scientific men. Its Metaphysical part, including ideas about the Spiritual portion of the universe, its being "Repulsion" while matter is "Attraction," whereas nevertheless Electricity is the Spiritual principle, and "Attraction and repulsion" (taken together), and "Matter" are convertible terms:—all this, we say, with much more of the same sort, is simply unintelligible, and smacks of the cuttle-fish. The Theological portion is intolerable. Mr. Poe has guessed. In some respects we may grant that we also "guess so." In others we most decidedly "guess *not."* We agree with him, that when his "theory has been corrected, reduced, sifted, cleared little by little, of its chaff of inconsistency—until at length there stands apparent an unincumbered *Consistency,"* it will be acknowledged "to be an absolute and unquestionable *Truth;"* but in this case, we opine, the sifters will discover an original, ingenious, profound, and abundant quantity of chaff.

—*The Literary World,* 3 (29 July 1848): 502

* * *

*Further than this, Mr. Poe's claim that he can account for the existence of all organized beings—man included— merely from those principles on which the origin and present appearance of suns and worlds, are explained, must be set down as mere bald assertion, without a particle of evidence. In other words, we should term it *arrant fudge,* were it not for a shrewd suspicion which haunts us, that the whole essay is nothing more nor less than an elaborate quiz upon some of the wild speculations of the day—a scientific hoax of the higher order which few men are capable of executing more cleverly than the ingenious author of "The Murders in the Rue Morgue, The Descent into the Maelstroom," &c., &c.

A Fable for Critics (1848)

G. P. Putnam published James Russell Lowell's A Fable for Critics, *the most famous spoof of antebellum letters and authors during its first year of operations. Putnam was delighted to have his name associated with the work of Lowell, whose first series of* Bigelow Papers *(1848) he was concurrently engaged in helping to distribute. Putnam did not have exaggerated expectations for* A Fable for Critics *and published probably one thousand copies, several hundred of which he shipped to his London dealer for sale overseas. Still, the poem caught the attention of the public and was the source of many imitations and parodies.*

* * *

In this excerpt from a 12 May 1848 letter, Lowell reports to friend Charles Frederick Briggs, who was acting as his unofficial agent in New York City, on his latest progress in composing A Fable for Critics. *The initials "L. M. C." and "S. M. F." refer to Lydia Maria Child and Sarah Margaret Fuller.*

I have begun upon the "Fable" again fairly, and am making some headway. I think with what I sent you (which I believe was about 500 lines) it will make something over a thousand. I have done, since I sent the first half, Willis, Longfellow, Bryant, Miss Fuller, and Mrs. Child. In Longfellow's case I have attempted no characterization. The same (in a degree) may be said of S. M. F. With her I have been perfectly good-humored, but I have a fancy that what I say will stick uncomfortably. It will make you laugh. So will L. M. C. After S. M. F. I make a short digression on bores in general, which has some drollery in it. Willis I think good. Bryant is funny, and as fair as I could make it, immitigably just. Indeed I have endeavored to be so in all. I am glad I did Bryant before I got your letter. The only verses I shall add regarding him are some complimentary ones, which I left for a happier mood after I had written the comic part. *I* steal from him indeed! If he knew me he would not say so. When I steal I shall go to a specie-vault, not to a till. Does he think that he *invented* the Past and has a prescription title to it? Do not think I am provoked. I am simply amused. If he had *riled* me, I might have knocked him into a cocked hat in my satire. But that, on second thought, would be no revenge, for it might make him President, a cocked hat being now the chief qualification. It would be more severe to knock him into the middle of next week, as that is in the future, and he has such a partiality towards the past. However, enough of him. My next volume will be enough revenge, for it will be better than my last. . . .

—*reproduced by permission of the Houghton Library, Harvard University, bMS AM 765 (6–17)*

* * *

Title page for James Russell Lowell's poem that assesses his generation's literary achievements and shortcomings (courtesy of Thomas Cooper Library, University of South Carolina)

In his 25 October 1848 letter to Lowell in Cambridge, Massachusetts, Briggs records the comedy of errors that delayed G. P. Putnam's publication and distribution of A Fable for Critics.

Octo: 25

My dear friend,

As you have promised me your unforgiveness I shall look for it as a matter of course; but, strike if you will but hear me first. I believe that there is no error in the Fable, typographically, but the title is most wretchedly printed, and by an accident the advertisement of Putnam which should have been placed on a fly leaf at the end of the volume was so printed as to face the title, and it was not discovered until the book was bound, and Putnam on board the steamer. By a strange succession of accidents it was delayed a fortnight and botched. But, as only

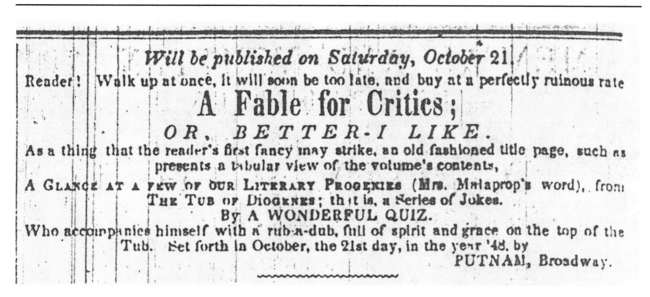

Advertisement in the 14 October 1848 issue of The Literary World. *Putnam promoted the book aggressively in New York and other American cities and sent off a shipment to his London partner, John Chapman, for sale in Great Britain.*

1000 copies have been printed, it shall be issued in the next edition, which I have little doubt will soon be called for. The literate have been itching for it the past month, and all who have had a glimpse of it are charmed with it. Putnam's leaving for London was a sudden move which discouraged matters so that the printing of the title page was given to the very person, and as he was anxious to take some copies with him he ordered the binder to send for it so that it was not seen, and I could not obtain it myself. Then it so happened that the order given for the paper was not for a sufficient quantity so that they had to wait near a week to get more from the mill. They advertised it for Saturday, but the copies were not obtained until this morning. They are mortified about it, but nobody was to blame, as they say when a steamboat blows up. I felt very much vexed about the matter on your account for I meant that the book should be elegantly got up. However, it has beauty enough, and goodness enough, to overcome much more serious blunders. 50 copies were boxed up and sent off to London by the steamer which succeeded the Hermann, together with Putnam's trunk, which, in his hurry he left behind. The Memorandum which I sent you in respect to the copies for Hosea [i.e., *The Biglow Papers*] was given to me by Putnam, but as I supposed that your publisher had attended to the matter I said nothing more about it to him. His men say that if he ordered 500 copies for New York it was probably with the expectation of being the distributing agent for the City.

—reproduced by permission of the Houghton Library, Harvard University, bMS AM 1191

Poole's Index to Periodical Literature (1848)

As a longtime compiler of lists of American publications, Putnam must have looked with special pleasure and patriotic pride on William Frederick Poole's pioneering compendium, which he published as An Alphabetical Index to Subjects, Treated in the Reviews, and Other Periodicals, to Which No Indexes Have Been Published. *It appeared at a time when relatively few individual periodicals were published with indexes and when general indexes of Americana were all but nonexistent. Putnam owed the opportunity to publish Poole's index to Henry Stevens, an old London friend and rare-book dealer who preceded Poole as a librarian of the Society of Brothers in Unity at Yale. Although eager to publish the book, Putnam had only modest commercial expectations for it, printing an unusually small edition of five hundred copies. In subsequent years, Poole updated the work and kept it in print, though with other publishers.*

* * *

Poole sent a circular advertising his index to periodicals even before he contracted to publish it with Putnam. The following excerpt was printed in The Literary World.

The Society of 'Brothers in Unity,' of Yale College, is preparing for its Library 'AN ALPHABETICAL INDEX TO SUBJECTS TREATED IN THE REVIEWS AND OTHER PERIODICALS TO WHICH NO INDEXES HAVE BEEN PUBLISHED.' The Periodicals that have been carefully examined, and referred to, in the work amount in all to five hundred and fifty volumes.

"The plan of the work is to furnish a *concise* and convenient reference to the contents of these volumes, and to this end, generally but a *single* reference is made to an article, under the most prominent *Word* of its *Subject*. It is termed an 'INDEX,' but the large number of volumes referred to, shows that the term is not used with its technical meaning in Bibliography; a reference to the minutiae of each article would so increase the size of the Work as to render the whole undertaking inpracticable. It does not claim to notice *every* article, but only such as will be of *utility* to a College community like ours. The light and fictitious articles in the Magazines have generally been omitted, as their titles would give no clue to their substance.

"We have long felt the need of such a work, and it is believed that a similar feeling exists in other Institutions. It is believed also, that the proposition we are about to make (dictated, as it is, by no motive of self-interest), will be received as a testimony of Friendship to, and Sympathy with, other similar Associations.

"This INDEX will be furnished to Literary Societies and Public Libraries (if taken in quantities) at *actual cost*. It will contain about one hundred and fifty pages, will be bound in a neat paper cover, and published about the 1st of June. An Introduction will contain a list of all the works referred to, the Editions, and the Abbreviations used. Five hundred copies only will be printed for this Institution; and as the first sheet is now in press, and as orders from Societies abroad have already been received, it is desirable to know *soon* the extent of the demand, that a sufficient number may be printed before the form is distributed. It is believed that the work can be furnished at fifty cents a copy, if *twenty* or more are taken. A smaller number will be furnished, but at a price advanced in proportion as the number is less.

"Communication may be addressed to
"WM. FRED POOLE"
–*The Literary World*, 3 (29 April 1848): 250

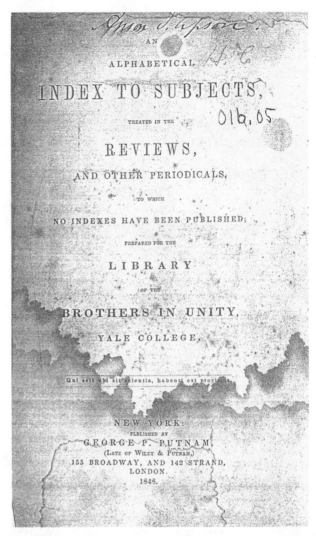

Title page for William Frederick Poole's index, which was soon regarded as a standard reference tool in Americana (courtesy of Special Collections, Thomas Cooper Library, University of South Carolina)

Index to Periodical Literature.

G. P. PUTNAM will publish next week,

In one volume, 8vo.

AN ALPHABETICAL INDEX TO SUBJECTS TREATED IN THE REVIEWS AND OTHER PERIODICALS TO WHICH NO INDEXES HAVE BEEN PUBLISHED. The Periodicals that have been carefully examined, and referred to, in the Work are, in part, the following:—

North American Review,	Vols. 26–66	41	Southern Review	complete	8	New England Magazine,	complete 6
American Quarterly "	complete	21	American Whig Review	"	6	Quarterly Christian Spectator	" 10
Foreign Quarterly, "	"	36	Walsh's American Review	"	4	New Englander,	" 5
Westminster "	"	48	Literary and Theolog. "	"	6	American Eclectic,	" 4
Edinburgh "	51–87	37	Edinburgh Monthly "	"	5	Museum of Foreign Literature,	" 37
London Quarterly "	60–81	22	Blackwood's Magazine,	"	62	Pamphleteer (London),	" 29
British and Foreign "	complete	16	Knickerbocker "	"	30	American Bib. Repository, 3d series,	" 3
Democratic "	"	22	Eclectic "	"	13	Bibliotheca Sacra,	" 4
New York "	"	10	Analectic "	"	12		

and many other Foreign and American Periodicals, amounting in all to five hundred and thirty-five volumes. To all the above works that are still published, the INDEX is brought down to January, 1848; and it is needless to add, that to those volumes of the North American, Edinburgh, and Quarterly, omitted in the above list, Indexes have been issued by their Publishers.

The plan of the work is to furnish a *concise* and convenient reference to the contents of these volumes, and to this end, generally but a *single* reference is made to an article, under the most prominent *Word* of its *Subject*. PUTNAM,

my27 (Of the Late Firm of Wiley & Putnam), 155 Broadway and Paternoster Row, London.

Advertisement in the 27 May 1848 issue of The Literary World

The California and Oregon Trail (1849)

Putnam published many travelogues during his years with Wiley and Putnam, and he remained keenly interested in the genre after forming his own publishing house. The first outstanding one he published under the G. P. Putnam imprint was Francis Parkman's The Oregon Trail, *which was originally titled* The California and Oregon Trail. *The Putnam edition appeared in March, just weeks after the two-year serialization of the work was completed in the* Knickerbocker Magazine. *The first printing of one thousand copies sold out within a month. Putnam then ordered two more printings, the first of five hundred copies (the quantity, he reported to Parkman, limited by paper shortages at the printing office) and the next probably of one thousand. Sales subsequently slowed markedly, however, and Parkman soon transferred his publishing connection to Boston.*

* * *

Putnam reports encouraging news to Parkman about sales of The California and Oregon Trail.

New York   March 30, 1849

My dear Parkman,

Again I must beg your indulgence for delay in replying to your letter that of 23d.–The Trade Sale, & my absence in Washington etc must beg my excuse. –

The 1st edn. (1000) of the Trail is now all sold–<u>including</u> paper covers–The second edn. (500) will be ready tomorrow–and will be <u>all</u> in cloth, with the plates. I think with you that the cloth copies are much preferable & that it is unnecessary to do any more in paper.–The paper books are fast going out of favor–& I dislike them particularly. I have printed but 500 of 2nd edn. simply on a/c of shortness of time & paper–but I hope to print another edn. of 1000 in a very short time. The book so far has 'sold' even better than I had hoped or anticipated.

We printed <u>1500</u> of the illustrations at first–so that we do not require any more until the 3d edn. is ready–I will then have the <u>reference</u> made which you mention[.] It certainly should have been done at first. Perhaps I can put in a <u>slip</u> to indicate the page illustrated.

I sent 6 copies to Editors in England, leaving the names for my agent to fill up–We usually send to the Athenaeum, Spectator, Douglas Jerrold, Lity. Gazette–Atlas & Examiner. I have never found it worth while to send to Blackwood for they do not <u>notice</u> one book in <u>100</u>–and if they wanted to review any particular book and to make it the text of an article they would buy it. The presentation makes no difference in their <u>Notices</u>. I will send one however if you wish it.

Very truly yours
G. P. Putnam

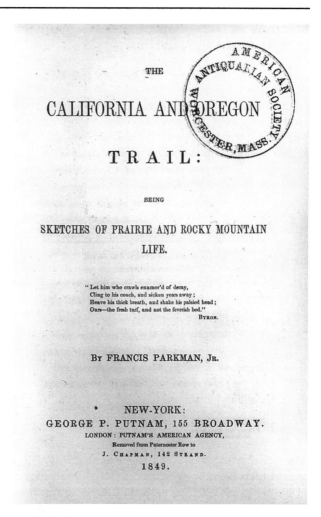

Title page for Francis Parkman's first book, a classic work, that went through several printings in its first months (courtesy of the American Antiquarian Society)

P. S.–and of course the most important part of the letter–in fact it shd. be a <u>separate</u> one on superfine paper–but you will pardon a desperately busy man like me: Permit me to congratulate you heartily on the very interesting & important 'engagement' which you have entered into: and forgive also my presumptuous egotism (?) in adding that if you are as fortunate in your matrimonial choice as I have been, you will be truly a happy man. That your taste & judgement is too critical & sound to permit any choice but the right one I feel very sure. The happy lady is unknown to <u>us</u>, but <u>Mrs Parkman</u> we know <u>must</u> be a <u>gem</u>.–My worthy spouse will give you her own congratulations.

Excuse this haste etc & believe me,
Truly yours
<u>G. P. Putnam</u>

–Francis Parkman Papers, Massachusetts Historical Society

* * *

Parkman wrote to Putnam to acknowledge royalties paid on the first two thousand copies of his book.

Lynn   Sept. 8th

My dear Sir,

I duly received the accounts & the draft for $167. I send you a receipt for the amount due on 2000 copies of the "Trail" & thank you for your liberal proposal with regard to the second illustration—Believe me in haste

Very truly your friend

F. Parkman p. by C.L.O.

Lynn   Sept. 8th, 1849

Received from G. P. Putnam in full the amount due on copyright of two thousand copies of the "Oregon Trail"

F. Parkman, Jr.

—Manuscripts Division, Department of Rare Books and Special Collections, Princeton University Library. Published with permission of the Princeton University Library.

* * *

Putnam reports slowing sales of The California and Oregon Trail. *He also mentions Washington Irving's disappointment at not having made Parkman's acquaintance when the two men crossed paths at Putnam's store.*

New York   Jany 3, 1850

My dear Parkman,

I recd. your note per "C. F. B." [Charles Frederick Briggs] of 30th [.] The title of the next edn shall be altered as you directed—I do not see any objection or any better title at present. The sale has been very slow of late and there are yet nearly the same number on hand as were mentioned in your a/c—but it may be practicable to give it a new start in the Spring.

I was thinking of so many different matters when you were here that you were gone before I was fairly aware of the fact that you were here. Mr Irving was quite vexed that he did not recognize you when we parted—He said he knew he seen [*sic*] you, but could not "place" you. He spoke of the "Trail" with much interest and said it was a capital book. He was full of anecdotes & reminiscences that day, & I was very sorry I had not insisted upon your dining with us. I hope you will stay longer next time.

We had a gathering of the literati at our rooms the other evening.—including Cooper, Bryant, Willis, Gliddon, Dr Robinson etc etc etc. You should have made one! I will certainly report when we come to Boston. Thine G P Putnam

—Francis Parkman Papers, Massachusetts Historical Society

In this letter to Parkman, Putnam discusses strategies, including a change of title, to improve sales of The California and Oregon Trail.

Francis Parkman Jr Esq.

(Boston)   Nov. 26th 1851

My dear Sir,

I have your note of 24th. You will remember that when the last a/c of the "Trail" was rendered & settled there were 288 copies on hand—It so happens—perhaps you will think it is my fault—that some of these still remain—I have no doubt that the title is partially at least the cause of this—although I have advertised the book as "Prairie & Rocky Mountain Life"—and have had a part of them bound up in leather for district School libraries, lettered with that title—about 80 copies are now left.

I certainly do not, any more than yourself, feel willing to let the work die out—It is a pity that the title "California & Oregon Trail" runs through each page of the book—but perhaps you can hit upon a new one which it will be better, even at some expense, to substitute—I dislike the idea of changing the title of a book, as, no doubt do you but in this case it seems needful—although one of the old titles should be retained as second title—so as to preserve the identity.

If you can hit upon a proper name, & will write a new preface or whatever you think desirable, I will have the plates altered & strike off an edn. of 500 for the early spring trade—which I hope may be soon repeated. –

I am glad to see such high praise of your new work, which has elevated you to a prominent niche as a historian. I hope you win a good many more laurels, and have no doubt you will.

This "still-beginning, never-ending" whirl of business has kept me of late more than ever in nervous excitement & anxiety—& I am sure you will excuse my business brevity—When shall you bring Mrs. Parkman to New York? Mrs Putnam would be delighted to see you both at the island [i. e., at the Putnams' Staten Island home]—She is well & would reciprocate your kind remembrances if she were here. Give my best respects to Mrs Parkman & believe me

dear sir faithfully yours

Geo P Putnam

F. Parkman Jr Esq

—Francis Parkman Papers, Massachusetts Historical Society

* * *

After Parkman left Putnam for Boston publishers, the two men lost touch. In this letter, written more than twenty years after the publication of The California and Oregon Trail, *Putnam responds to Parkman's inquiry about the location of the stereotype plates of the work. He ends the letter by encouraging Parkman to contribute to* Putnam's Magazine. *The four Putnam children mentioned are George Haven and John Bishop, partners in the firm; Irving, a student at Amherst College; and Mary, the first female student at the Ecole de Médecine.*

March 12 1870

Francis Parkman Esq
My Dear Sir

Your enquiry about the California Trail <u>shd</u> have been promptly answered–The reason it was not so, was simply the absence of the only person I knew of who could tell where the plates are–& whose return has been daily expected–but he is not yet here. In a day or two I will write again after learning all you ought to know.

I was very glad to see your familiar writing again and it has been a great gratification to Mrs Putnam (who has pleasant remembrances of our former acquaintance) and to myself to know of your important & successful contributions to History which have made the name of our former friend "familiar in our mouths as household words."

If you ever come to New York it would gratify us very much if you will let us have an opportunity of seeing you. My family are at present at a little seaside place in Connt.–our only homestead–where they have been all winter. <u>Two</u> of my sons are now my partners in business–a third is a student of Amherst College–My oldest daughter is an M. D.–but is now at the Ecole de Medicine in Paris–the first of the feminines who has ever been admitted there.–perhaps you may think she ought to be the <u>last</u>.

Cannot you send us a paper occasionally for our Magazine?

In haste, Dear Sir

faithfully yours

<u>G. P. Putnam</u>

–Francis Parkman Papers, Massachusetts Historical Society

Nineveh and Its Remains (1849)

Putnam owed his publication of Nineveh and Its Remains *to his good relations with John Murray, the London publisher of this book and of later works by the pioneering Assyriologist Austen Henry Layard. Putnam secured American rights to the work from Murray shortly after its London publication in 1849 and brought out an American edition that proved to be one of the better-selling works on his list not only that year but also for the next four years, with successive printings in a variety of formats required to satisfy public demand. Encouraged by that success, Putnam entered into a similar arrangement with Murray in 1851 for American rights to Layard's* Discoveries in the Ruins of Nineveh and Babylon, *which did not come out until 1853 in London and New York. G. P. Putnam did not enjoy the same degree of success with it as with its predecessor, however, because within months of its release Harper and Brothers published a rival, cheaper edition. The Harper edition, which Putnam publicly denounced as an act of piracy, effectively drove the Putnam edition out of the market.*

* * *

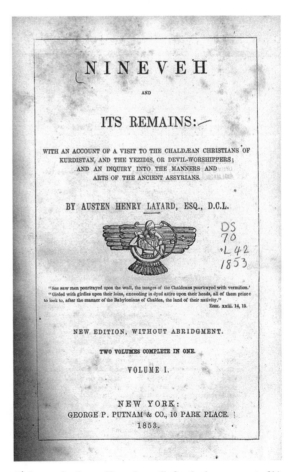

Title page for Austen Henry Layard's first book, an account of his excavations in Assyria (courtesy of Thomas Cooper Library, University of South Carolina)

This review in the form of a letter to Putnam was written by Edward Robinson, one of the leading scholarly authorities of his time on the Near East and a highly valued Wiley and Putnam author. Putnam, who had known Robinson for years and hosted him both in London and New York, probably initiated the idea of the review and then with Robinson's permission transmitted the letter to their common friend Evert Duyckinck, editor of The Literary World, *for publication.*

To G. P. PUTNAM, Esq.

My Dear Sir:—You request my opinion of Mr. LAYARD'S volumes entitled: NINEVEH AND ITS REMAINS; which you are about to introduce to the American public. I concur entirely with you in regarding this as a work of very high interest and importance; and as destined to mark an epoch in the wonderful progress of knowledge at the present day.

In this general progress the nineteenth century stands pre-eminent. In physical science, the brilliant discoveries of Davy and others have changed the whole face of Chemistry. The steam-engine, though in a measure earlier perfected, has first in our day been applied with its mighty energies to navigation, to locomotion on land, and (not least) to the printing-press. The flitting sunbeam has been grasped, and made to do man's bidding in place of painter's pencil. And although Franklin tamed the lightning, yet not until yesterday has its instantaneous flash been made the vehicle of language; thus, in the transmission of thought, annihilating space and time. The last forty years likewise bear witness to the exploration of many lands of ancient renown; and our present exact and full acquaintance with the regions and monuments of Greece and Egypt, of Asia Minor and the Holy Land, is the result of the awakened activity, coupled with the enlarged facilities, of the nineteenth century.—In all these discoveries and observations, it is not too much to say, that our country has borne at least her proportionate part.

. . . .

The work of Mr. Layard brings before us still another step of progress. Here we have to do, not with hoary ruins that have borne the brunt of centuries in the presence of the world, but with a resurrection of the monuments themselves. It is the disentombing of temple-palaces from the sepulchre of ages; the recovery of the metropolis of a powerful nation from the long night of oblivion. Nineveh, the great city of "three days' journey" that was "laid waste and there was none to bemoan her," whose greatness sank when that of Rome had just begun to rise, now stands forth again to testify to her own splendor, and to the civilization and power and magnificence of the Assyrian empire. This may be said, therefore, to be the crowning historical discovery of the nineteenth century. But the century as yet is only half elapsed.

. . . .

The volumes of Mr. Layard contain an account of the labors carried on by him at Nimroud, from November, 1845, until April, 1847; and also of the less extensive excavations made at Kalah Shegat and Kouyunjik. It has been truly said, that the narrative is like a romance. In its incidents and descriptions it does indeed remind one continually of an Arabian tale of wonders and genii. The style is simple and direct, without ornament and without effort; yet lively, vigorous, and graphic. Many difficulties did he have to encounter with Pashas and Sheikhs, Cadis and Ulemas, with Arabs of the plain

155 BROADWAY, NEW-YORK,

G. P. PUTNAM'S

NEW PUBLICATIONS.

Travels, Adventures, and Discoveries.

IN THE EAST.

Nineveh and its Remains;
With an Account of a Visit to the Chaldæan Christians of Kurdistan, and the Yezidis, or Devil-Worshippers; and an Inquiry into the Manners and Arts of the Ancient Assyrians.

BY AUSTEN HENRY LAYARD, ESQ., D. C. L.

WITH INTRODUCTORY NOTE BY PROF. E. ROBINSON, D. D., LL. D.

Illustrated with 13 Plates and Maps, and 90 Woodcuts. 2 vols. 8vo. Cloth. $4 50.

"We cannot doubt it will find its way into the hands of scholars and thinkers at once, and we shall be surprised if it does not prove to be one of the most popular, as it certainly is one of the most useful issues of the season."—*Evangelist.*

"As a record of discoveries it is equally wonderful and important; confirming in many particulars the incidental histories of Sacred Writ, disentombing temple-palaces from the sepulchre of ages, and recovering the metropolis of a wonderful nation from the long night of oblivion."—*Com. Advertiser.*

Advertisement from a catalogue bound into G. P. Putnam's books in 1850. Such an ornate notice was generally reserved for the firm's most promising books.

and Chaldeans of the mountains, in moulding them for accomplishments of his great purpose. These are often amusing, and are described with effect. In this way the work presents us with a better insight into oriental character and manners and customs, than is often to be found in volumes expressly devoted to these topics. The energy, skill, and perseverance everywhere displayed by Mr. Layard, as also his singular tact and judgment in the management of the Arabs, are worthy of all praise. This is probably the first instance, in which so many of this wild and excitable race, these sons of the desert, have been for so long a time brought under the influence of a single Frank, and led to follow regular and protracted labor.

In the latter portion of the second volume Mr. Layard gives a summary view of the results of his investigations, and of their bearing upon the history of the Assyrians. The monuments are yet too few to furnish full illustration; but they make us in many respects better acquainted with that powerful people, than all the accounts we have heretofore possessed. We may hope that Mr. Layard will yet be spared to prosecute like researches throughout the Assyrian and Mesopotamian plains, teeming as they do with similar mounds; and that the time will come, when all the monuments of those regions shall be laid open and deciphered.

. . . .

Ever truly yours,
E. Robinson.
Union Theological Seminary
New York, March, 1849
—The Literary World, 4 (17 March 1849): 242–244

Layard overseeing the removal of antiquities, which were transported to the British Museum

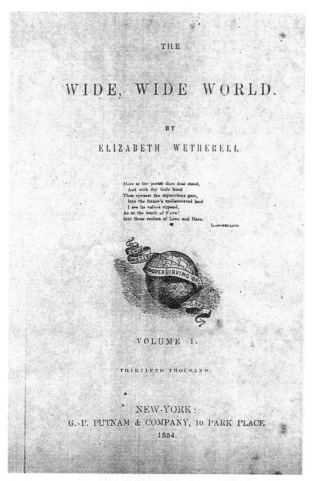

Title page for an 1854 printing of Susan Warner's still popular novel, which she first published pseudonymously in 1850 (courtesy of Thomas Cooper Library, University of South Carolina)

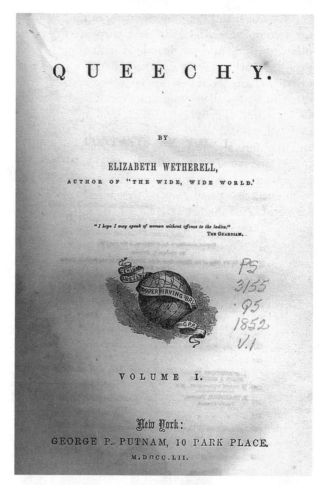

Title page for the successor to The Wide, Wide World *(courtesy of Thomas Cooper Library, University of South Carolina)*

The Wide, Wide World (1850)

Putnam had good personal and professional relations with many of the leading female writers of mid century–including Caroline Kirkland, Lydia Sigourney, Catharine Maria Sedgwick, Margaret Fuller, Susan Fenimore Cooper–but none of these authors approached Susan Warner for popularity. Indeed, he never handled another writer his entire career whose work commanded the public stage as did Warner's in the months following its publication just before Christmas 1850. Nor did he experience a bigger surprise.

The manuscript of The Wide, Wide World was offered to various New York City publishers before Warner's father brought it to G. P. Putnam. Putnam himself did not immediately see its possibilities, although he did–perhaps under family pressure–finally accept it for publication. Even though he and his wife hosted Warner in fall 1850 at their home as Warner read proof of the first of the two volumes, he plainly did not anticipate its potential as a best-seller, bringing it out in a conservative first printing of 750 copies. It took two months for that printing to sell out, but demand thereafter increased so rapidly that Putnam frequently had the pleasant task of ordering

repeated printings during the next few years, as sales mounted into the tens of thousands.

* * *

Queechy (1852)

The successor to The Wide, Wide World, Susan Warner's second novel, Queechy, also sold well, although it did not quite match the level of popular or critical success of its predecessor. Putnam was prepared this time for a hit, bringing out the largest first printing–seven thousand copies–he ever ordered for any of his firm's books in the belles lettres. With considerable publicity generated by The Wide, Wide World and Putnam's aggressive prepublication promotion campaign boosting it, that printing quickly sold out, as did a series of successive printings. Its staying power, however, proved limited. Queechy also sold well in England, although there too not equaling the runaway popularity of The Wide, Wide World.

* * *

This New-York Tribune *reviewer considers Warner's two immensely popular novels,* The Wide, Wide World *and* Queechy, *which for several years were widely discussed in the popular press.*

If we were disposed to pursue the inquiry how far the immediate success of a literary production is a proof of its intrinsic merits, we could scarcely have a more tempting occasion than is furnished by the writings of this new aspirant to public favor. Her previous novel entitled "The Wide, Wide World" attained a circulation in a short time almost without a parallel in the records of American authorship. But its extensive sale was only an expression of the admiration which it had called forth in a numerous circle of readers. There was nothing forced or artificial in its exceeding popularity. The name of the writer had never been heard of before. Wholly without pretension, it even gave no clue to her personality. Nor can it be said that her success has been greatly promoted by the influence of the press. The "Wide, Wide World" has been favorably, but not extensively, noticed by the public journals. It has found its way to the heart of the community purely by the force of its own character. The present work, in almost every respect, is a counterpart to the "Wide, Wide World." No one could mistake the identity of its origin with that unique production. It comes before the public with the brilliant prestige of its predecessor. It promises already to rival it in popularity. A large edition we understand, was sold, even before it appeared on the tables of the publisher. Readers were willing to take it on trust, in their grateful memories o[f] past enjoyment received from the pen of the gifted author.

If judged by the current rules of literary art, we confess, that we shall find it difficult to explain the remarkable success of these novels. They exhibit no striking originality of thought, nor any peculiar force or brilliancy of style. We should unhesitatingly pronounce them the work of an unpracticed writer—of one who had much to learn concerning the most effective resources of expression—and who was more indebted to a bold carelessness of composition, than to an artistic perception of the lights and shades of language. Nor is the construction of the plot in either of these works adapted to produce a powerful effect. There is no gradual accumulation of incident to pique the curiosity—the scenes pass over the stage with but faint consecutive relations—no mystery of concealment keeps the reader in breathless suspense—there is no intensity of passion—no exciting disclosures—none of the charm arising from the dramatic evolution of character—and the predestined approach to a harmonic denouement.

Still less is the secret of their success to be found in any condescension to popular taste. We acquit them

of everything like clap-trap. They have no writing for effect. Their tone is eminently pure, modest, refined, and elevated. They are equally free from inflation of sentiment and pomp of language. Often indeed they exhibit such a rare and beautiful simplicity that we might almost suppose them to have been written for the gratification of a private circle, rather than for the publicity of the press. The author is never guilty of excess of coloring—she indulges sparingly in ornament—and seldom uses any but chaste and appropriate imagery. With the prevailing love of the showy and impassioned, which is said to characterize our countrymen, we acknowledge that we should have predicted for works of this stamp quite a limited reception.

–New-York Tribune, 1 May 1852, p. 5

* * *

In a review of Warner's Karl Krisken and his Christmas Stocking *as well as her two novels, the* Southern Literary Messenger *critic takes note of and praises stories written for children, the "new literature" of the 1850s. Warner is, for this reviewer, an example of this new aesthetic.*

THE NEW LITERATURE

No trait in the literary development of the age is more striking than the importance which seems suddenly to have attached to what we call Juveniles—books for children, that is to say. At no former period has there been any movement of a similar description so observable as the present one. Children seem to rule; the nursery appears to have issued its edict, and straightway all that genius which once bent itself laboriously over history and polemics, and the severe tomes of serious thought, throws aside its important studies, smooths the wrinkled brow, and with a smile upon the lips, betakes itself to sporting in the flowery fields of juvenile romance. All the old water-courses seem broken up and obliterated—the stream runs in new channels; and, if we may be permitted to pursue the lame metaphor, the current which once bore up many ships now only serves to buoy the toy-boats of the child. Like all metaphor an exaggeration, but the truth is none the less striking. No one who has cast his eye over the catalogues of American publications during the year which has just elapsed, can have failed to observe the vast preponderance of books, whose avowed intent is to amuse and instruct the youthful hopes of our land; and the very best minds we have, wrote these volumes:—Hawthorne, and Miss Warner, and the poet Stoddard, and a host of other brilliant knights of the quill, who hearing the nursery edict, bowed their heads and obeyed.

Where will it end? What will become of those gentleman who are called "great authors" by the world, if the present flood of child-literature continues to overwhelm with a new deluge the "celebrated productions" of the magnates in Letters? There is no room for doubt—the child rules and leads in contented vassalage the best minds of the Old and the New World—Europe and America. Thackeray is compelled to chronicle the sayings and doings of "Doctor Birch and his young friends;"—Dickens must stop, in a measure, his great romances, and straightway write "A Child's History of England:"—Hans Anderson, that noble poet whose bright pen seems illuminated always by the internal light of noble thought, is no longer at liberty to compose brilliant "Improvisatores," but must expend his thoughts and time and toil upon fairy tales; upon "Wonder Books" and "Picture Books," and countless histories of Kay's and Gerdas, little match girls, and all the personages who people the bright realm of Faëry.

In America, Mr. Hawthorne is taken prisoner also; and is no longer permitted to write Scarlet Letters, or build his Seven Gabled Houses. The author of these works has yielded, and the world knows what delightful prose poems he has since produced for children—poems, which when his former works are dead, will live still; because Art forever vindicates herself and exalts what humbles itself, raising the true above that which is not true. Lastly, Miss Warner, the authoress of the "Wide-Wide World," and "Queechy," gives us the volumes whose titles we have copied at the commencement of this paper, and the triumph of the nursery is complete.

Where, we repeat, will it end? Will Mr. Macaulay take to editing a new and improved edition of the "History of Mother Goose;" Carlyle be constrained to write "Latter Day Pamphlets," on the isoteric significance of "Jack the Giant-Killer," and the "Princess Beautiful?" Will Lamartine stop writing histories to compose fairy tales, (like his "Confidences;") and Dumas and Sue find their vogue passed away, and the "Comtesse Berthe" and "Latourière" be considered the finest of their works? Where is all this flood going to have its debouchement? Will it irrigate the arid fields making them yield fruit, and blossom as the rose, or will it sweep before it every obstacle, and confound everything in its rush? Is it for good or for evil?

We think the answer is very plain. The movement is so full of promise, so worthy in itself that, for ourselves, we rejoice in it wholly and without reservation. It will improve letters. Intellect is above all too self-reliant, and is apt to exalt the brain above the heart—a great mistake, a fatal error. The pure intellect divorced from the heart, by which we mean the sympathies, impulses, feelings of every description, which characterise our moral nature, is a machine without the regulating wheel—a ship without a compass. The greater the power of the brain, the more fatal will be the absence of heart; and this is so true that we cannot ever conceive a gigantic intellect destitute of heart—for the world among all its monsters has never produced such a hideous abortion. Yet this is the tendency of that self-reliant intellect which treads all flowers under its feet, ignorant that it walks above fires concealed beneath deceitful ashes. Such natures want the crowning power of the brain—consciousness of weakness. They need humility—to understand that the Spring flower contains more beauty and purity and carries with it the proof of a power and strength greater than that of their most brilliant thoughts—their highest flights. All men need this lesson, for intellect reigns in our work-a-day world; and it is precisely because we are of opinion that the new literary movement has the desired tendency, that it is so much to our taste.

This is rather a prolonged introduction to the few words we have to say of that most charming of writers and purest of philosophers—if we may so designate a lady—the authoress of the "Wide Wide World." We have no intention of criticising any production of her pen, and only fear that we shall be guilty of extravagance in speaking of her writings. We well recollect our first perusal of the "Wide Wide World," and we then predicted its success. It deserved to succeed if a pure and beautiful work of Art, full of the most exalted piety, and as true to life and human nature as reality itself, deserve success. "Queechy," which followed it was its twin sister; and if the features were somewhat more arch and changeable and inviting, there was no such difference in the heart. The two books were dedicated to a single idea, and surely a grand idea! In both the object is to paint every-day life with its pleasures and annoyances, its sunshine and shadow, its joys and sufferings; and then, as a frame to the picture, a burden to the strain, to indicate the source from which humanity may gather strength to resist the trials of the world. Many sermons are preached in other places than the pulpit. We think that Miss Warner's works are among the strongest and most beautiful. Certain critics have taken exception to the variety of gifts united in her pictures of children, and, so, called the work unnatural. We dissent from this opinion, totally, in every point; but without pausing to discuss what is scarcely to our purpose, we may say without fear of dissent from any reader whatsoever, that the "moral" of these books is beyond criticism. We use the world *moral* in its familiar sense, and mean that Miss Warner's books make the reader purer, clear the atmosphere around him, open the blue sky above as the wind does when it sweeps away the clouds and vapors; when the purity and beauty of the world seems to revive, rising from sleep; when all is brighter for the clouds of trial. In the case of "Ellen," in the first work, the trial was in the form of a violent temper, and a tormenter who assailed the child on that weak-side with a relentless, never ceasing persecution. Against this persecution, assailing her systematically throughout every hour of the day, and driving her nearly mad with the conflict of emotions, pride and passion and self-condemnation—the child had her Bible only. Still that was quite enough. And how she at last overcame everything is all written there in the most delightful tale that has probably ever been written.

We have said that "Queechy" had the same theme—the dominant idea was identical in both; we may say as much of the two little works whose titles we have written at the commencement of this rambling paper,—which we have read quite through from title page to finis with the very greatest pleasure—and for which finally we return our thanks to the writers, and like Oliver ask for more. Miss Warner's co-worker in this little series is a character in her last work: the readers of Queechy will doubtless remember "Hugh;" and we only take notice of this circumstance to say that we should have suspected that the writer was a lady: and even possibly related to herself.

—*Southern Literary Messenger*, 20 (April 1854): 214–215

Homes of American Authors (1853)

One of the most important American gift books of the nineteenth century, Homes of American Authors *was an exercise in literary canonization. The book was produced at the same time that Putnam was reorganizing his house as G. P. Putnam and Company and working with his junior partner, John Leslie, to prepare for a variety of major initiatives, the most significant of which was the publication of* Putnam's Monthly. *In fact, the gift book and the magazine were separate but related ventures, both ambitious, expensive publications designed to exemplify the publisher's commitment to promote and publicize American authorship.*

Putnam initiated the Homes of American Authors *project and originally offered the position of editor to George William Curtis, perhaps expecting that Curtis would not only superintend the work but also compose all or some of its sketches. When Curtis declined the editorial component of the offer, Putnam turned for assistance to Charles Frederick Briggs and Frederick Saunders, but the main editorial work fell to Putnam. Through summer and fall 1852, he oversaw the operations of two separate teams, the writers who composed the biographical sketches and the artists who drew and engraved the depictions of the homes of the nation's leading authors.*

The work drew favorable attention following its December 1852 publication, but critical esteem outpaced actual sales. Putnam initially believed that the volume had not exhausted the subject and began projecting the contents of a second one. In summer 1853, however, he regretfully reached the conclusion that profits from the first volume were proving insufficient to justify a sequel.

* * *

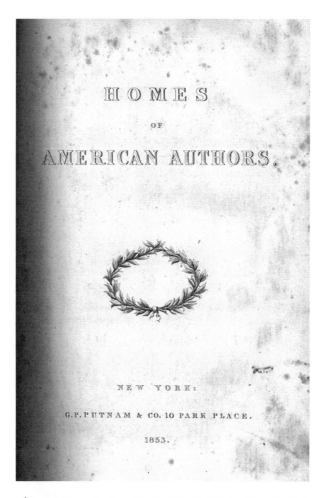

Title page for a critically acclaimed gift book initiated and largely edited by George Palmer Putnam. The book was published in time for the 1852 Christmas season but carried an 1853 imprint (Library of Congress).

In this undated 1852 letter George William Curtis declines Putnam's offer to oversee composition of Homes of American Authors.

Friday morning –
My dear Sir

Upon the whole I think I had better not undertake the work. Yet if you should finally conclude to have the articles written by various hands, I should be very glad to say what I could about Emerson, Longfellow & Hawthorne all of whom I have the good fortune to know quite well. Mr Bancroft, too, is a great friend of mine. –

In any case I am sure you will have no difficulty in finding a man for a duty so pleasant, and I am truly sorry that, in view of all the pros, and cons, I am unable to respond to your flattering preference.

    Believe me,
    Dear Sir
    Very truly Yours
    Geo. Wm. Curtis
27 Washington Place–
–Clifton Waller Barrett Library of American Literature, Special
Collections Department, University of Virginia Library

* * *

Hammat Billings, one of many artists engaged in the Homes of American Authors *project, reports to Putnam on his progress in preparing drawings of the homes of James Russell Lowell and Henry Wadsworth Longfellow.*

Boston July 2nd. 1852.

Dear Sir,

You will receive by to-day's express the drawing of Mr Lowell's residence. By reason of an accident to the drawing of Cragie [sic] House, I am obliged to redraw it but shall have it done tomorrow. Hoping the present one will prove satisfactory I am

    Respectfully yrs
    Hammat Billings
Geo. P. Putnam Esq.
–Clifton Waller Barrett Library of American Literature, Special
Collections Department, University of Virginia

* * *

Caroline Kirkland describes her progress in drafting a text to accompany the engraving of Catharine Maria Sedgwick's Berkshire house for the volume. She also contributed the sketch of her neighbor William Cullen Bryant's house.

Trenton Falls, Aug 21.

My dear Sir–Your letter requesting certain pages did not reach me until Thursday night–Yesterday, Friday was intolerably hot and wilting, and this morning, (Saturday) I am sick–So you must take these seven pages and make the best of them if they will do. You will see that I began on the supposition of what has been said about the Berkshire home–So if it does not fit in well you must put in a few dove-tailing words–
    Yours truly
    C. M. Kirkland
P. S.
I shall be at Utica next week

Kirkland adds an admonition in the left margin.

Do see that it is carefully read, for it is very badly written–on my knee as I sat on the rocks.

–Clifton Waller Barrett Library of American Literature, Special
Collections Department, University of Virginia Library

* * *

The reviewer for the Southern Literary Messenger *compares* Homes of American Authors *to G. P. Putnam's previous year's gift book,* Book of Home Beauty.

THE HOMES OF AMERICAN AUTHORS, *Comprising Anecdotal, Personal, and Descriptive Sketches.* Illustrated by Nineteen Fine Engravings on Steel, &c., &c., New York: G. P. Putnam & Co. 1853. [For sale by A. Morris, 97 Main Street.]

Who does not think, upon turning over the leaves of this delightful volume, how much better is such a testimonial to the country's intellect, than that showy tribute to female vanity–The Book of Home Beauty–and how much worthier of the soft incense of praise are the authors of a great nation than the belles of a great city? We therefore deem Mr. Putnam's "crack book" of the present season, entitled to far higher consideration than that of the last season. In republican America, where no Court Circle exists–giving laws to provincial society–no "earthly paradise of Ormolu," into which the million would stake their lives to be admitted–we do not care to read of the graces and accomplishments of any aristocratic set of beauties, but what man or woman who has been charmed by the Sketch Book into a feeling of personal regard for its author, or has learned to know Kennedy in Swallow Barn, or acquired from the Twice Told Tales an interest in anything relating to Hawthorne, will not be delighted with the *ana* given in "The Homes of American Authors"?

The Sketches contained in the volume are written with ease and elegance. "The Howadji" makes himself known here in his picturesque, Tennysonian sentences;—we recognize elsewhere in the book the finished and thoughtful manner of Tuckerman;—Griswold contributes to it a paper marked with his characteristic excellence, and Bryant gracefully appears in the description of the woodland haunt of his brother poet—William Gilmore Simms. We are disappointed in not finding in the work portraits of Simms and Kennedy, no satisfactory presentments of their fine faces having ever been given to the public. There are, however, very exquisite steel engravings of Irving, Cooper and Everett, and scattered throughout the entire work are numerous tinted illustrations on wood, and facsimiles of manuscripts. These latter seem to us singularly unfortunate as specimens of the author's autographs. Few men, who ever learned to sign their names, have written more legibly and beautifully than Mr. Everett or Mr. Kennedy—the latter's handwriting we consider the very perfection of caligraphy—yet from the facsimiles in this volume, both these gentlemen would appear to have acquired the art of penmmanship on Dogberry's plan who told us that "to *write* and read comes by nature." Surely the engraver must have picked out the worst leaf in the "Oration at Niblo's" and "Horse Shoe Robinson" for copying.

Altogether, we think "The Homes of American Authors" one of the pleasantest and prettiest books it has been our good fortune to meet with for many a day.

—*Southern Literary Messenger,* 18 (December 1852): 763

* * *

The reviewer in Graham's Magazine *affirms the cultural nationalism of* Homes of American Authors *and praises the stylish execution of its "pilgrimage" to the country's literary shrines.*

Homes of American Authors. New York: G. P. Putnam & Co.

This is the most delightful book we have perused for a long time—a combination of homestead sketches, portraits, autographs and gracefully written biographical reminiscences such as no American can read without feelings of interest and pleasure; interest, in the story of those who have furnished us with the first fruits of American literature, and pleasure, to know that the muses in this country have rewarded their votaries with such very comfortable quarters—attic residences, in fact, but *not* in the old Grub Street sense of the term. Absorbed in this book, we have allowed our feelings and ourselves to make pilgrimages to and fro, in the land of literary things, mindful only of the pleasant and picturesque of the routes. We have greeted Audubon, in his suburban parlor, in the midst of antlers, stuffed birds and drawings; and gazed at the Shawangunk and Katskill mountains from the terrace of Paulding's dwelling; and looked from the lawn at Sunny Side, on that Hudson scenery which Washington Irving has immortalized; and seen Bryant—without venturing too near that stern-looking *vates,* however—going about at Roslyn in a broad-brimmed hat; and keeping our own firmly on our head, looked away seaward from Dana's house at Cape Ann; and sat in Prescott's cottage at Nahant; and stared to see Fenimore Cooper carrying a string of onions in Broadway; and admired the elegance of Everett's library; and sat, "an earthly guest," in Emerson's parlor among the rigid and russet-eating philosophers who would not unbend. We have gone with a reverent recollection into the elegant and historic mansion of the Poet-Professor, Longfellow—

"Made famous by the pen
And glorious by the sword"—

to use the words of the great Marquis of Montrose; a place invested with the double charm of poetic interest and the renown of the most stainless soldier that ever drew a blade, and exercising henceforth, a double attraction for the pilgrims of glory and genius. We have also been wandering in the spirit through Concord and Salem, and trying to pick acquaintance with that shyest of men—Cowper scarcely excepted—Nathaniel Hawthorne; gazing anon, on the house where Daniel Webster came into the world, and that other in which he died, and admiring that aristocratic old house of Oliver's at Cambridge, where Lowell the poet was born. Before our eyes has passed a crowd of memorable and absorbing images, and after so much reverie in a charmed atmosphere, it is with a sort of depression that we come back into the light of common day.

These notices of the local habitations of our distinguished names are partly biographical and give glimpses of the careers of those they treat of. They are written in an animated and graphic style by some of the best American writers; and nothing is wanting to make the book an admired and popular one. The publishers have brought it out in an elegant typographical dress, and the portraits scattered throughout it—the fine, good-natured face of Irving, the massive head of Cooper, and the brave intellectual developments of Hawthorne—are executed in the most delicate style of art. Altogether, it is a choice book for any American library—having done in the most satisfactory style for American authors what the Howitts have done for those of England.

We are glad to perceive that there is to be another volume on the same themes—in which Halleck and others will find a place, and the possible Longfellows and Bryants of a future day, get a modicum of lithograph and typography, to cheer their motions as they climb the Parnassian pathways. We had marked so many portions of this book for extract that we find we have forgot the space at our disposal, and must omit them.

—*Graham's Magazine,* 42 (May 1853): 634–635

Homes of American Statesmen (1854)

Instead of publishing a sequel to Homes of American Authors, *Putnam initiated and supervised* Homes of American Statesmen *in time for the holiday season of 1853 (though copyrighted 1854). It repeated the formula used in the former, matching sketches of leading American statesmen to reproductions of their residences and manuscripts. Similarly, it replicated the earlier volume's idiosyncratic linking of class, culture, and patriotism.*

* * *

Putnam writes to author Nathaniel Parker Willis of his decision to drop the second volume of Homes of American Authors *and to reconceive the project.*

Feby 28, 1853

Dear Sir,

Your withdrawal, and some other difficulties in the way of a <u>suitable</u> selection of names have induced us to postpone for the present the 2nd volume of Houses of Living Authors. This year we propose to do the <u>departed</u> genius—both authors & statesmen.

I am glad to learn our "Monthly" finds favor in your region. Your "Society" notice <u>is</u> I think far more valuable than a mere fluff, even though we may not agree with your position & premises. That article seems to find strong favor in the right quarters.

In haste, truly yours

<u>G. P Putnam</u>

N. P. Willis Esq

—Manuscripts Division, Department of Rare Books and Special Collections, Princeton University Library. Published with permission of the Princeton University Library.

* * *

Putnam frequently introduced his firm's gift books and occasional books with a "Publishers' Notice" in which he pointed out the special features of the work. At the close of his introduction to Homes of American Statesmen *Putnam proudly announces his company's experiment in adapting the latest printing technology to publishing: the first printing in an American book of a photograph—the Hancock House in Boston—which was used as the frontispiece of the book.*

WE need hardly commend to the American public this attempt to describe and familiarize the habitual dwelling-places of some of the more eminent of our Statesmen. In bringing together such

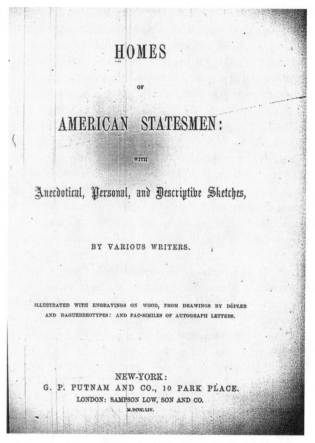

HOMES
OF
AMERICAN STATESMEN:
WITH
Anecdotical, Personal, and Descriptive Sketches,

BY VARIOUS WRITERS.

ILLUSTRATED WITH ENGRAVINGS ON WOOD, FROM DRAWINGS BY DÖPLER
AND DAGUERREOTYPES: AND FAC-SIMILES OF AUTOGRAPH LETTERS.

NEW-YORK:
G. P. PUTNAM AND CO., 10 PARK PLACE.
LONDON: SAMPSON LOW, SON AND CO.
M.DCCC.LIV.

Title page for the gift book G. P. Putnam published as the successor to Homes of American Authors *(Library of Congress)*

particulars as we could gather, of the homes of the men to whom we owe our own, we feel that we have performed an acceptable and not unnecessary service. The generation who were too well acquainted with these intimate personal circumstances to think of recording them, is fast passing away; and their successors, while acknowledging a vast debt of gratitude, might still forget to preserve and cherish the individual and private memories of the benefactors of our country and race. We therefore present our contribution to the national annals with confidence, hoping that in all respects the present volume will be found no unworthy or unwelcome successor of the "Homes of American Authors."

Dr. R. W. Griswold having been prevented by ill health from contributing an original paper on Marshall, we have availed ourselves, with his kind permission, of the sketch which he prepared for the "Prose Writers of America." All the other papers in the present volume have been written expressly for it: and the best acknowledgments of the publishers are due to the several contributors for the zealous interest and ability to which these sketches bear witness.

For several of the original letters which we have copied in *fac-simile,* we are indebted to the kindness of the Rev. Dr. Sprague of Albany.

Most of the illustrations in this volume have been engraved from original drawings, or daguerreotypes taken for the purpose. The frontispiece is somewhat of a curiosity, *each copy* being an *original sun-picture* on paper. The great luminary has here entered into direct competition with other artists in the engraving business—our readers can judge how well he has succeeded.

Life of George Washington (1855–1859)

Putnam had unusually high expectations for Washington Irving's Life of George Washington. *National veneration for George Washington remained great, and the prospect of a definitive Washington biography being written by his own leading author presented Putnam with an enticing prospect once Irving committed himself to the project in the early 1850s. The project, though, proved an all-but-unbearable burden for an aging author, particularly as it unexpectedly grew into a five-volume publication whose last volume was completed only months before Irving's death. A cobbled-together work, the biography earned only mixed reviews. It presented Putnam, however, with a non-pareil opportunity to promote the entire Irving canon and to do so over an extended period of time. He produced the* Life of George Washington *in styles that matched those of the various Irving editions he brought out over the course of the 1850s and marketed the work for years both as part of as well as distinct from those editions.*

* * *

The reviewer for Norton's Literary Gazette and Publishers' Circular *brought to this analysis the reverential attitude that Irving, then in his seventies, generally enjoyed in his last decade.*

THE LIFE OF GEORGE WASHINGTON, BY WASHINGTON IRVING. In 3 vols. Vol. 1. Putnam.

When Washington Irving, some years since, was understood to be engaged in writing the life of George Washington, it was felt by the public that no more appropriate labor could be found to crown a life of literary exertion, prolonged through a felicitous course seldom falling to the lot of authors. That the same pen which had given to the world

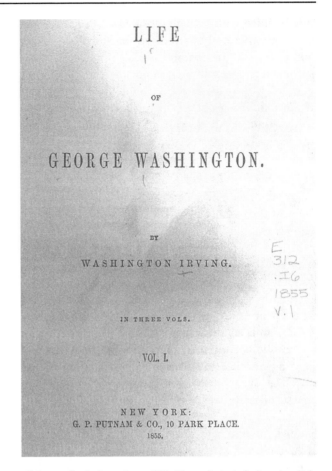

Title page for the first volume of Washington Irving's final work, which occupied nearly the entirety of his last decade (courtesy of Thomas Cooper Library, University of South Carolina)

the graceful, easy narrative of the discovery of America; which had traced the far beginnings of conquest and enterprise that waited on the track of Columbus, should, after a considerable interval—the lengthened period of human life, of three score and ten already accomplished—be once more at work unfolding the career of the second Columbus of the western sphere,—the founder of states and empire,—and with unabated powers of thought and happiness of style—this is poetic justice to the individual dedicated to the service of literature, rarely found in the broken, interrupted toils of that profession.

We have now to chronicle the appearance of the first instalment of this work, soon to be followed by the remaining portions which, we understand, are already mostly written.

It is a biography of Washington, of a semi-historic character, in which the personal interest and a certain degree of familiarity in the former, are happily blended with enough of the graver topics of the latter, to give body as well as sparkling life to the whole. The author-painter has selected a canvas of sufficient size upon which to portray the varied incident of historical narration, and thus far he has, while exhibiting the full length of his hero in the foreground, supplied with propriety and effect, the numerous accessories necessary to the adequate understanding, and, it may be added, the luxurious enjoyment of the scene.

Were we not aware that it is one of the privileges of the highest art to conceal its own means—*ars est celare artem*—we might readily be led into the error of supposing that the composition of the present work involved more skill than labor, that it was an adroit rendering of a difficult theme where the gentle and humorous author, by a happy knack of his profession, had escaped the proverbially wearisome toils of the historian. The narrative begins so simply, is continued so lightly; one incident succeeding another in so easy and natural an order; and the style, moreover, bearing such frequent marks of reflective enjoyment in the writer, that it appears but the holiday pastime of literature. So, indeed, in one sense, it is, for a genial, generous nature in such cases, relieves the student of half his toil; but the other half remains. The sun may shine, showers may fall, and the sweet influences of the seasons be all propitious; but, to secure the crop, the seed must first be sown and the land must be ploughed. Smooth as this book appears in its apparently negligent gracefulness, it may be safely conjectured that sometimes the furrowed brow, the aching head, the vexing perplexities of literary research presided over the reluctant felicities.

The qualities which Washington Irving has brought to this work should be fairly estimated for its full enjoyment. Foremost among these as giving secret life to his narrative, in which the charm and value of the book lies, and not especially in its original investigations or philosophy, is that certain vein of humor which has marked the compositions of Geoffrey Crayon—to the great satisfaction of the readers of this his native city, for more than half a century. When we speak of humor in this connection, we of course do not use the word in the limited vulgar sense of the comic or laughable; but in its deeper significance of a fine essence of the mind, which may here be well enough defined as an educated pleasurable instinct of observation, alive to every incident or act which is an external exhibition

of the character within. The possession of this trait is invaluable to the biographer who would interest the public. It is preëminently possessed by Irving. What other writers may compass by analysis, of hidden character and constitution, he seems to arrive at by a glance at the same person as he inevitably shows himself in his ordinary acts. There are critics who would despise this easy method, and call for something more profound; but, without undervaluing philosophy and profundity, we may invite such carpers to show any writer who has made fewer mistakes in his judgment of men and measures than Irving. The illustration and exhibition of character by his peculiar methods, on the very score of historic truthfulness is, indeed, one of the most valuable results which we look for in this Life of Washington, particularly when the author is thrown into the thicker throng of military and political actors, heroes, patriots, cowards, knaves, assistants, and malignants, in his subsequent volumes.

With this underlying truthful humor the narrative of Irving glides along pleasantly enough. It is quite an artistical affair in its getting up and arrangement. To secure its first requisite of clearness, it must be disencumbered of all superfluous and baser matters which would clog its progress; while, to be faithful and valuable, it must present the minute fact, and frequently the language of the times. It must be a good story, as well as an historical chronicle. No one can manage this more adroitly than Washington Irving. He knows exactly where to plant a telling fact, where to paint a wholesome moral, where to insinuate a gentle touch of sentiment; and he is also in possession of a secret known to very few writers, of reconciling the common mind to these refinements by frequently employing easy colloquial expressions. The author gives a hint of this in his preface, where he speaks of biography, "admitting of familiar anecdote, excursive digressions, and a flexible texture of narrative." The number of these idiomatic phrases is quite striking; and they seem admirably to convey the meaning, particularly in those portions relating to Washington's intercourse with the Indians, where stateliness of narrative would hardly be in keeping with the unsteady civilization.

—Norton's Literary Gazette and Publishers' Circular (1 June 1855): 227–229

Personal Narrative of a Pilgrimage to El-Medinah and Meccah (1856)

Putnam had previously published travelogues by British authors such as George Borrow, William Alexander Kinglake, and Austen Henry Layard when he brought out the first American edition of Lieutenant Richard F. Burton's Personal Narrative of a Pilgrimage to El-Medinah and Meccah. *Burton's was a particularly desirable volume; his reputation as explorer and author preceded him, and American interest in the Middle East and Islam was running high, in part because of the Crimean War. Produced in a far less expensive one-volume edition than the three-volume Longman edition published the previous year, the Putnam edition included an introduction by Bayard Taylor, whom Putnam quite likely saw as Burton's American peer. Proud of the appearance of the book, Putnam sent a copy to Burton in Zanzibar.*

* * *

Bayard Taylor, who had recently traveled through parts of the Middle East, discussed Burton's achievement in his introduction to the Putnam edition.

The present century is already remarkable beyond the last, for the extent and richness of its contributions of geographical knowledge; but the generation in which we live will be especially noted hereafter as that which has preeminently invaded the few lingering haunts of fable, and brought their cherished mysteries under the microscopic lenses of modern eyes. Within ten years the courageous M. Huc, has penetrated through the vast interior realms of China and Tartary, to the sacred city of Lha-Ssa, of which he has given the first satisfactory description; Lieutenant Lynch has exploded the superstitious terrors with which the Dead Sea was regarded; Dr. Barth has returned safely to Europe, after a residence of seven months at Timbuctoo; Dr. Krapf has looked upon the snowy pinnacles of the long lost Mountains of the Moon; and now, Lieutenant Burton, having penetrated to Medina and Mecca, and entered into the holiest sanctuaries of the Moslem faith, presents us with the picturesque story of his pilgrimage.

The extreme reverence in which these cities are held, and that jealousy which prevents all acknowledged followers of other religions from visiting, or even approaching them, undoubtedly grew out of the fierce and fanatical character of Mohammedanism in its earlier days. The violence of that fanaticism is now over. Except in Arabia, the cradle and stronghold of Islam, the Frank Christians mingle freely with the followers of the Prophet, not only without indignity, but in many places as their friends and

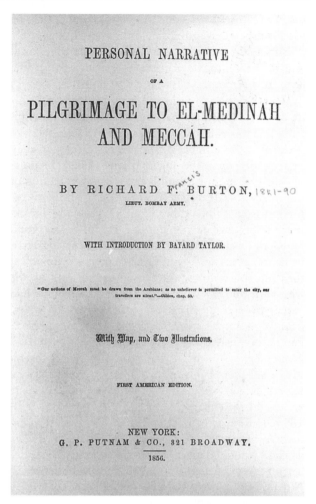

Title page for the first American edition of Richard F. Burton's book that was previously published in three volumes in London (courtesy of the American Antiquarian Society)

protectors. The rapid spread of intercourse between the East and the West, and, more than all, the recent alliance of Christian and Moslem powers in the war against Russia, has greatly weakened, and, in the course of time, may wholly obliterate, the bitterness of that religious prejudice which has hitherto been the characteristic of such intercourse. Its effect is already seen, in the facility with which travellers now obtain access to the sacred mosques of Constantinople and Cairo. Even the Mosque of Omar, at Jerusalem, where, five years ago, Christians were stoned for attempting to enter—whose gates would not open to a Frank for a firman of the Sultan himself—has alike become accessible to profane feet. The same challenge will eventually overtake the more bigoted population of the Hedjaz, and future travellers, perhaps, in green veils and spectacles, may languidly scrutinize the mosques of Mecca. The success of such men as Burckhardt and Burton should not be ascribed, however, to this circumstance. It is entirely due to their courage, prudence, and perseverance, and to their intimate acquaintance with eastern life, and the ceremonials of the Moslem faith.

The design of visiting Mecca has been a favorite one with travellers for centuries past, but the difficulties in the way of its prosecution have been so great, that the number of those who succeeded may be reckoned upon the fingers of one's hand. Lieutenant Burton, in an Appendix to the English edition of his work, gives extracts from the descriptions of his predecessors, which differ from his own and Burckhardt's in some telling particulars, but correspond much more nearly than might have been expected from travellers of such different epochs. Gibbon, at the time of writing his "Decline and Fall of the Roman Empire," was not aware any Christians had reached Mecca up to that time. It appears, however, from Mr. Burton's investigations, that two persons had accomplished the journey—Lodovico Bartema, a gentleman of Rome, in the year 1603; and Joseph Pitts, of Exon, England, in 1680. To these may be added, in later years, Giovanni Finati, an Italian renegade, and Burckhardt, both in 1814, and Burton, in 1853. The French apostates in the service of Mohammed Ali, some of whom made the usual pilgrimage, as good Mussulmans, need not be reckoned. Some of them have published accounts of their experiences, it is true; but, as new converts to the faith, they were regarded with distrust, and thereby prevented from making measurements or observations. Their accounts are therefore very inaccurate, and contribute nothing to our knowledge of the holy cities.

The first traveller on the list, Lodovico Bartema, visited Damascus in his wanderings through the East, and there won the friendship of a Mameluke captain, who was a renegade Christian. Disguising himself as a Mameluke, he accomplished the latter on a pilgrimage to Mecca, apparently conducting himself as a devout Mussulman, for his real character was not suspected, although he was afterwards imprisoned for a time in Yemen, on acknowledging himself a Christian. His narrative has all the quaint simplicity and picturesque character of those of the early travellers, with no more credulity than is necessary to give piquancy to his story. Lieutenant Burton, who of course is thoroughly competent to judge on this point, places him in the foremost rank of the old original travellers, for correctness of observation and readiness of wit.

Joseph Pitts was an English boy, who, for love of adventure going to sea in his fifteenth or sixteenth year, was captured by Algerine pirates and sold as a slave. His master, who had been a great sinner, determined to convert him, as an atonement for his own impiety, and achieved his object by means of the bastinado. Pitts submitted to this violent conversion, and performed all the external forms and ceremonies required of him; but hated the new faith in his heart, with a vehemence which was not in the least abated by fifteen years of Moslem life. He was taken to Mecca and El Medinah by his master, remained some months in the former city, and returned to Cairo. Having received his freedom, he determined to make his escape, in which, after various adventures, he succeeded, and returned safely to England. His descriptions of the Beit Allah (house of God) at Mecca, the ceremonies on Mount Arafat, the stoning of the devil, and other features of the pilgrimage, are very circumstantial and correct, considering that they were written from memory after a lapse of many years. Lieutenant Burton finds little fault with Pitts, except his hatred and bigotry, which the manner of his conversion may well explain.

Finati was an ignorant and unprincipled Italian renegade, who made the campaign against the Wahabees for the recovery of Mecca and Medina, in the army of Mohammed Ali. Mr. Bankes, the English traveller, afterwards took him into his service, and translated the narrative of his adventures, which was dictated in Italian, as he was unable to write. The particulars he gives concerning the holy places of Mecca are very imperfect and unsatisfactory. Burckhardt, who made his visit to Mecca and Medina in the same year as Finati, may be considered as the first enlightened and experienced traveller who describes those places. He ventured on the undertaking only after years of preparation in the East, and a familiarity with the language and the faith so complete, that, under his assumed name of Shekh Ibrahim, his real character was unsuspected. Only once, when visiting Mohammed Ali, at Tayf, was he subjected to a rigid examination on points of Mohammedan doctrine, by two learned *shekhs ul-Islam,* at the instance of the pasha, who had heard suspicions whispered against him in Cairo. Burckhardt passed the test triumphantly, the shekhs declaring, that he was not only a genuine Mussulman, but one of unusual learning and piety. After performing all the ceremonies of the pilgrimage, he returned to Mecca, where he remained three months, before visiting Medina. At the latter place he was too ill to make many observations, and his descriptions are more meagre than usual. His accounts of the holy edifices of Mecca, and the pilgrim ceremonies, however, are very complete, and Burton pays the highest tribute to his correctness, by copying entire his description of the Kaaba.

The present author, therefore, traverses a partly beaten track, but a track wherein the last success reflects as much honor as the first. His experiment, in fact, was even more daring than that of Burckhardt, whose assumed character was already recognised throughout the Orient, and who, after his examination at Tayf, was placed beyond the reach of suspicion. Burton, on the other hand, was a novice in this special field, and was obliged to disguise himself under a totally different character. He took his part with admirable boldness and skill, and when once suspected by the young Meccan rogue, Mohammed, whose travels had made his vision precociously keen, was defended by the remainder of the party, who completely silenced his accuser. Burton's narrative is especially valuable for his full and accurate particulars of the religious observances of the pilgrimage, and the various formulas of salutation and prayer. In this respect there is no other work of the kind equal to it. His descriptions of the holy edifices are scrupulously technical and careful; and he gives us, for the first time, sketches of the sacred cities which impress us with their fidelity to nature. We could have desired more ample pictures of the scenery through which he passed, and the spirited account of the voyage from Suez to Yambu shows that he is not deficient in descriptive power. But much allowance must be made for the night travels of the pilgrim caravan, and the consequent fatigue of the traveller. He has the advantage over Burckhardt of writing in his mother-tongue, and his narrative is much richer in those characteristic personal incidents and adventures which are the vital spirit of books of travel.

It is to be hoped that so prudent, daring, and intelligent a traveller will be permitted to carry out his original scheme of exploring the interior of the Arabian peninsula—one of the richest and most interesting fields of research now remaining. Certainly no one is better qualified for the undertaking.

B. T.

New York, *July* 1*st*, 1856.

* * *

The new interest in the Middle East then overtaking Western Europe and the United States permeates this Putnam's Monthly *review of Burton's experiences in Arabia.*

A similar contribution to geographical knowledge is to be found in LIEUTENANT BURTON'S *Personal Narrative of a Pilgrimage to El Medina and Mecca*. He was connected with the British army in Bombay, where he acquired a thorough acquaintance with the various dialects of Arabia and Persia, and where he learned to adopt the manners and even the looks of the Orientals so well, that he was afterwards enabled to pass everywhere in the East, not only without detection as a Frank, but with admirable helps for visiting tabooed places, and observing secluded customs. Having offered to the Royal Geographical Society of London, in 1852, his services, for the purpose of removing that opprobrium to modern adventure, the "huge white blot," which in our maps still notes the eastern and central regions of Arabia, they were accepted, and he, assuming the character of an old Persian wanderer, set out to cross the unknown Arabian peninsula, but particularly to visit El Medina and Mecca. At the time Gibbon wrote his "Decline and Fall," it was supposed that nobody, not of the Mohammedan faith, had ever reached Mecca; but Lieutenant Burton shows that two persons, at least, had accomplished the journey, first, an Italian named Bartema, 1603, and then an Englishman, named Joseph Potts, in 1680. Subsequently, another Italian named Fanati, and the celebrated Burckhardt, both in 1814, performed the feat. But though the track is thus shown not to be an entirely new one, it was never before traveled to so much purpose as by Burton, in 1853. In fact, El Medina is quite a virgin theme. His narrative contains more full and interesting particulars of the great pilgrimage to Mecca than have been before written; his descriptions of the holy edifices are scrupulously technical, and his sketches of the sacred cities, which we have, for the first time, faithful to the reality. What he says of the scenery is not very striking, but it was not for scenery that he undertook his wearisome and perilous adventures. It is the people, their manners and customs, their strange faiths and rites, their costumes and characters, which attract his attention, and which he portrays with singular vivacity, and yet, truthfulness. The interior life of Moslem he throws open to us, to afford, not a passing glance, but a full and steady look. By introducing himself into the very recesses of the harem and the caravan, as a practicing physician, he was enabled to behold mysteries which are sedulously guarded from the eyes of Christians, and which he exposes to all the world. Nor is he less amusing than instructive. Like the author of Eothen, or our own Howadji, he is not always grave, but mingles many a telling anecdote, many a laughter-moving incident among his more serious observations. A dramatic interest is thus given to his pages, and that truth of local color which is the greatest charm of travelers' stories.

—*Putnam's Monthly*, 8 (November 1856): 545–546

The Life and Letters of Washington Irving
(1862–1864)

Arguably the first major literary biography in American literary history, The Life and Letters of Washington Irving *grew out of the special relationship that Putnam enjoyed not only with Irving but also with his nephew and literary executor, Pierre M. Irving. Announced just months after the writer's death in November 1859, the biography grew into a four-volume project that G. P. Putnam published volume by volume. Although brought out during the Civil War years when book sales were slow, the biography sold so well that the firm published it in various formats and sold it both in conjunction with and apart from their editions of Washington Irving's works.*

* * *

Life and Letters of Washington Irving *was generally well received by the critics and sold well enough to prompt the publication of the new edition reviewed here in* Putnam's Magazine.

No biography of an American man of letters was ever received with such favor as "The Life and Letters of Washington Irving," by his nephew Pierre Irving, and, if the value of a work of the kind depends on the freedom with which the author delineates himself and his pursuits therein, no biography of an American man of letters ever deserved to be received with such favor. Of the many who have in some sort followed authorship here, few are worthy to be considered authors, and of those few Irving was the one above all others who was most an author. He lived and had his being in an atmosphere of books; his choicest companions were bookish men like himself. No American ever knew so many English authors, and no American was ever held in such high esteem by them. They were his friends as well as his correspondents, and his reputation was as dear to them as their own. The biography of such a man, even when the materials for it are scanty, is likely to be entertaining, and when they are as abundant as in Irving's case, it is certain to be so. Popular when it was first published, the biography of Irving is popular still, if the sale of several editions may be regarded as a test; and if the usual test of a cheap edition is to be trusted, it is destined to be still more popular. So, at

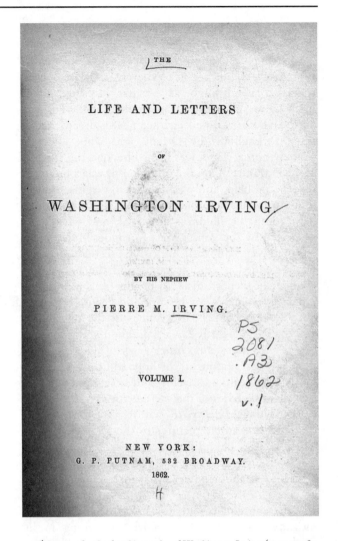

Title page for the first biography of Washington Irving (courtesy of Thomas Cooper Library, University of South Carolina)

least, think the publishers (G. P. Putnam & Son), who have just issued a new edition of *The Life and Letters of Washington Irving*. It is in three volumes (eighteen-mos, or thereabouts), each of which is illustrated with a portrait of Irving. The printing of these little volumes is every thing that ought to be looked for in a cheap edition of a favorite book: of this there are also two finer editions in different sizes.

–*Putnam's Magazine,* 5 (April 1870): 508

Book of the Artists. American Artist Life
(1867)

Book of the Artists was the result of Henry Tuckerman's lifelong engagement with the arts in the United States. It grew out of his 1847 Artist-Life: Or Sketches of American Painters and included sketches of the latest generation of artists, including Martin Johnson Heade, Winslow Homer, and James McNeill Whistler. For a publisher such as G. P. Putnam, committed for twenty years to the "progress" of the arts in the United States, Tuckerman's book carried a cachet matched by few other works on its list in the years following the Civil War. Putnam advertised it as a landmark study and brought it out in fall 1867 in both a regular trade edition and an expensive, subscription edition of 150 copies, printed on large paper.

* * *

Book of the Artists. American Artist Life, the most comprehensive overview of American art to date, attracted considerable attention upon its publication in 1867.

TUCKERMAN'S BOOK OF THE ARTISTS.
BOOK OF THE ARTISTS. AMERICAN ARTIST LIFE.
By HENRY T. TUCKERMAN. 8 vo. pp. 639. G. P. Putnam & Son.

Rarely has a more appropriate and generous preparation been brought to the composition of a literary work than is manifest in the present significant volume. Mr. Tuckerman has devoted many years of wise research and study to the most fruitful branches of modern culture; he has given the eye of a poet and the taste of a scholar to the contemplation of the noblest works of art; a long residence in the most polished European capitals has made him familiar with the world-celebrated productions of sculpture and painting; while an intimate personal intercourse with accomplished artists of the day has furnished him with a profusion of anecdotes and details in regard to the habits of artistic life, which he has turned to excellent account in the illustration of his work. He gives a history of the progress of art in this country from its early dawn in the East, before the Revolutionary War to its present comparatively golden flush; with ample biographical notices of its most distinguished representatives, and critical descriptions and estimates of their chief productions. The volume is written in an animated and flowing style, a little too elaborate, perhaps, for a superficial popular taste, and occasionally more diffuse than the subject requires; but always diversified with agreeable anecdotes, and personal sketches, which happily relieve the methodical course of critical aesthetic discussion.

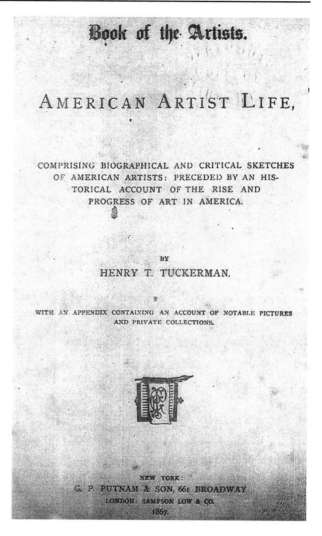

Title page for a work that reinforced the House of Putnam's longstanding commitment to books on American art (Library of Congress)

In the introductory chapter, Mr. Tuckerman treats of the historical development and present condition of American art, offering many valuable suggestions both to the artists as a body, and the portion of the public who are especially interested in their productions. A great change in the relations of art has taken place within the last ten years. In many instances, as Mr. Tuckerman tells us, artists among us have received a more liberal remuneration than would be justified by European prices. The vocation is no longer a precarious one, but affords a fair reward to talent and industry. But as yet, no uniform standard of excellence has been reached, even in the productions of the same artist.

–New-York Tribune, 12 December 1867, p. 6

Putnam Series

Publication in series format became a popular strategy among publishers in Great Britain, the European Continent, and the United States in the middle decades of the nineteenth century. Among the most popular series in their day were Bohn's Standard Library in England, Tauchnitz's Collection of British and American Authors in Germany, and the Harper's Family Library in the United States. This new movement toward publication of scale was made possible not only by the increased capitalization of publishing houses but also by their ability to employ the new technology of printing from stereotype plates, which allowed them to keep works in print cheaply and flexibly.

In 1845 Wiley and Putnam entered into this mode of publication by launching its Library of Choice Reading, followed almost immediately afterward by the Library of American Books. Though neither of these series, nor the ones that followed in the next decade, ever approached best-selling status at the level of either individual titles or the entire series, they helped to establish its position as a leading literary publisher and to solidify its reputation with the author and readers of serious literature.

Wiley and Putnam's Library of Choice Reading

Wiley and Putnam's Library of Choice Reading was planned in winter 1845 and launched in March by John Wiley and Evert Duyckinck, whom Wiley hired as its editor. The original idea was to produce a series of selected literary works—"the best books of Travels, Biographies, works of Classic Fiction"—well manufactured but inexpensive enough to allow for relatively wide distribution. The two men initially intended to include in the series both old works from Europe as well as new works from Europe and the United States but had barely sent the first work to press when they decided to launch a separate series for American books.

Duyckinck, who was one of the strongest advocates of an international copyright system, was eager not only to publish high-quality works but also to protect the interests of their European authors and publishers. He had a strong ideological and practical ally in this regard in Putnam, still the main American agent overseas in the international book trade, who scoured the London newspapers and bookstores and used his extensive network of relations with British authors and publishers to purchase American rights for a variety of attractive works. Despite the complicated logistics required to handle this transatlantic operation, the three men managed to channel works by leading authors of the 1840s smoothly into the Wiley and Putnam office on Broadway and rapidly from there to the print shop. They largely had their pick of works, and their library quickly gained the reputation as one of the finest series of belletristic works published to date in the United States.

The first work in the Library of Choice Reading, William Alexander Kinglake's Eothen (London, 1844), was published in March 1845. During the two years of the existence of the series, Wiley and Putnam brought out works new and old by leading contemporary writers such as Charles Dickens, William Makepeace Thackeray, Charles Lamb, Thomas Carlyle, William Hazlitt, Thomas Hook, Martin Farquhar Tupper, Anna Jameson, and Leigh Hunt. Despite the reputation of its authors and the generally impressive quality of their works, the series was not a major profit maker for the house. The experience of Carlyle—several of whose works in the Library of Choice Reading were brought out in unauthorized, cheaper editions by rival publishers—demonstrated that unusually attractive titles could not be protected in an era lacking effective international copyright laws.

* * *

This announcement of the Wiley and Putnam Library of Choice Reading states a common complaint about the low standards of American bookmaking in recent years and relief that the new series will help to reverse the decline. It appeared in the "New Publications" column of the New York Evening Post, the most literary daily newspaper in the city, a frequent supporter of Wiley and Putnam and G. P. Putnam publications.

Wiley & Putnam, of this city, have begun, under this name [Library of Choice Reading], a series of tasteful and entertaining books, which we hope is destined to supersede many of the "cheap publications," as badly printed pamphlets are falsely called. It will embrace works of sterling merit only, which will be uniformly printed in good large type, on fine paper, in a convenient form, and at as low a price as the actual cost of production will permit.

—New York Evening Post, 22 March 1845

* * *

WILEY AND PUTNAM'S

LIBRARY

OF

CHOICE READING.

{ 161 *Broadway, New York,*
{ March 1, 1845.

THE popular demand for works of a different class for general reading, than those which have latterly been exclusively furnished to the public, has been the inducement to the publishers to undertake a new series of publications which, it is believed, at this time, will be received with avidity and delight. While systematic provision has been made for books in the various departments of professional and business life—while the best treatises on Theology and Science abound, and the merchant has his useful dictionaries and encyclopædias, another and still most important field of literature has been comparatively neglected. The reading that especially cherishes a refined and cultivated taste—that instructs the head and the heart together—has been omitted, and its place frequently supplied by long drawn, vapid novels of an unprofitable, if not an injurious character. Between these two points of useful scientific knowledge, and the mass of the works of fiction of the day, there lies a middle ground to be cultivated, and one that will afford a rich harvest to all lovers of good literature. There is in fact a class of the most valuable books, which it has always been found expedient to collect together in a series for publication. The reader who owns but a shelf full of books, likes some unity and harmony among them in subject and appearance. Libraries or collections of books devoted to the preservation of what may be called the MINOR CLASSICS have been uniformly successful, as in the case of "Constable's Miscellany," "Dove's Classics," "The Library of Entertaining Knowledge," "Murray's Family Library," "Knight's Shilling Volume," &c.

Books, such as have formed the best portions of these series, are at present wanted in the American market. The so-called "Cheap Literature," while it has failed to supply good and sound reading, and has been attended with many publishing defects, has in some degree prepared the way for the new demand. It has shown the extent of the reading public in the country, and the policy of supplying that public with books at low prices proportioned to the extent. *Books in the United States must hereafter be cheap.* To reconcile the utmost possible cheapness with a proper attention to the literary and mechanical execution of the books published, will be the aim of the publishers in the present series. The book form, a legible

First page of a circular in which Wiley and Putnam describes its new series as seeking to "reconcile the utmost possible cheapness with a proper attention to the literary and mechanical execution of the books published" (Duyckinck Family Papers, Manuscripts and Archives Division, The New York Public Library, Astor, Lenox and Tilden Foundations)

This Broadway Journal *review was written by either Edgar Allan Poe or Charles Frederick Briggs and timed to the publication of* Eothen. *The reviewer's praise of the series as uniting good books and good, yet inexpensive, bookmaking was in keeping with the intent of the publishers, who launched their series under the phrase then current, "books which are books," as a means of distinguishing between their books and the cheap "extras" that had dominated American publishing during the previous half dozen years.*

If the days of "cheap and nasty" literature are not ended, we have proof before us that the day of cheap and elegant literature has at least dawned. Eöthen is the first of a series of reprints and original works, commenced by Wiley & Putnam, which is recommended by a novel elegance of form, and a tempting lowness of price. It argues little for the intelligence of our cheap publishers, that they should have allowed so attractive a work as Eöthen to escape their hands so long. Some of them have deluged the market with two shilling novels of every variety, Swedish, French, and English, since it appeared in England, but they have not thought it worth their while to offer it to the reading public; it shows very plainly their own want of intelligence or their want of faith in the intelligence of the people, the Native Americans, for whose benefit they publish their Countess Faustinas and Wandering Jews. The greater part of our publishers appear to have a singular taste in books: Scotch philosophy and French romance, watered with a pretty constant stream from Mr. James's pump, form the grand staple of their trade. Good English works, excepting in the shape of historical novels or novel-like histories, they carefully eschew, and were it not for the enterprise, or liberal daring of some of our publishers in Broadway, we should know nothing of many of the best books which are issued from the British press.

A gentleman asked one of the great publishers a few months since why they did not publish Dr. Arnold's life and correspondence? "Would you ruin us?" replied the sagacious book-dealer with a stare. But the Appletons have since done the public the service to publish this excellent work, and have risked the chance of ruin. Legally speaking, book-publishers have an unquestionable right to put forth only such books as they like, as a baker has an unquestionable right to sell nothing but sour bread, and we have no doubt that there are people all ready to snub us up, for pretending to insinuate that anybody, but especially publishers of books, should be called to account for doing what the law allows. We submit to the snub, begging the privilege of hinting that there are two kinds of law, the law of God, and the law of man, and that it is possible to break one while you observe the other.

Eöthen is a reprint of the most brilliant book of travels that has appeared in England since the time of Childe Harold. Teeming, as the English press does, with works on the East, the superior brilliancy of Eöthen has eclipsed them all. The author's name is not given, but he is known, as a matter of course, at home. The great marvel of his book is that it should have remained so long unpublished, and that the master of so fine a style and so lively an imagination should have kept his peace until now. It was nine years after his return from the East before his book was published; our travellers begin to publish the day after they leave home, and give us their sketches as they proceed. . . .

—Broadway Journal, 1 (22 March 1845): 177

* * *

This excerpt from an early notice of Eothen *was published in the* Democratic Review, *a periodical to which Duyckinck had close connections and which frequently gave the series favorable publicity as it evolved.*

It is a very elegant volume, of unexceptionable type and paper, and a very cheap one. It is published as the first of a series of books which it is promised shall equally delight the true scholar and the general reader—a high standard—but one warranted to be taken with such a book as Eöthen. The series, moreover, "Wiley & Putnam's Library of Choice Reading," is to contain new American Copyright Works, where there will be found greater difficulty in the selection, of course, than among the old Classic English treasures and the vast field of foreign contemporary literature. That we have as true and genuine men to write books here as anywhere is part of our belief, and it will be from lack of faithfulness rather than of opportunity if Messrs. Wiley and Putnam do not exhibit this in their "Library." Nothing is wanted for American Literature but good faith and due encouragement to ripen it to an early maturity.

—Democratic Review, 16 (April 1845): 375

* * *

In this letter to Evert Duyckinck, Putnam reacts enthusiastically to the news that his old friend is supervising his firm's Library of Choice Reading. Many of the volumes contracted for the series, including some mentioned here, came through Putnam's agency in London.

London May 19, 1845

My dear Duyckinck,

I am much obliged for your letter of 16th April.

I am right glad to find that we are enjoying the advantage of your valuable judgement in the new "library." It was quite evident from the first that some one of taste & common sense had had a hand [in] it, but in my very meagre advices respecting home operations, no particulars had been given of the origin, progress or direction of the enterprise. It was certainly a palpable hit–The form is just the thing–& the whole style is just what I would have wished as connected with our names. The selection of books so far is capital. There could scarcely have been a better pioneer than Eothen–It is a clever book written by a young man by the name of Kinglake–& not by Milnes, as some N. York paper rather blindly guessed. There are some flippancies in it–especially that note about Mr. Everett. Everett is evidently a good deal annoyed by it. He saw that we had re-pubd. the book & took some pains to explain to me (what I well knew before) that it was not true that he had sought for the degree,–He even tried to convince me that the book was a worthless one–that the supposed conversation with the Pasha of Semlin was quite absurd &c. You will say like many, probably that this is only a squib & can do no harm–but I think such flippant impertinencies ought to be castigated.

I shall be "wide awake" for new books, for as you suppose I like to have a finger in so good a pie– and those you suggest shall be secured. Thackeray's Tallyrand is not forthcoming as yet–but C[hapman]&

Hall promise his "Journey from Cowhill to Grand Cairo" by M. A. Titmarsh, which will probably be amusing & would do, if you don't provide enough Orientalism before. I send by this steamer the 2nd edn. of Warburton's "Crescent & the Cross"–which was proposed, probably for the library–It is a good book doubtless–if not too heavy for the purpose. I send also

> Tales from Tieck
> Fouque's Thiadoff the Icelander
> Tales from Eastern Land
> See "Spectator"

I hope the American series will succeed as well as the re-prints–I shall do my best to put it before the "candid British Public." I hope by the way it will include a volume of your own. If you light up so many tapers you should not leave your own candle under the bushels. Mary Clavers [pseudonym of Caroline Kirkland, whose Western Clearings was to appear that year in the library] will be good–& probably the others. I would trust your doctorship at any rate . . .

–*Duyckinck Family Papers, Manuscripts and Archives Division,*
The New York Public Library, Astor, Lenox and
Tilden Foundations

* * *

Putnam's handwritten offer of discounted wholesale orders in sheets of Library of Choice Reading titles. Putnam served as Duyckinck's man in the field in Europe lining up new works for the Wiley and Putnam libraries and attempting to market them there in various ways. Hector Bossange was his Paris agent (Duyckinck Family Papers, Manuscripts and Archives Division, The New York Public Library, Astor, Lenox and Tilden Foundations).

A Democratic Review critic praises Wiley and Putnam's Library of Choice Reading, then nearing its conclusion, as redeeming American book publishing from the low literary and manufacturing standards of the previous years. He finds the firm's Library of American Books wanting, however, when compared with the Library of Choice Reading.

The series of books placed at the head of this paper, has now reached its 91st number. Its success with the public may be inferred from the rapidity with which the publishers are still adding to a list already so extended. Almost every week puts us in possession of a new volume, similar in character to the works which have preceded it—the last of which we were about to say, always seems to us the best. The enterprising house to which we are indebted for them, certainly deserves the thanks as well as the more substantial rewards of the public, for the energy and taste with which they have prosecuted the undertaking. For, apart from the merits of the books themselves, which we shall speak of in the sequel—their influence upon the book trade has been of the most salutary kind.

At the time this series was begun, the business of book printing in this country was in an inexpressibly wretched condition. It was the day of what were termed cheap publications—Heaven save the mark! Generally, publications are very dear at any price, whether we consider their merits or their make. Printing could then scarcely be called an art; it was a manufacture, and that, too, of the rudest sort. A ream or two of dingy, unpressed paper, blackened by microscopic figures, said to resemble the letters of the alphabet, and folded into various heterogeneous shapes, with a stitch of pack-thread here and there—was all that then went to the making of that sacred and noble thing—a book. The consequence was, that respectable publishing was driven from the markets, and the whole subject was committed to the tender mercies of newspaper publishers and the agents of patent medicines. Even the regular trade were compelled to engage in the wholesale desecration of their art, in order to turn a penny where they could. Literature was overwhelmed with a deluge of pamphlets; choked to death by a surfeit of serials; or rather expired of a fit of apoplexy, brought on by a bad diet.

In this state of things Messrs. Wiley & Putnam determined to do something for the rescue of their trade and the public. At the suggestion of a literary gentleman of this city, who deserves well for his innumerable attempts to serve the cause of letters, they commenced the issue of the Library of Choice Reading. Their plan was to select the best foreign and domestic works, of a graceful and readable character, and publish them in a style which should be elegant as well as cheap. Their efforts were successful in every respect, so that the result has been, that other publishers have been induced to follow their example, and readers once more enjoy the luxury of "Books which are Books."

And now that we have so many numbers of this series before us, we can safely say that it is equal in merit, if not superior, to any other series that was ever presented. Now and then it is true, the editor's partialities, or the persuasions of injudicious friends, have led him to incorporate an inferior work into the collection; but as a whole, his labors have been not only unexceptionable, but highly praiseworthy. The volumes are generally of more than average excellence, while some may be regarded as among the finest specimens of modern book-writing. We confess, that we do not find any qualities in the works of the Headlong Hall set, or in Lady Duff Gordon's French in Algiers, or in the endless platitudes of one Martin Farquhar Tupper, who was silly enough once to attempt a sequel to Coleridge's Christabel, to entitle them to a place in such respectable company. But these are the exceptions to a general rule. Indeed, it is the unquestionable excellence of the rest of the series which brings out the comparative worthlessness of such as we have named, in a stronger relief. When publishers furnish us with "Eothen," and the "Crescent and the Cross," &c., among books of travels, we can afford to put up with the "French in Algiers;" and with Hazlitt's and Leigh Hunt's inestimable essays, and the tales of Zschokke, we will not make wry faces, even if compelled to swallow "Headlong Hall" and the "Crock of Gold," &c. One must not, we know, even in respect to books, be too fastidious; yet if we are so, Messrs. Wiley & Putnam must take part of the blame in having provided us with such elevated standards of judgment.

This series is now a library in itself, and contains several years of good reading in it—to say nothing of what is announced as yet to come. It is reading, too, adapted to all seasons, and to a great variety of cultivated tastes. The form of the numbers is such that they may be conveniently carried in the pocket, to annihilate time when one is also annihilating space in a rail car or steamboat, to add to the felicity of a summer sojourn in the country, or to enliven the comfort of the winter fireside. There are travels and essays, and sketches and biographies, and poems, embraced in the collection, with now and then a volume that aspires to all these titles. If you need something brilliant and racy, there is Eothen; something hearty and genial, there is Hunt; something suggestive though perverse, there is Hazlitt; something grand and striking, there is Beckford; something frolic and gentle, there is Lamb; something pretentious, there is the aforesaid Tupper; something wild, yet classic, there is Fouqué; something humorous or touching, there is Zschokke; or finally, something indescribable, there is Carlyle. And twinkling amid these larger lights, you will find the elegant Mrs. Jamieson, the pleasant Mrs. Southey, and the good Mary Howitt.

It is an unfortunate thing, we think, that Messrs. Wiley & Putnam took it into their heads to issue an American rival alongside of their foreign series. Not that it was not desirable to have an issue of well-printed American books, or that they may not have made money out of their project;

but because it has provoked comparisons rather unpleasant to our pride as Americans. The editor has not succeeded, it must be confessed, in procuring works fit to rank with the English selections, or that ought to be regarded as representative of American literature or genius. It must have been out of his power to get better, as such are to be had unquestionably, and he possesses taste enough to know them when he should see them. But it would have been a wiser policy, so far as the interests of our literature are concerned, to have published none at all, rather than put forth such imperfect efforts as those of Simms, Poe, Matthews, Headley, and last and worst, Cheever. Mr. Simm's magazine habits, or some other causes, have led him into an almost intolerable diffuseness, so that his naturally vigorous thought is overlaid by an endless drawl of words. Matthews possesses considerable talent, but it stands greatly in need of discipline and taste; Headley writes neither grammatically nor elegantly, but there is a certain intensity and fire about his manner which renders him popular, and which, if it were joined with scholarship and grace, would make him an effective writer. Of Mr. Poe we are not allowed to speak at present, and of Cheever's wretched sectarian sermonizings in the awful presence of the Jungfrau, we have no desire to speak. But there is not one of these writers whose books really do honor to our letters. Had they been retained in the posses-

sion of their authors, for ten years say, and submitted in the mean time to the severe castigations of some friendly but rigid critic, they might have had material and vitality enough in them to entitle them to an honorable midwifery. And we say this, not to injure the feelings of these gentlemen, for some of whom we have a high professional and personal respect, but to do our duty towards the public as critics. We are of opinion that the cause of our literature is greatly depreciated and damaged by the issues of injudicious books. It creates a wrong standard of judgment in the public mind, and retards the sale of more deserving attempts. Nor must it be supposed from these remarks, that the whole of this American series is of the same inadequate character. In the exquisite "Mosses" of Hawthorne, in the admirable tales of Mrs. Kirkland, in Calvert's "Scenes and Thoughts"—a book by no means sufficiently prized, in Melville's lively and picturesque "Typee," and Margaret Fuller's vigorous "Papers"—though these last require prunings and corrections, we find works which we should not only not scruple to send forth in the same coach with their foreign companions, but which we would send forth with some feeling of exultation . . .

—Democratic Review, 20 (March 1847): 238–239

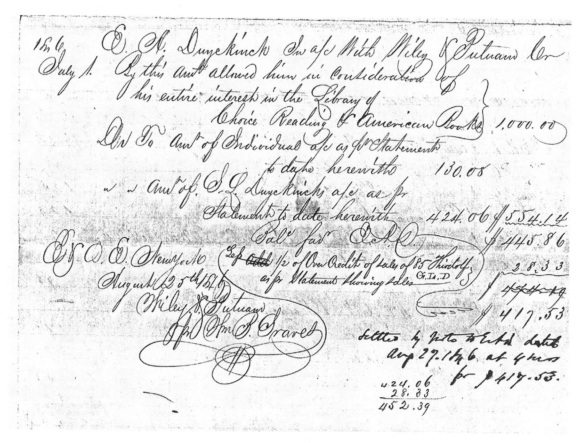

Statement of payment, dated 27 August 1846, for Evert Duyckinck's editorial work on Wiley and Putnam's Library of Choice Reading (Duyckinck Family Papers, Manuscripts and Archives Division, The New York Public Library, Astor, Lenox and Tilden Foundations)

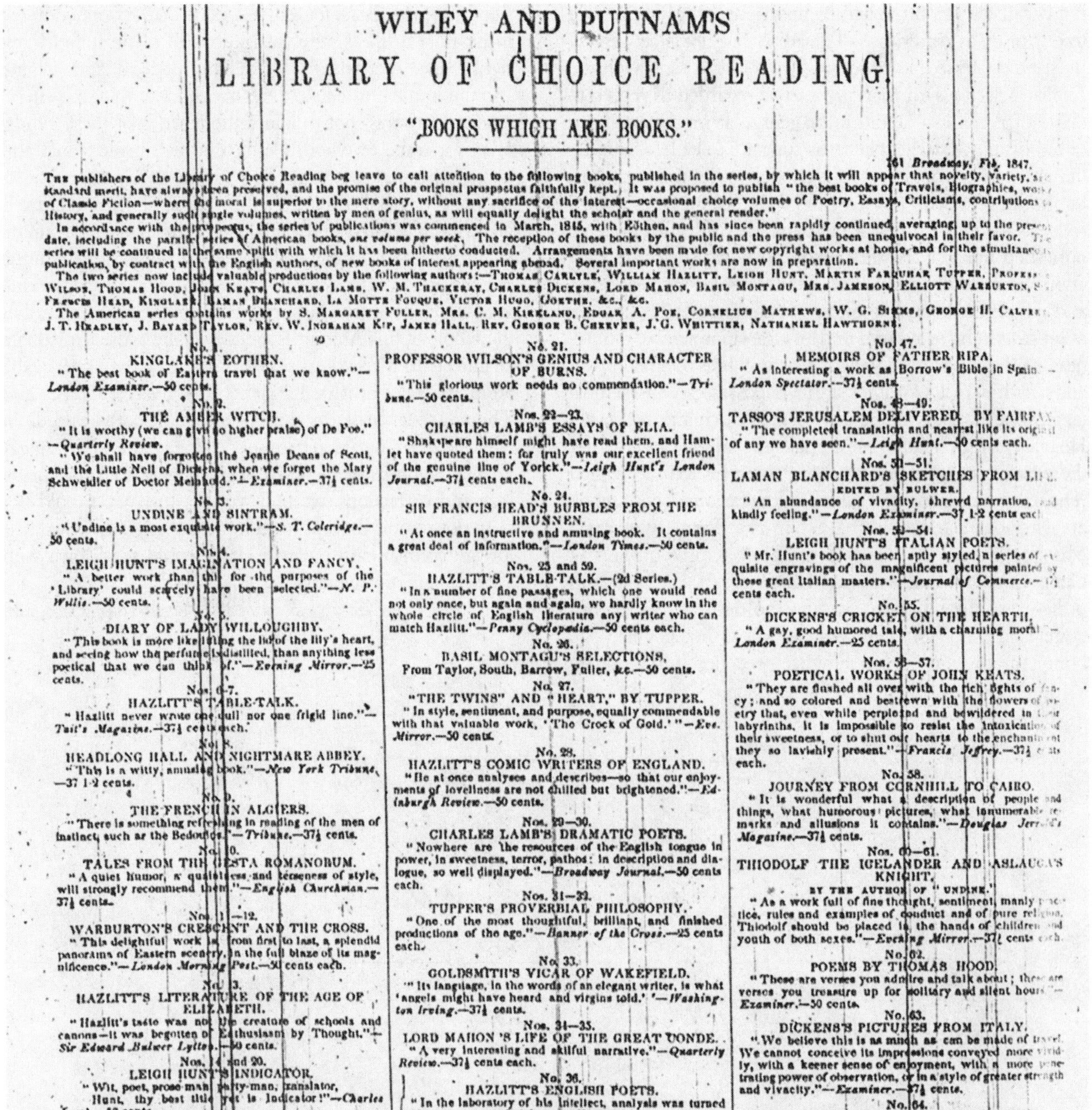

WILEY AND PUTNAM'S
LIBRARY OF CHOICE READING.

"BOOKS WHICH ARE BOOKS."

161 Broadway, Feb. 1847.

The publishers of the Library of Choice Reading beg leave to call attention to the following books, published in the series, by which it will appear that novelty, variety, standard merit, have always been preserved, and the promise of the original prospectus faithfully kept. It was proposed to publish "the best books of Travels, Biographies, works of Classic Fiction—where the moral is superior to the mere story, without any sacrifice of the interest—occasional choice volumes of Poetry, Essays, Criticism, contributions to History, and generally such single volumes, written by men of genius, as will equally delight the scholar and the general reader."

In accordance with their prospectus, the series of publications was commenced in March, 1845, with Eöthen, and has since been rapidly continued, averaging up to the present date, including the parallel series of American books, *one volume per week.* The reception of these books by the public and the press has been unequivocal in their favor. The series will be continued in the same spirit with which it has been hitherto conducted. Arrangements have been made for new copyright works at home, and for the simultaneous publication, by contract with the English authors, of new books of interest appearing abroad. Several important works are now in preparation.

The two series now include valuable productions by the following authors:—Thomas Carlyle, William Hazlitt, Leigh Hunt, Martin Farquhar Tupper, Professor Wilson, Thomas Hood, John Keats, Charles Lamb, W. M. Thackeray, Charles Dickens, Lord Mahon, Basil Montagu, Mrs. Jameson, Elliott Warburton, Sir Francis Head, Kinglake, Laman Blanchard, La Motte Fouqué, Victor Hugo, Goethe, &c., &c.

The American series contains works by S. Margaret Fuller, Mrs. C. M. Kirkland, Edgar A. Poe, Cornelius Mathews, W. G. Simms, George H. Calvert, J. T. Headley, J. Bayard Taylor, Rev. W. Ingraham Kip, James Hall, Rev. George B. Cheever, J. G. Whittier, Nathaniel Hawthorne.

No. 1.
KINGLAKE'S EOTHEN.
"The best book of Eastern travel that we know."—
London Examiner.—50 cents.

No. 2.
THE AMBER WITCH.
"It is worthy (we can give no higher praise) of De Foe."
—*Quarterly Review.*
"We shall have forgotten the Jeanie Deans of Scott, and the Little Nell of Dickens, when we forget the Mary Schweidler of Doctor Meinhold."—*Examiner.*—37½ cents.

No. 3.
UNDINE AND SINTRAM.
"Undine is a most exquisite work."—*S. T. Coleridge.*—50 cents.

No. 4.
LEIGH HUNT'S IMAGINATION AND FANCY.
"A better work than this for the purposes of the 'Library' could scarcely have been selected."—*N. P. Willis.*—50 cents.

No. 5.
DIARY OF LADY WILLOUGHBY.
"This book is more like reading the life of the lily's heart, and seeing how the perfume is distilled, than anything less poetical that we can think of."—*Evening Mirror.*—25 cents.

Nos. 6-7.
HAZLITT'S TABLE-TALK.
"Hazlitt never wrote one dull nor one frigid line."—*Tait's Magazine.*—37½ cents each.

No. 8.
HEADLONG HALL AND NIGHTMARE ABBEY.
"This is a witty, amusing book."—*New York Tribune.*—37 1-2 cents.

No. 9.
THE FRENCH IN ALGIERS.
"There is something refreshing in reading of the men of instinct, such as the Bedouins."—*Tribune.*—37½ cents.

No. 10.
TALES FROM THE GESTA ROMANORUM.
"A quiet humor, a quaintness and terseness of style, will strongly recommend them."—*English Churchman.*—37½ cents.

Nos. 11-12.
WARBURTON'S CRESCENT AND THE CROSS.
"This delightful work is from first to last, a splendid panorama of Eastern scenery, in the full blaze of its magnificence."—*London Morning Post.*—50 cents each.

No. 13.
HAZLITT'S LITERATURE OF THE AGE OF ELIZABETH.
"Hazlitt's taste was not the creature of schools and canons—it was begotten of Enthusiasm by Thought."—*Sir Edward Bulwer Lytton.*—50 cents.

Nos. 14 and 20.
LEIGH HUNT'S INDICATOR.
"Wit, poet, prose-man, party-man, translator, Hunt, thy best title yet is Indicator!"—*Charles Lamb.*—50 cents.

Nos. 15 and 37.
HEINRICH ZSCHOKKE'S TALES.
"Zschokke's Tales exhibit talent, grace and facility of style, and are particularly distinguished for their good moral tendency."—*Essy. Britannica.*—50 cents each.

Nos. 16 and 19.
HOOD'S PROSE AND VERSE.
"A very judicious selection, designed to embrace Hood's more earnest writings, those which were written most directly from the heart, which reflect most faithfully his life and opinions."—*Broadway Journal.*—37½ cents each.

No. 17.
HAZLITT'S CHARACTERS IN SHAKSPEARE'S PLAYS.
"An admirable book, full of simple, earnest, profound criticism, with an excellent tone of feeling."—*New York Evangelist.*—50 cents.

No. 18.
THE CROCK OF GOLD.
"A powerful tale by Martin Farquhar Tupper, author of 'Proverbial Philosophy.'"—*New York Observer.*—37 1-2 cents.

No. 21.
PROFESSOR WILSON'S GENIUS AND CHARACTER OF BURNS.
"This glorious work needs no commendation."—*Tribune.*—50 cents.

Nos. 22-23.
CHARLES LAMB'S ESSAYS OF ELIA.
"Shakspeare himself might have read them, and Hamlet have quoted them: for truly was our excellent friend of the genuine line of Yorick."—*Leigh Hunt's London Journal.*—37½ cents each.

No. 24.
SIR FRANCIS HEAD'S BUBBLES FROM THE BRUNNEN.
"At once an instructive and amusing book. It contains a great deal of information."—*London Times.*—50 cents.

Nos. 25 and 59.
HAZLITT'S TABLE-TALK.—(2d Series.)
"In a number of fine passages, which one would read not only once, but again and again, we hardly know in the whole circle of English literature any writer who can match Hazlitt."—*Penny Cyclopedia.*—50 cents each.

No. 26.
BASIL MONTAGU'S SELECTIONS,
From Taylor, South, Barrow, Fuller, &c.—50 cents.

No. 27.
"THE TWINS" AND "HEART," BY TUPPER.
"In style, sentiment, and purpose, equally commendable with that valuable work, 'The Crock of Gold.'"—*Eve. Mirror.*—50 cents.

No. 28.
HAZLITT'S COMIC WRITERS OF ENGLAND.
"He at once analyses and describes—so that our enjoyments of loveliness are not chilled but brightened."—*Edinburgh Review.*—50 cents.

Nos. 29-30.
CHARLES LAMB'S DRAMATIC POETS.
"Nowhere are the resources of the English tongue in power, in sweetness, terror, pathos: in description and dialogue, so well displayed."—*Broadway Journal.*—50 cents each.

Nos. 31-32.
TUPPER'S PROVERBIAL PHILOSOPHY.
"One of the most thoughtful, brilliant, and finished productions of the age."—*Banner of the Cross.*—25 cents each.

No. 33.
GOLDSMITH'S VICAR OF WAKEFIELD.
"Its language, in the words of an elegant writer, is what 'angels might have heard and virgins told.'"—*Washington Irving.*—37½ cents.

Nos. 34-35.
LORD MAHON'S LIFE OF THE GREAT CONDE.
"A very interesting and skilful narrative."—*Quarterly Review.*—37½ cents each.

No. 36.
HAZLITT'S ENGLISH POETS.
"In the laboratory of his intellect, analysis was turned to the sweet uses of alchemy.—He is seldom merely critical."—*Serjeant Talfourd.*—50 cents.

No. 38.
HERVEY'S BOOK OF CHRISTMAS.
"Every leaf of this book affords a feast worthy of the season."—*Dr. Hawk's Church Record.*—50 cents.

Nos. 39-42.
CROMWELL'S LETTERS AND SPEECHES BY CARLYLE.
"We believe it to be without precedent or example as a book of patient, honest, dignified research ; as a book of unwearied diligence and labor; and as a manly and high voiced appeal from the shows and shadows of ignorance and imposing judgment, to the eternal substance of Truth and History."—*London Examiner.*—50 cents each.

Nos. 43-44.
AUTOBIOGRAPHY OF BENVENUTO CELLINI.
"More amusing than any work I know!"—*Horace Walpole.*—50 cents each.

Nos. 45-46.
THE RHINE. BY VICTOR HUGO.
"His descriptions are wonderfully spirited."—*Quarterly Review.*—37½ cents each.

No. 47.
MEMOIRS OF FATHER RIPA.
"As interesting a work as Borrow's Bible in Spain."—*London Spectator.*—37½ cents.

Nos. 48-49.
TASSO'S JERUSALEM DELIVERED. BY FAIRFAX.
"The completest translation and nearest like its original of any we have seen."—*Leigh Hunt.*—50 cents each.

Nos. 50-51.
LAMAN BLANCHARD'S SKETCHES FROM LIFE.
EDITED BY BULWER.
"An abundance of vivacity, shrewd narration, and kindly feeling."—*London Examiner.*—37 1-2 cents each.

Nos. 52-54.
LEIGH HUNT'S ITALIAN POETS.
"Mr. Hunt's book has been aptly styled, a series of exquisite engravings of the magnificent pictures painted by these great Italian masters."—*Journal of Commerce.*—50 cents each.

No. 55.
DICKENS'S CRICKET ON THE HEARTH.
"A gay, good humored tale, with a charming moral."—*London Examiner.*—25 cents.

Nos. 56-57.
POETICAL WORKS OF JOHN KEATS.
"They are flushed all over with the rich lights of fancy; and so colored and besteewn with the flowers of poetry that, even while perplexed and bewildered in their labyrinths, it is impossible to resist the intoxication of their sweetness, or to shut our hearts to the enchantment they so lavishly present."—*Francis Jeffrey.*—37½ cents each.

No. 58.
JOURNEY FROM CORNHILL TO CAIRO.
"It is wonderful what a description of people and things, what humorous pictures, what innumerable remarks and allusions it contains."—*Douglas Jerrold's Magazine.*—37½ cents.

Nos. 60-61.
THIODOLF THE ICELANDER AND ASLAUGA'S KNIGHT.
BY THE AUTHOR OF "UNDINE."
"As a work full of fine thought, sentiment, manly practice, rules and examples of conduct and of pure religion, Thiodolf should be placed in the hands of children and youth of both sexes."—*Evening Mirror.*—37½ cents each.

No. 62.
POEMS BY THOMAS HOOD.
"These are verses you admire and talk about ; these are verses you treasure up for solitary and silent hours."—*Examiner.*—50 cents.

No. 63.
DICKENS'S PICTURES FROM ITALY.
"We believe this is as much as can be made of travel. We cannot conceive its impressions conveyed more vividly, with a keener sense of enjoyment, with a more penetrating power of observation, or in a style of greater strength and vivacity."—*Examiner.*—37½ cents.

No. 64.
MRS. JAMESON'S MEMOIRS AND ESSAYS
ILLUSTRATIVE OF ART, LITERATURE AND SOCIAL MORALS.
"We have here papers on Washington Allston and the Xanthian Marbles; an admirable essay on Woman's Mission and Woman's Position; another on Mothers and Governesses; and an enthusiastic diorama of Adelaide Kemble. But the paper which should be most popular is the House of Titian. Nothing can be more true in tone than this."—*London Athenæum.*—37½ cents.

Nos. 65-66.
BECKFORD'S ITALY, SPAIN, AND PORTUGAL.
"Glowing with genius."—*Gentleman's Magazine.*—50 cents each.

Nos. 67-68.
HOCHELAGA ; OR, ENGLAND IN THE NEW WORLD.
Edited by Warburton.
"A piece of fresh, lively, and instructive midsummer reading."—*London Athenæum.*—37½ cents each.

No. 69.
CARLYLE'S HEROES AND HERO WORSHIP.
"A book full of original, fiery thought, to stir the minds of men."—*Journal of Commerce.*—50 cents.

Advertisement in the 20 March 1847 issue of The Literary World. *The Library of Choice Reading grew quickly, reaching more than seventy volumes within two years of its inception.*

Wiley and Putnam Library of American Books

The Library of American Books was initiated in spring 1845 as the American twin of the European-based Library of Choice Reading. The impetus came from Duyckinck, who was eager to put the work of such talented American writers as Nathaniel Hawthorne, Ralph Waldo Emerson, Edgar Allan Poe, Margaret Fuller, James Russell Lowell, Henry Wadsworth Longfellow, John Greenleaf Whittier, and William Gilmore Simms—indeed, of American literature in general—into a wider circulation. With Wiley's backing, he went to work that spring writing letters of invitation to these and other writers to publish original works of fiction, nonfiction, and poetry in the series, offering in return to provide a national forum for their works and in most cases to pay 10–12 percent royalties after expenses. In addition, the firm planned to publish many of the books in the series in Great Britain, with Putnam importing them in sheets and retailing and wholesaling them from his London office.

Although Duyckinck failed to attract contributions from Emerson, Lowell, and Longfellow, he was nevertheless remarkably successful. With the appearance in June of Horatio Bridge's Journal of an African Cruiser, *edited by Hawthorne, which was soon followed by Poe's* Tales *and the immensely popular travel writer Joel Headley's* Letters from Italy, *it became clear that Duyckinck was attracting the leading writers in the country. During the series's two-year existence, he managed to bring into the Library of American Books Hawthorne's* Mosses from an Old Manse *(1846), Poe's* Tales *(1845) and* The Raven and Other Poems *(1845), Whittier's* Supernaturalism of New England *(1847), Simms's* The Wigwam and the Cabin *(1845–1846) and* Views and Reviews in American Literature, History and Fiction *(1846–1847), Melville's* Typee *(1846), Fuller's* Papers on Literature and Art *(1846), Caroline Kirkland's* Western Clearings, *and Bayard Taylor's* Views A-foot *(1846). Henry David Thoreau would have published his first work,* A Week on the Concord and Merrimack Rivers, *in the series had he not rejected Wiley's condition that it be published at the author's expense—an unusual condition for the series.*

The Library of American Books was the outstanding series of American letters of its time, but it was no more successful financially than was the Library of Choice Reading. Individual titles such as Typee *and* Views A-foot *sold well, but most of the books in the series apparently brought only marginal profits to publisher and author. Relatively few of the books remained long in print after the series was discontinued in mid 1847.*

* * *

This positive review of Journal of an African Cruiser, *the first book published in the Wiley and Putnam Library of American Books, and of the series itself appeared in the "Notices of Books" in the* New York Morning News, *a newspaper to which Duyckinck had close ties.*

This is published as the first number of a new copyright series of "American Books," uniform with the popular library of "Choice Reading," and destined, we trust, to attain an equal, if not greater degree of favor with the public. We hail the undertaking as the opening of a new channel by which our authors, particularly those of the refined class, may approach the public, guarded and protected by the vigilance and zeal of publishers pledged to their support. A want of faith in publishers, has, we honestly believe, done not a little to check the productiveness of American authors. There are inseparable difficulties between authors and publishers under any system, but in this country they have been aggravated a hundred fold by the false relations in which the writer has been placed by the injurious fact that the publisher has at his command, unpaid for, with a reputation ready made, all the wealth of the European book-trade. If he has a doubt of the value of an English book it is solved by an article in the Quarterly or a notice in the Examiner—while the home manuscript is misunderstood and rejected. Hence many of our best men are driven from the field of literature, and the exertions of those who remain discouraged and paralyzed. Hence, undoubtedly in a great measure, the absence of fresh original works and the prevalence of mediocrity.

Messrs. WILEY & PUTNAM have given a pledge in undertaking this American series, that they will assert and maintain the claims of the American author. If their series of American Books should become as voluminous as the parallel English one, and be sustained with care and discretion (and we see not why it should not be) their annual shelf full of books, written at home, informed with a genuine American spirit, fresh, original, characteristic of the authors, will redeem the pledge nobly. On the contrary, if there is any want of faith and courage in the measure, if the most devoted publishing diligence is not given to the work, and the wisest discrimination be not practised in the selection of the books, the undertaking will assuredly fail. The Press has given the publishers every facility in the establishment of their welcome library of English authors; it will not fail in making known the merits of the American volumes. Give us a score or two of American books worth praising, and they shall not want encouragement, Messrs. Publishers.

—New York Morning News, 21 June 1845

* * *

Duyckinck solicits a contribution from Ralph Waldo Emerson to Wiley and Putnam's Library of Choice Reading, the generic name here encompassing the Library of American Books. Emerson chose to retain his connections to Boston publishers and turned down this publication and all subsequent ones from Duyckinck.

To R W Emerson
Concord Mass.

Aug 13, 1845

Dear Sir,

I am requested by Mr Wiley to address you on the subject of a volume for his Library of Choice Reading. If you think well enough of the mode of publication, with which, I believe you are already acquainted through Mr Hawthorne and Mr Wiley be ready (as I believe he is) to pay liberally for a new work, I would urge the proposition as important to the literature of the country which needs the example of the few original authors. Messrs W & P would be glad to have a volume from you either 1st (which is most desirable) entirely new, written in a popular manner for the best class of readers <u>virginibus puerisque</u> or 2nd a collection from the Reviews with perhaps a lecture or two and 3rd your article in the Dial on Walter Savage Landor prefatory to a selection from his writings to be made by yourself. The latter has been already announced, without any editor's name but it would best proceed from your hands.

Hoping that these propositions may meet with favor at your hands I am

Respectfully
Your obedient Servant,
EAD.

–Duyckinck Family Papers, Manuscripts and Archives Division, The New York Public Library, Astor, Lenox and Tilden Foundations

* * *

In the "Notices of New Books" of the Democratic Review, *a reviewer encourages the publishers of the Library of American Books in terms nearly synonymous with Duyckinck's ambitions for the series.*

In thus recognizing the general claims of the "Library of Choice Literature," we cannot omit to hail with a special greeting the "American Series." It is to us a subject of congratulation that, at length, a highly respectable house, in spite of the non-existence of an international copyright law, with all its train of discouraging consequences, and in the face of the popular theory that the only books that will sell are the very entertaining and the very useful, have commenced the publication of a library neat and tasteful in its mechanical execution, reasonable in its price, claiming support chiefly on the ground of literary merit, and, best of all, composed of the writings of native authors. It is an experiment we shall watch with peculiar interest. We are not a little curious to observe to what efforts this new field of action will incite American writers, and how far such an opportunity of sustaining a home literary market, will excite the lukewarm patriotism and family pride of American readers. Let the publishers be true to their motto, and make the whole library *choice,*—let them have the courage to venture something for *intrinsic* merit, and not knuckle too much to merely popular catch-words or names,—let them be a little bold, a little liberal, a little truthful, and literature, in the true sense of the word, will acquire, under these auspices, fresh vitality, and a native character which will gladden the heart and extend the glory of the republic.

–Democratic Review, 17 (October 1845): 317–318

* * *

Putnam actively promoted the Library of American Books and kept a careful eye on its reception in the London press. Here he uses the house journal to provide a progress report on the first three titles. The literary man whom Putnam persuaded to read Poe's Tales *was Martin Farquhar Tupper, who also reviewed them favorably.*

The *Journal of an African Cruiser* has been largely quoted from in various English journals, with a unanimous verdict that it conveys much novel information in a very agreeable way. The very striking and powerful sketches of Poe have had less justice done them, simply for the reason that because they are *tales* merely, by a writer here but little known, the critics have not taken the trouble to read them. One literary man of high abilities, and as cool as a cucumber in his temperament, was induced, by my special request, to cut all the leaves and begin; next day he said, "a clever book–a very clever book–it made me hold my breath 'till I finished it at a sitting." The *Purloined Letter* was copied some time since by Chambers as a remarkable and original paper. By the way, has this or the *Gold Bug* any other basis than the writer's imagination? There is an air of what one might call *incredible* truth about several of these sketches; and the writer owns a pen of much more than ordinary power. Headley's *Letters from Italy* have received various kinds of treatment here–the Examiner and Atlas abusing the book.

–Wiley and Putnam's Literary News-Letter, 4 (October 1845): 366

* * *

As editor for the Brooklyn Daily Eagle, *Walt Whitman not only positively reviewed many individual titles in the Library of American Books but also endorsed the series itself.*

Wiley & Putnam's series of excellent Reading we have heretofore mentioned with commendation in our columns. Their *American* works we commend to especial notice and patronage. The more they give of them, the better. At their store in Broadway, N.Y. we may likewise mention, can always be found both the oldest and newest foreign works– their facilities enabling them to obtain the latter with unusual promptness.

–Brooklyn Daily Eagle, 21 February 1846

WILEY & PUTNAM'S
LIBRARY OF AMERICAN BOOKS.

No. 1.
JOURNAL OF AN AFRICAN CRUISER.
Edited by Hawthorne.

No. 2.
TALES BY EDGAR A. POE.

No. 3.
HEADLEY'S LETTERS FROM ITALY.

Nos. 4 and 12.
SIMMS'S WIGWAM AND THE CABIN.

No. 5.
MATHEWS'S BIG ABEL AND THE LITTLE MANHATTAN.

Nos. 6 and 11.
CHEEVER'S WANDERINGS OF A PILGRIM.
Under the Shadow of Mont Blanc and the Jungfrau.

No. 7.
MRS. KIRKLAND'S WESTERN CLEARINGS.

No. 8.
POE'S RAVEN, AND OTHER POEMS.

No. 9.
SIMMS'S VIEWS AND REVIEWS.

No. 10.
HEADLEY'S ALPS AND THE RHINE.

Nos. 13—14.
HERMAN MELVILLE'S TYPEE.

No. 15.
HALL'S WILDERNESS AND THE WAR-PATH.

No. 16.
CALVERT'S SCENES AND THOUGHTS IN EUROPE.

Nos. 17—18.
HAWTHORNE'S MOSSES FROM AN OLD MANSE.

Nos. 19—20.
MISS FULLER'S PAPERS ON LITERATURE AND ART.

Nos. 21—22.
KIP'S EARLY JESUIT MISSIONS.

Nos. 23—24.
BAYARD TAYLOR'S VIEWS A-FOOT.
WITH A PREFACE BY WILLIS.

No. 25.
SPENCER AND THE FAERY QUEEN.
By Mrs. C. M. Kirkland.

No. 26.
SELECTIONS FROM CHAUCER.

No. 27.
SUPERNATURALISM OF NEW ENGLAND.
By J. G. Whittier.

LIBRARY OF AMERICAN BOOKS.
IN VOLUMES.

WESTERN CLEARINGS, by Mrs. Kirkland; and Wilderness and War-Path, by Judge Hall. Two parts in 1 vol. ... $1 25

Wiley & Putnam, 161 Broadway.

LAMARTINE'S
HISTORY OF THE GIRONDINS.
Volume I.
THE ENGLISH EDITION.

WILEY & PUTNAM, 161 Broadway.

Advertisement in the 14 August 1847 issue of The Literary World, *near the time of the termination of the Library of American Books. Duyckinck was no longer working for the firm, and Wiley and Putnam was scaling back its publishing enterprises generally.*

161 Broadway, *October*, 1845.

WILEY AND PUTNAM'S

FOREIGN LIBRARY.

—

MESSRS. WILEY AND PUTNAM will publish immediately, uniformly with the "*Library of Choice Reading*," a series of Books of a Permanent Classical Character, with the elements of a wide popular circulation, drawn from the Literature of Foreign Languages. It is their intention to include in this Series, books, both old and new, from the Ancient and Modern Tongues. Translations of Classic Histories, Poems, Memoirs, Works of Fiction, Books of Travels, Criticism, will form part of the undertaking. Many of these will be original, the work of American scholars. In all cases the best accessible translations will be given. An enumeration of some of the early numbers of the FOREIGN LIBRARY, will show the capabilities of the undertaking. They will embrace The Rhine, by VICTOR HUGO; BENVENUTO CELLINI's Memoirs, the full and carefully annotated edition of Roscoe; Autobiographies of ZSCHOKKE, MARMONTEL, GOLDONI, and others; The Historical Works of SCHILLER; AUGUSTUS WILLIAM SCHLEGEL's Lectures on Dramatic Literature; MITCHELL's Translation of the Plays of Aristophanes; GOETHE's Wilhelm-Meister; FENELON's Telemachus; FOUQUE's Thiodolf and Magic Ring, &c.

It is believed that the public are prepared to receive the best works of the foreign authors, to whom, as a class, great injustice has been done by the carelessness of translators, and the selection of the most immoral works for publication. This Series it is hoped, while it will be welcomed by the general reader, will also take its place in the library of the scholar.

Circular describing the third Wiley and Putnam library, which proved to be the firm's shortest-lived and least successful literary series. Its contents more nearly reflected Evert Duyckinck's taste than that of the broader audience he hoped to reach with the other series.

Wiley and Putnam's Foreign Library

A fraction of the size of either the Library of Choice Reading or the Library of American Books, Wiley and Putnam's Foreign Library grew out of a business partnership between John Wiley and Evert and George Duyckinck, with the brothers investing in the project and Evert overseeing its development. Several of the titles, such as Parke Godwin's translation of Goethe's autobiography, came from the Library of Choice Reading. It also included editions of the autobiography of Benvenuto Cellini and Izaak Walton's Compleat Angler. *Such works were inexpensive to procure because they were long out of copyright protection, which might well have been a consideration in the undertaking and planning of the Foreign Library. The Duyckinck brothers were ultimately frustrated with the failure of the series to deliver profits—if there were profits at all—on a level with their expectations.*

* * *

One of the most valued works brought out by Wiley and Putnam was Parke Godwin's The Auto-Biography of Goethe, *the first English translation of the German text. Putnam, who kept the title on his list after separating from Wiley, warned the American trade against the Bohn edition of the autobiography.*

In consequence of portions of this work having been incorporated into the London Edition of *Goethe's Autobiography,* published in Bohn's Standard Library, the sale of that work will therefore be prohibited in this country, it being an infringement of the copyright.

—The Literary World, 6 (1 June 1850): 553

Title pages for the first English translation of Goethe's autobiography and the later Bohn edition that incorporated parts of Parke Godwin's work. Putnam was angered by the appearance of the autobiography in Bohn's Standard Library, a series that imitated the Wiley and Putnam edition model of producing classic works at prices affordable to general readers.

FIRST CLASS PASSENGERS.

Drawing from the 7 December 1844 issue of the Illustrated London News. *Reading on trains became
a common practice during the 1840s and 1850s as travel by rail proliferated.*

PUTNAM'S RAILWAY LIBRARY — In neat
pocket volumes:—

HOME AND SOCIAL PHILOSOPHY, ⎫ From Dickens'
HOME TRAVELS, ⎬ Household Words.
HOME NARRATIVES. ⎭
IDA PFEIFER'S TRAVELS IN ICELAND, SWEDEN AND
    NORWAY.
HOOD'S UP THE RHINE. With comic cuts.
HOOD'S WHIMS AND ODDITIES. With comic cuts.
MISS BREMER'S LETTERS FROM THE UNITED STATES,
    &c., &c. &c.

Advertisement in the 15 November 1851 issue of Norton's Literary Advertiser. *Impressed by what he had seen of George Routledge's railway series
in England, Putnam hoped with his own series to capitalize on rail travel in the United States.*

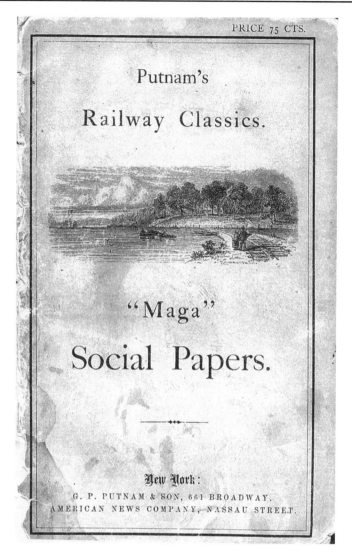

PRICE 75 CTS.

Putnam's

Railway Classics.

"Maga"

Social Papers.

New York:

G. P. PUTNAM & SON, 661 BROADWAY.
AMERICAN NEWS COMPANY, NASSAU STREET.

Title page for a post–Civil War addition to Putnam's railway series consisting of mostly humorous articles selected from Putnam's Monthly,
familiarly known as "Maga" (Library of Congress)

Putnam's Railway Classics

Putnam was well aware of the success being achieved by the inexpensive, small-sized "railway" books brought out by English publisher George Routledge when he elected to undertake his own such series in November 1851. He followed Routledge's lead in marketing belletristic reading matter at train stations, the newest gathering spots for public transportation. Putnam was not far ahead of his American competition; the New York City bookseller and literary agent Charles B. Norton was only a month behind with his own library. Putnam, though, was unusual in keeping his library running for most of the decade and then reconstituting it after he returned to publishing in 1867.

Putnam's Railway Classics opened with works by Thomas Hood and collections drawn from Charles Dickens's House-hold Words, which Putnam was then reprinting for the American market. He soon enlarged the series by printing cheap editions of works drawn from Washington Irving, George William Curtis, Henry Tuckerman, Oliver Goldsmith, William Alexander Kinglake, and other Putnam authors. He eventually added compilations drawn from his own Putnam's Monthly. Titles were brought out in inexpensive fashion in paper or cloth covers, measuring 7″ by 4 1/4″ and priced normally at 37 1/2¢–50¢ before the Civil War and 70¢–75¢ after it.

Putnam generally followed a policy of marketing his series in multiple formats in order to reach different sectors of the book-buying public.

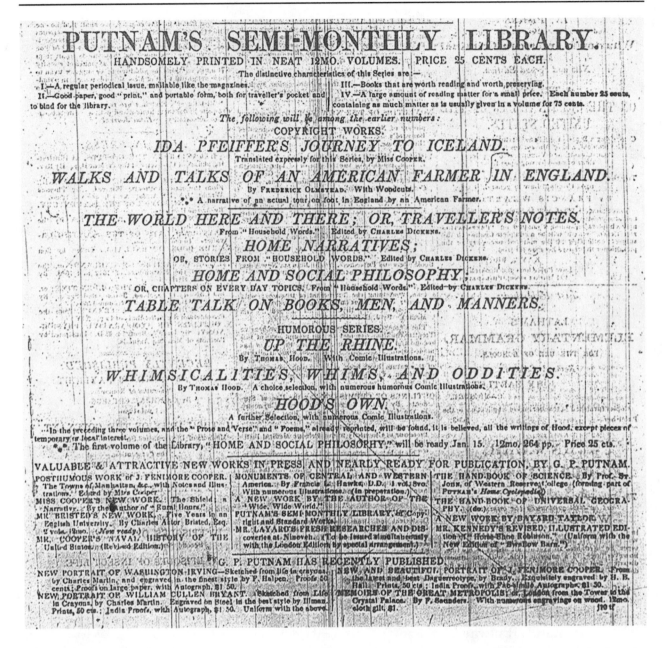

Advertisement in the 10 January 1852 issue of The Literary World. *G. P. Putnam rarely brought out its books in the 25¢ range; with its low price the Semi-Monthly Library was aimed at a more popular audience than the firm normally addressed.*

Putnam's Semi-Monthly Library

With his Semi-Monthly Library, Putnam initiated a plan similar to one Harper and Brothers had successfully employed in the 1840s. In its two-year history from 1852 to 1854, the series offered twenty-four volumes of what he advertised as "good and readable books" to the public at the unusually low price of 25¢ per volume ($6 collectively, $5 if paid in advance). There were various titles, including volumes from his Thomas Hood series, Layard's Nineveh and Its Remains, *Frederick Law Olmsted's* Walks and Talks of an American Farmer in England, *and a volume culled from Putnam's reprinted edition of Charles Dickens's* Household Words. *The literary quality of the series—featuring "books that are worth reading and worth preserving," according to the firm's advertisements—might well have overshot the mark for a publishing niche dictated by popularity, for the series was relatively short-lived. An "experiment" from its inception, Putnam's series clearly did not have the success of the Harpers's series.*

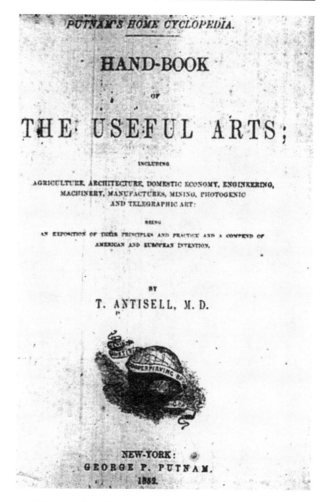

PUTNAM'S HOME CYCLOPÆDIA,

IN SIX VOLUMES;

Comprising the following:—each sold separately.

Hand-Book of Literature and Fine Arts.

By George Ripley, Esq., and Bayard Taylor, Esq.
1 vol. 8vo.

Hand-Book of Biography.

By Parke Godwin, Esq. 1 vol. 8vo.

Hand-Book of the Useful Arts, &c.

By Dr. Antisell. 1 vol. 8vo.

Hand-Book of the Sciences.

By Prof. St. John, of Western Reserve College. 1 vol.
8vo.

Hand-Book of Geography:

Or, UNIVERSAL GAZETTEER.

Hand-Book of History and Chronology:

Or, THE WORLD'S PROGRESS.   A Dictionary of
Dates.

In all 6 Vols., small 8vo., each containing from 600 to 800
pages, double columns, with Engravings. Cloth, each
vol., $2; sheep, $2 25; half morocco, $2 75; full moc-
rocco, $3 75.

Six volumes will complete the series, in which will be
comprised a comprehensive view of the whole circle of
human knowledge. For the preparation of a Hand-Book
of Literature and the Fine Arts, we know of no one
more competent than Mr. Ripley, the principal editor
and compiler of the work before us. A man of fine taste
and acute discrimination, and familiar, from his position
and pursuits, with the literature of all countries, he would
be able to enter upon such a work with a large amount
of valuable material already within his reach. Of the
scope of this volume, an idea may be formed from the
comprehensive title which we have copied above. It is
intended to furnish a thorough vocabulary of Art and
Literature, specially designed for schools, colleges, and
the great reading community of the United States. To
many portions of the text are given illustrative engravings.

The present series of popular manuals is intended not
for professional scholars, but for the great mass of American readers. No labor nor expense has been spared in
this preparation which could more perfectly adapt them
to their intended purpose. They have been edited with
great care by able scientific and literary men. The materials have been drawn from a great variety of sources.
In a small compass they contain the essence of many
large and valuable works. The subjects are brought
down to the latest dates, and presented with all the completeness and accuracy which could be secured by the
experience and industry of the editors.

The whole series furnishes a collection of manuals
adapted both for the use of classes and for general reference, presenting a lucid and comprehensive view of general History and Geography, Literature and the Fine
Arts, Biography, and the Sciences and Useful Arts.

"We know of no Biographical Dictionary which presents in so small a compass any thing like so comprehensive a list of names that have survived their owners, as
this of Mr. Godwin. It is especially full in reference to
Americans of distinction, and our only regret is that it

PUTNAM'S HOME CYCLOPEDIA.

HAND-BOOK

OF

THE USEFUL ARTS;

INCLUDING

AGRICULTURE, ARCHITECTURE, DOMESTIC ECONOMY, ENGINEERING,
MACHINERY, MANUFACTURES, MINING, PHOTOGENIC
AND TELEGRAPHIC ART:

BEING

AN EXPOSITION OF THEIR PRINCIPLES AND PRACTICE AND A COMPEND OF
AMERICAN AND EUROPEAN INVENTION.

BY

T. ANTISELL, M. D.

NEW-YORK:
GEORGE P. PUTNAM.
1852.

Title page of the third volume published in the Putnam's Home
Cyclopedia. *The "useful arts" were one of the main publishing
and cultural categories of a rapidly industrializing era.*
(Library of Congress)

Putnam's Home Cyclopedia

Putnam's Home Cyclopedia *was a six-volume set of reference manuals designed to present systematized general knowledge to
a middle-class readership. Brought out in 1852 and 1853, the series
was led off by Putnam himself, who updated his* Chronology; or,
An Introduction and Index to Universal History, Biography, and Useful Knowledge *(1833) as* Hand-Book of
Chronology *to fit in with the published titles of the other works in
the series: George Ripley and Bayard Taylor's* Hand-Book of Literature and the Fine Arts *(1852), Thomas Antisell's*
Hand-Book of the Useful Arts *(1852), Parke Godwin's*
Hand-Book of Universal Biography *(1852), T. Carey Calli-
cot's* Hand-Book of Universal Geography *(1853), and Samuel St. John's* Hand-Book of Science *(scheduled for publication
in 1853 but probably never completed).*

NEW YORK.

DIARY OF THE REBELLION.

NOT RUMORS, GUESSES, OR PREJUDICES, BUT FACTS.

Mr. G. P. PUTNAM,

Publisher, 532 Broadway, announces the
publication of

The REBELLION RECORD:

A DIARY OF AMERICAN EVENTS
(1860–1.)

Including the patriotic POETRY of the
time; a Digest of all verified FACTS; accurate copies of all essential documents, and a
reliable transcript of all notable and picturesque INCIDENTS. Carefully edited, as a
permanent digest for future reference.

WITH A PRELIMINARY, HISTORICAL
OUTLINE OF THE CAUSES OF
THE STRUGGLE.

Edited by FRANK MOORE,

Author of the "Diary of the American Revolution."

To be issued in handsome pamphlets of 48
pages. Royal 8vo.

No. I. will be issued immediately.

Newsmen and periodical dealers will
please send their orders.

Advertisement in the 27 April 1861 issue of American Publishers' Circular and Literary Gazette, *less than a week after
the Confederate shelling of Fort Sumter and the commencement of the Civil War*

Rebellion Record

Within two weeks of the firing on Fort Sumter, Putnam initiated publication of The Rebellion Record, *a compendium of newspaper articles, speeches, maps, songs, poems, and other Civil War–related material. Putnam and his partner, Frank Moore, did not envision a long, drawn out conflict; their weekly serial, however, eventually filled volumes. By the end of the war,* The Rebellion Record *constituted a veritable print archive of the conflict.*

Moore and Putnam formed a publishing partnership separate from G. P. Putnam that included a third investor, Putnam's former employee Charles T. Evans, by then an independent publisher. The three partners shared profits, with Moore serving as editor and Putnam as publisher. Putnam marketed The Rebellion Record *aggressively, offering it for sale in weekly and monthly numbers, as well as in bound volumes, and distributing the work via his firm and Evans's and through local news dealers and the trade. The three partners continued their relationship until December 1863, when Henry Holt, presumably brought in by his friend Putnam, purchased Evans's share. The arrangement did not last long, though, for both Holt and Putnam sold their interests to Moore the following year.*

* * *

In this undated note, Putnam writes to an unnamed printer or sign maker to prepare a placard advertising The Rebellion Record *to hang outside his Broadway office.*

Dear Sir   If you will get up a <u>big</u> board, to <u>project</u> from outside of the door & to be covered on both sides with bills of the Record & these lines <u>large</u> at the top–*viz*

> Down Town office of the
> Rebellion Record
> Published by Putnam 532 Broadway
> every Saturday

I will pay1/2 expense. It shd be done <u>at once</u>–& made bold & effective

Yours <u>G P Putnam</u>

—Clifton Waller Barrett Library of American Literature, Special Collections Department, University of Virginia Library

* * *

Susan Warner writes Putnam to request that he reprint in The Rebellion Record *a poem first published in the* New-York Tribune.

> The Island
> Oct. 10, 1862

Dear Mr Putnam,

I send you by this mail a No. of our little adventurous paper. If you will let me know the style & title of that young member of your family to whom the same would be likely to prove most acceptable; it shall in future go properly directed to him–or to her–whichever it may be.

A worse time certainly for the appearance of a new venture need not be desired. But it is a bad time also for books–& we must do something. And children, I suppose, will continue to read, if they can–whatever the older folks

are about. We can but try,–& leave our efforts in the Lord's hands. What a blessed thing it is to do that!

Anna promised to request you to insert a particular piece in the 'Record,' which has somehow escaped the notice of the Editor. It is called "A rainy day in camp"–was published in the Tribune of the 12th March 1862–& is, I think, one of the most beautiful things that have been written in connexion with this war-time. We do not know the author, nor anything about it, save its beauty.

In some haste, with love to the home circle, yours very truly, Susan Warner.

—Morristown National Historical Park

* * *

This retrospective notice of The Rebellion Record *in Putnam's Magazine assesses its pioneering status and place in the prolific literature produced as a consequence of the Civil War.* The Rebellion Record *realized a relatively modest circulation and profit compared to the wave of best-selling war-related biographies, histories, and campaign narratives.*

The first publication of any consequence undertaken in relation to it [literature about the Civil War] was the "Rebellion Record," projected by Mr. Putnam and conducted by Mr. Frank Moore. The calculation at the beginning was that one, or at most two volumes would suffice for this work. It has now reached eleven and will be cut short at twelve. Various narratives were begun in the same way, and lengthened their protracted series to the dismay of publishers and subscribers till new and condensed editions became necessary. Of course these works were for the most part compilations from necessarily imperfect materials; and will be resorted to only as quarries whence the future Bancrofts will pluck a block here and there for their more lasting literary edifices. But in the mean time their profitable sale has benefited authors and publishers, and afforded one among the thousand recent illustrations of the saying of Lucan, *bellum utile multis.* The war histories of Greeley, Abbott, and Headley have each exceeded a hundred thousand in circulation; and the biographies of Lincoln, of which Dr. Holland's takes the lead, stimulated by the agency and subscription system, have reaped a like harvest of popularity and profit. More than a hundred thousand dollars, we are told, has been received by the author of one of the "Lives," which exceeds the sum expected from, and thus far unhandsomely withheld by Congress, for the support of the widow of the illustrious subject of these volumes. If Senators and Representatives, to the scandal of the country, fail to do their duty in this matter, it might be well for Mrs. Lincoln, with Victoria for a precedent–for have we not here, too, our "Queens of Society"–to turn her attention to the booksellers. If, indeed, all who, directly or indirectly, have been indebted to Abraham Lincoln for the acquisition of a hundred thousand dollars, were to bestow upon his family a small percentage on this addition to their fortunes, there would be no occasion to expose the gifts of his friends for sale for the maintenance of his widow.

—Putnam's Magazine, 1 (January 1868): 121

Putnam Magazines

Wiley and Putnam's Literary News-Letter and Monthly Register and *The Literary World*

Wiley and Putnam's Literary News-Letter and Monthly Register of New Books, Foreign and American *(September 1841–April 1847), an early in-house, book-trade journal, was compiled jointly by the New York and London offices. In its nearly six years of existence, the* Literary News-Letter and Monthly Register *provided to the book-publishing industry in the United States a service it had lacked since Putnam suspended his own* Booksellers' Advertiser *five years before: a reliable source for news about the trade, authors, publishers, and book-related matters; lists of new books and journals; and a prime marketplace for advertisements. While Wiley and Putnam publications were naturally highlighted, the* Literary News-Letter and Monthly Register *nevertheless provided a wealth of information invaluable to American members of the trade, particularly because of Putnam's presence in London and his extensive ties to the book trade throughout Great Britain and the Continent. It proved to be a useful supplement to English journals such as* Publishers' Circular *and the* Athenaeum *and was sent free to literary professional organizations and individuals around the United States, including libraries, historical societies, colleges, and book collectors as well as publishers. In 1843 the rival New York publishing house of Appleton's began a look-alike trade paper,* Appleton's Literary News-Letter, *but the Wiley and Putnam newsletter remained the best source in the United States for professional information.*

In early 1847 John Wiley and William Appleton decided to disband their own periodicals in favor of The Literary World, *a magazine proposed by Evert A. Duyckinck that was modeled on the London* Athenaeum. *With the two houses subsidizing its publication and Duyckinck serving as editor,* The Literary World *first appeared on 6 February 1847. The publishers, however, shortly thereafter fired Duyckinck and replaced him for a year and a half with Charles Fenno Hoffman. In October 1848 Duyckinck and his brother George took both financial and editorial control over the journal and kept it in print until the end of 1853.*

* * *

The publishers formally dismissed Duyckinck from his editorship of The Literary World *just ten weeks after its inception.*

Evert A. Duyckinck Esqre.
New York
Dear Sir

We have repeatedly complained to you that in your performance of the duty of Editor of the Literary World you have thought proper to violate the agreement between you and ourselves in the only particular, in which, from delicacy towards you, we had refrained from inserting into our contract—a condition that was nevertheless expressly made between the parties. We apprized you after repeated breaches of this condition that we considered the contract between us to be rescinded by yourself, and we gave you the opportunity, if you chose, to become the sole proprietor of the Journal. This you declined. Finding that you still avowed a difference with us in the view you took of our agreement, we then proposed to submit any disagreement between us to the decisions of Referees. This you also peremptorily declined. You have therefore left us no alternative but to express our regret, that by your own act all connexion between you as the Editor, and ourselves as the proprietors of the Literary World is henceforth dissolved.

> Very Respectfully
> Yours,
> D. Appleton & Co
> Wiley & Putnam

New York April 21, 1847.
—Duyckinck Family Papers, Manuscripts and Archives Division, The New York Public Library, Astor, Lenox and Tilden Foundations

* * *

In this excerpt from a 14 June 1847 letter, Duyckinck explains to his brother George, absent in Europe, that the reason publishers Daniel Appleton and "glorious John" Wiley fired him as editor is that he involved his controversial friend Cornelius Mathews in editorial policy.

The main question of your letter received by the Hibernia (dated May 4) is rather a difficult one to

A CARD.

MESSRS. WILEY & PUTNAM's "Literary News-Letter" was commenced September 1, 1841, and Messrs. APPLETON & Co.'s "Literary Bulletin," June 1, 1843, since which periods thousands of copies of each have been distributed gratis throughout the country to Colleges, Literary Institutions, Schools and Academies, Public Libraries; to Clergymen, Lawyers, Physicians and others. The objects for which these journals were commenced, have become extended with the advance and growth of the trade, and the establishment of an enlarged journal, *in which all Publishers and Booksellers could unite*, and a full statement of the merits of the books of the day be presented to the public, has become an affair of importance. We have, therefore, discontinued the News-Letter and Bulletin, the usual contents of which will hereafter appear in the LITERARY WORLD. We warmly commend this undertaking to the support, by advertising and subscription, of all who have received the former journals.

D. APPLETON & Co.
WILEY & PUTNAM.

New York, Feb. 6, 1847.

Notice in the 6 February 1847 issue of The Literary World, *a periodical that was co-financed by the Appletons and Wiley and Putnam. The copy was probably written by founding editor Evert A. Duyckinck, who was also still overseeing the various Wiley and Putnam libraries.*

answer, more especially as I find my own course somewhat unsteadied from the shindy played by the publishers in the affair of the Literary World. The interruption of the latter was the most silly absurd thing of all grown Broadway merchants ever got their feet into and I believe some consciousness of this is dancing in the mind of "glorious John." You would have thought that Mathews had been a second Cataline.

—*Duyckinck Family Papers, Manuscripts and Archives Division, The New York Public Library, Astor, Lenox and Tilden Foundations*

Putnam's Monthly

The idea that book publishers might increase their revenues by also publishing general magazines was as old as the republic. The greatest book publisher in the early history of the nation, Mathew Carey, founded the American Museum *in 1787 and sustained it for six years. However, the idea of attaching a general magazine to a publishing house in such a way as to maximize their mutual advantage—serials in the magazine then published as books by the parent house, authors cultivated and published in two different formats, circulation of the firm's productions among*

(*Private*)

10 Park Place. New York
October 1st 1852.

Sir

We take the liberty of informing you of our intention to publish an Original periodical of a character different from any now in existence, and, as it is our wish to have the best talent of the Country to aid us in the undertaking, to solicit your assistance as a contributor.

We propose to publish <u>monthly</u> a work which shall combine the popular character of a Magazine, with the higher & graver aims of a Quarterly Review, but to preserve in all its departments an independent & elevated tone; and to make it as essentially an organ of American thought as possible. The want of such a publication, we believe, has long been felt in this Country, and it is only after mature consideration, and on the advice of some of the most eminent literary & scientific men of the Union who have offered us their aid that we have determined on the attempt to supply this want. We believe that the facilities connected with an established publishing business will enable us to place the work at once on a high footing, and beyond ordinary contingencies.

The work will be wholly original, and, as we are well aware that gratuitous contributions ought not to be relied on, even though they could be, we expect to pay as liberally as the nature of the work will allow for all articles that we may accept.

The first number of the work will be issued on the first of next January; it will contain about 144 pages, occasionally illustrated, printed in the best manner, and sold at $3. a year.

As it is desirable that we should know the extent of our literary resources, we shall be greatly obliged by as early an answer as may suit your convenience, whether or not you will be able to furnish us an occasional article, and if you will be willing that your name should be announced as a probable contributor. Business considerations making it important that no publicity should be given to our design before all our arrangements have been completed, you will oblige us by regarding this as a confidential communication until we make our public announcement.

We are Sir Yours very resp.y   G.P. Putnam & Co

Circular soliciting contributors to Putnam's Monthly *that was attached to a 5 November 1852 letter from Putnam to John Jay Smith.*
Such circulars were sent to dozens of American writers and survive in the collections of some of the era's leading writers
(George Palmer Putnam Collection, Manuscripts Division, Princeton University Library).

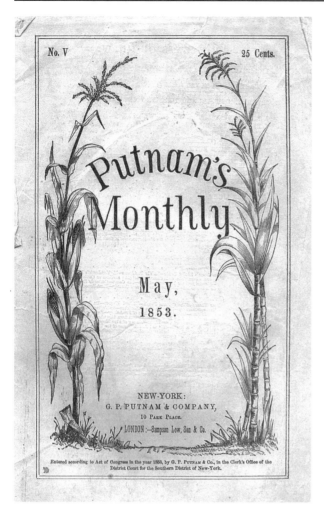

The cover for an issue of the first literary magazine published by
G. P. Putnam and Company. The pea-green color of the cover
made the magazine easily recognizable
(Collection of Ezra Greenspan).

two overlapping sets of readership—was more a nineteenth-century phenomenon. Like many American publishing practices, it was learned from British examples and adapted to American circumstances.

Harper and Brothers was able to attain unprecedented success in 1850 with Harper's Monthly by reprinting large quantities of popular British fiction and poetry and mixing in some original work. The circulation of the magazine quickly ascended through the tens into the hundreds of thousands, and its achievement became the envy of other publishers. Although no other American firm could match the advantages of the Harpers—who had not only the largest publishing list and collection of house authors but also a modern bookmaking plant—other publishers, such as Stringer and Townsend with their short-lived International, tried to duplicate the Harpers' model, but in vain.

Putnam, however, took another tack with Putnam's Monthly (January 1853–April 1855) by appealing to the mood of cultural nationalism with a magazine made up exclusively of the original work of American authors. The Putnam approach not only had no predecessor in the United States but also, more importantly, no immediate rival. In filling a void in the periodical market, Putnam was able to tap into the fast-growing reservoir of national talent, a fact he was clearly counting on when he sent out a 1 October 1852 circular inviting the leading writers in the country to contribute to his proposed magazine.

Putnam also enlisted the best editorial talent in New York City to operate the magazine. Charles Frederick Briggs, an experienced journalist and talented fiction writer, served as general editor; George William Curtis, one of the leading magazinists of the time, became the literary editor; and Parke Godwin, assistant editor to William Cullen Bryant at the New York Evening Post and gifted writer on current affairs, was the political editor. All outstanding writers in their own right, they proved doubly valuable to the magazine by also contributing frequently and notably to its contents.

Like most general magazines of the 1850s, Putnam's Monthly was published on a monthly basis at a price of 25¢ per issue or $3 (plus postage) for an annual subscription. Addressed to a sophisticated, middle-class readership, the magazine straddled an unoccupied market niche between the high-brow quarterlies, such as the North American Review, and the established general magazines, such as Harper's, Graham's, and Godey's, which were based heavily on foreign importations and addressed to a slightly less-sophisticated audience. In line with the increasing tendency toward professionalization, the formal policy of the magazine was to pay for all accepted contributions, generally at the rate of $3 per page for prose (or $5 for the work of the most highly regarded writers) and $10–$25 per poem depending on length. Authors' names were kept anonymous as was the normal practice in American magazine journalism until after the Civil War. Once established, the magazine became so attractive a place for publication that the ratio of acceptances to submissions was only one in ten.

Able to draw on the work of its talented editors and on the contributions of many of the leading American writers of the time, Putnam's Monthly achieved the status—recognized even contemporaneously—of being the best-written American magazine the country had yet seen. The fiction was particularly good. Herman Melville contributed such stories as "Bartleby, the Scrivener," "The Lightning-Rod Man," and "I and My Chimney"; he also serialized "The Encantadas" and Israel Potter. Three of the wittiest serials of the 1850s made their first appearance in the magazine: Curtis's Prue and I and The Potiphar Papers and Frederick Cozzens's Sparrowgrass Papers. Also serialized was the *fine novel by antislavery activist Edmund Quincy,* Wensley, *which Briggs commissioned for the magazine. Although poetry occupied relatively little space, the work of the country's most esteemed poet, Henry Wadsworth Longfellow, appeared frequently. Most of the poetry was sentimental or humorous and was clearly designed to appeal to a middle-class, family-oriented readership. Some of it even the editors dismissed as filler.*

The quality of the nonfiction equaled that of the fiction. Henry David Thoreau serialized Excursion to Canada *in four installments (and* Cape Cod *in summer 1855 shortly after Putnam had transferred the magazine). James Russell Lowell contributed "Moosehead Journals" and "Fireside Journal." Hardly a single number lacked a travelogue, one of the most popular forms of midcentury writing. Although not always up to the level of Thoreau or Lowell, many of the travelogues were memorable, in part because the editors were able to call upon the finest travel writers in the country, including Bayard Taylor, Richard Kimball, Charles Dudley Warner, Caroline Kirkland, and Curtis. Their geographical range covered the globe, including Cuba, Japan, and Russia. Political analysis was intelligent and serious, and book and art reviews matched the level of the best periodical journalism of the time.*

Sales figures suggest that the magazine had a circulation of approximately 30,000–35,000 while under the control of G. P. Putnam and Company—a healthy and profitable circulation for the time, especially for a periodical of its quality. Putnam's Monthly *won the regard of many leading writers as well as of readers and reviewers around the country and in England, where it was reprinted by Sampson Low. The magazine, however, lost at least a portion of its initial high regard after summer 1853 as Godwin increasingly set its editorial tone with a series of unusually forthright attacks on slavery, the South, and congressional and presidential ineptitude. The result, not surprisingly in the increasingly polarized, politicized atmosphere of the mid 1850s, was a marked tendency, especially in the South, to equate the magazine with antislavery and eventually with "Black Republicanism."*

Putnam's Monthly *might well have survived any storms incited by Godwin, whom in any case neither Briggs nor Putnam had any intention of silencing. It could not survive, however, the general financial debacle the parent company faced over the course of 1854, which obliged Putnam to jettison many assets in spring and summer before finally reaching the determination that he needed also to sell the magazine. His purchaser was the new publishing firm of Dix (a former G. P. Putnam employee) and Edwards, who assumed control beginning with the May 1855 issue and held it for two years before going bankrupt in summer 1857.*

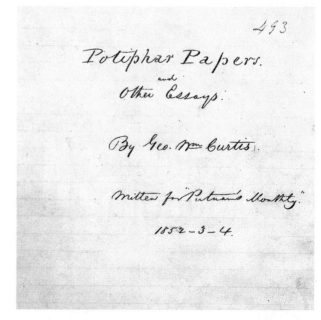

Title page for the manuscript of one of two popular serials George William Curtis wrote for Putnam's Monthly *(Courtesy of Pierpont Morgan Library)*

Selected List of Contributors to *Putnam's Monthly*

Clarence Cook (1828–1900)
James Fenimore Cooper (1789–1851)
Frederick Cozzens (1818–1869)
George William Curtis (1824–1892)
Charles Dana (1819–1897)
Parke Godwin (1816–1904)
Horace Greeley (1811–1872)
Edward Everett Hale (1822–1901)
Francis Hawks (1798–1866)
Henry James, Sr. (1811–1882)
Richard Kimball (1816–1892)
Caroline Kirkland (1801–1865)
Francis Lieber (1800–1872)
Henry Wadsworth Longfellow (1807–1882)
James Russell Lowell (1819–1891)
Herman Melville (1819–1891)
Charles Eliot Norton (1828–1908)
Fitz-James O'Brien (1828–1862)
Edmund Quincy (1810–1877)
George Ripley (1802–1880)
William Swinton (1833–1892)
Bayard Taylor (1825–1878)
Henry David Thoreau (1817–1862)
Charles Dudley Warner (1829–1900)
Nathaniel Willis (1806–1867)

* * *

* * *

Ralph Waldo Emerson responds favorably to the 1 October 1852 circular soliciting contributions to the forthcoming Putnam's Monthly.

Concord Mass. 11 Octr. 1852

Gentlemen,

Nothing could be more agreable [*sic*] to me than the establishment of an American Magazine of a truly elevated and independent tone, and if you shall really and perseveringly attempt that, you shall be sure of my hearty co-operation & aid. Perhaps my interest in such a project is even more serious than your own: but if I were nearer New York than I am, I should immediately seek an interview with you to name certain parties whose concurrence I think important; and now, I shall esteem it a favour if you will inform me who, if any there be, in Boston is acquainted with your design, or if none there, what literary man in New York.

Respectfully

R. W. Emerson.

—Manuscripts Division, Department of Rare Books and Special Collections, Princeton University Library. Published with permission of the Princeton University Library.

* * *

Henry James Sr. casts a few aspersions on Harper's Monthly, *the best-selling general magazine of the time and the presumed competition of* Putnam's Monthly, *in his response to Putnam.*

My dear Sir:

In answer to your circular letter, I may say that I shall be glad to contribute to your Magazine, and that you are at liberty to use my name to that effect if you think it worth the while.

Your project seems to me to have a very unobstructed prospect of success before it, so far at least as any domestic rivalry is concerned. Harper's Magazine is a mere stale and dishonest hash, where it is not a stupid vehicle of Methodism; and the Knickerbocker I presume will hardly stand in your way.

Yours very truly

H. James

New York Nov 5.

G. P. Putnam Esq

—Schaffer Library, Union College, Schenectady, New York

* * *

A writer for Graham's Magazine, *one of the leading magazines of the day, welcomes the appearance of* Putnam's Monthly. *The writer is less than forthright in identifying* Graham's *and* Godey's *with* Putnam's *as "American Magazines" but failing to name the "reprint" magazine with which his own was fighting a losing war for popular preeminence:* Harper's Monthly.

Putnam's Monthly.—This new candidate for public favor, comes to us with a very stately look—not a picture to catch the eye, nor a capital or italic to give emphasis to its voice. It is eminently sober, and quite modest. The articles are all original and well written. Putnam deserves success, if for nothing more than for his effort to sustain American authorship—and we cordially wish it to him—but he has a thorny road to travel. Sartain spent $16,000 for original articles in three years, and Graham $87,000 in the last ten years, but *great* success seems to follow the reprints—and, except Graham and Godey, we know of no American Magazines which have succeeded eminently. We give Putnam the right hand of fellowship nevertheless.

—Graham's Magazine, 42 (February 1853): 222

* * *

Acting on a tip provided by a common friend, antislavery activist Sydney Howard Gay, Charles Frederick Briggs solicits a fiction contribution to Putnam's Monthly *from Edmund Quincy, the noted antislavery journalist and writer. Quincy responded by serializing his novel* Wensley, *one of the finest narratives published in the magazine.*

C.F. Briggs—Feb. 20 /53

My dear Sir:

I have been intending the past three months, or rather, ever since I determined upon editing the new Magazine, to drop you a line and request the favor of an article from you. I know how facile your pen is, how just your thoughts, how free, pure, and forcible your style, and how well informed you keep yourself on the current topics of the day, and I had often regretted that you would not consent to make your mark in popular journalism, which I conceive to be the best arena for an American, that his country offers for the display of ability, although it is lamentably far from having the best Americans engaged upon it. I did not know, however, to your other talents you could add that of a story-teller, until our friend Gay informed me. He says that you have a tale, either finished, or nearly so, that you would be willing to send to "Putnam's Monthly" if it should be wanted. I have hardly a doubt that it would be most acceptable, and, if you have no objection to sending it with the understanding that I shall return it if it should not meet my approval, I shall be most happy to read it; and, if used, the publisher will pay you for it, when printed at the rate of three dollars a page. You of course know that in my position I can neither afford to insert an article on the ground of my esteem for the writer, nor because it may happen to please my individual taste. . . .

—Quincy Family Papers, Massachusetts Historical Society

* * *

Flushed with success after the first half-year of publication, Putnam included this optimistic statement at the end of the first volume of Putnam's Monthly.

CLOSE OF THE FIRST VOLUME.

ALTHOUGH we stated boldly and frankly in our first number, that we were not entering upon what we deemed an experiment, in projecting a new Magazine, yet we must now, at the close of the first volume, as frankly declare that our success has been much greater than we anticipated—that we have had more aid from both writers and readers than our previous knowledge of the literary resources of the country led us to hope for. We make this statement, and give the plain facts which will follow, because we know that our success will be alike gratifying to those who questioned the discretion of the undertaking, as to those who encouraged us by their counsel and promised assistance. Although, before publishing our prospectus, we made sure of abundant literary help, and gave the names of many of the distinguished writers who had assured us of their hearty sympathy, and promised us contributions, yet our conviction was, that our best aid would come from Young America, whose name had not yet been announced on Magazine covers. And so we determined not to give the names of the contributors to our Monthly, that each article might stand on its own merits, and the young unknown be presented to the public on a perfect equality with the illustrious contributor whose name, alone, would give him an audience; for, in literature, the new-comer is always treated as an intruder. By this course we missed the clapping of hands and bravos which we might have commanded by announcing the names of some of our contributors, but we are so well satisfied with the result of the experiment that we shall adhere to the rule hereafter.

Perhaps it is worth while to exhibit some of the mysteries of Magazine-making, and let our countrymen know how much intellectual activity there is among us. During the past six months we have received from voluntary contributors, four hundred and eighty-nine articles, the greater part from writers wholly unknown before. They came from every state and territory in the Union, with the single exception of Deseret, whose "Saints," probably, do not regard our Monthly as a fitting receptacle for their literary efforts. All of these articles we have read, and from them have been selected some of the most valuable papers that we have published; many of them we have been compelled, reluctantly, to return; some on account of their length, and many more, not so much from their lack of merit, as from the nature of their themes. Some articles have been curtailed of superfluous sentences, but the style

and sentiment have, in all cases, been given in their integrity. Every article that we have published has been paid for at a rate which their writers have thought "liberal," all have been original, the product of American pens, and with one exception, we believe that all were written for our columns.

We publish these facts with a feeling of pride, not only because they justify our undertaking, but because they afford abundant evidence of future success to our own and all kindred publications.

—*Putnam's Monthly,* 1 (June 1852)

* * *

The exchange system carried on among newspaper and magazine editors encouraged unpaid promotions of another's publications. The system of reviews was so frequently corrupted that the critic for the Washington National Era *feels compelled to state that his "unqualified praise" of* Putnam's Monthly *is genuine.*

Literary Notice
PUTNAM'S MONTHLY. August, 1853.

This is the eighth number of this capital publication and we have never yet *noticed* it as it deserves. Some unaccountable difficulty, postal or clerical, has hitherto prevented the receipt of it in the way that courtesy has established for the commerce of journalists. Even the number now on our table cost us a quarter. It is worth the money, indeed; but the habit of editorial *exchanges* generates a repugnance to purchasing books and papers, however valuable, desirable, and cheap, which we are glad our subscribers are not troubled with. If they knew and fully appreciated this communistic sentiment of the editorial fraternity, they would understand what a puff it is to say that we have actually bought *Putnam,* and paid for it with cash; and, what is more to the purpose, perhaps, they would value our unqualified praise something higher for knowing that it is not in any way purchased.

There are, luckily for reviewers, many ways of knowing enough about a book to estimate it fairly, without a regular and thorough perusal. By all of these, as well as by sufficient actual examination, we are satisfied that *Putnam's Monthly* deserves the best word we can say for it.

The *Tribune,* upon an evidently thorough examination, pronounces the June number, *upon the whole, the best American Magazine ever issued*—a judgment which we cordially and advisedly endorse. Its intrinsic qualities richly deserve this high praise; but there are other things about it which greatly increase our regard for the work. In size and character of contents it is a first class periodical, and its authorship is not stolen; it pays its contributors, and it does not humbug its readers with their reputation *otherwise* and *elsewhere* acquired and deserved; it is not engaged in the ugly business of breaking down our native periodical literature for the million, by glutting the market with more pages than Graham and Godey, while they pay for their matter, and afford it for the same money; and it is not so sneaking and slavish as the great Pecksniffian monthly with which it so generously and bravely contends for popular support.

Especially we like *Putnam,* because, while it does some sort of justice to American authorship, and something to encourage it, the pitch and drift of its articles put it into the place that is waiting to be well occupied. We do not say that its writers fully reach the mark that the publishers aim at, but we do see that the aim is well and steadily maintained, and we cheerfully acknowledge that the best talent of the country within their reach is employed.

Unfortunately, our *currency* literature is in the main, of the parisitic species; the colonial character still clings to it. The Putnams are doing what they can to deliver us from our dependency, and we give them our thanks and blessing for the effort. The editor seems to us to be all right, and growing at that; and the rank and file writers make a very fair show of metal and manhood. The author of the Potiphar Papers, for instance, *can't be beat* in his line, and the writer of "Works of American Statesmen" comes so near to statesmanship himself that he knows "there is no fixed political science, no absolute and unchangeable principles, that have yet been discovered." This is exactly true of the systems in vogue—of the systems for which the subjects of his article were renounced for knowing so much about! It was a bold, honest declaration of the French physiologist, Majendie, when, in his elementary book, he wrote the chapter on the Spleen in these words: "Functions *unknown,*" and there dropped it, and set about discovering something to teach, instead of going on with pages of nothing to say. It is absolutely funny to think of Clay, Calhoun, and Webster, getting an immortal fame out of an immortal wrangle—immortal *a parte post,* as well as *a parte ante!* The next best thing to giving us a system of "absolute and unchangeable principles," is owning up that we have none. That will put the boys on inquiry, and leave the oldsters to hurry up the monuments and get on the epitaphs—they will do for historical milestones. The Egyptians built pyramids to be wondered at, not used; and then they built palaces to lie in when they were mummied. That was their only chance for posthumous perpetuity. They didn't want to be "buried out of our sight"—they said, *we still live,* and they stuck to it. They are welcome to the spice, and may keep it

as it keeps them. The Barnums will attend to them. But we want men that will hold together without the bitumen and bandages of antiquity. So, "more power to your elbow," Messrs. Putnam & Company, and let us have the best you can do, for we need it badly.   E.

–*Washington National Era,* 7 (18 August 1853): 131

* * *

In this excerpt from a September 1853 letter, James Russell Lowell writes to his old friend Charles Frederick Briggs about his work for Putnam's Monthly.

I met Mr. Putnam in the street the other day. I am sorry I did not know he was in these parts. How is it about the sketch of Alston. I left it unfinished because you wrote me that the publication was deferred. What I have written (or part of it) would make a unique article for your Magazine—if the other thing is given up—It is a sketch of Cambridge as it was twenty-five years ago & is done as nobody but I could do it—for nobody knows the old town so well . . .

–*reproduced by permission of the Houghton Library, Harvard University bMS AM 765 (6–17)*

* * *

Buoyed by the success of the magazine after its first year, Putnam states the editorial policy of his magazine as one transcending party concerns and addressing the "national interest" candidly. He and his editors soon learned, however, that the magazine could not stand above the growing sectional divide, as it gradually became an object of derision in the South.

PUBLISHERS' NOTICE.

THE present number of "Putnam's Monthly" completes the second volume, and the first year of its existence.

In referring to the progress of the work so far, it is not worth while for the publishers to indulge in much self-glorification, or at least to do more than reiterate what was said at the close of the first volume; yet they have cause for honest congratulation in the successful establishment of "Putnam's Monthly" as a fixed fact. The character and extent of this success has been far beyond their most sanguine expectations. They have had the good fortune of enlisting in the enterprise some of the ablest pens in the country; and they deem it a special cause for satisfaction, not only that among their regular contributors and earnest co-operators are included many of the most eminent and respected of our literary men of various positions and shades of religious and political opinion—but also that the general management of the Magazine, and the character of its contents, have been such as to meet the cordial approval of a large majority of the most judicious and intelligent readers.

It is also pleasant to know, that while eminent and well-known writers have occupied a goodly portion of our pages, these pages have also been the means of introducing some younger writers of excellent promise, whose newly opened mines may doubtless yet produce as much pure metal as those which have been longer under contribution. Of the nine hundred and eighty articles which we have received, our two volumes could contain only about one in ten; and the most ungenial part of our task has been that of declining papers of interest and ability, which would fill half a dozen magazines as large as ours. Our space, and not our will, has been the arbiter in many of these instances. We would here return our cordial thanks to all those who have so zealously taken an interest in the plan and prospects of the Magazine; and to those who wish to make it a great deal better than it has been, we would say, Do so, by all means. Send us articles that are a great deal better, wiser, wittier, and every way more brilliant, and it shall go hard but they shall find a place and suitable reward.

The literary resources of our "Monthly," now so ample, will, in the coming year, be increased and elevated by all inducements in our power. With all its present general features, it is intended that the Magazine shall have new and varied attractions for all classes of its wide circle of readers. Each number will contain one or more entertaining and instructive papers, ILLUSTRATED from original designs, when such illustrations can add any thing to the value or interest of the text. Popular information on matters connected with practical science, and the useful arts and manufactures, will form a special feature.

A new and popular account of the public and private life of WASHINGTON, by one of our best writers, illustrated by the graphic pencil of DARLEY, will be commenced in the January number.

It is superfluous to repeat, that "Putnam's Monthly" is not a partisan or sectarian organ, and never has been so. Topics of national and general interest, or relating to the public welfare, will be discussed when there is occasion, with freedom, but not, it is believed, with reckless intentions, or from self-interested motives.

It has never been intended to restrict this Magazine to a character purely literary, but rather to extend as widely as possible its field of view, passing over no genuine human interest, and especially no genuine national interest. With the particular measures of Party, and above all, with the private aims and motives of parties, we not only will not, but *cannot* have any thing to do; inclination and policy alike forbid it. But, on the other hand, no fear of misrepresentation or abuse will deter us from untrammelled investigation of any matter

which may be deemed worthy of public attention. Whether this be done in a candid, honest, and impartial manner, or the contrary, our readers must judge.

—Putnam's Monthly, 2 (December 1853)

* * *

Putnam sends a check along with a typical note of thanks to William Cullen Bryant, a personal friend and professional ally, for a poem. Putnam also reports on the slow sales of his firm's edition of Bryant's Letters of a Traveller *(1850).*

Dec. 28, 1853

Dear Sir,

We have the pleasure of enclosing a cheque for $50 for your noble poem, "The Conqueror's Grave" with the Jany. number of our Magazine.

We hope we frequently have the similar pleasure.

On the 1st Feby. we shall report profits on the vol. of "Letters" though we fear the result for the past year has been very insignificant.

> With high respect
> Dear Sir,
> Yours very truly
> G. P. Putnam & Co.

W. C. Bryant, Esq.

—Manuscripts Division, Department of Rare Books and Special Collections, Princeton University Library. Published with permission of the Princeton University Library.

* * *

Briggs's blunt editorial on the sectional controversy in the March 1854 number of Putnam's Monthly *drew a critical response from the* Southern Literary Messenger.

We were greatly surprised to see in an editorial article of "Putnam's Monthly," for March, an unprovoked and wholly gratuitous attack upon the Messenger. In the course of some remarks intended specially "for the people South of Mason and Dixon's line," the editor says –

"We are accused of not being American because we are Northern. The South. . . . will not permit us to enjoy the common instincts of patriotism, but will cut us off of our inheritance, because we happen to live on the wrong side of Mason and Dixon's line. It was a son of New England who uttered the patriotic sentiment, 'I know no North, no South;' but our Southern friends say they 'know no North, only a South.' There are numberless publications calling themselves after the South, to indicate their social character and their antagonism to the North. *The Southern Quarterly,* the *Southern Literary Messenger,* and so on; but if there be a single periodical or other institution North of Mason and Dixon, whose title breathes such an un-American and sectional spirit, we are ignorant of its existence."

Now we must be permitted to say that a greater inconsistency than is involved in the first and last sentences of the foregoing paragraph has never fallen under our observation. Mr. Putnam complains that because he is Northern we say he is not American, and in the same breath accuses us of being unpatriotic for no other reason in the world than because we are Southern. Nor is it true that we call ourselves after the South to indicate antagonism to the North. No such reason operated to give this magazine its title, nor does anything that has appeared in our columns justify the assertion. We have not made, nor do we now make any war upon the Northern people or their literary journals, of our own accord. If we are engaged in sectional controversies, it is because of the aggressive spirit which has ever characterised Northern journalism with regard to our institutions; it is because Northern writers continue to malign and misrepresent us; it is because they would "*cut us off of our inheritance*"–and not from any real or fancied antagonism to our brethren "beyond the Tweed." To parry assaults directed at slavery and refute the falsehoods which find only too ready a currency among the Northern people concerning slaveholders, was recognized by the founder of the Messenger as one of the objects for which the work was established. To this extent we are sectional, so far we are unpatriotic, and shall ever continue to be, at least while the Messenger remains under our control. There are "numberless publications" we know, at the North, which if they would indicate truly by their titles the sentiments they cherish, would style themselves *Anti*-Southern. The difference between us is, that we frankly avow ourselves Southern, while they are constantly manifesting the most hostile feelings to us under titles which imply nationality.

We do not say "Putnam's Monthly" is one of these. We have seen articles in it which we thought decidedly obnoxious to Southern readers, but we acquit it of any systematic warfare upon our rights or traduction of our people, and certainly, its title is about as sectional as it well could be. It signifies that it is the exponent of a single individual, and represents only Park Row. If the magazine should look therefore only to local interests, and ignore the literary claims of distant portions of the country, it could not be said that it falsified its designation. But we are willing to believe its views are not so parochial. Let it be a little more careful for the future how it asperses its neighbours and we shall be pleased to witness its continued success.

–Southern Literary Messenger, 20 (April 1854): 253–254

* * *

In an attempt to preserve the good relations between the magazine and one of its most valued contributors, Putnam apologizes to Herman Melville for his editor's rejection the previous day of "The Two Temples," probably submitted for the June 1854 issue of Putnam's Monthly. *Melville remained a frequent contributor to the magazine.*

May 13 1854

Herman Melville of Pittsfield
Mass

Dear Sir,

There seems to be some reason to fear that some of our church leaders might be disturbed by the <u>point</u> of your sketch. I regret this very much, as we shd. have been glad to have had it in this number.– Do you think this could be avoided?–

We wish very much to have your <u>head</u> as one of our series of portraits. Curtis will be in the July no.– Have you not some drawing or daguerreotype that you can lend us?–Or can you oblige us by having a daguerreotype taken in Pittsfield & let us know the cost, which will be remitted at once?

We hope you will give us some more of your good things

In haste, Truly yours <u>G P Putnam & Co</u>
–*Herman Melville Collection, Houghton Library,*
Harvard University

* * *

In this undated, hastily written, and much corrected draft, Putnam prepares a statement for publication that points out the double thievery of Longfellow's "Two Angels." The poem was originally published in Putnam's Monthly *and reprinted in London in* Bentley's Miscellany *before being printed again in New York by* Littell's Living Age, *which mistakenly credited* Bentley's *as the original publisher. This incident typified for Putnam the injustices done to both authors and publishers by the lack of an international copyright.*

<u>Putnam's Monthly and Longfellow</u>
Littells' Living Age No 529 publishes Longfellow's poem of the "<u>Two Angels</u>," and credits it to <u>Bentley's Miscellany</u>. This poem, as most intelligent people know, was written for <u>Putnam's Monthly</u> & published in that magazine in April last. Bentley then appropriates it as original and shamefully omits to say where he took it from: and now Mr. Littell, (innocently of course, but <u>rather</u> carelessly) copies it with a credit to <u>Bentley</u>! "Encouragement to original genius" is a very laudable thing–but if choice bits of this kind are to be appropriated at once as public property & not only so but actually credited to a foreign journal that has stolen them, while the original publisher who alone has

THE TWO ANGELS.

BY PROFESSOR LONGFELLOW.

Two angels, one of Life and one of Death,
  Passed o'er the village as the morning broke;
The dawn was on their faces, and beneath,
  The sombre houses hearsed with plumes of
    smoke.

Their attitude and aspect were the same,
  Alike their features and their robes of white;
But one was crowned with amaranth, as with
  flame,
    And one with asphodels, like flakes of light.

I saw them pause on their celestial way;
  Then said I, with deep fear and doubt op-
    pressed:
"Beat not so loud, my heart, lest thou betray
  The place where thy beloved are at rest!"

And he, who wore the crown of asphodels,
  Descending, at my door began to knock,
And my soul sank within me, as in wells
  The waters sink before an earthquake's shock.

I recognized the nameless agony,
  The terror and the tremor and the pain,
That oft before had filled and haunted me,
  And now returned with threefold strength
    again.

The door I opened to my heavenly guest,
  And listened, for I thought I heard God's
    voice;
And knowing whatsoe'er He sent was best,
  Dared neither to lament nor to rejoice.

Then with a smile, that filled the house with
  light,
  "My errand is not Death, but Life," he said;
And ere I answered, passing out of sight
  On his celestial embassy he sped.

'T was at thy door, O friend! and not at mine,
  The angel with the amaranthine wreath,
Pausing descended, and with voice divine,
  Whispered a word that had a sound like Death.
Then fell upon the house a sudden gloom,

A shadow on those features fair and thin;
  And softly, from that hushed and darkened room,
    Two angels issued, where but one went in.

All is of God! If He but wave his hand
  The mists collect, the rain falls thick and loud,
Till with a smile of light on sea and land,
  Lo! He looks back from the departing cloud.

Angels of Life and Death alike are his;
  Without his leave they pass no threshold o'er;
Who, then, would wish or dare, believing this,
  Against his messengers to shut the door?
              Bentley's Miscellany.

DXXIX   LIVING AGE.   VOL. VI. 4

A poem by Henry Wadsworth Longfellow as it was reprinted in the 8 July 1854 issue of Littell's Living Age. *Putnam was angered that this poem, which originally appeared in his monthly, was credited to a London publication by the New York magazine.*

paid the author–& paid liberally–is <u>wholly ignored,</u> it is pretty evident that the publisher's "encouragement" is something less than the author's!

The meanness of sundry English Magazines in this particular–viz. appropriating as original, in their own pages original articles of American periodicals has been practised too long. As to the appropriation itself, they find, of course, abundant example, & provocation on this side–but it is not a general practice, to say the least, for American periodicals to take such things without acknowledging their origin. This is a meanness of which several popular & respectable English Magazines–especially Bentley's has been repeat-edly guilty–Indeed it is an every day matter with them. American re-publishers for English Magazines should be up early in the morning, therefore, with their eyes open, if they would avoid being liable for taking copyright matter belonging to their neighbours, who had paid for it in just the same way that they have paid for their pantaloons & bread & butter.

–Manuscripts Division, Department of Rare Books and Special Collections, Princeton University Library. Published with permission of the Princeton University Library.

* * *

G. P. Putnam & Co.,
American and Foreign Booksellers and Publishers, Purchasing Agents for the Trade and for Public Institutions.
GEORGE P. PUTNAM,
JOHN W. LESLIE.
Agencies at London, Paris, Brussels, and Leipsic.

10 Park Place, New York, ————— · 1854

List of Cuts of buildings &c in New York

belonging to ———— G. P. Putnam & Co.

			Cast.	Cost of Engraving, drawing &c long.
Feb. /54	No 1.	Birds-eye View of New York.	Steru.	2500. ✓
	– 2	Liberty St. in process of Rebuilding		69 00
	– 3	Store No 200 Broadway		20 00
	4	Trinity Buildings		27 00
	5	Wall Street		30 00
	6	Bank of the Republic		24 00
	7	Insurance Building		26 00
	8	Mercantile Bank		20 00
	9	Broadway Bank		26 00
	10	Merchants Exchange		56 50
April	11	Custom House		54 50
	12	Metropolitan Bank		22 00
	13	Stores cor. Broadway & Rector		31 00
	14	View of Dey St.		33 00 .
	15	Stewarts Store — front.		35 00
	16	——— " chambers St.		17 00
	17	Murray St.		31 00
	18	Astor House		29 00
	19	Delmonico's Hotel		35 00
	20	St Nicholas Hotel		41 00
	21	Taylor's Restaurant		35 25 .
	22	Prescott House		56 00
	23	Metropolitan Hotel	·	45 25
	24	St. Denis		53 00
			forward	$ 802 00

First of four pages in which Putnam lists the prices paid for engravings used in Putnam's Monthly *through its third volume (George Palmer Putnam Collection, Manuscripts and Archives Division, The New York Public Library, Astor, Lenox and Tilden Foundations)*

In his long, powerful essay "Our Parties and Politics," published in the September 1854 issue of Putnam's Monthly, *associate editor Parke Godwin analyzes the history of the American party system and argues that the parties have been degraded by the pressure of the slavery controversy. Responses to the essay divided sharply along sectional and ideological lines, revealing both the fracturing of American culture and the impossibility of the magazine serving as a truly national forum.*

FOREIGNERS complain that they cannot easily understand our political parties, and we do not wonder at it, because those parties do not always understand themselves. Their controversies like the old *homoousian* disputes of the church, often turn upon such niceties of distinction, that to discern their differences requires optics as sharp as those of Butler's hero, who could

————"Sever and divide
Betwixt north-west and north-west side."

What with whigs, democratic whigs, democrats, true democrats, barnburners, hunkers, silver grays, woolly heads, soft shells, hard shells, national reformers, fire-eaters, and filibusteros, it is not difficult to imagine how the exotic intellect should get perplexed! Even to our native and readier apprehensions, the diversity of principle hidden under the diversity of names, is not always palpable; while it must be confessed, that our parties are not universally so consistent with themselves as to enable us to write their distinctive creeds in a horn-book.

Yet, on a closer survey, it is found that parties here are very much the same, in their characteristic tendencies and aims, as parties elsewhere. They originate in that human nature, which is the same everywhere (modified by local circumstances only), and they exhibit under the various influences of personal constitution, ambition, interest, &c., the same contrasts of selfishness and virtue, of craft, audacity, genius, falsehood, wisdom and folly. It is true that our differences are not seemingly so fundamental and well-pronounced as those of older nations. We have no contests here as [to] the elementary principles of government. A monarchist is perhaps not to be found from the St. Lawrence to the Rio Grande, any more than a rhinoceros or lammergeyer. We are all republicans; we all believe in the supremacy of the people; and our convictions, as to the general nature and sphere of legislation, are as uniform as if they had been produced by a process of mental stereotype.

But within the range prescribed by this more general unanimity, there has been ample room and verge enough, for the evolution of many heated and distempered antagonisms. We have agreed that our governments should be republican, but as to what functions they should exercise, and what they should leave to the people, we have not always agreed; we have agreed that the separate States should be sovereign and independent, but to what extent they might carry that sovereignty and independence we have not agreed; we have agreed that the benefits of the federal union should be, from time to time, extended to new territories, but on what terms they should be extended, we have not agreed; we have agreed to keep aloof from the domestic affairs of other nations, but as to the details of foreign policy inside of this salutary rule, we have not agreed. There has been among us always, therefore, radical dissents and oppositions. We have had parties of many stripes and calibres,—some which favored, and some which opposed a large concentration of power in the federal government; some which have proposed to accomplish their social objects by legislative and others by voluntary action; some which have desired to restrict the elective franchise, and others to extend it; some which have opposed the acquisition of more territory, and others willing to run the risk of war for its sake; some which have aimed at the destruction of the Union, and others eager to sacrifice honor and liberty itself, to the preservation of the Union. In short, there has been an endless scope for parties.

It is a common saying, we know, that there can be but two parties in any nation,—the movement and the stationary parties,—and this is true as a philosophical generalisation, deduced from the changes of a certain period of time, but it is not true always as a contemporary and actual fact. In the long run, of course, all parties will be found to have advanced or retarded the progress of society, but in the immediate and present aspect of things, parties are more than two, are half a dozen at least, and they never lose their distinctions. Look where we will, provided free political discussion is allowed, and we shall find at least, to use the French mode of marking their relations, a centre, a right, a left, a right centre, and a left centre, besides a miscellaneous herd of eccentrics, all representing some contrast or gradation of opinion. In France, for instance, before France was reduced by the bayonet to a single man, there were the several branches of the legitimists, the Napoleonites, the republicans, the mountain, and the socialists; and in Great Britain, there are the tories, the whigs, the radicals, the chartists, &c. In the same way, in this country, we possess the several combinations to which we referred in the opening paragraph; and though their differences as we have said are not so marked, as those which prevail between the legitimists and the republicans of Europe, they are still as we shall see, valid, positive and important.

The earliest parties known to our history were those of the colonial times, when the grand debate as to the rights of the colonies was getting under way, and all men took sides, either as whigs or tories. They had imported their distinctive names, and to some extent their distinctive principles, from the mother country, from the iron times of Cromwell and the Puritans; but, in the progress of the controversy, as it often happens, they were led upon wholly new and vastly broader grounds of dispute than they had at first dreamed. The little squabble as to the limits and reaches of the imperial jurisdiction expanded into a war for national existence, nay, for the rights of humanity; and what was at the outset a violent talk only about stamp duties, and taxes on tea—mean and trivial even in its superficial aspects—concealed the noblest political theories, the sublimest political experiments, that had yet been recorded in the annals of our race. The whigs of the revolution, in crushing the tories of that day, touched the secret spring of a new creation. They gave to the world a new idea,—the American idea,—the conception of a state, founded upon the inherent freedom and dignity of the individual man. It seemed as if, gathering out of the ages all the aspirations of great and noble souls, all the yearnings of oppressed peoples, they had concentrated them into one grand act of emancipation. They actualised the dreams of Time, and in the latest age of the world, and on a new continent, introduced, as they fondly supposed, that reign of heavenly justice which the primitive golden ages had faintly foreshadowed, which patriots had so long struggled and sighed for in vain, which the political martyrs of every clime had welcomed only in beatific vision.

It was this patriot party of the revolution which gave the inspiration and impulse to the nation, which formed its character and sentiment, and erected the standard of opinion, destined, for some years, at least, to be the guide of all movements. It fused the national mind by the warmth of its convictions, or rather by the fiery earnestness with which it fought its way to success, into that single thought of democratic freedom, which has been the ground and substance of our national unity. The medley of settlers, chance-wafted hitherward, from the several corners of Europe, like seeds borne by the winds, were nourished by it into an organic whole, and have since been retained by its original influences, under all diversities of constitution, cli-

mate, and interest, in the coherence and uniformity of a national being. We are therefore infinitely indebted to our fathers, who were so not merely after the flesh, but after the spirit, who generated our minds as well as our bodies, and whose sublime thought of a free state, an inspiration greater than their knowledge, has been the fruitful germ of our best inward and outward life. No other people have had so grand a national origin, for we were born in a disinterested war for rights, and not for territory, and under the stimulus of an idea, which still transcends the highest practical achievements of our race.

It has been the greatness, the predominance, the profound inherency of this original American idea, which, forcing general conviction, has produced the uniformity of our later parties (to which we have alluded), and confined their divisions to transient or trivial and personal differences. But there is also another cause for that uniformity, in the fact that as societies advance in the career of civilization, their political divisions are less marked, but more subtle in principle, and less gross, but more indirect in the display of animosity and feeling. The rival chiefs of two factions of savages, who quarrel as to which shall eat the other, settle the matter with a blow of the tomahawk; but in a more refined community, the entire population may get at loggerheads, over the construction of a phrase in some dubious document, which they determine by vociferous clamours at a public meeting, or in able leading articles. One is sometimes amused, therefore, when a foreigner in the United States, an Englishman, for instance, complacently remarks that we have no great parties, no profound, radical, comprehensive questions, about which we may beat out each other's brains. "You have no question of church and state," he says; "no immense projects for parliamentary reform; no tremendous interests hanging upon some old law; no widely separated and powerful classes to be plunged into fierce and terrific conflicts. All that you quarrel about is summed up in the per centage of a tariff, the building of a road, or the possession of a few offices." In saying this, John imagines that he has reduced us to a lilliputian insignificance and littleness, especially by the side of his obese and ponderous magnitude. But we answer him, that those "great questions," about which he and his fellows, all the world over, are pummelling each other, or, at least, tearing their passions to tatters, were settled for us before we were born, and that we esteem it a happiness and glory to have got rid of them, even though they have left us little more to quarrel about than the cut of a neighbor's coat or the shape of his nose. We also hint to him, further, that the progress of nations, as we conceive it, consists in the gradual decay of political, and the growth of social questions, or, in other words, in the simplification and reduction of the machinery of government, with which politics has chiefly to do, and the consequent extinction of politicians, who become more and more a pernicious class, with, at the same time, a continuous aggrandizement of society itself, of its industry, its arts, its local improvements, and its freedom, as well as order. We are rather glad, then, on the whole, that our politics do not possess in foreign estimation, the importance, the dignity, and the vital sensibility, of those of other nations, and that our politicians, for the most part, are puny and contemptible specimens as statesmen. But we shall show in the sequel that we have our own difficulties nevertheless, some of them vital enough, and requiring for their adjustment the largest capacities and noblest impulses of great minds.

The most natural and the most permanent of our past political divisions have arisen out of the peculiar structure of the federal government, the nature and extent of its jurisdiction, and its relations to the States. As soon as the federal Constitution went into effect, the differences which had almost defeated its ratification before the people—the counteracting centripetal and centrifugal forces as we may call them—were developed into strong and positive party hostilities. The federalists and the anti-federalists took possession of the political field, and the noise of their conflicts sounded through many years, giving a sting not only to the debates of the Senate House, but embittering the intercourse of domestic life, and leaving deep scars of prejudice on the reputations of eminent men, as well as in the minds of their descendants. The mere disputes as to the authority of the general government might not, perhaps, have led to such earnest and envenomed battles, at the outset, if they had not been complicated, especially under the leadership of Jefferson and Hamilton, with the profounder questions of individual rights just then agitating the Old World, with an intensity of feeling which amounted to frenzy. Hamilton, a man of talent, bred in camps, distrustful of the masses, and admirer of the British constitution, and accustomed to rule, was disposed to rely upon the strong arm in government, and may be regarded as the representative of the sentiment of LAW; while Jefferson, on the other hand, a man of genius, self-confident, generous, sanguine, tolerant of theories, an acolyte, if not a teacher, of the French school of manners and thought, leaned to the spontaneous action of the people, and was

the representative of Liberty. Thus, the party of State rights and the party of liberty came to be identified, and took the name, after a time, of the democratic Republican party, while federalism, or the doctrine of a strong central government, jumped in naturally with the doctrine of law and order. There was a double pressure of tendencies separating the two parties, and intensifying their hatreds, and, in the exacerbations of the times, inducing them to accuse each other respectively of tyranny and licentiousness. A federalist, in the opinions of the republicans of those days, was only a monarchist in disguise, watching his opportunity to strangle the infant liberties of his country in the cradle, and to restore the emancipated colonies to their dependence upon Great Britain, while the federalist retorted the generous imputation of his adversary, by calling him a jacobin, a scoundrel and a demagogue, eager to uproot the foundations of order, and let loose the lees and scum of French infidelity and French immorality upon society. We, at this day, looking through the serener atmosphere of history, know that they were both mistaken in their extreme opinions, and that they were both good patriots after all, necessary to each other, as it now appears, in tempering the dangerous excesses which might have followed the unchecked predominance of either, and in giving a more uniform and stable action to our untried political system. But we can not conceal the deep significance of the contest in which they were engaged.

In all the subsequent changes of parties, the distinction of federalist and anti-federalist has been maintained, in theory at least, and sometimes in name, if not so rigidly in practice. It is a distinction that will only pass away with the final establishment of the truth, though it may often be obscured in the fluctuating movements of politics. During the war of 1812–15, the Federalists, as they were termed, were the most vigorous opponents of the use of power by the general government, and their most offensive acts, the proceedings of the Hartford Convention, were nothing worse than an attempt, as it was deemed, to arrest and restrain the encroachments of the central authority upon the rights and interests of the separate States; whilst, on the other hand, the most enormous exercise of that authority—the acquisition of Louisiana by Jefferson—the suppression of South Carolina nullification by Jackson—the annexation of Texas by Tyler—have been resorted to by the leaders of the so-called democratic or anti-federalist party. Indeed, so little consistency has been exhibited by parties in this respect, that it has been observed, that in general, whatever party was in possession of the federal government was disposed to push the use of its functions to the utmost practicable verge, while the party out of power has opposed this use, and assumed the virtue of continence. Under the administration of Jackson, when the struggle with the National Bank arose, the lines of demarcation between the principles of the federalists and anti-federalists were once more somewhat strictly drawn, and the shibboleths and rallying cries of that day have continued to be used by the politicians, for the most part impertinently, up to the present time. In the administrations of the States, too, there has been an undeniable line drawn, a gulf fixed, as we may say, between the friends of a strong and centralized government and the friends of social and popular freedom, but we may add, that as no party is now entitled to a monopoly of either class, this distinction has subsided. The feelings and convictions in which it originated have not passed away, and they will not speedily pass away, but there has been a lull in the public mind, in respect to them, partly produced by the decided gravitation of opinion to the democratic theory both of Federal and State government, and partly by the emergence of new grounds of conflict. The debris of former convulsions is all that the older parties have left us.

An anomaly in the social system of some of the States, however, not supposed to be so pregnant with consequences, as it has since proved, when the Federal Union was formed, has been developed into a chief cause of the complication of parties, and the principal incentive and danger of our more modern contests.

The primary idea of our institutions was, as we have seen, that of a free Democratic Republic. The liberty and equality of the people was the animating spirit of our revolution, and the inspiring genius of the constitutional structure to which it gave rise. But among the States, which form the elements of the confederacy, there are some not strictly democratic, and scarcely republican. They are aristocracies or oligarchies, built upon a diversity of races. Their political and social privileges are confined to a class, while all the rest of their inhabitants are slaves. The consequence has been a growing divergency, though it was not always apparent or even suspected, between the convictions, the interests and the tendencies of one half the Union, which was eminently free and democratic, and those of the other half, which was slave-holding and aristocratic. The reasons why this difference was not so strongly felt at the outset, were, because the slaves were few, and the great and good men who formed the Union, and helped to knit and bind together its primitive filaments, were almost unanimous in the sentiment that the system of bondage in which these were held would be only temporary. Like a growing youth in the flush and impulse of his formative period, they were scarcely conscious of the cancer lurking in the blood. But the vice, contrary to their expectations, was nurtured into strength, the sentiment in regard to it has changed, it has become interwoven with vast and intricate interests, and it is now sustained by certain political and philosophical convictions, so that the question of slavery is the controlling question in our politics.

Another reason why the radical vices of the federal relation were not more speedily extruded and discovered, was this; The slave-holders have been, for the most part, in alliance with the democratic or popular party. Devoted sticklers for equality among themselves, fierce lovers of their own liberties, only secured from the molestation of others by a rigid maintenance of the internal independence of the separate States, they have naturally sympathized with the party which appeared to be most devoted to these ends. Their sentiment of personal independence and right was the same sentiment which animates the masses of the free States in their opposition to the encroachments of power, and their necessity for security dictated the same doctrine of State-rights, to which the people adhered in their instinct for local self-government. Thus, the democratic party of the north, and the State-rights' party of the south, have formed what was called the great Republican party of the Union. The model democrats of the nation, Jefferson, who wrote the Declaration of Independence, Madison, who was one of the ablest expounders of the Constitution, Macon, who tolerated no injustice in legislation, were slave-holders in their local spheres; while the popular party of the north, clamoring against the pretensions of law and privilege for a larger liberty, were still, strange to say, their adherents and friends.

It was an alliance, however, which in the very nature of its components, could not endure for ever. An aristocracy is compelled by the exigencies of its position, to become defiant, aggressive, and prone to rule; while a democracy, on the other hand, is expansive, progressive, and no less apt to take the command. A league between them may be maintained, so long as they have certain objects in common,—an enemy to repulse, or a conquest to achieve,—but when these common objects are attained, their radical incompatibility will begin to be developed. It is impossible for men who sincerely believe in the equal rights of men, to coalesce permanently with others whose practice is an habitual invasion of those rights; it is impossible for an order of society, founded upon the most unlimited freedom of labor, to co-exist long in intimate relations with a society founded upon bond or forced labor; and it is no less impossible for political leaders, the breath of whose nostrils is popular emancipation and progress, to combine with leaders whose life is an utter denial of emancipation and progress. We have seen, consequently, that so long as the South and the North, in the earlier periods of national development, looked to the same ends,—to certain general organizing purposes,—to a strict construction of the Constitution, a denial of the schemes for enlarging the federal power—the independence of the States,—they have been able to act together, and the happiest results have been promoted by that unity; but when their mutual solicitude for these ends is outgrown—when in the progress of empire, the question arises, whether the social system of the one or the other shall prevail, to the exclusion, which is unavoidable, of its opponent; their friendship grows sultry, and a strenuous grapple and fight imminent.

If we were called upon then to describe the political parties of this nation, as they are, or as they have been gradually formed, by its developing circumstances, we should say that they were 1st. The Pro-slavery, unjustly called the Southern party, which is the propagandist of slavery. 2d. The Democrats, divided into the traditional or routine democrats, who masquerade in the faded wardrobe of democracy, but care more for office than principle, and the real democrats who still retain the inspirations of the Jefferson school. 3d. The Whigs, who are the legitimate depositories of federal principles crossed and improved by modern liberalism. 4th. The Fire-eaters, who seem to be opposed to the union of the Northern and Southern States under any circumstances, and 5th. The Abolitionists, who are rather a moral than a political combination, though a large branch of them are not opposed to decided political action. These we shall notice briefly in the reverse order in which they are named.

The Abolitionists and the Fire-eaters, representing the extremes of northern and southern feeling, have had no little influence on public opinion, but hardly any as yet in the direct action of the government. In eloquence, earnestness, and, we suspect, integrity of purpose, they are superior to the other parties (the abolitionists in particular, absorbing some of the finest ability of the country, oratorical and literary, and a great deal of the noblest aspiration), but they are both too extravagant in opinion, and too violent in procedure, to conciliate a large and effective alliance. Their denunciations of the Union, proceeding from contrary views of its effects,

the one condemning it because it is supposed to sanction, and the other, because it is supposed to interfere with slavery, neutralize each other and lead more tranquil minds,—minds whose brains are not boiling in their skulls to a conviction that they are both alike wrong. The federal Constitution does not recognise the existence of slavery as such, at all, and in no form except indirectly, nor does it, on the other hand, confer upon the government any authority for meddling with it, treating the subject wisely as a matter of exclusive state jurisdiction; yet the spirit and letter of that instrument are alike instinct with freedom, and rightly interpreted, set up an insuperable barrier against the extension of any form of servitude. The malice of its enemies finds its food, not in the legitimate operations of the organic law, as the framers of it intended it to operate, but in those deviations which the craft of politicians has superinduced upon its action, in those warpings and torturings of its structure, by which it has been made to cover selfish and flagitious local designs. It would be well, therefore, if some of the anathemas pronounced upon our factions of an extreme tincture and habit, upon the disunionists of either wing, should be occasionally levelled at those more formidable antagonists of our peace, the politicians to whose unjust and reckless schemes we owe nearly all these violent reactions.

It is no offence to the Whigs, we trust, for indeed it is only repeating the frequent avowals of their own leading exponents to say, that as a party they are pretty much defunct. Whatever uses their organization may have subserved in the course of our political history, and nobody will deny them some merits however splendid the talent by which their long but losing struggle has been illustrated, from the day in which their policy was inaugurated by Hamilton, until that in which its funeral discourse was uttered in "a fine rich brogue," by General Scott, it has never succeeded in becoming, for more than a year or two at a time, a predominant party. It has been able, on occasions, to carry its principles into effect, but not to the satisfaction of a permanent majority. Its distinguishing measures have been, on the other hand, repeatedly and unequivocally condemned. Not the most sanguine adherent can now hope to see them revived. The questions of a National Bank, of a Protective Tariff, of Internal Improvements, of the Distribution of the Public Lands, are adjudicated questions; no court exists wherein to bring an appeal; and the wisest thing for those who have been worsted in the controversy, is to do what the most of them have done—submit. Their once great and accomplished leaders sleep in honourable graves; no exigencies of state will ever again awaken the solemn eloquence of Webster, nor the clarion voice of Clay ever again summon his lieges to the battle. The masters are dead and their followers are dispersed or at feud; or should they rally again, it can only be, under other names and for deeper and nobler objects. A remnant of the camp of former times, a forlorn hope with Millard Fillmore as the drum-major, may strive to keep the old organism alive; but it is clear, in the present aspect of affairs, that it cannot possess more than a semi-vitality, useless for good and painful to behold. We do not say that the theory of politics which has hitherto animated the Whigs, is extinct, that Americans will no more be dazzled by visions of strong and splendid governments, nor seek to effect by unitary legislation what others hope to accomplish by voluntary effort; on the contrary, this tendency is perhaps as strong now as ever it was; but what we assert is, that the particular measures for which the whigs have been banded together, are obsolete, and the party, as a party, quite short of wind.

The Democrats of the purer stamp, the real Democrats as we have called them, are like the Whigs, in a state of comparative dissolution; or rather, they are scattered through their party at large, and elsewhere, as leaven through meal, without having an effective control in it, or perhaps connection. They may be described as democrats who still abide by the original principles of democracy, who represent the popular instincts, who cling to living ideas of justice, and equal rights and progress, and who refuse to follow their fellows in a *pell-mell* abandonment of themselves to the seductions of the slave holders. They are not few in number, as we are inclined to think, either at the north or the south, comprising, as we fain hope, a majority of the young men of the nation, yet uncorrupted by official contacts, as well as possessing the sympathies of many among parties which go by another name; but, having no separate organization anywhere, they are sadly overborne by the practised managers of the old organizations, who wield the machinery of party action, and consequently of power. In their external or immediate pretensions they are not formidable, but in the might of their sentiments they have already captured the future. A steady continuance in integrity, a deaf ear turned to the charmings of the adders of office, an eagerness to consult, amid all the shiftings of policy, the fresh impulses of the honest young heart of the nation, will, ere long, gather about them the intellect, the virtue, and the popular instinct of right, which are the redeeming elements of states.

The other class of Democrats, whom we denominate the official or machine-democrats, because they move and talk as they are wound up, mean as they appear, yet constitute, in reality, a distinct and powerful body in the state. It is not a new remark, we believe, that successful parties suck in and collect about them large squads of speculating politicians, who care nothing for truth or righteousness, while they have a ravenous appetite for distinction and provender. They are not precisely camp-followers, because they sometimes fight in the lines, but their interest in the contest is determined rather by the prospect of booty than by any convictions they may be imagined to entertain. Like Bunyan's By-ends, who followed Religion for the silver slippers she wore, they are patriots because it is profitable to be patriots. In other words, they are democrats because the democrats are generally in the ascendant, which means, in office. Sometimes they slip round to the whigs, when the whigs have a sure look for success; but they find it safer, in the long run, to be of the other side. No men more noisy than they in shouting the usual rallying cries, none more glib in the common-places of electioneering, and none so apparently earnest and sincere. But at heart they are among the greediest and shabbiest of scoundrels. It is upon their shoulders that incompetent and bad men are borne to places of high trust, and from them that the Prætorian guards of republics are selected in the hour of their eclipse and hastening decay.

This class of democrats (their innate flunkeyism would make them monarchists or satraps in other latitudes) flourish the best in those calm times when no great controversy agitates the nation, and no important emergency awakens strong and burning passions. In crises which call for lofty ambitions and abilities, they are of no use; in fact, they are shrivelled and consumed by the heat of them, and slink out of the way till the fiery storm is past. But in periods of comparative public indifference or reaction, when there are few who care to watch them, they swarm like maggots in a carrion. As the reins of power at those times are apt to fall into the hands of little men—of a Tyler or Pierce, for instance—the golden hour for narrow intellects and base hearts has arrived. The art of administration at once degenerates into mere trickery or management. Toads crawl into the seats of the eagles. Public policy fluctuates between the awkwardness of conscious incompetence and the blustering arrogance of bullyism. The possession of office becomes a badge, either of imbecility, or cunning, or insolence. It is won by services that elsewhere would warrant a halter, and it is conferred, not as the meed of patriotic deserts, but as the wages of supple and mercenary services. They who dispense patronage, do so in the conviction of Walpole, that every man has his price, and they who receive it, take it with a full knowledge that the stamp of venality is on every token of silver. Superiors in place are not superiors in merit, only superiors in craft and recklessness; while inferiors don the gilt lace and plush of their official varletism without a blush on their cheeks, or a sense of shame at their hearts. Government, in short, is converted into a vast conspiracy of placemen, managed by the adroiter villains of the set, controlling elections, dictating legislation, defeating reforms, and infusing gradually its own menial and muck-worm spirit into the very body of the community. The masses even, under the paralysis of such a domination, seem to be rendered insensible to the usual influences of honor and virtuous principle; are deadened almost to the heroic examples of their fathers; lose the inspiriting traditions of an earlier greatness and grandeur of conduct; and virtually, if not actually, sink into slaves. Then, schemers of wrong riot in the impunity of licence, and projects of gigantic wickedness are broached, which, a few years before, would have caused a shiver of indignation to run like a gathering earthquake through the whole land. But for a completer picture, a *tableau vivant* of the degradations of functionarism, of the sordure and meanness of stipendiary democracy,—the worst form of official corruption, since the best wine makes the sourest vinegar—let us say, in the words of Wren's epitaph, CIRCUMSPICE!

The Pro-Slavery Party, sometimes called the Southern Party, we are unwilling to speak of by this name, because we carefully distinguish between its southern members, who are the propagandists of slavery, and those gentlemen of the south who simply wish their peculiar domestic system to be let alone; while we do not distinguish between them and their northern coadjutors,—dough-faces are they hight,—who are their superserviceable instruments. The first distinction we make, because we know that there are large numbers of intelligent and conscientious people at the south, who do not believe that slavery is a good or a finality; on the contrary, who feel that it is a burden at best, and a sad and dreadful inheritance; who are anxious to manage it wisely, with a view to its ultimate extinction; and, consequently, would dread to see it strengthened or extended, looking with hope and Christian prayer to the day when the combined influences of modern Industrialism, and Democracy, and Christianity, shall have relieved them of their painful weight of responsibility. But we do not make the second distinction, because the most efficient, and by far the most despicable, branch of the Pro-Slavery Party, is that which, educated at the north, under all the genial inspirations of a free condition of existence, and without the necessity of an embarrassing involvement, still voluntarily casts itself at the feet of Slavery, to eat the dirt of its footmarks, and lick the sores on its limbs. For the first class of slaveholders, we

cherish not only a profound sympathy, but a genuine admiration and esteem; we have friends among them whose excellencies of character are themes for meditation and gratitude; and to the propagators of the system, even, we can attribute an entire honesty of purpose, though a mistaken one; but, for its cringing and adulatory northern sycophants we have no feeling but one of unmitigated pity and contempt. Could they be transferred, for a time, to the experience of the poor creatures whose fetters they help to bind, the most generous mind could hardly regard the change as less than a just and happy retribution.

The Pro-Slavery party, which grew mainly out of the old republican or democratic party, and which has never even taken a distinct name, has been the successful party of our history. It has achieved a more signal and longer ascendency than any other party, and it has done it, not by superior ability nor a more illustrious virtue, but by dint of its tact, and a compact and persistent determination. Its leaders, perceiving at an early day that they should play a losing game, if they attempted to stand alone, trusting to the ordinary means of success,—to the natural supremacy of talent, to the growth of numbers, and to the rectitude of their cause,—hit upon the available expedient of identifying themselves with the popular party of the North, and, then having accomplished that, of gradually directing that party to the defence and spread of their peculiar doctrines. Not satisfied with the concession, which every intelligent and judicious northerner was then glad to make, that slavery was a system exclusively within the control of the States, it first insinuated and then insisted that slavery was not to be discussed at all at the North, because a moral interference was quite as intolerable they said, as a direct political interference. This pretension, which was just the same as if Russia or Turkey should insist that the principles of absolutism should not be discussed in the United States, because Russia and Turkey had commercial treaties with the United States, yet found merchants sordid enough to instigate mobs against those who questioned it, and politicians wicked enough to entrench it behind the laws. Yet the taboo of sanctity did not stop there, but was drawn around regions in which all the states were clearly and equally interested,—as the District of Columbia and the public lands, while the Post Office, common to all, was forbidden to carry "incendiary documents," as every argument or appeal against the system was called, and petitions to Congress referring in the remotest manner to it, were treated with contumely and the utmost disdain. It was reserved, however, for an eminent leader of the South, for Mr. J. C. Calhoun, while acting as Secretary of State, to engage in an official defence of it before the tribunal of the world, and to disgrace the nation (we do not use too strong a term) by representing the Federal Republic as the apologist and defender of the most mean and most offensive species of despotism.

This point once reached, it was easy to take a bolder stand, and to clamor with all the vehemence of partizan heat, for the introduction of slavery into those new and virgin territories, which Providence had opened on our western borders, as we had fondly hoped, for the reception of the outcast republicans of Europe, and for a new and grander display of the beneficent influence of republicanism. And this impudent claim,—a claim which had no validity in law nor sanction in humanity,—the pretence that a local institution, existing entirely by municipal usage, and without an iota of validity beyond that,—should override all considerations of justice and policy under a threat of civil war, in case of its disallowance—was not too much (not to put too fine a point on it, as Mr. Snagsby says in Bleak House) for the forbearance of the North, in its ardent devotion to peace and the Union! Ah! how one submission begets another, until the chains of a crushing servitude are riveted around the necks of the victim! The Southern party thus triumphing in the territories, demanded in the next place that the free States should be made a hunting ground for slaves, that every man of the North should be compelled by law to do what no gentleman of the South would do for himself, or could be, under any circumstances, forced to do for others, *i.e.,* put himself on a level with blood hounds, and become a slave catcher, and the law was passed! Wresting the power from the States, that it might be exercised by Congress, which was not authorised to exercise it, it was passed; creating tribunals of justice which Congress was not authorised to create, rejecting from its provisions the most sacred rights of trial by jury and habeas corpus, this law was passed; imposing unusual and offensive penalties upon all who should refuse to take part in its execution, and bribing the officers appointed to administer it by offers of higher wages in the case of a decision adverse to the poor fugitive: this odious and disgraceful law was recorded on the statute books of the "Model Republic," in the central, the culminating year of the nineteenth century. Its passage, however, was not the worst feature of the transaction; the craven acceptance vouchsafed it by the pulpits and the commercial circles; the pliant ease with which the North bent to the insult, was the significant fact in the proceeding, which more than all others covered many an honest face with shame.

It is proper to say that one consideration prevailed in inducing this ready humiliation: the hope of removing the question from the sphere of political agitation. We are bound to believe, in justice to human nature, that the many who welcomed the compromises of 1850,

did so in the sincerest conviction that they would put an end to the difficulties between the North and South; and we must also confess that it seemed, for a time, as if that result were about to be effected. The national conventions of both the great parties acquiesced in the settlement; a President was chosen whose inaugural address was little more than a long proclamation of intended fidelity to it; and Congress came together and acted in a more fraternal spirit than had been manifested for years. Alas! the uncertainty of mortal expectations! In the midst of the apparent quietude, a bill, all bristling with outrages and dangers, is sprung upon the country. We mean, of course, the bill for the organization of Nebraska and Kansas territories, whose sole object was to repeal the solemn prohibition, erected thirty years ago, against the spread of slavery into those regions. At a time when there was not a citizen legitimately within those territories—when no part of the nation, save a few intriguers, was dreaming of such a measure; when not a single state, nay, not a single individual, had called for it—in the face of the most strenuous opposition from North and West, this bill was suddenly presented to a Congress, not elected in reference to it, and forced to a passage by all the tyrannical arts known to legislation, and all the sinister influences within the reach of an unscrupulous Executive. A grosser violation of all the requirements of honor—of all the safeguards and guarantees of republicanism—was seldom perpetrated.

This we shall show: and in the first place, let us remark, that the pretence by which the act was carried was fraudulent: a falsehood on the face of it, and designed only as a popular catch for the unreflecting. It purported to give the right of self-government to the people of the territories; but it did no such thing. It denied that right in the most important particulars, and mystified it so in others as to render it worthless. Nominally conceding the "non-intervention" of Congress in the local affairs of the territories, it yet intervenes in every form in which intervention is possible. It imposes the Governor and all other officers upon them; it prescribes the most unheard-of oaths to the people; it restricts the suffrage to actual citizens; it places in the hands of the President and his agents the power to mould the future character of the community; and it authorizes no legislation which is not subject, directly or indirectly, to the control of the federal government. The only non-intervention which it establishes is the permission to introduce slavery into a district where it was before forbidden, and the transfer of legislative control, hitherto exercised by the representatives of the whole people, to a body of judges appointed by the executive. It had no other end, from the beginning, and in that end it has succeeded.

Besides, this claim of absolute sovereignty for the people of the territories, is at war with our whole policy from the beginning, as well as with the most vital principles of just government. It was never contemplated by the framers of the Constitution, nor by the people of the states who ratified it, that the territories acquired under it, should instantly be placed upon a level with the original states. On the contrary, they were to be held in a state of pupilage, if we so express it, under the control of Congress, until they should have acquired population and stability enough to manage their affairs for themselves. The idea of "Squatter sovereignty," that a few accidental first-comers should determine the institutions of the future state, for all time, was one of the most offensive that could be uttered, and was unanimously condemned by the great statesmen of both the North and South. It was held, that if the whole people paid the expense of territorial acquisitions–whether by money or blood–if they were taxed for the support of their provisional governments; if they were liable for their defense against the aggressions of the bordering savages–then the whole people had also some right to a voice in their management. Taxation and representation must go together, said then Democracy; and this principle, we attest, is an older and better one than the miserable subterfuge of "non-intervention," by which the demagogues of Congress hope to supersede it. "Non-intervention!" forsooth, which means that the people of the states shall bear all the burdens of the territories, but have no power to protect them from the passage of injurious and infamous laws. It means that the parent must be responsible for all the debts and deeds of his child, and yet be divested of all the authority of a parent. It means, in short, that the perpetrators of the iniquity wanted some delusive pretext, and that "non-intervention," with all its absurdities, was the best they could find.

Again: this bill, in the method of its passage, nullified another fundamental principle of representative government, namely, that a representative is but the mouthpiece and organ of his constituents. Does anybody believe that, if the proposal to repeal the Missouri Compromise had been submitted to a direct vote of the people, that it would have commanded anywhere, north of Mason's and Dixon's line, a single majority in any district or township in any state? Was there a solitary petition for it sent in from either North or South? Was a single member of Congress, who voted for it, elected, with a view to such a question? Were not the tables of both Senate and House laden with remonstrances against it, forwarded not by politicians, nor enthusiasts, but by the most sober and conservative citizens? Did its friends, when challenged to do so, dare to postpone action upon it, for another year, until the people should be allowed to pass upon it? Was it suffered to take its

regular course in the progress of legislation? No!–no!–no! And yet, we are told, that ours is a representative government! A number of men, delegated for particular purposes to Washington, possessing not a particle of authority beyond that conferred upon them by the people, neglect the objects for which they were chosen, and proceed to accomplish other objects, which are not only not wished by their constituents, but are an outrage upon their sincerest and deepest convictions. Can we call them representatives? or, are they not rather usurpers, recreants, oligarchs, despots? What use is there in popular elections, when the persons chosen fancy themselves immediately exempted from all responsibility, and go on to act in the most independent and arbitrary manner? It is true, they may be dismissed afterwards for their criminal breach of trust, as the barn-door may be locked after the horse is stolen, but then the mischief is already done. We may discharge a clerk who robs the till, but will that restore us our money? We may punish a seducer when he is caught, but is that a recompense to our violated honor? Not at all. What we want in legislation, as in other trusts, are honest fiduciaries: men who will perform their duties according to our wishes, and not in pursuance of their own selfish objects; men who do not require to be watched at every step, and whose fidelity does not depend alone upon our ulterior privilege of breaking them when they have done wrong. A Congress of such men would be little better than an assemblage of cheats, and, for our parts, we should greatly prefer the rule of Nicholas or Louis Napoleon, to their heterogeneous frauds and oppressions. Now, there was hardly a man, who voted for the Nebraska Bill, who did not know that he was betraying the will of his constituents, and who should not be branded as utterly unworthy of confidence and support. He has done his share towards the conversion of our fair fabric of free government into a machine of office-holding despotism, and the only recourse that is left us, to mark his treachery, is to discharge him forever from every participation in its councils. He has wantonly provoked the reward, and let him have it, to his heart's content.

An open disregard of the will of the constituency is always a grave offence in a popular government, but how flagrant and unpardonable is it, when it is committed in furtherance of measures which look to the overthrow of popular liberty? Had the Nebraska bill been comparatively unexceptionable, had it contemplated some great and useful improvement or reform, there would even then have existed no excuse for the haste, the violence, and the audacity with which it was pressed to a vote; but when we reflect that its principal object was, to repeal a salutary ordinance against the diffusion of a pestilent and lamentable evil, we search dictionaries in vain for words to express our feeling of the magnitude and malignity of the wrong. For nearly half a century those fertile regions of the West had rejoiced in their prospective exemption from the outrages of slavery. The American, and the foreigner even, who rode over them, felt his heart dilate as he beheld in their rich fields, the future homes of an advancing and splendid civilization. He could already hear in the rustle of the grasses the hum of a prosperous industry; he saw magnificent cities rise on the borders of the streams, and pleasant villages dot the hills and a flourishing commerce whiten the ripples of the lakes; the laugh of happy children came up to him from the corn-fields, and as the glow of the evening sun tinged the distant plains, a radiant and kindling vision floated upon its beams, of myriads of men, escaped from the tyrannies of the old world, and gathered there in worshipping circles, to pour out their grateful hearts to God, for a redeemed and teeming earth. But, woe unto us now, this beautiful region, compared with which the largest principalities of Europe are but pin-folds, nay, compared with which the most powerful existing empires are of trivial extent, is opened to the blight, the hopelessness, the desolation of a form of society, which can never advance beyond a semi-barbarism, or whose highest achievement is a purchase of the wealth and freedom of one race, by the eternal subjection of another. Our vision of peaceful groups of free labourers is changed into the contemplation of black gangs of slaves. A single act of legislation, like Satan, when he entered Paradise, has reversed the destinies of a world. The fields seem to wither at its approach, the waters dry up, threatening clouds obscure the sky; and

"Nature, through all her works, gives signs of woe,
That all is lost."

It has been esteemed the special privilege and glory of this young republic that her future was in her own hands. Born to no inheritance of wrong and sorrow, like the nations of the older continents, and with an existence as fresh and unsullied as the fame of a ripening maiden, it was supposed that she might see the states which were soon to become the children of her family, growing up about her in prosperity, love and vigor. She could watch over their cradles and keep them from harm; she could nourish them with manly strength; she could form them by her wise and tender solicitude, to a career of exalted worth and greatness. A new page in the history of mankind appeared to be opened—a page unblotted by the blood-stains of tyranny, which mark the rubrics of the past, and destined to be written over only by the records of an ever-maturing nobleness and grandeur. This was the ambition of her fathers—of those who laid the beams of her habitation deep in the principles of virtuous freedom, and bequeathed to her the heroic precedent of single-hearted devotion to justice and right. But, alas, how are their hopes prostrated! Ere the first half century of her youth is passed, she finds herself not engaged in a hand-to-hand struggle for the preservation of her paternal acres, her unshorn and boundless prairies, from slavery, but yielding them almost without reluctance to the fatal blight. When Niobe saw her fair sons and daughters falling under the swift darts of the angry gods, she wept herself to stone, but the genius of America, whom it is the pride of her sculptors to represent as wearing the Phrygian cap of liberty on her brow, and trampling upon broken chains with her feet, and bearing aloft the ægis of eternal justice—surrenders her children, without remorse, to death. She belies her symbols, she suppresses her inspirations; she opens the gates of the coming centuries to the advent of a remediless bondage.

We are aware, it is often said, that slavery cannot be carried into the territories recently organized,—that their soil and climate are not adapted to its support, and that the sole aim, in removing the restriction of the Missouri compromise, is to erase a distinction which the South regards as dishonoring, and unjust. It has however, been sufficiently answered to this, that slavery thrives in Missouri, which is between nearly the same parallels of latitude, that Illinois, similarly situated, was only saved from it by a protracted and earnest struggle, and Indiana only by the immortal ordinance of 1787. But it is useless to adduce precedents and analogies in the face of current facts. The moment in which we write witnesses the proceedings of assemblages convened to keep free-emigration out of these territories by force of arms, if need be. Already slave holders are on their way to establish themselves and their "institution" there, nay they are already in possession of some of the choicest parts of the soil, and are resolved to maintain it, against all comers. Away, then, with the flimsy pretext that slavery is banned by what Mr. Webster called "the laws of God;" by natural position and circumstances! These we admit, have much to do with the prevalence and strength of the system,—but they are not omnipotent nor final,—they are only accessory, either for it or against it,—and the will of man, his determination to abide by the perennial principles of right, or to surrender them to a temporary and short-sighted spirit of gain,—is what gives character in this respect, to society. Nebraska and Kansas will be slave States if slave-holders go there, and they will be free States if freemen go there, and this is the long and short of the matter; let the soil woo and the climate smile encouragement upon whom it pleases. If the American people do not now—on the instant—rescue those lands to freedom, it is in vain that they will hereafter look to Nature or any other influences for their salvation.

We are, indeed, so far from being persuaded that it is not meant to take slavery into our new territories, that we begin to entertain the conviction, that the propagandists of the South, will not stop even with the territories. It is imputed to them, by authorities entitled to respect, that they cherish a policy which aims, not merely at its establishment within the limits of all the new states, but at the consolidation of it, by foreign conquests. We know that a movement has long been on foot in California for its legalization there; we know that Texas is considered as the nucleus of three or four slave-holding sovereignties; we know that schemes, open and secret, are prosecuted for the acquisition of Cuba, before Cuba shall have emancipated her blacks, as it is alleged she intends to do; we know that eager grasping eyes are set on Mexico; we know, that a Senator has called for the withdrawal of our naval squadron from the coast of Africa, that the slave-trade may be pursued in greater safety; we know that another Senator has broached the recognition of the Dominican republic, with an ulterior view to its annexation; and, we are told, that overtures have been made to Brazil for co-operation in the ultimate establishment of a vast slave-holding confederacy to the South. Of course, some of these designs are still in the gristle; they are not participated in by the judicious men of any section; but the remote conception of them should be monitory and waken us to vigilance. It is one of the dangers as well as glories, of this nation, that its plans are executed with the rapidity of magnetism. A thought is scarcely a thought before it becomes a deed. We scorn delays; we strike and parley afterwards; we actualize the dreams of the old philosophers, and impart to our abstract ideas an instant creative energy. The fact, then, that such comprehensive schemes of pro-slavery expansion, gain admittance into active minds, nay, that they are said to burrow in those of men of eminent station, should beget a timely and jealous watchfulness against their least beginnings. The meanest political swindle, which appeals to the avarice, the prejudice, and the restlessness of large numbers of men, may bear in its belly as foul a progeny of evils as were harboured by the Dragon of Wantley,—and how dangerous then, how pregnant and prolific may be even the germs of plans which embrace immense and complicated interests, and look to the dismemberment and control of empires?

It is one of the arrangements of Providence, by which it tests the reality of our virtue, and punishes the want of it, that we should be so insensible to joint or corporate responsibilities, and yet so intimately connected with the tremendous good or evil consequences of their infringement. We are apt to suppose that the offences of nations against the laws of integrity and right, can be laid to no man's charge, or rather that the criminality of them is dissipated, through the multitude of the offenders, and we do not feel in consenting or contributing to the commission of them that we contract any degree of personal guilt. On the contrary, we undervalue them as offences, and even laugh at the thought of national sins, as of some gigantic abstraction or chimera, the bodiless and impalpable act of one, who, as the adage expresses it, has neither a body to be kicked nor a soul to damn. But, measured by their actual effects, by the awful reach and deathless vitality of their workings, these national iniquities are they which are most to be struggled against, deprecated, dreaded. The evil done by a private individual spreads through a narrow circle only, and does not always live after him; the contagion of its virus may be speedily counteracted, and the worst results of it often are no more than the debasement of other individuals. But the evil done by the public man, which is sanctioned by a corporate authority, which gets embodied into a wicked law, and to that extent becomes the deed of many, either a family, an association, or tribe or a commonwealth, is augmented and multiplied, both in its criminality and its consequences, by the number of wills which may be supposed to have concurred in it, and is proportionably dreadful to contemplate. Its powers of mischief are infinitely increased; the potent enginery of the state is made its instrument; its blasting influences spread, not only through a single community, but over vast races, and travel downward to the remotest time. It may arrest the movements of nations, paralyse the very fertility of the earth, and stun the heart of humanity for ages. The vices of single men are the diseases by which they themselves suffer and are broken, or at most by which they communicate disease to those who come in contact with them, but the vices of states are a malaria which blisters in the air and festers in the soil, and sweeps away millions in horrible agonies to the tomb.

Oh! how much of good, may be done, or of evil prevented, by a little timely legislation. When Tiberius Gracchus, travelling through Italy, to join the army in Spain, saw how the multitude of his countrymen were impoverished and their fields laid desolate by the existence of slavery, he proposed to terminate its evils, and scatter the clouds of disaster that had already begun to gather and brood over the destinies of the Roman commonwealth, by a simple, just and practicable law which should build up, in the midst of the luxurious Roman nobles and their debased slaves, an independent Roman yeomanry. He perceived that the public domain, long usurped by the Patricians, if appropriated to the people, would prevent the concentration of wealth and stimulate the pride and industrial energies of the almost hopeless people; and, had his project been carried, he would have arrested the downward career of his country, and perpetuated for centuries, doubtless, the early Roman virtue, which still seems marvellous to us in its dignity and force. But the designs of Gracchus were defeated by his murder; the Patricians triumphed; the people grew poorer and corrupter, till they were at last fed like paupers from the public granaries; alternate insurrections of slaves swept the state like a whirlwind; despots like Sylla, and demagogues like Marius convulsed society by civil wars; and, finally, the tyrant Cæsar, arose to reap the harvest of previous distractions, and as the only salvation from profounder miseries, to erect on the ruins of the Republic an irresponsible monarchy.

We have dwelt upon the proceedings of the pro-slavery party so long, that we have left ourselves little space for urging upon other parties their duties in the crises. But we will not speak to them as parties. We will say to them as Americans, as freemen, as Christians, that the time has arrived when all divisions and animosities should be laid aside, in order to rescue this great, this beautiful, this glorious land from a hateful domination. As it now is, no man who expresses, however moderately, a free opinion of the slave-system of the south, is allowed to hold any office of profit or trust, under the General Government. No man can be President, no man a foreign minister, no man a tide-waiter, even, or the meanest scullion in the federal kitchen, who has not first bowed down and eaten the dirt of adherence to slavery. Oh! shameless debasement,—that under a Union formed for the establishment of liberty and justice,—under a Union born of the agonies and cemented by the blood of our parents,—a Union whose mission it was to set an example of republican freedom, and commend it to the panting nations of the world,—we freemen of the United States, should be suffocated by politicians into a silent acquiescence with despotism! That we should not dare to utter the words or breathe the aspirations of our fathers, or propagate their principles, on pain of ostracism and political death! just Heaven! into what depths of infamy and insensibility have we fallen!

We repeat, that until the sentiment of slavery is driven back to its original bounds, to the states to which it legitimately belongs, the people of the North are vassals. Yet their emancipation is practicable if not easy. They have only to evince a determination to be free, and they are free. They are to discard all past alliances, to put aside all present fears, to dread no future coalitions, in the single hope of carrying to speedy victory a banner inscribed with these devices:—THE REPEAL OF THE FUGITIVE SLAVE LAW,—THE RESTORATION OF THE MISSOURI COMPROMISE,—NO MORE SLAVE STATES,—NO MORE SLAVE TERRITORIES,—THE HOMESTEAD FOR FREE MEN ON THE PUBLIC LANDS.

—*Putnam's Monthly,* 4 (September 1854): 233–246

* * *

In an undated letter George Sumner, a close friend of Putnam's and the younger brother of Putnam's powerful political ally Charles Sumner, applauds Godwin's "Our Parties and Politics."

Boston, Thursday AM

All hail great Putnam!

–The article on Parties in the Sept. No. is <u>good</u>.– more than this, it is <u>true</u> . . True & pity tis, tis true

Go on, and save the nation.

Ever yours,

Geor Sumner

   —*Manuscripts Division, Department of Rare Books and Special Collections, Princeton University Library. Published with permission of the Princeton University Library.*

* * *

In perhaps the most outrageous letter in the Putnam's Monthly *archive, a potential contributor demands an exaggerated payment for his work.*

To the Editor of Putnam's Magazine

Dear Sir:

I enclose herewith an original poem, called "The Curse of Washington," for which if you are willing to pay me the sum of one thousand dollars, please enclose your check for that amount to me at Louisa Court-House P.O. Va. without unnecessary delay.

Yours etc.–

James Avis Bartley

David's Oak, Louisa, Va. Sep. 14th 1854

   —*Manuscripts Division, Department of Rare Books and Special Collections, Princeton University Library. Published with permission of the Princeton University Library.*

* * *

By the time the publisher's notice for the fourth volume was printed, Putnam had suffered financial problems and was trying to sell his magazine.

CLOSE OF THE FOURTH VOLUME

10 *Park Place, December* 1, 1854.

WITH the present Number, ends the Fourth Volume, and the second year of *Putnam's Monthly.*

In commencing the undertaking, the Publishers were fully aware that in a time of immense intellectual activity, and in a country of great and various literary rivalry, where, in the absence of an international copyright, the choicest works of the best foreign genius are to be had for the taking, the task was not easy, of founding and sustaining a Magazine, at once universal in its sympathies, and national in its tone.

The continued and increasing favor with which the *Monthly* has been received, is the best possible proof that the task has been in some degree fulfilled.

It was certainly impossible, with any just regard to the necessary differences of thought in a country like ours, to avoid all censure in the conduct of the Magazine, because it was not possible, with an equal regard for the liberty of the author, and the good sense of the reader, to trim every article to a certain level. Yet, both in the choice of topics, and in their treatment, the Publishers are confident that no thoughtful man has found anything unjustly partisan, since both sides of all the important social, moral, and political questions which have been discussed in these pages have had an equal chance, and an impartial consideration.

The New Volume of the Magazine commences under the best possible auspices. Its position is now assured. Two years have demonstrated the extent of its circle of friends, and that circle is constantly widening. The Magazine has not only the sympathy, but the actual literary support of the most eminent authors in the country. The greatest care is exercised in the selection of articles for its pages, from the immense number of MSS. received—a number now amounting to more than *eighteen hundred.* In so great a press of material to be considered, the Publishers appeal confidently for patience to all who favor them with their contributions, while they heartily thank them for their good will.

While care is taken that nothing in the remotest degree offensive to propriety or good taste defaces these pages, and the ablest talent is secured to make a Magazine, which, for variety of interest, and excellence of tone, shall be surpassed by no similar publication in the world, the Publishers assure the Public that their motto is still *onward,* and that every year's experience will enable them more fully to deserve the favor which they so gratefully acknowledge.

—Putnam's Monthly, 4 (December 1854)

* * *

Periodicals began to split along regional lines along with the nation during the 1850s. William Lloyd Garrison's antislavery Liberator *was pleased to cite the position of the proslavery* Richmond Enquirer *on* Putnam's Monthly.

PUTNAM'S MONTHLY

The Richmond (Va.) *Enquirer* speaks thus of this independent, out-spoken magazine:–

"Mr. G. P. Putnam is industriously writing down his magazine at the South. In the last number, he characterizes slavery in these words:–'From its very nature, it is a despotism of force, of law, and of opinion, combined—partially mitigated in practice by humane personal considerations, but in theory absolute. It is administered, for the most part, by the whip: it is sanctioned by legislation: and it admits of no scrutiny or discussion. All that can be said of it, in the regions where it prevails, even by those most deeply interested in its results, must be said in its favor, on pain of peremptory banishment or assassination.' If all Northern periodicals would speak in this spirit there would be some hope of a Southern literature. We are glad to learn from the booksellers here, that *Putnam* is rapidly vanishing from the market. The void should be supplied by the *Southern Quarterly Review,* the ablest periodical in the country."

—Liberator, 24 (8 December 1854): 193

* * *

Associate editor George William Curtis informs frequent contributor Longfellow of the sale of the magazine to the recently established firm of Dix and Edwards. Curtis stayed on at Putnam's Monthly, *which kept its name and signature look and style, as literary editor for several more years.*

New York–
March 8, 1855.

My dear Mr Longfellow –

"Putnam's Monthly" has changed hands—but it is a dead secret. P. found as I told him he would, (sagacious I!) that he could not edit & publish together. The two last numbers have edited and published themselves. But mismanaged in every way, as it has been, it still pays him a certain profit. Yet as he wants to devote himself to a few saleable books, he has parted with it. The purchasers are Dix & Edwards, a new firm, capital young men, full of business knowledge, enterprise and sagacity. They have some capital, & they have already made contacts for printing & manufacturing the mag. which, with nearly double the present estimate for copyright, leaves them a clear profit of $8000. This is contracted for; & is the profit upon the present circulation. But that ought to be run up ten thousand more, & could easily be so by proper editing & publishing.–& would then pay them very handsomely.

—reproduced by permission of the Houghton Library, Harvard University, bMS Am 1340.2 (1395)

Putnam's Magazine

The second general magazine published by the house of Putnam, Putnam's Magazine *(January 1868–November 1870), was born under radically different cultural, political, and publishing circumstances than was the first magazine. Whereas the antebellum* Putnam's Monthly *was the beneficiary of a mood of cultural nationalism, a lack of competition in the periodical market, and initially, at least, a wide pool of public goodwill, the postbellum* Putnam's Magazine *had none of these advantages. It was not the pioneering venture that its predecessor had been and it faced a formidable rival in the* Atlantic Monthly, *which had bought out the subscription list of the dying* Putnam's Monthly *in 1857 and had since taken its status as the leading literary magazine in the country (the same status occupied among publishing houses by its parent company, Ticknor and Fields). Altered, too, was the status of the parent publishing house. Whereas G. P. Putnam and Company had been a large, dynamic publisher in the field of the belles lettres, G. P. Putnam and Son was a relatively minor publisher in a more crowded field and had few connections to the rising generation of writers.*

What remained unchanged was the motivation of the publisher. Putnam reopened his publishing house in January 1867, eager to resuscitate the magazine but hesitant to do so without additional capital. Sharply improved financial prospects later that year persuaded him to risk the venture, and he spent much of the fall preparing for it. He brought back Charles Frederick Briggs as editor, sent out a circular designed to bring a new corps of writers to the magazine, and advertised for a small army of subscription agents with the goal of reaching a more nearly national readership than had been possible in the 1850s.

The new magazine followed customary magazine policies in a number of regards. It sold for 35¢ per issue or $4 a year, printed contributions without their authors' names, carried little or no outside advertising, and covered a wide range of the arts and sciences. The magazine was recognizably a Putnam production, not only because of its green covers and name but also because of its serious contents and self-referential editorializing. The first number opened with an article by Briggs entitled "The Old and the New. A Retrospect and a Prospect," which surveyed the glory days of Putnam's Monthly *and anticipated palmy days for* Putnam's Magazine. *Subsequent numbers also drew attention to the past, and the contents of the new periodical seemed as nearly nostalgic as farsighted.*

Putnam's Magazine *never succeeded in attracting many of the finest writers of the new generation. One reason it did not was financial: it simply could not afford to pay the best writers regularly according to the sharply risen postwar rate of compensation. Another reason was editorial stance, for the magazine lacked the timeliness and vibrancy that its predecessor exhibited; it also lacked the visual attractiveness of an increasing number of its competitors. Perhaps most seriously, Briggs and his successors did not have ties to the best writers comparable to those cultivated by the old editorial team. Nor, for that matter, did Putnam and the house have such connections.*

Putnam did have a circle of close personal and professional friends, including Richard and Elizabeth Stoddard, Bayard Taylor, and Edmund Stedman, who wrote with some frequency for the maga-zine. He also had a talented new resource right at hand, as his son John Bishop contributed a fascinating set of essays about his experiences in strife-ridden Japan, and his daughter Mary wrote an equally fine set of essays detailing her experiences in Paris during the Franco-Prussian War. Putnam also contributed good work himself, notably his publishing retrospective "Leaves from a Publisher's Letter-Book" and his travelogue "Some Things in London and Paris, 1836–1869."

The Putnam circle, though, could not compensate for the lack of a true authorial corps or a vibrant editorial policy. Lacking a firm literary or financial base, Putnam's Magazine *never had more than uncertain prospects. With a circulation that George Haven Putnam claimed ran between 15,000–20,000, the magazine could not have been sustainable indefinitely. Putnam tried to make various arrangements to raise capital to keep it going, but none of them worked out. In fall 1870 he gave in to the inevitable and sold the magazine to Charles Scribner, who merged it with his firm's new* Scribner's Monthly.

* * *

Selected List of Contributors to *Putnam's Magazine*

Louisa May Alcott (1832–1888)
Leonard Bacon (1802–1881)
Clarence Cook (1828–1900)
James Fenimore Cooper (1789–1851)
Susan Fenimore Cooper (1813–1894)
Frederick Cozzens (1818–1869)
Rebecca Harding Davis (1831–1910)
Van Buren Denslow (1834–1902)
Parke Godwin (1816–1904)
James Morgan Hart (1839–1916)
Julian Hawthorne (1846–1934)
Sophia Peabody Hawthorne (1811–1871)
John Hay (1838–1905)
William Dean Howells (1837–1920)
George Kennan (1845–1924)
Richard Kimball (1816–1892)
William Douglas O'Connor (1832–1889)
Frederic Beecher Perkins (1828–1899)
George Palmer Putnam (1814–1872)
John Bishop Putnam (1847–1915)
Mary Corinna Putnam (1842–1906)
Elie Réclus (1827–1904)
Maximilian Schele de Vere (1820–1898)
Edmund Stedman (1833–1908)
Frank Stockton (1834–1902)
Elizabeth Stoddard (1823–1902)
Richard Stoddard (1825–1903)
Bayard Taylor (1825–1878)
Henry Tuckerman (1813–1871)
Moses Coit Tyler (1835–1900)

* * *

G. P. Putnam's 4 September 1867 letter to Longfellow, one of many contributors to Putnam's Monthly *who were solicited to contribute to* Putnam's Magazine *(reproduced by permission of the Houghton Library, Harvard University, bMS Am 1340.2 [4554])*

Charles Frederick Briggs, the founding editor of both Putnam's Monthly and Putnam's Magazine, commemorates the first magazine and launches the new one with high expectations. One of the problems Briggs faced with Putnam's Magazine was reconciling the achievements of the past with the prospects of the present. He recognized the challenge, but he was unable to find a viable answer.

THE OLD AND THE NEW.
A RETROSPECT AND A PROSPECT.

In his notes to the republication of that tremendous screed which Mr. Carlyle calls "Shooting Niagara—and After," the troubled author declares his opinion that, "in fifty years hence, all serious souls will have quitted literature, and that for any noble man, or useful person, it will be a credit rather to declare, 'I never tried literature; believe me, I have never written any thing.'"

Mr. Carlyle may be endowed with the gift of prophecy; but, for our own part, we incline to the belief that fifty years hence will be very much like fifty years since, as far as literature is concerned, and that serious souls and noble men, as well as noble women, will be quite as ambitious of being known as the authors of something clever, as they ever were. It is just fourteen years since we had the honor to assist in getting out the first number of PUTNAM'S MONTHLY; and, so far from feeling at all ashamed of it, we confess to a feeling of pride, rather, in the part we took in it, and, on the whole, derive considerable satisfaction in remembering the cosy little dinner in a certain cosy house in Sixteenth-street, at which the plan of the work was discussed and the adventure determined upon. As this is only a gossippy little prelude, and not a grave essay, it will not be considered improper, we trust, if we mention, confidentially to the reader, that the little party consisted of Mrs. Caroline M. Kirkland, Mr. George Sumner, Mr. Parke Godwin, Mr. George W. Curtis, Mr. and Mrs. Putnam, and the present writer. It was but fifteen years ago, and of that little party two are already gone. The rest remain to assist in the revival of the work which was then so pleasantly and so auspiciously begun.

Fourteen years ago, the first number of PUTNAM'S MONTHLY was launched upon the troubled waters of this wayward world, as an experiment in literary navigation. Many predicted that it could not keep afloat, who yet hoped that it might, and did what they could to falsify their own predictions. But those who commenced it, and were responsible for its success, had no misgivings; and the result justified their faith and rewarded their efforts. The MONTHLY was in every respect not only a success, but a distinguished success. It earned not only a

decided reputation for itself, but for many youthful adventurers in literature, hitherto unknown, who contributed to its pages. The chief doubt in the minds of many was, whether the country could furnish the requisite number of writers to sustain an original magazine of the better class; but the experiment proved that there was plenty of latent talent which only required an opportunity for its development. The second question was, whether a public existed capable of appreciating and able to support a publication such as it was the aim of the projectors to furnish. These were strange doubts in a country that had produced writers like Irving and Cooper, and where every laborer was a reader. But the first number dispelled all doubts, and thenceforth all went well.

"But the work stopped," remarks some sagacious friend.

True enough. It did stop, but it did not die. Ships sometimes drop anchor and furl their sails, and then spread their canvas again and make prosperous voyages, as if nothing had happened; while other ships founder at sea and pass out of men's memories. But the MONTHLY was so strong and healthful in its constitution, so distinct in its individuality, and so much a necessity, that it could not well come to grief. Through certain misadventures, which need not be particularly noted here, the work stopped for a while, but anxious inquiries have constantly been heard as to when it would reappear; for no one seemed willing to believe that it had stopped for good. It was a strange thing, that the metropolis of the continent, the centre towards which the wealth, the intellect, the enterprise, the refinement, and the adventures of the New World all tend, should not be able to support its one original first-class magazine; and many have been the demands why this should be so.

When the old "PUTNAM" furled its sails for a season, the *Atlantic Monthly* was launched, and "took the flood" of public favor, sailing out upon the broad ocean, where it still floats prosperous. We have always and naturally been proud of that fellow-voyager, in whose build and trim we fondly recognize so much that is most familiar to us; and as "PUTNAM" again shakes out its sails, and heads for the open sea, it signals its consort "Good-morrow," and runs up its streamer with its old motto, "Excelsior."

One of the sincere friends and counsellors who most earnestly hoped for the success of the MONTHLY, and yet, with characteristic frankness, expressed his fears that its projectors were too sanguine in their expectations, was Washington Irving. The mention of this honored name sadly reminds us of other friends who were eager to help, by their counsel or contributions, in giving stability to the work, who are no longer here to aid or encourage us. As we glance over the names of the contributors to the earlier numbers of the MONTHLY, the black dashes which indicate the departures of those who helped us once, but can help us never more, are startling from their frequency. First on the list we find the name of William North, who wrote "The Living Corpse," in the first number. He was a young Englishman of good family, who had then but recently arrived in New York; a wild, impulsive creature, frank, generous, impatient of restraint, full of brilliant projects, hating routine, and bent on reforming mankind on the instant. He had published a periodical in London called "North's Magazine," and commenced various literary enterprises after his arrival in this country. But, after a brief career, he died by his own hand, and now lies in Greenwood Cemetery. Fitz-James O'Brien contributed "Our Young Authors" to the first number of the MONTHLY, and afterwards became better known by many brilliant contributions in prose and verse to various periodicals. He was a young Irishman, who landed in New York in the same week with William North. He was a man of remarkable gifts and of very comely presence, brave, generous, and impulsive. At the outbreak of the war he volunteered in defence of the Union, and, while serving on the staff of General Lander, in Western Virginia, was mortally wounded in an encounter in which he displayed great gallantry. His death, which did not occur until after he had undergone the amputation of his right arm, was remarkable for the heroic cheerfulness he displayed in his sufferings. The Rev. Dr. Francis L. Hawks, who wrote the article in the first number of the MONTHLY on "The Late John L. Stephens," and some others, died in the Autumn of 1866. Henry D. Thoreau, better known now than then, contributed "An Excursion to Canada," and was the author of several articles in subsequent numbers. He died in 1862. "Virginia in a Novel Form," a serial commenced in the first number, was the production of Mrs. Hicks, of Richmond; but whether she be living or dead, is more than we know. If still living, as we trust she is, the very novel form which Virginia has since assumed, might furnish a fresh theme for her very clever pen. The Rev. Dr. Bethune, who died in Florence, April 27, 1862, contributed the charming story of "Uncle Bernard," which appeared in the sixth number. This story had a very remarkable adventure. It was appropriated by a London magazine, without any hint being given of its origin, and republished here as original by one of our own magazines, without any suspicion of its American authorship; thus furnishing a very striking instance of the dangers encountered by literary pilferers in the absence of an international copyright-law. The Rev. Dr. Baird, who contributed an article on "Russia," which appeared in one of the early numbers, and which attracted great attention at the time by the accuracy with which the events of the war in the Crimea were predicted, died March 15, 1863. The Rev. J. H. Hanson (author of the article in the second number, the title of which, "Have we a Bourbon among us?" has passed into a proverb), as well as the subject of his ingenious essays, the supposed Bourbon, are both among the dead. William S. Thayer, one of the most promising and versatile of our younger brood of journalists, who contributed to the first volume a review of "Lowell's Poems," in conjunction with his friend and classmate, William Howland, died in Alexandria, Egypt, where he was United States Consul, about 1864.

Our necrological record is painfully long. It shows how many eminent names were on the list of our contributors, and how great a variety of talent is necessary to sustain the interest of a monthly magazine. In addition to those we have named, we can but briefly mention the names of others who well deserve a special commemoration; and chief among them is Caroline M. Kirkland, the vivacious, vigorous, genial, sensible, and erudite teacher and writer, who died as truly in the cause of the Union, as any of the heroes who gave their lives for their country on the battle-field; Richard Hildreth, the historian, who died a year ago in Italy, whither he had gone as Consul to Trieste; Henry W. Herbert, better known, perhaps, to American readers, as Frank Forrester, grandson of the Earl of Pembroke, who, like William North, died by his own hand; Prof. Charles W. Hackley, of Columbia College; Maj. E. B. Hunt, of the United States Army; Lieut. Bleecker, of the United States Navy; Dr. J. R. Orton, poet and novelist; Thomas Francis Meagher, who died Governor of Montana; C. M. Webber; Calvin W. Philleo, author of "Stage-Coach Stories;" and Maria Lowell, whose death was so tenderly commemorated by Longfellow, in the exquisite poem entitled "The Two Angels."

There are others, who have strangely disappeared from the world of letters, after letting their light shine for a brief while in the pages of the MONTHLY, who, we trust, are still among the living. What has become of "Jack Lantern" and his "railroad speculations?" Has he abandoned literature altogether for the law? The author of that sparkling essay on the "Pacific Railroad," which appeared in the ninth and eleventh numbers, has no right to wrap such talents as he possesses in a legal napkin. And what has become of Dick Tinto, and the author of

Full-page advertisement in the 15 November 1867 issue of American Literary Gazette and Publishers' Circular

"What is the Use?" Has Jervis McEntee, who once gave us such beautiful little landscapes in verse, entirely abandoned the pen for the pencil? And where, let us ask, is Herman Melville? Has that copious and imaginative author, who contributed so many brilliant articles to the MONTHLY, let fall his pen just where its use might have been so remunerative to himself, and so satisfactory to the public?

It is no small satisfaction to us to remember, that the MONTHLY first tempted several neophytes in literature to come out before the public, who have remained out to their own credit as well as to the public's satisfaction and profit. Among them were William Swinton, the accomplished historian of the Army of the Potomac, whose "Rambles among Verbs and Adjectives," which appeared in the twenty-third and twenty-fourth numbers, were written while he was a teacher in a school in North Carolina, and which he had to quit between two days to avoid the inevitable consequences of being suspected of abolitionism. Then there was Fred. B. Perkins, sufficiently well known now as a magazinist, whose "Connecticut Georgics" appeared in the sixteenth, and "Conversations with Miss Chester" in the twenty-sixth number. And Frederick S. Cozzens, the genial author of the "Sparrowgrass Papers," which were commenced in the twenty-fourth number.

Some remarkable volumes have been made up, too, from the early numbers of the MONTHLY, among which were "Shakespeare's Scholar," by Richard Grant White; Calvert's "Early Years in Europe;" Mackie's "Cosas de Espagna;" Mr. Curtis' "Potiphar Papers" and "Prue and I;" "Political Essays," by Parke Godwin; "The Sparrowgrass Papers," by F. S. Cozzens; "Washington," by Mrs. C. M. Kirkland; "Fireside Travels," by J. R. Lowell; "Twice Married," by C. W. Philleo; "Israel Potter," by Herman Melville; "The Lost Prince," by Hanson; "Cape Cod," by H. D. Thoreau; "Leaves from the Book of Nature," by Professor Schele de Vere; "The Criterion," by H. T. Tuckerman; and "Wensley," by that accomplished scholar and powerful writer, Edmund Quincy; besides the series of railroad volumes known as "Maga Stories," "Maga Social Papers," &c.

Can it with any justice be said, that a magazine which accomplished thus much was not a success? And, if such a success could be achieved fourteen years ago, is it at all unreasonable to anticipate less under the more favorable conditions which invite a similar enterprise now? Past experience has taught us many useful lessons, which we hope to turn to our advantage. We know exactly what the public need in a magazine, and we hope to be able to furnish it. Popular taste has not much changed. Fourteen years ago

it was considered an act of *hari-kari* for a popular periodical to express a political opinion, particularly if it was adverse to the "peculiar institution" of the South. But we ventured upon it without any harm coming of it, and we shall probably try it again. Certainly, we have no desire to publish a magazine for readers who are too feeble to endure a candid discussion, now and then, of political subjects. Stories are the life of a magazine, we are aware. One serial novel used to be considered sufficient for an English magazine; but so great is the general craving for stories, that no magazine ventures now to have less than two. Mrs. Todgers confessed, that the greatest difficulty in a commercial boarding-house, was to furnish a sufficiency of gravy for her guests. Stories are the gravy of a magazine, and this essential element to success shall not be wanting. American readers are accustomed almost entirely to foreign works of fiction; but we shall publish none but stories of native production. It is not possible that such devourers of stories should be incapable of producing the article so essential to their happiness. We have entire faith in our ability to bring out the required supply of American novels and romances. Like the gold in the gulches of the Rocky Mountains, they are only waiting for a little adventurous prospecting to bring them to light.

Once more, then, PUTNAM'S MAGAZINE takes its position in the literary firmament, with more "star-dust" in the atmosphere than there was at its first appearance, and with more luminaries to diminish its light, perhaps, by their superior brilliance.

Many excellent friends, who have favored us by their sage advice, have strangely insisted that it will be useless to expect good contributions, without good pay; as though a publisher or an editor were likely to have missed this special lesson in his dealings with authors. But there are two sides to this interesting question of pay. In order that a publisher should pay, he must himself be paid. One veteran author, by way of enforcing his views on this subject, demanded a retaining fee of five hundred dollars as an earnest of future payments, for whatever he might furnish. Experience has taught us, that in magazine-writing the best-paid authors are by no means necessarily the best. The young, fresh, vigorous, and original writers, who are yet unknown to fame, and whose names have no commercial value, are the least expensive and the most beneficial contributors to a magazine. We do not intend to delude the public by paying for the use of a name. We shall publish no articles except for their intrinsic merit, and shall always prefer a new writer to an old one.

None know better than our own authors what discouraging disadvantages the publisher of an original American magazine must contend against, in being obliged to compete with the unpaid British productions which are reproduced here almost simultaneously with their publication on the other side of the Atlantic. And while this unequal contest between the publisher who filches his matter, and the one who pays for it, almost prohibits the possibility of profit to the latter, the American author gauges his demand for compensation by the standard of his English brother. But we are touching, perhaps, on private rights by these allusions. The commercial value of any article depends upon what it will bring in the open market, and by that test we must be governed in the question of pay.

Something more we might add; but we cheerfully subside—to the reader's gratification, no doubt, as well as our own—to give place to the following note from our former coadjutor, GEORGE WILLIAM CURTIS.

MR. CURTIS' LETTER.

MY DEAR BRIGGS:—One bright day long and long ago,—it seems to me now that it must have been soon after the war of 1812, but, upon reflection, I discover that it was in 1852—I was dining with Mr. Harry Franco [*Briggs's pseudonym*] at Windust's, in Park Row. As we ate our simple repast and spoke of many things, Mr. Franco asked me what I thought of the prospect of a new and wholly American magazine; and immediately proceeded to set forth its possible character and brilliant promise so fully and conclusively, that I knew he was prophesying, and that, before many months, a phœnix would appear. That was my earliest knowledge of PUTNAM'S MONTHLY.

In the following Autumn, there was a little dinner at Mr. Publisher Putnam's cosy Sixteenth-street house, and the details of the enterprise were discussed at length. Mrs. Kirkland was there, and was, as usual, one of the most delightful of companions. When something was said of "pure literature" and "the classics," her genial face beamed with suppressed fun, as she said:

"Oh! the classics? They are in great repute at Washington. When I was there, last winter, a member of Congress sat beside me at dinner, and as he had been told that I was a *littery* woman, he evidently resolved to make the most of his opportunities; so, after a little while, he said to me:

" 'There's going to be a *lecter* to-morrow night.' "

"'Ah!' said I. 'Who is to lecture?' "

"'I disremember his name, but his subject,' said my neighbor slowly, to make sure, 'is The Age of Pericles'—pronouncing the last syllable as in the word miracles."

"My neighbor looked at me, as if he had not finished his remark, and repeated the words contemplatively, 'The Age of Pericles.' Then, with a kind of appealing expression, he suddenly asked me:

" 'What *are* Pericles?'—as if he supposed them to be a kind of shell-fish."

Of course, it had been long decided that the experiment of the magazine should be tried. It is safe to suppose, when advice is asked, that a resolution has been taken. When I arose from table at Windust's, on that long-vanished June afternoon, I was as sure that there would be a magazine as if Mr. Franco had told me that it was all in type; and now, after the other dinner in Sixteenth-street—for it is a beautiful provision of nature, that literary enterprises of great pith and moment should be matured under the benign influences of good eating and drinking—I found myself consulting, in a bare room in a deserted house in Park Place, where nobody could find us out, with Mr. Publisher Putnam, Mr. Harry Franco, editor-in-chief, and Mr. Parke Godwin, associate editor, upon the first number of PUTNAM'S MONTHLY.

We were an amiable triumvirate; and, although I say it, we put a great deal of conscience into our work. Our council-chamber was a third-story front room in a doomed house near to Mr. Putnam's headquarters, which were then in Park Place. I say doomed house; for, although a comfortable and staunch building, it was a dwelling-house, and as fashion had at last flown even from Park Place—the spot below Bleecker-street where it lingered longest—the house was patiently waiting to be demolished, and make way for a "store." Every day we met and looked over manuscripts. How many there were! And how good! And what piles of poetry! The country seemed to be an enormous nest of nightingales; or, perhaps, mocking-birds—certainly cat-birds. I can see now the philosophic Godwin tenderly opening a trembling sheet, traced with that feminine chirography so familiar to the editorial eye, and in a hopeful voice beginning to read. After a very few lines a voice is heard—methinks from Franco's chair: "Yes, yes; guess that's enough,"—Walter di Montreal, thy hour has come, and the familiar chirography flutters into the basket.

I suppose, my dear Briggs, you have long ago forgotten how many excellent suggestions Mr. Franco made. His nimble wit, his experience, his instinct of the popular taste, oiled all the dry and doubtful spots upon the ways, so that, when the stays were knocked away, the good ship of our hopes and fears slid smoothly out, and was at once launched in

Advertisement in the 5 December 1867 issue of The Nation. *The editors published the announced contents for the first number, but many of the promised articles did not appear.*

deep water. The Rev. Mr. Hanson brought his story about the Rev. Eleazar Williams, as the lost Bourbon. Mr. Franco instantly suggested the proper title, which has passed into current use, "Have we a Bourbon among us?" One day, after the first number was made up, Mr. Franco said, in his crisp way, "There must be an article upon the present state of parties, in the next number." Thereupon, Godwin, who was our statesman and political thinker, dropped his modest eyes; but Mr. Franco added, "I don't mean political parties; I mean Brown's." Alas! it was in that manner that "our best society" was described. The lovely maidens, whose exquisite draperies floated off Lyons looms; the polished youth, who encircled them in the modest waltz of the German, what time they placed bottles of champagne upon the floor beside their chairs for refreshment—these were described as "Brown's society." The result of Mr. Franco's hint was Mrs. Potiphar's first appearance. When she came out, it seems that somebody spoke of her, and of the person who had written about her, to Mr. Brown. "I don't know him," said Mr. Brown; and there was an end of that fine fellow.

The paper upon the Bourbon excited a curious interest. The subject was discussed every where, and in very many minds, the question soon became, *"Haven't* we a Bourbon among us?" One morning a message was sent up to the editorial rooms from headquarters, that the Bourbon was then and there visible in the flesh. Down we went, and found a tall, large-framed man, erect and portly, of a deep-bronze hue, and of a bland expression. His hands were soft, like a Prince's or an Indian's. The head was round, and receded from the forehead. The face was very full, and was certainly very like the face of the Bourbon kings upon the *Louis d'ors* of France. If he were not the Seventeenth Louis, there was no apparent reason why he should not be. He was quite as royal a looking gentleman as any king of his time; as mild of mien as his reputed father; and he undoubtedly led a much better life at Green Bay than his illustrious predecessor, the grand monarch, or his kinsman the Regent at Versailles. The reverend Prince died in 1858, and opinions still differ whether he were a full-blooded Prince royal or a half-breed Indian.

In one of the earlier numbers of PUTNAM'S MONTHLY—that for July, 1853—there is a letter "Number One" of Parepidemus. It is very short, only three pages, and the really attentive and perceptive reader must have felt that it was by none of the familiar writers of the magazine, and was both in a different vein and a different spirit from the usual magazine literature. The last sentence was suggestive of a foreign authorship: "Let me sign myself, my dear sir (as we are all 'strangers and pilgrims,' so myself in an especial sense), your obliged and faithful Parepidemus." The letter is a mere fragment, a brief expression of a divine doubt, a simple and sincere questioning of the nature and result of intellectual and moral effort and expression. One little characteristic sentence will reveal the writer to those who know him, or who knew his works. He is speaking of something more than mere self-relief in the work of the great artist, the high, inspired purpose, which may be detected in St. Peter's or in the Tempest, and then adds: "Imperfect, no doubt, both this and that is: short of the better thing to come—the thing that is. Yet not impotent, not wholly unavailing."

Parapidemus was Arthur Hugh Clough, the young English scholar and poet, whom Matthew Arnold mourns as sincerely as Milton mourned Lycidas, and whom the whole younger generation of thoughtful, cultivated Englishmen remember with affectionate regret, and deplore as a man whose remarkable powers should have made him a leader of the best. He was born in England, and was early brought to this country; then returned, and was one of the beloved scholars of Dr. Arnold at Rugby, with Tom Hughes, Dean Stanley, Palgrave, and others; and went from Rugby up to Oxford, and, as his companions all fondly believed, to still higher and higher influence and honors. His powers were indisputable, his attainments remarkable, and his character most lovely. But a conscience subtly sensitive, a mind too exquisitely balanced, held him in the incessant unrest of the deepest moral and intellectual inquiry. He had the ambition which is part of the dowry of genius. He knew, and valued, and desired the prizes in the career for which he was fitted. But something restrained his hand: "Ought I to take the crown?" he asked, as if unworthy, as if his title were not perfect, as if the very desire were a deceit; and while he asked, the crown grew shadowy and faded away. One little poem, printed originally in the very thin volume of his verses, which every owner dearly prizes, I will transcribe here, as singularly expressive of him:

"I have seen higher, holier things than those,
    And therefore must to those refuse my heart;
Yet I am panting for a little ease;
    I'll take, and so depart.

Ah, hold! The heart is prone to fall away,
    Her high and cherished visions to forget,
And, if thou takest, how wilt thou repay
    So vast, so dread a debt?

How will the heart, which now thou trustest, then
    Corrupt, yet in corruption mindful yet,

Turn with sharp stings upon itself! Again
    Bethink thee of the debt!

–Hast thou seen higher, holier things than these,
    And therefore must to these thy heart refuse?
With the true best, alack! how ill agrees
    The best that thou wouldst choose!

The Summum Pulchrum rests in heaven above;
    Do thou, as best thou may'st, thy duty do;
Amid the things allowed thee, live and love;
    Some day thou shalt it view."

Clough came to this country in 1852, with the intention of taking pupils in the higher studies, and lived at Cambridge. He was greatly beloved by those who knew best the rare qualities of his genius, and his friendships were with the best men and women. There was an attractive blending of scholarly shyness, melancholy, and geniality in the impression he made; and he had the fullest sympathy with the freedom and the promise of American life. But his sad self was relentless. He could not escape the old wonder and questioning. What he wrote in poetry and prose had a strain of sincere, child-like pathos, wholly unsurpassed in contemporary literature. And it characterizes all his writings. It is not a pathos of sighs and sobs, and elegiac weeping and wailing, but a melancholy like that of the Autumn in Nature, a primeval sadness. It was while he was in Cambridge that he wrote the two letters of Parepidemus, the second of which appeared in the August number of 1853. But he soon went back to England; was appointed to a position in the education department of the Privy Council; married; worked hard, and in 1859 finished a translation of Plutarch. In 1861 he was obliged to relinquish work; went to Greece and Constantinople; returned, and wandered about Europe, reaching Florence in the Autumn. There he died on the 13th of November, 1861, and there he lies buried under the beautiful cypresses of the Protestant cemetery.

Since his death, many of his letters and his manuscript poems have been privately printed in England, and an edition of the poems that he had already printed was published soon after his death. Clough's particular friend in this country was Charles Eliot Norton, of Cambridge, who edited a beautiful edition of his poems, which was published by Ticknor & Fields, in 1862. Mr. Norton prefaced them with a tender and modest memoir, and from that and an article by him in the *North American Review* for October, 1867, upon the privately printed volume, a very accurate impression of the rare and lovely genius of Clough may be obtained. His name is not yet very familiar in English literature, but it yearly becomes more so. His life seemed, of course, to many, a failure; but the union of real sincerity with real power never fails, however tardy be its recognition. It is refreshing to think of the antique nobility of soul, the true simplicity, the unshrinking devotion to the most celestial ideal, the patience, humility, and unselfishness of this thoroughly trained scholar and this true poet. A photograph of Clough hangs in Norton's study. It is a broad, balanced, serene, massive head, full of sweetness and wisdom, and of the child-like simplicity of modest genius. If I think of the pleasant and various society of our contributors, those who are living still, and those who are dead, there is no figure more significant and impressive, however modest and shadowy, and unknown to his companions, than that of Clough.

I suppose that Mr. Franco and Godwin, and the poor fellow who was snuffed out by Mr. Brown's brief remark, might fill many pages with their recollections of the pleasant cradle-and-crib days of the young "PUTNAM." Those three were the MONTHLY nurses. They saw that infant phenomenon safely through his prodigious childhood, and how rapidly he obtained his growth!

There are books in good standing, every where, which I can never see but with the feeling of the pedagogue towards his pupils, who have become illustrious. "*My* boys, sir; *my* boys!" he remarks with complacency, as the famous poets, or travellers, or novelists pass by. "Our books, sir; our books!" say the old triumvirate of "PUTNAM," as they hear the praises of the works, the manuscripts of which they luckily did not reject. Reject? I should say not. "I knew ye, Hal!" Their shrewd wits detected the signs at once, and saluted the genius unaided. And what editor ever does "reject" a manuscript? "Ladies, or fair ladies, I would wish you, or, I would request you, or, I would entreat you, not to fear, not to tremble," but to understand that when your manuscript returns, it is not because of any judgment upon its merits. Heaven forefend! It is only that, although nothing could be more, etc., etc., yet it is not exactly suitable to the pages of this magazine, and is, therefore, respectfully returned, or declined, with thanks. It is merely that this is a red rose—and very beautiful it is!—where a white lily was wanted. The enclosed pearl is returned with the most sincere thanks, because it was an opal which was needed to complete the necklace.

This, as we know, was the spirit of the original triumvirate of PUTNAM'S MONTHLY; and this, we are very sure (are we not?), will be the spirit of its more modern management. More modern? We,

then, are ancient! Among the fresh voices which now swell the blithe choir of our literature, we are as those who have come down from a former generation! How this latest-born into the Monthly world springs and sparkles! Ah! Mr. Franco, if it is not our child, let us submit, and believe it to be our grandchild. I seem to recognize our family likeness. Methinks I detect the air of the "PUTNAM" of long ago. May Heaven bless you, young stranger! May you live long and happily! Forgive an old-fashioned benediction, but may you be a better man than your father!

So prays, dear Briggs, your affectionate grandf––,

I mean, faithful friend,
GEORGE WILLIAM CURTIS.
–*Putnam's Magazine,* 1 (January 1868): 1–8

* * *

In this excerpt from an editorial in the first issue of Putnam's Magazine, *Briggs entrusts the success of the magazine to the laws of the marketplace even in an age of "magazine mania."*

The increased capital required to conduct a leading newspaper, will demand and obtain increased fidelity and responsibility. In a kindred walk, Periodical Literature has certainly increased in value and importance. The ability displayed in such publications as *The North American Review, The Atlantic Monthly, The Galaxy, Hours at Home,* and others which might be named; and in such weekly journals as *The Nation* and *The Round Table,* gives earnest that the intellectual resources of the country are likely to keep pace with its material prosperity.

. . . .

Every honest intellectual effort is to be welcomed. There may be too many physicians and too many lawyers in a community; but the evil, if it exist, of too many publishers or of too many publications will soon correct itself by the infallible agencies of the economy of trade. The point, we believe, is not yet reached of surplus intellectual activity and supply. The more the attention of the public is called to literature, the more readers there will be; and the rivalry of competition in this and in other instances must benefit the consumer in the quality and quantity of the article. It is said there are a great many magazines already, and the cry is, still they come. But there need be no fear on this head. The people, if any remedy is required, have it in their own hands. It is quite constitutional for one to buy them or not, as he may please. But in fact, to a great extent, the magazine mania, as it has been termed, is in many instances but another form of book publication, since it is mostly sustained by the serial novels of popular authors, whose works the public find it more convenient and agreeable to purchase in chapters than in volumes. Other considerations, as the convenience of an *unbound book,* which a magazine such as our own really is, the variety of entertainment, and the pleasure of a frequent visit from authors whose writings are esteemed, have much to do with it also. The model subscriber to a magazine, in fact, has a personal interest in the work; is a species of partner in the enterprise; has a community of interest with others, and enjoys a welcome sense of continuity, of a pleasure which ends not with the hour, but has a promise of renewal from month to month. We trust to have many such friendly appreciators of PUTNAM'S MAGAZINE.

–*Putnam's Magazine,* 1 (January 1868): 122

* * *

Notices such as this one in Putnam's Magazine *that offered advice to potential contributors were commonplace in American magazines during this era of emergent literary professionalism.*

COMPLETION OF THE SECOND VOLUME

OUR "Patrons," as the phrase used to be, and our contributors, will both please to accept our thanks for their increasing appreciation of each other.

Nearly all that we said in the customary formalities at the close of the first volume might be here repeated, with additional self-congratulations about our abundant success hitherto, and our "brilliant prospects" for the future. But these glittering generalities are pretty well understood and taken for granted. We may say in all modesty and with suitable deference to the daily and weekly critics who sit in judgment upon our "articles," that if these have not all been perfect models of excellence, we shall be delighted if our critics will send us better ones; and whenever we are guilty of rejecting better articles than we print, we shall be thankful for such information as will lead to the correction of the abuse.

It is needless for us to make new and glowing proclamations of the brilliant things we are going to do. The advertisement of our next volume mentions some of the contents and some of the writers for that volume; and our readers in future, as heretofore, will judge us by our fruits.

A few suggestions to contributors are given on the next page.

The growing activity and cosmopolitanism of the American mind is daily indicated by the excellent papers, on a wide range of subjects, which we receive. The very excellence of many of these essays, especially those giving sketches of travel and adventure, is a constant source of concern to the editor–an embarrassment of riches–for three magazines like ours could not contain all that we receive that is well worthy of publication.

But let no one be deterred from sending us their *best things.* We aim at a prompt and liberal appreciation of all good magazine literature, without partiality, or any question as to the personality or the fame of the writer. Both our readers and our "best writers" may be assured that we are always ready to make them "mutual friends;" and that BRIGHT, LIVELY, SENSIBLE, ENTERTAINING, and INSTRUCTIVE "READING MATTER" stands a good chance for mutually profitable use when it is sent to the editor of *Putnam's Magazine.*

TO CONTRIBUTORS.

Articles on all subjects of LIVE INTEREST, from writers known or unknown, short rather than long, terse and clear and crisp in style, will always receive prompt consideration.

New and significant facts and experiences are better than mere disquisitions and essays. Such, to be used, must be VERY well done.

Good short stories and poems are warmly welcomed.

All articles will be promptly examined and reported on, and if not used, returned on receipt of the necessary stamps.

The best way to prepare manuscript is to write on SMALL NOTE PAPER, (not on foolscap,) and to mail it in a flat package rather than a roll.

There must often be long delay in using an accepted MS., and changes in the course of events occasionally prevent the use of a MS. even after its acceptance. Such cases require a just indulgence from the author.

The publisher's statement that a theme proposed to him would furnish, if properly treated, a good article for the Magazine, is not a pledge to accept the article prepared in consequence, even if further alterations should be made by the author.

–*Putnam's Magazine,* 2 (December 1868)

* * *

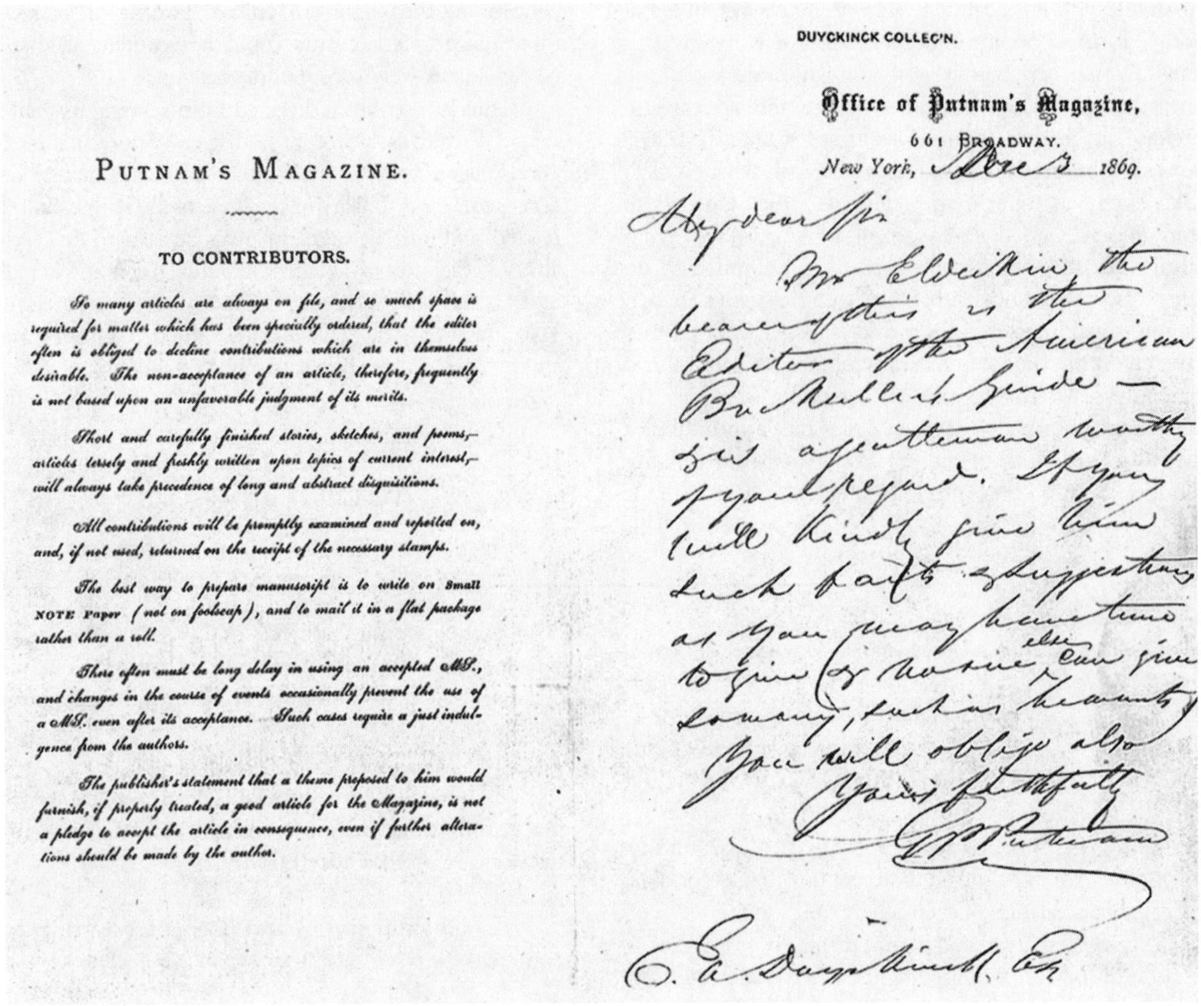

DUYCKINCK COLLEC'N.

PUTNAM'S MAGAZINE.

TO CONTRIBUTORS.

So many articles are always on file, and so much space is required for matter which has been specially ordered, that the editor often is obliged to decline contributions which are in themselves desirable. The non-acceptance of an article, therefore, frequently is not based upon an unfavorable judgment of its merits.

Short and carefully finished stories, sketches, and poems,—articles tersely and freshly written upon topics of current interest,—will always take precedence of long and abstract disquisitions.

All contributions will be promptly examined and reported on, and, if not used, returned on the receipt of the necessary stamps.

The best way to prepare manuscript is to write on SMALL NOTE Paper *(not on foolscap), and to mail it in a flat package rather than a roll.*

There often must be long delay in using an accepted MS., and changes in the course of events occasionally prevent the use of a MS. even after its acceptance. Such cases require a just indulgence from the authors.

The publisher's statement that a theme proposed to him would furnish, if properly treated, a good article for the Magazine, is not a pledge to accept the article in consequence, even if further alterations should be made by the author.

Office of Putnam's Magazine,
661 Broadway.
New York, Dec 3 1869.

My dear Sir

Mr Elderkin, the bearer of this is the Editor of the American Bookseller's Guide — & is a gentleman worthy of your regard. If you will kindly give him such facts & suggestions as you may have time to give (or anyone else can give so many, such as he wants) You will oblige also

Yours faithfully
G P Putnam

E. A. Duyckinck Esq

Guidelines for contributors to Putnam's Magazine. *Putnam here writes a letter of introduction to be given to Evert Duyckinck (Duyckinck Family Papers, Manuscripts and Archives Division, The New York Public Library, Astor, Lenox and Tilden Foundations)*

Despite the plural form of the possessive noun, this "Publishers' Notice," which appeared at the end of the last issue of Putnam's Magazine, *was Putnam's own admission of failure. The figures at its end indicate that the magazine was not a financial success, but what must have hurt Putnam more deeply was the fact that it had proved no more a literary or journalistic success.*

PUBLISHERS' NOTICE

A FEW words may be expected from the Publishers, in closing this second series of *Putnam's Magazine,* and in introducing the new periodical which will take its place.

It is not necessary for us to dilate upon the pleasures or the pains, the encouragements or the annoyances, connected with this department of a publisher's business.

The present Magazine was very generally and very kindly welcomed; for the earlier volumes, under the management of Messrs. Briggs, Curtis, and Godwin, were favorably and freshly remembered.

If we may take the verdict of perhaps ninety-nine out of a hundred of both our critics and our correspondents, during the last three years, we have the right to infer that the new series has given "general satisfaction" to its sensible readers, especially since it has had the supervision of Mr. Godwin. If a few *in*sensible critics—for any reason, good, bad, or indifferent—have now and then dissented from this general verdict, their right to do so in this free country may not be questioned. Probably not many have spied out our defects more keenly than we have ourselves. If our own ideal of a Magazine has not been in all respects achieved, perhaps the fault is not wholly ours.

Our friends and contemporaries who have given us words of cheer and kindly appreciation, and have expressed regret at our transformation–and their number is legion–will accept our hearty acknowledgments. Insignificant exceptions to this general good-will scarcely need mention.

This Magazine has had a larger circulation than several of its contemporaries at home, and much larger than a dozen of the English magazines whose names have been familiar for many years. Yet it is more and more evident that the *paying* popular taste calls for something *different;* it may be higher or lower, better or worse. But those who pay their money have a right to the choice.

We have aimed, from the first, to produce a Magazine *wholly* ORIGINAL, and essentially AMERI-CAN–*i.e.,* devoted largely to American topics as a specialty. We have avoided all temptations to *reprint* from foreign magazines, or to cater for any thing merely "sensational." In this we may have been Quixotic; but the aim, at least, was fair.

Doubtless better things may be done in this direction than we have been able to effect; but, so far, the best material sent to us–out of some 3,000 MSS.*–or, at least, those papers which were apparently most acceptable to our readers, have been printed in the six volumes now completed.

We now ask those who have expressed a friendly appreciation of the "pea green," to permit us to introduce its better-looking successor, and to give it a fair and candid reception. Retaining an interest in the sale of this new work (our edition bearing the name of PUTNAM'S as well as "SCRIBNER'S"), we ask our friends and correspondents to continue their subscriptions to us, in reasonable confidence that they will receive the full equivalent for their money.

* The exact number is 3,035 in three years: that is, about ten times as many as the six volumes could contain. Our contributors have all received their pecuniary compensation. We wish this had been a great deal larger; but we may state our *relative* reward thus:

Dr.–To cash paid contributors $30,000
Cr.– By compliments to publishers . . . .$? ? ?
    By profits on outlay of $100,000 . . . . 00 000

_____

By Balance–?
–*Putnam's Magazine,* 6 (November 1870)

George Palmer Putnam's Writings on the Profession of Publishing

A Few Preliminary Notes and Statistics

Putnam worked assiduously during the early 1840s to amass statistics and general information relating to the American book industry. To accomplish this research at a time when there was relatively little reliable information on the subject in the public realm, he mailed questionnaires to authors, editors, and publishers throughout North America, soliciting basic information about their publications. He then carefully examined and tabulated that information back home in London in preparation for publishing it in definitive form in American Facts *(1845). Before proceeding to book publication, however, he composed a succinct statement of his views and conclusions as the introduction to his firm's* American Book Circular *(1843). In this essay Putnam makes a strong case for the cultural nationalism that he and many others felt during a period when American bookmaking and culture were perceived on both sides of the Atlantic as inferior to their European counterparts. Putnam's original essay included footnotes, which have been converted into endnotes here.*

* * *

A FEW PRELIMINARY NOTES AND STATISTICS

"Literature and intellectual ability of the highest class meet with little encouragement in America. The names of Cooper, Channing, and Washington Irving, indeed, amply demonstrate that the American soil is not wanting in genius of the most elevated and fascinating character; but their works are almost all published in London—a decisive proof that European habits and ideas are necessary to their due development."
ALISON'S HISTORY OF EUROPE, vol. x. p. 624.

The above and other kindred passages in a recent elaborate work of high character have suggested the propriety of appending to a list of some of the principal American Books, a few Facts and Statistics, very briefly stated, respecting Literature, Publishing, etc., in the United States.

The logic of the conclusion of the above sentence from Mr. Alison appears somewhat doubtful. If the learned historian means that the works of the writers mentioned depended upon a foreign atmosphere for their birth,

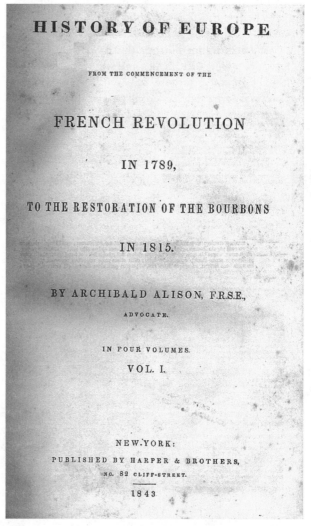

HISTORY OF EUROPE

FROM THE COMMENCEMENT OF THE

FRENCH REVOLUTION

IN 1789,

TO THE RESTORATION OF THE BOURBONS

IN 1815.

BY ARCHIBALD ALISON, F.R.S.E.,

ADVOCATE.

IN FOUR VOLUMES.
VOL. I.

NEW-YORK:
PUBLISHED BY HARPER & BROTHERS,
NO. 82 CLIFF-STREET.

1843

Title page for book that Putnam responded to in his introduction to the American Book Circular. *Putnam took pride in the fact that Harper and Brothers' American edition of* History of Europe *cost one-fifth the price of the English edition, but he conveniently overlooked the fact that the Harpers published the book without compensating the author.*

growth, and sustenance, the English publishers of them could easily have convinced him to the contrary. For Cooper—his early novels first saw the light from the press of an

APRIL, 1843.

No. 161,
BROADWAY,

NEW YORK.

AMERICAN
BOOK CIRCULAR.

STATIONERS'
HALL COURT,

LONDON.

WILEY AND PUTNAM.

CLASSIFIED LIST OF SOME OF THE MOST IMPORTANT
AND RECENT

AMERICAN PUBLICATIONS.

HISTORY, BIOGRAPHY, ETC.	EDUCATION.	MEDICINE, SURGERY.
VOYAGES, TRAVELS.	METAPHYSICS.	PHILOLOGY, CLASSICS.
SCIENCE, NATURAL HISTORY.	POLITICS, STATISTICS.	RELIGION AND ITS HISTORY.
USEFUL ARTS.	LAW, CONSTITUTIONS.	POETRY, FICTION, MISCELL.

PERIODICALS, ETC.—APPENDIX.

A FEW PRELIMINARY NOTES AND STATISTICS.

"*Literature and intellectual ability of the highest class meet with little encouragement in America. The names of Cooper, Channing, and Washington Irving, indeed, amply demonstrate that the American soil is not wanting in genius of the most elevated and fascinating character; but their works are almost all published in London—a decisive proof that European habits and ideas are necessary to their due development.*"
ALISON'S HISTORY OF EUROPE, vol. x. p. 624.

The above and other kindred passages in a recent elaborate work of high character have suggested the propriety of appending to a list of some of the principal American Books, a few Facts and Statistics, very briefly stated, respecting Literature, Publishing, etc., in the United States.

The logic of the conclusion of the above sentence from Mr. Alison appears somewhat doubtful. If the learned historian means that the works of the writers mentioned depended upon a foreign atmosphere for their birth, growth, and sustenance, the English publishers of them could easily have convinced him to the contrary. For Cooper—his early novels first saw the light from the press of an intelligent publisher of New York;* and all his works are now published simultaneously in Philadelphia and London, the American sale being at least equal to the English, and the amount paid the author equally great. The same is true also of Irving's works; except perhaps that one of them was first published in England during a temporary visit there. Of Channing—it is true that his fame is European; that his works have all, on being republished, had an immense circulation in Great Britain; of some of them, no less than seven rival editions have been reprinted, though it is not probable that the author received any pecuniary benefit from either of them; but neither of those authors was compelled to seek a publisher in Europe, or depended upon the European market for the "due development," or for the pecuniary avails, of his works. If European publishers

* C. Wiley, New York, 1818-19.

[London: Printed by Manning and Mason, Ivy Lane, St. Paul's.]

Cover for trade catalogue that featured Putnam's essay on publishing in North America intelligent publisher of New York;[1] and all his works are now published simultaneously in Philadelphia and London, the American sale being at least equal to the English, and the amount paid the author equally great. The same is true also of Irving's works; except perhaps that one of them was first published in England during a temporary visit there. Of Channing–it is true that his fame is European; that his works have all, on being republished, had an immense circulation in Great Britain; of some of them, no less than seven rival editions have been reprinted, though it is not probable that the author received any pecuniary benefit from either of them; but neither of those authors was compelled to seek a publisher in Europe, or depended upon the European market for the "due development," or for the pecuniary avails, of his works. If European publishers find it for their interest to reprint American works abroad, it surely does not follow from that, that those works are unappreciated at home.

The fact that *nine editions* of Prescott's "Ferdinand and Isabella" (an expensive work in three volumes octavo, equal to the London edition in style, etc.); that 12,000 copies of Stephens' "Central America" (also expensive–two octavos), and at least as many of his other works, have been sold in the United States in about four years, is perhaps sufficient proof that those two writers also are not entirely neglected by their own countrymen. We may also mention in this connexion the sale of more than 4000 sets of Washington's writings, in twelve octavo volumes; of about the same number of Franklin's works, in ten volumes; the publication of such books of travel as "Robinson's Researches in Palestine;" Stephens, and others; in Science: as the translation of the "Mecanique Céleste," with a commentary of nearly the same bulk, forming four large quartos, by a self-taught and practical man,[2] who rose from humble obscurity to fame and fortune by his own unaided exertions; "The Natural History of the State of New York," in ten quarto volumes, produced at an expense of 40,000*l.* (200,000 dol.); the publication for twenty-four years of a Scientific Quarterly Journal,[3] and of a Quarterly Literary Review,[4] both of the highest class, besides numerous minor works of the same character; the transactions of various scientific societies, etc.: the sale of *nine* editions of one expensive History of the United States;[5] and other elaborate works noticed elsewhere: and to refer to imaginative and elegant literature–the publication, chiefly within ten years, of no less than 120 different novels, original and copyright; (not all by Scotts and Bulwers, it is true; but the greater part at least deemed worthy of reprinting abroad); and of 110 different poetical works, besides collections:[6]–all of which would seem to indicate that "literature and intellectual ability" are not so *wholly* unencouraged in America as Mr. Alison appears to suppose.

As figures are useful in such matters, we annex a table, compiled from publishers' lists (necessarily incomplete), of American Publications, chiefly during the last fifteen years, as far as ascertained, and not including repeated editions; viz.

Subjects	Number of Works. Orign. Amer.	Reprints.
Biography	106	122
History and Geography (American)[7]	118	20
History and Geography of Foreign Countries	91	195
Literary History	–	12
Metaphysics	19	31
Poetry (besides collections)	103	76
Novels and Tales	115	***[8]
Greek and Latin Classics with original Notes, etc.	36	none
Ditto, Translations	–	36
Greek Latin and Hebrew Text Books, etc,	35	none
Medical, Law, and Miscellaneous	not ascertained	

The following is a table of American publications, in 1834.[9]

	Orig. Amer.	Reprints.
Education[10]	73	9
Divinity	37	18
Novels and Tales	19	95
History and Biography	19	17
Jurisprudence	20	3
Poetry	8	3
Travels	8	10
Fine Arts	8	–
Miscellaneous	59	43
	251	198

The aggregate cost of books published in 1834 and 1835, was estimated at 1,220,000 dol. The editions printed are larger and more frequent than is usual in England. The capital invested in printing, binding, and making paper, as returned by the census of 1840, is 10,619,054 dol.

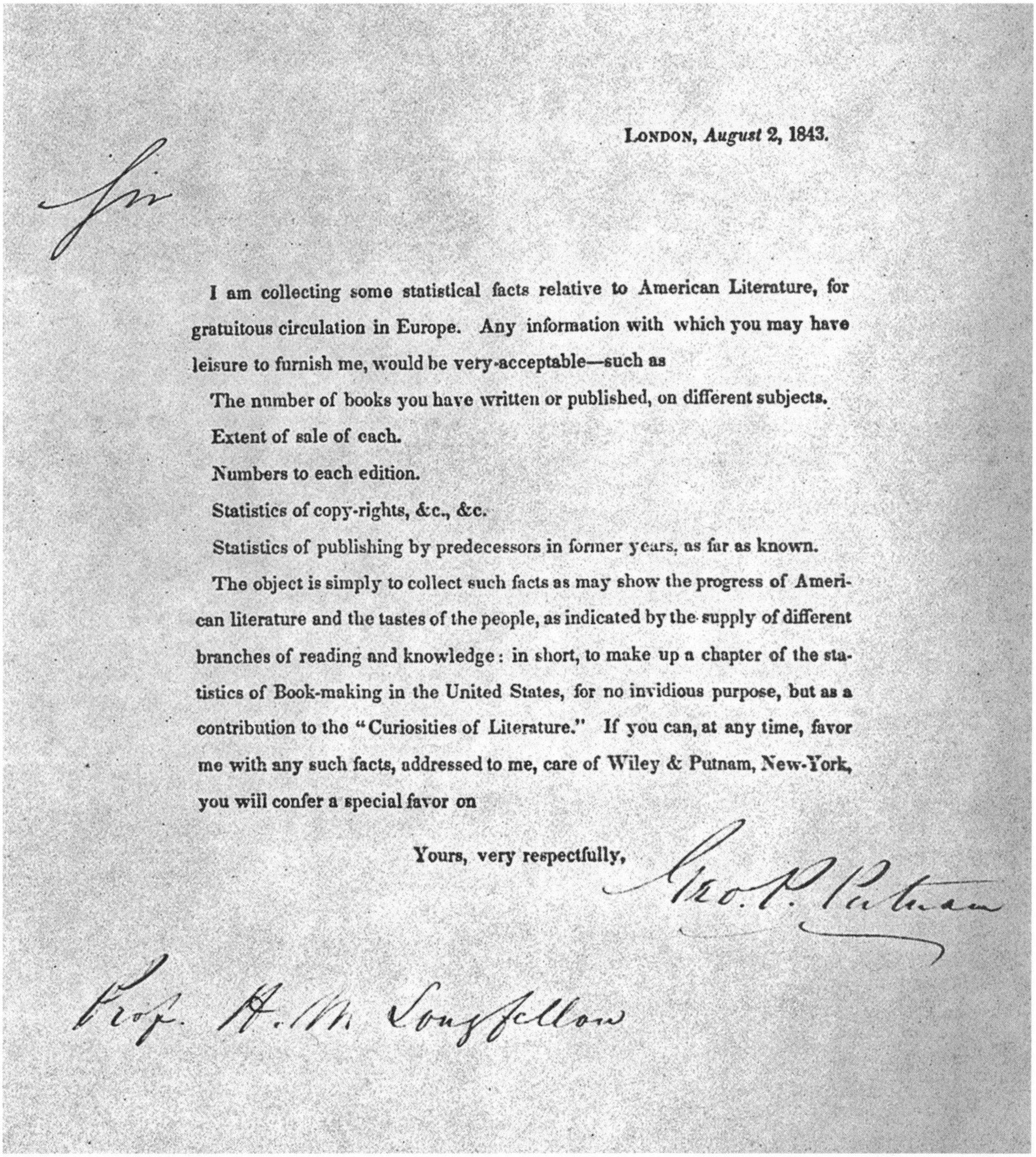

LONDON, *August 2, 1843.*

Sir,

I am collecting some statistical facts relative to American Literature, for gratuitous circulation in Europe. Any information with which you may have leisure to furnish me, would be very acceptable—such as

The number of books you have written or published, on different subjects.

Extent of sale of each.

Numbers to each edition.

Statistics of copy-rights, &c., &c.

Statistics of publishing by predecessors in former years, as far as known.

The object is simply to collect such facts as may show the progress of American literature and the tastes of the people, as indicated by the supply of different branches of reading and knowledge: in short, to make up a chapter of the statistics of Book-making in the United States, for no invidious purpose, but as a contribution to the "Curiosities of Literature." If you can, at any time, favor me with any such facts, addressed to me, care of Wiley & Putnam, New-York, you will confer a special favor on

Yours, very respectfully,

Geo. P. Putnam

Prof. H. W. Longfellow

A circular Putnam sent to Henry Wadsworth Longfellow, one of many letters to American writers Putnam addressed in order to compile statistical information about their publishing history (Longfellow Collection, Houghton Library, Harvard University)

Two voluminous Encyclopædias (Brewster's and Rees') were reprinted several years since; and the "Encyclopædia Americana" supplies the deficiencies of all others in American topics.

As proof that the people are not utterly and exclusively absorbed in "the present;" we may mention the demand for such works as "Scott's Commentary on the Bible," of which *three sets of stereotype plates* have produced not less than 60,000 copies; of "Henry's Commentary" the sale has been nearly as great; and not less than 100,000 large volumes of original compilations on Biblical Literature have been sent forth from one little village in the State of Vermont, where the whole process of book-making, from the paper-mill to the binder, is done under the same roof.

Though publishing is chiefly carried on in the Atlantic cities, it is not exclusively so, as we see Cincinnati (where fifty years since was a wilderness) producing quarto volumes on *American Antiquities,* in a style equal to that of the London press–while the *factory* town of Lowell, not yet thirty years old, produced editions of *Goethe's Faust* and a literary magazine, "written exclusively by females employed in the mills."[11]

While their own writings are not quite unknown elsewhere, these figures shew that the United States do not *entirely* rely upon foreign sources for their intellectual sustenance. Their elementary educational works are almost entirely written at home; and the number of school-books printed may be partly estimated from the fact, that of four or five geographical text-books from 100,000 to 300,000 copies have been issued in ten years.[12] A single publisher in Cincinnati, Ohio–a place of yesterday–has printed within six years, of six school-books, an aggregate of 650,000 copies.[13] The number of different school-books in use, each of which has a large sale, might surprise some; but the list is too long for this notice.

As to the character and value of these school-books, the fact that all foreign ones are *free* to the publishers, while they are paying large sums to their own authors, is a proof that they, at least, consider the domestic article better or more available than the imported. One may be mentioned–a Geography and Atlas of the Heavens,[14] extensively used in American common schools, which a competent British authority[15] has pronounced of a higher character than any similar compendium similarly used in England.

We have also good English authority for the opinion that the Hebrew Grammar, by Nordheimer; the Hebrew-English Lexicon, by Robinson; the Greek Lexicon to New Testament, by the same; the Commentary on Isaiah, by Barnes; System of Theology, by Dwight; Geography of Palestine, by Robinson;[16] Text-book Editions of Horace, etc., by Anthon; modern contribution to Spanish History (Ferdinand, etc.), by Prescott;[17] Medical Jurisprudence, by Dr. Beck; Medical Jurisprudence of Insanity, by Dr. Ray; Dictionary of the English Language (!!!), by Dr.

Webster[18]–are all the best Works in their several departments existing in the language.

And that American authors are not left to exist entirely upon *laurels* may be inferred from the fact, that a single publishing-house in Philadelphia[19] paid for copyrights in five years, ending 1837, the sum of 135,000 dol. (28,000L), of which 30,000 dol. was for *two* works. The author of "Notes on the New Testament" received for part of the copyright, about 5000 dol. in two years; a small musical compilation yielded the author nearly the same. Dr. Webster, it is said, has an income of 1000L per annum from a Spelling-book! Prescott, Stephens, Bancroft, etc., retaining their own copyrights, receive, of course, the pecuniary result of their labours, as do indeed, all *successful* writers, in spite of the *free* influx of European literature.

Mr. ALISON proceeds to say of the United States– "*Neither the future, nor the past, excites any sort of attention.*"[20] "*The classics are in little esteem,*" *etc.* vol. x. p. 624.

There are in the United States–[21]

103 Colleges, with 9936 Students, and 562,958 vols. in Libraries.

28 Medical Schools 3265 "

39 Theological do. 1305 " 123,600

The *alumni* of *seven* of the Colleges above, amount to 19,800. True, as Mr. Dickens says, many of the others, in the Western States are little more than Academies, and some as yet not fairly in oper-

Charles Dickens, one of the few authors with whom Putnam had bad relations. Dickens considered Putnam a pirate; Putnam considered Dickens a cultural chauvinist.

ation;[22] but for all these students, the Greek and Latin Classics and Mathematics form the chief part of the course of study.

For text-book editions of select classics, we need only refer to those of Anthon, Beck, Felton, Gould, Leverett, Kingsley, Stuart, Woolsey, etc., to shew that, for works "in little esteem," there is a marvellous deal of pains taken to drill them into the heads of 10,000 students, for each four long years.[23] *Translations* too are abundant, and at prices which render all the best works of the Ancients accessible to the million.

The works on Biblical and Oriental Philology, by Professors Stuart, Robinson, and others, are not unknown to English scholars: and the only translations[24] in English of the classical works of Eschenberg, Buttman, Gesenius, Jahn, Ramshorn, and Winer, are the American.

Again, the historian continues:–

"Works in the higher branches of philosophy or speculation are unknown." p. 624.

Jonathan Edwards, we supposed, was held in some repute as a metaphysician; and the recent treatises of Upham, Tappan, Schmucker, Rauch, Wayland, Day, Bowen, Adams, and others, indicate that this sort of "speculation" is not yet extinct in the country. But besides these original treatises, and translations of the works of Cousin, De Wette, Jouffroy, Gall, Spurzheim, etc.; the fact that the *first complete collections* ever made, of the works of Cudworth, Burke, Bolingbroke, Paley, and Dugald Stewart, have been printed in the United States;[25] and that they also have reprinted the works of Bacon, Dr. Thomas, Brown, Reid, Coleridge, Bentham, Abercrombie, Dymond, Adam Smith, Chalmers, Isaac Taylor, etc. etc.: all this we think has some bearing on Mr. Alison's assertion that, in America, *"the higher branches of speculation and philosophy are unknown."*

Again we are informed by Mr. ALISON, that–

"So wholly are they regardless of historical records or monuments, that half a century hence, its history, even of these times, could only be written from the archives of other States."–vol. x. p. 624.

The publication of more than fifty octavo volumes of the historical memoirs and correspondence of Washington, Franklin, Jay, Jefferson, Hamilton, Madison, Morris, Adams, and many other statesmen; of 20 vols. of Diplomatic Correspondence; of three or four biographical collections, and as many historical, statistical, and commercial Journals, continued for several years; the three folio volumes, commencing a series of "American Archives," arranged by Mr. Force, under Congressional authority; the collection of American State Papers, in about forty folio volumes; the existence of at least two thousand volumes of documents, published in successive years, by the two houses of Congress, and the various state legislatures; the systematic collection and arrangement of the *original* public archives, commenced in Massachusetts, under the direction of the government, and continued by other States;[26] the collections of the Historical Societies of Massachusetts, twenty-six volumes; of New York, of Pennsylvania, of Connecticut, of Rhode Island, of New Hampshire, of Georgia, of Ohio! all these and many more instances can be quoted in evidence, that the charge against the Americans of *wholly neglecting historical records,* is not more just, or true, than many other unfounded assertions respecting them.[27]

A nation, not yet seventy years old (as such), can scarcely be expected to possess a Bodleian Library, a Vatican, or a Bibliothèque du Roi–the growth of centuries: but it is *beginning* to collect libraries of moderate pretensions. In addition to the 562,000 volumes in the College libraries (*vide ante*), of which Harvard alone has 45,000: there are in

The Boston Athenaeum	32,000
" New York Society Library	40,000
" " Mercantile do..	26,000
Philadelphia Library	52,000
Library of Congress	25,000
Charleston Library	15,000

Besides these; books, etc. are to be found collected by the

Amer. Acad. Nat. Sciences, Philadelphia	
Amer. Philos. Society, do. founded	1769
Amer. Ac. Nat. Sciences, Boston,	1780
Conn. Acad. Arts and Sciences,	1799
Lit and Phil. Society, New York,	1815
National Institute, Washington,	1840
American Academy Fine Arts, N.Y.	
National Academy of Design, ditto.	
National Art Union, ditto.	
American Antiquarian Society, etc.[28]	

An immense number of local Lyceums, Societies, etc., would largely swell the list; while the cheapness of American editions places modern standard works much more generally in private houses than is usual in Europe. And may it not be presumed, that these 800,000 volumes, carefully chosen from the European accumulations of centuries, and brought within reach of all classes,[29] are at least more adapted for the *diffusion* of knowledge, than two or three times the amount of learned lumber, piled in folios and quartos on miles of dusty shelves, and rarely disturbed in their slumbering places (?) The scholar and the historian in the United States, doubtless, often find great deficiencies of material in their researches: the learning of the world cannot all be transplanted at once; and our *early* history being *colonial,* many of the original materials of it, are of course locked up in the Archives and State Paper Offices of England, France, and Holland. But these sources of information are not forgotten: by the liberal courtesy of those governments they have been thrown open to be examined and transcribed. The legislature of New York has appropriated 12,000 dols. for copying those relating to that State when a colony. Georgia and other States have also sent agents to Europe for this purpose; and American historians have appreciated the stores thus liberally opened to them, and which, from the nature of the case, *could not* previously have existed at home.[30]

That Science and Scientific Records are not neglected we have seen, as evidence the New York State appropriation of 200,000 dol. to develop its natural history; the Massachusetts' Legislative Survey and Publications, for the same purpose; the Transactions of the Geological Societies, and of the societies mentioned above; and the publication of several costly works of the highest scientific character.

But "Who reads an American book?"—*Edinburgh Review,* (old No.). A good many do so, without being themselves aware of it. The case of "the oldest" London Review appreciating the articles of the "North American" well enough to appropriate some of them entire, *as original, accidentally* omitting to mention their origin, is not a solitary one.[31] American periodicals have contributed "considerably" to some of those in England, in mutually innocent unconsciousness. Some few American writers would scarcely recognise their own offspring under their new names and foreign dress; and authors are apt to take some pride in their bantlings, whether clever or otherwise. Who, in looking over a list of titles, would suppose that "Quebec and New York, or the Three Beauties," was the same as "Burton, or the Sieges;" and "Cortes, or the Fall of Mexico," a reprint of "The Infidel;" that "The Last Days of Aurelian" is no other than Mr. Ware's "Probus, or Rome in the Third Century;" and "Montacute" only a new title for "A New Home;" that Mr. Muzzey's "Young Maiden" and "Young Wife" are *translated* into "The *English* Maiden," and the "*English* Wife!" and Mr. Sparks's "Life of Ledyard, the *American* Traveller," is only made more attractive as "The Memoirs of

Ledyard the *African* Traveller" (anon.); and two volumes of his "Writings of Washington," in twelve volumes, are reprinted with the original title, and apparently as if complete. Dr. Harris's "Natural History of the Bible;" Bancroft's Translation of Heeren's Politics of Greece; Mr. Everett's Translation of Buttman's Greek Grammar, were all reprinted and sold as English books. Judge Story's "Law of Bailments" was 'chopped into fragments,' and appended here and there, by Mr. Theobald, in his Notes on Sir William Jones.[32] These are a few specimens;—in most of them, the *preface,* etc., is sufficiently alerted to conceal their origin, and in several, the author's name is *suppressed.* One more may be mentioned:—Mr. Neal, of Philadelphia, published about 1839, a volume, called "Charcoal Sketches," with illustrations; his name appended in full. This volume appears *entire,* plates and all, in the *middle* of "Pic-Nic Papers," etc., "edited by C. Dickens, Esq.," 3 volumes, London, 1841. Mr. Neal, no doubt, would have been proud of his company, if his patron had not introduced him as a *nameless* person! "A volume has been appended," (to make the orthodox *three,*) "from an American source," says the editor; "but not a syllable about the name, either of author or book!"

The question of *copyright,* on either side, is quite another matter, and may be noticed elsewhere. Both omissions and additions have certainly been made in some American reprints of English works, and particularly in law books, where additional notes have been obviously indispensable; but we think it would be difficult to find many transatlantic cases of the sort of mangling above specified;[33] of such changing of titles and prefaces, and concealment of dates and origin; or of such *suppression* of author's *names,* condemning *them* to oblivion, while the publisher is reaping the benefit of his politic adaptation of the titles of their books, "the glory, more or less, all vanishing with the dash of the proof-reader's pen across the title-page," or a successful name appropriated for some dozens of books, which the original owner of the said name never saw.[34]

In "Bent's London Catalogue," we find the names of reprints of American books in England, chiefly within ten years, (not including American editions imported for sale), and all included, without distinction, in the general list, as English works. To give the different *editions* of Abbott, Channing, Stephens, Peter Parley, Barnes, Dana, etc., would be difficult.

AMERICAN BOOKMAN SCALPING AN ENGLISH AUTHOR.

Cartoon in the 29 May 1847 issue of the English magazine Punch.
*Putnam not only fought what he regarded as a one-sided
European view of American publishing but also
took a strong stand against American piracy.*

American books reprinted in England.

Theology,...	68 works.	History	22
Fiction	66 "	Poetry	12
Juvenile	56 "	Metaphysics ..	11
Travels.....	52 "	Philology....	10
Education...	41 "	Science	9
Biography ..	26 "	Law.........	9

This rapid glance at such facts as happen to be within reach at the moment, may, it is hoped, not be deemed impertinent or presumptuous by the many in England who take an interest in the subject. As the remarks of an American, and in such a connexion, they may be supposed, perhaps, to have exclusive reference to "the main chance," and "the almighty dollar;" and a claim to pure patriotism would not be worth while. As a people, we are certainly disposed to think well of ourselves, in spite of many *real* sins and peccadilloes, and of many more which are unjustly charged upon us; Bobadilism is said to be our *forte;* and love of country *will* degenerate into national vanity, which naturally puts the best face upon the matter, excuses the faults, and harmlessly boasts of the better points, especially when misrepresented. But as there is a deficiency abroad in available information, about the actual progress and condition of the United States,[35] we hope that these few figures may be of some service in suggesting some of the sources of such information.

We have referred to *specimens* only of the "impartiality" and fairness of Mr. ALISON, touching some topics; not a few of his other conclusions respecting the condition, etc., of the United States, are at least equally remarkable for those qualities: but we do not assume the office of reviewers. A brief allusion to one other specimen, elsewhere, may suffice as a suggestion, that an infallible judgment of a nation 3000 miles off cannot always be made from one-sided and garbled statements; or from *philosophical* and dogmatical dissertations on the social condition of seventeen millions of people from notes of a four months' railroad-steam-and-canal-boat "circulation," over an extent of country of perhaps sixteen times the surface of England.

The "Foreign Quarterly" article on the Newspaper Press of the United States (endorsed by Mr. Dickens), has at its head as text, the names of *eleven* newspapers (out of about 1600 in the country), while at least nine-tenths of the censurable extracts, to prove the writer's views, are from *one* paper, the New York Herald: and from *eight* out of the eleven, not a *single line* is quoted, either for praise or censure! The *candid* writer of the article forgets to mention that this same Herald, the disgrace and curse of the country, is entirely owned and conducted by *foreigners.* He refers to the *circulation,* as boasted for obvious purposes, by its editor, and doubtless much exaggerated. Do not the English stamp returns shew a greater circulation of the Weekly Dispatch than of almost any other paper? And are we then to infer that that paper is the best index of the tastes, opinions, and literature (!) of the English people?

Mr. Dickens refers all doubtful readers to the Papers themselves for proof of this "perfectly truthful" article. If any one took the trouble, did he find that either of those eight papers, with all their imperfections, deserved the atrocious character which is disingenuously fastened upon them by extracts—not from themselves, but from the New York Herald? We would second the suggestion—"let the malefactors be *examined.*" 1640 American newspapers are certainly not immaculate; deficiencies in ability, in courtesy, and in integrity, may, without question, be fairly charged upon many in this vast number, and in particular upon such as are blindly enlisted in political partizanship; but the Satirist is scarcely a fair specimen of the English press, nor is the New York Herald a representative either of the American newspapers or American people.

The courteous liberality which the writer, as an American, has received in England, induces the hope that these few remarks, although rather oddly introduced, may not give any cause of offence. At least no disrespect has been intended, either to individuals, or otherwise.

P.S.—We do not presume to meddle with politics, but *Maps* are not altogether out of place in connexion with books. The note on page 6 was in type before Sir Robert Peel, in putting a quietus on the famous "red line," had shewn the gross injustice of charging "perfidy," "fraud," "duplicity," "cheating," "dishonesty," "swindling," and all sorts of hard names, upon the American government, for not producing, as *decisive* against themselves, an *anonymous* line, without any direct authority whatever, *while their own claim coincided exactly with the line drawn at the time of the Treaty of 1783, by the "Geographer to the King!"*

* * *

1 C. Wiley, New York, 1818-19.

2 Dr. Bowditch.

3 Silliman's.

4 North American.

5 Bancroft.

6 From Publishers' Lists.

7 Including Travels.

8 Not ascertained.

9 From List of Titles in Booksellers' Adv. 1835, by G. P. Putnam, New York.

10 Including Theories and School Books.

11 Vide Mr. Dickens.

12 Viz. Parley's—Olney's—Woodbridge's—Goodrich, etc.

13 Truman and Smith.—See *American Publishers' Circular.*

14 Burritt's.

15 Dr. Thomas Dick.

16 Quarterly Review.

17 Edinburgh Review.

18 The Examiner, The Times, etc.

19 Carey, Lea & Co.

20 Barnes.

21 American Almanack.

22 The Census of 1840, returns 173 "Colleges," with 16,233 Students; and 3242 Academies and Grammar Schools, with 164,159 Students.

23 Under *Elementary Education,* the general statistics are thus returned by the same Census:—Primary and Common Schools, 47,209—number of Scholars, 1,845,244—Scholars at the Public Charge, 468,264.

The permanent available School Fund of the little State of Connecticut, one of the smallest of the twenty-six, is 2,240,000 dol. say 550,000*l*; and the amount paid from it, for forty-four years, is 2,609,315 dol. Out of a population of 301,000, in 1840, only 526 persons could be found, over twenty years of age, unable to read and write; and nearly all of these were Foreigners.

There are in the State of New York, 10,886 School District Libraries, containing 630,000 volumes, and the whole capital *permanently invested* for the support of education in that state, is ten-and-a-half millions of dollars; or more than *two millions sterling*.

24 Perhaps one or two exceptions.

25 Of more recent writers we may mention that the Essays of Carlyle, Macaulay, Jeffrey, Talfourd, and Professor Wilson, have all been *first* printed in a collected form, in the United States.

26 The State of New York as we are informed by its historical agent in Europe, J. R. Brodhead, Esq., has 250 folio volumes of MS. Records, copied or translated, and systematically arranged; and more than 900 pacquets of other state documents in the Secretary's office, all prior to 1775. Besides these all the counties and large towns have their own Records.

27 Even the great work of Mr. Alison himself, with all the hard things which he says in his American chapter, is considered worthy of being placed within reach of every man who can afford to pay 16*s.* for the entire ten volumes.

28 Mr. Astor of New York, has recently given the noble donation of 200,000 dol. for a free public library, to bear his name, in that city.

29 The subscription to the Mercantile (clerks) Library, of New York, is 2 dol. (8*s.* sterling per annum, which gives access to 25,000 selected standard books, and a reading-room filled with the periodicals of the world. A course of twenty lectures by the ablest scientific and literary men in the country is given at the same trifling expense—the number of members (4000) amply remunerating the lecturer. The same may be said of many similar institutions—composed *exclusively* of merchants' and tradesmen's '*clerks.*'

30 In the many censures touching a certain "red line," it is omitted to be noticed, that a large number of *British* maps exist with the line marked *as claimed by the United States;* that *ten* of these are in the British Museum; and that one of them, in the volume of Parliam. Debates for 1783! was engraved expressly to illustrate the Treaty. Why were these not taken to Washington in evidence?

31 See North American Review, Nos. 116 and 117.

32 See Comments on this in the North American Review, No. 116.

33 Much indignation was expressed by Mr. Dickens touching the "*dishonest*" opposition of Mr. Goodrich (Peter Parley), to international copyright, because it would not permit adaptations, etc. Was Mr. Dickens aware that an international copyright would have put some thousands of pounds into the pockets of this same Mr. Goodrich? Was this an entirely self-interested devotion to the "almighty dollar?" A word in connexion with Peter Parley. The Westminster Review favourably noticed those works, quoting, however, a series of "*Americanisms,*" which "disfigured" them. Can it be believed that every one of these quotations proved to be from the interpolations of the London publishers(!!)? Yet such is the fact. Not *one* was written by Peter himself, or is to be found in the American editions!

34 "Peter Parley," etc.

35 At least if we may judge from the many errors and erroneous inferences which disfigure the able and important work of Mr. Alison, to say nothing of the wholesale misrepresentations of newspapers and periodicals.

In a letter to historian George Bancroft, author of the well-regarded History of the United States *(1834–1874), Putnam discusses a variety of professional issues, including Wiley and Putnam's* American Book Circular. *At the beginning of the letter Putnam reports on his unsuccessful attempts to locate documents relating to North America necessary for Bancroft's research.*

New York Augt. 23d. 1843.

Dear Sir,

Your esteemed favor of 15th July was recd. in London just as I was leaving for a short visit at New York.

I regret that I am not able to inform you of the purchaser of the Virginia N York & New-England papers from Chalmers collectn.—Mr Brodhead recd. directions from the Govn. of New York to purchase the New York papers, but he found that they had been sold, and could not learn from Thorpe where they went. Thorpe's reply was that he presumed they were purchased "on speculation"—but that the purchaser requested that his name should not be mentioned—

I enquired of Col. Aspinwall & others but could learn nothing of them, and we concluded that Mr. Rich must have been the purchaser. Had I not left London the day after the rect. of your letter I should have taken more time to enquire into the matter—but I trust you will soon ascertain where the papers are, and have access to them, at least.

I am much gratified by your kind mention of the circular relating to American literature. It was very well recd. in London, & I trust it has had a good effect there & has given some impetus to the sale of American books in Europe. We have had several orders from it for historical & other standard works for France & Germany; & I am satisfied that American books have only to be made known in Europe & the demand for them must constantly increase.

I presume you are aware that a cheap edn. of your History is publishing in Glasgow in Nos.—This I fear will injure the sale of the American edn.—Mr Murray having had a supply from Little & Brown our own sales of the work have been very limited for some time past—but I still hope to do something more with it when the fourth vol. is ready.

Before I return to Europe I intend making an effort to induce all the Am[erica]n. <u>publishers</u> to unite in a petition for intentional copyright. I think the present state of the trade must convince them that as a matter of policy & self-interest merely, an international arrangement is highly desirable, if not absolutely necessary, to sustain American <u>publishers</u> as well as authors and if it can be brought about on this ground it would be much better than not having it done at all.

Any suggestions in reference to the subject which you might have leisure to make would be much valued. I expect to see the publishers in Philada., Boston, &c and hope to have the pleasure of calling on you.

With high respect

I remain Dear Sir,

Very faithfully yours

<u>Geo. P. Putnam</u>

George Bancroft Esq.

—*George Bancroft Papers, Massachusetts Historical Society*

* * *

One of Putnam's closest friends and allies of the mid 1840s, George Sumner congratulates the publisher on his American Book Circular *in this excerpt from a letter dated 18 December 1843.*

I need not tell you how delighted I am with the success of your circular and with the honorable reception it has had and honorable name it has won for you, at home as well as in England. It was an excellent thing and it came [?]. I have I think already told you, how much pleased Irving was with it, and how gratified he was that you had done the affair—He is a good friend of yours, and prizes you highly, though (if you will promise not to blush) I shall say no more than you justly deserve to be prized. When in Paris I heard of the enquiries made and flattering opinions uttered in consequence of your Circular. I sent a copy to Geo. W. Lafayette among others, and he was much delighted with it. . .

—*Manuscripts Division, Department of Rare Books and Special Collections, Princeton University Library. Published with permission of the Princeton University Library.*

Recollections of Irving

James T. Fields, publisher of the Atlantic Monthly, *writes to Putnam about the publication of "Recollections of Irving." His mention of "Lowell" is a reference to the editor of the magazine, James Russell Lowell. "Haven" is George Haven Putnam, who went to Europe to seek medical treatment for his eyes.*

Boston Sept. 29, 1860

135 Washington Street

My Dear Putnam,

Never mind about the heads of Andre. We will set them forward and so make them answer.

Your Irving article is in type but I fear Lowell will think there will be too much delay to send the proof as you wish, and as it should be sent. I do not urge it, as, if it were sent, the article might possibly be left out for the Dec. No. and I think it shd. go into the Nov. one without fail. Send your <u>paragraph</u> & we will try to get it in.

Touching the article on the recent Female novels, pray [have] it forwarded to me Lowell decided. I think I know the author; a clever girl she is.

Somebody said today that Haven is going abroad. Success & faithful progress.

Yours very truly,
James T. Fields

Bryant, Longfellow & Holmes breakfasted with us today in Charles St.
—*Manuscripts Division, Department of Rare Books and Special Collections, Princeton University Library. Published with permission of the Princeton University Library.*

* * *

This brief item titled "Letter from New York" was published in the 30 October 1860 Boston Post *just after Putnam's article appeared in the* Atlantic Monthly. *The writer apparently wished to protect Putnam's reputation, lest his motives in writing "Recollections of Irving" be somehow misconstrued. Putnam clipped out the item and pasted it in his scrapbook.*

Correspondence of the Boston Post.
NEW YORK, OCTOBER 27, 1860.

Putnam's Sunny Side Memories, (as they should have been entitled,) in the Atlantic Monthly for November, have warmed the hearts of hundreds of us Knickerbockers, to whom the name of Irving is a sort of sacred hereditament. The paper is one which no one besides Mr. Putnam could have written, and, considering the fact it is the first intimation in the pages of the Atlantic from which the readers of the magazine could learn of Mr Irving's death even–it was fit that so interesting a souvenir should impart the somewhat tardy information. The "article" ought to have been prefaced with the remark that it had been written at the earnest and repeated solicitation of Mr Fields, and that it was not, as it really seems to be, a *volunteered* tribute of personal esteem on the part of Mr Irving's publisher. Such a preliminary paragraph, or even, the letter which I know the writer of the reminiscences forwarded with his manuscript, would have placed Mr Putnam before the public in a manner more in accordance with that gentleman's well known modesty, and at the same time relieved his contribution from every shadow of suspicion as to the motives which prompted its publication.
—*Manuscripts Division, Department of Rare Books and Special Collections, Princeton University Library. Published with permission of the Princeton University Library.*

* * *

Putnam waited until a year after Washington Irving's death before giving this public testimony to their special relationship in the Atlantic Monthly. *In effect, he was not only offering legitimacy to Irving's status as the leading American author of his generation but also stating his own long-held belief in the symbiotic nature of author-publisher relations generally.*

RECOLLECTIONS OF IRVING.

BY HIS PUBLISHER.

YOU are aware that one of the most interesting reunions of men connected with literary pursuits in England is at the annual dinner of the "Literary Fund,"–the management of which has been so often dissected of late by Dickens and others. It is a fund for disabled authors; and, like most other British charities, requires to be fed annually by a public dinner. A notable occasion of this kind happened on the 11th of May, 1842. It was at this that I first met Mr. Irving in Europe. The president of the festival was no less than the Queen's young husband, Prince Albert,–his first appearance in that (presidential) capacity. His three speeches were more than respectable, for a prince; they were a *positive* success. In the course of the evening we had speeches by Hallam and Lord Mahon for the historians; Campbell and Moore for the poets; Talfourd for the dramatists and the bar; Sir Roderick Murchison for the *savans;* Chevalier Bunsen and Baron Brunnow for the diplomatists; G. P. R. James for the novelists; the Bishop of Gloucester; Gally Knight, the antiquary; and a goodly sprinkling of peers, *not* famed as authors. Edward Everett was present as American Minister; and Washington Irving (then on his way to Madrid in diplomatic capacity) represented American authors. Such an array of speakers in a single evening is rare indeed, and it was an occasion long to be remembered.

The toasts and speeches were, of course, very precisely arranged beforehand, as etiquette requires, I suppose, being in the presence of "His Royal Highness," yet most of them were animated and characteristic. When "Washington Irving and American Literature" was propounded by the fugleman at the elbow of H. R. H., the cheering was vociferously hearty and cordial, and the interest and curiosity to see and hear Geoffrey Crayon seemed to be intense. His name appeared to touch the finest chords of genial sympathy and good-will. The other famous men of the evening had been listened to with respect and deference, but Mr. Irving's name inspired genuine enthusiasm. We had been listening to the learned Hallam, and the sparkling Moore,–to the classic and fluent author of "Ion," and to the "Bard of Hope,"–to the historic and theologic diplomate from Prussia, and to the stately representative of the Czar. A dozen well-prepared sentiments had been responded to in as many different speeches. "The Mariners of England," "And doth not a meeting like this make amends," had been sung, to the evident satisfaction of the authors of those lyrics–(Campbell, by-the-way, who was near my seat, had to be "regulated" in his speech by his friend and publisher, Moxon, lest H. R. H. should be scandalized). And now everybody was on tiptoe for the author of "Bracebridge Hall." If his speech had been proportioned to the cheers which greeted him, it would have been the longest of the evening. When, therefore, he simply said, in his modest, beseeching manner, "I beg to return you my very sincere thanks," his brevity seemed almost ungracious to those who didn't know that it was physically impossible for him to make a speech. It was vexatious that routine had omitted from the list of speakers Mr. Everett, who was at Irving's side; but, as diplomate, the Prussian and Russian had precedence, and as American author, Irving, of course, was the representative man. An Englishman near me said to his neighbor,–"Brief?" "Yes, but you can tell the *gentleman* in the very tone of his voice."

In the hat-room I was amused to see "little Tom Moore" in the crowd, appealing, with mock-pathos, to Irving, as the biggest man, to pass his ticket, lest he should be demolished in the crush. They left the hall together to encounter a heavy shower; and Moore, in his "Diary," tells the following further incident.

"The best thing of the evening (as far as I was concerned) occurred after the whole grand show was over. Irving and I came away together, and we had hardly got into the street, when a most pelting shower came on, and cabs and umbrellas were in requisition in all directions. As we were provided with neither, our plight was becoming serious, when a common cad ran up to me, and said–"Shall I get you a cab Mr. Moore? Sure, a'n't I the man that patronizes your Melodies?" He then ran off in search of a vehicle, while Irving and I stood close up, like a pair of male caryatides, under the very narrow protection of a hall-door ledge, and thought, at last, that we were quite forgotten by my patron. But he came faithfully back, and while putting me into the cab, (without minding at all the trifle I gave him for his trouble,) he said confidentially in my ear,–'Now mind, whenever you want a cab, Misthur Moore, just call for Tim Flaherty, and I'm your man.'–Now, this I call *fame,* and of somewhat more agreeable kind than that of Dante, when the women in the street found him out by the marks of hell-fire on his beard."

When I said that Mr. Irving could not speak in public, I had forgotten that he did once get through

with a very nice little speech on such an occasion as that just alluded to. It was at an entertainment given in 1837, at the old City Hotel in New York, by the New York booksellers to American authors. Many of "the Trade" will remember the good things said on that evening, and among them Mr. Irving's speech about Halleck, and about Rogers the poet, as the "friend of American genius." At my request, he afterwards wrote out his remarks, which were printed in the papers of the day. Probably this was his last, if not his best effort in this line; for the Dickens-dinner remarks were not complete.

In 1845, Mr. Irving came to London from his post at Madrid, on a short visit to his friend, Mr. McLane, then American Minister to England. It was my privilege at that time to know him more domestically than before. It was pleasant to have him at my table at "Knickerbocker Cottage." With his permission, a quiet party of four was made up;–the others being Dr. Beattie, the friend and biographer of Campbell; Samuel Carter Hall, the *littérateur,* and editor of the "Art Journal"; and William Howitt. Irving was much interested in what Dr. Beattie had to tell about Campbell, and especially so in Carter Hall's stories of Moore and his patron, Lord Lansdowne. Moore, at this time, was in ill-health and shut up from the world. I need not attempt to quote the conversation. Irving had been somewhat intimate with Moore in former days, and found him doubtless an entertaining and lively companion,–but his replies to Hall about the "patronage" of my Lord Lansdowne, etc., indicated pretty clearly that he had no sympathy with the *small* traits and parasitical tendencies of Moore's character. If there was anything specially detestable to Irving and at variance with his very nature, it was that self-seeking deference to wealth and station which was so characteristic of the Irish poet.

I had hinted to one of my guests that Mr. Irving was sometimes "caught napping" even at the dinner-table, so that such an event should not occasion surprise. The conversation proved so interesting that I had almost claimed a victory, when, lo! a slight lull in the talk disclosed the fact that our respected guest was nodding. I believe it was a habit with him, for many years, thus to take "forty winks" at the dinner-table. Still, the conversation of that evening was a rich treat, and my English friends frequently thanked me afterwards for the opportunity of meeting "the man of all others whom they desired to know."

The term of Mr. Irving's contract with his Philadelphia publishers expired in 1843, and, for five years, his works remained in *statu quo,* no

American publisher appearing to think them of sufficient importance to propose definitely for a new edition. Surprising as this fact appears now, it is actually true that Mr. Irving began to think his works had "rusted out" and were "defunct,"–for nobody offered to reproduce them. Being, in 1848, again settled in New York, and apparently able to render suitable business-attention to the enterprise, I ambitiously proposed an arrangement to publish Irving's Works. My suggestion was made in a brief note, written on the impulse of the moment; but (what was more remarkable) it was promptly accepted without the change of a single figure or a single stipulation. It is sufficient to remark, that the number of volumes since printed of these works (including the later ones) amounts to about eight hundred thousand.

The relations of friendship–I cannot say intimacy–to which this arrangement admitted me were such as any man might have enjoyed with proud satisfaction. I had always too much earnest *respect* for Mr. Irving ever to claim familiar intimacy with him. He was a man who would unconsciously and quietly command deferential regard and consideration; for in all his ways and words there was the atmosphere of true refinement. He was emphatically a gentleman, in the best sense of that word. Never forbidding or morose, he was at times (indeed always, when quite well) full of genial humor,–sometimes overflowing with fun. But I need not, here at least, attempt to sum up his characteristics.

That "Sunnyside" home was too inviting to those who were privileged there to allow any proper opportunity for a visit to pass unimproved. Indeed, it became so attractive to strangers and lion-hunters, that some of those whose *entrée* was quite legitimate and acceptable refrained, especially during the last two years, from adding to the heavy tax which casual visitors began to levy upon the quiet hours of the host. Ten years ago, when Mr. Irving was in his best estate of health and spirits, when his mood was of the sunniest, and Wolfert's Roost was in the spring-time of its charms, it was my fortune to pass a few days there with my wife. Mr. Irving himself drove a snug pair of ponies down to the steamboat to meet us–(for, even then, Thackeray's "one old horse" was not the only resource in the Sunnyside stables). The drive of two miles from Tarrytown to that delicious lane which leads to the Roost,–who does not know all that, and how charming it is? Five hundred descriptions of the Tappan Sea and the region round about have not exhausted it. The modest cottage, almost buried under the luxuriant

Melrose ivy, was then just made what it is,–a picturesque and comfortable retreat for a man of tastes and habits like those of Geoffrey Crayon,–snug and modest, but yet, with all its surroundings, a fit residence for a gentleman who had means to make everything suitable as well as handsome about him. Of this a word anon.

I do not presume to write of the home-details of Sunnyside, further than to say that this delightful visit of three or four days gave us the impression that Mr. Irving's element seemed to be at home, as head of the family. He took us for a stroll over the grounds,–some twenty acres of wood and dell, with babbling brooks,–pointing out innumerable trees which he had planted with his own hands, and telling us anecdotes and reminiscences of his early life:–of his being taken in the Mediterranean by pirates;–of his standing on the pier at Messina, in Sicily, and looking at Nelson's fleet sweeping by on its way to the Battle of Trafalgar;–of his failure to see the interior of Milan Cathedral, because it was being decorated for the coronation of the first Napoleon;–of his adventures in Rome with Allston, and how near Geoffrey Crayon came to being an artist;–of Talleyrand, and many other celebrities;–and of incidents which seemed to take us back to a former generation. Often at this and subsequent visits I ventured to suggest, (not professionally,) after some of these reminiscences, "I hope you have taken time to make a note of these";–but the oracle nodded a sort of humorous No.–A drive to Sleepy Hollow–Mr. Irving again managing the ponies himself–crowned our visit; and with such a coachman and guide, in such regions, we were not altogether unable to appreciate the excursion.

You are aware that in "Knickerbocker," especially, Mr. Irving made copious revisions and additions, when the new edition was published in 1848. The original edition (1809) was dedicated with mock gravity to the New York Historical Society; and the preface to the revision explains the origin and intent of the work. Probably some of the more literal-minded grandsons of Holland were somewhat unappreciative of the precise scope of the author's genius and the bent of his humor; but if this "veritable history" really elicited any "doubts" or any hostility, at the time, such misapprehension has doubtless been long since removed. It has often been remarked that Diedrich Knickerbocker had really enlisted more practical interest in the early annals of his native State than all other historians together, down to his time. But for him we might never have had an O'Callaghan or a Brodhead.

The "Sketch-Book" also received considerable new matter in the revised edition; and the story, in the preface, of the author's connection with Scott and with Murray added new interest to the volume, which has always been *the* favorite with the public. You will remember Mr. Bryant's remark about the change in the tone of Mr. Irving's temperament shown in this work as contrasted with Knickerbocker, and the probable cause of this change. Mr. Bryant's very delicate and judicious reference to the fact of Mr. Irving's early engagement was undoubtedly correct. A miniature of a young lady, intellectual, refined, and beautiful, was handed me one day by Mr. Irving, with a request that I would have a slight injury repaired by an artist and a new case made for it, the old one being actually worn out by much use. The painting (on ivory) was exquisitely fine. When I returned it to him in a suitable velvet case, he took it to a quiet corner and looked intently on the face for some minutes, apparently unobserved, his tears falling freely on the glass as he gazed. That this was a miniature of the lady,—Miss Hoffman, a sister of Ogden Hoffman,—it is not now, perhaps, indelicate to surmise. It is for a poet to characterize the nature of an attachment so loyal, so fresh, and so fragrant, *forty years* after death had snatched away the mortal part of the object of affection.

During one of his visits to the city, Mr. Irving suddenly asked if I could give him a bed at my house at Staten Island. I could. So we had a nice chatty evening, and the next morning we took him on a charming drive over the hills of Staten Island. He seemed to enjoy it highly, for he had not been there, I believe, since he was stationed there in a military capacity, during the War of 1812, as aid of Governor Tompkins. He gave us a humorous account of some of his equestrian performances, and those of the Governor, while on duty at the island; but neither his valor nor the Governor's was tested by any actual contact with the enemy.

In facility of composition, Mr. Irving, I believe, was peculiarly influenced by "moods." When in his usual good health, and the spirit was on him, he wrote very rapidly; but at other times composition was an irksome task, or even an impossible one. Dr. Peters says, he frequently rose from his bed in the night and wrote for hours together. Then again he would not touch his pen for weeks. I believe his most rapidly written work was the one often pronounced his most spirited one, and a model as a biography, the "Life of Goldsmith." Sitting at my desk one day, he was looking at Forster's clever work, which I proposed to reprint. He remarked that it was a favorite theme of his, and he had half a

Washington Irving (seated, right center) surrounded by literary figures at his home, Sunnyside. This famous composite portrait positioned Irving at the center of the emergent literary canon of nineteenth-century America.

mind to pursue it, and extend into a volume a sketch he had once made for an edition of Goldsmith's Works. I expressed a hope that he would do so, and within sixty days the first sheets of Irving's "Goldsmith" were in the printer's hands. The press (as he says) was "dogging at his heels," for in two or three weeks the volume was published.

Visiting London shortly after the "Life of Mahomet" was prepared for the press, I arranged with Mr. Murray, on the author's behalf, for an English edition of "Mahomet," "Goldsmith," etc., and took a request from Mr. Irving to his old friend Leslie, that he would make a *true* sketch of the venerable Diedrich Knickerbocker. Mr. Irving insisted that the great historian of the Manhattoes was not the vulgar old fellow they would keep putting on the omnibuses and ice-carts; but that, though quaint and old-fashioned, he was still of gentle blood. Leslie's sketches, however, (he made two,) did not hit the mark exactly; Mr. Irving liked Darley's better.

Among the briefer visits to Sunnyside which I had the good-fortune to enjoy was one with the estimable compiler of the "Dictionary of Authors." Mr. Irving's amiable and hospitable nature prompted him always to welcome visitors so kindly, that no one, however dull, and however uncertain his claims, would fail to be pleased with his visit. But when the genial host was in good health and in his best moods, and the visitor had any magnetism in his composition, when he found, in short, a kindred spirit, his talk was of the choicest. Of Sir Walter Scott, especially, he would tell us much that was interesting. Probably no two writers ever appreciated each other more heartily than Scott and Irving. The sterling good sense, and quiet, yet rich humor of Scott, as well as his literary tastes and wonderful fund of legendary lore, would find no more intelligent and discriminating admirer than Irving; while the rollicking fun of the veritable Diedrich and the delicate fancy and pathos of Crayon were doubtless unaffectedly enjoyed by the great Scotsman. I wish I could tell you accurately one-half of the anecdotes which where so pleasantly related during those various brief visits at "the Cottage"; but I did not go there to take notes, and it is wicked to spoil good stories by misquotation. One story, however, I may venture to repeat.

You remember how the author of the "Pleasures of Hope" was once hospitably entertained by worthy people, under the supposition that he was the excellent missionary Campbell, just returned from Africa,—and how the massive man of state, Daniel Webster, had repeated occasion, in England, to disclaim honors meant for Noah, the man of words. Mr. Irving told, with great glee, a little story against himself, illustrating these uncertainties of distant fame. Making a small pur-

chase at a shop in England, not long after his second or third work had given currency to his name, he gave his address ("Mr. Irving, Number," etc.) for the parcel to be sent to his lodgings. The salesman's face brightened: "Is it possible," said he, "that I have the pleasure of serving Mr. Irving?" The question, and the manner of it, indicated profound respect and admiration. A modest and smiling acknowledgment was inevitable. A few more remarks indicated still more deferential interest on the part of the man of tape; and then another question, about Mr. Irving's "latest work," revealed the pleasant fact that he was addressed as the famous Edward Irving, of the Scotch Church,—the man of divers tongues. The very existence of the "Sketch-Book" was probably unknown to his intelligent admirer. "All I could do," added Mr. Crayon, with that rich twinkle in his eye,— "all I could do was to take my tail between my legs and slink away in the smallest possible compass."

A word more about Mr. Irving's manner of life. The impression given by Thackeray, in his notice (genial enough, and well-meant, doubtless) of Irving's death, is absurdly inaccurate. His picture of the "one old horse," the plain little house, etc., would lead one to imagine Mr. Irving a weak, good-natured old man, amiably, but parsimoniously, saving up his pennies for his "eleven nieces," (!) and to this end stinting himself, among other ways, to "a single glass of wine," etc., etc. Mr. Thackeray's notions of style and state and liveried retinues are probably not entirely un-English, notwithstanding he wields so sharp a pen against England's snobs; and he may naturally have looked for more display of greatness at the residence of an ex-ambassador. But he could scarcely appreciate that simple dignity and solid comfort, that unobtrusive *fitness,* which belonged to Mr. Irving's home-arrangements. There were no flunkies in gold and scarlet; but there were four or five good horses in the stable, and as many suitable carriages. Everything in the cottage was peculiarly and comfortably elegant, without the least pretension. As to the "single glass of wine," Mr. Irving, never a professed teetotaller, was always temperate on instinct both in eating and drinking; and in his last two years I believe he did not taste wine at all. In all financial matters, Mr. Irving's providence and preciseness were worthy of imitation by all professional literary men; but with exactness and punctuality he united a liberal disposition to make a suitable use of money, and to have all around him comfortable and appropriate. Knowing that he could leave a handsome independence for those nearest to him, he had no occasion for any such anxious care as Mr. Thackeray intimates.

Thackeray had been invited to Yonkers, to give his lecture on "Charity and Humor." At this "Ancient

Dorp" he was the guest of Cozzens, and I had the honor of accompanying the greater and lesser humorist in a drive to Sunnyside, nine miles. (This call of an hour, by-the-way, was Thackeray's only glimpse of the place he described.) The interview was in every way interesting. Mr. Irving produced a pair of antiquated spectacles, which had belonged to Washington, and Major Pendennis tried them on with evident reverence. The hour was well filled with rapid, pleasant chat; but no profound analysis of the characteristics of wit and humor was elicited either from the Stout Gentleman or from Vanity Fair. Mr. Irving went down to Yonkers, to hear Thackeray's lecture in the evening, after we had all had a slice of bear at Mr. Sparrowgrass's, to say nothing of sundry other courses, with a slight thread of conversation between. At the lecture, he was so startled by the eulogistic presentation of the lecturer to the audience, by the excellent chief of the committee, that I believe he did not once nod during the evening. We were, of course, proud to have as our own guest for the night such an embodiment of "Charity and Humor" as Mr. Thackeray saw in the front bench before him, but whom he considerately spared from holding up as an illustration of his subject.

Charity, indeed, practical "good-will toward men," was an essential part of Mr. Irving's Christianity,—and in this Christian virtue he was sometimes severely tested. Nothing was more irksome to him than to be compelled to endure calls of mere curiosity, or to answer letters either of fulsome eulogy of himself or asking for his eulogy of the MSS. or new work of the correspondent. Some letters of that kind he probably never did answer. Few had any idea of the *fagging* task they imposed on the distinguished victim. He would worry and fret over it trebly in anticipation, and the actual task itself was to him probably ten times as irksome as it would be to most others. Yet it would be curious to know how many letters of suggestion and encouragement he actually did write in reply to solicitations from young authors for his criticism and advice, and his recommendation, or, perhaps, his pecuniary aid. Always disposed to find merit, even where any stray grains of the article lay buried in rubbish, he would amiably say the utmost that could justly be said in favor of "struggling genius." Sometimes his readiness to aid meritorious young authors into profitable publicity was shamefully abused,—as in the case of Maitland, an Englishman, who deliberately forged an absurdly distorted paraphrase of a note of Mr. Irving's, besides other disreputable use of the signature which he had enticed from him in answer to urgent appeals. But these were among the penalties of honorable fame and influence which he might naturally expect to pay. The sunny aspect on the "even tenor of his way" still pre-

vailed; and until the hand of disease reached him in the last year of his life, very few probably enjoyed a more tranquil and unruffled existence.

It became almost a proverb, that Mr. Irving was a nearly solitary instance of a long literary career (half a century) untouched by even a breath of ill-will or jealousy on the part of a brother-author. The annals of the *genus irritabile* scarcely show a parallel to such a career. The most prominent American contemporary of Mr. Irving in imaginative literature, I suppose, was Fenimore Cooper,—whose genius raised the American name in Europe more effectively even than Irving's, at least on the Continent. Cooper had a right to claim respect and admiration, if not affection, from his countrymen, for his brilliant creations and his solid services to American literature; and he knew it. But, as we all know,—for it was patent,—when he returned from Europe, after sending his "Letter to his Countrymen," and gave us "Home as Found," his reception was much less marked with warmth and enthusiasm than Mr. Irving's was; and while he professed indifference to all such whims of popular regard, yet he evidently brooded a little over the relative amount of public attention extended to his brother-author. At any rate, he persistently kept aloof from Mr. Irving for many years; and not unfrequently discoursed, in his rather authoritative manner, about the humbuggery of success in this country, as exhibited in some shining instances of popular and official favor. With great admiration for Cooper, whose national services were never recognized as they deserved to be, I trust no injustice is involved in the above suggestion, which I make somewhat presumptuously,—especially as Mr. Irving more than once spoke to me in terms of strong admiration of the works and genius of Cooper, and regretted that the great novelist seemed to cherish some unpleasant feeling towards him. One day, some time after I had commenced a library edition of Cooper's best works, and while Irving's were in course of publication in companionship, Mr. Irving was sitting at my desk, with his back to the door, when Mr. Cooper came in, (a little bustlingly, as usual,) and stood at the office-entrance, talking. Mr. Irving did not turn, (for obvious reasons,) and Cooper did not see him. Remembering his "Mr. Sharp, Mr. Blunt,—Mr. Blunt, Mr. Sharp," I had acquired caution as to introductions without mutual consent; but with a brief thought of how matters stood, (they had not met for several years,) and a sort of instinct that reduced the real difference between the parties to a baseless fabric of misapprehension, I stoutly obeyed the impulse of the moment, and simply said,—"Mr. Cooper, here is Mr. Irving." The latter turned,—Cooper held out his hand cordially, dashed at once into an animated conversation, took a chair, and, to my surprise and delight, the two authors sat for an hour, chatting in their best manner about almost every topic of the day and some of former days. They parted with cordial good wishes, and Mr. Irving afterwards frequently alluded to the incident as being a very great gratification to him. He may have recalled it with new satisfaction, when, not many months afterwards, he sat on the platform at the "Cooper Commemoration," and joined in Bryant's tribute to the genius of the departed novelist.

Mr. Irving was never a systematic collector of books, and his little library at Sunnyside might have disappointed those who would expect to see there rich shelves of choice editions, and a full array of all the favorite authors among whom such a writer would delight to revel. Some rather antiquated tomes in Spanish,—indifferent sets of Calderon and Cervantes, and of some modern French and German authors,—a presentation-set of Cadell's "Waverley," as well as that more recent and elegant emanation from the classic press of Houghton,—a moderate amount of home-tools for the "Life of Washington," (rarer materials were consulted in the town-libraries and at Washington,)—and the remainder of his books were evidently a hap-hazard collection, many coming from the authors, with their respects, and thus sometimes costing the recipient their full (intrinsic) value in writing a letter of acknowledgment.

The little apartment had, nevertheless, become somewhat overcrowded, and a suggestion for a general renovation and pruning seemed to be gladly accepted,—so I went up and passed the night there for that purpose. Mr. Irving, in his easy-chair in the sitting-room, after dinner, was quite content to have me range at large in the library and to let me discard all the "lumber" as I pleased; so I turned out some hundred volumes of *un*-classic superfluity, and then called him in from his nap to approve or veto my proceedings. As he sat by, while I rapidly reported the candidates for exclusion, and he nodded assent, or as, here and there, he would interpose with "No, no, not *that*," and an anecdote or reminiscence would come in as a reason against the dismissal of the book in my hand, I could not help suggesting the scene in Don Quixote's library, when the priest and the barber entered upon their scrutiny of its contents. Mr. Irving seemed to be highly amused with this pruning process, and his running commentary on my "estimates of value" in weighing his literary collections was richly entertaining.

Observing that his library-table was somewhat antiquated and inadequate, I persuaded him to let me make him a present of a new one, with the modern conveniences of drawers and snug corners for keeping his stray papers. When I sent him such a one, my stipulation for the return of the old one as a present to me was pleasantly granted. This relic was of no great intrinsic value; but, as he had written on this table many of his later works, including "Mahomet," "Goldsmith," "Wolfert's Roost," and "Washington," I prize it, of course, as one of the most interesting momentos of Sunnyside.

As an illustration of habit, it may be added, that, some time after the new table had been installed, I was sitting with him in the library, when he searched long and fruitlessly for some paper which had been "so *very* carefully stowed away in some *very* safe drawer" that it was not to be found, and the search ended in a sort of half-humorous, half-earnest denunciation of all "modern conveniences";—the simple old table, with its primitive facilities, was, after all, worth a dozen of these elegant contrivances for memory-saving and neatness.

One rather curious characteristic of Mr. Irving was excessive, unaffected modesty and distrust of himself and of his own writings. Considering how many a *débutant* in letters, not yet out of his teens, is so demonstratively self-confident as to the prospective effect of his genius on an expecting and admiring world, it was always remarkable to hear a veteran, whose fame for half a century had been cosmopolitan, expressing the most timid doubts as to his latest compositions, and fearing they were unequal to their position,—so unwilling, too, to occupy an inch of ground to which any other writer might properly lay claim. Mr. Irving had planned and made some progress in a work on the Conquest of Mexico, when he learned of Mr. Prescott's intentions, and promptly laid his project aside. His "Life of Washington," originating more than thirty years ago, was repeatedly abandoned, as the successive works of Mr. Sparks, Mr. Paulding, and others, appeared; and though he was subsequently induced to proceed with his long-considered plan of a more dramatic and picturesque narrative from a new point of view, yet he was more than once inclined to put his MSS. into the fire, in the apprehension that the subject had been worn threadbare by the various compilations which were constantly coming out. When he ventured his first volume, the cordial and appreciative reception promptly accorded to it surprised as much as it cheered and pleased him; for though he despised hollow flattery, no young writer was more warmly sensitive than he to all discriminating, competent, and honest applause or criticism. When "Wolfert's Roost" was published, (I had to entice the papers of that volume from his drawers, for I doubt whether he would have collected them himself,) I saw him affected actually to tears, on reading some of the hearty and well-written personal tributes which that

Sunnyside Residence of Washington Irving

G.P. Putnam. & C°. N.Y.

Engraving of Irving's home in Homes of American Authors. *As Irving became a cultural icon by midcentury, Sunnyside became a cultural shrine.*

volume called forth. But though every volume was received in this spirit by the press and the public, he was to the last apprehensive of failure, until a reliable verdict should again reassure him. The very last volume of his works (the fifth of "Washington") was thus timidly permitted to be launched; and I remember well his expression of relief and satisfaction, when he said that Mr. Bancroft, Professor Felton, and Mr. Duyckinck had been the first to assure him the volume was all that it should be. His task on this volume had perhaps extended beyond the period of his robust health,—it had *fagged* him,—but he had been spared to write every line of it with his own hand, and my own copy is enriched by the autograph of his valedictory.

To refer, however briefly, to Mr. Irving's politics or religion, even if I had intimate knowledge of both, (which assuredly I had not,) would be, perhaps, to overstep decorous limits. It may, however,

properly be mentioned, that, in the face of all inherent probabilities as to his comfortable conservatism, and his earnest instincts in favor of fraternal conciliation and *justice,* (which was as marked a quality in him as in the great man whom he so faithfully portrayed,) in spite of all the considerations urged by timid gentlemen of the old school in favor of Fillmore and the *status quo,* he voted in 1856, as he told me, for Fremont. In speaking of the candidates then in the field, he said of Fremont, that his comparative youth and inexperience in party-politics were points in his favor; for he thought the condition of the country called for a man of nerve and energy, one in his prime, and unfettered by the party-traditions and bargains for "the spoils." His characterization of a more experienced functionary, who had once served in the State Department, was more severe than I ever heard from him of any other person; and severity from a man of his judicious and kindly impulses had a meaning in it.

Favored once with a quiet Sunday at "the Cottage," of course there was a seat for us all in the family-pew at Christ Church in the village (Tarrytown). Mr. Irving's official station as Church-Warden was indicated by the ex-ambassador's meek and decorous presentation of the plate for the silver and copper offerings of the parishioners. At subsequent successive meetings of the General (State) Convention of the Protestant Episcopal Church, (to which I had been delegated from a little parish on Staten Island,) the names of Washington Irving and Fenimore Cooper were both recorded,—the latter representing Christ Church, Cooperstown. Mr. Irving for several years served in this capacity, and as one of the Missionary Committee of the Convention. His name was naturally sought as honoring any organization. He was the last person to be demonstrative or conspicuous either as to his faith or his works; but no disciple of Christ, perhaps, felt more devoutly than he did the reverential aspiration of "Glory to God in the highest, and on earth peace, good-will toward men."

Passing a print-window in Broadway one day, his eye rested on the beautiful engraving of "Christus Consolator." He stopped and looked at it intently for some minutes, evidently much affected by the genuine inspiration of the artist in this remarkable representation of the Saviour as the consoler of sorrow-stricken humanity. His tears fell freely. "Pray, get me that print," said he; "I must have it framed for my sitting-room." When he examined it more closely and found the artist's name, "It's by my old friend Ary Scheffer!" said he,—remarking further, that he had known Scheffer intimately, and knew him to be a true artist, but had not expected from him anything so excellent as this. I afterwards sent him the companion, "Christus Remunerator"; and the pair remained his daily companions till the day of his death. To me, the picture of Irving, amid the noise and bustle of noon in Broadway, shedding tears as he studied that little print, so feelingly picturing human sorrow and the source of its alleviation, has always remained associated with the artist and his works. If Irving could enjoy wit and humor and give that enjoyment to others, no other writer of books had a heart more tenderly sensitive than his to the sufferings and ills which flesh is heir to.

Of his later days,—of the calmly received premonitions of that peaceful end of which only the precise moment was uncertain,—of his final departure, so gentle and so fitting,—of that "Washington-Irving-day" so dreamily, blandly still, and almost fragrant, December though it was, when with those simple and appropriate obsequies his mortal remains were placed by the side of his brothers and sisters in the burial-ground of Sleepy Hollow, while thousands from far and near silently looked for the last time on his genial face and mourned his loss as that of a personal friend and a national benefactor, yet could hardly for *his* sake desire any more enviable translation from mortality,—of the many beautiful and eloquent tributes of living genius to the life and character and writings of the departed author,—of all these you have already an ample record. I need not repeat or extend it. If you could have "assisted" at the crowning "Commemoration," on his birthday, (April 3d,) at the Academy of Music, you would have found it in many respects memorably in accordance with the intrinsic fitness of things. An audience of five thousand, so evidently and discriminatingly intelligent, addressed for two hours by Bryant, with all his cool, judicious, deliberate criticism, warmed into glowing appreciation of the most delicate and peculiar beauties of the character and literary services he was to delineate,—and this rich banquet fittingly *desserted* by the periods of Everett,—such an evening was worthy of the subject, and worthy to be remembered. The heartiness and the genial insight into Irving's best traits which the poet displayed were peculiarly gratifying to the nearer friends and relatives. His sketch and analysis, too, had a remarkable completeness for an address of that kind, while its style and manner were models of chaste elegance. Speaking of Irving's contemporaries and predecessors, he warms into poetry, thus:—

"We had but one novelist before the era of the 'Sketch-Book': their number is now beyond enumeration by any but a professed catalogue-maker, and many of them are read in every cultivated form of human speech. Those whom we acknowledge as our poets—one of whom is the special favorite of our brothers in language who dwell beyond the sea—appeared in the world of letters and won its attention after Irving had become famous. We have wits and humorists and amusing essayists, authors of some of the airiest and most graceful contributions of the present century,—and we owe them to the new impulse given to our literature in 1819. I look abroad on these stars of our literary firmament,—some crowded together with their minute points of light in a galaxy, some standing apart in glorious constellations; I recognize Arcturus and Orion and Perseus and the glittering jewels of the Southern Crown, and the Pleiades shedding sweet influences; but the Evening Star, the soft and serene light that glowed in their van, the precursor of them all, has sunk below the horizon. The spheres, meanwhile, perform their appointed courses; the same motion which lifted them up to the mid-sky bears them onward to their setting; and they, too, like their bright leader, must soon be carried by it below the earth."

Let me quote also Mr. Bryant's closing remarks:—

"Other hands will yet give the world a bolder, more vivid, and more exact portraiture. In the mean time, when I consider for how many years he stood before the world as an author, with still increasing fame,—half a century in this most changeful of centuries,—I cannot hesitate to predict for him a deathless renown. Since he began to write, empires have arisen and passed away; mighty captains have appeared on the stage of the world, performed their part, and been called to their account; wars have been fought and ended which have changed the destinies of the human race. New arts have been invented and adopted, and have pushed the old out of use; the household economy of half mankind has undergone a revolution. Science has learned a new dialect and forgotten the old; the chemist of 1807 would be a vain babbler among his brethren of the present day, and would in turn become bewildered in the attempt to understand them. Nation utters speech to nation in words that pass from realm to realm with the speed of light. Distant countries have been made neighbors; the Atlantic Ocean has become a narrow frith, and the Old World and the New shake hands across it; the East and the West look in at each other's windows. The new inventions bring new calamities, and men perish in crowds by the recoil of their own devices. War has learned more frightful modes of havoc, and armed himself with deadlier weapons; armies are borne to the battle-field on the wings of the wind, and dashed against each other and destroyed with infinite bloodshed. We grow giddy with this perpetual whirl of strange events, these rapid and ceaseless mutations; the earth seems to be reeling under our feet, and we turn to those who write like Irving for some assurance that we are still in the same world into which we were born; we read, and are quieted and consoled. In his pages we see that the language of the heart never becomes obsolete; that Truth and Good and Beauty, the offspring of God, are not subject to the changes which beset the inventions of men. We become satisfied that he whose works were the delight of our fathers, and are still ours, will be read with the same pleasure by those who come after us."

—*Atlantic Monthly,* 6 (November 1860): 601–612

Rough Notes of Thirty Years in the Trade

Putnam's experience over a period of four decades as a literary professional was more varied than that of any other contemporary American publisher. He had a decade of first-hand experience in the international book trade and extensive contacts and dealings with writers, publishers, printers, artists, and editors across the United States and overseas. He had, furthermore, an additional dimension of professional associations with politicians, diplomats, and librarians, arising out of his involvement in larger issues such as the organization of the profession and international copyright.

In short, Putnam had led a rich life in letters and had a compelling story to tell. Already the premier annalist of the publishing profession, he decided sometime around the outbreak of the Civil War to embark on a full-scale professional memoir and sounded out colleagues' opinions about the project. He had second thoughts, however, and instead composed a more modest set of sketches organized around his own professional experiences and memories. Though brief and unsystematic, "Rough Notes of Thirty Years in the Trade," which was published in three installments in American Publishers' Circular and Literary Gazette *in summer 1863, was his generation's best overview of the publishing industry during a period of remarkable development. The third installment included two footnotes, which have been converted into endnotes here.*

* * *

ROUGH NOTES OF THIRTY YEARS IN THE TRADE.

It was in 1829 that the book-trade and I were introduced to each other. Four years before that I had doubled Cape Ann on my sloop voyage from away down east, to take my chance in the wide world, or rather in the great city of Boston, which I imagined to be at least equal to all the rest of sublunary things. Four years' apprenticeship there in the business of supplying a footing for the understandings of the modern Athenians—in other words, selling them carpets—and then my fortunes were to be sought in what seemed at that period the remote El Dorado of New York. Two or three times a week the stages would start off hours before daylight to take passengers to "the splendid steamer Washington," at Providence—a longer and more tiresome journey than it is now to New York, six times the distance. Not, however, by the swift luxury of stage-coach, or railway, or steamer was my momentous journey to be performed, but by a week's voyage in Capt. Nickerson's "fast schooner" round Cape Cod, varied by a morning's call at Holmes' Hole and Hyannis, and by reiterated calms in the Sound. Coenties Slip and the wonders of Pearl Street were approached with suitable deference and awe, as one might now arrive at Moscow or Timbuctoo.

Thus, at the age of fifteen, afloat in the great metropolis, expected to make my own way in the world, my first studies consisted of paragraphs in the papers beginning "Boy wanted." With one of these cut from the "Courier" I promptly presented myself, as required, at the counting-room of the great mercantile house of Phelps, Peck, & Co., on the corner of Fulton and Cliff Streets.

A few questions from the rather awful personage at the head of the firm had so shaken my self-confidence or my nerves that when I essayed a specimen of handwriting, as he directed, the result was a failure: the great merchant shook his head, and I departed crestfallen. A year or two after this, it may be here mentioned, this great house tumbled down–not metaphorically, but literally–burying in its ruins every person in the building.

Vexed with the defeat of this first application for "a place," I was all the more ready for the next chance. At a little book and stationery store in Broadway near Maiden Lane, there was a notice in the window of "A boy wanted." I presented myself on the spot. "You are too old: only a small boy is wanted for errands, to sweep, &c., and to live in my family; wages twenty-five dollars a year and board." "That will suit me; if you choose to try me, I don't object to the work or the pay." The docility of the applicant seemed to please, and I was at once installed in the situation. This, my first master in the book trade, was Mr. GEORGE W. BLEECKER. He lived, London fashion, over his little store, a practice which in these days neither fashion nor economy would tolerate, at least in Broadway. He published a quarto monthly, called "The Euterpiad, an Album of Music, Poetry, and Prose." My first travel out of New York was a cruise up the Hudson to canvass for the interests of this creditable but rather short-lived periodical. The editor of the "Catskill Recorder" of that day, and perhaps some others in Hudson and Poughkeepsie, can testify to my zeal, if not to my success in this expedition.

An apprenticeship of a year or two as clerk-of-all-work in this little mart of school books, Andover theology, albums, stationery, and cheap pictures was not a severe ordeal. "J. & J. HARPER," then just beginning their successful career as publishers, were supplying the market with the new English novels on the whity-brown paper and in the rough paper-labelled boards which that era of the world deemed all-sufficient. In the production of many of these novels there was a lively competition between the Harpers and the old-established house of Carey & Lea, of Philadelphia. I well remember the almost frantic delight of poor McDonald Clarke, "the mad poet," our frequent visitor, when the enterprising printers of Cliff Street had ventured upon so great an investment as "Moore's Life of Byron," in a couple of very fair octavos. This amiable but erratic son of genius, I am sorry to add, used literally to swear by Byron, who appeared to be both in verse and in shirt collar his hero and his model; he would stand at the counter eagerly turning over Moore's leaves and quoting scraps. Whether his purse was finally equal to the coveted purchase is now uncertain.

To recall the unsolicited and mysterious promotion from this errand-boy position to the dignity of first clerk at the stately "Park Place House," "an emporium of literature and art" (since degraded into the vulgar purposes of a hotel), and the transfer to the less showy but more active duties of general clerk and messenger for Mr. JONATHAN LEAVITT in the two- story building on the corner of John Street and Broadway, and to tell of the incidents of trade in those times, might be tiresome and unprofitable. "Egotistical stuff" has already been muttered by the reader. I will try to drop the personal pronoun, only retaining it when needful for clearness and accuracy in these rough and rapid recollections.

No more worthy or conscientious man ever published or sold books than JONATHAN LEAVITT. Shrewdness and good sense made up for him the lack of even elementary book-learning, and he became the leading New York publisher of theological and religious books–particularly in connection with Crocker & Brewster, of Boston. What stacks of S. T. Armstrong's edition of Scott's Bible used to come weekly from Boston; what rows of Rosenmueller, and Calvin, and Tholuck from Leipsic; and what shelvesful of Calmet, and Lightfoot, and Baxter, and Owen, and Lardner, from that pioneer in "English remainders," Mr. W. C. Hall, the Yankee in London! The piles of these consignments from England and Germany grew so high that an extra room had to be hired for them in "Clinton Hall," the one now occupied by the Park Bank. Mr. DANIEL APPLETON, late of the "dry goods" interest, and brother-in-law of Mr. LEAVITT, was there installed in charge, to supply the "trade." This excellent gentleman, thus initiated among books, soon after became the founder of the great house of D. APPLETON & CO.

At this time (1832-3) the chief publishers of the land were these: In Boston, LINCOLN & EDMUNDS (succeeded by GOULD & LINCOLN), devoted especially to the views of the Baptists; CROCKER &

BREWSTER (still flourishing as the oldest book firm in the United States), the leading Orthodox Congregationalist publishers; CUMMINGS & HILLIARD, afterwards HILLIARD, GRAY & CO., chiefly engaged in school books; LILLY, WAIT, & CO., reprinters of the foreign reviews, &c.; R. P. & C. WILLIAMS, respectably rusty in the general trade; ALLEN & TICKNOR, predecessors of the present well-known firm of TICKNOR & FIELDS, on the classic corner of School Street, clinging with praiseworthy tenacity to the venerable old building which has survived some five or six generations; LITTLE & BROWN, still flourishing in strength, wealth, and respectability, though they have lost the original junior partner, Mr. Brown, one of the ablest and best-informed publishers this country has produced. PERKINS & MARVIN, and smaller concerns were also flourishing in Boston.

In New York, the old and most respectable firm of COLLINS & HANNAY carried on the best of the "jobbing trade" on Pearl Street, the sorted stock of Dabolls and Websters, and slates and sponges, and Ames' papers filling three or four lofts, supervised by the versatile and witty John Keese; T. & J. SWORDS, the "ancient" Episcopal publishers in Broadway, whose imprint may be found dated as early as 1792; EVERT DUYCKINCK, an estimable man, father of the well-known authors, E. A. and G. L. DUYCKINCK; S. WOOD and SONS (the sons worthily continuing); and JOSEPH B. COLLINS in the school book and jobbing trade; ELAM BLISS, the gentlemanly and popular literary caterer on Broadway (where Trinity Buildings now stand), whose elegant little "Talisman," edited by Bryant, Verplanck, and Robert C. Sands, was the father of American "Annuals," and a good deal better than some of the children; G. & C. CARVILL, the English successors of the still more famous Eastburn, on the corner of Wall Street and Broadway, the most extensive retail dealers in general literature (including English books), and like Bliss's, opposite, the lounging place of the *literati;* GEORGE DEARBORN, then a new star, also "gentlemanly" and intelligent, issuing double-column Byrons, Shakespeares, Johnsons, Burkes, and Rollins, besides the "American Monthly," the "Republic of Letters," and the "New York Review;" Jona. Leavitt, as aforesaid, taking charge especially of the department of theology; and the brothers Harper, as mentioned, were building up their gigantic business of producing general literature, then chiefly consisting of reprints from English authors. In Philadelphia, this main branch of the trade was then largely in the control of CAREY & LEA, successors of the famous Mathew Carey, a name that will always be remembered as an honor to our "craft," in the premises still occupied by the wealthy firm of BLANCHARD & LEA, the leading medical publishers. This house was then issuing, in quarterly volumes, the "Encyclopædia Americana," edited by Dr. Lieber, an enterprise of considerable magnitude for that day. CAREY & HART, in the same "corner of Fourth and Chesnut," rivalled the Harpers in their dispensations of the new novels, and also in more solid literature. JOHN GRIGG, a publisher and bookseller of remarkable ability, rare judgment, and tact, afterwards GRIGG & ELLIOT, published largely in medicine (as well as the Careys), [but "everybody knows Eberle's is the best *Practice*"], and the Standard Poets "in the best Philadelphia sheep," and "Weems' Washington," and "Gaston's Collections," and "Wirt's Patrick Henry," and the "Cases of Conscience," but doing a still greater trade in furnishing the "country dealers" in a thousand places, south and west, with their whole supplies of "books and stationery," thus founding the present extensive business of Lippincott & Co., besides one or two princely fortunes for the retiring partners. The rest of the trade in school and other books was divided between HOGAN & THOMPSON, URIAH HUNT, KEY & BIDDLE, and a few others.

In Andover, Massachusetts, Mr. FLAGG printed the learned works of Moses Stuart and Leonard Woods. In Hartford, "Uncle Silas" ANDRUS would grind out cords of Shakespeares, Byrons, Bunyans, and Alonzo and Melissas, suited for the country trade; and the HUNTINGTONS and ROBINSONS produced cart-loads of Olneys and Comstocks. In Springfield, the MERRIAMS printed Chitty's law books and others, but had not yet begun to work the golden mine of "Webster's unabridged." Here and there a book would come along with the imprint of Hyde of Portland, Kay of Pittsburg, Howe of New Haven, Metcalf of Cambridge, Gould of Albany, Armstrong of Baltimore; but the three great cities first named, then as now, monopolized the bulk of the book-making—Boston rather leading the van.

The importation of English books was almost wholly in the hands of THOMAS WARDLE, of Philadelphia, a sturdy Yorkshireman, who had served as porter at Longman's, in London.

Thus were all these names, thirty years since (and many of them happily remain), "familiar in our mouths as household words."

At this era, stereotyping was the exception (and in England is so yet). With us it is now the rule. Then, editions of 1,000 copies of new books from type were the average; those of 500 copies were as usual as any exceeding 2,000. Advertising was then an expense so trifling as to be scarcely taken into account; now, it frequently adds one-half to the cost of a book. Authors' fortunes were as rarely found in books as in gold mines; but then, as now, school text-books were often sources of large and steady income, both for author and publisher.

In process of time Mr. DANIEL APPLETON, after a short connection with Mr. Leavitt, opened his own separate business at No. 200 Broadway. Among the investments divided was one in an edition of 1,000 copies of a volume of my own, of some 400 pages, then just printed, entitled "Chronology, an Introduction and Index to Universal History." It was rather grand to have to say that two great publishing firms were required to produce my first work; for this little book of reference thus anonymously put forth by two (now rival) sponsors had been honestly compiled, originally, for my own benefit alone, from some 150 different volumes of historical works. In itself the book was "of no consequence," except as an ordinary manual of historical dates; but the origin of it I may be pardoned for noticing only as an encouragement for other lads in the same circumstances. It had so happened that although my father had graduated at Harvard, and my home influences were of the educated and cultivated sort, I had not received even the ordinary elementary "schooling," to say nothing of a college course; and further, I had been permitted even less than ordinary access to general reading.—It is therefore a pleasure to testify, as I can very heartily, to the usefulness of the New York Mercantile Library, then a few years old, and just located in the new Clinton Hall, in Beekman Street, the corner-stone of which I had seen laid by that liberal-minded citizen, Philip Hone. Now, in these degenerate days, boys in my position of sixteen or seventeen are usually dismissed from the "store" at six or seven o'clock; in 1831-2, we were kept till nine or ten; so that it was usually after nine when I could get up to the Mercantile and take out my book. It chanced that my tastes rather turned from the novels to the more solid interest of a course of history. Beginning with father Herodotus (in Beloe's English), I plodded on through Thucydides, Xenophon, Livy, Tacitus, Sallust; then Gibbon, Russell's Modern Europe, several histories of England, including Hume, Lingand, Smollett, and De Moleville. Crammed with some hundred and fifty octavos, rapidly mastered in succession, and with no clear guide at hand, personal or in book shape, to systematize and classify the stock of lore thus acquired, I began to take notes and make parallel tables. I copied and recopied, and collated and revised until I had written over a couple of reams. Much of this industry might have been spared if I had fallen in with any book of tables, such as now

Daniel Appleton, one of the first publishers Putnam came to know in New York. Putnam regarded Appleton's company, which was expanded by his sons, as a model of publishing imagination and integrity.

abound; but I look back upon this little exercise in amateur historical "research" as the best self-discipline and drilling I could have contrived. I can't imagine any more profitable self-instruction for a boy than something of this kind—a digest of what he has read or studied, prepared by himself, in systematic form, for easy reference and remembrance. The manual I refer to was commenced at the age of fifteen, and occupied me about three years, chiefly at night, between ten and two o'clock. When matured, as it appeared useful to me, I imagined it might be worth printing for others. Mr. Leavitt said, "Yes, if some learned man will examine and recommend it."

So I gathered pluck enough to present myself and my little wares to some of the literati. The first I called upon was Rev. Professor McVickar, of Columbia College. Looking at me somewhat sternly as he turned over the leaves, he asked, "Where were you educated, sir?"

"I have never had any education, sir."

"Ah!" (expressively.)

The MSS. was presently handed back to me with the *intimation* that it was not deemed expedient to promote and encourage any such presumption as my request and my statement implied.

The next *savant* approached was the late Rev. Dr. Schroeder, a man of extensive learning, whom I found in his library surrounded by Talmuds and Targums and scores of folios and quartos which would have put Dominie Sampson into ecstasies. Dr. S. was specially remarkable for courtesy and suavity of manners. Nothing could be kinder than my reception. His scrutiny was not very severe; but he gave me, nevertheless, a recommendation so cordial and emphatic that Mr. Leavitt was won over at once. Mr. Gray, of Cherry Street, was sent for, and the printing of the book was commenced. It took a whole year to be printed! In 1832 I carried home a bound copy, only quietly elated with my "authorship." The edition was soon sold out in both the rival houses, and for twenty-five years the book has been "O. P. Q." (the "Row" sign for "out of print quite").

I was still an underclerk at Mr. Leavitt's counter; but the habit of digesting and arranging facts and figures, acquired in making the "Chronology," spurred me on to attempt what seemed a *desideratum* in the trade—a periodical register of the publishing business. So I persuaded an enterprising firm of printers—West and Trow—(the latter still one of the leading printers of the country), to let me edit such an affair for them, and it was accordingly issued through the year 1834, under the title of the "Booksellers' Advertiser." In this, besides giving lists of new books, foreign and American, and statistics, I amused myself, if not others, in essaying an occasional "Notice," or short review of new books.

The audacity of this conduct on the part of a boy who could not give a single rule in English grammar, is sufficiently obvious to those who "know the ropes;" but it is not a solitary instance, I imagine, of a bray behind a lion's skin, and only reveals a small bit of the hollow pretension of the mysterious editorial "we." Thus, twenty-seven years ago, "we," the errand boy, actually reviewed with becoming gravity and decorous brevity, the first volume of "Bancroft's United States," "Knapp's Female Biography," "Jack Downing's Letters," "Abbott's Young Christian," "Mrs. Sigourney's Sketches," "Simms' Guy Rivers," "Cooper's Letter to his Countrymen," "Stewart's Great Britain," "Rapelye's Voyages," etc. etc.

In a brief notice of a volume by Mrs. Sigourney, "we" took care to embody a remark about the book which "we" had overheard in the store from the venerable "counsellor" George Griffin. When the paper was published the good old gentleman came in with a copy in his hand, took his accustomed chair, put up one of his long "continuations" to be nursed over the other,

adjusted his glasses, and began reading "our" notice as a remarkable corroboration of the opinion he had expressed, &c. Of course "we" demurely enjoyed the little joke none the less for its being harmless.

This little monthly—the grandfather of the present PUBLISHERS' CIRCULAR—I believe was the first attempt in this country to furnish a booksellers' journal with a statistical record of American publications. The scope of it was limited, of course, yet it was received with favor, and "promised to pay" in time, but I was unable to give it the needful attention. The editor's name was only given in the "Valedictory," in which it was stated that the paper "had been well received on both sides of the Atlantic," and had been "noticed in complimentary terms by various contemporaries. I resign it because it cannot be properly attended to without interfering with more legitimate duties, or infringing on midnight hours."

—*American Publishers' Circular and Literary Gazette*, n.s. 1 (15 July 1863): 242–245

* * *

[*Continued.*]

In the year 1836 I was invited to a junior partnership in the firm of W. & L., then beginning to cultivate the trade in English and foreign books. My "capital stock" contributed to the firm consisted of one hundred and fifty dollars, drawn from the Chambers' Street Savings Bank, and such knowledge of the business as I had picked up. Yet my new friends seemed to be content; and my first mission, after a laborious and dusty account of stock, was a trip to Europe to arrange foreign purchases and correspondence. This voyage and tour of eight months are referred to in another place. The errand was executed satisfactorily, and led to a business of considerable interest and value extending over several years.

The cultivation of friendly personal intercourse between the trade and between authors and publishers had already begun to be a topic of talk; and in March, 1837, George B. Collins, John Keese, and the writer of this started the idea of a Booksellers' Dinner to authors. A committee of a dozen or so was formed, and held meetings at David Felt's "Stationers' Hall," in Pearl Street, till they matured the plan of an entertainment, which "came off" at the old "City Hotel," on the 30th March. This, I suppose, was the first time American authors were ever recognized by the publishers as being worthy to be fed in public. The number of authors and editors present was about one hundred; these, with as many of the "Trade" from other places, were the guests of nearly one hundred booksellers of New York. Many will yet remember this as a creditable and pleasant

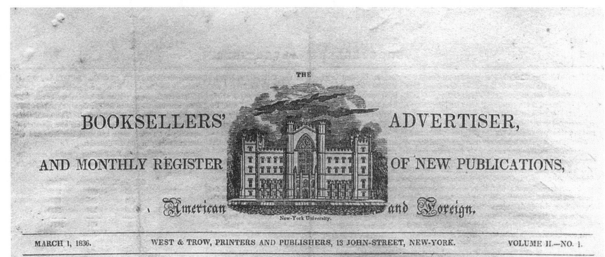

First page of an issue of the trade paper Putnam edited in 1834 and briefly in 1836 while he was a bookstore clerk. It was the first trade paper in American publishing history (courtesy of the American Antiquarian Society).

affair, and for several reasons interesting as significant of the progress of bookmaking. For a dignified president we resorted to the stationers, who furnished Mr. Felt. The sparkling Mr. Keese officiated as general aid, supervisor, and "toast-master," with an introductory speech. The speeches were by Col. Wm. L. Stone, of the "Commercial;" Charles King (now President of Columbia College), of the "American;" Philip Hone; Dr. J. W. Francis; Major Noah, of the "Star;" Matthew L. Davis, the biographer of Burr; Harrison Gray, for the Boston booksellers; James Harper, for those of Gotham; and Washington Irving.

The dinner-sayings and doings of twenty-five years ago would scarcely seem to be worth reproducing; yet, as one glances over the four columns of the report in the "N. Y. American" of April 1, 1837, it is pleasant to note the way they talked, and to think of those stars of the occasion that have since disappeared beneath the horizon. The genial and humorous Dr. Francis was, as usual, professional in his witty good sense, and abundant in his reminiscences. Chancellor Kent (of the "Commentaries") toasted "the Booksellers: they merit our gratitude, and especially when they zealously disseminate 'American Law.'" Ex-Mayor Hone gracefully complimented Irving, Halleck, and Bryant. The two poets were modestly silent; but Mr. Irving, in spite of himself, was enticed into a little speech, which he accomplished with positive success; it was a tribute to Rogers, the poet, as a friend of American genius, and (incidentally) to Halleck. Col. Stone, with "profitable length," supplied the solid facts and statistics, aided by the "Booksellers' Advertiser" before mentioned.

Among the notables present were Albert Gallatin, ex-Secretary of the Treasury; James K. Paulding, the novelist, whose speech, laudatory of J. Fenimore Cooper, was written, but not spoken; Col. John Trumbull, the venerable artist and aid of Washington. Toasts by the bushel were volunteered by Edgar A. Poe, Henry W. Herbert, Prof. Follen, Mr. Leggett, and others who have since passed away; and letters were read from Nicholas Biddle, the poet-financier; Mathew Carey and Gov. Armstrong, both ex-booksellers; Dr. Webster, the philologist; Dr. Bowditch, the mathematician; G. C. Verplanck; and others too tedious to mention. Cooper did not report himself. The occasion was pleasantly suggestive. In the "New York American," of next day, Mr. Charles King said that "the Booksellers' Festival was one of the best conducted, most spirited, and most agreeable entertainments it was ever our fortune to be present at." * * "This most successful festival will leave impressions which cannot but tend to good."

It is natural here to recall the next affair of the same kind seventeen years later, and in which it was again my fortune to have a rather excessive share of—

the *work;* and these things make work for some one. The cards for this occasion read thus:–

> The New York Publishers' Association
> Request the Honor of
> Mr. A. B.'s Company
> at a
> COMPLIMENTARY FRUIT FESTIVAL,
> at the
> New York Crystal Palace.
> Sept. 27, 1855.

This ovation (?) to pen-craft was effected at a cost (if I may descend to such statistics) of about $4000, all subscribed by that portion of the New York city booksellers who formed the "Publishers' Association." As far as numbers present were concerned, it was doubtless the most *extensive* attempt to entertain the literary world ever achieved. No less than seven hundred persons sat down to the innocent feast spread out on six immense tables in the north wing of the palace of glass. Of these, about one hundred and fifty belonged to the irritable *genus* of authors, including twenty of the female persuasion. To quote a tithe of their names, familiar as household words, would be tiresome. Here were Irving and Bryant, at the head of scores of the lesser luminaries of the world of letters; Morse, Davies, Olmsted, Loomis, and other *savans;* Bacon, Beecher, Chapin, Cheever, Dewey, Osgood, Prentiss, Spring, Tyng represented the clergy; Duer, Bradford, Jay, Daly appeared for the bar. Of the invited, who unavoidably were represented by "letters of regret," were Bancroft, Prescott, Longfellow, Everett, Kennedy, Simms, Emerson, Winthrop, Agassiz, Dana, Holmes, Halleck, Melville, Paulding, Sparks, etc.

Mr. W. H. Appleton, President of the Publishers' Association, and a munificent contributor to the festival, presided. The material entertainment, as promised in the cards, was simply a collation of fruit, with coffee, &c.; but as the whole affair was intrusted to that "prince of caterers," Mr. C. A. Stetson, of the Astor House, the display on the table was agreeable to the eye as well as to the taste. The most famous cultivators of pears and grapes in every part of the country were put under contribution, and the varieties obtained were choicer than the guests probably appreciated in the confusion. A full report of the speeches and letters was given in the *Publishers' Circular* of September and October, 1855, and a great part of them should be preserved in some permanent shape for future reference, for they were full of good things, and of special interest as illustrative of the progress of American bookmaking.

In 1838 my mission as partner in the firm seemed to be a foreign one. It was proposed to establish in London a branch of the house, there to import American books for the British market, and to purchase European books for this. It was with entire satisfaction that I again took passage with my old friend Captain Waite, in the packet ship England, to commence this inroad into the domains of our venerable Uncle John, for the purpose of an international change of ideas–a Yankee barter of our fresh young literature for the maturer and slower productions of fatherland. Elsewhere is chronicled the result of this enterprise. With several short visits home I remained in England nine years, returning in 1847.

In this interval my partner, Mr. W. (Mr. L. had retired), published a considerable number of books, original and reprinted. Among them were the works of Downing, the horticulturist, Professor Mahan, Professor Alexander, Ruskin, etc. But the most notable of his undertakings were the "Library of Choice Reading," reaching fifty volumes, and the "Library of American Books," including new works by Hawthorne, Bayard Taylor, Calvert, Mrs. Kirkland, Simms, Judge Hall, etc.; both series under the editorial supervision of Mr. E. A. Duyckinck. In the "Choice Library" were printed, in a style somewhat in advance of the previous average of cheap books, the works of Carlyle, Hood, Leigh Hunt, Lamb, Keats, Hazlitt, Coleridge, Kinglake, Warburton, Beckford, which the editor, with his proverbial discrimination, wisely judged would be a relief to many intelligent readers after the surfeit of "yellow-covered literature" which had afflicted the country. The success of this series was very encouraging, some volumes reaching a sale of six or seven thousand; but experience shows that collections of this kind, to be profitable, must not only be choice, but must be limited in extent.

The London agency was prosperous enough to *promise* permanence and solid advantage; and the continuance to this day of the business then and there founded, but transferred to two or three thriving firms, shows that its importance had not been overrated.

The amicable dissolution of our firm, in 1848, left me with my moderate portion of the "stock," but still without cash capital, to commence a separate business of my own.

The first year of this experiment proved successful in spite of several drawbacks; the balance of actual profit accrued having quadrupled the little capital invested. This result was, of course, largely owing to the new edition of Irving's works, started in August of this year, as referred to more particularly elsewhere. This was one of those comparatively rare enterprises in publishing aptly termed "a hit;" any reason, indeed, why it should not have been so is not very obvious.

It seems strange *now* that these works should have remained no less than five years in *statu-quo* waiting for a publisher to reprint them; and that our most eminent and most sagacious publishers should have pronounced that the only profitable edition of them would be a cheap one, in one or two large octavos, double columns! In another sketch, I have mentioned several little incidents of the pleasant, profitable, and honorable connection which my fortunate proposal for these works initiated. Much more might be said on such a theme; I merely add a word in regard to the mechanical part of the undertaking. Within a few years, an essential and creditable advance has been made in American book-manufacture. The press of the classic Houghton and others under the walls of old Harvard, and in New York have achieved wonders of neat elegance in typography; and the papermakers have well co-operated in the demonstration that the best issues of the English press can be equalled here when "we give our minds to it" (and our money). When the revised edition of Irving was commenced in 1848, we had no such models to imitate or excel. An epidemic of cheap pamphlets had prevailed; *these* works, classics though they were, now for the first time were presented in a snug and uniform shape, on fair paper and with neat externals–contrasting favorably with the rougher style of the last generation. The stereotyping by Mr. Trow was thought by Mr. Murray to be good enough for his market, and he purchased duplicates of the stereotypes of the new volumes; the octavo editions from Albemarle Street were printed from the American plates.

Up to that time the art of wood-engraving had not reached any marked excellence in this country; the cuts made in 1848 by Childs, Herrick, and others, from Darley's designs, were considered to be a material improvement on previous attempts of that sort. Of course, much better things have been done more recently; but designers have referred to these "cuts" of 1848 as giving a new impetus here to the business of wood engraving.

It may here be mentioned that the venerable father of American "Wood-cutting," Anderson, who practised the art more than "sixty years since," is (in 1863) still living, and continues to practise the art at the ripe age of 88. (!)

Referring to this art, I may here mention another affair in which the wood-cutters had a large and expensive share–the "Illustrated Record of the Crystal Palace Exhibition." Under the delusion that the Exhibition in 1854, managed by "our first citizens," was likely to prove a profitable as well as honorable success, after the manner of that in Hyde Park, I proposed, as did several other shrewder publishers, to produce a creditable volume, which should at least equal the "London Art Catalogue," and be in keeping with the character of the Crystal Palace and its contents. It would have been easy to send forth a cheap and showy book of superficial puffs, ornamented (?) with third-rate cuts at the expense of the exhibitors; but in an excess of simple confidence in the Directors and the Discriminating Public we went into the affair almost "without regard to expense." As a matter of curiosity to the initiated, and of warning to the inexperienced, I will record the dry facts that for this five-dollar quarto the daguerreotyping of the articles in the palace cost $1100; the drawings, engraving, and electrotyping cost $13,535 30 cts.; that the whole expense of 15,000 copies was nearly $40,000; 12,000 copies were sold at trade price, and the remainder at "a song;" and that the actual loss on the affair was about $20,000. Had the Exhibition been opened at the time appointed, and had all turned out as it was planned, perhaps the tables might have been turned; but the above result of a good deal of actual expense, besides time and labor taken from more profitable matters, was a sad lesson of the uncertainty of corporations, and especially of Crystal-Palace committees. I fear many of the "Board" were still more unlucky in their investments–and especially the stockholders, who purchased in the palmy days of promise at a premium of sixty-five per cent! At this price I knew of a positive sale by a gentleman who had only paid an instalment of ten per cent on his shares; and the net profits were some $3,000 on an investment of $300.

–*American Publishers' Circular and Literary Gazette,* n.s. 1
(1 August 1863): 258–259

* * *

[*Concluded.*]

In glancing back at such other publishing enterprises as my limited facilities permitted during the five years after the revised "Irving" was commenced, tiresome details may be avoided by giving only a brief reference to the *results* up to September, 1854, when, finding ourselves burdened with too much stock and too much responsibility, we decided suddenly to sell at auction the greater portion of all the stereotypes and stock accumulated. A few days' notice only was given, and the business was accomplished in a single extra day of the trade sale. Beginning at 9 A. M., and closing after midnight, this sale of stereotype plates and "sheet stock" produced the sum of $70,000. The oldest of the trade remembered no sale more successful, except that of Mr. Hart, of Philadelphia, a few months earlier. Without reproducing the catalogue, I may mention a few leading items. Considering the proverbial uncertainties of such investments, the result in these cases

shows that literary property sometimes has a tangible market value even in an auction room.

We had commenced a series of annotated British Classics in a snug "library" shape, the first being Addison, in six volumes, with notes by Prof. Greene, and Goldsmith, in four volumes, from Prior's edition. The metal plates for these ten volumes cost $5,900, and produced $3,900, after one edition of Addison and three of Goldsmith had been printed. These editions had been warmly welcomed, and have since formed the nucleus of Derby's long library of Classics. Downing's "Landscape Gardening" cost $471, and produced (after four editions) $2,050. His "Rural Essays" cost $500, and produced $900. The "Homes of American Authors," a volume which had been received with special favor (4,000 sold at $7), and which really merited success, produced $2,000–the plates, steels, and copyright having cost $2,370. The companion volumes of "Statesmen" cost $2,510, and sold for $1,800, after 2,000 had been printed. The twelve steels of the "Home Book of the Picturesque," an honest and I think a creditable attempt to produce a real work of art, from original pictures by *real* artists, were sold for $450–about one-fourth of their original value. The series of five "Home Cyclopedias," which several editors had compiled at my suggestion (my own compilation, "The World's Progress" being one), produced $6,500 for the plates and copyright, being nearly two-thirds of the first cost. 6,000 copies of "The World's Progress" had been sold. All these publications were such as one could regard with some satisfaction; and this might be said, too, of some others. "Layard's Nineveh," rather a bold venture for me at the time it was issued (1851), had cost for metal and illustrations some $1,250, but had yielded an actual profit of nearly $12,000, and now the plates produced three-fourths of the first cost–showing the advantage of substantial over ephemeral books. At that time, it will be remembered, we had no such precedents as "Uncle Tom's Cabin," or the 130,000 beautiful octavo volumes which our sagacious and liberal friend, of Brotherly Love, has so handsomely sent forth to tell the world of Kane's heroic endurance in the Polar seas. Four volumes of "Hood's Miscellanies" produced $1,000. These had been included in a collection of twenty-four semi-monthly volumes of "good and readable books," published, as an experiment, for twenty-five cents per volume.

After all this material transfer of "plates," we still retained the works of Bayard Taylor, Miss Warner, and (last, not least) Washington Irving; besides the "Monthly Magazine," the Crystal Palace work, and some others.

Besides the more costly ventures referred to, this sale also disposed of our interests in works of Bryant,

Olmsted, Dr. Hawks, Judge Hall, Parkman, Hawthorne, Kennedy, Prof. Silliman, Mayo, Godwin, Prof. Gray, Tuckerman, Mrs. Kirkland, Mrs. Gilman, Miss Sedgwick, Mrs. Robinson, Miss Cooper, Miss Wormeley; and in a number of reprints from Miss Bremer, Mrs. Howitt, Mrs. Moodie, Miss Murray, Dickens, Thackeray, Fouque, Warburton, Head, etc. At a little collation given to the buyers in the evening at the Astor House, some pleasant lines were improvised by the poet-publisher of Boston, whose genial kindness of heart is always as reliable as his ready wit and pure taste. Altogether this sale was a matter of some interest to the trade, and its success was noteworthy.

* * * * * * *

In October, 1852, a "private circular" was addressed to some hundred or more of the greater and lesser magnates in the American world of letters, inviting co-operation in a proposed new monthly magazine, which would "combine the popular character of a magazine with the higher and graver aims of the quarterly review;" "to preserve in all its departments an independent and elevated tone;" and to be "an organ of American thought." It was to be wholly original, and all contributions were to be paid for as liberally as the nature of the work would permit.

It would be both tedious and improper to reproduce even an outline of the correspondence which this scheme originated. This was but one of many attempts to establish an independent and high-toned magazine, and the promises and performances in all these attempts are perhaps scarcely expected to harmonize together with much nicety. This particular enterprise, moreover, did not prove to be of much more tenacious longevity than many of its predecessors. Still it is not too much, perhaps, to say, that this "Monthly" reached a reputation and success at least up to the average.

The volume of MS. responses to our circular would be entertaining to those who are curious in such matters; and so would be the quartos full of correspondence of contributors with the publisher–to say nothing of the editors' baskets-full. Mr. Everett, pleading engrossing cares, says: "If good wishes would help you, I could do you some good." Dr. Holmes "heartily approves of the design." Dr. Orville Dewey says, we promise "a magazine that the country wants." * * "Original writing to the purpose–to the business and bosoms of our American society, instead of the miserable trash," &c. Bishop Doane's "compliments to his old friend, and will be very happy," &c. Mr. Henry C. Carey speaks of the *specialites* which belong to individuals, and refers to certain essential obstacles in the way of independent treatment of themes, &c. Mr. Simms thinks "much will depend on the good sense, justice, and various resources of the editor;" but offers several tales. Prof. Tick-

Laying the Russ Pavement in Broadway, corner of Reade-street.

Illustration in the April 1853 issue of Putnam's Monthly. *Broadway was the main commercial street and the center of the publishing trade of antebellum New York, but its paving came late and lagged for years behind the northward movement of population up the island.*

nor has "not had time to do what he desired for the 'North American Review' and therefore," &c. Mr. Halleck sends "thanks for the honor you allow me, and will avail myself of it as soon as I can do aught which you may deem worthy of a place in your columns." Mr. Longfellow will be very happy to contribute, but wishes to do so anonymously, and will send a poem for the first number, if desired. Gen. Lewis Cass is "glad to find" we propose "such a periodical as we describe," and says "the literary condition of the country requires it;" as to contributions he "fears to undertake a task which may prove a failure." Rev. Dr. Chapin believes we shall obtain a wide circulation, and will aid. Rev. Dr. Wayland takes "great interest" in the work, and expresses "great confidence in your capacity for such an undertaking." Mr. Minister Theodore S. Fay will contribute articles on Switzerland.

A portion of other letters may be quoted freely, as giving ideas on magazinedom worth noting, as being from notable persons, several of whom have passed away.

Some of the incidents connected with the contributions to the magazine may be mentioned in further notes on the authors. A brief reference to the business statistics may be recorded here for the benefit of Monthlies of the next century.

The first edition of the first number was 10,000 copies. This had Longfellow's poem on Wellington–nothing else especially *notable*–yet the demand at once exhausted this and three or four successive editions, reaching an aggregate of 20,000. The second number, in which were the first "Bourbon" article, the first "Potiphar Papers," and several other "hits," at once attracted general attention, and insured a "paying" success. An edition of 30,000 was established as a minimum, and of some numbers 35,000 were printed. This number, compared to the circulation of that wonderfully cheap and excellent *popular* magazine from Cliff Street, then in the full tide of success, was insignificant; but it was in advance probably of any original magazine resting solely on its literary merits, either in this country or in Europe. In its palmiest days the world-famed "Blackwood" never claimed more than 9,000; and the "New Monthly," "Frazier," and "Metropolitan," from 750 to 4,000. (*Now,* to be sure, the "Cornhill," adopting the American idea of low price and large sales, is said to have a circulation of 100,000; but this is a new era in England.)

Each number of the "Monthly" was stereotyped. The amount paid to contributors and editors for the first two years was $12,819;[1] the cost of "illustrations," which were probably superfluous, was $3,000 more. When our successors in the publication made, in 1855, an unsolicited proposal to purchase the magazine, the circulation and statistics were fully exhibited, and the price offered and actually paid was $11,000. It had then been published two years and six months. A few *little* troubles and vexations had grown out of it; some jealousies, and perhaps positive ill-will had been excited in a few instances; but on the whole the affair was as agreeable and satisfactory in its personal relations as it was prosperous in its business results. The publishers' relations with the three gentlemen who were specially concerned, were always pleasant, and they still continue to be. I believe Maga continued to be equally fortunate in its new arrangements; but *other* business troubles caused its further transfer, until its whole character was changed, and it died of suffocation combined with lack of nutritious food.

A few specimens of the whims and oddities elicited by the delinquencies, delays, prejudices, and mistakes of editors and publishers, and the indignation and wrath of the contributors, may be quoted in another place. The two or three volumes of correspondence, saved from the editor's basket, is suggestive to future experimenters in Magazines;[2] but perhaps the most entertaining epistles were those from Southern "patrons," who were more or less incensed by the articles on national politics, and who politely invited the editor to come to Dixie to be throttled and lynched therefor. The fearful threats of the withdrawal of all Southern "patronage" would have been alarming if

the Magazine had built itself on this basis; but as the entire sale in what is now Secessia did not equal that in the single State of Ohio, we were not greatly moved; the author of "Parties and Politics" still continued his shots at Shams and his expositions of the corruptions of the times, North and South. These articles, next to the "Potiphar Papers," were the most effective and telling papers in the "Monthly."

To descend to the vulgar realities of dollars and cents–shall we say how all these instances of comparative success in publishing still fell short of permanent fortune? While a few judicious investments were unusually profitable, a much larger number produced no profit whatever; and though no great loss was incurred in any one case except that of the Exhibition Record, yet the mere absence of tangible return on so many publications, while the stern reality of large business expenses still existed, profit or no profit–this alone would account for unsatisfactory results. To show how a publisher in very moderate position is exposed to the temptation of going too fast, I may here mention that the number of new MS. works urgently offered us for publication during three years (in 1855–7) was more than 400. What must be the record of the *great* houses, the Harpers and Appletons, on this score?

In this "bank-note world" the "sum-total" and trial-balance of publishers' accounts *will,* sooner or later, become *the* topic for his consideration, whatever may be the pleasing insinuations of sanguine authors. Publishers have many sins to answer for, but not *all* the enormities which disappointed authors proverbially assess upon them. *Can* publishers be reasonably expected to furnish brains as well as cash? or should *they* always be responsible for dull books which the public won't buy?

I have always thought that no other business occupation offered equal attractions. But unfortunately these very allurements are the quicksands which imperil the craft, and swallow up all the profits of shrewder ventures. For a sanguine disposition and one interested in books, the most obvious danger in the trade is that of doing too much; and one of the most essential virtues is the courage to say "no." Other dangerous errors, closely akin, are "exchange paper," extra interest, favors to friends; hence, disaster, "extension," assignments.

To some of the pictures drawn in Kimball's "Revelations of Wall Street," I can testify as being within the modesty of nature; and how many victims endure hours, days, and months of anxiety, mortification, and distress never revealed to the selfish world around them! For myself, however, let me promptly, heartily, gratefully believe that "the world" is not so graspingly selfish as it is often painted. With a mere glimpse of such cases here and there, by way of foil, and in some instances where least excusable, I recall with more than satisfaction countless instances of liberal, generous consideration, and even most friendly and delicate courtesy, often, too, where I had the least possible claim to anything but strict business consid-erations. If these notes were meant to be full confessions, and of matters less strictly personal, it would be pleasant to chronicle facts and actions which go far to show the bright side of the trading world, and to prove that a magnani-mous and large-minded spirit may and does prevail where it is often least expected.

If I were to play Mentor to a young friend starting on the same career, I would say–in view of my own errors and bitter experience:–

Don't undertake more than you have time and means to do *well*.

Be ambitious about the quality rather than the quan-tity of your publications–remembering that two or three well-considered, thorough, and permanent works of high character, and suited to the market, are a better invest-ment, and are better for the community, than fifty tame or indifferent volumes, which will bring neither reputation, usefulness, nor profit–and–

Therefore, learn to resist the seductions of plausible and excellent authors, who are so very certain that their works are going to set the North River on fire, and that the world stands on tiptoes to receive the earliest copy.

Study independence of the world financially as far as practicable; avoid entanglements with responsibilities of others; don't spend all your profits on the brokers and note-shavers of Wall Street; and don't spend your money in any way faster than you make it.

So shall you hold your head erect; pay as you go; spend only what is fairly your own; and reach at last the brown-stone mansion and a comfortable retirement from the bustle of the world; with means to lighten your declin-ing years, and those of your fellow-men, by going about doing good!

* * * * * * *

A few notes about authors and booksellers in London and on the Continent may be given at another time.

–*American Publishers' Circular and Literary Gazette,* n.s. 1
(15 August 1863): 290–292

* * *

[1] Including $600 for thirteen short poems, by Longfellow, Bryant, Lowell, Bayard Taylor, Ellsworth and Buchanan Read, some of which actually appeared first in the daily papers, taken from our early copies; and yet perhaps they were a good investment as advertisements.

[2] 1800 MSS. were received in two years–enough to fill *ten* magazines of the same size. A Virginia contributor requested us to send him a check for $1,000 for a "poem" (?) of 30 lines.

Rough Notes of the English Book-Trade

True to his closing statement in "Rough Notes of Thirty Years in the Trade," Putnam composed a recollection of his decade in the London book trade. He notes a striking reversal in the English and American markets over the course of his career, for English books, which during his time in London were better made and higher priced than American books, have become cheaper and more plentiful, and American books, which used to be more poorly made and lower priced, have generally improved in quality and become higher priced, espe-cially as Civil War inflation affected the prices of all consumer goods. This reversal challenged the fundamental distinction Putnam habitu-ally drew between American "democracy" and English "aristocracy." Putnam's essay originally appeared in the American Publishers' Circular and Literary Gazette.

* * *

ROUGH NOTES OF THE ENGLISH BOOK-TRADE

The system which prevailed among English publish-ers when I first visited London, in 1836, has been consid-erably modified during the last ten years. Formerly small editions, not stereotyped, and at high prices, were the *rule;* and the exceptions were few. The interests of the wealthy aristocracy and of the circulating libraries only were con-sulted. To a great extent these comparatively small editions at high prices are still continued; but for several years the theory and practice of cheap books for the many, and good reading even for the million, have been making steady progress, until this feature in the trade has ceased to be an exception; it has almost become the general stan-dard. What was imperfectly foreshadowed by Constable's "Miscellany," in 1825, and by the Useful Knowledge Soci-ety's publications, a few years later, has been advanced by William and Robert Chambers, Charles Knight, Henry O. Bohn, George Routledge, and a host of others, until our boasted *cheapness* in book-making has been actually eclipsed; and many different series of popular and useful books are actually sold cheaper in England than books of the same character and equal mechanical excellence are sold in this country. The different "Libraries" published by Bohn, and now arrived at gigantic dimensions, form a remarkable and conspicuous example of this character and cheapness of price; but dozens of other cheap collections are also familiar to all who watch the book-market. The English progress in this direction is notable and suggestive. A few instances may show the character of the change. Twenty years ago such a book as Roscoe's "Leo the Tenth" cost $20; now the economical collector can have it for one-tenth of that sum. The same ratio of change is true of at least half the books printed in Bohn's collections. True, the editions are in small type and on ordinary paper;

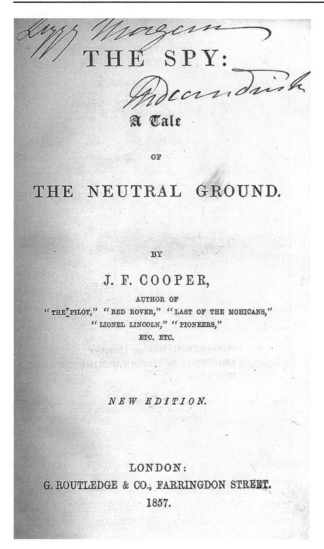

THE SPY:

A Tale

OF

THE NEUTRAL GROUND.

BY

J. F. COOPER,

AUTHOR OF

"THE PILOT," "RED ROVER," "LAST OF THE MOHICANS,"
"LIONEL LINCOLN," "PIONEERS,"
ETC. ETC.

NEW EDITION.

LONDON:
G. ROUTLEDGE & CO., FARRINGDON STREET.
1857.

Title page for a cheap English edition of James Fenimore Cooper's second book. George Routledge was one of the chief London pirates of the 1840s and 1850s, and Cooper, whose works were nearly as popular in England as in the United States, was a favorite author for his list of reprints (courtesy of Special Collections, Thomas Cooper Library, University of South Carolina).

but they are still passably readable. Thus hundreds of works of substantial value, which were *once* accessible to all but the select few, are now placed within the reach of "the people at large."

It is curious that progress on *our* side, meanwhile, has been rather in the direction of mechanical excellence than mere cheapness. The study of many of our publishers has been to improve the quality of the paper, the excellence of the type and presswork, and the general neatness of the externals. To a considerable extent our books have grown better in manufacture, and higher, proportionally, in price, while the English are becoming inferior in style and cheaper in price.

The first acquaintance I made among the English publishers was with the late D. A. Talboys, of Oxford. Arriving in that classic city on a Saturday afternoon, on my first journey from Liverpool to London in 1836, I made myself known to Mr. Talboys' manager as an American bookseller. I was immediately invited up stairs, and introduced to the family and to Mr. Whitaker, the London publisher here on a visit. I was made to feel at home at once; they fairly pressed me for the evening, and to dine with them next day, after taking me to the service at Magdalen Chapel. All day on Monday Mrs. Talboys devoted herself in the kindest and heartiest manner to ciceroning me through all the lions in Oxford; in short, the ordinary impressions of English coldness and distrust (especially without satisfactory introduction) were wholly dispelled by the really cordial treatment I received from this family, self-presented as I was two days after landing in Europe.

Another agreeable surprise here was the fact that Mr. Talboys, a leading publisher, under the very shadow of Oxford University, should be a warm admirer of American institutions, and, indeed, was a rather radical democrat himself. Without any college education, I believe, he was so far self-taught as to make a competent translation of Heeren's "Historical Works," in six volumes, and also to compile an elaborate folio volume known as the "Oxford Chronological Tables," besides editing several other publications. He was curiously free from the stiff formality and punctilious ceremony which are so characteristically English; I may say he was the most *American* Englishman I ever knew.

Another distinguished publisher of Oxford afforded a notable contrast—the very pink of formal politeness (and real courtesy, too), but reverently attached to English Church and State and every national institution, *because* it was English. He was the personification of that national loyalty which reveres the crown, as he said, even if it hangs on a bush. Kings and queens reign by Divine right; *ergo,* they must be obeyed, however wicked or imbecile they may be. Power coming from the people is rank heresy, if not blasphemy. Such was his creed.

In London my first introduction was to the *long* and ancient firm of Longman, Orme, Brown, Green, and Longman. This firm, as Longman and Co., originated more than a century ago; and English conservatism is illustrated by the fact that the business then established is still continued in the same premises—an old building cut up into rooms of all shapes and dimensions, in curious contrast to "modern improvements."[1] The senior Longman, then, was a thoroughly English gentleman of sixty-five; the fourth, I believe, in descent from the founder of the house. The active junior partner at that time was the eldest son, Thomas N., now at the head of the house, the father having died about seventeen years ago, leaving a handsome fortune. A younger brother, William, noted for literary and cultivated tastes, and the essence of courtesy in manner, is also in the firm. Excellent Mr. Brown managed the finances, and *English* Mr. Green conducted the home trading department.

Mr. John Murray, the elder, whose name is so linked with Byron's and Scott's, and the literature of the nineteenth century, was, in 1836, as his son is now, at the head of the fraternity in England. His name alone was a tower of strength to any book which acknowledged his sponsorship; probably it added one-third, at least, to the amount of the first orders of the trade for a new book; 300 would be taken when any other imprint would not command 200 for the same book. Such a reputation was, of course, a capital in itself. His place of business in Albemarle Street was on the ground floor of his own residence; and yet he entertained at this table not only the magnates of literature, but "noble lords" and statesmen, who were his willing guests. The portraits of authors which adorned his drawing and dining-rooms included Gifford, Southey, Byron, Crabbe, Irving; Parry and other Arctic navigators; Mrs. Somerville, the astronomer, etc. It was my fortune to share the old gentleman's hospitalities with the late Daniel Appleton, James Brown, and other American visitors, and the Byronic anecdotes and MSS. were among the notable things which linger in memory. Characteristic incidents of personal intercourse with these and other men of note in the English trade might be interesting to many, but I will not trespass either on the columns of the Circular, or the bounds of discretion and propriety. Brief reference only may be made to some of these magnates of the book world.

Mr. Bentley, "Her Majesty's Publisher in Ordinary," was a white-haired veteran of sixty odd when I lived in England; but even now, sixteen years later, he still vigorously conducts an extensive business in the gentlemanly manner of West End publishers—doing business in an office in his own dwelling-house in New Burlington Street. Bentley, as well as Murray, in the earlier days of our literature, was liberal in his payments to Irving, Cooper, Prescott, and a few other American authors, until the courts and the House of Lords decided that Americans cannot claim copyright in England until we reciprocate the compliment. Cooper was in the habit of drawing for £300 whenever he sent a

John Murray II, the leading literary publisher in the English-speaking world of his time. Putnam had extensive dealings with Murray and his son. The houses of Putnam and Murray brought out dozens of books cooperatively in their respective markets.

manuscript to Bentley. But, in process of time, all this was changed. American spoils became tempting; it was surmised that these popular books from Yankee-land could not be protected by English law; Bohn, Routledge, and others began to reprint them in shilling volumes. A considerable amount was expended among the lawyers in contesting the question, but the liberal publishers were beaten, and, at present, the defence of an American copyright in England, under any circumstances, is a foggy and uncertain affair. Unless the author resides temporarily in England, and prints there from manuscript, it seems to be useless to attempt any profitable protection there for American works. On this point more anon. We certainly should not grumble at this state of affairs so long as we refuse reciprocity of international literary interests.

Mr. Bentley, with all his courtesies to American authors, has been strangely blinded, like most of Uncle John's Islanders, about our present National struggle against rebellion. A postscript to a business note, received from him a few months ago, says: "Oh, that this miserable war would come to an end! Your once happy country is now reduced to misery and bankruptcy!" I couldn't resist the

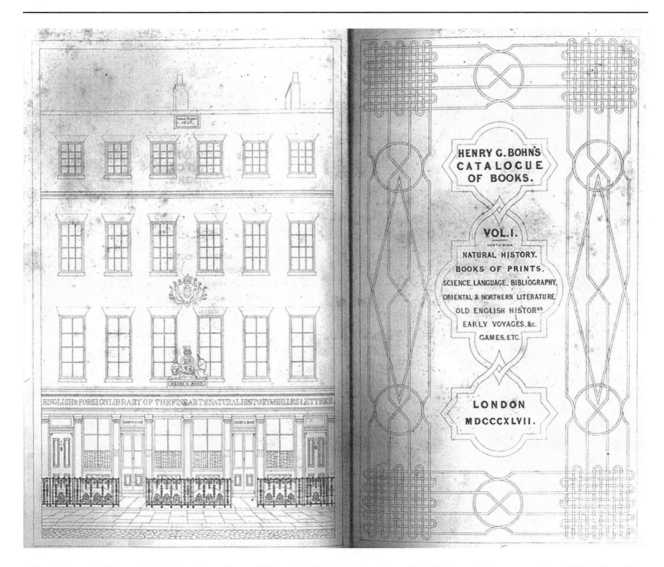

Frontispiece and title page for the first of two volumes of Henry G. Bohn's 1847 catalogue. Bohn built one of the most extensive publishing lists of his generation, and his catalogues ran into the hundreds of pages.

impulse to give him back a small broadside for that shot.

Mr. Henry G. Bohn, when I first met him in 1836, was an extensive dealer in the better class of old books for "gentlemen's libraries," and had just commenced the business of buying small "remainders" of editions sold off at the coffee-house sales by the "regular" publishers; but this was then a petty and insignificant business compared to that which he now conducts.

Bohn is the Napoleon of booksellers in ambition, ability, and energy. His energy is immense, and grasps his great business, both in bulk and in detail, with the comprehensiveness of a general who is master of the situation. Not content with daily purchases of tons of remainders and with printing shiploads of libraries—planning, selecting, editing,

translating, and annotating—he finds time withal to write books himself; and, in the midst of all this immense pressure of care and labor, he used scarcely to permit his most experienced clerk to sell a single old book from the shelves to the trade without consulting him as to the price. So enormous was the amount of work which he undertook that, though naturally strong and vigorous, it was said he had weekly visits from his surgeon to be examined as to how far endurance could be carried.

Mr. Bohn is not only a thorough bibliographer and editor, but has himself translated such things as Schiller's Plays from the German, and has prepared for the press a good many volumes of classical literature requiring industrious and learned research. His enterprise in starting and carrying on the various "Libraries," Standard, Classical, Historical,

Philological, Illustrated, &c., is one of the boldest and most remarkable in the whole annals of the book-trade. They are wonderful collections, especially when compared to expensive and inaccessible editions of the same works which were the only ones in existence before.

How far Mr. Bohn is justifiable in his aggressive warfare on those publishers who have been willing to recognize and reward American authors, I will not undertake to say.

When our "American Literary Agency" was placed among the club-houses of Waterloo Place, about twenty years ago, I used to have frequent calls from a pleasant, brisk, and active dealer in books from a little shop in one of the nooks near Leicester Square, who, in imitation of the larger operations of Bohn and Tegg, used to buy at the sales small lots of "remainders," say from twenty to five hundred copies, of the cheaper books, and would take under his arm a few "samples," and push round himself among the second-hand and other dealers to sell his bargains. So aptly did he fall into the American notion of barter or "dicker," that, when he found trade dull otherwise, he would propose a "swap" for any old lots of American importations that might chance to linger on our shelves. In process of time, he would venture larger "lots" and bigger books; then he began to reprint some American works, including Barnes' "Notes," and then some original works. Progress into bigger premises in Soho Square, and then into "the city," followed in due course, and now my quondam friend of the "job lots" is one of the magnates—no other than Mr. George Routledge of the extensive publishing house which makes £10,000 contracts with Sir Bulwer Lytton and the Right Hon. Chancellor of the Exchequer.

Progress of this kind, so peculiarly American, is just what any honest American would be proud to trace. It belongs to the chronicles of the "self-made men." Mr. R. was not of lordly kin, and boasted no University honors, but he had shrewdness, industry, intelligence, and *pluck*—and he has made his mark.

—*American Publishers' Circular and Literary Gazette*, n.s. 1 (15 October 1863): 418–419

* * *

[1]   I learn that it has just been replaced, at least, by a handsome edifice suited to the occasion.

Some Things in London and Paris

Putnam first crossed the Atlantic Ocean in 1836 as a young man recently admitted as a junior partner in the firm of Wiley and Long. His purpose in making what stretched into an eight-month tour of the major European book markets was to situate his firm more fully and advantageously in the transatlantic book trade. Putnam's initial excursion led to the establishment two years later of a branch office in London for the successor firm of Wiley and Putnam. He made many round-trips across the ocean during the decade of Wiley and Putnam's existence and continued to make such trips into the early 1850s, after he established his own company. Financial reverses and scaled-back operations after 1854 kept Putnam at home for the next fifteen years, giving a keener edge to his observations when he returned to London and Paris in 1869. Even the crossing of the ocean and the English Channel seemed to Putnam a transformed experience. His first trip from London to Paris took him nearly a week; in 1869 he remarked on the possibility of having lunch at the train station in London and arriving by midnight in Paris.

Altogether, Putnam was "startled" by the magnitude of the changes in the transportation system, architecture, and scale of urban life he saw all around him, but nothing more affected him—professional bookman that he was—than the utter transformation of the publishing industry and the culture of books in England. George Routledge, whom he remembered in the 1830s occupying a cramped stall near Leicester Square and dealing in remainders, now owned huge warehouses of books and owned one of the finest lists in the industry, and the scale and profitability of his operations were not unique. Book culture was similarly altered. Whereas books in England had once been far more expensive and scarce than in the United States, Putnam now found the English operating by the "American plan" of cheapness and ready availability to such an extent that he feared they were leaving his countrymen "almost out of sight." Putnam's sketch of the transformed publishing and civic scene in midcentury England and France was first published in Putnam's Magazine; *it was reprinted in George Haven Putnam's* A Memoir of George Palmer Putnam *(1903).*

* * *

Some Things in London and Paris–
1836–1869

Changes–The Voyage–English Notes–Travelling in Olden Time–Modern Improvements–Tabernacles and Cathedrals–Parliament–John Bright–Authors–Publishers–Cheap Books–Mercantile Honour–English Ethics on Rebellion–Museums of Art–Paris and its Renovations–The Emperor and Abraham Lincoln–Laboulaye–Doré, etc.

THIRTY-THREE years ago this month, I landed in Liverpool from the packet-ship *England,* from New York, and

The Hermann, *a Cunard vessel of the Hamburg line that spanned the ages of sail and steam. Putnam crossed the Atlantic nearly twenty times on a variety of ships, including the* Hermann.

made the most of six months in England and on the Continent. In a residence of ten years in London, interspersed with a dozen trips across the Atlantic, between 1836 and 1847, I had a chance to note some of the changes and comparative ills and advantages on both sides of the Atlantic, which a very dull person could hardly fail to observe with profit.

To revisit London and Paris after such an interval, and to compare 1869 with 1836, was to me a sensation—an item in one's personal remembrances of peculiar interest.

One of the first things to be remarked is the truism that the European trip of to-day has become so common as to require positive genius to place it in any new light. What was comparatively distant, novel, and mysterious in the last generation is now familiar in our mouths as household words. The full-grown man or woman who has not "done" the whole is becoming more of a novelty than the lions themselves. These notes, then, simply refer to some of the changes and signs of progress during the "generation" last past.

And, first, of the vessels that take you. In 1836, the bright-sided "liners," the sailing packet-ships of New York, were our pride and boast. Ranging from 600 to 900 tons (a mere yacht in these days), their fine models, excellent accommodations, and wide-awake, "gentlemanly" captains, were proverbial all over the world. Where are they now?

Two trips in the *England,* with the well-known Captain Waite, and two in the *Margaret Evans,* with the always popular E. G. Tinker (both now retired with honourable independence), then in the *St. James,* then another in the

grade of vessels next afloat—the Collins line—and then good-bye to sailing vessels. A new era commences. It was my fortune to have a trial of nearly all the rival lines for the passenger trade between 1839 and 1851: the *Caledonia, Canada,* and *Cambria* of the Cunarders, the *Great Western* (second vessel of all in the field), the *Great Liverpool,*—a peninsular steamer, recklessly sent across the Atlantic in a winter voyage and narrowly escaping the bottom,—the ill-fated *President* on her last trip to New York, two trips in the American steamers *Hermann* in 1849 and the *Franklin* in 1851.

These sufficed to give one a specimen of progressive improvements in "floating palaces," so called, and in some of the perils of navigation. Six of these vessels were afterwards utterly lost; and of two, the *England* (sailing) and the *President* (steamer), no tidings whatever were ever received. Probably the loss of life at sea, at least in "regular" packets, is not much greater in average than on railways, but there is enough to show that no human skill is infallible.

With but little knowledge of the merits of recent lines, I found myself almost at random aboard the *Westphalia,* of the Hamburg line. A greater advance over the vessels of olden time, which I had known, could not be expected even with these twenty years of experiment.

The older Cunarders and the *Hermann* and *Franklin* were about 1200 tons, and were then the marvels of genius. The ships of this Hamburg line are of 3000 tons, all "screws," most substantially built (on the Clyde, by the way) of iron, and fitted up comfortably and luxuriously enough for a prince, and admirably managed. I write this in the *Hammonia,* on my return.

The *Westphalia* is still finer, and the *Cimbria* and *Holsatia* are of the same grade. Officers and stewards civil and attentive, in notable contrast to the martinet ways of the Cunarders; and the table superabundantly provided with delicacies by a French cook. Our trip, though in February, was but nine days and eight hours to Cowes, and, compared with any of the fourteen trips of former years, it was as superior in comfort as it was in speed.

That superb morning when we passed the Needles, with a full moon in a clear sky on one side, and the red light on those picturesque rocks on the other, was a delicious surprise, especially as one is so apt to be met on these coasts by a cold, raw fog or drizzling rain. This agreeable reception was enhanced half an hour later off Cowes, where her Majesty's steam yacht appeared as if all ready to greet us, and the Queen herself, with the whole household, left Osborne House (off which we had anchored) and preceded us in said yacht to Southampton, and thence on the railway to London—blocking us, by the way, on the track for a couple of hours. While listening to the impatient jokes of our German neighbour in the cars during this delay, it was natural to look back to 1836, when I first saw the fair young Princess Victoria, just seventeen, with her mother, at a musical festival in Exeter Hall—then "the expectancy and rose of the fair state"—but attracting no very marked observation, and looking like many other damsels of her age in the audience. Five years later, sitting in the gardens of the Temple on the 9th November, to see the Lord Mayor's gingerbread barge, I heard the guns which proclaimed the birth of her first son, the Prince of Wales. I had been permitted meanwhile to "assist" at a soirée, and also at a public dinner, both attended in a sort of "state" by H.R.H. Prince Albert—and what a handsome, well-formed, sensibly behaved young man he was! The sables still worn by the stout, matronly Queen, and the monuments everywhere erected to her worthy and useful consort, show that he is freshly remembered—and his works do follow him. The *ci-devant* maiden of sweet seventeen is now fat if not fair, and some dozen children call her "Grandmother."

Towns like Southampton continue to be as essentially and distinctively English as they were in the last generation—the same substantial stone piers, the same snug, compact streets and shops, the same cosey inns, with their cold joints and muffins and excellent tea for breakfast, the same threepence to the waiter and the "boots," the same general air of decent *comfort* in the snug-looking houses of the "trades-people," without a particle of superfluous ornament or frippery. Coming to the railway station, a "N. Y. & New Haven" passenger remarks rather the freedom and absence of red tape, and the quiet, easy fashion of things, less show and even less comfort in

the famous "first-class" compartments than one remembers of the first days of English railways. But to go back still farther, when railways were *not,* one cannot help remembering the slower but more picturesque and exhilarating locomotion of olden time,—even as late as 1836,—when we mounted to the box or sat with the guard on the top of the "Royal Mail" coach, and the coachman, cracking his whip over his spirited "team" of four unexceptionable bays, groomed and harnessed to a nicety, we bowled along over the hard, smooth roads at the rate of ten to twelve miles an hour, and absurdly supposed the perfection of travelling had been reached. Or, again, when on a dewy morning we enjoyed the luxury of a drive in an English post-chaise (*à la milord*), with four horses and a postilion to each pair, and dashed with gentlemanly speed along those delicious byways and hedge-lined cross-roads, to do the "lions" in Derbyshire and Warwickshire—to "realise" our schoolboy dreams of Shakespearean Stratford-on-Avon, and lordly Blenheim, and monastic Oxford, and baronial Warwick, and magnificent Chatsworth, and romantic Haddon Hall; or when we used to roam over the softly carpeted hills of Kent and read Boswell at Tunbridge Wells and Sidney's *Arcadia* at Penshurst, and Chaucer at Canterbury, and *King Lear* under Shakespeare's Cliff at Dover; or imbibed Gray's *Odes* and *Elegy* at Windsor and Stoke Park, and Pope's couplets at Twickenham, and *The Lady of the Lake* at Loch Katrine. All these remembrances of real enjoyment of former days in rural England—away from the iron track, and even before iron tracks existed—all these rose up in memory like an exhalation, as we took our seats to ride to London in the modern humdrum compartment from which the "country" and the chimney-tops can be seen at the rate of from thirty to sixty miles per hour.

At Waterloo Station, cabs in abundance stand by the platform ready for yourself and your luggage, and a plainly printed card of their lawful fares—6d. (12 cents) per mile, or 2s. (50 cents) per hour—is posted in each cab. Observe: you pay for yourself and luggage for the first mile, say 25 cents, and 12 cents for each additional mile; and no grumbling about it. In this point London cabbies have improved. When will New York follow suit?

Whirling over Waterloo Bridge, through the Strand, Trafalgar Square, and Regent Street, my first impression was that even the latter appeared less stately than of yore. In fact, our recent mercantile marble, iron, and brownstone palaces of Broadway have dwarfed the stuccoed grandeur of the famous street of George the Fourth—and I began to wonder whether this was really the great Babylon of my

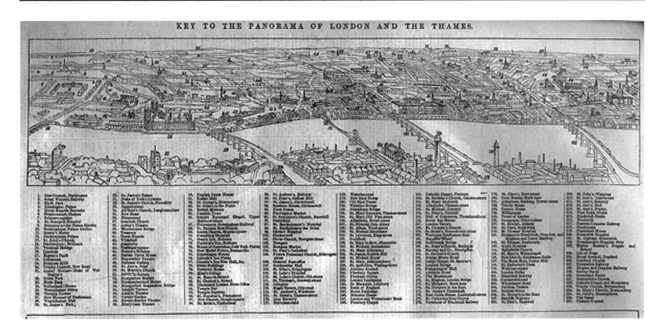

Central London, as depicted in the 6 July 1844 issue of the Illustrated London News. *It was the most populous city in the world during the period in which Putnam ran the overseas office of Wiley and Putnam.*

romantic days. Only the more deliberate comparisons of recent architectural improvements of this vast metropolis sufficed to prove its enormous advances—outstripping in proportion even our wide-awake cities of the West. Chicago herself has scarcely grown more in the last quarter of a century than this ancient and unweildy "metropolis of the world."

The "Langham" and the "Charing Cross" are the new hotels for the times, and so I tried them both. Stately as the former appears as you look down Portland Place, the Londoners say it has spoiled the symmetry of that lordly street. Where it stands, the famous Lord Mansfield used to live, and the Czar Nicholas, whom I had seen in London in 1844-'5, "put up" at Mansfield House. The Langham, with its six stories of solid masonry, already well smoked, and its American manager (Mr. Sanderson), has not yet, they say, paid large dividends to its company (limited). Its cost was large, and the results have not justified the outlay, even after all the advantage of Yo-semitic-Hiawathan-entertainment. The "plan" of this house promised a combination of the excellencies of the English, French, and American systems. Let us hope that in attempting all, the company may not fail to reach either. Of course the house is *comfortable;*—any English country inn is that; but it lacks something of the cheerful conveniences and elegant economies of the best French and American hotels. The dull dimness of the stately corridors gives one the blues. It caters, apparently, to American customers, and takes the N. Y. *Times*—but the latest number on the files was a month older than that I had myself brought.

A new hotel of the same class, apparently, is the Alexandra,—in Piccadilly, opposite Hyde Park,—a more lively and equally convenient situation, where one sees more of the outside world at a glance.

The Charing Cross—a huge structure at the railway-station of that name—is another "novelty" to me—substantial, bustling, almost dizzying by its constant whirl of active life—for it is at the very heart of London. Looking from my fourth-floor window out upon the familiar tail of the lion on Northumberland House—(town-home of "the Percy's high-born race")—I could not help wondering how the present owner of this ancient and wealthy dukedom likes being jostled so briskly and so closely by modern improvements—locomotives smoking and wheezing and cabs rumbling under his very windows.

At the immense "station" immediately adjoining this hotel, trains with locomotives arrive and depart every few minutes—either on the Dover track or to the Crystal Palace and the suburbs, or to the other stations of the metropolitan or underground railway. But the comparative order and quiet, the absence of all loud calls or locomotive shrieks, the smooth, easy gliding of the cars, without any needless noise or confusion, are in such strong contrast to the aspect of one of our large "depots" (when shall we quash this word and say "station"?) that one can hardly realise at first how much business is going on. A mere glance at these operations at Charing Cross—with all its details and surroundings—such as a first-rate hotel, a restaurant, a lunch-room, where you are well and civilly served with appetising bits (Mugby Junction is defunct) and at "prices to suit"—the railway library and news-stand on the platform, where you buy a good novel for a shilling, and your *Daily News* or *Telegraph* for one penny, your *Echo* for a ha'penny (a well-printed *double* evening journal), and your *Judy* and *Echoes* for twopence, and are thanked for doing it—with every other suggestion for the agreeable and comfortable start on your journey, whether it is to London Bridge, or to Australia—all these systematic arrangements are so nearly perfect as to make an American growl with disgust when he thinks of the miserable shanties of the Jersey ferry, whence one starts on the great national route to the American metropolis—and where a Senator and an apple-woman or bootblack are huddled together in a scramble for the first squeeze in the wooden hut, six feet or so square, where your ticket or your life (almost) is the consideration. "They manage these things better in France," and so they do in England—whatever tyrannies and despotism there may be behind the scenes. If that amiable, gracious, and obliging Cerberus who watches for lapdogs and parcels and anxious fathers at the ladies' room of the N. Y. & New Haven would come and take a look at the Charing Cross Station—or rather, if his masters, the directors, would do so—possibly a useful hint or two might be gained, which in the course of a few years might be of advantage to our long-suffering people. How is it that while our River and Sound steamers eclipse those of all the world, our railway system is so imperfect—in many conspicuous places so utterly mean and disgraceful?

One thing is objectionable in these stations—at least for a stranger—and that is the display of hundreds of large advertisements and posters—some of them enormous—on the walls, utterly confusing, with their big letters, any one looking for *needful* information. The *profit* of these to the company must be large, to justify or excuse the nuisance; and as they are repeated in every station, large and small, all over the kingdom, the expense to advertisers must be enormous. Thus the newer journals and magazines post bills eight feet long on all the dead walls in London, and many of these are done in all sizes, in cast-iron plates with enamelled letters. If full-size double daily papers like the *Standard, News, Star,* etc., can be sold for two cents, and the *Echo* (larger than our *Evening Mail*) for one cent, how can they afford to pay thousands of pounds a year for street advertisements? and how is it that with all this heavy incubus of expense of publicity the supply of reading for the million has so wonderfully increased in England and its cheapness in proportion? Thirty years ago, English newspapers cost 10 cents to 15 cents each—and new books were a luxury for the select few, while ours cost comparatively nothing. Now, both papers and books may be had for less than half the price of ours.

Probably Mr. Carey can explain. This turning of the tables is easily accounted for to a certain extent—but the complete revolution and reversal of proportions seems at first to be mysterious.

Even the gilt-edged "Guide" which they give you at the Langham suggests the expediency of your hearing Mr. Spurgeon and of going early and that the cab-fare is 2s.; but it does *not* hint that you can go on the top of an omnibus for 4d., and that the ride may be more instructive. My first observation in the course of this lofty survey was the apparent change in Sabbath observance in London. Not only the gin-palaces, but a great many shops of all kinds were in active business—and in one street on the Surrey side some thousands of rough-looking people were holding high change—apparently a Jewish holi-, not holy, day. Near the famed Elephant and Castle, my omnibus-neighbour, learning my destination, said he was one of that congregation, and invited me (as a stranger) to his seat—otherwise the chance would have been "limited." For a rarity, as I was told, Mr. Spurgeon had exchanged with a brother-minister from the other side of the river, who began by sympathising with the disappointment of the thousands before him. In reality, I liked the substitute better than I expected to like the more renowned preacher. But neither could be half so impressive as the immense audience itself—said to be over 8000, of which 5000 are in rented seats, placed in three galleries and on the floor of the gigantic Tabernacle so adroitly that every one could see and hear: and when the multitude rose as one man, and followed the precentor at the side of the preacher's table in singing a familiar psalm, the effect was far more touching and solemn than any preaching could possibly be.

In the evening I returned and heard Spurgeon himself: the crowd was greater, every seat filled and every aisle thronged—and the preacher's power over the vast assembly was indeed a marvel. I can't quite forget my prejudice against his heavy face; but his wonderful executive ability and his immense influence for good over so many thousands of regular hearers, and tens of thousands of casual ones, can hardly be overestimated. Boxes for coins for the "Pastors' College" in Regent's Park, placed everywhere in sight, were labelled to the effect that last week's contribution was some £35.

Next Sunday morning, the service at Westminster Abbey was impressive, and notable for other things. This glorious old edifice has not only had care and renovation in its outward aspects, but also in its practical uses. The ding-dong of its ancient dozing vergers, who lay in wait for strangers' sixpences, seems to have been lulled; and on Saturday I was actually permitted to walk about where I pleased, everywhere but in Henry VII.'s Chapel, without any hint of guides or pennies. On Sunday, too, instead of the monotonous homily of a drowsy pluralist, to a handful of people in the choir, a large part of the whole edifice is filled with an interested audience in comfortable seats (graded, of course, for the gentle and simple), the music and chanting are of the best, and a man of real ability preaches a practical and excellent sermon, which gentle and simple may profit by alike. At least this was what I saw and heard. The preacher seemed to be of a different mould from the canons of olden time. Has the Church come down to the people? From the text, "Where shall we buy bread that these may eat?" he not only expounded spiritual food for the hearers on both sides of the railing which separated the chairs from the benches, but he discussed, for the plainer people, the simple but often urgent wants and anxieties for the wherewithal to *live*–the daily problem, "how to make both ends meet," which many, even of those not classed as "poor," find it often difficult to solve. The excellent sense and earnest feeling of the sermon surprised as well as instructed a listener who had come to the Abbey from the last generation. The rich tones of the organ, and some good voices echoing through those long-drawn aisles and lofty arches, were as impressive, in their way, as the 8000 human voices singing in unison at the Tabernacle, without even a bass-viol or melodeon to guide them. Why may not both modes of worship be acceptable, if fervently and honestly rendered, to Him who regardeth the spirit and not the letter of such service?

The huge St. Paul's also is now turned to other uses besides a Pantheon for big monuments. In the evening, I attended service there, when some 5000 people were comfortably seated under the great dome and in the nave as well as the choir, to listen to the choral service and fine anthems, and to hear a really able and interesting discourse by the Bishop of Derry. I don't know who he may be, but he is not one of the drones. These services are held every Sunday evening, and are always crowded,–for they make a point, I am told, of having the ablest and most effective preachers from all quarters of the Establishment. The English Church is evidently waking up to the expediency of *doing* something besides enjoying its immense revenues and fat sinecures. The Taits, Trenches, and Stanleys appreciate the situation.

In a week-day visit to the two cathedrals, I noted some of the new monuments which mark the eminences who have passed away since I saw England. In St. Paul's they have put up the usual style of marble to several military notabilities. In Westminster, a full-length Peel, and a ditto Palmerston; and in a modest niche of Poets' Corner is a simple bust of Thackeray, looking toward the wits and poets whom he had revivified, as though he were not quite sure whether he was there

merely on sufferance. "Tom Campbell," Hallam, Wordsworth, and Macaulay are more conspicuously honoured, for as the man in Sheridan's play says, "I'm told there's snug lying in the Abbey," and even men of genius dream of that apotheosis. The whole building is evidently cared for and renovated with suitable reverence–and St. Paul's, too, is in the hands of skilful restorers, who are gradually completing the ornamentation so long left unfinished. Appeals for pennies to aid this renovation are posted, and it is pleasant to know that these grand memorials of bygone ages are not to be permitted to fall into ruin.

Street monuments to England's great men continue to prevail, but do not improve much in grace. Havelock and C. J. Napier stand on each side of Nelson's big lions in Trafalgar Square, with the ambling steed of Charles I., and the pigtail of George III. in near proximity. England's earlier chivalry is embodied in an equestrian Richard Cœur de Lion, near the House of Lords. In Waterloo Place, one of the finest sites of the metropolis is filled with a very heavy if not ugly group of iron grenadiers placed against a granite pile on which is inscribed "Crimea." The only symmetrical and satisfactory recent attempt at the monumental is the Gothic structure in Hyde Park, on the site of the Palace of '51, to the honour of Prince Albert.

The gorgeous Gothic pile built by Barry for the Houses of Parliament has been completed since my residence in London. With a card for the "Speaker's Gallery" from our very polite Secretary of Legation, Mr Moran, I had good opportunity to observe the *manner* of the present Ministry–especially Mr. Gladstone, who spoke twice, briefly, but with peculiar clearheaded tact, courtesy, and dignity, which showed the secret of his influence and power. It was the night after the first great debate on the Irish Church Bill. Everybody knows what the House of Commons is–the only remark I need make is to wonder why the architect of this enormous building, whose halls and corridors and towers are on a superb scale in size and elegance, could not have provided a little more room for the most important object of the building, viz., the sessions of the House? Why should the 650 members be forced to sit like so many schoolboys crowded on "forms," or forced in a full house to take refuge in the galleries?–(for there are not seats for all the members on the floor). Why should the spectators' galleries be limited to 100 seats? and why should the ladies be limited to a score or so, caged behind a glass screen, to peep like Tom of Coventry at a dumb show, without hearing a word of what is said? Probably all this has been asked and answered scores of times, but each newcomer, who has seen the ample scope of our Capitol, will be sure to wonder over again at these and other of our Uncle's little anomalies.

The one name in England which perhaps excites most interest in an American–after Dickens and Tennyson–is that of John Bright. As I had been privileged with two or three notes from him during the war, in reference to his portrait, and to certain "rebellion" documents, I ventured to send him a card, though half ashamed of the intrusion on a Cabinet Minister as busy as the President of the Board of Trade must necessarily be. A pleasant, familiar note from him within a few hours asked me to call between the hours of 10 and 11 next day–which I did not fail to do. His lodgings in Clarges Street were so much like the modest apartments I had once occupied near by, that I imagined I had blundered in the number. No,–Mr. Bright was in, and I was shown to a plain room on the second floor. "Is there a room below where one can wait if he calls?" Mr. Bright asked of the damsel after he had cordially greeted and seated me. "No, sir," says the servant, "*it* is occupied." A word or two of apology for intruding on his valuable time–which I feared my countrymen were too apt to do–was kindly and simply cut short, and for half an hour he made me entirely "at home" in a rapid talk about certain points on which, as it happened, I was able to give him some information. The servant meanwhile announced "Mr. Livingstone." Again the question about the room below. "No, sir, he is still there." "No matter," said Mr. B., turning to me, "you won't mind his coming up here–he is a brother of Dr. Livingstone, the traveller. *We* have no secrets to talk about." Of course I could but again apologise and propose to take leave–but he kept me some twenty minutes longer, Mr. Livingstone, meanwhile, meekly waiting for his turn–and when I left him I was again invited with some emphasis to call on my return from Paris. All this is a trifle, but it is mentioned simply to illustrate the unassuming, simple, hearty good nature of this noble man, so different in his manners and his surroundings from our tradition of an English Cabinet Minister. Portraits do not do him justice. His face is a model of the best English type–rosy health without grossness[,] intelligence, good sense, and *bonhomie* happily united. If I might quote some of his sayings, they would show that he has some pickle and *spice* in his composition, also, and that he is a shrewd and independent thinker.

The next call I had to make was on the author of *Foul Play* and *Never Too Late to Mend*. His domicile and its peculiarities were not less interesting for being those of a man of genius who had such marvellous facility in dramatic stories; but one is scarcely justified in relating private conversation, even of a famous author, or in describing his dressing-gown

H. G. Bohn, whom Putnam came to regard as one of the greatest figures in publishing. In his earlier years, though, Putnam considered Bohn a menace for his widespread piracy against foreign authors, including Putnam's.

and pet cat. Mr. Charles Reade is a good deal cosmopolitan as well as English in his notions, and his shrewd independence and self-reliance seem to belong to what is usually termed "a man of the world."

A short visit to Miss Thackeray, the charming daughter of the great novelist, and herself a bright and sensible storyteller, was an agreeable episode in the day's doings. Her grace of manner–wholly free from pedantry or pretence, as simple as a child and as polished as a duchess–is quite winning. To express satisfaction in knowing any one who "had known her father" was very easy, but the evident sincerity of the cordial greeting was not to be doubted.

The author of *The Woman in White* has everything handsome about him, and is evidently a gentleman, and a very agreeable man.

My old friends, Mr. and Mrs. Hall, Mr. and Mrs. Howitt, and others with whom we used to exchange visits in olden time, are still flourishing in hale and healthy maturity, I was told, but there was no time to seek them.

The elders of the houses of Murray, Longman, and Whittaker, who had hospitably received me in

1836, have passed away, but the business of the first two is vigorously pursued by the present generation. The new and elegant premises of the Longmans, and the newer and handsome palace of the rising Nelsons are both lost in the narrow lane, where booksellers most do congregate–Paternoster Row. Many of the wealthy, older publishers whose names are familiar in our mouths, are conservatively pursuing their vocation exactly as they were thirty years ago. Baldwin, Moxon, Tilt, the elder Bohn, Pickering, and others, have passed off the stage. Henry Bohn, "the Napoleon of remainders," partially retired, after printing 500 Library volumes and editing many of them himself, now amuses himself with knick-knacks like old china, for which hobby they say he has expended £50,000 of his well-earned fortune. The name of Bentley, who is now quite advanced and in poor health, is kept in title-pages by his son, and so is Pickering's, in a moderate way.

But the newer men who have risen up to fame and fortune in this responsible vocation are rapidly eclipsing the old fogies in the magnitude and activity if not respectability of their operations. Of these, Routledge, Warne, Strahan, Macmillan, and Low & Marston, are the most notable–the progress of some of these having been more on our American plan than in the ordinary English habit. In my younger days in London, Routledge had a little box near Leicester Square whence he would sally forth himself with samples of "trade-sale job-lots" under his arm and sell "13–12 at 1s."–or make a "dicker" for Yankee books if he couldn't do better.

Now his warehouses are "big things," and his list of publications numbers many hundreds. His first noted contract was with Bulwer–to give him £2000 a year for ten years for the use of his works, printing them in tens of thousands "for the million," at a nominal price. The cheapness of his publications, and others of their class in England, has distanced American competition marvellously. Warne, Nelson, Strahan, Low, and others do an immense business in the same department. Books for five, three, two shillings, and one shilling, and even for sixpence–(a very decent copy of Cooper's novels, for example)–were published originally at a guinea or a guinea and a half. Apparently they find their account in this system, for it is common to hear of editions of tens of thousands; and Hotten told me that of one of Artemus Ward's books he had sold a quarter of a million! *We* boast of the universality of our book-reading, but where does the English reading public come from? Look at their periodical literature! To say nothing of their merely "popular" serials like *Good Words, All the Year Round,* and *Once a Week,* ranging from 50,000 to 130,000, the number of shilling magazines is startling to think of–three times as many in proportion as we have, and most people would say ours are too many. Then the penny issues, such as *British Workman,* etc., are marvellous for the excellence of their illustrations as well as their literature. In all this matter of instruction and entertainment for the million, our English contemporaries are leaving us very far astern–almost out of sight.

Here, again, one of "the trade" of thirty years ago is startled with the differences. Then the cheapness of American books was proverbial, and English editions were luxuries which few could afford. The stately quartos and octavos, priced in guineas instead of pence, are still issued when important new books are to be launched for the first time; but, the nabobs and the libraries once supplied, the "people" are then cared for with compact duodecimos at prices to suit.

The good old aristocratic days of the elder Murray and his kin are passing away. How he used to entertain the American bibliopoles, the rarity of whose advent, thirty years ago, rendered them objects of curiosity! James Brown and Daniel Appleton and one or two others comprised the whole American delegation for many years. The two named are gone; but others are now familiar with the Albemarle Street mahogany on which the portraits of Scott and Byron and Southey and Crabbe and Irving and the Arctic navigators looked down approvingly. How the old gentleman used to produce his *Childe Harold* and other choice MSS., with half-earnest apprehension lest these wild Americans should slip them into their pockets! (The present Mr. John Murray, who makes the red-books for travellers, sometimes styled the British tourist's Bible, is now absent on his first visit to Italy; oddly enough, although all these guide-books were supposed to be actually prepared by him, and those on Germany really were so, he has never till now even seen Rome or Florence.) How the *long* firm of Longmans used to give us a hospitable chair at their long table in the Row, where the excellent Brown's bachelor-hall in the warehouse used to provide a hot joint for their authors and business friends! How the Napoleonic Bohn used to give us holiday dinners at the "Star & Garter" of Richmond Hill, and ex-Sheriff Whittaker used to tell us how many men he had hanged when "the City" had the advantage of his services! How democratic Talboys, under the very shadow of the ancient university on the Isis, used to surprise us with his admiration for American institutions, even more strange to us than the superultra loyalty of the official publisher, Mr. Parker, who taught us that "the Crown must be respected if it only hangs on a bush!" But such gossip of old times might be extended *ad nauseam*.

Among the nooks and corners which an American in England, thirty years ago, was apt to "mouse out" were the old Dr. Johnson tavern in Bolt Court, where we used to pay for a pint of ale for the sake of a peep at the Lumber Troop Hall, once the library of the growling old lexicographer; then the rather doubtful respectability of the "Judge and Jury Society," in Covent Garden, where mock "appeals from the Lord Chancellor's Court below, at Westminster," were gravely argued by big-wigs at the bar before a bigger wig "on the bench"–the price of a "pot of 'alf and 'alf" being the admission fee. But I did not fail to revisit and take my "chop and Cheshire" at the little smoky room of Dolly's chop-house in Paternoster Row, which for three hundred years last past has dispensed those comforts to bibliopoles and others who have haunted the place since the time of Spenser and Shakespeare and Ben Jonson.

While the old "haunts" and curiosities remain, the renovations and improvements going on in London are wonderful in their extent and costly excellence. The Thames Embankment, and new bridges, to say nothing of the enormous railway system, the viaduct at Holborn Valley, and the complete transformation of Smithfield and its old cattle market of John Rogers's memory; the new buildings in the city, the immense demolition of rookeries between the Strand and Holborn for the new law courts; the new hotels; the amazing growth of the suburbs; the new horticultural gardens and museums; the wonderful Museum in progress at Kensington and the completion of that at Bloomsbury, are among the signs that London not only "still lives," but that this "huge, overgrown metropolis," as it was called when half its present size, is advancing in apparent prosperity quite as fast as any of our growing Western cities. It is true that in the matter of dwelling-houses in the suburbs the speculative builders seem to have "overdone it" for the time–for Overend & Gurney's failure, and other things of that sort, were a terrible shock to English credit, and sadly contracted the incomes of multitudes of the middle classes. Here again I found a difference from the tone of olden time–in the days when every American in England was pharisaically lectured about the shortcomings of his countrymen, culminating in the national crime of repudiation, and we were kindly told to observe that "an Englishman's word is his bond the world over." Truly, we deserved the lecture somewhat; and Englishmen had a right to a good deal of self-complacency. They have still; for, as a nation, their phariseeism is based on a sturdy, downright foundation of honest candour and integrity. And yet there are exceptions–strange to say. Such cases as that of Overend & Gurney, where thousands were ruined by unsuspicious confidence which proved for a series of years to have been betrayed, have not been so very rare; and one finds a difference in the whole tone in which business operations are referred to. To speak of a contemporary in trade as "slippery," or something worse, is a frequent habit, and it was not at all pleasant to notice so much jealousy and disparagement of each other, even among the prosperous portion of our own fraternity.

The earnest, hearty hospitality and genuine kindness which I met among English acquaintances of former years were enough to revive the heartiest liking for Old England and to make one feel at home there with enduring friends. Once established in the good-will of such people and they grapple you to their hearts with hooks of steel. Their practical friendliness was so pleasant to think of, that I could not but wonder the more when a passing allusion to our recent national struggle betrayed the fact that the bitterest of the "unreconstructed"–the haughtiest of the unrepentant "secesh"–are not more thoroughly tainted with the poison of Southern doctrine than some of our kindest and most warm-hearted and intelligent personal friends in England. Not all the stubborn events of the war itself and its great results, not all the magnanimous treatment of the leaders of the great conspiracy, has apparently changed or softened in the least the prejudices of many even moderate, well-bred, liberal-minded English men and women which were nursed and fed in the out set by the lies of the London *Times*. Even now, some of the most excellent people, who would do all sorts of hospitable things for you personally, will hold up their hands and roll their eyes in horror at "the abominable treatment of Mr. Davis," and of "that excellent, noble-hearted man, General Lee." Of course this view of things is not universal–but what there is yet, even among the "middle classes," would surprise a simple-minded Northern Republican. The way the sturdy, downright John Bright spoke of a certain famous "admiral" who had eclipsed Captain Kidd, was not much like the tone of Mr. Davis's admirers. But it will take some time yet for the simple truth of our great struggle to be appreciated in the various circles of English life.

After all, however, the American name in England is treated with more consideration than in the time when Lynch Law, Repudiation, Slavery, and the Oregon and the North-eastern Boundary Questions used to be poked at American visitors and residents in a patronisingly offensive style. Some curious illustrations of the spirit of thirty years since, which it was my fortune to encounter, might be quoted–but it is scarcely worth while. Mr. George Peabody, now the great dispenser of millions for the London poor, was then a modest merchant, keeping bachelor-hall with a friend in a small £80-house in Devonshire Street,– where the chums occasionally dined some of the American residents or visitors, and he now and then joined a similar little gathering at Knickerbocker Cottage, where it was my fortune to entertain, in a small way, three successive envoys,–Mr. Everett, Mr. McLane, and Mr. Bancroft,–besides our Spanish Minister, Mr. Irving; the little

American circle being mixed sometimes with some of our English literary friends. It was delicious to take another look at the semi-detached snuggeries and gardens in St. John's Wood and north of Regent's Park, and to remember the good old times when we enjoyed the luxuries of the "Zoölogical and Botanical" and the immediate proximity to Primrose Hill and Hampstead Heath and the magnificent slopes of the Park itself. No street walk in the world, perhaps, is more agreeable than that from Primrose Hill along the terraces of Regent's Park and gardens, and down Portland Place and Regent Street to Waterloo Place–the central point of London grandeur.

But one of the crowning glories of London of recent growth is that superb collection of rare things in the yet unfinished museum at South Kensington. The old British Museum in Bloomsbury, now wholly reconstructed on the site of the old brick pile of the 17th century, is a world of itself, an amazing collection of illustrations of the wonders of nature, ancient art, and the literature of all nations. But the newly built galleries at South Kensington already con-

tain relics and models of ancient and mediæval art which are eclipsing those of the Louvre–while the collections of paintings of the English school, including those made by Sheepshanks, Vernon, Bell, and others, are the most delicious things in modern art to be seen in Europe. Of course, thousands of American visitors in Europe for the last twenty years are aware of all this, but how many of them appreciate fully the immense wealth of art in this building? How many of those who have ample means in lucre to make their names immortal, are disposed to do so by even laying the foundation of such an institution in New York,–so thoroughly constructed, so perfectly warmed and ventilated, so fully furnished with every luxurious convenience for the *people*–rich and poor, learned and ignorant–to study art in its purest and highest forms, to cultivate their taste and their intellect, to enjoy at all times and in the most liberal manner the advantage of communion with genius of all ages and nations, and to drink in the richest inspirations of art with as much freedom as the air itself?

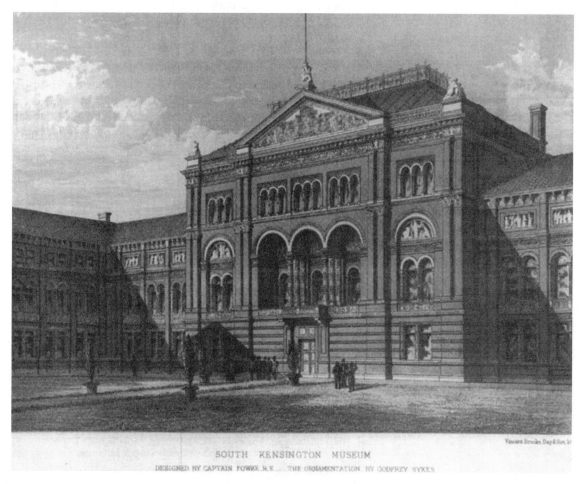

SOUTH KENSINGTON MUSEUM
DESIGNED BY CAPTAIN FOWKE R.E.   THE ORNAMENTATION BY GODFREY SYKES

The Victoria and Albert Museum in Kensington, which Putnam saw being built during his 1869 London visit, was a model for the great art museum he wished to see built in Manhattan. Putnam was instrumental in the founding of the Metropolitan Museum and served as its first superintendent.

PARIS

On my first visit to France, in 1836, I was a whole week on the way from London to Paris, including four days at Boulogne waiting for a chance seat in the diligence. Returning, four days at Havre waiting for a steamer, and then a twenty-four hours' passage in a gale to Southampton, left impressions of the trip between the two cities which dozens of subsequent visits only partially modified. When one now takes his cushioned seat at Cannon Street, at 1 P.M., after a good lunch in the station, and at twelve the same evening finds himself comfortably in bed on the Boulevards with his *douaned* portmanteau in the corner, without the least shade of fatigue or discomfort (except somewhat in that cramped Folkestone steamer, which is no bigger and no better than thirty years since), it is safe to conclude that in some particulars the world has advanced since the days of our youth.

But when you sally forth into the glazed courtyard of the Grand Hotel and thence into the Boulevard and take a glance at "N. & E.'s" gigantic new Opera House and the superb new streets diverging therefrom; when you follow these from block to block until you discover in every direction miles and miles of broad, palace-lined, asphaltum-paved streets, newly built where narrow lanes and uncouth rookeries only existed at the time of your last visit; when you find these superb avenues, which have risen like an exhalation, stretching along not in one or two central localities merely, but in every quarter of the great capital, built on a uniform scale of substantial elegance which shows at a glance that some central power—despotic or other—has devised and directed the whole operation; when you look in vain for the old lanterns suspended across from house to house, and the dirty gutters splashing you from the centre of ill-paved, sidewalkless streets, such as there were in the good old days of Louis Philippe—but find instead smoothly-paved streets with well-made *trottoirs,* and perfect neatness and cleanliness wherever you go, even in the old Latin quarter; when you study without and within the wonderful pile of palaces restored and completed where the Louvre and the Tuileries were sundered by unsightly nuisances; when you look at these and scores of similar improvements on a large scale, is it strange that American visitors should join others in admiring the energy and taste, "imperial" though it be, which has effected such a magnificent transformation? It is true that the people are now called upon to "pay the piper" (there's the rub), and Hausmanised Paris is on the *qui-vive* at this moment for the verdict of the Corps Législatif on the legality and the justice of these enormous expenditures and high-handed seizures of individual property. But, after all the grumbling, Paris likes her new holiday

The broad avenues and great public intersections of Paris, the result of the improvements supervised by French administrator
Baron Georges-Eugène Haussmann, came as a revelation to Putnam,
who remembered a much different city fifteen years before.

dress too well to quarrel with the Emperor for insisting upon her wearing it—and paying for it too; and so when the Ministers the other day confessed to the deputies that the improvements had been illegally made—but they "would n't do so any more," the deputies voted that his Imperial Majesty and his advisers should be excused and forgiven—just this once. The radicals growled, but the bankers and merchants applauded, and all again "goes merry as a marriage bell."

It was curious to note the different shades of feeling in regard to the government and to the prospects of France. Some of the shrewdest and most active of the "reds" whom I had a favourable chance to know are so bitter in their hostility to the "upstart" Emperor, that one wonders as to the chances of his head. But, going from these to the prosperous men of business, one may imagine universal contentment and security for the dynasty to an unlimited extent. As to the Orleanists and Legitimists, if they still exist in any strength, they do not appear to be demonstrative.

In 1851, during a flying visit to Paris, one of the members of the Chamber of Deputies was pointed out to me as Prince Louis Napoleon—"the adventurer" who had come over from England and got himself elected to the legislature, but who appeared to be looked upon as of small account. Eleven years before, by an odd chance I had, with an American friend, taken the very rooms in St. James Street which this same adventurous prince had vacated only a day or two before, when he went over to Boulogne, with thirty men and a tame eagle, for his second attempt at the conquest of France. The freak was not, probably, so utterly insane as it then appeared; but if a prophet had then recorded, in advance, his imperial reign, in apparent strength for seventeen years (whatever yet may come), and all the immense progress of France and the astounding growth and magnificent renovation of Paris, which is even now an accomplished fact, how many would have believed the prediction?

The moderate republicans, led by such men as Laboulaye, Martin, Cochin, and Jules Simon, make occasional demonstrations, in the shape of *conferences,* or public lectures. I was fortunate in hearing one of these, of notable interest. There was an assembly of 3500 intelligent-looking men and women, in one of the largest theatres of Paris,—Prince Imperial,—at two o'clock in the afternoon—admission three francs—proceeds for some charity. Laboulaye presided, and made an introductory address of half an hour, and then came an oration of more than two hours by Auguste Cochin, the handsome and wealthy member of the Institute, who wrote those excellent books on slavery. His theme was the life and character of Abraham Lincoln—and the address was a very interesting and comprehensive account of that remarkable man, with all the lights and shades of his early and later life, from flatboatman to President and Commander-in-Chief. The sly parallels with Imperialism were, apparently, capital hits, for the interest seemed to be intense, and the applause frequent and earnest. Probably the idea was a compound one—the running fire on the Government was as much the purpose as the eulogy of our martyred President. The tone, however, was moderate and dignified, warming occasionally into real eloquence, as when he quoted the famous Second Inaugural—"With malice toward none, with charity for all." The oration is to be published, probably, for it was most interesting and significant under the circumstances.

An evening with M. Laboulaye—at one of his "receptions"—was another pleasant incident to remember. The republican leader (as he may be called) is a gentleman of winning address,—calm, dignified, yet kind and genial,—inspiring at once a good deal of respectful regard. Among his visitors were members of the Corps Législatif, and notable men from various parts of Europe. It was curious, by the way, to observe that at French "receptions" of this sort, the sterner sex appear to do the talking among themselves, leaving the ladies to their own resources. The charming Madame Laboulaye entertained the feminine visitors in the same room, but in a group by themselves.

M. Laboulaye's *Paris in America* has so many clever and shrewd hits at our most creditable national traits and habits, that one can scarcely believe the author knows us only through books. His keen appreciation of the good points in American theories and practice shows him to be a skilful observer, and a judicious and able friend of constitutional liberty and progress.

A visit to the great warerooms of Hachette, the Harper of France, was another matter of quite as much interest, to a publisher at least, as many of the lions in the programme. Besides the immense piles—some hundreds of tons—of cheap, popular books, educational and other, this house issues those famous folios which Doré has illustrated with that magician's pencil which he wields with such marvellous facility: and the "royals" of popular science, such as *La Terre,* by Réclus, and the famous serial called *Autour du Monde*—an illustrated quarto which reproduces and illustrates notable travels in

Gustave Doré, circa 1870. Putnam frequently visited artists' studios during trips in the United States and overseas.

all parts of the world. They are now preparing, in a series of sumptuous folios, an edition of the four Gospels, the production of which will cost some $200,000. One of the artists engaged on this stays two years in Jerusalem, simply to make the sketches. This *œuvre de luxe* is done for the love of art and of fame alone, and not for profit in lucre.

"Would you like to visit Gustave Doré's studio?" Wouldn't I ! With a card from Hachette's, we were not long in finding it—even without a number or name to indicate it—for probably it is the only isolated studio in Paris built for the purpose—it must certainly be the largest. An artist who paints pictures 30 feet long and 22 feet high must have a studio of his own: and these are the dimensions of the last great work of Doré, which we saw on his easel (?), nearly or quite finished. The subject is Christ coming down from the Judgment Hall of Pilate—some twenty or more life-size figures fill the canvas. The competition for such a work must be somewhat limited—for what galleries less extensive than the Louvre can hold such a canvas? In the spacious studio, at this moment, there were also more than a dozen large pictures, all recently painted by this almost miraculous artist—(marvellous, at least; so far as facility and amount of work are concerned)—including figure-pieces from Dante and from *A Midsummer Night's Dream,* Rossini in his bed after death, and two very beautiful forest scenes, all

these being about six or eight feet high. One would think that Doré's pencil drawings might have occupied any one man for a lifetime, but to see these enormous and elaborate works in oil going on simultaneously, causes one's wonder to grow in proportion to their square feet. But for the janitor's assurance that no one but the master himself touched the canvas, we might guess that a large part of the work was done by pupils. Doré himself is a surprise, for he is, apparently, still on the sunny side of thirty-five. In feature he is not very unlike Thomas Nast, whose pencil comes nearest on our side to that of the French prodigy. M. Doré received us with that quiet and unpretending manner which marks the modesty of true merit: and though we avoided using minutes that must be money—and much money—to a man who can do such things as he does, yet he kindly explained the chief points in his recent works in a simple and sensible fashion, and gave us the impression that he was a true son of genius. And yet even a novice may guess that his drawings are not all faultless.

A fortnight in Paris and another in London, actively employed, gave ample material for rambling notes to an indefinite extent, but too much of our space is already filled.

—*Putnam's Magazine,* 3 (June 1869): 733–743

Leaves from a Publisher's Letter-Book

Only scattered documents from the early years of the House of Putnam have survived. There are some caches of extant material, however, from what was once surely one of the premier nineteenth-century collections of publishing papers and accounts. Most notably, the letters George Haven Putnam selected for the purpose of writing his father's biography are now housed at Princeton University Library. As George Haven Putnam knew, his father had likewise sorted through his professional correspondence on various occasions for aid in composing sketches about the world of letters and publishing. Though limited by discretion and seemingly informal in method, those sketches are valuable pieces of American literary history. One of the most important such pieces was "Leaves from a Publisher's Letter-Book," a file of correspondence that Putnam culled from the company's incoming letter-books and published in three installments in Putnam's Magazine *in the last three months of 1869. The original footnotes have been converted to endnotes.*

* * *

LEAVES FROM A PUBLISHER'S LETTER-BOOK.

I.

In the course of a "somewhat busy" experience of thirty-three years, as publisher and bookseller on both sides of the Atlantic, it has been my fortune to know, more or less intimately, several authors and artists of the period, whose names have become, in some sort, the world's heritage.

Looking over the earlier letter-files of such a business, one is reminded of personal interviews and incidents, trivial enough, perhaps, but often characteristic and suggestive as being connected with men who have left their mark in the reading world, and "whose works do follow them." Personal references to living men would be questionable, if not improper. Of others who have passed away, it may not be amiss to recall a fact or two—for life is made up of little things, and slight touches may aid in filling up an outline portrait. In some slight "Recollections of Irving," a few years ago, a few other authors were briefly mentioned. Some others may be here referred to in connection with a scrap or two from their correspondence.

The name of FENIMORE COOPER in American authorship was a prominent one during his life. It is not yet wholly eclipsed—but whether it will continue to fill a place in proportion to the bulk of his writings may have ceased, perhaps, to be a question. He was as conspicuous in person as in intellect; standing over six feet in height—strong, erect, well proportioned—with the air and manner of one who claimed the right to be listened to, and to have his *dictum* respected. A man who had seen so much of the world, whose opinions were so well fortified by reading and observation, and who had done so much for his country's fame in letters, was well entitled to respectful attention—yet it was not always pleasant to hear his rather tart criticisms of notable contemporaries. One of his axioms appeared to be, that the very possession of office or of popular favor in this country, was *prima-facie* evidence of incompetency, superficial attainment, or positive dishonesty. [It is rather sad to think, that if he had lived longer, this estimate of popular and official success might have been strengthened rather than diminished.] He loved to demonstrate this by examples—and would even include such names as Edward Everett, and others, whose fame and position were beyond ordinary question.

His views on *personal* rights were very decided, and often decidedly expressed. Coming from my house at Staten Island, he took occasion,—having been brusquely jostled by a carman driving on to the ferry boat,—to give him a five-minutes' lecture on the inherent rights of foot-passengers as against all vehicles whatsoever. The dignity and force of the argument evidently impressed both the carman and the bystanders.

Mr. Cooper was a good story-teller. At my house he gave a sketch of a scene in court with a thick-headed witness, which was rich in graphic humor, and was often afterwards quoted by our neighbors who heard it. For his book copyrights, he was fond of constructing his own agreements with all provisos and conditions. Eleven of his thirty-three novels were included in one library edition as those best worthy of preservation; and only one other was suggested by the author as being thus worthy of a fine edition. The only original work of his, first published by us, was his last, "The Ways of the Hour," intended to show the dangers and evils of our Jury system. Referring to the London edition of this, he wrote the following. [Mr. Bentley, "Her Majesty's publisher," had been in the habit of accepting his drafts for £300 on the receipt of the MS. of each of his novels; but the lighter craft in London, cruising about for free spoils in books, had discovered that there was, at least, a question whether an American author could *convey* a right to an English publisher which he did not first possess himself;—and so they had boldly seized Mr. Bentley's guinea and a half "copyright edition," and printed them for a shilling,—in defiance both of courtesy and tradition. As to the English *law,* that still remains in *in*glorious uncertainty, while *our* law is still ingloriously *certain*—on the wrong side.]

HALL, COOPERSTOWN, July 23, 1849.
MY DEAR SIR: *   *   *   *

Mr. Bentley has sent me a recent decision of an English court, which, as he asserts, goes to affect his interest in my books. He sends me a new proposition for the publication of "The Ways of the Hour" that I have declined accepting. Now, I wish to know if you cannot dispose of this book for me to some English publisher. * * *

I shall expect somewhere about £400 for the book, to be paid in drafts on the publishers at sixty days, £100 on sending vol. I, £100 on sending vol. II, and balance on sending the last volume of the work. I did think of asking £500 for this particular book, which is more elaborated than most of its companions; but this difficulty may compel me to accept even £300. There has certainly been a decision adverse to American copyrights, but it is evident that Bentley himself does not think it will stand.

Under no circumstances will I sell a book to share the profits. This is of the nature of Bentley's last proposition, though he proposes paying me down for a certain number of copies.

*   *   *   *   *

Yours, very truly,
FENIMORE COOPER.

When the volume on the "Homes of American Authors" was planned, those who were designated for it were applied to for some of the facts needed to complete

William Hickling Prescott, whom Putnam included in Homes of
American Authors

symmetrical sketches of their literary biography. Mr. PRESCOTT, the historian (who had volunteered some kind words respecting a pamphlet of what he called "curious and interesting statistics" of American authorship, which I had compiled and printed in London) sent us several notes in regard to his residences and his mode of composition–in addition to the particulars given to Mr. George S. Hillard, who wrote the sketch. Some of these may be quoted.

BOSTON, April 15, 1852.

MY DEAR SIR: I am very sorry that I cannot do better than to send you a pencil outline of a cottage I occupy on the seashore in the summer. The truth is, I have three places of residence, among which I contrive to distribute my year. Six months I pass in town, where my house is in Beacon street, looking on the Common, which, you may recollect, is an uncommonly fine situation, commanding a noble view of land and water. There is more than one engraving of these situations round the Boston Common, though none of my own house in particular. Here is my library, etc., which makes it the residence of the most importance to me. I have, about forty miles from town, in Pepperell, Massachusetts, an old family property, called the Highlands. * * *

The other place is a cottage,–what Lady Emmeline Wortley calls in her "Travels" "a charming *country* villa"–at Nahant, where for more than twenty years I have passed the summer months, as it is the coolest spot in New England. The house stands on a bold cliff, overlooking the ocean, so near, that in a storm the spray is thrown over the piazza: and as it stands on the entrance point of the peninsula, is many miles out at sea. There is more than one printed account of Nahant, which is a remarkable watering-place, from the bold formation of the coast and the exposure to the ocean. It is not a bad place–the sea-girt citadel– for reverie and writing, with the music of the winds and the waters, incessantly beating on the rocks and broad beaches below. This place is called "Fitful Head"–and Norna's was not wilder.

I am sorry I can send you nothing better than the enclosed sketch, made last summer by the pencil of a friend to amuse an idle hour.

The idea of your book seems to me to be a good one, if well executed, and I wish it may come to something in your hands. Do not take the trouble to return the sketch. I will only add that if there is any further information you desire respecting these matters, I shall be happy to communicate it as far as in my power.

I remain, my dear sir,
Very truly yours,
WM. H. PRESCOTT.
G. P. PUTNAM, ESQ.

BOSTON, May 12, 1852.

MY DEAR SIR: At your suggestion, I have found an artist and sent him to Pepperell. The result is the sketch which I enclose to you.

I am very well pleased to have this old place, to which I am attached by many associations and recollections, thus preserved; and I shall not, therefore, charge you with the expense of the sketch as you proposed, but only desire that, in case you do not use it, you will return the drawings to me.

The place at Pepperell has been in the family for more than a century and a half—an uncommon event among our locomotive people.

The house is about a century old—the original building having been greatly enlarged, by my father first, and since by me. It is here that my grandfather, Col. Wm. Prescott, who commanded at Bunker Hill, was born and died, and in the village churchyard he lies buried, under a simple slab, containing only the record of his name and age. My father, Wm. Prescott, the best and wisest of the name, was also born, and passed his earlier days here. And from my own infancy not a year has passed that I have not spent more or less of in these shades, now hallowed to me by the recollections of happy hours and friends that are gone.

The place which is called the "Highlands" consists of some two hundred and fifty acres about forty-two miles from Boston, on the border line of Massachusetts and New Hampshire. It is a fine rolling country, and the house stands on a rising ground that descends with a gentle sweep to the Nissitisset, a clear and very pretty river, affording picturesque views in its winding course. A bold mountain chain on the north-west, among which is the grand Monadnoc of New Hampshire, makes a dark frame to the picture. The land is well studded with trees—oak, walnut, chestnut, and maple—distributed in clumps and avenues, so as to produce an excellent effect. The maple, in particular, in the autumn season, when the family are there, makes a brave show with its gay livery when touched by the frost.

As I have mentioned to you, I usually pass the hot months in the cottage at Nahant, of which I sent you a sketch, and then migrate to the Highlands until winter brings us back to town. The ample accommodations of the house are put into requisition; for I have endeavored to keep up the good name for hospitality which the old dwelling has had for many a year. And yet it is the spot where I often do most work; and many a chapter of "Ferdinand" and "Mexico" have I composed while galloping over the hills, or wandering among the chestnut shades of my favorite walk in autumn.

I have been thus particular at your suggestion; and if more than you desire, I suppose it is because I love the theme better than you can.

I remain,　　　*　*　*

WM. H. PRESCOTT.

BOSTON, July 3, 1852.

MY DEAR SIR: Mr. Hillard, who went with me to my old place in the country the other day, tells me that he is to ruralize about the matter, to the extent of some dozen pages, more or less, for you. In your note to him, you ask if I have any objection to your printing the notes I sent to you about Pepperell and Nahant. I have no copy of them, and, of course, cannot recall the contents with any accuracy. But they were written as *Mémoires pour servir,* to supply the necessary material, and you can use your judgment as to using them or not after you have seen Hillard's performance, which perhaps may contain much of what is in them, and told in a better way.

I remain,　　　*　*　*

WM. H. PRESCOTT.

NAHANT, July 9, 1852.

MY DEAR SIR: As you desire, I send you a specimen of my autograph. It is the concluding page of one of the chapters of the "Conquest of Peru," Book III., chap. 3. The writing is not, as you may imagine, made by a pencil, but is indelible, being made with an apparatus used by the blind. This is a very simple affair, consisting of a frame of the size of a common sheet of letter-paper, with brass wires inserted in it, to correspond with the number of lines wanted. On one side of this frame is pasted a leaf of thin carbonated paper, such as is used to obtain duplicates.

Instead of a pen the writer makes use of a stylus of ivory or agate, the last being better or harder. The great difficulties in the way of a blind man's writing in the usual manner arise from his not knowing when the ink is exhausted in his pen, and when his lines run into one another. Both difficulties are obviated by this simple writing case, which enables one to do his work as well in the dark as in the light.

Though my trouble is not blindness, but a disorder of the nerve of the eye, the effect, so far as this is concerned, is the same, and I am wholly incapacitated for writing in the ordinary way.

In this manner I have written every word of my *historicals.* This *modus operandi* exposes one to some embarrassments. For as one cannot see what he is doing on the other side of the paper, any more than a performer in the treadmill sees what he is grinding on the other side of the wall, it becomes very difficult to make corrections. This requires the subject to be pretty thoroughly canvassed in the mind; and all the blots and erasures to be made there before taking up the pen–or rather the stylus. This compels me to go over my composition–to the extent of a whole chapter, however long it may be–several times in my head, before sitting down to my desk. When there, the work becomes one of memory, rather than of creation, and the writing is apt to run off glibly enough.

A letter which I received some years since from the French historian Thierry, who is totally blind, urged me, by all means, to cultivate the habit of dictation, to which he had resorted. And James, the eminent novelist, who has adopted this habit, finds it favorable to facility of composition. But I have been too long accustomed to my own way to change. And to say truth, I never dictated a sentence in my life for publication, without its falling so flat on my ear, that I felt almost ashamed to send it to the press. I suppose it is habit.

One thing I may add. My MS. is usually too illegible (I have sent you a favorable specimen) for the press; and it is always fairly copied by an amanuensis before it is consigned to the printer. I have accompanied the autograph with these explanations, which are at your service, if you think they will have interest for your reader. My *modus operandi* has the merit of novelty. At least, I have never heard of any history-monger who has adopted it besides myself.

I remain,   *   *   *

WM. H. PRESCOTT

In one of many letters which I received in England from Mr. Tupper, the poet-proverbialist, he says, "Shall we make EDGAR POE famous by a notice in the Literary Gazette?" referring to the volumes of Poe's Tales which Mr. Wiley had printed in our Library of American Books, and which I had given to the poet as novelties. These tales have a weird kind of fascination, which made me curiously interested in the author, whom I had never seen. Another incident enhanced this interest. At our London office we had received, about 1840, a volume called "The Narrative of Arthur Gordon Pym, of Nantucket," which in a long title-page purported to describe sundry veritable voyages, ending with one in which the author had reached the eighty-fourth parallel of southern latitude. The late Mr. D. Appleton was sitting in our office in Paternoster Row. "Here is an American contribution to geographical science," I said to him. "This man has reached a higher latitude than any European navigator. Let us reprint this for the benefit of Mr. Bull." He assented, and took half share in the venture. The grave particularity of the title and of the narrative misled many of the critics as well as ourselves, and whole columns of these new "discoveries," including the hieroglyphics (!) found on the rocks, were copied by many of the English country papers as sober historical truth. Whether such a book were as justifiable as Robinson Crusoe may be questioned–it was certainly ingenious and skilful.

Some years after, when my desk was in Broadway, in separate quarters, a gentleman with a somewhat nervous and excited manner claimed attention on a subject which he said was of the highest importance. Seated at my desk, and looking at me a full minute with his "glittering eye," he at length said: "I am Mr. Poe." I was "all ear," of course, and sincerely interested. It was the author of "The Raven," and of "The Gold Bug!" "I hardly know," said the poet, after a pause, "how to begin what I have to say. It is a matter of profound importance." After another pause, the poet seeming to be in a tremor of excitement, he at length went on to say that the publication he had to propose was of momentous interest. Newton's discovery of gravitation was a mere incident compared to the discoveries revealed in this book. It would at once command such universal and intense attention that the publisher might give up all other enterprises, and make this one book the business of his lifetime. An edition of fifty thousand copies might be sufficient to begin with, but it would be but a small beginning. No other scientific event in the history of the world approached in importance the original developments of this book. All this and more, not in irony or in jest, but in *intense* earnest, for he held me with his eye, like the Ancient Mariner. I was really impressed–but not overcome. Promising a decision on Monday (it was late Saturday, P.M.), the poet had to rest so long in uncertainty about the *extent* of the edition–partly reconciled, by a small loan, meanwhile. We *did* venture, not upon fifty thousand, but five hundred.[1]

This little book of "great expectations" was simply "Eureka–a new Theory of the Universe"–which Mr. Poe had read as a lecture to a small audience at the Society Library. A Southern magazine, "The Nineteenth Century," gave recently a high estimate of the theory or discovery announced in "Eureka"–but it has never, apparently, caused any profound interest either to popular or scientific readers.

Edward Everett, whose serious advocacy for international copyright in his various public capacities as ambassador, senator, and secretary of state brought him into close relations with Putnam

During Mr. EDWARD EVERETT'S residence in London as American Minister, the few American families residing there were always made "at home" at the Legation receptions, where we sometimes met English notabilities, such as Sydney Smith, who was a firm friend of our Minister, even while he was writing epigrams on Pennsylvania bonds—and whose rather burly figure and good-humored wit-lighted face were frequently visible among Mr. Everett's visitors. Mr. Everett's interest in the progress of American letters was evidenced in many inquiries received from him respecting book-making statistics. He kindly made suggestions in regard to some facts and figures which I had collected in answer to a chapter of Alison's Europe referring to American authorship, which he "had read, with pleasure," and which would "be of great value to the candid Englishman."

When Mr. Everett was Secretary of State, he arranged with Mr. Crampton (British Minister) the plan of a treaty for international copyright; but this treaty, by some opposing influence, was withheld and never presented to the Senate. At Mr. Everett's request, I had prepared a schedule of the American books that had been reprinted in England up to that time—most of them being more or less disguised in their English costume—the whole number being about seven hundred and fifty.

WASHINGTON, March 25, 1853.

DEAR SIR: I duly received yours of the 16th, with the list of American works published in England, for which I am greatly indebted to you.

It is a very important document, and when properly made use of will have its effect on the public mind.

I do not think we shall be able to take up the Copy-Right Convention at this session. The Senate is greatly preoccupied with other subjects, and there is an indisposition to take up business of this kind.

Great pains have been taken by outsiders to prejudice the Senate against the treaty; and not much to counteract these efforts. It is the universal opinion, as far as I know, of the friends of the measure, that it would be unwise to take it up this Spring.

Let this, however, be *entre nous*. You must get some able, temperate, and skilful friend of the measure to advocate it in a series of articles in your magazine. It would be worth while to have something in each number during the recess of Congress.

With great regard, faithfully yours,
EDWARD EVERETT.

Mr. PAULDING was already a veteran at the time these notes begin—having retired from the duties of Navy Agent and Secretary of the Navy to the shades of Hyde Park, on the Hudson. For our booksellers' dinner to authors at the City Hotel in 1837, he had prepared a short speech about Cooper; but, for some reason, it was not spoken, and he sent it to me. The letter quoted relates to a proposed publication.

HYDE PARK, DUCHESS COUNTY, December 14, 1851.

DEAR SIR: You may probably recollect that some time since a negotiation took place between us on the subject of a work entitled "The New and the Old World; or, the Balance of Power," and that you agreed to publish it on certain conditions. For reasons which it is not necessary to specify, I delayed sending you the MS., knowing that you consented to publish it more to oblige me than yourself.

The times are now favorable to its publication, as the subject has become one of great interest; and I now offer the work to you again for publication, without considering you in the least bound by any former agreement, and without asking any thing for the copy-right for five years.

Though a political, it is not a party work, but, in fact, devoted to the interests of the world. It will make a couple of hundred pages, I presume; and I don't contemplate putting my name to it, as I believe it will be better received as written by "A retired Statesman."

I shall be obliged to you for a prompt reply, as the present period is peculiarly favorable for the appearance of such a work, and I should wish it to be published as early as possible.

I am very respectfully your friend and servant,

J. K. PAULDING

HYDE PARK, DUCHESS COUNTY, July 14, 1852.

DEAR SIR: I have received your letter, and regret that I have no materials in preparation with which I can furnish you.

With respect to my biography, I have always had an insuperable objection to writing the life of a man while he is living, conceiving it little better than a fraud on posterity by forestalling its decision. Besides, the incidents of my life are of the most ordinary kind; of no interest except to my family and friends, and not worth communicating to the public. I have therefore always declined furnishing them to persons who have occasionally applied to me, except in private communications to friends, without, of course, any view to publication.

A gentleman of South Carolina has, however, lately, in the spirit of friendship, published a sketch of my life, which was copied a few days ago in the "*Southern Press,*" which is pretty correct in its details, and to which I refer Mr. Griswold, in whose candor, discretion, and judgment I implicitly confide, and in whose hands I am perfectly willing to trust myself.

The sketch is compiled from information communicated by me, in a friendly correspondence; but the opinions of the writer as to myself and my writings are, of course, his own, and I am not in any way responsible for them. Mr. Griswold will, if he expresses any on the subject, be governed by his own judgment.

I would, however, advise him in all cases to abstain from any thing but mere facts, and thus avoid ruffling the plumage of us literary peacocks, by any appearance of preference.

Exaggerated praise does a man more harm than unjust censure. The first excites envy or disgust, the second calls forth our indignation at its injustice, and our sympathies in behalf of the victim. I would send you the paper containing the article, but that I cannot lay my hand on it, as I believe it has been destroyed. I will, if you wish it, give you a short sketch of the scenery in my neighborhood and the views from my piazza, which are thought very fine. As they are not my works, I can praise them without any violation of modesty.

I am, dear sir,

Yours very truly,

J. K. PAULDING

———

PARIS, November 28, 1846.

DEAR SIR: *   *   *   *

Proposals have been made to me for translating some fragments of my writings into the French journals, and I think that, at least, the sketch of American literature and some part of "Woman in the Nineteenth Century" might be interesting here. Will you have the kindness to send me five copies of the "Papers on Literature and Art," and to purchase for me as many of "Woman," etc., to send with them. I can give them away much to my advantage and pleasure to the persons with whom I am making acquaintance. As I have already given away the copies I brought with me, would you have the kindness to send the parcel as early as possible, and in some safe way, to my address here.   * * *

We are enjoying a great deal here; it is truly the city of pleasures.

Mademoiselle Rachel I have seen with the greatest delight. I go whenever she acts, and when I have seen the entire range of her parts, intend to write a detailed critique, which shall also comprehend comments on the high French tragedy.   * * *

With compliments,

MARGARET FULLER.

During her visit to London, on her way to Italy, Margaret Fuller passed an evening at Knickerbocker Cottage; and I had also an opportunity to study her peculiar manner when she made an address at the anniversary of an Italian school, at which Mazzini, Gallenga, and others made speeches. In this address (1847) Miss Fuller said that it was quite customary in her own country for women to speak in public. This seemed to me to be not a very accurate, though it might be a prophetic remark.

It so happened that our party in Genoa, Leghorn, Naples, and Rome, was a good deal with that of Miss Fuller. Between Leghorn and Civita Vecchia our steamer, an English one, was run down in the night by a French steamer. As they were going in opposite directions, at the rate of twelve miles an hour, such a shock in the dead of night, knocking us out of our berths, was not fitted to soothe an anxious spirit. The first impulse was to rush on deck to see if we were actually sinking. Fortunately the bow of the Frenchman had merely smashed one of our paddle-boxes, and the wheel itself, but had not injured the hull; so I jumped down to the ladies' cabin, to re-assure my wife and the other ladies. The door was opened by Miss Fuller in her night-dress. Instead of hysterical fright, as I expected, my hurried report that there would be time to dress before we went to the bottom, was met by Miss Fuller by the remark that seemed to me superhuman in its quiet calmness: "Oh, we–had not–made up our minds, that it was–worth while–to be at all–alarmed!" Verily woman–American woman, at least–is wonderful for her cool philosophy and strong-nerved stoicism in great danger!

The narration in the memoirs of Miss Fuller of her first meeting with her future husband, the Marquis d'Ossoli, is not accurate. Her party had been attending some of the services of Holy Week in St. Peter's–ours had heard the miserère in the Sistine Chapel. As we came away from the Chapel, and met the throng from the great church on the steps, Miss Fuller stepped out quickly to overtake us, saying she had lost her friends; and as it was nearly dark, she seemed quite bewildered–more alarmed, indeed, than when we were really in danger of being drowned in the Mediterranean. She had taken the arm of a young gentleman in the crowd, who had politely offered to escort her home, or to a cab; but on joining us, she took leave of him, as we thought, rather ungraciously. She certainly did not give her address to him, but left him in the crowd, and we ourselves took her to her lodgings. How and when they met again, we do not know. But this was the first time the Marquis had seen her, and he left her in the confusion, without knowing who she was or where she lived.

At a notable private concert at the Palazzo—, Miss Fuller appeared with us one evening, rather unconsciously, in the character of Madame. The superb music, from some of the best artists in Europe, with cardinals and other grandees for fellow-guests, was pleasant to remember, rather than the question of identity suggested by the very magnificent hostess and her chief of staff.

–*Putnam's Magazine,* 4 (October 1869): 467–474

II.

STOCKHOLM, May 4, 1854.

MY DEAR SIR: The moment is come when I can fulfill the promise given to my friend A. J. Downing, and to yourself, that you, and no other publisher in America, should be the publisher of my first novel after my work, "Homes of the New World." That work, and many cares both private and public, have taken up my thoughts and my time since, so that I had no time to write a novel; until lately the pressure of the spirit has had the upper hand, and made me bring forth a novel, not of large size, but, as I presume to-day, of no small or narrow mind. I shall have it published leisurely during the summer, so as to have it ready to be published in November or December. Every printed sheet I shall send (reduced to its smallest dimensions) to England, to France, Germany, and to America, all at the same time, and so that the different publications may all be issued at the same time. I do not think that the size of this new book will exceed that of my little novel, the "Midnight Sun." I leave it to you if you will have the translation done in America, in case of which I wish you would try to engage Mrs. ––– to do it; or, if you will, make an agreement with Mrs. Mary Howitt to have a copy of her English translation. Her genial mind and manner of writing will always make her translations in many ways unsurpassed; and her growing knowledge of the Swedish language will hereafter make mistakes of words very rare; nor will they matter much in a work of fiction. I leave to you to make the pecuniary terms of the agreement between us, perfectly sure that they will be honorable; and I am ready to subscribe to any mode you shall propose. Only I wish that you will pay the postage, in case you want me to send the printed sheets over to America, and I cannot get them free of post by the legation of the United States in Stockholm, which I fear will not be possible. I do not think it safe to send any thing with travellers; these are apt to be forgetful, and leave the things behind them.

My friend Downing wrote to me, in the last letter that I received from him (shortly before his most tragical death), that he would send to me several books–I think called "American Stories"–all written by women. I have also heard of travellers being charged with some books for me, which I supposed to be these; yet they have never come to me. I am sure, also, that you have forwarded to me that last work of my friend for which I had written a biographical sketch, and sent from Sweden the daguerreotype after which the portrait in the book was drawn. I am sure that Mrs. Downing would not that I should be without this last dear memory of her husband and my friend. . . .

Many changes, most of them sorrowful, have taken place among my friends in America since I was with them. Some of these friends have blessed me with their visits in my land and home; some I hope still to see here. My dear friends of ——— Cottage are still in Europe, and gave several weeks last summer to Scandinavia, which made me happy, as I was there with them. I hope, my dear sir, that the happy and beautiful family that I saw at your house on Staten Island is so still, only growing, as all good things should.–Give my kind regards to my lovely hostess there, and remember me to common friends.

I remain, my dear sir,

Yours faithfully,

FREDRIKA BREMER.

P.S.–Do me the favor, my dear sir, to put the adjoined little notice, as an extract out of my letter, in some popular magazine or newspaper in New York, as it may possibly be of some benefit to the excellent family of which it treats, and for whom I have the greatest regard and friendship.

——— Many changes among my friends in America have taken place since I was with them, some of them too painful to me here to speak of. One there is which gives me both pain and pleasure. I mean the removal of the family of Mr. ——— from its beautiful home in Charleston, S. C., to ——— *Seminary,* near New York. I grieve to see this change of circumstances in a family so well deserving all the boons of fortune, whose home was my dear delightful home during many weeks in the sunny South, and whose prosperity was so nobly used; but I must rejoice when I reflect that this turn of fortune is going to widen the sphere of influence and activity of this excellent family, and that its home, now and henceforward, will be the home of many a young girl during her years of development from girlhood to womanhood. This will be a blessing to many. Then, in this home they will not only acquire the knowledge and talents requisite for a good education, but, what is much more, they will, by that influence of all the most irresistible–the influence of example and strong persuasion–be led to acquire true piety, strength of principle, the love of duty, of labor, and kindness, the character and refinement of true womanliness. Yea, if I had a daughter, and could not well educate her at home, I would be happy to take her to that new home on the Hudson, knowing, were I to do it, that in its superintendent, excellent Mrs. ———, "whose whole life has been so good" (to speak in the words of a noble lady in Charleston), my child would not only find a monitress, but also a careful mother; and in her daughters not only teachers, but also kind and noble minds.

As the charcoal is the mother of the diamond, so, in this case, may misfortune be the mother of fortune in a larger and a higher meaning than ever before enjoyed by the members of this family. "Then they loved to do good."

CRAVEN HILL COTTAGE, BAYSWATER,
January 15, 1852.

DEAR SIR: Let me thank you very cordially for the pleasure with which I beheld your name among the list of subscribers forwarded to me by the kind consideration of our most amiable and thoughtful friend, Mr. Balmanno. His chief delight seems to be in conferring gratification; and he knew what a surpassing one it would be to me to see the several names on that treasured list. I have also to tell you how much pleased I have been by your having promoted *our* book to the dignity of large-paper copies. Pray accept my warm thanks for the many instances of courtesy and liberality I have met with at your hands, and believe me to be, dear sir, yours faithfully and obliged,

MARY COWDEN CLARKE.[2]

LONDON, Dec. 9, 1851.

SIR: I have a bad habit, sometimes, of not opening parcels which are addressed to me; and I am appropriately punished by not having till now discovered the very neat edition of my lectures which you have had the great kindness to send me. Late as it is, and uncertain as I am whether this will find you, I cannot forbear from expressing my gratification well at the fact of my production having been deemed worthy of republication in a country to which I feel so many ties of attachment, and at your own personal courtesy in the matter. I have the honor to be your obliged servant,

CARLISLE.[3]

48 DOUGHTY STREET,
Friday, Aug. 31, 1838.

–I beg to thank you for the books you have been so obliging as to forward me. I have only had time to glance at them, but have been already much pleased, and hope to be more so. I assure you that nothing would yield me greater pleasure than to be the humble means of introducing any American writer to this part of the world. I would only entreat you to remember that our means do not always keep pace with our inclination, and that the claims upon the very limited space of such a magazine as the *Miscellany* are necessarily more than it is possible to answer with any speed or regularity. I should be very happy to write something for the *Knickerbocker* and *American Monthly;* but I do assure you I have scarcely time to complete my existing engagements. So I think I must defer this pleasure until I visit America, which I hope to do before very long; and then I shall be more independent and free, which will be more in keeping. I am your very obedient servant,

CHARLES DICKENS.

3 KING STREET, GREENWICH
Jan. 2, 1845.

GENTLEMEN: As you are now publishers both for the Old as well as the New World, I take leave to offer you the manuscript of a work edited, translated, and partly written by me, under the following circumstances. During the last three years, I have passed much time in the north of Germany, particularly in Holstein, where I met, at the home of a learned friend, an old Swedish officer, who, for reasons of state, preferred living in obscurity under the protection of the Danish government. Being there at the time of opening the iron chests at Upsala, which were not to be unclosed until fifty years after the death of Gustavus III., it naturally excited much conversation, and many discussions took place thereon. The old soldier had written a sort of memoir of the events which led to the assassination of that monarch, which he permitted me to translate; to add much from books in our friend's library, much from his own mouth, and some, during my stay in London, from books within my own reach. When this was done, he destroyed his own memorandum, and returned to his country retirement. He much admired and zealously vindicated the patriotism and ability of his murdered sovereign, which he declared was as much as high treason in Sweden, and dangerous in Denmark, but declared his satisfaction at entrusting his views to a native of a country which feared not the vindication of any one who required it. The weather not permitting me to return to Denmark for the present, I have revised my manuscript, which will make about ten sheets octave of such type and page as the historical novels of the present day. If this comes within your views, I will send you the manuscript for a moderate remuneration and for some copies for my friends, as I must make my ancient friend a present. I am, gentlemen, your very obedient servant,

JAMES ELMES.[4]

19 Austen Friars, City.

MY DEAR SIR: This letter will be presented to you by Mr. H––, a German by birth, who is soon to be an American by choice. He comes to settle in the United States, with a young wife and a small family. He is a relation to my wife's family—in fact, first cousin to my wife. He is a good engineer, and will look for employment in his profession either in New York or in any other of your States. If he does not succeed in that line of business, he will become a settler in some of your new agricultural districts. He comes sufficiently provided with means. I beg, for "auld lang syne," that you will help him with your advice and friendly assistance in every thing that may be in your power, both by taking him by the hand in New York itself, so long as he stays there, and supplying him with good introductions and recommendations wherever his fortune may lead him. I am sure you must have agents and correspondents all over.

And now to ourselves. I hope you are happy in your own native Broadway. . . . I repeat to you my great regret that you should just have absconded yourself from London, when I brought into it a wife of my own whom I wanted to introduce to Mrs. –––, and who would have suited her to perfection. I am now made glad in the house by the presence of a little child, by name Romeo, something less than thirty months old, and a little prodigy—in his mother's estimation.

I published, since your absence, a volume entitled "Scenes from Italian Life," 1840 (Newby), and "Italy in 1848," London, Chapman & Hall, 1851. I am now finishing a two-volume novel, entitled "Days of Hope," which I intend offering to the same Chapman & Hall. It is an Italian romance, somewhat drawn out of my own life. I suppose you know I was in Italy and Germany in 1848 and 1849, and had some political, military, diplomatical, revolutionary business in those countries. Likewise you must know that I had published a second edition of "Italy Past and Present," in November, 1848, half of which was new matter. . . .

Why are you not here, and your lady? Let me hear one word—only one—from you, and believe me, ever yours truly,

A. GALLENGA.
(L. MARIOTTI.)
21 THURLOW SQUARE, LONDON, July 9, 1851.

13 KENSINGTON GATE, LONDON,
August 5, 1854.

MY DEAR FRIEND: The bearer will be Mr. –––, from Stuttgart, who has been driven from one to another of the petty German towns in consequence of the political convulsions which are rapidly draining that country of all its talent and industry. Mr. –––has all the advantages of a good German education, and had lately been employed by several first-rate publishers in his country. He is well versed in your business, and would be glad to make himself useful in your land of refuge. His wife is intimately acquainted with a good friend of mine, a lady whom I greatly wish to oblige. I have before recommended to you other persons in the same situation; as I never received any answer, and, indeed, never any news from you, I might be left to think either that you consider my frequent applications to your kindness as importunate, or that you are dead and buried—or that you are (and that is the most likely hypothesis) sunk over head and ears in work. I have seen several numbers of your magazine, which is universally well received in England. Has any body in Yankee-land heard of a new work of mine—published anonymously—entitled "Castelamonte," and which appeared last January, published by Westerton, in two volumes? I am now printing a work on the "History of Piedmont," which Chapman & Hall have undertaken to publish. It will be in three volumes, and two volumes are ready now; but we will put off the publication till next Christmas or spring. I should offer it to you for joint publication, and most happy should I be to come to an understanding with you. But, alas! what cares Yankee-land for our musty Old World?

Believe me, my dear Putnam, with the kindest remembrances to –––, yours truly,

A. GALLENGA.

(MARIOTTI.[5])

. . . Seriously, if by chance you wish to take my "Piedmont" into consideration, I will gladly send you the two first volumes for inspection. They will be ready by the end of April; but you must let me have your letter by the end of May. You shall have the two volumes, and take the whole autumn to make up your mind—only say the word. In May I leave London for Turin, where I mean to make arrangements for an Italian translation. As I said, even in London the book is not to appear before Christmas, or before March, 1855.

PRESCOTT HOUSE.

Ivan Golovin presents his compliments to Mr. Putnam, and begs him to undertake the publication of his MS. "Stars and Stripes, or Russian Letters and American Impressions"–a volume like "The Potiphar Papers."

CORPUS CHRISTI COLLEGE,
OXFORD, Nov. 10.

Dr. Giles presents his compliments to Messrs., and writes to inform them that he has just completed an original work entitled ––– "Life and Letters of Thomas à Becket," which is now very nearly printed by Messrs. Gilbert & Rivington, in two volumes, 8vo, usual type and paper.

Dr. Giles is desirous that the work should appear at the same time in America, and would be glad to know whether Mr. ––– will enter into any arrangement with him to that effect. If so, Dr. Giles will immediately revise the impression before the work is published here, and add a dozen other letters of Becket, and make such additions as may render the American reprint to all intents and purposes a second edition. This arrangement can be effected by means of a sale of the copyright, or of an edition of five hundred copies, or by any other mode which Messrs. ––– can suggest.

RECTORY HOUSE, 4 NICHOLAS LANE,
LOMBARD STREET, April 14, 1836.

DEAR SIR: Prof. Bush informs me that you are desirous of information respecting our London bookstores. I shall be very happy to give you any assistance in this matter in my power, and also with reference to the Continent.

If you pass the British Museum tomorrow, you will find me there from 10 till 4. I am there every day in the week, except Sunday. I propose to leave this note at our lodgings on my way to the Museum. If you are not better engaged next Sunday, Mrs. Horne and myself will have much pleasure in seeing you here, to take a plain family-dinner with us. We dine at the unfashionably early hour of half-past one, that our servants may each have the opportunity of attending Divine worship. I remain, dear sir, very truly yours,

THOMAS HARTWELL HORNE.[6]

ROYAL ACADEMY, May 10, 1845.

Mr. Howard presents his compliments to Mr. Putnam, and assures him that the error of which he complains with regard to Mr. Edmonds' picture shall be corrected as quickly as possible; but he cannot authorize any addition to the description, or the placing such a label on the picture as Mr. P. proposes. The word "Honorary" is applied to all such artists as are not professional–the word "Amateur" never being used. In Mr. Putnam's letter there was no mention of price with regard to Mr. Cropsey's picture, which excludes it from any benefit from the Art Union. It shall, however, be entered in the record-book. Mr. H. requests, that when any of the pictures sent by Mr. Putnam are to be removed from the Academy, he will send a written order, as no works are ever delivered to –––, or carriers, without orders from artists or their agents.[7]

MY DEAR SIR: You are indeed extremely kind, and both Mr. Howitt and myself feel greatly indebted to you.

We shall like to have, as early as convenient, the materials for the memoirs of Daniel Webster and Mr. Bancroft. We shall thank you for the portrait of Webster. I do not exactly understand from your note whether you have sent it, or will send it; but we have not received it. Mr. Howitt will write to Mr. Bancroft about having a sketch made for the Journal. He will thank Mr. Brodhead for any hints he can give him from which he will draw up a memoir, which Mr. Bancroft shall then see, so that it may be made as complete and perfect as possible. Have you any memoir of Abby Kelly? We have a portrait of her,

William and Mary Howitt, who were friends with Putnam during the years of his London residence. Putnam patterned Homes of American Authors *after William Howitt's* Homes and Haunts of the Most Eminent British Poets.

which we mean to give some time, accompanied by a memoir, for she is really a noble woman. I am greatly interested in the "Views A-foot," much of the ground is so familiar to us; so many of the persons mentioned in the work are known to us. You shall find a notice of it before long. It is to Mr. Dennett, I believe, that we are indebted for the sight of the Album. Pray thank him. It is really very interesting. With kind regards to Mrs. –––, I am, dear sir, yours very truly,

MARY HOWITT.

 UPPER CLAPTON, April 12, 1844.
DEAR SIR: Many thanks for the card of admittance to your Reading Room,[8] which, should we have occasion to avail ourselves of at any time, we shall not fail to do. Yours very truly,
W. HOWITT.

ISLINGTON, March 19.
DEAR SIR: In forwarding the accompanying letter, I beg to mention that the writer, the Rev. Dr. Beard, of Manchester, is a gentleman of the highest respectability,

and a great book-buyer; and as he begins to feel a desire to cultivate an acquaintance with American theological literature, which he has means of bringing into notice in this country, there will be much benefit in your affording him such facilities and information as he may require. Dr. Beard writes in the *Cyclopædia of Biblical Literature,* and in various influential periodicals. I am, dear sir, most truly yours,
JOHN KITTO.[9]

NEW YORK, November 16, 1850.
DEAR SIR: I received, yesterday, your note, with an enclosed letter from England, and beg hereby to return to you my best thanks for the same. I feel exceedingly sorry to hear that you have not received my acknowledgment of the receipt of the beautiful books which you so kindly presented to me when last in New York, and may thus have been led to think that I did not fully appreciate your splendid gift; but beg you to be assured that such is not the case, as, on the contrary, they have afforded me great enjoyment. Believe me, dear sir, yours, truly obliged,
JENNY LIND.

OFFICE OF COMMITTEE OF PRIVY COUNCIL FOR TRADE, Whitehall, Dec. 13, 1844.
GENTLEMEN: With reference to your application of the 31st October last, on the subject of the duty on a series of engravings imported in the ship Northumberland from New York, which are intended to illustrate a work on "Weaving," originally published in New York, and reprinting in this country, I am directed, by the Lords of the Committee of Privy Council for Trade, to acquaint you that the Commissioners of the Customs have been informed that, provided the work for which these plates are stated to be intended be one which might be legally imported at the low duty of the cwt., and there be no doubt that the plates are really intended to illustrate the work reprinted in this country, the plates should be admitted at the lower rate of duty by weight, as requested by you. I am, gentlemen, your obedient servant,
J. MACGREGOR.[10]
₊ The engravings and parts of the work left at this office are herewith returned to you.

OFFICE OF COMMITTEE OF PRIVY COUNCIL FOR TRADE, Whitehall, Nov. 4, 1844.
GENTLEMEN: I am directed by the Lords of the Committee of Privy Council for Trade to acquaint you that your application on the subject of being prevented by the Post-office authorities from sending by the steamers, to the

United States of America, newspapers more than seven days old, has been referred to the Lords Commissioners of Her Majesty's Treasury. I am, gentlemen, your obedient servant,

JOHN MACGREGOR.

HEIDELBERG, July 23.

DEAR SIR: I hope to hear that the proofs of my "Life of Shelley" were despatched by the packet of the 18th, and that you urged the expediency of despatch in the publication.

I learned from Bentley that he had made copyright of Prescott's "Conquest of Peru," although republished in America; and in the still stronger precedent in my case, I am led to augur an equally favorable result.

I trust that your firm will exert themselves to accomplish this. I enclose you a letter of Shelley, to form an autograph-lithograph to embellish the work. On looking over my MSS., I find that, singularly enough, in the first page of the introduction to the ———, a line was omitted in the transcript, which must be supplied. After speaking of the steamer that plied from Marseilles to Genoa, and before mentioning my departure from one place to another, the following words should be introduced: "But before I take the reader with me on my voyage, I will transcribe from my journals the first impression which my entrance into the dark blue Mediterranean, some months before, made on me. And now," &c.

The "Life of Shelley" will not appear in England till after the elections are over—probably the latter end of August—which will give Messrs. Wiley & Putnam ample time to print the work. I will trouble you, as soon as you hear from them, to give me a line, and am, dear sir, yours truly,

W. MEDWIN.

P. S.–I have marked in inverted commas the passages from the letter which may form the autograph. Pray send the note by the first opportunity. I should wish to have the letter from Shelley returned. Send also the enclosed "Corrected Translation of the Death of Ugolino."

BROUGH HALL, NORFOLK, ENGLAND,
February 19, 1856.

Dear Sir: I am obliged by your communication, forwarded through Mr. Parker. If you have not sent me any copy of the American edition of my book, it would please me to see the Letters in the form they have been published in by you. I wish you may have corrected some of the errors of the type in this country, which are more numerous from the printing having been done from the original letters, with the disadvantage of my not being in London to correct the proofs.

I observe ——— is always spelt with an *e*. I cannot accuse the English papers of having treated this publication with indifference–by a few it has been favorably, by many severely treated–but a very bitter review in the *Times* newspaper, I am convinced by internal evidence, emanated from your side the Atlantic; an acquaintance of yours as well as mine, I feel sure (in return for my refusal to minister to his wish for popularity), took this opportunity of being even with me. This was not either wise or generous, because the criticisms were so over-done as to excite a reaction in my favor. I have not sought approbation in either country, but have simply told the truth as far as my judgment could discover it; and I have been duly prepared for all the hard words which may be given. Yours faithfully,

AMELIA M. MURRAY.[11]

4 VANE STREET, BATH, ENGLAND,
November 3, 1856.

DEAR SIR: I have just received safely your letter of the 18th of last month, with the two bills[12] enclosed; and while acknowledging the receipt of them, I must express my sense of the honorable manner in which the business has been conducted.

I have not yet received Professor Gray's work, but no doubt it will be duly forwarded. I remain, dear sir, yours, truly obliged,

AMELIA M. MURRAY.

PARLIAMENT STREET, LONDON.

SIR: I am sorry I cannot communicate any particulars relative to Mrs. Charlotte Lennox, except what appears in "Nichols' Literary Anecdotes," the "Gentleman's Magazine," "Chalmers' Biographical Dictionary," &c. She was an active member of the literary world for a long series of years. Her history, in brief, appears to have been this:

Barbara Charlotte Lennox was the daughter of Lieutenant-General George Ramsay, Lieutenant-Governor of New York, and was born about 1719 or 1720. At the age of fifteen she came to England to visit a wealthy aunt; but on her arrival her aunt was out of her senses, and never recovered them, and about the same time her father died.

From this period she depended on her literary talents for support. In 1747 she published a volume of poems; in 1752, "The Female Quixote" and "Memoirs of Harriet Stuart;" in 1753, "Shakespeare," illustrated, 2 vols.; in 1756, "Memoirs of the Countess of Berci" and "Sully's Memoirs;" in 1758, "Philander; a Dramatic Pastoral," and "Henrietta," a novel. In 1760, with the assistance of the Earl of Cork and Orrery and Dr. Johnson, a translation of "Father Brumoy's Greek Theatre," 3 vols. In 1762 she published "Sophia," a novel, and in 1769 brought out at Covent Garden "The Sisters," a comedy, from her novel of "Henrietta." This comedy was not successful. In 1773 she produced, at Drury Lane, another comedy called "Old

City Manners." She afterwards wrote (it is believed) "Euphemia," a novel.

Her latter years were clouded by distress; and it is mentioned in the printed notices of her, that she was relieved by the Literary Fund; but no additional particulars of her are to be gleaned from their books. The Literary Fund seems also to have assisted to fit out her son for an employment in America. Dr. Johnson's high opinion of her may be learned by the following extract from "Boswell's Life:" "I dined yesterday at Mr. Garrick's, with Mrs. Carter, Miss Hannah More, and Miss Fanny Burney. Three such women are not to be found. I know not where to find a fourth, *except Mrs. Lennox, who is superior to them all.*"

Besides the works before noticed, she published "Memoirs of Madame de Maintenon," 2 vols.; translated "The Age of Louis XIV.;" "Eliza," erroneously attributed to Dr. Young; "Harriet and Sophia," 2 vols.; and translated "The Devotions of Madame de Valiere, Mistress of Louis XIV.;" and the three first numbers of "The Trifler." She died in Dean's Yard, in the parish of St. Margaret, and is buried in the parochial ground; but no stone marks the spot where she was interred. Your very obedient servant,

B. NICHOLS.[13]

Amelia Opie requests Mr. Putnam will be so good as to send down to her "The Religious Souvenir," intended for her by its editor in Philadelphia, according to the following address: "Mrs Opie, Lady's Lane, Norwich."

11th Mo., 9th, 1838.

ABINGDON, February 28, 1844.

SIR: Your note found me on the eve of my departure for the Oxford Circuit, and too much pressed by business to answer it before leaving town. In reply to your inquiry, I beg to inform you that the copyright act, 5th and 6th inst., *is* that which you refer to as *mine*—that which I endeavored to pass for four sessions; but it is not purely mine, as I was not in Parliament when it was passed.

It does not affect the question of international copyright, as I relinquished the clause I had prepared to the conduct of Government, by whom the bill of 1838 was carried.

I have no objection to the publication of my letter to you. It was written very hastily, and is not, therefore, in point of style what I should desire to see published; but as it contains the substance of my opinion on the existing position of the law, I will not on that account desire to suppress it.

Accept my thanks for the books which accompanied your last note; and believe me to remain, sir, yours faithfully,

T. N. TALFOURD.[14]

3 THAVIES INN, February 23, 1844.[15]

SIR: I am happy to furnish any information which may, in the smallest degree, assist the endeavors of those who are laboring in the cause of literature and of justice. In my judgment, no further legislation is required on the part of England to secure to American authors the reciprocity which ought to accompany the acknowledgment of the rights of English authors by the United States.

Before the passing of my act on the subject of international copyright, Lord Abinger decided in the case of D'Almaine *vs.* Boosey, reported in 1 Young and Collyer's Reports, 288, that a foreigner, publishing his work in this country within a reasonable time after its first publication in his own, may acquire for himself, or his assignee, a copyright within the protection of the law of England. I believe this decision to be correct; but finding that doubts existed on the subject, I was desirous of setting them at rest by a declaratory clause in my own bill, and therefore introduced the subject in my first speech in the House of Commons, and a clause in the bill to effect the object. When, however, the bill was discussed in a following session, Mr. Powlett Thompson, on the part of Government, requested me to leave that part of my scheme in the hands of Ministers, who proposed to deal with it themselves. I acquiesced; and the result was the passing of an act of 2d and 3d Vict., c. 59: "For securing to Authors, in certain cases, the benefit of International Copyright." Already the Queen is empowered, by Order in Council, to direct that the authors of books published in foreign countries shall secure copyright here, in their works, on registering them at Stationers' Hall.

The object of this Act was to enable our Government to regulate with foreign powers on terms of reciprocity; and therefore, if I am wrong in thinking that the law now gives absolutely the right which this Act enables the Crown to confer as matter of bargain, there can be no doubt that, upon the understanding that the copyright of English authors would be acknowledged in America, the benefits of this Act would be at once and cordially extended to American authors. This Act, of course, assumes an opinion contrary to that of Lord Abinger, as to the existing law, but it does not vary it; and perhaps, practically, it is not material whether it was necessary or not, as there can be no doubt that it would be liberally applied to the purpose for which it was enacted.

Heartily wishing success to your endeavors to do justice to authors of both countries, I have the honor to be, sir, your obedient and faithful servant,

T. N. TALFOURD.

P. S.—I send you the only copy I have left of my speeches on "Copyright," in which, page 26, you will find the subject of international copyright referred to.

ALBURY, December 23, 1845.[16]

MY DEAR SIR: Your "American Facts" have at once delighted and instructed me. I have just finished the book; and it is a pleasure to be able so warmly to commend it, as in all sincerity I can and do.

To praise a man to his face, is but clumsy courtesy; and therefore I will spare your modesty respecting the mere "manner" of the work, however creditable to you: but its "matter" is the point on which, without offence, I may dwell in honest approbation. You have stated, in a temperate, just, and pleasant spirit, Facts which may well make you proud of your native land; and Facts which may render the philanthropists of every shore your debtors. I regret, and have for years regretted, the many printed insults offered to America by a certain forward race amongst us: my only astonishment has been that they are so warmly and sensitively taken up: it has always appeared to me that you might well afford to laugh at or neglect them. Not but that there is something generous in your acknowledged "thin-skinnishness:" America, like a right-hearted youth, earnestly though secretly looks to parental England for praise in doing well; and the fraud of praise withheld, or (worse) perverted into censure, is an aching disappointment. Apathy would argue disrespect and disaffection: these be far from you, and far from us, as towards each other.

You have by no means overrated the popular ignorance of all that concerns your New World amongst us; but we have one really fair excuse in mitigation: to wit, your very Newness. Ten years ago, haply, Cincinnati was not: possibly ten years hence you may have an enormous Timbuctoo with a hundred churches in the middle of Missouri. My old country-house here was built when New York and New Orleans were swamp and forest: and you know how philosophically suitable to the veneration of such creatures of change and chance as we are, is the magic of Antiquity.

If your Athens, somewhere in Arkansas, was all built of Parthenons and Acropolises, still it never could attain one thousandth of the glory of the attic-town.

Old Time makes all the difference. Our ignorance then is not merely that we cannot keep pace with the race of your prosperities, but that, on archæological principles, we even feel an inward disinclination to believe such "facts" unseen. After all is said—and call each other what we may—America and England are one people: language, laws, religion, literature, identity of origin, and history—goodsooth, here are ties enough: moreover, you are not black, nor we cannibals.

For my own part, I boast myself a genuine Anglo-Saxon: in 1550, the Emperor Charles V. complimented my direct ancestor in the tenth generation by expelling him from Germany for Protestantism; so that, whilst I dearly love England and her institutions, I claim to be a bit of a cosmopolite.

Therefore, as one of the great Anglo-Saxon family, I have sympathy with you as brethren; and if ever my good star sent me to visit you over the Atlantic, my verdict (I am clear) would be far other and truer than that of Dickens, Trollope, and the like.

I am scribbling this at midnight, somewhat loosely and egotistically, too, I fear; but, as I perceive you to be a man of sense and feeling, I am sure you will not take my note amiss.

Mr. Willis and yourself are the only Americans I have personally encountered; and you make me respect your country. With reference to your literature, it may interest your patriotism to be told that Moses Stuart and Dr. Robinson taught me my little Hebrew—that Abbott helped my early Christian course—that I found Anthon a vast improvement on old classical Lempriere—and that Peter Parley now instructs my children. Having prosed sufficiently, and not as yet having thanked you for the book itself (which therefore I request now to do), I remain, My dear Sir, Very faithfully yours,

MARTIN FARQUHAR TUPPER.

4 ROBERT STREET, BEDFORD ROW,
May 10, 1843.

SIR:—Before I leave town—for a day or two only, however—I think it best to write to state my acceptance of the terms offered for the publication of the "Letters," namely, that your firm will defray the cost of paper, printing, advertisements, and every expense connected

Martin F. Tupper, a major Wiley and Putnam author during the years in which his reputation was at its height

with publishing both in London and New York; and that, after the sale of the first edition, the profits accruing to be divided equally between your firm and myself.[17]

You would greatly oblige me if you would forward me, to this address, with as little delay as suits your convenience, a copy of the agreement to be signed, and perhaps a printed specimen or proof of the form in which you would publish the work.

In case of further editions being required, I feel so obliged by your courtesy and favorable opinion, that, as a matter of course, the publication shall be offered to you in the first instance.

I readily adopt your recommendation in regard to the title, and will make the "amende honorable" to the charities of England, either in a closing letter containing a summary of the British character, or in the preface.

Any further hints your knowledge, taste, and experience may suggest, I shall gladly act upon. I mean, as to the subject of future letters; and really no time should be lost. I have the honor to be, sir, Your obedient servant,

M. L. BATTLEY.

MY DEAR MISS PEABODY:—I now write to ask the favor of you to transmit a message to Mr. P., of London, by the earliest conveyance you may have. Will you say to him that his communication to my father, of the 18th of April, by the Cambria, reached us on the day of my father's death—a few hours only before his death, when he was so weak as to be apparently unconscious.

We were thus debarred the satisfaction of communicating to him this testimony of Mr. Putnam's regard for my father's just rights and literary reputation. As we are denied the privilege of knowing and communicating my father's views and wishes on this subject, which possessed for him so deep an interest, will you thank Mr. Putnam in our name for the regard he has thus manifested?

It will be gratifying to Mr. Putnam to be assured that the course which he took in England in relation to the Greek Lexicon, has met with the approbation of two of my father's most intimate friends, Mr. William H. Prescott and Professor Edward Robinson.

Yours very truly,
MARY O. PICKERING.[18]

Rowe St., July 1, 1846.
—*Putnam's Magazine,* 4 (November 1869): 551–561

III.

BERNARD BARTON, the Quaker-poet, had been visited by Bayard Taylor in the days of "Views A-Foot,"

and after that volume was published he sent me copies of two little privately-printed books—one about himself—to send to his "friend Bayard Taylor," and one for my "acceptance." The change from "yours" to "thine" in the two notes will be observed:

WOODBRIDGE, SUFFOLK, 2 mo. 2d., 1847.

RESPECTED FRIEND:—May I trouble you to let me know the price of my friend Bayard Taylor's "Travels in Europe?" . . . It is reviewed, as I hear, in the *Literary Gazette* of the 30th ult.; and they tell me I am chronicled in its pages. The author must have belied a very pleasing exterior, if he have said aught ill-natured of me; but of that I am not much afraid. At any rate, I should like to read his book, and to possess it, if not too dear. Yours respectfully,

BERNARD BARTON.

WOODBRIDGE, 2 mo. 10d., 1847.

MY DEAR FRIEND:—I know nothing whatever of the frequency or mode of your transmissions to America, but I send two little trifles of mine, for thy acceptance;—of which I should like to forward duplicates for Bayard Taylor, if worthy of his having. I only printed one hundred and fifty or two hundred copies of them for private circulation, so they cannot be bought or very common.

I have a few copies of each left; so, if the Memorial should have reached thee, and be about going off, these may go with it; and I will send thee a couple more, either by post, or some free conveyance, very shortly, shouldst thou wish for copies of them. Thine affectionately,

B. BARTON.

During Miss BREMER'S visit to this country, I had the pleasure of meeting her at Mr. Downing's, on the Hudson, and she was also a guest for a few days at our house at Staten Island. "Why not publish a decent library edition of Miss Bremer's works while she is here?" said Mr. Downing one evening while we were sitting together in his library. "If Miss Bremer will sanction it, and write a preface and revise the translations, we shall be glad to do so." All this was done. But, unfortunately, the "rights" arising from previous reprints [sold at one eighth of the price, by the Great House] were made the pretext for hostilities against us, because we had dared thus to meet the wishes of the author and her friends.

STOCKHOLM, October 14, 1844.

MY DEAR SIR:—After a residence of several months in the country, far away from Stockholm, I have returned to my capital, and there received your note of the 10th July, and the bill for the case of books you have had the kindness to send to me with the Brig Beate to Gotheborg. Of the brig and the bookcase I have as yet no kind of intimation from Gotheborg, but will write to ask for them. I thank you very much for the good and valuable books that you have given me by this and before this, and look upon them as a fair retribution * * *

I have written to Mrs. Howitt, according to your first letter, to ask her to send you the printed sheets of her translation; but it seems that she is not free to do it, as Messrs. Chapman, Hall & Virtue pay her for the translation. It is also, if I understand it right, with these gentlemen that you must make arrangements if you wish to have Mrs. Howitt's translation, which certainly will be the very best translation possible to be had, and greatly favorable to your publication. Then, though she makes occasional mistakes, her style is full of life, and her genial mind shows itself even in the translation; and the knowledge which she has now gained of the Swedish language will make her less subject than ever to mistakes; and Mr. Howitt, being now at home, will be able to correct these. My advice is, therefore, my dear sir, that you should write to Messrs. Virtue & Hall, and make them propositions about the translation, and to enable you to compete in these with the Harpers, you shall *owe me nothing,* and I will write for your publication a special introduction, as I want to dedicate the book to the memory of my friend A. J. Downing; so that your publication will be sure to have a good run in America. I have written to Messrs. Virtue & Hall how much I want you to publish this book, asking them to let you have it on the best possible terms. . . .

As the book has been much detained (by various causes), and is not yet finished, I have but last week sent to Mrs. Howitt the first sheet (printed) for translation, so that you will be in good time to have the printed sheets from England for your publication, and be able to keep ahead with the English publishers.

I shall take a special delight in the dedication and introduction; and all I ask of you is, to write to me and tell me how the affair has succeeded, and how you are satisfied. As soon as I have your answer and approbation of the course I have suggested, I shall sit down and write what I have promised, and immediately send it to you. I remain, my dear sir, yours faithfully,

FREDRIKA BREMER.

Mr. GREENOUGH'S heroic statue of Washington was placed in the Capitol grounds at Washington in 1843. Probably the criticisms upon it, especially those of the more unsophisticated Western visitors, were not all jubilant in its favor. The sculptor seemed to think his ideas needed explanation and defence—and the letter annexed relates to a publication proposed for this purpose.

After Mr. Greenough's return from Europe he placed in our hands a volume which he had printed, containing some rather severe strictures on the American standards of taste in art and literature. A few copies were circulated among friends; but the main part of the edition was suppressed and destroyed, I believe, by the advice of friends just before Mr. Greenough's death.

FLORENCE, December 5, 1843.

* * * –I send herewith three impressions of a plate engraved from my statue of Washington, which I intend to publish, that such of my countrymen and others as have not the opportunity of seeing the original may become acquainted with the work. The fact that the statue in question is the first work of importance in that walk of art by an American citizen, gives it an importance in the history of transatlantic culture which its own intrinsic merits cannot be expected to equal. This plate will be accompanied by two others of equal size and not inferior workmanship, representing on a larger scale the bas-reliefs and devices of the chair.

I propose to furnish eight or ten sheets of letterpress to accompany these plates, in which I will give the Act of Congress authorizing the creation of the statue, the correspondence between the Secretary of State and myself relating to it, and selections of speeches made on the floor of Congress in regard to it.

This memoir, though brief, may, I think, be made *piquant* in a high degree. I shall not spare myself in reporting the ridicule and vituperation with which I have been assailed by those who differ from me on a point of *taste;* and I believe that the result of such openness and publicity will be less mortifying to me than instructive to those who will come after me; while gentlemen in Congress will feel that it is necessary to speak warily of that which we have studied superficially.

It has occurred to me that you may be willing to undertake the publication of this work—and I request that you will give me as early as convenient some account of your disposition in regard to it. I should tell you that I cannot afford the plates at less than one pound sterling the set. The letter-press should, of course, be of a size and execution to match the plates. A few copies might be made on a more expensive plan, and charged accordingly.

If you see any hope of procuring subscribers, I request that you will take steps immediately to set the matter in motion.

My address is,
"Florence, G. Duchy of Tuscany. Palazzo Pucci. Via dei Pucci."

Your obedient servant,
HORATIO GREENOUGH.

Mr. HALLECK was a frequent visitor at our "book-store" in Broadway, always with the same sunny smile and courteous greeting, and always ready with his pleasant chat about books, authors, politics, theology, metaphysics, or æsthetics.

Whether he was a Romanist or not, at that time, he used, perhaps just for the sake of argument, to defend the chief "Catholic" tenets, and I remember his apparently earnest exposition of the necessity of worshipping the Virgin as the Mother of God. His conversion to Catholicism we never doubted at the time, and it was frequently referred to by visitors; but as Halleck was rather fond of paradoxes, he may possibly have intended merely to puzzle his listeners.

At the notable dinner to authors, given by the New York booksellers at the old City Hotel, in 1837, Halleck was of course in one of the places of honor; and Irving in his single successful dinner-speech quoted a letter from Rogers complimentary to the author of "Marco Bozzaris," and gracefully turned the current of courtesies to the *speechless* poet.

The courtly Philip Hone also managed to hit the genial "Croaker" with his sugar-plums, and Halleck often referred afterward to the overwhelming laurels forced on his modest brow.

The letter annexed is his response to an extra invitation to the Fruit Festival to Authors at the New York Crystal Palace, in 1853.

Genial, interesting, and fluent as he was in conversation, he could say nothing in public, and his dread of being called upon even for a word, prompted refusal of all such invitations.

In his later days, I used to meet him occasionally in Broadway, when he came to town; and he seemed to enjoy a short chat even on the sidewalk, and to be glad of a listener; but his growing deafness was his excuse for refusing all enticements where more than two or three were present. He had been a valued member of the "Century," and a frequent visitor there; but his infirmity made him shrink from all assemblies even in this favorite haunt.

GUILFORD, CONNECTICUT, September 19, 1853 [*sic*].

MY DEAR SIR:—I feel highly flattered by the renewed expression of your kind wishes, more particularly as you are aware that I have no talent, either as a hearer or speaker, that can aid your good cause, or make my presence or absence noticed on such an occasion.

Believe me, I am as anxious to enjoy your hospitalities as you in your large benevolence are to bestow it.

I very reluctantly wrote you my unsatisfactory note, and fear that I cannot make this much less so; but

I hasten to assure you that, if it be possible for me to escape from my present engagements, I will do my utmost to be with you.

I remain, my dear sir, most truly yours,
FITZ-GREENE HALLECK.

———

In 1841, I crossed to England with Dr. ASAHEL GRANT, missionary to the Nestorians, and author of a book about them. Dr. Grant will be remembered by many as a man of pure and earnest devotion to his philanthropic work, and worthy of all honor as an intelligent physician who took his life in his hands to carry civilization and Christianity into ancient Mesopotamia.

The letter quoted is one of several I received in London, giving some interesting incidents of facts about the Nestorians and the wilder people in the neighborhood of ancient Nineveh. Dr. Grant died at his post in 185––.

MOSUL, MESOPOTAMIA, October 5, 1843.

MY DEAR SIR:—I have been looking for a long time for a letter from you in answer to mine of last November and last February or March. Perhaps you have been absent in America. I see from the *New York Observer* that Murray, my publisher, is dead! How far will this sad event affect the prospects of my book? The second edition, it appears, had been some months out of the press. How far has the sale proceeded and what are the prospects? Will young Murray carry on his father's business? Is it probable that another edition of my book will be demanded, and if so, what arrangements would you make? * * *

Please send us also any thing you may see from Rev. Mr. Badger, Episcopal (high-church) missionary at this place, or any thing in relation to him.

Perhaps I am already indebted to you for the London Record, containing some notice of him. I hear that he is likely to be recalled. As we have now a regular-service monthly *post* from Constantinople, our means of intelligence and communication are greatly increased. We get news, letters, and papers from America in *two* months. We ought to have news from London in little more than a month. * * *

You will doubtless have learned that the Mountain Nestorians have at length been subdued by their Mohammedan foes. The strongest parts of their heretofore inaccessible mountains are quite desolated; hundreds killed, hundreds more driven into captivity; churches demolished, villages burned, their flocks driven away, and the people reduced to a state of destitution which leaves room to fear that famine may boast more victims than the sword during their long, cold, mountain winter. The patriarch's mother, a brother, an appointed successor, and many relatives, are among the killed. His sister and three brothers were taken captives. He has escaped to this place, and I have just got the promise of his *autograph* for you, which I hope to receive in time to enclose in this. Has Mr. Perkins' book on Persia and the Nestorians found its way into England, and does it circulate there?

And now, my dear sir, how is it with you * * *

I have been exposed to some dangers from the commotions in the mountains since my last, but providentially made good my escape after the work of death had seriously begun. When I may be able to return to that wild region and wilder people again, I know not. Should the country long remain disturbed, I may perhaps make another visit to America. But this is uncertain. The threatened war between Persia and Turkey is at a truce for the winter, but as the ground of difficulty remains, it may break out at a future day. Poor, ill-fated countries! Could the powers of Europe agree upon the division of the spoils, they would fall into other hands before another year!

With affectionate regards to * * *

Yours most truly and faithfully,

ASAHEL GRANT.

Mr. S. C. HALL, editor of the *Art Journal,* and of many tasteful illustrated works,–a genial and agreeable man, who has been all his life devoted to popularizing a pleasant combination of art and literature, used with his accomplished wife to exchange a cosy little party with us at their snug little "Rosery," where we would meet an American here and there sandwiched between some of the literary notabilities. Mrs. Hall took great interest in the Hutchinson family, who were then giving concerts in London.

THE ROSERY, OLD BROMPTON,
(Close to the Turnpike), April 30.

MY DEAR SIR:–During my recent visit to Paris, I fell in with a very agreeable countryman of yours. He is now in London, and I expect will dine with me on Saturday–5 o'clock. Will you kindly come and meet him? Faithfully yours,

S.C. HALL.

THE ROSERY.

DEAR SIR:–It occurred to me that you might find some pleasure (as you are so much interested for the Hutchinson family[19]), in reading the accompanying note and notice, which Miss Douglass sent me. I am very sorry she was not at Birmingham, as she would have rejoiced to pay that most interesting girl any attention in her power. I hope they will give a morning entertainment. I dare not take my beloved mother out at

night; but if the morning was fine, she might venture. Dear sir, your obliged,

ANNA MARIA HALL.

*₊*I have just been looking over some very charming publications you have been so good as to send to "The Art Journal." I shall not complain of one of my violent colds, which will give me time to read them.

Among the few really able men in the London pulpit, while we lived in England, was the somewhat famous HENRY MELVILLE, whose published sermons are well known to churchmen. His church at Clapham was usually crowded, especially on Sunday evenings, and his audience seemed almost spell-bound by his peculiar eloquence; but it seemed to me this was rather on account of the rarity of any life or character in English sermonizing, at least in "the Church," than because it was intrinsically so very excellent.

At this time I frequently heard Dr. Croly, author of "Salathiel;" Hon. and Rev. Baptist Noel; "Satan" Montgomery; W. J. Fox, the "Nothingarian" M. P.; and Wiseman, afterwards Cardinal.

EAST INDIA COLLEGE, HERTFORD,
February 8, 1847.

Some time ago I received a letter from Mr. G. Griffin, of New York, stating that he had forwarded to you a copy of his work, "The Sufferings of Christ, by a Layman," said copy being intended for me. If this copy have reached you, I shall feel much obliged by your taking the trouble of sending it to my address by the Eastern Counties Railway, as parcels are received in the ——— or at the Golden Cross. This will not, I hope, cause you much inconvenience. I remain, very faithfully yours,

HENRY MELVILLE.

When Mr. MCLANE was a second time Minister to England, I was honored with some intimacy with his amiable family at the Legation and at Knickerbocker Cottage. Mr. Irving, who had been Secretary of Legation with Mr. McLane at the same post in 1830, and was now Minister to Spain, visited his old friend when he came to London, about the time the Oregon question was most hotly discussed. During Mr. McLane's visit to Paris, when this negotiation was in the most delicate condition and a war seemed to many inevitable, I was told that the Minister was invited by Lord Aberdeen to a formal diplomatic dinner, given to the leading foreign Ministers.

In his absence, the Secretary, Mr. M——, appeared in his place. Replying to a formal toast, "The President of the United States," the Secretary electrified the diplomatic circle by a Tammany speech, winding up somewhat thus: "I was one who helped to place Mr. Polk where he now is, and I know that he will not *dare* to recede from 54.40!"

The late Archbishop Hughes (then only Bishop) was the chief guest at a breakfast given by the Secretary soon after. I was much impressed with his mildly dignified and genial manner; so different was it from previous notions of this energetic prelate.

In order to dispense a little sound information on the Oregon question, which had become *the* exciting topic of the day, I proposed to the Minister to print the documents for general circulation. His reply is annexed.

> December 30, 1845.
>
> DEAR SIR:—Being engaged out last evening, I was not able to attend to your note earlier.
>
> All the documents relating to the Oregon question—at least all that are any way necessary to an understanding of the subject—are contained in the *Times* newspaper of yesterday. Among them you will find not only the letters of Mr. Calhoun, but those of Mr. Buchanan also; and after reading them, you can well form a judgment which to select for publication, or whether to publish the whole. The whole would be best, unless you should find them too voluminous for the bulk of your pamphlet.
>
> Believe me to be, dear sir, with great respect,
>
> LOUIS MCLANE.

> BUCKINGHAM PALACE, June 29, 1844.
>
> SIR:—You would oblige me much if you would secure and send to me any review or periodical published in America, in which there appears a notice of my novel called "Prairie-Bird," which was published in London this spring. I am not aware whether it has found its way to the United States or been reprinted there; but if it has, I should be glad to learn what was thought of it by those who are nearer to the scene of action, and on that account, at least, better judges of the accuracy of its description than the generality of English readers. I am, sir, your very obedient servant,
>
> CH. A. MURRAY.[20]

> ALBEMARLE ST.,[21] Monday, July 19.
>
> Mr. and Mrs. Murray request the pleasure of Mr. and Mrs. P——'s company at dinner on Tuesday, the 20th, at quarter before 7 o'clock.

Our advertisement in the London *Times* of some American publications was noticed by an old gentleman, who seemed to be curious about the name of the advertiser. His name was Sir FREDERICK ROBINSON—and it appeared that he was a general in the British army; that he was now ninety-five years old; that he had been an officer in the British army during our revolution, and had been taken prisoner on the Hudson by General Putnam, in whose custody he remained for some time, and for whom, as he wrote in one of his notes to me, he "had learned to cherish great respect," which gave him a special interest in the General's descendants. It was a pleasant incident,—this little connecting link with a former generation. The old General wrote several notes, in which he seemed glad to recall memories of our great struggle and his rough old captor; but I find only these:

> 33 BEDFORD SQUARE, BRIGHTON,[22]
> August 11, 1845.
>
> The descendants of General Putnam and all his well-wishers will find many very satisfactory passages in Stedman's "History of the Revolutionary War," particularly in the first volume.
>
> Sir Frederick Robinson has very great pleasure in communicating the above to Mr. P——.
>
> 39 [*sic*] BEDFORD SQUARE, BRIGHTON,
> October 3, 1845.
>
> Sir F. Robinson presents his compliments to Mr. Putnam, and requests to know whether Mr. P. has the History of New York, or of the State of New York, in his library, and if so, what the price may be.
>
> Mr. P. will perceive that Sir Frederick has moved from No. 33 to 39 Bedford Square.

WILLIS' ROOMS
King Street, St. James's.
Mr. THACKERAY'S LECTURES
On the English Humorists of the 18th Century.

MR. THACKERAY
will deliver a series of Six Lectures, on
"The English Humorists of the 18th Century
Their Lives and Writings, their Friends
and Associates."

The course will contain notices of Swift, Pope, and Gay, Addison, Steele, and Congreve, Fielding and Hogarth, Smollett, Sterne, and Goldsmith.

The First Lecture will be given on Thursday Morning, May 22d. To be continued each succeeding Thursday. Commencing at Three o'clock.

Tickets for the Course of Six Lectures £2 2s.; for which the seats will be numbered and reserved. Single Tickets 7s. 6d. Family Tickets, to admit four, 21s. Which may be secured at Mr. Mitchel's Royal Library, 33 Old Bond Street, &c.

This course of lectures, given during the great Exhibition of 1851, at the "fashionable" rooms of "Almack's," was attended by a brilliant audience. The most notable of the aristocracy both of birth and of intellect were eager listeners. Macaulay, Bulwer, and scores of the poets and novelists, were sprinkled among the dukes and duchesses; the stairs were lined with liveried "Jeameses," and Jermyn-street was completely blocked with lordly equipages. What specially amused an American was the apparently indifferent and nonchalant coolness of the lecturer: he seemed less deferential and more completely at his ease than when he repeated the same course to a *republican* audience at Dr. Chapin's church, in Broadway.

While I was living at Yonkers, Mr. Thackeray accepted an invitation to give his lecture on "Charity and Humor" at the Lyceum at that place. In the morning the great novelist, with Mr. F. S. Cozzens and myself, drove up to Sunnyside to call on Mr. Irving, and to bring him down to the lecture. The hour passed at Sunnyside was delicious, for the talk of the two humorists was free, cordial, and interesting; even more so than at Mr. Sparrowgrass' dinner-party later in the day. At the lecture the Lyceum-President was overwhelming in his introduction of the author of "Vanity Fair," who fairly blushed under the eulogiums heaped upon him; but he had the good taste to make no reference to it, or to the living representative of the theme of his discourse, who sat before him as a listener.

At one of the little gatherings of book-men, editors, and artists at my house in New York, Mr. Thackeray was talking with a lady, when Dr. Rufus W. Griswold came up and asked me to introduce him, which of course was done. Thackeray bowed slightly, and went on talking to the lady. Presently, the Doctor having slipped away for the moment, the novelist said to me, inquiringly, "That's Rufus, is it?" "Yes—that's he." "He's been abusing me in the *Herald,*" pursued the satirist. "I've a mind to charge him with it." "By all means," I replied; "if you are sure he did it." "Positive." So he stalked across to the corner where Griswold stood, and I observed him looking down from his six-foot elevation on to the Doctor's bald head and glaring at him in half-earnest anger through his glasses, while he pummeled him with his charge of the *Herald* articles. The Doctor,

William Makepeace Thackeray, whom Putnam invited several times to publish with his firm in the United States. Thackeray, however, preferred not to upset his lucrative connection with the Harpers.

after a while, escaping, quoted him thus: "Thackeray came and said to me: 'Doctor, you've been writing ugly things about me in the *Herald*–you called me a SNOB; do I look like a SNOB?' and he drew himself up and looked thunder-gusts at me. Now I didn't write those articles." "Yes, but he did though," said the big satirist, when I quoted to him this denial; and so he persisted in saying, weeks after, at the *Century.*

CLARENDON HOTEL, NEW YORK,
November 27, 1852.

DEAR SIR:–Messrs.———, who have published my larger books and have paid my London publisher for my last work, have offered me a sum of money for the republication of my lectures; and all things considered, I think it is best that I should accept their liberal proposal. I thank you very much for your very generous offer; and for my own sake, as well as that of my literary brethren in England, I am sincerely rejoiced to find how very kindly the American publishers are disposed towards us.

Believe me most faithfully yours,

W. M. THACKERAY.

–*Putnam's Magazine,* 4 (December 1869)

* * *

1 Even after this small edition was in type, the poet proposed to punish us by giving a duplicate of the MS. to another publisher, because a third little advance was deemed inexpedient.

2 Author of "Concordance to Shakespeare," "Girlhood of Shakespeare's Heroines," &c. The reference is to a handsome library-chair, which was sent to Mrs. Clarke as a gift from some fifty gentlemen, including Daniel Webster, Irving, Bryant, and others who appreciated her laborious and important work, the "Concordance to Shakespeare."

3 Earl of Carlisle–Lord-Lieutenant of Ireland; better known in the United States as Lord Morpeth. His two Lectures–one on "America" and the other on the "Poetry of Pope"–had been reprinted in New York by G. P. P. & Co.

4 Surveyor of the Port of London, author of "Memoirs of Sir Christopher Wren."

5 Under the name of Mariotti, a young Professor Gallenga of the University of Parma, who had been one of the "Young Italy" or "Carbonari" patriots, was exiled and came to Boston about 1837. He resided some time at Cambridge, and wrote for the *North American Review* several papers on Italian Literature of History. During his subsequent residence in England he was intimate in my family. He was gently esteemed by prominent literary men in England, such as Carlyle, Bulwer, Macaulay. With Mazzini, who was then his close friend, we used to take maccaroni together and abuse Sir James Graham for opening letters–(said to be treasonable against somebody). He was a contributor to *Frazer, N. Monthly, Foreign Quarterly,* etc. A few years later, after his marriage with an English lady, he returned to Lombardy, and was elected member of the Italian Parliament. His quarrel with Mazzini was a curious episode. On the first day of the riots in New York, in July, 1863, he landed in New York, in the capacity of confidential correspondent of the *London Times.*

6 Author of "Introduction to the Study of the Bible." Died 1862.

7 Paintings by A. B. Durand, J. F. Cropsey, and the late F. W. Edmonds, C. C. Ingham, and Henry Inman, were sent through our agency to the Exhibition of the Royal Academy in 1845. With characteristic liberality two or three of these were placed in an upper corner of the "architectural" room, and the remainder in a little octagon usually called the "dark hole." Since then American art has had better treatment.

8 A large room at the "American Literary Agency," in Waterloo Place, Pall Mall, near the Athenæum and U. Service Club, established by W. & P. for the special purpose of introducing to the M. P.s, and nabobs of the "West End," some specimens of American books, paintings, maps, newspapers, magazines &c. Being on the way to Parliament St., my Lord Duke, the Rt. Rev. Bishop, and the Right Honorable Baronet, were frequent visitors, showing considerable interest and curiosity in "American facts."

9 Author of "Cyclopædia of Biblical Literature," the "Lost Senses," &c. In this little volume the learned author, who was *wholly* deaf, contended that blindness was preferable to deafness. He was self-taught; but his acquirements, especially in biblical literature, were very extensive. He was a frequent visitor in search of American contributions to this branch of learning.

10 Author of *"Commercial Statistics, Progress of America,* &c., died 1857.

He was the Scotch Secretary of the "Board of Trade,"–and a man of liberal views and immense energy. He was a constant visitor at the American Literary Agency in search of the latest information. The case referred to above was a notable instance of how red tape may be cut by a man of practical good sense.

11 Hon. Miss Murray, Maid of Honor to Queen Victoria; author of "Letters from America," republished by special arrangement.

12 Exchange of about £200, for "copyright" on sales of the New York edition of her *Letters from America.*

13 Author of *"Literary Anecdotes of the Eighteenth Century,* in 16 vols. 8vo. At this time he was about eighty years old, and remained as a connecting link with the days of Dr. Johnson, Goldsmith, and Reynolds.

14 Sergeant Talfourd, M.P., author of "Ion"–an active promoter of the interests of authors.

George Haven Putnam added to this note when he edited his father's letters: The question of the rights belonging to foreigners under the Act of Victoria (1838) came into discussion in various suits of later date. *Murray vs. Bohn, Low vs. Rutledge,* etc. It was passed upon by law officers of the Crown in July, 1891,–who accepted the conclusions of Talfourd. Their decision has since been questioned by McGillivray (1902). G. H. P.

15 *This letter was excluded by George Haven Putnam in reprinting his father's original articles.*

16 *This letter was excluded by George Haven Putnam in reprinting his father's original articles.*

17 Referring to *Change for American Notes*–(in answer to Dickens)–published by W. & P., London, 1844, post 8vo. 10s. 6d., and by Harper & Bro., New York. The author was a lady, evidently more Hiberian than Yankee; indeed, it was rather evident she had never been in the United States; but, with a certain intuitive perception and a facile pen, she had volunteered as a champion of American ideas and practices against the criticisms of Boz's *Notes,* then passing current in the English book-market. The various "suggestions" which this chivalric undertaking occasioned, absorbed some quires of note-paper exchanged with the publisher. The book received very fair treatment in England in spite of the Yankee-isms (?) which the Dublin critics discovered in it. And Messrs. Harper sent the author a liberal draft for their early copy.

18 Daughter of the late John Pickering, author of a Greek Lexicon. Referring to a correspondence with Prof. Dunbar of Edinburgh, who was charged, in *American Facts,* with using Pickering's work in his own Lexicon, without any proper credit. His angry denial was replied to in the *Scotsman.*

19 The American vocalists.

20 Master of the Queen's Household–author of the "Prairie-Bird," "Travels in America," &c. Brother of Hon. Miss Murray, who wrote also "Travels in America."

21 Merely recalling some notable and pleasant evenings amidst the lions at this headquarters of literature, in the days when the elder "dear Mr. Murray" of Byron, used to entertain greater and lesser authors and members of the craft.

22 *This letter was excluded by George Haven Putnam in reprinting his father's original articles.*

George Palmer Putnam's Public Statements

Dispute on International Copyright

The following exchange of letters pitted two of the most respected publishers in the profession and two of the most outspoken spokesmen on the divisive issue of international copyright: Putnam in favor, Abraham Hart against. Hart had challenged Putnam at a recent trade sale to debate the issue on the spot, but Putnam demurred. Instead, they expressed their views in open letters printed in Norton's Literary Gazette *and* Publishers' Circular.

The issue of copyright, they and their colleagues all knew, was central to the profession of publishing in midcentury America. Because of the lack of an international copyright agreement between the United States and England, foreign authors and publishers could lay no legal claim to their works published in the United States. That lack of protection, conversely, made their works especially attractive to American publishers, who could print and sell them more cheaply and therefore more profitably than copyright-protected American works. Firms such as Hart's (Carey and Hart) engaged heavily in the reprint trade, bringing out many English and European works in American editions, sometimes without compensating the author or publisher and sometimes paying something, though rarely at a level commensurate with the royalties paid to domestic authors. G. P. Putnam, by contrast, had made its reputation primarily as a publisher of American works; when his firm did reprint foreign works, Putnam made a point of coming to a satisfactory arrangement with the foreign publisher. Little wonder, then, that Hart and Putnam emerged on opposite sides of this issue.

The debate was timely because earlier in 1853 the United States and England had been negotiating a copyright treaty. Stories were appearing in the press and rumors were flying through the trade. By the time of the New York spring trade sale, Putnam had been apprized by Secretary of State Edward Everett that there was little chance a treaty would be signed, but Hart perhaps did not yet know. The exchange is reprinted as it was published—first Putnam's letter and then Hart's rejoinder.

* * *

Letter from Mr. Putnam upon International Copyright.

To A. Hart, *Esq., Publisher, Philadelphia*

My Dear Sir:—When, at the last Trade Sale, you challenged me, somewhat suddenly, to a discussion before the audience, touching the question of international copyright, you took me at disadvantage. "I am no orator, as Brutus is," for my modesty forbids me even to "speak right on," much less play the rhetorician. It was not to be supposed that even an orator could do justice to himself and his cause, under such circumstances, amid the noise, hurry, and impatience of "knock-down argument;" and of course you knew that my self-confidence, at such a time especially, was not equal to the task of removing the impression which had been created by your well-known ability, in a few courteous and well-pointed words. I give you full credit, my dear Hart, for the courtesy as well as the adroitness of this "hit;" but, at the same time, I am unwilling that a good cause should suffer by any real or apparent inability on the part of its friends to defend it. You had the *ear* of our brethren in the trade, and I am sure you will permit me (being "unaccustomed to public speaking") to make a brief reply in print. The circumstances referred to seem to justify my printing it in the shape of a letter to you, the more especially as it happens that no one connected with American publishing enjoys more worthily the respect and confidence of his compeers.

And here let me briefly premise, that I trust you will give me credit for sincere deference to your opinion, and that of the two or three other intelligent and high-standing "leaders" of the trade, who oppose the project in question. You will not suppose that I presume to set up my humble judgment above that of far more able, more experienced, and more interested men, who are much more competent to argue and decide the question at issue. All I aim to do is simply to bring forward some suggestions which appear to have been lost sight of, and to remove, as far as possible, certain illogical mystifications which have been connected with the supposed effect of International Copyright. And 1st: The point which you so adroitly (I will not say uncandidly) alluded to, at the Trade Sale, viz.: *the protection of*

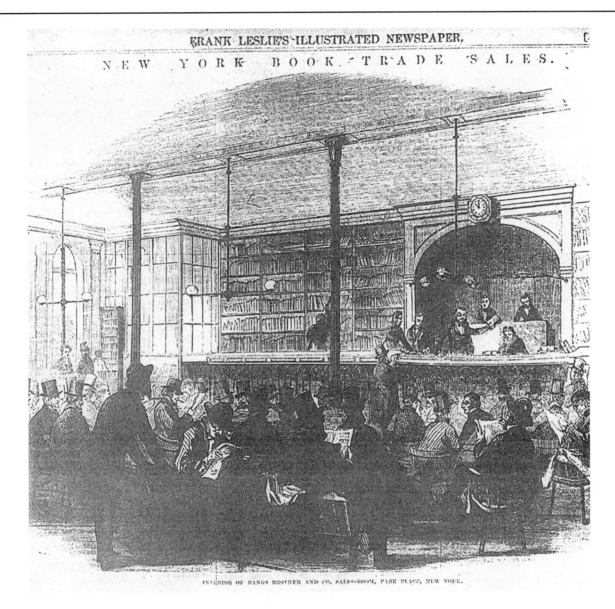

A New York Book Trade Sale, as depicted in the 5 April 1856 issue of Frank Leslie's Illustrated Newspaper.
Trade sales in major cities grew in importance as the publishing profession became more centralized. G. P. Putnam
was often one of the most active participants in selling its publications in lots.

the interests of American paper-makers, printers and binders. You referred to what you kindly styled my "able advocacy," etc., and then proceeded to illustrate the practical *effect* of what I advocated, by pointing to the edition of Layard's Babylon, which I had *imported,* instead of printing here. But you omitted to state that I had expressly urged, as an equitable condition of the international arrangement, that the *manufacture* of books, on either side, should be reciprocally and mutually protected. What I said was this:

"It seems to me but equitable that this measure should be strictly for the benefit of English and Ameri-

can *authors,* and that it should not give to English publishers the right to force us to import *their* editions, or else have none. American authors will be ready to sell their manuscripts to English publishers, to be printed in England in the English modes and dress. Let English authors be required, when claiming protection, to do the same with us; and the American mode of making *books for the people—books at MODERATE PRICES for general circulation—will not only yield the English author the most profitable returns, but it will give employment and protection to the very large number of men and women engaged in the manufacture of books in this country:* in the paper mills, the type foundries, the printing-offices, and the binderies. Thus the author will be paid on each side of the Atlantic; industry protected in its proper place; the publisher enabled to manufacture books in a respectable and economical manner, free from the petty rivalries resulting from the present unsound state of things; and the reading public will be supplied with fairly-printed books, which yield the author his equitable per centage, without any essential addition to the price."

The claim of printers, etc., for protection, at least so long as the book manufacture is immature in this country, and so long as it does not stand on an equal footing, relatively, with other interests, may be a very proper claim. I yield to no one in respect for the rights and interests of those engaged in this important manufacture in this country (and I hope to see, ere long, some movement in behalf of the *physical* welfare of the men, women, and children employed in the close, ill-ventilated printing offices and binderies, especially in New York). I am not quite sure that the printing interest can reasonably expect a greater protection than is given to other manufacturers, or that they should be supported at all hazards, while those of the authors of the very books which *create* the business in question are *wholly ignored,* and treated as unworthy of consideration. Surely, if we should look carefully after the interests of those who cast and set the types, make the paper, and bind the book, we should not wholly forget those whose daily bread is to be earned by their services in writing the very book which sets all this machinery in motion, and gives employment to the hundreds who take part in its mechanical execution. In the production of an ordinary edition of any book, it is safe to estimate that employment is given to one hundred individuals, to say nothing of those who get their living by selling the book. Now, shall all these be protected, and the single individual, who has *created* all this employment, and is perhaps often as much in need of his pittance as any one of the artizans thus employed,—shall *he,* no matter who he is and where he lives,—shall the *author,* who has given a living to hundreds and pleasure to tens of thousands, be utterly disregarded as a thing of no account?

However, these enquiries are merely incidental, and not essential to the main point, though I think even you, my dear Hart, with all your tender care for the "craft" (which I know to be in earnest), will admit, on reflection, that there may be at least a reasonable doubt said craft should have *all* the protection. Further than this, I imagine that the members of the craft themselves, if they possess half the spirit of enterprise and independence for which I give them credit, would be ashamed to admit that they *need* protection, or that they cannot beat John Bull on *any* tack. If we cannot already make books in this country as cheaply as they are made in England, I see no reason why we should not begin to learn how to do so. It is true that uncle John has been waking up lately, and, *imitating OUR example,* has published books within a year or two, which, in the current phrase, almost "defy competition," especially the cheap "libraries" and cheap Bibles (which, however, don't happen to be copyright on either side). But still I think you will agree with me that we have all the elements of success here with us, and that, on the *same footing,* we may challenge the world's competition. I, for one, believe in "free trade" as well as *author's* rights; and, in the long run, I believe that the printing interest would flourish here just as well if a Custom House did not exist; and, as a publisher, I would vote for their abolition to-morrow. But to the point.

As an illustration of the effect of the copyright which I advocated, you held up a copy of Layard's new work, the importation of which, by us, had deprived our paper makers and printers (not binders) of so much employment. Now, I cannot suppose you were really and candidly in earnest, although it was evident the audience thought so. In the first place, what had the case to do with copyright? The sin charged (if it be a sin) was committed *without* copyright, in the entire absence of the law proposed. Why, then, if there was any odium in the proceeding,—why attach it to a measure that was in no way responsible for it?

The simple fact, as you know, was this: in this particular instance, it was *safer* to import the book than to re-print it. The large number of costly illustrations would require so much time and expense to be reproduced, that it became a simple matter of *policy* to purchase a large impression struck off from the English plates; and the fact that the price, low as it was, still yielded something to the *author,* was not considered a necessary objection. We, therefore, accepted the proposal in this form. The fact that we did so, *we* consider entirely our own affair. So long as we produce and publish a book in good style, at a suitable price, and with the author's approval, we do not think it to be the business of our neighbors whether we should have it printed here or in St. Petersburgh, or in Hong Kong. It is true that in this, as in other cases under the present system, we have no protection; and any one else who can produce the same book better or cheaper, has a perfect *legal* right to do so. We considered this, and counted the cost, leaving the result to be determined by courtesy, policy, or the actual ability of others to produce a better article.

The sin, therefore, is admitted. "The very head and front of our offending hath this extent." I confess the whole—and now, friend Hart, what of it? You point out an instance so rare—perhaps unique—as to excite remark—where the edition of a book issued in this country has been printed in England—and you say, "thus much work have American printers lost!" Now, if this *be* the issue, and if it be wicked for us to use any but our own manufactures, let it be understood. But, surely, a man of your well-known candor, courtesy, fairness, and liberality, won't advocate the Irish system of reciprocity, all on one side? It is a poor rule that won't work both ways; and I want you to read a lecture to Murray, Longman, Bentley, and others in London who may have been guilty of the same sin as ourselves. Your near neighbor and very able fellow-advocate on your side of this cause, published Lynch's Dead Sea Expedition—a handsome octavo, with many illustrations. Her Majesty's "publisher in ordinary" wished to publish this work in England, and, if I mistake not, instead of re-printing it there he imported 1,000 or 2,000 copies of the American edition; simply because (as in our case with 'Babylon'), there were so many illustrations that he could import it better than he could re-print it. Precisely the same case occurred with Squier's Nicaragua; Appleton & Co. supplying Longman and Co. with an edition printed in New York. Again, and to a still greater extent, Messrs. Harpers supplied Murray with large editions of Stephens's two works, 'Yucatan' and 'Central America,' each in two large volumes; and the Boston publishers did the same with an edition of Robinson's three large vols. of Travels in Palestine. Messrs. Little & Brown printed editions of Judge Story's, and other valuable Law Books, which are introduced as English editions by the London publisher Maxwell. We, ourselves, have manufactured, for Mr. Murray, stereotype plates of some of Irving's works; and have supplied him, Bentley, and Bogue, with entire editions of Spencer's Travels in the East, Taylor's Eldorado, Bryant's Letters of a Traveler, Kimball's St. Leger, Turnbull's Genius of Italy, Olmsted's American Farmer, and other books.

All these, bear in mind, are not small quantities merely imported for sale, but entire and often large editions, which are published in London with English title-pages, as English books; and all these are stereotyped and most of them printed in *this* country on American paper. Now, why don't the English printers and type founders complain? As far as I know, the instances of editions imported into England from us, are as *ten to one* compared with our importations, like Layard's Babylon; and that, too, in spite of the fact that the duty there is at least double ours. In other words, the *present* mode of reciprocity and exchange, has given American printers and paper-makers *ten* times as much work in *exports* as they have lost by imports. Now, friend Hart, is not this so? And do you not feel a little conscience-stricken on the score of your one-sided claim for protection? And do you not

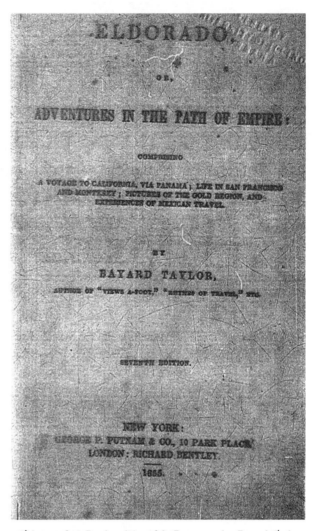

Title page for a Bentley edition of the Putnam author Bayard Taylor. Often Putnam's transatlantic partner, Bentley printed his first edition of Eldorado *from Putnam's sheets in 1850 and continued to reprint the work despite a competing Routledge edition.*

believe that, with copyright or without it, an open free trade in books between this country and England, would be very shortly, if it is not at this moment, as much for us as against us? Pray consider this. If I am wrong, I am ready to be corrected; but what is stated as facts, so far, I believe is beyond question.

But I have already trespassed too long, while the main topic remains untouched. I have only tried to show that while *expediency* and due regard for existing interests might call for provisions requiring American *printing* for all books, claiming protection here, and although I have urged the propriety of such provisions— yet I believe that they are far less *essential* than many have supposed, and that however doubtful might be the effect at first, yet in the long run we should gain as much as we should lose by a perfectly open free-trade. Let me add a few facts and figures.

In 1834 the *original American* books published
in this country were, ...240
The reprints of foreign books, ...260
Now mark the difference.
In 1852 the reprints remained about the same as
nineteen years ago, being 240
The original American books published
in 1852, were 760
(An increase of 300 per cent, in nineteen years).

Some will remark, perhaps, that this increase is owing to the *absence* of international copyright, and is an argument against it. This I do not believe; although it shows that American literature can increase and multiply whether protected or not—and I never have given much weight to the plaintive cry of some small authorlings that their genius was obscured and trampled down by the influx of uncopyrighted foreign books. A man of real genius is pretty sure of a hearing in this country whether protected or not—and all the international treaties in the world can never elevate into fame a weak or dull individual who has mistaken his vocation. But whether American authors have or have not a fair chance at home, under the present state of things, you are, I am sure, too good a patriot and too warm a friend of home genius not to advocate a measure which should add anything, however small, to their generally limited incomes,—especially if it should come from the pockets of another country. You will admit that as a rule, our authors, if not poor, are at least far from being in affluent circumstances. The few *exceptions,* where other causes besides books have lodged some of our authors in picturesque and comfortable "homes" with a competence,—these exceptions only prove the rule. You would not then grudge our authors any little remittances produced by their books over the water, if they could reach any such. Perhaps you are not aware how many such remittances might be expected even *now* under an international arrangement. I have ascertained from authentic printed lists that the number of American books reprinted in England up to December, 1852, and chiefly within the last ten years (including *rival* editions of the same work, but not including *importations* of American books), is not less than

850.

Of many of these books, many thousands have been and are still being printed; and the number of reprints is rapidly and constantly increasing. Now suppose that each of these books produced for the author the moderate sum, on an average of $50 per annum; there would be the respectable sum of $42,500 a year distributed among our authors as a reward and an encouragement for the labors of their brains.

It is true that in some instances,—Irving's, Cooper's, and a few others—a handsome copyright was paid by English publishers some years ago, even in the absence of a definite law—and it is also true that since Lord Campbell's decision in 1851, *all* American books published simultaneously in London, are even now protected and paid for, and very liberal sums have been received by several of our authors from English publishers. But I suggest to your sense of magnanimity and common justice, friend Hart, whether this is not a strong additional reason why we should reciprocate the *compliment?*

This word, by the way, suggests the nice abstract question, "Has an author a moral and equitable right to *claim* property in his works reprinted in another country?" Now I am not prepared, for one, to say yea or nay to this—I am not a logician or a jurist—and much wiser men than myself have differed on this point. But this I do say; that there is a sort of innate sense of propriety, an internal satisfaction, in the idea of permitting an author to control his works everywhere, and reaping from them a fair proportion of all gains they produce. Waive the "*right,*" both legal and moral—shall we not pay the author as a matter of courtesy, as a suitable acknowledgment of benefit received? Publishers, after all, only stand in the capacity of mediators between the author and his readers; and if the readers are ready to pay the author, why should the publisher object? Now what proportion, think you, of the ten thousand American *purchasers* of a popular English book, sold at a dollar for instance,—what proportion of those who have derived instruction or amusement from such a work, would not, if asked, cheerfully and promptly add a shilling to the price of the book as his (the reader's) payment to the author? Talk of its being a burdensome tax on a reading community? The reading community would scorn such an absurdity. Supposing Macaulay, or a poorer author should say personally to an American reader of his book, "will you not give me one shilling as my share of the benefit you have received from me?" Show me the man—the *thing* that would say "No, I will not. I have got your book and read it, and you have no legal right to demand a penny. Therefore I will pay nothing." No, they would not say this *singly,* why should they in the aggregate? Ten thousand readers paying each *ten cents*—say for an ordinary duodecimo—will give the author $1000. Now would this be a burdensome tax? I do not believe that one in one hundred of intelligent American readers, if asked to decide whether they would add one-tenth to their book expenses, for the sake of the authors, would hesitate one moment. Who would not read his books with ten times the satisfaction, after knowing that the author was paid, and was in comfortable circumstances, ready to produce another and a better work? Observe: the *individual* "tax" (if it *be* a tax,) of *ten cents,* might produce an *aggregate* for the author of $1,000—perhaps a great deal more.

In the business of re-printing English books without paying copyright, I have some sins of my own to answer for. I have re-printed several such; and the more I think of them, the less satisfactory is the reflection. I can say, however, very sincerely, that even as a matter of policy, I should have *preferred* in these instances to pay the English authors for a full copyright, with the sanction and protection therein involved.

But this query, as to the burden proposed to be laid on the reading community, and whether they will assent to it, leads me to the last question which I wished to suggest, viz.:

Would an International Copyright Law necessarily and materially increase the price of books in this country?

I may be mistaken: but my observation and whatever shrewdness of guessing my limited experience warrants, leads me to answer, *no!* Do you not agree with me in this?

It may be possible, I will admit, that in the first offset of such a new system of things, there might be individual instances of short-sighted policy, clinging to high prices and a narrow market. I leave out of the question any control of this matter by English *publishers,* because it is not probable that any law would be passed which would leave it in their hands; although, as I said before, I would not individually object to leaving it open on both sides to fill each other's markets, as each instance might render expedient. But if publishing is to be carried on, as it now is, by American publishers, is it not self-evident that it is for their interest to make all their books, copyright or not, *suited to the market?* Now, what kind of books does our market require and call for? Novels at eight dollars per copy? Certainly not.

A great deal of nonsense has been written about this bugbear of high prices, as a necessary consequence of copyright. "A printer" in the *Times,* parades in parallel columns the prices of certain books in England, and reprints of the same in New York, thus:

	London Price	N. Y. Price
Bulwer's "My Novel,"	$10.50	$ .75
Alison's Europe,	25.00	5.00
Macaulay's England,	4.50	.40
Layard's Nineveh,	9.00	1.75

And others in proportion.

Now, what does all this prove? Anything against copyright? You, friend Hart, are too shrewd and candid a man to say so. The reasons for the high prices of certain classes of books in England are various, and some of them are obvious enough. England is still behind the age in many things, and she still clings to many usages which are more fitted to her people than to ours. The circulating-library system there, for instance, is still greatly in vogue;

and these librarians would rather have a novel published at a guinea and a half than at half a crown. Why? Nineteen-twentieths of all readers must come to the libraries for the book. They cannot afford to buy it. So, also, with other expensive books printed for a comparatively small audience of wealthy people. But even England is learning wisdom from us on this point; and the records of the publishing world, in London, for the last three years, show quite as many cheap books as our own; aye, even copyright books too: and the whole system of publishing there is very rapidly being assimilated to ours.

Now, as I said before, and as I think you will admit, it is certain that in this country, with copyright or without it, the *interests* of publishers will prompt them to make books cheap—suited in price to the character of the market. It is more *profitable* to publish books at moderate prices, within the means of the largest number of readers, than it is to make them expensive. More than this—the publisher can afford to pay the author, whether American or Foreign, a reasonable per centage for the protection afforded, and still sell the books without *any* increase of price. Even now, we publish *numerous original works, for which we pay the author, and yet sell at the same price as others of the same size which pay no copyright. Is it not so?* I repeat, that in publishing a book at our present average prices, I would *rather* pay ten per cent to the author for *copyright,* than to have it without copyright, still selling it at the same price.

But this epistle is already too prosy; and you and I both have little time to waste in writing or reading long-winded arguments, unless they have a useful practical bearing. I have attempted to show—

1. That American printers have *not* suffered, as you intimated, by foreign importations; but, on the contrary, they have gained ten to one by the reciprocity, unrestricted by anything but importation duty.

2. That a copyright law can and will protect American printers; although their claim to special protection is at least doubtful, if not unnecessary.

3. That there is an *inherent* and *natural* claim for protection on the part of the author, whether American or foreign, as well founded, at least, as that of the printer.

4. That American authors would gain by the measure *now,* almost, and very soon, *quite* as much as English authors.

5. That a reciprocal protection of English authors here is called for *equitably* by the present English practices of protecting and paying American authors.

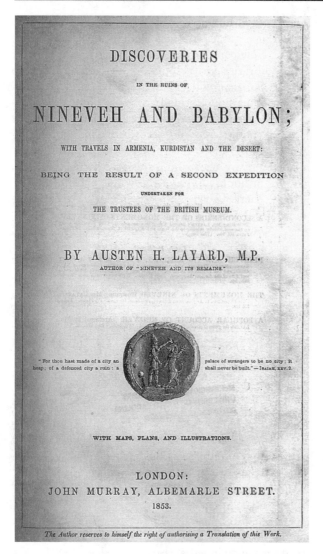

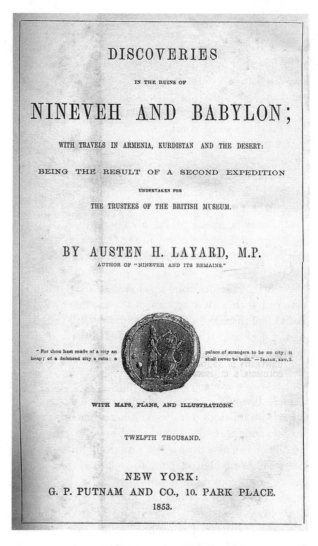

Title pages for the second book by Layard that Putnam published through an arrangement with John Murray. Abraham Hart charged that the sale of this book, and others like it printed by American publishers from imported sheets, cost American workers jobs.

6. And generally, that there is no danger that such a protection would materially increase the price of books, or prove a burdensome tax on the reading community, or any tax at all which would not be cheerfully assented to by book-buyers; that cheap publishing would continue as it does now:—and, finally, that the measure, while it would materially benefit authors, will not injure printers, much less publishers. It will add to the security and respectability of the Trade; and it will do no harm to any one.

Some points here stated may call for further remark; but, meanwhile, if I have mis-stated any question of fact, or made any wrong inferences, I shall be glad if you will point them out. I do not write you this to make myself conspicuous or promote individual interests; though I will not hesitate to add, that I believe I am right in this matter, and am anxious to convince those who think otherwise. At any rate, you will believe me, dear Hart,

Yours, very truly,
GEO. P. PUTNAM
(G. P. Putnam & Co., Publishers.)

———

Note.—It will be gratifying, and perhaps useful, if every bookseller or publisher who takes an interest in this subject will communicate his *yea* or *nay* to the question with any comment which may seem called for—addressed either to the Publisher of the Literary Gazette or to the writer of the above article.—Edr's.

—*Norton's Literary Gazette and Publishers' Circular,* 3 (15 April 1853): 62–64

* * *

Abraham Hart, one of many American publishers who profited from free access to foreign works

Mr. Hart's Reply to Mr. Putnam on the International Copyright Law.

Philadelphia, May 31st, 1853.
To G. P. Putnam, Esq., *Publisher,* New York.

MY DEAR SIR:–When, at the Trade Sale in your city, I exhibited to the company a volume with your imprint, "Layard's last work on Nineveh and Babylon," but *printed in London,* as embodying labor and skill that should have given employment to our own artists and manufacturers, I then little expected to be called upon to answer *six* columns of close print, or to be placed as an opponent to compensating authors; my object being merely to exhibit to the Trade there assembled, the probable practical effect of conceding an *unrestricted* copyright to foreigners. And, as you were then present, I desired that you should understand what I knew to be the fact, that the Trade were not nineteen-twentieths in favor of a modification of the copyright law by *treaty,* and on the terms said to be embodied in the one presented to the Senate, which idea had been sent out through the newspapers, under the sanction of your name, far and wide, (and allowed by you to stand, I believe, without contradiction). You, I think, were satisfied that you should have corrected the assertion directly on its appearance, and have stated precisely to the public what you intended to convey by that remark.

I am not the opponent of compensating authors; my practice is the reverse. I delight in knowing that authors participate with me in the profits arising from their labors; there is no great merit or liberality in this; nor am I alone in this feeling, I may say that it is an universal one among the Book Trade of this country. But I am opposed to any modification of the Copyright Law by *treaty*–it is an abuse of the power–and that, with all deference to greater men who think otherwise, I do not object to a change in our Copyright Act by the House of Representatives and Senate, or ordinary power, that will grant protection to the works of Foreign Authors who sell them outright to American citizens, with a proviso that all works should be actually printed in this country, and that within some given time after their appearance abroad; this will be legislating *for our own citizens,* and *Foreign authors* will be incidentally benefited. I think the Trade generally have the same views.

Practically, things are at present to some extent so managed, without any International Copyright Law; and, if Foreign authors would more generally seek to find publishers in this country for first or early sheets of their works, to be issued here and in London on the same day, independent of their London publishers, they would find their interest promoted by it, for large sums are constantly paid for early sheets, but unfortunately for them, English authors generally permit this to accrue to the London publisher, who would be most benefited by an unrestricted change of the law as designed by *The Treaty.*

I have not stood forth as the peculiar and particular champion of the rights of authors, (they being perfectly capable of taking care of themselves,)–you have that honor; but, if I understand your *present position,* you have certainly come over to my way of thinking, that legislation, if done at all in relation to Copyright, should be for *our own citizens,* through which *foreign authors* may be benefited: i. e., *that only American citizens shall hold copyrights of foreign works, and that all works so held shall be bona fide printed in this country.* It is not, therefore, necessary to follow your argument or refute your statements; the public generally care little about practical facts or figures, and the *Book Trade* understand them perhaps as well as you or I. I shall, therefore, pass over your further remarks and draw to a conclusion, observing, that as you say you are "no orator," I, on the other hand, deny all claim to be considered "a writer," and shall, therefore, as I dislike public controversy, decline appearing in print again on this subject. But before closing I would remark, that it is rather a matter of surprise than otherwise to me, that the Publishers in this country should look upon any change of the Copyright Law with the least favor, as people do not generally cling with pleasure to those who abuse them. The epithets that have been heaped upon the trade by many writers in favor of authors' rights, and the terms of reproach used, such as "Pirates," "Robbers," "Thieves," and "Highwaymen," would rather drive them, I should think, to oppose than support any change of the law.

The legal right to reprint English Books is not questioned, nor is the moral right; it is and has been done by as good and pure citizens as ever wrote books or articles on the copyright question. It is a mere question of expediency; England has set us the example of limiting the right of an author over his works, we have followed it; this decision at once settles the difference between property in copyright and property in the paper on which the book is printed. The reprinting of English Works is a legitimate and honorable trade, and whilst in the Publishing business I expect to continue it, and will be happy if authors shall participate with me in the profits, which can be done with or without an International Copyright Law; if with such a law most certainly at the expense of the reading public, for you understand as well as any one the convenience of small or moderate editions, with selected customers in the Trade at an advanced price, to cheap and large editions with forced sales. Every man will seek his own interest and convenience if protected by law in his business. The Book Trade will, of course, not be an exception. Again, allow me to say, that the Book Trade make many enemies with those who wield a pen, to one who does an active business, from the necessity of refusing so many works. You are as well aware as any other in the Trade, that the refusal to print works offered is the most disagreeable portion of our business, and certainly does not add to the number of our friends; the public may understand through this why it is the Trade is abused in joke and earnest, when they or their doings are the subject of remark.

From the foregoing you will readily perceive that I am in favor of compensating, and have generally compensated Foreign Authors, without any obligation on my part so to do by any existing Copyright Law, and without even having received early copies to print from. And with these remarks I take leave of the subject, and remain, with respect,

Yours, very truly,

A. HART

P. S. What prevented the $42,500 from being received by the authors in this country, on the 850 American books which you state were issued abroad? Was it inattention *to their own interests,* or did they refuse compensation? for you know, according to the English Copyright Law they were entitled to it, merely by the publisher depositing 6 copies of each publication, without any further expense.

—Norton's Literary Gazette and Publishers' Circular, 3 (15 June 1853): 99

Crystal Palace Speech

In 1855 Putnam played a leading role in organizing his fellow publishers into the New York Book Publishers' Association and accepted the position of secretary. In that role, he initiated the idea and supervised the planning of the authors-publishers dinner that took place on 27 September at the Crystal Palace in the course of the association's fall trade sale. It was designed to be the largest gathering of authors and publishers in American history and an occasion to celebrate the accomplishments of American culture.

Putnam took particular pride in delivering the main speech of the evening, arguably the central public moment of his career. He prepared his speech carefully, having proof set by a printer and asking the advice of trusted friends. His speech at the Crystal Palace expressed the faith in progress and culture that characterized "official" antebellum American attitudes. It was printed in American Publishers' Circular and Literary Gazette, *the trade paper launched weeks before by the Publishers' Association.*

* * *

INTRODUCTORY STATISTICAL SKETCH.

In proposing the regular toasts prepared for this occasion, Mr. President, we do not, with these "Our Sentiments," offer our respected guests choice Johannisberger, or Imperial Tokay, or Sparkling Catawba with which to pledge us, for we booksellers are law-abiding citizens. But though we provide only such juice of the grape as is pure, beyond suspicion, and in its *original packages;* yet *that,* we trust,—or the flavor of the Mocha,—or the Celestial beverage,—or the crystal Croton,—or, better than all, the inspiration of the proposed sentiments themselves, and the presence here to-night of those who so eminently illustrate them, will touch responsive chords in generous hearts, and prompt the eloquent tongues of some of those whose names are "familiar in our mouths as household words."

Eighteen years ago, Mr. President, a gathering like this, of authors and booksellers, took place at the old City Hotel. Our recently formed Association of Publishers came to the conclusion,—a sensible one, we hope our guests think,—that it was quite time to have another such caucus, or rather mass meeting:—perhaps it may be voted that this should not be the last. The interests of the writers, and publishers, and sellers of books, in this great and thriving country; are daily growing in magnitude and importance;—and these interests are, or should be, mutual and identical. Friendly social intercourse between ourselves is one of the prominent objects of the Association of Publishers; and surely it is both pleasant, and proper, and profitable

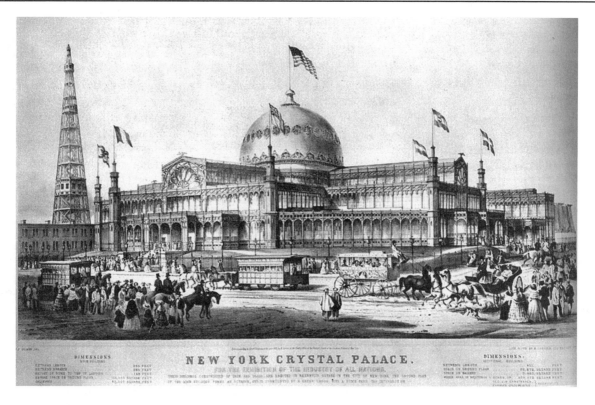

The New York Crystal Palace, which Putnam saw as a monument to the twin values of progress and free enterprise

to extend and strengthen this intercourse between publishers and authors.

On the occasion alluded to, in March, 1837, Mr. Keese, referring in terms excusably glowing and exultant, to the progress of American literature and the Book Trade to that time, remarked that "our once infant intellect now walk with giant strides." I do not, Mr. President, propose to inflict on our guests full details of dry statistics of progress since then. The details are at hand, and would be curious to many,—but you, sir, and all of us, will be jealous of every moment that keeps us from metal more attractive,—from those who speak with "thoughts that breathe, and words that burn." I will merely refer very briefly to one or two prominent outlines of our progress.

The records of American Publications (*) for the twelve years ending in 1842 show an aggregate of 1115 different works. Of these 623 were original, and 492 were reprinted from foreign books. The full list of reprints would show very nearly the same number as the originals,—viz., an average of 52 of each, per annum.

In the year 1853 there were 733 new works published in the United States; of which 278 were reprints of English works, 35 were translations of foreign authors, and 420 (a large preponderance) were original American works—thus showing an increase of about 800 per cent. in less than twenty years. As the average increase of the population of the United States in the same time,—great as it was,—scarcely reached 80 per cent., it appears that literature and the book trade advanced ten times as fast as the population. If we compare the *numbers* printed of each edition, the growth is still greater; for, 20 years ago who *imagined* editions of 300,000, or 75,000, or 30,000, or even the now common number of 10,000? Who would then believe in reaching 150,000 with a magazine or newspaper?

In 1844, the learned Scotch historian, Mr. Alison, pronounced in his great work, the dictum "that literature and intellectual ability of the highest class meet but little encouragement in America;" a sentence which he has graciously seen fit to modify in the edition of 1850, making it read thus: "Literary and intellectual abilities of the highest class are comparatively rare in America." We all know, Mr. President, that whatever may be the defects in our national character, excessive modesty about our greatness is not the most notable. If this *is* a great country, we are not apt to lose sight of the fact, or to let the world forget to recognize our grandeur and our virtues. Our national vanity is in no lack of sustenance. And we should not forget, Mr. President, in summing up the 'total' of our book-*manufacture,* and of the reams of paper we consume, that *Mind* is *not* always equivalent to Matter.

But making all allowances for superfluous patriotism, we cannot but think that our censorial friend the learned Glasgow sheriff, and others of his stamp on the other side, when they scrutinize us again, should be provided with glasses a little less covered with the dust of ignorance and prejudice. Both in quantity and in quality our literature may prove to be entitled to some better consideration from 'the honorable gentlemen on the opposition benches.' If some portion of those huge issues from the Press of the day, that count by tens of thousands, are *not* entitled to the highest niche in the temple of intellect, what then? *Are* "literary and intellectual abilities comparatively rare in America?" and do they "meet with but little encouragement?" And is it true, as Mr. Alison says, that we are "so wholly regardless of historical records?" To answer these questions, Mr. President, seems almost superfluous: to do so at large would more than exhaust the whole evening. By way of suggestion merely, permit me to call a rapid roll of names, 'here and there,' as representative men. Such, in theology and biblical literature, as the Dwights, the Edwardses, the Alexanders and the Beechers, Emmons, Hopkins, Barnes, Buckminster, Bushnell, Hodge, M'Ilvaine, Norton, Robinson, Moses Stuart, Woods, and fifty others, scarcely less eminent. In jurisprudence and politics we need not be reminded of Calhoun, Curtis, Duer, Greenleaf, Hoffman, Hamilton, Jay, Kent, Livingston, Marshall, Wheaton, Webster, Story; nor, in medicine of Beck, Chapman, Dewess, Dunglison, Eberle, Morton, Mott, Warren, and Wood. In Science has not something been achieved by such men as Audubon, Bachman, Beck, Bowditch, Silliman, Dana, Godman, Gray, Hitchcock, Holbrook, Hall, DeKay, Mitchell, Morton, Nuttall, Olmsted, Pierce, Pickering, Torrey; to say nothing of those we are so proud to 'adopt' and 'develope,'–need I name Guyot and Agassiz?–to say nothing also of other contributors to such works as the New York State Natural History in twenty quartos; the Exploring Expeditions and other Government Surveys, filling not less than one hundred volumes, chiefly quartos and folios, unexcelled by royal presses in style of execution;–and the publications of Scientific Institutes, and Societies, and of the State Governments;–in all, not less than 500 volumes of original research in Science and Natural History.

In Metaphysics, it would suffice to claim Jonathan Edwards,–in himself a host–and such thinkers as Henry, Hickok, James, Tappan, Upham, and Wayland, know how to speak for themselves on the "Science of Mind." The principles of education have been discussed by writers like Henry Barnard, Horace Mann, Bishop Potter [observe I am not reading a catalogue, but names almost at random]. As to the writers of text books, their name is legion and too numerous to mention here, even at random; but we may remember that even Young England receives lessons in its own language from Lindley Murray, an American; and that our 120 colleges and 100,000 schools, are taught from books almost entirely prepared by our own countrymen. Philology and Ethnology have been illustrated by the researches of Duponceau, Gallatin, Pickering, Andrews, Hale, Robinson, Stuart, Leverett, Worcester, Squier, Bartlett (from our own fraternity), and last not least, Noah Webster, whose great work, with all its sins, while giving law in orthography to twenty millions of his countrymen is rapidly becoming authority to mother England herself.

In *History,* the names of John Adams, and indeed many of our statesmen who '*made* history;' and Winthrop, Prescott, Bancroft, Cooper, Hildreth, Irving, Schoolcraft, Sparks, Ingersoll, and a hundred others, together with the issues of the Historical Societies, Congress, and the legislatures, have produced an aggregate of nearly four thousand volumes, to show Mr. Alison how 'wholly regardless' we are 'of historical records.'

From the section of Geography and Travels, you will at once think of some scores; and not forget the adventurous explorers of our western wilderness-empire and the Isthmus, from Lewis and Clarke down to Fremont, Schoolcraft, Catlin, Gunnison, Bartlett, Squier and Stephens;–the hundred pioneers of light and knowledge in the isles of the Pacific and the old kingdoms of the East, who have brought back light and knowledge in their books:–Wilkes, who gives us a New Continent at the South Pole; and Kane, who we hope has ere this written his own name and Henry Grinnell's on the shores of that open sea which circles the other Pole at the north.

In the useful arts of engineering, ship building, navigation, architecture, agriculture, gardening, the works of our Mahans, Bowditchs, Griffiths, Overmans, Minifies and Downings, are admitted to be unsurpassed in their kind, in the world.

As to *Belles-Lettres* and general literature, I must be content to allude to perhaps one in 20 of names we cherish, such as Channing and Cooper, and Brockden Brown, Paulding, Irving, Kennedy; Fay, Halleck, Hawthorne, Hoffman; Longfellow, Lowell, Mitchell, Curtis, Whittier, Bayard Taylor, Willis: and from the brilliant circle of our female writers–(where else is it equalled?)–if I quote the names of Caroline Kirkland, Maria Mackintosh, Alice Cary, Lydia Sigourney, Catherine [*sic*] Sedgewick, Elizabeth Warner, or Harriet Stowe, should I exhaust the list? Far from it. These names, Mr. President, lighted upon almost at random, (I do not presume upon invidious distinctions–if you seek for other monuments, look around you!)–these names are merely representatives of American authors, justly entitled to be called original in their works;–who have made positive, and in many cases very important additions to the stock of human knowledge, or who have extended and adorned the realms of Fancy and Imagination. It is safe to estimate from the data before us, that the original works produced in this country up to this time, and more or less entitled to credit, as advances upon what had been done

AMERICAN PUBLISHERS' CIRCULAR
AND
Literary Gazette.

ISSUED WEEKLY BY THE BOOK PUBLISHERS' ASSOCIATION.

Temporary Committee. WILLIAM H. APPLETON, GEORGE P. PUTNAM.

Communications should be addressed to C. B. Norton, Assistant Secretary and Librarian, No. 3 Appletons' Building, Broadway.

VOL. I.—No. V.   NEW YORK, SEPTEMBER 29, 1855.   PRICE $2 A YEAR.

Complimentary Fruit Festival
OF THE
NEW YORK BOOK PUBLISHERS' ASSOCIATION
TO AUTHORS AND BOOKSELLERS,
AT THE CRYSTAL PALACE, SEPTEMBER 27, 1855.

[From the N. Y. Daily Times.]

AUTHORS AMONG FRUITS—GENIUS IN THE CRYSTAL PALACE—SEVEN HUNDRED GUESTS AT TABLE—LETTERS—TOASTS—SPEECHES—A TEETOTAL ENTERTAINMENT.

The long promised Banquet tendered by the Book Publishers' Association of this city to the Authors, came off at the Crystal Palace last evening. In the arrangements for the event, the Publishers spared no pains. Every thing was ordered upon a scale of great variety and elegance. The viands consisted almost wholly of fruits. The beverages were altogether destitute of alcoholic stimulant. The ladies were admitted among the guests—the gentlemen refrained from indulgence in cigars and wine—the place was kept at a temperature unusually comfortable for such an occasion—the tables were graced with the presence of wit and wisdom, and the evening passed off in a very successful manner.

APPEARANCE OF THE HALL.

The entire north nave of the Crystal Palace was given up to the Association. It was enclosed in the form of a pavilion, with longitudinal strips of red, white, and blue, alternating. Six long tables, stretching from north to south, were flanked at the southern extremity by a dais, upon which rested the table for the officers of the evening and the speakers. Covers were laid for six hundred and fifty persons, but the number who actually took part in the destruction of the viands, and afterward were within ear shot of the speakers, was about seven hundred. Upon each plate was placed a card, bearing the name of a guest. The caterers of the occasion were COLEMAN & STETSON, whose entire force of waiters—one hundred and fifty—was transferred from the Astor House.

In front of the President's chair, resting upon a small platform, was placed a Cornucopia, from the mouth of which poured a luscious flood of the gifts of Pomona. From the other extremity hung a card, inscribed with the words: "May plenty crown the humblest board."

At each lady's place at table lay a small bouquet, wrapped in filigree. The number of ladies who occupied seats in the main Hall was very small—probably there were not above fifty in all. In the galleries there were many spectators, and nine tenths of them ladies. All the points in the Palace from which a view of the Banqueting Hall could be obtained were occupied.

A strong force of police was present in uniform, and excellent order was preserved upon the floor by a detailed force under command of Sergeant JONES.

THE BANQUET.

Gentlemen with ladies, and gentlemen without that privilege, alike endeavored to be polite, and displayed excellent capabilities of enjoyment. The beverages were coffee, tea, and the simplest and earliest of liquids.

The President's table was honored by the presence of many familiar faces. WASHINGTON IRVING was there—fresh and genial, and the object of universal remark. Dr. VALENTINE MOTT sat on the left of Mr. APPLETON, and near him Rev. GARDINER SPRING, Professor WEBSTER, Principal of the Free Academy; President WOOLSEY, of Yale College; Hon. CHARLES KING, President of Columbia College; Judge DUER, HENRY C. CAREY, Rev. Dr. ROBINSON and his lady, ("Talvi,") Professor DENISON OLMSTED, Judge JAY. Towards the eastern end of the table were Mayor WOOD and Hon. J. V. C. SMITH, Mayor of Boston, Rev. Dr. TYNG, Rev. H. WARD BEECHER, Rev. E. H. CHAPIN, Rev. Dr. OSGOOD, WM. C. BRYANT, WASHINGTON IRVING, and Prof. S. F. B. MORSE. Among the persons at table we noticed, in the list of ladies, Miss LESLIE, Miss MACKINTOSH, Mrs. KIRKLAND, Mrs. BOTTA, (late Miss ANNE C. LYNCH,) "MINNIE MYRTLE," ALICE CARY, and the Misses WARNER.[*] Ex-Mayor HARPER, Rev. Mr.

[*] A corrected list is given elsewhere.

MILBURN, N. P. WILLIS, and a host of well-known faces—publishers, authors, and paper men—were among the party. It was altogether a brilliant assemblage of the literary people of the city and its vicinity. On no former occasion has there been an opportunity to enjoy the sight of so many very great men at once.

[New York Express.]

The unrivalled assemblage of literary celebrities, invited to attend the grand Fruit and Flower Festival, given by the New York Publishers' Association to the authors of America, convened last evening at the Crystal Palace.

The north naive of this edifice was enclosed for the occasion, with hangings of red and white cloth. Six parallel tables, with one transverse table at the head, were spread for the guests, within this enclosure. Upon the wainscoting around the enclosure were disposed an array of various greenhouse plants, together with a magnificent profusion of flowers in vases, &c. The Chairman and chief guests, some fifty in number, were seated at the transverse head tables which was raised on a dais, and visible from all parts of the house. Behind these, and reaching towards the great dome of the Palace, an amphitheatre was raised, with seats for ladies. Here, and in the overhanging galleries, a brilliant and crowded collection of spectators were assembled.

The whole edifice was fully illuminated, the gas working admirably. The great chandelier of jets under the dome, and the lengthy and brilliant array of lights in the picture gallery were all ablaze. In the naive, where the festivities were prepared, the appearance was magnificent. Besides the tasteful arrangement of flowers and draperies, an extraordinary illumination of gas jets was prepared for the occasion. From under the stained roof depended an illumination of gas jets, exhibiting, within the dimensions of 20 by 25 feet, in large letters, the inscription:

> COMPLIMENTARY FRUIT AND FLOWER FESTIVAL
> GIVEN TO AUTHORS,
> BY THE
> NEW YORK PUBLISHERS' ASSOCIATION,
> SEPTEMBER 27, 1855.

Beneath this, affixed to the gallery, was a statue of Clio, the Muse of History, enclosed in an illumination, above which was the inscription, in letters of light:

> HONOR TO GENIUS.

In the space behind the chief guests was a large number of growing plants, trees, &c.

On the tables, besides the profusion of splendid fruit, were silver and other rich ware, varieties of cake and pastry, devices of books in singular bindings, and other suggestive decorations, together with a large number of chandeliers of wax tapers, and vases of gorgeous flowers.

In view of the brilliant and splendid array presented by the assembled guests, no doubt much of the singular beauty of the ornamental arrangements and their novelty as a public entertainment, were lost upon those who witnessed and enjoyed them. Nothing we have ever seen, however, could be in better taste, and few occasions could have elicited a more genial or thorough satisfaction.

At a little after six, the guests formed beneath the rotunda, and entered two by two to the banquet. A band in attendance, stationed in the gallery, played throughout the evening, during the intermissions of speaking.

The repast consisted of a profusion of rich and varied fruits, cold meats, salads, jellies, teas, coffee, ices, &c. Mr. Stetson, caterer for the occasion, had provided a splendid abundance of every thing that could give beauty or zest to the display on the tables.

When the guests were all seated, the scene presented was one of the most striking. The floor crowded and animated, the amphitheatre and galleries packed, the effect of the painted dome and roof, the brilliant illumination, all presented a scene which perhaps no other public occasion in this country has surpassed.

Front page of the issue of the New York Book Publishers' Association trade paper given over to coverage of the Authors-Publishers Dinner before, amount to not less than eight thousand different volumes, of which at least three fourths have been issued within the last twenty years. And yet our sage critics across the water profess to be sadly grieved because we have, (or have *not,* shall we say?) done more to increase and diffuse knowledge among men in our brief National existence of 80 years, than has been accomplished by some of the old States of Europe in a thousand!

The queries of Sydney Smith in the Edinburgh, of 1820, have been so often referred to, that further answer becomes hackneyed and superfluous. If he then so despondingly, (or triumphantly) asked where is their Fox or Burke, their Scott, or Byron or Siddons?—or, in the four quarters of the globe who reads an American book? or goes to an American play? or looks at an American picture or statue? or what have they done in mathematics or science? If that excellent wit and liberal-minded philanthropist asked these questions thirty years ago, perhaps, after all he was excusable, though even *then,* Jonathan Edwards, the first metaphysician of the age had given his works to the world; Franklin, Rittenhouse, Godfrey, and others had achieved most important discoveries in Science: Jefferson, Hamilton, Madison and Jay, had produced works on political science; Gilbert Stuart had painted some of the best portraits of the age; and Benjamin West of Pennsylvania, had won for himself the presidency of even the British Royal Academy of Art—as the successor of Sir Joshua Reynolds.

But it is the reiteration of the *spirit,* at least, of those queries of 1820 by historians of writers and the present day, that we must protest against:—if we have not done enough already to earn a better estimate than they have given us, there are those here to-night that will redeem the country yet.

As to the query about American pictures and statues, probably a fair answer might be made to that also by some who know how to appreciate an Allston, a Cole, a Vanderlyn, a Greenough, or Powers, or Crawford; and the respected president of our Academy, could, I think, give a good account of his Academicians, though he is too modest to mention himself. But this is not our province now. "What we have done in science" has already been alluded to in the names of some of those who have *written* science—and has not our own MORSE improved upon the achievements of our own FRANKLIN, and given to the world the first practical demonstration of that wonderful application of natural laws, which literally annihilates time and space, and promises to realize in sober earnest the fairy doings of Puck, and enable us to put a girdle round about the earth in forty minutes? And has not MAURY conferred a boon on humanity, and lessened both danger and distance for the mariner the world over, by mapping shortcuts and turnpikes on the broad ocean?

But, Mr. President, even this glance at landmarks is trespassing on your time. One word about the Mechanical aspects of our progress in book-making. We have yet much to achieve. *Excelsior* is our motto. But, sir, even now, we may point with pride to specimens of the "black art," not a whit behind the best across the sea. If *every* specimen is not perfect, let it be remembered that the aggregate of the NEW books first manufactured in a single year is not less than two millions four hundred thousand. Putting aside school-books, Bibles, and society publications, the number of volumes printed and reprinted will reach eight millions! The school-books alone will swell the number twelve millions more. The number of volumes issued yearly from the gigantic establishment of Messrs. Harper alone has been estimated at more than a million of volumes; and the Philadelphia house of Lippincott sends forth books at an average of fifty cases per day the year round. Specimens, these, though large ones. And then consider, besides, the enormous bulk of reading matter issued by our two hundred periodicals and two thousand newspapers! Think of the eighteen thousand double, or thirty-six thousand single reams of paper, required yearly for a single magazine, which courses over the country, unprecedented in cheapness and attraction, at the rate of one hundred and fifty thousand per month. The wildest imaginings, at home or abroad, twenty years ago, would not have stretched so far as this. Why, sir, the sheets from our book-presses alone, in a single year, would reach nearly twice round the globe; and if we add the periodicals and newspapers, the issues of our presses in about eighteen months would make a belt, two feet wide, printed on both sides, which would stretch from New York to the Moon!

In the *machinery* for this great manufacture, our artisans, I will venture to say, are not yet excelled, if equalled, elsewhere. The printing presses of Hoe and of Adams are said to surpass any used in Europe. The important art of Stereotyping, which there is reason to believe originated in this country, has certainly been brought to greater perfection here than it has reached abroad—and naturally so; for our wide market requires this permanent form, for nearly all we print. And by a recent beautiful invention of another of those citizens, whom we are proud to 'adopt' and 'develope,' the types themselves are set up by steam, aided by rapid girlish fingers, touching keys like those of a piano, and sliding words of thought into 'form,' about four times as fast as the quickest compositor.

The learned historian already quoted, remarks of Cooper, Channing, and Irving, that "their works are all published in London; a decisive proof" (he sagely adds) "that European habits and ideas are necessary to their due development." This remark also he modifies in 1850, thus: "So great is the influence of English popularity in America, that the highest class of American authors, such as Cooper, Prescott, and Irving, publish all their works in London, in preference to their own country." The historian's logic may be sound, but his premises and facts are not, and I fear he knows it. With one or two unessential exceptions, all the works of the authors mentioned were first published at home; and we might say, with equal propriety, "the works of Byron, Scott, and Dickens are all published in New York: a decisive proof that American habits and ideas are necessary for their due developement." It is true that the American authors mentioned, and some others, received a suitable compensation for the English circulation of their works. We only wish that more of our author friends could do likewise; and far be it from me to depreciate or lose sight of the large debt which we have yet to repay our 'fatherland' for the intellectual supplies to which we have so long and so freely helped ourselves. But to show that reciprocity in this justice to literature on *both* sides is rapidly becoming even more important to us than to England, let me mention one or two significant facts, and I will detain you but a moment longer. In 1834, American publications stood thus: 252 original, and 198 reprints. Even *that* proportion would surprise some who imagined that we relied chiefly on England for intellectual novelties,–as indeed we *did* within the present generation. In 1853, the originals were 420, and the reprints 278. On the other hand, the number of American books reprinted in England in our whole history, up to 1842, was 382, not including rival editions. In 1854 these had increased to 950, of which, including rival editions, no less than 119 were reprinted in 1853, and 185 in 1854– nearly as many in these two years as there had been in sixty, up to twelve years ago. Comment is unnecessary. Some of these reprints appear, it is true, in somewhat doubtful guise and uncertain paternity–making it evident that our English cousins of this day not only do read American books, but read them sometimes without knowing it. But, sir, we have our own sins to answer for, and there is doubtless room for mutual improvement in that generous and honorable emulation which prompts us to promote our own interests, but never disregards the courtesy and justice due to our neighbors. Mr. President, I have detained our guests too long over these dry figures and dates,–dry, but I hope, to our guests, suggestive of richer and more genial products. I proceed to read the first of the

REGULAR TOASTS.

1. *The Republic of Letters*–Boundless as the world, it should guarantee equal rights to every section: pure genius should be its only badge of honor, and the sure passport to substantial reward.

AIR–Behold how brightly breaks the morning.

2. *American Literature*–Its youth gives brilliant promise of an honorable future: may its riper years show that it has been trained in the right schools.

3. *Literature and Statesmanship*–When we are governed at home or represented abroad by a WHEATON, a BANCROFT, an EVERETT, an IRVING, a MARSH, a HAWTHORNE, a KENNEDY; there is hope for the dignity of the country and the interests of letters.

4. *Our Lady-guests and their Writings*–The *New England Tale* is re-echoed from the *New Home* of the Far West; and from a *Cabin* on the banks of the Ohio, a touch of Nature vibrates among *The Lofty and the Lowly* through the *Wide, Wide World*.

5. *The Clergy*–Promoters of useful intelligence and Christian patriotism, their influence on the minds of men should entitle them to the gratitude of all sensible booksellers.

6. *Our Men of Science*–The ends of the earth and the depths of the sea have been explored by their skill and energy, and the world looks with admiration on the results.

7. *The Fine Arts*–The offspring of Free Institutions, and the ornament of a Practical People; their Use lies in their Beauty, and their Beauty lies in their Truth.

8. *The Bench and the Bar*–Illustrated by a Marshall, a Story, a Kent and a Webster, they prove that Literature and Law may mutually adorn each other.

9. *Institutions of Learning*–The best operators for an active demand in the book market–they will never permit our judicious investments to fall belowpar.

10. *The Printing Press* of the Age of Steam and Electricity.

11. *Editors of the Newspaper Press*–Guardians of our literature and sentinels on the watch-towers of our liberties, they wield a power which might dethrone a monarch or elevate a people.

12. *Periodical Literature*.

13. *English Literature and our Guests who illustrate it.*

14. *The sister cities of Boston, Philadelphia, and New York,* whose chief magistrates honor us to-night:–While each aims to produce the best books of the best authors, and best regulated homes for them, the more rivalry the better.

15. *The Publishers of Boston*–A Fraternity that has been illustrated by the patriotism of KNOX, and the practical intelligence of an ARMSTRONG, a LINCOLN and a BROWN, may still be proud of the products of their cultivated FIELDS.

Washington Street, the center of the antebellum publishing trade in Boston. Firms located on the street included Little and Brown, Phillips and Sampson, and Ticknor and Fields.

16. *The Publishers of Philadelphia*—Who by honorable enterprise have so magnified the business that numbers BENJAMIN FRANKLIN among its founders, and which has since been adorned by the CAREYS, the THOMASES, the GRIGGS and the HARTS of the city of Brotherly Love.

17. *The Booksellers of the Union*—So long as they are the mediums for diffusing sound intelligence and the pure products of true genius, they deserve an honorable position in the community; for, in the ordinary business of their lives, they become benefactors to their country.

—*American Publishers' Circular and Literary Gazette*, 1 (29 September 1855): 67–69

* * *

*Incomplete in the list of reprints.

Speech at Boston Harbor

Putnam made the following remarks while on a day outing during the August 1859 Boston trade sale. Although he protested his limited speaking ability, Putnam had no peer for expressing his profession's esprit de corps. A clipping from a Boston newspaper containing the text of his speech, which he gave from the main deck of a steamer transporting the assembled publishers into Boston Harbor, is pasted in his scrapbook.

"The Boston Book Trade Sale."
The Excursion in Boston Harbor—Speech of Mr. George P. Putnam

The members of the book trade now visiting Boston took a steamboat excursion in Boston Harbor last Friday, under the auspices of the city government. The steamer Nantasket was chartered, and about five hundred persons joined in the festivities. At Deer Island they visited the public institutions, and on the return trip a collation was served on the steamer. Of course, it was attended with toasts and speeches. Among the speakers were J. H.

Underwood and Thomas Drew of Boston; George P. Putnam, Lowell Mason and J. F. Zebley of New York; Mr. Bliss and James Challen of Philadelphia; Mr. Z. Pratt of Baltimore; Mr. McCarter of Charleston, S. C.; Mr. Blanchard of Cincinnati; J. M. Usher of Medford; and Messrs. W. C. Wyman, Perkins, Moses Kimball, Moses Tenney and P. Donahoe of Boston.

Mr. Putnam being called upon to respond for New York, said:

"The New York booksellers are unfortunate if they are to be represented by the one least able to speak for them—the one whose oratorical abilities are not yet developed. Booksellers, sir, are very modest men; but who ever saw a modest orator? We know that we are really amongst the most important persons in the community, and that the country is indebted to us for its ample supplies of learning, intelligence and virtue; but then we don't like to say so.

"But I will say, on behalf of the 'trade' of New York, that we really like Boston and New England, for more reasons than one. Whether that essential 'hub of the universe' be located in Beacon street or not, we do know that a large proportion of *our* best authors of *our* best books originate in New England; and we also find here the best market for our own books.

"We have plenty of other reasons for admiring New England and its great metropolis—but they would alone fill a big book. Many of us claim close kindred with you. Indeed a Knickerbocker historian has recently proved (quite conclusively, I believe,) that Dutchmen and Yankees are the *same people*—English Lincolnshire having sheltered, 700 years ago, the Dutch colony whose descendants in 1620 sent out the fathers of New England. However this may be, many of us are proud of New England progress as a part of our own birthright. We are proud of the substantial advancement of you 'solid men of Boston,' who 'drink no strong potations'—proud of your growing commerce, literature and arts—your noble public institutions—of your massive palaces of trade—more than realizing, in durable granite, the fairy wonders of Alladin. We are proud of the neatness, order, enterprize, shrewd intelligence everywhere manifested in your noble city; and not a few of us may look about us here and say, with honest enthusiasm, 'I, too, am a full-blooded Yankee,' and repeat the verse of our nursery days—

'Mayn't Massachusetts boast as great
As any other sister state?'

"We are glad, too—not pharasically, we hope, but in the spirit of hearty brotherly love—that our southern friends should come here and see your energetic advance.

"Yesterday, sir, some of us saw, at the rooms of your Historical Society, a portion of the identical tea which, at a certain tea party of the olden time, was mixed with the waters of this beautiful harbor. On that occasion an ancestor of my own assisted to do the honors. Probably our tea to-day, sir, is somewhat stronger than that of our grandfathers, for they used an excessive proportion of water. But though their tea was weak, they themselves waxed strong. If, to-day, we seek for their monument, we need only 'look around us.'

The occasion which has called us to Boston has been emphatically a success. We always believed that Boston would do thoroughly whatever she deliberately resolved upon—now we *know* it. Our English cousins, Murray or Longman, would marvel greatly at the tons of books which have here found a 'paying' and ready market. The liberal hospitality, too, of your managers and committee, will be '*freshly* remembered.' But when we consider the attractive pleasure provided for us to-day by your honorable body—representing the great city itself—we are reluctantly compelled to make some 'odorous comparisons.' New York, sir, we think, is a growing seaport of some considerable importance. But if *our* Common Council ever spontaneously originate a compliment so intelligent and discriminating as this of yours to-day, it is probable that the Millennium will follow shortly after. The poet Campbell's toast—"The memory of Napoleon—he once ordered a bookseller to be shot"—was very well in its way, especially as he had never seen our Boston boy, *our* poet publisher, the firm friend and favorite of all good authors, on both sides of the Atlantic. But I would apologize for detaining you so long and merely remind you of "*Our Fields*—The 'Admirable Crichton' of American Publishers."

—*George Palmer Putnam Collection. Manuscripts Division. Princeton University Library.*

Eulogy for Charles Scribner

Putnam and Scribner knew and dealt with each other as colleagues for nearly three decades, a period during which they grew to be two of the most respected men in publishing. Putnam eulogized Scribner, a man he plainly admired, at a meeting of publishers and booksellers held on 22 September 1871 at the store of Sheldon and Company, New York City. His speech was published as "In Memoriam" in Scribner's Monthly.

* * *

GENTLEMEN:—I am sure that all present, and especially those who were personally acquainted with Mr. Scribner, are united in feeling that the expression of this meeting should not be a cold formality—a routine task, simply decent, and properly in unison with time-honored custom; but that we all feel sincerely in earnest when we thus come together as members of a business fraternity, from various States in the Union, to express our heart-felt sorrow in our common loss,—well knowing that it is a loss of more than ordinary magnitude. Mr. Scribner's very prominent and honorable place in the guild of book-publishers; his well-earned and conspicuous success and eminent position as a business manager; the exceptionally pure tendency and high importance of the numerous publications issued by the prosperous house which he founded; and, above all, his own personal character—so proverbial not merely for sagacity and sound judgment, but for liberal culture, for his kind and courteous disposition, and his sensitive integrity, were all so marked and distinguished, that his departure from us seems to be to each of us a personal affliction. It may be described as, in some sense, even a national calamity. For is not the nation itself influenced for its best welfare by the books which our late friend has been the means of scattering broadcast over the country?

In a brief but judicious notice of our friend, in the printed circular of the house, his business associates speak of him as "a man to whom meanness seemed impossible; he was high-minded, generous, genial; a friend, the very soul of sympathy and tenderness; a Christian, devout, humble, and sincere. But his tenderness never turned to weakness, and he was ever quick to detect shams. Gentle and modest as a woman, there was a manliness and nobility about him that embarrassed subterfuge and commanded the instant respect and confidence of all with whom he came in contact." I quote these words because they are peculiarly fitting, and I am sure they will be adopted and indorsed by every one of us who had the best opportunities to test their truth.

Mr. Scribner's singularly modest, quiet, retiring manner did not, perhaps, encourage much personal intimacy, except with a few chosen friends and associates; but, so far as any of us were privileged with his acquaintance, I do not doubt that we can all share heartily in the genial tribute of his friend Dr. Holland—one of many who can speak understandingly about our late friend. "Few publishers," says this very popular author, "have been able to bring to their business the education and

Charles Scribner, who, like Putnam, was a central figure in the professionalization of publishing in nineteenth-century America and the founder of a major family-operated publishing house

culture which enabled Mr. Scribner to achieve his large success. . . . The relations that existed between him and those authors for whom he published, were the most cordial that can be imagined. Every author who had these personal relations with him must feel personally bereft by his death, for he was social, and brotherly, and considerate almost beyond parallel. . . . His literary judgment was remarkable—probably no other publisher living who has done an equal amount of business has done it with fewer mistakes. . . . While disliking the details of business, and shunning contact with the asperities of trade, his ideas and plans of business were large, far-sighted, and liberal, in an eminent degree." I am told also by one of his partners, that he almost invariably read the entire MS. of every book published by the firm; and though he always declined everything that he thought might *possibly* do harm, he sometimes accepted others as likely to serve a worthy cause rather than for pecuniary results. The remarkable success of that very serious undertaking, the great Biblical Commentary of Lange, was a source of very great satisfaction to him, which he frequently dilated upon—more, I do not doubt, because it was a substantial service to Biblical literature than on account of its profits in money, large as they may have been.

In his last letter from Switzerland to his partners he uses these words, which I have been permitted to quote:—

"Having been so long connected with our publishing business—a quarter of a century—and having seen its present magnitude and usefulness, I desire with you to consecrate it to the service of our Saviour."

I have reason to know that Mr. Scribner declined tempting offers of a very profitable connection with another branch of business, because he desired to use this more congenial trade in good books, in conferring a substantial benefit on the community. My friends, is it not worth our while to derive some practical benefit in this brief contemplation of such an example? Cannot those of us who are engaged in the responsible vocation of publishers learn some useful lessons by looking back upon the business career of Charles Scribner? As one of the least of the fraternity—though one of those longest connected with it—I feel humiliated when I consider how much permanent benefit has been conferred upon his fellow-men by the liberal enterprise and conscientious judgment of our late friend, while so much time and money and influence *may* be wasted in printing books, not including those positively harmful, but those which are simply *indifferent;* which add nothing to the common stock of sound knowledge, which contribute nothing to elevate the intellectual, moral, or religious character of our fellow-men. I do not mean that we must publish only dogmatic theology, or religious homilies; for there may be "religious books," so called, which are as useless in their way as the many inane or "so-so" attempts in other departments. But may not the community as well as our own pockets be benefited, by greater care in avoiding any and every book that is not *both* morally pure and intellectually worthy to *claim* public attention? I hope these remarks are not tainted with Pecksniffian cant: none of us are so innocent as to be worthy to cast the first stone. But for one, I simply suggest, with all deference, the query, whether this occasion may not be practically useful to us all, and whether the character and career of our eminent friend who has gone to a better world may not serve for the encouragement and example of those of us who are left.

It is often evident that we do not sufficiently appreciate the high responsibility resting upon men who disseminate, if they do not create, the intellectual food of a nation. Let us imitate Charles Scribner; and while we work for honorable independence, let us, at the same time, seek to serve the cause of sound literature, pure religion, and public morals.

—Scribner's Monthly, 3 (November 1871): 110–111

Nineteenth-Century Assessments of Putnam and His Company

Sketches of the Publishers Series

By midcentury the American publishing industry had developed to such an extent that it became a prominent subject for journalists. One of the best specimens of this interest is the Sketches of the Publishers series in the New York monthly The Round Table, *from which this sketch of Putnam is taken. In a footnote at the beginning of the article, the unnamed writer comments that in this "sketch of this veteran publisher we have made free use not only of the facts kindly placed by him at our disposal, but of his genial and interesting series of papers which appeared in the 'American Publishers' Circular,' in 1863, under the title of 'Rough Notes of Thirty Years in the Trade.'" In fact, entire paragraphs are taken verbatim from "Rough Notes of Thirty Years in the Book Trade." Such sketches were influential in establishing the content of early histories of American publishing.*

* * *

SKETCHES OF THE PUBLISHERS.
GEORGE P. PUTNAM.
I.

GEORGE P. PUTNAM, a native of Brunswick, Maine, was born in the year 1814, and at the age of eleven commenced his business as "boy" in a carpet-store in Boston. Four years later, in the year 1829, and at the age of fifteen, he found himself an amazed and unknown, yet hopeful, stranger in the city of New York, busily conning those advertisements in the *Courier* which began with "boy wanted." After some rebuffs, he found employment in a little book and stationery store in Broadway, near Maiden Lane, kept by George W. Bleecker, his duties being to run errands, sweep, etc., for which he was to receive $25 a year, and live in the family of his employer, who resided, London fashion, over his little store. Mr. Bleecker then published a quarto monthly, called "The Euterpiad: an Album of Music, Poetry, and Prose," and young Putnam was occasionally sent up the North River, or to other rural districts in the neighborhood of the city, as canvasser for this "creditable but rather short-lived periodical." After an apprenticeship of a year or two as clerk-of-

all-work in "this little mart of school-books, Andover theology, albums, stationery, and cheap pictures," he received and accepted what he denominates "an unsolicited and mysterious promotion" to the dignity of first clerk at the "Park Place House," "an emporium of literature and art," which has long since been metamorphosed into a hotel. His next stage of progress was to the "less showy but more active duties of general clerk and messenger" for the excellent Jonathan Leavitt, the "leading New York publisher of theological and religious books, particularly in connection with Crocker & Brewster, of Boston." In his "Rough Notes" Mr. Putnam has so pleasantly sketched "the trade" as it then (1832-3) existed in the United States that we are tempted to reproduce it for the benefit of those of our readers who have not seen it in the pages of the "Circular." The trade in those days were: In Boston, Lincoln & Edmonds (succeeded by Gould & Lincoln), devoted especially to the views of the Baptists; Crocker & Brewster (still flourishing as the oldest book firm in the United States), the leading Orthodox Congregationalist publishers; Cummings & Hilliard (afterwards Hilliard, Gray & Co.), chiefly engaged in school-books; Lilly, Wait & Co., reprinters of the foreign reviews, etc.; R. P. & C. Williams, in the general trade; Allen & Ticknor (predecessors of the present well-known firm of Ticknor & Fields), on the classic corner of School Street, clinging with praiseworthy tenacity to the venerable old building which has survived some five or six generations; Little & Brown, still flourishing in strength, wealth, and respectability, though they have lost the original junior partner, Mr. Brown, one of the ablest and best-informed publishers this country has produced; Perkins & Marvin, and some smaller concerns, were also flourishing in Boston.

In New York, the old and most respectable firm of Collins & Hannay carried on the best of the jobbing trade on Pearl Street, the sorted stock of Dabolls, and Websters, and slates, and sponges, and Ames's papers, filling three or four lofts, supervised by the versatile and witty John Keese; T. & J. Swords, the "ancient" Episcopal publishers in Broadway, whose imprint may be found dated as early as 1792; Evert Duyckinck, an estimable man, father of the well-known authors, E. A. and G. L. Duyckinck; S. Wood & Sons (the sons worthily continuing), and Joseph B. Collins in the school-book and jobbing trade; Elam Bliss, the gentlemanly and popular literary caterer on Broadway (where Trinity Buildings now stand), whose elegant little "Talisman," edited by Bryant, Verplanck, and Robert C. Sands was the father of American "Annuals," and a good deal better than some of the children; G. & C. Carvill, the English successors of the still more famous Eastburn, on the corner of Wall Street and Broadway, the most extensive retail dealers in general literature (including English books), and, like Bliss's opposite, the lounging place of the *literati;* George Dearborn, then a new star, also "gentlemanly" and intelligent, issuing double-column Byrons, Shakespeares, Johnsons, Brookses, and Rollinses, besides the "American Monthly," the "Republic of Letters," and the "New York Review;" Jonathan Leavitt, as aforesaid, taking charge especially of the department of theology; and the Brothers Harper were building up their gigantic business of producing general literature, then chiefly consisting of reprints from English authors.

In Philadelphia this main branch of the trade was then largely in the control of Carey & Lea, successors of the famous Mathew Carey, a name that will always be remembered as an honor to our craft, in the premises still occupied by the wealthy firm of Blanchard & Lea, the leading medical publishers. This house was then issuing, in quarterly volumes, the "Encyclopedia Americana," edited by Dr. Lieber, an enterprise of considerable magnitude for that day. Carey & Hart, in the same "corner of Sixth and Chestnut," rivaled the Harpers in their dispensations of the new novels, and also in more solid literature. John Grigg, a publisher and bookseller of remarkable ability, rare judgment, and tact, afterwards Grigg & Elliot, published largely in medicine (as well as the Careys) [but "everybody knows Eberic's is the best 'Practice' "], and the standard poets "in the best Philadelphia sheep," and "Weems's Washington," and "Gaston's Collections," and "Wirt's Patrick Henry," and the "Cases of Conscience," but doing a still greater trade in furnishing the country dealers in a thousand places, South and West, with their whole supplies of books and stationery, thus founding the present extensive business of Lippincott & Co., besides one or two princely fortunes for the retiring partners. The rest of the trade in school and other books was divided between Hogan & Thompson, Uriah Hunt, Key & Biddle, and a few others.

In Andover, Mass., Mr. Flagg printed the learned works of Moses Stuart and Leonard Woods. In Hartford, "Uncle Silas" Andrus would grind out cords of

Shakespeares, Byrons, Bunyans, and Alonzo and Melissas, suited for the country trade; and the Huntingtons and Robinsons produced cart-loads of Olneys and Comstocks. In Springfield, the Merriams printed Chitty's law-books and others, but had not yet begun to work the golden mine of "Webster's Unabridged." Here and there a book would come along with the imprint of Hyde of Portland, Kay of Pittsburg, Howe of New Haven, Metcalf of Cambridge, Gould of Albany, Armstrong of Baltimore; but the three great cities first named, then as now monopolized the bulk of the book-making: Boston rather leading the van. The importation of English books was almost wholly in the hands of Thomas Wardle, of Philadelphia, a sturdy Yorkshireman, who had served as a porter at Longmans' in London.

About this time (1832) Mr. Putnam modestly appeared before the world as the author of a volume of some 400 pages, entitled "Chronology, an Introduction and Index to Universal History." This manual, commenced at the age of fifteen, was a well-digested collation of the various histories, some 150 in number, which he had read during his evenings after he was dismissed from the shop—and that, in those days, was not until 9 o'clock P.M. The edition of 1,000 copies was among the stock divided between Daniel Appleton and Jonathan Leavitt when they separated and set up business independently of one another, and was soon sold out, much to the surprise and pleasure of its juvenile author, who had originally compiled it simply for his own benefit. His native Yankee "push," and, perhaps, also, the success of his first venture at book-making now led young Putnam to attempt what then seemed a *desideratum* in the trade—a periodical register of the publishing business. So he coaxed an enterprising firm of printers, West & Trow (the latter of whom is still an eminent landmark in his profession), to let him edit such a paper for them. It was accordingly issued through the year 1834, under the title of the "Bookseller's Advertiser," and though its scope was limited, it was received with favor, and promised to pay. Other duties, however, prevented its youthful projector and editor from devoting the requisite time to it, and it was, in consequence, discontinued.

In the year 1836, Mr. Putnam was invited to become a junior partner in the house of Wiley & Long, of 161 Broadway, then just beginning to cultivate the trade in English and foreign books; the capital stock which he contributed to the firm being only $150, and such experience in the trade as he had picked up. The same year he was dispatched to Europe for the purpose of arranging foreign purchases and correspondence; his tour of eight months resulted satisfactorily, and led to a business of considerable interest and value. In 1837, Mr.

Putnam, together with George B. Collins and John Keese, conceived the idea of a booksellers' dinner to authors, which came off at the Old City Hotel on the 30th of March. It was the first affair of the kind ever attempted in America, and deserved the success which it met with; one hundred authors and editors, as well as many of the trade from other cities, being the guests of nearly one hundred booksellers of New York. About this time the firm to which Mr. Putnam belonged proposed to establish a branch of their house in the city of London, there to import American books for the English market, and to purchase European books for this. The duty was again devolved upon Mr. P., who, in the spring of 1838, established in London the first permanent agency for American literature in England—thus laying the foundation of the trade in American books which has since been so extensively and successfully carried on by Low, Greene & Co., Trübner & Co., Joseph Chapman, and others. His location was at 67 Paternoster Row, and afterwards at "Amen Corner" and Stationer's Hall Court, adjoining Whittaker's and Simpkin & Marshall's, and near Longmans'. Subsequently (induced by a laudable desire to display his Yankee literary wares before the "West End," and under the very noses of the "M.P.'s"), Mr. Putnam took possession of premises in Regent Street which had formerly been occupied by a club, and in the immediate vicinity of the United Service and the Athenæum club-houses. On the handsome portico of this new and aristocratic shop were brilliantly displayed the words, "American Literary Agency;" and it soon became a pleasant resort for the literati, the trade, and last, but not least, for some of the prominent statesmen of the day, who were more or less curious about American progress in literature, and who not infrequently dropped in to look around. It was in answer to questions from many of these visitors, and to sneers and misstatements of American affairs in the newspapers, that Mr. Putnam compiled and published, in 1844, a small octavo volume entitled "American Facts," which elicited a good deal of favorable, and even courteous, notice from the English press, even from that portion of it which had been most abusive of our institutions. It was a vindication of his native country against the prejudices, abuse, and misrepresentations which were at that time thrown at her by the English journals, on the score of slavery, repudiation, liquor laws, etc., and evinced an extensive acquaintance with the history, statistics, etc., of the United States, and an intelligent appreciation of our institutions and character.

In 1847 Mr. Putnam returned to New York, where, during his absence, his partner, Mr. Wiley (Mr. Long having retired), had published a considerable number of books, original and reprinted. Among them were the works of Downing, the horticulturist, and Professors Mahan, Alexander, and Ruskin. The most notable publications of the firm, however, were the "Library of Choice Reading," a series of fifty volumes printed in a style somewhat better than the average of the cheap literature of the day, and comprising such works as those of Carlyle, Leigh Hunt, Hood, Lamb, Keats, Hazlitt, and others, and of which the success was very remarkable, some volumes reaching a sale of 6,000 or 7,000 copies. There was, also, the "Library of American Books," including works by Hawthorne, Bayard Taylor, Simms, Judge Hall, etc., and, like the "Choice Library," issued under the supervision and editorship of the accomplished E. A. Duyckinck.

The amicable dissolution of the firm of Wiley & Putnam, in 1848, left Mr. Putnam with his moderate portion of the stock, but without much cash capital, to commence a separate business of his own, which he established at 155 Broadway. Nothing daunted, however, he set himself about the preparation and publication of a "revised edition" of Irving's works in a style of typography and appearance far in advance of anything which had then been attempted in this country. It was in all respects a hazardous enterprise—one at which the most eminent and sagacious publishers here looked somewhat askance; but it was a perfect success. These American *classics* were, for the first time, presented in a neat and uniform shape, on fair paper and with neat externals, and the stereotyping, by Mr. Trow, was thought by Murray, the well-known English publisher, to be good enough for his market, and he purchased duplicates of the plates, from which the London edition was printed. Artists and designers, also, have referred to the cuts which illustrated these works as giving a new impetus here to the art and business of wood-engraving. Irving's works have proved to be a remarkably remunerative piece of literary property. The revised edition, commenced in 1848, reached a sale of about 10,000 copies of each volume, while, in the course of publication, prior to 1865, the sale amounted to nearly 50,000 sets. The first edition of "Irving's Life of Washington," in five vols. octavo, was sold by subscription to the extent of about 18,000 sets. An edition of 110 copies was also published in quarto form, with 100 proof plates; a copy of this, illustrated with 1,036 extra portraits, autographs, and views, brought, at the sale of Mr. Andrew Wight's library, of Philadelphia, in 1864, the sum of $775 00. Another edition, in numbers, with steel plates (costing nearly $10,000), was also completed in five volumes royal octavo. Of a large-paper edition of "Irving's Complete Works" and the "Life," in 26 volumes, 100 copies were printed for subscribers, and these sets are now valued at double the original price. An illustrated edition of the "Sketch Book," "Knickerbocker," and "Traveler," with designs by Darley, each in octavo, had a sale of some 2,500 copies. The "Artist's Edition" of the "Sketch Book" was commenced in 1860 and issued in 1863. It was illustrated from the designs of about fifty of the leading American artists; and, in respect to paper, engraving, presswork, and binding, it was an attempt fully equaling, if not rivaling, the choicest productions of our home or foreign presses. The cost of production of the first edition of 1,000 copies was $15,000. The "National Edition" of Irving's works was issued in monthly volumes to subscribers, commencing in 1860, and 3,500 sets were printed. The "Riverside Edition," in 16mo, commenced in 1863, and now in course of publication, is becoming very popular. The "Regular" or "Library Edition" now in the market is called the "Sunnyside Edition," and comprises the whole of Irving's works in 26 volumes. Over 40,000 volumes of Irving's works are now sold every year. The "Sketch Book" seems to be, from the publisher's stand-point, the most popular of all of Irving's works, closely followed, however, by "Knickerbocker's New York," "Bracebridge Hall," and "The Traveler." The reader will find, in an appendix to the fourth volume of the "Life and Letters of Irving," an interesting statement of the amount of copyright paid to the author and his executors by Mr. Putnam prior to 1864.

Among Mr. Putnam's other publications, Bayard Taylor's works have attained no inconsiderable pecuniary value. The sales of "Views Afoot" have reached about 30,000 copies; the other "Travels" from 12,000 to 15,000—the demand for the series continuing steadily. Of his later works, "Hannah Thurston" 18,000, and of "John Godfrey's Fortunes" 13,000, copies have been sold thus far.

In 1853, having removed from 155 Broadway to 10 Park Place, he received Mr. John M. Leslie as a partner, and the firm took the style of Geo. P. Putnam & Co. In January of this year they issued the first number of "Putnam's Monthly Magazine," designed—as a private circular issued to the *literati* in October, 1852, expressed it—"to combine the popular character of a magazine with the higher and graver aims of the quarterly review;" to "preserve, in all its departments, an independent and elevated tone," and to be an original "organ of American thought." The plan was acceptable, and the magazine immediately assumed a prominent stand in the world of literature. The first edition of the first number was 10,000 copies. This had Longfellow's poem on Wellington—nothing else specially notable—yet the demand at once exhausted this and three or four successive editions, reaching an aggregate of 20,000. The second number, in which was the first "Bourbon" article, the first of the "Potiphar Papers," and several other hits, at

AMERICAN LITERARY AGENCY IN LONDON.

G EORGE P. PUTNAM begs to inform his friends and correspondents that his interest in the above Agency, originally established by him in 1838, has *not* passed into the hands of any other person.

Orders for English and Foreign Books of all kinds, *if sent to Mr. Putnam at New York*, will be sure of receiving prompt and careful attention in the most economical manner. Mr. Putnam has special Agents also in Paris, Leghorn, Brussels, Hamburgh, and St. Petersburgh.

Consignments of AMERICAN BOOKS SUITED for the London Market should also be sent as above, to 155 Broadway, New York.

G. P. PUTNAM, relying upon his long experience in this business in Europe, will continue to give thorough and personal attention to it, and is prepared to receive Orders of PUBLIC LIBRARIES, as well as from Individuals and the Trade, for large numbers or single books.

Address, in all cases,

☞ G. P. PUTNAM, 155 *Broadway, New York,*

who will send out orders by every Steamer up to the hour of closing the Mail, and give all information required.

Advertisement in the 15 June 1850 issue of The Literary World. *Although he ceded the Wiley and Putnam London office to Wiley at the time of their separation, Putnam maintained his own overseas commission agency for supplying customers with European books and periodicals.*

once attracted general attention and insured a paying success. An edition of 30,000 was established as a minimum, and of some successive numbers 35,000 were printed. This number, compared to that wonderfully cheap and excellent popular magazine from Cliff Street, then in the full tide of success, was insignificant, but it was in advance, probably, of any original magazine, resting solely on its literary merits, either in this country or in Europe. Each number of the "Monthly" was stereotyped; and the amount paid to contributors and editors for the first two years was $12,819, besides the sum of $3,000, cost of illustrations, which, perhaps, were superfluous. In 1855 the magazine, then two and a half years old, was sold to Messrs. Dix & Edwards, a new firm, and on their own unsolicited proposals, for the snug sum of $11,000. Previously, however, to this, in September, 1854, Putnam & Co., finding themselves incumbered with too much stock, and too heavy a load of responsibility, suddenly decided to sell at auction the larger portion of their stock and stereotypes. A few days' notice only was given; and the business was effected in a single extra day of the trade sale then in session. Beginning at 9 A.M. and closing at midnight of the same day, this sale brought the handsome sum of $70,000. Among the books of their publication thus suddenly disposed of were the plates of snug library editions of "Addison" and "Goldsmith;" Downing's "Landscape Gardening" and "Rural Essays;" "Homes of American Authors" and "Homes of American Statesmen," choice illustrated volumes; the series of five "Home Cyclopedias;" Layard's "Nineveh;" "Hood's Miscellaneous Works," and a host of other works by American and foreign authors. After all this cleaning out of stock and plates, the firm still retained the works of Irving, Bayard Taylor, Miss Warner, the "Monthly Magazine," the "Illustrated Record of the Crystal Palace Exhibition," and others.

This Crystal Palace book was one of the most creditable undertakings which was ever assumed by an American publisher. Under the delusion that the Exhibition of 1854 would prove a profitable as well as honorable success, Mr. Putnam conceived the idea of producing an illustrated book which should be at least equal, in mechanical execution, to the "London Art Catalogue" of the English exhibition. He accordingly got it up in a manner highly creditable to his taste and generosity, but entirely regardless of expense; the result being that the whole cost of 15,000 copies was nearly $40,000, and the actual loss on the affair was about $20,000! In 1855 Mr. Putnam removed to 321 Broadway, where he remained until his removal, in 1862, to 441 Broadway.

–*The Round Table,* 3 (10 February 1866): 90–91

* * *

II.

IN April, 1861, Mr. Charles T. Evans, who had previously had charge of the subscription and canvassing department of Messrs. G. P. Putnam & Co.'s business, suggested the expediency of publishing a serial which should contain a register of current events connected with the war then just commenced. Mr. Putnam undertook this enterprise, although somewhat reluctantly, under the impression that it would be completed in one, or at most two, volumes. The title of the work, as well as its plan and arrangement, were also suggested by him. As it happened, the same paper which contained the first announcement of this projected enterprise also contained the proposals for a similar work by Mr. Frank H. Moore, and intended to be on the plan of his "Diary of the American Revolution." Negotiations ensued, by which it was arranged that Mr. Moore, abandoning his own plan, should become the editor of "The Rebellion Record," sharing the profits with Mr. Evans and the publisher. In December, 1863, Mr. Evans's interest was purchased by Mr. Henry Holt, a graduate of Yale, and thus, for the first time, introduced to the book-publishing fraternity; in January, 1865, the interests of both Mr. Putnam and Mr. Holt were purchased by Mr. D. Van Nostrand for the sum of $12,000. The work is approaching completion, and will probably fill 12 volumes. Of the first volume of this "Record" nearly 10,000 copies were sold.

In the year 1862 Mr. Putnam received the appointment of Collector of the U. S. Internal Revenue for the Eighth District of the State of New York, which position he still continues to hold. This was in no sense a political appointment, but was granted in response to the application of Mr. William Cullen Bryant, Hon. George Bancroft, and other prominent citizens of New York, who requested it as a personal favor to themselves. The gift, though valuable in itself (the Eighth being an important income district), received an additional value from the graceful manner in which it was bestowed by Secretary Chase, who pleasantly assured the recipient, in reply to an expression of thanks, that he "must thank 'Putnam's Monthly' for that."

In 1864 Mr. Putnam farmed out his stereotype plates (comprising Irving's works, Taylor's travels, etc.) and publishing business for a limited time to Hurd & Houghton, thus forming a partial connection with that new and enterprising house.

We deem it proper to conclude our notice of Mr. Putnam with a brief notice of the books written by him during his long and busy career as a publisher:

1. "Chronology: An Introduction and Index to Universal History, Biography, and Useful Knowledge," etc., etc. 12mo, pp. 352. New York: Jonathan Leavitt & Daniel Appleton. 1832.

2. "The Tourist in Europe." 12mo. Wiley & Putnam. 1837. [Intended as a guide-book, as well as a record of a brief tour.]

3. "American Facts. Notes and Statistics relative to the Government, Resources, Engagements, Manufactures, etc., etc., of the United States. With Map." London: Wiley & Putnam. 1844. Pp. 292. With portraits.

4. "The World's Progress: A Dictionary of Dates." 8vo, pp. 859. New York: G. P. Putnam. 1850.

[This volume, of which about 10,000 copies have been sold, was founded partly on the "Chronology" compiled by Mr. Putnam in 1832, and partly on Hayden's "Dictionary of Dates," which was freely used.]

5. "A Pocket Memorandum Book in Italy and Germany in 1847." Privately printed. 16mo quarto. 1848.

[This is, in fact, a reprint of notes first issued in the "Literary World." A copy of this little work, belonging to the late John Allan, inlaid and illustrated, was sold, at the sale of his library, for $82 50.]

Besides these, "The American Book Circular," 8vo, pp. 32, issued in London 1840–41, contained a compilation of facts on the progress of American literature, which received considerable attention from the London *Athenæum* and other English journals. Mr. Putnam is also the author of a "Statistical Address prepared for the Publishers' Fruit Festival," held at the New York Crystal Palace in 1854, and an article in the "Knickerbocker Magazine" for September, 1861, on the battle of Bull Run. He has been, moreover, a frequent contributor to the columns of the *New World, Commercial Advertiser,* and *Evening Post.*

—*The Round Table,* 3 (17 February 1866): 106

Notes on Books and Booksellers

The following appreciative account of G. P. Putnam's operations originally appeared in 1868 in the New York Evening Post, *whose publisher, William Cullen Bryant, and editor, Parke Godwin, were longtime Putnam friends and colleagues; it was reprinted in the* American Literary Gazette and Publishers' Circular. *Bryant used his considerable political influence in the Republican Party to lobby President Abraham Lincoln's administration to get Putnam a government patronage office. He also collaborated with Putnam in founding the International Copyright Association and occasionally contributed to G. P. Putnam publications.*

* * *

PUTNAM & SON.—Mr. George P. Putnam has been engaged in the book trade for thirty-five years. His business is now very prosperous, and steadily increasing under the management of himself and his son. Their salesrooms at No. 661 Broadway present a cosy retreat for those desirous of either purchasing or examining the works of standard authors, or the current literature of the day. Their sale of Irving's works continues to be immensely large. For some weeks back they have not been able to supply the demand for them, so great has it been. This circumstance, together with the fact that Hurd & Houghton have sold during the year more of Cooper's novels than ever before, proves that they are mistaken who assert that the writings of our old American authors are less sought after as time goes by. More than a million copies of "Geoffrey Crayon" works have thus far been disposed of. Messrs. Putnam & Son are now publishing three editions of these works, which are to be issued punctually on the first day of each month until completed. They began with "Bracebridge Hall" in October. The editions are known as "The Knickerbocker," "The Riverside," and "The People's." The "Sunnyside" edition is now published complete in 28 volumes.

The favorable reception everywhere extended to "Putnam's Monthly," indicates that the public were not only ready but eager for its reappearance. The demand for the first number gives assurance to believe that it will shoot rapidly ahead of some of the periodicals which have sprung up during the period of its suspension, and quickly attain its former circulation and popularity.

—*American Literary Gazette and Publishers' Circular,*
octavo series 10 (1 January 1868): 155–156

William Cullen Bryant at sixty

Mary Putnam, the oldest Putnam child, in 1866, shortly before she left home to study medicine in Paris (courtesy of the Library of Congress)

A Daughter's Appreciation

The author of "George P. Putnam: An Appreciation" was his oldest child, Mary Putnam Jacobi (1842–1906). She was born in England during her parents' London residence and was educated in various schools in the United States before becoming the first woman admitted to the School of Medicine at the Sorbonne, from which she graduated with her medical degree in 1871. She returned to the United States and went into private practice, earning a national reputation as a medical practitioner, researcher, and crusader for women's medical education.

Mary Putnam's choice of career put her into conflict with her father, who considered medicine unfeminine. Despite that disagreement and a difference of temperaments, their relationship was cordial, as her remarks here demonstrate. In a footnote to this essay, which George Haven Putnam included in his 1903 memoir of his father, he writes, "This graceful and discriminating appreciation, which was originally printed anonymously, may now properly be credited to its author, my sister Minnie."

* * *

George P. Putnam: An Appreciation

At the funeral services of George P. Putnam, when, as is the custom, an attempt was made to sum up the character of the life that had closed, Mr. Elder, his pastor, called it "pure, patient, gentle, self-sacrificing." No words could have been more fitly chosen, and not one could have been spared. The purity of his nature was so perfect, so childlike, that I think he was hardly ever called upon to resist a temptation, for many things that would have seemed such to other men were regarded by him as simple impossibilities. I remember, however, one vanquished in his boyhood. He was hardly twelve years old, a fatherless lad, trying to make his way in commercial life as youngest clerk or errand-boy in a Boston store. He was living with very strict relatives, whose religious principles forbade the indulgence of any "worldly" amusements. The little fellow, however, whose imagination was hungry and craved nourishment, contrived two means of satisfying it. He carried a volume of Miss Edgeworth's tales about with him, and read them whenever sent on an errand; afterwards, stimulated to greater daring by this first nibble at forbidden fruit, he managed to make several secret visits to the theatre. But this last concealment was too serious a strain upon his conscience, and one evening a sudden self-reproach arrested him in what then seemed a "mad career,"—on the road to the theatre. He turned round, walked home, and voluntarily renounced the enticing pleasure; even the innocent dissipation of Miss Edgeworth's stories was for a while given up, under the pressure of remorse. I do not know that he ever suffered remorse again in his life.

Mr. Putnam's judgments of things were formed from their sunny and kindly, but also superficial aspect. Worldly superficiality is common, but unworldly superficiality is rare. The reason is, that most men who escape from the world do so in virtue of a profounder reflection that pierces its illusions and seeks more solid ground than its sham supports. But he escaped, even to the end of his life, by the same instinctive purity and naïveté of feeling that we fancy we detect in a child who prefers flowers to diamonds. He had, indeed, a naïve delight in the sheen and glitter of certain worldlinesses, but this always took one shape,—the sense of pleasure of belonging to a social institution, or a group, or an individuality wider than his own. He was so completely destitute of arrogance or self-assertion that he habitually thought of what he was or what he did as quite insignificant, but attached a rather whimsical importance to the occasions which had brought him in contact with notable things, events, or men. I have heard him relate many times, and with the utmost glee, the account of some public banquet to which he was invited in London, which was graced by the presence of many eminent men, and over which Prince Albert presided.

Early in life, when Mr. Putnam was principally associated with men of letters and of the world, he never forgot to lend his share of support to the Church. During the last fifteen years, when religious belief had become a matter of profound personal experience with him, and he was associated with many who "dreaded the world," he entered with even more earnestness into schemes for the general improvement of society by means of political reforms in cities, or the establishment of reading-rooms and lecture associations in country places—of innocent enjoyment everywhere. Within my recollection of him, though now long ago, he did active battle for Frémont, in the great campaign of '56, that virtually forbade the extension of slavery into the Territories; and during the last year of his life he was an active though unostentatious member of the Council for Political Reform, that he helped to found. As a young man, hewing a way for himself in London, he wrote his volume of *American Facts,* proud to vindicate the reputation of his country in Europe. And it is well known to many of his fellow- citizens, that almost his latest and most enjoyed efforts were in behalf of their Metropolitan Art Museum, which seemed to him to foreshadow European glories for New York, which opened an illimitable vista to his imagination, and about which he dreamed fondly, in the quaint, shy, reticent manner in which he always dreamed.

His interest in art was, indeed, chiefly the expression of his general interest in the moral welfare of society. He had, as had been said, an almost human fondness for pictures and books, such fondness as we sometimes have for dumb animals, for their own sake, and not for what they cannot say to us. He never received the intellectual training requisite for the thorough study of any one thing, and his was not a powerfully concentrated nature, able to dispense with such training and grasp a subject for himself. But without the knowledge requisite for real intellectual culture, his innate refinement and natural taste gave him a love for beautiful things that he desired to see propagated as a humanizing influence. He had that craving for harmony and orderly fitness which, carried further, becomes an artistic faculty, but which with him predominantly suggested his love of peace and good-will. He was so thoroughly gentle himself that he always

believed that men only had to be soothed in order to be purified; and his desire for purity gave a latent enthusiasm to his social efforts, and tinged many things for him with a certain romantic ideality. By the side of the restless activity that distinguished his youth was another nature, quiet and dreamy, such as characterizes men who have spent their lives as custodians in the cloistered libraries of great museums of the Old World. It was this that gained ground as he grew older (for he did not live to grow old), and when those who stood nearest to him could mark that the pulses of his life were beating with greater stillness. He was looking forward, I think, to a quiet old age, to an afternoon of beneficent leisure, filled with social plannings, such as has the legitimate reward of a broad and sympathetic and reverent life. It seems hard that this should have been denied him.

His beneficence, however, did not wait for old age or for leisure; it was so spontaneous with him that it imitated none other, but was always characteristic of himself. He made no researches, he originated no missions,—he shrank from those departments of philanthropic work that unmask depths of wretchedness and degradation. He left to others the task of digging painfully at the roots of things, but devoted himself all the more earnestly to his own work of diffusing brightness, and pleasantness, and sunniness on the surface. It has always seemed to me rather whimsically typical of him, that the one general mission among the poor with which I knew him to be connected was an enterprise for establishing public baths and wash-houses. He used to laugh over this himself. He perfectly illustrated the rather subtle distinction that exists between a thoroughly public-spirited man and a philanthropist. Both are good, but few men can be everything.

His public spirit was the result both of instinct and principle; his kindness was always personal, and so natural that it seemed scarcely to require the intervention of principle. It was both in social beneficence and in individual kindness that he habitually sought refuge from personal care. I remember once, when some financial crisis had just inflicted upon him losses that he could ill afford to sustain, and when he might be well supposed to be absorbed in the future of his own family, he took a poor widow with her children from a wretched tenement house in the city, found a home for them in the country near his own, and for months watched over them with unforgetting solicitude. He believed very practically in the doctrine, "As ye do unto them, so also will your heavenly Father do unto you."

Other kindnesses, however, he did not recognize to be such. His business brought him into frequent relation with a class for whom he always had the most profound and chivalrous sympathy,—poor and solitary women struggling to maintain themselves by the uncertain profits of the pen. I do not know that anything touched him so much,—and this never failed to touch him. To refuse the manuscript of such a one, when he had once made personal acquaintance with her, was a positive pain to him; and the care with which he tried to soften such refusal and render it "less ungracious" has certainly been appreciated by many with whom he has had to do. This word "ungracious" was very frequently on his lips, and was one of his strongest expressions of disapproval. I think the idea of showing indifference or rudeness to the personal presence of another human being struck him as something like blasphemy, of which he was indeed literally incapable. He would sometimes say at a distance, "So-and-so is a queer genius,—I should like to give him a piece of my mind"; but, once brought in contact with the offender, the suavity which was the literal expression of the goodness of his heart, and never disguised his independence, always prevented the threatened verbal retribution.

He theorized so little, that it was easy for him to be consistent. His philosophy was wonderfully homogeneous, and stood the test of every trial, great or small. He believed in the first place in the most absolute liberty for every human being, and had a perfect horror of every kind of coercion or tyranny, temporal or spiritual, social or domestic. The large indulgence that outsiders noticed in his treatment of children from infancy upward was regarded by himself as a matter of simple justice. He disclaimed all right to interfere with the individuality of another human being, which seemed to him sacred, though it were that of his own children. He always showed a fastidious delicacy in regard to speech with them on topics of intimate personal experience, and his rare words of counsel and admonition were generally conveyed by letter, and with an eloquence unsuspected by those who knew the hesitancy with which he spoke.

His general elastic confidence in the integrity and good intentions of mankind was absolute in regard to those in whose veins ran his own blood. Whatever the disagreement, either in theoretical belief or in practical preferences, he never allowed it to become a cause of separation or of distrust; but with a rare sweetness and magnanimity of feeling himself set it aside, and acted as though it never had been. He really dreaded imposing his own opinions even upon those who were naturally bound to be guided by them; and was always ready to further their plans because they were theirs, even when in themselves they crossed his wishes, or seemed to him absurd.

He was thus endeared to his children by the very things that so often introduce alienation and discord into families, and he had the satisfaction in many cases of seeing the final triumph of his own wishes, whose silent weight he had not deigned to enforce by command or exhortation.

His second fundamental belief was certainly in Providence. Even in the space of my recollection of him, I can trace the gradual evolution of this belief from the general conviction "that everything would turn out for the best," a conviction at first originating in the constitutional elasticity and animal spirits of his youth and younger manhood. When he was young, he looked persistently on the bright side of things because it attracted him; when he was older, he kept his eyes steadily fixed in the same direction, because he would have esteemed it a wicked unthankfulness to have done otherwise. The name of God was rarely upon his lips, but it was frequently in his heart, and his constant watchword in any trouble or misfortune was, "We have had so many mercies, we have no right to complain." He was indeed spared a long catalogue of the worst misfortunes that fall so thickly on many, and which never even menaced him, but a man's judgment of his own fortunes depends more upon his own nature than on theirs. And into minute daily affairs—those that often torment people as by a rack of pins, so unnecessarily we think, yet so inevitably—he carried the same patience with which he confronted greater trials. It was touching to see in later years how his patience gained upon his hope,—to learn to recognize by a certain look that crossed his face at times, that the vivacity of his enjoyment had begun to lessen, and his sensitiveness to pain to increase. This transition is the common fate of all; its details may seem trivial, yet they are not so, for according to their nature they foretell the approach of a genial and loving or of a selfish and querulous old age. This last never could have been his, whose sympathies continually widened and deepened as he grew older,—with whom one amiable instinct after another became converted into a fixed principle, and who could thus be rightly ranked with those just men whose light shineth more and more unto the perfect day.

This was moral light. Intellectually, he accomplished his best work long before he died. Perhaps his period of greatest mental activity was the two years of his boyhood, from fifteen to seventeen, when, after working as a clerk until nine o'clock in the evening, he then studied until two, arranging material for *The World's Progress,* whose publication gave him a just title to precocious authorship. On account of its precocity, of the disadvantages in regard to leisure and previous education under which the boy labored, this book affords proof of a certain originality and boldness of mental conception which could not be fairly inferred from it were it the work of a mature man, or of one professing to be a ripe scholar. It is a proof, too, of the patient persistency that characterized him, and which was rather moral than intellectual. He had no capacity for intellectual research or analysis; he had a great deal for the grouping of things together in a manner to be most effective,—that is, to convey the most intelligible meaning to some one else, and I consider this preference another proof that his interest in literature, as in art, was, unconsciously to himself, chiefly moral. While he loved refinement, he hated subtleties; he admired a pithy sentence, even though it contained a loose thought, and, it must be acknowledged, he frequently failed to comprehend a pithy thought, especially if clothed in vague language. Associated with so many books, he really, after the one great effort of his boyhood, read few, and his taste lay very definitely in one direction—for the calm, even, harmonious style that we associate with Addison and Goldsmith and Irving.

His association with the latter writer has been so intimate, and is so well known, that to many it is perhaps the principal fact suggested by the mention of his own name. The association is not fortuitous, but, I think, really means all that it seems to imply. It has always been said that one peculiar charm of Irving's life of Goldsmith arises from the evident kinship that exists between the genius of the author and that of his hero. The devotion of one life to the interpretation of another always implies the consciousness of some such kinship between the two, even when the mode of expression of the genius be quite different, as in the case of Turner and Ruskin; or when the genius is all on one side, and on the other belongs only what Carlyle has well called "the genius of appreciation" in Boswell for Johnson. To this latter class of appreciative friendship belongs that which for so many years existed between Mr. Putnam and Washington Irving. This was much more than the ordinary relations between a publisher and author who share each other's success. Mr. Putnam was one of the first to appreciate Irving, and immediately devoted himself to the task of hewing out a road for his future reputation, with a zeal

and generous confidence that was certainly most generously recognized, and has been amply recompensed.

But this divination of Irving's possibilities for success, to whose external conditions he largely contributed, was not the mere insight of a man of business trained to detect what will succeed. It was rather that joyful perception of a person who meets in another the full and graceful and adequate expression of what he would like to say himself, and said in just the way in which he would wish to say it.

The serenity, the openness, the facility, the limpid clearness of Irving's style, and of Irving's not too deep thought, not less than the gentleness and geniality of his character, with its quaintness, its shy delicacy, its fastidious reserve, its unspoken depth of sentiment, its stainless honor, irresistibly attracted a nature, that, though intellectually inferior, was morally akin. A sketch of Irving that Mr. Putnam wrote for *Harper's Weekly,* about two years ago, shows distinctly the points at which he had attached himself to him,—the details upon which he most loved to dwell. Irving was, indeed, his hero, his ideal in the world of letter in which he lived, his type of the region of that world which he most preferred.

Irving has a national fame which will last, at least for a while; that of his friend, in the hurry of events, and in the urgent proportion of other things, must be sooner forgotten. It is for that very reason that I, as one of his nearest and dearest friends, have tried to gather up into an imperfect portrait these few traits of a man that I loved, not merely from habit and association, but because his character has always impressed me as winning and touching and lovely. He was nearly always inadequate fully to express himself; who is not that is worth the expression? He lacked grace and presence, so that his real depth and force were frequently concealed or misunderstood. But when these had once been felt, they were not easily forgotten. Nor, in a world thronged at once with louder merit and with vices yet more loud, can pass unprized and unmissed this life, which, though so energetic in action, possessed its greatest power in silence; and which, though so vivacious in worldly activity, yet through singleness of purpose and sincerity of belief ever kept itself at heart unspotted from the world.

M. P. J.

January, 1873.

—*A Memoir of George Palmer Putnam,* pp. 393–407

Eng.^d by Geo E. Perine, N.York

J. C. Derby, whose publishing house went under in the recession of 1857, worked for Putnam's firm in the early 1860s.

James C. Derby on Putnam

James Cephas Derby in Fifty Years among Authors, Books and Publishers *(1884) gave the fullest nineteenth-century treatment of the generation of literary professionals involved in the creation of the American publishing industry. Derby was the head of a middle-sized New York City publishing house that in its heyday in the mid 1850s published the works of Fanny Fern, and he was personally acquainted with many of his subjects. He knew Putnam especially well, since they were Yonkers neighbors in the 1850s, and Derby worked for G. P. Putnam for a time in the early 1860s while Putnam was active in government service.*

Derby's chapter on Putnam is as revealing about the terms and categories of mid-nineteenth-century literary publishing as it is about Putnam. What he knows about Putnam was presumably cobbled from various sources: his personal knowledge, conversations with George Haven Putnam, and Putnam's published writings, especially "Rough Notes of Thirty Years in the Trade."

* * *

GEORGE PALMER PUTNAM.

In the Front Rank of Publishers—Fellow Clerk with William H. Appleton—Becomes an Author at Eighteen—Starts a Branch in London—Effectually refutes Alison, the Historian—Bayard Taylor applies for Aid—Beginning of a long-lived Friendship—Edgar A. Poe astonishes the Natives—James Russell Lowell's Fables—The "Wide Wide World" and "Providence"—Becomes Irving's Publisher—Astonishes John Bull with "Sketch-Book"—Establishes Putnam's Magazine—First Advocate of International Copyright—Prince Albert, Irving and Putnam—Irving's First and only Love—Thackeray Lectures at Yonkers—Mr. Putnam's Sudden Death Mourned and Greatly Regretted—G. P. Putnam's Sons.

IN the front rank of our distinguished book-publishers belongs the honored name of George P. Putnam, who for nearly half a century gave lustre to the world of letters and books. From a very early age to the day of his lamented death, he devoted his business life to the vocation of his choice.

He was first employed, when about fourteen years of age, by George W. Bleecker, in a small book-store in New York, at a yearly salary of twenty-five dollars, exclusive of board and lodging. He afterwards took a position under Jonathan Leavitt, where he had special charge of the publications of Crocker & Brewster of Boston, Mr. Leavitt being their New York agent, and where at one time William H. Appleton was a fellow clerk.

In the year 1832, young Putnam began his first literary work, the compilation of an "Index to Universal History," which was the foundation of the important work—"The World's Progress," referred to hereafter. It was printed and published by Mr. Leavitt, who at that time had associated with him as a special partner, the late Daniel Appleton. The young author was much delighted at the success of his first venture, the small edition being readily disposed of.

His next undertaking was a monthly register of new publications called *The Bookseller's Advertiser*. This was commenced in January, 1834, when still in his teens, and was printed by John F. Trow, and lasted until December of the same year, in which number appeared the following valedictory:

"With the present number this little journal expires. It was commenced with the idea that it would be useful, not only to publishers, but to all who are interested in the literature of the day, and it is a satisfaction to know that however imperfectly it has been conducted amidst other responsibilities, it has been well received on both sides of the Atlantic, and has been noticed in complimentary terms by various contemporaries. I resign it because it cannot be properly attended to without interfering with more legitimate duties or infringing on midnight hours."

In the year 1836, Mr. Putnam became a partner in the publishing-house of Wiley & Long, contributing to the capital stock the sum of one hundred and fifty dollars in cash ; but what was more important than capital to them at that time, was his thorough acquaintance with authors and publishers, which, to the new firm, was invaluable. He was soon sent to Europe, where he made the acquaintance of many authors and the more important members of the book-trade. Establishing on one of his visits to London, in 1838, a branch-house—Mr. Long having retired—the new firm continued in both places as Wiley & Putnam. This was the first American house ever established in London for the publication of books, Mr. Putnam becoming a zealous representative of American interests. It became a favorite resort for all Americans residing or traveling in Europe, who were interested in literary matters.

About that time Alison, the celebrated historian, published his "History of Europe," in which appeared many passages regarding the progress of literature in America, which were anything but friendly or true. To the statements and assertions made by Alison, Mr. Putnam made a most effectual reply, in a published volume prepared by him entitled "American Facts," in which he proved conclusively the ignorance of the famous historian as to the real condition of American literature. The circulation of this volume did much to increase respect for the people of the United States in Europe. Mr. Putnam remained in charge of the London house until 1848, having resided there seven consecutive years, after which he returned to New York.

In the year 1847 Mr. Putnam received a call at his office in Waterloo Place from a young American printer, who had been making a journey through the continent, and whose funds were exhausted. Some remittances he had expected had not come to hand, and he was entirely destitute of the means of support, endeavoring to secure work at his trade in a London printing office, where he succeeded temporarily, but was thrown out of the first position he secured through the jealousy of English compositors, who were not willing to have in the office a foreigner not belonging to their typographical guild. Mr. Putnam sympathizing with the young American, gave him temporary clerical work. This timely assistance laid the foundation of a friendship, a very close one, which lasted as long as their lives.

Within a year after the acquaintance thus formed, Mr. Putnam had the pleasure of publishing the narrative of this young printer's trip over the continent under the title of "Views Afoot, or Europe seen with Knapsack and Staff," by Bayard Taylor. On its publication, the English reviews gave it unstinted praise. The London *Athenæum* said:

"That among the hundreds of volumes already issued on the same subject, Mr. Bayard Taylor's is the best and the liveliest. We too are richer for his travels by the amount of an earnest, manly and sensible book. There is nothing more graphic in De Foe."

At this time young Taylor was but twenty-one years of age. This, the first volume of his travels, has continued in demand for more than forty years, reaching a sale of over one hundred thousand copies. Mr. Putnam continued the publication of Bayard Taylor's Travels as they appeared from time to time, all of which met with unvarying success.

Another visit of a singular character which Mr. Putnam received about this time, was from Edgar A. Poe. The latter had brought some notes of introduction to Mr. Putnam to whom he represented that he had accidentally secured from a family in Nantucket, the narrative of a Nantucket seaman, containing his adventures in the Arctic regions. As the London public were specially excited at that time in consequence of the expedition of Sir John Franklin to the polar seas, Mr. Putnam, after glancing over the MS., which bore on its face an air of realism and made the story of the discovery of the MS. plausible enough, accepted and published the book. It was written in good but rather rough style, such as a Nantucket seaman might naturally use. In the haste to get the matter into type before a certain date, having a connection with this Arctic expedition, Mr. Putnam had not time to complete the reading of the MS, but sent it at once to the compositors. It was not until after the book was published and he had read the criticism of the volume in the *Saturday Review* and other influential journals, that he found it necessary to read the concluding page which ends as my readers may remember with the drowning of all, leaving no possibility for the narrator to reach home to tell the story, and the *Saturday Review* naturally inquired, "What is this Yankee publisher giving us?" The narrative of Arthur Gordon Pym was one of the improbable creations so prolific in Mr. Poe's brain.

After this, Mr. Putnam never published a book bearing his imprint without first completing the reading of it, or having it read by a trusty reader, with one exception, which will be referred to hereafter. In this connection, it may be well to mention another call made by Mr. Poe on Mr. Putnam in 1849, soon after the latter's return to New York. Poe called at his Broadway book-store after he had apparently dined a little heavily, sat down and wrote furiously until long after business hours, when the porter was obliged to close the store, thus virtually turning him out.

The next morning Poe brought to Mr. Putnam the MS. he had just written, and with a good deal of solemnity declared he had arrived at the solution of the secret of the Universe, which, when published, would make millions of dollars for both author and publisher. The millions were only in Poe's brain, for the first edition of Eureka, the work in question, was never exhausted by the current sales.

It is an interesting fact to state that the name of Putnam is yet connected with the publication of Poe's works. The present firm is now issuing a limited edition *de luxe* for subscribers only. The specimen volumes indicate that it will not only be the handsomest edition of Poe which has yet appeared, but one of the most elegant of the much sought after *de luxe* editions of standard authors.

In 1848, Mr. Putnam issued James Russell Lowell's Fable for Critics which created at that time something of a literary sensation.

The volume was affectionately inscribed to Charles F. Briggs, whose nom de plume "Harry Franco" was then well known in the literary world. Mr. Briggs was a great admirer of Mr. Lowell's genius. It was through him that I had the pleasure of an introduc-

James Russell Lowell in 1857 (photograph by Mathew Brady)

tion to that distinguished gentleman now so famous as an author and diplomat, representing the United States at the court of St. James, with credit to himself and honor to his country. The unique title-page is well worth reproducing here:

A

FABLE FOR CRITICS;

OR, BETTER,

A GLANCE

AT A FEW OF OUR LITERARY PROGENIES

(Mrs. Malaprop's word)

FROM

THE TUB OF DIOGENES;

A VOCAL AND MUSICAL MEDLEY,

THAT IS,

A SERIES OF JOKES

By a Wonderful Quiz,

who accompanies himself with a rub-a-dub-dub, full of spirit and grace, on the top of the tub.

Set forth in October, the 31st day,

In the year '48, G. P. Putnam, Broadway.

That popular novel "The Wide Wide World," by Miss Warner, had a singular advent into book form. Mr. Putnam was interested in the story, but thought it did not possess the qualities likely to insure its popularity, while its great length (it contained matter enough for two volumes) was not favorable to its success. His literary advisers all counselled him against it. His mother, however, happened to get hold of the MS. and after reading it, said to her son, "George, that is too good a book not to come into print, you must print it!" He took his mother's advice and published it. For months after it was issued, Mr. Putnam began to think he would have to charge the loss account to the score of filial obedience. The book remained stocked upon the shelves apparently without commercial value. His mother tried to cheer him by saying "that the book was so good, she was sure that Providence would aid him in the sale of it." As a matter of fact, Providence did help the matter out. The first favorable review of the work appeared in a Providence paper, and the first large order that was received was from a Providence bookseller. The sale in a few months amounted to over 40,000 copies, which yielded, of course, a large profit to both author and publisher. Miss Warner's next novel, "Queechy," was nearly as successful; although these two books were published more than thirty years ago, they have been selling steadily ever since. They are almost the only American novels published one-third of a century ago, that have a continued sale.

Mr. Putnam about this time published Dr. J. G. Holland's novel "Bay Path," which was as much a failure as his later works published by Scribner, have been successes.

In the year 1854, Mr. David A. Wells became associated with Mr. Putnam as a special partner. Mr. Wells is the well known writer on Political Economy and author of The Year's Book of Facts. He had had no experience in bookselling, but wanting to make himself useful as a member of the firm, and finding on the books certain uncollected accounts against prominent New York citizens, he asked his senior in a general way, whether it would not be a good thing to collect all of the over-due accounts. Mr. Putnam naturally replied it was a very desirable thing to do. Thereupon his energetic junior wrote sharp letters to the delinquents, among whom unfortunately, were a number of prominent people, including some literary men, who although responsible, were not generally prompt in the payment of their accounts, and with whom it was of course important to keep on good terms. Mr. Putnam was horrified during the next few days to receive indignant calls from old and responsible citizens to know why they were thus threatened with the terrors of the law. Most of them he was of course able to appease with satisfactory explanation. Mr. John Wiley, who was present, said it was the only time in which he ever saw Mr. Putnam angry, during the whole of their lifelong acquaintance. It is not supposed that this incident was incorporated in the next edition of Mr. Wells' Year Book of Facts. The latter soon retired from the firm to the more congenial atmosphere of authorship, in which he now holds a high rank.

The publication of the works of Washington Irving was the first important undertaking of Mr. Putnam after he established himself alone in 1848. The volumes which had previously appeared from Irving's pen had for three years been out of print. As previously stated, the Philadelphia publishers who had had charge of them had not felt sufficient encouragement to undertake the preparation of new editions. In fact they had practically advised Mr. Irving, that while his material was certainly very pleasant, and had met with a fair success, it would hardly be considered as belonging to permanent literature. Mr. Irving had become so completely discouraged as to his literary prospects, that he told one of his nephews, he supposed he would have to turn his hands to something else for a living, and as his previous business experience had not given him a very good idea of his own capacity, he was very much in doubt which way to turn. At this time of his despondency, came a proposition from Mr. Putnam to undertake the publication of the books then in existence, which Mr. Irving readily accepted. The following are the terms agreed upon as stated by Pierre M. Irving, in his interesting "Life of Washington Irving:"

"The agreement with Mr. George P. Putnam, by which Mr. Irving was to prepare revised copies of all his works for publication, bears date July 26th, 1848. By this arrangement, which was to continue for five years, Mr. Putnam was to have the exclusive right of publishing his already published works and writings, in uniform duodecimo volumes until the whole series was completed, at such intervals as the publisher might find most advantageous for the mutual interest of the parties. He had the right also to publish one or more of the works in a larger size and illustrated. Mr. Putnam was to be at the whole charge of publication 'including all the expenses thereto incident,' and was to pay Mr. Irving twelve and a half per cent. on the retail price of all the copies sold. The accounts of sales were to be balanced at the end of the year commencing with July, 1849; and the author was to receive in notes at four months, the amount accruing to him at the above rate; but, as Mr. Putnam agreed to pay him in quarterly payments, one thousand dollars for the first year, fifteen hundred for the second, and two thousand for the third, fourth and fifth years, all of which payments were to be made on account of the percentage above specified, in the confident expectation of the publisher that the year's receipts would overrun the amount advanced, and that the author would have a surplus to receive at the stated period of settlement. In case of a disappointment in this particular, and that the percentage within the year should not amount to the sum or sums advanced, the author was not called upon to refund any part of the advance. In other words, by this agreement, Mr. Putnam was answerable for the payment of eight thousand five hundred dollars, the sum provided for in the several annual advances, whatever be the amount of the percentage; but whenever this guarantee of eight thousand five hundred dollars should be covered by the gross amount of profits received by Mr. Irving, the advances were to cease; or, if continued at the stipulated rate, and at the annual settlement, it should appear that they had overrun the percentage, the author was to refund the difference."

It may be interesting to know that at no subsequent period, did the actual payments for royalty fail to considerably exceed the minimum above-named. Before the death of Mr. Irving he took pains to make a complete revision of nearly all of his works, adding, omitting and largely altering them.

In 1857, when Mr. Putnam was in business difficulties, Mr. Irving stepped forward and took control of the stereotype plates which had been Mr. Putnam's property, advancing upon these plates what money was needed. Mr. Irving was in a position to purchase the plates, if he desired, and such purchase would have been very advantageous to him. He preferred, however, simply to hold them for Mr. Putnam, replacing the latter in control, a few years later. During this time he received numerous propositions for the transfer of his writings to different houses in Boston and Philadelphia, but he told Mr. Putnam subsequently, that as long as a Putnam was in position to publish, Irving's writings should be in his hands, thus repaying ten years later, the confidence shown by Mr. Putnam in 1848.

In 1852, the author wrote his publisher as follows:

"Sunnyside, Dec. 27, '52.

* * * * * * * *

"For my own especial part let me say how sensibly I appreciate the kind tone and expressions of your letter, but as you talk of obligations to me, I am conscious of none that have not been fully counter-balanced on your part, and I take pleasure in expressing the great satisfaction I have derived throughout all our intercourse, from your amiable, obliging and honorable conduct. Indeed, I never had dealings with any man, whether in the way of business or friendship, more perfectly free from any alloy. That these dealings have been profitable is merely owing to your own sagacity and enterprise. You had confidence in the continued vitality of my writings when my former publishers had almost persuaded me they were defunct. You called them again into active existence and gave them a circulation that I believe has surprised yourself. In rejoicing at their success, my satisfaction is doubly enhanced by the idea that you share in the benefits derived from it.

"Wishing you that continued prosperity in business which your upright, enterprising, truthful and liberal mode of conducting its merits is calculated to ensure, I again invoke on you and yours a happy New Year."

A letter like this from Mr. Irving, is one that Mr. Putnam's sons may well be proud to inherit.

On going up to Sunnyside one afternoon and finding Mr. Irving writing at his little pine table, covered with papers in apparent confusion, there being evidently much need of space, Mr. Putnam said, "Mr. Irving, you ought to have a proper desk for arranging and sifting your materials. I am going to ask you to let me send you one." "Well, Putnam," said he, "I am afraid it will trouble me to get accustomed to anything but my old-fashioned table." However, Mr. Putnam sent up the desk with the stipulation that the old table should be given to him. At Mr. Putnam's next visit, the author was found fumbling over his manuscripts puzzled to know where he had disposed of his numerous papers, and grumbling dreadfully at his publisher's liberality. This historic table on which the works of the great author were written, was given to one of Mr. Putnam's sons.

When the artist's edition of the Sketch-book, which was so admirably illustrated by Daniel Huntington, F. O. C. Darley and other well known artists, was published, it was considered the most beautiful book that had yet been issued by an American publisher. There were several applications from the London trade who desired an edition with their imprint. Among them was the well known firm of Bell & Daldy, who ordered

one thousand copies on which their name appeared according to arrangement, as publishers. Soon after this order was given, Mr. Putnam met another London publisher, who, in a boastful tone, said to him, "You Americans do fair work, but it takes an English house to issue a book like this," as he took down a copy of the artist's edition of Irving's Sketch-book. "Such beautiful printing and wood drawing I have never seen." Mr. Putnam was of course delighted, and after he had explained that it was his own edition issued in America, the British bookseller enjoyed a laugh at his own expense. It is estimated that one hundred and seventy-five thousand dollars have been paid to Washington Irving and his heirs by George P. Putnam and his sons, for copyright.

The most important of Mr. Putnam's literary efforts was the completion of a large octavo volume, entitled, "The World's Progress, an Index to Universal History and a Cyclopedia of facts, Dates, and General Information."

This immense volume is the outgrowth of the small undertaking in 1832, before referred to, and is a lasting monument to Mr. Putnam's literary intelligence.

Mr. Putnam first met Washington Irving in Europe, on the 11th of May, 1842, on which occasion there was a notable gathering of distinguished authors to attend the annual dinner of the "Literary Fund," an organization for dispensing charities to disabled authors; this was the first appearance of Queen Victoria's young husband Prince Albert, in his presidential capacity; he made three speeches which Mr. Putnam says were more than respectable for a Prince, they were a positive success.

Among those present who made speeches were Hallam and Lord Mahon, the historians, and Campbell and Moore, the poets. Edward Everett was then the United States Minister at the Court of St. James, and Washington Irving was then on his way to Madrid, as Minister to Spain. Mr. Putnam says the speeches made on that occasion were long to be remembered; when the toast to the author of "Bracebridge Hall" was given the whole audience greeted that gentleman with rousing cheers. Mr. Irving, as was well-known by his friends, was anything but a speaker; when, therefore, he arose and in his modest and beseeching manner simply said, "I beg to return you my sincere thanks" his brevity seemed almost ungracious to those who did not know it was physically impossible for him to make a speech. Mr. Putnam says an Englishman, who sat near him said to his neighbor, "Brief!" "Yes," was the reply, "but you can tell the gentleman in the very tone of his voice."

Mr. Putnam in speaking of Mr. Irving's early engagement, says, that on one occasion a miniature of a young lady, intellectual, refined and beautiful, was handed to him by Mr. Irving, with the request that he would have a slight injury repaired by an artist and a new case made for it, the old one being actually worn out by much use; the painting, which was on ivory, was exquisitely fine. When Mr. Putnam returned it to him in a suitable velvet case, he took it to a quiet corner and looked intently on the face some minutes, apparently unobserved, his tears falling freely on the glass as he gazed. This was the miniature of the sister of the eloquent Ogden Hoffman. Mr. Putnam delicately suggests that it is for a poet to characterize the nature of an attachment so loyal, so fresh, and so fragrant forty years after death had snatched away the mortal part of the object of affection. It was generally known among the friends of J. Fenimore Cooper and Mr. Irving that there was for a time some estrangement between them, but from what cause it was not known.

Mr. Putnam says that one day after he had commenced the publication of the library edition of Cooper's works, Mr. Irving was sitting at his desk with his back to the door, when Mr. Cooper suddenly came in, in his usual bustling manner, standing at the office entrance talking. Mr. Irving did not turn and Mr. Cooper did not see him. Mr. Putnam, acting on the impulse of the moment, simply said, "Mr. Cooper, here is Mr. Irving;" the latter turned, Cooper held out his hand, cordially dashed at once into an animated conversation, and to Mr. Putnam's surprise and delight, took a chair and chatted for an hour on the topics of the day and some former days. They parted with cordial good wishes, and Mr. Irving afterwards frequently alluded to the incident as being a great gratification to him.

Mr. Putnam relates on another occasion, that as Mr. Irving and himself, while walking up Broadway, were passing a print window, Mr. Irving's eyes rested on the beautiful engraving "Christus Consolator." He stopped and looked at it intently for some minutes, evidently much affected by the genuine inspiration of the artist, in this remarkable representation of the Saviour as the Consoler of sorrow-stricken humanity. His tears fell freely. "Pray, get me that print," said he; "I must have it framed for my sitting-room." When he examined it more closely and found the artist's name, "It's by my old friend Ary Scheffer," said he, remarking further, that he had known Scheffer intimately, and knew him to be a true artist, but had not expected from him anything so excellent as this. Mr. Putnam afterwards sent him the companion, "Christus Remunerator," and the pair remained his daily companions till the day of his death.

Another incident in Mr. Putnam's recollections of Mr. Irving, which I find in the *Atlantic Monthly* of 1860, is doubly interesting to me. Mr. Thackeray had been invited to deliver his lecture on "Charity and Humor" at Yonkers, on the Hudson, of which place I

was at that time a resident. Mr. Thackeray was the guest of Mr. Frederick S. Cozzens, whose humorous "Sparrowgrass Papers" my firm had recently published. Mr. Irving, who had already met Mr. Thackeray, was present at the lecture. I can well remember that enjoyable occasion and the circumstances attending it. These well-known characters are all dead, first Mr. Irving, then Mr. Thackeray, next Mr. Cozzens, and last Mr. Putnam. Each died suddenly, without a moment's warning.

One of the most important enterprises inaugurated by Mr. Putnam was the publication of Putnam's *Monthly Magazine*. The idea was conceived by him in the year 1852 of establishing a monthly magazine both entertaining and practical; one suited to the family as well as to scholars. The contents were to consist entirely of original matter, contributed by the best writers in the country, and Mr. Parke Godwin and Mr. Charles F. Briggs to be the editors. The magazine was well received, and proved both a literary and commercial success. I have been looking over more than seventy letters from distinguished American poets and prose writers, promising to contribute to the new magazine in answer to Mr. Putnam's prospective circular. Among others, those of Edward Everett, James K. Paulding, William Cullen Bryant, Fitz Greene Halleck, William Gilmore Simms, Edwin P. Whipple, Richard H. Dana, Theodore S. Fay, Ralph Waldo Emerson and Henry W. Longfellow. The following from the poet Longfellow is a fair specimen of those received by the publisher.

> "Cambridge, October 22, 1852.
>
> "DEAR SIR:
>
> "I shall be very happy to contribute occasionally to the pages of your magazine, but will do so anonymously. At the same time I have no objection to have my name mentioned among the list of contributors if you think it worth while. If you like, I will send you a poem for your first number. How soon shall you want it?
>
> "Yours, very truly,
> HENRY W. LONGFELLOW."

The letter from T. Buchanan Read, the poet-painter, will be interesting, especially the portion relating to the Brownings—alluding, as it does, to Mrs. Browning's forthcoming poetic novel, "Aurora Leigh."

> "Florence, Italy, September 20th, 1854.
>
> "DEAR MR. PUTNAM:
>
> "The Brownings, the poets, having made inquiries of me in regard to American publishers, I took pride and pleasure in speaking of your house, as the most desirable in my estimation, especially for works such as theirs. They told me that they would both have new volumes ready for the press by the

next Spring, and that they would like to make some arrangements with an American publisher to bring them out simultaneously with their appearance in London, and desired me if I knew you, to inquire what terms you would be willing to allow them, if you thought worth while to enter into any arrangement. I promised them to do this, and if you think it worth while to reply, I will communicate to them anything you may desire; or if you prefer, you might address them directly. Mrs. Browning's poem is a romance in verse, which with her reputation in America would sell well. Mr. Browning's is a volume of lyrics, all new. In addressing you I am merely fulfilling a request on their part and a promise on mine. I gather from what they said that they would be glad also to contribute to your magazine. . . . I sincerely hope your magazine is still successful as it deserves to be. If I can be of any assistance, you have only to command me. I am happy to state, that I find at last success attending my studio. I am full of orders for pictures, so that I feel much more independent of the pen than heretofore! I never did write for money, but I have before now, been compelled to publish for it. I am now, I think, beyond the necessity of that. When I sent you that last poem, you may remember I set no price, intending that you might pay what you felt inclined to. I will, as soon as I can, get something not too long for your pages, and send you again on the same terms. If you were as rich as the Harpers, I might stand on the price, but under present circumstances, I am willing to write for you, as it is necessary, on your own terms, for something or nothing, as you may afford, until you find yourself fairly afloat again.

"Very truly,
T. BUCHANAN READ."

George W. Curtis' celebrated "Potiphar Papers" and Frederick S. Cozzens' equally celebrated "Sparrowgrass Papers" were originally contributions to Putnam's *Monthly Magazine*.

Mr. Putnam was the first American publisher of whom we have any account who took action on the question of International Copyright. In 1840, soon after his arrival in London, he prepared what seems to be the first printed argument in behalf of that measure, which appeared in this country. It was issued in pamphlet form under the title "An Argument in behalf of International Copyright." In 1843, Mr. Putnam obtained the signatures of nearly a hundred publishers, including those interested in the manufacture of books, to a petition he had prepared and which was duly presented to Congress. It took the broad ground that the absence of International Copyright was actually injurious to the interest of publishing and to the best interest of the people at large. Shortly afterwards, Henry C. Carey published his "Letters on International Copyright," in which he took the position that the facts and ideas in a book are the common property of society, and that property in copyright is indefensible. These antagonistic positions are still defended with much persistency,

the former by George Haven Putnam, and the latter by Henry Carey Baird. In a recent conversation with each of these intelligent gentlemen I found them firm in their belief that each had the right of the argument.

The death of Mr. Putnam occurred at Christmas time in 1872, when the booksellers annually reap their harvest in the sales of the holiday books. Mr. Putnam had provided unusual attractions in the way of attractive books, when he was suddenly stricken down in death, while actively engaged in his own store. Authors and readers felt that a prop and guide was taken from them; the doors of the crowded store were closed; the mourning family in their grief cared not that the holiday sales were the event of the year, but the ever-generous guild of booksellers grasped the sad moment to illustrate their affection for the dead. Henry Holt, Andrew Armstrong and Alfred Houghton published a card stating that to the affliction of the family should not be added the serious financial embarrassment of having in that busy season the store of the late publisher closed, and they took upon themselves the work of re-opening the store and carrying on the business for the family.

As an indication of the respect in which Mr. Putnam was held the following resolutions were passed by the Publishers' Board of Trade:

"Resolved: That this Board regards with deep sorrow, the death of G. P. Putnam, a publisher whose life added dignity to our calling and whose memory is among the best traditions.

"Resolved: That we, as his business associates, wish to give our testimony to that already so copiously given by the press, that Mr. Putnam's career was one of great advantage to American letters, and that his example is worthy the emulation of those whose function it is to decide what literature shall go before the public.

"Resolved: That while his sudden death reminds us of the uncertainty of our tenure of active effort it equally reminds us that it is impossible entirely to obliterate the influence of a good and useful life.

HENRY IVISON, *Pres.*
HENRY HOLT, *Secretary."*

The funeral was largely attended by representative men, especially those of the literary world. An eloquent sermon was delivered on the occasion by his pastor, Rev. Dr. J. F. Elder, who characterized Mr. Putnam's life as "pure, patient, gentle, self-sacrificing."

I am permitted to make public the following letters to the bereaved widow and son, from the late Bayard Taylor, who knew the deceased more intimately perhaps, than any other man then living, outside of the family.

344

Horace Greeley in 1872. Both longtime New York City publishers with roots in New England, Putnam and Greeley knew each other from the 1830s until their deaths, less than a month apart—Greeley on 29 November and Putnam on 20 December 1872.

"Lausanne, Switzerland,
Jan. 17, 1873.

"MY DEAR MRS. PUTNAM:

"With the sorrow for Mr. Greeley's loss still upon me, I can hardly tell you how much I have been shocked and grieved by this additional blow. . . . It seemed incredible that a man like Mr. Putnam, with so much freshness and energy for his years, such an active habit of life, such temperance and regularity, *could* be stricken down so suddenly; to you and your children the blow must have been awful in its swiftness. . . . I remember when Washington Irving was called away by as sudden a summons, how Mr. Putnam spoke of it as a fortunate death, saying that if men were allowed to choose, the most would prefer to die as Irving did. He now has been equally fortunate, and we who have known him so long and intimately, know that he was always ready for the call. His nature had that transparent goodness and purity which cannot be hidden: it was seen of all, and the only thing which seemed disparagement that I ever heard said of him was: 'He's too good a man to be successful in business!' But I consider such a life successful and noble in the highest sense. Mr. Putnam's personal and moral influence extended further and was more enduring than he or even his family could know; and it does not cease with his death. There is, there must be,

some consolation in contemplating the stainless record of his life even to those who have lost the most in losing him."

"MY DEAR HAVEN:

"I did not get the sad news until only three days ago. . . . This swift death coming so close upon Kensett's (who was also a dear old friend) and Greeley's shocks me inexpressibly. At my age one makes friends slowly and clings all the more strongly to those with whom so many past experiences have been shared. Twenty-six years of friendship as well as business relations, taught me how perfectly I could confide in your father."

The loss of Mr. Putnam was deeply felt by his many attached friends, none more so than by William Cullen Bryant, who wrote the following letter:

"Here, too, the closing days of the year (1872) have been saddened by the deaths of those whom we much prized, suddenly removed in the midst of their usefulness. Kensett, the amiable and generous artist; Putnam, the liberal minded and kindly bookseller, and the promoter of every good work; and the much esteemed treasurer of the Century Association, Priestley, a man of great worth and intelligence. It is not often we lose, so near to each other so many deeply and widely mourned. What a fleeting thing human life is!– like the shadows of a cloud passing swiftly over the fields leaving behind the flowers which it visits but for an instant, and the prattling brooks and the pools that give back the image of the sky, and the song sparrow warbling on its perch, and the meadow-lark brooding on its nest in the grass–leaving all, all,–and hurrying to be lost on the dim distant hills where the sight can no longer follow it. I miss Putnam greatly. He published two of my books and I employed him to get together my Cummington Library– about four thousand volumes. What he did for me beyond my special directions was judiciously and disinterestedly done."

It can be truly said that Mr. Putnam's life was always spent more for the benefit of others than for his own aggrandizement, more for the dissemination of good ideas than for the accumulation of wealth. Generous and untiring in his devotion to the objects which aroused his enthusiasm, the very effort to subordinate his personality to the general good of booksellers and book-readers will ever make his name brightly conspicuous in their annals.

In Rev. Dr. Ward's Review of Thomas Hughes' "Memoir of Macmillan," headed "The Publisher's Vocation," the following tribute to Mr. Putnam is given:

"One recalls the name of several Americans, who have stood in such relations to authors and readers that their imprint carried immense influence, making them not only benefactors to authors, but the purveyors of the best books to those for whom they were written. Eminent among these was George P. Putnam, who brought a sensitive conscience and excellent literary taste to the business of a bookseller and publisher and is always to be named as one of the best friends American authors ever had. He published books on their merits and drew around him the men who had something to say to the public; and the magazine which he started in 1853 is still remembered, although long ago discontinued, for the noble character and excellent quality of the contents. He filled out the idea of what the public needed and had the largeness of conception requisite to the undertaking, and the proper business capacity to make it a success. No man knew better how to help authors forward, or how to furnish the public with readable books of the best character."

The present firm consists of George Haven, John Bishop and Irving Putnam, all of whom inherit the literary qualities of their father under the firm style "G. P. Putnam's Sons," and conduct with great success the business founded by their father a half a century ago. Since the death of the latter they have added to their catalogue of works in general literature, lists of medical and educational publications, and have also extended their business so as to include bookselling and importing as well as publishing. In connection with their importing business they now have a branch house in London, not far from the original headquarters of G. P. Putnam, from which, in 1848 "American Facts" was published.

The talent in the Putnam family is not all confined to the male branches. Dr. Mary Putnam Jacobi was the first woman who ever secured admission into the Paris Ecole de Medecine (in 1864), from which she was graduated with honors in 1870. She was doing work as a medical student in Paris during both the Prussian and Communists' sieges, and in the interim, while the lecture courses were closed, she busied herself with work in the hospitals.

She was the first woman who was ever elected a member of the Pathological Society, as well as of the New York Academy of Medicine. All of which seems strange enough to the writer, who knew her when a young school girl, more than thirty years ago, while a near neighbor of her father's at Yonkers, on the Hudson.

The following incident will serve as an example of the kind of responsibility which sometimes attaches to the business of supplying libraries. Not long since, a pastor in a country town wrote G. P. Putnam's Sons to say that two hundred dollars had been raised for the town library, and that, as chairman of the committee, the duty of selecting books devolved upon him. He asked the firm to use their own judgment as to the list, stipulating only that it should include the writings of Mrs.–, one of the most "sensational" novelists of the day. As her pen was prolific as well as sensational, a set of her books would have absorbed a very large proportion of the appropriation, and it was thought best therefore to *query* the necessity for sending this particular set, and to suggest in its place a selection of really standard works of fiction. A note in reply was received, somewhat as follows:–

"Dear Sirs:

"I am exceedingly indebted for your kind advice in this matter. Please send in place of Mrs.–'s books the volumes suggested by yourselves. Being a minister, I have never read any fiction in my life and know nothing about it, and when some of my young men mentioned the novels referred to as indispensable, I supposed they were better than any others."

For the purpose of presenting in convenient form the class of information required by such inquirers, a volume entitled "The Best Reading," which is of great assistance to all those needing advice in selecting libraries, was planned by G. H. Putnam, and prepared by himself, F. B. Perkins, and L. E. Jones. The firm has also recently published a book by two of the brothers, entitled "Authors and Publishers," a manual of suggestions to beginners in literature, which is considered of great value to all those who have written, or expect to become authors of books.

–*Fifty Years among Authors, Books and Publishers,*
pp. 299–320

Books for Further Reading

Ballou, Ellen. *The Building of the House: Houghton Mifflin's Formative Years* (Boston: Houghton Mifflin, 1970).

Charvat, William. *Literary Publishing in America, 1790–1850* (Philadelphia: University of Pennsylvania Press, 1959).

Charvat. *The Profession of Authorship in America, 1800–1870,* edited by Matthew J. Bruccoli (Columbus: Ohio State University Press, 1968).

Coultrap-McQuin, Susan. *Doing Literary Business: American Women Writers in the Nineteenth Century* (Chapel Hill: University of North Carolina Press, 1990).

Dzwonkoski, Peter Z., ed. *American Literary Publishing Houses, 1638–1899,* volume 49 of *Dictionary of Literary Biography* (Detroit, Mich.: Gale Research Company, 1986).

Exman, Eugene. *The Brothers Harper: A Unique Publishing Partnership and Its Impact upon the Cultural Life of America from 1817 to 1853* (New York: Harper & Row, 1965).

Exman. *The House of Harper: One Hundred and Fifty Years of Publishing* (New York: Harper & Row, 1967).

Greenspan, Ezra. *George Palmer Putnam: Representative American Publisher* (University Park: Penn State University Press, 2000).

Moore, John Hammond. *Wiley: One Hundred and Seventy-five Years of Publishing* (New York: John Wiley and Sons, 1982).

Putnam, George Haven. *A Memoir of George Palmer Putnam,* 2 volumes (New York: G. P. Putnam's Sons, 1903); reprinted, with slight changes, as *George Palmer Putnam: A Memoir* (New York: G. P. Putnam's Sons, 1912).

Tebbel, John. *A History of Book Publishing in the United States,* volume 1, *The Creation of an Industry, 1630–1895* (New York: R. R. Bowker, 1972).

Tryon, Warren S. *Parnassus Corner: A Life of James T. Fields, Publisher to the Victorians* (Boston: Houghton Mifflin, 1963).

Tryon and Charvat, eds. *The Cost Books of Ticknor and Fields, and Their Predecessors, 1832–1858* (New York: Bibliographical Society of America, 1949).

Winship, Michael. *American Literary Publishing in the Mid-Nineteenth Century: The Business of Ticknor and Fields* (Cambridge, U.K. & New York: Cambridge University Press, 1996).

Cumulative Index

Dictionary of Literary Biography, Volumes 1-254
Dictionary of Literary Biography Yearbook, 1980-2000
Dictionary of Literary Biography Documentary Series, Volumes 1-19
Concise Dictionary of American Literary Biography, Volumes 1-7
Concise Dictionary of British Literary Biography, Volumes 1-8
Concise Dictionary of World Literary Biography, Volumes 1-4

Cumulative Index

DLB before number: *Dictionary of Literary Biography,* Volumes 1-254
Y before number: *Dictionary of Literary Biography Yearbook,* 1980-2000
DS before number: *Dictionary of Literary Biography Documentary Series,* Volumes 1-19
CDALB before number: *Concise Dictionary of American Literary Biography,* Volumes 1-7
CDBLB before number: *Concise Dictionary of British Literary Biography,* Volumes 1-8
CDWLB before number: *Concise Dictionary of World Literary Biography,* Volumes 1-4

A

Aakjær, Jeppe 1866-1930 . . . . .DLB-214

Abbey, Edwin Austin 1852-1911 . . . . . . .DLB-188

Abbey, Maj. J. R. 1894-1969 . . . . .DLB-201

Abbey Press DLB-49

The Abbey Theatre and Irish Drama,
 1900-1945 . . . . .DLB-10

Abbot, Willis J. 1863-1934 . . . . .DLB-29

Abbott, Jacob 1803-1879 . . . . .DLB-1, 243

Abbott, Lee K. 1947- DLB-130

Abbott, Lyman 1835-1922 . . . . .DLB-79

Abbott, Robert S. 1868-1940 . . . . .DLB-29, 91

Abe Kōbō 1924-1993 . . . . .DLB-182

Abelard, Peter circa 1079-1142? DLB-115, 208

Abelard-Schuman DLB-46

Abell, Arunah S. 1806-1888 . . . . .DLB-43

Abell, Kjeld 1901-1961 . . . . .DLB-214

Abercrombie, Lascelles 1881-1938 . . . . . . .DLB-19

Aberdeen University Press Limited DLB-106

Abish, Walter 1931- DLB-130, 227

Ablesimov, Aleksandr Onisimovich
 1742-1783 . . . . .DLB-150

Abraham à Sancta Clara 1644-1709 . . . . . .DLB-168

Abrahams, Peter
 1919- DLB-117, 225; CDWLB-3

Abrams, M. H. 1912- DLB-67

Abramson, Jesse 1904-1979 . . . . .DLB-241

Abrogans circa 790-800 . . . . .DLB-148

Abschatz, Hans Aßmann von
 1646-1699 . . . . .DLB-168

Abse, Dannie 1923- DLB-27, 245

Abutsu-ni 1221-1283 . . . . .DLB-203

Academy Chicago Publishers DLB-46

Accius circa 170 B.C.-circa 80 B.C. DLB-211

Accrocca, Elio Filippo 1923- DLB-128

Ace Books DLB-46

Achebe, Chinua 1930- DLB-117; CDWLB-3

Achtenberg, Herbert 1938- DLB-124

Ackerman, Diane 1948- DLB-120

Ackroyd, Peter 1949- DLB-155, 231

Acorn, Milton 1923-1986 . . . . .DLB-53

Acosta, Oscar Zeta 1935?- DLB-82

Acosta Torres, José 1925- DLB-209

Actors Theatre of Louisville DLB-7

Adair, Gilbert 1944- DLB-194

Adair, James 1709?-1783? DLB-30

Adam, Graeme Mercer 1839-1912 . . . . . . .DLB-99

Adam, Robert Borthwick II 1863-1940 . . .DLB-187

Adame, Leonard 1947- DLB-82

Adameşteanu, Gabriel 1942- DLB-232

Adamic, Louis 1898-1951 . . . . .DLB-9

Adams, Abigail 1744-1818 . . . . .DLB-200

Adams, Alice 1926-1999 . . . . DLB-234, Y-86

Adams, Bertha Leith (Mrs. Leith Adams,
 Mrs. R. S. de Courcy Laffan)
 1837?-1912 .DLB-240

Adams, Brooks 1848-1927 . . . . .DLB-47

Adams, Charles Francis, Jr. 1835-1915 . . . .DLB-47

Adams, Douglas 1952- Y-83

Adams, Franklin P. 1881-1960 . . . . .DLB-29

Adams, Hannah 1755-1832 . . . . .DLB-200

Adams, Henry 1838-1918 . . . . DLB-12, 47, 189

Adams, Herbert Baxter 1850-1901 . . . . . . .DLB-47

Adams, J. S. and C. [publishing house] DLB-49

Adams, James Truslow
 1878-1949 . . . . DLB-17; DS-17

Adams, John 1735-1826 . . . . .DLB-31, 183

Adams, John 1735-1826 and
 Adams, Abigail 1744-1818 . . . . .DLB-183

Adams, John Quincy 1767-1848 . . . . .DLB-37

Adams, Léonie 1899-1988 . . . . .DLB-48

Adams, Levi 1802-1832 . . . . .DLB-99

Adams, Samuel 1722-1803 . . . . .DLB-31, 43

Adams, Sarah Fuller Flower
 1805-1848 . . . . .DLB-199

Adams, Thomas 1582 or 1583-1652 . . . . .DLB-151

Adams, William Taylor 1822-1897 . . . . . . .DLB-42

Adamson, Sir John 1867-1950 . . . . .DLB-98

Adcock, Arthur St. John 1864-1930 . . . . . .DLB-135

Adcock, Betty 1938- DLB-105

"Certain Gifts" DLB-105

Adcock, Fleur 1934- DLB-40

Addison, Joseph 1672-1719 . . .DLB-101; CDBLB-2

Ade, George 1866-1944 . . . . .DLB-11, 25

Adeler, Max (see Clark, Charles Heber)

Adonias Filho 1915-1990 . . . . .DLB-145

Adorno, Theodor W. 1903-1969 . . . . . . .DLB-242

Advance Publishing Company DLB-49

Ady, Endre 1877-1919 . . . . . . DLB-215; CDWLB-4

AE 1867-1935 . . . . DLB-19; CDBLB-5

Ælfric circa 955-circa 1010 . . . . .DLB-146

Aeschines
 circa 390 B.C.-circa 320 B.C. DLB-176

Aeschylus 525-524 B.C.-456-455 B.C.
 . . . . DLB-176; CDWLB-1

Afro-American Literary Critics:
 An Introduction DLB-33

After Dinner Opera Company Y-92

Agassiz, Elizabeth Cary 1822-1907 . . . . . .DLB-189

Agassiz, Louis 1807-1873 . . . . .DLB-1, 235

Agee, James
 1909-1955 . . . . .DLB-2, 26, 152; CDALB-1

The Agee Legacy: A Conference at the University
 of Tennessee at Knoxville Y-89

Aguilera Malta, Demetrio 1909-1981 . . . .DLB-145

Ai 1947- DLB-120

Aichinger, Ilse 1921- DLB-85

Aidoo, Ama Ata 1942- DLB-117; CDWLB-3

Aiken, Conrad
 1889-1973 . . . . .DLB-9, 45, 102; CDALB-5

Aiken, Joan 1924- DLB-161

Aikin, Lucy 1781-1864 . . . . .DLB-144, 163

Ainsworth, William Harrison 1805-1882 . .DLB-21

Aistis, Jonas 1904-1973 . . . . . DLB-220; CDWLB-4

Aitken, George A. 1860-1917 . . . . .DLB-149

Aitken, Robert [publishing house] DLB-49

Akenside, Mark 1721-1770 . . . . .DLB-109

Akins, Zoë 1886-1958 . . . . .DLB-26

Aksahov, Sergei Timofeevich
 1791-1859 . . . . .DLB-198

Akutagawa, Ryūnsuke 1892-1927 . . . . . . .DLB-180

Alabaster, William 1568-1640 . . . . .DLB-132

Alain de Lille circa 1116-1202/1203 . . . . .DLB-208

Alain-Fournier 1886-1914 . . . . .DLB-65

Alanus de Insulis (see Alain de Lille)

Alarcón, Francisco X. 1954- DLB-122

Alarcón, Justo S. 1930- DLB-209

Alba, Nanina 1915-1968 .... DLB-41

Albee, Edward 1928- DLB-7; CDALB-1

Albert the Great circa 1200-1280 ...... DLB-115

Albert, Octavia 1853-ca. 1889 .... DLB-221

Alberti, Rafael 1902-1999 .... DLB-108

Albertinus, Aegidius circa 1560-1620 .... DLB-164

Alcaeus born circa 620 B.C. DLB-176

Alcott, Bronson 1799-1888 .... DLB-1, 223

Alcott, Louisa May 1832-1888
  ... DLB-1, 42, 79, 223, 239; DS-14; CDALB-3

Alcott, William Andrus 1798-1859 .... DLB-1, 243

Alcuin circa 732-804 .... DLB-148

Alden, Beardsley and Company DLB-49

Alden, Henry Mills 1836-1919 .... DLB-79

Alden, Isabella 1841-1930 .... DLB-42

Alden, John B. [publishing house] DLB-49

Aldington, Richard
  1892-1962 .... DLB-20, 36, 100, 149

Aldis, Dorothy 1896-1966 .... DLB-22

Aldis, H. G. 1863-1919 .... DLB-184

Aldiss, Brian W. 1925- DLB-14

Aldrich, Thomas Bailey
  1836-1907 .... DLB-42, 71, 74, 79

Alegría, Ciro 1909-1967 .... DLB-113

Alegría, Claribel 1924- DLB-145

Aleixandre, Vicente 1898-1984 .... DLB-108

Aleksandravičius, Jonas (see Aistis, Jonas)

Aleksandrov, Aleksandr Andreevich
  (see Durova, Nadezhda Andreevna)

Aleramo, Sibilla 1876-1960 .... DLB-114

Alexander, Cecil Frances 1818-1895 ..... DLB-199

Alexander, Charles 1868-1923 .... DLB-91

Alexander, Charles Wesley
  [publishing house] DLB-49

Alexander, James 1691-1756 .... DLB-24

Alexander, Lloyd 1924- DLB-52

Alexander, Sir William, Earl of Stirling
  1577?-1640 .... DLB-121

Alexie, Sherman 1966- DLB-175, 206

Alexis, Willibald 1798-1871 .... DLB-133

Alfred, King 849-899 .... DLB-146

Alger, Horatio, Jr. 1832-1899 .... DLB-42

Algonquin Books of Chapel Hill DLB-46

Algren, Nelson
  1909-1981 ..... DLB-9; Y-81, Y-82; CDALB-1

Nelson Algren: An International
  Symposium Y-00

Allan, Andrew 1907-1974 .... DLB-88

Allan, Ted 1916- DLB-68

Allbeury, Ted 1917- DLB-87

Alldritt, Keith 1935- DLB-14

Allen, Ethan 1738-1789 .... DLB-31

Allen, Frederick Lewis 1890-1954 ...... DLB-137

Allen, Gay Wilson 1903-1995 ..... DLB-103; Y-95

Allen, George 1808-1876 .... DLB-59

Allen, George [publishing house] DLB-106

Allen, George, and Unwin Limited DLB-112

Allen, Grant 1848-1899 .... DLB-70, 92, 178

Allen, Henry W. 1912- Y-85

Allen, Hervey 1889-1949 .... DLB-9, 45

Allen, James 1739-1808 .... DLB-31

Allen, James Lane 1849-1925 .... DLB-71

Allen, Jay Presson 1922- DLB-26

Allen, John, and Company DLB-49

Allen, Paula Gunn 1939- DLB-175

Allen, Samuel W. 1917- DLB-41

Allen, Woody 1935- DLB-44

Allende, Isabel 1942- DLB-145; CDWLB-3

Alline, Henry 1748-1784 .... DLB-99

Allingham, Margery 1904-1966 .... DLB-77

Allingham, William 1824-1889 .... DLB-35

Allison, W. L. [publishing house] DLB-49

The *Alliterative Morte Arthure and the Stanzaic
  Morte Arthur* circa 1350-1400 .... DLB-146

Allott, Kenneth 1912-1973 .... DLB-20

Allston, Washington 1779-1843 ...... DLB-1, 235

Almon, John [publishing house] DLB-154

Alonzo, Dámaso 1898-1990 .... DLB-108

Alsop, George 1636-post 1673 .... DLB-24

Alsop, Richard 1761-1815 .... DLB-37

Altemus, Henry, and Company DLB-49

Altenberg, Peter 1885-1919 .... DLB-81

Althusser, Louis 1918-1990 .... DLB-242

Altolaguirre, Manuel 1905-1959 .... DLB-108

Aluko, T. M. 1918- DLB-117

Alurista 1947- DLB-82

Alvarez, A. 1929- DLB-14, 40

Alver, Betti 1906-1989 ..... DLB-220; CDWLB-4

Amadi, Elechi 1934- DLB-117

Amado, Jorge 1912- DLB-113

Ambler, Eric 1909-1998 .... DLB-77

American Conservatory Theatre DLB-7

American Fiction and the 1930s DLB-9

American Humor: A Historical Survey
  East and Northeast
  South and Southwest
  Midwest
  West DLB-11

The American Library in Paris Y-93

American News Company DLB-49

The American Poets' Corner: The First
  Three Years (1983-1986) Y-86

American Publishing Company DLB-49

American Stationers' Company DLB-49

American Sunday-School Union DLB-49

American Temperance Union DLB-49

American Tract Society DLB-49

The American Trust for the
  British Library Y-96

The American Writers Congress
  (9-12 October 1981) Y-81

The American Writers Congress: A Report
  on Continuing Business Y-81

Ames, Fisher 1758-1808 .... DLB-37

Ames, Mary Clemmer 1831-1884 .... DLB-23

Amiel, Henri-Frédéric 1821-1881 .... DLB-217

Amini, Johari M. 1935- DLB-41

Amis, Kingsley 1922-1995
  .... DLB-15, 27, 100, 139, Y-96; CDBLB-7

Amis, Martin 1949- DLB-194

Ammianus Marcellinus
  circa A.D. 330-A.D. 395 .... DLB-211

Ammons, A. R. 1926- DLB-5, 165

Amory, Thomas 1691?-1788 .... DLB-39

Anania, Michael 1939- DLB-193

Anaya, Rudolfo A. 1937- DLB-82, 206

Ancrene Riwle circa 1200-1225 .... DLB-146

Andersch, Alfred 1914-1980 .... DLB-69

Andersen, Benny 1929- DLB-214

Anderson, Alexander 1775-1870 .... DLB-188

Anderson, David 1929- DLB-241

Anderson, Frederick Irving 1877-1947 ... DLB-202

Anderson, Margaret 1886-1973 .... DLB-4, 91

Anderson, Maxwell 1888-1959 .... DLB-7, 228

Anderson, Patrick 1915-1979 .... DLB-68

Anderson, Paul Y. 1893-1938 .... DLB-29

Anderson, Poul 1926- DLB-8

Anderson, Robert 1750-1830 .... DLB-142

Anderson, Robert 1917- DLB-7

Anderson, Sherwood
  1876-1941 ..... DLB-4, 9, 86; DS-1; CDALB-4

Andreae, Johann Valentin 1586-1654 .... DLB-164

Andreas Capellanus
  flourished circa 1185 .... DLB-208

Andreas-Salomé, Lou 1861-1937 .... DLB-66

Andres, Stefan 1906-1970 .... DLB-69

Andreu, Blanca 1959- DLB-134

Andrewes, Lancelot 1555-1626 ..... DLB-151, 172

Andrews, Charles M. 1863-1943 .... DLB-17

Andrews, Miles Peter ?-1814 .... DLB-89

Andrian, Leopold von 1875-1951 .... DLB-81

Andrić, Ivo 1892-1975 ...... DLB-147; CDWLB-4

Andrieux, Louis (see Aragon, Louis)

Andrus, Silas, and Son DLB-49

Andrzejewski, Jerzy 1909-1983 .... DLB-215

Angell, James Burrill 1829-1916 .... DLB-64

Angell, Roger 1920- DLB-171, 185

Angelou, Maya 1928- DLB-38; CDALB-7

Anger, Jane flourished 1589 .... DLB-136

Angers, Félicité (see Conan, Laure)

Anglo-Norman Literature in the Development
  of Middle English Literature DLB-146

The *Anglo-Saxon Chronicle* circa 890-1154 .. DLB-146

The "Angry Young Men" DLB-15

Angus and Robertson (UK) Limited DLB-112

Anhalt, Edward 1914-2000 .... DLB-26

Anners, Henry F. [publishing house] DLB-49

Annolied between 1077 and 1081 .... DLB-148

Annual Awards for *Dictionary of Literary Biography*
Editors and Contributors Y-98, Y-99, Y-00

Anselm of Canterbury 1033-1109 . . . . DLB-115

Anstey, F. 1856-1934 . . . . DLB-141, 178

Anthony, Michael 1932- DLB-125

Anthony, Piers 1934- DLB-8

Anthony, Susanna 1726-1791 . . . . DLB-200

Antin, David 1932- DLB-169

Antin, Mary 1881-1949 . . . . DLB-221; Y-84

Anton Ulrich, Duke of Brunswick-Lüneburg
1633-1714 . . . . DLB-168

Antschel, Paul (see Celan, Paul)

Anyidoho, Kofi 1947- DLB-157

Anzaldúa, Gloria 1942- DLB-122

Anzengruber, Ludwig 1839-1889 . . . . DLB-129

Apess, William 1798-1839 . . . . DLB-175, 243

Apodaca, Rudy S. 1939- DLB-82

Apollonius Rhodius third century B.C. DLB-176

Apple, Max 1941- DLB-130

Appleton, D., and Company DLB-49

Appleton-Century-Crofts DLB-46

Applewhite, James 1935- DLB-105

Applewood Books DLB-46

Apuleius circa A.D. 125-post A.D. 164
. . . . DLB-211; CDWLB-1

Aquin, Hubert 1929-1977 . . . . DLB-53

Aquinas, Thomas 1224 or 1225-1274 . . . . DLB-115

Aragon, Louis 1897-1982 . . . . DLB-72

Aralica, Ivan 1930- DLB-181

Aratus of Soli
circa 315 B.C.-circa 239 B.C. DLB-176

Arbasino, Alberto 1930- DLB-196

Arbor House Publishing Company DLB-46

Arbuthnot, John 1667-1735 . . . . DLB-101

Arcadia House DLB-46

Arce, Julio G. (see Ulica, Jorge)

Archer, William 1856-1924 . . . . DLB-10

Archilochhus
mid seventh century B.C.E. DLB-176

The Archpoet circa 1130?-? DLB-148

Archpriest Avvakum (Petrovich)
1620?-1682 . . . . DLB-150

Arden, John 1930- DLB-13, 245

Arden of Faversham DLB-62

Ardis Publishers Y-89

Ardizzone, Edward 1900-1979 . . . . DLB-160

Arellano, Juan Estevan 1947- DLB-122

The Arena Publishing Company DLB-49

Arena Stage DLB-7

Arenas, Reinaldo 1943-1990 . . . . DLB-145

Arendt, Hannah 1906-1975 . . . . DLB-242

Arensberg, Ann 1937- Y-82

Arghezi, Tudor 1880-1967 . . . DLB-220; CDWLB-4

Arguedas, José María 1911-1969 . . . . DLB-113

Argueta, Manlio 1936- DLB-145

Arias, Ron 1941- DLB-82

Arishima, Takeo 1878-1923 . . . . DLB-180

Aristophanes circa 446 B.C.-circa 386 B.C.
. . . . DLB-176; CDWLB-1

Aristotle 384 B.C.-322 B.C.
. . . . DLB-176; CDWLB-1

Ariyoshi Sawako 1931-1984 . . . . DLB-182

Arland, Marcel 1899-1986 . . . . DLB-72

Arlen, Michael 1895-1956 . . . . . . DLB-36, 77, 162

Armah, Ayi Kwei 1939- . . . DLB-117; CDWLB-3

Armantrout, Rae 1947- DLB-193

Der arme Hartmann ?-after 1150 . . . . DLB-148

Armed Services Editions DLB-46

Armstrong, Martin Donisthorpe
1882-1974 . . . . DLB-197

Armstrong, Richard 1903- DLB-160

Arndt, Ernst Moritz 1769-1860 . . . . DLB-90

Arnim, Achim von 1781-1831 . . . . DLB-90

Arnim, Bettina von 1785-1859 . . . . DLB-90

Arnim, Elizabeth von (Countess Mary
Annette Beauchamp Russell)
1866-1941 . . . . DLB-197

Arno Press DLB-46

Arnold, Edward [publishing house] DLB-112

Arnold, Edwin 1832-1904 . . . . DLB-35

Arnold, Edwin L. 1857-1935 . . . . DLB-178

Arnold, Matthew
1822-1888 . . . . DLB-32, 57; CDBLB-4

Preface to *Poems* (1853) DLB-32

Arnold, Thomas 1795-1842 . . . . DLB-55

Arnott, Peter 1962- DLB-233

Arnow, Harriette Simpson 1908-1986 . . . . . DLB-6

Arp, Bill (see Smith, Charles Henry)

Arpino, Giovanni 1927-1987 . . . . DLB-177

Arreola, Juan José 1918- DLB-113

Arrian circa 89-circa 155 . . . . DLB-176

Arrowsmith, J. W. [publishing house] DLB-106

The Art and Mystery of Publishing:
Interviews Y-97

Arthur, Timothy Shay
1809-1885 . . . . DLB-3, 42, 79; DS-13

The Arthurian Tradition and
Its European Context DLB-138

Artmann, H. C. 1921-2000 . . . . DLB-85

Arvin, Newton 1900-1963 . . . . DLB-103

Asch, Nathan 1902-1964 . . . . DLB-4, 28

Ascham, Roger 1515 or 1516-1568 . . . . . DLB-236

Ash, John 1948- DLB-40

Ashbery, John 1927- DLB-5, 165; Y-81

Ashbridge, Elizabeth 1713-1755 . . . . DLB-200

Ashburnham, Bertram Lord
1797-1878 . . . . DLB-184

Ashendene Press DLB-112

Asher, Sandy 1942- Y-83

Ashton, Winifred (see Dane, Clemence)

Asimov, Isaac 1920-1992 . . . . DLB-8; Y-92

Askew, Anne circa 1521-1546 . . . . DLB-136

Aspazija 1865-1943 . . . . DLB-220; CDWLB-4

Asselin, Olivar 1874-1937 . . . . DLB-92

The Association of American Publishers Y-99

The Association for Documentary Editing . . . Y-00

Astley, William (see Warung, Price)

Asturias, Miguel Angel
1899-1974 . . . . DLB-113; CDWLB-3

At Home with Albert Erskine Y-00

Atheneum Publishers DLB-46

Atherton, Gertrude 1857-1948 . . . . . DLB-9, 78, 186

Athlone Press DLB-112

Atkins, Josiah circa 1755-1781 . . . . DLB-31

Atkins, Russell 1926- DLB-41

Atkinson, Louisa 1834-1872 . . . . DLB-230

The Atlantic Monthly Press DLB-46

Attaway, William 1911-1986 . . . . DLB-76

Atwood, Margaret 1939- DLB-53

Aubert, Alvin 1930- DLB-41

Aubert de Gaspé, Phillipe-Ignace-François
1814-1841 . . . . DLB-99

Aubert de Gaspé, Phillipe-Joseph
1786-1871 . . . . DLB-99

Aubin, Napoléon 1812-1890 . . . . DLB-99

Aubin, Penelope
1685-circa 1731 . . . . DLB-39

Preface to *The Life of Charlotta
du Pont* (1723) DLB-39

Aubrey-Fletcher, Henry Lancelot (see Wade, Henry)

Auchincloss, Louis 1917- DLB-2, 244; Y-80

Auden, W. H. 1907-1973 . . . DLB-10, 20; CDBLB-6

Audio Art in America: A Personal Memoir . . . Y-85

Audubon, John James 1785-1851 . . . . DLB-248

Audubon, John Woodhouse
1812-1862 . . . . DLB-183

Auerbach, Berthold 1812-1882 . . . . DLB-133

Auernheimer, Raoul 1876-1948 . . . . DLB-81

Augier, Emile 1820-1889 . . . . DLB-192

Augustine 354-430 . . . . DLB-115

Responses to Ken Auletta Y-97

Aulus Cellius
circa A.D. 125-circa A.D. 180? DLB-211

Austen, Jane
1775-1817 . . . . DLB-116; CDBLB-3

Auster, Paul 1947- DLB-227

Austin, Alfred 1835-1913 . . . . DLB-35

Austin, Jane Goodwin 1831-1894 . . . . DLB-202

Austin, Mary 1868-1934 . . . . . DLB-9, 78, 206, 221

Austin, William 1778-1841 . . . . DLB-74

Australie (Emily Manning)
1845-1890 . . . . DLB-230

Author-Printers, 1476–1599 . . . . DLB-167

Author Websites Y-97

Authors and Newspapers Association DLB-46

Authors' Publishing Company DLB-49

Avallone, Michael 1924-1999 . . . . Y-99

Avalon Books DLB-46

Avancini, Nicolaus 1611-1686 . . . . DLB-164

Avendaño, Fausto 1941- DLB-82

Averroëö 1126-1198 . . . . DLB-115

Avery, Gillian 1926- DLB-161

Avicenna 980-1037 . . . . DLB-115

Avison, Margaret 1918- DLB-53

Avon Books DLB-46

Avyžius, Jonas 1922-1999 . . . . DLB-220

Awdry, Wilbert Vere 1911-1997 . . . . DLB-160

Awoonor, Kofi 1935- DLB-117

Ayckbourn, Alan 1939- DLB-13, 245

Aymé, Marcel 1902-1967 . . . . DLB-72

Aytoun, Sir Robert 1570-1638 . . . . DLB-121

Aytoun, William Edmondstoune
    1813-1865 . . . . DLB-32, 159

B

B. V. (see Thomson, James)

Babbitt, Irving 1865-1933 . . . . DLB-63

Babbitt, Natalie 1932- DLB-52

Babcock, John [publishing house] DLB-49

Babits, Mihály 1883-1941 . . . DLB-215; CDWLB-4

Babrius circa 150-200 . . . . .DLB-176

Baca, Jimmy Santiago 1952- DLB-122

Bache, Benjamin Franklin 1769-1798 . . . . . DLB-43

Bacheller, Irving 1859-1950 . . . . DLB-202

Bachmann, Ingeborg 1926-1973 . . . . DLB-85

Bačinskaitė-Bučienė, Salomėja (see Nėris, Salomėja)

Bacon, Delia 1811-1859 . . . . DLB-1, 243

Bacon, Francis
    1561-1626 . . . . DLB-151, 236; CDBLB-1

Bacon, Sir Nicholas circa 1510-1579 . . . . . DLB-132

Bacon, Roger circa 1214/1220-1292 . . . . . DLB-115

Bacon, Thomas circa 1700-1768 . . . . DLB-31

Bacovia, George
    1881-1957 . . . . DLB-220; CDWLB-4

Badger, Richard G., and Company DLB-49

Bagaduce Music Lending Library Y-00

Bage, Robert 1728-1801 . . . . DLB-39

Bagehot, Walter 1826-1877 . . . . DLB-55

Bagley, Desmond 1923-1983 . . . . DLB-87

Bagley, Sarah G. 1806-1848 . . . . DLB-239

Bagnold, Enid 1889-1981 . . .DLB-13, 160, 191, 245

Bagryana, Elisaveta
    1893-1991 . . . . .DLB-147; CDWLB-4

Bahr, Hermann 1863-1934 . . . . DLB-81, 118

Bailey, Abigail Abbot 1746-1815 . . . . DLB-200

Bailey, Alfred Goldsworthy 1905- DLB-68

Bailey, Francis [publishing house] DLB-49

Bailey, H. C. 1878-1961 . . . . DLB-77

Bailey, Jacob 1731-1808 . . . . DLB-99

Bailey, Paul 1937- DLB-14

Bailey, Philip James 1816-1902 . . . . DLB-32

Baillargeon, Pierre 1916-1967 . . . . DLB-88

Baillie, Hugh 1890-1966 . . . . DLB-29

Baillie, Joanna 1762-1851 . . . . DLB-93

Bailyn, Bernard 1922- DLB-17

Bainbridge, Beryl 1933- DLB-14, 231

Baird, Irene 1901-1981 . . . . DLB-68

Baker, Augustine 1575-1641 . . . . DLB-151

Baker, Carlos 1909-1987 . . . . DLB-103

Baker, David 1954- DLB-120

Baker, Herschel C. 1914-1990 . . . . DLB-111

Baker, Houston A., Jr. 1943- DLB-67

Baker, Nicholson 1957- DLB-227

Baker, Samuel White 1821-1893 . . . . DLB-166

Baker, Thomas 1656-1740 . . . . DLB-213

Baker, Walter H., Company
    ("Baker's Plays") DLB-49

The Baker and Taylor Company DLB-49

Bakhtin, Mikhail Mikhailovich
    1895-1975 . . . . DLB-242

Balaban, John 1943- DLB-120

Bald, Wambly 1902- DLB-4

Balde, Jacob 1604-1668 . . . . DLB-164

Balderston, John 1889-1954 . . . . DLB-26

Baldwin, James 1924-1987
    . . . . DLB-2, 7, 33, 249; Y-87; CDALB-1

Baldwin, Joseph Glover
    1815-1864 . . . . DLB-3, 11, 248

Baldwin, Louisa (Mrs. Alfred Baldwin)
    1845-1925 . . . . DLB-240

Baldwin, Richard and Anne
    [publishing house] DLB-170

Baldwin, William circa 1515-1563 . . . . . DLB-132

Bale, John 1495-1563 . . . . DLB-132

Balestrini, Nanni 1935- DLB-128, 196

Balfour, Sir Andrew 1630-1694 . . . . DLB-213

Balfour, Arthur James 1848-1930 . . . . DLB-190

Balfour, Sir James 1600-1657 . . . . DLB-213

Ballantine Books DLB-46

Ballantyne, R. M. 1825-1894 . . . . DLB-163

Ballard, J. G. 1930- DLB-14, 207

Ballard, Martha Moore 1735-1812 . . . . . . DLB-200

Ballerini, Luigi 1940- DLB-128

Ballou, Maturin Murray
    1820-1895 . . . . .DLB-79, 189

Ballou, Robert O. [publishing house] DLB-46

Balzac, Honoré de 1799-1855 . . . . DLB-119

Bambara, Toni Cade
    1939- DLB-38, 218; CDALB-7

Bamford, Samuel 1788-1872 . . . . DLB-190

Bancroft, A. L., and Company DLB-49

Bancroft, George 1800-1891 . . . DLB-1, 30, 59, 243

Bancroft, Hubert Howe 1832-1918 . . .DLB-47, 140

Bandelier, Adolph F. 1840-1914 . . . . DLB-186

Bangs, John Kendrick 1862-1922 . . . . .DLB-11, 79

Banim, John 1798-1842 . . . . . . .DLB-116, 158, 159

Banim, Michael 1796-1874 . . . . DLB-158, 159

Banks, Iain 1954- DLB-194

Banks, John circa 1653-1706 . . . . DLB-80

Banks, Russell 1940- DLB-130

Bannerman, Helen 1862-1946 . . . . DLB-141

Bantam Books DLB-46

Banti, Anna 1895-1985 . . . . .DLB-177

Banville, John 1945- DLB-14

Banville, Théodore de 1823-1891 . . . . . . .DLB-217

Baraka, Amiri
    1934- DLB-5, 7, 16, 38; DS-8; CDALB-1

Barańczak, Stanisław 1946- DLB-232

Baratynsky, Evgenii Abramovich
    1800-1844 . . . . DLB-205

Barbauld, Anna Laetitia
    1743-1825 . . . . DLB-107, 109, 142, 158

Barbeau, Marius 1883-1969 . . . . DLB-92

Barber, John Warner 1798-1885 . . . . DLB-30

Bàrberi Squarotti, Giorgio 1929- DLB-128

Barbey d'Aurevilly, Jules-Amédée
    1808-1889 . . . . DLB-119

Barbier, Auguste 1805-1882 . . . . .DLB-217

Barbilian, Dan (see Barbu, Ion)

Barbour, John circa 1316-1395 . . . . DLB-146

Barbour, Ralph Henry 1870-1944 . . . . DLB-22

Barbusse, Henri 1873-1935 . . . . DLB-65

Barclay, Alexander circa 1475-1552 . . . . . DLB-132

Barclay, E. E., and Company DLB-49

Bardeen, C. W. [publishing house] DLB-49

Barham, Richard Harris 1788-1845 . . . . . DLB-159

Barich, Bill 1943- DLB-185

Baring, Maurice 1874-1945 . . . . DLB-34

Baring-Gould, Sabine
    1834-1924 . . . . DLB-156, 190

Barker, A. L. 1918- DLB-14, 139

Barker, Arthur, Limited DLB-112

Barker, George 1913-1991 . . . . DLB-20

Barker, Harley Granville 1877-1946 . . . . . . DLB-10

Barker, Howard 1946- DLB-13, 233

Barker, James Nelson 1784-1858 . . . . DLB-37

Barker, Jane 1652-1727 . . . . DLB-39, 131

Barker, Lady Mary Anne 1831-1911 . . . . DLB-166

Barker, William circa 1520-after 1576 . . . DLB-132

Barkov, Ivan Semenovich 1732-1768 . . . . DLB-150

Barks, Coleman 1937- DLB-5

Barlach, Ernst 1870-1938 . . . . DLB-56, 118

Barlow, Joel 1754-1812 . . . . DLB-37

The Prospect of Peace (1778) DLB-37

Barnard, John 1681-1770 . . . . DLB-24

Barne, Kitty (Mary Catherine Barne)
    1883-1957 . . . . DLB-160

Barnes, A. S., and Company DLB-49

Barnes, Barnabe 1571-1609 . . . . DLB-132

Barnes, Djuna 1892-1982 . . . . DLB-4, 9, 45

Barnes, Jim 1933- DLB-175

Barnes, Julian 1946- DLB-194; Y-93

Barnes, Margaret Ayer 1886-1967 . . . . DLB-9

Barnes, Peter 1931- DLB-13, 233

Barnes, William 1801-1886 . . . . DLB-32

Barnes and Noble Books DLB-46

Barnet, Miguel 1940- DLB-145

Barney, Natalie 1876-1972 . . . . .DLB-4

Barnfield, Richard 1574-1627 . . . . .DLB-172

Baron, Richard W.,
    Publishing Company. DLB-46

Barr, Amelia Edith Huddleston
    1831-1919 . . . . .DLB-202, 221

Barr, Robert 1850-1912 . . . . .DLB-70, 92

Barral, Carlos 1928-1989 . . . . .DLB-134

Barrax, Gerald William 1933- DLB-41, 120

Barrès, Maurice 1862-1923 . . . . .DLB-123

Barrett, Eaton Stannard 1786-1820 . . . . . .DLB-116

Barrie, J. M.
    1860-1937 . . . . . .DLB-10, 141, 156; CDBLB-5

Barrie and Jenkins DLB-112

Barrio, Raymond 1921- DLB-82

Barrios, Gregg 1945- DLB-122

Barry, Philip 1896-1949 . . . . .DLB-7, 228

Barry, Robertine (see Françoise)

Barry, Sebastian 1955- DLB-245

Barse and Hopkins. DLB-46

Barstow, Stan 1928- DLB-14, 139

Barth, John 1930- DLB-2, 227

Barthelme, Donald
    1931-1989 . . . . DLB-2, 234; Y-80, Y-89

Barthelme, Frederick 1943- DLB-244; Y-85

Bartholomew, Frank 1898-1985. . . . . . . .DLB-127

Bartlett, John 1820-1905 . . . . .DLB-1, 235

Bartol, Cyrus Augustus 1813-1900 . . . .DLB-1, 235

Barton, Bernard 1784-1849 . . . . .DLB-96

Barton, John ca. 1610-1675 . . . . .DLB-236

Barton, Thomas Pennant 1803-1869 . . . . .DLB-140

Bartram, John 1699-1777 . . . . .DLB-31

Bartram, William 1739-1823 . . . . .DLB-37

Basic Books DLB-46

Basille, Theodore (see Becon, Thomas)

Bass, Rick 1958- DLB-212

Bass, T. J. 1932- Y-81

Bassani, Giorgio 1916- DLB-128, 177

Basse, William circa 1583-1653 . . . . .DLB-121

Bassett, John Spencer 1867-1928 . . . . .DLB-17

Bassler, Thomas Joseph (see Bass, T. J.)

Bate, Walter Jackson 1918-1999 . . . . . DLB-67, 103

Bateman, Christopher
    [publishing house] DLB-170

Bateman, Stephen circa 1510-1584 . . . . . .DLB-136

Bates, H. E. 1905-1974. . . . . .DLB-162, 191

Bates, Katharine Lee 1859-1929 . . . . .DLB-71

Batiushkov, Konstantin Nikolaevich
    1787-1855. .DLB-205

Batsford, B. T. [publishing house] DLB-106

Battiscombe, Georgina 1905- DLB-155

The Battle of Maldon circa 1000 . . . . .DLB-146

Baudelaire, Charles 1821-1867 . . . . .DLB-217

Bauer, Bruno 1809-1882 . . . . .DLB-133

Bauer, Wolfgang 1941- DLB-124

Baum, L. Frank 1856-1919 . . . . .DLB-22

Baum, Vicki 1888-1960 . . . . .DLB-85

Baumbach, Jonathan 1933- Y-80

Bausch, Richard 1945- DLB-130

Bausch, Robert 1945- DLB-218

Bawden, Nina 1925- DLB-14, 161, 207

Bax, Clifford 1886-1962 . . . . .DLB-10, 100

Baxter, Charles 1947- DLB-130

Bayer, Eleanor (see Perry, Eleanor)

Bayer, Konrad 1932-1964 . . . . .DLB-85

Baynes, Pauline 1922- DLB-160

Baynton, Barbara 1857-1929 . . . . .DLB-230

Bazin, Hervé 1911-1996. . . . . .DLB-83

Beach, Sylvia 1887-1962. . . . . .DLB-4; DS-15

Beacon Press DLB-49

Beadle and Adams. DLB-49

Beagle, Peter S. 1939- Y-80

Beal, M. F. 1937- Y-81

Beale, Howard K. 1899-1959. . . . . .DLB-17

Beard, Charles A. 1874-1948 . . . . .DLB-17

A Beat Chronology: The First Twenty-five
    Years, 1944-1969. . . . . .DLB-16

Periodicals of the Beat Generation. DLB-16

The Beats in New York City DLB-237

The Beats in the West DLB-237

Beattie, Ann 1947- DLB-218; Y-82

Beattie, James 1735-1803 . . . . .DLB-109

Beatty, Chester 1875-1968 . . . . .DLB-201

Beauchemin, Nérée 1850-1931 . . . . .DLB-92

Beauchemin, Yves 1941- DLB-60

Beaugrand, Honoré 1848-1906 . . . . .DLB-99

Beaulieu, Victor-Lévy 1945- DLB-53

Beaumont, Francis circa 1584-1616
    and Fletcher, John 1579-1625
    . . . . DLB-58; CDBLB-1

Beaumont, Sir John 1583?-1627. . . . . . . .DLB-121

Beaumont, Joseph 1616-1699. . . . . .DLB-126

Beauvoir, Simone de 1908-1986 . . . . DLB-72; Y-86

Becher, Ulrich 1910- DLB-69

Becker, Carl 1873-1945 . . . . .DLB-17

Becker, Jurek 1937-1997. . . . . .DLB-75

Becker, Jurgen 1932- DLB-75

Beckett, Samuel 1906-1989
    . . . . .DLB-13, 15, 233; Y-90; CDBLB-7

Beckford, William 1760-1844 . . . . .DLB-39

Beckham, Barry 1944- DLB-33

Becon, Thomas circa 1512-1567 . . . . .DLB-136

Becque, Henry 1837-1899 . . . . .DLB-192

Beddoes, Thomas 1760-1808. . . . . .DLB-158

Beddoes, Thomas Lovell 1803-1849 . . . . . .DLB-96

Bede circa 673-735 . . . . .DLB-146

Beecher, Catharine Esther 1800-1878 . .DLB-1, 243

Beecher, Henry Ward 1813-1887 . . . . . .DLB-3, 43

Beer, George L. 1872-1920 . . . . .DLB-47

Beer, Johann 1655-1700 . . . . .DLB-168

Beer, Patricia 1919-1999 . . . . .DLB-40

Beerbohm, Max 1872-1956 . . . . .DLB-34, 100

Beer-Hofmann, Richard 1866-1945 . . . . . .DLB-81

Beers, Henry A. 1847-1926 . . . . .DLB-71

Beeton, S. O. [publishing house] DLB-106

Bégon, Elisabeth 1696-1755 . . . . .DLB-99

Behan, Brendan
    1923-1964 . . . . .DLB-13, 233; CDBLB-7

Behn, Aphra 1640?-1689 . . . . .DLB-39, 80, 131

Behn, Harry 1898-1973 . . . . .DLB-61

Behrman, S. N. 1893-1973. . . . . .DLB-7, 44

Belaney, Archibald Stansfeld (see Grey Owl)

Belasco, David 1853-1931 . . . . .DLB-7

Belford, Clarke and Company DLB-49

Belinksy, Vissarion Grigor'evich
    1811-1848 . . . . .DLB-198

Belitt, Ben 1911- DLB-5

Belknap, Jeremy 1744-1798 . . . . DLB-30, 37

Bell, Adrian 1901-1980 . . . . .DLB-191

Bell, Clive 1881-1964. . . . . DS-10

Bell, Daniel 1919- DLB-246

Bell, George, and Sons. DLB-106

Bell, Gertrude Margaret Lowthian
    1868-1926 . . . . .DLB-174

Bell, James Madison 1826-1902. . . . . .DLB-50

Bell, Madison Smartt 1957- DLB-218

Bell, Marvin 1937- DLB-5

Bell, Millicent 1919- DLB-111

Bell, Quentin 1910-1996 . . . . .DLB-155

Bell, Robert [publishing house] DLB-49

Bell, Vanessa 1879-1961 . . . . DS-10

Bellamy, Edward 1850-1898 . . . . .DLB-12

Bellamy, John [publishing house]. DLB-170

Bellamy, Joseph 1719-1790 . . . . .DLB-31

La Belle Assemblée 1806-1837 . . . . .DLB-110

Bellezza, Dario 1944-1996 . . . . .DLB-128

Belloc, Hilaire 1870-1953 . . . .DLB-19, 100, 141, 174

Belloc, Madame (see Parkes, Bessie Rayner)

Bellonci, Maria 1902-1986. . . . . .DLB-196

Bellow, Saul
    1915- DLB-2, 28; Y-82; DS-3; CDALB-1

Belmont Productions DLB-46

Bels, Alberts 1938- DLB-232

Belševica, Vizma 1931- DLB-232; CDWLB-4

Bemelmans, Ludwig 1898-1962. . . . . .DLB-22

Bemis, Samuel Flagg 1891-1973. . . . . .DLB-17

Bemrose, William [publishing house] DLB-106

Ben no Naishi 1228?-1271? DLB-203

Benchley, Robert 1889-1945 . . . . .DLB-11

Bencúr, Matej (see Kukučin, Martin)

Benedetti, Mario 1920- DLB-113

Benedict, Pinckney 1964- DLB-244

Benedict, Ruth 1887-1948 . . . . .DLB-246

Benedictus, David 1938- DLB-14

Benedikt, Michael 1935- DLB-5

Benediktov, Vladimir Grigor'evich
    1807-1873 . . . . .DLB-205

Cumulative Index

Benét, Stephen Vincent
    1898-1943 . . . . DLB-4, 48, 102, 249

Benét, William Rose 1886-1950 . . . . DLB-45

Benford, Gregory 1941- Y-82

Benjamin, Park 1809-1864 . . . . DLB-3, 59, 73

Benjamin, S. G. W. 1837-1914 . . . . DLB-189

Benjamin, Walter 1892-1940 . . . . DLB-242

Benlowes, Edward 1602-1676 . . . . DLB-126

Benn Brothers Limited DLB-106

Benn, Gottfried 1886-1956 . . . . DLB-56

Bennett, Arnold
    1867-1931 . . . . DLB-10, 34, 98, 135; CDBLB-5

Bennett, Charles 1899-1995 . . . . DLB-44

Bennett, Emerson 1822-1905 . . . . DLB-202

Bennett, Gwendolyn 1902- DLB-51

Bennett, Hal 1930- DLB-33

Bennett, James Gordon 1795-1872 . . . . DLB-43

Bennett, James Gordon, Jr. 1841-1918 . . . . DLB-23

Bennett, John 1865-1956 . . . . DLB-42

Bennett, Louise 1919- DLB-117; CDWLB-3

Benni, Stefano 1947- DLB-196

Benoit, Jacques 1941- DLB-60

Benson, A. C. 1862-1925 . . . . DLB-98

Benson, E. F. 1867-1940 . . . . DLB-135, 153

Benson, Jackson J. 1930- DLB-111

Benson, Robert Hugh 1871-1914 . . . . DLB-153

Benson, Stella 1892-1933 . . . . DLB-36, 162

Bent, James Theodore 1852-1897 . . . . DLB-174

Bent, Mabel Virginia Anna ?-? DLB-174

Bentham, Jeremy 1748-1832 . . . . DLB-107, 158

Bentley, E. C. 1875-1956 . . . . DLB-70

Bentley, Phyllis 1894-1977 . . . . DLB-191

Bentley, Richard [publishing house] DLB-106

Benton, Robert 1932- and Newman,
    David 1937- DLB-44

Benziger Brothers DLB-49

Beowulf circa 900-1000 or 790-825
    . . . . DLB-146; CDBLB-1

Berent, Wacław 1873-1940 . . . . DLB-215

Beresford, Anne 1929- DLB-40

Beresford, John Davys
    1873-1947 . . . . DLB-162, 178, 197

"Experiment in the Novel" (1929) DLB-36

Beresford-Howe, Constance 1922- DLB-88

Berford, R. G., Company DLB-49

Berg, Stephen 1934- DLB-5

Bergengruen, Werner 1892-1964 . . . . DLB-56

Berger, John 1926- DLB-14, 207

Berger, Meyer 1898-1959 . . . . DLB-29

Berger, Thomas 1924- DLB-2; Y-80

Berkeley, Anthony 1893-1971 . . . . DLB-77

Berkeley, George 1685-1753 . . . . DLB-31, 101

The Berkley Publishing Corporation DLB-46

Berlin, Lucia 1936- DLB-130

Berman, Marshall 1940- DLB-246

Bernal, Vicente J. 1888-1915 . . . . DLB-82

Bernanos, Georges 1888-1948 . . . . DLB-72

Bernard, Harry 1898-1979 . . . . DLB-92

Bernard, John 1756-1828 . . . . DLB-37

Bernard of Chartres circa 1060-1124? . . . DLB-115

Bernard of Clairvaux 1090-1153 . . . . . . DLB-208

The Bernard Malamud Archive at the
    Harry Ransom Humanities
    Research Center Y-00

Bernard Silvestris
    flourished circa 1130-1160 . . . . DLB-208

Bernari, Carlo 1909-1992 . . . . .DLB-177

Bernhard, Thomas
    1931-1989 . . . . .DLB-85, 124; CDWLB-2

Bernstein, Charles 1950- DLB-169

Berriault, Gina 1926-1999 . . . . DLB-130

Berrigan, Daniel 1921- DLB-5

Berrigan, Ted 1934-1983 . . . . DLB-5, 169

Berry, Wendell 1934- DLB-5, 6, 234

Berryman, John 1914-1972 . . . . DLB-48; CDALB-1

Bersianik, Louky 1930- DLB-60

Berthelet, Thomas [publishing house] DLB-170

Berto, Giuseppe 1914-1978 . . . . .DLB-177

Bertolucci, Attilio 1911- DLB-128

Berton, Pierre 1920- DLB-68

Bertrand, Louis "Aloysius"
    1807-1841 . . . . DLB-217

Besant, Sir Walter 1836-1901 . . . . . . DLB-135, 190

Bessette, Gerard 1920- DLB-53

Bessie, Alvah 1904-1985 . . . . DLB-26

Bester, Alfred 1913-1987 . . . . DLB-8

Besterman, Theodore 1904-1976 . . . . DLB-201

The Bestseller Lists: An Assessment Y-84

Bestuzhev, Aleksandr Aleksandrovich
    (Marlinsky) 1797-1837 . . . . DLB-198

Bestuzhev, Nikolai Aleksandrovich
    1791-1855 . . . . DLB-198

Betham-Edwards, Matilda Barbara (see Edwards,
    Matilda Barbara Betham-)

Betjeman, John
    1906-1984 . . . . DLB-20; Y-84; CDBLB-7

Betocchi, Carlo 1899-1986 . . . . DLB-128

Bettarini, Mariella 1942- DLB-128

Betts, Doris 1932- DLB-218; Y-82

Beùkoviù, Matija 1939- DLB-181

Beveridge, Albert J. 1862-1927 . . . . DLB-17

Beverley, Robert circa 1673-1722 . . . . . DLB-24, 30

Bevilacqua, Alberto 1934- DLB-196

Bevington, Louisa Sarah 1845-1895 . . . . . DLB-199

Beyle, Marie-Henri (see Stendhal)

Białoszewski, Miron 1922-1983 . . . . . . DLB-232

Bianco, Margery Williams 1881-1944 . . . DLB-160

Bibaud, Adèle 1854-1941 . . . . DLB-92

Bibaud, Michel 1782-1857 . . . . DLB-99

Bibliographical and Textual Scholarship
    Since World War II Y-89

Bichsel, Peter 1935- DLB-75

Bickerstaff, Isaac John 1733-circa 1808 . . . . DLB-89

Biddle, Drexel [publishing house] DLB-49

Bidermann, Jacob
    1577 or 1578-1639 . . . . DLB-164

Bidwell, Walter Hilliard 1798-1881 . . . . . . DLB-79

Bienek, Horst 1930- DLB-75

Bierbaum, Otto Julius 1865-1910 . . . . DLB-66

Bierce, Ambrose 1842-1914?
    . . . . . . .DLB-11, 12, 23, 71, 74, 186; CDALB-3

Bigelow, William F. 1879-1966 . . . . DLB-91

Biggle, Lloyd, Jr. 1923- DLB-8

Bigiaretti, Libero 1905-1993 . . . . .DLB-177

Bigland, Eileen 1898-1970 . . . . DLB-195

Biglow, Hosea (see Lowell, James Russell)

Bigongiari, Piero 1914- DLB-128

Billinger, Richard 1890-1965 . . . . DLB-124

Billings, Hammatt 1818-1874 . . . . DLB-188

Billings, John Shaw 1898-1975 . . . . .DLB-137

Billings, Josh (see Shaw, Henry Wheeler)

Binding, Rudolf G. 1867-1938 . . . . DLB-66

Bingay, Malcolm 1884-1953 . . . . DLB-241

Bingham, Caleb 1757-1817 . . . . DLB-42

Bingham, George Barry 1906-1988 . . . . . .DLB-127

Bingham, Sallie 1937- DLB-234

Bingley, William [publishing house] DLB-154

Binyon, Laurence 1869-1943 . . . . DLB-19

Biographia Brittanica DLB-142

Biographical Documents I Y-84

Biographical Documents II Y-85

Bioren, John [publishing house] DLB-49

Bioy Casares, Adolfo 1914- DLB-113

Bird, Isabella Lucy 1831-1904 . . . . DLB-166

Bird, Robert Montgomery 1806-1854 . . . DLB-202

Bird, William 1888-1963 . . . . DLB-4; DS-15

Birken, Sigmund von 1626-1681 . . . . DLB-164

Birney, Earle 1904- DLB-88

Birrell, Augustine 1850-1933 . . . . DLB-98

Bisher, Furman 1918- DLB-171

Bishop, Elizabeth
    1911-1979 . . . . DLB-5, 169; CDALB-6

Bishop, John Peale 1892-1944 . . . . . . DLB-4, 9, 45

Bismarck, Otto von 1815-1898 . . . . DLB-129

Bisset, Robert 1759-1805 . . . . DLB-142

Bissett, Bill 1939- DLB-53

Bitzius, Albert (see Gotthelf, Jeremias)

Bjørnvig, Thorkild 1918- DLB-214

Black, David (D. M.) 1941- DLB-40

Black, Walter J. [publishing house] DLB-46

Black, Winifred 1863-1936 . . . . DLB-25

The Black Aesthetic: Background DS-8

Black Theaters and Theater Organizations in
    America, 1961-1982:
    A Research List DLB-38

Black Theatre: A Forum [excerpts] DLB-38

Blackamore, Arthur 1679-? DLB-24, 39

Blackburn, Alexander L. 1929- Y-85

Blackburn, Paul 1926-1971 . . . . .DLB-16; Y-81

Blackburn, Thomas 1916-1977 ....DLB-27

Blackmore, R. D. 1825-1900 ....DLB-18

Blackmore, Sir Richard 1654-1729......DLB-131

Blackmur, R. P. 1904-1965 ....DLB-63

Blackwell, Basil, Publisher DLB-106

Blackwood, Algernon Henry
1869-1951 .... DLB-153, 156, 178

Blackwood, Caroline 1931-1996 .....DLB-14, 207

Blackwood, William, and Sons, Ltd......DLB-154

Blackwood's Edinburgh Magazine
1817-1980 ....DLB-110

Blades, William 1824-1890 ....DLB-184

Blaga, Lucian 1895-1961 ....DLB-220

Blagden, Isabella 1817?-1873 ....DLB-199

Blair, Eric Arthur (see Orwell, George)

Blair, Francis Preston 1791-1876 ....DLB-43

Blair, James circa 1655-1743.............DLB-24

Blair, John Durburrow 1759-1823 ....DLB-37

Blais, Marie-Claire 1939- DLB-53

Blaise, Clark 1940- DLB-53

Blake, George 1893-1961..............DLB-191

Blake, Lillie Devereux 1833-1913 ...DLB-202, 221

Blake, Nicholas 1904-1972..............DLB-77
(see Day Lewis, C.)

Blake, William
1757-1827.......DLB-93, 154, 163; CDBLB-3

The Blakiston Company DLB-49

Blandiana, Ana 1942- DLB-232; CDWLB-4

Blanchot, Maurice 1907- DLB-72

Blanckenburg, Christian Friedrich von
1744-1796........................DLB-94

Blaser, Robin 1925- DLB-165

Blaumanis, Rudolfs 1863-1908 ....DLB-220

Bleasdale, Alan 1946- DLB-245

Bledsoe, Albert Taylor 1809-1877 ..DLB-3, 79, 248

Bleecker, Ann Eliza 1752-1783 ....DLB-200

Blelock and Company DLB-49

Blennerhassett, Margaret Agnew
1773-1842 ....DLB-99

Bles, Geoffrey [publishing house].......DLB-112

Blessington, Marguerite, Countess of
1789-1849 ....DLB-166

The Blickling Homilies circa 971 ....DLB-146

Blind, Mathilde 1841-1896 ....DLB-199

Blish, James 1921-1975.................DLB-8

Bliss, E., and E. White
[publishing house] DLB-49

Bliven, Bruce 1889-1977 ....DLB-137

Blixen, Karen 1885-1962 ....DLB-214

Bloch, Robert 1917-1994 ....DLB-44

Block, Lawrence 1938- DLB-226

Block, Rudolph (see Lessing, Bruno)

Blondal, Patricia 1926-1959 ....DLB-88

Bloom, Harold 1930- DLB-67

Bloomer, Amelia 1818-1894 ....DLB-79

Bloomfield, Robert 1766-1823 ....DLB-93

Bloomsbury Group DS-10

Blotner, Joseph 1923- DLB-111

Blount, Thomas 1618?-1679 ....DLB-236

Bloy, Léon 1846-1917 ....DLB-123

Blume, Judy 1938- DLB-52

Blunck, Hans Friedrich 1888-1961 ....DLB-66

Blunden, Edmund 1896-1974 ...DLB-20, 100, 155

Blundeville, Thomas 1522?-1606 ....DLB-236

Blunt, Lady Anne Isabella Noel
1837-1917 ....DLB-174

Blunt, Wilfrid Scawen 1840-1922 ....DLB-19, 174

Bly, Nellie (see Cochrane, Elizabeth)

Bly, Robert 1926- DLB-5

Blyton, Enid 1897-1968 ....DLB-160

Boaden, James 1762-1839 ....DLB-89

Boas, Frederick S. 1862-1957...........DLB-149

The Bobbs-Merrill Archive at the
Lilly Library, Indiana University Y-90

Boborykin, Petr Dmitrievich 1836-1921 ..DLB-238

The Bobbs-Merrill Company DLB-46

Bobrov, Semen Sergeevich
1763?-1810 ....DLB-150

Bobrowski, Johannes 1917-1965 ....DLB-75

The Elmer Holmes Bobst Awards in Arts
and Letters Y-87

Bodenheim, Maxwell 1892-1954.......DLB-9, 45

Bodenstedt, Friedrich von 1819-1892 ....DLB-129

Bodini, Vittorio 1914-1970.............DLB-128

Bodkin, M. McDonnell 1850-1933 ....DLB-70

Bodley, Sir Thomas 1545-1613 ....DLB-213

Bodley Head DLB-112

Bodmer, Johann Jakob 1698-1783 ....DLB-97

Bodmershof, Imma von 1895-1982 ....DLB-85

Bodsworth, Fred 1918- DLB-68

Boehm, Sydney 1908- DLB-44

Boer, Charles 1939- DLB-5

Boethius circa 480-circa 524 ....DLB-115

Boethius of Dacia circa 1240-? DLB-115

Bogan, Louise 1897-1970 ....DLB-45, 169

Bogarde, Dirk 1921- DLB-14

Bogdanovich, Ippolit Fedorovich
circa 1743-1803 ....DLB-150

Bogue, David [publishing house].......DLB-106

Böhme, Jakob 1575-1624 ....DLB-164

Bohn, H. G. [publishing house] DLB-106

Bohse, August 1661-1742..............DLB-168

Boie, Heinrich Christian 1744-1806.......DLB-94

Bok, Edward W. 1863-1930 .....DLB-91; DS-16

Boland, Eavan 1944- DLB-40

Boldrewood, Rolf (Thomas Alexander Browne)
1826?-1915 ....DLB-230

Bolingbroke, Henry St. John, Viscount
1678-1751 ....DLB-101

Böll, Heinrich
1917-1985 .... DLB-69; Y-85; CDWLB-2

Bolling, Robert 1738-1775 ....DLB-31

Bolotov, Andrei Timofeevich
1738-1833 ....DLB-150

Bolt, Carol 1941- DLB-60

Bolt, Robert 1924-1995 ....DLB-13, 233

Bolton, Herbert E. 1870-1953 ....DLB-17

Bonaventura DLB-90

Bonaventure circa 1217-1274 ....DLB-115

Bonaviri, Giuseppe 1924- DLB-177

Bond, Edward 1934- DLB-13

Bond, Michael 1926- DLB-161

Boni, Albert and Charles
[publishing house].................DLB-46

Boni and Liveright...................DLB-46

Bonner, Marita 1899-1971 ....DLB-228

Bonner, Paul Hyde 1893-1968...........DS-17

Bonner, Sherwood (see McDowell, Katharine
Sherwood Bonner)

Robert Bonner's Sons DLB-49

Bonnin, Gertrude Simmons (see Zitkala-Ša)

Bonsanti, Alessandro 1904-1984 ....DLB-177

Bontemps, Arna 1902-1973 ....DLB-48, 51

The Book Arts Press at the University
of Virginia........................Y-96

The Book League of America DLB-46

Book Publishing Accounting: Some Basic
Concepts Y-98

Book Reviewing in America: I.............Y-87

Book Reviewing in America: II............Y-88

Book Reviewing in America: III Y-89

Book Reviewing in America: IV Y-90

Book Reviewing in America: V............Y-91

Book Reviewing in America: VI Y-92

Book Reviewing in America: VII Y-93

Book Reviewing in America: VIII..........Y-94

Book Reviewing in America and the
Literary Scene.....................Y-95

Book Reviewing and the
Literary Scene...............Y-96, Y-97

Book Supply Company DLB-49

The Book Trade History Group Y-93

The Book Trade and the Internet Y-00

The Booker Prize.....................Y-96

Address by Anthony Thwaite,
Chairman of the Booker Prize Judges
Comments from Former Booker
Prize Winners Y-86

The Books of George V. Higgins:
A Checklist of Editions and Printings....Y-00

Boorde, Andrew circa 1490-1549 ....DLB-136

Boorstin, Daniel J. 1914- DLB-17

Booth, Franklin 1874-1948.............DLB-188

Booth, Mary L. 1831-1889 ....DLB-79

Booth, Philip 1925- Y-82

Booth, Wayne C. 1921- DLB-67

Booth, William 1829-1912..............DLB-190

Borchardt, Rudolf 1877-1945 ....DLB-66

Borchert, Wolfgang 1921-1947 ......DLB-69, 124

Borel, Pétrus 1809-1859...............DLB-119

Borges, Jorge Luis
1899-1986 ...... DLB-113; Y-86; CDWLB-3

Börne, Ludwig 1786-1837 . . . . DLB-90

Bornstein, Miriam 1950- DLB-209

Borowski, Tadeusz
1922-1951 . . . . DLB-215; CDWLB-4

Borrow, George 1803-1881 . . . . . DLB-21, 55, 166

Bosch, Juan 1909- DLB-145

Bosco, Henri 1888-1976 . . . . DLB-72

Bosco, Monique 1927- DLB-53

Bosman, Herman Charles 1905-1951. . . . DLB-225

Bostic, Joe 1908-1988 . . . . DLB-241

Boston, Lucy M. 1892-1990 . . . . DLB-161

Boswell, James
1740-1795 . . . . DLB-104, 142; CDBLB-2

Boswell, Robert 1953- DLB-234

Bote, Hermann
circa 1460-circa 1520 . . . . .DLB-179

Botev, Khristo 1847-1876 . . . . DLB-147

Botta, Anne C. Lynch 1815-1891 . . . . DLB-3

Botto, Ján (see Krasko, Ivan)

Bottome, Phyllis 1882-1963 . . . . DLB-197

Bottomley, Gordon 1874-1948 . . . . DLB-10

Bottoms, David 1949- DLB-120; Y-83

Bottrall, Ronald 1906- DLB-20

Bouchardy, Joseph 1810-1870. . . . . DLB-192

Boucher, Anthony 1911-1968. . . . . DLB-8

Boucher, Jonathan 1738-1804 . . . . DLB-31

Boucher de Boucherville, George
1814-1894. DLB-99

Boudreau, Daniel (see Coste, Donat)

Bourassa, Napoléon 1827-1916. . . . . DLB-99

Bourget, Paul 1852-1935 . . . . DLB-123

Bourinot, John George 1837-1902. . . . . . . DLB-99

Bourjaily, Vance 1922- DLB-2, 143

Bourne, Edward Gaylord
1860-1908 . . . . DLB-47

Bourne, Randolph 1886-1918. . . . . DLB-63

Bousoño, Carlos 1923- DLB-108

Bousquet, Joë 1897-1950. . . . . DLB-72

Bova, Ben 1932- Y-81

Bovard, Oliver K. 1872-1945 . . . . DLB-25

Bove, Emmanuel 1898-1945. . . . . DLB-72

Bowen, Elizabeth
1899-1973. . . . . DLB-15, 162; CDBLB-7

Bowen, Francis 1811-1890 . . . . DLB-1, 59, 235

Bowen, John 1924- DLB-13

Bowen, Marjorie 1886-1952 . . . . DLB-153

Bowen-Merrill Company DLB-49

Bowering, George 1935- DLB-53

Bowers, Bathsheba 1671-1718. . . . . DLB-200

Bowers, Claude G. 1878-1958 . . . . DLB-17

Bowers, Edgar 1924-2000. . . . . DLB-5

Bowers, Fredson Thayer
1905-1991 . . . . .DLB-140; Y-80, 91

Bowles, Paul 1910-1999 . . . . . .DLB-5, 6, 218; Y-99

Bowles, Samuel III 1826-1878 . . . . DLB-43

Bowles, William Lisles 1762-1850 . . . . DLB-93

Bowman, Louise Morey 1882-1944 . . . . . DLB-68

Boyd, James 1888-1944 . . . . DLB-9; DS-16

Boyd, John 1919- DLB-8

Boyd, Thomas 1898-1935 . . . . DLB-9; DS-16

Boyd, William 1952- DLB-231

Boyesen, Hjalmar Hjorth
1848-1895 . . . . .DLB-12, 71; DS-13

Boyle, Kay 1902-1992 . . . . .DLB-4, 9, 48, 86; Y-93

Boyle, Roger, Earl of Orrery 1621-1679. . . DLB-80

Boyle, T. Coraghessan 1948- DLB-218; Y-86

Božić, Mirko 1919- DLB-181

Brackenbury, Alison 1953- DLB-40

Brackenridge, Hugh Henry
1748-1816. . . . . .DLB-11, 37

Brackett, Charles 1892-1969. . . . . DLB-26

Brackett, Leigh 1915-1978 . . . . DLB-8, 26

Bradburn, John [publishing house] DLB-49

Bradbury, Malcolm 1932-2000. . . . . . .DLB-14, 207

Bradbury, Ray 1920- DLB-2, 8; CDALB-6

Bradbury and Evans. DLB-106

Braddon, Mary Elizabeth
1835-1915 . . . . .DLB-18, 70, 156

Bradford, Andrew 1686-1742 . . . . DLB-43, 73

Bradford, Gamaliel 1863-1932 . . . . DLB-17

Bradford, John 1749-1830. . . . . DLB-43

Bradford, Roark 1896-1948 . . . . DLB-86

Bradford, William 1590-1657. . . . . . . DLB-24, 30

Bradford, William III 1719-1791 . . . . . DLB-43, 73

Bradlaugh, Charles 1833-1891 . . . . DLB-57

Bradley, David 1950- DLB-33

Bradley, Ira, and Company DLB-49

Bradley, J. W., and Company DLB-49

Bradley, Katherine Harris (see Field, Michael)

Bradley, Marion Zimmer 1930-1999 . . . . . . DLB-8

Bradley, William Aspenwall 1878-1939 . . . . DLB-4

Bradshaw, Henry 1831-1886 . . . . DLB-184

Bradstreet, Anne
1612 or 1613-1672 . . . . . . DLB-24; CDABL-2

Bradūnas, Kazys 1917- DLB-220

Bradwardine, Thomas circa
1295-1349 . . . . DLB-115

Brady, Frank 1924-1986. . . . . DLB-111

Brady, Frederic A. [publishing house] DLB-49

Bragg, Melvyn 1939- DLB-14

Brainard, Charles H. [publishing house] . . DLB-49

Braine, John 1922-1986 . DLB-15; Y-86; CDBLB-7

Braithwait, Richard 1588-1673 . . . . DLB-151

Braithwaite, William Stanley
1878-1962. . . . . DLB-50, 54

Braker, Ulrich 1735-1798 . . . . DLB-94

Bramah, Ernest 1868-1942. . . . . DLB-70

Branagan, Thomas 1774-1843 . . . . DLB-37

Branch, William Blackwell 1927- DLB-76

Branden Press. DLB-46

Branner, H.C. 1903-1966 . . . . DLB-214

Brant, Sebastian 1457-1521. . . . . .DLB-179

Brassey, Lady Annie (Allnutt)
1839-1887 . . . . DLB-166

Brathwaite, Edward Kamau
1930- DLB-125; CDWLB-3

Brault, Jacques 1933- DLB-53

Braun, Matt 1932- DLB-212

Braun, Volker 1939- DLB-75

Brautigan, Richard
1935-1984 . . . . DLB-2, 5, 206; Y-80, Y-84

Braxton, Joanne M. 1950- DLB-41

Bray, Anne Eliza 1790-1883 . . . . DLB-116

Bray, Thomas 1656-1730 . . . . DLB-24

Brazdžionis, Bernardas 1907- DLB-220

Braziller, George [publishing house] DLB-46

The Bread Loaf Writers' Conference 1983 . . . Y-84

Breasted, James Henry 1865-1935 . . . . DLB-47

Brecht, Bertolt
1898-1956 . . . . .DLB-56, 124; CDWLB-2

Bredel, Willi 1901-1964 . . . . DLB-56

Bregendahl, Marie 1867-1940. . . . . DLB-214

Breitinger, Johann Jakob 1701-1776 . . . . . DLB-97

Bremser, Bonnie 1939- DLB-16

Bremser, Ray 1934- DLB-16

Brennan, Christopher 1870-1932 . . . . DLB-230

Brentano, Bernard von 1901-1964 . . . . DLB-56

Brentano, Clemens 1778-1842 . . . . DLB-90

Brentano's. DLB-49

Brenton, Howard 1942- DLB-13

Breslin, Jimmy 1929-1996 . . . . DLB-185

Breton, André 1896-1966. . . . . DLB-65

Breton, Nicholas circa 1555-circa 1626. . . DLB-136

The Breton Lays
1300-early fifteenth century DLB-146

Brewer, Luther A. 1858-1933. . . . . .DLB-187

Brewer, Warren and Putnam. DLB-46

Brewster, Elizabeth 1922- DLB-60

Breytenbach, Breyten 1939- DLB-225

Bridge, Ann (Lady Mary Dolling Sanders
O'Malley) 1889-1974 . . . . DLB-191

Bridge, Horatio 1806-1893. . . . . DLB-183

Bridgers, Sue Ellen 1942- DLB-52

Bridges, Robert
1844-1930 . . . . DLB-19, 98; CDBLB-5

The Bridgewater Library DLB-213

Bridie, James 1888-1951 . . . . DLB-10

Brieux, Eugene 1858-1932 . . . . DLB-192

Brigadere, Anna 1861-1933 . . . . DLB-220

Bright, Mary Chavelita Dunne (see Egerton, George)

Brimmer, B. J., Company. DLB-46

Brines, Francisco 1932- DLB-134

Brink, André 1935- DLB-225

Brinley, George, Jr. 1817-1875 . . . . DLB-140

Brinnin, John Malcolm 1916-1998 . . . . DLB-48

Brisbane, Albert 1809-1890 . . . . DLB-3

Brisbane, Arthur 1864-1936. . . . . DLB-25

British Academy. DLB-112

The British Critic 1793-1843 . . . . .DLB-110

The British Library and the Regular
    Readers' Group Y-91

British Literary Prizes Y-98

*The British Review and London Critical
    Journal 1811-1825* DLB-110

British Travel Writing, 1940-1997 . . . . . . .DLB-204

Brito, Aristeo 1942- DLB-122

Brittain, Vera 1893-1970 . . . . .DLB-191

Brizeux, Auguste 1803-1858 . . . . .DLB-217

Broadway Publishing Company DLB-46

Broch, Hermann
    1886-1951 . . . . .DLB-85, 124; CDWLB-2

Brochu, André 1942- DLB-53

Brock, Edwin 1927- DLB-40

Brockes, Barthold Heinrich 1680-1747 . . . .DLB-168

Brod, Max 1884-1968 . . . . .DLB-81

Brodber, Erna 1940- DLB-157

Brodhead, John R. 1814-1873 . . . . .DLB-30

Brodkey, Harold 1930-1996 . . . . .DLB-130

Brodsky, Joseph 1940-1996 . . . . .Y-87

Brodsky, Michael 1948- DLB-244

Broeg, Bob 1918- DLB-171

Brøgger, Suzanne 1944- DLB-214

Brome, Richard circa 1590-1652 . . . . .DLB-58

Brome, Vincent 1910- DLB-155

Bromfield, Louis 1896-1956 . . . . .DLB-4, 9, 86

Bromige, David 1933- DLB-193

Broner, E. M. 1930- DLB-28

Bronk, William 1918-1999 . . . . .DLB-165

Bronnen, Arnolt 1895-1959 . . . . .DLB-124

Brontë, Anne 1820-1849 . . . . .DLB-21, 199

Brontë, Charlotte
    1816-1855 . . . . . .DLB-21, 159, 199; CDBLB-4

Brontë, Emily
    1818-1848 . . . . . .DLB-21, 32, 199; CDBLB-4

Brook, Stephen 1947- DLB-204

Brook Farm 1841-1847 . . . . .DLB-223

Brooke, Frances 1724-1789 . . . . .DLB-39, 99

Brooke, Henry 1703?-1783 . . . . .DLB-39

Brooke, L. Leslie 1862-1940 . . . . .DLB-141

Brooke, Margaret, Ranee of Sarawak
    1849-1936 . . . . .DLB-174

Brooke, Rupert
    1887-1915 . . . . .DLB-19, 216; CDBLB-6

Brooker, Bertram 1888-1955 . . . . .DLB-88

Brooke-Rose, Christine 1923- DLB-14, 231

Brookner, Anita 1928- DLB-194; Y-87

Brooks, Charles Timothy 1813-1883 . . .DLB-1, 243

Brooks, Cleanth 1906-1994 . . . . . . .DLB-63; Y-94

Brooks, Gwendolyn
    1917-2000 . . . . .DLB-5, 76, 165; CDALB-1

Brooks, Jeremy 1926- DLB-14

Brooks, Mel 1926- DLB-26

Brooks, Noah 1830-1903 . . . . .DLB-42; DS-13

Brooks, Richard 1912-1992 . . . . .DLB-44

Brooks, Van Wyck
    1886-1963 . . . . .DLB-45, 63, 103

Brophy, Brigid 1929-1995 . . . . .DLB-14

Brophy, John 1899-1965 . . . . .DLB-191

Brossard, Chandler 1922-1993 . . . . .DLB-16

Brossard, Nicole 1943- DLB-53

Broster, Dorothy Kathleen 1877-1950 . . . .DLB-160

Brother Antoninus (see Everson, William)

Brotherton, Lord 1856-1930 . . . . .DLB-184

Brougham and Vaux, Henry Peter Brougham,
    Baron 1778-1868 . . . . .DLB-110, 158

Brougham, John 1810-1880 . . . . .DLB-11

Broughton, James 1913-1999 . . . . .DLB-5

Broughton, Rhoda 1840-1920 . . . . .DLB-18

Broun, Heywood 1888-1939 . . . . .DLB-29, 171

Brown, Alice 1856-1948 . . . . .DLB-78

Brown, Bob 1886-1959 . . . . .DLB-4, 45

Brown, Cecil 1943- DLB-33

Brown, Charles Brockden
    1771-1810 . . . . .DLB-37, 59, 73; CDALB-2

Brown, Christy 1932-1981 . . . . .DLB-14

Brown, Dee 1908- Y-80

Brown, Frank London 1927-1962 . . . . .DLB-76

Brown, Fredric 1906-1972 . . . . .DLB-8

Brown, George Mackay
    1921-1996 . . . . DLB-14, 27, 139

Brown, Harry 1917-1986 . . . . .DLB-26

Brown, Larry 1951- DLB-234

Brown, Marcia 1918- DLB-61

Brown, Margaret Wise 1910-1952 . . . . . . .DLB-22

Brown, Morna Doris (see Ferrars, Elizabeth)

Brown, Oliver Madox 1855-1874 . . . . .DLB-21

Brown, Sterling 1901-1989 . . . . . .DLB-48, 51, 63

Brown, T. E. 1830-1897 . . . . .DLB-35

Brown, Thomas Alexander (see Boldrewood, Rolf)

Brown, Warren 1894-1978 . . . . .DLB-241

Brown, William Hill 1765-1793 . . . . .DLB-37

Brown, William Wells
    1815-1884 . . . . .DLB-3, 50, 183, 248

Browne, Charles Farrar 1834-1867 . . . . . . .DLB-11

Browne, Frances 1816-1879 . . . . .DLB-199

Browne, Francis Fisher 1843-1913 . . . . . . .DLB-79

Browne, Howard 1908-1999 . . . . .DLB-226

Browne, J. Ross 1821-1875 . . . . .DLB-202

Browne, Michael Dennis 1940- DLB-40

Browne, Sir Thomas 1605-1682 . . . . .DLB-151

Browne, William, of Tavistock
    1590-1645 . . . . .DLB-121

Browne, Wynyard 1911-1964 . . . . . . .DLB-13, 233

Browne and Nolan DLB-106

Brownell, W. C. 1851-1928 . . . . .DLB-71

Browning, Elizabeth Barrett
    1806-1861 . . . . .DLB-32, 199; CDBLB-4

Browning, Robert
    1812-1889 . . . . .DLB-32, 163; CDBLB-4

Introductory Essay: *Letters of Percy
    Bysshe Shelley* (1852) DLB-32

Brownjohn, Allan 1931- DLB-40

Brownson, Orestes Augustus
    1803-1876 . . . . .DLB-1, 59, 73, 243

Bruccoli, Matthew J. 1931- DLB-103

Bruce, Charles 1906-1971 . . . . .DLB-68

John Edward Bruce: Three Documents DLB-50

Bruce, Leo 1903-1979 . . . . .DLB-77

Bruce, Mary Grant 1878-1958 . . . . .DLB-230

Bruce, Philip Alexander 1856-1933 . . . . . . .DLB-47

Bruce Humphries [publishing house] DLB-46

Bruce-Novoa, Juan 1944- DLB-82

Bruckman, Clyde 1894-1955 . . . . .DLB-26

Bruckner, Ferdinand 1891-1958 . . . . .DLB-118

Brundage, John Herbert (see Herbert, John)

Brutus, Dennis
    1924- DLB-117, 225; CDWLB-3

Bryan, C. D. B. 1936- DLB-185

Bryant, Arthur 1899-1985 . . . . .DLB-149

Bryant, William Cullen
    1794-1878 . . . . .DLB-3, 43, 59, 189; CDALB-2

Bryce Echenique, Alfredo
    1939- DLB-145; CDWLB-3

Bryce, James 1838-1922 . . . . .DLB-166, 190

Bryden, Bill 1942- DLB-233

Brydges, Sir Samuel Egerton 1762-1837 . .DLB-107

Bryskett, Lodowick 1546?-1612 . . . . .DLB-167

Buchan, John 1875-1940 . . . . DLB-34, 70, 156

Buchanan, George 1506-1582 . . . . .DLB-132

Buchanan, Robert 1841-1901 . . . . .DLB-18, 35

"The Fleshly School of Poetry and Other
    Phenomena of the Day" (1872), by
    Robert Buchanan DLB-35

"The Fleshly School of Poetry: Mr. D. G.
    Rossetti" (1871), by Thomas Maitland
    (Robert Buchanan) DLB-35

Buchman, Sidney 1902-1975 . . . . .DLB-26

Buchner, Augustus 1591-1661 . . . . .DLB-164

Büchner, Georg 1813-1837 . .DLB-133; CDWLB-2

Bucholtz, Andreas Heinrich 1607-1671 . . .DLB-168

Buck, Pearl S. 1892-1973 . . .DLB-9, 102; CDALB-7

Bucke, Charles 1781-1846 . . . . .DLB-110

Bucke, Richard Maurice 1837-1902 . . . . . . .DLB-99

Buckingham, Joseph Tinker 1779-1861 and
    Buckingham, Edwin 1810-1833 . . . . . .DLB-73

Buckler, Ernest 1908-1984 . . . . .DLB-68

Buckley, William F., Jr. 1925- . . . DLB-137; Y-80

Buckminster, Joseph Stevens
    1784-1812 . . . . .DLB-37

Buckner, Robert 1906- DLB-26

Budd, Thomas ?-1698 . . . . .DLB-24

Budrys, A. J. 1931- DLB-8

Buechner, Frederick 1926- Y-80

Buell, John 1927- DLB-53

Bufalino, Gesualdo 1920-1996 . . . . .DLB-196

Buffum, Job [publishing house] DLB-49

Bugnet, Georges 1879-1981 . . . . .DLB-92

Buies, Arthur 1840-1901 . . . . .DLB-99

Building the New British Library
  at St Pancras. Y-94

Bukowski, Charles 1920-1994 . . . DLB-5, 130, 169

Bulatović, Miodrag
  1930-1991 . . . . DLB-181; CDWLB-4

Bulgarin, Faddei Venediktovich
  1789-1859. . . . . DLB-198

Bulger, Bozeman 1877-1932 . . . . .DLB-171

Bullein, William
  between 1520 and 1530-1576. . . . . . . DLB-167

Bullins, Ed 1935- DLB-7, 38, 249

Bulwer, John 1606-1656 . . . . DLB-236

Bulwer-Lytton, Edward (also Edward Bulwer)
  1803-1873. . . . . DLB-21

"On Art in Fiction "(1838) DLB-21

Bumpus, Jerry 1937- Y-81

Bunce and Brother DLB-49

Bunner, H. C. 1855-1896 . . . . .DLB-78, 79

Bunting, Basil 1900-1985 . . . . DLB-20

Buntline, Ned (Edward Zane Carroll Judson)
  1821-1886 . . . . DLB-186

Bunyan, John 1628-1688 . . . . . DLB-39; CDBLB-2

Burch, Robert 1925- DLB-52

Burciaga, José Antonio 1940- DLB-82

Bürger, Gottfried August 1747-1794 . . . . . . DLB-94

Burgess, Anthony
  1917-1993 . . . . DLB-14, 194; CDBLB-8

The Anthony Burgess Archive at
  the Harry Ransom Humanities
  Research Center. Y-98

Anthony Burgess's 99 Novels:
  An Opinion Poll. Y-84

Burgess, Gelett 1866-1951 . . . . DLB-11

Burgess, John W. 1844-1931 . . . . DLB-47

Burgess, Thornton W. 1874-1965 . . . . DLB-22

Burgess, Stringer and Company DLB-49

Burick, Si 1909-1986. . . . . .DLB-171

Burk, John Daly circa 1772-1808 . . . . DLB-37

Burk, Ronnie 1955- DLB-209

Burke, Edmund 1729?-1797 . . . . DLB-104

Burke, James Lee 1936- DLB-226

Burke, Kenneth 1897-1993 . . . . DLB-45, 63

Burke, Thomas 1886-1945 . . . . DLB-197

Burley, Dan 1907-1962 . . . . DLB-241

Burlingame, Edward Livermore
  1848-1922 . . . . DLB-79

Burnet, Gilbert 1643-1715 . . . . DLB-101

Burnett, Frances Hodgson
  1849-1924 . . . . DLB-42, 141; DS-13, 14

Burnett, W. R. 1899-1982 . . . . DLB-9, 226

Burnett, Whit 1899-1973 and
  Martha Foley 1897-1977 . . . . DLB-137

Burney, Fanny 1752-1840. . . . . DLB-39

Dedication, *The Wanderer* (1814) DLB-39

Preface to *Evelina* (1778) DLB-39

Burns, Alan 1929- DLB-14, 194

Burns, John Horne 1916-1953 . . . . .Y-85

Burns, Robert 1759-1796. . . . . DLB-109; CDBLB-3

Burns and Oates. DLB-106

Burnshaw, Stanley 1906- DLB-48

Burr, C. Chauncey 1815?-1883 . . . . DLB-79

Burr, Esther Edwards 1732-1758 . . . . . . DLB-200

Burroughs, Edgar Rice 1875-1950 . . . . DLB-8

Burroughs, John 1837-1921 . . . . DLB-64

Burroughs, Margaret T. G. 1917- DLB-41

Burroughs, William S., Jr. 1947-1981 . . . . . DLB-16

Burroughs, William Seward 1914-1997
  . . . . DLB-2, 8, 16, 152, 237; Y-81, Y-97

Burroway, Janet 1936- DLB-6

Burt, Maxwell Struthers
  1882-1954 . . . . DLB-86; DS-16

Burt, A. L., and Company DLB-49

Burton, Hester 1913- DLB-161

Burton, Isabel Arundell 1831-1896. . . . . . DLB-166

Burton, Miles (see Rhode, John)

Burton, Richard Francis
  1821-1890 . . . . DLB-55, 166, 184

Burton, Robert 1577-1640. . . . . DLB-151

Burton, Virginia Lee 1909-1968 . . . . DLB-22

Burton, William Evans 1804-1860 . . . . DLB-73

Burwell, Adam Hood 1790-1849 . . . . DLB-99

Bury, Lady Charlotte 1775-1861 . . . . DLB-116

Busch, Frederick 1941- DLB-6, 218

Busch, Niven 1903-1991. . . . . DLB-44

Bushnell, Horace 1802-1876. . . . . .DS-13

Bussieres, Arthur de 1877-1913. . . . . DLB-92

Butler, Charles ca. 1560-1647. . . . . DLB-236

Butler, Guy 1918- DLB-225

Butler, E. H., and Company. DLB-49

Butler, Josephine Elizabeth 1828-1906 . . . DLB-190

Butler, Juan 1942-1981. . . . . DLB-53

Butler, Judith 1956- DLB-246

Butler, Octavia E. 1947- DLB-33

Butler, Pierce 1884-1953. . . . . DLB-187

Butler, Robert Olen 1945- DLB-173

Butler, Samuel 1613-1680. . . . . DLB-101, 126

Butler, Samuel 1835-1902. . . . . . . DLB-18, 57, 174

Butler, William Francis 1838-1910 . . . . . . DLB-166

Butor, Michel 1926- DLB-83

Butter, Nathaniel [publishing house]. DLB-170

Butterworth, Hezekiah 1839-1905 . . . . DLB-42

Buttitta, Ignazio 1899- DLB-114

Butts, Mary 1890-1937 . . . . DLB-240

Buzzati, Dino 1906-1972. . . . . .DLB-177

Byars, Betsy 1928- DLB-52

Byatt, A. S. 1936- DLB-14, 194

Byles, Mather 1707-1788 . . . . DLB-24

Bynneman, Henry
  [publishing house] DLB-170

Bynner, Witter 1881-1968 . . . . DLB-54

Byrd, William circa 1543-1623. . . . . .DLB-172

Byrd, William II 1674-1744 . . . . DLB-24, 140

Byrne, John Keyes (see Leonard, Hugh)

Byron, George Gordon, Lord
  1788-1824. . . . . DLB-96, 110; CDBLB-3

Byron, Robert 1905-1941. . . . . DLB-195

C

Caballero Bonald, José Manuel
  1926- DLB-108

Cabañero, Eladio 1930- DLB-134

Cabell, James Branch 1879-1958 . . . . . . .DLB-9, 78

Cabeza de Baca, Manuel 1853-1915. . . . . DLB-122

Cabeza de Baca Gilbert, Fabiola
  1898- DLB-122

Cable, George Washington
  1844-1925 . . . . .DLB-12, 74; DS-13

Cable, Mildred 1878-1952 . . . . DLB-195

Cabrera, Lydia 1900-1991 . . . . DLB-145

Cabrera Infante, Guillermo
  1929- DLB-113; CDWLB-3

Cadell [publishing house] DLB-154

Cady, Edwin H. 1917- DLB-103

Caedmon flourished 658-680 . . . . DLB-146

Caedmon School circa 660-899 . . . . DLB-146

Cafés, Brasseries, and Bistros DS-15

Cage, John 1912-1992 . . . . DLB-193

Cahan, Abraham 1860-1951 . . . . . . DLB-9, 25, 28

Cain, George 1943- DLB-33

Cain, James M. 1892-1977 . . . . DLB-226

Caird, Mona 1854-1932 . . . . .DLB-197

Čaks, Aleksandrs
  1901-1950 . . . . DLB-220; CDWLB-4

Caldecott, Randolph 1846-1886 . . . . DLB-163

Calder, John (Publishers), Limited DLB-112

Calderón de la Barca, Fanny
  1804-1882 . . . . DLB-183

Caldwell, Ben 1937- DLB-38

Caldwell, Erskine 1903-1987 . . . . DLB-9, 86

Caldwell, H. M., Company DLB-49

Caldwell, Taylor 1900-1985. . . . . .DS-17

Calhoun, John C. 1782-1850 . . . . DLB-3, 248

Călinescu, George 1899-1965. . . . . DLB-220

Calisher, Hortense 1911- DLB-2, 218

A Call to Letters and an Invitation
  to the Electric Chair,
  by Siegfried Mandel. DLB-75

Callaghan, Mary Rose 1944- DLB-207

Callaghan, Morley 1903-1990 . . . . DLB-68

Callahan, S. Alice 1868-1894 . . . . . . .DLB-175, 221

Callaloo Y-87

Callimachus circa 305 B.C.-240 B.C. DLB-176

Calmer, Edgar 1907- DLB-4

Calverley, C. S. 1831-1884. . . . . DLB-35

Calvert, George Henry
  1803-1889 . . . . DLB-1, 64, 248

Calvino, Italo 1923-1985 . . . . DLB-196

Cambridge, Ada 1844-1926 . . . . DLB-230

Cambridge Press DLB-49

Cambridge Songs (Carmina Cantabrigensia)
  circa 1050. . . . . DLB-148

Cambridge University Press DLB-170

Camden, William 1551-1623 . . . . DLB-172

Camden House: An Interview with
James Hardin Y-92

Cameron, Eleanor 1912- DLB-52

Cameron, George Frederick
1854-1885 . . . . DLB-99

Cameron, Lucy Lyttelton 1781-1858 . . . . . DLB-163

Cameron, Peter 1959- DLB-234

Cameron, William Bleasdell 1862-1951 . . . DLB-99

Camm, John 1718-1778 . . . . DLB-31

Camon, Ferdinando 1935- DLB-196

Camp, Walter 1859-1925 . . . . DLB-241

Campana, Dino 1885-1932 . . . . DLB-114

Campbell, Bebe Moore 1950- DLB-227

Campbell, Gabrielle Margaret Vere
(see Shearing, Joseph, and Bowen, Marjorie)

Campbell, James Dykes 1838-1895 . . . . . . DLB-144

Campbell, James Edwin 1867-1896 . . . . . . DLB-50

Campbell, John 1653-1728 . . . . DLB-43

Campbell, John W., Jr. 1910-1971 . . . . DLB-8

Campbell, Roy 1901-1957 . . . . DLB-20, 225

Campbell, Thomas 1777-1844 . . . . DLB-93, 144

Campbell, William Wilfred 1858-1918 . . . . DLB-92

Campion, Edmund 1539-1581 . . . . DLB-167

Campion, Thomas
1567-1620 . . . . DLB-58, 172; CDBLB-1

Campton, David 1924- DLB-245

Camus, Albert 1913-1960 . . . . DLB-72

The Canadian Publishers' Records
Database Y-96

Canby, Henry Seidel 1878-1961 . . . . DLB-91

Candelaria, Cordelia 1943- DLB-82

Candelaria, Nash 1928- DLB-82

Canetti, Elias
1905-1994 . . . . DLB-85, 124; CDWLB-2

Canham, Erwin Dain 1904-1982 . . . . DLB-127

Canitz, Friedrich Rudolph Ludwig von
1654-1699 . . . . DLB-168

Cankar, Ivan 1876-1918 . . . . . DLB-147; CDWLB-4

Cannan, Gilbert 1884-1955 . . . . DLB-10, 197

Cannan, Joanna 1896-1961 . . . . DLB-191

Cannell, Kathleen 1891-1974 . . . . DLB-4

Cannell, Skipwith 1887-1957 . . . . DLB-45

Canning, George 1770-1827 . . . . DLB-158

Cannon, Jimmy 1910-1973 . . . . DLB-171

Cano, Daniel 1947- DLB-209

Cantú, Norma Elia 1947- DLB-209

Cantwell, Robert 1908-1978 . . . . DLB-9

Cape, Jonathan, and Harrison Smith
[publishing house] DLB-46

Cape, Jonathan, Limited DLB-112

Čapek, Karel 1890-1938 . . . . DLB-215; CDWLB-4

Capen, Joseph 1658-1725 . . . . DLB-24

Capes, Bernard 1854-1918 . . . . DLB-156

Capote, Truman 1924-1984
. . . . . DLB-2, 185, 227; Y-80, Y-84; CDALB-1

Caproni, Giorgio 1912-1990 . . . . DLB-128

Caragiale, Mateiu Ioan 1885-1936 . . . . . . DLB-220

Cardarelli, Vincenzo 1887-1959 . . . . DLB-114

Cárdenas, Reyes 1948- DLB-122

Cardinal, Marie 1929- DLB-83

Carew, Jan 1920- DLB-157

Carew, Thomas 1594 or 1595-1640 . . . . . DLB-126

Carey, Henry circa 1687-1689-1743 . . . . . . DLB-84

Carey, M., and Company DLB-49

Carey, Mathew 1760-1839 . . . . DLB-37, 73

Carey and Hart DLB-49

Carlell, Lodowick 1602-1675 . . . . DLB-58

Carleton, William 1794-1869 . . . . DLB-159

Carleton, G. W. [publishing house] DLB-49

Carlile, Richard 1790-1843 . . . . DLB-110, 158

Carlson, Ron 1947- DLB-244

Carlyle, Jane Welsh 1801-1866 . . . . DLB-55

Carlyle, Thomas
1795-1881 . . . . DLB-55, 144; CDBLB-3

"The Hero as Man of Letters: Johnson,
Rousseau, Burns" (1841) [excerpt] DLB-57

The Hero as Poet. Dante;
Shakspeare (1841) DLB-32

Carman, Bliss 1861-1929 . . . . DLB-92

Carmina Burana circa 1230 . . . . DLB-138

Carnero, Guillermo 1947- DLB-108

Carossa, Hans 1878-1956 . . . . DLB-66

Carpenter, Humphrey
1946- DLB-155; Y-84, Y-99

The Practice of Biography III: An Interview
with Humphrey Carpenter Y-84

Carpenter, Stephen Cullen ?-1820? DLB-73

Carpentier, Alejo
1904-1980 . . . . DLB-113; CDWLB-3

Carr, Marina 1964- DLB-245

Carrier, Roch 1937- DLB-53

Carrillo, Adolfo 1855-1926 . . . . DLB-122

Carroll, Gladys Hasty 1904- DLB-9

Carroll, John 1735-1815 . . . . DLB-37

Carroll, John 1809-1884 . . . . DLB-99

Carroll, Lewis
1832-1898 . . . . . . DLB-18, 163, 178; CDBLB-4

The Lewis Carroll Centenary Y-98

Carroll, Paul 1927- DLB-16

Carroll, Paul Vincent 1900-1968 . . . . DLB-10

Carroll and Graf Publishers DLB-46

Carruth, Hayden 1921- DLB-5, 165

Carryl, Charles E. 1841-1920 . . . . DLB-42

Carson, Anne 1950- DLB-193

Carswell, Catherine 1879-1946 . . . . DLB-36

Cărtărescu, Mirea 1956- DLB-232

Carter, Angela 1940-1992 . . . . DLB-14, 207

Carter, Elizabeth 1717-1806 . . . . DLB-109

Carter, Henry (see Leslie, Frank)

Carter, Hodding, Jr. 1907-1972 . . . . DLB-127

Carter, John 1905-1975 . . . . DLB-201

Carter, Landon 1710-1778 . . . . DLB-31

Carter, Lin 1930- Y-81

Carter, Martin 1927-1997 . . . . DLB-117; CDWLB-3

Carter, Robert, and Brothers DLB-49

Carter and Hendee DLB-49

Cartwright, Jim 1958- DLB-245

Cartwright, John 1740-1824 . . . . DLB-158

Cartwright, William circa 1611-1643 . . . . DLB-126

Caruthers, William Alexander
1802-1846 . . . . DLB-3, 248

Carver, Jonathan 1710-1780 . . . . DLB-31

Carver, Raymond
1938-1988 . . . . DLB-130; Y-83, Y-88

First Strauss "Livings" Awarded to Cynthia
Ozick and Raymond Carver
An Interview with Raymond Carver Y-83

Cary, Alice 1820-1871 . . . . DLB-202

Cary, Joyce 1888-1957 . . . . DLB-15, 100; CDBLB-6

Cary, Patrick 1623?-1657 . . . . DLB-131

Casey, Juanita 1925- DLB-14

Casey, Michael 1947- DLB-5

Cassady, Carolyn 1923- DLB-16

Cassady, Neal 1926-1968 . . . . DLB-16, 237

Cassell and Company DLB-106

Cassell Publishing Company DLB-49

Cassill, R. V. 1919- DLB-6, 218

Cassity, Turner 1929- DLB-105

Cassius Dio circa 155/164-post 229 . . . . . . DLB-176

Cassola, Carlo 1917-1987 . . . . DLB-177

The Castle of Perserverance circa 1400-1425 . . DLB-146

Castellano, Olivia 1944- DLB-122

Castellanos, Rosario
1925-1974 . . . . DLB-113; CDWLB-3

Castillo, Ana 1953- DLB-122, 227

Castillo, Rafael C. 1950- DLB-209

Castlemon, Harry (see Fosdick, Charles Austin)

Čašule, Kole 1921- DLB-181

Caswall, Edward 1814-1878 . . . . DLB-32

Catacalos, Rosemary 1944- DLB-122

Cather, Willa
1873-1947 . . . . DLB-9, 54, 78; DS-1; CDALB-3

Catherine II (Ekaterina Alekseevna), "The Great,"
Empress of Russia 1729-1796 . . . . DLB-150

Catherwood, Mary Hartwell 1847-1902 . . . DLB-78

Catledge, Turner 1901-1983 . . . . DLB-127

Catlin, George 1796-1872 . . . . DLB-186, 189

Cato the Elder 234 B.C.-149 B.C. DLB-211

Cattafi, Bartolo 1922-1979 . . . . DLB-128

Catton, Bruce 1899-1978 . . . . DLB-17

Catullus circa 84 B.C.-54 B.C.
. . . . DLB-211; CDWLB-1

Causley, Charles 1917- DLB-27

Caute, David 1936- DLB-14, 231

Cavendish, Duchess of Newcastle,
Margaret Lucas 1623-1673 . . . . DLB-131

Cawein, Madison 1865-1914 . . . . DLB-54

Caxton, William [publishing house] DLB-170

The Caxton Printers, Limited DLB-46

Caylor, O. P. 1849-1897. . . . . DLB-241

Cayrol, Jean 1911- DLB-83

Cecil, Lord David 1902-1986. . . . . DLB-155

Cela, Camilo José 1916- Y-89

Celan, Paul 1920-1970 . . . . . DLB-69; CDWLB-2

Celati, Gianni 1937- DLB-196

Celaya, Gabriel 1911-1991 . . . . DLB-108

A Celebration of Literary Biography Y-98

Céline, Louis-Ferdinand 1894-1961 . . . . . . DLB-72

The Celtic Background to Medieval English
    Literature DLB-146

Celtis, Conrad 1459-1508. . . . . .DLB-179

Center for Bibliographical Studies and
    Research at the University of
    California, Riverside Y-91

The Center for the Book in the Library
    of Congress Y-93

Center for the Book Research Y-84

Centlivre, Susanna 1669?-1723. . . . . DLB-84

The Centre for Writing, Publishing and
    Printing History at the University
    of Reading .Y-00

The Century Company DLB-49

Cernuda, Luis 1902-1963 . . . . DLB-134

Cervantes, Lorna Dee 1954- DLB-82

Ch., T. (see Marchenko, Anastasiia Iakovlevna)

Chaadaev, Petr Iakovlevich
    1794-1856. . . . . DLB-198

Chacel, Rosa 1898- DLB-134

Chacón, Eusebio 1869-1948. . . . . DLB-82

Chacón, Felipe Maximiliano 1873-? DLB-82

Chadwick, Henry 1824-1908 . . . . DLB-241

Chadwyck-Healey's Full-Text Literary Databases:
    Editing Commercial Databases of
    Primary Literary Texts Y-95

Challans, Eileen Mary (see Renault, Mary)

Chalmers, George 1742-1825 . . . . DLB-30

Chaloner, Sir Thomas 1520-1565. . . . . . . DLB-167

Chamberlain, Samuel S. 1851-1916 . . . . . DLB-25

Chamberland, Paul 1939- DLB-60

Chamberlin, William Henry 1897-1969 . . . DLB-29

Chambers, Charles Haddon 1860-1921 . . . DLB-10

Chambers, María Cristina (see Mena, María Cristina)

Chambers, Robert W. 1865-1933. . . . . . . DLB-202

Chambers, W. and R.
    [publishing house] DLB-106

Chamisso, Albert von 1781-1838 . . . . DLB-90

Champfleury 1821-1889. . . . . DLB-119

Chandler, Harry 1864-1944 . . . . DLB-29

Chandler, Norman 1899-1973 . . . . DLB-127

Chandler, Otis 1927- DLB-127

Chandler, Raymond
    1888-1959 . . . . DLB-226; DS-6; CDALB-5

Raymond Chandler Centenary Tributes
    from Michael Avallone, James Ellroy,
    Joe Gores, and William F. Nolan Y-88

Channing, Edward 1856-1931 . . . . DLB-17

Channing, Edward Tyrrell
    1790-1856. . . . . DLB-1, 59, 235

Channing, William Ellery
    1780-1842 . . . . DLB-1, 59, 235

Channing, William Ellery II
    1817-1901. . . . . DLB-1, 223

Channing, William Henry
    1810-1884 . . . . DLB-1, 59, 243

Chaplin, Charlie 1889-1977 . . . . DLB-44

Chapman, George
    1559 or 1560-1634. . . . . DLB-62, 121

Chapman, John. DLB-106

Chapman, Olive Murray 1892-1977. . . . . DLB-195

Chapman, R. W. 1881-1960 . . . . DLB-201

Chapman, William 1850-1917 . . . . DLB-99

Chapman and Hall. DLB-106

Chappell, Fred 1936- DLB-6, 105

    "A Detail in a Poem" DLB-105

Chappell, William 1582-1649. . . . . DLB-236

Charbonneau, Jean 1875-1960 . . . . DLB-92

Charbonneau, Robert 1911-1967 . . . . DLB-68

Charles, Gerda 1914- DLB-14

Charles, William [publishing house]. DLB-49

Charles d'Orléans 1394-1465. . . . . DLB-208

Charley (see Mann, Charles)

Charteris, Leslie 1907-1993. . . . . DLB-77

Chartier, Alain circa 1385-1430 . . . . DLB-208

Charyn, Jerome 1937- Y-83

Chase, Borden 1900-1971. . . . . DLB-26

Chase, Edna Woolman 1877-1957 . . . . . . DLB-91

Chase, Mary Coyle 1907-1981 . . . . DLB-228

Chase-Riboud, Barbara 1936- DLB-33

Chateaubriand, François-René de
    1768-1848. . . . . DLB-119

Chatterton, Thomas 1752-1770. . . . . DLB-109

Essay on Chatterton (1842), by
    Robert Browning DLB-32

Chatto and Windus DLB-106

Chatwin, Bruce 1940-1989. . . . . . . DLB-194, 204

Chaucer, Geoffrey
    1340?-1400. . . . . DLB-146; CDBLB-1

Chauncy, Charles 1705-1787 . . . . DLB-24

Chauveau, Pierre-Joseph-Olivier
    1820-1890 . . . . DLB-99

Chávez, Denise 1948- DLB-122

Chávez, Fray Angélico 1910- DLB-82

Chayefsky, Paddy 1923-1981. . . . . DLB-7, 44; Y-81

Cheesman, Evelyn 1881-1969 . . . . DLB-195

Cheever, Ezekiel 1615-1708 . . . . DLB-24

Cheever, George Barrell 1807-1890 . . . . . DLB-59

Cheever, John 1912-1982
    . . . . . .DLB-2, 102, 227; Y-80, Y-82; CDALB-1

Cheever, Susan 1943- Y-82

Cheke, Sir John 1514-1557 . . . . DLB-132

Chelsea House DLB-46

Chênedollé, Charles de 1769-1833 . . . . . DLB-217

Cheney, Ednah Dow 1824-1904 . . . . . DLB-1, 223

Cheney, Harriet Vaughn 1796-1889. . . . . DLB-99

Chénier, Marie-Joseph 1764-1811. . . . . . DLB-192

Chernyshevsky, Nikolai Gavrilovich
    1828-1889 . . . . DLB-238

Cherry, Kelly 1940. . . . . .Y-83

Cherryh, C. J. 1942- Y-80

Chesebro', Caroline 1825-1873 . . . . DLB-202

Chesney, Sir George Tomkyns
    1830-1895 . . . . DLB-190

Chesnut, Mary Boykin 1823-1886. . . . . . DLB-239

Chesnutt, Charles Waddell
    1858-1932 . . . . .DLB-12, 50, 78

Chesson, Mrs. Nora (see Hopper, Nora)

Chester, Alfred 1928-1971 . . . . DLB-130

Chester, George Randolph 1869-1924 . . . DLB-78

The Chester Plays circa 1505-1532;
    revisions until 1575 . . . . DLB-146

Chesterfield, Philip Dormer Stanhope,
    Fourth Earl of 1694-1773 . . . . DLB-104

Chesterton, G. K. 1874-1936
    . . .DLB-10, 19, 34, 70, 98, 149, 178; CDBLB-6

Chettle, Henry circa 1560-circa 1607 . . . . DLB-136

Cheuse, Alan 1940- DLB-244

Chew, Ada Nield 1870-1945. . . . . DLB-135

Cheyney, Edward P. 1861-1947. . . . . DLB-47

Chiara, Piero 1913-1986. . . . . .DLB-177

Chicano History. DLB-82

Chicano Language DLB-82

Child, Francis James 1825-1896 . . . DLB-1, 64, 235

Child, Lydia Maria 1802-1880. . . . .DLB-1, 74, 243

Child, Philip 1898-1978 . . . . DLB-68

Childers, Erskine 1870-1922. . . . . DLB-70

Children's Book Awards and Prizes DLB-61

Children's Illustrators, 1800-1880 . . . . . . DLB-163

Childress, Alice 1916-1994. . . . . . . .DLB-7, 38, 249

Childs, George W. 1829-1894 . . . . DLB-23

Chilton Book Company. DLB-46

Chin, Frank 1940- DLB-206

Chinweizu 1943- DLB-157

Chitham, Edward 1932- DLB-155

Chittenden, Hiram Martin 1858-1917 . . . . DLB-47

Chivers, Thomas Holley 1809-1858 . . DLB-3, 248

Cholmondeley, Mary 1859-1925 . . . . .DLB-197

Chomsky, Noam 1928- DLB-246

Chopin, Kate 1850-1904. . . DLB-12, 78; CDALB-3

Chopin, Rene 1885-1953 . . . . DLB-92

Choquette, Adrienne 1915-1973. . . . . DLB-68

Choquette, Robert 1905- DLB-68

Chrétien de Troyes
    circa 1140-circa 1190 . . . . DLB-208

Christensen, Inger 1935- DLB-214

The Christian Publishing Company. DLB-49

Christie, Agatha
    1890-1976. . . . . . . .DLB-13, 77, 245; CDBLB-6

Christine de Pizan
    circa 1365-circa 1431 . . . . DLB-208

Christus und die Samariterin circa 950. . . . . . DLB-148

Christy, Howard Chandler 1873-1952 . . .DLB-188

Chulkov, Mikhail Dmitrievich
1743?-1792. .DLB-150

Church, Benjamin 1734-1778. . . . . .DLB-31

Church, Francis Pharcellus 1839-1906 . . . .DLB-79

Church, Peggy Pond 1903-1986 . . . . . . .DLB-212

Church, Richard 1893-1972. . . . . .DLB-191

Church, William Conant 1836-1917 . . . . . .DLB-79

Churchill, Caryl 1938- DLB-13

Churchill, Charles 1731-1764. . . . . .DLB-109

Churchill, Winston 1871-1947. . . . . .DLB-202

Churchill, Sir Winston
1874-1965 . . . . . . .DLB-100; DS-16; CDBLB-5

Churchyard, Thomas 1520?-1604. . . . . . .DLB-132

Churton, E., and Company. DLB-106

Chute, Marchette 1909-1994 . . . . .DLB-103

Ciardi, John 1916-1986 . . . . .DLB-5; Y-86

Cibber, Colley 1671-1757. . . . . .DLB-84

Cicero
106 B.C.-43 B.C.. . . . . . .DLB-211, CDWLB-1

Cima, Annalisa 1941- DLB-128

Čingo, Živko 1935-1987 . . . . .DLB-181

Cioran, E. M. 1911-1995. . . . . .DLB-220

Čipkus, Alfonsas (see Nyka-Niliūnas, Alfonsas)

Cirese, Eugenio 1884-1955 . . . . .DLB-114

Cīrulis, Jānis (see Bels, Alberts)

Cisneros, Sandra 1954- DLB-122, 152

City Lights Books DLB-46

Cixous, Hélène 1937- DLB-83, 242

Clampitt, Amy 1920-1994 . . . . .DLB-105

Clancy, Tom 1947- DLB-227

Clapper, Raymond 1892-1944. . . . . .DLB-29

Clare, John 1793-1864 . . . . .DLB-55, 96

Clarendon, Edward Hyde, Earl of
1609-1674 .DLB-101

Clark, Alfred Alexander Gordon (see Hare, Cyril)

Clark, Ann Nolan 1896- DLB-52

Clark, C. E. Frazer Jr. 1925- DLB-187

Clark, C. M., Publishing Company. DLB-46

Clark, Catherine Anthony 1892-1977 . . . . .DLB-68

Clark, Charles Heber 1841-1915. . . . . . . .DLB-11

Clark, Davis Wasgatt 1812-1871 . . . . .DLB-79

Clark, Eleanor 1913- DLB-6

Clark, J. P. 1935- DLB-117; CDWLB-3

Clark, Lewis Gaylord 1808-1873. . . .DLB-3, 64, 73

Clark, Walter Van Tilburg
1909-1971 . . . . .DLB-9, 206

Clark, William (see Lewis, Meriwether)

Clark, William Andrews Jr. 1877-1934 . . .DLB-187

Clarke, Austin 1896-1974. . . . . .DLB-10, 20

Clarke, Austin C. 1934- DLB-53, 125

Clarke, Gillian 1937- DLB-40

Clarke, James Freeman
1810-1888 . . . . .DLB-1, 59, 235

Clarke, Lindsay 1939- DLB-231

Clarke, Marcus 1846-1881. . . . . .DLB-230

Clarke, Pauline 1921- DLB-161

Clarke, Rebecca Sophia 1833-1906 . . . . . . .DLB-42

Clarke, Robert, and Company DLB-49

Clarkson, Thomas 1760-1846 . . . . .DLB-158

Claudel, Paul 1868-1955 . . . . .DLB-192

Claudius, Matthias 1740-1815 . . . . .DLB-97

Clausen, Andy 1943- DLB-16

Clawson, John L. 1865-1933 . . . . .DLB-187

Claxton, Remsen and Haffelfinger DLB-49

Clay, Cassius Marcellus 1810-1903. . . . . . .DLB-43

Cleage, Pearl 1948- DLB-228

Cleary, Beverly 1916- DLB-52

Cleary, Kate McPhelim 1863-1905 . . . . . .DLB-221

Cleaver, Vera 1919- and
Cleaver, Bill 1920-1981. . . . . .DLB-52

Cleland, John 1710-1789 . . . . .DLB-39

Clemens, Samuel Langhorne (Mark Twain)
1835-1910 . . . . .DLB-11, 12, 23, 64, 74,
186, 189; CDALB-3

Mark Twain on Perpetual Copyright Y-92

Clement, Hal 1922- DLB-8

Clemo, Jack 1916- DLB-27

Clephane, Elizabeth Cecilia
1830-1869 . . . . .DLB-199

Cleveland, John 1613-1658 . . . . .DLB-126

Cliff, Michelle 1946- DLB-157; CDWLB-3

Clifford, Lady Anne 1590-1676. . . . . .DLB-151

Clifford, James L. 1901-1978 . . . . .DLB-103

Clifford, Lucy 1853?-1929. . . . .DLB-135, 141, 197

Clifton, Lucille 1936- DLB-5, 41

Clines, Francis X. 1938- DLB-185

Clive, Caroline (V) 1801-1873. . . . . .DLB-199

Clode, Edward J. [publishing house] DLB-46

Clough, Arthur Hugh 1819-1861 . . . . .DLB-32

Cloutier, Cécile 1930- DLB-60

Clouts, Sidney 1926-1982 . . . . .DLB-225

Clutton-Brock, Arthur 1868-1924 . . . . . . .DLB-98

Coates, Robert M. 1897-1973. . . . . .DLB-4, 9, 102

Coatsworth, Elizabeth 1893- DLB-22

Cobb, Charles E., Jr. 1943- DLB-41

Cobb, Frank I. 1869-1923 . . . . .DLB-25

Cobb, Irvin S. 1876-1944. . . . . . .DLB-11, 25, 86

Cobbe, Frances Power 1822-1904 . . . . . . .DLB-190

Cobbett, William 1763-1835 . . . . .DLB-43, 107

Cobbledick, Gordon 1898-1969 . . . . .DLB-171

Cochran, Thomas C. 1902- DLB-17

Cochrane, Elizabeth 1867-1922 . . . . . .DLB-25, 189

Cockerell, Sir Sydney 1867-1962 . . . . . . .DLB-201

Cockerill, John A. 1845-1896. . . . . .DLB-23

Cocteau, Jean 1889-1963 . . . . .DLB-65

Coderre, Emile (see Jean Narrache)

Coe, Jonathan 1961- DLB-231

Coetzee, J. M. 1940- DLB-225

Coffee, Lenore J. 1900?-1984. . . . . .DLB-44

Coffin, Robert P. Tristram 1892-1955. . . . .DLB-45

Coghill, Mrs. Harry (see Walker, Anna Louisa)

Cogswell, Fred 1917- DLB-60

Cogswell, Mason Fitch 1761-1830 . . . . . . .DLB-37

Cohan, George M. 1878-1942 . . . . .DLB-249

Cohen, Arthur A. 1928-1986. . . . . .DLB-28

Cohen, Leonard 1934- DLB-53

Cohen, Matt 1942- DLB-53

Colbeck, Norman 1903-1987. . . . . .DLB-201

Colden, Cadwallader 1688-1776 . . . . . .DLB-24, 30

Colden, Jane 1724-1766 . . . . .DLB-200

Cole, Barry 1936- DLB-14

Cole, George Watson 1850-1939 . . . . . . .DLB-140

Colegate, Isabel 1931- DLB-14, 231

Coleman, Emily Holmes 1899-1974 . . . . . . .DLB-4

Coleman, Wanda 1946- DLB-130

Coleridge, Hartley 1796-1849 . . . . .DLB-96

Coleridge, Mary 1861-1907. . . . . .DLB-19, 98

Coleridge, Samuel Taylor
1772-1834 . . . . .DLB-93, 107; CDBLB-3

Coleridge, Sara 1802-1852. . . . . .DLB-199

Colet, John 1467-1519 . . . . .DLB-132

Colette 1873-1954 . . . . .DLB-65

Colette, Sidonie Gabrielle (see Colette)

Colinas, Antonio 1946- DLB-134

Coll, Joseph Clement 1881-1921 . . . . .DLB-188

Collier, John 1901-1980. . . . . .DLB-77

Collier, John Payne 1789-1883 . . . . .DLB-184

Collier, Mary 1690-1762 . . . . .DLB-95

Collier, P. F. [publishing house]. DLB-49

Collier, Robert J. 1876-1918. . . . . .DLB-91

Collin and Small DLB-49

Collingwood, W. G. 1854-1932 . . . . .DLB-149

Collins, An floruit circa 1653. . . . . .DLB-131

Collins, Isaac [publishing house] DLB-49

Collins, Merle 1950- DLB-157

Collins, Mortimer 1827-1876 . . . . .DLB-21, 35

Collins, Tom (see Furphy, Joseph)

Collins, Wilkie
1824-1889 . . . . . . .DLB-18, 70, 159; CDBLB-4

Collins, William 1721-1759 . . . . .DLB-109

Collins, William, Sons and Company DLB-154

Collis, Maurice 1889-1973. . . . . .DLB-195

Collyer, Mary 1716?-1763? DLB-39

Colman, Benjamin 1673-1747 . . . . .DLB-24

Colman, George, the Elder 1732-1794 . . . . .DLB-89

Colman, George, the Younger
1762-1836 . . . . .DLB-89

Colman, S. [publishing house] DLB-49

Colombo, John Robert 1936- DLB-53

Colquhoun, Patrick 1745-1820 . . . . .DLB-158

Colter, Cyrus 1910- DLB-33

Colum, Padraic 1881-1972. . . . . .DLB-19

Columella fl. first century A.D.. . . . . .DLB-211

Colvin, Sir Sidney 1845-1927 . . . . .DLB-149

Colwin, Laurie 1944-1992. . . . . . . .DLB-218; Y-80

Comden, Betty 1919-   and
   Green, Adolph 1918- DLB-44

Come to Papa Y-99

Comi, Girolamo 1890-1968 . . . . DLB-114

The Comic Tradition Continued
   [in the British Novel] DLB-15

Commager, Henry Steele 1902-1998 . . . . . DLB-17

The Commercialization of the Image of
   Revolt, by Kenneth Rexroth DLB-16

Community and Commentators: Black
   Theatre and Its Critics DLB-38

Commynes, Philippe de
   circa 1447-1511 . . . . DLB-208

Compton-Burnett, Ivy 1884?-1969 . . . . . . DLB-36

Conan, Laure 1845-1924 . . . . DLB-99

Concord History and Life DLB-223

Concord Literary History of a Town DLB-223

Conde, Carmen 1901- DLB-108

Conference on Modern Biography Y-85

Congreve, William
   1670-1729 . . . . DLB-39, 84; CDBLB-2

Preface to *Incognita* (1692) DLB-39

Conkey, W. B., Company DLB-49

Conn, Stewart 1936- DLB-233

Connell, Evan S., Jr. 1924- DLB-2; Y-81

Connelly, Marc 1890-1980 . . . . DLB-7; Y-80

Connolly, Cyril 1903-1974 . . . . DLB-98

Connolly, James B. 1868-1957 . . . . DLB-78

Connor, Ralph 1860-1937 . . . . DLB-92

Connor, Tony 1930- DLB-40

Conquest, Robert 1917- DLB-27

Conrad, John, and Company DLB-49

Conrad, Joseph
   1857-1924 . . . . DLB-10, 34, 98, 156; CDBLB-5

Conroy, Jack 1899-1990 . . . . Y-81

Conroy, Pat 1945- DLB-6

Considine, Bob 1906-1975 . . . . DLB-241

The Consolidation of Opinion: Critical
   Responses to the Modernists DLB-36

Consolo, Vincenzo 1933- DLB-196

Constable, Archibald, and Company DLB-154

Constable, Henry 1562-1613 . . . . DLB-136

Constable and Company Limited DLB-112

Constant, Benjamin 1767-1830 . . . . DLB-119

Constant de Rebecque, Henri-Benjamin de
   (see Constant, Benjamin)

Constantine, David 1944- DLB-40

Constantin-Weyer, Maurice 1881-1964 . . . DLB-92

Contempo Caravan: Kites in a Windstorm . . . Y-85

A Contemporary Flourescence of Chicano
   Literature Y-84

Continental European Rhetoricians,
   1400-1600 . . . . DLB-236

The Continental Publishing Company DLB-49

Conversations with Editors Y-95

Conversations with Publishers I: An Interview
   with Patrick O'Connor Y-84

Conversations with Publishers II: An Interview
   with Charles Scribner III Y-94

Conversations with Publishers III: An Interview
   with Donald Lamm Y-95

Conversations with Publishers IV: An Interview
   with James Laughlin Y-96

Conversations with Rare Book Dealers I: An
   Interview with Glenn Horowitz Y-90

Conversations with Rare Book Dealers II: An
   Interview with Ralph Sipper Y-94

Conversations with Rare Book Dealers
   (Publishers) III: An Interview with
   Otto Penzler Y-96

The Conversion of an Unpolitical Man,
   by W. H. Bruford DLB-66

Conway, Moncure Daniel
   1832-1907 . . . . DLB-1, 223

Cook, David C., Publishing Company DLB-49

Cook, Ebenezer circa 1667-circa 1732 . . . . . DLB-24

Cook, Edward Tyas 1857-1919 . . . . DLB-149

Cook, Eliza 1818-1889 . . . . DLB-199

Cook, Michael 1933- DLB-53

Cooke, George Willis 1848-1923 . . . . DLB-71

Cooke, Increase, and Company DLB-49

Cooke, John Esten 1830-1886 . . . . DLB-3, 248

Cooke, Philip Pendleton
   1816-1850 . . . . DLB-3, 59, 248

Cooke, Rose Terry 1827-1892 . . . . DLB-12, 74

Cook-Lynn, Elizabeth 1930- DLB-175

Coolbrith, Ina 1841-1928 . . . . DLB-54, 186

Cooley, Peter 1940- DLB-105

"Into the Mirror" DLB-105

Coolidge, Clark 1939- DLB-193

Coolidge, George [publishing house] DLB-49

Coolidge, Susan (see Woolsey, Sarah Chauncy)

Cooper, Anna Julia 1858-1964 . . . . DLB-221

Cooper, Edith Emma (see Field, Michael)

Cooper, Giles 1918-1966 . . . . DLB-13

Cooper, J. California 19??- DLB-212

Cooper, James Fenimore
   1789-1851 . . . . DLB-3, 183; CDALB-2

Cooper, Kent 1880-1965 . . . . DLB-29

Cooper, Susan 1935- DLB-161

Cooper, Susan Fenimore 1813-1894 . . . . . DLB-239

Cooper, William [publishing house] DLB-170

Coote, J. [publishing house] DLB-154

Coover, Robert 1932- DLB-2, 227; Y-81

Copeland and Day DLB-49

Ćopić, Branko 1915-1984 . . . . DLB-181

Copland, Robert 1470?-1548 . . . . DLB-136

Coppard, A. E. 1878-1957 . . . . DLB-162

Coppée, François 1842-1908 . . . . DLB-217

Coppel, Alfred 1921- Y-83

Coppola, Francis Ford 1939- DLB-44

Copway, George (Kah-ge-ga-gah-bowh)
   1818-1869 . . . . DLB-175, 183

Corazzini, Sergio 1886-1907 . . . . DLB-114

Corbett, Richard 1582-1635 . . . . DLB-121

Corbière, Tristan 1845-1875 . . . . DLB-217

Corcoran, Barbara 1911- DLB-52

Cordelli, Franco 1943- DLB-196

Corelli, Marie 1855-1924 . . . . DLB-34, 156

Corle, Edwin 1906-1956 . . . . Y-85

Corman, Cid 1924- DLB-5, 193

Cormier, Robert 1925-2000 . . . DLB-52; CDALB-6

Corn, Alfred 1943- DLB-120; Y-80

Cornford, Frances 1886-1960 . . . . DLB-240

Cornish, Sam 1935- DLB-41

Cornish, William circa 1465-circa 1524 . . DLB-132

Cornwall, Barry (see Procter, Bryan Waller)

Cornwallis, Sir William, the Younger
   circa 1579-1614 . . . . DLB-151

Cornwell, David John Moore (see le Carré, John)

Corpi, Lucha 1945- DLB-82

Corrington, John William
   1932-1988 . . . . DLB-6, 244

Corrothers, James D. 1869-1917 . . . . DLB-50

Corso, Gregory 1930- DLB-5, 16, 237

Cortázar, Julio 1914-1984 . . . . DLB-113; CDWLB-3

Cortéz, Carlos 1923- DLB-209

Cortez, Jayne 1936- DLB-41

Corvinus, Gottlieb Siegmund
   1677-1746 . . . . DLB-168

Corvo, Baron (see Rolfe, Frederick William)

Cory, Annie Sophie (see Cross, Victoria)

Cory, William Johnson 1823-1892 . . . . DLB-35

Coryate, Thomas 1577?-1617 . . . . . . DLB-151, 172

Ćosić, Dobrica 1921- DLB-181; CDWLB-4

Cosin, John 1595-1672 . . . . DLB-151, 213

Cosmopolitan Book Corporation DLB-46

Costain, Thomas B. 1885-1965 . . . . DLB-9

Coste, Donat 1912-1957 . . . . DLB-88

Costello, Louisa Stuart 1799-1870 . . . . . . DLB-166

Cota-Cárdenas, Margarita 1941- DLB-122

Cotten, Bruce 1873-1954 . . . . DLB-187

Cotter, Joseph Seamon, Sr. 1861-1949 . . . . DLB-50

Cotter, Joseph Seamon, Jr. 1895-1919 . . . . DLB-50

Cottle, Joseph [publishing house] DLB-154

Cotton, Charles 1630-1687 . . . . DLB-131

Cotton, John 1584-1652 . . . . DLB-24

Cotton, Sir Robert Bruce 1571-1631 . . . . . DLB-213

Coulter, John 1888-1980 . . . . DLB-68

Cournos, John 1881-1966 . . . . DLB-54

Courteline, Georges 1858-1929 . . . . DLB-192

Cousins, Margaret 1905-1996 . . . . DLB-137

Cousins, Norman 1915-1990 . . . . DLB-137

Couvreur, Jessie (see Tasma)

Coventry, Francis 1725-1754 . . . . DLB-39

Dedication, *The History of Pompey
   the Little* (1751) DLB-39

Coverdale, Miles 1487 or 1488-1569 . . . . DLB-167

Coverly, N. [publishing house] DLB-49

Covici-Friede DLB-46

Coward, Noel
1899-1973 . . . . .DLB-10, 245; CDBLB-6

Coward, McCann and Geoghegan DLB-46

Cowles, Gardner 1861-1946 . . . . .DLB-29

Cowles, Gardner "Mike" Jr.
1903-1985 . . . . DLB-127, 137

Cowley, Abraham 1618-1667 . . . . . .DLB-131, 151

Cowley, Hannah 1743-1809 . . . . .DLB-89

Cowley, Malcolm
1898-1989 . . . . DLB-4, 48; Y-81, Y-89

Cowper, William 1731-1800 . . . . . . .DLB-104, 109

Cox, A. B. (see Berkeley, Anthony)

Cox, James McMahon 1903-1974 . . . . . . .DLB-127

Cox, James Middleton 1870-1957 . . . . . . .DLB-127

Cox, Leonard ca. 1495-ca. 1550 . . . . . . .DLB-236

Cox, Palmer 1840-1924 . . . . .DLB-42

Coxe, Louis 1918-1993 . . . . .DLB-5

Coxe, Tench 1755-1824 . . . . .DLB-37

Cozzens, Frederick S. 1818-1869 . . . . . . .DLB-202

Cozzens, James Gould
1903-1978 . . . . .DLB-9; Y-84; DS-2; CDALB-1

James Gould Cozzens—A View from Afar Y-97

James Gould Cozzens Case Re-opened Y-97

James Gould Cozzens: How to Read Him. . . . Y-97

Cozzens's *Michael Scarlett* Y-97

James Gould Cozzens Symposium and
Exhibition at the University of
South Carolina, Columbia Y-00

Crabbe, George 1754-1832 . . . . .DLB-93

Crace, Jim 1946- DLB-231

Crackanthorpe, Hubert 1870-1896 . . . . . .DLB-135

Craddock, Charles Egbert (see Murfree, Mary N.)

Cradock, Thomas 1718-1770 . . . . .DLB-31

Craig, Daniel H. 1811-1895 . . . . .DLB-43

Craik, Dinah Maria 1826-1887 . . . . .DLB-35, 136

Cramer, Richard Ben 1950- DLB-185

Cranch, Christopher Pearse
1813-1892 . . . . .DLB-1, 42, 243

Crane, Hart 1899-1932 . . . . .DLB-4, 48; CDALB-4

Crane, R. S. 1886-1967 . . . . .DLB-63

Crane, Stephen
1871-1900 . . . . . . .DLB-12, 54, 78; CDALB-3

Crane, Walter 1845-1915 . . . . .DLB-163

Cranmer, Thomas 1489-1556 . . . . . .DLB-132, 213

Crapsey, Adelaide 1878-1914. . . . . .DLB-54

Crashaw, Richard 1612 or 1613-1649 . . . .DLB-126

Craven, Avery 1885-1980 . . . . .DLB-17

Crawford, Charles 1752-circa 1815 . . . . . . .DLB-31

Crawford, F. Marion 1854-1909 . . . . .DLB-71

Crawford, Isabel Valancy 1850-1887. . . . . .DLB-92

Crawley, Alan 1887-1975 . . . . .DLB-68

Crayon, Geoffrey (see Irving, Washington)

Crayon, Porte (see Strother, David Hunter)

Creamer, Robert W. 1922- DLB-171

Creasey, John 1908-1973 . . . . .DLB-77

Creative Age Press. DLB-46

Creech, William [publishing house] DLB-154

Creede, Thomas [publishing house] DLB-170

Creel, George 1876-1953 . . . . .DLB-25

Creeley, Robert 1926- . . . DLB-5, 16, 169; DS-17

Creelman, James 1859-1915 . . . . .DLB-23

Cregan, David 1931- DLB-13

Creighton, Donald Grant 1902-1979. . . . .DLB-88

Cremazie, Octave 1827-1879 . . . . .DLB-99

Crémer, Victoriano 1909?- DLB-108

Crescas, Hasdai circa 1340-1412? DLB-115

Crespo, Angel 1926- DLB-134

Cresset Press DLB-112

Cresswell, Helen 1934- DLB-161

Crèvecoeur, Michel Guillaume Jean de
1735-1813 . . . . .DLB-37

Crewe, Candida 1964- DLB-207

Crews, Harry 1935- DLB-6, 143, 185

Crichton, Michael 1942- Y-81

A Crisis of Culture: The Changing Role
of Religion in the New Republic DLB-37

Crispin, Edmund 1921-1978 . . . . .DLB-87

Cristofer, Michael 1946- DLB-7

Crnjanski, Miloš
1893-1977 . . . . .DLB-147; CDWLB-4

Crocker, Hannah Mather 1752-1829. . . . .DLB-200

Crockett, David (Davy)
1786-1836 . . . . .DLB-3, 11, 183, 248

Croft-Cooke, Rupert (see Bruce, Leo)

Crofts, Freeman Wills 1879-1957. . . . . . . .DLB-77

Croker, John Wilson 1780-1857 . . . . .DLB-110

Croly, George 1780-1860. . . . . .DLB-159

Croly, Herbert 1869-1930 . . . . .DLB-91

Croly, Jane Cunningham 1829-1901. . . . . .DLB-23

Crompton, Richmal 1890-1969 . . . . .DLB-160

Cronin, A. J. 1896-1981. . . . . .DLB-191

Cros, Charles 1842-1888 . . . . .DLB-217

Crosby, Caresse 1892-1970 . . . . .DLB-48

Crosby, Caresse 1892-1970
and Crosby, Harry
1898-1929 . . . . .DLB-4; DS-15

Crosby, Harry 1898-1929 . . . . .DLB-48

Crosland, Camilla Toulmin
(Mrs. Newton Crosland)
1812-1895 . . . . .DLB-240

Cross, Gillian 1945- DLB-161

Cross, Victoria 1868-1952 . . . . DLB-135, 197

Crossley-Holland, Kevin 1941- DLB-40, 161

Crothers, Rachel 1878-1958. . . . . .DLB-7

Crowell, Thomas Y., Company DLB-49

Crowley, John 1942- Y-82

Crowley, Mart 1935- DLB-7

Crown Publishers .DLB-46

Crowne, John 1641-1712 . . . . .DLB-80

Crowninshield, Edward Augustus
1817-1859 . . . . .DLB-140

Crowninshield, Frank 1872-1947. . . . . . . .DLB-91

Croy, Homer 1883-1965 . . . . .DLB-4

Crumley, James 1939- DLB-226; Y-84

Cruse, Mary Anne 1825?-1910 . . . . .DLB-239

Cruz, Migdalia 1958- DLB-249

Cruz, Victor Hernández 1949- DLB-41

Csokor, Franz Theodor 1885-1969 . . . . . .DLB-81

Csoóri, Sándor 1930- DLB-232; CDWLB-4

Cuala Press DLB-112

Cullen, Countee
1903-1946 . . . . .DLB-4, 48, 51; CDALB-4

Culler, Jonathan D. 1944- DLB-67, 246

Cullinan, Elizabeth 1933- DLB-234

The Cult of Biography
Excerpts from the Second Folio Debate:
"Biographies are generally a disease of
English Literature" – Germaine Greer,
Victoria Glendinning, Auberon Waugh,
and Richard Holmes. Y-86

Cumberland, Richard 1732-1811. . . . . . . .DLB-89

Cummings, Constance Gordon
1837-1924 . . . . .DLB-174

Cummings, E. E.
1894-1962 . . . . .DLB-4, 48; CDALB-5

Cummings, Ray 1887-1957 . . . . .DLB-8

Cummings and Hilliard DLB-49

Cummins, Maria Susanna
1827-1866 . . . . .DLB-42

Cumpián, Carlos 1953- DLB-209

Cunard, Nancy 1896-1965 . . . . .DLB-240

Cundall, Joseph [publishing house] DLB-106

Cuney, Waring 1906-1976. . . . . .DLB-51

Cuney-Hare, Maude 1874-1936. . . . . .DLB-52

Cunningham, Allan 1784-1842 . . . . .DLB-116, 144

Cunningham, J. V. 1911- DLB-5

Cunningham, Peter F.
[publishing house] DLB-49

Cunquiero, Alvaro 1911-1981 . . . . .DLB-134

Cuomo, George 1929- Y-80

Cupples, Upham and Company DLB-49

Cupples and Leon .DLB-46

Cuppy, Will 1884-1949. . . . . .DLB-11

Curiel, Barbara Brinson 1956- DLB-209

Curll, Edmund [publishing house]. DLB-154

Currie, James 1756-1805 . . . . .DLB-142

Currie, Mary Montgomerie Lamb Singleton,
Lady Currie
(see Fane, Violet)

Cursor Mundi circa 1300 . . . . .DLB-146

Curti, Merle E. 1897- DLB-17

Curtis, Anthony 1926- DLB-155

Curtis, Cyrus H. K. 1850-1933 . . . . .DLB-91

Curtis, George William
1824-1892 . . . . .DLB-1, 43, 223

Curzon, Robert 1810-1873. . . . . .DLB-166

Curzon, Sarah Anne 1833-1898 . . . . .DLB-99

Cushing, Harvey 1869-1939 . . . . .DLB-187

Custance, Olive (Lady Alfred Douglas)
1874-1944 . . . . .DLB-240

Cynewulf circa 770-840 . . . . .DLB-146

Czepko, Daniel 1605-1660. . . . . .DLB-164

Czerniawski, Adam 1934- DLB-232

D

Dabit, Eugène 1898-1936 . . . . DLB-65

Daborne, Robert circa 1580-1628 . . . . DLB-58

Dąbrowska, Maria
1889-1965 . . . . DLB-215; CDWLB-4

Dacey, Philip 1939- DLB-105

"Eyes Across Centuries: Contemporary
Poetry and 'That Vision Thing,'" DLB-105

Dach, Simon 1605-1659 . . . . DLB-164

Daggett, Rollin M. 1831-1901 . . . . DLB-79

D'Aguiar, Fred 1960- DLB-157

Dahl, Roald 1916-1990 . . . . DLB-139

Dahlberg, Edward 1900-1977 . . . . DLB-48

Dahn, Felix 1834-1912 . . . . DLB-129

Dal', Vladimir Ivanovich (Kazak Vladimir
Lugansky) 1801-1872 . . . . DLB-198

Dale, Peter 1938- DLB-40

Daley, Arthur 1904-1974 . . . . .DLB-171

Dall, Caroline Healey 1822-1912 . . . . . DLB-1, 235

Dallas, E. S. 1828-1879 . . . . DLB-55

From The Gay Science (1866) DLB-21

The Dallas Theater Center DLB-7

D'Alton, Louis 1900-1951 . . . . DLB-10

Daly, Carroll John 1889-1958 . . . . DLB-226

Daly, T. A. 1871-1948 . . . . DLB-11

Damon, S. Foster 1893-1971 . . . . DLB-45

Damrell, William S. [publishing house] . . . DLB-49

Dana, Charles A. 1819-1897 . . . . DLB-3, 23

Dana, Richard Henry, Jr.
1815-1882 . . . . DLB-1, 183, 235

Dandridge, Ray Garfield DLB-51

Dane, Clemence 1887-1965 . . . . .DLB-10, 197

Danforth, John 1660-1730 . . . . DLB-24

Danforth, Samuel, I 1626-1674 . . . . DLB-24

Danforth, Samuel, II 1666-1727 . . . . DLB-24

Dangerous Years: London Theater,
1939-1945 . . . . DLB-10

Daniel, John M. 1825-1865 . . . . DLB-43

Daniel, Samuel 1562 or 1563-1619 . . . . . . DLB-62

Daniel Press DLB-106

Daniells, Roy 1902-1979 . . . . DLB-68

Daniels, Jim 1956- DLB-120

Daniels, Jonathan 1902-1981 . . . . DLB-127

Daniels, Josephus 1862-1948 . . . . DLB-29

Daniels, Sarah 1957- DLB-245

Danilevsky, Grigorii Petrovich
1829-1890 . . . . DLB-238

Dannay, Frederic 1905-1982 and
Manfred B. Lee 1905-1971 . . . . DLB-137

Danner, Margaret Esse 1915- DLB-41

Danter, John [publishing house] DLB-170

Dantin, Louis 1865-1945 . . . . DLB-92

Danzig, Allison 1898-1987 . . . . .DLB-171

D'Arcy, Ella circa 1857-1937 . . . . DLB-135

Darke, Nick 1948- DLB-233

Darley, Felix Octavious Carr 1822-1888 . DLB-188

Darley, George 1795-1846 . . . . DLB-96

Darmesteter, Madame James
(see Robinson, A. Mary F.)

Darwin, Charles 1809-1882 . . . . .DLB-57, 166

Darwin, Erasmus 1731-1802 . . . . DLB-93

Daryush, Elizabeth 1887-1977 . . . . DLB-20

Dashkova, Ekaterina Romanovna
(née Vorontsova) 1743-1810 . . . . DLB-150

Dashwood, Edmée Elizabeth Monica de la Pasture
(see Delafield, E. M.)

Daudet, Alphonse 1840-1897 . . . . DLB-123

d'Aulaire, Edgar Parin 1898- and
d'Aulaire, Ingri 1904- DLB-22

Davenant, Sir William 1606-1668 . . . DLB-58, 126

Davenport, Guy 1927- DLB-130

Davenport, Marcia 1903-1996 . . . . .DS-17

Davenport, Robert ?-? DLB-58

Daves, Delmer 1904-1977 . . . . DLB-26

Davey, Frank 1940- DLB-53

Davidson, Avram 1923-1993 . . . . DLB-8

Davidson, Donald 1893-1968 . . . . DLB-45

Davidson, John 1857-1909 . . . . DLB-19

Davidson, Lionel 1922- DLB-14

Davidson, Robyn 1950- DLB-204

Davidson, Sara 1943- DLB-185

Davie, Donald 1922- DLB-27

Davie, Elspeth 1919- DLB-139

Davies, Sir John 1569-1626 . . . . .DLB-172

Davies, John, of Hereford 1565?-1618 . . . DLB-121

Davies, Peter, Limited DLB-112

Davies, Rhys 1901-1978 . . . . DLB-139, 191

Davies, Robertson 1913- DLB-68

Davies, Samuel 1723-1761 . . . . DLB-31

Davies, Thomas 1712?-1785 . . . . DLB-142, 154

Davies, W. H. 1871-1940 . . . . .DLB-19, 174

Daviot, Gordon 1896?-1952 . . . . DLB-10
(see also Tey, Josephine)

Davis, Arthur Hoey (see Rudd, Steele)

Davis, Charles A. 1795-1867 . . . . DLB-11

Davis, Clyde Brion 1894-1962 . . . . DLB-9

Davis, Dick 1945- DLB-40

Davis, Frank Marshall 1905-? DLB-51

Davis, H. L. 1894-1960 . . . . DLB-9, 206

Davis, John 1774-1854 . . . . DLB-37

Davis, Lydia 1947- DLB-130

Davis, Margaret Thomson 1926- DLB-14

Davis, Ossie 1917- DLB-7, 38, 249

Davis, Owen 1874-1956 . . . . DLB-249

Davis, Paxton 1925-1994 . . . . .Y-89

Davis, Rebecca Harding 1831-1910 . . DLB-74, 239

Davis, Richard Harding 1864-1916
. . . . .DLB-12, 23, 78, 79, 189; DS-13

Davis, Samuel Cole 1764-1809 . . . . DLB-37

Davis, Samuel Post 1850-1918 . . . . DLB-202

Davison, Peter 1928- DLB-5

Davydov, Denis Vasil'evich
1784-1839 . . . . DLB-205

Davys, Mary 1674-1732 . . . . DLB-39

Preface to The Works of
Mrs. Davys (1725) DLB-39

DAW Books DLB-46

Dawson, Ernest 1882-1947 . . . . DLB-140

Dawson, Fielding 1930- DLB-130

Dawson, Sarah Morgan 1842-1909 . . . DLB-239

Dawson, William 1704-1752 . . . . DLB-31

Day, Angel flourished 1583-1599 . . . .DLB-167, 236

Day, Benjamin Henry 1810-1889 . . . . DLB-43

Day, Clarence 1874-1935 . . . . DLB-11

Day, Dorothy 1897-1980 . . . . DLB-29

Day, Frank Parker 1881-1950 . . . . DLB-92

Day, John circa 1574-circa 1640 . . . . DLB-62

Day, John [publishing house] DLB-170

Day, The John, Company DLB-46

Day Lewis, C. 1904-1972 . . . . DLB-15, 20
(see also Blake, Nicholas)

Day, Mahlon [publishing house] DLB-49

Day, Thomas 1748-1789 . . . . DLB-39

Dazai Osamu 1909-1948 . . . . DLB-182

Deacon, William Arthur 1890-1977 . . . . . . DLB-68

Deal, Borden 1922-1985 . . . . DLB-6

de Angeli, Marguerite 1889-1987 . . . . DLB-22

De Angelis, Milo 1951- DLB-128

De Bow, J. D. B.
1820-1867 . . . . .DLB-3, 79, 248

de Bruyn, Günter 1926- DLB-75

de Camp, L. Sprague 1907-2000 . . . . DLB-8

De Carlo, Andrea 1952- DLB-196

De Casas, Celso A. 1944- DLB-209

Dechert, Robert 1895-1975 . . . . .DLB-187

Dee, John 1527-1608 or 1609 . . . . . . DLB-136, 213

Deeping, George Warwick 1877-1950 . . . DLB 153

Defoe, Daniel
1660-1731 . . . . DLB-39, 95, 101; CDBLB-2

Preface to Colonel Jack (1722) DLB-39

Preface to The Farther Adventures of
Robinson Crusoe (1719) DLB-39

Preface to Moll Flanders (1722) DLB-39

Preface to Robinson Crusoe (1719) DLB-39

Preface to Roxana (1724) DLB-39

de Fontaine, Felix Gregory 1834-1896 . . . . DLB-43

De Forest, John William 1826-1906 . . DLB-12, 189

DeFrees, Madeline 1919- DLB-105

"The Poet's Kaleidoscope: The Element
of Surprise in the Making of
the Poem" DLB-105

DeGolyer, Everette Lee 1886-1956 . . . . . .DLB-187

de Graff, Robert 1895-1981 . . . . Y-81

de Graft, Joe 1924-1978 . . . . .DLB-117

De Heinrico circa 980? DLB-148

Deighton, Len 1929- DLB-87; CDBLB-8

DeJong, Meindert 1906-1991 . . . . DLB-52

Dekker, Thomas
circa 1572-1632 . . . . . .DLB-62, 172; CDBLB-1

Delacorte, Jr., George T. 1894-1991 . . . . . .DLB-91

Delafield, E. M. 1890-1943 . . . . .DLB-34

Delahaye, Guy 1888-1969 . . . . .DLB-92

de la Mare, Walter
1873-1956 . . . . . .DLB-19, 153, 162; CDBLB-6

Deland, Margaret 1857-1945 . . . . .DLB-78

Delaney, Shelagh 1939- DLB-13; CDBLB-8

Delano, Amasa 1763-1823 . . . . .DLB-183

Delany, Martin Robinson 1812-1885. . . . .DLB-50

Delany, Samuel R. 1942- DLB-8, 33

de la Roche, Mazo 1879-1961 . . . . .DLB-68

Delavigne, Jean François Casimir
1793-1843 . . . . .DLB-192

Delbanco, Nicholas 1942- DLB-6, 234

Del Castillo, Ramón 1949- DLB-209

De León, Nephtal 1945- DLB-82

Delgado, Abelardo Barrientos 1931- DLB-82

Del Giudice, Daniele 1949- DLB-196

De Libero, Libero 1906-1981. . . . . .DLB-114

DeLillo, Don 1936- DLB-6, 173

de Lisser H. G. 1878-1944 . . . . .DLB-117

Dell, Floyd 1887-1969 . . . . .DLB-9

Dell Publishing Company DLB-46

delle Grazie, Marie Eugene 1864-1931 . . . .DLB-81

Deloney, Thomas died 1600 . . . . .DLB-167

Deloria, Ella C. 1889-1971. . . . . .DLB-175

Deloria, Vine, Jr. 1933- DLB-175

del Rey, Lester 1915-1993 . . . . .DLB-8

Del Vecchio, John M. 1947- DS-9

Del'vig, Anton Antonovich 1798-1831. . . .DLB-205

de Man, Paul 1919-1983 . . . . .DLB-67

DeMarinis, Rick 1934- DLB-218

Demby, William 1922- DLB-33

Deming, Philander 1829-1915 . . . . .DLB-74

Deml, Jakub 1878-1961 . . . . .DLB-215

Demorest, William Jennings 1822-1895. . . .DLB-79

De Morgan, William 1839-1917 . . . . .DLB-153

Demosthenes 384 B.C.-322 B.C. DLB-176

Denham, Henry [publishing house]. DLB-170

Denham, Sir John 1615-1669. . . . . . .DLB-58, 126

Denison, Merrill 1893-1975 . . . . .DLB-92

Denison, T. S., and Company DLB-49

Dennery, Adolphe Philippe 1811-1899 . . .DLB-192

Dennie, Joseph 1768-1812 . . . . . DLB-37, 43, 59, 73

Dennis, John 1658-1734. . . . . .DLB-101

Dennis, Nigel 1912-1989 . . . . . . .DLB-13, 15, 233

Denslow, W. W. 1856-1915 . . . . .DLB-188

Dent, J. M., and Sons. DLB-112

Dent, Tom 1932-1998 . . . . .DLB-38

Denton, Daniel circa 1626-1703. . . . . .DLB-24

DePaola, Tomie 1934- DLB-61

Department of Library, Archives, and Institutional
Research, American Bible Society Y-97

De Quille, Dan 1829-1898. . . . . .DLB-186

De Quincey, Thomas
1785-1859 . . . . .DLB-110, 144; CDBLB-3

"Rhetoric" (1828; revised, 1859)
[excerpt]. DLB-57

Derby, George Horatio 1823-1861 . . . . . .DLB-11

Derby, J. C., and Company DLB-49

Derby and Miller. DLB-49

De Ricci, Seymour 1881-1942 . . . . .DLB-201

Derleth, August 1909-1971 . . . . . . .DLB-9; DS-17

Derrida, Jacques 1930- DLB-242

The Derrydale Press DLB-46

Derzhavin, Gavriil Romanovich
1743-1816 . . . . .DLB-150

Desaulniers, Gonsalve 1863-1934 . . . . . . .DLB-92

Desbordes-Valmore, Marceline
1786-1859 . . . . .DLB-217

Deschamps, Emile 1791-1871. . . . . .DLB-217

Deschamps, Eustache 1340?-1404. . . . . . .DLB-208

Desbiens, Jean-Paul 1927- DLB-53

des Forêts, Louis-Rene 1918- DLB-83

Desiato, Luca 1941- DLB-196

Desnica, Vladan 1905-1967. . . . . .DLB-181

DesRochers, Alfred 1901-1978. . . . . .DLB-68

Desrosiers, Léo-Paul 1896-1967. . . . . .DLB-68

Dessì, Giuseppe 1909-1977 . . . . .DLB-177

Destouches, Louis-Ferdinand
(see Céline, Louis-Ferdinand)

De Tabley, Lord 1835-1895 . . . . .DLB-35

Deutsch, André, Limited DLB-112

Deutsch, Babette 1895-1982 . . . . .DLB-45

Deutsch, Niklaus Manuel (see Manuel, Niklaus)

Deveaux, Alexis 1948- DLB-38

The Development of the Author's Copyright
in Britain DLB-154

The Development of Lighting in the Staging
of Drama, 1900-1945 . . . . .DLB-10

"The Development of Meiji Japan" DLB-180

De Vere, Aubrey 1814-1902 . . . . .DLB-35

Devereux, second Earl of Essex, Robert
1565-1601 . . . . .DLB-136

The Devin-Adair Company. DLB-46

De Vinne, Theodore Low 1828-1914 . . . .DLB-187

Devlin, Anne 1951- DLB-245

De Voto, Bernard 1897-1955. . . . . .DLB-9

De Vries, Peter 1910-1993. . . . . .DLB-6; Y-82

Dewdney, Christopher 1951- DLB-60

Dewdney, Selwyn 1909-1979. . . . . .DLB-68

Dewey, John 1859-1952. . . . . .DLB-246

Dewey, Orville 1794-1882 . . . . .DLB-243

Dewey, Thomas B. 1915-1981 . . . . .DLB-226

DeWitt, Robert M., Publisher DLB-49

DeWolfe, Fiske and Company DLB-49

Dexter, Colin 1930- DLB-87

de Young, M. H. 1849-1925 . . . . .DLB-25

Dhlomo, H. I. E. 1903-1956 . . . . . DLB-157, 225

Dhuoda circa 803-after 843 . . . . .DLB-148

The Dial 1840-1844 . . . . .DLB-223

The Dial Press. DLB-46

Diamond, I. A. L. 1920-1988 . . . . .DLB-26

Dibble, L. Grace 1902-1998. . . . . .DLB-204

Dibdin, Thomas Frognall 1776-1847 . . . . .DLB-184

Di Cicco, Pier Giorgio 1949- DLB-60

Dick, Philip K. 1928-1982 . . . . .DLB-8

Dick and Fitzgerald DLB-49

Dickens, Charles 1812-1870
. . . . .DLB-21, 55, 70, 159, 166; CDBLB-4

Dickey, James 1923-1997
. . . . .DLB-5, 193; Y-82, Y-93, Y-96;
DS-7, DS-19; CDALB-6

James Dickey Tributes. Y-97

The Life of James Dickey: A Lecture to
the Friends of the Emory Libraries,
by Henry Hart Y-98

Dickey, William 1928-1994. . . . . .DLB-5

Dickinson, Emily
1830-1886 . . . . .DLB-1, 243; CDWLB-3

Dickinson, John 1732-1808 . . . . .DLB-31

Dickinson, Jonathan 1688-1747 . . . . .DLB-24

Dickinson, Patric 1914- DLB-27

Dickinson, Peter 1927- DLB-87, 161

Dicks, John [publishing house]. DLB-106

Dickson, Gordon R. 1923- DLB-8

Dictionary of Literary Biography Yearbook Awards
. . . . .Y-92, Y-93, Y-97, Y-98, Y-99, Y-00

The Dictionary of National Biography. DLB-144

Didion, Joan 1934-
. . . . . DLB-2, 173, 185; Y-81, Y-86; CDALB-6

Di Donato, Pietro 1911- DLB-9

Die Fürstliche Bibliothek Corvey Y-96

Diego, Gerardo 1896-1987 . . . . .DLB-134

Digges, Thomas circa 1546-1595. . . . . . .DLB-136

The Digital Millennium Copyright Act:
Expanding Copyright Protection in
Cyberspace and Beyond Y-98

Dillard, Annie 1945- Y-80

Dillard, R. H. W. 1937- DLB-5, 244

Dillingham, Charles T., Company DLB-49

The Dillingham, G. W., Company DLB-49

Dilly, Edward and Charles
[publishing house] DLB-154

Dilthey, Wilhelm 1833-1911 . . . . .DLB-129

Dimitrova, Blaga 1922- . . . DLB-181; CDWLB-4

Dimov, Dimitr 1909-1966 . . . . .DLB-181

Dimsdale, Thomas J. 1831?-1866 . . . . . . .DLB-186

Dinescu, Mircea 1950- DLB-232

Dinesen, Isak (see Blixen, Karen)

Dingelstedt, Franz von 1814-1881 . . . . . . .DLB-133

Dintenfass, Mark 1941- Y-84

Diogenes, Jr. (see Brougham, John)

Diogenes Laertius circa 200. . . . . .DLB-176

DiPrima, Diane 1934- DLB-5, 16

Disch, Thomas M. 1940- DLB-8

Disney, Walt 1901-1966 . . . . .DLB-22

Disraeli, Benjamin 1804-1881 . . . . .DLB-21, 55

D'Israeli, Isaac 1766-1848 . . . . DLB-107

Ditlevsen, Tove 1917-1976 . . . . DLB-214

Ditzen, Rudolf (see Fallada, Hans)

Dix, Dorothea Lynde 1802-1887 . . . . . DLB-1, 235

Dix, Dorothy (see Gilmer, Elizabeth Meriwether)

Dix, Edwards and Company DLB-49

Dix, Gertrude circa 1874-? DLB-197

Dixie, Florence Douglas 1857-1905 . . . . . .DLB-174

Dixon, Ella Hepworth
1855 or 1857-1932 . . . . DLB-197

Dixon, Paige (see Corcoran, Barbara)

Dixon, Richard Watson 1833-1900 . . . . . . DLB-19

Dixon, Stephen 1936- DLB-130

Dmitriev, Ivan Ivanovich 1760-1837 . . . . . DLB-150

Dobell, Bertram 1842-1914 . . . . DLB-184

Dobell, Sydney 1824-1874 . . . . DLB-32

Dobie, J. Frank 1888-1964 . . . . DLB-212

Döblin, Alfred 1878-1957 . . . . DLB-66; CDWLB-2

Dobson, Austin 1840-1921 . . . . DLB-35, 144

Doctorow, E. L.
1931- DLB-2, 28, 173; Y-80; CDALB-6

Documents on Sixteenth-Century
Literature DLB-167, 172

Dodd, Anne [publishing house] DLB-154

Dodd, Mead and Company DLB-49

Dodd, Susan M. 1946- DLB-244

Dodd, William E. 1869-1940 . . . . DLB-17

Doderer, Heimito von 1896-1968 . . . . DLB-85

Dodge, B. W., and Company DLB-46

Dodge, Mary Abigail 1833-1896 . . . . DLB-221

Dodge, Mary Mapes
1831?-1905 . . . . DLB-42, 79; DS-13

Dodge Publishing Company DLB-49

Dodgson, Charles Lutwidge (see Carroll, Lewis)

Dodsley, R. [publishing house] DLB-154

Dodsley, Robert 1703-1764 . . . . DLB-95

Dodson, Owen 1914-1983 . . . . DLB-76

Dodwell, Christina 1951- DLB-204

Doesticks, Q. K. Philander, P. B.
(see Thomson, Mortimer)

Doheny, Carrie Estelle 1875-1958 . . . . . . DLB-140

Doherty, John 1798?-1854 . . . . DLB-190

Doig, Ivan 1939- DLB-206

Doinaş, Ştefan Augustin 1922- DLB-232

Domínguez, Sylvia Maida 1935- DLB-122

Donahoe, Patrick [publishing house] DLB-49

Donald, David H. 1920- DLB-17

The Practice of Biography VI: An
Interview with David Herbert Donald Y-87

Donaldson, Scott 1928- DLB-111

Doni, Rodolfo 1919- DLB-177

Donleavy, J. P. 1926- DLB-6, 173

Donnadieu, Marguerite (see Duras, Marguerite)

Donne, John
1572-1631 . . . . DLB-121, 151; CDBLB-1

Donnelley, R. R., and Sons Company DLB-49

Donnelly, Ignatius 1831-1901 . . . . DLB-12

Donohue and Henneberry DLB-49

Donoso, José 1924-1996 . . . . .DLB-113; CDWLB-3

Doolady, M. [publishing house] DLB-49

Dooley, Ebon (see Ebon)

Doolittle, Hilda 1886-1961 . . . . DLB-4, 45

Doplicher, Fabio 1938- DLB-128

Dor, Milo 1923- DLB-85

Doran, George H., Company DLB-46

Dorgelès, Roland 1886-1973 . . . . DLB-65

Dorn, Edward 1929-1999 . . . . DLB-5

Dorr, Rheta Childe 1866-1948 . . . . DLB-25

Dorris, Michael 1945-1997 . . . . .DLB-175

Dorset and Middlesex, Charles Sackville,
Lord Buckhurst, Earl of 1643-1706 . . . .DLB-131

Dorst, Tankred 1925- DLB-75, 124

Dos Passos, John 1896-1970
. . . . DLB-4, 9; DS-1, DS-15; CDALB-5

John Dos Passos: Artist Y-99

John Dos Passos: A Centennial
Commemoration Y-96

Dostoevsky, Fyodor 1821-1881 . . . . DLB-238

Doubleday and Company DLB-49

Dougall, Lily 1858-1923 . . . . DLB-92

Doughty, Charles M.
1843-1926 . . . . DLB-19, 57, 174

Douglas, Lady Alfred (see Custance, Olive)

Douglas, Gavin 1476-1522 . . . . DLB-132

Douglas, Keith 1920-1944 . . . . DLB-27

Douglas, Norman 1868-1952 . . . . DLB-34, 195

Douglass, Frederick 1818-1895
. . . . DLB-1, 43, 50, 79, 243; CDALB-2

Douglass, William circa 1691-1752 . . . . . . DLB-24

Dourado, Autran 1926- DLB-145

Dove, Arthur G. 1880-1946 . . . . DLB-188

Dove, Rita 1952- DLB-120; CDALB-7

Dover Publications DLB-46

Doves Press DLB-112

Dowden, Edward 1843-1913 . . . . DLB-35, 149

Dowell, Coleman 1925-1985 . . . . DLB-130

Dowland, John 1563-1626 . . . . .DLB-172

Downes, Gwladys 1915- DLB-88

Downing, J., Major (see Davis, Charles A.)

Downing, Major Jack (see Smith, Seba)

Dowriche, Anne
before 1560-after 1613 . . . . .DLB-172

Dowson, Ernest 1867-1900 . . . . DLB-19, 135

Doxey, William [publishing house] DLB-49

Doyle, Sir Arthur Conan
1859-1930 . . .DLB-18, 70, 156, 178; CDBLB-5

Doyle, Kirby 1932- DLB-16

Doyle, Roddy 1958- DLB-194

Drabble, Margaret
1939- DLB-14, 155, 231; CDBLB-8

Drach, Albert 1902- DLB-85

Dragojević, Danijel 1934- DLB-181

Drake, Samuel Gardner 1798-1875 . . . . . . DLB-187

The Dramatic Publishing Company DLB-49

Dramatists Play Service DLB-46

Drant, Thomas early 1540s?-1578 . . . . . . DLB-167

Draper, John W. 1811-1882 . . . . DLB-30

Draper, Lyman C. 1815-1891 . . . . DLB-30

Drayton, Michael 1563-1631 . . . . DLB-121

Dreiser, Theodore 1871-1945
. . . . . . .DLB-9, 12, 102, 137; DS-1; CDALB-3

Dresser, Davis 1904-1977 . . . . DLB-226

Drewitz, Ingeborg 1923-1986 . . . . DLB-75

Drieu La Rochelle, Pierre 1893-1945 . . . . . DLB-72

Drinker, Elizabeth 1735-1807 . . . . DLB-200

Drinkwater, John
1882-1937 . . . . .DLB-10, 19, 149

Droste-Hülshoff, Annette von
1797-1848 . . . . .DLB-133; CDWLB-2

The Drue Heinz Literature Prize
Excerpt from "Excerpts from a Report
of the Commission," in David
Bosworth's *The Death of Descartes*
An Interview with David Bosworth Y-82

Drummond, William, of Hawthornden
1585-1649 . . . . DLB-121, 213

Drummond, William Henry
1854-1907 . . . . DLB-92

Druzhinin, Aleksandr Vasil'evich
1824-1864 . . . . DLB-238

Dryden, Charles 1860?-1931 . . . . .DLB-171

Dryden, John
1631-1700 . . . . . . DLB-80, 101, 131; CDBLB-2

Držić, Marin
circa 1508-1567 . . . . .DLB-147; CDWLB-4

Duane, William 1760-1835 . . . . DLB-43

Dubé, Marcel 1930- DLB-53

Dubé, Rodolphe (see Hertel, François)

Dubie, Norman 1945- DLB-120

Dubois, Silvia 1788 or 1789?-1889 . . . . . . DLB-239

Du Bois, W. E. B.
1868-1963 . . . .DLB-47, 50, 91, 246; CDALB-3

Du Bois, William Pène 1916-1993 . . . . DLB-61

Dubrovina, Ekaterina Oskarovna
1846-1913 . . . . DLB-238

Dubus, Andre 1936-1999 . . . . DLB-130

Ducange, Victor 1783-1833 . . . . DLB-192

Du Chaillu, Paul Belloni 1831?-1903 . . . . DLB-189

Ducharme, Réjean 1941- DLB-60

Dučić, Jovan 1871-1943 . . . . .DLB-147; CDWLB-4

Duck, Stephen 1705?-1756 . . . . DLB-95

Duckworth, Gerald, and Company
Limited DLB-112

Duclaux, Madame Mary (see Robinson, A. Mary F.)

Dudek, Louis 1918- DLB-88

Duell, Sloan and Pearce DLB-46

Duerer, Albrecht 1471-1528 . . . . .DLB-179

Duff Gordon, Lucie 1821-1869 . . . . DLB-166

Dufferin, Helen Lady, Countess of Gifford
1807-1867 . . . . DLB-199

Duffield and Green DLB-46

Duffy, Maureen 1933- DLB-14

Dufief, Nicholas Gouin 1776-1834 . . . . DLB-187
Dugan, Alan 1923- DLB-5
Dugard, William [publishing house] DLB-170
Dugas, Marcel 1883-1947 . . . . DLB-92
Dugdale, William [publishing house] DLB-106
Duhamel, Georges 1884-1966 . . . . DLB-65
Dujardin, Edouard 1861-1949 . . . . DLB-123
Dukes, Ashley 1885-1959 . . . . DLB-10
Dumas, Alexandre *père* 1802-1870 . . . . . DLB-119, 192
Dumas, Alexandre *fils* 1824-1895 . . . . DLB-192
Dumas, Henry 1934-1968 . . . . DLB-41
du Maurier, Daphne 1907-1989 . . . . DLB-191
Du Maurier, George 1834-1896 . . . . . DLB-153, 178
Dunbar, Paul Laurence
    1872-1906 . . . . DLB-50, 54, 78; CDALB-3
Dunbar, William
    circa 1460-circa 1522 . . . . DLB-132, 146
Duncan, Norman 1871-1916 . . . . DLB-92
Duncan, Quince 1940- DLB-145
Duncan, Robert 1919-1988 . . . . DLB-5, 16, 193
Duncan, Ronald 1914-1982 . . . . DLB-13
Duncan, Sara Jeannette 1861-1922 . . . . DLB-92
Dunigan, Edward, and Brother DLB-49
Dunlap, John 1747-1812 . . . . DLB-43
Dunlap, William 1766-1839 . . . . . . DLB-30, 37, 59
Dunn, Douglas 1942- DLB-40
Dunn, Harvey Thomas 1884-1952 . . . . . . DLB-188
Dunn, Stephen 1939- DLB-105
"The Good, The Not So Good" DLB-105
Dunne, Finley Peter 1867-1936 . . . . . . DLB-11, 23
Dunne, John Gregory 1932- Y-80
Dunne, Philip 1908-1992 . . . . DLB-26
Dunning, Ralph Cheever 1878-1930 . . . . . . DLB-4
Dunning, William A. 1857-1922 . . . . DLB-17
Dunsany, Lord (Edward John Moreton
    Drax Plunkett, Baron Dunsany)
    1878-1957 . . . . DLB-10, 77, 153, 156
Duns Scotus, John circa 1266-1308 . . . . . . DLB-115
Dunton, John [publishing house] DLB-170
Dunton, W. Herbert 1878-1936 . . . . DLB-188
Dupin, Amantine-Aurore-Lucile (see Sand, George)
Dupuy, Eliza Ann 1814-1880 . . . . DLB-248
Durand, Lucile (see Bersianik, Louky)
Duranti, Francesca 1935- DLB-196
Duranty, Walter 1884-1957 . . . . DLB-29
Duras, Marguerite 1914-1996 . . . . DLB-83
Durfey, Thomas 1653-1723 . . . . DLB-80
Durova, Nadezhda Andreevna
    (Aleksandr Andreevich Aleksandrov)
    1783-1866 . . . . DLB-198
Durrell, Lawrence 1912-1990
    . . . . DLB-15, 27, 204; Y-90; CDBLB-7
Durrell, William [publishing house] DLB-49
Dürrenmatt, Friedrich
    1921-1990 . . . . DLB-69, 124; CDWLB-2
Duston, Hannah 1657-1737 . . . . DLB-200
Dutt, Toru 1856-1877 . . . . DLB-240

Dutton, E. P., and Company DLB-49
Duvoisin, Roger 1904-1980 . . . . DLB-61
Duyckinck, Evert Augustus
    1816-1878 . . . . DLB-3, 64
Duyckinck, George L. 1823-1863 . . . . DLB-3
Duyckinck and Company DLB-49
Dwight, John Sullivan 1813-1893 . . . . . DLB-1, 235
Dwight, Timothy 1752-1817 . . . . DLB-37
Dybek, Stuart 1942- DLB-130
Dyer, Charles 1928- DLB-13
Dyer, Sir Edward 1543-1607 . . . . DLB-136
Dyer, George 1755-1841 . . . . DLB-93
Dyer, John 1699-1757 . . . . DLB-95
Dyk, Viktor 1877-1931 . . . . DLB-215
Dylan, Bob 1941- DLB-16

E

Eager, Edward 1911-1964 . . . . DLB-22
Eagleton, Terry 1943- DLB-242
Eames, Wilberforce 1855-1937 . . . . DLB-140
Earle, Alice Morse 1853-1911 . . . . DLB-221
Earle, James H., and Company DLB-49
Earle, John 1600 or 1601-1665 . . . . DLB-151
Early American Book Illustration,
    by Sinclair Hamilton DLB-49
Eastlake, William 1917-1997 . . . . DLB-6, 206
Eastman, Carol ?- DLB-44
Eastman, Charles A. (Ohiyesa)
    1858-1939 . . . . DLB-175
Eastman, Max 1883-1969 . . . . DLB-91
Eaton, Daniel Isaac 1753-1814 . . . . DLB-158
Eaton, Edith Maude 1865-1914 . . . . DLB-221
Eaton, Winnifred 1875-1954 . . . . DLB-221
Eberhart, Richard 1904- DLB-48; CDALB-1
Ebner, Jeannie 1918- DLB-85
Ebner-Eschenbach, Marie von
    1830-1916 . . . . DLB-81
Ebon 1942- DLB-41
E-Books Turn the Corner Y-98
Ecbasis Captivi circa 1045 . . . . DLB-148
Ecco Press DLB-46
Eckhart, Meister circa 1260-circa 1328 . . . DLB-115
The Eclectic Review 1805-1868 . . . . DLB-110
Eco, Umberto 1932- DLB-196, 242
Edel, Leon 1907-1997 . . . . DLB-103
Edes, Benjamin 1732-1803 . . . . DLB-43
Edgar, David 1948- DLB-13, 233
Edgeworth, Maria
    1768-1849 . . . . DLB-116, 159, 163
The Edinburgh Review 1802-1929 . . . . DLB-110
Edinburgh University Press DLB-112
The Editor Publishing Company DLB-49
Editorial Institute at Boston University Y-00
Editorial Statements DLB-137
Edmonds, Randolph 1900- DLB-51
Edmonds, Walter D. 1903-1998 . . . . DLB-9

Edschmid, Kasimir 1890-1966 . . . . DLB-56
Edson, Russell 1935- DLB-244
Edwards, Amelia Anne Blandford
    1831-1892 . . . . DLB-174
Edwards, Dic 1953- DLB-245
Edwards, Edward 1812-1886 . . . . DLB-184
Edwards, James [publishing house] DLB-154
Edwards, Jonathan 1703-1758 . . . . DLB-24
Edwards, Jonathan, Jr. 1745-1801 . . . . DLB-37
Edwards, Junius 1929- DLB-33
Edwards, Matilda Barbara Betham
    1836-1919 . . . . DLB-174
Edwards, Richard 1524-1566 . . . . DLB-62
Edwards, Sarah Pierpont 1710-1758 . . . . . DLB-200
Effinger, George Alec 1947- DLB-8
Egerton, George 1859-1945 . . . . DLB-135
Eggleston, Edward 1837-1902 . . . . DLB-12
Eggleston, Wilfred 1901-1986 . . . . DLB-92
Eglītis, Anšlavs 1906-1993 . . . . DLB-220
Ehrenreich, Barbara 1941- DLB-246
Ehrenstein, Albert 1886-1950 . . . . DLB-81
Ehrhart, W. D. 1948- DS-9
Ehrlich, Gretel 1946- DLB-212
Eich, Günter 1907-1972 . . . . DLB-69, 124
Eichendorff, Joseph Freiherr von
    1788-1857 . . . . DLB-90
Eifukumon'in 1271-1342 . . . . DLB-203
1873 Publishers' Catalogues DLB-49
Eighteenth-Century Aesthetic
    Theories DLB-31
Eighteenth-Century Philosophical
    Background DLB-31
Eigner, Larry 1926-1996 . . . . DLB-5, 193
Eikon Basilike 1649 . . . . DLB-151
Eilhart von Oberge
    circa 1140-circa 1195 . . . . DLB-148
Einhard circa 770-840 . . . . DLB-148
Eiseley, Loren 1907-1977 . . . . DS-17
Eisenberg, Deborah 1945- DLB-244
Eisenreich, Herbert 1925-1986 . . . . DLB-85
Eisner, Kurt 1867-1919 . . . . DLB-66
Eklund, Gordon 1945- Y-83
Ekwensi, Cyprian
    1921- DLB-117; CDWLB-3
Elaw, Zilpha circa 1790-? DLB-239
Eld, George [publishing house] DLB-170
Elder, Lonne III 1931- DLB-7, 38, 44
Elder, Paul, and Company DLB-49
The Electronic Text Center and the Electronic
    Archive of Early American Fiction at the
    University of Virginia Library Y-98
Eliade, Mircea 1907-1986 . . . . DLB-220; CDWLB-4
Elie, Robert 1915-1973 . . . . DLB-88
Elin Pelin 1877-1949 . . . . DLB-147; CDWLB-4
Eliot, George
    1819-1880 . . . . DLB-21, 35, 55; CDBLB-4
Eliot, John 1604-1690 . . . . DLB-24

Eliot, T. S. 1888-1965
.... DLB-7, 10, 45, 63, 245; CDALB-5

T. S. Eliot Centennial.................. Y-88

Eliot's Court Press DLB-170

Elizabeth I 1533-1603................ DLB-136

Elizabeth of Nassau-Saarbrücken
after 1393-1456...................DLB-179

Elizondo, Salvador 1932- DLB-145

Elizondo, Sergio 1930- DLB-82

Elkin, Stanley 1930-1995 ....DLB-2, 28, 218; Y-80

Elles, Dora Amy (see Wentworth, Patricia)

Ellet, Elizabeth F. 1818?-1877 .... DLB-30

Elliot, Ebenezer 1781-1849 .... DLB-96, 190

Elliot, Frances Minto (Dickinson)
1820-1898 .... DLB-166

Elliott, Charlotte 1789-1871 .... DLB-199

Elliott, George 1923- DLB-68

Elliott, George P. 1918-1980........... DLB-244

Elliott, Janice 1931- DLB-14

Elliott, Sarah Barnwell 1848-1928 ...... DLB-221

Elliott, Thomes and Talbot DLB-49

Elliott, William III 1788-1863....... DLB-3, 248

Ellis, Alice Thomas (Anna Margaret Haycraft)
1932- DLB-194

Ellis, Edward S. 1840-1916............ DLB-42

Ellis, Frederick Staridge
[publishing house] DLB-106

The George H. Ellis Company......... DLB-49

Ellis, Havelock 1859-1939 .... DLB-190

Ellison, Harlan 1934- DLB-8

Ellison, Ralph
1914-1994....DLB-2, 76, 227; Y-94; CDALB-1

Ellmann, Richard 1918-1987 ......DLB-103; Y-87

Ellroy, James 1948- DLB-226; Y-91

Elyot, Thomas 1490?-1546........... DLB-136

Emanuel, James Andrew 1921- DLB-41

Emecheta, Buchi 1944- DLB-117; CDWLB-3

Emendations for *Look Homeward, Angel*....... Y-00

The Emergence of Black Women Writers DS-8

Emerson, Ralph Waldo 1803-1882
.... DLB-1, 59, 73, 183, 223; CDALB-2

Ralph Waldo Emerson in 1982 ....Y-82

Emerson, William 1769-1811 .... DLB-37

Emerson, William 1923-1997 ....Y-97

Emin, Fedor Aleksandrovich
circa 1735-1770.................. DLB-150

Empedocles fifth century B.C. DLB-176

Empson, William 1906-1984 .... DLB-20

Enchi Fumiko 1905-1986 .... DLB-182

"Encounter with the West"........... DLB-180

The End of English Stage Censorship,
1945-1968 .... DLB-13

Ende, Michael 1929-1995............. DLB-75

Endō Shūsaku 1923-1996............. DLB-182

Engel, Marian 1933-1985............. DLB-53

Engels, Friedrich 1820-1895.......... DLB-129

Engle, Paul 1908- DLB-48

English, Thomas Dunn 1819-1902...... DLB-202

English Composition and Rhetoric (1866),
by Alexander Bain [excerpt]........ DLB-57

The English Language: 410 to 1500..... DLB-146

Ennius 239 B.C.-169 B.C. DLB-211

Enright, D. J. 1920- DLB-27

Enright, Elizabeth 1909-1968 .... DLB-22

Epic and Beast Epic DLB-208

Epictetus circa 55-circa 125-130 ....DLB-176

Epicurus 342/341 B.C.-271/270 B.C. DLB-176

Epps, Bernard 1936- DLB-53

Epstein, Julius 1909- and
Epstein, Philip 1909-1952 .... DLB-26

Equiano, Olaudah
circa 1745-1797 .... DLB-37, 50; DWLB-3

Olaudah Equiano and Unfinished Journeys:
The Slave-Narrative Tradition and
Twentieth-Century Continuities, by
Paul Edwards and Pauline T.
Wangman DLB-117

The E-Researcher: Possibilities and Pitfalls ... Y-00

Eragny Press..................... DLB-112

Erasmus, Desiderius 1467-1536 .... DLB-136

Erba, Luciano 1922- DLB-128

Erdrich, Louise
1954- DLB-152, 175, 206; CDALB-7

Erichsen-Brown, Gwethalyn Graham
(see Graham, Gwethalyn)

Eriugena, John Scottus circa 810-877 .... DLB-115

Ernst, Paul 1866-1933 .... DLB-66, 118

Ershov, Petr Pavlovich
1815-1869 .... DLB-205

Erskine, Albert 1911-1993 ....Y-93

Erskine, John 1879-1951........... DLB-9, 102

Erskine, Mrs. Steuart ?-1948 .... DLB-195

Ertel', Aleksandr Ivanovich
1855-1908 .... DLB-238

Ervine, St. John Greer 1883-1971........ DLB-10

Eschenburg, Johann Joachim 1743-1820... DLB-97

Escoto, Julio 1944- DLB-145

Esdaile, Arundell 1880-1956........... DLB-201

Eshleman, Clayton 1935- DLB-5

Espriu, Salvador 1913-1985 .... DLB-134

Ess Ess Publishing Company DLB-49

Essex House Press DLB-112

Essop, Ahmed 1931- DLB-225

Esterházy, Péter 1950- DLB-232; CDWLB-4

Estes, Eleanor 1906-1988 .... DLB-22

Estes and Lauriat DLB-49

Estleman, Loren D. 1952- DLB-226

Eszterhas, Joe 1944- DLB-185

Etherege, George 1636-circa 1692 .... DLB-80

Ethridge, Mark, Sr. 1896-1981........ DLB-127

Ets, Marie Hall 1893- DLB-22

Etter, David 1928- DLB-105

Ettner, Johann Christoph 1654-1724 .... DLB-168

Eupolemius flourished circa 1095....... DLB-148

Euripides circa 484 B.C.-407/406 B.C.
.... DLB-176; CDWLB-1

Evans, Augusta Jane 1835-1909 .... DLB-239

Evans, Caradoc 1878-1945 .... DLB-162

Evans, Charles 1850-1935 ....DLB-187

Evans, Donald 1884-1921 .... DLB-54

Evans, George Henry 1805-1856....... DLB-43

Evans, Hubert 1892-1986............. DLB-92

Evans, M., and Company............. DLB-46

Evans, Mari 1923- DLB-41

Evans, Mary Ann (see Eliot, George)

Evans, Nathaniel 1742-1767 .... DLB-31

Evans, Sebastian 1830-1909 .... DLB-35

Evaristi, Marcella 1953- DLB-233

Everett, Alexander Hill 1790-1847 ...... DLB-59

Everett, Edward 1794-1865 ...... DLB-1, 59, 235

Everson, R. G. 1903- DLB-88

Everson, William 1912-1994 ......DLB-5, 16, 212

Ewart, Gavin 1916-1995.............. DLB-40

Ewing, Juliana Horatia 1841-1885 ... DLB-21, 163

The Examiner 1808-1881............. DLB-110

Exley, Frederick 1929-1992 ......DLB-143; Y-81

von Eyb, Albrecht 1420-1475 ....DLB-179

Eyre and Spottiswoode............... DLB-106

Ezera, Regīna 1930- DLB-232

Ezzo ?-after 1065 .... DLB-148

F

Faber, Frederick William 1814-1863 ..... DLB-32

Faber and Faber Limited............. DLB-112

Faccio, Rena (see Aleramo, Sibilla)

Fagundo, Ana María 1938- DLB-134

Fair, Ronald L. 1932- DLB-33

Fairfax, Beatrice (see Manning, Marie)

Fairlie, Gerard 1899-1983............. DLB-77

Fallada, Hans 1893-1947 .... DLB-56

Fancher, Betsy 1928- Y-83

Fane, Violet 1843-1905................ DLB-35

Fanfrolico Press DLB-112

Fanning, Katherine 1927 ....DLB-127

Fanshawe, Sir Richard 1608-1666 ...... DLB-126

Fantasy Press Publishers.............. DLB-46

Fante, John 1909-1983 ....DLB-130; Y-83

Al-Farabi circa 870-950............... DLB-115

Farabough, Laura 1949- DLB-228

Farah, Nuruddin 1945- DLB-125; CDWLB-3

Farber, Norma 1909-1984 .... DLB-61

Farigoule, Louis (see Romains, Jules)

Farjeon, Eleanor 1881-1965 .... DLB-160

Farley, Harriet 1812-1907 .... DLB-239

Farley, Walter 1920-1989............. DLB-22

Farmborough, Florence 1887-1978 ...... DLB-204

Farmer, Penelope 1939- DLB-161

Farmer, Philip José 1918- DLB-8

Farnaby, Thomas 1575?-1647 . . . . .DLB-236

Farningham, Marianne (see Hearn, Mary Anne)

Farquhar, George circa 1677-1707 . . . . . . .DLB-84

Farquharson, Martha (see Finley, Martha)

Farrar, Frederic William 1831-1903 . . . . . .DLB-163

Farrar and Rinehart DLB-46

Farrar, Straus and Giroux DLB-46

Farrell, J. G. 1935-1979 . . . . .DLB-14

Farrell, James T. 1904-1979 . . . .DLB-4, 9, 86; DS-2

Fast, Howard 1914- DLB-9

Faulkner, George [publishing house] DLB-154

Faulkner, William 1897-1962
    . . .DLB-9, 11, 44, 102; DS-2; Y-86; CDALB-5

William Faulkner Centenary Y-97

"Faulkner 100–Celebrating the Work,"
    University of South Carolina, Columbia . Y-97

Impressions of William Faulkner Y-97

Faulkner and Yoknapatawpha Conference,
    Oxford, Mississippi Y-97

Faulks, Sebastian 1953- DLB-207

Fauset, Jessie Redmon 1882-1961 . . . . . . .DLB-51

Faust, Irvin 1924- DLB-2, 28, 218; Y-80

Fawcett, Edgar 1847-1904 . . . . .DLB-202

Fawcett, Millicent Garrett 1847-1929 . . . . .DLB-190

Fawcett Books DLB-46

Fay, Theodore Sedgwick 1807-1898 . . . . .DLB-202

Fearing, Kenneth 1902-1961 . . . . .DLB-9

Federal Writers' Project DLB-46

Federman, Raymond 1928- Y-80

Fedorov, Innokentii Vasil'evich
    (see Omulevsky, Innokentii Vasil'evich)

Feiffer, Jules 1929- DLB-7, 44

Feinberg, Charles E. 1899-1988 . . . . DLB-187; Y-88

Feind, Barthold 1678-1721 . . . . .DLB-168

Feinstein, Elaine 1930- DLB-14, 40

Feiss, Paul Louis 1875-1952 . . . . .DLB-187

Feldman, Irving 1928- DLB-169

Felipe, Léon 1884-1968 . . . . .DLB-108

Fell, Frederick, Publishers DLB-46

Felltham, Owen 1602?-1668 . . . . . . .DLB-126, 151

Felman, Soshana 1942- DLB-246

Fels, Ludwig 1946- DLB-75

Felton, Cornelius Conway 1807-1862 . .DLB-1, 235

Fenn, Harry 1837-1911 . . . . .DLB-188

Fennario, David 1947- DLB-60

Fenner, Dudley 1558?-1587? DLB-236

Fenno, Jenny 1765?-1803 . . . . .DLB-200

Fenno, John 1751-1798 . . . . .DLB-43

Fenno, R. F., and Company DLB-49

Fenoglio, Beppe 1922-1963 . . . . DLB-177

Fenton, Geoffrey 1539?-1608 . . . . .DLB-136

Fenton, James 1949- DLB-40

Ferber, Edna 1885-1968 . . . . .DLB-9, 28, 86

Ferdinand, Vallery III (see Salaam, Kalamu ya)

Ferguson, Sir Samuel 1810-1886 . . . . .DLB-32

Ferguson, William Scott 1875-1954 . . . . . . .DLB-47

Fergusson, Robert 1750-1774 . . . . .DLB-109

Ferland, Albert 1872-1943 . . . . .DLB-92

Ferlinghetti, Lawrence
    1919- DLB-5, 16; CDALB-1

Fermor, Patrick Leigh 1915- DLB-204

Fern, Fanny (see Parton, Sara Payson Willis)

Ferrars, Elizabeth 1907- DLB-87

Ferré, Rosario 1942- DLB-145

Ferret, E., and Company DLB-49

Ferrier, Susan 1782-1854 . . . . .DLB-116

Ferril, Thomas Hornsby 1896-1988 . . . . .DLB-206

Ferrini, Vincent 1913- DLB-48

Ferron, Jacques 1921-1985 . . . . .DLB-60

Ferron, Madeleine 1922- DLB-53

Ferrucci, Franco 1936- DLB-196

Fetridge and Company DLB-49

Feuchtersleben, Ernst Freiherr von
    1806-1849 . . . . .DLB-133

Feuchtwanger, Lion 1884-1958 . . . . .DLB-66

Feuerbach, Ludwig 1804-1872 . . . . .DLB-133

Feuillet, Octave 1821-1890 . . . . .DLB-192

Feydeau, Georges 1862-1921 . . . . .DLB-192

Fichte, Johann Gottlieb 1762-1814 . . . . . . .DLB-90

Ficke, Arthur Davison 1883-1945 . . . . .DLB-54

Fiction Best-Sellers, 1910-1945 . . . . .DLB-9

Fiction into Film, 1928-1975: A List of Movies
    Based on the Works of Authors in
    British Novelists, 1930-1959 . . . . .DLB-15

Fiedler, Leslie A. 1917- DLB-28, 67

Field, Barron 1789-1846 . . . . .DLB-230

Field, Edward 1924- DLB-105

Field, Joseph M. 1810-1856 . . . . .DLB-248

Field, Michael
    (Katherine Harris Bradley [1846-1914]
    and Edith Emma Cooper
    [1862-1913]) .DLB-240

"The Poetry File" DLB-105

Field, Eugene
    1850-1895 . . . . .DLB-23, 42, 140; DS-13

Field, John 1545?-1588 . . . . .DLB-167

Field, Marshall, III 1893-1956 . . . . .DLB-127

Field, Marshall, IV 1916-1965 . . . . .DLB-127

Field, Marshall, V 1941- DLB-127

Field, Nathan 1587-1619 or 1620 . . . . .DLB-58

Field, Rachel 1894-1942 . . . . .DLB-9, 22

A Field Guide to Recent Schools of American
    Poetry Y-86

Fielding, Helen 1958- DLB-231

Fielding, Henry
    1707-1754 . . . . . .DLB-39, 84, 101; CDBLB-2

"Defense of *Amelia*" (1752) DLB-39

From *The History of the Adventures of
    Joseph Andrews* (1742) DLB-39

Preface to *Joseph Andrews* (1742) DLB-39

Preface to Sarah Fielding's *The Adventures
    of David Simple* (1744) DLB-39

Preface to Sarah Fielding's *Familiar Letters*
    (1747) [excerpt] DLB-39

Fielding, Sarah 1710-1768 . . . . .DLB-39

Preface to *The Cry* (1754) DLB-39

Fields, Annie Adams 1834-1915 . . . . .DLB-221

Fields, James T. 1817-1881 . . . . .DLB-1, 235

Fields, Julia 1938- DLB-41

Fields, Osgood and Company DLB-49

Fields, W. C. 1880-1946 . . . . .DLB-44

Fifty Penguin Years Y-85

Figes, Eva 1932- DLB-14

Figuera, Angela 1902-1984 . . . . .DLB-108

Filmer, Sir Robert 1586-1653 . . . . .DLB-151

Filson, John circa 1753-1788 . . . . .DLB-37

Finch, Anne, Countess of Winchilsea
    1661-1720 . . . . .DLB-95

Finch, Robert 1900- DLB-88

Findley, Timothy 1930- DLB-53

Finlay, Ian Hamilton 1925- DLB-40

Finley, Martha 1828-1909 . . . . .DLB-42

Finn, Elizabeth Anne (McCaul)
    1825-1921 . . . . .DLB-166

Finnegan, Seamus 1949- DLB-245

Finney, Jack 1911-1995 . . . . .DLB-8

Finney, Walter Braden (see Finney, Jack)

Firbank, Ronald 1886-1926 . . . . .DLB-36

Firmin, Giles 1615-1697 . . . . .DLB-24

First Edition Library/Collectors'
    Reprints, Inc. Y-91

Fischart, Johann
    1546 or 1547-1590 or 1591 . . . . DLB-179

Fischer, Karoline Auguste Fernandine
    1764-1842 . . . . .DLB-94

Fischer, Tibor 1959- DLB-231

Fish, Stanley 1938- DLB-67

Fishacre, Richard 1205-1248 . . . . .DLB-115

Fisher, Clay (see Allen, Henry W.)

Fisher, Dorothy Canfield 1879-1958 . . .DLB-9, 102

Fisher, Leonard Everett 1924- DLB-61

Fisher, Roy 1930- DLB-40

Fisher, Rudolph 1897-1934 . . . . .DLB-51, 102

Fisher, Steve 1913-1980 . . . . .DLB-226

Fisher, Sydney George 1856-1927 . . . . .DLB-47

Fisher, Vardis 1895-1968 . . . . .DLB-9, 206

Fiske, John 1608-1677 . . . . .DLB-24

Fiske, John 1842-1901 . . . . .DLB-47, 64

Fitch, Thomas circa 1700-1774 . . . . .DLB-31

Fitch, William Clyde 1865-1909 . . . . .DLB-7

FitzGerald, Edward 1809-1883 . . . . .DLB-32

Fitzgerald, F. Scott 1896-1940
    . . . . .DLB-4, 9, 86, 219; Y-81, Y-92;
        DS-1, 15, 16; CDALB-4

F. Scott Fitzgerald Centenary
    Celebrations Y-96

F. Scott Fitzgerald Inducted into the American
    Poets' Corner at St. John the Divine;
    Ezra Pound Banned Y-99

"F. Scott Fitzgerald: St. Paul's Native Son
   and Distinguished American Writer":
   University of Minnesota Conference,
   29-31 October 1982 . . . . Y-82

First International F. Scott Fitzgerald
   Conference Y-92

Fitzgerald, Penelope 1916- DLB-14, 194

Fitzgerald, Robert 1910-1985 . . . . Y-80

Fitzgerald, Thomas 1819-1891 . . . . DLB-23

Fitzgerald, Zelda Sayre 1900-1948 . . . . Y-84

Fitzhugh, Louise 1928-1974 . . . . DLB-52

Fitzhugh, William circa 1651-1701 . . . . DLB-24

Flagg, James Montgomery 1877-1960 . . . . DLB-188

Flanagan, Thomas 1923- Y-80

Flanner, Hildegarde 1899-1987 . . . . DLB-48

Flanner, Janet 1892-1978 . . . . DLB-4

Flannery, Peter 1951- DLB-233

Flaubert, Gustave 1821-1880 . . . . DLB-119

Flavin, Martin 1883-1967 . . . . DLB-9

Fleck, Konrad
   (flourished circa 1220) DLB-138

Flecker, James Elroy 1884-1915 . . . . . . DLB-10, 19

Fleeson, Doris 1901-1970 . . . . DLB-29

Fleißer, Marieluise 1901-1974 . . . . DLB-56, 124

Fleischer, Nat 1887-1972 . . . . DLB-241

Fleming, Abraham 1552?-1607 . . . . DLB-236

Fleming, Ian 1908-1964 . . DLB-87, 201; CDBLB-7

Fleming, Paul 1609-1640 . . . . DLB-164

Fleming, Peter 1907-1971 . . . . DLB-195

Fletcher, Giles, the Elder 1546-1611 . . . . . DLB-136

Fletcher, Giles, the Younger
   1585 or 1586-1623 . . . . DLB-121

Fletcher, J. S. 1863-1935 . . . . DLB-70

Fletcher, John (see Beaumont, Francis)

Fletcher, John Gould 1886-1950 . . . . DLB-4, 45

Fletcher, Phineas 1582-1650 . . . . DLB-121

Flieg, Helmut (see Heym, Stefan)

Flint, F. S. 1885-1960 . . . . DLB-19

Flint, Timothy 1780-1840 . . . . DLB-73, 186

Flores-Williams, Jason 1969- DLB-209

Florio, John 1553?-1625 . . . . DLB-172

Fo, Dario 1926- Y-97

Foix, J. V. 1893-1987 . . . . DLB-134

Foley, Martha (see Burnett, Whit, and Martha Foley)

Folger, Henry Clay 1857-1930 . . . . DLB-140

Folio Society DLB-112

Follen, Charles 1796-1840 . . . . DLB-235

Follen, Eliza Lee (Cabot) 1787-1860 . . . DLB-1, 235

Follett, Ken 1949- DLB-87; Y-81

Follett Publishing Company DLB-46

Folsom, John West [publishing house] DLB-49

Folz, Hans
   between 1435 and 1440-1513 . . . . DLB-179

Fontane, Theodor
   1819-1898 . . . . DLB-129; CDWLB-2

Fontes, Montserrat 1940- DLB-209

Fonvisin, Denis Ivanovich
   1744 or 1745-1792 . . . . DLB-150

Foote, Horton 1916- DLB-26

Foote, Mary Hallock
   1847-1938 . . . . DLB-186, 188, 202, 221

Foote, Samuel 1721-1777 . . . . DLB-89

Foote, Shelby 1916- DLB-2, 17

Forbes, Calvin 1945- DLB-41

Forbes, Ester 1891-1967 . . . . DLB-22

Forbes, Rosita 1893?-1967 . . . . DLB-195

Forbes and Company DLB-49

Force, Peter 1790-1868 . . . . DLB-30

Forché, Carolyn 1950- DLB-5, 193

Ford, Charles Henri 1913- DLB-4, 48

Ford, Corey 1902-1969 . . . . DLB-11

Ford, Ford Madox
   1873-1939 . . . . DLB-34, 98, 162; CDBLB-6

Ford, J. B., and Company DLB-49

Ford, Jesse Hill 1928-1996 . . . . DLB-6

Ford, John 1586-? DLB-58; CDBLB-1

Ford, R. A. D. 1915- DLB-88

Ford, Richard 1944- DLB-227

Ford, Worthington C. 1858-1941 . . . . DLB-47

Fords, Howard, and Hulbert DLB-49

Foreman, Carl 1914-1984 . . . . DLB-26

Forester, C. S. 1899-1966 . . . . DLB-191

Forester, Frank (see Herbert, Henry William)

Forman, Harry Buxton 1842-1917 . . . . . . DLB-184

Fornés, María Irene 1930- DLB-7

Forrest, Leon 1937-1997 . . . . DLB-33

Forster, E. M.
   1879-1970 . . . . DLB-34, 98, 162, 178, 195;
                                         DS-10; CDBLB-6

Forster, Georg 1754-1794 . . . . DLB-94

Forster, John 1812-1876 . . . . DLB-144

Forster, Margaret 1938- DLB-155

Forsyth, Frederick 1938- DLB-87

Forten, Charlotte L. 1837-1914 . . . . . . DLB-50, 239

Charlotte Forten: Pages from
   her Diary DLB-50

Fortini, Franco 1917- DLB-128

Fortune, Mary ca. 1833-ca. 1910 . . . . . . DLB-230

Fortune, T. Thomas 1856-1928 . . . . DLB-23

Fosdick, Charles Austin 1842-1915 . . . . . DLB-42

Foster, Genevieve 1893-1979 . . . . DLB-61

Foster, Hannah Webster 1758-1840 . . . DLB-37, 200

Foster, John 1648-1681 . . . . DLB-24

Foster, Michael 1904-1956 . . . . DLB-9

Foster, Myles Birket 1825-1899 . . . . DLB-184

Foucault, Michel 1926-1984 . . . . DLB-242

Foulis, Robert and Andrew / R. and A.
   [publishing house] DLB-154

Fouqué, Caroline de la Motte
   1774-1831 . . . . DLB-90

Fouqué, Friedrich de la Motte
   1777-1843 . . . . DLB-90

Four Seas Company DLB-46

Four Winds Press DLB-46

Fournier, Henri Alban (see Alain-Fournier)

Fowler and Wells Company DLB-49

Fowles, John
   1926- DLB-14, 139, 207; CDBLB-8

Fox, John 1939- DLB-245

Fox, John, Jr. 1862 or 1863-1919 . . . DLB-9; DS-13

Fox, Paula 1923- DLB-52

Fox, Richard K. [publishing house] DLB-49

Fox, Richard Kyle 1846-1922 . . . . DLB-79

Fox, William Price 1926- DLB-2; Y-81

Foxe, John 1517-1587 . . . . DLB-132

Fraenkel, Michael 1896-1957 . . . . DLB-4

France, Anatole 1844-1924 . . . . DLB-123

France, Richard 1938- DLB-7

Francis, C. S. [publishing house] DLB-49

Francis, Convers 1795-1863 . . . . DLB-1, 235

Francis, Dick 1920- DLB-87

Francis, Sir Frank 1901-1988 . . . . DLB-201

Francis, Jeffrey, Lord 1773-1850 . . . . DLB-107

François 1863-1910 . . . . DLB-92

François, Louise von 1817-1893 . . . . DLB-129

Franck, Sebastian 1499-1542 . . . . DLB-179

Francke, Kuno 1855-1930 . . . . DLB-71

Frank, Bruno 1887-1945 . . . . DLB-118

Frank, Leonhard 1882-1961 . . . . DLB-56, 118

Frank, Melvin (see Panama, Norman)

Frank, Waldo 1889-1967 . . . . DLB-9, 63

Franken, Rose 1895?-1988 . . . . . . DLB-228, Y-84

Franklin, Benjamin
   1706-1790 . . . . DLB-24, 43, 73, 183; CDALB-2

Franklin, James 1697-1735 . . . . DLB-43

Franklin, Miles 1879-1954 . . . . DLB-230

Franklin Library DLB-46

Frantz, Ralph Jules 1902-1979 . . . . DLB-4

Franzos, Karl Emil 1848-1904 . . . . DLB-129

Fraser, G. S. 1915-1980 . . . . DLB-27

Fraser, Kathleen 1935- DLB-169

Frattini, Alberto 1922- DLB-128

Frau Ava ?-1127 . . . . DLB-148

Fraunce, Abraham 1558?-1592 or 1593 . . DLB-236

Frayn, Michael 1933- DLB-13, 14, 194, 245

Frederic, Harold
   1856-1898 . . . . DLB-12, 23; DS-13

Freeling, Nicolas 1927- DLB-87

Freeman, Douglas Southall
   1886-1953 . . . . DLB-17; DS-17

Freeman, Legh Richmond 1842-1915 . . . . DLB-23

Freeman, Mary E. Wilkins
   1852-1930 . . . . DLB-12, 78, 221

Freeman, R. Austin 1862-1943 . . . . DLB-70

Freidank circa 1170-circa 1233 . . . . DLB-138

Freiligrath, Ferdinand 1810-1876 . . . . . . DLB-133

Frémont, John Charles 1813-1890 . . . . . . DLB-186

Frémont, John Charles 1813-1890 and
   Frémont, Jessie Benton 1834-1902 . . . DLB-183

French, Alice 1850-1934 . . . . DLB-74; DS-13

French Arthurian Literature. DLB-208

French, David 1939- DLB-53

French, Evangeline 1869-1960. . . . . .DLB-195

French, Francesca 1871-1960 . . . . .DLB-195

French, James [publishing house]. DLB-49

French, Samuel [publishing house]. DLB-49

Samuel French, Limited DLB-106

Freneau, Philip 1752-1832 . . . . DLB-37, 43

Freni, Melo 1934- DLB-128

Freshfield, Douglas W. 1845-1934. . . . . . .DLB-174

Freytag, Gustav 1816-1895 . . . . .DLB-129

Fried, Erich 1921-1988. . . . . .DLB-85

Friedan, Betty 1921- DLB-246

Friedman, Bruce Jay 1930- DLB-2, 28, 244

Friedrich von Hausen circa 1171-1190. . . .DLB-138

Friel, Brian 1929- DLB-13

Friend, Krebs 1895?-1967? DLB-4

Fries, Fritz Rudolf 1935- DLB-75

Fringe and Alternative Theater in
    Great Britain DLB-13

Frisch, Max
    1911-1991 . . . . DLB-69, 124; CDWLB-2

Frischlin, Nicodemus 1547-1590 . . . . DLB-179

Frischmuth, Barbara 1941- DLB-85

Fritz, Jean 1915- DLB-52

Froissart, Jean circa 1337-circa 1404. . . . . .DLB-208

Fromentin, Eugene 1820-1876 . . . . .DLB-123

Frontinus circa A.D. 35-A.D. 103/104 . . . .DLB-211

Frost, A. B. 1851-1928. . . . . .DLB-188; DS-13

Frost, Robert
    1874-1963 . . . . .DLB-54; DS-7; CDALB-4

Frothingham, Octavius Brooks
    1822-1895 .DLB-1, 243

Froude, James Anthony
    1818-1894 . . . . DLB-18, 57, 144

Fruitlands 1843-1844 . . . . .DLB-223

Fry, Christopher 1907- DLB-13

Fry, Roger 1866-1934 . . . . DS-10

Fry, Stephen 1957- DLB-207

Frye, Northrop 1912-1991 . . . . . . DLB-67, 68, 246

Fuchs, Daniel 1909-1993 . . . . . DLB-9, 26, 28; Y-93

Fuentes, Carlos 1928- DLB-113; CDWLB-3

Fuertes, Gloria 1918- DLB-108

Fugard, Athol 1932- DLB-225

The Fugitives and the Agrarians:
    The First Exhibition Y-85

Fujiwara no Shunzei 1114-1204 . . . . .DLB-203

Fujiwara no Tameaki 1230s?-1290s? DLB-203

Fujiwara no Tameie 1198-1275 . . . . .DLB-203

Fujiwara no Teika 1162-1241 . . . . .DLB-203

Fulbecke, William 1560-1603?. DLB-172

Fuller, Charles H., Jr. 1939- DLB-38

Fuller, Henry Blake 1857-1929. . . . . .DLB-12

Fuller, John 1937- DLB-40

Fuller, Margaret (see Fuller, Sarah)

Fuller, Roy 1912-1991 . . . . .DLB-15, 20

Fuller, Samuel 1912- DLB-26

Fuller, Sarah 1810-1850
    . . . . .DLB-1, 59, 73, 183, 223, 239; CDALB-2

Fuller, Thomas 1608-1661. . . . . .DLB-151

Fullerton, Hugh 1873-1945 . . . . .DLB-171

Fullwood, William flourished 1568 . . . . . .DLB-236

Fulton, Alice 1952- DLB-193

Fulton, Len 1934- Y-86

Fulton, Robin 1937- DLB-40

Furbank, P. N. 1920- DLB-155

Furman, Laura 1945- Y-86

Furness, Horace Howard
    1833-1912 .DLB-64

Furness, William Henry
    1802-1896 . . . . .DLB-1, 235

Furnivall, Frederick James
    1825-1910 .DLB-184

Furphy, Joseph
    (Tom Collins) 1843-1912 . . . . .DLB-230

Furthman, Jules 1888-1966 . . . . .DLB-26

Furui Yoshikichi 1937- DLB-182

Fushimi, Emperor 1265-1317. . . . . .DLB-203

Futabatei, Shimei
    (Hasegawa Tatsunosuke)
    1864-1909 .DLB-180

The Future of the Novel (1899), by
    Henry James DLB-18

Fyleman, Rose 1877-1957. . . . . .DLB-160

G

Gadda, Carlo Emilio 1893-1973 . . . . DLB-177

Gaddis, William 1922-1998. . . . . DLB-2, Y-99

Gág, Wanda 1893-1946. . . . . .DLB-22

Gagarin, Ivan Sergeevich 1814-1882 . . . . .DLB-198

Gagnon, Madeleine 1938- DLB-60

Gaine, Hugh 1726-1807 . . . . .DLB-43

Gaine, Hugh [publishing house] DLB-49

Gaines, Ernest J.
    1933- DLB-2, 33, 152; Y-80; CDALB-6

Gaiser, Gerd 1908-1976 . . . . .DLB-69

Gaitskill, Mary 1954- DLB-244

Galarza, Ernesto 1905-1984. . . . . .DLB-122

Galaxy Science Fiction Novels. DLB-46

Gale, Zona 1874-1938 . . . . DLB-9, 228, 78

Galen of Pergamon 129-after 210 . . . . DLB-176

Gales, Winifred Marshall 1761-1839 . . . . .DLB-200

Gall, Louise von 1815-1855. . . . . .DLB-133

Gallagher, Tess 1943- DLB-120, 212, 244

Gallagher, Wes 1911- DLB-127

Gallagher, William Davis 1808-1894. . . . . .DLB-73

Gallant, Mavis 1922- DLB-53

Gallegos, María Magdalena 1935- DLB-209

Gallico, Paul 1897-1976 . . . . DLB-9, 171

Gallop, Jane 1952- DLB-246

Galloway, Grace Growden 1727-1782 . . . .DLB-200

Gallup, Donald 1913- DLB-187

Galsworthy, John 1867-1933
    . . . . .DLB-10, 34, 98, 162; DS-16; CDBLB-5

Galt, John 1779-1839 . . . . .DLB-99, 116

Galton, Sir Francis 1822-1911 . . . . .DLB-166

Galvin, Brendan 1938- DLB-5

Gambit. DLB-46

Gamboa, Reymundo 1948- DLB-122

Gammer Gurton's Needle DLB-62

Gan, Elena Andreevna (Zeneida R-va)
    1814-1842 .DLB-198

Gannett, Frank E. 1876-1957 . . . . .DLB-29

Gao Xingjian 1940- Y-00

Gaos, Vicente 1919-1980. . . . . .DLB-134

García, Andrew 1854?-1943 . . . . .DLB-209

García, Lionel G. 1935- DLB-82

García, Richard 1941- DLB-209

García-Camarillo, Cecilio 1943- DLB-209

García Lorca, Federico 1898-1936. . . . . . .DLB-108

García Márquez, Gabriel
    1928- DLB-113; Y-82; CDWLB-3

Gardam, Jane 1928- DLB-14, 161, 231

Garden, Alexander circa 1685-1756. . . . . .DLB-31

Gardiner, John Rolfe 1936- DLB-244

Gardiner, Margaret Power Farmer
    (see Blessington, Marguerite, Countess of)

Gardner, John
    1933-1982 . . . . .DLB-2; Y-82; CDALB-7

Garfield, Leon 1921-1996 . . . . .DLB-161

Garis, Howard R. 1873-1962. . . . . .DLB-22

Garland, Hamlin 1860-1940 . . DLB-12, 71, 78, 186

Garneau, Francis-Xavier 1809-1866 . . . . . .DLB-99

Garneau, Hector de Saint-Denys
    1912-1943 .DLB-88

Garneau, Michel 1939- DLB-53

Garner, Alan 1934- DLB-161

Garner, Hugh 1913-1979 . . . . .DLB-68

Garnett, David 1892-1981 . . . . .DLB-34

Garnett, Eve 1900-1991. . . . . .DLB-160

Garnett, Richard 1835-1906 . . . . .DLB-184

Garrard, Lewis H. 1829-1887 . . . . .DLB-186

Garraty, John A. 1920- DLB-17

Garrett, George
    1929- DLB-2, 5, 130, 152; Y-83

Fellowship of Southern Writers Y-98

Garrett, John Work 1872-1942 . . . . .DLB-187

Garrick, David 1717-1779. . . . . .DLB-84, 213

Garrison, William Lloyd
    1805-1879 . . . . .DLB-1, 43, 235; CDALB-2

Garro, Elena 1920-1998. . . . . .DLB-145

Garth, Samuel 1661-1719. . . . . .DLB-95

Garve, Andrew 1908- DLB-87

Gary, Romain 1914-1980 . . . . .DLB-83

Gascoigne, George 1539?-1577 . . . . .DLB-136

Gascoyne, David 1916- DLB-20

Gaskell, Elizabeth Cleghorn
    1810-1865 . . . . . .DLB-21, 144, 159; CDBLB-4

Gaspey, Thomas 1788-1871 . . . . .DLB-116

Gass, William H. 1924- DLB-2, 227

Gates, Doris 1901- DLB-22

Gates, Henry Louis, Jr. 1950- DLB-67

Gates, Lewis E. 1860-1924 .... DLB-71

Gatto, Alfonso 1909-1976 .... DLB-114

Gault, William Campbell 1910-1995 .... DLB-226

Gaunt, Mary 1861-1942 ....DLB-174, 230

Gautier, Théophile 1811-1872 .... DLB-119

Gauvreau, Claude 1925-1971 .... DLB-88

The *Gawain*-Poet
flourished circa 1350-1400 .... DLB-146

Gay, Ebenezer 1696-1787 .... DLB-24

Gay, John 1685-1732 .... DLB-84, 95

Gayarré, Charles E. A. 1805-1895 .... DLB-30

Gaylord, Charles [publishing house] DLB-49

Gaylord, Edward King 1873-1974 ...... DLB-127

Gaylord, Edward Lewis 1919- DLB-127

Geda, Sigitas 1943- DLB-232

Geddes, Gary 1940- DLB-60

Geddes, Virgil 1897- DLB-4

Gedeon (Georgii Andreevich Krinovsky)
circa 1730-1763 .... DLB-150

Gee, Maggie 1948- DLB-207

Gee, Shirley 1932- DLB-245

Geßner, Salomon 1730-1788 .... DLB-97

Geibel, Emanuel 1815-1884 .... DLB-129

Geiogamah, Hanay 1945- DLB-175

Geis, Bernard, Associates DLB-46

Geisel, Theodor Seuss 1904-1991 ... DLB-61; Y-91

Gelb, Arthur 1924- DLB-103

Gelb, Barbara 1926- DLB-103

Gelber, Jack 1932- DLB-7, 228

Gelinas, Gratien 1909- DLB-88

Gellert, Christian Füerchtegott
1715-1769 .... DLB-97

Gellhorn, Martha 1908-1998 .... Y-82, Y-98

Gems, Pam 1925- DLB-13

Genet, Jean 1910-1986 ....DLB-72; Y-86

Genette, Gérard 1930- DLB-242

Genevoix, Maurice 1890-1980 .... DLB-65

Genovese, Eugene D. 1930- DLB-17

Gent, Peter 1942- Y-82

Geoffrey of Monmouth
circa 1100-1155 .... DLB-146

George, Henry 1839-1897 .... DLB-23

George, Jean Craighead 1919- DLB-52

George, W. L. 1882-1926 .... DLB-197

George III, King of Great Britain and Ireland
1738-1820 .... DLB-213

George V. Higgins to Julian Symons Y-99

Georgslied 896? DLB-148

Gerber, Merrill Joan 1938- DLB-218

Gerhardie, William 1895-1977 .... DLB-36

Gerhardt, Paul 1607-1676 .... DLB-164

Gérin, Winifred 1901-1981 .... DLB-155

Gérin-Lajoie, Antoine 1824-1882 .... DLB-99

German Drama 800-1280 .... DLB-138

German Drama from Naturalism
to Fascism: 1889-1933 .... DLB-118

German Literature and Culture from Charlemagne
to the Early Courtly Period
.... DLB-148; CDWLB-2

German Radio Play, The DLB-124

German Transformation from the Baroque
to the Enlightenment, The DLB-97

The Germanic Epic and Old English
Heroic Poetry: *Widsith, Waldere,*
and *The Fight at Finnsburg* DLB-146

Germanophilism, by Hans Kohn DLB-66

Gernsback, Hugo 1884-1967 ....DLB-8, 137

Gerould, Katharine Fullerton
1879-1944 .... DLB-78

Gerrish, Samuel [publishing house] DLB-49

Gerrold, David 1944- DLB-8

The Ira Gershwin Centenary Y-96

Gerson, Jean 1363-1429 .... DLB-208

Gersonides 1288-1344 .... DLB-115

Gerstäcker, Friedrich 1816-1872 .... DLB-129

Gerstenberg, Heinrich Wilhelm von
1737-1823 .... DLB-97

Gervinus, Georg Gottfried
1805-1871 .... DLB-133

Geston, Mark S. 1946- DLB-8

Al-Ghazali 1058-1111 .... DLB-115

Gibbings, Robert 1889-1958 .... DLB-195

Gibbon, Edward 1737-1794 .... DLB-104

Gibbon, John Murray 1875-1952 .... DLB-92

Gibbon, Lewis Grassic (see Mitchell, James Leslie)

Gibbons, Floyd 1887-1939 .... DLB-25

Gibbons, Reginald 1947- DLB-120

Gibbons, William ?-? DLB-73

Gibson, Charles Dana
1867-1944 .... DLB-188; DS-13

Gibson, Graeme 1934- DLB-53

Gibson, Margaret 1944- DLB-120

Gibson, Margaret Dunlop 1843-1920 .....DLB-174

Gibson, Wilfrid 1878-1962 .... DLB-19

Gibson, William 1914- DLB-7

Gide, André 1869-1951 .... DLB-65

Giguère, Diane 1937- DLB-53

Giguère, Roland 1929- DLB-60

Gil de Biedma, Jaime 1929-1990 .... DLB-108

Gil-Albert, Juan 1906- DLB-134

Gilbert, Anthony 1899-1973 .... DLB-77

Gilbert, Sir Humphrey 1537-1583 .... DLB-136

Gilbert, Michael 1912- DLB-87

Gilbert, Sandra M. 1936- DLB-120, 246

Gilchrist, Alexander 1828-1861 .... DLB-144

Gilchrist, Ellen 1935- DLB-130

Gilder, Jeannette L. 1849-1916 .... DLB-79

Gilder, Richard Watson 1844-1909 ... DLB-64, 79

Gildersleeve, Basil 1831-1924 .... DLB-71

Giles of Rome circa 1243-1316 .... DLB-115

Giles, Henry 1809-1882 .... DLB-64

Gilfillan, George 1813-1878 .... DLB-144

Gill, Eric 1882-1940 .... DLB-98

Gill, Sarah Prince 1728-1771 .... DLB-200

Gill, William F., Company DLB-49

Gillespie, A. Lincoln, Jr. 1895-1950 ...... DLB-4

Gilliam, Florence ?-? DLB-4

Gilliatt, Penelope 1932-1993 .... DLB-14

Gillott, Jacky 1939-1980 .... DLB-14

Gilman, Caroline H. 1794-1888 .... DLB-3, 73

Gilman, Charlotte Perkins 1860-1935 ... DLB-221

Gilman, W. and J. [publishing house]..... DLB-49

Gilmer, Elizabeth Meriwether 1861-1951.. DLB-29

Gilmer, Francis Walker 1790-1826....... DLB-37

Gilroy, Frank D. 1925- DLB-7

Gimferrer, Pere (Pedro) 1945- DLB-134

Gingrich, Arnold 1903-1976..........DLB-137

Ginsberg, Allen
1926-1997 ....DLB-5, 16, 169, 237; CDALB-1

Ginzburg, Natalia 1916-1991 ....DLB-177

Ginzkey, Franz Karl 1871-1963 .... DLB-81

Gioia, Dana 1950- DLB-120

Giono, Jean 1895-1970 .... DLB-72

Giotti, Virgilio 1885-1957............ DLB-114

Giovanni, Nikki 1943- DLB-5, 41; CDALB-7

Gipson, Lawrence Henry 1880-1971 ......DLB-17

Girard, Rodolphe 1879-1956 .... DLB-92

Giraudoux, Jean 1882-1944 .... DLB-65

Gissing, George 1857-1903 ......DLB-18, 135, 184

The Place of Realism in Fiction (1895).... DLB-18

Giudici, Giovanni 1924- DLB-128

Giuliani, Alfredo 1924- DLB-128

Glackens, William J. 1870-1938 .... DLB-188

Gladstone, William Ewart
1809-1898 ....DLB-57, 184

Glaeser, Ernst 1902-1963 .... DLB-69

Glancy, Diane 1941- DLB-175

Glanville, Brian 1931- DLB-15, 139

Glapthorne, Henry 1610-1643? DLB-58

Glasgow, Ellen 1873-1945 .... DLB-9, 12

Glasier, Katharine Bruce 1867-1950 ..... DLB-190

Glaspell, Susan 1876-1948 ......DLB-7, 9, 78, 228

Glass, Montague 1877-1934 .... DLB-11

Glassco, John 1909-1981 .... DLB-68

Glauser, Friedrich 1896-1938........... DLB-56

F. Gleason's Publishing Hall............ DLB-49

Gleim, Johann Wilhelm Ludwig
1719-1803 .... DLB-97

Glendinning, Victoria 1937- DLB-155

The Cult of Biography
Excerpts from the Second Folio Debate:
"Biographies are generally a disease of
English Literature" Y-86

Glinka, Fedor Nikolaevich 1786-1880.... DLB-205

Glover, Keith 1966- DLB-249

Glover, Richard 1712-1785 .... DLB-95

Glück, Louise 1943- DLB-5

Glyn, Elinor 1864-1943 . . . . .DLB-153

Gnedich, Nikolai Ivanovich 1784-1833 . . .DLB-205

Gobineau, Joseph-Arthur de
1816-1882 . . . . .DLB-123

Godber, John 1956- DLB-233

Godbout, Jacques 1933- DLB-53

Goddard, Morrill 1865-1937 . . . . .DLB-25

Goddard, William 1740-1817 . . . . .DLB-43

Godden, Rumer 1907-1998 . . . . .DLB-161

Godey, Louis A. 1804-1878 . . . . .DLB-73

Godey and McMichael DLB-49

Godfrey, Dave 1938- DLB-60

Godfrey, Thomas 1736-1763 . . . . .DLB-31

Godine, David R., Publisher DLB-46

Godkin, E. L. 1831-1902 . . . . .DLB-79

Godolphin, Sidney 1610-1643 . . . . .DLB-126

Godwin, Gail 1937- DLB-6, 234

Godwin, M. J., and Company DLB-154

Godwin, Mary Jane Clairmont
1766-1841 . . . . .DLB-163

Godwin, Parke 1816-1904 . . . . .DLB-3, 64

Godwin, William 1756-1836
. . . . . .DLB-39, 104, 142, 158, 163; CDBLB-3

Preface to *St. Leon* (1799) DLB-39

Goering, Reinhard 1887-1936 . . . . .DLB-118

Goes, Albrecht 1908- DLB-69

Goethe, Johann Wolfgang von
1749-1832 . . . . .DLB-94; CDWLB-2

Goetz, Curt 1888-1960 . . . . .DLB-124

Goffe, Thomas circa 1592-1629 . . . . .DLB-58

Goffstein, M. B. 1940- DLB-61

Gogarty, Oliver St. John 1878-1957 . . . .DLB-15, 19

Gogol, Nikolai Vasil'evich 1809-1852 . . . .DLB-198

Goines, Donald 1937-1974 . . . . .DLB-33

Gold, Herbert 1924- DLB-2; Y-81

Gold, Michael 1893-1967 . . . . .DLB-9, 28

Goldbarth, Albert 1948- DLB-120

Goldberg, Dick 1947- DLB-7

Golden Cockerel Press DLB-112

Golding, Arthur 1536-1606 . . . . .DLB-136

Golding, Louis 1895-1958 . . . . .DLB-195

Golding, William
1911-1993 . . . . .DLB-15, 100; Y-83; CDBLB-7

Goldman, Emma 1869-1940 . . . . .DLB-221

Goldman, William 1931- DLB-44

Goldring, Douglas 1887-1960 . . . . .DLB-197

Goldsmith, Oliver 1730?-1774
. . . . . .DLB-39, 89, 104, 109, 142; CDBLB-2

Goldsmith, Oliver 1794-1861 . . . . .DLB-99

Goldsmith Publishing Company DLB-46

Goldstein, Richard 1944- DLB-185

Gollancz, Sir Israel 1864-1930 . . . . .DLB-201

Gollancz, Victor, Limited DLB-112

Gombrowicz, Witold
1904-1969 . . . . .DLB-215; CDWLB-4

Gómez-Quiñones, Juan 1942- DLB-122

Gomme, Laurence James
[publishing house] DLB-46

Goncharov, Ivan Aleksandrovich
1812-1891 . . . . .DLB-238

Goncourt, Edmond de 1822-1896 . . . . . . .DLB-123

Goncourt, Jules de 1830-1870 . . . . .DLB-123

Gonzales, Rodolfo "Corky" 1928- DLB-122

González, Angel 1925- DLB-108

Gonzalez, Genaro 1949- DLB-122

Gonzalez, Ray 1952- DLB-122

Gonzales-Berry, Erlinda 1942- DLB-209

"Chicano Language" DLB-82

González de Mireles, Jovita
1899-1983 . . . . .DLB-122

González-T., César A. 1931- DLB-82

Goodbye, Gutenberg? A Lecture at the
New York Public Library,
18 April 1995, by Donald Lamm Y-95

Goodis, David 1917-1967 . . . . .DLB-226

Goodison, Lorna 1947- DLB-157

Goodman, Allegra 1967- DLB-244

Goodman, Paul 1911-1972 . . . . .DLB-130, 246

The Goodman Theatre DLB-7

Goodrich, Frances 1891-1984 and
Hackett, Albert 1900-1995 . . . . .DLB-26

Goodrich, Samuel Griswold
1793-1860 . . . . .DLB-1, 42, 73, 243

Goodrich, S. G. [publishing house] DLB-49

Goodspeed, C. E., and Company DLB-49

Goodwin, Stephen 1943- Y-82

Googe, Barnabe 1540-1594 . . . . .DLB-132

Gookin, Daniel 1612-1687 . . . . .DLB-24

Goran, Lester 1928- DLB-244

Gordimer, Nadine 1923- DLB-225; Y-91

Gordon, Adam Lindsay 1833-1870 . . . . . .DLB-230

Gordon, Caroline
1895-1981 . . . . . . .DLB-4, 9, 102; DS-17; Y-81

Gordon, Giles 1940- DLB-14, 139, 207

Gordon, Helen Cameron, Lady Russell
1867-1949 . . . . .DLB-195

Gordon, Lyndall 1941- DLB-155

Gordon, Mary 1949- DLB-6; Y-81

Gordone, Charles 1925-1995 . . . . .DLB-7

Gore, Catherine 1800-1861 . . . . .DLB-116

Gore-Booth, Eva 1870-1926 . . . . .DLB-240

Gores, Joe 1931- DLB-226

Gorey, Edward 1925-2000 . . . . .DLB-61

Gorgias of Leontini
circa 485 B.C.-376 B.C. DLB-176

Görres, Joseph 1776-1848 . . . . .DLB-90

Gosse, Edmund 1849-1928 . . . . .DLB-57, 144, 184

Gosson, Stephen 1554-1624 . . . . .DLB-172

The Schoole of Abuse (1579) DLB-172

Gotlieb, Phyllis 1926- DLB-88

Go-Toba 1180-1239 . . . . .DLB-203

Gottfried von Straßburg
died before 1230 . . . . . . .DLB-138; CDWLB-2

Gotthelf, Jeremias 1797-1854 . . . . .DLB-133

Gottschalk circa 804/808-869 . . . . .DLB-148

Gottsched, Johann Christoph
1700-1766 . . . . .DLB-97

Götz, Johann Nikolaus 1721-1781 . . . . .DLB-97

Goudge, Elizabeth 1900-1984 . . . . .DLB-191

Gough, John B. 1817-1886 . . . . .DLB-243

Gould, Wallace 1882-1940 . . . . .DLB-54

Govoni, Corrado 1884-1965 . . . . .DLB-114

Gower, John circa 1330-1408 . . . . .DLB-146

Goyen, William 1915-1983 . . . . .DLB-2, 218; Y-83

Goytisolo, José Augustín 1928- DLB-134

Gozzano, Guido 1883-1916 . . . . .DLB-114

Grabbe, Christian Dietrich 1801-1836 . . . .DLB-133

Gracq, Julien 1910- DLB-83

Grady, Henry W. 1850-1889 . . . . .DLB-23

Graf, Oskar Maria 1894-1967 . . . . .DLB-56

Graf Rudolf
between circa 1170 and circa 1185 . . .DLB-148

Graff, Gerald 1937- DLB-246

Grafton, Richard [publishing house] DLB-170

Grafton, Sue 1940- DLB-226

Graham, Frank 1893-1965 . . . . .DLB-241

Graham, George Rex 1813-1894 . . . . .DLB-73

Graham, Gwethalyn 1913-1965 . . . . .DLB-88

Graham, Jorie 1951- DLB-120

Graham, Katharine 1917- DLB-127

Graham, Lorenz 1902-1989 . . . . .DLB-76

Graham, Philip 1915-1963 . . . . .DLB-127

Graham, R. B. Cunninghame
1852-1936 . . . . .DLB-98, 135, 174

Graham, Shirley 1896-1977 . . . . .DLB-76

Graham, Stephen 1884-1975 . . . . .DLB-195

Graham, W. S. 1918- DLB-20

Graham, William H. [publishing house] . . .DLB-49

Graham, Winston 1910- DLB-77

Grahame, Kenneth
1859-1932 . . . . .DLB-34, 141, 178

Grainger, Martin Allerdale 1874-1941 . . . . .DLB-92

Gramatky, Hardie 1907-1979 . . . . .DLB-22

Grand, Sarah 1854-1943 . . . . .DLB-135, 197

Grandbois, Alain 1900-1975 . . . . .DLB-92

Grandson, Oton de circa 1345-1397 . . . . .DLB-208

Grange, John circa 1556-? DLB-136

Granich, Irwin (see Gold, Michael)

Granovsky, Timofei Nikolaevich
1813-1855 . . . . .DLB-198

Grant, Anne MacVicar 1755-1838 . . . . . . .DLB-200

Grant, Duncan 1885-1978 . . . . .DS-10

Grant, George 1918-1988 . . . . .DLB-88

Grant, George Monro 1835-1902 . . . . .DLB-99

Grant, Harry J. 1881-1963 . . . . .DLB-29

Grant, James Edward 1905-1966 . . . . .DLB-26

Grass, Günter 1927- . . .DLB-75, 124; CDWLB-2

Grasty, Charles H. 1863-1924 . . . . .DLB-25

Grau, Shirley Ann 1929- DLB-2, 218

Graves, John 1920- Y-83

Graves, Richard 1715-1804. . . . . DLB-39

Graves, Robert 1895-1985
. . . .DLB-20, 100, 191; DS-18; Y-85; CDBLB-6

Gray, Alasdair 1934- DLB-194

Gray, Asa 1810-1888 . . . . DLB-1, 235

Gray, David 1838-1861 . . . . DLB-32

Gray, Simon 1936- DLB-13

Gray, Thomas 1716-1771 . . . . DLB-109; CDBLB-2

Grayson, Richard 1951- DLB-234

Grayson, William J. 1788-1863. . . . DLB-3, 64, 248

The Great Bibliographers Series. Y-93

The Great Modern Library Scam. Y-98

The Great War and the Theater, 1914-1918
[Great Britain] DLB-10

The Great War Exhibition and Symposium at
the University of South Carolina. Y-97

Grech, Nikolai Ivanovich 1787-1867 . . . . . DLB-198

Greeley, Horace 1811-1872 . . . . . . DLB-3, 43, 189

Green, Adolph (see Comden, Betty)

Green, Anna Katharine
1846-1935 . . . . DLB-202, 221

Green, Duff 1791-1875 . . . . DLB-43

Green, Elizabeth Shippen 1871-1954 . . . . DLB-188

Green, Gerald 1922- DLB-28

Green, Henry 1905-1973 . . . . DLB-15

Green, Jonas 1712-1767. . . . . DLB-31

Green, Joseph 1706-1780. . . . . DLB-31

Green, Julien 1900-1998 . . . . DLB-4, 72

Green, Paul 1894-1981. . . . . . .DLB-7, 9, 249; Y-81

Green, T. and S. [publishing house] DLB-49

Green, Thomas Hill 1836-1882 . . . . DLB-190

Green, Timothy [publishing house] DLB-49

Greenaway, Kate 1846-1901. . . . . DLB-141

Greenberg: Publisher DLB-46

Green Tiger Press. DLB-46

Greene, Asa 1789-1838. . . . . DLB-11

Greene, Belle da Costa 1883-1950 . . . . . . DLB-187

Greene, Benjamin H.
[publishing house] DLB-49

Greene, Graham 1904-1991
. . . . .DLB-13, 15, 77, 100, 162, 201, 204;
Y-85, Y-91; CDBLB-7

Greene, Robert 1558-1592 . . . . DLB-62, 167

Greene, Robert Bernard (Bob) Jr.
1947- DLB-185

Greenfield, George 1917-2000. . . . . .Y-00

Greenhow, Robert 1800-1854 . . . . DLB-30

Greenlee, William B. 1872-1953. . . . . . . DLB-187

Greenough, Horatio 1805-1852 . . . . . . DLB-1, 235

Greenwell, Dora 1821-1882 . . . . DLB-35, 199

Greenwillow Books DLB-46

Greenwood, Grace (see Lippincott, Sara Jane Clarke)

Greenwood, Walter 1903-1974. . . . . . DLB-10, 191

Greer, Ben 1948- DLB-6

Greflinger, Georg 1620?-1677. . . . . DLB-164

Greg, W. R. 1809-1881 . . . . DLB-55

Greg, W. W. 1875-1959 . . . . DLB-201

Gregg, Josiah 1806-1850. . . . . DLB-183, 186

Gregg Press. DLB-46

Gregory, Isabella Augusta Persse, Lady
1852-1932 . . . . DLB-10

Gregory, Horace 1898-1982. . . . . DLB-48

Gregory of Rimini circa 1300-1358 . . . . . DLB-115

Gregynog Press DLB-112

Greiffenberg, Catharina Regina von
1633-1694 . . . . DLB-168

Greig, Noël 1944- DLB-245

Grenfell, Wilfred Thomason
1865-1940 . . . . .DLB-92

Gress, Elsa 1919-1988 . . . . DLB-214

Greve, Felix Paul (see Grove, Frederick Philip)

Greville, Fulke, First Lord Brooke
1554-1628 . . . . .DLB-62, 172

Grey, Sir George, K.C.B. 1812-1898 . . . . DLB-184

Grey, Lady Jane 1537-1554 . . . . DLB-132

Grey Owl 1888-1938 . . . . DLB-92; DS-17

Grey, Zane 1872-1939 . . . . DLB-9, 212

Grey Walls Press DLB-112

Griboedov, Aleksandr Sergeevich
1795?-1829. . . . . DLB-205

Grier, Eldon 1917- DLB-88

Grieve, C. M. (see MacDiarmid, Hugh)

Griffin, Bartholomew flourished 1596 . . . .DLB-172

Griffin, Gerald 1803-1840 . . . . DLB-159

The Griffin Poetry Prize. Y-00

Griffith, Elizabeth 1727?-1793. . . . . . . DLB-39, 89

Preface to The Delicate Distress (1769) DLB-39

Griffith, George 1857-1906. . . . . .DLB-178

Griffiths, Ralph [publishing house]. DLB-154

Griffiths, Trevor 1935- DLB-13, 245

Griggs, S. C., and Company. DLB-49

Griggs, Sutton Elbert 1872-1930. . . . . DLB-50

Grignon, Claude-Henri 1894-1976 . . . . . . DLB-68

Grigorovich, Dmitrii Vasil'evich
1822-1899 . . . . DLB-238

Grigson, Geoffrey 1905- DLB-27

Grillparzer, Franz
1791-1872. . . . . DLB-133; CDWLB-2

Grimald, Nicholas
circa 1519-circa 1562 . . . . DLB-136

Grimké, Angelina Weld 1880-1958 . . . DLB-50, 54

Grimké, Sarah Moore 1792-1873 . . . . DLB-239

Grimm, Hans 1875-1959 . . . . DLB-66

Grimm, Jacob 1785-1863 . . . . DLB-90

Grimm, Wilhelm
1786-1859. . . . . DLB-90; CDWLB-2

Grimmelshausen, Johann Jacob Christoffel von
1621 or 1622-1676 . . . . . DLB-168; CDWLB-2

Grimshaw, Beatrice Ethel 1871-1953 . . . . .DLB-174

Grindal, Edmund 1519 or 1520-1583. . . . DLB-132

Griswold, Rufus Wilmot 1815-1857. . . . DLB-3, 59

Grosart, Alexander Balloch 1827-1899 . . . DLB-184

Gross, Milt 1895-1953 . . . . DLB-11

Grosset and Dunlap DLB-49

Grossman, Allen 1932- DLB-193

Grossman Publishers DLB-46

Grosseteste, Robert circa 1160-1253. . . . . DLB-115

Grosvenor, Gilbert H. 1875-1966. . . . . . . DLB-91

Groth, Klaus 1819-1899. . . . . DLB-129

Groulx, Lionel 1878-1967. . . . . DLB-68

Grove, Frederick Philip 1879-1949. . . . . . DLB-92

Grove Press DLB-46

Grubb, Davis 1919-1980 . . . . DLB-6

Gruelle, Johnny 1880-1938. . . . . DLB-22

von Grumbach, Argula
1492-after 1563? DLB-179

Grymeston, Elizabeth
before 1563-before 1604 . . . . DLB-136

Gryphius, Andreas
1616-1664 . . . . .DLB-164; CDWLB-2

Gryphius, Christian 1649-1706. . . . . DLB-168

Guare, John 1938- DLB-7, 249

Guerra, Tonino 1920- DLB-128

Guest, Barbara 1920- DLB-5, 193

Guèvremont, Germaine 1893-1968 . . . . . . DLB-68

Guidacci, Margherita 1921-1992 . . . . DLB-128

Guide to the Archives of Publishers, Journals,
and Literary Agents in North American
Libraries. Y-93

Guillén, Jorge 1893-1984 . . . . DLB-108

Guilloux, Louis 1899-1980. . . . . DLB-72

Guilpin, Everard
circa 1572-after 1608? DLB-136

Guiney, Louise Imogen 1861-1920 . . . . . . DLB-54

Guiterman, Arthur 1871-1943 . . . . DLB-11

Günderrode, Caroline von
1780-1806. DLB-90

Gundulić, Ivan
1589-1638 . . . . .DLB-147; CDWLB-4

Gunn, Bill 1934-1989. . . . . DLB-38

Gunn, James E. 1923- DLB-8

Gunn, Neil M. 1891-1973. . . . . DLB-15

Gunn, Thom 1929- DLB-27; CDBLB-8

Gunnars, Kristjana 1948- DLB-60

Günther, Johann Christian
1695-1723. DLB-168

Gurik, Robert 1932- DLB-60

Gustafson, Ralph 1909- DLB-88

Gütersloh, Albert Paris 1887-1973 . . . . . . DLB-81

Guthrie, A. B., Jr. 1901-1991 . . . . DLB-6, 212

Guthrie, Ramon 1896-1973 . . . . DLB-4

The Guthrie Theater DLB-7

Guthrie, Thomas Anstey (see Anstey, FC)

Gutzkow, Karl 1811-1878. . . . . DLB-133

Guy, Ray 1939- DLB-60

Guy, Rosa 1925- DLB-33

Guyot, Arnold 1807-1884. . . . . .DS-13

Gwynne, Erskine 1898-1948 . . . . DLB-4

Gyles, John 1680-1755 . . . . DLB-99

Gysin, Brion 1916- DLB-16

H

H.D. (see Doolittle, Hilda)

Habermas, Jürgen 1929- DLB-242

Habington, William 1605-1654 ....DLB-126

Hacker, Marilyn 1942- DLB-120

Hackett, Albert (see Goodrich, Frances)

Hacks, Peter 1928- DLB-124

Hadas, Rachel 1948- DLB-120

Hadden, Briton 1898-1929 ....DLB-91

Hagedorn, Friedrich von 1708-1754.....DLB-168

Hagelstange, Rudolf 1912-1984........DLB-69

Haggard, H. Rider
  1856-1925 ....DLB-70, 156, 174, 178

Haggard, William 1907-1993 ....Y-93

Hagy, Alyson 1960- DLB-244

Hahn-Hahn, Ida Gräfin von
  1805-1880 ....DLB-133

Haig-Brown, Roderick 1908-1976 ....DLB-88

Haight, Gordon S. 1901-1985 ....DLB-103

Hailey, Arthur 1920- DLB-88; Y-82

Haines, John 1924- DLB-5, 212

Hake, Edward flourished 1566-1604 .....DLB-136

Hake, Thomas Gordon 1809-1895 ....DLB-32

Hakluyt, Richard 1552?-1616 ....DLB-136

Halas, František 1901-1949 ....DLB-215

Halbe, Max 1865-1944 ....DLB-118

Halberstam, David 1934- DLB-241

Haldane, J. B. S. 1892-1964 ....DLB-160

Haldeman, Joe 1943- DLB-8

Haldeman-Julius Company DLB-46

Haldone, Charlotte 1894-1969 ....DLB-191

Hale, E. J., and Son DLB-49

Hale, Edward Everett
  1822-1909 .... DLB-1, 42, 74, 235

Hale, Janet Campbell 1946- DLB-175

Hale, Kathleen 1898- DLB-160

Hale, Leo Thomas (see Ebon)

Hale, Lucretia Peabody 1820-1900 ....DLB-42

Hale, Nancy
  1908-1988 .... DLB-86; DS-17; Y-80, Y-88

Hale, Sarah Josepha (Buell)
  1788-1879..........DLB-1, 42, 73, 243

Hale, Susan 1833-1910................DLB-221

Hales, John 1584-1656................DLB-151

Halévy, Ludovic 1834-1908............DLB-192

Haley, Alex 1921-1992 ....DLB-38; CDALB-7

Haliburton, Thomas Chandler
  1796-1865 ....DLB-11, 99

Hall, Anna Maria 1800-1881 ....DLB-159

Hall, Donald 1928- DLB-5

Hall, Edward 1497-1547...............DLB-132

Hall, Halsey 1898-1977 ....DLB-241

Hall, James 1793-1868 ....DLB-73, 74

Hall, Joseph 1574-1656 ....DLB-121, 151

Hall, Radclyffe 1880-1943 ....DLB-191

Hall, Samuel [publishing house].........DLB-49

Hall, Sarah Ewing 1761-1830..........DLB-200

Hall, Stuart 1932- DLB-242

Hallam, Arthur Henry 1811-1833 ....DLB-32

On Some of the Characteristics of Modern
  Poetry and On the Lyrical Poems of
  Alfred Tennyson (1831) DLB-32

Halleck, Fitz-Greene 1790-1867 ....DLB-3

Haller, Albrecht von 1708-1777 ....DLB-168

Halliday, Brett (see Dresser, Davis)

Halliwell-Phillipps, James Orchard
  1820-1889 ....DLB-184

Hallmann, Johann Christian
  1640-1704 or 1716? DLB-168

Hallmark Editions DLB-46

Halper, Albert 1904-1984 ....DLB-9

Halperin, John William 1941- DLB-111

Halstead, Murat 1829-1908 ....DLB-23

Hamann, Johann Georg 1730-1788 ....DLB-97

Hamburger, Michael 1924- DLB-27

Hamilton, Alexander 1712-1756..........DLB-31

Hamilton, Alexander 1755?-1804 ....DLB-37

Hamilton, Cicely 1872-1952 ....DLB-10, 197

Hamilton, Edmond 1904-1977...........DLB-8

Hamilton, Elizabeth 1758-1816 .....DLB-116, 158

Hamilton, Gail (see Corcoran, Barbara)

Hamilton, Gail (see Dodge, Mary Abigail)

Hamilton, Hamish, Limited............DLB-112

Hamilton, Ian 1938- DLB-40, 155

Hamilton, Janet 1795-1873............DLB-199

Hamilton, Mary Agnes 1884-1962 ......DLB-197

Hamilton, Patrick 1904-1962........DLB-10, 191

Hamilton, Virginia 1936- DLB-33, 52

Hammett, Dashiell
  1894-1961 ....DLB-226; DS-6; CDALB-5

The Glass Key and Other Dashiell Hammett
  Mysteries Y-96

Dashiell Hammett: An Appeal in *TAC* Y-91

Hammon, Jupiter 1711-died between
  1790 and 1806.................DLB-31, 50

Hammond, John ?-1663................DLB-24

Hamner, Earl 1923- DLB-6

Hampson, John 1901-1955 ....DLB-191

Hampton, Christopher 1946- DLB-13

Handel-Mazzetti, Enrica von 1871-1955 ...DLB-81

Handke, Peter 1942- DLB-85, 124

Handlin, Oscar 1915- DLB-17

Hankin, St. John 1869-1909...........DLB-10

Hanley, Clifford 1922- DLB-14

Hanley, James 1901-1985 ....DLB-191

Hannah, Barry 1942- DLB-6, 234

Hannay, James 1827-1873 ....DLB-21

Hano, Arnold 1922- DLB-241

Hansberry, Lorraine
  1930-1965 ....DLB-7, 38; CDALB-1

Hansen, Martin A. 1909-1955 ....DLB-214

Hansen, Thorkild 1927-1989 ....DLB-214

Hanson, Elizabeth 1684-1737 ....DLB-200

Hapgood, Norman 1868-1937 ....DLB-91

Happel, Eberhard Werner 1647-1690 ....DLB-168

The Harbinger 1845-1849 ....DLB-223

Harcourt Brace Jovanovich DLB-46

Hardenberg, Friedrich von (see Novalis)

Harding, Walter 1917- DLB-111

Hardwick, Elizabeth 1916- DLB-6

Hardy, Thomas
  1840-1928.......DLB-18, 19, 135; CDBLB-5

"Candour in English Fiction" (1890)......DLB-18

Hare, Cyril 1900-1958 ....DLB-77

Hare, David 1947- DLB-13

Hargrove, Marion 1919- DLB-11

Häring, Georg Wilhelm Heinrich
  (see Alexis, Willibald)

Harington, Donald 1935- DLB-152

Harington, Sir John 1560-1612 ....DLB-136

Harjo, Joy 1951- DLB-120, 175

Harkness, Margaret (John Law)
  1854-1923 ....DLB-197

Harley, Edward, second Earl of Oxford
  1689-1741 ....DLB-213

Harley, Robert, first Earl of Oxford
  1661-1724 ....DLB-213

Harlow, Robert 1923- DLB-60

Harman, Thomas flourished 1566-1573 ..DLB-136

Harness, Charles L. 1915- DLB-8

Harnett, Cynthia 1893-1981 ....DLB-161

Harper, Edith Alice Mary (see Wickham, Anna)

Harper, Fletcher 1806-1877 ....DLB-79

Harper, Frances Ellen Watkins
  1825-1911 ....DLB-50, 221

Harper, Michael S. 1938- DLB-41

Harper and Brothers DLB-49

Harpur, Charles 1813-1868............DLB-230

Harraden, Beatrice 1864-1943.........DLB-153

Harrap, George G., and Company
  Limited DLB-112

Harriot, Thomas 1560-1621 ....DLB-136

Harris, Alexander 1805-1874...........DLB-230

Harris, Benjamin ?-circa 1720 ......DLB-42, 43

Harris, Christie 1907- DLB-88

Harris, Frank 1856-1931 ....DLB-156, 197

Harris, George Washington
  1814-1869 ....DLB-3, 11, 248

Harris, Joel Chandler
  1848-1908 ....DLB-11, 23, 42, 78, 91

Harris, Mark 1922- DLB-2; Y-80

Harris, Wilson 1921- DLB-117; CDWLB-3

Harrison, Mrs. Burton
  (see Harrison, Constance Cary)

Harrison, Charles Yale 1898-1954........DLB-68

Harrison, Constance Cary 1843-1920....DLB-221

Harrison, Frederic 1831-1923 ....DLB-57, 190

"On Style in English Prose" (1898).......DLB-57

Harrison, Harry 1925- DLB-8

Harrison, James P., Company DLB-49

Harrison, Jim 1937- Y-82

Harrison, Mary St. Leger Kingsley
(see Malet, Lucas)

Harrison, Paul Carter 1936- DLB-38

Harrison, Susan Frances 1859-1935 ..... DLB-99

Harrison, Tony 1937- DLB-40, 245

Harrison, William 1535-1593 .... DLB-136

Harrison, William 1933- DLB-234

Harrisse, Henry 1829-1910 .... DLB-47

The Harry Ransom Humanities
Research Center at the University
of Texas at Austin Y-00

Harryman, Carla 1952- DLB-193

Harsdörffer, Georg Philipp 1607-1658 ... DLB-164

Harsent, David 1942- DLB-40

Hart, Albert Bushnell 1854-1943 .... DLB-17

Hart, Anne 1768-1834 .... DLB-200

Hart, Elizabeth 1771-1833 .... DLB-200

Hart, Julia Catherine 1796-1867 .... DLB-99

The Lorenz Hart Centenary Y-95

Hart, Moss 1904-1961 .... DLB-7

Hart, Oliver 1723-1795 .... DLB-31

Hart-Davis, Rupert, Limited DLB-112

Harte, Bret 1836-1902
.... DLB-12, 64, 74, 79, 186; CDALB-3

Harte, Edward Holmead 1922- DLB-127

Harte, Houston Harriman 1927- DLB-127

Hartlaub, Felix 1913-1945 .... DLB-56

Hartlebon, Otto Erich 1864-1905 .... DLB-118

Hartley, L. P. 1895-1972 .... DLB-15, 139

Hartley, Marsden 1877-1943 .... DLB-54

Hartling, Peter 1933- DLB-75

Hartman, Geoffrey H. 1929- DLB-67

Hartmann, Sadakichi 1867-1944 .... DLB-54

Hartmann von Aue
circa 1160-circa 1205 ... DLB-138; CDWLB-2

Harvey, Gabriel 1550?-1631 .... DLB-167, 213, 236

Harvey, Jean-Charles 1891-1967 .... DLB-88

Harvill Press Limited DLB-112

Harwood, Lee 1939- DLB-40

Harwood, Ronald 1934- DLB-13

Hašek, Jaroslav 1883-1923 .. DLB-215; CDWLB-4

Haskins, Charles Homer 1870-1937 ...... DLB-47

Haslam, Gerald 1937- DLB-212

Hass, Robert 1941- DLB-105, 206

Hastings, Michael 1938- DLB-233

Hatar, Győző 1914- DLB-215

The Hatch-Billops Collection DLB-76

Hathaway, William 1944- DLB-120

Hauff, Wilhelm 1802-1827 .... DLB-90

A Haughty and Proud Generation (1922),
by Ford Madox Hueffer DLB-36

Haugwitz, August Adolph von
1647-1706 .... DLB-168

Hauptmann, Carl 1858-1921 .... DLB-66, 118

Hauptmann, Gerhart
1862-1946 .... DLB-66, 118; CDWLB-2

Hauser, Marianne 1910- Y-83

Havel, Václav 1936- DLB-232; CDWLB-4

Havergal, Frances Ridley 1836-1879 .... DLB-199

Hawes, Stephen 1475?-before 1529 ..... DLB-132

Hawker, Robert Stephen 1803-1875 ..... DLB-32

Hawkes, John
1925-1998 .... DLB-2, 7, 227; Y-80, Y-98

John Hawkes: A Tribute Y-98

Hawkesworth, John 1720-1773 .... DLB-142

Hawkins, Sir Anthony Hope (see Hope, Anthony)

Hawkins, Sir John 1719-1789 ...... DLB-104, 142

Hawkins, Walter Everette 1883-? DLB-50

Hawthorne, Nathaniel
1804-1864 ... DLB-1, 74, 183, 223; CDALB-2

Hawthorne, Nathaniel 1804-1864 and
Hawthorne, Sophia Peabody
1809-1871 .... DLB-183

Hawthorne, Sophia Peabody
1809-1871 .... DLB-183, 239

Hay, John 1835-1905 .... DLB-12, 47, 189

Hayashi, Fumiko 1903-1951 .... DLB-180

Haycox, Ernest 1899-1950 .... DLB-206

Haycraft, Anna Margaret (see Ellis, Alice Thomas)

Hayden, Robert
1913-1980 .... DLB-5, 76; CDALB-1

Haydon, Benjamin Robert
1786-1846 .... DLB-110

Hayes, John Michael 1919- DLB-26

Hayley, William 1745-1820 .... DLB-93, 142

Haym, Rudolf 1821-1901 .... DLB-129

Hayman, Robert 1575-1629 .... DLB-99

Hayman, Ronald 1932- DLB-155

Hayne, Paul Hamilton
1830-1886 .... DLB-3, 64, 79, 248

Hays, Mary 1760-1843 .... DLB-142, 158

Hayward, John 1905-1965 .... DLB-201

Haywood, Eliza 1693?-1756 .... DLB-39

From the Dedication, *Lasselia* (1723) DLB-39

From *The Tea-Table* *DLB-39*

From the Preface to *The Disguis'd
Prince* (1723) DLB-39

Hazard, Willis P. [publishing house] DLB-49

Hazlitt, William 1778-1830 .... DLB-110, 158

Hazzard, Shirley 1931- Y-82

Head, Bessie
1937-1986 .... DLB-117, 225; CDWLB-3

Headley, Joel T. 1813-1897 .. DLB-30, 183; DS-13

Heaney, Seamus
1939- DLB-40; Y-95; CDBLB-8

Heard, Nathan C. 1936- DLB-33

Hearn, Lafcadio 1850-1904 ...... DLB-12, 78, 189

Hearn, Mary Anne (Marianne Farningham,
Eva Hope) 1834-1909 .... DLB-240

Hearne, John 1926- DLB-117

Hearne, Samuel 1745-1792 .... DLB-99

Hearne, Thomas 1678?-1735 .... DLB-213

Hearst, William Randolph 1863-1951 .... DLB-25

Hearst, William Randolph, Jr.
1908-1993 .... DLB-127

Heartman, Charles Frederick
1883-1953 .... DLB-187

Heath, Catherine 1924- DLB-14

Heath, James Ewell 1792-1862 .... DLB-248

Heath, Roy A. K. 1926- DLB-117

Heath-Stubbs, John 1918- DLB-27

Heavysege, Charles 1816-1876 .... DLB-99

Hebbel, Friedrich
1813-1863 .... DLB-129; CDWLB-2

Hebel, Johann Peter 1760-1826 ...... DLB-90

Heber, Richard 1774-1833 .... DLB-184

Hébert, Anne 1916-2000 .... DLB-68

Hébert, Jacques 1923- DLB-53

Hecht, Anthony 1923- DLB-5, 169

Hecht, Ben 1894-1964 .... DLB-7, 9, 25, 26, 28, 86

Hecker, Isaac Thomas 1819-1888 .... DLB-1, 243

Hedge, Frederic Henry
1805-1890 .... DLB-1, 59, 243

Hefner, Hugh M. 1926- DLB-137

Hegel, Georg Wilhelm Friedrich
1770-1831 .... DLB-90

Heide, Robert 1939- DLB-249

Heidish, Marcy 1947- Y-82

Heißenbüttel, Helmut 1921-1996 .... DLB-75

Heike monogatari DLB-203

Hein, Christoph 1944- DLB-124; CDWLB-2

Hein, Piet 1905-1996 .... DLB-214

Heine, Heinrich 1797-1856 ... DLB-90; CDWLB-2

Heinemann, Larry 1944- DS-9

Heinemann, William, Limited DLB-112

Heinesen, William 1900-1991 .... DLB-214

Heinlein, Robert A. 1907-1988 .... DLB-8

Heinrich Julius of Brunswick
1564-1613 .... DLB-164

Heinrich von dem Türlîn
flourished circa 1230 .... DLB-138

Heinrich von Melk
flourished after 1160 .... DLB-148

Heinrich von Veldeke
circa 1145-circa 1190 .... DLB-138

Heinrich, Willi 1920- DLB-75

Heinse, Wilhelm 1746-1803 .... DLB-94

Heinz, W. C. 1915- DLB-171

Heiskell, John 1872-1972 .... DLB-127

Hejinian, Lyn 1941- DLB-165

Heliand circa 850 .... DLB-148

Heller, Joseph
1923-1999 .... DLB-2, 28, 227; Y-80, Y-99

Heller, Michael 1937- DLB-165

Hellman, Lillian 1906-1984 ..... DLB-7, 228; Y-84

Hellwig, Johann 1609-1674 .... DLB-164

Helprin, Mark 1947- Y-85; CDALB-7

Helwig, David 1938- DLB-60

Hemans, Felicia 1793-1835 .... DLB-96

Hemenway, Abby Maria 1828-1890 . . . . .DLB-243

Hemingway, Ernest 1899-1961
. . . . .DLB-4, 9, 102, 210; Y-81, Y-87, Y-99;
DS-1, DS-15, DS-16; CDALB-4

The Hemingway Centenary Celebration at the
JFK Library. Y-99

Ernest Hemingway: A Centennial
Celebration Y-99

The Ernest Hemingway Collection at the
John F. Kennedy Library. Y-99

Ernest Hemingway's Reaction to James Gould
Cozzens. Y-98

Ernest Hemingway's Toronto Journalism
Revisited: With Three Previously
Unrecorded Stories Y-92

Falsifying Hemingway Y-96

Hemingway: Twenty-Five Years Later Y-85

Not Immediately Discernible . . . but Eventually
Quite Clear: The *First Light* and *Final Years*
of Hemingway's Centenary. Y-99

Hemingway Salesmen's Dummies Y-00

Second International Hemingway Colloquium:
Cuba Y-98

Hémon, Louis 1880-1913 . . . . .DLB-92

Hempel, Amy 1951- DLB-218

Hemphill, Paul 1936- Y-87

Hénault, Gilles 1920- DLB-88

Henchman, Daniel 1689-1761 . . . . .DLB-24

Henderson, Alice Corbin 1881-1949 . . . . . .DLB-54

Henderson, Archibald 1877-1963. . . . . . . .DLB-103

Henderson, David 1942- DLB-41

Henderson, George Wylie 1904- DLB-51

Henderson, Zenna 1917-1983 . . . . .DLB-8

Henisch, Peter 1943- DLB-85

Henley, Beth 1952- Y-86

Henley, William Ernest 1849-1903 . . . . . . .DLB-19

Henning, Rachel 1826-1914. . . . . .DLB-230

Henningsen, Agnes 1868-1962 . . . . .DLB-214

Henniker, Florence 1855-1923. . . . . .DLB-135

Henry, Alexander 1739-1824. . . . . .DLB-99

Henry, Buck 1930- DLB-26

Henry VIII of England 1491-1547 . . . . . .DLB-132

Henry of Ghent
circa 1217-1229 - 1293. . . . . .DLB-115

Henry, Marguerite 1902-1997 . . . . .DLB-22

Henry, O. (see Porter, William Sydney)

Henry, Robert Selph 1889-1970. . . . . .DLB-17

Henry, Will (see Allen, Henry W.)

Henryson, Robert
1420s or 1430s-circa 1505. . . . . .DLB-146

Henschke, Alfred (see Klabund)

Hensley, Sophie Almon 1866-1946 . . . . . . .DLB-99

Henson, Lance 1944- DLB-175

Henty, G. A. 1832?-1902. . . . . .DLB-18, 141

Hentz, Caroline Lee 1800-1856 . . . . . .DLB-3, 248

Heraclitus
flourished circa 500 B.C.. . . . . .DLB-176

Herbert, Agnes circa 1880-1960. . . . . . . .DLB-174

Herbert, Alan Patrick 1890-1971 . . . . .DLB-10, 191

Herbert, Edward, Lord, of Cherbury
1582-1648 . . . . .DLB-121, 151

Herbert, Frank 1920-1986 . . . . . .DLB-8; CDALB-7

Herbert, George 1593-1633. . .DLB-126; CDBLB-1

Herbert, Henry William 1807-1858 . . . . .DLB-3, 73

Herbert, John 1926- DLB-53

Herbert, Mary Sidney, Countess of Pembroke
(see Sidney, Mary)

Herbert, Zbigniew
1924-1998 . . . . .DLB-232; CDWLB-4

Herbst, Josephine 1892-1969 . . . . .DLB-9

Herburger, Gunter 1932- DLB-75, 124

Hercules, Frank E. M. 1917-1996. . . . . . . .DLB-33

Herder, Johann Gottfried 1744-1803 . . . . . .DLB-97

Herder, B., Book Company. DLB-49

Heredia, José-María de 1842-1905. . . . . .DLB-217

Herford, Charles Harold 1853-1931 . . . . .DLB-149

Hergesheimer, Joseph 1880-1954. . . . . .DLB-9, 102

Heritage Press DLB-46

Hermann the Lame 1013-1054 . . . . .DLB-148

Hermes, Johann Timotheus
1738-1821 . . . . .DLB-97

Hermlin, Stephan 1915-1997 . . . . .DLB-69

Hernández, Alfonso C. 1938- DLB-122

Hernández, Inés 1947- DLB-122

Hernández, Miguel 1910-1942. . . . . .DLB-134

Hernton, Calvin C. 1932- DLB-38

Herodotus circa 484 B.C.-circa 420 B.C.
. . . . DLB-176; CDWLB-1

Heron, Robert 1764-1807. . . . . .DLB-142

Herr, Michael 1940- DLB-185

Herrera, Juan Felipe 1948- DLB-122

Herrick, E. R., and Company DLB-49

Herrick, Robert 1591-1674 . . . . .DLB-126

Herrick, Robert 1868-1938 . . . . . . .DLB-9, 12, 78

Herrick, William 1915- Y-83

Herrmann, John 1900-1959. . . . . .DLB-4

Hersey, John 1914-1993 . . .DLB-6, 185; CDALB-7

Hertel, François 1905-1985 . . . . .DLB-68

Hervé-Bazin, Jean Pierre Marie (see Bazin, Hervé)

Hervey, John, Lord 1696-1743 . . . . .DLB-101

Herwig, Georg 1817-1875. . . . . .DLB-133

Herzog, Emile Salomon Wilhelm
(see Maurois, André)

Hesiod eighth century B.C.. . . . . DLB-176

Hesse, Hermann
1877-1962 . . . . .DLB-66; CDWLB-2

Hessus, Helius Eobanus 1488-1540. . . . . .DLB-179

Hewat, Alexander circa 1743-circa 1824 . . .DLB-30

Hewitt, John 1907- DLB-27

Hewlett, Maurice 1861-1923 . . . . .DLB-34, 156

Heyen, William 1940- DLB-5

Heyer, Georgette 1902-1974 . . . . . . .DLB-77, 191

Heym, Stefan 1913- DLB-69

Heyse, Paul 1830-1914 . . . . .DLB-129

Heytesbury, William
circa 1310-1372 or 1373. . . . . .DLB-115

Heyward, Dorothy 1890-1961. . . . . . . .DLB-7, 249

Heyward, DuBose 1885-1940 . . .DLB-7, 9, 45, 249

Heywood, John 1497?-1580?. DLB-136

Heywood, Thomas
1573 or 1574-1641. . . . . .DLB-62

Hibbs, Ben 1901-1975 . . . . .DLB-137

Hichens, Robert S. 1864-1950. . . . . .DLB-153

Hickey, Emily 1845-1924 . . . . .DLB-199

Hickman, William Albert 1877-1957 . . . . . .DLB-92

Hicks, Granville 1901-1982. . . . . .DLB-246

Hidalgo, José Luis 1919-1947 . . . . .DLB-108

Hiebert, Paul 1892-1987 . . . . .DLB-68

Hieng, Andrej 1925- DLB-181

Hierro, José 1922- DLB-108

Higgins, Aidan 1927- DLB-14

Higgins, Colin 1941-1988 . . . . .DLB-26

Higgins, George V.
1939-1999 . . . . .DLB-2; Y-81, Y-98, Y-99

George V. Higgins to Julian Symons. Y-99

Higginson, Thomas Wentworth
1823-1911 . . . . .DLB-1, 64, 243

Highwater, Jamake 1942?- DLB-52; Y-85

Hijuelos, Oscar 1951- DLB-145

Hildegard von Bingen 1098-1179. . . . . . .DLB-148

Das Hildesbrandslied
circa 820 . . . . .DLB-148; CDWLB-2

Hildesheimer, Wolfgang
1916-1991 . . . . .DLB-69, 124

Hildreth, Richard 1807-1865 . . .DLB-1, 30, 59, 235

Hill, Aaron 1685-1750 . . . . .DLB-84

Hill, Geoffrey 1932- DLB-40; CDBLB-8

Hill, George M., Company DLB-49

Hill, "Sir" John 1714?-1775. . . . . .DLB-39

Hill, Lawrence, and Company,
Publishers. DLB-46

Hill, Leslie 1880-1960 . . . . .DLB-51

Hill, Susan 1942- DLB-14, 139

Hill, Walter 1942- DLB-44

Hill and Wang. .DLB-46

Hillberry, Conrad 1928- DLB-120

Hillerman, Tony 1925- DLB-206

Hilliard, Gray and Company DLB-49

Hills, Lee 1906- DLB-127

Hillyer, Robert 1895-1961. . . . . .DLB-54

Hilton, James 1900-1954 . . . . .DLB-34, 77

Hilton, Walter died 1396. . . . . .DLB-146

Hilton and Company. DLB-49

Himes, Chester 1909-1984 . . .DLB-2, 76, 143, 226

Hindmarsh, Joseph [publishing house] . . .DLB-170

Hine, Daryl 1936- DLB-60

Hingley, Ronald 1920- DLB-155

Hinojosa-Smith, Rolando 1929- DLB-82

Hinton, S. E. 1948- CDALB-7

Hippel, Theodor Gottlieb von
1741-1796 . . . . .DLB-97

Hippocrates of Cos flourished circa 425 B.C.
. . . . DLB-176; CDWLB-1

Hirabayashi, Taiko 1905-1972 . . . . DLB-180

Hirsch, E. D., Jr. 1928- DLB-67

Hirsch, Edward 1950- DLB-120

Hoagland, Edward 1932- DLB-6

Hoagland, Everett H., III 1942- DLB-41

Hoban, Russell 1925- DLB-52; Y-90

Hobbes, Thomas 1588-1679 . . . . DLB-151

Hobby, Oveta 1905- DLB-127

Hobby, William 1878-1964 . . . . DLB-127

Hobsbaum, Philip 1932- DLB-40

Hobson, Laura Z. 1900- DLB-28

Hobson, Sarah 1947- DLB-204

Hoby, Thomas 1530-1566 . . . . DLB-132

Hoccleve, Thomas
    circa 1368-circa 1437 . . . . DLB-146

Hochhuth, Rolf 1931- DLB-124

Hochman, Sandra 1936- DLB-5

Hocken, Thomas Morland
    1836-1910 . . . . DLB-184

Hodder and Stoughton, Limited DLB-106

Hodgins, Jack 1938- DLB-60

Hodgman, Helen 1945- DLB-14

Hodgskin, Thomas 1787-1869 . . . . DLB-158

Hodgson, Ralph 1871-1962 . . . . DLB-19

Hodgson, William Hope
    1877-1918 . . . . DLB-70, 153, 156, 178

Hoe, Robert III 1839-1909 . . . . DLB-187

Hoeg, Peter 1957- DLB-214

Højholt, Per 1928- DLB-214

Hoffenstein, Samuel 1890-1947 . . . . DLB-11

Hoffman, Charles Fenno 1806-1884 . . . . . DLB-3

Hoffman, Daniel 1923- DLB-5

Hoffmann, E. T. A.
    1776-1822 . . . . DLB-90; CDWLB-2

Hoffman, Frank B. 1888-1958 . . . . DLB-188

Hoffman, William 1925- DLB-234

Hoffmanswaldau, Christian Hoffman von
    1616-1679 . . . . DLB-168

Hofmann, Michael 1957- DLB-40

Hofmannsthal, Hugo von
    1874-1929 . . . . DLB-81, 118; CDWLB-2

Hofstadter, Richard 1916-1970 . . . . . . DLB-17, 246

Hogan, Desmond 1950- DLB-14

Hogan, Linda 1947- DLB-175

Hogan and Thompson DLB-49

Hogarth Press DLB-112

Hogg, James 1770-1835 . . . . DLB-93, 116, 159

Hohberg, Wolfgang Helmhard Freiherr von
    1612-1688 . . . . DLB-168

von Hohenheim, Philippus Aureolus
    Theophrastus Bombastus (see Paracelsus)

Hohl, Ludwig 1904-1980 . . . . DLB-56

Holbrook, David 1923- DLB-14, 40

Holcroft, Thomas 1745-1809 . . . . DLB-39, 89, 158

Preface to Alwyn (1780) DLB-39

Holden, Jonathan 1941- DLB-105

"Contemporary Verse Story-telling" DLB-105

Holden, Molly 1927-1981 . . . . DLB-40

Hölderlin, Friedrich 1770-1843 DLB-90; CDWLB-2

Holiday House DLB-46

Holinshed, Raphael died 1580 . . . . DLB-167

Holland, J. G. 1819-1881 . . . . DS-13

Holland, Norman N. 1927- DLB-67

Hollander, John 1929- DLB-5

Holley, Marietta 1836-1926 . . . . DLB-11

Hollinghurst, Alan 1954- DLB-207

Hollingsworth, Margaret 1940- DLB-60

Hollo, Anselm 1934- DLB-40

Holloway, Emory 1885-1977 . . . . DLB-103

Holloway, John 1920- DLB-27

Holloway House Publishing Company . . . DLB-46

Holme, Constance 1880-1955 . . . . DLB-34

Holmes, Abraham S. 1821?-1908 . . . . DLB-99

Holmes, John Clellon 1926-1988 . . . . DLB-16, 237

"Four Essays on the Beat Generation" . . . DLB-16

Holmes, Mary Jane 1825-1907 . . . . . DLB-202, 221

Holmes, Oliver Wendell
    1809-1894 . . . . . . DLB-1, 189, 235; CDALB-2

Holmes, Richard 1945- DLB-155

The Cult of Biography
    Excerpts from the Second Folio Debate:
    "Biographies are generally a disease of
    English Literature" Y-86

Holmes, Thomas James 1874-1959 . . . . . DLB-187

Holroyd, Michael 1935- DLB-155; Y-99

Holst, Hermann E. von 1841-1904 . . . . . DLB-47

Holt, Henry, and Company DLB-49

Holt, John 1721-1784 . . . . DLB-43

Holt, Rinehart and Winston DLB-46

Holtby, Winifred 1898-1935 . . . . DLB-191

Holthusen, Hans Egon 1913- DLB-69

Hölty, Ludwig Christoph Heinrich
    1748-1776 . . . . DLB-94

Holub, Miroslav
    1923-1998 . . . . DLB-232; CDWLB-4

Holz, Arno 1863-1929 . . . . DLB-118

Home, Henry, Lord Kames
    (see Kames, Henry Home, Lord)

Home, John 1722-1808 . . . . DLB-84

Home, William Douglas 1912- DLB-13

Home Publishing Company DLB-49

Homer circa eighth-seventh centuries B.C.
    . . . . DLB-176; CDWLB-1

Homer, Winslow 1836-1910 . . . . DLB-188

Homes, Geoffrey (see Mainwaring, Daniel)

Honan, Park 1928- DLB-111

Hone, William 1780-1842 . . . . DLB-110, 158

Hongo, Garrett Kaoru 1951- DLB-120

Honig, Edwin 1919- DLB-5

Hood, Hugh 1928- DLB-53

Hood, Mary 1946- DLB-234

Hood, Thomas 1799-1845 . . . . DLB-96

Hook, Theodore 1788-1841 . . . . DLB-116

Hooker, Jeremy 1941- DLB-40

Hooker, Richard 1554-1600 . . . . DLB-132

Hooker, Thomas 1586-1647 . . . . DLB-24

hooks, bell 1952- DLB-246

Hooper, Johnson Jones
    1815-1862 . . . . DLB-3, 11, 248

Hope, Anthony 1863-1933 . . . . DLB-153, 156

Hope, Christopher 1944- DLB-225

Hope, Eva (see Hearn, Mary Anne)

Hope, Laurence (Adela Florence
    Cory Nicolson) 1865-1904 . . . . DLB-240

Hopkins, Ellice 1836-1904 . . . . DLB-190

Hopkins, Gerard Manley
    1844-1889 . . . . DLB-35, 57; CDBLB-5

Hopkins, John (see Sternhold, Thomas)

Hopkins, John H., and Son DLB-46

Hopkins, Lemuel 1750-1801 . . . . DLB-37

Hopkins, Pauline Elizabeth 1859-1930 . . . . DLB-50

Hopkins, Samuel 1721-1803 . . . . DLB-31

Hopkinson, Francis 1737-1791 . . . . DLB-31

Hopper, Nora (Mrs. Nora Chesson)
    1871-1906 . . . . DLB-240

Hoppin, Augustus 1828-1896 . . . . DLB-188

Hora, Josef 1891-1945 . . . . . . DLB-215; CDWLB-4

Horace 65 B.C.-8 B.C. DLB-211; CDWLB-1

Horgan, Paul 1903-1995 . . . . . . DLB-102, 212; Y-85

Horizon Press DLB-46

Hornby, C. H. St. John 1867-1946 . . . . . . DLB-201

Hornby, Nick 1957- DLB-207

Horne, Frank 1899-1974 . . . . DLB-51

Horne, Richard Henry (Hengist)
    1802 or 1803-1884 . . . . DLB-32

Horney, Karen 1885-1952 . . . . DLB-246

Hornung, E. W. 1866-1921 . . . . DLB-70

Horovitz, Israel 1939- DLB-7

Horton, George Moses 1797?-1883? DLB-50

Horváth, Ödön von 1901-1938 . . . . . DLB-85, 124

Horwood, Harold 1923- DLB-60

Hosford, E. and E. [publishing house] DLB-49

Hoskens, Jane Fenn 1693-1770? DLB-200

Hoskyns, John 1566-1638 . . . . DLB-121

Hosokawa Yūsai 1535-1610 . . . . DLB-203

Hostovský, Egon 1908-1973 . . . . DLB-215

Hotchkiss and Company DLB-49

Hough, Emerson 1857-1923 . . . . DLB-9, 212

Houghton, Stanley 1881-1913 . . . . DLB-10

Houghton Mifflin Company DLB-49

Household, Geoffrey 1900-1988 . . . . DLB-87

Housman, A. E. 1859-1936 . . . DLB-19; CDBLB-5

Housman, Laurence 1865-1959 . . . . DLB-10

Houston, Pam 1962- DLB-244

Houwald, Ernst von 1778-1845 . . . . DLB-90

Hovey, Richard 1864-1900 . . . . DLB-54

Howard, Donald R. 1927-1987 . . . . DLB-111

Howard, Maureen 1930- Y-83

Howard, Richard 1929- DLB-5

Howard, Roy W. 1883-1964 . . . . DLB-29

Howard, Sidney 1891-1939 . . . . . . DLB-7, 26, 249

Howard, Thomas, second Earl of Arundel
1585-1646 . . . . DLB-213

Howe, E. W. 1853-1937 . . . . DLB-12, 25

Howe, Henry 1816-1893 . . . . DLB-30

Howe, Irving 1920-1993 . . . . DLB-67

Howe, Joseph 1804-1873 . . . . DLB-99

Howe, Julia Ward 1819-1910 . . . . DLB-1, 189, 235

Howe, Percival Presland 1886-1944 . . . . . DLB-149

Howe, Susan 1937- DLB-120

Howell, Clark, Sr. 1863-1936 . . . . DLB-25

Howell, Evan P. 1839-1905 . . . . DLB-23

Howell, James 1594?-1666. . . . . DLB-151

Howell, Soskin and Company DLB-46

Howell, Warren Richardson
1912-1984 . . . . DLB-140

Howells, William Dean 1837-1920
. . . . DLB-12, 64, 74, 79, 189; CDALB-3

Introduction to Paul Laurence Dunbar,
Lyrics of Lowly Life (1896). DLB-50

Howitt, Mary 1799-1888 . . . . DLB-110, 199

Howitt, William 1792-1879 and
Howitt, Mary 1799-1888 . . . . DLB-110

Hoyem, Andrew 1935- DLB-5

Hoyers, Anna Ovena 1584-1655 . . . . DLB-164

Hoyos, Angela de 1940- DLB-82

Hoyt, Henry [publishing house] DLB-49

Hoyt, Palmer 1897-1979. . . . . DLB-127

Hrabal, Bohumil 1914-1997. . . . . DLB-232

Hrabanus Maurus 776?-856. . . . . DLB-148

Hronský, Josef Cíger 1896-1960 . . . . DLB-215

Hrotsvit of Gandersheim
circa 935-circa 1000. . . . . DLB-148

Hubbard, Elbert 1856-1915 . . . . DLB-91

Hubbard, Kin 1868-1930. . . . . DLB-11

Hubbard, William circa 1621-1704 . . . . . . DLB-24

Huber, Therese 1764-1829. . . . . DLB-90

Huch, Friedrich 1873-1913. . . . . DLB-66

Huch, Ricarda 1864-1947 . . . . DLB-66

Huck at 100: How Old Is
Huckleberry Finn? Y-85

Huddle, David 1942- DLB-130

Hudgins, Andrew 1951- DLB-120

Hudson, Henry Norman 1814-1886 . . . . . . DLB-64

Hudson, Stephen 1868?-1944 . . . . DLB-197

Hudson, W. H. 1841-1922 . . . . . DLB-98, 153, 174

Hudson and Goodwin DLB-49

Huebsch, B. W. [publishing house] DLB-46

Oral History: B. W. Huebsch Y-99

Hueffer, Oliver Madox 1876-1931. . . . . . . DLB-197

Hugh of St. Victor circa 1096-1141 . . . . . DLB-208

Hughes, David 1930- DLB-14

Hughes, Dusty 1947- DLB-233

Hughes, Hatcher 1881-1945 . . . . DLB-249

Hughes, John 1677-1720. . . . . DLB-84

Hughes, Langston 1902-1967
. . . . DLB-4, 7, 48, 51, 86, 228; CDALB-5

Hughes, Richard 1900-1976. . . . . DLB-15, 161

Hughes, Ted 1930-1998 . . . . DLB-40, 161

Hughes, Thomas 1822-1896 . . . . DLB-18, 163

Hugo, Richard 1923-1982 . . . . DLB-5, 206

Hugo, Victor 1802-1885 . . . . . DLB-119, 192, 217

Hugo Awards and Nebula Awards DLB-8

Hull, Richard 1896-1973 . . . . DLB-77

Hulme, T. E. 1883-1917 . . . . DLB-19

Hulton, Anne ?-1779? DLB-200

Humboldt, Alexander von 1769-1859 . . . . . DLB-90

Humboldt, Wilhelm von 1767-1835. . . . . . DLB-90

Hume, David 1711-1776. . . . . DLB-104

Hume, Fergus 1859-1932. . . . . DLB-70

Hume, Sophia 1702-1774 . . . . DLB-200

Hume-Rothery, Mary Catherine
1824-1885 . . . . DLB-240

Humishuma (see Mourning Dove)

Hummer, T. R. 1950- DLB-120

Humorous Book Illustration DLB-11

Humphrey, Duke of Gloucester
1391-1447 . . . . DLB-213

Humphrey, William 1924-1997 . . . DLB-6, 212, 234

Humphreys, David 1752-1818. . . . . DLB-37

Humphreys, Emyr 1919- DLB-15

Huncke, Herbert 1915-1996 . . . . DLB-16

Huneker, James Gibbons 1857-1921 . . . . . DLB-71

Hunold, Christian Friedrich 1681-1721 . . . DLB-168

Hunt, Irene 1907- DLB-52

Hunt, Leigh 1784-1859 . . . . DLB-96, 110, 144

Hunt, Violet 1862-1942. . . . . DLB-162, 197

Hunt, William Gibbes 1791-1833 . . . . DLB-73

Hunter, Evan 1926- Y-82

Hunter, Jim 1939- DLB-14

Hunter, Kristin 1931- DLB-33

Hunter, Mollie 1922- DLB-161

Hunter, N. C. 1908-1971 . . . . DLB-10

Hunter-Duvar, John 1821-1899. . . . . DLB-99

Huntington, Henry E. 1850-1927 . . . . DLB-140

Huntington, Susan Mansfield
1791-1823 . . . . DLB-200

Hurd and Houghton DLB-49

Hurst, Fannie 1889-1968 . . . . DLB-86

Hurst and Blackett. DLB-106

Hurst and Company DLB-49

Hurston, Zora Neale
1901?-1960 . . . . DLB-51, 86; CDALB-7

Husson, Jules-François-Félix (see Champfleury)

Huston, John 1906-1987 . . . . DLB-26

Hutcheson, Francis 1694-1746. . . . . DLB-31

Hutchinson, Ron 1947- DLB-245

Hutchinson, R. C. 1907-1975. . . . . DLB-191

Hutchinson, Thomas 1711-1780
. . . . DLB-30, 31

Hutchinson and Company
(Publishers) Limited DLB-112

Hutton, Richard Holt 1826-1897. . . . . DLB-57

von Hutton, Ulrich 1488-1523 . . . . DLB-179

Huxley, Aldous 1894-1963
. . . . DLB-36, 100, 162, 195; CDBLB-6

Huxley, Elspeth Josceline
1907-1997 . . . . DLB-77, 204

Huxley, T. H. 1825-1895 . . . . DLB-57

Huyghue, Douglas Smith 1816-1891. . . . . DLB-99

Huysmans, Joris-Karl 1848-1907 . . . . DLB-123

Hwang, David Henry
1957- DLB-212, 228

Hyde, Donald 1909-1966 and
Hyde, Mary 1912- DLB-187

Hyman, Trina Schart 1939- DLB-61

I

Iavorsky, Stefan 1658-1722 . . . . DLB-150

Iazykov, Nikolai Mikhailovich
1803-1846 . . . . DLB-205

Ibáñez, Armando P. 1949- DLB-209

Ibn Bajja circa 1077-1138 . . . . DLB-115

Ibn Gabirol, Solomon
circa 1021-circa 1058. . . . . DLB-115

Ibuse, Masuji 1898-1993 . . . . DLB-180

Ichijō Kanera
(see Ichijō Kaneyoshi)

Ichijō Kaneyoshi (Ichijō Kanera)
1402-1481 . . . . DLB-203

The Iconography of Science-Fiction Art DLB-8

Iffland, August Wilhelm 1759-1814. . . . . . DLB-94

Ignatow, David 1914-1997. . . . . DLB-5

Ike, Chukwuemeka 1931- DLB-157

Ikkyū Sōjun 1394-1481 . . . . DLB-203

Iles, Francis (see Berkeley, Anthony)

Illich, Ivan 1926- DLB-242

The Illustration of Early German Literar
Manuscripts, circa 1150-circa 1300 . . . DLB-148

Illyés, Gyula 1902-1983 . . . . . DLB-215; CDWLB-4

Imbs, Bravig 1904-1946. . . . . DLB-4

Imbuga, Francis D. 1947- DLB-157

Immermann, Karl 1796-1840. . . . . DLB-133

Inchbald, Elizabeth 1753-1821 . . . . DLB-39, 89

Inge, William 1913-1973 . . . DLB-7, 249; CDALB-1

Ingelow, Jean 1820-1897 . . . . DLB-35, 163

Ingersoll, Ralph 1900-1985 . . . . DLB-127

The Ingersoll Prizes. Y-84

Ingoldsby, Thomas (see Barham, Richard Harris)

Ingraham, Joseph Holt 1809-1860. . . . . DLB-3, 248

Inman, John 1805-1850 . . . . DLB-73

Innerhofer, Franz 1944- DLB-85

Innis, Harold Adams 1894-1952 . . . . DLB-88

Innis, Mary Quayle 1899-1972 . . . . DLB-88

Inō Sōgi 1421-1502 . . . . DLB-203

Inoue Yasushi 1907-1991 . . . . DLB-181

International Publishers Company DLB-46

Interviews:

Anastas, Benjamin Y-98

Baker, Nicholson Y-00

Bank, Melissa Y-98

Bernstein, Harriet Y-82

Betts, Doris Y-82

Bosworth, David Y-82

Bottoms, David Y-83

Bowers, Fredson Y-80

Burnshaw, Stanley Y-97

Carpenter, Humphrey Y-84, Y-99

Carr, Virginia Spencer Y-00

Carver, Raymond Y-83

Cherry, Kelly Y-83

Coppel, Alfred Y-83

Cowley, Malcolm Y-81

Davis, Paxton Y-89

De Vries, Peter Y-82

Dickey, James Y-82

Donald, David Herbert Y-87

Ellroy, James Y-91

Fancher, Betsy Y-83

Faust, Irvin Y-00

Fulton, Len Y-86

Garrett, George Y-83

Greenfield, George Y-91

Griffin, Bryan Y-81

Guilds, John Caldwell Y-92

Hardin, James Y-92

Harrison, Jim Y-82

Hazzard, Shirley Y-82

Higgins, George V Y-98

Hoban, Russell Y-90

Holroyd, Michael Y-99

Horowitz, Glen Y-90

Jakes, John Y-83

Jenkinson, Edward B Y-82

Jenks, Tom Y-86

Kaplan, Justin Y-86

King, Florence Y-85

Klopfer, Donald S. Y-97

Krug, Judith Y-82

Lamm, Donald Y-95

Laughlin, James Y-96

Lindsay, Jack Y-84

Mailer, Norman Y-97

Manchester, William Y-85

McCormack, Thomas Y-98

McNamara, Katherine Y-97

Mellen, Joan Y-94

Menaher, Daniel Y-97

Mooneyham, Lamarr Y-82

Nosworth, David Y-82

O'Connor, Patrick Y-84, Y-99

Ozick, Cynthia Y-83

Penner, Jonathan Y-83

Pennington, Lee Y-82

Penzler, Otto Y-96

Plimpton, George Y-99

Potok, Chaim Y-84

Prescott, Peter S. Y-86

Rabe, David Y-91

Rallyson, Carl Y-97

Rechy, John Y-82

Reid, B. L. Y-83

Reynolds, Michael Y-95, Y-99

Schlafly, Phyllis Y-82

Schroeder, Patricia Y-99

Schulberg, Budd Y-81

Scribner, Charles III Y-94

Sipper, Ralph Y-94

Staley, Thomas F. Y-00

Styron, William Y-80

Toth, Susan Allen Y-86

Tyler, Anne Y-82

Vaughan, Samuel Y-97

Von Ogtrop, Kristin Y-92

Wallenstein, Barry Y-92

Weintraub, Stanley Y-82

Williams, J. Chamberlain Y-84

Editors, Conversations with Y-95

Interviews on E-Publishing Y-00

Irving, John 1942- DLB-6; Y-82

Irving, Washington 1783-1859
. . . . DLB-3, 11, 30, 59, 73, 74,
183, 186; CDALB-2

Irwin, Grace 1907- DLB-68

Irwin, Will 1873-1948 . . . . DLB-25

Iser, Wolfgang 1926- DLB-242

Isherwood, Christopher
1904-1986 . . . . .DLB-15, 195; Y-86

The Christopher Isherwood Archive,
The Huntington Library Y-99

Ishiguro, Kazuo
1954- DLB-194

Ishikawa Jun
1899-1987 . . . . DLB-182

The Island Trees Case: A Symposium on
School Library Censorship
An Interview with Judith Krug
An Interview with Phyllis Schlafly
An Interview with Edward B. Jenkinson
An Interview with Lamarr Mooneyham
An Interview with Harriet Bernstein Y-82

Islas, Arturo
1938-1991 . . . . DLB-122

Issit, Debbie 1966- DLB-233

Ivanišević, Drago
|1907-1981 . . . . DLB-181

Ivaska, Astrīde 1926- DLB-232

Ivers, M. J., and Company DLB-49

Iwaniuk, Wacław 1915- DLB-215

Iwano, Hōmei 1873-1920 . . . . DLB-180

Iwaszkiewicz, Jarosław 1894-1980 . . . . . . DLB-215

Iyayi, Festus 1947- DLB-157

Izumi, Kyōka 1873-1939 . . . . DLB-180

J

Jackmon, Marvin E. (see Marvin X)

Jacks, L. P. 1860-1955 . . . . DLB-135

Jackson, Angela 1951- DLB-41

Jackson, Charles 1903-1968 . . . . DLB-234

Jackson, Helen Hunt
1830-1885 . . . . DLB-42, 47, 186, 189

Jackson, Holbrook 1874-1948 . . . . DLB-98

Jackson, Laura Riding 1901-1991 . . . . DLB-48

Jackson, Shirley
1916-1965 . . . . DLB-6, 234; CDALB-1

Jacob, Naomi 1884?-1964 . . . . DLB-191

Jacob, Piers Anthony Dillingham
(see Anthony, Piers)

Jacob, Violet 1863-1946 . . . . DLB-240

Jacobi, Friedrich Heinrich 1743-1819 . . . . . DLB-94

Jacobi, Johann Georg 1740-1841 . . . . DLB-97

Jacobs, George W., and Company DLB-49

Jacobs, Harriet 1813-1897 . . . . DLB-239

Jacobs, Joseph 1854-1916 . . . . DLB-141

Jacobs, W. W. 1863-1943 . . . . DLB-135

Jacobsen, Jørgen-Frantz 1900-1938 . . . . . . DLB-214

Jacobsen, Josephine 1908- DLB-244

Jacobson, Dan 1929- DLB-14, 207, 225

Jacobson, Howard 1942- DLB-207

Jacques de Vitry circa 1160/1170-1240 . . . DLB-208

Jæger, Frank 1926-1977 . . . . DLB-214

Jaggard, William [publishing house] DLB-170

Jahier, Piero 1884-1966 . . . . DLB-114

Jahnn, Hans Henny 1894-1959 . . . . . DLB-56, 124

Jakes, John 1932- Y-83

Jakobson, Roman 1896-1982 . . . . DLB-242

James, Alice 1848-1892 . . . . DLB-221

James, C. L. R. 1901-1989 . . . . DLB-125

James, George P. R. 1801-1860 . . . . DLB-116

James, Henry 1843-1916
. . . . . .DLB-12, 71, 74, 189; DS-13; CDALB-3

James, John circa 1633-1729 . . . . DLB-24

James, M. R. 1862-1936 . . . . DLB-156, 201

James, Naomi 1949- DLB-204

James, P. D. 1920- . . DLB-87; DS-17; CDBLB-8

James VI of Scotland, I of England
1566-1625 . . . . .DLB-151, 172

*Ane Schort Treatise Conteining Some Revlis
and Cautelis to Be Obseruit and Eschewit
in Scottis Poesi* (1584) DLB-172

James, Thomas 1572?-1629 . . . . DLB-213

James, U. P. [publishing house] DLB-49

James, Will 1892-1942 . . . . .DS-16

Jameson, Anna 1794-1860 . . . . DLB-99, 166

Jameson, Fredric 1934- DLB-67

Jameson, J. Franklin 1859-1937 . . . . .DLB-17

Jameson, Storm 1891-1986 . . . . DLB-36

Jančar, Drago 1948- DLB-181

Janés, Clara 1940- DLB-134

Janevski, Slavko 1920- DLB-181; CDWLB-4

Janvier, Thomas 1849-1913. . . . . .DLB-202

Jaramillo, Cleofas M. 1878-1956 . . . . . . .DLB-122

Jarman, Mark 1952- DLB-120

Jarrell, Randall 1914-1965 . .DLB-48, 52; CDALB-1

Jarrold and Sons. DLB-106

Jarry, Alfred 1873-1907 . . . . .DLB-192

Jarves, James Jackson 1818-1888 . . . . . . .DLB-189

Jasmin, Claude 1930- DLB-60

Jaunsudrabiņš, Jānis 1877-1962 . . . . .DLB-220

Jay, John 1745-1829 . . . . .DLB-31

Jean de Garlande (see John of Garland)

Jefferies, Richard 1848-1887 . . . . . . .DLB-98, 141

Jeffers, Lance 1919-1985 . . . . .DLB-41

Jeffers, Robinson
  1887-1962 . . . . .DLB-45, 212; CDALB-4

Jefferson, Thomas
  1743-1826 . . . . .DLB-31, 183; CDALB-2

Jégé 1866-1940. . . . . .DLB-215

Jelinek, Elfriede 1946- DLB-85

Jellicoe, Ann 1927- DLB-13, 233

Jemison, Mary circa 1742-1833 . . . . .DLB-239

Jenkins, Dan 1929- DLB-241

Jenkins, Elizabeth 1905- DLB-155

Jenkins, Robin 1912- DLB-14

Jenkins, William Fitzgerald (see Leinster, Murray)

Jenkins, Herbert, Limited. DLB-112

Jennings, Elizabeth 1926- DLB-27

Jens, Walter 1923- DLB-69

Jensen, Johannes V. 1873-1950 . . . . .DLB-214

Jensen, Merrill 1905-1980 . . . . .DLB-17

Jensen, Thit 1876-1957. . . . . .DLB-214

Jephson, Robert 1736-1803 . . . . .DLB-89

Jerome, Jerome K. 1859-1927 . . . .DLB-10, 34, 135

Jerome, Judson 1927-1991 . . . . .DLB-105

Jerrold, Douglas 1803-1857 . . . . . . .DLB-158, 159

Jesse, F. Tennyson 1888-1958 . . . . .DLB-77

Jewel, John 1522-1571 . . . . .DLB-236

Jewett, John P., and Company. DLB-49

Jewett, Sarah Orne 1849-1909 . . . .DLB-12, 74, 221

The Jewish Publication Society DLB-49

Jewitt, John Rodgers 1783-1821 . . . . .DLB-99

Jewsbury, Geraldine 1812-1880. . . . . .DLB-21

Jewsbury, Maria Jane 1800-1833 . . . . .DLB-199

Jhabvala, Ruth Prawer 1927- DLB-139, 194

Jiménez, Juan Ramón 1881-1958. . . . . . . .DLB-134

Jin, Ha 1956- DLB-244

Joans, Ted 1928- DLB-16, 41

Jōha 1525-1602 . . . . .DLB-203

Johannis de Garlandia (see John of Garland)

John, Errol 1924-1988 . . . . .DLB-233

John, Eugenie (see Marlitt, E.)

John of Dumbleton
  circa 1310-circa 1349. . . . . .DLB-115

John of Garland (Jean de Garlande, Johannis de
  Garlandia) circa 1195-circa 1272 . . . . .DLB-208

Johns, Captain W. E. 1893-1968 . . . . . . .DLB-160

Johnson, Mrs. A. E. ca. 1858-1922 . . . . . .DLB-221

Johnson, Amelia (see Johnson, Mrs. A. E.)

Johnson, B. S. 1933-1973 . . . . .DLB-14, 40

Johnson, Benjamin [publishing house]. DLB-49

Johnson, Benjamin, Jacob, and
  Robert [publishing house] DLB-49

Johnson, Charles 1679-1748. . . . . .DLB-84

Johnson, Charles R. 1948- DLB-33

Johnson, Charles S. 1893-1956 . . . . . . .DLB-51, 91

Johnson, Denis 1949- DLB-120

Johnson, Diane 1934- Y-80

Johnson, Dorothy M. 1905–1984 . . . . . . .DLB-206

Johnson, E. Pauline (Tekahionwake)
  1861-1913 . . . . .DLB-175

Johnson, Edgar 1901-1995. . . . . .DLB-103

Johnson, Edward 1598-1672 . . . . .DLB-24

Johnson, Fenton 1888-1958 . . . . .DLB-45, 50

Johnson, Georgia Douglas
  1877?-1966 . . . . .DLB-51, 249

Johnson, Gerald W. 1890-1980 . . . . .DLB-29

Johnson, Greg 1953- DLB-234

Johnson, Helene 1907-1995 . . . . .DLB-51

Johnson, Jacob, and Company. DLB-49

Johnson, James Weldon
  1871-1938 . . . . .DLB-51; CDALB-4

Johnson, John H. 1918- DLB-137

Johnson, Joseph [publishing house] DLB-154

Johnson, Linton Kwesi 1952- DLB-157

Johnson, Lionel 1867-1902. . . . . .DLB-19

Johnson, Nunnally 1897-1977 . . . . .DLB-26

Johnson, Owen 1878-1952. . . . . Y-87

Johnson, Pamela Hansford 1912- DLB-15

Johnson, Pauline 1861-1913. . . . . .DLB-92

Johnson, Ronald 1935-1998. . . . . .DLB-169

Johnson, Samuel 1696-1772 . . . DLB-24; CDBLB-2

Johnson, Samuel
  1709-1784 . . . . DLB-39, 95, 104, 142, 213

Johnson, Samuel 1822-1882. . . . . .DLB-1, 243

Johnson, Susanna 1730-1810 . . . . .DLB-200

Johnson, Terry 1955- DLB-233

Johnson, Uwe 1934-1984. . . . . DLB-75; CDWLB-2

Johnston, Annie Fellows 1863-1931. . . . . . .DLB-42

Johnston, Basil H. 1929- DLB-60

Johnston, David Claypole 1798?-1865. . . .DLB-188

Johnston, Denis 1901-1984 . . . . .DLB-10

Johnston, Ellen 1835-1873 . . . . .DLB-199

Johnston, George 1913- DLB-88

Johnston, Sir Harry 1858-1927 . . . . .DLB-174

Johnston, Jennifer 1930- DLB-14

Johnston, Mary 1870-1936. . . . . .DLB-9

Johnston, Richard Malcolm 1822-1898 . . . .DLB-74

Johnstone, Charles 1719?-1800? DLB-39

Johst, Hanns 1890-1978 . . . . .DLB-124

Jolas, Eugene 1894-1952 . . . . .DLB-4, 45

Jones, Alice C. 1853-1933 . . . . .DLB-92

Jones, Charles C., Jr. 1831-1893 . . . . .DLB-30

Jones, D. G. 1929- DLB-53

Jones, David 1895-1974 . . .DLB-20, 100; CDBLB-7

Jones, Diana Wynne 1934- DLB-161

Jones, Ebenezer 1820-1860 . . . . .DLB-32

Jones, Ernest 1819-1868. . . . . .DLB-32

Jones, Gayl 1949- DLB-33

Jones, George 1800-1870 . . . . .DLB-183

Jones, Glyn 1905- DLB-15

Jones, Gwyn 1907- DLB-15, 139

Jones, Henry Arthur 1851-1929 . . . . .DLB-10

Jones, Hugh circa 1692-1760 . . . . .DLB-24

Jones, James 1921-1977 . . . . DLB-2, 143; DS-17

James Jones Papers in the Handy Writers'
  Colony Collection at the University of
  Illinois at Springfield Y-98

The James Jones Society Y-92

Jones, Jenkin Lloyd 1911- DLB-127

Jones, John Beauchamp 1810-1866 . . . . . .DLB-202

Jones, LeRoi (see Baraka, Amiri)

Jones, Lewis 1897-1939 . . . . .DLB-15

Jones, Madison 1925- DLB-152

Jones, Major Joseph
  (see Thompson, William Tappan)

Jones, Marie 1955- DLB-233

Jones, Preston 1936-1979 . . . . .DLB-7

Jones, Rodney 1950- DLB-120

Jones, Thom 1945- DLB-244

Jones, Sir William 1746-1794 . . . . .DLB-109

Jones, William Alfred 1817-1900 . . . . .DLB-59

Jones's Publishing House. DLB-49

Jong, Erica 1942- DLB-2, 5, 28, 152

Jonke, Gert F. 1946- DLB-85

Jonson, Ben
  1572?-1637 . . . . .DLB-62, 121; CDBLB-1

Jordan, June 1936- DLB-38

Joseph and George. Y-99

Joseph, Jenny 1932- DLB-40

Joseph, Michael, Limited DLB-112

Josephson, Matthew 1899-1978 . . . . .DLB-4

Josephus, Flavius 37-100. . . . . .DLB-176

Josiah Allen's Wife (see Holley, Marietta)

Josipovici, Gabriel 1940- DLB-14

Josselyn, John ?-1675 . . . . .DLB-24

Joudry, Patricia 1921- DLB-88

Jovine, Giuseppe 1922- DLB-128

Joyaux, Philippe (see Sollers, Philippe)

Joyce, Adrien (see Eastman, Carol)

Joyce, James 1882-1941
  . . . . DLB-10, 19, 36, 162, 247; CDBLB-6

James Joyce Centenary: Dublin, 1982. . . . . . Y-82

James Joyce Conference. Y-85

A Joyce (Con)Text: Danis Rose and the
  Remaking of *Ulysses* Y-97

The New *Ulysses* Y-84

Jozsef, Attila 1905-1937..... DLB-215; CDWLB-4

Judd, Orange, Publishing Company...... DLB-49

Judd, Sylvester 1813-1853 .... DLB-1, 243

Judith circa 930....................... DLB-146

Julian of Norwich
1342-circa 1420 .... DLB-1146

Julius Caesar
100 B.C.-44 B.C. DLB-211; CDWLB-1

June, Jennie
(see Croly, Jane Cunningham)

Jung, Franz 1888-1963 .... DLB-118

Jünger, Ernst 1895- DLB-56; CDWLB-2

Der jüngere Titurel circa 1275 .... DLB-138

Jung-Stilling, Johann Heinrich
1740-1817........................ DLB-94

Justice, Donald 1925- Y-83

Juvenal circa A.D. 60-circa A.D. 130
.... DLB-211; CDWLB-1

The Juvenile Library
(see Godwin, M. J., and Company)

K

Kacew, Romain (see Gary, Romain)

Kafka, Franz 1883-1924 ..... DLB-81; CDWLB-2

Kahn, Roger 1927- DLB-171

Kaikō Takeshi 1939-1989............. DLB-182

Kaiser, Georg 1878-1945.... DLB-124; CDWLB-2

Kaiserchronik circca 1147............... DLB-148

Kaleb, Vjekoslav 1905- DLB-181

Kalechofsky, Roberta 1931- DLB-28

Kaler, James Otis 1848-1912............ DLB-12

Kames, Henry Home, Lord
1696-1782.................. DLB-31, 104

Kamo no Chōmei (Kamo no Nagaakira)
1153 or 1155-1216 .... DLB-203

Kamo no Nagaakira (see Kamo no Chōmei)

Kampmann, Christian 1939-1988....... DLB-214

Kandel, Lenore 1932- DLB-16

Kanin, Garson 1912-1999.............. DLB-7

Kant, Hermann 1926- DLB-75

Kant, Immanuel 1724-1804............. DLB-94

Kantemir, Antiokh Dmitrievich
1708-1744.................... DLB-150

Kantor, MacKinlay 1904-1977 .... DLB-9, 102

Kanze Kōjirō Nobumitsu 1435-1516 .... DLB-203

Kanze Motokiyo (see Zeami)

Kaplan, Fred 1937- DLB-111

Kaplan, Johanna 1942- DLB-28

Kaplan, Justin 1925- DLB-111; Y-86

The Practice of Biography V:
An Interview with Justin Kaplan Y-86

Kaplinski, Jaan 1941- DLB-232

Kapnist, Vasilii Vasilevich 1758?-1823 ... DLB-150

Karadžić, Vuk Stefanović
1787-1864 ....DLB-147; CDWLB-4

Karamzin, Nikolai Mikhailovich
1766-1826.................... DLB-150

Karinthy, Frigyes 1887-1938.......... DLB-215

Karsch, Anna Louisa 1722-1791 .... DLB-97

Kasack, Hermann 1896-1966.......... DLB-69

Kasai, Zenzō 1887-1927 .... DLB-180

Kaschnitz, Marie Luise 1901-1974 ...... DLB-69

Kassák, Lajos 1887-1967............. DLB-215

Kaštelan, Jure 1919-1990 .... DLB-147

Kästner, Erich 1899-1974 .... DLB-56

Katenin, Pavel Aleksandrovich
1792-1853.................... DLB-205

Kattan, Naim 1928- DLB-53

Katz, Steve 1935- Y-83

Kauffman, Janet 1945- DLB-218; Y-86

Kauffmann, Samuel 1898-1971......... DLB-127

Kaufman, Bob 1925- DLB-16, 41

Kaufman, George S. 1889-1961 .... DLB-7

Kavanagh, P. J. 1931- DLB-40

Kavanagh, Patrick 1904-1967........ DLB-15, 20

Kawabata, Yasunari 1899-1972.......... DLB-180

Kaye-Smith, Sheila 1887-1956........... DLB-36

Kazin, Alfred 1915-1998.............. DLB-67

Keane, John B. 1928- DLB-13

Keary, Annie 1825-1879............. DLB-163

Keary, Eliza 1827-1918............... DLB-240

Keating, H. R. F. 1926- DLB-87

Keatley, Charlotte 1960- DLB-245

Keats, Ezra Jack 1916-1983 .... DLB-61

Keats, John 1795-1821 ... DLB-96, 110; CDBLB-3

Keble, John 1792-1866 .... DLB-32, 55

Keckley, Elizabeth 1818?-1907 .... DLB-239

Keeble, John 1944- Y-83

Keeffe, Barrie 1945- DLB-13, 245

Keeley, James 1867-1934 .... DLB-25

W. B. Keen, Cooke and Company DLB-49

Keillor, Garrison 1942- Y-87

Keith, Marian 1874?-1961 .... DLB-92

Keller, Gary D. 1943- DLB-82

Keller, Gottfried
1819-1890 .... DLB-129; CDWLB-2

Kelley, Edith Summers 1884-1956....... DLB-9

Kelley, Emma Dunham ?-?............ DLB-221

Kelley, William Melvin 1937- DLB-33

Kellogg, Ansel Nash 1832-1886 .... DLB-23

Kellogg, Steven 1941- DLB-61

Kelly, George E. 1887-1974...........DLB-7, 249

Kelly, Hugh 1739-1777 .... DLB-89

Kelly, Piet and Company DLB-49

Kelly, Robert 1935- DLB-5, 130, 165

Kelman, James 1946- DLB-194

Kelmscott Press DLB-112

Kemble, E. W. 1861-1933 .... DLB-188

Kemble, Fanny 1809-1893 .... DLB-32

Kemelman, Harry 1908- DLB-28

Kempe, Margery circa 1373-1438....... DLB-146

Kempner, Friederike 1836-1904 .... DLB-129

Kempowski, Walter 1929- DLB-75

Kendall, Claude [publishing company].... DLB-46

Kendall, Henry 1839-1882............. DLB-230

Kendall, May 1861-1943............. DLB-240

Kendell, George 1809-1867 .... DLB-43

Kenedy, P. J., and Sons DLB-49

Kenkō circa 1283-circa 1352 .... DLB-203

Kennan, George 1845-1924 .... DLB-189

Kennedy, Adrienne 1931- DLB-38

Kennedy, John Pendleton 1795-1870 .. DLB-3, 248

Kennedy, Leo 1907- DLB-88

Kennedy, Margaret 1896-1967......... DLB-36

Kennedy, Patrick 1801-1873........... DLB-159

Kennedy, Richard S. 1920- DLB-111

Kennedy, William 1928- DLB-143; Y-85

Kennedy, X. J. 1929- DLB-5

Kennelly, Brendan 1936- DLB-40

Kenner, Hugh 1923- DLB-67

Kennerley, Mitchell [publishing house] ... DLB-46

Kenny, Maurice 1929- DLB-175

Kent, Frank R. 1877-1958............. DLB-29

Kenyon, Jane 1947-1995............. DLB-120

Keough, Hugh Edmund 1864-1912.....DLB-171

Keppler and Schwartzmann DLB-49

Ker, John, third Duke of Roxburghe
1740-1804.................... DLB-213

Ker, N. R. 1908-1982................ DLB-201

Kerlan, Irvin 1912-1963 ....DLB-187

Kermode, Frank 1919- DLB-242

Kern, Jerome 1885-1945..............DLB-187

Kerner, Justinus 1776-1862............ DLB-90

Kerouac, Jack
1922-1969 .. DLB-2, 16, 237; DS-3; CDALB-1

The Jack Kerouac Revival Y-95

"Re-meeting of Old Friends":
The Jack Kerouac Conference..........Y-82

Kerouac, Jan 1952-1996.............. DLB-16

Kerr, Charles H., and Company DLB-49

Kerr, Orpheus C. (see Newell, Robert Henry)

Kesey, Ken 1935- ... DLB-2, 16, 206; CDALB-6

Kessel, Joseph 1898-1979 .... DLB-72

Kessel, Martin 1901- DLB-56

Kesten, Hermann 1900- DLB-56

Keun, Irmgard 1905-1982 .... DLB-69

Key and Biddle...................... DLB-49

Keynes, Sir Geoffrey 1887-1982 .... DLB-201

Keynes, John Maynard 1883-1946.........DS-10

Keyserling, Eduard von 1855-1918 ...... DLB-66

Khan, Ismith 1925- DLB-125

Khaytov, Nikolay 1919- DLB-181

Khemnitser, Ivan Ivanovich
1745-1784...................... DLB-150

Kheraskov, Mikhail Matveevich
1733-1807..................... DLB-150

Khomiakov, Aleksei Stepanovich
1804-1860 .... DLB-205

Khristov, Boris 1945- DLB-181

Khvoshchinskaia, Nadezhda Dmitrievna
   1824-1889 . . . . .DLB-238

Khvostov, Dmitrii Ivanovich
   1757-1835. . . . . .DLB-150

Kidd, Adam 1802?-1831 . . . . .DLB-99

Kidd, William [publishing house] DLB-106

Kidder, Tracy 1945- DLB-185

Kiely, Benedict 1919- DLB-15

Kieran, John 1892-1981. . . . . .DLB-171

Kiggins and Kellogg. DLB-49

Kiley, Jed 1889-1962 . . . . .DLB-4

Kilgore, Bernard 1908-1967. . . . . .DLB-127

Killens, John Oliver 1916- DLB-33

Killigrew, Anne 1660-1685 . . . . .DLB-131

Killigrew, Thomas 1612-1683 . . . . .DLB-58

Kilmer, Joyce 1886-1918 . . . . .DLB-45

Kilroy, Thomas 1934- DLB-233

Kilwardby, Robert circa 1215-1279 . . . . . .DLB-115

Kimball, Richard Burleigh 1816-1892 . . . .DLB-202

Kincaid, Jamaica 1949-
   . . . . . . DLB-157, 227; CDALB-7; CDWLB-3

King, Charles 1844-1933 . . . . .DLB-186

King, Clarence 1842-1901 . . . . .DLB-12

King, Florence 1936. . . . . Y-85

King, Francis 1923- DLB-15, 139

King, Grace 1852-1932 . . . . .DLB-12, 78

King, Harriet Hamilton 1840-1920 . . . . . .DLB-199

King, Henry 1592-1669 . . . . .DLB-126

King, Solomon [publishing house] DLB-49

King, Stephen 1947- DLB-143; Y-80

King, Susan Petigru 1824-1875 . . . . .DLB-239

King, Thomas 1943- DLB-175

King, Woodie, Jr. 1937- DLB-38

Kinglake, Alexander William
   1809-1891 . . . . .DLB-55, 166

Kingsley, Charles
   1819-1875 . . . . DLB-21, 32, 163, 178, 190

Kingsley, Henry 1830-1876 . . . . .DLB-21, 230

Kingsley, Mary Henrietta 1862-1900. . . . .DLB-174

Kingsley, Sidney 1906- DLB-7

Kingsmill, Hugh 1889-1949. . . . . .DLB-149

Kingsolver, Barbara
   1955- DLB-206; CDALB-7

Kingston, Maxine Hong
   1940- DLB-173, 212; Y-80; CDALB-7

Kingston, William Henry Giles
   1814-1880 . . . . .DLB-163

Kinnan, Mary Lewis 1763-1848. . . . . . . .DLB-200

Kinnell, Galway 1927- DLB-5; Y-87

Kinsella, Thomas 1928- DLB-27

Kipling, Rudyard 1865-1936
   . . . . .DLB-19, 34, 141, 156; CDBLB-5

Kipphardt, Heinar 1922-1982 . . . . .DLB-124

Kirby, William 1817-1906 . . . . .DLB-99

Kircher, Athanasius 1602-1680 . . . . .DLB-164

Kireevsky, Ivan Vasil'evich 1806-1856 . . .DLB-198

Kireevsky, Petr Vasil'evich 1808-1856 . . .DLB-205

Kirk, Hans 1898-1962 . . . . .DLB-214

Kirk, John Foster 1824-1904 . . . . .DLB-79

Kirkconnell, Watson 1895-1977. . . . . .DLB-68

Kirkland, Caroline M.
   1801-1864 . . . . DLB-3, 73, 74; DS-13

Kirkland, Joseph 1830-1893. . . . . .DLB-12

Kirkman, Francis [publishing house] DLB-170

Kirkpatrick, Clayton 1915- DLB-127

Kirkup, James 1918- DLB-27

Kirouac, Conrad (see Marie-Victorin, Frère)

Kirsch, Sarah 1935- DLB-75

Kirst, Hans Hellmut 1914-1989. . . . . .DLB-69

Kiš, Danilo 1935-1989 . . . . . .DLB-181; CDWLB-4

Kita Morio 1927- DLB-182

Kitcat, Mabel Greenhow 1859-1922 . . . . .DLB-135

Kitchin, C. H. B. 1895-1967 . . . . .DLB-77

Kittredge, William 1932- DLB-212, 244

Kiukhel'beker, Vil'gel'm Karlovich
   1797-1846. . . . . .DLB-205

Kizer, Carolyn 1925- DLB-5, 169

Klabund 1890-1928 . . . . .DLB-66

Klaj, Johann 1616-1656 . . . . .DLB-164

Klappert, Peter 1942- DLB-5

Klass, Philip (see Tenn, William)

Klein, A. M. 1909-1972 . . . . .DLB-68

Kleist, Ewald von 1715-1759 . . . . .DLB-97

Kleist, Heinrich von
   1777-1811. . . . . .DLB-90; CDWLB-2

Klinger, Friedrich Maximilian
   1752-1831 . . . . .DLB-94

Klíma, Ivan 1931- DLB-232; CDWLB-4

Kliushnikov, Viktor Petrovich
   1841-1892 . . . . .DLB-238

Oral History Interview with Donald S.
   Klopfer Y-97

Klopstock, Friedrich Gottlieb
   1724-1803 . . . . .DLB-97

Klopstock, Meta 1728-1758 . . . . .DLB-97

Kluge, Alexander 1932- DLB-75

Knapp, Joseph Palmer 1864-1951 . . . . . . .DLB-91

Knapp, Samuel Lorenzo 1783-1838 . . . . . .DLB-59

Knapton, J. J. and P.
   [publishing house] DLB-154

Kniazhnin, Iakov Borisovich
   1740-1791 . . . . .DLB-150

Knickerbocker, Diedrich (see Irving, Washington)

Knigge, Adolph Franz Friedrich Ludwig,
   Freiherr von 1752-1796 . . . . .DLB-94

Knight, Charles, and Company. DLB-106

Knight, Damon 1922- DLB-8

Knight, Etheridge 1931-1992. . . . . .DLB-41

Knight, John S. 1894-1981 . . . . .DLB-29

Knight, Sarah Kemble 1666-1727 . . . . .DLB-24, 200

Knight-Bruce, G. W. H. 1852-1896 . . . . . .DLB-174

Knister, Raymond 1899-1932 . . . . .DLB-68

Knoblock, Edward 1874-1945 . . . . .DLB-10

Knopf, Alfred A. 1892-1984 . . . . Y-84

Knopf, Alfred A. [publishing house] DLB-46

Knopf to Hammett: The Editoral
   Correspondence Y-00

Knorr von Rosenroth, Christian
   1636-1689 . . . . .DLB-168

"Knots into Webs: Some Autobiographical
   Sources," by Dabney Stuart DLB-105

Knowles, John 1926- DLB-6; CDALB-6

Knox, Frank 1874-1944 . . . . .DLB-29

Knox, John circa 1514-1572. . . . . .DLB-132

Knox, John Armoy 1850-1906 . . . . .DLB-23

Knox, Lucy 1845-1884 . . . . .DLB-240

Knox, Ronald Arbuthnott 1888-1957 . . . . .DLB-77

Knox, Thomas Wallace 1835-1896. . . . . . .DLB-189

Kobayashi Takiji 1903-1933 . . . . .DLB-180

Kober, Arthur 1900-1975. . . . . .DLB-11

Kobiakova, Aleksandra Petrovna
   1823-1892 . . . . .DLB-238

Kocbek, Edvard 1904-1981 . . . DLB-147; CDWB-4

Koch, Howard 1902- DLB-26

Koch, Kenneth 1925- DLB-5

Kōda, Rohan 1867-1947. . . . . .DLB-180

Koenigsberg, Moses 1879-1945 . . . . .DLB-25

Koeppen, Wolfgang 1906-1996 . . . . .DLB-69

Koertge, Ronald 1940- DLB-105

Koestler, Arthur 1905-1983 . . . . . . Y-83; CDBLB-7

Kohn, John S. Van E. 1906-1976 and
   Papantonio, Michael 1907-1978. . . . . .DLB-187

Kokoschka, Oskar 1886-1980 . . . . .DLB-124

Kolb, Annette 1870-1967 . . . . .DLB-66

Kolbenheyer, Erwin Guido
   1878-1962 . . . . .DLB-66, 124

Kolleritsch, Alfred 1931- DLB-85

Kolodny, Annette 1941- DLB-67

Kol'tsov, Aleksei Vasil'evich
   1809-1842 . . . . .DLB-205

Komarov, Matvei circa 1730-1812. . . . . . .DLB-150

Komroff, Manuel 1890-1974 . . . . .DLB-4

Komunyakaa, Yusef 1947- DLB-120

Koneski, Blaže 1921-1993 . . . DLB-181; CDWLB-4

Konigsburg, E. L. 1930- DLB-52

Konparu Zenchiku 1405-1468?. DLB-203

Konrád, György 1933- DLB-232; CDWLB-4

Konrad von Würzburg
   circa 1230-1287 . . . . .DLB-138

Konstantinov, Aleko 1863-1897. . . . . .DLB-147

Konwicki, Tadeusz 1926- DLB-232

Kooser, Ted 1939- DLB-105

Kopit, Arthur 1937- DLB-7

Kops, Bernard 1926?- DLB-13

Kornbluth, C. M. 1923-1958. . . . . .DLB-8

Körner, Theodor 1791-1813 . . . . .DLB-90

Kornfeld, Paul 1889-1942 . . . . .DLB-118

Kosinski, Jerzy 1933-1991 . . . . DLB-2; Y-82

Kosmač, Ciril 1910-1980 . . . . .DLB-181

Kosovel, Srečko 1904-1926 . . . . .DLB-147

Kostrov, Ermil Ivanovich 1755-1796..... DLB-150

Kotzebue, August von 1761-1819 .... DLB-94

Kotzwinkle, William 1938- DLB-173

Kovačić, Ante 1854-1889 .... DLB-147

Kovič, Kajetan 1931- DLB-181

Kozlov, Ivan Ivanovich 1779-1840 ...... DLB-205

Kraf, Elaine 1946- Y-81

Kramer, Jane 1938- DLB-185

Kramer, Larry 1935- DLB-249

Kramer, Mark 1944- DLB-185

Kranjčević, Silvije Strahimir
    1865-1908 .... DLB-147

Krasko, Ivan 1876-1958 .... DLB-215

Krasna, Norman 1909-1984 .... DLB-26

Kraus, Hans Peter 1907-1988 .... DLB-187

Kraus, Karl 1874-1936 .... DLB-118

Krauss, Ruth 1911-1993 .... DLB-52

Kreisel, Henry 1922- DLB-88

Krestovsky V. (see Khvoshchinskaia,
    Nadezhda Dmitrievna)

Krestovsky, Vsevolod Vladimirovich
    1839-1895 .... DLB-238

Kreuder, Ernst 1903-1972............ DLB-69

Krėvė-Mickevičius, Vincas 1882-1954 ... DLB-220

Kreymborg, Alfred 1883-1966 .... DLB-4, 54

Krieger, Murray 1923- DLB-67

Krim, Seymour 1922-1989 .... DLB-16

Kristensen, Tom 1893-1974 .... DLB-214

Kristeva, Julia 1941- DLB-242

Krleža, Miroslav 1893-1981 ..DLB-147; CDWLB-4

Krock, Arthur 1886-1974 .... DLB-29

Kroetsch, Robert 1927- DLB-53

Kross, Jaan 1920- DLB-232

Krúdy, Gyula 1878-1933 .... DLB-215

Krutch, Joseph Wood
    1893-1970.................. DLB-63, 206

Krylov, Ivan Andreevich
    1769-1844................... DLB-150

Kubin, Alfred 1877-1959.............. DLB-81

Kubrick, Stanley 1928-1999 .... DLB-26

Kudrun circa 1230-1240.............. DLB-138

Kuffstein, Hans Ludwig von
    1582-1656 .... DLB-164

Kuhlmann, Quirinus 1651-1689........ DLB-168

Kuhnau, Johann 1660-1722 .... DLB-168

Kukol'nik, Nestor Vasil'evich
    1809-1868 .... DLB-205

Kukučín, Martin
    1860-1928 .... DLB-215; CDWLB-4

Kumin, Maxine 1925- DLB-5

Kuncewicz, Maria 1895-1989 .... DLB-215

Kundera, Milan 1929- DLB-232; CDWLB-4

Kunene, Mazisi 1930- DLB-117

Kunikida, Doppo 1869-1908 .... DLB-180

Kunitz, Stanley 1905- DLB-48

Kunjufu, Johari M. (see Amini, Johari M.)

Kunnert, Gunter 1929- DLB-75

Kunze, Reiner 1933- DLB-75

Kupferberg, Tuli 1923- DLB-16

Kurahashi Yumiko 1935- DLB-182

Kureishi, Hanif 1954- DLB-194, 245

Kürnberger, Ferdinand 1821-1879 ..... DLB-129

Kurz, Isolde 1853-1944................ DLB-66

Kusenberg, Kurt 1904-1983 .... DLB-69

Kushchevsky, Ivan Afanas'evich
    1847-1876.................... DLB-238

Kushner, Tony 1956- DLB-228

Kuttner, Henry 1915-1958 .... DLB-8

Kyd, Thomas 1558-1594 .... DLB-62

Kyffin, Maurice circa 1560?-1598....... DLB-136

Kyger, Joanne 1934- DLB-16

Kyne, Peter B. 1880-1957............. DLB-78

Kyōgoku Tamekane 1254-1332 .... DLB-203

L

L. E. L. (see Landon, Letitia Elizabeth)

Laberge, Albert 1871-1960 .... DLB-68

Laberge, Marie 1950- DLB-60

Labiche, Eugène 1815-1888 .... DLB-192

Labrunie, Gerard (see Nerval, Gerard de)

La Capria, Raffaele 1922- DLB-196

Lacombe, Patrice
    (see Trullier-Lacombe, Joseph Patrice)

Lacretelle, Jacques de 1888-1985 .... DLB-65

Lacy, Ed 1911-1968 .... DLB-226

Lacy, Sam 1903- DLB-171

Ladd, Joseph Brown 1764-1786 ...... DLB-37

La Farge, Oliver 1901-1963 .... DLB-9

Laffan, Mrs. R. S. de Courcy (see Adams,
    Bertha Leith)

Lafferty, R. A. 1914- DLB-8

La Flesche, Francis 1857-1932..........DLB-175

Laforge, Jules 1860-1887.............. DLB-217

Lagorio, Gina 1922- DLB-196

La Guma, Alex
    1925-1985 .... DLB-117, 225; CDWLB-3

Lahaise, Guillaume (see Delahaye, Guy)

Lahontan, Louis-Armand de Lom d'Arce,
    Baron de 1666-1715? DLB-99

Laing, Kojo 1946- DLB-157

Laird, Carobeth 1895- Y-82

Laird and Lee..................... DLB-49

Lalić, Ivan V. 1931-1996 .... DLB-181

Lalić, Mihailo 1914-1992 .... DLB-181

Lalonde, Michèle 1937- DLB-60

Lamantia, Philip 1927- DLB-16

Lamartine, Alphonse de 1790-1869 ..... DLB-217

Lamb, Lady Caroline 1785-1828 .... DLB-116

Lamb, Charles
    1775-1834.......DLB-93, 107, 163; CDBLB-3

Lamb, Mary 1764-1874............... DLB-163

Lambert, Betty 1933-1983 .... DLB-60

Lamming, George 1927- ...DLB-125; CDWLB-3

L'Amour, Louis 1908-1988 ....DLB-206; Y-80

Lampman, Archibald 1861-1899 ..... DLB-92

Lamson, Wolffe and Company DLB-49

Lancer Books DLB-46

Landesman, Jay 1919- and
    Landesman, Fran 1927- DLB-16

Landolfi, Tommaso 1908-1979..........DLB-177

Landon, Letitia Elizabeth 1802-1838 ..... DLB-96

Landor, Walter Savage 1775-1864 ....DLB-93, 107

Landry, Napoléon-P. 1884-1956 .... DLB-92

Lane, Charles 1800-1870 .... DLB-1, 223

Lane, F. C. 1885-1984 .... DLB-241

Lane, John, Company DLB-49

Lane, Laurence W. 1890-1967 .... DLB-91

Lane, M. Travis 1934- DLB-60

Lane, Patrick 1939- DLB-53

Lane, Pinkie Gordon 1923- DLB-41

Laney, Al 1896-1988 ....DLB-4, 171

Lang, Andrew 1844-1912......DLB-98, 141, 184

Langevin, André 1927- DLB-60

Langgässer, Elisabeth 1899-1950 .... DLB-69

Langhorne, John 1735-1779 .... DLB-109

Langland, William
    circa 1330-circa 1400 .... DLB-146

Langton, Anna 1804-1893 .... DLB-99

Lanham, Edwin 1904-1979.............. DLB-4

Lanier, Sidney 1842-1881........ DLB-64; DS-13

Lanyer, Aemilia 1569-1645 .... DLB-121

Lapointe, Gatien 1931-1983 .... DLB-88

Lapointe, Paul-Marie 1929- DLB-88

Larcom, Lucy 1824-1893 .... DLB-221, 243

Lardner, John 1912-1960 ....DLB-171

Lardner, Ring 1885-1933
    ......DLB-11, 25, 86, 171; DS-16; CDALB-4

Lardner 100: Ring Lardner
    Centennial Symposium Y-85

Lardner, Ring, Jr. 1915-2000 ....DLB-26, Y-00

Larkin, Philip 1922-1985 ..... DLB-27; CDBLB-8

La Roche, Sophie von 1730-1807 .... DLB-94

La Rocque, Gilbert 1943-1984 .... DLB-60

Laroque de Roquebrune, Robert
    (see Roquebrune, Robert de)

Larrick, Nancy 1910- DLB-61

Larsen, Nella 1893-1964.............. DLB-51

La Sale, Antoine de
    circa 1386-1460/1467............. DLB-208

Lasch, Christopher 1932-1994 .... DLB-246

Lasker-Schüler, Else 1869-1945 ..... DLB-66, 124

Lasnier, Rina 1915- DLB-88

Lassalle, Ferdinand 1825-1864 .... DLB-129

Latham, Robert 1912-1995........... DLB-201

Lathrop, Dorothy P. 1891-1980........ DLB-22

Lathrop, George Parsons 1851-1898 ..... DLB-71

Lathrop, John, Jr. 1772-1820.......... DLB-37

Latimer, Hugh 1492?-1555........... DLB-136

Latimore, Jewel Christine McLawler
  (see Amini, Johari M.)

Latymer, William 1498-1583 . . . . DLB-132

Laube, Heinrich 1806-1884 . . . . DLB-133

Laud, William 1573-1645 . . . . DLB-213

Laughlin, James 1914-1997 . . . . DLB-48; Y-96

James Laughlin Tributes Y-97

Conversations with Publishers IV:
  An Interview with James Laughlin Y-96

Laumer, Keith 1925- DLB-8

Lauremberg, Johann 1590-1658 . . . . DLB-164

Laurence, Margaret 1926-1987 . . . . DLB-53

Laurentius von Schnüffis 1633-1702 . . . . . DLB-168

Laurents, Arthur 1918- DLB-26

Laurie, Annie (see Black, Winifred)

Laut, Agnes Christiana 1871-1936 . . . . DLB-92

Lauterbach, Ann 1942- DLB-193

Lautreamont, Isidore Lucien Ducasse, Comte de
  1846-1870 . . . . DLB-217

Lavater, Johann Kaspar 1741-1801 . . . . DLB-97

Lavin, Mary 1912-1996 . . . . DLB-15

Law, John (see Harkness, Margaret)

Lawes, Henry 1596-1662 . . . . DLB-126

Lawless, Anthony (see MacDonald, Philip)

Lawless, Emily (The Hon. Emily Lawless) 1845-1913
  DLB-240

Lawrence, D. H. 1885-1930
  . . . . . DLB-10, 19, 36, 98, 162, 195; CDBLB-6

Lawrence, David 1888-1973 . . . . DLB-29

Lawrence, Jerome 1915- and
  Lee, Robert E. 1918-1994 . . . . DLB-228

Lawrence, Seymour 1926-1994 . . . . Y-94

Lawrence, T. E. 1888-1935 . . . . DLB-195

Lawson, George 1598-1678 . . . . DLB-213

Lawson, Henry 1867-1922 . . . . DLB-230

Lawson, John ?-1711 . . . . DLB-24

Lawson, John Howard 1894-1977 . . . . DLB-228

Lawson, Louisa Albury 1848-1920 . . . . . . DLB-230

Lawson, Robert 1892-1957 . . . . DLB-22

Lawson, Victor F. 1850-1925 . . . . DLB-25

Layard, Sir Austen Henry
  1817-1894 . . . . DLB-166

Layton, Irving 1912- DLB-88

LaZamon flourished circa 1200 . . . . DLB-146

Lazarević, Laza K. 1851-1890 . . . . DLB-147

Lazarus, George 1904-1997 . . . . DLB-201

Lazhechnikov, Ivan Ivanovich
  1792-1869 . . . . DLB-198

Lea, Henry Charles 1825-1909 . . . . DLB-47

Lea, Sydney 1942- DLB-120

Lea, Tom 1907- DLB-6

Leacock, John 1729-1802 . . . . DLB-31

Leacock, Stephen 1869-1944 . . . . DLB-92

Lead, Jane Ward 1623-1704 . . . . DLB-131

Leadenhall Press DLB-106

Leakey, Caroline Woolmer 1827-1881 . . . DLB-230

Leapor, Mary 1722-1746 . . . . DLB-109

Lear, Edward 1812-1888 . . . . DLB-32, 163, 166

Leary, Timothy 1920-1996 . . . . DLB-16

Leary, W. A., and Company DLB-49

Léautaud, Paul 1872-1956 . . . . DLB-65

Leavis, F. R. 1895-1978 . . . . DLB-242

Leavitt, David 1961- DLB-130

Leavitt and Allen DLB-49

Le Blond, Mrs. Aubrey 1861-1934 . . . . . . DLB-174

le Carré, John 1931- DLB-87; CDBLB-8

Lécavelé, Roland (see Dorgeles, Roland)

Lechlitner, Ruth 1901- DLB-48

Leclerc, Félix 1914- DLB-60

Le Clézio, J. M. G. 1940- DLB-83

Lectures on Rhetoric and Belles Lettres (1783),
  by Hugh Blair [excerpts] DLB-31

Leder, Rudolf (see Hermlin, Stephan)

Lederer, Charles 1910-1976 . . . . DLB-26

Ledwidge, Francis 1887-1917 . . . . DLB-20

Lee, Dennis 1939- DLB-53

Lee, Don L. (see Madhubuti, Haki R.)

Lee, George W. 1894-1976 . . . . DLB-51

Lee, Harper 1926- DLB-6; CDALB-1

Lee, Harriet (1757-1851) and
  Lee, Sophia (1750-1824) DLB-39

Lee, Laurie 1914-1997 . . . . DLB-27

Lee, Li-Young 1957- DLB-165

Lee, Manfred B. (see Dannay, Frederic, and
  Manfred B. Lee)

Lee, Nathaniel circa 1645-1692 . . . . DLB-80

Lee, Sir Sidney 1859-1926 . . . . DLB-149, 184

Lee, Sir Sidney, "Principles of Biography," in
  Elizabethan and Other Essays DLB-149

Lee, Vernon
  1856-1935 . . . . DLB-57, 153, 156, 174, 178

Lee and Shepard DLB-49

Le Fanu, Joseph Sheridan
  1814-1873 . . . . DLB-21, 70, 159, 178

Leffland, Ella 1931- Y-84

le Fort, Gertrud von 1876-1971 . . . . DLB-66

Le Gallienne, Richard 1866-1947 . . . . DLB-4

Legaré, Hugh Swinton
  1797-1843 . . . . DLB-3, 59, 73, 248

Legaré, James Mathewes 1823-1859 . . . DLB-3, 248

The Legends of the Saints and a Medieval
  Christian Worldview DLB-148

Léger, Antoine-J. 1880-1950 . . . . DLB-88

Le Guin, Ursula K.
  1929- DLB-8, 52; CDALB-6

Lehman, Ernest 1920- DLB-44

Lehmann, John 1907- DLB-27, 100

Lehmann, John, Limited DLB-112

Lehmann, Rosamond 1901-1990 . . . . DLB-15

Lehmann, Wilhelm 1882-1968 . . . . DLB-56

Leiber, Fritz 1910-1992 . . . . DLB-8

Leibniz, Gottfried Wilhelm 1646-1716 . . . . DLB-168

Leicester University Press DLB-112

Leigh, W. R. 1866-1955 . . . . DLB-188

Leinster, Murray 1896-1975 . . . . DLB-8

Leiser, Bill 1898-1965 . . . . DLB-241

Leisewitz, Johann Anton 1752-1806 . . . . . DLB-94

Leitch, Maurice 1933- DLB-14

Leithauser, Brad 1943- DLB-120

Leland, Charles G. 1824-1903 . . . . DLB-11

Leland, John 1503?-1552 . . . . DLB-136

Lemay, Pamphile 1837-1918 . . . . DLB-99

Lemelin, Roger 1919- DLB-88

Lemercier, Louis-Jean-Népomucène
  1771-1840 . . . . DLB-192

Le Moine, James MacPherson
  1825-1912 . . . . DLB-99

Lemon, Mark 1809-1870 . . . . DLB-163

Le Moyne, Jean 1913- DLB-88

Lemperly, Paul 1858-1939 . . . . DLB-187

L'Engle, Madeleine 1918- DLB-52

Lennart, Isobel 1915-1971 . . . . DLB-44

Lennox, Charlotte
  1729 or 1730-1804 . . . . DLB-39

Lenox, James 1800-1880 . . . . DLB-140

Lenski, Lois 1893-1974 . . . . DLB-22

Lentricchia, Frank 1940- DLB-246

Lenz, Hermann 1913-1998 . . . . DLB-69

Lenz, J. M. R. 1751-1792 . . . . DLB-94

Lenz, Siegfried 1926- DLB-75

Leonard, Elmore 1925- DLB-173, 226

Leonard, Hugh 1926- DLB-13

Leonard, William Ellery 1876-1944 . . . . . . DLB-54

Leonowens, Anna 1834-1914 . . . . . DLB-99, 166

LePan, Douglas 1914- DLB-88

Lepik, Kalju 1920-1999 . . . . DLB-232

Leprohon, Rosanna Eleanor 1829-1879 . . . DLB-99

Le Queux, William 1864-1927 . . . . DLB-70

Lermontov, Mikhail Iur'evich
  1814-1841 . . . . DLB-205

Lerner, Max 1902-1992 . . . . DLB-29

Lernet-Holenia, Alexander 1897-1976 . . . . DLB-85

Le Rossignol, James 1866-1969 . . . . DLB-92

Lescarbot, Marc circa 1570-1642 . . . . DLB-99

LeSeur, William Dawson 1840-1917 . . . . . DLB-92

LeSieg, Theo. (see Geisel, Theodor Seuss)

Leskov, Nikolai Semenovich 1831-1895 . . DLB-238

Leslie, Doris before 1902-1982 . . . . DLB-191

Leslie, Eliza 1787-1858 . . . . DLB-202

Leslie, Frank 1821-1880 . . . . DLB-43, 79

Leslie, Frank, Publishing House DLB-49

Leśmian, Bolesław 1878-1937 . . . . DLB-215

Lesperance, John 1835?-1891 . . . . DLB-99

Lessing, Bruno 1870-1940 . . . . DLB-28

Lessing, Doris
  1919- DLB-15, 139; Y-85; CDBLB-8

Lessing, Gotthold Ephraim
  1729-1781 . . . . DLB-97; CDWLB-2

Lettau, Reinhard 1929- DLB-75

Letter from Japan Y-94, Y-98

Letter from London Y-96

Letter to [Samuel] Richardson on *Clarissa* (1748), by Henry Fielding DLB-39

A Letter to the Editor of *The Irish Times* Y-97

Lever, Charles 1806-1872 . . . . DLB-21

Lever, Ralph ca. 1527-1585 . . . . DLB-236

Leverson, Ada 1862-1933 . . . . DLB-153

Levertov, Denise 1923-1997 . . . . DLB-5, 165; CDALB-7

Levi, Peter 1931- DLB-40

Levi, Primo 1919-1987 . . . . .DLB-177

Lévi-Strauss, Claude 1908- DLB-242

Levien, Sonya 1888-1960 . . . . DLB-44

Levin, Meyer 1905-1981 . . . . . . .DLB-9, 28; Y-81

Levine, Norman 1923- DLB-88

Levine, Philip 1928- DLB-5

Levis, Larry 1946- DLB-120

Levy, Amy 1861-1889 . . . . DLB-156, 240

Levy, Benn Wolfe 1900-1973 . . . . . . .DLB-13; Y-81

Lewald, Fanny 1811-1889 . . . . DLB-129

Lewes, George Henry 1817-1878 . . . . DLB-55, 144

"Criticism In Relation To Novels" (1863) DLB-21

The Principles of Success in Literature (1865) [excerpt] DLB-57

Lewis, Agnes Smith 1843-1926 . . . . .DLB-174

Lewis, Alfred H. 1857-1914 . . . . DLB-25, 186

Lewis, Alun 1915-1944 . . . . DLB-20, 162

Lewis, C. Day (see Day Lewis, C.)

Lewis, C. S. 1898-1963 . . . . . DLB-15, 100, 160; CDBLB-7

Lewis, Charles B. 1842-1924 . . . . DLB-11

Lewis, Henry Clay 1825-1850 . . . . DLB-3, 248

Lewis, Janet 1899-1999 . . . . Y-87

Lewis, Matthew Gregory 1775-1818 . . . . .DLB-39, 158, 178

Lewis, Meriwether 1774-1809 and Clark, William 1770-1838 . . . . . DLB-183, 186

Lewis, Norman 1908- DLB-204

Lewis, R. W. B. 1917- DLB-111

Lewis, Richard circa 1700-1734 . . . . DLB-24

Lewis, Sinclair 1885-1951 . . . . . DLB-9, 102; DS-1; CDALB-4

Sinclair Lewis Centennial Conference Y-85

Lewis, Wilmarth Sheldon 1895-1979 . . . . DLB-140

Lewis, Wyndham 1882-1957 . . . . DLB-15

Lewisohn, Ludwig 1882-1955 . . DLB-4, 9, 28, 102

Leyendecker, J. C. 1874-1951 . . . . DLB-188

Lezama Lima, José 1910-1976 . . . . DLB-113

L'Heureux, John 1934- DLB-244

Libbey, Laura Jean 1862-1924 . . . . DLB-221

The Library of America DLB-46

The Licensing Act of 1737 . . . . DLB-84

Lichfield, Leonard I [publishing house] . . .DLB-170

Lichtenberg, Georg Christoph 1742-1799 . . DLB-94

The Liddle Collection Y-97

Lieb, Fred 1888-1980 . . . . .DLB-171

Liebling, A. J. 1904-1963 . . . . .DLB-4, 171

Lieutenant Murray (see Ballou, Maturin Murray)

Lighthall, William Douw 1857-1954 . . . . . DLB-92

Lilar, Françoise (see Mallet-Joris, Françoise)

Lili'uokalani, Queen 1838-1917 . . . . DLB-221

Lillo, George 1691-1739 . . . . DLB-84

Lilly, J. K., Jr. 1893-1966 . . . . DLB-140

Lilly, Wait and Company DLB-49

Lily, William circa 1468-1522 . . . . DLB-132

Limited Editions Club DLB-46

Limón, Graciela 1938- DLB-209

Lincoln and Edmands DLB-49

Lindesay, Ethel Forence (see Richardson, Henry Handel)

Lindsay, Alexander William, Twenty-fifth Earl of Crawford 1812-1880 . . . . DLB-184

Lindsay, Sir David circa 1485-1555 . . . . . DLB-132

Lindsay, Jack 1900- Y-84

Lindsay, Lady (Caroline Blanche Elizabeth Fitzroy Lindsay) 1844-1912 . . . . DLB-199

Lindsay, Vachel 1879-1931 . . . . DLB-54; CDALB-3

Linebarger, Paul Myron Anthony (see Smith, Cordwainer)

Link, Arthur S. 1920-1998 . . . . DLB-17

Linn, Ed 1922-2000 . . . . DLB-241

Linn, John Blair 1777-1804 . . . . DLB-37

Lins, Osman 1924-1978 . . . . DLB-145

Linton, Eliza Lynn 1822-1898 . . . . DLB-18

Linton, William James 1812-1897 . . . . DLB-32

Lintot, Barnaby Bernard [publishing house] DLB-170

Lion Books DLB-46

Lionni, Leo 1910-1999 . . . . DLB-61

Lippard, George 1822-1854 . . . . DLB-202

Lippincott, J. B., Company DLB-49

Lippincott, Sara Jane Clarke 1823-1904 . . . DLB-43

Lippmann, Walter 1889-1974 . . . . DLB-29

Lipton, Lawrence 1898-1975 . . . . DLB-16

Liscow, Christian Ludwig 1701-1760 . . . . . DLB-97

Lish, Gordon 1934- DLB-130

Lisle, Charles-Marie-René Leconte de 1818-1894 . . . . DLB-217

Lispector, Clarice 1925-1977 . . . . .DLB-113; CDWLB-3

A Literary Archaelogist Digs On: A Brief Interview with Michael Reynolds by Michael Rogers Y-99

The Literary Chronicle and Weekly Review 1819-1828 . . . . DLB-110

Literary Documents: William Faulkner and the People-to-People Program Y-86

Literary Documents II: *Library Journal*—Statements and Questionnaires from First Novelists Y-87

Literary Effects of World War II [British novel] DLB-15

Literary Prizes Y-00

Literary Prizes [British] DLB-15

Literary Research Archives: The Humanities Research Center, University of Texas Y-82

Literary Research Archives II: Berg Collection of English and American Literature of the New York Public Library Y-83

Literary Research Archives III: The Lilly Library Y-84

Literary Research Archives IV: The John Carter Brown Library Y-85

Literary Research Archives V: Kent State Special Collections Y-86

Literary Research Archives VI: The Modern Literary Manuscripts Collection in the Special Collections of the Washington University Libraries Y-87

Literary Research Archives VII: The University of Virginia Libraries Y-91

Literary Research Archives VIII: The Henry E. Huntington Library Y-92

Literary Research Archives IX: Special Collections at Boston University . . Y-99

The Literary Scene and Situation and . . . Who (Besides Oprah) Really Runs American Literature? Y-99

Literary Societies Y-98, Y-99, Y-00

"Literary Style" (1857), by William Forsyth [excerpt] DLB-57

Literatura Chicanesca: The View From Without DLB-82

Literature at Nurse, or Circulating Morals (1885), by George Moore DLB-18

Littell, Eliakim 1797-1870 . . . . DLB-79

Littell, Robert S. 1831-1896 . . . . DLB-79

Little, Brown and Company DLB-49

Little Magazines and Newspapers DS-15

The Little Review 1914-1929 . . . . .DS-15

Littlewood, Joan 1914- DLB-13

Lively, Penelope 1933- DLB-14, 161, 207

Liverpool University Press DLB-112

The Lives of the Poets DLB-142

Livesay, Dorothy 1909- DLB-68

Livesay, Florence Randal 1874-1953 . . . . . DLB-92

"Living in Ruin," by Gerald Stern DLB-105

Livings, Henry 1929-1998 . . . . DLB-13

Livingston, Anne Howe 1763-1841 . . .DLB-37, 200

Livingston, Myra Cohn 1926-1996 . . . . . . DLB-61

Livingston, William 1723-1790 . . . . DLB-31

Livingstone, David 1813-1873 . . . . DLB-166

Livingstone, Douglas 1932-1996 . . . . DLB-225

Livy 59 B.C.-A.D. 17 . . . . . . .DLB-211; CDWLB-1

Liyong, Taban lo (see Taban lo Liyong)

Lizárraga, Sylvia S. 1925- DLB-82

Llewellyn, Richard 1906-1983 . . . . DLB-15

Lloyd, Edward [publishing house] DLB-106

Lobel, Arnold 1933- DLB-61

Lochridge, Betsy Hopkins (see Fancher, Betsy)

Locke, David Ross 1833-1888 . . . . DLB-11, 23

Locke, John 1632-1704 . . . . .DLB-31, 101, 213

Locke, Richard Adams 1800-1871 . . . . DLB-43

Locker-Lampson, Frederick
1821-1895 . . . . .DLB-35, 184

Lockhart, John Gibson
1794-1854 . . . . DLB-110, 116 144

Lockridge, Ross, Jr. 1914-1948 . . . . DLB-143; Y-80

Locrine and Selimus .DLB-62

Lodge, David 1935- DLB-14, 194

Lodge, George Cabot 1873-1909 . . . . .DLB-54

Lodge, Henry Cabot 1850-1924 . . . . .DLB-47

Lodge, Thomas 1558-1625 . . . . .DLB-172

From *Defence of Poetry* (1579) DLB-172

Loeb, Harold 1891-1974 . . . . .DLB-4

Loeb, William 1905-1981 . . . . .DLB-127

Lofting, Hugh 1886-1947. . . . . .DLB-160

Logan, Deborah Norris 1761-1839 . . . . . .DLB-200

Logan, James 1674-1751. . . . . .DLB-24, 140

Logan, John 1923- DLB-5

Logan, Martha Daniell 1704?-1779 . . . . . .DLB-200

Logan, William 1950- DLB-120

Logau, Friedrich von 1605-1655 . . . . .DLB-164

Logue, Christopher 1926- DLB-27

Lohenstein, Daniel Casper von
1635-1683 .DLB-168

Lomonosov, Mikhail Vasil'evich
1711-1765. .DLB-150

London, Jack
1876-1916 . . . . .DLB-8, 12, 78, 212; CDALB-3

The London Magazine 1820-1829 . . . . .DLB-110

Long, David 1948- DLB-244

Long, H., and Brother DLB-49

Long, Haniel 1888-1956 . . . . .DLB-45

Long, Ray 1878-1935. . . . . .DLB-137

Longfellow, Henry Wadsworth
1807-1882 . . . . .DLB-1, 59, 235; CDALB-2

Longfellow, Samuel 1819-1892 . . . . .DLB-1

Longford, Elizabeth 1906- DLB-155

Longinus circa first century DLB-176

Longley, Michael 1939- DLB-40

Longman, T. [publishing house] DLB-154

Longmans, Green and Company DLB-49

Longmore, George 1793?-1867 . . . . .DLB-99

Longstreet, Augustus Baldwin
1790-1870. . . . . DLB-3, 11, 74, 248

Longworth, D. [publishing house] DLB-49

Lonsdale, Frederick 1881-1954 . . . . .DLB-10

A Look at the Contemporary Black Theatre
Movement. DLB-38

Loos, Anita 1893-1981. . . . . DLB-11, 26, 228; Y-81

Lopate, Phillip 1943- Y-80

López, Diana
(see Isabella, Ríos)

López, Josefina 1969- DLB-209

Loranger, Jean-Aubert 1896-1942 . . . . .DLB-92

Lorca, Federico García 1898-1936 . . . . . .DLB-108

Lord, John Keast 1818-1872. . . . . .DLB-99

The Lord Chamberlain's Office and Stage
Censorship in England DLB-10

Lorde, Audre 1934-1992 . . . . .DLB-41

Lorimer, George Horace 1867-1939 . . . . . .DLB-91

Loring, A. K. [publishing house] DLB-49

Loring and Mussey DLB-46

Lorris, Guillaume de (see *Roman de la Rose*)

Lossing, Benson J. 1813-1891 . . . . .DLB-30

Lothar, Ernst 1890-1974 . . . . .DLB-81

Lothrop, D., and Company. DLB-49

Lothrop, Harriet M. 1844-1924. . . . . .DLB-42

Loti, Pierre 1850-1923 . . . . .DLB-123

Lotichius Secundus, Petrus 1528-1560 . . .DLB-179

Lott, Emeline ?-? DLB-166

Louisiana State University Press Y-97

The Lounger, no. 20 (1785), by Henry
Mackenzie DLB-39

Lounsbury, Thomas R. 1838-1915 . . . . . . .DLB-71

Louÿs, Pierre 1870-1925 . . . . .DLB-123

Lovelace, Earl 1935- DLB-125; CDWLB-3

Lovelace, Richard 1618-1657. . . . . .DLB-131

Lovell, Coryell and Company DLB-49

Lovell, John W., Company DLB-49

Lover, Samuel 1797-1868. . . . . .DLB-159, 190

Lovesey, Peter 1936- DLB-87

Lovinescu, Eugen
1881-1943 . . . . .DLB-220; CDWLB-4

Lovingood, Sut
(see Harris, George Washington)

Low, Samuel 1765-? DLB-37

Lowell, Amy 1874-1925. . . . . .DLB-54, 140

Lowell, James Russell 1819-1891
. . . . . . DLB-1, 11, 64, 79, 189, 235; CDALB-2

Lowell, Robert 1917-1977. . .DLB-5, 169; CDALB-7

Lowenfels, Walter 1897-1976. . . . . .DLB-4

Lowndes, Marie Belloc 1868-1947. . . . . . .DLB-70

Lowndes, William Thomas 1798-1843 . . .DLB-184

Lownes, Humphrey [publishing house] . . .DLB-170

Lowry, Lois 1937- DLB-52

Lowry, Malcolm 1909-1957. . . .DLB-15; CDBLB-7

Lowther, Pat 1935-1975. . . . . .DLB-53

Loy, Mina 1882-1966 . . . . .DLB-4, 54

Lozeau, Albert 1878-1924 . . . . .DLB-92

Lubbock, Percy 1879-1965. . . . . .DLB-149

Lucan A.D. 39-A.D. 65 . . . . .DLB-211

Lucas, E. V. 1868-1938 . . . . .DLB-98, 149, 153

Lucas, Fielding, Jr. [publishing house] DLB-49

Luce, Clare Booth 1903-1987 . . . . .DLB-228

Luce, Henry R. 1898-1967 . . . . .DLB-91

Luce, John W., and Company. DLB-46

Lucian circa 120-180 . . . . .DLB-176

Lucie-Smith, Edward 1933- DLB-40

Lucilius circa 180 B.C.-102/101 B.C. DLB-211

Lucini, Gian Pietro 1867-1914 . . . . .DLB-114

Lucretius circa 94 B.C.-circa 49 B.C.
. . . . .DLB-211; CDWLB-1

Luder, Peter circa 1415-1472 . . . . DLB-179

Ludlum, Robert 1927- Y-82

Ludus de Antichristo circa 1160 . . . . .DLB-148

Ludvigson, Susan 1942- DLB-120

Ludwig, Jack 1922- DLB-60

Ludwig, Otto 1813-1865 . . . . .DLB-129

Ludwigslied 881 or 882 . . . . .DLB-148

Luera, Yolanda 1953- DLB-122

Luft, Lya 1938- DLB-145

Lugansky, Kazak Vladimir
(see Dal', Vladimir Ivanovich)

Lukács, Georg (see Lukács, György)

Lukács, György
1885-1971 . . . . .DLB-215, 242; CDWLB-4

Luke, Peter 1919- DLB-13

Lummis, Charles F. 1859-1928 . . . . .DLB-186

Lupton, F. M., Company. DLB-49

Lupus of Ferrières
circa 805-circa 862 . . . . .DLB-148

Lurie, Alison 1926- DLB-2

Lustig, Arnošt 1926- DLB-232

Luther, Martin 1483-1546 . . . DLB-179; CDWLB-2

Luzi, Mario 1914- DLB-128

L'vov, Nikolai Aleksandrovich 1751-1803 . .DLB-150

Lyall, Gavin 1932- DLB-87

Lydgate, John circa 1370-1450. . . . . .DLB-146

Lyly, John circa 1554-1606 . . . . .DLB-62, 167

Lynch, Patricia 1898-1972 . . . . .DLB-160

Lynch, Richard flourished 1596-1601 . . . .DLB-172

Lynd, Robert 1879-1949 . . . . .DLB-98

Lyon, Matthew 1749-1822. . . . . .DLB-43

Lyotard, Jean-François 1924-1998 . . . . . . .DLB-242

Lysias circa 459 B.C.-circa 380 B.C. DLB-176

Lytle, Andrew 1902-1995 . . . . DLB-6; Y-95

Lytton, Edward
(see Bulwer-Lytton, Edward)

Lytton, Edward Robert Bulwer
1831-1891. . . . . .DLB-32

M

Maass, Joachim 1901-1972. . . . . .DLB-69

Mabie, Hamilton Wright 1845-1916 . . . . . .DLB-71

Mac A'Ghobhainn, Iain (see Smith, Iain Crichton)

MacArthur, Charles 1895-1956. . . . . DLB-7, 25, 44

Macaulay, Catherine 1731-1791. . . . . .DLB-104

Macaulay, David 1945- DLB-61

Macaulay, Rose 1881-1958 . . . . .DLB-36

Macaulay, Thomas Babington
1800-1859 . . . . .DLB-32, 55; CDBLB-4

Macaulay Company DLB-46

MacBeth, George 1932- DLB-40

Macbeth, Madge 1880-1965 . . . . .DLB-92

MacCaig, Norman 1910-1996 . . . . DLB-27

MacDiarmid, Hugh
1892-1978 . . . . .DLB-20; CDBLB-7

MacDonald, Cynthia 1928- DLB-105

MacDonald, George 1824-1905 . . . .DLB-18, 163, 178

MacDonald, John D. 1916-1986 . . . . .DLB-8; Y-86

MacDonald, Philip 1899?-1980 . . . . DLB-77

Macdonald, Ross (see Millar, Kenneth)

MacDonald, Sharman 1951- DLB-245

MacDonald, Wilson 1880-1967 . . . . DLB-92

Macdonald and Company (Publishers) . . DLB-112

MacEwen, Gwendolyn 1941- DLB-53

Macfadden, Bernarr 1868-1955 . . . . . . DLB-25, 91

MacGregor, John 1825-1892 . . . . DLB-166

MacGregor, Mary Esther (see Keith, Marian)

Machado, Antonio 1875-1939 . . . . DLB-108

Machado, Manuel 1874-1947 . . . . DLB-108

Machar, Agnes Maule 1837-1927 . . . . DLB-92

Machaut, Guillaume de
circa 1300-1377 . . . . DLB-208

Machen, Arthur Llewelyn Jones
1863-1947 . . . . DLB-36, 156, 178

MacInnes, Colin 1914-1976 . . . . DLB-14

MacInnes, Helen 1907-1985 . . . . DLB-87

Mac Intyre, Tom 1931- DLB-245

Mačiulis, Jonas (see Maironis, Jonas)

Mack, Maynard 1909- DLB-111

Mackall, Leonard L. 1879-1937 . . . . DLB-140

MacKaye, Percy 1875-1956 . . . . DLB-54

Macken, Walter 1915-1967 . . . . DLB-13

Mackenzie, Alexander 1763-1820 . . . . DLB-99

Mackenzie, Alexander Slidell
1803-1848 . . . . DLB-183

Mackenzie, Compton 1883-1972 . . . . DLB-34, 100

Mackenzie, Henry 1745-1831 . . . . DLB-39

Mackenzie, William 1758-1828 . . . . DLB-187

Mackey, Nathaniel 1947- DLB-169

Mackey, Shena 1944- DLB-231

Mackey, William Wellington
1937- DLB-38

Mackintosh, Elizabeth (see Tey, Josephine)

Mackintosh, Sir James 1765-1832 . . . . DLB-158

Maclaren, Ian (see Watson, John)

Macklin, Charles 1699-1797 . . . . DLB-89

MacLean, Katherine Anne 1925- DLB-8

Maclean, Norman 1902-1990 . . . . DLB-206

MacLeish, Archibald 1892-1982
. . . . DLB-4, 7, 45, 228; Y-82; CDALB-7

MacLennan, Hugh 1907-1990 . . . . DLB-68

MacLeod, Alistair 1936- DLB-60

Macleod, Fiona (see Sharp, William)

Macleod, Norman 1906-1985 . . . . DLB-4

Mac Low, Jackson 1922- DLB-193

Macmillan and Company DLB-106

The Macmillan Company DLB-49

Macmillan's English Men of Letters,
First Series (1878-1892) DLB-144

MacNamara, Brinsley 1890-1963 . . . . DLB-10

MacNeice, Louis 1907-1963 . . . . DLB-10, 20

MacPhail, Andrew 1864-1938 . . . . DLB-92

Macpherson, James 1736-1796 . . . . DLB-109

Macpherson, Jay 1931- DLB-53

Macpherson, Jeanie 1884-1946 . . . . DLB-44

Macrae Smith Company DLB-46

MacRaye, Lucy Betty (see Webling, Lucy)

Macrone, John [publishing house] DLB-106

MacShane, Frank 1927-1999 . . . . DLB-111

Macy-Masius DLB-46

Madden, David 1933- DLB-6

Madden, Sir Frederic 1801-1873 . . . . DLB-184

Maddow, Ben 1909-1992 . . . . DLB-44

Maddux, Rachel 1912-1983 . . . . . . DLB-234; Y-93

Madgett, Naomi Long 1923- DLB-76

Madhubuti, Haki R. 1942- DLB-5, 41; DS-8

Madison, James 1751-1836 . . . . DLB-37

Madsen, Svend Åge 1939- DLB-214

Maeterlinck, Maurice 1862-1949 . . . . DLB-192

Mafūz, Najīb 1911- Y-88

Magee, David 1905-1977 . . . . DLB-187

Maginn, William 1794-1842 . . . . DLB-110, 159

Magoffin, Susan Shelby 1827-1855 . . . . . . DLB-239

Mahan, Alfred Thayer 1840-1914 . . . . DLB-47

Maheux-Forcier, Louise 1929- DLB-60

Mahin, John Lee 1902-1984 . . . . DLB-44

Mahon, Derek 1941- DLB-40

Maikov, Vasilii Ivanovich 1728-1778 . . . . DLB-150

Mailer, Norman 1923-
. . . . DLB-2, 16, 28, 185; Y-80, Y-83, Y-97;
DS-3; CDALB-6

Maillart, Ella 1903-1997 . . . . DLB-195

Maillet, Adrienne 1885-1963 . . . . DLB-68

Maillet, Antonine 1929- DLB-60

Maillu, David G. 1939- DLB-157

Maimonides, Moses 1138-1204 . . . . DLB-115

Main Selections of the Book-of-the-Month
Club, 1926-1945 . . . . DLB-9

Main Trends in Twentieth-Century Book
Clubs DLB-46

Mainwaring, Daniel 1902-1977 . . . . DLB-44

Mair, Charles 1838-1927 . . . . DLB-99

Maironis, Jonas
1862-1932 . . . . DLB-220; CDWLB-4

Mais, Roger 1905-1955 . . . . DLB-125; CDWLB-3

Major, Andre 1942- DLB-60

Major, Charles 1856-1913 . . . . DLB-202

Major, Clarence 1936- DLB-33

Major, Kevin 1949- DLB-60

Major Books DLB-46

Makemie, Francis circa 1658-1708 . . . . . . DLB-24

The Making of Americans Contract Y-98

The Making of a People, by
J. M. Ritchie DLB-66

Maksimović, Desanka
1898-1993 . . . . DLB-147; CDWLB-4

Malamud, Bernard 1914-1986
. . . . . . DLB-2, 28, 152; Y-80, Y-86; CDALB-1

Mălăncioiu, Ileana 1940- DLB-232

Malerba, Luigi 1927- DLB-196

Malet, Lucas 1852-1931 . . . . DLB-153

Mallarmé, Stéphane 1842-1898 . . . . .DLB-217

Malleson, Lucy Beatrice (see Gilbert, Anthony)

Mallet-Joris, Françoise 1930- DLB-83

Mallock, W. H. 1849-1923 . . . . .DLB-18, 57

"Every Man His Own Poet; or,
The Inspired Singer's Recipe
Book" (1877) DLB-35

Malone, Dumas 1892-1986 . . . . .DLB-17

Malone, Edmond 1741-1812 . . . . DLB-142

Malory, Sir Thomas
circa 1400-1410 - 1471 . . . DLB-146; CDBLB-1

Malpede, Karen 1945- DLB-249

Malraux, André 1901-1976 . . . . DLB-72

Malthus, Thomas Robert
1766-1834 . . . . .DLB-107, 158

Maltz, Albert 1908-1985 . . . . DLB-102

Malzberg, Barry N. 1939- DLB-8

Mamet, David 1947- DLB-7

Mamin, Dmitrii Narkisovich 1852-1912 . . DLB-238

Manaka, Matsemela 1956- DLB-157

Manchester University Press DLB-112

Mandel, Eli 1922- DLB-53

Mandeville, Bernard 1670-1733 . . . . DLB-101

Mandeville, Sir John
mid fourteenth century DLB-146

Mandiargues, André Pieyre de 1909- . . . DLB-83

Manea, Norman 1936- DLB-232

Manfred, Frederick 1912-1994 . . . .DLB-6, 212, 227

Manfredi, Gianfranco 1948- DLB-196

Mangan, Sherry 1904-1961 . . . . DLB-4

Manganelli, Giorgio 1922-1990 . . . . DLB-196

Manilius fl. first century A.D. DLB-211

Mankiewicz, Herman 1897-1953 . . . . DLB-26

Mankiewicz, Joseph L. 1909-1993 . . . . . . DLB-44

Mankowitz, Wolf 1924-1998 . . . . DLB-15

Manley, Delarivière 1672?-1724 . . . . . DLB-39, 80

Preface to *The Secret History, of Queen Zarah,
and the Zarazians* (1705) DLB-39

Mann, Abby 1927- DLB-44

Mann, Charles 1929-1998 . . . . Y-98

Mann, Heinrich 1871-1950 . . . . DLB-66, 118

Mann, Horace 1796-1859 . . . . DLB-1, 235

Mann, Klaus 1906-1949 . . . . DLB-56

Mann, Mary Peabody 1806-1887 . . . . DLB-239

Mann, Thomas 1875-1955 . . . DLB-66; CDWLB-2

Mann, William D'Alton 1839-1920 . . . . . .DLB-137

Mannin, Ethel 1900-1984 . . . . DLB-191, 195

Manning, Emily (see Australie)

Manning, Marie 1873?-1945 . . . . DLB-29

Manning and Loring DLB-49

Mannyng, Robert
flourished 1303-1338 . . . . DLB-146

Mano, D. Keith 1942- DLB-6

Manor Books DLB-46

Mansfield, Katherine 1888-1923 . . . . DLB-162

Manuel, Niklaus circa 1484-1530 . . . . . . .DLB-179

Manzini, Gianna 1896-1974 . . . . DLB-177

Mapanje, Jack 1944- DLB-157

Maraini, Dacia 1936- DLB-196

Marcel Proust at 129 and the Proust Society
of America Y-00

Marcel Proust's *Remembrance of Things Past:*
The Rediscovered Galley Proofs Y-00

March, William 1893-1954 . . . . DLB-9, 86

Marchand, Leslie A. 1900-1999 . . . . DLB-103

Marchant, Bessie 1862-1941 . . . . DLB-160

Marchant, Tony 1959- DLB-245

Marchenko, Anastasiia Iakovlevna
1830-1880 . . . . DLB-238

Marchessault, Jovette 1938- DLB-60

Marcinkevičius, Justinas 1930- DLB-232

Marcus, Frank 1928- DLB-13

Marcuse, Herbert 1898-1979 . . . . DLB-242

Marden, Orison Swett 1850-1924 . . . . DLB-137

Marechera, Dambudzo 1952-1987 . . . . DLB-157

Marek, Richard, Books DLB-46

Mares, E. A. 1938- DLB-122

Margulies, Donald 1954- DLB-228

Mariani, Paul 1940- DLB-111

Marie de France flourished 1160-1178 . . . . DLB-208

Marie-Victorin, Frère 1885-1944 . . . . DLB-92

Marin, Biagio 1891-1985 . . . . DLB-128

Marincovič, Ranko
1913- DLB-147; CDWLB-4

Marinetti, Filippo Tommaso
1876-1944 . . . . DLB-114

Marion, Frances 1886-1973 . . . . DLB-44

Marius, Richard C. 1933-1999 . . . . Y-85

Markevich, Boleslav Mikhailovich
1822-1884 . . . . DLB-238

Markfield, Wallace 1926- DLB-2, 28

Markham, Edwin 1852-1940 . . . . DLB-54, 186

Markle, Fletcher 1921-1991 . . . . DLB-68; Y-91

Marlatt, Daphne 1942- DLB-60

Marlitt, E. 1825-1887 . . . . DLB-129

Marlowe, Christopher
1564-1593 . . . . DLB-62; CDBLB-1

Marlyn, John 1912- DLB-88

Marmion, Shakerley 1603-1639 . . . . DLB-58

Der Marner before 1230-circa 1287 . . . . . . DLB-138

Marnham, Patrick 1943- DLB-204

The *Marprelate Tracts* 1588-1589 . . . . DLB-132

Marquand, John P. 1893-1960 . . . . DLB-9, 102

Marqués, René 1919-1979 . . . . DLB-113

Marquis, Don 1878-1937 . . . . DLB-11, 25

Marriott, Anne 1913- DLB-68

Marryat, Frederick 1792-1848 . . . . . . DLB-21, 163

Marsh, Capen, Lyon and Webb DLB-49

Marsh, George Perkins
1801-1882 . . . . DLB-1, 64, 243

Marsh, James 1794-1842 . . . . DLB-1, 59

Marsh, Narcissus 1638-1713 . . . . DLB-213

Marsh, Ngaio 1899-1982 . . . . DLB-77

Marshall, Edison 1894-1967 . . . . DLB-102

Marshall, Edward 1932- DLB-16

Marshall, Emma 1828-1899 . . . . DLB-163

Marshall, James 1942-1992 . . . . DLB-61

Marshall, Joyce 1913- DLB-88

Marshall, Paule 1929- DLB-33, 157, 227

Marshall, Tom 1938- DLB-60

Marsilius of Padua
circa 1275-circa 1342 . . . . DLB-115

Mars-Jones, Adam 1954- DLB-207

Marson, Una 1905-1965 . . . . DLB-157

Marston, John 1576-1634 . . . . DLB-58, 172

Marston, Philip Bourke 1850-1887 . . . . . . DLB-35

Martens, Kurt 1870-1945 . . . . DLB-66

Martial circa A.D. 40-circa A.D. 103
. . . . DLB-211; CDWLB-1

Martien, William S. [publishing house] DLB-49

Martin, Abe (see Hubbard, Kin)

Martin, Catherine ca. 1847-1937 . . . . DLB-230

Martin, Charles 1942- DLB-120

Martin, Claire 1914- DLB-60

Martin, Jay 1935- DLB-111

Martin, Johann (see Laurentius von Schnüffis)

Martin, Thomas 1696-1771 . . . . DLB-213

Martin, Violet Florence (see Ross, Martin)

Martin du Gard, Roger 1881-1958 . . . . DLB-65

Martineau, Harriet
1802-1876 . . . . DLB-21, 55, 159, 163, 166, 190

Martínez, Demetria 1960- DLB-209

Martínez, Eliud 1935- DLB-122

Martínez, Max 1943- DLB-82

Martínez, Rubén 1962- DLB-209

Martone, Michael 1955- DLB-218

Martyn, Edward 1859-1923 . . . . DLB-10

Marvell, Andrew
1621-1678 . . . . DLB-131; CDBLB-2

Marvin X 1944- DLB-38

Marx, Karl 1818-1883 . . . . DLB-129

Marzials, Theo 1850-1920 . . . . DLB-35

Masefield, John
1878-1967 . . . DLB-10, 19, 153, 160; CDBLB-5

Mason, A. E. W. 1865-1948 . . . . DLB-70

Mason, Bobbie Ann
1940- DLB-173; Y-87; CDALB-7

Mason, William 1725-1797 . . . . DLB-142

Mason Brothers DLB-49

Massey, Gerald 1828-1907 . . . . DLB-32

Massey, Linton R. 1900-1974 . . . . DLB-187

Massinger, Philip 1583-1640 . . . . DLB-58

Masson, David 1822-1907 . . . . DLB-144

Masters, Edgar Lee
1868-1950 . . . . DLB-54; CDALB-3

Masters, Hilary 1928- DLB-244

Mastronardi, Lucio 1930-1979 . . . . DLB-177

Matevski, Mateja 1929- . . . DLB-181; CDWLB-4

Mather, Cotton
1663-1728 . . . . DLB-24, 30, 140; CDALB-2

Mather, Increase 1639-1723 . . . . DLB-24

Mather, Richard 1596-1669 . . . . DLB-24

Matheson, Annie 1853-1924 . . . . DLB-240

Matheson, Richard 1926- DLB-8, 44

Matheus, John F. 1887- DLB-51

Mathews, Cornelius 1817?-1889 . . . . DLB-3, 64

Mathews, Elkin [publishing house] DLB-112

Mathews, John Joseph 1894-1979 . . . . DLB-175

Mathias, Roland 1915- DLB-27

Mathis, June 1892-1927 . . . . DLB-44

Mathis, Sharon Bell 1937- DLB-33

Matković, Marijan 1915-1985 . . . . DLB-181

Matoš, Antun Gustav 1873-1914 . . . . DLB-147

Matsumoto Seichō 1909-1992 . . . . DLB-182

The Matter of England 1240-1400 . . . . . . DLB-146

The Matter of Rome early twelfth to late
fifteenth century DLB-146

Matthew of Vendôme
circa 1130-circa 1200 . . . . DLB-208

Matthews, Brander
1852-1929 . . . . DLB-71, 78; DS-13

Matthews, Jack 1925- DLB-6

Matthews, Victoria Earle 1861-1907 . . . . . DLB-221

Matthews, William 1942-1997 . . . . DLB-5

Matthiessen, F. O. 1902-1950 . . . . DLB-63

Matthiessen, Peter 1927- DLB-6, 173

Maturin, Charles Robert 1780-1824 . . . . . DLB-178

Maugham, W. Somerset 1874-1965
. . . . DLB-10, 36, 77, 100, 162, 195; CDBLB-6

Maupassant, Guy de 1850-1893 . . . . DLB-123

Mauriac, Claude 1914-1996 . . . . DLB-83

Mauriac, François 1885-1970 . . . . DLB-65

Maurice, Frederick Denison
1805-1872 . . . . DLB-55

Maurois, André 1885-1967 . . . . DLB-65

Maury, James 1718-1769 . . . . DLB-31

Mavor, Elizabeth 1927- DLB-14

Mavor, Osborne Henry (see Bridie, James)

Maxwell, Gavin 1914-1969 . . . . DLB-204

Maxwell, H. [publishing house] DLB-49

Maxwell, John [publishing house] DLB-106

Maxwell, William 1908- DLB-218; Y-80

May, Elaine 1932- DLB-44

May, Karl 1842-1912 . . . . DLB-129

May, Thomas 1595 or 1596-1650 . . . . DLB-58

Mayer, Bernadette 1945- DLB-165

Mayer, Mercer 1943- DLB-61

Mayer, O. B. 1818-1891 . . . . DLB-3, 248

Mayes, Herbert R. 1900-1987 . . . . DLB-137

Mayes, Wendell 1919-1992 . . . . DLB-26

Mayfield, Julian 1928-1984 . . . . DLB-33; Y-84

Mayhew, Henry 1812-1887 . . . . . . DLB-18, 55, 190

Mayhew, Jonathan 1720-1766 . . . . DLB-31

Mayne, Ethel Colburn 1865-1941 . . . . DLB-197

Mayne, Jasper 1604-1672 . . . . DLB-126

Mayne, Seymour 1944- DLB-60

Mayor, Flora Macdonald 1872-1932 . . . . . DLB-36

Mayrocker, Friederike 1924- DLB-85

Mazrui, Ali A. 1933- DLB-125

Mažuranić, Ivan 1814-1890 . . . . DLB-147

Mazursky, Paul 1930- DLB-44

McAlmon, Robert
    1896-1956 . . . . DLB-4, 45; DS-15

McArthur, Peter 1866-1924 . . . . DLB-92

McBride, Robert M., and Company DLB-46

McCabe, Patrick 1955- DLB-194

McCaffrey, Anne 1926- DLB-8

McCarthy, Cormac 1933- DLB-6, 143

McCarthy, Mary 1912-1989 . . . . DLB-2; Y-81

McCay, Winsor 1871-1934 . . . . DLB-22

McClane, Albert Jules 1922-1991 . . . . . . .DLB-171

McClatchy, C. K. 1858-1936 . . . . DLB-25

McClellan, George Marion 1860-1934 . . . . DLB-50

McCloskey, Robert 1914- DLB-22

McClung, Nellie Letitia 1873-1951 . . . . . . DLB-92

McClure, Joanna 1930- DLB-16

McClure, Michael 1932- DLB-16

McClure, Phillips and Company DLB-46

McClure, S. S. 1857-1949 . . . . DLB-91

McClurg, A. C., and Company DLB-49

McCluskey, John A., Jr. 1944- DLB-33

McCollum, Michael A. 1946 . . . . Y-87

McConnell, William C. 1917- DLB-88

McCord, David 1897-1997 . . . . DLB-61

McCord, Louisa S. 1810-1879 . . . . DLB-248

McCorkle, Jill 1958- DLB-234; Y-87

McCorkle, Samuel Eusebius
    1746-1811 . . . . DLB-37

McCormick, Anne O'Hare 1880-1954 . . . . DLB-29

Kenneth Dale McCormick Tributes Y-97

McCormick, Robert R. 1880-1955 . . . . . . DLB-29

McCourt, Edward 1907-1972 . . . . DLB-88

McCoy, Horace 1897-1955 . . . . DLB-9

McCrae, John 1872-1918 . . . . DLB-92

McCullagh, Joseph B. 1842-1896 . . . . DLB-23

McCullers, Carson
    1917-1967 . . . . . .DLB-2, 7, 173, 228; CDALB-1

McCulloch, Thomas 1776-1843 . . . . DLB-99

McDonald, Forrest 1927- DLB-17

McDonald, Walter 1934- DLB-105, DS-9

"Getting Started: Accepting the Regions
    You Own—or Which Own You," . . . DLB-105

McDougall, Colin 1917-1984 . . . . DLB-68

McDowell, Katharine Sherwood Bonner
    1849-1883 . . . . DLB-202, 239

McDowell, Obolensky DLB-46

McEwan, Ian 1948- DLB-14, 194

McFadden, David 1940- DLB-60

McFall, Frances Elizabeth Clarke
    (see Grand, Sarah)

McFarlane, Leslie 1902-1977 . . . . DLB-88

McFee, William 1881-1966 . . . . DLB-153

McGahern, John 1934- DLB-14, 231

McGee, Thomas D'Arcy 1825-1868 . . . . . DLB-99

McGeehan, W. O. 1879-1933 . . . . . . .DLB-25, 171

McGill, Ralph 1898-1969 . . . . DLB-29

McGinley, Phyllis 1905-1978 . . . . DLB-11, 48

McGinniss, Joe 1942- DLB-185

McGirt, James E. 1874-1930 . . . . DLB-50

McGlashan and Gill DLB-106

McGough, Roger 1937- DLB-40

McGrath, John 1935- DLB-233

McGrath, Patrick 1950- DLB-231

McGraw-Hill DLB-46

McGuane, Thomas 1939- DLB-2, 212; Y-80

McGuckian, Medbh 1950- DLB-40

McGuffey, William Holmes 1800-1873 . . . DLB-42

McGuinness, Frank 1953- DLB-245

McHenry, James 1785-1845 . . . . DLB-202

McIlvanney, William 1936- DLB-14, 207

McIlwraith, Jean Newton 1859-1938 . . . . . DLB-92

McIntosh, Maria Jane 1803-1878 . . . DLB-239, 248

McIntyre, James 1827-1906 . . . . DLB-99

McIntyre, O. O. 1884-1938 . . . . DLB-25

McKay, Claude 1889-1948 . . . . .DLB-4, 45, 51, 117

The David McKay Company DLB-49

McKean, William V. 1820-1903 . . . . DLB-23

McKenna, Stephen 1888-1967 . . . . DLB-197

The McKenzie Trust Y-96

McKerrow, R. B. 1872-1940 . . . . DLB-201

McKinley, Robin 1952- DLB-52

McKnight, Reginald 1956- DLB-234

McLachlan, Alexander 1818-1896 . . . . . . DLB-99

McLaren, Floris Clark 1904-1978 . . . . DLB-68

McLaverty, Michael 1907- DLB-15

McLean, John R. 1848-1916 . . . . DLB-23

McLean, William L. 1852-1931 . . . . DLB-25

McLennan, William 1856-1904 . . . . DLB-92

McLoughlin Brothers DLB-49

McLuhan, Marshall 1911-1980 . . . . DLB-88

McMaster, John Bach 1852-1932 . . . . DLB-47

McMurtry, Larry
    1936- . . .DLB-2, 143; Y-80, Y-87; CDALB-6

McNally, Terrence 1939- DLB-7, 249

McNeil, Florence 1937- DLB-60

McNeile, Herman Cyril 1888-1937 . . . . . . DLB-77

McNickle, D'Arcy 1904-1977 . . . . . . .DLB-175, 212

McPhee, John 1931- DLB-185

McPherson, James Alan 1943- DLB-38, 244

McPherson, Sandra 1943- Y-86

McWhirter, George 1939- DLB-60

McWilliams, Carey 1905-1980 . . . . DLB-137

Mda, Zakes 1948- DLB-225

Mead, L. T. 1844-1914 . . . . DLB-141

Mead, Matthew 1924- DLB-40

Mead, Taylor ?- DLB-16

Meany, Tom 1903-1964 . . . . .DLB-171

Mechthild von Magdeburg
    circa 1207-circa 1282 . . . . DLB-138

Medieval French Drama DLB-208

Medieval Travel Diaries DLB-203

Medill, Joseph 1823-1899 . . . . DLB-43

Medoff, Mark 1940- DLB-7

Meek, Alexander Beaufort
    1814-1865 . . . . DLB-3, 248

Meeke, Mary ?-1816? DLB-116

Meinke, Peter 1932- DLB-5

Mejia Vallejo, Manuel 1923- DLB-113

Melanchthon, Philipp 1497-1560 . . . . . . .DLB-179

Melançon, Robert 1947- DLB-60

Mell, Max 1882-1971 . . . . DLB-81, 124

Mellow, James R. 1926-1997 . . . . DLB-111

Mel'nikov, Pavel Ivanovich 1818-1883 . . DLB-238

Meltzer, David 1937- DLB-16

Meltzer, Milton 1915- DLB-61

Melville, Elizabeth, Lady Culross
    circa 1585-1640 . . . . .DLB-172

Melville, Herman
    1819-1891 . . . . DLB-3, 74; CDALB-2

Memoirs of Life and Literature (1920),
    by W. H. Mallock [excerpt] DLB-57

Mena, María Cristina 1893-1965 . . . DLB-209, 221

Menander 342-341 B.C.-circa 292-291 B.C.
    .DLB-176; CDWLB-1

Menantes (see Hunold, Christian Friedrich)

Mencke, Johann Burckhard
    1674-1732 . . . . DLB-168

Mencken, H. L. 1880-1956
    . . . . DLB-11, 29, 63, 137, 222; CDALB-4

H. L. Mencken's "Berlin, February, 1917" Y-00

Mencken and Nietzsche: An Unpublished
    Excerpt from H. L. Mencken's *My Life
    as Author and Editor* Y-93

Mendelssohn, Moses 1729-1786 . . . . DLB-97

Mendes, Catulle 1841-1909 . . . . .DLB-217

Méndez M., Miguel 1930- DLB-82

Mens Rea (or Something) Y-97

The Mercantile Library of New York Y-96

Mercer, Cecil William (see Yates, Dornford)

Mercer, David 1928-1980 . . . . DLB-13

Mercer, John 1704-1768 . . . . DLB-31

Meredith, George
    1828-1909 . . . .DLB-18, 35, 57, 159; CDBLB-4

Meredith, Louisa Anne 1812-1895 . . DLB-166, 230

Meredith, Owen
    (see Lytton, Edward Robert Bulwer)

Meredith, William 1919- DLB-5

Mergerle, Johann Ulrich
    (see Abraham ä Sancta Clara)

Mérimée, Prosper 1803-1870 . . . . . . .DLB-119, 192

Merivale, John Herman 1779-1844 . . . . . . DLB-96

Meriwether, Louise 1923- DLB-33

Merlin Press DLB-112

Merriam, Eve 1916-1992 . . . . DLB-61

The Merriam Company DLB-49

Merrill, James 1926-1995. . . . . . DLB-5, 165; Y-85

Merrill and Baker. DLB-49

The Mershon Company DLB-49

Merton, Thomas 1915-1968 . . . . . . .DLB-48; Y-81

Merwin, W. S. 1927- DLB-5, 169

Messner, Julian [publishing house]. DLB-46

Mészöly, Miklós 1921- DLB-232

Metcalf, J. [publishing house]. DLB-49

Metcalf, John 1938- DLB-60

The Methodist Book Concern. DLB-49

Methuen and Company. DLB-112

Meun, Jean de (see *Roman de la Rose*)

Mew, Charlotte 1869-1928 . . . . .DLB-19, 135

Mewshaw, Michael 1943- Y-80

Meyer, Conrad Ferdinand 1825-1898 . . . .DLB-129

Meyer, E. Y. 1946- DLB-75

Meyer, Eugene 1875-1959 . . . . .DLB-29

Meyer, Michael 1921-2000 . . . . .DLB-155

Meyers, Jeffrey 1939- DLB-111

Meynell, Alice 1847-1922. . . . . .DLB-19, 98

Meynell, Viola 1885-1956 . . . . .DLB-153

Meyrink, Gustav 1868-1932 . . . . .DLB-81

Mézières, Philipe de circa 1327-1405 . . . . .DLB-208

Michael, Ib 1945- DLB-214

Michaëlis, Karen 1872-1950. . . . . .DLB-214

Michaels, Leonard 1933- DLB-130

Micheaux, Oscar 1884-1951 . . . . .DLB-50

Michel of Northgate, Dan
    circa 1265-circa 1340. . . . . .DLB-146

Micheline, Jack 1929-1998. . . . . .DLB-16

Michener, James A. 1907?-1997. . . . . .DLB-6

Micklejohn, George
    circa 1717-1818 . . . . .DLB-31

Middle English Literature:
    An Introduction. DLB-146

The Middle English Lyric DLB-146

Middle Hill Press. DLB-106

Middleton, Christopher 1926- DLB-40

Middleton, Richard 1882-1911 . . . . .DLB-156

Middleton, Stanley 1919- DLB-14

Middleton, Thomas 1580-1627 . . . . .DLB-58

Miegel, Agnes 1879-1964. . . . . .DLB-56

Mieželaitis, Eduardas 1919-1997 . . . . . . .DLB-220

Mihailović, Dragoslav 1930- DLB-181

Mihalić, Slavko 1928- DLB-181

Mikhailov, A. (see Sheller, Aleksandr
    Konstantinovich)

Mikhailov, Mikhail Larionovich
    1829-1865 . . . . .DLB-238

Miles, Josephine 1911-1985 . . . . .DLB-48

Miles, Susan (Ursula Wyllie Roberts)
    1888-1975 . . . . .DLB-240

Miliković, Branko 1934-1961 . . . . .DLB-181

Milius, John 1944- DLB-44

Mill, James 1773-1836 . . . . DLB-107, 158

Mill, John Stuart
    1806-1873 . . . . .DLB-55, 190; CDBLB-4

Millar, Andrew [publishing house] DLB-154

Millar, Kenneth
    1915-1983 . . . . .DLB-2, 226; Y-83; DS-6

Millay, Edna St. Vincent
    1892-1950 . . . . .DLB-45, 249; CDALB-4

Millen, Sarah Gertrude 1888-1968 . . . . . .DLB-225

Miller, Arthur 1915- DLB-7; CDALB-1

Miller, Caroline 1903-1992 . . . . .DLB-9

Miller, Eugene Ethelbert 1950- DLB-41

Miller, Heather Ross 1939- DLB-120

Miller, Henry
    1891-1980 . . . . . . .DLB-4, 9; Y-80; CDALB-5

Miller, Hugh 1802-1856 . . . . .DLB-190

Miller, J. Hillis 1928- DLB-67

Miller, James [publishing house] DLB-49

Miller, Jason 1939- DLB-7

Miller, Joaquin 1839-1913 . . . . .DLB-186

Miller, May 1899- DLB-41

Miller, Paul 1906-1991 . . . . .DLB-127

Miller, Perry 1905-1963 . . . . DLB-17, 63

Miller, Sue 1943- DLB-143

Miller, Vassar 1924-1998. . . . . .DLB-105

Miller, Walter M., Jr. 1923- DLB-8

Miller, Webb 1892-1940 . . . . .DLB-29

Millett, Kate 1934- DLB-246

Millhauser, Steven 1943- DLB-2

Millican, Arthenia J. Bates 1920- DLB-38

Milligan, Alice 1866-1953 . . . . .DLB-240

Mills and Boon DLB-112

Milman, Henry Hart 1796-1868 . . . . . . .DLB-96

Milne, A. A. 1882-1956 . . . . . DLB-10, 77, 100, 160

Milner, Ron 1938- DLB-38

Milner, William [publishing house] DLB-106

Milnes, Richard Monckton (Lord Houghton)
    1809-1885 . . . . .DLB-32, 184

Milton, John
    1608-1674 . . . . .DLB-131, 151; CDBLB-2

Miłosz, Czesław 1911- DLB-215; CDWLB-4

Minakami Tsutomu 1919- DLB-182

Minamoto no Sanetomo 1192-1219. . . . . .DLB-203

The Minerva Press DLB-154

Minnesang circa 1150-1280 . . . . .DLB-138

Minns, Susan 1839-1938 . . . . .DLB-140

Minor Illustrators, 1880-1914 . . . . .DLB-141

Minor Poets of the Earlier Seventeenth
    Century. .DLB-121

Minton, Balch and Company DLB-46

Mirbeau, Octave 1848-1917. . . . . . .DLB-123, 192

Mirk, John died after 1414?. DLB-146

Miron, Gaston 1928- DLB-60

A Mirror for Magistrates DLB-167

Mishima Yukio 1925-1970. . . . . .DLB-182

Mitchel, Jonathan 1624-1668. . . . . .DLB-24

Mitchell, Adrian 1932- DLB-40

Mitchell, Donald Grant
    1822-1908 . . . . .DLB-1, 243; DS-13

Mitchell, Gladys 1901-1983. . . . . .DLB-77

Mitchell, James Leslie 1901-1935. . . . . . . .DLB-15

Mitchell, John (see Slater, Patrick)

Mitchell, John Ames 1845-1918. . . . . .DLB-79

Mitchell, Joseph 1908-1996 . . . . . . .DLB-185; Y-96

Mitchell, Julian 1935- DLB-14

Mitchell, Ken 1940- DLB-60

Mitchell, Langdon 1862-1935 . . . . .DLB-7

Mitchell, Loften 1919- DLB-38

Mitchell, Margaret 1900-1949 . . .DLB-9; CDALB-7

Mitchell, S. Weir 1829-1914 . . . . .DLB-202

Mitchell, W. J. T. 1942- DLB-246

Mitchell, W. O. 1914- DLB-88

Mitchison, Naomi Margaret (Haldane)
    1897-1999. . . . . .DLB-160, 191

Mitford, Mary Russell 1787-1855. . . . DLB-110, 116

Mitford, Nancy 1904-1973. . . . . .DLB-191

Mittelholzer, Edgar
    1909-1965 . . . . DLB-117; CDWLB-3

Mitterer, Erika 1906- DLB-85

Mitterer, Felix 1948- DLB-124

Mitternacht, Johann Sebastian
    1613-1679 . . . . .DLB-168

Miyamoto, Yuriko 1899-1951 . . . . .DLB-180

Mizener, Arthur 1907-1988 . . . . .DLB-103

Mo, Timothy 1950- DLB-194

Modern Age Books DLB-46

"Modern English Prose" (1876),
    by George Saintsbury DLB-57

The Modern Language Association of America
    Celebrates Its Centennial Y-84

The Modern Library. DLB-46

"Modern Novelists – Great and Small" (1855),
    by Margaret Oliphant DLB-21

"Modern Style" (1857), by Cockburn
    Thomson [excerpt] DLB-57

The Modernists (1932),
    by Joseph Warren Beach. DLB-36

Modiano, Patrick 1945- DLB-83

Moffat, Yard and Company DLB-46

Moffet, Thomas 1553-1604 . . . . .DLB-136

Mohr, Nicholasa 1938- DLB-145

Moix, Ana María 1947- DLB-134

Molesworth, Louisa 1839-1921 . . . . .DLB-135

Möllhausen, Balduin 1825-1905 . . . . .DLB-129

Molnár, Ferenc
    1878-1952 . . . . .DLB-215; CDWLB-4

Molnár, Miklós (see Mészöly, Miklós)

Momaday, N. Scott
    1934- DLB-143, 175; CDALB-7

Monkhouse, Allan 1858-1936 . . . . .DLB-10

Monro, Harold 1879-1932 . . . . .DLB-19

Monroe, Harriet 1860-1936. . . . . DLB-54, 91

Monsarrat, Nicholas 1910-1979 . . . . .DLB-15

Montagu, Lady Mary Wortley
    1689-1762 . . . . .DLB-95, 101

Montague, C. E. 1867-1928 . . . . DLB-197

Montague, John 1929- DLB-40

Montale, Eugenio 1896-1981 . . . . DLB-114

Montalvo, José 1946-1994 . . . . DLB-209

Monterroso, Augusto 1921- DLB-145

Montesquiou, Robert de 1855-1921 . . . . . DLB-217

Montgomerie, Alexander
circa 1550?-1598 . . . . DLB-167

Montgomery, James 1771-1854 . . . . . . DLB-93, 158

Montgomery, John 1919- DLB-16

Montgomery, Lucy Maud
1874-1942. . . . . DLB-92; DS-14

Montgomery, Marion 1925- DLB-6

Montgomery, Robert Bruce (see Crispin, Edmund)

Montherlant, Henry de 1896-1972 . . . . DLB-72

The Monthly Review 1749-1844 . . . . DLB-110

Montigny, Louvigny de 1876-1955. . . . . . . DLB-92

Montoya, José 1932- DLB-122

Moodie, John Wedderburn Dunbar
1797-1869 . . . . DLB-99

Moodie, Susanna 1803-1885. . . . . DLB-99

Moody, Joshua circa 1633-1697 . . . . DLB-24

Moody, William Vaughn 1869-1910 . . . .DLB-7, 54

Moorcock, Michael 1939- DLB-14, 231

Moore, Catherine L. 1911- DLB-8

Moore, Clement Clarke 1779-1863 . . . . DLB-42

Moore, Dora Mavor 1888-1979 . . . . DLB-92

Moore, George 1852-1933 . . . . DLB-10, 18, 57, 135

Moore, Lorrie 1957- DLB-234

Moore, Marianne
1887-1972 . . . . DLB-45; DS-7; CDALB-5

Moore, Mavor 1919- DLB-88

Moore, Richard 1927- DLB-105

Moore, T. Sturge 1870-1944 . . . . DLB-19

Moore, Thomas 1779-1852. . . . . DLB-96, 144

Moore, Ward 1903-1978 . . . . DLB-8

Moore, Wilstach, Keys and Company DLB-49

Moorehead, Alan 1901-1983 . . . . DLB-204

Moorhouse, Geoffrey 1931- DLB-204

The Moorland-Spingarn Research
Center DLB-76

Moorman, Mary C. 1905-1994 . . . . DLB-155

Mora, Pat 1942- DLB-209

Moraga, Cherríe 1952- DLB-82, 249

Morales, Alejandro 1944- DLB-82

Morales, Mario Roberto 1947- DLB-145

Morales, Rafael 1919- DLB-108

Morality Plays: Mankind circa 1450-1500 and
Everyman circa 1500 . . . . DLB-146

Morante, Elsa 1912-1985 . . . . .DLB-177

Morata, Olympia Fulvia 1526-1555 . . . . . .DLB-179

Moravia, Alberto 1907-1990 . . . . .DLB-177

Mordaunt, Elinor 1872-1942 . . . . .DLB-174

Mordovtsev, Daniil Lukich 1830-1905. . . DLB-238

More, Hannah
1745-1833. . . . . DLB-107, 109, 116, 158

More, Henry 1614-1687 . . . . DLB-126

More, Sir Thomas
1477 or 1478-1535 . . . . DLB-136

Moreno, Dorinda 1939- DLB-122

Morency, Pierre 1942- DLB-60

Moretti, Marino 1885-1979. . . . . DLB-114

Morgan, Berry 1919- DLB-6

Morgan, Charles 1894-1958. . . . . . . DLB-34, 100

Morgan, Edmund S. 1916- DLB-17

Morgan, Edwin 1920- DLB-27

Morgan, John Pierpont 1837-1913 . . . . . . DLB-140

Morgan, John Pierpont, Jr. 1867-1943 . . . DLB-140

Morgan, Robert 1944- DLB-120

Morgan, Sydney Owenson, Lady
1776?-1859 . . . . DLB-116, 158

Morgner, Irmtraud 1933- DLB-75

Morhof, Daniel Georg 1639-1691 . . . . . . DLB-164

Mori, Ōgai 1862-1922 . . . . DLB-180

Móricz, Zsigmond 1879-1942 . . . . DLB-215

Morier, James Justinian
1782 or 1783?-1849 . . . . DLB-116

Mörike, Eduard 1804-1875. . . . . DLB-133

Morin, Paul 1889-1963. . . . . DLB-92

Morison, Richard 1514?-1556 . . . . DLB-136

Morison, Samuel Eliot 1887-1976 . . . . DLB-17

Morison, Stanley 1889-1967. . . . . DLB-201

Moritz, Karl Philipp 1756-1793 . . . . DLB-94

Moriz von Craûn circa 1220-1230 . . . . DLB-138

Morley, Christopher 1890-1957 . . . . DLB-9

Morley, John 1838-1923. . . . . . . DLB-57, 144, 190

Morris, George Pope 1802-1864 . . . . DLB-73

Morris, James Humphrey (see Morris, Jan)

Morris, Jan 1926- DLB-204

Morris, Lewis 1833-1907 . . . . DLB-35

Morris, Margaret 1737-1816 . . . . DLB-200

Morris, Richard B. 1904-1989 . . . . DLB-17

Morris, William 1834-1896
. . . . DLB-18, 35, 57, 156, 178, 184; CDBLB-4

Morris, Willie 1934-1999 . . . . .Y-80

Morris, Wright
1910-1998 . . . . .DLB-2, 206, 218; Y-81

Morrison, Arthur 1863-1945 . . . .DLB-70, 135, 197

Morrison, Charles Clayton 1874-1966 . . . . DLB-91

Morrison, Toni 1931-
. . . . . . .DLB-6, 33, 143; Y-81, Y-93; CDALB-6

Morrow, William, and Company. DLB-46

Morse, James Herbert 1841-1923. . . . . . . DLB-71

Morse, Jedidiah 1761-1826 . . . . DLB-37

Morse, John T., Jr. 1840-1937 . . . . DLB-47

Morselli, Guido 1912-1973 . . . . .DLB-177

Mortimer, Favell Lee 1802-1878 . . . . DLB-163

Mortimer, John
1923- DLB-13, 245; CDBLB-8

Morton, Carlos 1942- DLB-122

Morton, H. V. 1892-1979 . . . . DLB-195

Morton, John P., and Company. DLB-49

Morton, Nathaniel 1613-1685 . . . . DLB-24

Morton, Sarah Wentworth 1759-1846 . . . . DLB-37

Morton, Thomas circa 1579-circa 1647 . . . DLB-24

Moscherosch, Johann Michael
1601-1669 . . . . DLB-164

Moseley, Humphrey
[publishing house] DLB-170

Möser, Justus 1720-1794. . . . . DLB-97

Mosley, Nicholas 1923- DLB-14, 207

Moss, Arthur 1889-1969 . . . . DLB-4

Moss, Howard 1922-1987 . . . . DLB-5

Moss, Thylias 1954- DLB-120

The Most Powerful Book Review
in America
[New York Times Book Review] Y-82

Motion, Andrew 1952- DLB-40

Motley, John Lothrop
1814-1877. . . . . DLB-1, 30, 59, 235

Motley, Willard 1909-1965 . . . . .DLB-76, 143

Mott, Lucretia 1793-1880 . . . . DLB-239

Motte, Benjamin Jr. [publishing house]. . . DLB-154

Motteux, Peter Anthony 1663-1718 . . . . . . DLB-80

Mottram, R. H. 1883-1971 . . . . DLB-36

Mount, Ferdinand 1939- DLB-231

Mouré, Erin 1955- DLB-60

Mourning Dove (Humishuma) between
1882 and 1888?-1936. . . . . . . .DLB-175, 221

Movies from Books, 1920-1974 . . . . DLB-9

Mowat, Farley 1921- DLB-68

Mowbray, A. R., and Company,
Limited. DLB-106

Mowrer, Edgar Ansel 1892-1977 . . . . DLB-29

Mowrer, Paul Scott 1887-1971 . . . . DLB-29

Moxon, Edward [publishing house] DLB-106

Moxon, Joseph [publishing house] DLB-170

Mphahlele, Es'kia (Ezekiel)
1919- DLB-125; CDWLB-3

Mrożek, Sławomir 1930- . . DLB-232; CDWLB-4

Mtshali, Oswald Mbuyiseni 1940- DLB-125

Mucedorus DLB-62

Mudford, William 1782-1848 . . . . DLB-159

Mueller, Lisel 1924- DLB-105

Muhajir, El (see Marvin X)

Muhajir, Nazzam Al Fitnah (see Marvin X)

Mühlbach, Luise 1814-1873 . . . . DLB-133

Muir, Edwin 1887-1959 . . . . . . .DLB-20, 100, 191

Muir, Helen 1937- DLB-14

Muir, John 1838-1914 . . . . DLB-186

Muir, Percy 1894-1979 . . . . DLB-201

Mujū Ichien 1226-1312. . . . . DLB-203

Mukherjee, Bharati 1940- DLB-60, 218

Mulcaster, Richard
1531 or 1532-1611. . . . . DLB-167

Muldoon, Paul 1951- DLB-40

Müller, Friedrich (see Müller, Maler)

Müller, Heiner 1929-1995 . . . . DLB-124

Müller, Maler 1749-1825 . . . . DLB-94

Muller, Marcia 1944- DLB-226

Müller, Wilhelm 1794-1827 ....DLB-90

Mumford, Lewis 1895-1990 ....DLB-63

Munby, A. N. L. 1913-1974...........DLB-201

Munby, Arthur Joseph 1828-1910 ....DLB-35

Munday, Anthony 1560-1633 .... DLB-62, 172

Mundt, Clara (see Mühlbach, Luise)

Mundt, Theodore 1808-1861 ....DLB-133

Munford, Robert circa 1737-1783........DLB-31

Mungoshi, Charles 1947- DLB-157

Munk, Kaj 1898-1944 ....DLB-214

Munonye, John 1929- DLB-117

Munro, Alice 1931- DLB-53

Munro, George [publishing house] DLB-49

Munro, H. H.
  1870-1916 ....DLB-34, 162; CDBLB-5

Munro, Neil 1864-1930 ....DLB-156

Munro, Norman L.
  [publishing house] DLB-49

Munroe, James, and Company DLB-49

Munroe, Kirk 1850-1930..............DLB-42

Munroe and Francis..................DLB-49

Munsell, Joel [publishing house] DLB-49

Munsey, Frank A. 1854-1925 ......DLB-25, 91

Munsey, Frank A., and Company.......DLB-49

Murakami Haruki 1949- DLB-182

Murav'ev, Mikhail Nikitich
  1757-1807......................DLB-150

Murdoch, Iris
  1919-1999 .....DLB-14, 194, 233; CDBLB-8

Murdoch, Rupert 1931- DLB-127

Murfree, Mary N. 1850-1922 ....DLB-12, 74

Murger, Henry 1822-1861............DLB-119

Murger, Louis-Henri (see Murger, Henry)

Murner, Thomas 1475-1537 ....DLB-179

Muro, Amado 1915-1971...............DLB-82

Murphy, Arthur 1727-1805 ....DLB-89, 142

Murphy, Beatrice M. 1908- DLB-76

Murphy, Dervla 1931- DLB-204

Murphy, Emily 1868-1933...........DLB-99

Murphy, Jack 1923-1980 ....DLB-241

Murphy, John, and Company DLB-49

Murphy, John H., III 1916- DLB-127

Murphy, Richard 1927-1993 ....DLB-40

Murray, Albert L. 1916- DLB-38

Murray, Gilbert 1866-1957 ....DLB-10

Murray, Jim 1919-1998 ....DLB-241

Murray, John [publishing house] DLB-154

Murry, John Middleton 1889-1957 ......DLB-149

"The Break-Up of the Novel" (1922).....DLB-36

Murray, Judith Sargent 1751-1820.... DLB-37, 200

Murray, Pauli 1910-1985 ....DLB-41

Musäus, Johann Karl August 1735-1787....DLB-97

Muschg, Adolf 1934- DLB-75

The Music of *Minnesang*..............DLB-138

Musil, Robert
  1880-1942 ....DLB-81, 124; CDWLB-2

Muspilli circa 790-circa 850............DLB-148

Musset, Alfred de 1810-1857 ...... DLB-192, 217

Mussey, Benjamin B., and Company DLB-49

Mutafchieva, Vera 1929- DLB-181

Mwangi, Meja 1948- DLB-125

Myers, Frederic W. H. 1843-1901......DLB-190

Myers, Gustavus 1872-1942 ....DLB-47

Myers, L. H. 1881-1944 ....DLB-15

Myers, Walter Dean 1937- DLB-33

Mykolaitis-Putinas, Vincas 1893-1967....DLB-220

Myles, Eileen 1949- DLB-193

N

Na Prous Boneta circa 1296-1328 ....DLB-208

Nabl, Franz 1883-1974.................DLB-81

Nabokov, Vladimir 1899-1977
  .... DLB-2, 244; Y-80, Y-91; DS-3; CDALB-1

The Vladimir Nabokov Archive
  in the Berg Collection Y-91

Nabokov Festival at Cornell Y-83

Nádaši, Ladislav (see Jégé)

Naden, Constance 1858-1889 ....DLB-199

Nadezhdin, Nikolai Ivanovich
  1804-1856 ....DLB-198

Naevius circa 265 B.C.-201 B.C........DLB-211

Nafis and Cornish DLB-49

Nagai, Kafū 1879-1959................DLB-180

Naipaul, Shiva 1945-1985 .... DLB-157; Y-85

Naipaul, V. S. 1932-
  ....DLB-125, 204, 207; Y-85;
  CDBLB-8; CDWLB-3

Nakagami Kenji 1946-1992 ....DLB-182

Nakano-in Masatada no Musume (see Nijō, Lady)

Nałkowska, Zofia 1884-1954...........DLB-215

Nancrede, Joseph [publishing house] DLB-49

Naranjo, Carmen 1930- DLB-145

Narezhny, Vasilii Trofimovich
  1780-1825 ....DLB-198

Narrache, Jean 1893-1970 ....DLB-92

Nasby, Petroleum Vesuvius (see Locke, David Ross)

Nash, Eveleigh [publishing house] DLB-112

Nash, Ogden 1902-1971................DLB-11

Nashe, Thomas 1567-1601?.............DLB-167

Nason, Jerry 1910-1986..............DLB-241

Nast, Conde 1873-1942 ....DLB-91

Nast, Thomas 1840-1902..............DLB-188

Nastasijević, Momčilo 1894-1938 ....DLB-147

Nathan, George Jean 1882-1958 ....DLB-137

Nathan, Robert 1894-1985 ....DLB-9

National Book Critics Circle Awards 2000 ... Y-00

The National Jewish Book Awards Y-85

The National Theatre and the Royal
  Shakespeare Company: The
  National Companies DLB-13

Natsume, Sōseki 1867-1916 ....DLB-180

Naughton, Bill 1910- DLB-13

Navarro, Joe 1953- DLB-209

Naylor, Gloria 1950- DLB-173

Nazor, Vladimir 1876-1949 ....DLB-147

Ndebele, Njabulo 1948- DLB-157

Neagoe, Peter 1881-1960.................DLB-4

Neal, John 1793-1876.........DLB-1, 59, 243

Neal, Joseph C. 1807-1847 ....DLB-11

Neal, Larry 1937-1981.................DLB-38

The Neale Publishing Company DLB-49

Nebel, Frederick 1903-1967............DLB-226

Neely, F. Tennyson [publishing house] DLB-49

Negoiţescu, Ion 1921-1993 ....DLB-220

Negri, Ada 1870-1945 ....DLB-114

"The Negro as a Writer," by
  G. M. McClellan...................DLB-50

"Negro Poets and Their Poetry," by
  Wallace Thurman..................DLB-50

Neidhart von Reuental
  circa 1185-circa 1240...............DLB-138

Neihardt, John G. 1881-1973..........DLB-9, 54

Neilson, John Shaw 1872-1942 ....DLB-230

Neledinsky-Meletsky, Iurii Aleksandrovich
  1752-1828 ....DLB-150

Nelligan, Emile 1879-1941 ....DLB-92

Nelson, Alice Moore Dunbar 1875-1935 ...DLB-50

Nelson, Antonya 1961- DLB-244

Nelson, Kent 1943- DLB-234

Nelson, Thomas, and Sons [U.K.].......DLB-106

Nelson, Thomas, and Sons [U.S.] DLB-49

Nelson, William 1908-1978 ....DLB-103

Nelson, William Rockhill 1841-1915.....DLB-23

Nemerov, Howard 1920-1991 ..... DLB-5, 6; Y-83

Németh, László 1901-1975.............DLB-215

Nepos circa 100 B.C.-post 27 B.C........DLB-211

Nėris, Salomėja
  1904-1945 ....DLB-220; CDWLB-4

Nerval, Gerard de 1808-1855 ....DLB-217

Nesbit, E. 1858-1924 .... DLB-141, 153, 178

Ness, Evaline 1911-1986 ....DLB-61

Nestroy, Johann 1801-1862 ....DLB-133

Neugeboren, Jay 1938- DLB-28

Neukirch, Benjamin 1655-1729 ....DLB-168

Neumann, Alfred 1895-1952 ....DLB-56

Neumann, Ferenc (see Molnár, Ferenc)

Neumark, Georg 1621-1681 ....DLB-164

Neumeister, Erdmann 1671-1756........DLB-168

Nevins, Allan 1890-1971 .... DLB-17; DS-17

Nevinson, Henry Woodd 1856-1941 ....DLB-135

The New American Library DLB-46

New Approaches to Biography: Challenges
  from Critical Theory, USC Conference
  on Literary Studies, 1990 .... Y-90

New Directions Publishing Corporation ...DLB-46

A New Edition of *Huck Finn*...............Y-85

New Forces at Work in the American Theatre:
  1915-1925 ....DLB-7

New Literary Periodicals:
A Report for 1987 . . . . Y-87

New Literary Periodicals:
A Report for 1988 . . . . Y-88

New Literary Periodicals:
A Report for 1989 . . . . Y-89

New Literary Periodicals:
A Report for 1990 . . . . Y-90

New Literary Periodicals:
A Report for 1991 . . . . Y-91

New Literary Periodicals:
A Report for 1992 . . . . Y-92

New Literary Periodicals:
A Report for 1993 . . . . Y-93

The New Monthly Magazine
1814-1884 . . . . DLB-110

The New Variorum Shakespeare Y-85

A New Voice: The Center for the Book's First
Five Years Y-83

The New Wave [Science Fiction] DLB-8

New York City Bookshops in the 1930s and 1940s:
The Recollections of Walter Goldwater . . . Y-93

Newbery, John [publishing house] DLB-154

Newbolt, Henry 1862-1938 . . . . DLB-19

Newbound, Bernard Slade (see Slade, Bernard)

Newby, Eric 1919- DLB-204

Newby, P. H. 1918- DLB-15

Newby, Thomas Cautley
[publishing house] DLB-106

Newcomb, Charles King 1820-1894 . . . DLB-1, 223

Newell, Peter 1862-1924 . . . . DLB-42

Newell, Robert Henry 1836-1901 . . . . DLB-11

Newhouse, Samuel I. 1895-1979 . . . . DLB-127

Newman, Cecil Earl 1903-1976 . . . . DLB-127

Newman, David (see Benton, Robert)

Newman, Frances 1883-1928 . . . . Y-80

Newman, Francis William 1805-1897 . . . . DLB-190

Newman, John Henry
1801-1890 . . . . DLB-18, 32, 55

Newman, Mark [publishing house] DLB-49

Newmarch, Rosa Harriet 1857-1940 . . . . . DLB-240

Newnes, George, Limited DLB-112

Newsome, Effie Lee 1885-1979 . . . . DLB-76

Newspaper Syndication of American
Humor DLB-11

Newton, A. Edward 1864-1940 . . . . DLB-140

Nexø, Martin Andersen 1869-1954 . . . . . DLB-214

Nezval, Vítěslav
1900-1958 . . . . DLB-215; CDWLB-4

Ngugi wa Thiong'o
1938- DLB-125; CDWLB-3

Niatum, Duane 1938- DLB-175

The *Nibelungenlied* and the *Klage*
circa 1200 . . . . DLB-138

Nichol, B. P. 1944- DLB-53

Nicholas of Cusa 1401-1464 . . . . DLB-115

Nichols, Ann 1891?-1966 . . . . DLB-249

Nichols, Beverly 1898-1983 . . . . DLB-191

Nichols, Dudley 1895-1960 . . . . DLB-26

Nichols, Grace 1950- DLB-157

Nichols, John 1940- Y-82

Nichols, Mary Sargeant (Neal) Gove
1810-1884 . . . . DLB-1, 243

Nichols, Peter 1927- DLB-13, 245

Nichols, Roy F. 1896-1973 . . . . DLB-17

Nichols, Ruth 1948- DLB-60

Nicholson, Edward Williams Byron
1849-1912 . . . . DLB-184

Nicholson, Norman 1914- DLB-27

Nicholson, William 1872-1949 . . . . DLB-141

Ní Chuilleanáin, Eiléan 1942- DLB-40

Nicol, Eric 1919- DLB-68

Nicolai, Friedrich 1733-1811 . . . . DLB-97

Nicolas de Clamanges circa 1363-1437 . . . DLB-208

Nicolay, John G. 1832-1901 and
Hay, John 1838-1905 . . . . DLB-47

Nicolson, Adela Florence Cory (see Hope, Laurence)

Nicolson, Harold 1886-1968 . . . . . . .DLB-100, 149

Nicolson, Nigel 1917- DLB-155

Niebuhr, Reinhold 1892-1971 . . . . . .DLB-17; DS-17

Niedecker, Lorine 1903-1970 . . . . DLB-48

Nieman, Lucius W. 1857-1935 . . . . DLB-25

Nietzsche, Friedrich
1844-1900 . . . . DLB-129; CDWLB-2

Nievo, Stanislao 1928- DLB-196

Niggli, Josefina 1910- Y-80

Nightingale, Florence 1820-1910 . . . . . . DLB-166

Nijō, Lady (Nakano-in Masatada no Musume)
1258-after 1306 . . . . DLB-203

Nijō Yoshimoto 1320-1388 . . . . DLB-203

Nikolev, Nikolai Petrovich
1758-1815 . . . . DLB-150

Niles, Hezekiah 1777-1839 . . . . DLB-43

Nims, John Frederick 1913-1999 . . . . DLB-5

Nin, Anaïs 1903-1977 . . . . DLB-2, 4, 152

1985: The Year of the Mystery:
A Symposium Y-85

The 1997 Booker Prize Y-97

The 1998 Booker Prize Y-98

Niño, Raúl 1961- DLB-209

Nissenson, Hugh 1933- DLB-28

Niven, Frederick John 1878-1944 . . . . DLB-92

Niven, Larry 1938- DLB-8

Nixon, Howard M. 1909-1983 . . . . DLB-201

Nizan, Paul 1905-1940 . . . . DLB-72

Njegoš, Petar II Petrović
1813-1851 . . . . .DLB-147; CDWLB-4

Nkosi, Lewis 1936- DLB-157

"The No Self, the Little Self, and the Poets,"
by Richard Moore DLB-105

Nobel Peace Prize

The 1986 Nobel Peace Prize: Elie Wiesel Y-86

The Nobel Prize and Literary Politics Y-86

Nobel Prize in Literature

The 1982 Nobel Prize in Literature:
Gabriel García Márquez Y-82

The 1983 Nobel Prize in Literature:
William Golding Y-83

The 1984 Nobel Prize in Literature:
Jaroslav Seifert Y-84

The 1985 Nobel Prize in Literature:
Claude Simon Y-85

The 1986 Nobel Prize in Literature:
Wole Soyinka Y-86

The 1987 Nobel Prize in Literature:
Joseph Brodsky Y-87

The 1988 Nobel Prize in Literature:
Najīb Mahfūz Y-88

The 1989 Nobel Prize in Literature:
Camilo José Cela Y-89

The 1990 Nobel Prize in Literature:
Octavio Paz Y-90

The 1991 Nobel Prize in Literature:
Nadine Gordimer Y-91

The 1992 Nobel Prize in Literature:
Derek Walcott Y-92

The 1993 Nobel Prize in Literature:
Toni Morrison Y-93

The 1994 Nobel Prize in Literature:
Kenzaburō Ōe Y-94

The 1995 Nobel Prize in Literature:
Seamus Heaney Y-95

The 1996 Nobel Prize in Literature:
Wisława Szymborsha Y-96

The 1997 Nobel Prize in Literature:
Dario Fo Y-97

The 1998 Nobel Prize in Literature:
José Saramago Y-98

The 1999 Nobel Prize in Literature:
Günter Grass Y-99

The 2000 Nobel Prize in Literature:
Gao Xingjian Y-00

Nodier, Charles 1780-1844 . . . . DLB-119

Noel, Roden 1834-1894 . . . . DLB-35

Nogami, Yaeko 1885-1985 . . . . DLB-180

Nogo, Rajko Petrov 1945- DLB-181

Nolan, William F. 1928- DLB-8

Noland, C. F. M. 1810?-1858 . . . . DLB-11

Noma Hiroshi 1915-1991 . . . . DLB-182

Nonesuch Press DLB-112

Noonan, Robert Phillipe (see Tressell, Robert)

Noonday Press DLB-46

Noone, John 1936- DLB-14

Nora, Eugenio de 1923- DLB-134

Nordan, Lewis 1939- DLB-234

Nordbrandt, Henrik 1945- DLB-214

Nordhoff, Charles 1887-1947 . . . . DLB-9

Norman, Charles 1904-1996 . . . . DLB-111

Norman, Marsha 1947- Y-84

Norris, Charles G. 1881-1945 . . . . DLB-9

Norris, Frank
1870-1902 . . . . DLB-12, 71, 186; CDALB-3

Norris, Leslie 1921- DLB-27

Norse, Harold 1916- DLB-16

Norte, Marisela 1955- DLB-209

North, Marianne 1830-1890 . . . . .DLB-174

North Point Press DLB-46

Nortje, Arthur 1942-1970 . . . . DLB-125

Norton, Alice Mary (see Norton, Andre)

Norton, Andre 1912- DLB-8, 52

Norton, Andrews 1786-1853 . . . . DLB-1, 235

Norton, Caroline 1808-1877 . . . . DLB-21, 159, 199

Norton, Charles Eliot 1827-1908 . . . DLB-1, 64, 235

Norton, John 1606-1663 . . . . DLB-24

Norton, Mary 1903-1992 . . . . DLB-160

Norton, Thomas (see Sackville, Thomas)

Norton, W. W., and Company DLB-46

Norwood, Robert 1874-1932 . . . . DLB-92

Nosaka Akiyuki 1930- DLB-182

Nossack, Hans Erich 1901-1977 . . . . DLB-69

Not Immediately Discernible . . . but Eventually
    Quite Clear: The *First Light* and *Final Years*
    of Hemingway's Centenary Y-99

A Note on Technique (1926), by
    Elizabeth A. Drew [excerpts] DLB-36

Notker Balbulus circa 840-912 . . . . DLB-148

Notker III of Saint Gall
    circa 950-1022 . . . . DLB-148

Notker von Zweifalten ?-1095 . . . . DLB-148

Nourse, Alan E. 1928- DLB-8

Novak, Slobodan 1924- DLB-181

Novak, Vjenceslav
    1859-1905 . . . . DLB-147

Novakovich, Josip 1956- DLB-244

Novalis 1772-1801 . . . . DLB-90; CDWLB-2

Novaro, Mario 1868-1944 . . . . DLB-114

Novás Calvo, Lino
    1903-1983 . . . . DLB-145

"The Novel in [Robert Browning's] 'The Ring and
    the Book'" (1912), by Henry James . . . DLB-32

The Novel of Impressionism,
    by Jethro Bithell DLB-66

Novel-Reading: *The Works of Charles Dickens,*
    The Works of W. Makepeace Thackeray
    (1879), by Anthony Trollope DLB-21

Novels for Grown-Ups Y-97

The Novels of Dorothy Richardson (1918),
    by May Sinclair DLB-36

Novels with a Purpose (1864), by
    Justin M'Carthy DLB-21

Noventa, Giacomo 1898-1960 . . . . DLB-114

Novikov, Nikolai
    Ivanovich 1744-1818 . . . . DLB-150

Novomeský, Laco
    1904-1976 . . . . DLB-215

Nowlan, Alden 1933-1983 . . . . DLB-53

Noyes, Alfred 1880-1958 . . . . DLB-20

Noyes, Crosby S. 1825-1908 . . . . DLB-23

Noyes, Nicholas 1647-1717 . . . . DLB-24

Noyes, Theodore W. 1858-1946 . . . . DLB-29

N-Town Plays circa 1468 to early
    sixteenth century DLB-146

Nugent, Frank 1908-1965 . . . . DLB-44

Nugent, Richard Bruce 1906- DLB-151

Nušić, Branislav
    1864-1938 . . . . DLB-147; CDWLB-4

Nutt, David [publishing house] DLB-106

Nwapa, Flora 1931-1993 . . . . DLB-125; CDWLB-3

Nye, Bill 1850-1896 . . . . DLB-186

Nye, Edgar Wilson (Bill) 1850-1896 . . . DLB-11, 23

Nye, Naomi Shihab 1952- DLB-120

Nye, Robert 1939- DLB-14

Nyka-Niliūnas, Alfonsas
    1919- DLB-220

O

Oakes Smith, Elizabeth
    1806-1893 . . . . DLB-1, 239, 243

Oakes, Urian circa 1631-1681 . . . . DLB-24

Oakley, Violet 1874-1961 . . . . DLB-188

Oates, Joyce Carol 1938- . . . DLB-2, 5, 130; Y-81

Ōba Minako 1930- DLB-182

Ober, Frederick Albion 1849-1913 . . . . . . DLB-189

Ober, William 1920-1993 . . . . Y-93

Oberholtzer, Ellis Paxson 1868-1936 . . . . . . DLB-47

Obradović, Dositej 1740?-1811 . . . . DLB-147

O'Brien, Charlotte Grace 1845-1909 . . . . . DLB-240

O'Brien, Edna 1932- . . . DLB-14, 231; CDBLB-8

O'Brien, Fitz-James 1828-1862 . . . . DLB-74

O'Brien, Flann (see O'Nolan, Brian)

O'Brien, Kate 1897-1974 . . . . DLB-15

O'Brien, Tim
    1946- DLB-152; Y-80; DS-9; CDALB-7

O'Casey, Sean 1880-1964 . . . . . DLB-10; CDBLB-6

Occom, Samson 1723-1792 . . . . DLB-175

Ochs, Adolph S. 1858-1935 . . . . DLB-25

Ochs-Oakes, George Washington
    1861-1931 . . . . DLB-137

O'Connor, Flannery 1925-1964
    . . . . DLB-2, 152; Y-80; DS-12; CDALB-1

O'Connor, Frank 1903-1966 . . . . DLB-162

Octopus Publishing Group DLB-112

Oda Sakunosuke 1913-1947 . . . . DLB-182

Odell, Jonathan 1737-1818 . . . . DLB-31, 99

O'Dell, Scott 1903-1989 . . . . DLB-52

Odets, Clifford 1906-1963 . . . . DLB-7, 26

Odhams Press Limited DLB-112

Odoevsky, Aleksandr Ivanovich
    1802-1839 . . . . DLB-205

Odoevsky, Vladimir Fedorovich
    1804 or 1803-1869 . . . . DLB-198

O'Donnell, Peter 1920- DLB-87

O'Donovan, Michael (see O'Connor, Frank)

O'Dowd, Bernard 1866-1953 . . . . DLB-230

Ōe Kenzaburō 1935- DLB-182; Y-94

O'Faolain, Julia 1932- DLB-14, 231

O'Faolain, Sean 1900- DLB-15, 162

Off Broadway and Off-Off Broadway DLB-7

Off-Loop Theatres DLB-7

Offord, Carl Ruthven 1910- DLB-76

O'Flaherty, Liam 1896-1984 . . . DLB-36, 162; Y-84

Ogilvie, J. S., and Company DLB-49

Ogilvy, Eliza 1822-1912 . . . . DLB-199

Ogot, Grace 1930- DLB-125

O'Grady, Desmond 1935- DLB-40

Ogunyemi, Wale 1939- DLB-157

O'Hagan, Howard 1902-1982 . . . . DLB-68

O'Hara, Frank 1926-1966 . . . . DLB-5, 16, 193

O'Hara, John
    1905-1970 . . . . DLB-9, 86; DS-2; CDALB-5

John O'Hara's Pottsville Journalism Y-88

O'Hegarty, P. S. 1879-1955 . . . . DLB-201

Okara, Gabriel 1921- DLB-125; CDWLB-3

O'Keeffe, John 1747-1833 . . . . DLB-89

Okes, Nicholas [publishing house] DLB-170

Okigbo, Christopher
    1930-1967 . . . . DLB-125; CDWLB-3

Okot p'Bitek 1931-1982 . . . . . DLB-125; CDWLB-3

Okpewho, Isidore 1941- DLB-157

Okri, Ben 1959- DLB-157, 231

Olaudah Equiano and Unfinished Journeys:
    The Slave-Narrative Tradition and
    Twentieth-Century Continuities, by
    Paul Edwards and Pauline T.
    Wangman DLB-117

Old English Literature:
    An Introduction DLB-146

Old English Riddles
    eighth to tenth centuries DLB-146

Old Franklin Publishing House DLB-49

Old German Genesis and *Old German Exodus*
    circa 1050-circa 1130 . . . . DLB-148

Old High German Charms and
    Blessings DLB-148; CDWLB-2

The *Old High German Isidor*
    circa 790-800 . . . . DLB-148

The Old Manse DLB-223

Older, Fremont 1856-1935 . . . . DLB-25

Oldham, John 1653-1683 . . . . DLB-131

Oldman, C. B. 1894-1969 . . . . DLB-201

Olds, Sharon 1942- DLB-120

Olearius, Adam 1599-1671 . . . . DLB-164

O'Leary, Ellen 1831-1889 . . . . DLB-240

Oliphant, Laurence 1829?-1888 . . . . . DLB-18, 166

Oliphant, Margaret 1828-1897 . . . . . . DLB-18, 190

Oliver, Chad 1928- DLB-8

Oliver, Mary 1935- DLB-5, 193

Ollier, Claude 1922- DLB-83

Olsen, Tillie 1912 or 1913-
    . . . . DLB-28, 206; Y-80; CDALB-7

Olson, Charles 1910-1970 . . . . DLB-5, 16, 193

Olson, Elder 1909- DLB-48, 63

Omotoso, Kole 1943- DLB-125

Omulevsky, Innokentii Vasil'evich
    1836 [or 1837]-1883 . . . . DLB-238

On Learning to Write Y-88

Ondaatje, Michael 1943- DLB-60

O'Neill, Eugene 1888-1953 . . . . . DLB-7; CDALB-5

Eugene O'Neill Memorial Theater
    Center DLB-7

Eugene O'Neill's Letters: A Review Y-88

Onetti, Juan Carlos
    1909-1994 . . . . DLB-113; CDWLB-3

Onions, George Oliver 1872-1961 . . . . . . DLB-153

Onofri, Arturo 1885-1928 . . . . DLB-114

O'Nolan, Brian 1911-1966 . . . . DLB-231

Opie, Amelia 1769-1853 . . . . DLB-116, 159

Opitz, Martin 1597-1639 . . . . DLB-164

Oppen, George 1908-1984 . . . . DLB-5, 165

Oppenheim, E. Phillips 1866-1946 . . . . . . DLB-70

Oppenheim, James 1882-1932 . . . . DLB-28

Oppenheimer, Joel 1930-1988 . . . . DLB-5, 193

Optic, Oliver (see Adams, William Taylor)

Oral History: B. W. Huebsch. Y-99

Oral History Interview with Donald S.
    Klopfer. Y-97

Orczy, Emma, Baroness 1865-1947 . . . . . . DLB-70

Oregon Shakespeare Festival Y-00

Origo, Iris 1902-1988 . . . . DLB-155

Orlovitz, Gil 1918-1973 . . . . DLB-2, 5

Orlovsky, Peter 1933- DLB-16

Ormond, John 1923- DLB-27

Ornitz, Samuel 1890-1957 . . . . DLB-28, 44

O'Rourke, P. J. 1947- DLB-185

Orten, Jiří 1919-1941 . . . . DLB-215

Ortese, Anna Maria 1914- DLB-177

Ortiz, Simon J. 1941- DLB-120, 175

Ortnit and Wolfdietrich circa 1225-1250 . . . . DLB-138

Orton, Joe 1933-1967 . . . . DLB-13; CDBLB-8

Orwell, George
    1903-1950 . . . . . . DLB-15, 98, 195; CDBLB-7

The Orwell Year. Y-84

(Re-)Publishing Orwell Y-86

Ory, Carlos Edmundo de 1923- DLB-134

Osbey, Brenda Marie 1957- DLB-120

Osbon, B. S. 1827-1912. . . . . DLB-43

Osborn, Sarah 1714-1796 . . . . DLB-200

Osborne, John 1929-1994. . . . . DLB-13; CDBLB-8

Osgood, Herbert L. 1855-1918. . . . . DLB-47

Osgood, James R., and Company DLB-49

Osgood, McIlvaine and Company DLB-112

O'Shaughnessy, Arthur 1844-1881. . . . . . DLB-35

O'Shea, Patrick [publishing house] DLB-49

Osipov, Nikolai Petrovich
    1751-1799 . . . . DLB-150

Oskison, John Milton 1879-1947. . . . . . . .DLB-175

Osler, Sir William 1849-1919 . . . . DLB-184

Osofisan, Femi 1946- DLB-125; CDWLB-3

Ostenso, Martha 1900-1963 . . . . DLB-92

Ostrauskas, Kostas 1926- DLB-232

Ostriker, Alicia 1937- DLB-120

Osundare, Niyi 1947- DLB-157; CDWLB-3

Oswald, Eleazer 1755-1795 . . . . DLB-43

Oswald von Wolkenstein
    1376 or 1377-1445 . . . . .DLB-179

Otero, Blas de 1916-1979 . . . . DLB-134

Otero, Miguel Antonio 1859-1944 . . . . . . DLB-82

Otero, Nina 1881-1965. . . . . DLB-209

Otero Silva, Miguel 1908-1985. . . . . DLB-145

Otfried von Weißenburg
    circa 800-circa 875? DLB-148

Otis, Broaders and Company DLB-49

Otis, James (see Kaler, James Otis)

Otis, James, Jr. 1725-1783 . . . . DLB-31

Ottaway, James 1911- DLB-127

Ottendorfer, Oswald 1826-1900. . . . . DLB-23

Ottieri, Ottiero 1924- DLB-177

Otto-Peters, Louise 1819-1895 . . . . DLB-129

Otway, Thomas 1652-1685 . . . . DLB-80

Ouellette, Fernand 1930- DLB-60

Ouida 1839-1908 . . . . DLB-18, 156

Outing Publishing Company DLB-46

Outlaw Days, by Joyce Johnson. DLB-16

Overbury, Sir Thomas
    circa 1581-1613 . . . . DLB-151

The Overlook Press DLB-46

Overview of U.S. Book Publishing,
    1910-1945 . . . . DLB-9

Ovid 43 B.C.-A.D. 17 . . . . . . DLB-211; CDWLB-1

Owen, Guy 1925- DLB-5

Owen, John 1564-1622. . . . . DLB-121

Owen, John [publishing house]. DLB-49

Owen, Peter, Limited DLB-112

Owen, Robert 1771-1858 . . . . .DLB-107, 158

Owen, Wilfred
    1893-1918 . . . . DLB-20; DS-18; CDBLB-6

The Owl and the Nightingale
    circa 1189-1199 . . . . DLB-146

Owsley, Frank L. 1890-1956 . . . . DLB-17

Oxford, Seventeenth Earl of, Edward
    de Vere 1550-1604. . . . . .DLB-172

Ozerov, Vladislav Aleksandrovich
    1769-1816. DLB-150

Ozick, Cynthia 1928- DLB-28, 152; Y-83

First Strauss "Livings" Awarded to Cynthia
    Ozick and Raymond Carver
    An Interview with Cynthia Ozick Y-83

P

Pace, Richard 1482?-1536 . . . . DLB-167

Pacey, Desmond 1917-1975 . . . . DLB-88

Pack, Robert 1929- DLB-5

Packaging Papa: The Garden of Eden Y-86

Padell Publishing Company DLB-46

Padgett, Ron 1942- DLB-5

Padilla, Ernesto Chávez 1944- DLB-122

Page, L. C., and Company. DLB-49

Page, Louise 1955- DLB-233

Page, P. K. 1916- DLB-68

Page, Thomas Nelson
    1853-1922 . . . . .DLB-12, 78; DS-13

Page, Walter Hines 1855-1918. . . . . . . DLB-71, 91

Paget, Francis Edward 1806-1882 . . . . . . DLB-163

Paget, Violet (see Lee, Vernon)

Pagliarani, Elio 1927- DLB-128

Pain, Barry 1864-1928 . . . . .DLB-135, 197

Pain, Philip ?-circa 1666 . . . . DLB-24

Paine, Robert Treat, Jr. 1773-1811 . . . . . . DLB-37

Paine, Thomas
    1737-1809 . . . . DLB-31, 43, 73, 158; CDALB-2

Painter, George D. 1914- DLB-155

Painter, William 1540?-1594 . . . . DLB-136

Palazzeschi, Aldo 1885-1974. . . . . DLB-114

Paley, Grace 1922- DLB-28, 218

Palfrey, John Gorham 1796-1881 . . DLB-1, 30, 235

Palgrave, Francis Turner 1824-1897. . . . . . DLB-35

Palmer, Joe H. 1904-1952. . . . . .DLB-171

Palmer, Michael 1943- DLB-169

Paltock, Robert 1697-1767 . . . . DLB-39

Paludan, Jacob 1896-1975. . . . . DLB-214

Pan Books Limited DLB-112

Panama, Norman 1914- and
    Frank, Melvin 1913-1988. . . . . DLB-26

Panaev, Ivan Ivanovich 1812-1862. . . . . . DLB-198

Panaeva, Avdot'ia Iakovlevna
    1820-1893 . . . . DLB-238

Pancake, Breece D'J 1952-1979. . . . . DLB-130

Panduro, Leif 1923-1977 . . . . DLB-214

Panero, Leopoldo 1909-1962 . . . . DLB-108

Pangborn, Edgar 1909-1976 . . . . DLB-8

"Panic Among the Philistines": A Postscript,
    An Interview with Bryan Griffin Y-81

Panizzi, Sir Anthony 1797-1879. . . . . DLB-184

Panneton, Philippe (see Ringuet)

Panshin, Alexei 1940- DLB-8

Pansy (see Alden, Isabella)

Pantheon Books DLB-46

Papadat-Bengescu, Hortensia
    1876-1955. DLB-220

Papantonio, Michael (see Kohn, John S. Van E.)

Paperback Library DLB-46

Paperback Science Fiction. DLB-8

Paquet, Alfons 1881-1944. . . . . DLB-66

Paracelsus 1493-1541 . . . . .DLB-179

Paradis, Suzanne 1936- DLB-53

Páral, Vladimír, 1932- DLB-232

Pardoe, Julia 1804-1862 . . . . DLB-166

Paredes, Américo 1915-1999 . . . . DLB-209

Pareja Diezcanseco, Alfredo 1908-1993 . . DLB-145

Parents' Magazine Press DLB-46

Parise, Goffredo 1929-1986 . . . . .DLB-177

Parisian Theater, Fall 1984: Toward
    A New Baroque Y-85

Parizeau, Alice 1930- DLB-60

Parke, John 1754-1789 . . . . DLB-31

Parker, Dan 1893-1967. . . . . DLB-241

Parker, Dorothy 1893-1967 . . . . . . DLB-11, 45, 86

Parker, Gilbert 1860-1932 . . . . DLB-99

Parker, J. H. [publishing house] DLB-106

Parker, James 1714-1770. . . . . .DLB-43

Parker, John [publishing house]. DLB-106

Parker, Matthew 1504-1575. . . . . .DLB-213

Parker, Stewart 1941-1988. . . . . .DLB-245

Parker, Theodore 1810-1860. . . . . .DLB-1, 235

Parker, William Riley 1906-1968 . . . . . . .DLB-103

Parkes, Bessie Rayner (Madame Belloc)
   1829-1925 . . . . .DLB-240

Parkman, Francis
   1823-1893 . . . . .DLB-1, 30, 183, 186, 235

Parks, Gordon 1912- DLB-33

Parks, Tim 1954- DLB-231

Parks, William 1698-1750 . . . . .DLB-43

Parks, William [publishing house] DLB-49

Parley, Peter (see Goodrich, Samuel Griswold)

Parmenides
   late sixth-fifth century B.C. DLB-176

Parnell, Thomas 1679-1718 . . . . .DLB-95

Parnicki, Teodor 1908-1988 . . . . .DLB-215

Parr, Catherine 1513?-1548. . . . . .DLB-136

Parrington, Vernon L. 1871-1929 . . . . . DLB-17, 63

Parrish, Maxfield 1870-1966 . . . . .DLB-188

Parronchi, Alessandro 1914- DLB-128

Parton, James 1822-1891 . . . . .DLB-30

Parton, Sara Payson Willis
   1811-1872 . . . . DLB-43, 74, 239

Partridge, S. W., and Company. DLB-106

Parun, Vesna 1922- DLB-181; CDWLB-4

Pasinetti, Pier Maria 1913- DLB-177

Pasolini, Pier Paolo 1922- DLB-128, 177

Pastan, Linda 1932- DLB-5

Paston, George (Emily Morse Symonds)
   1860-1936 . . . . .DLB-149, 197

The Paston Letters 1422-1509 . . . . .DLB-146

Pastorius, Francis Daniel
   1651-circa 1720 . . . . .DLB-24

Patchen, Kenneth 1911-1972 . . . . .DLB-16, 48

Pater, Walter
   1839-1894 . . . . .DLB-57, 156; CDBLB-4

Aesthetic Poetry (1873) DLB-35

Paterson, A. B. "Banjo" 1864-1941 . . . . . .DLB-230

Paterson, Katherine 1932- DLB-52

Patmore, Coventry 1823-1896. . . . . . .DLB-35, 98

Paton, Alan 1903-1988. . . . . DS-17

Paton, Joseph Noel 1821-1901. . . . . .DLB-35

Paton Walsh, Jill 1937- DLB-161

Patrick, Edwin Hill ("Ted") 1901-1964 . . .DLB-137

Patrick, John 1906-1995. . . . . .DLB-7

Pattee, Fred Lewis 1863-1950 . . . . .DLB-71

Pattern and Paradigm: History as
   Design, by Judith Ryan DLB-75

Patterson, Alicia 1906-1963 . . . . .DLB-127

Patterson, Eleanor Medill 1881-1948. . . . . .DLB-29

Patterson, Eugene 1923- DLB-127

Patterson, Joseph Medill 1879-1946. . . . . . .DLB-29

Pattillo, Henry 1726-1801 . . . . .DLB-37

Paul, Elliot 1891-1958 . . . . .DLB-4

Paul, Jean (see Richter, Johann Paul Friedrich)

Paul, Kegan, Trench, Trubner and
   Company Limited DLB-106

Paul, Peter, Book Company DLB-49

Paul, Stanley, and Company Limited DLB-112

Paulding, James Kirke 1778-1860. . . . DLB-3, 59, 74

Paulin, Tom 1949- DLB-40

Pauper, Peter, Press. DLB-46

Pavese, Cesare 1908-1950 . . . . DLB-128, 177

Pavić, Milorad 1929- DLB-181; CDWLB-4

Pavlov, Konstantin 1933- DLB-181

Pavlov, Nikolai Filippovich 1803-1864. . . . .DLB-198

Pavlova, Karolina Karlovna 1807-1893 . . . .DLB-205

Pavlović, Miodrag
   1928- DLB-181; CDWLB-4

Paxton, John 1911-1985. . . . . .DLB-44

Payn, James 1830-1898 . . . . .DLB-18

Payne, John 1842-1916 . . . . .DLB-35

Payne, John Howard 1791-1852 . . . . .DLB-37

Payson and Clarke. DLB-46

Paz, Octavio 1914-1998. . . . . .Y-90, Y-98

Pazzi, Roberto 1946- DLB-196

Peabody, Elizabeth Palmer 1804-1894. .DLB-1, 223

Peabody, Elizabeth Palmer
   [publishing house] DLB-49

Peabody, Josephine Preston 1874-1922 . . .DLB-249

Peabody, Oliver William Bourn
   1799-1848 . . . . .DLB-59

Peace, Roger 1899-1968 . . . . .DLB-127

Peacham, Henry 1578-1644? DLB-151

Peacham, Henry, the Elder
   1547-1634 . . . . DLB-172, 236

Peachtree Publishers, Limited DLB-46

Peacock, Molly 1947- DLB-120

Peacock, Thomas Love 1785-1866 . . .DLB-96, 116

Pead, Deuel ?-1727. . . . . .DLB-24

Peake, Mervyn 1911-1968. . . . . DLB-15, 160

Peale, Rembrandt 1778-1860 . . . . .DLB-183

Pear Tree Press .DLB-112

Pearce, Philippa 1920- DLB-161

Pearson, H. B. [publishing house] DLB-49

Pearson, Hesketh 1887-1964 . . . . .DLB-149

Pechersky, Andrei (see Mel'nikov, Pavel Ivanovich)

Peck, George W. 1840-1916 . . . . DLB-23, 42

Peck, H. C., and Theo. Bliss
   [publishing house] DLB-49

Peck, Harry Thurston 1856-1914 . . . . .DLB-71, 91

Peden, William 1913-1999. . . . . .DLB-234

Peele, George 1556-1596 . . . . .DLB-62, 167

Pegler, Westbrook 1894-1969 . . . . .DLB-171

Pekić, Borislav 1930-1992 . . .DLB-181; CDWLB-4

Pellegrini and Cudahy. DLB-46

Pelletier, Aimé (see Vac, Bertrand)

Pemberton, Sir Max 1863-1950. . . . . .DLB-70

de la Peña, Terri 1947- DLB-209

Penfield, Edward 1866-1925 . . . . .DLB-188

Penguin Books [U.K.] DLB-112

Penguin Books [U.S.]. DLB-46

Penn Publishing Company DLB-49

Penn, William 1644-1718. . . . . .DLB-24

Penna, Sandro 1906-1977 . . . . .DLB-114

Pennell, Joseph 1857-1926 . . . . .DLB-188

Penner, Jonathan 1940- Y-83

Pennington, Lee 1939- Y-82

Pepys, Samuel
   1633-1703 . . . . .DLB-101, 213; CDBLB-2

Percy, Thomas 1729-1811 . . . . .DLB-104

Percy, Walker 1916-1990 . . . . . DLB-2; Y-80, Y-90

Percy, William 1575-1648 . . . . .DLB-172

Perec, Georges 1936-1982 . . . . .DLB-83

Perelman, Bob 1947- DLB-193

Perelman, S. J. 1904-1979 . . . . .DLB-11, 44

Perez, Raymundo "Tigre" 1946- DLB-122

Peri Rossi, Cristina 1941- DLB-145

Perkins, Eugene 1932- DLB-41

Perkoff, Stuart Z. 1930-1974 . . . . .DLB-16

Perley, Moses Henry 1804-1862 . . . . .DLB-99

Permabooks. DLB-46

Perovsky, Aleksei Alekseevich
   (Antonii Pogorel'sky) 1787-1836 . . . . .DLB-198

Perri, Henry 1561-1617 . . . . .DLB-236

Perrin, Alice 1867-1934 . . . . .DLB-156

Perry, Bliss 1860-1954. . . . . .DLB-71

Perry, Eleanor 1915-1981 . . . . .DLB-44

Perry, Henry (see Perri, Henry)

Perry, Matthew 1794-1858. . . . . .DLB-183

Perry, Sampson 1747-1823 . . . . .DLB-158

Persius A.D. 34-A.D. 62 . . . . .DLB-211

Perutz, Leo 1882-1957. . . . . .DLB-81

Pesetsky, Bette 1932- DLB-130

Pestalozzi, Johann Heinrich 1746-1827 . . . .DLB-94

Peter, Laurence J. 1919-1990. . . . . .DLB-53

Peter of Spain circa 1205-1277. . . . . .DLB-115

Peterkin, Julia 1880-1961. . . . . .DLB-9

Peters, Lenrie 1932- DLB-117

Peters, Robert 1924- DLB-105

"Foreword to *Ludwig of Bavaria*". DLB-105

Petersham, Maud 1889-1971 and
   Petersham, Miska 1888-1960 . . . . . . .DLB-22

Peterson, Charles Jacobs 1819-1887 . . . . . .DLB-79

Peterson, Len 1917- DLB-88

Peterson, Levi S. 1933- DLB-206

Peterson, Louis 1922-1998 . . . . .DLB-76

Peterson, T. B., and Brothers DLB-49

Petitclair, Pierre 1813-1860 . . . . .DLB-99

Petrescu, Camil 1894-1957 . . . . .DLB-220

Petronius circa A.D. 20-A.D. 66
   . . . . DLB-211; CDWLB-1

Petrov, Aleksandar 1938- DLB-181

Petrov, Gavriil 1730-1801 . . . . .DLB-150

Petrov, Valeri 1920- DLB-181

Petrov, Vasilii Petrovich 1736-1799 . . . . . DLB-150

Petrović, Rastko
 1898-1949 . . . . .DLB-147; CDWLB-4

Petruslied circa 854? DLB-148

Petry, Ann 1908-1997 . . . . DLB-76

Pettie, George circa 1548-1589 . . . . DLB-136

Peyton, K. M. 1929- DLB-161

Pfaffe Konrad flourished circa 1172 . . . . . DLB-148

Pfaffe Lamprecht flourished circa 1150 . . DLB-148

Pfeiffer, Emily 1827-1890 . . . . DLB-199

Pforzheimer, Carl H. 1879-1957 . . . . DLB-140

Phaedrus circa 18 B.C.-circa A.D. 50 . . . . DLB-211

Phaer, Thomas 1510?-1560 . . . . DLB-167

Phaidon Press Limited DLB-112

Pharr, Robert Deane 1916-1992 . . . . DLB-33

Phelps, Elizabeth Stuart 1815-1852 . . . . . DLB-202

Phelps, Elizabeth Stuart 1844-1911 . . . DLB-74, 221

Philander von der Linde
 (see Mencke, Johann Burckhard)

Philby, H. St. John B. 1885-1960 . . . . DLB-195

Philip, Marlene Nourbese 1947- DLB-157

Philippe, Charles-Louis 1874-1909 . . . . . . DLB-65

Philips, John 1676-1708 . . . . DLB-95

Philips, Katherine 1632-1664 . . . . DLB-131

Phillipps, Sir Thomas 1792-1872 . . . . . . DLB-184

Phillips, Caryl 1958- DLB-157

Phillips, David Graham 1867-1911 . . . . . DLB-9, 12

Phillips, Jayne Anne 1952- Y-80

Phillips, Robert 1938- DLB-105

 "Finding, Losing, Reclaiming: A Note
 on My Poems" DLB-105

Phillips, Sampson and Company DLB-49

Phillips, Stephen 1864-1915 . . . . DLB-10

Phillips, Ulrich B. 1877-1934 . . . . DLB-17

Phillips, Wendell 1811-1884 . . . . DLB-235

Phillips, Willard 1784-1873 . . . . DLB-59

Phillips, William 1907- DLB-137

Phillpotts, Adelaide Eden (Adelaide Ross)
 1896-1993 . . . . DLB-191

Phillpotts, Eden 1862-1960 . . .DLB-10, 70, 135, 153

Philo circa 20-15 B.C.-circa A.D. 50 . . . . . .DLB-176

Philosophical Library DLB-46

Phinney, Elihu [publishing house] DLB-49

Phoenix, John (see Derby, George Horatio)

PHYLON (Fourth Quarter, 1950),
 The Negro in Literature:
 The Current Scene DLB-76

Physiologus circa 1070-circa 1150 . . . . DLB-148

Piccolo, Lucio 1903-1969 . . . . DLB-114

Pickard, Tom 1946- DLB-40

Pickering, William [publishing house] . . . DLB-106

Pickthall, Marjorie 1883-1922 . . . . DLB-92

Pictorial Printing Company DLB-49

Piercy, Marge 1936- DLB-120, 227

Pierro, Albino 1916- DLB-128

Pignotti, Lamberto 1926- DLB-128

Pike, Albert 1809-1891 . . . . DLB-74

Pike, Zebulon Montgomery
 1779-1813 . . . . DLB-183

Pillat, Ion 1891-1945 . . . . DLB-220

Pilon, Jean-Guy 1930- DLB-60

Pinckney, Eliza Lucas 1722-1793 . . . . . . DLB-200

Pinckney, Josephine 1895-1957 . . . . DLB-6

Pindar circa 518 B.C.-circa 438 B.C.
 . . . . DLB-176; CDWLB-1

Pindar, Peter (see Wolcot, John)

Pineda, Cecile 1942- DLB-209

Pinero, Arthur Wing 1855-1934 . . . . DLB-10

Pinget, Robert 1919-1997 . . . . DLB-83

Pinkney, Edward Coote 1802-1828 . . . . . DLB-248

Pinnacle Books DLB-46

Piñon, Nélida 1935- DLB-145

Pinsky, Robert 1940- Y-82

 Robert Pinsky Reappointed Poet Laureate Y-98

Pinter, Harold 1930- DLB-13; CDBLB-8

Piontek, Heinz 1925- DLB-75

Piozzi, Hester Lynch [Thrale]
 1741-1821 . . . . DLB-104, 142

Piper, H. Beam 1904-1964 . . . . DLB-8

Piper, Watty DLB-22

Pirckheimer, Caritas 1467-1532 . . . . .DLB-179

Pirckheimer, Willibald 1470-1530 . . . . . .DLB-179

Pisar, Samuel 1929- Y-83

Pisemsky, Aleksai Feofilaktovich
 1821-1881 . . . . DLB-238

Pitkin, Timothy 1766-1847 . . . . DLB-30

The Pitt Poetry Series: Poetry Publishing
 Today Y-85

Pitter, Ruth 1897- DLB-20

Pix, Mary 1666-1709 . . . . DLB-80

Pixerécourt, René Charles Guilbert de
 1773-1844 . . . . DLB-192

Plaatje, Sol T. 1876-1932 . . . . DLB-125, 225

Plante, David 1940- Y-83

Platen, August von 1796-1835 . . . . DLB-90

Plath, Sylvia
 1932-1963 . . . . DLB-5, 6, 152; CDALB-1

Plato circa 428 B.C.-348-347 B.C.
 . . . . DLB-176; CDWLB-1

Plato, Ann 1824?-? DLB-239

Platon 1737-1812 . . . . DLB-150

Platt and Munk Company DLB-46

Plautus circa 254 B.C.-184 B.C.
 . . . . DLB-211; CDWLB-1

Playboy Press DLB-46

Playford, John [publishing house] DLB-170

Plays, Playwrights, and Playgoers DLB-84

Playwrights on the Theater DLB-80

Der Pleier flourished circa 1250 . . . . DLB-138

Plenzdorf, Ulrich 1934- DLB-75

Plessen, Elizabeth 1944- DLB-75

Pletnev, Petr Aleksandrovich
 1792-1865 . . . . DLB-205

Pliekšāne, Elza Rozenberga (see Aspazija)

Pliekšāns, Jānis (see Rainis, Jānis)

Plievier, Theodor 1892-1955 . . . . DLB-69

Plimpton, George 1927- DLB-185, 241; Y-99

Pliny the Elder A.D. 23/24-A.D. 79 . . . . . DLB-211

Pliny the Younger
 circa A.D. 61-A.D. 112 . . . . DLB-211

Plomer, William
 1903-1973 . . . . .DLB-20, 162, 191, 225

Plotinus 204-270 . . . . .DLB-176; CDWLB-1

Plume, Thomas 1630-1704 . . . . DLB-213

Plumly, Stanley 1939- DLB-5, 193

Plumpp, Sterling D. 1940- DLB-41

Plunkett, James 1920- DLB-14

Plutarch
 circa 46-circa 120 . . . . . . .DLB-176; CDWLB-1

Plymell, Charles 1935- DLB-16

Pocket Books DLB-46

Poe, Edgar Allan 1809-1849
 . . . . .DLB-3, 59, 73, 74, 248; CDALB-2

Poe, James 1921-1980 . . . . DLB-44

The Poet Laureate of the United States
 Statements from Former Consultants
 in Poetry Y-86

Pogodin, Mikhail Petrovich
 1800-1875 . . . . DLB-198

Pogorel'sky, Antonii
 (see Perovsky, Aleksei Alekseevich)

Pohl, Frederik 1919- DLB-8

Poirier, Louis (see Gracq, Julien)

Poláček, Karel 1892-1945 . . . .DLB-215; CDWLB-4

Polanyi, Michael 1891-1976 . . . . DLB-100

Pole, Reginald 1500-1558 . . . . DLB-132

Polevoi, Nikolai Alekseevich
 1796-1846 . . . . DLB-198

Polezhaev, Aleksandr Ivanovich
 1804-1838 . . . . DLB-205

Poliakoff, Stephen 1952- DLB-13

Polidori, John William 1795-1821 . . . . . . DLB-116

Polite, Carlene Hatcher 1932- DLB-33

Pollard, Alfred W. 1859-1944 . . . . DLB-201

Pollard, Edward A. 1832-1872 . . . . DLB-30

Pollard, Graham 1903-1976 . . . . DLB-201

Pollard, Percival 1869-1911 . . . . DLB-71

Pollard and Moss DLB-49

Pollock, Sharon 1936- DLB-60

Polonsky, Abraham 1910-1999 . . . . DLB-26

Polotsky, Simeon 1629-1680 . . . . DLB-150

Polybius circa 200 B.C.-118 B.C. DLB-176

Pomialovsky, Nikolai Gerasimovich
 1835-1863 . . . . DLB-238

Pomilio, Mario 1921-1990 . . . . .DLB-177

Ponce, Mary Helen 1938- DLB-122

Ponce-Montoya, Juanita 1949- DLB-122

Ponet, John 1516?-1556 . . . . DLB-132

Poniatowski, Elena
 1933- DLB-113; CDWLB-3

Ponsard, François 1814-1867 . . . . DLB-192

Ponsonby, William [publishing house] . . . DLB-170

Pontiggia, Giuseppe 1934- DLB-196

Pony Stories DLB-160

Poole, Ernest 1880-1950 . . . . DLB-9

Poole, Sophia 1804-1891 . . . . DLB-166

Poore, Benjamin Perley 1820-1887 . . . . DLB-23

Popa, Vasko 1922-1991 . . . . . DLB-181; CDWLB-4

Pope, Abbie Hanscom 1858-1894 . . . . DLB-140

Pope, Alexander
1688-1744 . . . . . . DLB-95, 101, 213; CDBLB-2

Popov, Mikhail Ivanovich
1742-circa 1790 . . . . DLB-150

Popović, Aleksandar 1929-1996 . . . . DLB-181

Popular Library DLB-46

Porete, Marguerite ?-1310 . . . . DLB-208

Porlock, Martin (see MacDonald, Philip)

Porpoise Press DLB-112

Porta, Antonio 1935-1989 . . . . DLB-128

Porter, Anna Maria 1780-1832 . . . . . DLB-116, 159

Porter, David 1780-1843 . . . . DLB-183

Porter, Eleanor H. 1868-1920 . . . . DLB-9

Porter, Gene Stratton (see Stratton-Porter, Gene)

Porter, Henry ?-? DLB-62

Porter, Jane 1776-1850 . . . . DLB-116, 159

Porter, Katherine Anne 1890-1980
. . . . . DLB-4, 9, 102; Y-80; DS-12; CDALB-7

Porter, Peter 1929- DLB-40

Porter, William Sydney
1862-1910 . . . . DLB-12, 78, 79; CDALB-3

Porter, William T. 1809-1858 . . . . DLB-3, 43

Porter and Coates DLB-49

Portillo Trambley, Estela 1927-1998 . . . . . DLB-209

Portis, Charles 1933- DLB-6

Posey, Alexander 1873-1908 . . . . DLB-175

Postans, Marianne circa 1810-1865 . . . . . . DLB-166

Postl, Carl (see Sealsfield, Carl)

Poston, Ted 1906-1974 . . . . DLB-51

Potekhin, Aleksei Antipovich 1829-1908 . . DLB-238

Potok, Chaim 1929- DLB-28, 152

A Conversation with Chaim Potok Y-84

Potter, Beatrix 1866-1943 . . . . DLB-141

Potter, David M. 1910-1971 . . . . DLB-17

Potter, Dennis 1935-1994 . . . . DLB-233

The Harry Potter Phenomenon Y-99

Potter, John E., and Company DLB-49

Pottle, Frederick A. 1897-1987 . . . . . DLB-103; Y-87

Poulin, Jacques 1937- DLB-60

Pound, Ezra 1885-1972
. . . . DLB-4, 45, 63; DS-15; CDALB-4

Poverman, C. E. 1944- DLB-234

Povich, Shirley 1905-1998 . . . . DLB-171

Powell, Anthony 1905-2000 . . . DLB-15; CDBLB-7

Dawn Powell, Where Have You Been All
Our Lives? Y-97

Powell, John Wesley 1834-1902 . . . . DLB-186

Powell, Padgett 1952- DLB-234

Powers, J. F. 1917-1999 . . . . DLB-130

Powers, Jimmy 1903-1995 . . . . DLB-241

Pownall, David 1938- DLB-14

Powys, John Cowper 1872-1963 . . . . DLB-15

Powys, Llewelyn 1884-1939 . . . . DLB-98

Powys, T. F. 1875-1953 . . . . DLB-36, 162

Poynter, Nelson 1903-1978 . . . . DLB-127

The Practice of Biography: An Interview
with Stanley Weintraub Y-82

The Practice of Biography II: An Interview
with B. L. Reid Y-83

The Practice of Biography III: An Interview
with Humphrey Carpenter Y-84

The Practice of Biography IV: An Interview with
William Manchester Y-85

The Practice of Biography VI: An Interview with
David Herbert Donald Y-87

The Practice of Biography VII: An Interview with
John Caldwell Guilds Y-92

The Practice of Biography VIII: An Interview
with Joan Mellen Y-94

The Practice of Biography IX: An Interview
with Michael Reynolds Y-95

Prados, Emilio 1899-1962 . . . . DLB-134

Praed, Mrs. Caroline (see Praed, Rosa)

Praed, Rosa (Mrs. Caroline Praed)
1851-1935 . . . . DLB-230

Praed, Winthrop Mackworth 1802-1839 . . . DLB-96

Praeger Publishers DLB-46

Praetorius, Johannes 1630-1680 . . . . DLB-168

Pratolini, Vasco 1913-1991 . . . . DLB-177

Pratt, E. J. 1882-1964 . . . . DLB-92

Pratt, Samuel Jackson 1749-1814 . . . . DLB-39

Preciado Martin, Patricia 1939- DLB-209

Preface to *The History of Romances* (1715), by
Pierre Daniel Huet [excerpts] DLB-39

Préfontaine, Yves 1937- DLB-53

Prelutsky, Jack 1940- DLB-61

Premisses, by Michael Hamburger DLB-66

Prentice, George D. 1802-1870 . . . . DLB-43

Prentice-Hall DLB-46

Prescott, Orville 1906-1996 . . . . Y-96

Prescott, William Hickling
1796-1859 . . . . DLB-1, 30, 59, 235

The Present State of the English Novel (1892),
by George Saintsbury DLB-18

Prešeren, Francè
1800-1849 . . . . DLB-147; CDWLB-4

Preston, Margaret Junkin
1820-1897 . . . . DLB-239, 248

Preston, May Wilson 1873-1949 . . . . DLB-188

Preston, Thomas 1537-1598 . . . . DLB-62

Price, Reynolds 1933- DLB-2, 218

Price, Richard 1723-1791 . . . . DLB-158

Price, Richard 1949- Y-81

Prideaux, John 1578-1650 . . . . DLB-236

Priest, Christopher 1943- DLB-14, 207

Priestley, J. B. 1894-1984
. . . DLB-10, 34, 77, 100, 139; Y-84; CDBLB-6

Primary Bibliography: A Retrospective Y-95

Prime, Benjamin Young 1733-1791 . . . . . . DLB-31

Primrose, Diana floruit circa 1630 . . . . . . DLB-126

Prince, F. T. 1912- DLB-20

Prince, Nancy Gardner 1799-? DLB-239

Prince, Thomas 1687-1758 . . . . DLB-24, 140

Pringle, Thomas 1789-1834 . . . . DLB-225

Printz, Wolfgang Casper 1641-1717 . . . . . DLB-168

Prior, Matthew 1664-1721 . . . . DLB-95

Prisco, Michele 1920- DLB-177

Pritchard, William H. 1932- DLB-111

Pritchett, V. S. 1900-1997 . . . . DLB-15, 139

Probyn, May 1856 or 1857-1909 . . . . DLB-199

Procter, Adelaide Anne 1825-1864 . . . DLB-32, 199

Procter, Bryan Waller 1787-1874 . . . . . DLB-96, 144

Proctor, Robert 1868-1903 . . . . DLB-184

*Producing Dear Bunny, Dear Volodya: The Friendship
and the Feud* Y-97

The Profession of Authorship:
Scribblers for Bread Y-89

Prokopovich, Feofan 1681?-1736 . . . . DLB-150

Prokosch, Frederic 1906-1989 . . . . DLB-48

The Proletarian Novel DLB-9

Pronzini, Bill 1943- DLB-226

Propertius circa 50 B.C.-post 16 B.C.
. . . . DLB-211; CDWLB-1

Propper, Dan 1937- DLB-16

Prose, Francine 1947- DLB-234

Protagoras circa 490 B.C.-420 B.C. DLB-176

Proud, Robert 1728-1813 . . . . DLB-30

Proust, Marcel 1871-1922 . . . . DLB-65

Prynne, J. H. 1936- DLB-40

Przybyszewski, Stanislaw 1868-1927 . . . . . DLB-66

Pseudo-Dionysius the Areopagite floruit
circa 500 . . . . DLB-115

Public Domain and the Violation of Texts Y-97

The Public Lending Right in America Statement by
Sen. Charles McC. Mathias, Jr. PLR and the
Meaning of Literary Property Statements on
PLR by American Writers Y-83

The Public Lending Right in the United Kingdom
Public Lending Right: The First Year in the
United Kingdom Y-83

The Publication of English
Renaissance Plays DLB-62

Publications and Social Movements
[Transcendentalism] DLB-1

Publishers and Agents: The Columbia
Connection Y-87

Publishing Fiction at LSU Press Y-87

The Publishing Industry in 1998:
Sturm-und-drang.com Y-98

The Publishing Industry in 1999 . . . . Y-99

Pückler-Muskau, Hermann von
1785-1871 . . . . DLB-133

Pufendorf, Samuel von 1632-1694 . . . . . . DLB-168

Pugh, Edwin William 1874-1930 . . . . DLB-135

Pugin, A. Welby 1812-1852 . . . . DLB-55

Puig, Manuel 1932-1990 . . . . DLB-113; CDWLB-3

Pulitzer, Joseph 1847-1911 . . . . DLB-23

Pulitzer, Joseph, Jr. 1885-1955 . . . . DLB-29

Pulitzer Prizes for the Novel, 1917-1945 . . . . DLB-9

Pulliam, Eugene 1889-1975. . . . . DLB-127

Purchas, Samuel 1577?-1626. . . . . DLB-151

Purdy, Al 1918-2000. . . . . DLB-88

Purdy, James 1923- DLB-2, 218

Purdy, Ken W. 1913-1972 . . . . DLB-137

Pusey, Edward Bouverie 1800-1882. . . . . DLB-55

Pushkin, Aleksandr Sergeevich
    1799-1837 . . . . DLB-205

Pushkin, Vasilii L'vovich 1766-1830. . . . . DLB-205

Putnam, George Palmer
    1814-1872. . . . . DLB-3, 79, 254

G. P. Putnam [publishing house] DLB-254

G. P. Putnam's Sons [U.K.] DLB-106

G. P. Putnam's Sons [U.S.]. DLB-49

A Publisher's Archives: G. P. Putnam Y-92

Putnam, Samuel 1892-1950 . . . . DLB-4

Puzo, Mario 1920-1999 . . . . DLB-6

Pyle, Ernie 1900-1945. . . . . DLB-29

Pyle, Howard 1853-1911 . . . . DLB-42, 188; DS-13

Pym, Barbara 1913-1980 . . . . . DLB-14, 207; Y-87

Pynchon, Thomas 1937- DLB-2, 173

Pyramid Books DLB-46

Pyrnelle, Louise-Clarke 1850-1907. . . . . . DLB-42

Pythagoras circa 570 B.C.-? DLB-176

Q

Quad, M. (see Lewis, Charles B.)

Quaritch, Bernard 1819-1899. . . . . DLB-184

Quarles, Francis 1592-1644 . . . . DLB-126

The Quarterly Review 1809-1967 . . . . . . DLB-110

Quasimodo, Salvatore 1901-1968. . . . . . . DLB-114

Queen, Ellery (see Dannay, Frederic, and
    Manfred B. Lee)

Queen, Frank 1822-1882 . . . . DLB-241

The Queen City Publishing House DLB-49

Queneau, Raymond 1903-1976 . . . . DLB-72

Quennell, Sir Peter 1905-1993 . . . . . DLB-155, 195

Quesnel, Joseph 1746-1809. . . . . DLB-99

The Question of American Copyright
    in the Nineteenth Century
    Preface, by George Haven Putnam
    The Evolution of Copyright, by
        Brander Matthews
    Summary of Copyright Legislation in
        the United States, by R. R. Bowker
    Analysis of the Provisions of the
        Copyright Law of 1891, by
        George Haven Putnam
    The Contest for International Copyright,
        by George Haven Putnam
    Cheap Books and Good Books,
        by Brander Matthews. DLB-49

Quiller-Couch, Sir Arthur Thomas
    1863-1944 . . . . DLB-135, 153, 190

Quin, Ann 1936-1973 . . . . DLB-14, 231

Quincy, Samuel, of Georgia ?-? DLB-31

Quincy, Samuel, of Massachusetts
    1734-1789 . . . . DLB-31

Quinn, Anthony 1915- DLB-122

The Quinn Draft of James Joyce's
    Circe Manuscript Y-00

Quinn, John 1870-1924. . . . . DLB-187

Quiñónez, Naomi 1951- DLB-209

Quintana, Leroy V. 1944- DLB-82

Quintana, Miguel de 1671-1748
    A Forerunner of Chicano Literature . DLB-122

Quintillian
    circa A.D. 40-circa A.D. 96 . . . . DLB-211

Quintus Curtius Rufus fl. A.D. 35 . . . . . . DLB-211

Quist, Harlin, Books. DLB-46

Quoirez, Françoise (see Sagan, Françoise)

R

R-va, Zeneida (see Gan, Elena Andreevna)

Raabe, Wilhelm 1831-1910 . . . . DLB-129

Raban, Jonathan 1942- DLB-204

Rabe, David 1940- DLB-7, 228

Raboni, Giovanni 1932- DLB-128

Rachilde 1860-1953 . . . . DLB-123, 192

Racin, Kočo 1908-1943 . . . . DLB-147

Rackham, Arthur 1867-1939. . . . . DLB-141

Radauskas, Henrikas
    1910-1970. . . . . DLB-220; CDWLB-4

Radcliffe, Ann 1764-1823 . . . . .DLB-39, 178

Raddall, Thomas 1903- DLB-68

Radford, Dollie 1858-1920 . . . . DLB-240

Radichkov, Yordan 1929- DLB-181

Radiguet, Raymond 1903-1923 . . . . DLB-65

Radishchev, Aleksandr Nikolaevich
    1749-1802. . . . . DLB-150

Radnóti, Miklós
    1909-1944 . . . . DLB-215; CDWLB-4

Radványi, Netty Reiling (see Seghers, Anna)

Rahv, Philip 1908-1973. . . . . DLB-137

Raich, Semen Egorovich 1792-1855 . . . . . DLB-205

Raičković, Stevan 1928- DLB-181

Raimund, Ferdinand Jakob 1790-1836 . . . . DLB-90

Raine, Craig 1944- DLB-40

Raine, Kathleen 1908- DLB-20

Rainis, Jānis 1865-1929. . . . . DLB-220; CDWLB-4

Rainolde, Richard
    circa 1530-1606 . . . . DLB-136, 236

Rakić, Milan 1876-1938 . . . . .DLB-147; CDWLB-4

Rakosi, Carl 1903- DLB-193

Ralegh, Sir Walter
    1554?-1618. . . . . DLB-172; CDBLB-1

Ralin, Radoy 1923- DLB-181

Ralph, Julian 1853-1903 . . . . DLB-23

Ramat, Silvio 1939- DLB-128

Rambler, no. 4 (1750), by Samuel Johnson
    [excerpt] DLB-39

Ramée, Marie Louise de la (see Ouida)

Ramírez, Sergío 1942- DLB-145

Ramke, Bin 1947- DLB-120

Ramler, Karl Wilhelm 1725-1798. . . . . . DLB-97

Ramon Ribeyro, Julio 1929- DLB-145

Ramos, Manuel 1948- DLB-209

Ramous, Mario 1924- DLB-128

Rampersad, Arnold 1941- DLB-111

Ramsay, Allan 1684 or 1685-1758 . . . . . . DLB-95

Ramsay, David 1749-1815 . . . . DLB-30

Ramsay, Martha Laurens 1759-1811 . . . . DLB-200

Ranck, Katherine Quintana 1942- DLB-122

Rand, Avery and Company DLB-49

Rand, Ayn 1905-1982. . . . . . DLB-227; CDALB-7

Rand McNally and Company DLB-49

Randall, David Anton 1905-1975. . . . . . DLB-140

Randall, Dudley 1914- DLB-41

Randall, Henry S. 1811-1876 . . . . DLB-30

Randall, James G. 1881-1953 . . . . .DLB-17

The Randall Jarrell Symposium:
    A Small Collection of Randall Jarrells
    Excerpts From Papers Delivered at the
    Randall Jarrel Symposium Y-86

Randolph, A. Philip 1889-1979. . . . . DLB-91

Randolph, Anson D. F.
    [publishing house] DLB-49

Randolph, Thomas 1605-1635. . . . . DLB-58, 126

Random House DLB-46

Ranlet, Henry [publishing house] DLB-49

Ransom, Harry 1908-1976 . . . . .DLB-187

Ransom, John Crowe
    1888-1974. . . . . DLB-45, 63; CDALB-7

Ransome, Arthur 1884-1967 . . . . DLB-160

Raphael, Frederic 1931- DLB-14

Raphaelson, Samson 1896-1983. . . . . DLB-44

Rashi circa 1040-1105. . . . . DLB-208

Raskin, Ellen 1928-1984. . . . . DLB-52

Rastell, John 1475?-1536. . . . . .DLB-136, 170

Rattigan, Terence
    1911-1977. . . . . DLB-13; CDBLB-7

Rawlings, Marjorie Kinnan 1896-1953
    . . . . .DLB-9, 22, 102; DS-17; CDALB-7

Rawlinson, Richard 1690-1755. . . . . DLB-213

Rawlinson, Thomas 1681-1725 . . . . DLB-213

Raworth, Tom 1938- DLB-40

Ray, David 1932- DLB-5

Ray, Gordon Norton 1915-1986 . . . .DLB-103, 140

Ray, Henrietta Cordelia 1849-1916 . . . . . DLB-50

Raymond, Ernest 1888-1974 . . . . DLB-191

Raymond, Henry J. 1820-1869. . . . . . .DLB-43, 79

Michael M. Rea and the Rea Award for the
    Short Story. Y-97

Reach, Angus 1821-1856 . . . . DLB-70

Read, Herbert 1893-1968. . . . . DLB-20, 149

Read, Herbert, "The Practice of Biography," in
    The English Sense of Humour and
    Other Essays DLB-149

Read, Martha Meredith DLB-200

Read, Opie 1852-1939 . . . . DLB-23

Read, Piers Paul 1941- DLB-14

Reade, Charles 1814-1884. . . . . .DLB-21

Reader's Digest Condensed Books DLB-46

Readers Ulysses Symposium Y-97

Reading, Peter 1946- DLB-40

Reading Series in New York City Y-96

The Reality of One Woman's Dream:
The de Grummond Children's
Literature Collection Y-99

Reaney, James 1926- DLB-68

Rebhun, Paul 1500?-1546 . . . . DLB-179

Rèbora, Clemente 1885-1957. . . . . .DLB-114

Rebreanu, Liviu 1885-1944 . . . . .DLB-220

Rechy, John 1934- DLB-122; Y-82

The Recovery of Literature:
Criticism in the 1990s: A Symposium. . . . Y-91

Redding, J. Saunders 1906-1988 . . . . . . DLB-63, 76

Redfield, J. S. [publishing house] DLB-49

Redgrove, Peter 1932- DLB-40

Redmon, Anne 1943- Y-86

Redmond, Eugene B. 1937- DLB-41

Redpath, James [publishing house] DLB-49

Reed, Henry 1808-1854. . . . . .DLB-59

Reed, Henry 1914- DLB-27

Reed, Ishmael
1938- DLB-2, 5, 33, 169, 227; DS-8

Reed, Rex 1938- DLB-185

Reed, Sampson 1800-1880. . . . . .DLB-1, 235

Reed, Talbot Baines 1852-1893 . . . . .DLB-141

Reedy, William Marion 1862-1920 . . . . . .DLB-91

Reese, Lizette Woodworth 1856-1935. . . . .DLB-54

Reese, Thomas 1742-1796 . . . . .DLB-37

Reeve, Clara 1729-1807 . . . . .DLB-39

Preface to *The Old English Baron* (1778) DLB-39

The Progress of Romance (1785) [excerpt]. DLB-39

Reeves, James 1909-1978 . . . . .DLB-161

Reeves, John 1926- DLB-88

"Reflections: After a Tornado,"
by Judson Jerome DLB-105

Regnery, Henry, Company DLB-46

Rehberg, Hans 1901-1963 . . . . .DLB-124

Rehfisch, Hans José 1891-1960 . . . . .DLB-124

Reich, Ebbe Kløvedal 1940- DLB-214

Reid, Alastair 1926- DLB-27

Reid, B. L. 1918-1990 . . . . DLB-111; Y-83

The Practice of Biography II:
An Interview with B. L. Reid Y-83

Reid, Christopher 1949- DLB-40

Reid, Forrest 1875-1947 . . . . .DLB-153

Reid, Helen Rogers 1882-1970. . . . . .DLB-29

Reid, James ?-?. .DLB-31

Reid, Mayne 1818-1883. . . . . .DLB-21, 163

Reid, Thomas 1710-1796 . . . . .DLB-31

Reid, V. S. (Vic) 1913-1987 . . . . .DLB-125

Reid, Whitelaw 1837-1912 . . . . .DLB-23

Reilly and Lee Publishing Company DLB-46

Reimann, Brigitte 1933-1973 . . . . .DLB-75

Reinmar der Alte
circa 1165-circa 1205. . . . . .DLB-138

Reinmar von Zweter
circa 1200-circa 1250. . . . . .DLB-138

Reisch, Walter 1903-1983 . . . . .DLB-44

Reizei Family DLB-203

Remarks at the Opening of "The Biographical
Part of Literature" Exhibition, by
William R. Cagle Y-98

Remarque, Erich Maria
1898-1970 . . . . DLB-56; CDWLB-2

Remington, Frederic
1861-1909 . . . . DLB-12, 186, 188

Reminiscences, by Charles Scribner Jr. DS-17

Renaud, Jacques 1943- DLB-60

Renault, Mary 1905-1983 . . . . Y-83

Rendell, Ruth 1930- DLB-87

Rensselaer, Maria van Cortlandt van
1645-1689 . . . . .DLB-200

Repplier, Agnes 1855-1950 . . . . .DLB-221

Representative Men and Women: A Historical
Perspective on the British Novel,
1930-1960 . . . . .DLB-15

Research in the American Antiquarian Book
Trade Y-97

Reshetnikov, Fedor Mikhailovich
1841-1871 . . . . .DLB-238

Rettenbacher, Simon 1634-1706. . . . . . . .DLB-168

Reuchlin, Johannes 1455-1522. . . . . .DLB-179

Reuter, Christian 1665-after 1712 . . . . . . .DLB-168

Revell, Fleming H., Company DLB-49

Reuter, Fritz 1810-1874 . . . . .DLB-129

Reuter, Gabriele 1859-1941. . . . . .DLB-66

Reventlow, Franziska Gräfin zu
1871-1918 . . . . .DLB-66

Review of Nicholson Baker's *Double Fold:
Libraries and the Assault on Paper*. Y-00

Review of Reviews Office DLB-112

Review of [Samuel Richardson's] *Clarissa* (1748),
by Henry Fielding DLB-39

The Revolt (1937), by Mary Colum
[excerpts]. DLB-36

Rexroth, Kenneth 1905-1982
. . . . . . DLB-16, 48, 165, 212; Y-82; CDALB-1

Rey, H. A. 1898-1977 . . . . .DLB-22

Reynal and Hitchcock DLB-46

Reynolds, G. W. M. 1814-1879 . . . . .DLB-21

Reynolds, John Hamilton 1794-1852 . . . . .DLB-96

Reynolds, Sir Joshua 1723-1792. . . . . . . .DLB-104

Reynolds, Mack 1917- DLB-8

A Literary Archaeologist Digs On: A Brief
Interview with Michael Reynolds by
Michael Rogers Y-99

Reznikoff, Charles 1894-1976 . . . . . .DLB-28, 45

Rhett, Robert Barnwell 1800-1876. . . . . . .DLB-43

Rhode, John 1884-1964. . . . . .DLB-77

Rhodes, James Ford 1848-1927 . . . . .DLB-47

Rhodes, Richard 1937- DLB-185

Rhys, Jean 1890-1979
. . . . . DLB-36, 117, 162; CDBLB-7; CDWLB-3

Ricardo, David 1772-1823 . . . . DLB-107, 158

Ricardou, Jean 1932- DLB-83

Rice, Elmer 1892-1967. . . . . .DLB-4, 7

Rice, Grantland 1880-1954 . . . . DLB-29, 171

Rich, Adrienne 1929- DLB-5, 67; CDALB-7

Richard de Fournival
1201-1259 or 1260 . . . . .DLB-208

Richard, Mark 1955- DLB-234

Richards, David Adams 1950- DLB-53

Richards, George circa 1760-1814 . . . . . . .DLB-37

Richards, Grant [publishing house] DLB-112

Richards, I. A. 1893-1979 . . . . .DLB-27

Richards, Laura E. 1850-1943 . . . . .DLB-42

Richards, William Carey 1818-1892 . . . . .DLB-73

Richardson, Charles F. 1851-1913. . . . . . .DLB-71

Richardson, Dorothy M. 1873-1957 . . . . . .DLB-36

Richardson, Henry Handel
(Ethel Florence Lindesay
Robertson) 1870-1946 . . . . DLB-197, 230

Richardson, Jack 1935- DLB-7

Richardson, John 1796-1852 . . . . .DLB-99

Richardson, Samuel
1689-1761 . . . . .DLB-39, 154; CDBLB-2

Introductory Letters from the Second
Edition of *Pamela* (1741) DLB-39

Postscript to [the Third Edition of]
Clarissa (1751) DLB-39

Preface to the First Edition of
Pamela (1740) DLB-39

Preface to the Third Edition of
Clarissa (1751) [excerpt] DLB-39

Preface to Volume 1 of *Clarissa* (1747) DLB-39

Preface to Volume 3 of *Clarissa* (1748) DLB-39

Richardson, Willis 1889-1977 . . . . .DLB-51

Riche, Barnabe 1542-1617 . . . . .DLB-136

Richepin, Jean 1849-1926 . . . . .DLB-192

Richler, Mordecai 1931- DLB-53

Richter, Conrad 1890-1968 . . . . .DLB-9, 212

Richter, Hans Werner 1908- DLB-69

Richter, Johann Paul Friedrich
1763-1825 . . . . .DLB-94; CDWLB-2

Rickerby, Joseph [publishing house] DLB-106

Rickword, Edgell 1898-1982 . . . . .DLB-20

Riddell, Charlotte 1832-1906. . . . . .DLB-156

Riddell, John (see Ford, Corey)

Ridge, John Rollin 1827-1867 . . . . .DLB-175

Ridge, Lola 1873-1941 . . . . .DLB-54

Ridge, William Pett 1859-1930 . . . . .DLB-135

Riding, Laura (see Jackson, Laura Riding)

Ridler, Anne 1912- DLB-27

Ridruego, Dionisio 1912-1975 . . . . .DLB-108

Riel, Louis 1844-1885 . . . . .DLB-99

Riemer, Johannes 1648-1714 . . . . .DLB-168

Rifbjerg, Klaus 1931- DLB-214

Riffaterre, Michael 1924- DLB-67

Riggs, Lynn 1899-1954 . . . . DLB-175

Riis, Jacob 1849-1914 . . . . DLB-23

Riker, John C. [publishing house] DLB-49

Riley, James 1777-1840 . . . . DLB-183

Riley, John 1938-1978 . . . . DLB-40

Rilke, Rainer Maria
   1875-1926 . . . . DLB-81; CDWLB-2

Rimanelli, Giose 1926- DLB-177

Rimbaud, Jean-Nicolas-Arthur
   1854-1891 . . . . DLB-217

Rinehart and Company DLB-46

Ringuet 1895-1960 . . . . DLB-68

Ringwood, Gwen Pharis 1910-1984 . . . . . . DLB-88

Rinser, Luise 1911- DLB-69

Ríos, Alberto 1952- DLB-122

Ríos, Isabella 1948- DLB-82

Ripley, Arthur 1895-1961 . . . . DLB-44

Ripley, George 1802-1880 . . . . DLB-1, 64, 73, 235

The Rising Glory of America:
   Three Poems DLB-37

The Rising Glory of America:
   Written in 1771 (1786),
   by Hugh Henry Brackenridge and
   Philip Freneau DLB-37

Riskin, Robert 1897-1955 . . . . DLB-26

Risse, Heinz 1898- DLB-69

Rist, Johann 1607-1667 . . . . DLB-164

Ristikivi, Karl 1912-1977 . . . . DLB-220

Ritchie, Anna Mowatt 1819-1870 . . . . DLB-3

Ritchie, Anne Thackeray 1837-1919 . . . . . . DLB-18

Ritchie, Thomas 1778-1854 . . . . DLB-43

Rites of Passage [on William Saroyan] Y-83

The Ritz Paris Hemingway Award Y-85

Rivard, Adjutor 1868-1945 . . . . DLB-92

Rive, Richard 1931-1989 . . . . DLB-125, 225

Rivera, José 1955- DLB-249

Rivera, Marina 1942- DLB-122

Rivera, Tomás 1935-1984 . . . . DLB-82

Rivers, Conrad Kent 1933-1968 . . . . DLB-41

Riverside Press DLB-49

Rivington, Charles [publishing house] . . . DLB-154

Rivington, James circa 1724-1802 . . . . DLB-43

Rivkin, Allen 1903-1990 . . . . DLB-26

Roa Bastos, Augusto 1917- DLB-113

Robbe-Grillet, Alain 1922- DLB-83

Robbins, Tom 1936- Y-80

Roberts, Charles G. D. 1860-1943 . . . . . . DLB-92

Roberts, Dorothy 1906-1993 . . . . DLB-88

Roberts, Elizabeth Madox
   1881-1941 . . . . DLB-9, 54, 102

Roberts, James [publishing house] DLB-154

Roberts, Kenneth 1885-1957 . . . . DLB-9

Roberts, Michèle 1949- DLB-231

Roberts, Ursula Wyllie (see Miles, Susan)

Roberts, William 1767-1849 . . . . DLB-142

Roberts Brothers DLB-49

Robertson, A. M., and Company DLB-49

Robertson, Ethel Florence Lindesay
   (see Richardson, Henry Handel)

Robertson, William 1721-1793 . . . . DLB-104

Robins, Elizabeth 1862-1952 . . . . DLB-197

Robinson, A. Mary F. (Madame James
   Darmesteter, Madame Mary
   Duclaux) 1857-1944 . . . . DLB-240

Robinson, Casey 1903-1979 . . . . DLB-44

Robinson, Edwin Arlington
   1869-1935 . . . . DLB-54; CDALB-3

Robinson, Henry Crabb 1775-1867 . . . . . .DLB-107

Robinson, James Harvey 1863-1936 . . . . . DLB-47

Robinson, Lennox 1886-1958 . . . . DLB-10

Robinson, Mabel Louise 1874-1962 . . . . . . DLB-22

Robinson, Marilynne 1943- DLB-206

Robinson, Mary 1758-1800 . . . . DLB-158

Robinson, Richard circa 1545-1607 . . . . . DLB-167

Robinson, Therese 1797-1870 . . . . DLB-59, 133

Robison, Mary 1949- DLB-130

Roblès, Emmanuel 1914-1995 . . . . DLB-83

Roccatagliata Ceccardi, Ceccardo
   1871-1919 . . . . DLB-114

Roche, Billy 1949- DLB-233

Rochester, John Wilmot, Earl of
   1647-1680 . . . . DLB-131

Rock, Howard 1911-1976 . . . . DLB-127

Rockwell, Norman Perceval 1894-1978 . . DLB-188

Rodgers, Carolyn M. 1945- DLB-41

Rodgers, W. R. 1909-1969 . . . . DLB-20

Rodney, Lester 1911- DLB-241

Rodríguez, Claudio 1934-1999 . . . . DLB-134

Rodríguez, Joe D. 1943- DLB-209

Rodríguez, Luis J. 1954- DLB-209

Rodriguez, Richard 1944- DLB-82

Rodríguez Julia, Edgardo 1946- DLB-145

Roe, E. P. 1838-1888 . . . . DLB-202

Roethke, Theodore
   1908-1963 . . . . DLB-5, 206; CDALB-1

Rogers, Jane 1952- DLB-194

Rogers, Pattiann 1940- DLB-105

Rogers, Samuel 1763-1855 . . . . DLB-93

Rogers, Will 1879-1935 . . . . DLB-11

Rohmer, Sax 1883-1959 . . . . DLB-70

Roiphe, Anne 1935- Y-80

Rojas, Arnold R. 1896-1988 . . . . DLB-82

Rolfe, Frederick William
   1860-1913 . . . . DLB-34, 156

Rolland, Romain 1866-1944 . . . . DLB-65

Rolle, Richard circa 1290-1300 - 1340 . . . DLB-146

Rölvaag, O. E. 1876-1931 . . . . DLB-9, 212

Romains, Jules 1885-1972 . . . . DLB-65

Roman, A., and Company DLB-49

Roman de la Rose: Guillaume de Lorris
   1200 to 1205-circa 1230, Jean de Meun
   1235-1240-circa 1305 . . . . DLB-208

Romano, Lalla 1906- DLB-177

Romano, Octavio 1923- DLB-122

Romero, Leo 1950- DLB-122

Romero, Lin 1947- DLB-122

Romero, Orlando 1945- DLB-82

Rook, Clarence 1863-1915 . . . . DLB-135

Roosevelt, Theodore 1858-1919 . . . . . .DLB-47, 186

Root, Waverley 1903-1982 . . . . DLB-4

Root, William Pitt 1941- DLB-120

Roquebrune, Robert de 1889-1978 . . . . . . DLB-68

Rorty, Richard 1931- DLB-246

Rosa, João Guimarães 1908-1967 . . . . . . DLB-113

Rosales, Luis 1910-1992 . . . . DLB-134

Roscoe, William 1753-1831 . . . . DLB-163

Danis Rose and the Rendering of *Ulysses* Y-97

Rose, Reginald 1920- DLB-26

Rose, Wendy 1948- DLB-175

Rosegger, Peter 1843-1918 . . . . DLB-129

Rosei, Peter 1946- DLB-85

Rosen, Norma 1925- DLB-28

Rosenbach, A. S. W. 1876-1952 . . . . DLB-140

Rosenbaum, Ron 1946- DLB-185

Rosenberg, Isaac 1890-1918 . . . . DLB-20, 216

Rosenfeld, Isaac 1918-1956 . . . . DLB-28

Rosenthal, Harold 1914-1999 . . . . DLB-241

Rosenthal, M. L. 1917-1996 . . . . DLB-5

Rosenwald, Lessing J. 1891-1979 . . . . . . .DLB-187

Ross, Alexander 1591-1654 . . . . DLB-151

Ross, Harold 1892-1951 . . . . .DLB-137

Ross, Leonard Q. (see Rosten, Leo)

Ross, Lillian 1927- DLB-185

Ross, Martin 1862-1915 . . . . DLB-135

Ross, Sinclair 1908- DLB-88

Ross, W. W. E. 1894-1966 . . . . DLB-88

Rosselli, Amelia 1930-1996 . . . . DLB-128

Rossen, Robert 1908-1966 . . . . DLB-26

Rossetti, Christina 1830-1894 . . . DLB-35, 163, 240

Rossetti, Dante Gabriel
   1828-1882 . . . . DLB-35; CDBLB-4

Rossner, Judith 1935- DLB-6

Rostand, Edmond 1868-1918 . . . . DLB-192

Rosten, Leo 1908-1997 . . . . DLB-11

Rostenberg, Leona 1908- DLB-140

Rostopchina, Evdokiia Petrovna
   1811-1858 . . . . DLB-205

Rostovsky, Dimitrii 1651-1709 . . . . DLB-150

Rota, Bertram 1903-1966 . . . . DLB-201

   Bertram Rota and His Bookshop Y-91

Roth, Gerhard 1942- DLB-85, 124

Roth, Henry 1906?-1995 . . . . DLB-28

Roth, Joseph 1894-1939 . . . . DLB-85

Roth, Philip 1933-
   . . . . .DLB-2, 28, 173; Y-82; CDALB-6

Rothenberg, Jerome 1931- DLB-5, 193

Rothschild Family DLB-184

Rotimi, Ola 1938- DLB-125

Routhier, Adolphe-Basile 1839-1920 . . . . . .DLB-99

Routier, Simone 1901-1987 . . . . .DLB-88

Routledge, George, and Sons. DLB-106

Roversi, Roberto 1923- DLB-128

Rowe, Elizabeth Singer 1674-1737 . . . . .DLB-39, 95

Rowe, Nicholas 1674-1718 . . . . .DLB-84

Rowlands, Samuel circa 1570-1630 . . . . . .DLB-121

Rowlandson, Mary
    circa 1637-circa 1711 . . . . .DLB-24, 200

Rowley, William circa 1585-1626 . . . . . . .DLB-58

Rowse, A. L. 1903-1997 . . . . .DLB-155

Rowson, Susanna Haswell
    circa 1762-1824 . . . . DLB-37, 200

Roy, Camille 1870-1943 . . . . .DLB-92

Roy, Gabrielle 1909-1983 . . . . .DLB-68

Roy, Jules 1907- DLB-83

The G. Ross Roy Scottish Poetry Collection
    at the University of South Carolina Y-89

The Royal Court Theatre and the English
    Stage Company DLB-13

The Royal Court Theatre and the New
    Drama DLB-10

The Royal Shakespeare Company
    at the Swan Y-88

Royall, Anne Newport 1769-1854 . . . .DLB-43, 248

The Roycroft Printing Shop DLB-49

Royde-Smith, Naomi 1875-1964 . . . . . . .DLB-191

Royster, Vermont 1914- DLB-127

Royston, Richard [publishing house] DLB-170

Różewicz, Tadeusz 1921- DLB-232

Ruark, Gibbons 1941- DLB-120

Ruban, Vasilii Grigorevich 1742-1795 . . . .DLB-150

Rubens, Bernice 1928- DLB-14, 207

Rudd and Carleton DLB-49

Rudd, Steele (Arthur Hoey Davis) DLB-230

Rudkin, David 1936- DLB-13

Rudolf von Ems circa 1200-circa 1254 . . .DLB-138

Ruffin, Josephine St. Pierre
    1842-1924 . . . . .DLB-79

Ruganda, John 1941- DLB-157

Ruggles, Henry Joseph 1813-1906 . . . . . . .DLB-64

Ruiz de Burton, María Amparo
    1832-1895 . . . . .DLB-209, 221

Rukeyser, Muriel 1913-1980 . . . . .DLB-48

Rule, Jane 1931- DLB-60

Rulfo, Juan 1918-1986 . . . . . . DLB-113; CDWLB-3

Rumaker, Michael 1932- DLB-16

Rumens, Carol 1944- DLB-40

Rummo, Paul-Eerik 1942- DLB-232

Runyon, Damon 1880-1946 . . . . . DLB-11, 86, 171

Ruodlieb circa 1050-1075 . . . . .DLB-148

Rush, Benjamin 1746-1813 . . . . .DLB-37

Rush, Rebecca 1779-? DLB-200

Rushdie, Salman 1947- DLB-194

Rusk, Ralph L. 1888-1962 . . . . .DLB-103

Ruskin, John
    1819-1900 . . . . . .DLB-55, 163, 190; CDBLB-4

Russ, Joanna 1937- DLB-8

Russell, B. B., and Company DLB-49

Russell, Benjamin 1761-1845 . . . . .DLB-43

Russell, Bertrand 1872-1970 . . . . .DLB-100

Russell, Charles Edward 1860-1941 . . . . . .DLB-25

Russell, Charles M. 1864-1926 . . . . .DLB-188

Russell, Fred 1906- DLB-241

Russell, George William (see AE)

Russell, Countess Mary Annette Beauchamp
    (see Arnim, Elizabeth von)

Russell, R. H., and Son DLB-49

Russell, Willy 1947- DLB-233

Rutebeuf flourished 1249-1277 . . . . .DLB-208

Rutherford, Mark 1831-1913 . . . . .DLB-18

Ruxton, George Frederick 1821-1848 . . . .DLB-186

Ryan, Michael 1946- Y-82

Ryan, Oscar 1904- DLB-68

Ryder, Jack 1871-1936 . . . . .DLB-241

Ryga, George 1932- DLB-60

Rylands, Enriqueta Augustina Tennant
    1843-1908 . . . . .DLB-184

Rylands, John 1801-1888 . . . . .DLB-184

Ryleev, Kondratii Fedorovich
    1795-1826 . . . . .DLB-205

Rymer, Thomas 1643?-1713 . . . . .DLB-101

Ryskind, Morrie 1895-1985 . . . . .DLB-26

Rzhevsky, Aleksei Andreevich
    1737-1804 . . . . .DLB-150

S

The Saalfield Publishing Company DLB-46

Saba, Umberto 1883-1957 . . . . .DLB-114

Sábato, Ernesto 1911- DLB-145; CDWLB-3

Saberhagen, Fred 1930- DLB-8

Sabin, Joseph 1821-1881 . . . . .DLB-187

Sacer, Gottfried Wilhelm 1635-1699 . . . . .DLB-168

Sachs, Hans 1494-1576 . . . . . DLB-179; CDWLB-2

Sack, John 1930- DLB-185

Sackler, Howard 1929-1982 . . . . .DLB-7

Sackville, Lady Margaret 1881-1963 . . . . .DLB-240

Sackville, Thomas 1536-1608 . . . . .DLB-132

Sackville, Thomas 1536-1608
    and Norton, Thomas 1532-1584 . . . . . .DLB-62

Sackville-West, Edward 1901-1965 . . . . . .DLB-191

Sackville-West, V. 1892-1962 . . . . . . .DLB-34, 195

Sadlier, D. and J., and Company DLB-49

Sadlier, Mary Anne 1820-1903 . . . . .DLB-99

Sadoff, Ira 1945- DLB-120

Sadoveanu, Mihail 1880-1961 . . . . .DLB-220

Sáenz, Benjamin Alire 1954- DLB-209

Saenz, Jaime 1921-1986 . . . . .DLB-145

Saffin, John circa 1626-1710 . . . . .DLB-24

Sagan, Françoise 1935- DLB-83

Sage, Robert 1899-1962 . . . . .DLB-4

Sagel, Jim 1947- DLB-82

Sagendorph, Robb Hansell 1900-1970 . . . .DLB-137

Sahagún, Carlos 1938- DLB-108

Sahkomaapii, Piitai (see Highwater, Jamake)

Sahl, Hans 1902- DLB-69

Said, Edward W. 1935- DLB-67

Saigyō 1118-1190 . . . . .DLB-203

Saiko, George 1892-1962 . . . . .DLB-85

St. Dominic's Press DLB-112

Saint-Exupéry, Antoine de 1900-1944 . . . .DLB-72

St. John, J. Allen 1872-1957 . . . . .DLB-188

St. Johns, Adela Rogers 1894-1988 . . . . . . .DLB-29

The St. John's College Robert Graves Trust . . Y-96

St. Martin's Press DLB-46

St. Omer, Garth 1931- DLB-117

Saint Pierre, Michel de 1916-1987 . . . . . . .DLB-83

Sainte-Beuve, Charles-Augustin
    1804-1869 . . . . .DLB-217

Saints' Lives DLB-208

Saintsbury, George 1845-1933 . . . . DLB-57, 149

Saiokuken Sōchō 1448-1532 . . . . .DLB-203

Saki (see Munro, H. H.)

Salaam, Kalamu ya 1947- DLB-38

Šalamun, Tomaž 1941- . . . DLB-181; CDWLB-4

Salas, Floyd 1931- DLB-82

Sálaz-Marquez, Rubén 1935- DLB-122

Salemson, Harold J. 1910-1988 . . . . .DLB-4

Salinas, Luis Omar 1937- DLB-82

Salinas, Pedro 1891-1951 . . . . .DLB-134

Salinger, J. D.
    1919- DLB-2, 102, 173; CDALB-1

Salkey, Andrew 1928- DLB-125

Sallust circa 86 B.C.-35 B.C.
    . . . . DLB-211; CDWLB-1

Salt, Waldo 1914- DLB-44

Salter, James 1925- DLB-130

Salter, Mary Jo 1954- DLB-120

Saltus, Edgar 1855-1921 . . . . .DLB-202

Saltykov, Mikhail Evgrafovich
    1826-1889 . . . . .DLB-238

Salustri, Carlo Alberto (see Trilussa)

Salverson, Laura Goodman 1890-1970 . . . .DLB-92

Samain, Albert 1858-1900 . . . . .DLB-217

Sampson, Richard Henry (see Hull, Richard)

Samuels, Ernest 1903-1996 . . . . .DLB-111

Sanborn, Franklin Benjamin
    1831-1917 . . . . .DLB-1, 223

Sánchez, Luis Rafael 1936- DLB-145

Sánchez, Philomeno "Phil" 1917- DLB-122

Sánchez, Ricardo 1941-1995 . . . . .DLB-82

Sánchez, Saúl 1943- DLB-209

Sanchez, Sonia 1934- DLB-41; DS-8

Sand, George 1804-1876 . . . . DLB-119, 192

Sandburg, Carl
    1878-1967 . . . . DLB-17, 54; CDALB-3

Sanders, Edward 1939- DLB-16, 244

Sandoz, Mari 1896-1966 . . . . DLB-9, 212

Sandwell, B. K. 1876-1954 . . . . .DLB-92

Sandy, Stephen 1934- DLB-165

Sandys, George 1578-1644 . . . . DLB-24, 121

Sangster, Charles 1822-1893 . . . . DLB-99

Sanguineti, Edoardo 1930- DLB-128

Sanjōnishi Sanetaka 1455-1537 . . . . DLB-203

Sansay, Leonora ?-after 1823 . . . . DLB-200

Sansom, William 1912-1976 . . . . DLB-139

Santayana, George
1863-1952 . . . . DLB-54, 71, 246; DS-13

Santiago, Danny 1911-1988 . . . . DLB-122

Santmyer, Helen Hooven 1895-1986 . . . . Y-84

Sanvitale, Francesca 1928- DLB-196

Sapidus, Joannes 1490-1561 . . . . .DLB-179

Sapir, Edward 1884-1939 . . . . DLB-92

Sapper (see McNeile, Herman Cyril)

Sappho circa 620 B.C.-circa 550 B.C.
. . . . .DLB-176; CDWLB-1

Saramago, José 1922- Y-98

Sardou, Victorien 1831-1908 . . . . DLB-192

Sarduy, Severo 1937- DLB-113

Sargent, Pamela 1948- DLB-8

Saro-Wiwa, Ken 1941- DLB-157

Saroyan, William
1908-1981 . . . . .DLB-7, 9, 86; Y-81; CDALB-7

Sarraute, Nathalie 1900-1999 . . . . DLB-83

Sarrazin, Albertine 1937-1967 . . . . DLB-83

Sarris, Greg 1952- DLB-175

Sarton, May 1912-1995 . . . . DLB-48; Y-81

Sartre, Jean-Paul 1905-1980 . . . . DLB-72

Sassoon, Siegfried
1886-1967 . . . . DLB-20, 191; DS-18

Siegfried Loraine Sassoon:
A Centenary Essay
Tributes from Vivien F. Clarke and
Michael Thorpe .Y-86

Sata, Ineko 1904- DLB-180

Saturday Review Press DLB-46

Saunders, James 1925- DLB-13

Saunders, John Monk 1897-1940 . . . . DLB-26

Saunders, Margaret Marshall
1861-1947. . . . . DLB-92

Saunders and Otley DLB-106

Saussure, Ferdinand de 1857-1913 . . . . . . DLB-242

Savage, James 1784-1873. . . . . DLB-30

Savage, Marmion W. 1803?-1872. . . . . . . DLB-21

Savage, Richard 1697?-1743 . . . . DLB-95

Savard, Félix-Antoine 1896-1982 . . . . DLB-68

Savery, Henry 1791-1842 . . . . DLB-230

Saville, (Leonard) Malcolm 1901-1982. . . DLB-160

Sawyer, Ruth 1880-1970. . . . . DLB-22

Sayers, Dorothy L.
1893-1957. . . . .DLB-10, 36, 77, 100; CDBLB-6

Sayle, Charles Edward 1864-1924 . . . . . . DLB-184

Sayles, John Thomas 1950- DLB-44

Sbarbaro, Camillo 1888-1967 . . . . DLB-114

Scalapino, Leslie 1947- DLB-193

Scannell, Vernon 1922- DLB-27

Scarry, Richard 1919-1994 . . . . DLB-61

Schaefer, Jack 1907-1991. . . . . DLB-212

Schaeffer, Albrecht 1885-1950 . . . . DLB-66

Schaeffer, Susan Fromberg 1941- DLB-28

Schaff, Philip 1819-1893 . . . . .DS-13

Schaper, Edzard 1908-1984 . . . . DLB-69

Scharf, J. Thomas 1843-1898 . . . . DLB-47

Schede, Paul Melissus 1539-1602 . . . . . . .DLB-179

Scheffel, Joseph Viktor von 1826-1886. . . DLB-129

Scheffler, Johann 1624-1677 . . . . DLB-164

Schelling, Friedrich Wilhelm Joseph von
1775-1854 . . . . DLB-90

Scherer, Wilhelm 1841-1886 . . . . DLB-129

Scherfig, Hans 1905-1979 . . . . DLB-214

Schickele, René 1883-1940 . . . . DLB-66

Schiff, Dorothy 1903-1989 . . . . DLB-127

Schiller, Friedrich
1759-1805 . . . . DLB-94; CDWLB-2

Schirmer, David 1623-1687 . . . . DLB-164

Schlaf, Johannes 1862-1941 . . . . DLB-118

Schlegel, August Wilhelm 1767-1845 . . . . . DLB-94

Schlegel, Dorothea 1763-1839. . . . . DLB-90

Schlegel, Friedrich 1772-1829 . . . . DLB-90

Schleiermacher, Friedrich 1768-1834 . . . . . DLB-90

Schlesinger, Arthur M., Jr. 1917- DLB-17

Schlumberger, Jean 1877-1968 . . . . DLB-65

Schmid, Eduard Hermann Wilhelm
(see Edschmid, Kasimir)

Schmidt, Arno 1914-1979 . . . . DLB-69

Schmidt, Johann Kaspar (see Stirner, Max)

Schmidt, Michael 1947- DLB-40

Schmidtbonn, Wilhelm August
1876-1952. . . . . DLB-118

Schmitz, James H. 1911- DLB-8

Schnabel, Johann Gottfried
1692-1760. . . . . DLB-168

Schnackenberg, Gjertrud 1953- DLB-120

Schnitzler, Arthur
1862-1931 . . . . .DLB-81, 118; CDWLB-2

Schnurre, Wolfdietrich 1920-1989 . . . . DLB-69

Schocken Books DLB-46

Scholartis Press DLB-112

Scholderer, Victor 1880-1971 . . . . DLB-201

The Schomburg Center for Research
in Black Culture DLB-76

Schönbeck, Virgilio (see Giotti, Virgilio)

Schönherr, Karl 1867-1943 . . . . DLB-118

Schoolcraft, Jane Johnston 1800-1841 . . . . .DLB-175

School Stories, 1914-1960 . . . . DLB-160

Schopenhauer, Arthur 1788-1860 . . . . DLB-90

Schopenhauer, Johanna 1766-1838 . . . . . . DLB-90

Schorer, Mark 1908-1977 . . . . DLB-103

Schottelius, Justus Georg 1612-1676 . . . . . DLB-164

Schouler, James 1839-1920 . . . . DLB-47

Schrader, Paul 1946- DLB-44

Schreiner, Olive
1855-1920 . . . . .DLB-18, 156, 190, 225

Schroeder, Andreas 1946- DLB-53

Schubart, Christian Friedrich Daniel
1739-1791 . . . . DLB-97

Schubert, Gotthilf Heinrich 1780-1860 . . . . DLB-90

Schücking, Levin 1814-1883. . . . . DLB-133

Schulberg, Budd 1914- DLB-6, 26, 28; Y-81

Schulte, F. J., and Company DLB-49

Schulz, Bruno 1892-1942 . . . .DLB-215; CDWLB-4

Schulze, Hans (see Praetorius, Johannes)

Schupp, Johann Balthasar 1610-1661 . . . . DLB-164

Schurz, Carl 1829-1906 . . . . DLB-23

Schuyler, George S. 1895-1977 . . . . DLB-29, 51

Schuyler, James 1923-1991 . . . . DLB-5, 169

Schwartz, Delmore 1913-1966 . . . . DLB-28, 48

Schwartz, Jonathan 1938- Y-82

Schwartz, Lynne Sharon 1939- DLB-218

Schwarz, Sibylle 1621-1638 . . . . DLB-164

Schwerner, Armand 1927-1999. . . . . DLB-165

Schwob, Marcel 1867-1905. . . . . DLB-123

Sciascia, Leonardo 1921-1989 . . . . .DLB-177

Science Fantasy DLB-8

Science-Fiction Fandom and Conventions . . DLB-8

Science-Fiction Fanzines: The Time
Binders DLB-8

Science-Fiction Films DLB-8

Science Fiction Writers of America and the
Nebula Awards DLB-8

Scot, Reginald circa 1538-1599. . . . . DLB-136

Scotellaro, Rocco 1923-1953 . . . . DLB-128

Scott, Alicia Anne (Lady John Scott)
1810-1900 . . . . DLB-240

Scott, Catharine Amy Dawson
1865-1934 . . . . DLB-240

Scott, Dennis 1939-1991 . . . . DLB-125

Scott, Dixon 1881-1915 . . . . DLB-98

Scott, Duncan Campbell 1862-1947 . . . . . . DLB-92

Scott, Evelyn 1893-1963 . . . . DLB-9, 48

Scott, F. R. 1899-1985. . . . . DLB-88

Scott, Frederick George 1861-1944. . . . . . . DLB-92

Scott, Geoffrey 1884-1929 . . . . DLB-149

Scott, Harvey W. 1838-1910 . . . . DLB-23

Scott, Lady Jane (see Scott, Alicia Anne)

Scott, Paul 1920-1978 . . . . .DLB-14, 207

Scott, Sarah 1723-1795 . . . . DLB-39

Scott, Tom 1918- DLB-27

Scott, Sir Walter 1771-1832
. . . . . . .DLB-93, 107, 116, 144, 159; CDBLB-3

Scott, Walter, Publishing
Company Limited DLB-112

Scott, William Bell 1811-1890 . . . . DLB-32

Scott, William R. [publishing house] DLB-46

Scott-Heron, Gil 1949- DLB-41

Scribe, Eugene 1791-1861. . . . . DLB-192

Scribner, Arthur Hawley 1859-1932 . . . .DS-13, 16

Scribner, Charles 1854-1930 . . . . .DS-13, 16

Scribner, Charles, Jr. 1921-1995. . . . . .Y-95

Reminiscences DS-17

Charles Scribner's Sons DLB-49; DS-13, 16, 17

Scripps, E. W. 1854-1926 . . . . DLB-25

Scudder, Horace Elisha 1838-1902 . . . . DLB-42, 71

Scudder, Vida Dutton 1861-1954 . . . . DLB-71

Scupham, Peter 1933- DLB-40

Seabrook, William 1886-1945 . . . . DLB-4

Seabury, Samuel 1729-1796 . . . . DLB-31

Seacole, Mary Jane Grant 1805-1881. . . . . DLB-166

The Seafarer circa 970 . . . . DLB-146

Sealsfield, Charles (Carl Postl)
    1793-1864 . . . . DLB-133, 186

Sears, Edward I. 1819?-1876 . . . . DLB-79

Sears Publishing Company DLB-46

Seaton, George 1911-1979 . . . . DLB-44

Seaton, William Winston 1785-1866 . . . . . . DLB-43

Secker, Martin [publishing house] DLB-112

Secker, Martin, and Warburg Limited. . . . DLB-112

The Second Annual New York Festival
    of Mystery. Y-00

Second-Generation Minor Poets of the
    Seventeenth Century DLB-126

Sedgwick, Arthur George 1844-1915. . . . . . DLB-64

Sedgwick, Catharine Maria
    1789-1867 . . . . DLB-1, 74, 183, 239, 243

Sedgwick, Ellery 1872-1930 . . . . DLB-91

Sedgwick, Eve Kosofsky 1950- DLB-246

Sedley, Sir Charles 1639-1701 . . . . DLB-131

Seeberg, Peter 1925-1999. . . . . DLB-214

Seeger, Alan 1888-1916 . . . . DLB-45

Seers, Eugene (see Dantin, Louis)

Segal, Erich 1937- Y-86

Šegedin, Petar 1909- DLB-181

Seghers, Anna 1900-1983. . . . . DLB-69; CDWLB-2

Seid, Ruth (see Sinclair, Jo)

Seidel, Frederick Lewis 1936- Y-84

Seidel, Ina 1885-1974 . . . . DLB-56

Seifert, Jaroslav
    1901-1986 . . . . DLB-215; Y-84; CDWLB-4

Seigenthaler, John 1927- DLB-127

Seizin Press DLB-112

Séjour, Victor 1817-1874 . . . . DLB-50

Séjour Marcou et Ferrand, Juan Victor
    (see Séjour, Victor)

Sekowski, Józef-Julian, Baron Brambeus
    (see Senkovsky, Osip Ivanovich)

Selby, Bettina 1934- DLB-204

Selby, Hubert, Jr. 1928- DLB-2, 227

Selden, George 1929-1989 . . . . DLB-52

Selden, John 1584-1654 . . . . DLB-213

Selected English-Language Little Magazines
    and Newspapers [France, 1920-1939] . . . DLB-4

Selected Humorous Magazines
    (1820-1950) DLB-11

Selected Science-Fiction Magazines and
    Anthologies DLB-8

Selenić, Slobodan 1933-1995 . . . . DLB-181

Self, Edwin F. 1920- DLB-137

Self, Will 1961- DLB-207

Seligman, Edwin R. A. 1861-1939. . . . . . . DLB-47

Selimović, Meša
    1910-1982 . . . . DLB-181; CDWLB-4

Selous, Frederick Courteney
    1851-1917 . . . . DLB-174

Seltzer, Chester E. (see Muro, Amado)

Seltzer, Thomas [publishing house] DLB-46

Selvon, Sam 1923-1994 . . . . . DLB-125; CDWLB-3

Semmes, Raphael 1809-1877 . . . . DLB-189

Senancour, Etienne de 1770-1846 . . . . . . DLB-119

Sendak, Maurice 1928- DLB-61

Seneca the Elder
    circa 54 B.C.-circa A.D. 40 . . . . DLB-211

Seneca the Younger
    circa 1 B.C.-A.D. 65 . . . . DLB-211; CDWLB-1

Senécal, Eva 1905- DLB-92

Sengstacke, John 1912- DLB-127

Senior, Olive 1941- DLB-157

Senkovsky, Osip Ivanovich
    (Józef-Julian Sekowski, Baron Brambeus)
    1800-1858 . . . . DLB-198

Šenoa, August 1838-1881 . . . DLB-147; CDWLB-4

"Sensation Novels" (1863), by
    H. L. Manse DLB-21

Sepamla, Sipho 1932- DLB-157, 225

Seredy, Kate 1899-1975 . . . . DLB-22

Sereni, Vittorio 1913-1983. . . . . DLB-128

Seres, William [publishing house] DLB-170

Serling, Rod 1924-1975 . . . . DLB-26

Serote, Mongane Wally 1944- DLB-125, 225

Serraillier, Ian 1912-1994. . . . . DLB-161

Serrano, Nina 1934- DLB-122

Service, Robert 1874-1958 . . . . DLB-92

Sessler, Charles 1854-1935 . . . . DLB-187

Seth, Vikram 1952- DLB-120

Seton, Elizabeth Ann 1774-1821. . . . . DLB-200

Seton, Ernest Thompson
    1860-1942 . . . . DLB-92; DS-13

Setouchi Harumi 1922- DLB-182

Settle, Mary Lee 1918- DLB-6

Seume, Johann Gottfried 1763-1810. . . . . . DLB-94

Seuse, Heinrich 1295?-1366. . . . . DLB-179

Seuss, Dr. (see Geisel, Theodor Seuss)

The Seventy-fifth Anniversary of the Armistice:
    The Wilfred Owen Centenary and
    the Great War Exhibit
    at the University of Virginia Y-93

Severin, Timothy 1940- DLB-204

Sewall, Joseph 1688-1769 . . . . DLB-24

Sewall, Richard B. 1908- DLB-111

Sewell, Anna 1820-1878. . . . . DLB-163

Sewell, Samuel 1652-1730 . . . . DLB-24

Sex, Class, Politics, and Religion [in the
    British Novel, 1930-1959] DLB-15

Sexton, Anne 1928-1974 . . . DLB-5, 169; CDALB-1

Seymour-Smith, Martin 1928-1998 . . . . . . DLB-155

Sgorlon, Carlo 1930- DLB-196

Shaara, Michael 1929-1988 . . . . Y-83

Shabel'skaia, Aleksandra Stanislavovna
    1845-1921 . . . . DLB-238

Shadwell, Thomas 1641?-1692 . . . . DLB-80

Shaffer, Anthony 1926- DLB-13

Shaffer, Peter 1926- DLB-13, 233; CDBLB-8

Shaftesbury, Anthony Ashley Cooper,
    Third Earl of 1671-1713 . . . . DLB-101

Shairp, Mordaunt 1887-1939 . . . . DLB-10

Shakespeare, Nicholas 1957- DLB-231

Shakespeare, William
    1564-1616 . . . . DLB-62, 172; CDBLB-1

The Shakespeare Globe Trust Y-93

Shakespeare Head Press DLB-112

Shakhovskoi, Aleksandr Aleksandrovich
    1777-1846. DLB-150

Shange, Ntozake 1948- DLB-38, 249

Shapiro, Karl 1913-2000 . . . . DLB-48

Sharon Publications DLB-46

Sharp, Margery 1905-1991 . . . . DLB-161

Sharp, William 1855-1905. . . . . DLB-156

Sharpe, Tom 1928- DLB-14, 231

Shaw, Albert 1857-1947 . . . . DLB-91

Shaw, George Bernard
    1856-1950 . . . . DLB-10, 57, 190, CDBLB-6

Shaw, Henry Wheeler 1818-1885 . . . . DLB-11

Shaw, Joseph T. 1874-1952 . . . . DLB-137

Shaw, Irwin
    1913-1984 . . . . . . DLB-6, 102; Y-84; CDALB-1

Shaw, Mary 1854-1929 . . . . DLB-228

Shaw, Robert 1927-1978. . . . . DLB-13, 14

Shaw, Robert B. 1947- DLB-120

Shawn, William 1907-1992 . . . . DLB-137

Shay, Frank [publishing house] DLB-46

Shchedrin, N. (see Saltykov, Mikhail Evgrafovich)

Shea, John Gilmary 1824-1892 . . . . DLB-30

Sheaffer, Louis 1912-1993 . . . . DLB-103

Shearing, Joseph 1886-1952. . . . . DLB-70

Shebbeare, John 1709-1788 . . . . DLB-39

Sheckley, Robert 1928- DLB-8

Shedd, William G. T. 1820-1894. . . . . DLB-64

Sheed, Wilfred 1930- DLB-6

Sheed and Ward [U.S.] DLB-46

Sheed and Ward Limited [U.K.] DLB-112

Sheldon, Alice B. (see Tiptree, James, Jr.)

Sheldon, Edward 1886-1946 . . . . DLB-7

Sheldon and Company DLB-49

Sheller, Aleksandr Konstantinovich
    1838-1900 . . . . DLB-238

Shelley, Mary Wollstonecraft 1797-1851
    . . . . DLB-110, 116, 159, 178; CDBLB-3

Shelley, Percy Bysshe
    1792-1822 . . . . . . DLB-96, 110, 158; CDBLB-3

Shelnutt, Eve 1941- DLB-130

Shenstone, William 1714-1763 . . . . DLB-95

Shepard, Clark and Brown DLB-49

Shepard, Ernest Howard 1879-1976 . . . . . DLB-160

Shepard, Sam 1943- DLB-7, 212

Shepard, Thomas I, 1604 or 1605-1649 . . . DLB-24

Shepard, Thomas II, 1635-1677 . . . . DLB-24

Shepherd, Luke
   flourished 1547-1554 . . . . DLB-136

Sherburne, Edward 1616-1702 . . . . DLB-131

Sheridan, Frances 1724-1766 . . . . DLB-39, 84

Sheridan, Richard Brinsley
   1751-1816 . . . . DLB-89; CDBLB-2

Sherman, Francis 1871-1926 . . . . DLB-92

Sherman, Martin 1938- DLB-228

Sherriff, R. C. 1896-1975 . . . . . DLB-10, 191, 233

Sherrod, Blackie 1919- DLB-241

Sherry, Norman 1935- DLB-155

Sherry, Richard 1506-1551 or 1555 . . . . . DLB-236

Sherwood, Mary Martha 1775-1851 . . . . . DLB-163

Sherwood, Robert E. 1896-1955 . . .DLB-7, 26, 249

Shevyrev, Stepan Petrovich
   1806-1864 . . . . DLB-205

Shiel, M. P. 1865-1947 . . . . DLB-153

Shiels, George 1886-1949 . . . . DLB-10

Shiga, Naoya 1883-1971 . . . . DLB-180

Shiina Rinzō 1911-1973 . . . . DLB-182

Shikishi Naishinnō 1153?-1201 . . . . DLB-203

Shillaber, Benjamin Penhallow
   1814-1890 . . . . DLB-1, 11, 235

Shimao Toshio 1917-1986 . . . . DLB-182

Shimazaki, Tōson 1872-1943 . . . . DLB-180

Shine, Ted 1931- DLB-38

Shinkei 1406-1475 . . . . DLB-203

Ship, Reuben 1915-1975 . . . . DLB-88

Shirer, William L. 1904-1993 . . . . DLB-4

Shirinsky-Shikhmatov, Sergii Aleksandrovich
   1783-1837 . . . . DLB-150

Shirley, James 1596-1666 . . . . DLB-58

Shishkov, Aleksandr Semenovich
   1753-1841 . . . . DLB-150

Shockley, Ann Allen 1927- DLB-33

Shōno Junzō 1921- DLB-182

Shore, Arabella 1820?-1901 and
   Shore, Louisa 1824-1895 . . . . DLB-199

Short, Peter [publishing house] DLB-170

Shorter, Dora Sigerson 1866-1918 . . . . . . DLB-240

Shorthouse, Joseph Henry 1834-1903 . . . . DLB-18

Shōtetsu 1381-1459 . . . . DLB-203

Showalter, Elaine 1941- DLB-67

Shulevitz, Uri 1935- DLB-61

Shulman, Max 1919-1988 . . . . DLB-11

Shute, Henry A. 1856-1943 . . . . DLB-9

Shuttle, Penelope 1947- DLB-14, 40

Sibbes, Richard 1577-1635 . . . . DLB-151

Sibiriak, D. (see Mamin, Dmitrii Narkisovich)

Siddal, Elizabeth Eleanor 1829-1862 . . . . DLB-199

Sidgwick, Ethel 1877-1970 . . . . DLB-197

Sidgwick and Jackson Limited DLB-112

Sidney, Margaret (see Lothrop, Harriet M.)

Sidney, Mary 1561-1621 . . . . DLB-167

Sidney, Sir Philip
   1554-1586 . . . . DLB-167; CDBLB-1

An Apologie for Poetrie (the Olney
   edition, 1595, of *Defence of Poesie*) DLB-167

Sidney's Press DLB-49

Sierra, Rubén 1946- DLB-122

Sierra Club Books DLB-49

Siger of Brabant circa 1240-circa 1284 . . . DLB-115

Sigourney, Lydia Huntley
   1791-1865 . . . . . . .DLB-1, 42, 73, 183, 239, 243

Silkin, Jon 1930- DLB-27

Silko, Leslie Marmon 1948- DLB-143, 175

Silliman, Benjamin 1779-1864 . . . . DLB-183

Silliman, Ron 1946- DLB-169

Silliphant, Stirling 1918- DLB-26

Sillitoe, Alan 1928- DLB-14, 139; CDBLB-8

Silman, Roberta 1934- DLB-28

Silva, Beverly 1930- DLB-122

Silverberg, Robert 1935- DLB-8

Silverman, Kaja 1947- DLB-246

Silverman, Kenneth 1936- DLB-111

Simak, Clifford D. 1904-1988 . . . . DLB-8

Simcoe, Elizabeth 1762-1850 . . . . DLB-99

Simcox, Edith Jemima 1844-1901 . . . . DLB-190

Simcox, George Augustus 1841-1905 . . . . . DLB-35

Sime, Jessie Georgina 1868-1958 . . . . DLB-92

Simenon, Georges 1903-1989 . . . . . . .DLB-72; Y-89

Simic, Charles 1938- DLB-105

   "Images and 'Images,'" DLB-105

Simionescu, Mircea Horia 1928- DLB-232

Simmel, Johannes Mario 1924- DLB-69

Simmes, Valentine [publishing house] DLB-170

Simmons, Ernest J. 1903-1972 . . . . DLB-103

Simmons, Herbert Alfred 1930- DLB-33

Simmons, James 1933- DLB-40

Simms, William Gilmore
   1806-1870 . . . . .DLB-3, 30, 59, 73, 248

Simms and M'Intyre DLB-106

Simon, Claude 1913- DLB-83; Y-85

Simon, Neil 1927- DLB-7

Simon and Schuster DLB-46

Simons, Katherine Drayton Mayrant
   1890-1969 . . . . Y-83

Simović, Ljubomir 1935- DLB-181

Simpkin and Marshall
   [publishing house] DLB-154

Simpson, Helen 1897-1940 . . . . DLB-77

Simpson, Louis 1923- DLB-5

Simpson, N. F. 1919- DLB-13

Sims, George 1923- DLB-87; Y-99

Sims, George Robert 1847-1922 . . .DLB-35, 70, 135

Sinán, Rogelio 1904- DLB-145

Sinclair, Andrew 1935- DLB-14

Sinclair, Bertrand William 1881-1972 . . . . . DLB-92

Sinclair, Catherine 1800-1864 . . . . DLB-163

Sinclair, Jo 1913-1995 . . . . DLB-28

Sinclair, Lister 1921- DLB-88

Sinclair, May 1863-1946 . . . . DLB-36, 135

Sinclair, Upton 1878-1968 . . . . . DLB-9; CDALB-5

Sinclair, Upton [publishing house] DLB-46

Singer, Isaac Bashevis
   1904-1991 . . . DLB-6, 28, 52; Y-91; CDALB-1

Singer, Mark 1950- DLB-185

Singmaster, Elsie 1879-1958 . . . . DLB-9

Sinisgalli, Leonardo 1908-1981 . . . . DLB-114

Siodmak, Curt 1902-2000 . . . . DLB-44

Sîrbu, Ion D. 1919-1989 . . . . DLB-232

Siringo, Charles A. 1855-1928 . . . . DLB-186

Sissman, L. E. 1928-1976 . . . . DLB-5

Sisson, C. H. 1914- DLB-27

Sitwell, Edith 1887-1964 . . . . . . DLB-20; CDBLB-7

Sitwell, Osbert 1892-1969 . . . . .DLB-100, 195

Skácel, Jan 1922-1989 . . . . DLB-232

Skalbe, Kārlis 1879-1945 . . . . DLB-220

Skármeta, Antonio
   1940- DLB-145; CDWLB-3

Skavronsky, A. (see Danilevsky, Grigorii Petrovich)

Skeat, Walter W. 1835-1912 . . . . DLB-184

Skeffington, William
   [publishing house] DLB-106

Skelton, John 1463-1529 . . . . DLB-136

Skelton, Robin 1925- DLB-27, 53

Škėma, Antanas 1910-1961 . . . . DLB-220

Skinner, Constance Lindsay
   1877-1939 . . . . DLB-92

Skinner, John Stuart 1788-1851 . . . . DLB-73

Skipsey, Joseph 1832-1903 . . . . DLB-35

Skou-Hansen, Tage 1925- DLB-214

Škvorecký, Josef 1924- DLB-232; CDWLB-4

Slade, Bernard 1930- DLB-53

Slamnig, Ivan 1930- DLB-181

Slančeková, Božena (see Timrava)

Slater, Patrick 1880-1951 . . . . DLB-68

Slaveykov, Pencho 1866-1912 . . . . .DLB-147

Slaviček, Milivoj 1929- DLB-181

Slavitt, David 1935- DLB-5, 6

Sleigh, Burrows Willcocks Arthur
   1821-1869 . . . . DLB-99

A Slender Thread of Hope:
   The Kennedy Center Black
   Theatre Project DLB-38

Slesinger, Tess 1905-1945 . . . . DLB-102

Slick, Sam (see Haliburton, Thomas Chandler)

Sloan, John 1871-1951 . . . . DLB-188

Sloane, William, Associates DLB-46

Small, Maynard and Company DLB-49

Small Presses in Great Britain and Ireland,
   1960-1985 . . . . DLB-40

Small Presses I: Jargon Society Y-84

Small Presses II: The Spirit That Moves
   Us Press Y-85

Small Presses III: Pushcart Press Y-87

Smart, Christopher 1722-1771 . . . . DLB-109

Smart, David A. 1892-1957 . . . . DLB-137

Smart, Elizabeth 1913-1986 . . . . DLB-88

Smedley, Menella Bute 1820?-1877 . . . . . DLB-199

Smellie, William [publishing house] DLB-154

Smiles, Samuel 1812-1904 . . . . DLB-55

Smiley, Jane 1949- DLB-227, 234

Smith, A. J. M. 1902-1980 . . . . DLB-88

Smith, Adam 1723-1790 . . . . DLB-104

Smith, Adam (George Jerome Waldo Goodman)
1930- DLB-185

Smith, Alexander 1829-1867 . . . . DLB-32, 55

"On the Writing of Essays" (1862) DLB-57

Smith, Amanda 1837-1915 . . . . DLB-221

Smith, Betty 1896-1972 . . . . Y-82

Smith, Carol Sturm 1938- Y-81

Smith, Charles Henry 1826-1903 . . . . DLB-11

Smith, Charlotte 1749-1806 . . . . DLB-39, 109

Smith, Chet 1899-1973 . . . . DLB-171

Smith, Cordwainer 1913-1966 . . . . DLB-8

Smith, Dave 1942- DLB-5

Smith, Dodie 1896- DLB-10

Smith, Doris Buchanan 1934- DLB-52

Smith, E. E. 1890-1965 . . . . DLB-8

Smith, Elder and Company DLB-154

Smith, Elihu Hubbard 1771-1798 . . . . DLB-37

Smith, Elizabeth Oakes (Prince)
(see Oakes Smith, Elizabeth)

Smith, Eunice 1757-1823 . . . . DLB-200

Smith, F. Hopkinson 1838-1915 . . . . DS-13

Smith, George D. 1870-1920 . . . . DLB-140

Smith, George O. 1911-1981 . . . . DLB-8

Smith, Goldwin 1823-1910 . . . . DLB-99

Smith, H. Allen 1907-1976 . . . . DLB-11, 29

Smith, Harrison, and Robert Haas
[publishing house] DLB-46

Smith, Harry B. 1860-1936 . . . . DLB-187

Smith, Hazel Brannon 1914- DLB-127

Smith, Henry circa 1560-circa 1591 . . . . . DLB-136

Smith, Horatio (Horace) 1779-1849 . . . . . DLB-116

Smith, Horatio (Horace) 1779-1849 and
James Smith 1775-1839 . . . . DLB-96

Smith, Iain Crichton 1928- DLB-40, 139

Smith, J. Allen 1860-1924 . . . . DLB-47

Smith, J. Stilman, and Company DLB-49

Smith, Jessie Willcox 1863-1935 . . . . DLB-188

Smith, John 1580-1631 . . . . DLB-24, 30

Smith, Josiah 1704-1781 . . . . DLB-24

Smith, Ken 1938- DLB-40

Smith, Lee 1944- DLB-143; Y-83

Smith, Logan Pearsall 1865-1946 . . . . DLB-98

Smith, Margaret Bayard 1778-1844 . . . . . DLB-248

Smith, Mark 1935- Y-82

Smith, Michael 1698-circa 1771 . . . . DLB-31

Smith, Pauline 1882-1959 . . . . DLB-225

Smith, Red 1905-1982 . . . . DLB-29, 171

Smith, Roswell 1829-1892 . . . . DLB-79

Smith, Samuel Harrison 1772-1845 . . . . . . DLB-43

Smith, Samuel Stanhope 1751-1819 . . . . . . DLB-37

Smith, Sarah (see Stretton, Hesba)

Smith, Sarah Pogson 1774-1870 . . . . DLB-200

Smith, Seba 1792-1868 . . . . DLB-1, 11, 243

Smith, Stevie 1902-1971 . . . . DLB-20

Smith, Sydney 1771-1845 . . . . DLB-107

Smith, Sydney Goodsir 1915-1975 . . . . DLB-27

Smith, Sir Thomas 1513-1577 . . . . DLB-132

Smith, W. B., and Company DLB-49

Smith, W. H., and Son DLB-106

Smith, Wendell 1914-1972 . . . . DLB-171

Smith, William flourished 1595-1597 . . . . DLB-136

Smith, William 1727-1803 . . . . DLB-31

A General Idea of the College of Mirania
(1753) [excerpts] DLB-31

Smith, William 1728-1793 . . . . DLB-30

Smith, William Gardner 1927-1974 . . . . . . DLB-76

Smith, William Henry 1808-1872 . . . . DLB-159

Smith, William Jay 1918- DLB-5

Smithers, Leonard [publishing house] DLB-112

Smollett, Tobias
1721-1771 . . . . DLB-39, 104; CDBLB-2

Dedication, Ferdinand Count
Fathom (1753) DLB-39

Preface to Ferdinand Count Fathom (1753) DLB-39

Preface to Roderick Random (1748) DLB-39

Smythe, Francis Sydney 1900-1949 . . . . . DLB-195

Snelling, William Joseph 1804-1848 . . . . . DLB-202

Snellings, Rolland (see Touré, Askia Muhammad)

Snodgrass, W. D. 1926- DLB-5

Snow, C. P.
1905-1980 . . . . . DLB-15, 77; DS-17; CDBLB-7

Snyder, Gary 1930- . . . DLB-5, 16, 165, 212, 237

Sobiloff, Hy 1912-1970 . . . . DLB-48

The Society for Textual Scholarship and
TEXT Y-87

The Society for the History of Authorship,
Reading and Publishing Y-92

Soffici, Ardengo 1879-1964 . . . . DLB-114

Sofola, 'Zulu 1938- DLB-157

Solano, Solita 1888-1975 . . . . DLB-4

Soldati, Mario 1906-1999 . . . . DLB-177

Šoljan, Antun 1932-1993 . . . . DLB-181

Sollers, Philippe 1936- DLB-83

Sollogub, Vladimir Aleksandrovich
1813-1882 . . . . DLB-198

Sollors, Werner 1943- DBL-246

Solmi, Sergio 1899-1981 . . . . DLB-114

Solomon, Carl 1928- DLB-16

Solway, David 1941- DLB-53

Solzhenitsyn and America Y-85

Somerville, Edith Œnone 1858-1949 . . . . DLB-135

Somov, Orest Mikhailovich
1793-1833 . . . . DLB-198

Sønderby, Knud 1909-1966 . . . . DLB-214

Song, Cathy 1955- DLB-169

Sono Ayako 1931- DLB-182

Sontag, Susan 1933- DLB-2, 67

Sophocles 497/496 B.C.-406/405 B.C.
. . . . DLB-176; CDWLB-1

Šopov, Aco 1923-1982 . . . . DLB-181

Sørensen, Villy 1929- DLB-214

Sorensen, Virginia 1912-1991 . . . . DLB-206

Sorge, Reinhard Johannes 1892-1916 . . . . DLB-118

Sorrentino, Gilbert 1929- DLB-5, 173; Y-80

Sotheby, James 1682-1742 . . . . DLB-213

Sotheby, John 1740-1807 . . . . DLB-213

Sotheby, Samuel 1771-1842 . . . . DLB-213

Sotheby, Samuel Leigh 1805-1861 . . . . . . DLB-213

Sotheby, William 1757-1833 . . . . DLB-93, 213

Soto, Gary 1952- DLB-82

Sources for the Study of Tudor and Stuart
Drama DLB-62

Souster, Raymond 1921- DLB-88

The South English Legendary circa thirteenth-fifteenth
centuries DLB-146

Southerland, Ellease 1943- DLB-33

Southern, Terry 1924-1995 . . . . DLB-2

Southern Illinois University Press Y-95

Southern Writers Between the Wars DLB-9

Southerne, Thomas 1659-1746 . . . . DLB-80

Southey, Caroline Anne Bowles
1786-1854 . . . . DLB-116

Southey, Robert 1774-1843 . . . . . DLB-93, 107, 142

Southwell, Robert 1561?-1595 . . . . DLB-167

Southworth, E. D. E. N. 1819-1899 . . . . . DLB-239

Sowande, Bode 1948- DLB-157

Sowle, Tace [publishing house] DLB-170

Soyfer, Jura 1912-1939 . . . . DLB-124

Soyinka, Wole
1934- DLB-125; Y-86, Y-87; CDWLB-3

Spacks, Barry 1931- DLB-105

Spalding, Frances 1950- DLB-155

Spark, Muriel 1918- . . . DLB-15, 139; CDBLB-7

Sparke, Michael [publishing house] DLB-170

Sparks, Jared 1789-1866 . . . . DLB-1, 30, 235

Sparshott, Francis 1926- DLB-60

Späth, Gerold 1939- DLB-75

Spatola, Adriano 1941-1988 . . . . DLB-128

Spaziani, Maria Luisa 1924- DLB-128

Special Collections at the University of Colorado
at Boulder Y-98

The Spectator 1828- DLB-110

Spedding, James 1808-1881 . . . . DLB-144

Spee von Langenfeld, Friedrich
1591-1635 . . . . DLB-164

Speght, Rachel 1597-after 1630 . . . . DLB-126

Speke, John Hanning 1827-1864 . . . . DLB-166

Spellman, A. B. 1935- DLB-41

Spence, Catherine Helen 1825-1910..... DLB-230

Spence, Thomas 1750-1814 .... DLB-158

Spencer, Anne 1882-1975 .... DLB-51, 54

Spencer, Charles, third Earl of Sunderland
1674-1722 .... DLB-213

Spencer, Elizabeth 1921- DLB-6, 218

Spencer, George John, Second Earl Spencer
1758-1834 .... DLB-184

Spencer, Herbert 1820-1903 .... DLB-57

"The Philosophy of Style" (1852) DLB-57

Spencer, Scott 1945- Y-86

Spender, J. A. 1862-1942 .... DLB-98

Spender, Stephen 1909-1995... DLB-20; CDBLB-7

Spener, Philipp Jakob 1635-1705 .... DLB-164

Spenser, Edmund
circa 1552-1599 .... DLB-167; CDBLB-1

Envoy from *The Shepheardes Calender*..... DLB-167

"The Generall Argument of the
Whole Booke," from
The Shepheardes Calender........... DLB-167

"A Letter of the Authors Expounding
His Whole Intention in the Course
of this Worke: Which for that It Giueth
Great Light to the Reader, for the Better
Vnderstanding Is Hereunto Annexed,"
from *The Faerie Qveene* (1590) DLB-167

"To His Booke," from
The Shepheardes Calender (1579) DLB-167

"To the Most Excellent and Learned Both
Orator and Poete, Mayster Gabriell Haruey,
His Verie Special and Singular Good Frend
E. K. Commendeth the Good Lyking of
This His Labour, and the Patronage of
the New Poete," from
The Shepheardes Calender........... DLB-167

Sperr, Martin 1944- DLB-124

Spicer, Jack 1925-1965 .... DLB-5, 16, 193

Spielberg, Peter 1929- Y-81

Spielhagen, Friedrich 1829-1911....... DLB-129

"Spielmannsepen" (circa 1152-circa 1500) .. DLB-148

Spier, Peter 1927- DLB-61

Spillane, Mickey 1918- DLB-226

Spink, J. G. Taylor 1888-1962 .... DLB-241

Spinrad, Norman 1940- DLB-8

Spires, Elizabeth 1952- DLB-120

Spitteler, Carl 1845-1924 .... DLB-129

Spivak, Lawrence E. 1900- DLB-137

Spofford, Harriet Prescott
1835-1921 .... DLB-74, 221

Spring, Howard 1889-1965........... DLB-191

Squibob (see Derby, George Horatio)

Squier, E. G. 1821-1888 .... DLB-189

Stacpoole, H. de Vere 1863-1951 .... DLB-153

Staël, Germaine de 1766-1817...... DLB-119, 192

Staël-Holstein, Anne-Louise Germaine de
(see Staël, Germaine de)

Stafford, Jean 1915-1979 ....DLB-2, 173

Stafford, William 1914-1993........ DLB-5, 206

Stage Censorship: "The Rejected Statement"
(1911), by Bernard Shaw [excerpts] ... DLB-10

Stallings, Laurence 1894-1968 ....DLB-7, 44

Stallworthy, Jon 1935- DLB-40

Stampp, Kenneth M. 1912- DLB-17

Stănescu, Nichita 1933-1983.......... DLB-232

Stanev, Emiliyan 1907-1979 .... DLB-181

Stanford, Ann 1916- DLB-5

Stangerup, Henrik 1937-1998 .... DLB-214

Stanitsky, N. (see Panaeva, Avdot'ia Iakovlevna)

Stankevich, Nikolai Vladimirovich
1813-1840 .... DLB-198

Stanković, Borisav ("Bora")
1876-1927.............DLB-147; CDWLB-4

Stanley, Henry M. 1841-1904 ... DLB-189; DS-13

Stanley, Thomas 1625-1678 .... DLB-131

Stannard, Martin 1947- DLB-155

Stansby, William [publishing house]......DLB-170

Stanton, Elizabeth Cady 1815-1902 ...... DLB-79

Stanton, Frank L. 1857-1927........... DLB-25

Stanton, Maura 1946- DLB-120

Stapledon, Olaf 1886-1950 .... DLB-15

Star Spangled Banner Office........... DLB-49

Stark, Freya 1893-1993............... DLB-195

Starkey, Thomas circa 1499-1538 ...... DLB-132

Starkie, Walter 1894-1976 .... DLB-195

Starkweather, David 1935- DLB-7

Starrett, Vincent 1886-1974 .... DLB-187

The State of Publishing.................... Y-97

Statements on the Art of Poetry DLB-54

Stationers' Company of London, The DLB-170

Statius circa A.D. 45-A.D. 96 .... DLB-211

Stead, Robert J. C. 1880-1959 .... DLB-92

Steadman, Mark 1930- DLB-6

The Stealthy School of Criticism (1871), by
Dante Gabriel Rossetti............. DLB-35

Stearns, Harold E. 1891-1943.......... DLB-4

Stebnitsky, M. (see Leskov, Nikolai Semenovich)

Stedman, Edmund Clarence 1833-1908... DLB-64

Steegmuller, Francis 1906-1994 .... DLB-111

Steel, Flora Annie 1847-1929 ...... DLB-153, 156

Steele, Max 1922- Y-80

Steele, Richard
1672-1729.......... DLB-84, 101; CDBLB-2

Steele, Timothy 1948- DLB-120

Steele, Wilbur Daniel 1886-1970 .... DLB-86

Steere, Richard circa 1643-1721 .... DLB-24

Stefanovski, Goran 1952- DLB-181

Stegner, Wallace 1909-1993 ....DLB-9, 206; Y-93

Stehr, Hermann 1864-1940 .... DLB-66

Steig, William 1907- DLB-61

Stein, Gertrude 1874-1946
...... DLB-4, 54, 86, 228; DS-15; CDALB-4

Stein, Leo 1872-1947................... DLB-4

Stein and Day Publishers DLB-46

Steinbeck, John
1902-1968 ....DLB-7, 9, 212; DS-2; CDALB-5

John Steinbeck Research Center........... Y-85

Steinem, Gloria 1934- DLB-246

Steiner, George 1929- DLB-67

Steinhoewel, Heinrich 1411/1412-1479....DLB-179

Steloff, Ida Frances 1887-1989 ....DLB-187

Stendhal 1783-1842.................. DLB-119

Stephen Crane: A Revaluation Virginia
Tech Conference, 1989 .... Y-89

Stephen, Leslie 1832-1904 ...... DLB-57, 144, 190

Stephen Vincent Benét Centenary Y-97

Stephens, A. G. 1865-1933............. DLB-230

Stephens, Alexander H. 1812-1883 ...... DLB-47

Stephens, Alice Barber 1858-1932 ...... DLB-188

Stephens, Ann 1810-1886........... DLB-3, 73

Stephens, Charles Asbury 1844?-1931.... DLB-42

Stephens, James 1882?-1950.....DLB-19, 153, 162

Stephens, John Lloyd 1805-1852 .... DLB-183

Stephens, Michael 1946- DLB-234

Sterling, George 1869-1926 .... DLB-54

Sterling, James 1701-1763 .... DLB-24

Sterling, John 1806-1844 .... DLB-116

Stern, Gerald 1925- DLB-105

Stern, Gladys B. 1890-1973 ....DLB-197

Stern, Madeleine B. 1912- DLB-111, 140

Stern, Richard 1928- DLB-218; Y-87

Stern, Stewart 1922- DLB-26

Sterne, Laurence
1713-1768.............. DLB-39; CDBLB-2

Sternheim, Carl 1878-1942........ DLB-56, 118

Sternhold, Thomas ?-1549 and
John Hopkins ?-1570 .... DLB-132

Steuart, David 1747-1824 .... DLB-213

Stevens, Henry 1819-1886 .... DLB-140

Stevens, Wallace 1879-1955 ... DLB-54; CDALB-5

Stevenson, Anne 1933- DLB-40

Stevenson, D. E. 1892-1973 .... DLB-191

Stevenson, Lionel 1902-1973 .... DLB-155

Stevenson, Robert Louis
1850-1894 ....DLB-18, 57, 141, 156, 174;
DS-13; CDBLB-5

"On Style in Literature:
Its Technical Elements" (1885) DLB-57

Stewart, Donald Ogden
1894-1980 .... DLB-4, 11, 26

Stewart, Dugald 1753-1828............. DLB-31

Stewart, George, Jr. 1848-1906.......... DLB-99

Stewart, George R. 1895-1980 .... DLB-8

Stewart, Maria W. 1803?-1879......... DLB-239

Stewart, Randall 1896-1964 .... DLB-103

Stewart and Kidd Company........... DLB-46

Stickney, Trumbull 1874-1904 .... DLB-54

Stieler, Caspar 1632-1707 .... DLB-164

Stifter, Adalbert
1805-1868 ....DLB-133; CDWLB-2

Stiles, Ezra 1727-1795 .... DLB-31

Still, James 1906- DLB-9

Stirner, Max 1806-1856 .... DLB-129

Stith, William 1707-1755 .... DLB-31

Stock, Elliot [publishing house]........ DLB-106

Stockton, Frank R.
1834-1902 . . . . DLB-42, 74; DS-13

Stockton, J. Roy 1892-1972 . . . . DLB-241

Stoddard, Ashbel [publishing house] DLB-49

Stoddard, Charles Warren
1843-1909 . . . . DLB-186

Stoddard, Elizabeth 1823-1902 . . . . DLB-202

Stoddard, Richard Henry
1825-1903 . . . . DLB-3, 64; DS-13

Stoddard, Solomon 1643-1729 . . . . DLB-24

Stoker, Bram
1847-1912 . . . . DLB-36, 70, 178; CDBLB-5

Stokes, Frederick A., Company DLB-49

Stokes, Thomas L. 1898-1958 . . . . DLB-29

Stokesbury, Leon 1945- DLB-120

Stolberg, Christian Graf zu 1748-1821 . . . . . DLB-94

Stolberg, Friedrich Leopold Graf zu
1750-1819 . . . . DLB-94

Stone, Herbert S., and Company DLB-49

Stone, Lucy 1818-1893 . . . . DLB-79, 239

Stone, Melville 1848-1929 . . . . DLB-25

Stone, Robert 1937- DLB-152

Stone, Ruth 1915- DLB-105

Stone, Samuel 1602-1663 . . . . DLB-24

Stone, William Leete 1792-1844 . . . . DLB-202

Stone and Kimball DLB-49

Stoppard, Tom
1937- DLB-13, 233; Y-85; CDBLB-8

Playwrights and Professors DLB-13

Storey, Anthony 1928- DLB-14

Storey, David 1933- DLB-13, 14, 207, 245

Storm, Theodor 1817-1888 . . DLB-129; CDWLB-2

Story, Thomas circa 1670-1742 . . . . DLB-31

Story, William Wetmore 1819-1895 . . . DLB-1, 235

Storytelling: A Contemporary Renaissance . . . Y-84

Stoughton, William 1631-1701 . . . . DLB-24

Stow, John 1525-1605 . . . . DLB-132

Stowe, Harriet Beecher 1811-1896
. . DLB-1, 12, 42, 74, 189, 239, 243; CDALB-3

Stowe, Leland 1899- DLB-29

Stoyanov, Dimitr Ivanov (see Elin Pelin)

Strabo 64 or 63 B.C.-circa A.D. 25 . . . . . . DLB-176

Strachey, Lytton 1880-1932 . . . . . DLB-149; DS-10

Strachey, Lytton, Preface to Eminent
Victorians DLB-149

Strahan, William [publishing house] DLB-154

Strahan and Company DLB-106

Strand, Mark 1934- DLB-5

The Strasbourg Oaths 842 . . . . DLB-148

Stratemeyer, Edward 1862-1930 . . . . DLB-42

Strati, Saverio 1924- DLB-177

Stratton and Barnard DLB-49

Stratton-Porter, Gene
1863-1924 . . . . DLB-221; DS-14

Straub, Peter 1943- Y-84

Strauß, Botho 1944- DLB-124

Strauß, David Friedrich 1808-1874 . . . . . . DLB-133

The Strawberry Hill Press DLB-154

Streatfeild, Noel 1895-1986 . . . . DLB-160

Street, Cecil John Charles (see Rhode, John)

Street, G. S. 1867-1936 . . . . DLB-135

Street and Smith DLB-49

Streeter, Edward 1891-1976 . . . . DLB-11

Streeter, Thomas Winthrop 1883-1965 . . . DLB-140

Stretton, Hesba 1832-1911 . . . . DLB-163, 190

Stribling, T. S. 1881-1965 . . . . DLB-9

Der Stricker circa 1190-circa 1250 . . . . . . DLB-138

Strickland, Samuel 1804-1867 . . . . DLB-99

Stringer, Arthur 1874-1950 . . . . DLB-92

Stringer and Townsend DLB-49

Strittmatter, Erwin 1912- DLB-69

Strniša, Gregor 1930-1987 . . . . DLB-181

Strode, William 1630-1645 . . . . DLB-126

Strong, L. A. G. 1896-1958 . . . . DLB-191

Strother, David Hunter (Porte Crayon)
1816-1888 . . . . DLB-3, 248

Strouse, Jean 1945- DLB-111

Stuart, Dabney 1937- DLB-105

Stuart, Jesse 1906-1984 . . . . . DLB-9, 48, 102; Y-84

Stuart, Lyle [publishing house] DLB-46

Stuart, Ruth McEnery 1849?-1917 . . . . . . DLB-202

Stubbs, Harry Clement (see Clement, Hal)

Stubenberg, Johann Wilhelm von
1619-1663 . . . . DLB-164

Studio DLB-112

The Study of Poetry (1880), by
Matthew Arnold DLB-35

Stump, Al 1916-1995 . . . . DLB-241

Sturgeon, Theodore 1918-1985 . . . . . DLB-8; Y-85

Sturges, Preston 1898-1959 . . . . DLB-26

"Style" (1840; revised, 1859), by
Thomas de Quincey [excerpt] DLB-57

"Style" (1888), by Walter Pater DLB-57

Style (1897), by Walter Raleigh
[excerpt] DLB-57

"Style" (1877), by T. H. Wright
[excerpt] DLB-57

"Le Style c'est l'homme" (1892), by
W. H. Mallock DLB-57

Styron, William
1925- DLB-2, 143; Y-80; CDALB-6

Suárez, Mario 1925- DLB-82

Such, Peter 1939- DLB-60

Suckling, Sir John 1609-1641? DLB-58, 126

Suckow, Ruth 1892-1960 . . . . DLB-9, 102

Sudermann, Hermann 1857-1928 . . . . DLB-118

Sue, Eugène 1804-1857 . . . . DLB-119

Sue, Marie-Joseph (see Sue, Eugène)

Suetonius circa A.D. 69-post A.D. 122 . . . DLB-211

Suggs, Simon (see Hooper, Johnson Jones)

Sui Sin Far (see Eaton, Edith Maude)

Suits, Gustav 1883-1956 . . . . DLB-220; CDWLB-4

Sukenick, Ronald 1932- DLB-173; Y-81

Suknaski, Andrew 1942- DLB-53

Sullivan, Alan 1868-1947 . . . . DLB-92

Sullivan, C. Gardner 1886-1965 . . . . DLB-26

Sullivan, Frank 1892-1976 . . . . DLB-11

Sulte, Benjamin 1841-1923 . . . . DLB-99

Sulzberger, Arthur Hays 1891-1968 . . . . . DLB-127

Sulzberger, Arthur Ochs 1926- DLB-127

Sulzer, Johann Georg 1720-1779 . . . . DLB-97

Sumarokov, Aleksandr Petrovich
1717-1777 . . . . DLB-150

Summers, Hollis 1916- DLB-6

A Summing Up at Century's End Y-99

Sumner, Charles 1811-1874 . . . . DLB-235

Sumner, Henry A. [publishing house] DLB-49

Surtees, Robert Smith 1803-1864 . . . . DLB-21

Survey of Literary Biographies Y-00

A Survey of Poetry Anthologies,
1879-1960 . . . . DLB-54

Surveys: Japanese Literature,
1987-1995 . . . . DLB-182

Sutherland, Efua Theodora
1924-1996 . . . . DLB-117

Sutherland, John 1919-1956 . . . . DLB-68

Sutro, Alfred 1863-1933 . . . . DLB-10

Svendsen, Hanne Marie 1933- DLB-214

Swados, Harvey 1920-1972 . . . . DLB-2

Swain, Charles 1801-1874 . . . . DLB-32

Swallow Press DLB-46

Swan Sonnenschein Limited DLB-106

Swanberg, W. A. 1907- DLB-103

Swenson, May 1919-1989 . . . . DLB-5

Swerling, Jo 1897- DLB-44

Swift, Graham 1949- DLB-194

Swift, Jonathan
1667-1745 . . . . DLB-39, 95, 101; CDBLB-2

Swinburne, A. C.
1837-1909 . . . . DLB-35, 57; CDBLB-4

Swineshead, Richard
floruit circa 1350 . . . . DLB-115

Swinnerton, Frank 1884-1982 . . . . DLB-34

Swisshelm, Jane Grey 1815-1884 . . . . DLB-43

Swope, Herbert Bayard 1882-1958 . . . . DLB-25

Swords, T. and J., and Company DLB-49

Swords, Thomas 1763-1843 and
Swords, James ?-1844 . . . . DLB-73

Sykes, Ella C. ?-1939 . . . . DLB-174

Sylvester, Josuah
1562 or 1563-1618 . . . . DLB-121

Symonds, Emily Morse (see Paston, George)

Symonds, John Addington
1840-1893 . . . . DLB-57, 144

"Personal Style" (1890) DLB-57

Symons, A. J. A. 1900-1941 . . . . DLB-149

Symons, Arthur 1865-1945 . . . . . . DLB-19, 57, 149

Symons, Julian
1912-1994 . . . . DLB-87, 155; Y-92

Julian Symons at Eighty Y-92

Symons, Scott 1933- DLB-53

A Symposium on *The Columbia History of the Novel* Y-92

Synge, John Millington 1871-1909 .... DLB-10, 19; CDBLB-5

Synge Summer School: J. M. Synge and the Irish Theater, Rathdrum, County Wiclow, Ireland Y-93

Syrett, Netta 1865-1943 ....DLB-135, 197

Szabó, Lőrinc 1900-1957......................... DLB-215

Szabó, Magda 1917- DLB-215

Szymborska, Wisława 1923- DLB-232, Y-96; CDWLB-4

T

Taban lo Liyong 1939?- DLB-125

Tabori, George 1914- DLB-245

Tabucchi, Antonio 1943- DLB-196

Taché, Joseph-Charles 1820-1894 .... DLB-99

Tachihara Masaaki 1926-1980 .... DLB-182

Tacitus circa A.D. 55-circa A.D. 117 .... DLB-211; CDWLB-1

Tadijanović, Dragutin 1905- DLB-181

Tafdrup, Pia 1952- DLB-214

Tafolla, Carmen 1951- DLB-82

Taggard, Genevieve 1894-1948 .... DLB-45

Taggart, John 1942- DLB-193

Tagger, Theodor (see Bruckner, Ferdinand)

Taiheiki late fourteenth century DLB-203

Tait, J. Selwin, and Sons.............. DLB-49

Tait's Edinburgh Magazine 1832-1861 ..... DLB-110

The Takarazaka Revue Company Y-91

Talander (see Bohse, August)

Talese, Gay 1932- DLB-185

Talev, Dimitr 1898-1966 .... DLB-181

Taliaferro, H. E. 1811-1875 .... DLB-202

Tallent, Elizabeth 1954- DLB-130

TallMountain, Mary 1918-1994........ DLB-193

Talvj 1797-1870.................... DLB-59, 133

Tamási, Áron 1897-1966.............. DLB-215

Tammsaare, A. H. 1878-1940........... DLB-220; CDWLB-4

Tan, Amy 1952- DLB-173; CDALB-7

Tandori, Dezső 1938- DLB-232

Tanner, Thomas 1673/1674-1735 .... DLB-213

Tanizaki Jun'ichirō 1886-1965 .... DLB-180

Tapahonso, Luci 1953- DLB-175

The Mark Taper Forum............... DLB-7

Taradash, Daniel 1913- DLB-44

Tarbell, Ida M. 1857-1944 .... DLB-47

Tardivel, Jules-Paul 1851-1905......... DLB-99

Targan, Barry 1932- DLB-130

Tarkington, Booth 1869-1946 ...... DLB-9, 102

Tashlin, Frank 1913-1972.............. DLB-44

Tasma (Jessie Couvreur) 1848-1897 .... DLB-230

Tate, Allen 1899-1979......DLB-4, 45, 63; DS-17

Tate, James 1943- DLB-5, 169

Tate, Nahum circa 1652-1715.......... DLB-80

Tatian circa 830..................... DLB-148

Taufer, Veno 1933- DLB-181

Tauler, Johannes circa 1300-1361....... DLB-179

Tavčar, Ivan 1851-1923 .... DLB-147

Taverner, Richard ca. 1505-1575 .... DLB-236

Taylor, Ann 1782-1866.............. DLB-163

Taylor, Bayard 1825-1878 .... DLB-3, 189

Taylor, Bert Leston 1866-1921.......... DLB-25

Taylor, Charles H. 1846-1921 .... DLB-25

Taylor, Edward circa 1642-1729 .... DLB-24

Taylor, Elizabeth 1912-1975........... DLB-139

Taylor, Henry 1942- DLB-5

Taylor, Sir Henry 1800-1886.......... DLB-32

Taylor, Jane 1783-1824.............. DLB-163

Taylor, Jeremy circa 1613-1667 .... DLB-151

Taylor, John 1577 or 1578 - 1653....... DLB-121

Taylor, Mildred D. ?- DLB-52

Taylor, Peter 1917-1994.....DLB-218; Y-81, Y-94

Taylor, Susie King 1848-1912 .... DLB-221

Taylor, William Howland 1901-1966 ... DLB-241

Taylor, William, and Company........ DLB-49

Taylor-Made Shakespeare? Or Is "Shall I Die?" the Long-Lost Text of Bottom's Dream?..... Y-85

Teasdale, Sara 1884-1933.............. DLB-45

Telles, Lygia Fagundes 1924- DLB-113

Temple, Sir William 1628-1699 .... DLB-101

Temrizov, A. (see Marchenko, Anastasia Iakovlevna)

Tench, Watkin ca. 1758-1833.......... DLB-230

Tenn, William 1919- DLB-8

Tennant, Emma 1937- DLB-14

Tenney, Tabitha Gilman 1762-1837....................DLB-37, 200

Tennyson, Alfred 1809-1892 .... DLB-32; CDBLB-4

Tennyson, Frederick 1807-1898 .... DLB-32

Tenorio, Arthur 1924- DLB-209

Tepliakov, Viktor Grigor'evich 1804-1842 .... DLB-205

Terence circa 184 B.C.-159 B.C. or after DLB-211; CDWLB-1

Terhune, Albert Payson 1872-1942 .... DLB-9

Terhune, Mary Virginia 1830-1922 ....DS-13, DS-16

Terry, Megan 1932- DLB-7, 249

Terson, Peter 1932- DLB-13

Tesich, Steve 1943-1996..................Y-83

Tessa, Delio 1886-1939 .... DLB-114

Testori, Giovanni 1923-1993 ....DLB-128, 177

Tey, Josephine 1896?-1952............. DLB-77

Thacher, James 1754-1844 .... DLB-37

Thackeray, William Makepeace 1811-1863 .. DLB-21, 55, 159, 163; CDBLB-4

Thames and Hudson Limited.......... DLB-112

Thanet, Octave (see French, Alice)

Thatcher, John Boyd 1847-1909....... DLB-187

Thaxter, Celia Laighton 1835-1894 ..... DLB-239

Thayer, Caroline Matilda Warren 1785-1844...................... DLB-200

The Theatre Guild.................... DLB-7

The Theater in Shakespeare's Time...... DLB-62

Thegan and the Astronomer flourished circa 850 .... DLB-148

Thelwall, John 1764-1834.......... DLB-93, 158

Theocritus circa 300 B.C.-260 B.C. DLB-176

Theodorescu, Ion N. (see Arghezi, Tudor)

Theodulf circa 760-circa 821 .... DLB-148

Theophrastus circa 371 B.C.-287 B.C.....DLB-176

Theriault, Yves 1915-1983 .... DLB-88

Thério, Adrien 1925- DLB-53

Theroux, Paul 1941- DLB-2, 218; CDALB-7

Thesiger, Wilfred 1910- DLB-204

They All Came to Paris DS-16

Thibaudeau, Colleen 1925- DLB-88

Thielen, Benedict 1903-1965 .... DLB-102

Thiong'o Ngugi wa (see Ngugi wa Thiong'o)

Third-Generation Minor Poets of the Seventeenth Century............. DLB-131

This Quarter 1925-1927, 1929-1932........DS-15

Thoma, Ludwig 1867-1921 .... DLB-66

Thoma, Richard 1902- DLB-4

Thomas, Audrey 1935- DLB-60

Thomas, D. M. 1935- .. DLB-40, 207; CDBLB-8

D. M. Thomas: The Plagiarism Controversy........................Y-82

Thomas, Dylan 1914-1953 ...... DLB-13, 20, 139; CDBLB-7

The Dylan Thomas Celebration Y-99

Thomas, Edward 1878-1917............DLB-19, 98, 156, 216

Thomas, Frederick William 1806-1866 .. DLB-202

Thomas, Gwyn 1913-1981........ DLB-15, 245

Thomas, Isaiah 1750-1831 ......DLB-43, 73, 187

Thomas, Isaiah [publishing house]....... DLB-49

Thomas, Johann 1624-1679 .... DLB-168

Thomas, John 1900-1932.............. DLB-4

Thomas, Joyce Carol 1938- DLB-33

Thomas, Lorenzo 1944- DLB-41

Thomas, R. S. 1915-2000..... DLB-27; CDBLB-8

Thomasîn von Zerclære circa 1186-circa 1259 .... DLB-138

Thomasius, Christian 1655-1728 .... DLB-168

Thompson, Daniel Pierce 1795-1868 .... DLB-202

Thompson, David 1770-1857 .... DLB-99

Thompson, Dorothy 1893-1961........ DLB-29

Thompson, E. P. 1924-1993........... DLB-242

Thompson, Flora 1876-1947.......... DLB-240

Thompson, Francis 1859-1907 .... DLB-19; CDBLB-5

Thompson, George Selden (see Selden, George)

Thompson, Henry Yates 1838-1928 .... DLB-184

Thompson, Hunter S. 1939- DLB-185

Thompson, Jim 1906-1977 .... DLB-226

Thompson, John 1938-1976. . . . . .DLB-60

Thompson, John R. 1823-1873 . . . .DLB-3, 73, 248

Thompson, Lawrance 1906-1973. . . . . . .DLB-103

Thompson, Maurice 1844-1901. . . . . . DLB-71, 74

Thompson, Ruth Plumly 1891-1976 . . . . .DLB-22

Thompson, Thomas Phillips 1843-1933 . . .DLB-99

Thompson, William 1775-1833 . . . . .DLB-158

Thompson, William Tappan
1812-1882 . . . . .DLB-3, 11, 248

Thomson, Edward William 1849-1924. . . .DLB-92

Thomson, James 1700-1748 . . . . .DLB-95

Thomson, James 1834-1882 . . . . .DLB-35

Thomson, Joseph 1858-1895 . . . . .DLB-174

Thomson, Mortimer 1831-1875. . . . . . . .DLB-11

Thon, Melanie Rae 1957- DLB-244

Thoreau, Henry David
1817-1862 . . . . . . .DLB-1, 183, 223; CDALB-2

The Thoreauvian Pilgrimage: The Structure of an
American Cult. DLB-223

Thorpe, Adam 1956- DLB-231

Thorpe, Thomas Bangs
1815-1878 . . . . .DLB-3, 11, 248

Thorup, Kirsten 1942- DLB-214

Thoughts on Poetry and Its Varieties (1833),
by John Stuart Mill DLB-32

Thrale, Hester Lynch
(see Piozzi, Hester Lynch [Thrale])

Thubron, Colin 1939- DLB-204, 231

Thucydides
circa 455 B.C.-circa 395 B.C. DLB-176

Thulstrup, Thure de 1848-1930 . . . . . . .DLB-188

Thümmel, Moritz August von
1738-1817 . . . . .DLB-97

Thurber, James
1894-1961 . . . . .DLB-4, 11, 22, 102; CDALB-5

Thurman, Wallace 1902-1934. . . . . .DLB-51

Thwaite, Anthony 1930- DLB-40

The Booker Prize
Address by Anthony Thwaite,
Chairman of the Booker Prize Judges
Comments from Former Booker
Prize Winners Y-86

Thwaites, Reuben Gold 1853-1913 . . . . . .DLB-47

Tibullus circa 54 B.C.-circa 19 B.C. DLB-211

Ticknor, George 1791-1871 . . . DLB-1, 59, 140, 235

Ticknor and Fields. DLB-49

Ticknor and Fields (revived) DLB-46

Tieck, Ludwig 1773-1853. . . . .DLB-90; CDWLB-2

Tietjens, Eunice 1884-1944 . . . . .DLB-54

Tilghman, Christopher circa 1948. . . . . .DLB-244

Tilney, Edmund circa 1536-1610. . . . . . .DLB-136

Tilt, Charles [publishing house]. DLB-106

Tilton, J. E., and Company DLB-49

Time and Western Man (1927), by Wyndham
Lewis [excerpts]. DLB-36

Time-Life Books DLB-46

Times Books DLB-46

Timothy, Peter circa 1725-1782 . . . . . . .DLB-43

Timrava 1867-1951 . . . . .DLB-215

Timrod, Henry 1828-1867. . . . . .DLB-3, 248

Tindal, Henrietta 1818?-1879. . . . . .DLB-199

Tinker, Chauncey Brewster 1876-1963 . . .DLB-140

Tinsley Brothers DLB-106

Tiptree, James, Jr. 1915-1987. . . . . .DLB-8

Tišma, Aleksandar 1924- DLB-181

Titus, Edward William
1870-1952 . . . . .DLB-4; DS-15

Tiutchev, Fedor Ivanovich 1803-1873 . . . .DLB-205

Tlali, Miriam 1933- DLB-157, 225

Todd, Barbara Euphan 1890-1976. . . . . .DLB-160

Todorov, Tzvetan 1939- DLB-242

Tofte, Robert
1561 or 1562-1619 or 1620. . . . . . . .DLB-172

Toklas, Alice B. 1877-1967. . . . . .DLB-4

Tokuda, Shūsei 1872-1943. . . . . .DLB-180

Tolkien, J. R. R.
1892-1973 . . . . .DLB-15, 160; CDBLB-6

Toller, Ernst 1893-1939. . . . . .DLB-124

Tollet, Elizabeth 1694-1754 . . . . .DLB-95

Tolson, Melvin B. 1898-1966 . . . . . . .DLB-48, 76

Tolstoy, Aleksei Konstantinovich
1817-1875. . . . . .DLB-238

Tolstoy, Leo 1828-1910. . . . . .DLB-238

Tom Jones (1749), by Henry Fielding
[excerpt]. DLB-39

Tomalin, Claire 1933- DLB-155

Tomasi di Lampedusa, Giuseppe
1896-1957 .DLB-177

Tomlinson, Charles 1927- DLB-40

Tomlinson, H. M. 1873-1958 . . .DLB-36, 100, 195

Tompkins, Abel [publishing house]. DLB-49

Tompson, Benjamin 1642-1714 . . . . .DLB-24

Tomson, Graham R.
(see Watson, Rosamund Marriott)

Ton'a 1289-1372 . . . . .DLB-203

Tondelli, Pier Vittorio 1955-1991 . . . . . .DLB-196

Tonks, Rosemary 1932- DLB-14, 207

Tonna, Charlotte Elizabeth 1790-1846 . . .DLB-163

Tonson, Jacob the Elder
[publishing house] DLB-170

Toole, John Kennedy 1937-1969 . . . . .Y-81

Toomer, Jean 1894-1967 . . .DLB-45, 51; CDALB-4

Tor Books DLB-46

Torberg, Friedrich 1908-1979 . . . . .DLB-85

Torrence, Ridgely 1874-1950. . . . . . .DLB-54, 249

Torres-Metzger, Joseph V. 1933- DLB-122

Toth, Susan Allen 1940- Y-86

Tottell, Richard [publishing house] DLB-170

"The Printer to the Reader," (1557)
by Richard Tottell. DLB-167

Tough-Guy Literature. DLB-9

Touré, Askia Muhammad 1938- DLB-41

Tourgée, Albion W. 1838-1905. . . . . . . .DLB-79

Tournemir, Elizaveta Sailhas de (see Tur, Evgeniia)

Tourneur, Cyril circa 1580-1626. . . . . . . .DLB-58

Tournier, Michel 1924- DLB-83

Tousey, Frank [publishing house] DLB-49

Tower Publications DLB-46

Towne, Benjamin circa 1740-1793 . . . . . . .DLB-43

Towne, Robert 1936- DLB-44

The Townely Plays fifteenth and sixteenth
centuries DLB-146

Townshend, Aurelian
by 1583-circa 1651 . . . . .DLB-121

Toy, Barbara 1908- DLB-204

Tracy, Honor 1913- DLB-15

Traherne, Thomas 1637?-1674 . . . . .DLB-131

Traill, Catharine Parr 1802-1899 . . . . . . .DLB-99

Train, Arthur 1875-1945 . . . . .DLB-86; DS-16

The Transatlantic Publishing Company . . .DLB-49

The Transatlantic Review 1924-1925 . . . . .DS-15

The Transcendental Club 1836-1840 . . . .DLB-223

Transcendentalism. DLB-223

Transcendentalists, American DS-5

A Transit of Poets and Others: American
Biography in 1982. . . . . Y-82

transition 1927-1938. . . . . .DS-15

Translators of the Twelfth Century: Literary Issues
Raised and Impact Created. DLB-115

Travel Writing, 1837-1875 . . . . .DLB-166

Travel Writing, 1876-1909 . . . . .DLB-174

Travel Writing, 1910-1939 . . . . .DLB-195

Traven, B. 1882? or 1890?-1969? DLB-9, 56

Travers, Ben 1886-1980 . . . . .DLB-10, 233

Travers, P. L. (Pamela Lyndon)
1899-1996 .DLB-160

Trediakovsky, Vasilii Kirillovich
1703-1769 .DLB-150

Treece, Henry 1911-1966 . . . . .DLB-160

Trejo, Ernesto 1950- DLB-122

Trelawny, Edward John
1792-1881 . . . . DLB-110, 116, 144

Tremain, Rose 1943- DLB-14

Tremblay, Michel 1942- DLB-60

Trends in Twentieth-Century
Mass Market Publishing DLB-46

Trent, William P. 1862-1939. . . . . .DLB-47

Trescot, William Henry 1822-1898. . . . . .DLB-30

Tressell, Robert (Robert Phillipe Noonan)
1870-1911 .DLB-197

Trevelyan, Sir George Otto
1838-1928 .DLB-144

Trevisa, John circa 1342-circa 1402. . . . . .DLB-146

Trevor, William 1928- DLB-14, 139

Trierer Floyris circa 1170-1180 . . . . .DLB-138

Trillin, Calvin 1935- DLB-185

Trilling, Lionel 1905-1975 . . . . .DLB-28, 63

Trilussa 1871-1950. . . . . .DLB-114

Trimmer, Sarah 1741-1810 . . . . .DLB-158

Triolet, Elsa 1896-1970 . . . . .DLB-72

Tripp, John 1927- DLB-40

Trocchi, Alexander 1925- DLB-15

Troisi, Dante 1920-1989 . . . . .DLB-196

Trollope, Anthony
1815-1882.......DLB-21, 57, 159; CDBLB-4

Trollope, Frances 1779-1863........ DLB-21, 166

Trollope, Joanna 1943- DLB-207

Troop, Elizabeth 1931- DLB-14

Trotter, Catharine 1679-1749 .... DLB-84

Trotti, Lamar 1898-1952 .... DLB-44

Trottier, Pierre 1925- DLB-60

Troubadours, *Trobaíritz,* and Trouvères .. DLB-208

Troupe, Quincy Thomas, Jr. 1943- DLB-41

Trow, John F., and Company........... DLB-49

Trowbridge, John Townsend 1827-1916 . DLB-202

Truillier-Lacombe, Joseph-Patrice
1807-1863........................ DLB-99

Trumbo, Dalton 1905-1976 .... DLB-26

Trumbull, Benjamin 1735-1820 .... DLB-30

Trumbull, John 1750-1831 .... DLB-31

Trumbull, John 1756-1843 .... DLB-183

Truth, Sojourner 1797?-1883 .... DLB-239

Tscherning, Andreas 1611-1659........ DLB-164

Tsubouchi, Shōyō 1859-1935.......... DLB-180

Tucholsky, Kurt 1890-1935 .... DLB-56

Tucker, Charlotte Maria
1821-1893 .... DLB-163, 190

Tucker, George 1775-1861 ...... DLB-3, 30, 248

Tucker, James 1808?-1866? DLB-230

Tucker, Nathaniel Beverley
1784-1851.................... DLB-3, 248

Tucker, St. George 1752-1827 .... DLB-37

Tuckerman, Frederick Goddard
1821-1873.................... DLB-243

Tuckerman, Henry Theodore 1813-1871.. DLB-64

Tumas, Juozas (see Vaižgantas)

Tunis, John R. 1889-1975..........DLB-22, 171

Tunstall, Cuthbert 1474-1559......... DLB-132

Tuohy, Frank 1925- DLB-14, 139

Tupper, Martin F. 1810-1889 .... DLB-32

Tur, Evgeniia 1815-1892 .... DLB-238

Turbyfill, Mark 1896- DLB-45

Turco, Lewis 1934- Y-84

Turgenev, Aleksandr Ivanovich
1784-1845...................... DLB-198

Turgenev, Ivan Sergeevich 1818-1883 ... DLB-238

Turnball, Alexander H. 1868-1918...... DLB-184

Turnbull, Andrew 1921-1970 .... DLB-103

Turnbull, Gael 1928- DLB-40

Turner, Arlin 1909-1980 .... DLB-103

Turner, Charles (Tennyson)
1808-1879...................... DLB-32

Turner, Ethel 1872-1958............. DLB-230

Turner, Frederick 1943- DLB-40

Turner, Frederick Jackson
1861-1932 ....DLB-17, 186

Turner, Joseph Addison 1826-1868 ..... DLB-79

Turpin, Waters Edward 1910-1968 ..... DLB-51

Turrini, Peter 1944- DLB-124

Tutuola, Amos 1920-1997 .. DLB-125; CDWLB-3

Twain, Mark (see Clemens, Samuel Langhorne)

Tweedie, Ethel Brilliana
circa 1860-1940 ....DLB-174

The 'Twenties and Berlin, by Alex Natan . DLB-66

Two Hundred Years of Rare Books and
Literary Collections at the
University of South Carolina.......... Y-00

Twombly, Wells 1935-1977 .... DLB-241

Twysden, Sir Roger 1597-1672........ DLB-213

Tyler, Anne
1941- DLB-6, 143; Y-82; CDALB-7

Tyler, Mary Palmer 1775-1866........ DLB-200

Tyler, Moses Coit 1835-1900........DLB-47, 64

Tyler, Royall 1757-1826 .... DLB-37

Tylor, Edward Burnett 1832-1917 .... DLB-57

Tynan, Katharine 1861-1931 ..... DLB-153, 240

Tyndale, William circa 1494-1536..... DLB-132

U

Uchida, Yoshika 1921-1992 ....CDALB-7

Udall, Nicholas 1504-1556............. DLB-62

Ugrêsić, Dubravka 1949- DLB-181

Uhland, Ludwig 1787-1862............. DLB-90

Uhse, Bodo 1904-1963............... DLB-69

Ujević, Augustin ("Tin") 1891-1955..... DLB-147

Ulenhart, Niclas flourished circa 1600 ... DLB-164

Ulibarrí, Sabine R. 1919- DLB-82

Ulica, Jorge 1870-1926 .... DLB-82

Ulivi, Ferruccio 1912- DLB-196

Ulizio, B. George 1889-1969 .... DLB-140

Ulrich von Liechtenstein
circa 1200-circa 1275 .... DLB-138

Ulrich von Zatzikhoven
before 1194-after 1214 .... DLB-138

Ulysses, Reader's Edition................. Y-97

Unaipon, David 1872-1967............ DLB-230

Unamuno, Miguel de 1864-1936 ...... DLB-108

Under, Marie 1883-1980
.... DLB-220; CDWLB-4

Under the Microscope (1872), by
A. C. Swinburne DLB-35

Underhill, Evelyn 1875-1941 .... DLB-240

Ungaretti, Giuseppe 1888-1970 .... DLB-114

Unger, Friederike Helene 1741-1813 ..... DLB-94

United States Book Company DLB-49

Universal Publishing and Distributing
Corporation..................... DLB-46

The University of Iowa Writers' Workshop
Golden Jubilee Y-86

The University of South Carolina Press...... Y-94

University of Wales Press DLB-112

University Press of Florida................ Y-00

University Press of Kansas................ Y-98

University Press of Mississippi............. Y-99

"The Unknown Public" (1858), by
Wilkie Collins [excerpt] DLB-57

Uno, Chiyo 1897-1996 .... DLB-180

Unruh, Fritz von 1885-1970 .... DLB-56, 118

Unspeakable Practices II: The Festival of Vanguard
Narrative at Brown University Y-93

Unsworth, Barry 1930- DLB-194

Unt, Mati 1944- DLB-232

The Unterberg Poetry Center of the
92nd Street Y...................... Y-98

Unwin, T. Fisher [publishing house] DLB-106

Upchurch, Boyd B. (see Boyd, John)

Updike, John 1932-
........DLB-2, 5, 143, 218, 227; Y-80, Y-82;
DS-3; CDALB-6

John Updike on the Internet............. Y-97

Upīts, Andrejs 1877-1970 .... DLB-220

Upton, Bertha 1849-1912 .... DLB-141

Upton, Charles 1948- DLB-16

Upton, Florence K. 1873-1922 .... DLB-141

Upward, Allen 1863-1926 .... DLB-36

Urban, Milo 1904-1982 .... DLB-215

Urista, Alberto Baltazar (see Alurista)

Urquhart, Fred 1912- DLB-139

Urrea, Luis Alberto 1955- DLB-209

Urzidil, Johannes 1896-1976........... DLB-85

The Uses of Facsimile................... Y-90

Usk, Thomas died 1388.............. DLB-146

Uslar Pietri, Arturo 1906- DLB-113

Ussher, James 1581-1656 .... DLB-213

Ustinov, Peter 1921- DLB-13

Uttley, Alison 1884-1976 .... DLB-160

Uz, Johann Peter 1720-1796 .... DLB-97

V

Vac, Bertrand 1914- DLB-88

Vācietis, Ojārs 1933-1983........... DLB-232

Vaičiulaitis, Antanas 1906-1992 ...... DLB-220

Vaculík, Ludvík 1926- DLB-232

Vaičiūnaite, Judita 1937- DLB-232

Vail, Laurence 1891-1968 .... DLB-4

Vailland, Roger 1907-1965 .... DLB-83

Vaižgantas 1869-1933 .... DLB-220

Vajda, Ernest 1887-1954............. DLB-44

Valdés, Gina 1943- DLB-122

Valdez, Luis Miguel 1940- DLB-122

Valduga, Patrizia 1953- DLB-128

Valente, José Angel 1929-2000......... DLB-108

Valenzuela, Luisa 1938- ..DLB-113; CDWLB-3

Valeri, Diego 1887-1976 .... DLB-128

Valerius Flaccus fl. circa A.D. 92 .... DLB-211

Valerius Maximus fl. circa A.D. 31 ..... DLB-211

Valesio, Paolo 1939- DLB-196

Valgardson, W. D. 1939- DLB-60

Valle, Víctor Manuel 1950- DLB-122

Valle-Inclán, Ramón del 1866-1936..... DLB-134

Vallejo, Armando 1949- DLB-122

Vallès, Jules 1832-1885.............. DLB-123

Vallette, Marguerite Eymery (see Rachilde)

Valverde, José María 1926-1996 . . . . . . .DLB-108

Van Allsburg, Chris 1949- DLB-61

Van Anda, Carr 1864-1945 . . . . .DLB-25

van der Post, Laurens 1906-1996 . . . . . . .DLB-204

Van Dine, S. S. (see Wright, Williard Huntington)

Van Doren, Mark 1894-1972 . . . . .DLB-45

van Druten, John 1901-1957 . . . . .DLB-10

Van Duyn, Mona 1921- DLB-5

Van Dyke, Henry 1852-1933 . . . . .DLB-71; DS-13

Van Dyke, Henry 1928- DLB-33

Van Dyke, John C. 1856-1932 . . . . .DLB-186

van Gulik, Robert Hans 1910-1967 . . . . DS-17

van Itallie, Jean-Claude 1936- DLB-7

Van Loan, Charles E. 1876-1919 . . . . .DLB-171

Van Rensselaer, Mariana Griswold
    1851-1934 . . . . .DLB-47

Van Rensselaer, Mrs. Schuyler
    (see Van Rensselaer, Mariana Griswold)

Van Vechten, Carl 1880-1964 . . . . .DLB-4, 9

van Vogt, A. E. 1912-2000 . . . . .DLB-8

Vanbrugh, Sir John 1664-1726 . . . . .DLB-80

Vance, Jack 1916?- DLB-8

Vančura, Vladislav
    1891-1942 . . . . .DLB-215; CDWLB-4

Vane, Sutton 1888-1963 . . . . .DLB-10

Vanguard Press DLB-46

Vann, Robert L. 1879-1940 . . . . .DLB-29

Vargas Llosa, Mario
    1936- DLB-145; CDWLB-3

Varley, John 1947- Y-81

Varnhagen von Ense, Karl August
    1785-1858 . . . . .DLB-90

Varnhagen von Ense, Rahel
    1771-1833 . . . . .DLB-90

Varro 116 B.C.-27 B.C. DLB-211

Vasiliu, George (see Bacovia, George)

Vásquez, Richard 1928- DLB-209

Vásquez Montalbán, Manuel 1939- DLB-134

Vassa, Gustavus (see Equiano, Olaudah)

Vassalli, Sebastiano 1941- DLB-128, 196

Vaughan, Henry 1621-1695 . . . . .DLB-131

Vaughan, Thomas 1621-1666 . . . . .DLB-131

Vaughn, Robert 1592?-1667 . . . . .DLB-213

Vaux, Thomas, Lord 1509-1556 . . . . .DLB-132

Vazov, Ivan 1850-1921 . . . . .DLB-147; CDWLB-4

Véa Jr., Alfredo 1950- DLB-209

Veblen, Thorstein 1857-1929 . . . . .DLB-246

Vega, Janine Pommy 1942- DLB-16

Veiller, Anthony 1903-1965 . . . . .DLB-44

Velásquez-Trevino, Gloria 1949- DLB-122

Veley, Margaret 1843-1887 . . . . .DLB-199

Velleius Paterculus
    circa 20 B.C.-circa A.D. 30 . . . . .DLB-211

Veloz Maggiolo, Marcio 1936- DLB-145

Vel'tman Aleksandr Fomich
    1800-1870 . . . . .DLB-198

Venegas, Daniel ?-? DLB-82

Venevitinov, Dmitrii Vladimirovich
    1805-1827 . . . . .DLB-205

Vergil, Polydore circa 1470-1555 . . . . . . .DLB-132

Veríssimo, Erico 1905-1975 . . . . .DLB-145

Verlaine, Paul 1844-1896 . . . . .DLB-217

Verne, Jules 1828-1905 . . . . .DLB-123

Verplanck, Gulian C. 1786-1870 . . . . .DLB-59

Very, Jones 1813-1880 . . . . .DLB-1, 243

Vian, Boris 1920-1959 . . . . .DLB-72

Viazemsky, Petr Andreevich
    1792-1878 . . . . .DLB-205

Vicars, Thomas 1591-1638 . . . . .DLB-236

Vickers, Roy 1888?-1965 . . . . .DLB-77

Vickery, Sukey 1779-1821 . . . . .DLB-200

Victoria 1819-1901 . . . . .DLB-55

Victoria Press .DLB-106

Vidal, Gore 1925- DLB-6, 152; CDALB-7

Vidal, Mary Theresa 1815-1873 . . . . .DLB-230

Vidmer, Richards 1898-1978 . . . . .DLB-241

Viebig, Clara 1860-1952 . . . . .DLB-66

Viereck, George Sylvester
    1884-1962 . . . . .DLB-54

Viereck, Peter 1916- DLB-5

Viets, Roger 1738-1811 . . . . .DLB-99

Viewpoint: Politics and Performance, by
    David Edgar DLB-13

Vigil-Piñon, Evangelina 1949- DLB-122

Vigneault, Gilles 1928- DLB-60

Vigny, Alfred de
    1797-1863 . . . . .DLB-119, 192, 217

Vigolo, Giorgio 1894-1983 . . . . .DLB-114

The Viking Press DLB-46

Vilde, Eduard 1865-1933 . . . . .DLB-220

Vilinskaia, Mariia Aleksandrovna
    (see Vovchok, Marko)

Villanueva, Alma Luz 1944- DLB-122

Villanueva, Tino 1941- DLB-82

Villard, Henry 1835-1900 . . . . .DLB-23

Villard, Oswald Garrison
    1872-1949 . . . . .DLB-25, 91

Villarreal, Edit 1944- DLB-209

Villarreal, José Antonio 1924- DLB-82

Villaseñor, Victor 1940- DLB-209

Villegas de Magnón, Leonor
    1876-1955 . . . . .DLB-122

Villehardouin, Geoffroi de
    circa 1150-1215 . . . . .DLB-208

Villemaire, Yolande 1949- DLB-60

Villena, Luis Antonio de 1951- DLB-134

Villiers, George, Second Duke
    of Buckingham 1628-1687 . . . . .DLB-80

Villiers de l'Isle-Adam, Jean-Marie Mathias
    Philippe-Auguste, Comte de
    1838-1889 . . . . .DLB-123, 192

Villon, François 1431-circa 1463? DLB-208

Vine Press DLB-112

Viorst, Judith ?- DLB-52

Vipont, Elfrida (Elfrida Vipont Foulds,
    Charles Vipont) 1902-1992 . . . . .DLB-160

Viramontes, Helena María 1954- DLB-122

Virgil 70 B.C.-19 B.C. DLB-211; CDWLB-1

Virtual Books and Enemies of Books Y-00

Vischer, Friedrich Theodor 1807-1887 . . .DLB-133

Vitruvius circa 85 B.C.-circa 15 B.C. DLB-211

Vitry, Philippe de 1291-1361 . . . . .DLB-208

Vivanco, Luis Felipe 1907-1975 . . . . .DLB-108

Viviani, Cesare 1947- DLB-128

Vivien, Renée 1877-1909 . . . . .DLB-217

Vizenor, Gerald 1934- DLB-175, 227

Vizetelly and Company DLB-106

Voaden, Herman 1903- DLB-88

Voß, Johann Heinrich 1751-1826 . . . . . . .DLB-90

Voigt, Ellen Bryant 1943- DLB-120

Vojnović, Ivo 1857-1929 . . . .DLB-147; CDWLB-4

Volkoff, Vladimir 1932- DLB-83

Volland, P. F., Company DLB-46

Vollbehr, Otto H. F.
    1872?-1945 or 1946 . . . . .DLB-187

Vologdin (see Zasodimsky, Pavel Vladimirovich)

Volponi, Paolo 1924- DLB-177

von der Grün, Max 1926- DLB-75

Vonnegut, Kurt 1922-
    . . . . . . .DLB-2, 8, 152; Y-80; DS-3; CDALB-6

Voranc, Prežihov 1893-1950 . . . . .DLB-147

Vovchok, Marko 1833-1907 . . . . .DLB-238

Voynich, E. L. 1864-1960 . . . . .DLB-197

Vroman, Mary Elizabeth
    circa 1924-1967 . . . . .DLB-33

W

Wace, Robert ("Maistre")
    circa 1100-circa 1175 . . . . .DLB-146

Wackenroder, Wilhelm Heinrich
    1773-1798 . . . . .DLB-90

Wackernagel, Wilhelm 1806-1869 . . . . . .DLB-133

Waddell, Helen 1889-1965 . . . . .DLB-240

Waddington, Miriam 1917- DLB-68

Wade, Henry 1887-1969 . . . . .DLB-77

Wagenknecht, Edward 1900- DLB-103

Wagner, Heinrich Leopold 1747-1779 . . . . .DLB-94

Wagner, Henry R. 1862-1957 . . . . .DLB-140

Wagner, Richard 1813-1883 . . . . .DLB-129

Wagoner, David 1926- DLB-5

Wah, Fred 1939- DLB-60

Waiblinger, Wilhelm 1804-1830 . . . . .DLB-90

Wain, John
    1925-1994 . . . DLB-15, 27, 139, 155; CDBLB-8

Wainwright, Jeffrey 1944- DLB-40

Waite, Peirce and Company DLB-49

Wakeman, Stephen H. 1859-1924 . . . . . . .DLB-187

Wakoski, Diane 1937- DLB-5

Walahfrid Strabo circa 808-849 . . . . .DLB-148

Walck, Henry Z. DLB-46

Walcott, Derek
1930- DLB-117; Y-81, Y-92; CDWLB-3

Waldegrave, Robert [publishing house] ...DLB-170

Waldman, Anne 1945- DLB-16

Waldrop, Rosmarie 1935- DLB-169

Walker, Alice 1900-1982 .... DLB-201

Walker, Alice
1944- DLB-6, 33, 143; CDALB-6

Walker, Annie Louisa (Mrs. Harry Coghill)
circa 1836-1907 .... DLB-240

Walker, George F. 1947- DLB-60

Walker, John Brisben 1847-1931 .... DLB-79

Walker, Joseph A. 1935- DLB-38

Walker, Margaret 1915- DLB-76, 152

Walker, Ted 1934- DLB-40

Walker and Company DLB-49

Walker, Evans and Cogswell Company... DLB-49

Wallace, Alfred Russel 1823-1913 ...... DLB-190

Wallace, Dewitt 1889-1981 and
Lila Acheson Wallace 1889-1984.... DLB-137

Wallace, Edgar 1875-1932 .... DLB-70

Wallace, Lew 1827-1905 .... DLB-202

Wallace, Lila Acheson
(see Wallace, Dewitt, and Lila Acheson Wallace)

Wallace, Naomi 1960- DLB-249

Wallant, Edward Lewis
1926-1962 .... DLB-2, 28, 143

Waller, Edmund 1606-1687 .... DLB-126

Walpole, Horace 1717-1797.... DLB-39, 104, 213

Preface to the First Edition of
The Castle of Otranto (1764) DLB-39

Preface to the Second Edition of
The Castle of Otranto (1765) DLB-39

Walpole, Hugh 1884-1941 .... DLB-34

Walrond, Eric 1898-1966 .... DLB-51

Walser, Martin 1927- DLB-75, 124

Walser, Robert 1878-1956 .... DLB-66

Walsh, Ernest 1895-1926 .... DLB-4, 45

Walsh, Robert 1784-1859 .... DLB-59

Walters, Henry 1848-1931 .... DLB-140

Waltharius circa 825 .... DLB-148

Walther von der Vogelweide
circa 1170-circa 1230 .... DLB-138

Walton, Izaak
1593-1683 .... DLB-151, 213; CDBLB-1

Wambaugh, Joseph 1937- DLB-6; Y-83

Wand, Alfred Rudolph 1828-1891 ...... DLB-188

Waniek, Marilyn Nelson 1946- DLB-120

Wanley, Humphrey 1672-1726 .... DLB-213

Warburton, William 1698-1779 .... DLB-104

Ward, Aileen 1919- DLB-111

Ward, Artemus (see Browne, Charles Farrar)

Ward, Arthur Henry Sarsfield (see Rohmer, Sax)

Ward, Douglas Turner 1930- DLB-7, 38

Ward, Mrs. Humphry 1851-1920 .... DLB-18

Ward, Lynd 1905-1985 .... DLB-22

Ward, Lock and Company DLB-106

Ward, Nathaniel circa 1578-1652 .... DLB-24

Ward, Theodore 1902-1983........... DLB-76

Wardle, Ralph 1909-1988 .... DLB-103

Ware, Henry, Jr. 1794-1843 .... DLB-235

Ware, William 1797-1852 .... DLB-1, 235

Warfield, Catherine Ann 1816-1877 ......DLB-248

Waring, Anna Letitia 1823-1910 .... DLB-240

Warne, Frederick, and Company [U.K.]... DLB-106

Warne, Frederick, and Company [U.S.] ... DLB-49

Warner, Anne 1869-1913............ DLB-202

Warner, Charles Dudley 1829-1900 ..... DLB-64

Warner, Marina 1946- DLB-194

Warner, Rex 1905- DLB-15

Warner, Susan 1819-1885 .... DLB-3, 42, 239

Warner, Sylvia Townsend
1893-1978................. DLB-34, 139

Warner, William 1558-1609............DLB-172

Warner Books DLB-46

Warr, Bertram 1917-1943............. DLB-88

Warren, John Byrne Leicester (see De Tabley, Lord)

Warren, Lella 1899-1982 ....Y-83

Warren, Mercy Otis 1728-1814 ..... DLB-31, 200

Warren, Robert Penn 1905-1989
.......DLB-2, 48, 152; Y-80, Y-89; CDALB-6

Warren, Samuel 1807-1877........... DLB-190

Die Wartburgkrieg circa 1230-circa 1280... DLB-138

Warton, Joseph 1722-1800 ....DLB-104, 109

Warton, Thomas 1728-1790.......DLB-104, 109

Warung, Price (William Astley)
1855-1911 .... DLB-230

Washington, George 1732-1799 .... DLB-31

Wassermann, Jakob 1873-1934 .... DLB-66

Wasserstein, Wendy 1950- DLB-228

Wasson, David Atwood 1823-1887 ... DLB-1, 223

Watanna, Onoto (see Eaton, Winnifred)

Waterhouse, Keith 1929- DLB-13, 15

Waterman, Andrew 1940- DLB-40

Waters, Frank 1902-1995.........DLB-212; Y-86

Waters, Michael 1949- DLB-120

Watkins, Tobias 1780-1855 .... DLB-73

Watkins, Vernon 1906-1967 .... DLB-20

Watmough, David 1926- DLB-53

Watson, James Wreford (see Wreford, James)

Watson, John 1850-1907 .... DLB-156

Watson, Rosamund Marriott
(Graham R. Tomson) 1860-1911.... DLB-240

Watson, Sheila 1909- DLB-60

Watson, Thomas 1545?-1592.......... DLB-132

Watson, Wilfred 1911- DLB-60

Watt, W. J., and Company DLB-46

Watten, Barrett 1948- DLB-193

Watterson, Henry 1840-1921.......... DLB-25

Watts, Alan 1915-1973 .... DLB-16

Watts, Franklin [publishing house]....... DLB-46

Watts, Isaac 1674-1748 .... DLB-95

Waugh, Alec 1898-1981............. DLB-191

Waugh, Auberon 1939-2000 ...DLB-14, 194; Y-00

The Cult of Biography
Excerpts from the Second Folio Debate:
"Biographies are generally a disease of
English Literature"................. Y-86

Waugh, Evelyn
1903-1966 ..... DLB-15, 162, 195; CDBLB-6

Way and Williams DLB-49

Wayman, Tom 1945- DLB-53

We See the Editor at Work Y-97

Weatherly, Tom 1942- DLB-41

Weaver, Gordon 1937- DLB-130

Weaver, Robert 1921- DLB-88

Webb, Beatrice 1858-1943 and
Webb, Sidney 1859-1947.......... DLB-190

Webb, Frank J. ?-? DLB-50

Webb, James Watson 1802-1884 .... DLB-43

Webb, Mary 1881-1927 .... DLB-34

Webb, Phyllis 1927- DLB-53

Webb, Walter Prescott 1888-1963 ....DLB-17

Webbe, William ?-1591 .... DLB-132

Webber, Charles Wilkins 1819-1856? ... DLB-202

Webling, Lucy (Lucy Betty MacRaye)
1877-1952........................ DLB-240

Webling, Peggy (Arthur Weston)
1871-1949....................... DLB-240

Webster, Augusta 1837-1894 .... DLB-35, 240

Webster, Charles L., and Company...... DLB-49

Webster, John
1579 or 1580-1634? DLB-58; CDBLB-1

John Webster: The Melbourne
Manuscript........................Y-86

Webster, Noah
1758-1843......... DLB-1, 37, 42, 43, 73, 243

Weckherlin, Georg Rodolf 1584-1653 ... DLB-164

Wedekind, Frank
1864-1918 .... DLB-118; CDBLB-2

Weeks, Edward Augustus, Jr.
1898-1989 ....DLB-137

Weeks, Stephen B. 1865-1918 ....DLB-187

Weems, Mason Locke 1759-1825...DLB-30, 37, 42

Weerth, Georg 1822-1856 .... DLB-129

Weidenfeld and Nicolson............. DLB-112

Weidman, Jerome 1913-1998........... DLB-28

Weiß, Ernst 1882-1940................ DLB-81

Weigl, Bruce 1949- DLB-120

Weinbaum, Stanley Grauman 1902-1935 .. DLB-8

Weintraub, Stanley 1929- DLB-111; Y82

The Practice of Biography: An Interview
with Stanley Weintraub............... Y-82

Weise, Christian 1642-1708 .... DLB-168

Weisenborn, Gunther 1902-1969.... DLB-69, 124

Weiss, John 1818-1879 .... DLB-1, 243

Weiss, Peter 1916-1982 .... DLB-69, 124

Weiss, Theodore 1916- DLB-5

Weisse, Christian Felix 1726-1804 .... DLB-97

Weitling, Wilhelm 1808-1871......... DLB-129

Welch, James 1940- DLB-175

Welch, Lew 1926-1971?. DLB-16

Weldon, Fay 1931- DLB-14, 194; CDBLB-8

Wellek, René 1903-1995 . . . . .DLB-63

Wells, Carolyn 1862-1942. . . . . .DLB-11

Wells, Charles Jeremiah circa 1800-1879. . .DLB-32

Wells, Gabriel 1862-1946 . . . . .DLB-140

Wells, H. G.
 1866-1946 . . . DLB-34, 70, 156, 178; CDBLB-6

Wells, Helena 1758?-1824 . . . . .DLB-200

Wells, Robert 1947- DLB-40

Wells-Barnett, Ida B. 1862-1931 . . . . .DLB-23, 221

Welty, Eudora 1909-
 . . . . DLB-2, 102, 143; Y-87; DS-12; CDALB-1

Eudora Welty: Eye of the Storyteller. Y-87

Eudora Welty Newsletter Y-99

Eudora Welty's Ninetieth Birthday Y-99

Wendell, Barrett 1855-1921. . . . . .DLB-71

Wentworth, Patricia 1878-1961 . . . . .DLB-77

Wentworth, William Charles
 1790-1872 .DLB-230

Werder, Diederich von dem 1584-1657. . .DLB-164

Werfel, Franz 1890-1945 . . . . .DLB-81, 124

Werner, Zacharias 1768-1823 . . . . .DLB-94

The Werner Company DLB-49

Wersba, Barbara 1932- DLB-52

Wescott, Glenway 1901- DLB-4, 9, 102

Wesker, Arnold 1932- DLB-13; CDBLB-8

Wesley, Charles 1707-1788. . . . . .DLB-95

Wesley, John 1703-1791. . . . . .DLB-104

Wesley, Mary 1912- DLB-231

Wesley, Richard 1945- DLB-38

Wessels, A., and Company DLB-46

Wessobrunner Gebet circa 787-815 . . . . .DLB-148

West, Anthony 1914-1988. . . . . .DLB-15

West, Cornel 1953- DLB-246

West, Dorothy 1907-1998 . . . . .DLB-76

West, Jessamyn 1902-1984 . . . . .DLB-6; Y-84

West, Mae 1892-1980 . . . . .DLB-44

West, Nathanael
 1903-1940 . . . . .DLB-4, 9, 28; CDALB-5

West, Paul 1930- DLB-14

West, Rebecca 1892-1983 . . . . .DLB-36; Y-83

West, Richard 1941- DLB-185

West and Johnson DLB-49

Westcott, Edward Noyes 1846-1898 . . . . .DLB-202

The Western Messenger 1835-1841 . . . . .DLB-223

Western Publishing Company. DLB-46

Western Writers of America Y-99

The Westminster Review 1824-1914 . . . . . . .DLB-110

Weston, Arthur (see Webling, Peggy)

Weston, Elizabeth Jane circa 1582-1612 . .DLB-172

Wetherald, Agnes Ethelwyn 1857-1940. . . .DLB-99

Wetherell, Elizabeth (see Warner, Susan)

Wetherell, W. D. 1948- DLB-234

Wetzel, Friedrich Gottlob 1779-1819 . . . . . .DLB-90

Weyman, Stanley J. 1855-1928 . . . . .DLB-141, 156

Wezel, Johann Karl 1747-1819 . . . . .DLB-94

Whalen, Philip 1923- DLB-16

Whalley, George 1915-1983 . . . . .DLB-88

Wharton, Edith 1862-1937
 . . . . . DLB-4, 9, 12, 78, 189; DS-13; CDALB-3

Wharton, William 1920s?- Y-80

"What You Lose on the Swings You Make Up
 on the Merry-Go-Round" Y-99

Whately, Mary Louisa 1824-1889. . . . . . .DLB-166

Whately, Richard 1787-1863 . . . . .DLB-190

From *Elements of Rhetoric* (1828;
 revised, 1846) .DLB-57

What's Really Wrong With Bestseller Lists . . Y-84

Wheatley, Dennis Yates 1897-1977 . . . . . . .DLB-77

Wheatley, Phillis
 circa 1754-1784 . . . . . . .DLB-31, 50; CDALB-2

Wheeler, Anna Doyle 1785-1848?. DLB-158

Wheeler, Charles Stearns 1816-1843. . .DLB-1, 223

Wheeler, Monroe 1900-1988. . . . . .DLB-4

Wheelock, John Hall 1886-1978 . . . . .DLB-45

Wheelwright, J. B. 1897-1940 . . . . .DLB-45

Wheelwright, John circa 1592-1679 . . . . . .DLB-24

Whetstone, George 1550-1587 . . . . .DLB-136

Whetstone, Colonel Pete (see Noland, C. F. M.)

Whicher, Stephen E. 1915-1961 . . . . .DLB-111

Whipple, Edwin Percy 1819-1886. . . . . .DLB-1, 64

Whitaker, Alexander 1585-1617 . . . . .DLB-24

Whitaker, Daniel K. 1801-1881. . . . . .DLB-73

Whitcher, Frances Miriam
 1812-1852 . . . . .DLB-11, 202

White, Andrew 1579-1656. . . . . .DLB-24

White, Andrew Dickson 1832-1918 . . . . . .DLB-47

White, E. B. 1899-1985 . . . .DLB-11, 22; CDALB-7

White, Edgar B. 1947- DLB-38

White, Edmund 1940- DLB-227

White, Ethel Lina 1887-1944 . . . . .DLB-77

White, Hayden V. 1928- DLB-246

White, Henry Kirke 1785-1806 . . . . .DLB-96

White, Horace 1834-1916 . . . . .DLB-23

White, Phyllis Dorothy James (see James, P. D.)

White, Richard Grant 1821-1885 . . . . . . .DLB-64

White, T. H. 1906-1964 . . . . .DLB-160

White, Walter 1893-1955 . . . . .DLB-51

White, William, and Company DLB-49

White, William Allen 1868-1944. . . . . . .DLB-9, 25

White, William Anthony Parker
 (see Boucher, Anthony)

White, William Hale (see Rutherford, Mark)

Whitechurch, Victor L. 1868-1933 . . . . . . .DLB-70

Whitehead, Alfred North 1861-1947 . . . . .DLB-100

Whitehead, James 1936- Y-81

Whitehead, William 1715-1785 . . . . .DLB-84, 109

Whitfield, James Monroe 1822-1871 . . . . . .DLB-50

Whitfield, Raoul 1898-1945. . . . . .DLB-226

Whitgift, John circa 1533-1604 . . . . .DLB-132

Whiting, John 1917-1963 . . . . .DLB-13

Whiting, Samuel 1597-1679 . . . . .DLB-24

Whitlock, Brand 1869-1934 . . . . .DLB-12

Whitman, Albert, and Company. DLB-46

Whitman, Albery Allson 1851-1901 . . . . . .DLB-50

Whitman, Alden 1913-1990 . . . . Y-91

Whitman, Sarah Helen (Power)
 1803-1878 . . . . .DLB-1, 243

Whitman, Walt
 1819-1892 . . . . .DLB-3, 64, 224; CDALB-2

Whitman Publishing Company. DLB-46

Whitney, Geoffrey 1548 or 1552?-1601 . .DLB-136

Whitney, Isabella flourished 1566-1573. . .DLB-136

Whitney, John Hay 1904-1982 . . . . .DLB-127

Whittemore, Reed 1919-1995 . . . . .DLB-5

Whittier, John Greenleaf
 1807-1892 . . . . .DLB-1, 243; CDALB-2

Whittlesey House DLB-46

Who Runs American Literature? Y-94

Whose *Ulysses*? The Function of Editing Y-97

Wickham, Anna (Edith Alice Mary Harper)
 1884-1947 .DLB-240

Wicomb, Zoë 1948- DLB-225

Wideman, John Edgar 1941- DLB-33, 143

Widener, Harry Elkins 1885-1912 . . . . . .DLB-140

Wiebe, Rudy 1934- DLB-60

Wiechert, Ernst 1887-1950. . . . . .DLB-56

Wied, Martina 1882-1957 . . . . .DLB-85

Wiehe, Evelyn May Clowes (see Mordaunt, Elinor)

Wieland, Christoph Martin 1733-1813 . . . .DLB-97

Wienbarg, Ludolf 1802-1872. . . . . .DLB-133

Wieners, John 1934- DLB-16

Wier, Ester 1910- DLB-52

Wiesel, Elie
 1928- DLB-83; Y-86, 87; CDALB-7

Wiggin, Kate Douglas 1856-1923 . . . . .DLB-42

Wigglesworth, Michael 1631-1705. . . . . . .DLB-24

Wilberforce, William 1759-1833 . . . . .DLB-158

Wilbrandt, Adolf 1837-1911 . . . . .DLB-129

Wilbur, Richard
 1921- DLB-5, 169; CDALB-7

Wild, Peter 1940- DLB-5

Wilde, Lady Jane Francesca Elgee
 1821?-1896 .DLB-199

Wilde, Oscar 1854-1900
 . . . . DLB-10, 19, 34, 57, 141, 156, 190;
 CDBLB-5

"The Critic as Artist" (1891) DLB-57

Oscar Wilde Conference at Hofstra
 University. Y-00

From "The Decay of Lying" (1889) DLB-18

"The English Renaissance of
 Art" (1908) DLB-35

"L'Envoi" (1882) DLB-35

Wilde, Richard Henry 1789-1847 . . . . . .DLB-3, 59

Wilde, W. A., Company DLB-49

Wilder, Billy 1906- DLB-26

Wilder, Laura Ingalls 1867-1957........ DLB-22

Wilder, Thornton
1897-1975 ....DLB-4, 7, 9, 228; CDALB-7

Thornton Wilder Centenary at Yale Y-97

Wildgans, Anton 1881-1932.......... DLB-118

Wiley, Bell Irvin 1906-1980 .... DLB-17

Wiley, John, and Sons DLB-49

Wilhelm, Kate 1928- DLB-8

Wilkes, Charles 1798-1877 .... DLB-183

Wilkes, George 1817-1885 .... DLB-79

Wilkins, John 1614-1672............. DLB-236

Wilkinson, Anne 1910-1961........... DLB-88

Wilkinson, Eliza Yonge
1757-circa 1813 .... DLB-200

Wilkinson, Sylvia 1940- Y-86

Wilkinson, William Cleaver 1833-1920... DLB-71

Willard, Barbara 1909-1994.......... DLB-161

Willard, Emma 1787-1870............ DLB-239

Willard, Frances E. 1839-1898 .... DLB-221

Willard, L. [publishing house] DLB-49

Willard, Nancy 1936- DLB-5, 52

Willard, Samuel 1640-1707........... DLB-24

Willeford, Charles 1919-1988......... DLB-226

William of Auvergne 1190-1249........ DLB-115

William of Conches
circa 1090-circa 1154 .... DLB-115

William of Ockham circa 1285-1347 .... DLB-115

William of Sherwood
1200/1205-1266/1271............. DLB-115

The William Chavrat American Fiction Collection
at the Ohio State University Libraries Y-92

Williams, A., and Company........... DLB-49

Williams, Ben Ames 1889-1953 .... DLB-102

Williams, C. K. 1936- DLB-5

Williams, Chancellor 1905- DLB-76

Williams, Charles 1886-1945 ..... DLB-100, 153

Williams, Denis 1923-1998........... DLB-117

Williams, Emlyn 1905-1987 ....DLB-10, 77

Williams, Garth 1912-1996 .... DLB-22

Williams, George Washington
1849-1891 .... DLB-47

Williams, Heathcote 1941- DLB-13

Williams, Helen Maria 1761-1827 ...... DLB-158

Williams, Hugo 1942- DLB-40

Williams, Isaac 1802-1865 .... DLB-32

Williams, Joan 1928- DLB-6

Williams, Joe 1889-1972............. DLB-241

Williams, John A. 1925- DLB-2, 33

Williams, John E. 1922-1994 .... DLB-6

Williams, Jonathan 1929- DLB-5

Williams, Miller 1930- DLB-105

Williams, Nigel 1948- DLB-231

Williams, Raymond 1921- ... DLB-14, 231, 242

Williams, Roger circa 1603-1683 .... DLB-24

Williams, Rowland 1817-1870......... DLB-184

Williams, Samm-Art 1946- DLB-38

Williams, Sherley Anne 1944-1999 ...... DLB-41

Williams, T. Harry 1909-1979 .... DLB-17

Williams, Tennessee
1911-1983 .... DLB-7; Y-83; DS-4; CDALB-1

Williams, Terry Tempest 1955- DLB-206

Williams, Ursula Moray 1911- DLB-160

Williams, Valentine 1883-1946 .... DLB-77

Williams, William Appleman 1921- DLB-17

Williams, William Carlos
1883-1963 ..... DLB-4, 16, 54, 86; CDALB-4

Williams, Wirt 1921- DLB-6

Williams Brothers................... DLB-49

Williamson, Henry 1895-1977 .... DLB-191

Williamson, Jack 1908- DLB-8

Willingham, Calder Baynard, Jr.
1922-1995 .... DLB-2, 44

Williram of Ebersberg circa 1020-1085 .. DLB-148

Willis, Nathaniel Parker
1806-1867 .....DLB-3, 59, 73, 74, 183; DS-13

Willkomm, Ernst 1810-1886 .... DLB-133

Willumsen, Dorrit 1940- DLB-214

Wills, Garry 1934- DLB-246

Wilmer, Clive 1945- DLB-40

Wilson, A. N. 1950- DLB-14, 155, 194

Wilson, Angus 1913-1991 ......DLB-15, 139, 155

Wilson, Arthur 1595-1652 .... DLB-58

Wilson, August 1945- DLB-228

Wilson, Augusta Jane Evans 1835-1909... DLB-42

Wilson, Colin 1931- DLB-14, 194

Wilson, Edmund 1895-1972........... DLB-63

Wilson, Effingham [publishing house] ... DLB-154

Wilson, Ethel 1888-1980 .... DLB-68

Wilson, F. P. 1889-1963 .... DLB-201

Wilson, Harriet E.
1827/1828?-1863? DLB-50, 239, 243

Wilson, Harry Leon 1867-1939 .... DLB-9

Wilson, John 1588-1667.............. DLB-24

Wilson, John 1785-1854 .... DLB-110

Wilson, John Dover 1881-1969 .... DLB-201

Wilson, Lanford 1937- DLB-7

Wilson, Margaret 1882-1973 .... DLB-9

Wilson, Michael 1914-1978 .... DLB-44

Wilson, Mona 1872-1954............. DLB-149

Wilson, Robley 1930- DLB-218

Wilson, Romer 1891-1930............ DLB-191

Wilson, Thomas 1524-1581....... DLB-132, 236

Wilson, Woodrow 1856-1924 .... DLB-47

Wimsatt, William K., Jr. 1907-1975 ...... DLB-63

Winchell, Walter 1897-1972 .... DLB-29

Winchester, J. [publishing house] DLB-49

Winckelmann, Johann Joachim
1717-1768 .... DLB-97

Winckler, Paul 1630-1686 .... DLB-164

Wind, Herbert Warren 1916- DLB-171

Windet, John [publishing house] DLB-170

Windham, Donald 1920- DLB-6

Wing, Donald Goddard 1904-1972 ......DLB-187

Wing, John M. 1844-1917 ....DLB-187

Wingate, Allan [publishing house] DLB-112

Winnemucca, Sarah 1844-1921 ....DLB-175

Winnifrith, Tom 1938- DLB-155

Winning an Edgar Y-98

Winsloe, Christa 1888-1944........... DLB-124

Winslow, Anna Green 1759-1780....... DLB-200

Winsor, Justin 1831-1897.............. DLB-47

John C. Winston Company DLB-49

Winters, Yvor 1900-1968............. DLB-48

Winterson, Jeanette 1959- DLB-207

Winthrop, John 1588-1649.......... DLB-24, 30

Winthrop, John, Jr. 1606-1676 .... DLB-24

Winthrop, Margaret Tyndal 1591-1647.. DLB-200

Winthrop, Theodore 1828-1861 .... DLB-202

Wirt, William 1772-1834 .... DLB-37

Wise, John 1652-1725............... DLB-24

Wise, Thomas James 1859-1937 .... DLB-184

Wiseman, Adele 1928- DLB-88

Wishart and Company............... DLB-112

Wisner, George 1812-1849............. DLB-43

Wister, Owen 1860-1938 ....DLB-9, 78, 186

Wister, Sarah 1761-1804.............. DLB-200

Wither, George 1588-1667........... DLB-121

Witherspoon, John 1723-1794 .... DLB-31

Withrow, William Henry 1839-1908..... DLB-99

Witkacy (see Witkiewicz, Stanisław Ignacy)

Witkiewicz, Stanisław Ignacy
1885-1939 ....DLB-215; CDWLB-4

Wittig, Monique 1935- DLB-83

Wodehouse, P. G.
1881-1975......... DLB-34, 162; CDBLB-6

Wohmann, Gabriele 1932- DLB-75

Woiwode, Larry 1941- DLB-6

Wolcot, John 1738-1819.............. DLB-109

Wolcott, Roger 1679-1767 .... DLB-24

Wolf, Christa 1929- DLB-75; CDWLB-2

Wolf, Friedrich 1888-1953 .... DLB-124

Wolfe, Gene 1931- DLB-8

Wolfe, John [publishing house] DLB-170

Wolfe, Reyner (Reginald)
[publishing house] DLB-170

Wolfe, Thomas
1900-1938 .... DLB-9, 102, 229; Y-85;
DS-2, DS-16; CDALB-5

The Thomas Wolfe Collection at the University
of North Carolina at Chapel Hill........ Y-97

Thomas Wolfe Centennial
Celebration in Asheville.............. Y-00

Fire at Thomas Wolfe Memorial Y-98

The Thomas Wolfe Society Y-97

Wolfe, Tom 1931- DLB-152, 185

Wolfenstein, Martha 1869-1906........ DLB-221

Wolff, Helen 1906-1994................ Y-94

Wolff, Tobias 1945- DLB-130

Wolfram von Eschenbach
circa 1170-after 1220 . . . . DLB-138; CDWLB-2

Wolfram von Eschenbach's *Parzival:*
Prologue and Book 3. . . . . .DLB-138

Wolker, Jiří 1900-1924 . . . . .DLB-215

Wollstonecraft, Mary
1759-1797. . . . . .DLB-39, 104, 158; CDBLB-3

Wondratschek, Wolf 1943- DLB-75

Wood, Anthony à 1632-1695 . . . . .DLB-213

Wood, Benjamin 1820-1900 . . . . .DLB-23

Wood, Charles 1932- DLB-13

Wood, Mrs. Henry 1814-1887. . . . . .DLB-18

Wood, Joanna E. 1867-1927. . . . . .DLB-92

Wood, Sally Sayward Barrell Keating
1759-1855 .DLB-200

Wood, Samuel [publishing house] DLB-49

Wood, William ?-? DLB-24

The Charles Wood Affair:
A Playwright Revived Y-83

Woodberry, George Edward
1855-1930 . . . . .DLB-71, 103

Woodbridge, Benjamin 1622-1684 . . . . . . .DLB-24

Woodcock, George 1912-1995 . . . . .DLB-88

Woodhull, Victoria C. 1838-1927 . . . . . . .DLB-79

Woodmason, Charles circa 1720-?. DLB-31

Woodress, Jr., James Leslie 1916- DLB-111

Woods, Margaret L. 1855-1945. . . . . . . .DLB-240

Woodson, Carter G. 1875-1950. . . . . .DLB-17

Woodward, C. Vann 1908-1999 . . . . .DLB-17

Woodward, Stanley 1895-1965 . . . . .DLB-171

Wooler, Thomas 1785 or 1786-1853 . . . . .DLB-158

Woolf, David (see Maddow, Ben)

Woolf, Douglas 1922-1992 . . . . .DLB-244

Woolf, Leonard 1880-1969 . . . . . .DLB-100; DS-10

Woolf, Virginia 1882-1941
. . . . . . .DLB-36, 100, 162; DS-10; CDBLB-6

Woolf, Virginia, "The New Biography," *New York
Herald Tribune,* 30 October 1927 . . . . .DLB-149

Woollcott, Alexander 1887-1943 . . . . . . .DLB-29

Woolman, John 1720-1772. . . . . .DLB-31

Woolner, Thomas 1825-1892 . . . . .DLB-35

Woolrich, Cornell 1903-1968 . . . . .DLB-226

Woolsey, Sarah Chauncy 1835-1905. . . . . .DLB-42

Woolson, Constance Fenimore
1840-1894 . . . . DLB-12, 74, 189, 221

Worcester, Joseph Emerson
1784-1865 . . . . .DLB-1, 235

Worde, Wynkyn de [publishing house]. . .DLB-170

Wordsworth, Christopher 1807-1885 . . . .DLB-166

Wordsworth, Dorothy 1771-1855 . . . . . . .DLB-107

Wordsworth, Elizabeth 1840-1932 . . . . . .DLB-98

Wordsworth, William
1770-1850 . . . . .DLB-93, 107; CDBLB-3

Workman, Fanny Bullock 1859-1925 . . . .DLB-189

The Works of the Rev. John Witherspoon
(1800-1801) [excerpts] DLB-31

A World Chronology of Important Science
Fiction Works (1818-1979) DLB-8

World Publishing Company DLB-46

World War II Writers Symposium
at the University of South Carolina,
12–14 April 1995. . . . . Y-95

Worthington, R., and Company DLB-49

Wotton, Sir Henry 1568-1639. . . . . .DLB-121

Wouk, Herman 1915- Y-82; CDALB-7

Wreford, James 1915- DLB-88

Wren, Sir Christopher 1632-1723 . . . . . . .DLB-213

Wren, Percival Christopher
1885-1941 . . . . .DLB-153

Wrenn, John Henry 1841-1911 . . . . . . .DLB-140

Wright, C. D. 1949- DLB-120

Wright, Charles 1935- DLB-165; Y-82

Wright, Charles Stevenson 1932- DLB-33

Wright, Frances 1795-1852 . . . . .DLB-73

Wright, Harold Bell 1872-1944 . . . . .DLB-9

Wright, James
1927-1980 . . . . .DLB-5, 169; CDALB-7

Wright, Jay 1935- DLB-41

Wright, Louis B. 1899-1984 . . . . .DLB-17

Wright, Richard
1908-1960 . . . . .DLB-76, 102; DS-2; CDALB-5

Wright, Richard B. 1937- DLB-53

Wright, Sarah Elizabeth 1928- DLB-33

Wright, Willard Huntington ("S. S. Van Dine")
1888-1939 . . . . DS-16

A Writer Talking: A Collage. Y-00

Writers and Politics: 1871-1918,
by Ronald Gray DLB-66

Writers and their Copyright Holders:
the WATCH Project. Y-94

Writers' Forum Y-85

Writing for the Theatre,
by Harold Pinter DLB-13

Wroth, Lawrence C. 1884-1970. . . . . . . .DLB-187

Wroth, Lady Mary 1587-1653. . . . . .DLB-121

Wurlitzer, Rudolph 1937- DLB-173

Wyatt, Sir Thomas circa 1503-1542 . . . . .DLB-132

Wycherley, William
1641-1715 . . . . DLB-80; CDBLB-2

Wyclif, John
circa 1335-31 December 1384. . . . . . . .DLB-146

Wyeth, N. C. 1882-1945 . . . . DLB-188; DS-16

Wylie, Elinor 1885-1928 . . . . .DLB-9, 45

Wylie, Philip 1902-1971. . . . . .DLB-9

Wyllie, John Cook 1908-1968 . . . . .DLB-140

Wyman, Lillie Buffum Chace
1847-1929 . . . . .DLB-202

Wymark, Olwen 1934- DLB-233

Wynne-Tyson, Esmé 1898-1972 . . . . .DLB-191

X

Xenophon circa 430 B.C.-circa 356 B.C. . . . DLB-176

Y

Yasuoka Shōtarō 1920- DLB-182

Yates, Dornford 1885-1960 . . . . DLB-77, 153

Yates, J. Michael 1938- DLB-60

Yates, Richard
1926-1992 . . . . DLB-2, 234; Y-81, Y-92

Yau, John 1950- DLB-234

Yavorov, Peyo 1878-1914 . . . . .DLB-147

The Year in Book Publishing Y-86

The Year in Book Reviewing and the Literary
Situation Y-98

The Year in British Drama Y-99, Y-00

The Year in British Fiction Y-99, Y-00

The Year in Children's
Books Y-92–Y-96, Y-98, Y-99, Y-00

The Year in Children's Literature Y-97

The Year in Drama Y-82-Y-85, Y-87–Y-96

The Year in Fiction . . .Y-84–Y-86, Y-89, Y-94–Y-99

The Year in Fiction: A Biased View Y-83

The Year in Literary Biography . . Y-83–Y-98, Y-00

The Year in Literary Theory. Y-92–Y-93

The Year in London Theatre Y-92

The Year in the Novel. Y-87, Y-88, Y-90–Y-93

The Year in Poetry Y-83–Y-92, Y-94–Y-00

The Year in Science Fiction and Fantasy Y-00

The Year in Short Stories Y-87

The Year in the Short Story. Y-88, Y-90–Y-93

The Year in Texas Literature Y-98

The Year in U.S. Drama Y-00

The Year in U.S. Fiction Y-00

The Year's Work in American Poetry. Y-82

The Year's Work in Fiction: A Survey Y-82

Yearsley, Ann 1753-1806. . . . . .DLB-109

Yeats, William Butler
1865-1939 . . . .DLB-10, 19, 98, 156; CDBLB-5

Yep, Laurence 1948- DLB-52

Yerby, Frank 1916-1991 . . . . .DLB-76

Yezierska, Anzia
1880-1970 . . . . .DLB-28, 221

Yolen, Jane 1939- DLB-52

Yonge, Charlotte Mary
1823-1901 . . . . .DLB-18, 163

The York Cycle circa 1376-circa 1569. . . .DLB-146

A Yorkshire Tragedy DLB-58

Yoseloff, Thomas [publishing house]. DLB-46

Young, A. S. "Doc" 1919-1996 . . . . .DLB-241

Young, Al 1939- DLB-33

Young, Arthur 1741-1820 . . . . .DLB-158

Young, Dick 1917 or 1918 - 1987 . . . . . .DLB-171

Young, Edward 1683-1765 . . . . .DLB-95

Young, Frank A. "Fay" 1884-1957. . . . . . .DLB-241

Young, Francis Brett 1884-1954 . . . . . . .DLB-191

Young, Gavin 1928- DLB-204

Young, Stark 1881-1963 . . . . . . DLB-9, 102; DS-16

Young, Waldeman 1880-1938. . . . . .DLB-26

Young, William
publishing house] DLB-49

Young Bear, Ray A. 1950- DLB-175

Yourcenar, Marguerite
1903-1987 . . . . DLB-72; Y-88

"You've Never Had It So Good," Gusted by
"Winds of Change": British Fiction in the
1950s, 1960s, and After. DLB-14

Yovkov, Yordan 1880-1937. . DLB-147; CDWLB-4

Z

Zachariä, Friedrich Wilhelm 1726-1777 . . . .DLB-97

Zagajewski, Adam 1945- DLB-232

Zagoskin, Mikhail Nikolaevich
   1789-1852 . . . . DLB-198

Zajc, Dane 1929- DLB-181

Zālīte, Māra 1952- DLB-232

Zamora, Bernice 1938- DLB-82

Zand, Herbert 1923-1970 . . . . DLB-85

Zangwill, Israel 1864-1926 . . . . . DLB-10, 135, 197

Zanzotto, Andrea 1921- DLB-128

Zapata Olivella, Manuel 1920- DLB-113

Zasodimsky, Pavel Vladimirovich
   1843-1912 . . . . DLB-238

Zebra Books DLB-46

Zebrowski, George 1945- DLB-8

Zech, Paul 1881-1946 . . . . DLB-56

Zeidner, Lisa 1955- DLB-120

Zeidonis, Imants 1933- DLB-232

Zeimi (Kanze Motokiyo) 1363-1443 . . . . . DLB-203

Zelazny, Roger 1937-1995 . . . . DLB-8

Zenger, John Peter 1697-1746 . . . . DLB-24, 43

Zepheria DLB-172

Zesen, Philipp von 1619-1689 . . . . DLB-164

Zhukovsky, Vasilii Andreevich
   1783-1852 . . . . DLB-205

Zieber, G. B., and Company DLB-49

Ziedonis, Imants 1933- CDWLB-4

Zieroth, Dale 1946- DLB-60

Zigler und Kliphausen, Heinrich
   Anshelm von 1663-1697 . . . . DLB-168

Zimmer, Paul 1934- DLB-5

Zinberg, Len (see Lacy, Ed)

Zindel, Paul 1936- DLB-7, 52; CDALB-7

Zingref, Julius Wilhelm 1591-1635 . . . . . . DLB-164

Zinnes, Harriet 1919- DLB-193

Zinzendorf, Nikolaus Ludwig von
   1700-1760 . . . . DLB-168

Zitkala-Ša 1876-1938 . . . . DLB-175

Zīverts, Mārtiņš 1903-1990 . . . . DLB-220

Zlatovratsky, Nikolai Nikolaevich
   1845-1911 . . . . DLB-238

Zola, Emile 1840-1902 . . . . DLB-123

Zolla, Elémire 1926- DLB-196

Zolotow, Charlotte 1915- DLB-52

Zschokke, Heinrich 1771-1848 . . . . DLB-94

Zubly, John Joachim 1724-1781 . . . . DLB-31

Zu-Bolton II, Ahmos 1936- DLB-41

Zuckmayer, Carl 1896-1977 . . . . DLB-56, 124

Zukofsky, Louis 1904-1978 . . . . DLB-5, 165

Zupan, Vitomil 1914-1987 . . . . DLB-181

Župančič, Oton 1878-1949 . . . DLB-147; CDWLB-4

zur Mühlen, Hermynia 1883-1951 . . . . DLB-56

Zweig, Arnold 1887-1968 . . . . DLB-66

Zweig, Stefan 1881-1942 . . . . DLB-81, 118

ISBN 0-7876-5248-2

90000